Canada

Yukon Territory p767

Northwest Territories p791

Nunavut p811

British Columbia p631

Alberta p558

Manitoba p512

Saskatchewan p534

Ontario p66

Québec p227

Newfoundland & Labrador p459

Prince Edward Island p431

New Brunswick p391

Nova Scotia p330

Brendan Sainsbury, Oliver Berry, John Lee, Regis St Louis,
Ray Bartlett, Gregor Clark, Shawn Duthie, Steve Fallon, Carolyn B
Heller, Anna Kaminski, Adam Karlin, Craig McLachlan, Korina Miller,
Liza Prado, Phillip Tang

PLAN YOUR TRIP

POUTINE P284

TORONTO P71

ON THE ROAD

Contents

ON THE ROAD

COVID-19

We have re-checked every business in this book before publication to ensure that it is still open after the COVID-19 outbreak. However, the economic and social impacts of COVID-19 will continue to be felt long after the outbreak has been contained, and many businesses, services and events referenced in this guide may experience ongoing restrictions. Some businesses may be temporarily closed, have changed their opening hours and services, or require bookings; some unfortunately could have closed permanently. We suggest you check with venues before visiting for the latest information.

Contents

Right: Bow Lake near the Icefields Parkway (p592)

TRPHOTOS/SHUTTERSTOCK ©

WELCOME TO
Canada

Along with over 20% of Canada's population, I was born overseas, gravitating to British Columbia in my 30s where I was quickly seduced by a country whose personality is rooted to the noble tenets of peace, order, and good government. I love Canada for its cultural diversity, liberal freedoms, fondness for outdoor life, and pure, unsullied wilderness. After over a decade living here, I'm still only scratching the surface.

By Brendan Sainsbury, Writer

🐦 @sainsburyb

For more about our writers, see p896

Canada

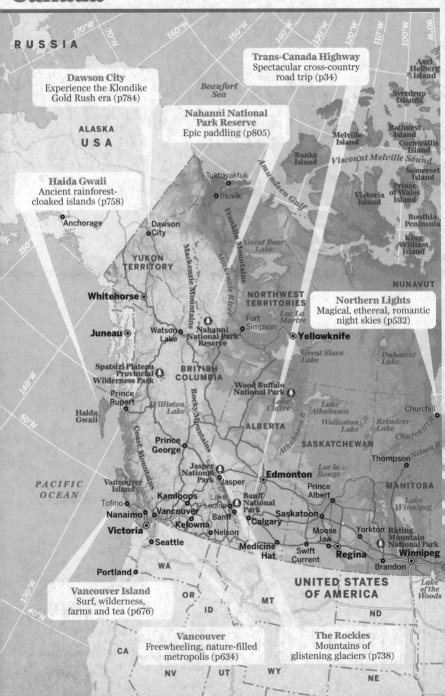

Dawson City
Experience the Klondike
Gold Rush era (p784)

Trans-Canada Highway
Spectacular cross-country
road trip (p34)

**Nahanni National
Park Reserve**
Epic paddling (p805)

Haida Gwaii
Ancient rainforest-
cloaked islands (p758)

Northern Lights
Magical, ethereal, romantic
night skies (p532)

Vancouver Island
Surf, wilderness,
farms and tea (p676)

Vancouver
Freewheeling, nature-filled
metropolis (p634)

The Rockies
Mountains of
glistening glaciers (p738)

0 ___ 500 km
0 ___ 250 miles

GREENLAND

DENMARK

ICELAND

Ellesmere Island

Nares Strait

Devon Island

Davis Strait

ELEVATION

	3000m
	2500m
	2000m
	1500m
	1000m
	600m
	300m
	100m
	0

Churchill
Polar bear central by Hudson Bay (p529)

Baffin Island

Gulf of Boothia

Prince Charles Island

Nettiling Lake

Melville Peninsula

Foxe Basin

Amadjuak Lake

⊙ **Iqaluit**

Québec City
Stroll the atmospheric Old Town (p272)

ATLANTIC OCEAN

Southampton Island

Hudson Strait

Coats Island

Cabot Trail
Coastal scenery and Celtic culture (p379)

Hudson Bay

Charlevoix
Orchards, farms, and fresh, fresh food (p290)

George River

Labrador Sea

Montréal
World's largest Jazz Fest (p231)

Belcher Islands

Feuilles R.

Mélèzes R.

Caniapiscau R.

Labrador

Smallwood Reservoir

Churchill R.

NEWFOUNDLAND & LABRADOR

Lac Bienville

Lac Caniapiscau

Reservoir Manicouagan

Northern Peninsula

St John's ⊙

James Bay

Severn River

Winisk R.

Reservoir Robert-Bourassa

Lac Mistassini

Île d'Anticosti

Corner Brook

Newfoundland

Port aux Basques

Îles de la Madeleine

Cape Breton Highlands National Park

ONTARIO

Moosonee ⊙

QUÉBEC

Tadoussac

Rivière-du-Loup

Fredericton ⊙

NEW BRUNSWICK

Moncton ⊙ ⊙ Amherst

PEI ⊙ **Charlottetown**

Lac Seul

Lake Nipigon

Reservoir Gouin

Québec City

St Stephen

Saint John

⊙ **Halifax**

Thunder Bay

North Bay

OTTAWA ☆

Montréal

NOVA SCOTIA

Yarmouth

ATLANTIC OCEAN

MN

Sudbury

Lake Superior

Sault Ste Marie

Georgian Bay

Kingston

Boston

ME

VT NH

WI

Lake Huron

Toronto

Lake Ontario

MA

Stratford ⊙

Niagara Falls

NY CT RI

Minneapolis

Lake Michigan

London ⊙

Detroit

Lake Erie

PA

New York

Toronto
Canada's multicultural megacity (p71)

IA

Chicago

Niagara Falls
North America's most voluminous cascade (p119)

Canada's Top Experiences

1 WORLD-CLASS NATIONAL PARKS

While Italy has ornate churches and France has gourmet food, Canada tops the ratings with its world-class national parks. The substantial network of 48 protected enclaves represents the cream of Canada's diverse, largely unspoiled landscapes. Don't leave before you've visited at least one.

Banff

The world's third old-est national park (pic-tured left and right) is an integral slice of Canadian history and a dramatic introduc-tion to the majesty of the Rocky Mountains. Banff is where tourism in Canada first took off in the 19th century, inspired by the redis-covery of a natural hot springs and the building of a cross-continental railroad. p585

Right: Inkpots (p598)

Pacific Rim

A narrow but dramatic strip of wave-whipped beaches, brooding forests, and weather-beaten sea-stacks on the west coast of Vancouver Island, this park is esteemed for kayaking, sublime sunsets, and the best surf breaks in Canada. p700

Above: Tofino (p702)

Kluane

Kluane is an imposing empire of mountain and ice that's home to Can-ada's highest peak, Mt Logan, and sits flush up against humongous Wrangell-St Elias national park in Alaska to form one of the largest protected wil-derness areas in the world. p780

Above: Kluane Lake

WINTER SPORTS

2

If you had to pick a motif to personify the essence of Canada, chances are it would be a winter sport. Picture a stick-wielding teenager chasing a hockey puck across a frozen lake, a skillful snowboarder etching artistic grooves onto an impossibly steep mountainside, or thousands of Ottawa citizens skating en masse along the Rideau Canal. When temperatures dive and snow starts to fall, Canadians don't hibernate; they embrace the cold.

Whistler

One of the world's largest and finest ski resorts (pictured above left) melds tasteful nouveau Alpine architecture with spectacular gondola rides, an Olympic nordic park, spine-chilling black diamond runs and the chance to partake in a bobsled ride. p665

Montréal Canadiens

Hockey is the national passion, and if you're visiting between October and April, going to a game is practically mandatory. Pick a team – such as the Montréal Canadiens (flag pictured top right) – and work out how such a polite country embraces such a ferocious sport. p254

Rideau Canal

This well-established 200km-long waterway (pictured above) is at its finest in Ottawa in the winter, when it becomes the world's largest skating rink. People swoosh by on a special 7.8km section of groomed ice, pausing for hot chocolate and delicious slabs of fried dough called beavertails. p217

3 WATCHING WILD FAUNA

While other countries have hunted their wild animals to extinction or corralled what remains of them into zoos and wildlife parks, Canada has preserved a semblance of its original ecosystems. Bears rummage around Vancouver's crinkled North Shore, musk oxen roam by the herd across the arctic tundra and cougars stalk the craggy peaks of the Rockies. Walk carefully through the mountains and valleys and establish your place in the food chain.

Jasper National Park

Seeing big fauna in Jasper (pictured below) is more a guarantee than a possibility. Elks graze on railway tracks, bears poke their noses around alpine meadows, and wolves and caribou occasionally frequent the park's central valleys in the winter. p607

CHERYLRAMALHO/SHUTTERSTOCK ©

BENNEKOM/SHUTTERSTOCK ©

WEEKEND WARRIOR PHOTOS/SHUTTERSTOCK ©

Grasslands National Park

This semi-arid sea of grass and prairie in Saskatchewan is the habitat for two important animal species: black-tailed prairie dogs and plains bison. The latter beasts, once ubiquitous in North America, were successfully reintroduced into the park (pictured above left) two decades ago. p546

Churchill

This lone Manitoba outpost (pictured above right) is right in the middle of a polar bear migration path. From late September to early November, tundra buggies head out in search of the razor-clawed beasts, sometimes getting you close enough to lock eyes. p529

COOL CITIES

4

While not as old or culture heavy as their metro cousins in Europe, Canadian cities are notable for their diversity and cosmopolitanism. Places like Toronto and Vancouver pulsate with a United Nations of neighborhoods and ethnic cuisines while slick skyscrapers and modern infrastructure consistently rank them at the top of global livability indices. There's art and festivals too and, when you tire of the urban bustle, the uncrowded countryside is never far away.

SHAWN.CCF/SHUTTERSTOCK ©

CATHERINE ZIBO/SHUTTERSTOCK ©

FRANKLIN MCKAY/SHUTTERSTOCK ©

Vancouver

Regularly trumpeted as one of the world's prettiest 21st century cities, Vancouver (pictured above left) mixes a diverse Asian-influenced food culture with a penchant for glassy streamlined architecture and an abundance of urban beaches. p634

Montréal

Bilingual Montréal (pictured top right) is a jubilant juxtaposition of Anglo-French culture where bohemian street poets share cafe space with city slickers, and comparisons with Paris aren't exaggerations. p231

Toronto

One of the most cosmopolitan cities on the planet, Toronto (pictured above right) is Canada's 'big apple', a hyperactive stew of cultures and neighborhoods that will blind you with its sheer urban awe. p71

5 NORTH OF THE 60TH PARALLEL

Only a tiny percentage of visitors to Canada make it north of the 60th parallel. Yet, this bleak, beautiful land accounts for over 40% of the country's total area and is laced with some of its more esoteric attractions. Come in winter to see the Northern Lights in all their glory or decamp in summer and drive all the way to the Arctic Ocean on one of Canada's newest roads.

Dawson City

The wonderfully preserved hub of Canada's legendary gold rush, Dawson (pictured below left) is one of the nation's most compelling small towns where false-fronted streets and buildings reek with the essence of a lost era. p784

PIERRE JEAN DURIEU/SHUTTERSTOCK ©

Nahanni National Park

Thirty-storey waterfalls, towering canyons and legends of lost gold await in this Northwest Territories nirvana. Visit on a day trip or spend a week paddling (pictured top right). p805

Baffin Island

The forlorn, brutal landscape of the Inuit, Baffin is a siren call for hardcore hikers and climbers, and more than a few polar bears. p817

Bottom right: Akshayuk Pass (p818)

6 DIVERSE INDIGENOUS CULTURE

ARCHITECT: ROBERT LEBLOND. IMAGE: PECOLD/SHUTTERSTOCK ©

GROGL/SHUTTERSTOCK ©

PETR KAHANEK/SHUTTERSTOCK ©

Scratch the surface of Canada's indigenous culture – a mix of Inuit, Métis and over 600 First Nations groups – and a complex web of layered history will reveal itself. Herein lie thousands of years of different stories, struggles, languages, and creation myths as vast and diverse as the country that shelters them. You'll find it in art, music, place names and landscapes, reflecting the complicated vicissitudes of Canada's soul.

Gwaii Haanas National Park Reserve

In the Haida Gwaii archipelago you'll find the soul of the Haida people, best known for their war-canoe and totem-pole carvings. This national park combines lost villages, burial caves and hot springs. p759

Museum of Anthropology

The best museum in Vancouver is stuffed with art from cultures around the world with an obvious bias for masterpieces plucked from the First Nations of the Pacific Northwest. p639

Head-Smashed-In Buffalo Jump

A superb museum and Unesco World Heritage Site (pictured above) in Southern Alberta documenting the Blackfoot people and their legendary buffalo hunts on the cliffs near the town of Fort McLeod. p617

7 ISLAND CULTURE

From the fifth largest island in the world (Baffin) to the 63 tiny landfalls scattered around Georgian Bay in Lake Huron protected in a national park, Canada has an incredible variety of islands. Prince Edward Island is a province in its own right, Cape Breton has a rich Celtic and Acadian heritage that sets it apart, while Ellesmere Island in the far north is the same size as Great Britain but harbors a population of just 191.

Manitoulin

The largest freshwater island in the world (pictured top left) is situated in the middle of Lake Huron and is replete with beaches, summery cottages and numerous First Nations communities. p168

Vancouver Island

With its forested mountains and storm-whipped beaches, Vancouver Island (pictured above left) is rugged but easy-going, and unsullied by excessive development. p676

PEI

Canada's smallest province is home to gentle pastures, sweeping sand dunes (pictured above right) and the woods that inspired Lucy Maud Montgomery's *Anne of Green Gables*. p431

8 HITTING THE ROAD

Cabot Trail

A 300km-long highway (pictured top left) that winds and climbs over stunning coastal mountains, with heart-stopping sea views, moose nibbling on the roadside and plenty of trails to stop and hike. p379

Viking Trail

This highway connects Newfoundland's Gros Morne National Park and its fjord-like lakes and geological oddities with the sublime, 1000-year-old Viking settlement at L'Anse aux Meadows. p494

Icefields Parkway

Known more romantically as the 'Promenade des Glaciers' in French, this super-smooth highway (pictured bottom left) through the Rocky Mountains invites vigorous head-twists every few kilometers as you glide past lakes, glaciers and grazing wildlife. p592

Distances can be long in the world's second largest country but the scenery is more often than not spectacular. To absorb the best of it at ground level, hire a car and hit the road for a week or three. Classic drives abound on the well-maintained highways and byways of Canada, many of them meticulously mapped with recommended stop-off points and overnight stays en route.

9 LONG-DISTANCE HIKING

A vast country replete with national parks and numerous other protected areas: Canada is a hiker's paradise. Day walks are all very well (and plentiful), but to get an eye-full of the country's most photogenic panoramas, you'll need to disconnect yourself from social media and immerse yourself in Canada's rural splendor with a tent, some bear spray and the other essential (dis)comforts of backcountry living.

West Coast Trail

Tracking the so-called graveyard of the Pacific (courtesy of its shipwrecks), this 75km trail (pictured below left) is laced together by a mix of ladders, rocky scrambles, tidal pools and old First Nations paths. p701

CHESS OCAMPO/SHUTTERSTOCK ©

Bruce Trail

The granddaddy of all Canadian trails (pictured top right) was conceived in 1959 and runs for 900km across Ontario's Niagara escarpment to Tobermory on the tip of the Bruce peninsula. p120

East Coast Trail

Wrapped around Newfoundland's Avalon peninsula where steep cliffs rise from the ocean, this 265km (and growing) trail (pictured right) is made up of 25 linked paths which can be done separately. p476

10 HISTORIC SITES

STEVE CUKROV/SHUTTERSTOCK ©

/KSIMAGE/SHUTTERSTOCK © ©

SF PHOTO/SHUTTERSTOCK ©

It's not as new as it looks. Loaded with millennia of Indigenous narratives, Canada's history pierces the past with widely spread roots. Historic sites incorporate Viking vestiges, Métis battlegrounds, erstwhile Gold Rush boomtowns and – star of the show – the handsome walled city of Québec. Discovering them takes you from the colonial squabbles of 18th century Europe, to the building of a cross-continental railroad and the settlement of Canada's 'wild' west.

Québec City

Québec's capital is more than 400 years old, and its ancient stone walls, glinting spired cathedrals and jazz-filled corner cafes suffuse it with atmosphere, romance, melancholy and intrigue on par with any European city. p272

L'Anse aux Meadows

Though there are few physical remains of Leif Erikson's Viking voyage to Newfoundland in 1000 CE, the story of the improbable settlement and its 1960 rediscovery never cease to fascinate. p498

Louisbourg

Endure soldiers' rations, bribe guards and camp out 18th-century style at this re-creation of a 1744 French fort in Nova Scotia (pictured above). p388

Need to Know

For more information, see Survival Guide (p849)

Currency
Canadian dollar ($)

Languages
English, French

Visas
Visitors may require a visa to enter Canada. Those exempt require an Electronic Travel Authorization (eTA; $7), with the exception of Americans.

Money
ATMs are widely available. Credit cards are accepted in nearly all hotels and restaurants.

Cell Phones
Local SIM cards can be used in unlocked GSM 850/1900 compatible phones. Other phones must be set to roaming.

Time
Atlantic Standard Time (GMT/UTC minus four hours)
Eastern Standard Time (GMT/UTC minus five hours)
Central Standard Time (GMT/UTC minus six hours)
Pacific Standard Time (GMT/UTC minus eight hours)

When to Go

- Dry climate
- Warm to hot summers, mild winters
- Summers – mild to warm (north & east) & warm to hot (south), cold winters
- Polar climate

Churchill
GO Sep–Nov

Banff
GO Jul–Sep

Vancouver
GO Jun–Aug

Montréal
GO Jun–Aug

Halifax
GO Jul–Sep

High Season
(Jun–Aug)

➡ Sunshine and warm weather prevail; far northern regions briefly thaw.

➡ Accommodation prices peak (up 30% on average).

➡ December through March is equally busy and expensive in ski resort towns.

Shoulder
(May, Sep & Oct)

➡ Crowds and prices drop off.

➡ Temperatures are cool but comfortable.

➡ Attractions keep shorter hours.

➡ Fall foliage areas (eg Cape Breton Island and Québec) remain busy.

Low Season
(Nov–Apr)

➡ Places outside the big cities and ski resorts close.

➡ Darkness and cold take over.

➡ April and November are particularly good for bargains.

Useful Websites

Destination Canada (en.des tinationcanada.com) Official tourism site.

Environment Canada Weather (www.weather.gc.ca) Forecasts for any town.

Lonely Planet (www.lonely planet.com/canada) Destination information, hotel reviews and more.

Government of Canada (www. gc.ca) National and regional information.

Parks Canada (www.pc.gc.ca) Lowdown on national parks.

Canadian Broadcasting Corporation (www.cbc.ca) National and provincial news.

Important Numbers

Country code	☏1
International access code	☏011
Emergency	☏911
Directory assistance	☏411

Exchange Rates

Australia	A$1	C$0.90
Europe	€1	C$1.46
Japan	¥100	C$1.21
New Zealand	NZ$1	C$0.86
UK	UK£1	C$1.71
USA	US$1	C$1.33

For current exchange rates see www.xe.com.

Daily Costs

Budget: Less than $100

➡ Dorm bed: $25–40

➡ Campsite: $25–35

➡ Self-catered meals from markets and supermarkets: $12–20

Midrange: $100–250

➡ B&B or room in a midrange hotel: $80–180 ($100–250 in major cities)

➡ Meal in a good local restaurant: from $20 plus drinks

➡ Rental car: $45–70 per day

➡ Attraction admissions: $5–25

Top end: More than $250

➡ Four-star hotel room: from $180 (from $250 in major cities)

➡ Three-course meal in a top restaurant: from $65 plus drinks

➡ Skiing day pass: $50–90

Opening Hours

Opening hours vary throughout the year. We've provided high-season opening hours; hours will generally decrease in the shoulder and low seasons.

Banks 10am–5pm Monday to Friday; some open 9am–noon Saturday

Restaurants breakfast 8–11am, lunch 11:30am–2:30pm Monday to Friday, dinner 5–9:30pm daily; some open for brunch 8am to 1pm Saturday and Sunday

Bars 5pm–2am daily

Clubs 9pm–2am Wednesday to Saturday

Shops 10am–6pm Monday to Saturday, noon–5pm Sunday; some open to 8pm or 9pm Thursday and/or Friday

Supermarkets 9am–8pm; some open 24 hours

Arriving in Canada

Toronto Pearson International Airport Trains (adult/child $12.35/free) run downtown every 15 minutes from 5:30am to 1am; taxis cost around $60 (45 minutes).

Montréal Trudeau International Airport A 24-hour airport shuttle bus ($10) runs downtown. Taxis cost a flat $40 (30 to 60 minutes).

Vancouver International Airport Trains ($7.95 to $10.70) run downtown every six to 20 minutes; taxis cost around $40 (30 minutes).

Land Border Crossings Visit the website of the Canadian Border Services Agency (www. cbsa-asfc.gc.ca) for the latest info on border crossings.

Getting Around

Car An extensive highway system links most towns. The Trans-Canada Hwy stretches from Newfoundland to Vancouver Island. Outside cities, distances can be deceivingly long and travel times slow due to single-lane highways. All the major rental car companies are readily available.

Train Outside the Toronto–Montréal corridor, train travel is mostly for scenic journeys.

Ferry Public ferry systems operate extensively in British Columbia, Québec and the Maritime provinces.

Air Regional and national carriers crisscross the country, taking days off travel time and reaching northern towns inaccessible by road.

Bus Greyhound Canada is no longer operating. Bus travel is still possible with other operators for shorter, regional trips.

For much more on **getting around**, see p863

What's New

Canada has juggled the trials of COVID-19 with several other existential challenges over the last couple of years. With the economy and health system surviving pandemic-related shocks in 2020, emphasis has subsequently shifted to climate change and indigenous relations.

Best in Travel

Vancouver Island was listed in Lonely Planet's Top 10 regions to visit in 2022. What was once dismissed as a regional backwater where British Columbians went to retire, has morphed into a cool hub of surfing beaches, boutique vineyards, community-led trail-building projects and locavore restaurants. If you're into riding whitecapped Pacific breakers, getting from A to B by human-powered transport, or frequenting a ski resort that isn't called 'Whistler', this could be your post-pandemic nirvana.

With a population of less than one million spread over a jagged landmass the size of Taiwan, the island has ample room for visitors to spread out and explore its forested mountains and storm-whipped beaches while reveling in the spontaneity of life on Canada's wild west coast.

Royal Tyrrell Museum, Drumheller

A massive, multi-million-dollar expansion that opened in 2019 makes a great dinosaur experience (p614) even more amazing, with interactive exhibits, fossil-casting workshops, and all the dinos you know and love.

Mosaic Stadium, Saskatchewan

Regina's CFL team – the much loved Roughriders (p540) – have a new home where 33,000 of their closest fans can cheer them on.

LOCAL KNOWLEDGE

WHAT'S HAPPENING IN CANADA

Brendan Sainsbury, Lonely Planet writer

Canada was relatively successful in mitigating the worst effects of the coronavirus pandemic in 2020-21, especially compared to its American neighbor in the south. Furthermore, after a sluggish start, its vaccination campaign morphed into one of the world's fastest and most comprehensive.

But as COVID-19 subsided and restrictions gradually eased in mid-2021, a couple of new problems reared their ugly heads. In June 2021, the remains of 215 indigenous children were found at the site of a former residential school in Kamloops, BC. The discovery quickly sent shockwaves across the country and reopened the bitter wounds of Canada's colonial past and its deplorable treatment of indigenous people.

Later the same month, a meteorological 'heat dome' installed itself over the Pacific Northwest, prompting record-breaking temperatures in British Columbia which topped a life-threatening 49°C in the village of Lytton. The heat led to a spate of more than 500 sudden unexpected deaths and sparked off numerous forest fires that destroyed whole communities.

Thaidene Nëné National Park Reserve, Northwest Territories

Canada's newest national park was officially inaugurated in August 2019 and inhabits over 14,000 sq km of boreal uplands on the eastern arm of Great Slave Lake.

Biodôme renovation, Montréal

The kid-friendly interactive science museum (p239) becomes more immersive with a renovation bringing in more natural light and raised walkways.

Vancouver Island Trail

A community campaign is putting the finishing touches to a 770km-long multi-use trail running the full length of Vancouver Island. Juxtaposing existing paths with newer sections over rugged terrain, the task of knitting the route together should be mostly complete by 2022.

Grand Prix du Canada, Montréal

The new three-story Grand Prix du Canada pit building has been revealed at Circuit Gilles Villeneuve (p240).

Fireworks Feast, Prince Edward Island

Food Network star and celebrity chef Michael Smith took over the upscale Inn at Bay Fortune (p444) in 2015, and recently added a gargantuan 25ft-long brick-lined stove, where he cooks up summertime feasts for hungry guests and diners.

Polygon Gallery, Vancouver

North Vancouver's sparkling contemporary art space (p643) occupies a dramatic sawtooth-roof building on the waterfront. Check out the artworks plus the views of downtown's glass-towered cityscape.

Remai Modern, Saskatoon

Part of the River Landing redevelopment by the South Saskatchewan River, Remai Modern (p550) is a museum of modern and contemporary art for Saskatoon. Approach

LISTEN, WATCH & FOLLOW

For inspiration, visit www.lonelyplanet.com/canada/travel-tips-and-articles.

Explore (www.explore-mag.com) Popular Canadian outdoor magazine with an online podcast and blog.

Ski Canada Magazine (www.skicanadamag.com) For the latest on what's happening in the snowy north.

I Backpack Canada (ibackpackcanada.com) Independent website and blog with good tips on budget travel in Canada.

Canadian Geographic (www.canadiangeographic.ca) Published by the Royal Canadian Geographical Society, this illustrious magazine has been running since 1930.

FAST FACTS

Food trend Plant-based food

Black bear population approx 380,000

Percentage of population that is indigenous 3%

Population 38 million

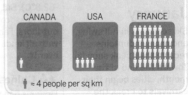

CANADA   USA   FRANCE

↑ ≈ 4 people per sq km

it along the newly named Joni Mitchell Promenade.

Pacific Rim Cycle Path, BC

A superb new 25km-long cycling path running between the surfing towns of Ucluelet and Tofino will officially open in 2022. The trail closely tracks the coast through the Pacific Rim National Park.

Pangea Pod Hotel, Whistler

Claiming to be Canada's first capsule hotel (p668), this funky place has added an affordable flourish to Whistler's pricey hotel scene.

Month by Month

January

Ski season is in full swing, and many mountains receive their peak snowfall. Toward the end of the month, cities begin their carnivals to break the shackles of cold, dark days.

🍷 Ice Wine Festivals

British Columbia's Okanagan Valley (www. thewinefestivals.com) and Ontario's Niagara Peninsula (www.niagarawinefesti val.com) celebrate their ice wines with good-time festivals. The distinctive, sweet libations go down the hatch alongside chestnut roasts, cocktail competitions and cozy alpine-lodge ambience.

🍴 Eat Drink Halifax

Hosted by the local Halifax magazine *Curated*, this winter celebration of all things epicurean brings together some of the city's top chefs, brewers, cider makers and cocktail shakers (www.curatedmagazine.ca/ events/eat-drink-halifax).

February

Yes it's cold, as in 'coldest temperature ever recorded in Canada' cold (Snag – Yukon, on February 3, 1947: -62.8°C). But that doesn't stop folks from being outdoors; February is filled with all kinds of wintry events.

🎆 Chinese New Year

Dragons dance, firecrackers burst and food sizzles in the country's Chinatowns. Vancouver (www.vancou ver-chinatown.com) hosts the biggest celebration, but Toronto, Calgary, Ottawa and Montréal also have festivities. The lunar calendar determines the date.

☆ Québec City's Winter Carnival

Revelers watch ice-sculpture competitions, hurtle down snow slides, go ice fishing and cheer on their favorite paddlers in an insane canoe race on the half-frozen, ice-floe-filled St Lawrence River. It's the world's biggest winter fest (www.carnaval. qc.ca). (p279)

🏃 Winterlude in Ottawa

A snowy bash along the Rideau Canal, where skaters glide by on the 7.8km of groomed ice. When they're not sipping hot chocolate and eating beavertails (fried-dough pastry), the townsfolk build massive sculptures entirely of ice (www.canada.ca/en/canadi an-heritage). (p218)

🏃 Yukon Quest

This legendary 1600km dogsled race (www.yukon quest.com) goes from Whitehorse to Fairbanks, Alaska, through February darkness and -50°C temperatures. It's the ultimate test of musher and husky. Record time: eight days, 14 hours, 21 minutes.

☆ World Pond Hockey Tournament

Plaster Rock, New Brunswick, plows 20 rinks on Roulston Lake, rings them with straw-bale seating for 8000-odd spectators and invites 120 four-person teams to hit the puck. Teams travel from as far as the UK, Egypt and the Cayman Islands (www.world pondhockey.ca). (p400)

☃ Northern Manitoba Trappers' Festival

The Pas, Manitoba, puts on a weekend of frosty anarchy featuring dogsled races, snowmobiling, ice sculptures, torchlight parades and trapping games (www.trappersfestival.ca). Bundle up: the daily mean temperature is -16.1°C. (p529)

♟ Vancouver International Wine Festival

Vancouver uncorks 1700 wines from 200 vintners at the Vancouver International Wine Festival (www.vanwinefest.ca), a rite of spring for oenophiles. You're drinking for art's sake, since the event raises funds for the city's Bard on the Beach summer Shakespeare festival. (p645)

March

Snow lessens and temperatures moderate from the brunt of winter. Ski resorts still do brisk business, especially mid-month when kids typically have a school break.

✘ Sugar Shacks

Québec produces three-quarters of the world's maple syrup, and March is when trees get tapped. Head out to a local sugar shack and do the tire d'érable (taffy pull), where steaming maple syrup is poured onto snow and wound around a popsicle stick once it's cooled.

☃ Regina Powwow

Students at First Nations University of Canada initiated this Saskatchewan powwow (www.fnuniv.

ca/pow-wow) more than 40 years ago to celebrate spring and give thanks for the land's rebirth. Dancers arrive from around North America, and traditional crafts and foods abound.

April

Apart from in the far north, winter's chill fades and spring sprouts. It's a good time for bargains, as ski season is winding down but the summer influx hasn't yet begun.

☆ Stratford Festival

Canada's Stratford, a few hours outside Toronto, nearly outdoes England's Stratford-upon-Avon. This festival (www.stratfordfestival.ca) plays a monster season from April to November. Four theaters stage contemporary drama, music, operas and, of course, works by Shakespeare. Productions are first-rate and feature well-known actors. (p144)

☃ World Ski & Snowboard Festival

Ski bums converge on Whistler for 10 days of adrenaline events, outdoor rock and hip-hop concerts, film screenings, dog parades and a whole lotta carousing (www.wssf.com). Heed the motto: party in April, sleep in May. (p668)

☆ Hot Docs

Want to learn more about Ontario's Hwy 7? Millionaires who live in Mumbai's slums? Belly dancers working in Cairo? Toronto hosts North America's largest documentary film festival (www.hotdocs.ca), screening 170-plus documentaries from around the globe. (p92)

May

This is a fine time for shoulder-season bargains and wildflower vistas. The weather is warm by day, though nippy at night. Victoria Day (called 'National Patriots' Day' in Québec), in the third week of May, marks the official start of summer.

☃ Tiptoe through the Tulips

Ottawa bursts with color – more than three million tulips of 200 types blanket the city for the Canadian Tulip Festival (www.tulipfestival.ca). Festivities include parades, regattas, car rallies, dances, concerts and fireworks. (p218)

✘ Chocolate Festival

Plays about chocolate, painting with chocolate, jewelry making with chocolate – are you sensing a theme? Québec's Fête du Chocolat de Bromont (www.facebook.com/Feteduchocolat.Bromont) is all about the sweet stuff. The best part: eating the chocolate. Bromont lies 75km east of Montréal.

June

Take advantage of long, warm days to hike, paddle and soak up the great outdoors (but bring repellent for black flies). Attractions don't get mega-busy until later in the month, when school's out for summer.

☆ Luminato

For 10 days in early June, big-name musicians,

artists, dancers, writers, actors and filmmakers descend on Toronto for a celebration of creativity that reflects the city's diversity (www.luminatofestival. com). Many performances are free. (p92)

☆ North by Northeast

Over more than 25 years, NXNE (www.nxne.com) has become a must on the music-industry calendar, with around 1000 emerging indie bands taking to the stages of Toronto's coolest clubs. You might catch the rock stars of tomorrow. Film screenings and comedy shows add to the mix. (p93)

☆ Montréal Jazz Festival

Two million music lovers descend on Montréal in late June, when the heart of downtown explodes with jazz and blues for 11 straight days (www.mon trealjazzfest.com). Most concerts are outdoors and free, and the party goes on round the clock. (p243)

☆ Pride Toronto

Toronto's most flamboyant event (www.pridetoronto. com) celebrates diversity of sexuality and gender identity with a month of festivities, climaxing with a triple whammy: the Trans March, Dyke March and Pride Parade. Rainbow-coated Church-Wellesley Village is ground zero. (p92)

☆ Saskatchewan Jazz Festival

Come show your soul patch at this jazzy 10-day festival (www.saskjazz.com) at venues throughout Saskatoon. Blues, funk, pop and world

music are also on the agenda. Herbie Hancock and Ziggy Marley are among the acts that have trekked to the prairie. (p552)

☆ Alianait Arts Festival

Iqaluit's summer fest celebrates Inuit culture through a series of events, including music and talent shows, held at various venues around town. (p815)

July

This is prime time for visiting most provinces, with the weather at its warmest, a bounty of fresh produce and seafood filling plates, and festivals rockin' the nights away. Crowds are thick.

☆ Country Music in Cavendish

Some of the biggest names in country music come to Prince Edward Island for the Cavendish Beach Festival (www.cavendishbeachmusic. com). This is one of the largest outdoor music festivals in North America, and the island swells with people.

☆ Montréal Comedy Festival

Everyone gets giddy for two weeks at the Just for Laughs Festival (www.ha haha.com), which features hundreds of comedy shows, including free ones in the Quartier Latin. The biggest names in the biz yuck it up for this one. (p243)

☆ Calgary Stampede

Raging bulls, chuckwagon racing and bad-ass, boot-

wearing cowboys unite for the 'Greatest Outdoor Show on Earth.' A midway of rides and games makes it a family affair well beyond the usual rodeo event, attracting up to 1.5 million yee-hawin' fans (www.cal garystampede.com). (p576)

☆ Winnipeg Fringe Festival

North America's second-largest fringe fest (www. winnipegfringe.com) stages creative, raw and oddball works from a global lineup of performers. Comedy, drama, music, cabaret and even musical memoirs are on tap over 12 days. (p519)

☆ Arctic Art

The Great Northern Arts Festival (www.gnaf.org) in Inuvik, Northwest Territories, draws scores of carvers, painters and other creators from across the circumpolar world. It's an ideal place to buy Arctic art, watch it being made, or participate in workshops.

☆ Stan Rogers Folk Festival

Honoring a legendary Canadian folk singer, the three-day Stanfest (www. stanfest.com) in Canso, Nova Scotia, has drawn dozens of artists for over two decades. Over 10,000 fans flock to the tiny town to strum, dance and croon. (p390)

☆ Festival d'Été de Québec

With 300 shows on 10 stages, the 11-day Summer Festival (www.infofestival. com) attracts musicians and top new talent from all over the world to Québec City. (p279)

Top: Bonhomme, ambassador of Québec City's Winter Carnival (p28)

Bottom: Chinese New Year (p28) in Vancouver

August

The sunny days and shindigs continue. Visitors throng most provinces, and prices reflect it. It can get downright hot and humid away from the coasts.

☆ Festival Acadien

Acadians tune their fiddles and unleash their Franco-Canadian spirit for the Festival Acadien (www.festival acadien.ca) in Caraquet, New Brunswick. It's the biggest event on the Acadian calendar, with singers, musicians and dancers letting loose for two weeks in early August. (p428)

🏃 Newfoundland Rowing Regatta

The streets are empty, the stores are closed and everyone migrates to the shores of Quidi Vidi Lake for the Royal St John's Regatta (www.stjohnsregatta.org). The rowing race began in 1825 and is now the continent's oldest continuously held sporting event. (p466)

☆ Edmonton Fringe Festival

Edmonton Fringe Festival (www.fringetheatre.ca) is North America's largest fringe bash, staging some 1600 performances of wild, uncensored shows over 11 days in mid-August. Acts are democratically chosen by lottery.

🎪 Canadian National Exhibition

Akin to a state fair in the USA, 'The Ex' (www.theex.com) features more than 700 exhibitors, agricultural shows, lumberjack competitions and outdoor concerts at Toronto's Exhibition

Place. The carnivalesque 18-day event runs through Labour Day and ends with a bang-up fireworks display. (p93)

September

Labour Day in early September heralds the end of summer, after which crowds (and prices) diminish. But the weather is still decent in most places, making it an excellent time to visit. Plus, moose mating season begins!

PEI Fall Flavours

This island-wide kitchen party merges toe-tapping traditional music with incredible seafood over the course of three weeks (www.fallflavours.ca). In Charlottetown, don't miss the oyster-shucking championships or the chowder challenge. (p437)

☆ Toronto International Film Festival

Toronto's prestigious 10-day celebration (www.tiff.net) is a major cinematic event. Films of all lengths and styles are screened, as celebs shimmy between gala events and the Bell Lightbox building. Buy tickets well in advance. (p93)

Newfoundland Coastal Cookout

The wee town of Elliston in eastern Newfoundland gathers many of Canada's best chefs and has them cook at stations set up along a gorgeous 5km coastal trail. Foodies flock in to eat and hike and eat some more (www.rootsrantsandroars.ca).

☆ Canadian Deep Roots Festival

Tune in to Mi'kmaw, Acadian, African–Nova Scotian and other unique music – all with local roots – in the fun university town of Wolfville, Nova Scotia (www.deeprootsmusic.ca). Workshops are available with some of the performers, so you can learn to drum, strum or fiddle. (p369)

October

With fall foliage flaming bright and the weather cool but comfortable, October welcomes lots of visitors. Grab a stick, because hockey season gets underway.

Celtic Colours

With foot-stompin' music amid riotous foliage, this roving festival in Cape Breton attracts top musicians from Scotland, Spain and other countries with Celtic connections (www.celtic-colours.com). Community suppers, step-dancing classes and tin-whistle lessons round out the cultural celebration. (p377)

Oktoberfest in Ontario

Willkommen to this nine-day beery Bavarian bash in Kitchener, supposedly the largest Oktoberfest outside of Germany (www.oktoberfest.ca). The sauerkraut, oompah bands, lederhosen and biergartens bring 500,000 people to clink steins under the tents. (p139)

Dark Sky Festival

In late October, Jasper's Dark Sky Festival (jasperdarksky.travel) fills 10 days and nights with events celebrating space. Hear talks by astronauts, astronomers and astrophotographers, listen to the symphony under the stars, see the aurora borealis reflected in a glacial lake and gaze through a telescope into the great beyond. (p612)

November

After fall color but still early in the ski season, this is an offbeat time to visit. It's cold, but just a tease as to what's coming over the next three months.

Niagara Festival of Lights

From November to January, the family-friendly Winter Festival of Lights (www.wfol.com) gets everyone in the holiday spirit with two million twinkling bulbs and 125 animated displays brightening the town and the waterfalls themselves. Fireworks occasionally light up the skies, too. (p124)

December

Get out the parka. Winter begins in earnest as snow falls, temperatures drop and ski resorts ramp up for the masses. 'Tis the holiday season, too.

Mountain Time

Powder hounds hit the slopes from east to west. Whistler in British Columbia, Mont-Tremblant in Québec and the Canadian Rockies around Banff, Alberta, pull the biggest crowds, but there's downhill action – and cross-country – going on in every province.

Itineraries

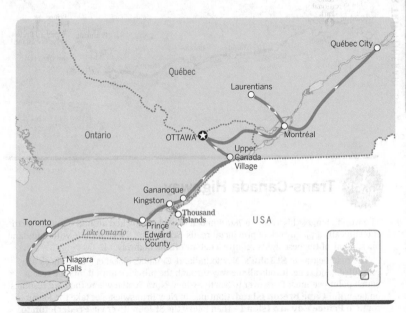

 The Central Corridor

This 1450km route from Toronto to Québec City encompasses Canada's largest cities, mightiest waterfalls and prettiest islands.

Spend two days in multicultural **Toronto**, wallowing in the wealth of architecture, art museums, restaurants and nightclubs. Spend day three at **Niagara Falls**, then begin your eastward haul. The Loyalist Parkway (Hwy 33) rambles shoreside in winery-laden **Prince Edward County** and pulls into colonial **Kingston**. From there, the misty, mansion-covered **Thousand Islands** dot the St Lawrence River; **Gananoque** makes a good break for a day in their midst. Make a half-day stop at **Upper Canada Village**, a recreated 1860s town, before heading to **Ottawa** for a couple of days to get your culture fix at the national museums.

Save room for your next stop, **Montréal**, where the French exuberance seduces via Euro-cool clubs and foodie-beloved cafes. Had your fill? Swing over to the **Laurentians** to spend a day or two and hike, cycle or ski yourself back into shape. Finish in **Québec City** – its charismatic walled Old Town, dramatically poised on a bluff over the St Lawrence, will leave an impression long after you return home.

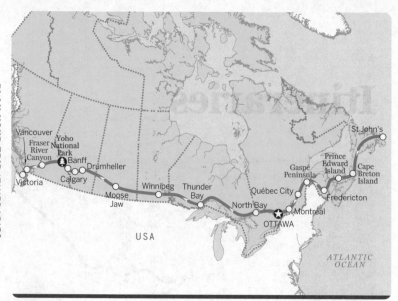

Trans-Canada Highway

The world's longest highway – a 7800km belt of asphalt cinched around Canada's girth – is technically a patchwork of provincial roads. Scenic stretches alternate with mundane ones; many of the best sights require a detour off the highway.

The road begins in **St John's**, Newfoundland, Canada's oldest city and a heck of a pub-filled good time. It rolls all the way through the province until it hits the sea, at which point you must ferry over to North Sydney, Nova Scotia, where the road resumes on beautiful **Cape Breton Island**. Continue to New Brunswick – or take the longer route to **Prince Edward Island** – then follow the St John River via **Fredericton** to Québec. The **Gaspé Peninsula** entices as a pastoral side-trip east. Otherwise, the highway follows the mighty St Lawrence River and reaches romantic **Québec City**.

Carry on the urban theme in **Montréal**, where the *pâtisseries* and *café* will keep you lingering, before plunging into Ontario at museum-fortified **Ottawa**. From there, follow in the fur traders' footsteps to **North Bay**, the gateway to the Algoma wilderness that inspired the Group of Seven painters. Savor the superb stretch of road skirting Lake Superior to **Thunder Bay** and voilà, there goes week two.

Next the highway enters the prairie flatlands of Manitoba, where **Winnipeg** rockets up and provides an enlivening patch of cafes and culture. The road dawdles under Saskatchewan's big skies until reaching bad-ass **Moose Jaw**, where Al Capone used to hide his bootlegged booze. In Alberta, dinosaur junkies can detour to **Drumheller**. And put on your cowboy boots before arriving in **Calgary**, a former cow town that's become one of Canada's fastest-growing cities. So passes week three...

You're in the Rockies now. They offer a dramatic change of scenery as the highway meanders through **Banff** before entering British Columbia at **Yoho National Park** and reaching its highest point (1627m) at Kicking Horse Pass. The mountains eventually give way to river country. The most memorable section leads through the **Fraser River Canyon**, from where it's only a quick jaunt to mod, multicultural **Vancouver** and the ferry to **Victoria**. Snap a picture at the Mile 0 sign. You made it!

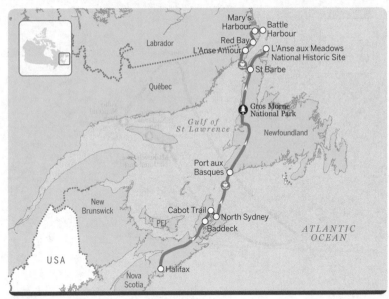

 Cabot & Viking Trails

Wild, windswept and whale-riddled, this 1700km route through Nova Scotia, Newfoundland, Labrador and Québec unfurls sea-and-cliff vistas, Viking vestiges and much more.

Start in **Halifax** and spend a few days enjoying the beer, farmers markets and cosmopolitan life. Then hit the road to Celtic-tinged Cape Breton Island for two days. It's about a five-hour drive, and there's no ferry involved, as a causeway connects the mainland to the island. You won't have time to traverse Cape Breton in depth, but you can certainly get a feel for its beauty in pastoral **Baddeck** and along the art-studio-dotted **Cabot Trail**. Industrial **North Sydney** is nearby for the ferry to Newfoundland.

It's a six-hour sail over the Cabot Strait to **Port aux Basques**. The ferry goes daily, but be sure to book in advance. Spend a day in the sleepy town, then steer for **Gros Morne National Park**, about four hours north on the Trans-Canada Hwy. This World Heritage site is rich with mountain hikes, sea-kayak tours, fjord-like lakes and weird rock formations. After soaking it up for three days, continue on the Viking Trail to its awe-inspiring endpoint: **L'Anse aux Meadows**. This was North America's first European settlement, where Leif Eriksson and his Viking pals homesteaded 1000 years ago. Poke around for a day before backtracking about two hours to **St Barbe**, where the ferry for Labrador departs. Reservations are wise for the daily, two-hour crossing.

And then you're in the Big Land. (Actually, the ferry lands in Québec, but more on that province later.) Turn your wheels northeast and head for **L'Anse Amour**, intriguing for its tall lighthouse and shipwreck-strewn hiking trail. Further along is **Red Bay**, Canada's newest World Heritage site, which preserves a massive, 16th-century whaling port. To really get away from it all, drive 90km onward to **Mary's Harbour** and spend the night on the offshore island that holds **Battle Harbour**, a restored village. After a few days in Labrador, it's time to head back. Before getting on the ferry, detour for a few hours down Rte 138 in Québec. It makes a beautiful drive past waterfalls and overlooks the crashing surf. Afterward, you'll need a couple of (long) days to retrace your path to Halifax.

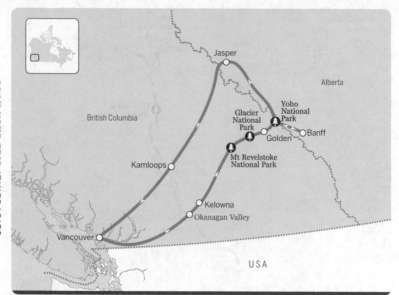

2 WEEKS The Rockies

Prepare to feast on a smorgasbord of scenic delights on this 2000km trek, which loops through British Columbia and Alberta.

Start with a couple of days in mountain-meets-the-sea **Vancouver**, where you'll be spoiled by urban hiking, biking and other activities, plus western Canada's best culinary scene. Make the wine pilgrimage east through rolling hills to the lake-studded **Okanagan Valley**, famous for its fruit orchards, crisp whites and bold reds. **Kelowna** makes a good sipping base in the area if you fancy tippling for a night or two.

Next it's time to get high in BC's Rocky Mountains. A trio of national parks pops up in quick succession, each providing plenty of 'ah'-inspiring vistas: **Mt Revelstoke** has a cool scenic drive and hikes; **Glacier** has 430 of its namesake ice fields; and **Yoho** is home to looming peaks and crashing waterfalls. **Golden** is a convenient base to take these in, with a decent array of tourist facilities, restaurants and stores.

Cross the border into Alberta, and park it in **Banff**. You won't be able to stop the clichés from flying forth. Grand! Majestic! Awe-inspiring! Allot plenty of time – at least three days – for hiking, paddling, gawking at glaciers and spotting grizzly bears (best done from a distance). Sapphire-blue Lake Louise is a must, with a pair of alpine-style teahouses to fuel your hikes with scones, beer and hot chocolate.

From Banff, the Icefields Pkwy (Hwy 93) parallels the Continental Divide for 230km to **Jasper**. Try to keep your eyes at least partially on the road as you drive by the humongous Columbia Icefield and its numerous fanning glaciers. Foaming waterfalls, dramatic mountains and the sudden dart of a bear (Or was that a moose? Or was it a wolverine?!) are also part of the journey. Jasper itself is bigger and less crowded than Banff, and offers superb hiking, horseback riding, rock climbing, mountain biking and rafting.

It's a shame to have to leave, but we must return to Vancouver. The Yellowhead Hwy (Hwy 5) plows south to **Kamloops**, a handy spot to spend the night before motoring back to the City of Glass.

Top: Upper Canada Village (p210), Ontario

Bottom: Confederation Bridge (p434), Prince Edward Island

MMACKILLOP/GETTY IMAGES ©

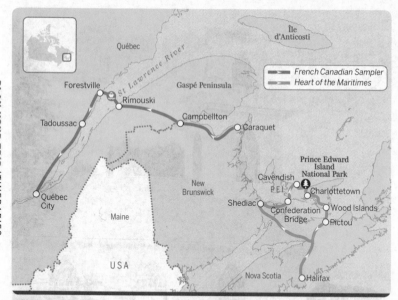

1 WEEK French Canadian Sampler

Get a taste of Gallic Canada on this 700km jaunt through New Brunswick and Québec.

Start in **Caraquet** and immerse yourself in Acadian culture at the historic sites and via local foods such as *pets de sœur* ('nun's farts' in English – try one to see if you can figure out why). If you visit in August, the fiddle-fueled Festival Acadien takes over the town.

Ramble east through **Campbellton** and cross into Québec. **Rimouski**, on the St Lawrence River, is your target. Explore its intriguing museums and delicious cafes, and day-trip east up the Gaspé Peninsula on Rte 132, where fluttering Acadian flags, tidy farming hamlets and rocky shores flash by.

From Rimouski, a ferry crosses the river to **Forestville**, from where you can head south to welcoming **Tadoussac**. It's all about whale-watching in this boho little town; Zodiacs motor out to see the blue whales that patrol the area.

Finish your trip in atmospheric **Québec City**. Check in at a cozy inn in the Old Town, wander its labyrinth of lanes and stop often to sip in the corner cafes.

1 WEEK Heart of the Maritimes

This 650km loop lassos the core of the Maritime provinces (Nova Scotia, New Brunswick and Prince Edward Island).

Eat and drink your way through **Halifax**, then make a break northwest for New Brunswick. Festive **Shediac** is home to the world's biggest lobster sculpture and – no surprise – the cooked version of the creature gets served in eateries all over town.

Barrel over the 12.9km **Confederation Bridge** that links New Brunswick to PEI and begin the pilgrimage to Anne's Land. Anne, of course, is the fictional red-headed orphan of Green Gables fame, and **Cavendish** is the wildly developed town that pays homage to her.

Continue the red theme by exploring the red sandstone bluffs at **Prince Edward Island National Park**; there's birdwatching, beach walking and swimming, too. Stop in PEI's compact, colonial capital **Charlottetown**, before taking the ferry from **Wood Islands** back to **Pictou** in Nova Scotia. You can stroll Pictou's boardwalk and, if you're lucky, the town might be hosting its First Nations Powwow. It's about two hours from here back to Halifax.

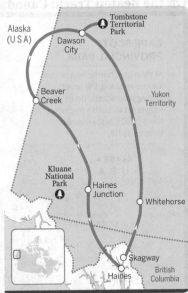

Bite of British Columbia
1 WEEK

You don't have to drive far to experience a range of heart-leaping landscapes in southern BC. Ocean, mountains, forests, islands – all are present and accounted for in roughly 550km.

Begin in **Vancouver** and take a couple of days to check out the indie shops, the foodie fare and the forested-seawall vistas of Stanley Park. On day three, drive to the **Tsawwassen ferry terminal** for the dreamy boat trip to Swartz Bay on Vancouver Island. Zip over to **Victoria**, spending an overnight stay exploring the picture-perfect capital and its historic buildings. On day four, drive north up the island on Hwy 1, stopping off at **Chemainus**, a former logging settlement that's reinvented itself as an art town. Continue north for a late lunch and an overnight in **Nanaimo**, then, next morning, catch the ferry back to the mainland's Horseshoe Bay terminal in **West Vancouver**.

From here, the Sea to Sky Hwy (Hwy 99) runs cliffside through formidable mountains to **Whistler**. The resort town has heaps of adrenaline activities and fun, ski-bum bars to occupy your final few days. It's 120km back to Vancouver.

Klondike Highway & Around
1 WEEK

Heed the call of the wild, and set your wheels for this epic roadway. Know it'll be a lot of driving for one week (approximately 30 hours), but the road *is* the main attraction of the trip.

Start in **Skagway**, Alaska, as the Klondike Hwy does. Soon you'll leave the cruise ships behind and enter the rugged land Jack London wrote so much about. Follow the road to lively **Whitehorse**, which has groovy arts and organic bakeries. From there continue north to offbeat **Dawson City**. Linger a few days and check out the gold rush historic sites, take a mine tour and blow a kiss to the dancing girls. Day-trip to **Tombstone Territorial Park** for its wide, steep grandeur.

Next, follow the Top of the World Hwy (Hwy 9) across mountaintops to the Alaskan border, and connect down through the US and onto the Alaska Hwy in the Yukon at **Beaver Creek**. The road between here and well-stocked **Haines Junction** is sublime, paralleling Kluane National Park and the St Elias Mountains. The gawk-worthy Haines Hwy rolls into **Haines**, Alaska, where your journey ends.

CAPE SCOTT PROVINCIAL PARK

At the rugged northern tip of Vancouver Island, this remote, logging-road-accessed park is not easy to get to, but it's (arguably) home to BC's best wilderness beaches. (p715)

UKKUSIKSALIK NATIONAL PARK

Nunavut's frontier on the frontier, this remote national park juxtaposes bleak tundra landscapes with an abundance of unusual wildlife spearheaded by polar bears. (p821)

BLACKFOOT CROSSING HISTORICAL PARK

The Siksika (Blackfoot) First Nations have opened a superb historical center on their reservation. There's a museum, plus guided tours and trails through quintessential prairie landscapes. (p620)

VEREGIN

A small prairie village and national historic site cataloging the history and culture of the Doukhobors, a religious sect (championed by Leo Tolstoy) who settled here after their exile from Russia in 1897. (p549)

Ellesmere Island
Axel Heiberg Island
Sverdrup Islands
Melville Island
Bathurst Island
Devon Island

Beaufort Sea

ALASKA
U S A
Anchorage
Dawson City
Tuktoyaktuk
Inuvik
Franklin Mountains
Great Bear Lake

YUKON TERRITORY
Whitehorse
Mackenzie Mountains
Mackenzie River
Nahanni National Park Reserve
NORTHWEST TERRITORIES
Fort Simpson
Yellowknife
Thelon River
Dubawent Lake

Juneau
Watson Lake
Great Slave Lake
UKKUSIKSALIK NATIONAL PARK
NUNAVUT

Spatsizi Plateau Provincial Wilderness Park
Prince Rupert
BRITISH COLUMBIA
Rocky Mountains
Wood Buffalo National Park
Lake Claire
Lake Athabasca
Churchill

Haida Gwaii
Prince George
ALBERTA
Jasper National Park
Athabasca R.
SASKATCHEWAN
Churchill R.
Nelson R.
Thompson

Jasper
Edmonton
Prince Albert
MANITOBA
Lake Winnipeg

CAPE SCOTT PROVINCIAL PARK
Vancouver Island
Nanaimo
Victoria
Vancouver
Banff National Park
Banff
Calgary
Saskatoon
VEREGIN
Riding Mountain National Park
Regina
Winnipeg

BLACKFOOT CROSSING HISTORICAL PARK
Swift Current

PACIFIC OCEAN
Seattle
Portland
WA
OR
ID
MT
UNITED STATES OF AMERICA
ND
MN

Minneapolis
IA

ST JOSEPH ISLAND

This wooded island, tucked away in the northwest corner of Lake Huron flush up against the US border, holds the fascinating ruins of an erstwhile British fort. (p170)

TORNGAT MOUNTAINS NATIONAL PARK

You'll have to fly or boat in to Labrador's chilly tip, home to polar bears and some of the highest peaks east of the Rockies. Local Inuit guides lead the way for otherworldly hiking and flightseeing. (p510)

GASPÉ PENINSULA

This is the windswept, rocky spot where Jacques Cartier landed in 1534, surrounded by steep limestone cliffs, pebble beaches, whales, seals and the ever-crashing sea. (p307)

TAYLOR HEAD PROVINCIAL PARK

This beachy park on Nova Scotia's undeveloped eastern shore juts out into the Atlantic, offering trails of wildflowers and beach grass and plenty of perfect sheltered coves for kayaking. (p389)

Stawamus Chief Provincial Park (p663), Squamish

Plan Your Trip
Scenic Drives & Train Trips

Canada is made for road-tripping, with a huge expanse of wild landscapes that have highways unfurling right through the good parts. Spiky mountains, ocean vistas, moose and Tim Hortons doughnut shops flash by. Even if you have just one day, you can take an incredible journey. With more time you can really roll.

HAILSHADOW/GETTY IMAGES ©

Need to Know

Best Experiences

➡ Dance at a traditional ceilidh on the Cabot Trail

➡ Visit a misty, Gothic castle on the Thousand Islands Parkway

➡ Hike and bike on the Sea to Sky Hwy

➡ See whales from shore on the Cabot Trail

➡ Gape at dazzling mountain views on the Rockies Rail Route

Major Sights

➡ Jasper National Park (Rockies Rail Route)

➡ The Chief (Sea to Sky Hwy)

➡ Thousand Islands National Park (Thousand Islands Pkwy)

➡ Cape Breton Highlands National Park (Cabot Trail)

Key Starting Points

➡ Vancouver or Whistler, British Columbia (Sea to Sky Hwy)

➡ Gananoque or Brockville, Ontario (Thousand Islands Pkwy)

➡ Chéticamp or Baddeck, Nova Scotia (Cabot Trail)

➡ Jasper, Alberta or Prince Rupert, British Columbia (Rockies Rail Route)

Sea to Sky Highway

Otherwise known as Hwy 99, this cliffside roadway offers a heart-leaping, humbling drive from Vancouver's ocean to Whistler's peaks. It begins at sea level, clasping the shore of Howe Sound, before twisting into the Coast Mountains and climbing through old-growth rainforests. You'll rise 670m (2200ft) during the 120km route, with plenty of opportunities for scenic vistas, waterfall gaping and outdoor activities along the way.

Highlights

In West Vancouver, not long after you cross the Lion's Gate Bridge, drop by Lighthouse Park to see the namesake structure along with shimmering sea views. Next you'll pass Horseshoe Bay, where ferries glide in and out for the 20-minute ride to Bowen Island – a rustically charming retreat populated by writers and artists.

Back on Hwy 99, about 30km north is the kid-friendly Britannia Mine Museum. Descend into the former copper pit for an underground train tour, followed by gold panning. About 6km onward you'll hear the rushing waters of Shannon Falls Provincial Park. Pull into the parking lot and stroll the 10-minute trail to British Columbia's third-highest waterfall, which gushes 335m down the rock face.

Continuing your drive, you'll soon see a sheer, 652m-high granite rock face looming ahead. It's called the Chief and it's the highlight of Stawamus Chief Provincial Park. Climbers go gaga over it. The town just beyond is Squamish, a haven for mountain bikers, hikers, kiteboarders and microbrew aficionados. It's a great spot to hang out for a day.

Nearby Brackendale attracts thousands of salmon-hungry eagles in winter. Hikers will want to pit stop at Garibaldi Provincial Park. Pull over at any of the designated trailheads to meander past scenic alpine meadows and breathtaking mountain views.

Back on the road, you'll be in Whistler before you know it. Canada's favorite ski resort combines a gabled, Christmas-card village with some jaw-dropping dual-mountain terrain. Skiers and snowboarders will be in their glory in winter, while summer is almost as busy with mountain bikers and hikers.

When to Go

This is a beautiful, well-maintained drive any time of year.

Time & Mileage

It's 120km from Vancouver to Whistler on the Sea to Sky Hwy. You can drive it in under two hours. But why hurry? It works best when stretched into a two- or three-day jaunt.

Resources

Tourism BC (www.hellobc.com/road-trips/sea-to-sky-highway-route) Driving directions for the route and stop-off points along the way.

Western Road & Rail

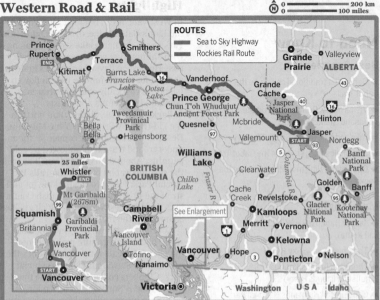

Mountain FM Radio (107.1) Provides handy traffic and road-condition updates en route.

Drive BC (www.drivebc.ca) Driving conditions and alerts.

Rockies Rail Route

Rail buffs consider the **Jasper to Prince Rupert** train a must-do journey. It traverses epic Canadian scenery, from the cloud-wrapped peaks and glacial streams in Alberta's Rockies to the hauntingly beautiful Pacific coast of British Columbia. In between a whole lot of pine, spruce and hemlock trees whiz by, as do rustic settlements, rivers and sawmills. But then – did you see it? A black bear loping trackside. And totem poles that mark an ancient indigenous village veiled by trees. And unbelievably turquoise lakes glistening in the valleys...

Highlights

The train – a retro silver bullet from the 1950s – chugs during daylight hours only, so you see the landscape in all its glory. (You spend the night in Prince George, a long-standing lumber town at roughly the halfway point.)

The route traces an old indigenous trading path. It climbs over the Yellowhead Pass at 1130m, and follows the Skeena River to the ocean. The train gently sways and fabled images flash by: the ancient red cedars of Chun T'oh Whudujut Park, daring bridges, deep canyons, dark tunnels and snowy mountains.

The trip starts and ends with a scenic bang. Jasper National Park has the white-dipped peaks and glistening glaciers you see on postcards, while Prince Rupert is a misty, unspoiled town with an intriguing indigenous heritage. Both are hot spots for adventure seekers.

When to Go

Mid-June to late September is the peak period, when 'touring class' tickets (which include tour guides, meals and access to the train carriage with a panoramic dome) are available. The rest of the year only 'economy class' seats are available.

Time & Mileage

The train runs year-round, departing three times a week on Wednesday, Friday and Sunday. The 1160km trip between Jasper

Britannia Mine Museum (p663), near Squamish

and Prince Rupert, including an overnight stay in Prince George, takes 33 hours.

Resources

Via Rail (www.viarail.ca) Prices and specifics on train routes.

Prince George Tourism (http://tourismpg.com) Lodging listings for your overnight stay.

Prince Rupert Tourism (www.visitprincerupert. com) For help planning onward adventures.

Thousand Islands Parkway

The Thousand Islands Pkwy rolls along a pastoral strip by the St Lawrence River, where a fog-cloaked constellation of 1800 islands floats between Kingston and Brockville, Ontario. The road offers dreamy vistas and dainty Victorian towns, where you can pull over to spend the night at an inn or take a boat ride through the isles, many of which hold rambling old mansions and castles. It's a mist-kissed trip into a slower, gentler era.

GO BIG OR GO HOME

Canada is a big place – and not every little town has a lot going for it. In a bid to attract tourists, communities across the country have created sights that may not be grand, but are certainly BIG, proving that size does matter to Canadians. Here's just a few of the World's Biggest that you might encounter:

Hockey Stick 62.5m (Duncan, BC)

Cuckoo Clock 6.7m (Kimberley, BC)

Pierogi 7.6m (Glendon, Alberta)

T-rex 26.2m (Drumheller, Alberta)

Mac the Moose 9.7m (Moose Jaw, Saskatchewan)

Nickel 9.1m (Sudbury, Ontario)

Axe 14.9 (Nackawic, NB)

Goose 6.7m (Wawa, Ontario)

Eastern Excursions

Highlights

Even though the islands start around Kingston – a pretty, historical town with loads of museums on everything from shipbuilding to penitentiaries – the scenic drive doesn't really pick up until the town of Gananoque, some 33km east along Hwy 401. That's where the parkway dips south of the highway and rolls into gorgeous territory.

Gananoque is the area's star for ambience, filled with quaint inns and manicured gardens. It's also the jump-off point for boat cruises through the islands, especially to Boldt Castle, a turreted, Gothic palace. Built by the gent who was the original proprietor of New York City's famous Waldorf Astoria Hotel, it's technically in the USA, so bring your passport.

Ivylea is 22km onward, where soaring bridges link Ontario to New York State over several islands. Halfway across there's an observation deck with killer views (mists permitting). If boat tours aren't your thing, you can keep driving over the bridges and reach Boldt Castle by car.

Back on the parkway, the road continues to snake along the river, with furry green islands dotting the water beside it. In 18km

you'll come to Mallorytown, the home base for Thousand Islands National Park. Twenty rugged, pine-laden islands are protected homes to lumbering turtles and peregrine falcons. It's a sublime area for backcountry camping and kayaking.

The parkway moseys on, hugging the river for a few more kilometers before rejoining Hwy 401 for the final approach into Brockville. This is another atmospheric town, with opulent 19th-century manors and vintage-looking streets where you can imagine the clip-clop sounds of carriage horses that used to ring through the area.

When to Go

June through September is peak season, when the weather is most pleasant. May and October are good shoulder-season times. Many boat companies and activity outfitters close between November and April.

Time & Mileage

The parkway runs for 40km between Gananoque and just north of Mallorytown. The islands themselves stretch from Kingston to Brockville (about 90km). With boat trips or detours into the USA, you'll need a full day, and it's well worthwhile to spend the night along the way.

Top: Boldt Castle (p206)

Bottom: Rockies Rail Route (p44) between Jasper and Prince Rupert

Resources

1000 Islands Gananoque Visitor Services Centre (www.1000islandstourism.com) Activity, restaurant and lodging info.

Cabot Trail

The Cabot Trail rings Cape Breton Island, Nova Scotia's lush tip. Driving it is a singular, brake-smoking journey. The road twists and climbs over coastal mountains, and around every bend something awesome reveals itself: ocean views, dramatic cliffs, breaching whales just offshore or moose snacking by the roadside. Celtic and Acadian communities dot the area, and their crazy-fiddlin' music vibrates through local pubs. Their unique foods get heaped on local plates, too, so loosen the belt for a full cultural immersion.

Highlights

Most road trippers start at Chéticamp, a deeply Acadian fishing community known for its crafty hooked rugs and lively music. It's also the gateway into Cape Breton Highlands National Park, where moose and bald eagle sightings are common. To stretch your legs, the park's hiking trails zigzag to spectacular, edge-of-cliff sea vistas. And how about some Acadian stewed chicken and potato pancakes with molasses? Chéticamp's eateries are prime for sampling.

Next along the roadway you'll reach Pleasant Bay, known for its whale-watching tours and Tibetan Buddhist monastery, where the monks give tours. Little fishing towns, world-famous golf courses, lighthouses and divine seafood houses pop up as you keep heading around the Cabot Trail. Keep your eyes peeled for pods of frolicking pilot whales, and the area around St Ann's is a center for Celtic arts. Baddeck is the unofficial end of the road, a beautiful spot to wind down and take in a traditional ceilidh (gathering for fiddling and dancing) in the town parish hall.

When to Go

July and August are peak season, with the best weather. September and October are good months to go, especially the latter for the Celtic Colours festival. Many places close from November through May.

Time & Mileage

The Cabot Trail winds for 300km around Cape Breton Island's northeastern tip. The highlights lie on the coastal portion between Chéticamp and Baddeck. You can do the drive in a day, but that's pushing it, as the road is narrow, hilly and slow-going most of the way.

Resources

Cabot Trail (www.cabottrail.travel) Lists accommodations, restaurants and events for towns along the way and has a useful interactive map.

Cape Breton Island (www.cbisland.com) Great resource covering the whole of the cape.

Tourism Nova Scotia (www.novascotia.com/explore/top-25/cabot-trail) Useful background info from the official source.

Cabot Trail through Cape Breton National Park

TOP ROAD TRIP ALBUMS

These Canadian artists – some old, some new, spanning genres and provinces – will provide the proper soundtrack for your trip. Load up your favorites, hit shuffle and 'keep the car running,' as the first group on our list sings.

➡ Arcade Fire *Neon Bible*
➡ Tragically Hip *Fully Completely*
➡ Neil Young *Massey Hall 1971*
➡ The New Pornographers *Mass Romantic*
➡ Drake *Hotline Bling*
➡ Rush *Moving Pictures*
➡ Great Big Sea *Road Rage*
➡ Feist *The Reminder*
➡ Bachman-Turner Overdrive *Bachman-Turner Overdrive II*
➡ Stompin' Tom Connors *Ballad of Stompin' Tom*
➡ Jill Barber *Chansons*
➡ Great Lake Swimmers *Where in the World Are You*
➡ Drake *Take Care*
➡ The Weeknd *Beauty Behind the Madness*
➡ Gilles Vigneault *Gilles Vigneault Collection*
➡ Les Soeurs Boulay *Le Poids des Confettis (The Weight of Confetti)*
➡ Joni Mitchell *Blue*

Plan Your Trip

Outdoor Activities

While the great Canadian outdoors is undeniably postcard pretty, the wilderness here has more than good looks, with activities ranging from hiking and kayaking to biking and climbing. There are countless operators across the country that can help you gear up and get out there.

Top Skiing

Whistler-Blackcomb, Whistler, British Columbia (BC)

North America's most comprehensive ski resort, with two mountains joined by a spectacular gondola ride.

Le Massif de Charlevoix, Baie St Paul, Québec

Spectacular views on this descent of nearly 800m overlooking the St Lawrence River.

Sunshine Village, Banff, Alberta

Expansive Continental Divide vistas to enjoy as you schuss or slalom down Sunshine's 100-plus runs.

Big White, Kelowna, BC

Top family skiing, beginner slopes and terrain park east of Kelowna.

Fernie Alpine Resort, Fernie, BC

Endless dumps of snow only a five-minute drive from town.

Revelstoke Mountain Resort, Revelstoke, BC

The greatest vertical drop at a ski resort in North America.

Skiing & Snowboarding

It seems like almost everyone in Canada was born to ski. Visitors will find some of the world's most renowned resorts here – British Columbia (BC), Alberta and Québec host the premier ones – but it's also worth asking the locals where they like to hit the slopes: for every big-time swanky resort, there are several smaller spots where the terrain and the welcome can be even better.

Québec boasts some big slopes – Le Massif de Charlevoix, 80km northeast of Québec City, has a vertical drop of 770m (2526ft) – located handily close to the cities. Most of these lower-elevation resorts, such as Mont-Tremblant, are a day's drive from Toronto and an hour from Québec City and Montréal. Ski areas in Québec's Eastern Townships offer renowned gladed runs that weave through a thinned forest.

Head west and you'll hit the big mountains and vast alpine terrains. Glide down gargantuan slopes at Whistler-Blackcomb, which has North America's highest vertical drop and most impressive terrain variation. You'll also slide through stunning postcard landscapes in the Canadian Rockies, especially at Sunshine in Banff National Park.

In BC's Okanagan Valley, resorts such as Apex and Big White boast good snow year after year. Snowpack ranges from 2m to 6m-plus, depending on how close the resort is to the Pacific Ocean. The deepest, driest snow in the world piles up in BC's Kootenay Region. Ski it at Nelson's Whitewater, Rossland's Red Mountain, Fernie Alpine Resort or Revelstoke Mountain Resort.

For nordic skiers, Canmore Nordic Centre (p589) in Alberta – host of the 1988 Winter Olympics – offers more than 65km of cross-country trails.

For further information and resources covering the national scene, check the website of the Canadian Ski Council (www.skicanada.org).

RESOURCES
....

Parks Canada (www.pc.gc.ca) National park action.

Alpine Club of Canada (www.alpine clubofcanada.ca) Climbing and mountaineering.

Canada Trails (www.canadatrails. ca) Hiking, biking and cross-country skiing.

Canadian Ski Council (www.skican ada.org) Skiing and snowboarding.

Paddle Canada (www.paddlecan ada.com) Kayaking and canoeing.

Hiking

You don't have to be a hiker to hike in Canada. While there are plenty of multiday jaunts for those who like tramping through the wilderness equipped only with a Swiss Army knife, there are also innumerable opportunities for those who prefer a gentle stroll around a lake with a pub at the end.

The country's hiking capital is Banff National Park, crisscrossed with stupefying vistas accessible to both hard and soft eco-adventurers. Near Lake Louise, for example, you can march through dense spruce and pine forests, then ascend into alpine meadows carpeted with wildflowers and surrounded by rugged glaciers and azure lakes. Also in the Rockies region, Wilcox Ridge and Parker Ridge offer breathtaking glacier views.

In BC's provincial parks system (www. bcparks.ca), you'll have a choice of more than 100 parks, each with distinct landscapes to hike through: check out Garibaldi Park's landscape of ancient volcanoes (not far from Whistler) and Mt Robson Park's popular Berg Lake alpine trail. Vancouver's North Shore is home to the Grouse Grind, a steep forest hike that's also known as 'Mother Nature's Stairmaster.' Across the water in Vancouver Island's Pacific Rim Park, the lush 75km West Coast Trail (www.westcoasttrail.com) is undoubtedly one of the country's most breathtaking, combining traditional First Nations trails and life-saving routes used by shipwreck survivors.

Out east, awe-inspiring trails pattern the landscape. In southern Ontario, the Bruce Trail (www.brucetrail.org) tracks from Niagara Falls to Tobermory. It's the oldest and longest continuous footpath in Canada and spans more than 850km. Though portions are near cities such as Hamilton and Toronto, it's surprisingly serene. Cape Breton Highlands National Park offers exquisite hiking over stark, dramatic coastline. Newfoundland's trails make for fantastic shoreline hiking and often provide whale views. The East Coast Trail (www.eastcoasttrail.ca) on the Avalon Peninsula is particularly renowned for its vistas, and Skerwink Trail in eastern Newfoundland has been named one of the best walks in North America.

And don't forget the cities. Canada's major metropolises offer some great urban hikes, an ideal way to get to know the communities you're visiting. Slip into your runners for a stroll (or a jog) with the locals in Montréal's Parc du Mont Royal or in Vancouver's gemlike Stanley Park, where the idyllic seawall winds alongside towering trees and lapping ocean.

Top Day Hikes

Lake Louise, Banff, Alberta Hike to historic Lake Agnes Teahouse, then climb the Big Beehive for dazzling panoramic views.

Skyline Trail, Cape Breton Highlands, Nova Scotia The Cabot Trail's classic ridge hike offers majestic vistas of sea and mountain.

Parker Ridge, Jasper, Alberta An hour-long uphill jaunt into Jasper's backcountry brings you face-to-face with the magnificent Saskatchewan Glacier.

GROGL/SHUTTERSTOCK ©

Top: Rock climbing in Squamish (p54), British Columbia

Bottom: Paddling on the Nahanni River, Northwest Territories

Stanley Park, Vancouver, BC Forested seawall in the watery heart of one of the world's greenest cities.

Bruce Trail, Ontario From Niagara-on-the-Lake's vineyards to Tobermory's shimmering waters, the epic Bruce Trail inspires and delights.

Othello Tunnels, Hope, BC Walk the old tunnels and bridges of the Kettle Valley Rail Trail.

Sea to Sky Trail, Squamish, BC An adventurous climb to Squamish's top cable-car station, with the promise of cold drinks and poutine on top.

Kayaking & Canoeing

The Canadian Arctic, kayaking's motherland, still remains one of its special places: cruise the polar fjords of Ellesmere Island and watch narwhals and walruses during the short summer. In the Yukon, paddle down the Yukon River from Whitehorse and spot bald eagles. Further south, slide silently past ancient forests and totem poles in BC's Gwaii Haanas National Park Reserve, or watch orcas breaching in the province's Johnstone Strait. The east coast has sea kayaking galore: the seaside adjunct of Kejimkujik National Park is a superb place to paddle. Paddlers in Witless Bay or Gros Morne, Newfoundland, often glide alongside whales.

If you're on a tight schedule and don't have time for multiday odysseys, there are plenty of more accessible ways to get your kayaking fix. Big cities such as BC's Vancouver and Victoria offer tours and lessons near town, while the province's Sunshine Coast and Salt Spring Island have crenulated coastlines combined with tranquil sea inlets.

As old as kayaking, and equally as Canadian, is the canoe. Experienced paddlers can strike out on one of 33 Canadian Heritage Rivers (www.chrs.ca). Some of the best include the Northwest Territories' South Nahanni River (near Fort Simpson) and Ontario's French River (near Sudbury).

Top Places to Paddle

South Nahanni River, Northwest Territories The majestic center of Nahanni National Park, pristine and beautiful and everything paddling should be.

Gros Morne National Park, Newfoundland Paddle in a World Heritage–designated site, the second largest in Canada.

Telegraph Cove, Vancouver Island, BC Dip a paddle into the calm waters of this former fishing village, where kayak trips double as wildlife-watching excursions.

Gwaii Haanas National Park Reserve, BC Extraordinary wilderness experiences await paddling around Haida Gwaii.

Killarney Provincial Park, Ontario Sea kayaking and paddling in backcountry so beautiful that artists petitioned to make it a park.

Kejimkujik Seaside Adjunct, Nova Scotia As Mi'kmaw people have known for centuries, this coastal park is best explored by kayak or canoe.

Yukon River, YT Paddle for half a day or two weeks downriver from Whitehorse.

Mountain Biking & Cycling

Mountain biking is a big deal in Canada. While cycling enthusiasts in Europe might be into trundling around town or along a gentle riverside trail, in Canada you're more likely to find them hurtling down a mountainside covered in mud. Given the landscape, of course, it was just a matter of time before the wheels went off-road here.

If you need to ease yourself in, start gently with BC's Kettle Valley Rail Trail (www.kettlevalleyrailway.ca), near Kelowna. This dramatic segment of converted railway barrels across picturesque wooden trestle bridges and through canyon tunnels.

Looking for more of an adrenaline rush? In Vancouver's North Shore area, you'll be riding on much narrower and steeper trestles. Birthplace of freeride mountain biking (which combines downhill and dirt jumping), this area offers some unique innovations: elevated bridges, log rides and skinny planks that loft over the wet undergrowth. It's a similar story up at Whistler, where the melted ski slopes are transformed into a summertime bike park that draws thousands every year – especially during the annual Crankworx Mountain Bike Festival (www.crankworx.com/whistler) in August.

A rising star in Canada's mountain biking scene is the extensive trail network located a mere pedal-turn from the village of Cumberland on Vancouver Island. The network is run and maintained by a local community group called the United Riders of Cumberland (www.unitedridersofcumberland.com)

For road touring, Canada's east coast, with more small towns and less emptiness, is a fantastic place to pedal, either as a single-day road ride or a multiday trip. Circle Québec's Lac St-Jean; try any part of the 4000km Route Verte (www.routeverte.com), the longest network of bicycle paths in the Americas; or follow Prince Edward Island's bucolic red roads and its Confederation Trail (www.tourismpei.com/pei-cycling).

Also worthwhile is the 48km Corridor du Littoral (p277), starting southwest of Québec City at Cap-Rouge and extending northeast via the Old Lower Town to Montmorency Falls. The heart of the path is the Promenade Samuel-de-Champlain, an especially beautiful 2.5km section.

Top Biking

Confederation Trail, Prince Edward Island (PEI) Cruise forests, farmland, fields and beautiful coastline along the course of PEI's decommissioned railway.

Kettle Valley Rail Trail, Kelowna, BC Ride the train trestles and cool, eerie tunnels of lovely Myra Canyon near Kelowna.

North Shore, Vancouver, BC Great trails for all experience levels amid the spectacular backdrop of the Pacific rainforest.

Route Verte, Québec The longest chain of biking trails in North America, with off-road, mountain and paved options. What's not to like?

Cumberland, Vancouver Island, BC A relatively new attraction for cyclists, this community-run bike network is a pedal-turn from Cumberland's funky main street.

Rock Climbing & Mountaineering

All those inviting crags you've spotted on your trip are an indication that Canada is a major climbing capital, ideal for both short sport climbs and epic big-wall ascents.

BC's Squamish region, located between Vancouver and Whistler, is a climbing center, with dozens of accessible (and not so accessible) cracks, faces, arêtes and overhangs. Tap into the scene via **Squamish Rock Guides** (☑604-892-7816; www.squamishrockguides.com; guided rock climbs half-day/day from $100/140). Canmore, near Banff, is another ideal destination for rock climbers, no matter what your skill level. For the adventure of a lifetime, the Northwest Territories' Cirque of the Unclimbables is certainly near the top of the list. If your trip takes you out east instead, Ontario's favorite climbing havens dot the Bruce Peninsula.

If mountaineering is more your thing, the Rockies are the recommended first stop. Yamnuska (www.yamnuska.com) is one company that offers ice climbing, ski mountaineering and avalanche training in the region. The Matterhorn of Canada is BC's Mt Assiniboine, located between the Kootenay and Banff National Parks. Other western classics include Alberta's Mt Edith Cavell, in Jasper; BC's Mt Robson and Sir Donald in the Rockies; and Garibaldi Peak, in Garibaldi Provincial Park, near Whistler. If you need a guide, check in with the excellent Alpine Club of Canada (www.alpineclubofcanada.ca).

HOCKEY: THE NATIONAL PASTIME

Canadians aren't fooling around when it comes to hockey. They play hard and well and if they're not playing, they cheer and catcall like they mean it.

Grassroots hockey, aka pond hockey, takes place in communities across the country every night on a frozen surface. All you need is a puck, a hockey stick and a few friends to live the dream.

If you'd rather watch than play, Vancouver, Edmonton, Calgary, Toronto, Ottawa, Winnipeg and Montréal all have NHL (www.nhl.com) teams who skate tough and lose the odd tooth. Minor pro teams and junior hockey clubs fill many more arenas with rabid fans; check the Canadian Hockey League (www.chl.ca) and American Hockey League (www.theahl.com) for local stick wielders.

Top Climbs

The Chief, Squamish, BC Attempt multiple climbs on the Chief's sheer rock wall or hike up a steep trail around the back for some impressive views.

Canmore, Alberta Scale Mt Rundle's iconic cliffs or the crags above Grassi Lakes in Canada's climbing capital.

Pont-Rouge, Québec Challenge yourself on often soft, sometimes crumbling, ice pillars in the Jacques-Cartier River.

Skaha Bluffs, Okanagan Valley, BC Choose from a near-bewildering number (more than 400!) of bolted routes for all experience levels near Penticton.

Bugaboo Spire, near Golden, BC Part of beautiful Bugaboo Provincial Park, this climb has stunning vistas above glaciers and steep, hard granite walls.

Fishing

Built on its indigenous and pioneer past, Canada has a strong tradition of fishing and you can expect to come across plenty of opportunities to hook walleye, pike, rainbow or lake trout on your travels. Among the best fishing holes to head for are Lunenburg in Nova Scotia and the Miramichi River in New Brunswick. And while salmon are the usual draw on the Pacific coastline, hopping aboard a local vessel for some sea fishing off Haida Gwaii can deliver the kind of giant catches you'll be bragging about for years to come.

Surfing & Windsurfing

If you're aiming to become a beach bum on your Canada trip, head to the wild west coast of BC's Vancouver Island and hang out on the beaches around Tofino. Surfing schools and gear-rental operations stud this region and you'll have an awesome time riding the swells (or just watching everyone else as you stretch out on the sand). Backed by verdant rainforest, it's an idyllic spot to spend some time.

June to September is the height of the season here, but serious surfers also like to drop by in winter to face down the lashing waves. Check Surfing Vancouver Island (www.surfingvancouverisland.com) for a taste of what to expect.

Some 6000km away, the east coast of Nova Scotia can also dish out some formidable swells. The US south coast's hurricane season (August to November) brings Canadians steep fast breaks, snappy right and left point breaks, and offshore reef and shoal breaks in areas such as Lawrencetown, just outside Halifax, as well as across the entire South Shore region. There are also a couple of surf schools here. SANS (Surfing Association of Nova Scotia; www.surfns.com) is a good place to start your research on the swells.

Windsurfers set their sails for Howe Sound in Squamish, BC, and for Québec's Îles de la Madeleine (Magdalen Islands), a small chain in the Gulf of St Lawrence.

Top Places to Surf & Windsurf

Tofino, Vancouver Island, BC Canada's surfing capital harnesses the wild white-capped waves of Vancouver Island's beautiful and broad western beaches.

Lawrencetown, Nova Scotia Didn't know you could surf in Nova Scotia? This beach east of Halifax will set you straight, though even in summer the water temperatures will chill you.

Îles de la Madeleine (Magdalen Islands), Québec Great breezes and beautiful island scenery make this stringy archipelago a top spot for windsurfing in the Gulf of St Lawrence.

Howe Sound, Squamish, BC Launch off wind-licked Squamish Spit into the breezy waters of this triangular-mountain-rimmed fjord for some of BC's best windsurfing.

Plan Your Trip
Family Travel

Deciding where to go with your kids in Canada can be a daunting decision. Mountains, prairies, beaches and easygoing cities are strewn across six time zones. Luckily, between wildlife sightings, cowboy encounters, hands-on pirate history, hunting for dinosaur fossils and ice-skating on mountain lakes, it's impossible to make a bad choice.

Best Regions for Kids

Drumheller
No kid on the planet can be ho-hum about seeing T-rex and his friends brought vividly to life, or yawn about finding real-life dino fossils in the multicolored clay hills.

Vancouver
Sandwiched between sea and mountains, build a sandcastle one day and go snowboarding the next while enjoying the comforts of the city.

Canadian Rockies
Hike, ski, camp or snowshoe while looking out for moose, bear, elk and whistling marmot.

Montréal
Get a taste of Québécois *bonheur* in the historic streets, year-round ice-skating, inner-city beach and the Biôdome full of critters.

Maritime Provinces
Climb a lighthouse, sail on a pirate ship, whale-watch and beach hop in summer; see the trees turn red, orange and gold in fall.

Canada for Kids

As if seeing moose, eagles and whales or running around in the snow, on the beach or in the woods all day isn't fun enough, everywhere you turn, those crafty Canadians have cooked up some hands-on learning experience, living history lesson or child-oriented theater.

Outdoor Activities

Canada is all about open spaces, fresh air, rivers, lakes and mountains, snow, sand and wildlife. Kids are often admitted free or at reduced prices.

➡ Most Canadian cities are endowed with parks and promenades set up for even the tiniest **cyclists**, but finding a child-sized bike rental can be hit or miss. For a cycling-oriented holiday, try the mostly flat Confederation Trail, which traverses bucolic Prince Edward Island, or the traffic-free Kettle Valley Trail (KVR; British Columbia) that's one of the least strenuous stretches of the Trans Canada Trail. You will likely want to bring along your child's bike helmet.

➡ The Canadian National Park system contains easy strolls as well as longer **hiking trails** that teens might enjoy. **Horseback riding** is widely on offer and can be especially fun in cowboy country around Calgary.

➡ Most lake areas offer **canoe** rentals perfect for leisurely family outings, while seafront regions are packed with **kayak** outfits. For a bigger adrenaline rush for older kids, try **white-water rafting** or **'playboating'** spots, particularly on the Ottawa River in Beechburg.

➡ There are plenty of **fishing** lodges, but you'd be surprised at how lucky you can get just casting into any lake or river. Likewise, try **clamming** (Prince Edward Island and British Columbia are tops) – ask locals where to go and bring a shovel and a bucket.

➡ On the coasts and the Bay of Fundy, **whale-watching** can be thrilling, but be prepared with seasickness pills, extra snacks, sunscreen and warm clothes.

➡ The tiny summer waves on the east and west coast are an excellent way to start learning to **surf**; rent a board or wet suit or take a class.

➡ Heading out **skiing** or **snowboarding** is an obvious family choice. Children under six often ski for free, ages six to 12 usually pay around 12% to 50% of the adult price and ages 12 to 18 pay a little more, 33% to 75% of the adult price. Then, of course, there's also **ice-skating**, **sledding** and **snowshoeing**.

Museums & Monuments

Most large Canadian cities have science museums that specialize in hands-on activities, while at historic sites strewn across the country, costumed thespians get you right into the period and often give demonstrations of everything from blacksmithing to cooking. At some of these places there are also puppet or theatrical performances for children and other events, such as hayrides. Teens usually enjoy these sites as well, since they are often large and diverse enough for self-exploration and they touch on subjects studied at school.

Children's Highlights

Lessons in History

Dinosaurs Royal Tyrrell Museum of Palaeontology, Drumheller (Alberta), Dinosaur National Park (Alberta)

Indigenous Peoples Haida Gwaii (British Columbia), Head-Smashed-In Buffalo Jump World Heritage site (Alberta), Indigenous Experiences (Ottawa), Wanuskewin Heritage Park (Saskatchewan), Huronia Museum (Ontario)

European Colonization L'Anse aux Meadows (Newfoundland), Louisbourg National Historic Site (Nova Scotia), Fort William Historical Park (Ontario), Fort Edmonton (Alberta), Ste-Marie among the Hurons (Ontario), Fort Langley (southern BC)

Winter Wonderlands

Winter Carnivals Québec City Winter Carnival, Cavalcade of Lights (Toronto), Vancouver Festival of Lights

Ice-skating Rideau Canal (Ottawa), Lake Louise (Alberta), Harbourfront Centre (Toronto), Lac des Castors (Montréal)

Skiing, Snowboarding & Sledding Whistler-Blackcomb (British Columbia), Norquay (Banff), Mont-Ste-Anne (Québec)

Dogsledding Yellowknife (Northwest Territories), Iqaluit (Nunavut)

Critters of the Great North

Moose Nearly everywhere but especially Algonquin National Park (Eastern Ontario), Gros Morne National Park (Newfoundland), the Maligne Lake area in Jasper National Park (Alberta)

Polar Bears Churchill (Manitoba)

Whales & Orcas Vancouver Island (British Columbia), Québec, Bay of Fundy (New Brunswick and Nova Scotia), Newfoundland

Bald Eagles Brackendale (British Columbia), Jasper and Banff (Alberta), southern Vancouver Island (British Columbia), Cape Breton Island (Nova Scotia)

Wet & Wild

Beaches Prince Edward Island, British Columbia

Surfing Lawrencetown Beach (Nova Scotia), Tofino (British Columbia)

Kayaking Salt Spring (British Columbia), Georgian Bay (Ontario)

Canoeing Algonquin National Park (Ontario), Bowron Lakes (British Columbia), Kejimkujik National Park (Nova Scotia)

Fishing Lunenburg, Nova Scotia (lobster), Point Prim, Prince Edward Island (clams), Northern Saskatchewan (freshwater fish), Maritime Provinces (deep-sea fish)

Snorkeling Fathom Five National Marine Park (Ontario)

Top: Canada's Wonderland (p89), Toronto

Bottom: Canoeing in Alberta

HERO IMAGES/GETTY IMAGES ©

Urban Adventures

Vancouver's outside action Capilano Suspension Bridge Park, Stanley Park

Ottawa's museum mission Canada Agricultural Museum, Museum of Nature, Science & Technology Museum, Canadian Museum of History

Toronto's heights & depths CN Tower to the subterranean corridors connecting downtown

Montréal's culture infusion Old Montréal, Little Italy

Halifax's Titanic connection Maritime Museum of the Atlantic, *Titanic* graveyards

Saskatchewan's discoveries Wonderhub Children's Discovery Museum, Saskatoon

Theme Park Delights

Canada's Wonderland (www.canadaswonderland.com) Amusement and water park, Toronto

Galaxy Land (www.wem.ca/play/attractions/galaxyland) World's largest indoor amusement park, Edmonton

La Ronde (www.laronde.com) Amusement park, Montréal

Calaway Park (www.calawaypark.com) Amusement park and campground, Calgary

Playland (www.pne.ca/playland) Oldest amusement park in Canada, Vancouver

Planning

Traveling around Canada with the tots can be child's play. Lonely Planet's *Travel with Children* offers a wealth of tips and tricks. The website **Travel For Kids** (http://travelforkids.com) is another good, general resource.

When to Go

Festivals fill Canadian calendars year-round and most are very family-oriented. Summer is the most festival-heavy time, with lots of outdoor get-togethers from jazz festivals to rodeos. Fall is a lovely time to visit Canada if you can arrange it around your children's school schedule. At this time the trees are changing colors, daytime temperatures are still manageably warm and most of the crowds have gone.

The best time for fresh snow and snow sports is January to April. Santa Claus

parades usually kick off the holiday season in November and early December. Around the same time or just after, you can expect fireworks, parades and Christmas tree lightings at the festivals of light.

Accommodations

Hotels and motels commonly have rooms with two double beds. Even those that don't have enough beds may bring in rollaways or cots, usually for a small extra charge. Some properties offer 'kids stay free' promotions, while others (particularly B&Bs) may not accept children. Ask when booking.

Another good option is cabins, which are usually rented out by the week and come with kitchens, any number of bedrooms, and other perks such as barbecues. You can find full listings with each province's visitors' guides online and in print (order them for free at each province's tourism website).

Camping is huge in Canada and many campgrounds also offer rustic cabins (bring your own bedding) that sometimes have kitchens, fire pits or barbecues. Some grounds offer exotic options such as tipis or yurts, while others have swimming pools or mini-golf, or might be located on a lake. Bring bug spray.

Eating Out

Everywhere you turn in Canada you'll find fast food and fried fare. If you're health-conscious, a hurdle can be finding more wholesome options in small towns; however, you can usually find at least one cafe with sandwiches and wraps or you can self-cater. Fortunately, there are plenty of cabin- and family-suite-style options that allow you to cook for yourself, and some B&Bs will also let you cook. In cities, every restaurant option is available from vegan to steakhouses.

EXTRAS BY AGE

Babies & Toddlers

➡ Kids' car seats: car-hire companies rent them for high rates; in Canada babies need a rear-facing infant safety seat, while children under 18kg (40lb) must be in a forward-facing seat.

➡ A front or back sling for baby and toddler if you're planning on hiking and a stroller for city jaunts (nearly everywhere is stroller-accessible).

➡ Sandcastle- or snowman-making tools.

Six to 12 years

➡ Kids' car seats: children between 18kg (40lb) and 36kg (80lb) should have a booster seat. Seat belts can be used as soon as a child is either 36kg, 145cm (4ft 9in) tall or eight years old.

➡ Binoculars for young explorers to zoom in on wildlife.

➡ A bear bell for hikes.

➡ Field guides about Canada's flora and fauna.

➡ A camera to inject newfound fun into 'boring' grown-up sights and walks.

➡ Kite (for beaches).

➡ Bike helmet that fits well.

Teens

➡ Canada-related iPhone or Android apps.

➡ Canada-related novels (find a list of Young Adult Canadian Book Award winners at www.cla.ca).

➡ French-Canadian phrasebook or translation app.

Easy-to-find Canadian foods your kids will love if you let them include poutine (French fries topped with brown gravy and cheese curds), fish and chips, Montréal-style bagels (wood-fired, dense and slightly sweet), pancakes or French toast with maple syrup, bear-claw doughnuts, butter tarts, and Nanaimo bars (crumb crust topped with custard and then melted chocolate). You may all gain a few kilos on this trip!

Most Canadian restaurants offer booster seats and child-friendly servers as soon as you steer your progeny through the door. However, families with even the most well-behaved children may not feel comfortable at fine-dining establishments.

What to Pack

Canada is very family-friendly so anything you forget can probably be purchased in-country. Breastfeeding in public is legal and tolerated, although most women are discreet about it. Most facilities can accommodate a child's needs; public toilets usually have diaper-changing tables.

What you will need is layered clothing for everyone, as it can get spontaneously cool even during the summer months. Sunscreen is a must – you'd be surprised how much you can burn on the greyest of days – as are rain gear and bug spray. It's also a good idea to bring activities for lengthy car rides, since getting anywhere in Canada can involve very long distances.

Regions at a Glance

You can't go wrong in Canada, where each region has eye-catching landscapes and a slew of activities to match. Ontario, Québec and British Columbia (BC) – the most populated provinces – are the ones with the most going on. In addition to outdoor action, they hold Canada's largest cities – Toronto, Montréal and Vancouver – with multicultural museums, sophisticated eateries and wee-hours nightlife. Alberta booms in the Rockies with parks and oil-rich towns, while Manitoba and Saskatchewan in the Plains hold big wildlife and arty surprises. The salty Atlantic provinces are tops for seafood munching and whale-watching. And the far north is the place to lose the crowds (and roads) and get totally off the beaten path.

Ontario

Cuisine
Parks
Culture

Farms & Vineyards

At a geological and climactic nexus, Ontario is ripe with agriculture and viticulture. The province's wines are internationally recognized, pairing well with the delicious farm-to-table fare.

Fresh Air

If you're looking for a simple stroll, a multiday backpacking trip or some time on the water, Ontario supplies everything from green city spaces to massive provincial parks. This is the place to bring your binoculars and break in your hiking boots.

Museums

From tiny sports-memorabilia shrines to world-class collections of ancient artifacts and geological remnants, Ontario offers myriad museums in Ottawa, Toronto and beyond.

p66

Québec

Cuisine
Winter Sports
Architecture

Joie de Vivre

Imagine sipping a *café au lait* and eating a buttery croissant on a sidewalk terrace while the murmurs of Canadian French waft through the air. It's easy to be charmed by the Québécois way of life when fine wines and superb food play such a large role.

Snowy Fun

Most of the undulating Laurentians offer skiing and snowboarding opportunities, but it's the French panache and small-town feel of Mont-Tremblant in particular that draws the international crowds.

Historic Style

Nowhere are the vestiges of Canada's colonial past more apparent than in the cobbled streets and grandiose facades of Old Montréal and within the fortified city walls of Québec City's Old Town.

p227

Nova Scotia

Culture
Nature Activities
History

Cultural Mishmash

Tartan shops, French-speaking villages and First Nations communities are all within kilometers of each other, rendering the province one big cultural mosaic.

Coves, Cliffs & Tides

Coastal coves rich in flora and fauna beg you to go paddling. Cape Breton Island's vertiginous cliffs and the Fundy Coast with its mega-high tides are gorgeous areas for adventure and wildlife.

Time Warp

Nova Scotians don't just preserve their historical vestiges, they get in period costume and reenact old-time activities from lace making to blacksmithing, letting you experience the scene as it was hundreds of years ago.

p330

New Brunswick

Canoeing
Fishing
Wildlife

Paddling Culture

From the tranquil Nictau and Nepisiguit chains of lakes to the Tobique River, New Brunswick is absolutely tops for canoeing, surely the most Canadian of activities. You can even meet the artisans who make canoes.

Tie your Flies

New Brunswick's famed rivers are the kind anglers dream of – where they fly-cast into the current and, within minutes, reel in a fat silvery salmon or speckled trout.

Puffin Lovin'

Whether you're a hardcore birdwatcher or you just want to glimpse a moose, New Brunswick's got plenty of animal action to go around. Your best bet: observing rare Atlantic puffin on desolate Machias Seal Island.

p391

Prince Edward Island

Culture
Cuisine
Beaches

It's All About Anne

PEI's culture is intrinsically linked to the novel *Anne of Green Gables* and scattered with sights relating directly to the book and the life of its author, Lucy Maud Montgomery.

Lobsters & Spuds

The province vies with Idaho as potato capital of the Americas. Seek out town halls serving supersized suppers of the island's famous lobster – alongside PEI spud salad!

White & Pink Sands

PEI showcases sienna beach flats topped by red-and-white lighthouses, cream-colored dunes and stretches of white sand that 'sing' when you walk on them.

p431

Newfoundland & Labrador

Seascapes
Culture
History

Great Big Sea

'There's one!' someone shouts, and sure enough, a big, barnacled humpback steams through the water, with a backdrop of hulking icebergs. Whether you're hiking alongshore or out in a boat, Newfoundland's sea delivers.

Strange Brew

The brogue is vaguely Irish and the slang indecipherable. Plates arrive with cod tongues, bakeapple jam and figgy duff. This place is so offbeat it even has its own time zone: a *half*-hour ahead of the mainland.

Viking Vestiges

Feel the Vikings' edge-of-the-world isolation at L'Anse aux Meadows, Leif Eriksson's 1000-year-old settlement set on a bare, forlorn sweep of land.

p459

Manitoba

Wildlife
Open Spaces
Culture

Polar Bears & Whales

Polar bears prowling the ice: that's what subarctic Churchill is all about. The hemisphere's biggest predators turn up by the hundreds in the fall. Out on the water in summer, expect to see scores of beluga whales.

Muskeg & Wheat

Drive through the south and you'll be mesmerized by kilometer after kilometer of wheat, punctuated by giant grain elevators. In the subarctic north, a year-round evergreen swath grows in the rich muskeg – think marshy soil from eons of plants.

Oh Winnipeg!

This surprising oasis of world-class museums and galleries, great dining, fun nightlife, craft beer and hip culture rises up from the prairies around it.

p512

Saskatchewan

Wildlife
History
Nightlife

Moose & Critters

Although remote, the web of back roads that stretch across this huge province are not empty. Saskatchewan is alive with Canada's iconic critters, especially moose, which love roadside salt pools.

Revolution Rocks

In 1885 Louis Riel fought the law and, while the law won, he and a band of followers almost beat the army at Batoche. The indigenous town declared independence after the national government broke treaties.

The Good Twins

Regina and Saskatoon both offer plenty to do after dark. Inventive restaurants using the province's produce combine with pubs serving regional microbrews.

p534

Alberta

Activities
History
Festivals

National Park Hiking

Banff and Jasper parks are filled with wildlife, glacial lakes and hundreds of miles of trails. If you're ever going to fulfill your latent hiking ambitions, this is the place to do it.

Dinosaurs & Fossils

In the Badlands, seemingly endless prairies cut majestically away into coulees and canyons that take you back in time. Fossils poke out of painted cliff sides, and Drumheller's Royal Tyrrell Museum brings dinosaurs to life.

Fringe Theater

Edinburgh invented it, but Edmonton has taken the concept of 'alternative theater' and given it a Canadian twist. At the International Fringe Festival, cutting-edge performers offer comedy, satire and weirdness.

p558

British Columbia

Landscapes
Cuisine
Wildlife

Breathtaking Vistas

From jaw-dropping mountains and multi-fjorded coastlines to dense old-growth forest and lush islands, BC is a vista-packed idyll for landscape lovers.

Dine-around Delights

Local flavors are a foodie focus here, from North America's best Asian dining scene to a cornucopia of regional seafood and produce – accompanied, of course, by a BC wine or microbrewery beer.

Wildlife Wonderland

The Inside Passage is alive. Hop a ferry along the coast and stay glued to the deck for orca, whale, seal and birdlife sightings. On shore, the entire cast of Canadian animal characters is here, especially huge grizzlies in the north.

p631

Yukon Territory

Wildlife
Parks
History

Bears, Oh My!

The Alaska Hwy cuts across the lower Yukon on its twisting journey to its namesake state. But stop to admire the wildlife and you may not bother reaching your destination. Keep your eyes peeled for bear, moose, wolf and elk.

Unimaginable Beauty

Kluane National Park is a Unesco-recognized wilderness of glaciers cleaving through granite peaks. You'll feel minute surrounded by all this giant beauty.

Gold!

The Klondike gold rush of 1898 still shapes the Yukon with its spirited sense of adventure. Paddle your way to Dawson City, a time-capsule town that's almost as lively now as then.

p767

Northwest Territories

Northern Lights
Kayaking
Winter Sports

Nocturnal Tours

Fantastically remote and light-pollution-free, NWT is prime for seeing the green-draped flickerings of the aurora borealis. Outfitters take you far into the night, with heated viewing areas to fend off the chill.

Remote Paddling

Nahanni National Park is a Unesco World Heritage site that offers some of the most spectacular river kayaking in Canada. With no road access, it is a true back-of-beyond adventure.

Dogsledding

With zero ski resorts, NWT specializes in more esoteric winter activities, such as dogsledding. This traditional form of arctic transportation is a thrilling way to travel.

p791

Nunavut

Wildlife
Culture
Parks

Arctic Outfitters

Yes, animals live up here, it's just that they're not easy to spot. Hook up with a professional arctic outfitter for rare viewings of polar bear, caribou, walrus, narwhals and musk oxen.

Indigenous Art

Genuine Inuit art is one of the region's biggest draws. Look for stone and bone carvings, prints, tapestries and more in Cape Dorset, Pangnirtung and Iqaluit.

Untamed Wilderness

With each of them having annual visitation numbers that rarely hit three figures, Nunavut's four national parks guarantee an extreme wilderness experience. Sky-high costs are tempered by the moonlike emptiness of the incredible terrain.

p811

On the Road

Ontario

Best Places to Eat

➡ Lee (p101)

➡ Beckta Dining & Wine Bar (p222)

➡ Buoys Eatery (p169)

➡ Pan Chancho (p204)

➡ Tomlin (p184)

Best Places to Stay

➡ Clarence Park (p94)

➡ Taboo Muskoka (p158)

➡ Three Houses Bed & Breakfast (p144)

➡ Fairmont Château Laurier (p219)

➡ Planet Travelers Hostel (p97)

Why Go?

The breathtaking four-seasonal palette of Ontario's vast wilderness, endless forests and abundant wildlife awaits. Around 40% of Canada's population lives here for good reason: Ontario is larger than France and Spain combined. Over 250,000 lakes contain a fifth of the planet's fresh water.

Most Ontarians call behemoth Toronto or Ottawa, the nation's cosmopolitan capital, home. Foodies, fashionistas and funsters converge on Toronto's vibrant multicultural neighborhoods, where immigrants from far and wide live in hockey-following harmony. Both cities have hopping arts and entertainment scenes, kept current by the neighborly influences of New York and Montréal.

Whether you want to reconnect with nature or lose yourself in the excitement of the most multiculturally diverse and socially cohesive region on Earth, you've come to the right place. Let Ontario surprise you with the beauty of her scenery and welcome you with the warmth of her people.

When to Go
Toronto, ON

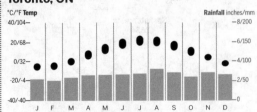

May & Jun
Celebrate spring and marvel at moose, trilliums and loons in Ontario's parks.

Jul–Sep
Join the frenzy of Toronto's festival mania or savor summer in cottage country.

Oct & Nov
Unleash your inner artist as fall colors the leaves throughout the province.

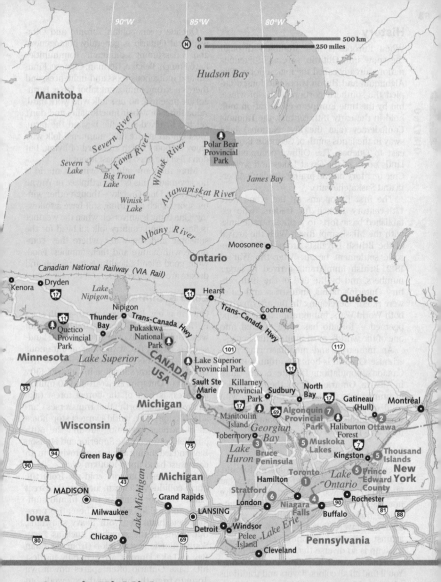

Ontario Highlights

1 Toronto (p71) Discovering what fashionistas and foodies adore about the city's diverse neighborhoods.

2 Ottawa (p211) Getting cultured in the capital, with its French flavors, world-class museums and ByWard Market.

3 Bruce Peninsula (p165) Exploring beautiful Tobermory,

then catching the ferry to Manitoulin Island.

4 Niagara Falls (p119) Marveling at the sheer power of the falls aboard a boat, riding straight into the mist.

5 Cottage Country (p207) Drooling over cottages-cum-mansions and rocky island retreats as you cruise

around the Thousand Islands, Muskoka Lakes and Prince Edward Island.

6 Stratford (p142) Wining, dining and heading back in time in this cultured town.

7 Algonquin Provincial Park (p190) Hiking or canoeing into this 7600-sq-km wilderness.

History

When Europeans first stumbled through the snow into Ontario, several indigenous nations already called the region home. The Algonquin and Huron tribes had long occupied the southern portion of the province, but by the time European colonization took hold in the early 18th century, the Iroquois Confederacy (aka the Five Nations) held sway in the lands south of Georgian Bay and east to Québec. The Ojibwe occupied the lands north of the Great Lakes and west to Cree territory on the prairies (today's Alberta and Saskatchewan).

The first Europeans on the scene were 17th-century French fur traders, who established basic forts to facilitate trade links with the Mississippi River. With the arrival of the British Loyalists around 1775, large-scale settlement began. After the War of 1812, British immigrants arrived in larger numbers, and by the end of the 19th century Ontario's farms, industries and cities were rapidly developing. In the aftermath of both World Wars, immigration from Europe boomed – Toronto has since evolved into one of the world's most multicultural cities.

An industrial and manufacturing powerhouse, Ontario is home to around 40% of Canada's population. Despite boom times in Alberta, Ontario remains the first choice of immigrants from across the globe, with solid employment prospects and Toronto's well-established immigrant support services proving a powerful draw.

Local Culture

There's something for everyone in Toronto. Locals love their city and seem somewhat blinded to its flaws: bitter winters, expensive housing, congested roads and inadequate public transit. They smile through gritted teeth as if it were their duty to defend the city against criticism. Toronto's ethnocultural makeup is so diverse that it defies attempts to define or resist it: people just get along. You'll find all all colors, flavors and traditions of the world represented here.

Outside cosmopolitan Toronto and Ottawa, rural Ontario is generally homogenous and unassuming, although communities have French, Belgian, German, Chinese, Finnish and indigenous roots and influences, and there's a strong immigrant labor force. Farmers are practical, no-fuss folk who work hard, value things for their functionality and don't get too involved with life beyond the farm. Most Ontarians are mild-mannered folk who enjoy a good to high standard of living, but don't feel the need to boast about it.

More than any other province, Ontario is hockey-mad – this is the birthplace of Wayne 'The Great One' Gretzky – though other winter sports such as curling still have a following. One thing is universal: when the weather is fine, city and country folk all head for the sunshine and the water, where they commune with nature and their families. Food, wine, good friends, healthy conversation and debate are all valued here.

Land & Climate

Ontario is big. Its longest north–south span is 1730km, and 1568km separate east from west. Unlike Canada's rugged west, the landscape is largely flat, with some mountainous regions and lots of lakes: four of the five Great Lakes have shoreline in Ontario. Fifty percent of Ontario's area (around 50 million hectares) is part of the boreal forest (aka 'Amazon of the North') that transverses Canada. It's one of the world's largest storehouses of carbon, beginning around the 50th parallel, between Lake Superior and Hudson Bay, and extending across the province in an east–west band up to 1000km wide.

In southern Ontario, cold air from the north collides with warm air from the Great Lakes, causing plenty of rain, humid summers and milder winters. The entire province gets blanketed with heavy snowfalls, but towns in the snowbelt, such as Parry Sound, Barrie and London (from Georgian Bay to Lake Huron), are generally hardest hit. Lake Ontario often spares downtown Toronto from the brunt of the snowfall, but winter storms have been known to shut down the city. January averages around -4°C on the Niagara Peninsula and -18°C in the north.

As summer draws closer, southwestern Ontario and the Niagara Peninsula get increasingly hot and sticky. It can feel oppressively humid in Toronto, where pollution can be stifling, and Ottawa. Summer storms are common along the Niagara Escarpment and conditions sometimes produce torna-

ONTARIO ITINERARIES

Four Days

Get yourself oriented in Toronto (p71) with a visit to Yonge & Dundas Sq, then scoot down to scan the scene from atop the CN Tower (p76). When you've got your bearings, head out to explore the sights, sounds and smells of Toronto's neighborhoods, starting with Queen Street West and Kensington Market (p81). On day two, focus on King St: from the Entertainment District to St Lawrence Market (p77) and the Distillery District (p77). You'll barely scratch the surface of what's on offer.

On your third day, take a tour with Chariots of Fire (p91) for the most comfortable and affordable way to cram the best of Niagara Falls (p119) and Niagara-on-the-Lake (p129) into a single day. Or rent a car, drive yourself and stay a night. On day four, head west to the pretty riverside villages of Elora and Fergus (p140), step back in time to the Mennonite community of St Jacobs (p140) and head onward to arty-foody Stratford (p142) for the night, catching a play at the festival before hotfooting it back to Toronto.

Two Weeks

In the warmer months, Ontario does road trips well. You could combine both our Nature Loop and Culture Loop itineraries, but you'll be covering a lot of ground.

NATURE LOOP

Head north to explore the beauty of the Muskoka Lakes (p157), then through the West Gate of Algonquin Provincial Park (p190) for a few days' canoeing and moose spotting, before crossing toward Georgian Bay. Avid kayakers, hikers and campers should follow the peninsula to Killarney Provincial Park (p170), while those who prefer creature comforts with their isolation will delight in Manitoulin Island (p168). If you're feeling adventurous, head north to parks such as Lake Superior Provincial Park (p178), but you'll have to backtrack to catch the Chi-Cheemaun ferry down to magical Tobermory (p166), the magnificent Bruce Peninsula (p165) and back to Toronto, via Collingwood (p164).

CULTURE LOOP

Start with a few days in vibrant Toronto (p71), and don't miss the nearby highlights of Niagara Falls (p119), Niagara-on-the-Lake (p129) and Stratford (p142), before heading east along Lake Ontario. Stop first to sample the rustic charm of a Prince Edward County B&B (p197) and the region's fine food and wine. Stop by the county's Sandbanks Provincial Park (p197) for a swim, then spend a night or two in historic Kingston (p200). Journey on to Gananoque (p206) for a cruise around the delightful Thousand Islands (p205), then continue along the St Lawrence River through quaint Brockville (p208) and the historic Upper Canada Village (p210). Finally, turn north to Ottawa (p211), the nation's proud capital, for a bounty of museums, gourmet restaurants, hip bars and the 185-year-old Rideau Canal (p217), a Unesco World Heritage site for its cultural significance.

---

does. July averages around 23°C here and 15°C in the north. Late spring and early fall are the best times to visit, when temperatures are mild, and days long and sunny.

National & Provincial Parks

Ontario contains six of Canada's national parks: Georgian Bay Islands National Park, Bruce Peninsula National Park (p166), Fathom Five National Marine Park (p166), Point Pelee National Park (p155) (the southernmost point of the Canadian mainland), Pukaskwa National Park (p180) and Thousand Islands National Park (p206). There are also more than 330 provincial parks here, many of which offer hiking and camping facilities. Campsites for up to six people cost between $36 and $53 per night. They range from basic sites without showers or electricity to well-located powered plots with showers. Make reservations with **Ontario Parks** (☑ 800-668-2746; www.ontarioparks.com).

❶ Getting There & Away

AIR

Most Canadian airlines and major international carriers arrive at Toronto Pearson International Airport (p117). From here, **Air Canada** (www.air canada.com) and **WestJet** (www.westjet.com) operate extensive services within the province and beyond. From the downtown Billy Bishop Toronto City Airport (p117), Porter Airlines

ONTARIO

Greater Toronto Area (GTA)

Toronto Pearson International Airport

Mimico Creek

McMichael Canadian Art Collection (17km)

Weston Golf & Country Club

St George's Golf & Country Club

Islington Golf Club

Humber River

Humber Bay

LEGOLAND Discovery Centre (13km); Canada's Wonderland (15km)

Jane St

Weston Rd

Black Creek Dr

Keele St

Scarlett Rd

Royal York Rd

Islington Ave

Kipling Ave

Rathburn Rd

Burnhamthorpe Rd

Bloor St

Eglinton Ave W

Macdonald–Cartier Fwy

Dundas St E

Browline

Toronto Golf Club

Lake Shore Blvd W

The Queensway

Gardiner Expwy

Queensway East

Mimico Creek

Etobicoke Creek

Bloor St W

High Park

Humber Marshes Park

Dundas St W

Bloor St

Bathurst St

Wilson Ave

Lawrence Ave W

Allen Expwy

Eglinton Ave W

St Clair Ave W

Davenport Rd

Queen St W

Dundas St W

Avenue Rd

Yonge St

Mt Pleasant Rd

Mount Pleasant Cemetery

Sunnybrook Park

Don Mills Rd

Don Valley Pkwy

David Dunlap Observatory (13km)

Sharon Temple (42km)

Ellesmere Rd

Warden Ave

Lawrence Ave E

Eglinton Ave E

St Clair Ave E

O'Connor Dr

Woodbine Ave

Danforth Ave

Kingston Rd

Cathedral Bluffs Park (1km); Toronto Zoo (17km)

Pine Hills Cemetery

Charles Sauriol Conservation Reserve

Edwards Gardens

Evergreen Brick Works

Gerrard St E

Queen St E

Ivan Forrest Gardens

Balmy Beach

Lake Ontario

Tommy Thompson Park

Woodbine Park

Ward's Island Beach

Toronto Islands

Billy Bishop Airport Tunnel

Billy Bishop Toronto City Airport

See East End Map (p90)

See Downtown Toronto North Map (p78)

See Downtown Toronto South Map (p82)

See West Toronto Map (p86)

Bay St

5 km
2.5 miles

(p174) services Northern Ontario as well as Ottawa, Montréal, Chicago, New York, Boston, Washington and more.

The John C Munro Hamilton International Airport (p135) is an alternative for budget US flights if Toronto is booked out. Distant Northern Ontario (p170) has a useful network of airports, including Moosonee, North Bay, Sault Ste Marie, Sudbury, Timmins and Thunder Bay.

Useful services from the small **Ottawa Mac-Donald-Cartier International Airport** (YOW; ☑ 613-248-2125; www.yow.ca; 1000 Airport Pkwy) include flights to Iqaluit (Nunavut) and Yellowknife (Northwest Territories), operated by **Canadian North** (☑ 800-661-1505; www.canadiannorth.com), First Air (https://firstair.ca) and Air North (www.flyairnorth.com), with connections throughout the far north.

TRAIN

VIA Rail (☑ 888-842-7245; www.viarail.ca) trains service the busy Ontario–Québec corridor, from Windsor in the southwest all the way to Montréal. VIA Rail also operates Trans-Canada services, which stop in Northern Ontario en route to Manitoba and beyond.

TORONTO

POP 5.9 MILLION

Where to begin? Toronto is itself a cultural phenomenon, with residents from around the world and scores of languages, foods, customs and celebrations – they're what make the city great. As Canada's largest city, Toronto has outstanding museums and galleries, from the Frank Gehry–redesigned Art Gallery of Ontario to the delightful Bata Shoe Museum (yes, shoes). The same goes for theaters; the gorgeous Elgin & Winter Garden Theatre has backstage tours as well as regular shows, and Shakespeare in High Park channels the Bard every summer. Then there's live music, poetry readings, comedy shows and LGBTIQ+ spots, too. But nowhere is Toronto's remarkable diversity more evident than in its food and restaurants. There's Pakistani, Persian, and Portuguese; indigenous and new fusion; Japanese pancakes and Korean barbecue; and fresh pasta in Little Italy, shawarmas in Greektown and the best damn dumplings in Chinatown.

History

In the 17th century, present-day Toronto was Seneca Indigenous land. Frenchman Étienne Brûlé was the first European here, in 1615, but unwelcoming locals impeded French invasion until 1720 when the French established a fur-trading post in what's now the west end. In 1763 the British took over, and John Simcoe, lieutenant governor of the new Upper Canada, moved the capital from Niagara-on-the-Lake and founded the town of York. On April 27, 1813, during the War of 1812, American forces looted and razed York, but were only able to hold sway for six days before Canadian troops hounded them back to Washington.

Toronto was born in 1834, when Mayor William Lyon Mackenzie renamed the town from an indigenous name meaning 'gathering place.' The Victorian city, controlled by conservative politicians, became known as 'Toronto the Good.' Religious restraints and strong antivice laws were such that on Sundays it was illegal to hire a horse, the curtains of department-store windows were drawn (window-shopping was sinful!) and film screenings prohibited.

In 1904 Toronto had a great fire, which burned about 5 hectares of the inner city and leveled 122 buildings. Amazingly no one was killed, and by the 1920s Bay St was booming, in part due to gold, silver and uranium discoveries in Northern Ontario. Prior to WWII, 80% of the population was Anglo-Celtic. After the war, then Prime Minister Lester B Pearson introduced the world's first points-based immigration system. Since then Toronto has welcomed millions of skilled immigrants and refugees from all corners of the globe.

The Anglo-Celtic figure is now closer to 50%. In 1998 five sprawling Toronto suburbs – York, East York, North York, Etobicoke and Scarborough – fused to become the Greater Toronto Area (GTA). As the fifth-largest city in North America, contemporary Toronto is gloriously diverse – half of its current residents were born outside Canada – and it is a place that grapples with urban issues with passion, intelligence and heart.

◉ Sights

Downtown Toronto is an easy-to-navigate grid bounded by a hodgepodge of bohemian, cultural and historic neighborhoods. Yonge St, the world's longest thoroughfare, dissects the city: an East or West designation indicates a street's position relative to Yonge.

Most sights are found in the Waterfront, Entertainment and Financial Districts at the southern end of downtown. Just north, Yorkville and the Annex have a cache of museums. Due south, locals retreat to the Toronto Islands for beaches and hands-down the best skyline views.

Back on the mainland, the pocket between Yonge and the Don Valley Pkwy enfolds some of Toronto's oldest and best-preserved neighborhoods: St Lawrence Market, the Distillery District and Cabbagetown. Many argue that West is best: Kensington Market and Queen West are edgy and artsy. Meanwhile, the East is full of flavor: Leslieville, Greektown and the Beaches, slightly San Franciscan in their sensibilities, are the main draws.

◉ Waterfront

★ Harbourfront Centre   ARTS CENTER
(Map p82; ☑416-973-4000; www.harbourfront centre.com; 235 Queens Quay W; ⊙10am-11pm Mon-Sat, to 9pm Sun; P♿; ➌509, 510) An artistic powerhouse, this 4-hectare complex educates and entertains Toronto's community through a variety of year-round performances, events and exhibits. The center is made up of more than two dozen waterfront venues, including parks, outdoor stages, theaters and galleries. The main building alone houses the well-respected **Craft & Design Studios**, open studios where the public can watch artists-in-residence at work; the 1300-seat **Concert Stage**; and even a lakeside rink (p89) where you can slice up the winter ice.

★ Power Plant
Contemporary Art Gallery   GALLERY
(Map p82; ☑416-973-4949; www.thepowerplant. org; 231 Queens Quay W; ⊙10am-5pm Tue, Wed & Fri-Sun, to 8pm Thu; P♿; ➌509, 510) FREE Easily recognized by its painted smokestack, the Power Plant gallery is just that: a former power plant transformed into Toronto's premier gallery of contemporary art. Best of all, it's free and exhibitions change regularly. Free kid-centered tours and workshops are offered throughout the month; call to reserve a spot. It's part of the Harbourfront Centre complex.

Toronto Music Garden
GARDENS

(Map p82; ☑416-973-4000; www.harbourfront centre.com; 479 Queens Quay W; ⌷509, 510) Delicately strung along the western harbor front, the Toronto Music Garden was designed in collaboration with cellist Yo-Yo Ma. It expresses Bach's *Suite No 1 for Unaccompanied Cello* through landscape, with an arc-shaped grove of conifers, a swirling path through a wildflower meadow and a grass-stepped amphitheater where free concerts are held, including **Summer Music in the Garden**, a classical series presented every Thursday (7pm) and Sunday (4pm) from June to September.

Spadina Quay Wetlands
PARK

(Map p82; ☑416-392-1111; www.toronto.ca; 479 Queens Quay W; ☺dawn-dusk; ⌷509, 510) A former lakeside parking lot has been transformed into the 2800-sq-meter Spadina Quay Wetlands, a thriving, sustainable ecosystem full of frogs, birds, fish and butterflies. When lakeside fishers noticed that northern pike were spawning here each spring, the city took it upon itself to create this new habitat. Complete with flowering heath plants, poplar trees and a birdhouse, it's a little gem that led the way in the harborfront's redevelopment.

Fort York National Historic Site
HISTORIC SITE

(Map p70; ☑416-392-6907; www.fortyork.ca; 250 Fort York Blvd; adult/child $14/6; ☺10am-5pm Jun-Aug, 10am-4pm Mon-Fri, to 5pm Sat & Sun Sep-May; ℗♿; ⌷509, 511) Established by the British in 1793 to defend the then town of York, Fort York was almost entirely destroyed during the War of 1812 when a small band of Ojibwe warriors and British troops were unable to defeat their US attackers. Several structures – barracks, block houses and powder magazines – were immediately rebuilt and still stand on the 17-hectare site. From May to September, men decked out in 19th-century British military uniforms carry out marches and drills, firing musket volleys into the sky.

⊙ Toronto Islands

For independent travelers the Toronto Islands' main sights are the beaches, situated along the islands' southern, lake-facing shore. Each beach has its own appeal – family friendly, less busy and even clothing optional – though all are worth visiting if you have the time. The harbor side has no beaches but terrific views of Toronto's skyline. Travelers with young children will likely want to visit the amusement park on Centre Island.

Ward's Island
ISLAND

(Map p70; www.torontoisland.com; ⛴Ward's Island) The most residential of the Toronto Islands, Ward's has funky old houses crowded together and narrow pedestrian- and cyclist-only streets. At the island's western end is an 18-hole **Disc Golf Course** (Map p70; www.discgolfontario.com; ☺dawn-dusk) **FREE**. An old-fashioned boardwalk runs the length of the southern shore, starting at Ward's Island Beach and passing the back gate of **Riviera cafe** (Map p70; ☑416-203-2152; www.island riviera.com; 102 Lakeshore Ave,; mains $12-17; ☺11am-11pm; ☎♿) with its lovely patio.

★ Ward's Island Beach
BEACH

(Map p70; ☑ beach hotline 416-392-7161; Lakeshore Ave, Ward's Island; ⛴Ward's Island) Arguably the prettiest beach on the Toronto Islands, this is a long, curving shoreline with tawny sand and views of boats sailing past. Lifeguards are on duty from 11:30am to 6:30pm daily (May to September). It's on the south side of Ward's Island.

Gibraltar Point Beach
BEACH

(Map p70; Lakeshore Ave, Hanlan's Point; ⛴Centre Island) Gibraltar Point is a pleasant little beach backed by small sand dunes and beach grass. It's less frequented than other island beaches, making it a bit more tranquil. Stop by the 1808 **Gibraltar Lighthouse** as you arrive; it's the oldest lighthouse on the Great Lakes and said to be haunted by its first keeper, JP Rademuller, who was allegedly killed for his bootlegged beer. It's at the southwestern corner of Hanlan's Point.

Hanlan's Point
ISLAND

(Map p70; ⛴Hanlan's Point) West of Centre Island, the island of Hanlan's Point is named after world-champion sculler 'Ned' Hanlan (1855–1904), a member of the first family to permanently settle here; his statue overlooks the ferry dock. Babe Ruth hit his first professional home run here in 1914 while playing minor-league baseball in the long-since-demolished stadium – the ball drowned in Lake Ontario, the ultimate souvenir lost forever! The island is also home to Billy Bishop Toronto City Airport (p117) and the clothing-optional **Hanlan's Point Beach** (Map p70; ☑ beach hotline 416-392-8196; Lakeshore Ave).

JAVEN/SHUTTERSTOCK © ARCHITECT: DANIEL LIBESKIND

IMAGIXIAN/GETTY IMAGES ©

JON ANDRASZ/GETTY IMAGES ©

1. Royal Ontario Museum (p81)
The multidisciplinary ROM, located in Toronto, is Canada's biggest natural-history museum and one of the largest museums in North America.

2. Bruce Peninsula (p165)
The Bruce is a 100km limestone outcrop that separates the cooler crystal waters of Georgian Bay from warmer Lake Huron.

3. Muskoka Lakes (p157)
Originally rich in lumber production and shipbuilding, this area is at the heart of 'cottage country'.

4. ByWard Market (p225)
In summer, over 260 stalls fill the streets of this popular market in Ottawa, but in winter the weather drastically reduces the number of businesses.

Centreville
Amusement Park AMUSEMENT PARK

(Map p70; ☑ 416-203-0405; www.centreisland. ca; Centre Island; all-day ride passes adult/child/ family $36/27/118; ☺ 10:30am-8pm Jun-Aug, Sat & Sun only with earlier closing May & Sep; ♠; ⬟ Centre Island) From Centre Island ferry terminal, wander past the information booth to quaint Centreville's antique carousel, goofy golf course, miniature train and little-kids' rides. **Far Enough Farm** petting zoo presents plenty of opportunities to cuddle something furry and step in something sticky. There's no admission fee to the park, but you need to purchase a pass to use the rides. It's most fun for families with kids aged seven and under.

⊙ Entertainment & Financial Districts

Downtown is where many of the best-known tourist sights are, from the CN Tower to the Hockey Hall of Fame. It's also where you go to catch a Maple Leafs (p113), Blue Jays (p114) or Raptors (p113) game, or take the kids to the aquarium. But there are also plenty of pocket-sized galleries and attractions to be sought out, like the **Gallery of Inuit Art** (Map p82; ☑ 416-982-8473; www.td.com/corporate-responsibility/art.jsp; 79 Wellington St W, ground fl & mezzanine, TD Centre south tower; ☺ 8am-6pm Mon-Fri, 10am-4pm Sat & Sun; ⬟ St Andrew) 𝗙𝗥𝗘𝗘 on the bottom floor of a skyscraper, and a cool little **museum and exhibit** (Map p82; ☑ 416-214-9229; www.torontorailwaymuseum.com; 255 Bremner Blvd; adult/child $5/3; ☺ noon-5pm Jun-Sep, closed Mon & Tue Oct-Apr; ♠; ⬟ Union, 🚋 509, 510) on trains.

★ CN Tower TOWER

(La Tour CN; Map p82; ☑ 416-868-6937; www.cntower.ca; 301 Front St W; Tower Experience adult/child $38/28; ☺ 8:30am-11pm; ♠; ⬟ Union) Toronto's iconic CN Tower, a communications spire and a marvel of 1970s engineering, looks like a giant concrete hypodermic needle. Riding one of the glass elevators up what was once the world's highest free-standing structure (553m) is one of those things you just *have* to do in Toronto. Even if you don't, you're bound to catch a glimpse of the tower at night: the entire structure puts on a brilliant (free) light show year-round.

On a clear day the vista from the top is astounding – a bird's-eye view of the city and lake, Niagara Falls in the distance, even helicopters flying *below* you; if it's hazy you won't see a thing. Queues for the elevator can be up to two hours long in each direction. During summer, you can pay a little more ($7) for a timed ride to the top...though not back down. Buying tickets online, or using the CN Tower app, saves 15%. There's the obligatory revolving restaurant (called 360°): it's expensive, but the elevator price is waived for diners. Cashed-up daredevils (13 years plus) can now do the EdgeWalk ($195), a 20-minute outdoor walk around the unbounded perimeter of the main pod (356m). It's not for the fainthearted. For an even loftier, though indoor, view, opt for the SkyPod (447m; an extra $15) – though you may not notice much difference to the regular view.

The best street-level vantage point for the tower is at the intersection of McCaul St and Queen St W, due north.

★ 401 Richmond GALLERY

(Map p78; ☑ 416-595-5900; www.401richmond. com; 401 Richmond St W; ☺ 9am-7pm Mon-Fri, to 6pm Sat; 🚋 510) 𝗙𝗥𝗘𝗘 Inside an early-20th-century lithographer's warehouse, restored in 1994, this 18,500-sq-meter New York–style artists collective hums with the creative vibes of more than 140 contemporary galleries, exhibition spaces, studios and shops representing works in almost any medium you can think of. Speaker series and film fests are held throughout the year. Grab a snack at the ground-floor cafe (open 9am to 5pm Monday to Friday) and enjoy it on the expansive roof garden, a little-known oasis in summer.

★ Ripley's
Aquarium of Canada AQUARIUM

(Map p82; ☑ 647-351-3474; www.ripleysaquariumofcanada.com; 288 Bremner Blvd; adult/child $32/22; ☺ 9am-11pm; ♠; ⬟ Union) Arguably one of Toronto's best attractions for both young and old, it has more than 16,000 aquatic animals and 5.7 million liters of water in the combined tanks. There are touch tanks, a glass tunnel with a moving walkway, educational dive presentations...and even live jazz on the second Friday of each month. Open 365 days a year. Peak hours are 11am to 4pm.

★ Hockey Hall of Fame MUSEUM

(Map p82; ☑ 416-360-7765; www.hhof.com; Brookfield Place, 30 Yonge St; adult/child $20/14; ☺ 9:30am-6pm Mon-Sat, 10am-6pm Sun Jun-Sep, 10am-5pm Mon-Fri, 9:30am-6pm Sat, 10:30am-5pm Sun Oct-May; ♠; ⬟ Union) Inside the rococo gray-stone Bank of Montreal building (c 1885), the Hockey Hall of Fame is a Canadian institution. Even those unfamiliar with the rough, super-fast sport are likely to be impressed by this, the world's largest collection of hockey memorabilia. Check out the *Texas Chainsaw Massacre*–esque goalkeeping masks or go head to head with the great Wayne Gretzky, virtual-reality style. And, of course, be sure to take a pic with the beloved Stanley Cup.

Graffiti Alley   PUBLIC ART
(Rush Lane; Map p86; Graffiti Alley, btwn Spadina Ave & Portland St; 301, 501) Possibly the most popular place to check out street art in Toronto (and there are many), this back alley has a magnificent collection of colorful murals and street art. Spanning three blocks (about 400m), the alley was popularized as the location of Rick Mercer's rants on CBC comedy program the *Rick Mercer Report*. Great for photo ops.

Design Exchange   MUSEUM
(DX; Map p82; 416-363-6121; www.dx.org; 234 Bay St; 9am-5pm Tue-Fri, noon-4:30pm Sat; King) FREE The original Toronto Stock Exchange now houses eye-catching industrial-design exhibits. The permanent collection of this rather tiny museum includes more than 1000 Canadian pieces that span six decades. There are free one-hour tours the last Friday of each month, starting at noon.

Old Town, Corktown & Distillery District

This area is where the village of York, later renamed Toronto, was founded. Sights here are historical in nature, naturally, but with stylish updates. The two main destinations – St Lawrence Market and the Distillery District – have their roots in the early 1800s. Anything but stodgy, they're home to shops, eateries and galleries that are packed with locals and visitors.

★St Lawrence Market Complex   MARKET
(Map p82; 416-392-7219; www.stlawrencemarket.com; 92-95 Front St E; 8am-6pm Tue-Thu, to 7pm Fri, 5am-5pm Sat; P; 503, 504) Old York's sensational St Lawrence Market has been a neighborhood meeting place for over two centuries. The restored, high-trussed 1845 **South Market** houses more than 120 specialty food stalls and shops: cheese vendors, fishmongers, butchers, bakers and pasta makers. The **Carousel Bakery** is famed

for its peameal-bacon sandwiches and **St Urbain** for its authentic Montréal-style bagels.

Inside the old council chambers upstairs, the **Market Gallery** (Map p82; 416-392-0572; www.toronto.ca/marketgallery; St Lawrence Market, 95 Front St E, 2nd fl; adult/child $8/5, Fri $4/2.50; 10am-4pm Tue-Fri, 9am-4pm Sat; 503, 504) has rotating displays of paintings, photographs, documents and historical relics. Next door, cooking workshops and special events are held at the **Market Kitchen**.

On the opposite side of Front St, the **North Market** building, a concrete bunker built in the late 1960s, was demolished after years of delays due to budget restraints and archaeological finds. Completion of the new North Market building is estimated for late 2022. In the meantime, the temporary site for the **Saturday farmers market** (5am to 5pm) and the fantastic Sunday antique market (p114) is one block south at 125 The Esplanade.

Just a few steps north of the construction site, check out the glorious **St Lawrence Hall** (1850), topped by a mansard roof and a copper-clad clock tower that can be seen for blocks; once a public gathering place, it now houses shops and city offices.

★Distillery District   AREA
(Map p90; 416-364-1177; www.thedistillerydistrict.com; 9 Trinity St; 10am-7pm Mon-Wed, to 8pm Thu-Sat, 11am-6pm Sun; 72, 503, 504) Centered on the 1832 Gooderham and Worts distillery – once the British Empire's largest – the 5-hectare Distillery District is one of Toronto's best downtown attractions. Its Victorian industrial warehouses have been converted into soaring galleries, artists studios, design boutiques, cafes and eateries. On weekends newlyweds pose before a backdrop of red brick and cobblestone, young families walk their dogs and the fashionable shop for art beneath charmingly decrepit gables and gantries. In summer expect live jazz, activities, exhibitions and foodie events.

Flatiron Building   HISTORIC BUILDING
(Gooderham Building; Map p82; 49 Wellington St E; 503) An iconic sight in the heart of the old town, the Flatiron is impossible to miss. Built in 1892, it's a five-story iron-shaped building with a steep copper roof and turret; in the background, Toronto's skyscrapers provide a beautiful contrast. Be sure to check out the mural on the building's western side; created by Canadian artist Derek Michael Besant,

Downtown Toronto North

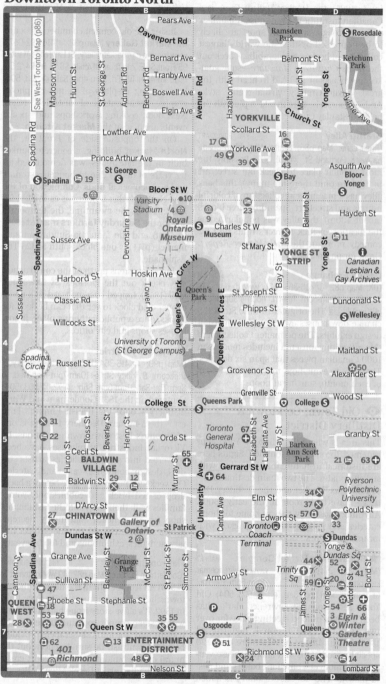

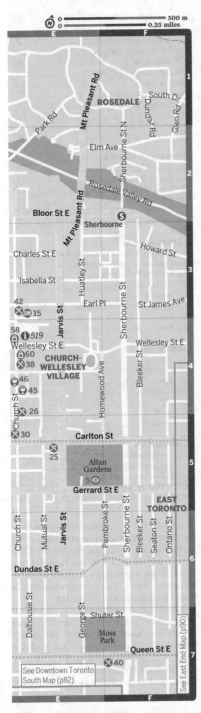

it integrates with the existing structure to make it appear that a curtain of windows has not been properly tacked up.

◉ The Beaches

The name says it all: this neighborhood is all about its beaches and beachfront parks. There's tawny sand, clear water and a relaxed vibe. Come for a day to unwind with a blanket and book or to walk along the water's edge, on the boardwalk or on the paths of a human-made nature preserve.

★ Tommy Thompson Park   PARK

(Map p70; ☑416-661-6600; www.tommythomp sonpark.ca; Leslie St; ◷4-9pm Mon-Fri, 5:30am-9pm Sat & Sun; ◙83 Jones S, ◙501) A 5km-long artificial peninsula between the Harbourfront and the Beaches, Tommy Thompson Park reaches further into Lake Ontario than the Toronto Islands. This 'accidental wilderness' – constructed from Outer Harbour dredgings – has become a phenomenal wildlife success. It's one of the world's largest nesting places for ring-billed gulls, and is a haven for terns, black-crowned night herons, turtles, owls, foxes and even coyotes.

It's open to the public on weekends and after 4pm on weekdays; vehicles and pets are prohibited. Summer schedules offer interpretive programs and guided walks, usually with an ecological theme. At the end of the park there's a lighthouse and great city views. To get here, take any streetcar along Queen St E to Leslie St, then walk 800m south to the gates, or follow the Martin Goodman Trail (p89).

Kew Beach   BEACH

(Map p70; www.toronto.ca/parks/beaches; cnr Lee Ave & boardwalk; ◷dawn-dusk; ⊞; ◙501) Of all the beaches, Kew is the most popular stretch of sand, with a wide boardwalk running east to Balmy Beach and west to Woodbine Beach. Restrooms and a snack bar in adjacent **Kew Gardens** (Map p70; 2075 Queen St E; ◷dawn-dusk; ⊞) make it easy to spend the day here. For more food options, head to nearby Queen St E for picnic supplies and restaurants.

◉ Downtown Yonge

The must-see sight in Downtown Yonge is the venerable Elgin & Winter Garden Theatre, with tours available of its sumptuous

Downtown Toronto North

interior. There are also the two iterations of Toronto's city government – gargoyled Old City Hall and flying-saucer-ish new City Hall – located across the street from one another, plus a small textile museum and a historic church.

★Elgin & Winter
Garden Theatre   THEATER
(Map p78; ☎416-314-2871; www.heritage
trust.on.ca/ewg; 189 Yonge St; tours adult/student
$12/10; ⓢQueen) This restored masterpiece
is the world's last operating Edwardian double-decker theater. Celebrating its centenni-

al in 2013, the Winter Garden was built as the flagship for a vaudeville chain that never really took off, while the downstairs Elgin was converted into a movie house in the 1920s. Today it serves as a stage for traveling Broadway shows. Fascinating tours run at 5pm Monday and 10am Saturday.

Saved from demolition in 1981, the theat-ers received a $29 million face-lift: bread dough was used to uncover rose-garden frescoes, the Belgian company that made the original carpet was contacted for fresh rugs, and the floral Winter Garden ceiling was re-placed, leaf by painstaking leaf.

City Hall　　　　HISTORIC BUILDING

(Map p78; ☑416-392-2489, 311; www.toronto.ca; 100 Queen St W; ☺8:30am-4:30pm Mon-Fri; Ⓟ; ⓈQueen) FREE Much-maligned City Hall was Toronto's bold leap into architectural modernity. Its twin clamshell towers, central 'flying saucer', ramps and mosaics were completed in 1965 to Finnish architect Viljo Revell's award-winning design. An irritable Frank Lloyd Wright compared it to a gravestone; Revell died before construction was finished. At the info desk you can collect a self-guided tour pamphlet with points of interest in the complex, including a stunning artwork by Norval Morrisseau, one of Canada's most revered Indigenous painters.

Out front is **Nathan Phillips Square** (though most just call it City Hall, too), a magnet for skaters, demonstrators, fast-food trucks, and tourists taking selfies with the lit-up 'Toronto' letters day and night. In summer, check out the **Fresh Wednesdays** farmers market, free concerts, special events and office workers on their lunch breaks, up the ramp on the green roof. Look for a tourist-information pop-up at the corner of Bay and Queen. The fountain pool becomes a fun-filled **ice-skating rink** in winter (10am to 10pm).

◉ Kensington Market & Chinatown

There's really just one sight in Kensington Market and Chinatown: the superlative Art Gallery of Ontario. AGO is spectacular inside and out, and one of the true must-sees of Toronto. Beyond that, the sights of the neighborhoods are mostly sublime in nature: a striking mural, a unique street performer, a lovely old building turned into a record store.

★**Art Gallery of Ontario**　　　GALLERY

(AGO; Map p78; ☑416-979-6648; www.ago.net; 317 Dundas St W; adult/under 25yr $25/free, 6-9pm Wed free; ☺10:30am-5pm Tue & Thu, to 9pm Wed & Fri, to 5:30pm Sat & Sun; ☐505) The AGO houses collections both excellent and extensive (bring your stamina). Renovations of the facade, designed by the revered Frank Gehry and completed in 2008, impress at street level: it's like looking at a huge crystal ship docked on a busy city street. Inside, highlights of the permanent collection include rare Québecois religious statuary, Inuit carvings, stunningly presented works by Canadian greats the Group of Seven, the Henry

Moore sculpture pavilion, and restored Georgian house The Grange.

There's a surcharge for special exhibits, but visits to the permanent collection on Wednesday evenings are free. Several highly recommended – and free – tours are offered throughout the week, all leaving from the Walker Court. The most popular? Daily one-hour tours leaving on the hour from 11am to 3pm and on Wednesdays and Fridays at 7pm. If you don't want to commit that much time, 10-minute pop-up 'On the Dot' art chats are held in front of different works every day on the half-hour from 11:30am to 3:30pm and on Wednesdays and Fridays at 7:30pm.

◉ Yorkville & the Annex

One of Toronto's must-sees is in this area: the Royal Ontario Museum. It's a massive space with an equally massive collection, covering natural history and world cultures. Nearby are more museums, one focusing on shoes (p83), another on **ceramics** (Map p78; ☑416-586-8080; www.gardinermuseum.on.ca; 111 Queen's Park; adult/child $15/free, 4-9pm Wed half price; ☺10am-6pm Mon, Tue, Thu & Fri, to 9pm Wed, to 5pm Sat & Sun; ⓈMuseum). And then there's Casa Loma (p83) – the huge, famous and rather strange castle of an eccentric Torontonian of yesteryear.

★**Royal Ontario Museum**　　　MUSEUM

(ROM; Map p78; ☑416-586-8000; www.rom.on.ca; 100 Queen's Park; adult/child $23/14, 5:30-8:30pm 3rd Mon of month free; ☺10am-5:30pm, to 8:30pm 3rd Mon of month; ⓈMuseum) Opened in 1914, the multidisciplinary ROM is Canada's biggest natural-history museum and one of the largest museums in North America. You'll either love or loathe the synergy between the original heritage buildings at the main entrance on Bloor St and the 2007 addition of 'the Crystal,' which appears to pierce the original structure and juts out into the street like a massive shard. There are free docent-led tours daily.

The permanent collection features more than six million specimens and artifacts, divided between two main galleries: the Natural History Galleries (all on the 2nd floor) and the World Culture Galleries (on the 1st, 3rd and 4th floors). The Chinese temple sculptures, Gallery of Korean Art, and costumes and textile collections are some of the best in the world. Kids rush to the dinosaur rooms, Egyptian mummies and Jamaican

Downtown Toronto South

500 m
0.25 miles

See Downtown Toronto North Map (p78)

See West Toronto Map (p86)

Wellington St W

Camden St

Spadina Ave

Adelaide St W

King St W

Clarence
Square
Park

Front St W

Spadina Ave

Lake Shore Blvd W

Queens Quay W

Bremner Blvd

Gardiner Expwy

Peter St

Widmer St

Nelson St

Adelaide St W

King St W

Pearl St

THEATRE
BLOCK

John St

Blue Jays Way

Bremner Blvd

ENTERTAINMENT
DISTRICT

Simcoe St

Emily St

St Andrew

King St W

Wellington St W

Piper St

University Ave

Station St

CN Tower

Metro
Convention
Centre

Lower Simcoe St

Bremner Blvd

Bobbie
Rosenfield
Park

Ripley's
Aquarium
of Canada

Queens Quay W

Rees St
Slip

Peter St
Slip

Spadina
Ave Slip

Tiki
Taxi

Lake Shore Blvd W

Queens Quay W

Stinson St
Slip

HARBOURFRONT

Harbourfront
Centre

Power Plant
Contemporary
Art Gallery

York St
Slip

FINANCIAL
DISTRICT

York St

Bremner Blvd

Travellers
Aid Society
of Toronto

Union
Station

Front St W

Bay St

The Esplanade

Gardiner Expwy

Queens
Quay

Harbour St

Harbour
Square
Park

Yonge St
Slip

Toronto
Islands
Ferries

Yonge St

Freeland St

Cooper St

Queens Quay E

Lower
Jarvis St

Jarvis St
Slip

Toronto
Inner Harbour

Lake Shore Blvd E

Harbour St

Jarvis St

Market St

St Lawrence
Market Complex

The Esplanade

George St

Frederick St

Wellington St E

Front St E

Colborne St

King St E

St James
Park

Adelaide St E

Jarvis St

St James
Park

Lombard St

King St E

Victoria St

King St

Yonge St

Hockey
Hall of
Fame

Bay St

Downtown Toronto South

◎ Top Sights
1 CN Tower	C3
2 Harbourfront Centre	C4
3 Hockey Hall of Fame	E2
4 Power Plant Contemporary Art Gallery	D4
5 Ripley's Aquarium of Canada	C3
6 St Lawrence Market Complex	G2

◎ Sights
7 Design Exchange	E1
8 Flatiron Building	F2
Market Gallery	(see 6)
9 Rogers Centre	C3
10 Spadina Quay Wetlands	A4
11 TD Gallery of Inuit Art	D1
12 Toronto Music Garden	A4
13 Toronto Railway Museum	C3
14 Toronto's First Post Office	F1

◎ Activities, Courses & Tours
15 Chariots of Fire	E2
16 Heritage Toronto	G1
17 Martin Goodman Trail	C4
18 Natrel Rink	D4
19 Wheel Excitement	C4

◎ Sleeping
20 Bisha Hotel	B1
21 Clarence Park	B1
22 Executive Cosmopolitan Hotel	F1
23 Fairmont Royal York	D2
24 Hostelling International Toronto	F1
25 Shangri-La Hotel	D1
26 Westin Harbour Castle	E4

◎ Eating
27 Boxcar Social	D4
28 Bymark	E2
29 Harbour 60	E3
30 Khao San Road	B1
31 King Taps	E1
32 La Carnita	C1
33 Pai	C1
34 Patrician Grill	G1
35 Pearl Diver	F1
36 Ravi Soups	B1
37 Sud Forno	E1
38 Terroni	F1
39 WORKS Gourmet Burger Bistro	F2

◎ Drinking & Nightlife
40 Against the Grain Urban Tavern	G4
41 C'est What	F2
42 Dineen Coffee Company	E1

◎ Entertainment
43 Adelaide Hall	C1
44 Reservoir Lounge	F2
Scotiabank Arena	(see 47)
45 TIFF Bell Lightbox	C1
46 Toronto Blue Jays	B3
47 Toronto Maple Leafs	E3
Toronto Raptors	(see 47)
Toronto Rock	(see 47)
48 Toronto Symphony Orchestra	C1
49 Young People's Theatre	G2

◎ Shopping
50 Sunday Antique Market	G2

ONTARIO TORONTO

bat-cave replica. The cedar crest totem poles carved by Indigenous tribes in British Columbia are wonderful.

Each year the ROM hosts a variety of big temporary exhibits from around the world (special exhibit surcharges apply). Keep an eye out for the Friday Night Live programs, when the museum opens its doors, stocks its bars and calls in the DJs for a makeshift dance party.

Casa Loma　　　　　　　　HISTORIC BUILDING
(Map p70; ☑416-923-1171; www.casaloma.org; 1 Austin Tce; adult/child $33/23; ⊗9:30am-5pm, last entry 4pm; P; ☒127, ⑤Dupont) Toronto's only castle may never have housed royalty, but it certainly has grandeur, lording over the Annex from a cliff that was once the shoreline of the glacial Lake Iroquois, from which Lake Ontario derived. A self-guided audio tour leads visitors through the four levels of the Edwardian mansion as well as the 800ft tunnel to the stables; the top floor

houses a military museum. Head to the pool turned theater first, where a short film provides a good overview.

The 98-room mansion – an architectural hurricane of castellations, chimneys, flagpoles, turrets and Rapunzel-esque balconies – was built between 1911 and 1914 for Sir Henry Pellatt, a wealthy financier who made bags of cash from his contract to provide Toronto with electricity. He later lost everything in land speculation, the resultant foreclosure forcing the Pellatts to downsize, eventually to a single room in the home of their former chauffeur. To reach the *casa,* climb the 27m **Baldwin Steps** up the slope from Spadina Ave, north of Davenport Rd.

Bata Shoe Museum　　　　　　MUSEUM
(Map p78; ☑416-979-7799; www.batashoemu seum.ca; 327 Bloor St W; adult/child $14/5, 5-8pm Thu suggested donation $5; ⊗10am-5pm Mon-Wed, Fri & Sat, to 8pm Thu, noon-5pm Sun; ⑤St George) It's important in life to be well shod,

a stance the Bata Shoe Museum takes seriously. Impressively designed by Raymond Moriyama to resemble a stylized shoebox, the museum houses a collection of 13,000 'pedi-artifacts' from around the globe, spanning 4500 years; only 3% to 4% are on view at any given time. Peruse 19th-century French chestnut-crushing clogs, Canadian indigenous polar boots or famous modern pairs worn by Elton John, Indira Gandhi and Pablo Picasso. Come along for something truly different.

Spadina Museum   MUSEUM
(Map p70; ☏416-392-6910; www.toronto.ca/museums; 285 Spadina Rd; tours adult/child $10/6, grounds free; ⊙noon-5pm Tue-Sun Apr-Aug, noon-4pm Mon-Fri, to 5pm Sat & Sun Sep-Dec; ℗; Ⓢ Dupont) Atop the Baldwin Steps, this gracious home and its Victorian-Edwardian gardens were built in 1866 as a country estate for financier James Austin and his family. Donated to the city in 1978, it became a museum in 1984 and was painstakingly transformed to evoke the heady age of the 1920s and '30s. Knowledgeable guides lead visitors through the estate, sharing the history of the home and the Austen family along the way – highly recommended.

◉ West End

The West End's sights are somewhat off the beaten track, but they're well worth a visit to take in art, the outdoors and a historic neighborhood all in one part of town.

★High Park   PARK
(Map p70; www.toronto.ca/parks; 1873 Bloor St W; ⊙dawn-dusk; ℗; Ⓢ High Park, ☒501, 506, 508) Toronto's favorite green space is a wonderful spot to unfurl a picnic blanket, swim, play tennis, bike around, skate on 14-hectare **Grenadier Pond** or – in spring – meander through the groves of cherry blossoms donated by the Japanese ambassador in 1959. Several nature walks, workshops and talks are organized by the Nature Centre (https://highparknaturecentre.com) and led by rangers. Shakespeare in High Park (p113) has been produced in the park's amphitheater for almost 40 years.

If you have small kids, check out the children's **zoo** or take a **train ride** through the park (adult/child $4.50/3.50, 30 minutes, April to October). And be sure to peek into **Colborne Lodge**, built in 1836 by the How-

ard family, who donated much of High Park to the city in 1873.

On weekends and holidays from mid-June to early September, bus 30B picks up at High Park subway station and then loops through the park. Otherwise it's a 200m walk from the subway station to the north gates. The 506 High Park streetcar drops off on the eastern side of the park. If you exit the park by Colborne Lodge at the south gates, walk down to Lake Shore Blvd W and catch any eastbound streetcar to downtown.

Museum of Contemporary Art Toronto   MUSEUM
(MOCA Toronto; Map p70; ☏416-530-2500; http://museumofcontemporaryart.ca; 158 Sterling Rd; adult/child $10/free, 10am-2pm last Sun of month free; ⊙10am-5pm Wed-Mon, to 9pm Fri; ℗◨; Ⓢ Lansdowne, ☒306, 506) Housed in what was once Toronto's tallest building – a factory producing aluminum parts – MOCA exhibits innovative works by Canadian and international artists that address themes of contemporary relevance. Exhibits change four times per year, but all seek to provoke and engage viewers, whether they like what they see or not.

◉ East Toronto & Rosedale

All but one of the major sights on the east side are on or within walking distance of the Don River Valley. Sidewalks, trails and roadways lead visitors from one place to the next in minutes, making it easy to explore several in just a day.

★Evergreen Brick Works   PARK
(Map p70; ☏416-596-7670; www.evergreen.ca; 550 Bayview Ave; ⊙9am-5pm Mon-Fri, 8am-5pm Sat, 10am-5pm Sun; ℗◨; ☒28A, Ⓢ Broadview) ✔FREE Famed for the transformation of its once-deteriorating heritage buildings into a prime location for all things geotourism, this dynamic, LEED-certified environmental center and park hosts interactive workshops and community festivals on the themes of ecology, technology and the environment. There's a garden market, an ice rink and lots of nature trails, which can be explored on foot or by bike (rentals are available). Check the website to see what's going on. Take the free shuttle bus from Broadview subway station.

★Riverdale Farm   MUSEUM
(Map p90; ☏416-392-6794; http://riverdalefarm toronto.ca; 201 Winchester St; ⊙9am-5pm; ℗◨;

🏠506) FREE On the site of the Riverdale Zoo, where from 1888 to 1974 prairie wolves howled at night and spooked the Cabbagetown kids, Riverdale Farm is a downtown rural oasis. Now a working farm and museum, it has two barns, a summer wading pool, and pens of feathered and furry friends. Kids follow the farmers around as they do their daily chores, including milking goats and collecting eggs. Visitors can learn about a particular animal during the daily 'Farmer Demo' at 11:30am.

Allan Gardens Conservatory   GARDENS
(Map p78; 🗷416-392-7288; www.toronto.ca/explore-enjoy/parks-gardens-beaches/gardens-and-horticulture/conservatories/allan-gardens-conservatory; 160 Gerrard St E; ⊙10am-4:45pm; 🚹; 🏠506) FREE Dating from 1858, Allan Gardens is one of Toronto's oldest parks. The highlight is its indoor botanical garden and conservatory, filled with plants from all around the world (and even some turtles in the orchid section). Housed in a stunning, historical cast-iron and glass building, it's a lovely little escape in the city, especially on a cold winter day.

Todmorden Mills Heritage Site   HISTORIC SITE
(Map p70; 🗷416-396-2819; www.toronto.ca/todmordenmills; 67 Pottery Rd; adult/child $8/5, gallery free; ⊙10am-4:30pm Tue-Fri, noon-5pm Sat & Sun Jun-Aug, noon-4pm Wed-Sun Sep-May; 🅿; 🆂Broadview) In an idyllic setting by the Don River, Todmorden Mills is a late-18th-century grist mill turned saw mill, then brewery and distillery, then paper mill. Historical relics are on display inside. Enthusiastic guides show visitors around old millers' houses and the petite Don train station. To get here, take the subway to Broadview station, then board any bus. Alight at Mortimer/Pottery Rd (Dairy Queen), turn left and walk down Pottery Rd.

◉ **Greater Toronto Area (GTA)**

Further afield, in outlying areas of the Greater Toronto Area (GTA), where Toronto's neighborhoods start to become suburbs and begin to look the same, there are a number of worthy attractions: the Scarborough Bluffs (p87), the Aga Khan Museum (p87) and the spectacular McMichael Canadian Art Collection (p87). The downer? Public

ONTARIO TORONTO

LGBTIQ+ TORONTO

To say Toronto is LGBTIQ+ friendly is an understatement. That it embraces diversity more fully than most other centers of its size is closer to the mark. In 2003 Toronto became the first city in North America to legalize same-sex marriage. Just over a year later, an Ontario Court also recognized the first legal same-sex divorce.

Toronto's Pride festival (p92) is one of the largest in the world, and lasts a month. On Parade day, the streets around Church and Wellesley swell with over a million happy LGBTIQ+ folks and their friends and families. If Pride is your bag, be sure to book accommodations well in advance. At other times of the year, the Church St strip of the Village draws everyone from biker bears to lipstick lesbians to its modest smattering of sunny patios, pubs, cafes and restaurants for promenading and people-watching. After dark it's all about the dancing: whether for cabaret or drag, thumping top-40 and R & B or queer alterna-punk, late-night revelers spill onto the streets, especially on weekends.

Other gay-friendly neighborhoods include the Annex, Kensington, Queen West, Cabbagetown and Leslieville (aka 'Lesbianville'). Gay nightlife venues are abundant, and although men's bars and clubs vastly outnumber lesbian venues, Toronto is also home to drag kings, women-only bathhouse nights and lesbian reading series.

Toronto is a great place to be gay or to explore your sexuality. Head to the *Daily Xtra* (www.dailyxtra.com) internet magazine for the latest scoop on LGBTIQ+ issues in the Village. There are also plenty of fantastic free community resources and support groups:

519 (Church St Community Centre; Map p78; 🗷416-392-6874; www.the519.org; 519 Church St; ⊙8:30am-10pm Mon-Fri, 9am-5pm Sat, 10am-5pm Sun; 🆂Wellesley)

Canadian Lesbian & Gay Archives (Map p78; 🗷416-777-2755; www.clga.ca; 34 Isabella St; ⊙6:30-9pm Tue-Thu, 1-5pm Fri; 🆂Wellesley)

Hassle Free Clinic (Map p78; 🗷416-922-0566; www.hasslefreeclinic.org; 2nd fl, 66 Gerrard St E; ⊙10am-3pm & 4-8pm Mon-Thu, to 7pm Fri, 10am-2pm Sat; 🆂College)

Queer West (www.queerwest.org)

West Toronto

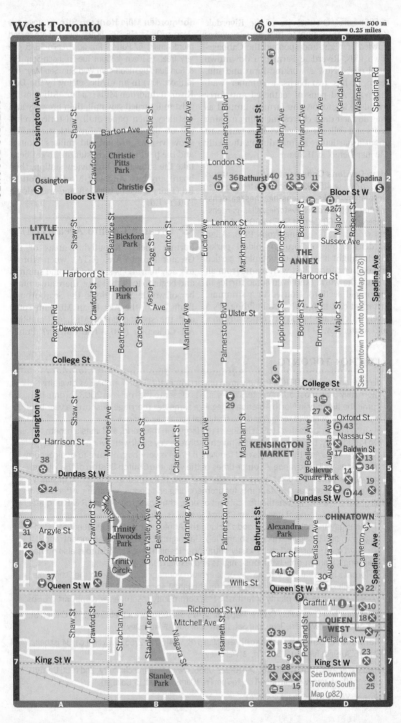

0 — 500 m
0 — 0.25 miles

West Toronto

transportation isn't the easiest and driving means traffic.

⭐**McMichael Canadian Art Collection** GALLERY
(☏905-893-1121; www.mcmichael.com; 10365 Islington Ave, Kleinburg; adult/child $18/15, Tue $15/12; ⊙10am-5pm May-Oct, to 4pm Tue-Sun Nov-Apr; 🅿; 🚌13) Handcrafted buildings (including painter Tom Thomson's cabin, moved from its original location), set amid 40 hectares of conservation trails, contain works by Canada's best-known landscape painters, the Group of Seven, as well as works by First Nations, Inuit, Métis and other acclaimed Canadian artists. It's a 34km, 45-minute drive from Toronto and totally worth the trip. A sculpture garden and the graves of gallery co-founders Robert and Signe McMichaels and six of the Group of Seven artists are also on-site.

Aga Khan Museum MUSEUM
(Map p70; ☏416-646-4677; https://agakhanmu seum.org; 77 Wynford Dr, North York; adult/child $20/10, 4-8pm Wed free; ⊙10am-6pm Tue, to 8pm Wed, to 6pm Thu-Sun; 🅿; 🚌34C, 100A) Located just outside Toronto, the Aga Khan is the first museum in North America dedicated to Islamic art. The magnificent building houses the extensive collection of the late Prince Sadruddin Aga Khan, including works originating from places as diverse as the Iberian peninsula and China, created over a span of 1000 years. Tours of the collection, special exhibits and grounds are available for an additional fee. Music and dance performances regularly held – check the website for the calendar. Parking $10.

Scarborough Bluffs PARK
(The Bluffs; ☏416-392-1111; www.toronto.ca; Scarborough; ⊙dawn-dusk; 🅿; 🚌12, Ⓢ Victoria Park) **FREE** Lakeshore cliffs with cathedral-spire formations expose evidence of five glacial periods at Scarborough Bluffs. Spanning 14km, from **Rosetta McClain Gardens** to **East Point Park**, this is a stunning landscape as well as an important stopover for migrating birds. Several trails allow visitors to enjoy meadows, forests, beaches, wetlands and spectacular views across Lake Ontario. The

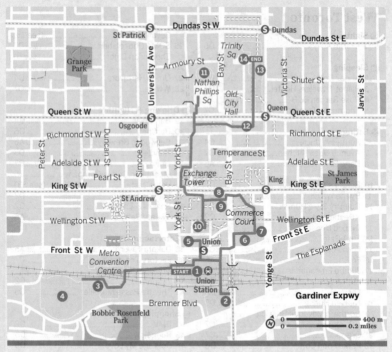

City Walk
Subterranean Toronto

START UNION STATION
END TRINITY SQ
LENGTH 2.5KM; THREE TO FIVE HOURS

When it's just too cold to be outside, duck into Toronto's underground PATH (www.toronto.ca/path) system, a 28km labyrinth of subterranean corridors connecting downtown sights, skyscrapers and shops. You'll be surprised at how much is interconnected. Allow yourself a full day if you want to do all of the below.

From ❶**Union Station** (p117) you can head southeast to ❷**Scotiabank Arena** (p114) or follow the tubular SkyWalk over the train tracks, emerging outdoors at the iconic ❸**CN Tower** (p76), next to the ❹**Rogers Centre** (p113). The tower is a must-see, even if just from the outside.

Back at Union Station PATH, cross beneath Front St and up the staircase into the ❺**Fairmont Royal York** (p96). From here, follow the color-coded arrows to ❻**Brookfield Place** and the ❼**Hockey Hall of Fame** (p76). Wander through Commerce Court to the ❽**TD Centre**. Beyond the digital stock-market displays, go left and emerge at the ❾**Design Exchange** (p77).

From back beneath the TD Centre, follow signs for the TD Waterhouse Tower to the ❿**Toronto Gallery of Inuit Art** (p76). Next, head toward the Standard Life Centre, the Exchange Tower and then the Richmond-Adelaide complex. You'll pass the Sheraton Centre to reach ⓫**City Hall** (p81) and Nathan Phillips Sq, which in winter becomes an ice-skating rink with a cheery mood.

From City Hall you can head back underground and follow the signs for ⓬**Hudson's Bay** (Canada's oldest department store) and shop till you drop. The PATH continues to the ⓭**Eaton Centre** (p114), whose large atrium plazas bring the feeling of outside in. From here, it's easy to reach Trinity Sq in the shadow of the ⓮**Church of the Holy Trinity** (Map p78; ☑416-598-4521; www.holytrinitytoronto.org; 10 Trinity Sq; ⊙11am-3pm Mon-Fri, 8am-2pm Sun, services 12:15pm Wed, 10:30am & 2pm Sun; Ⓢ Dundas) or pick up the subway at Dundas station for your onward journey.

highest section, grassy **Cathedral Bluffs Park** (65m), makes a great photo op. Below, **Bluffers Park Beach** is the best place to appreciate the jutting cliffs and spires.

About 6km east is **Guild Park**, a serene 36-hectare lakefront forest filled with architectural relics and sculptures collected from the 1950s to the 1970s by the forward-thinking Rosa and Spencer Clark.

Without wheels, getting to the Bluffs can be a drag. Take the subway to Victoria Park, then bus 12 along Kingston Rd to Cathedral Bluffs Dr, east of the St Clair Ave E intersection. If you're driving, Kingston Rd (Hwy 2) runs parallel to the lakeshore; turn south onto Brimley Rd for Bluffers Park Beach, south at Cathedral Bluffs Dr to reach Cathedral Bluffs Park, or south on Guildwood Pkwy for Guild Park.

Canada's Wonderland   AMUSEMENT PARK
([✓] 905-832-8131; www.canadaswonderland.com; 9580 Jane St, Vaughan; day passes $66; ⊙ 10am-10pm Jun-Aug, Sat & Sun only with earlier closing May & Sep; [P]; [S] Vaughan) Amusement-park lovers will want to trek to this, Canada's largest, featuring more than 60 rides, including the mammoth Leviathan, with a peak height of 93m! There's also an exploding volcano, the 20-hectare Splash Works water park and a white-water canyon. Queues can be lengthy. Most rides operate no matter the weather; tickets are cheaper online. From the Vaughan subway stop, catch the 20 bus (operated by York Region Transit).

 Activities

They're often muffled in winter layers, but Torontonians still like to keep fit. Outdoor activities abound: folks walk, cycle and jog along the lakeshore and hike up the city's ravines. They kayak and paddleboard on Lake Ontario. Ice-skating and hockey are winter faves.

Cycling

For cyclists, the **Martin Goodman Trail** (Map p82; Queens Quay W), a 56km paved recreational trail running along the Beaches and the Waterfront to the Humber River in the west, is the place to go. Head for the lake and you'll find it. On the way you can connect to the Don Valley mountain-bike trails at Cherry St as well as leafy High Park (p84) in the West End. On the Toronto Islands, the south-shore boardwalk and the interconnecting paved paths are car free. For a longer trek, the Martin Goodman Trail is part of the Lake Ontario Waterfront Trail (www.waterfronttrail.org), stretching 450km from east of Toronto to Niagara-on-the-Lake.

If you choose to explore Toronto by bike, stick to marked cycling trails when possible. Although many locals cycle to work, downtown is fraught with peril: aggressive drivers, streetcars and phone-blinded pedestrians. Cyclists do get hit by car doors, and rider accidents from connecting with streetcar tracks aren't uncommon. Though there's no legal requirement that adults wear a helmet in Ontario, anyone 17 and younger must wear one.

Essential information for cyclists can be found at www.toronto.ca/cycling/map. For real-time route planning, go to www.ridethecity.com.

Toronto Islands
Bicycle Rental   CYCLING
(Map p70; [✓] 416-203-0009; www.torontoislandbicyclerental.com; Centre Island; per hour bicycles/tandems $9/16, 2-/4-seat quadricycles $18/32; ⊙ 11am-5pm May-Sep; [🚗]; [🚊] Centre Island) One of the best ways to explore the islands is by bike. A variety of options are offered here, including tandems, quadricycles and smaller frames for kids. Helmets are provided. Look for the shop next to Outlook Pier.

Hiking

Feel like stretching your legs? Delve into Toronto's city parks, nature reserves or ravines, such as Tommy Thompson Park (p79), Evergreen Brick Works (p84) or High Park (p84). Alternatively, hook up with a group such as Hike Ontario (www.hikeontario.com) or the Toronto Bruce Trail Club (www.torontobrucetrailclub.org) for hardy day hikes.

Ice Skating

Locals love to skate. When the weather's freezing and the snow's falling lightly, downtown Toronto's outdoor ice rinks come alive. The best-known rinks are at **Nathan Phillips Square** outside City Hall (p81) and the **Natrel Rink** (Map p82; [✓] 416-954-9866; www.harbourfrontcentre.com; Harbourfront Centre, 235 Queens Quay W; ⊙ 9am-10pm Sun-Thu, to 11pm Fri & Sat Nov-Mar; [🚗]; [🚊] 509, 510) at the Harbourfront Centre. These artificial rinks are open daily (weather permitting) from 10am to 10pm from mid-November to March. Admission is free; skate rental is available. Toronto Parks & Recreation (www.toronto.ca/parks) has info on other rinks around town, including those at Kew Gardens (p79) in the Beaches and **Trinity Bellwoods Park**

East End

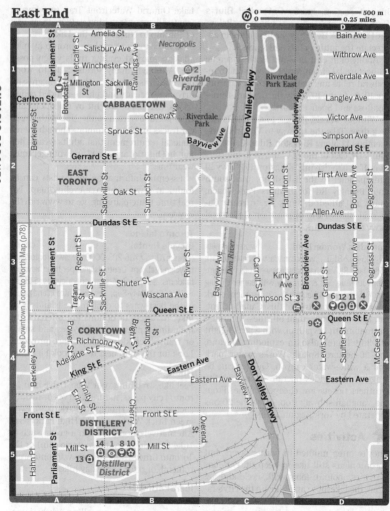

in the West End. If it's been *really* cold, you can skate on **Grenadier Pond** in High Park (p84). Beginners might prefer the lesser-known **Ryerson Rink**, tucked away just north of Yonge & Dundas Sq at 25 Gould St – in summer the rink is a water feature.

Swimming

Torontonians generally avoid swimming in Lake Ontario, despite the presence of a dozen city beaches tended by lifeguards from July to August, eight of which are Blue Flag certified. Before taking the plunge, check with the Beach Water Quality Hotline (app.toronto.ca/tpha/beaches.

html), as water quality deteriorates after heavy rain and the presence of *E. coli* bacteria is a potential risk.

From June to September the City of Toronto operates more than 50 outdoor swimming pools, generally open from dawn to dusk. The complete list is found at www.toronto.ca.

Water Sports

★ **Toronto Island SUP**   WATER SPORTS
(Map p70; ☑ 416-899-1668; www.torontoislandsup.com; 13 Algonquin Bridge Rd, Algonquin Island; 2hr tours from $79, yoga $49, rental 1st/additional hour $30/10; ⊙10:30am-before sunset Mon-Fri,

East End

ONTARIO TORONTO

10am-6pm Sat & Sun; 🚢 Ward's Island) 🏄 Join a paddleboard tour to explore the 14 islands that make up the Toronto Islands archipelago. Morning and afternoon excursions focus on flora and fauna, while night tours (with illuminated paddles) let you take in the city views. There are whimsical ukulele tours (yep, paddle and play) and yoga classes on the water, too. Rentals available. Launches are from Algonquin Bridge.

Boat House KAYAKING
(Map p70; 🗹 416-397-5166; Centre Island; 1/3hr single kayak $19/43, double kayak $38/99, canoe $30/76; ☺11am-6pm Mon-Fri, to 7pm Sat & Sun; 🚶; 🚢 Centre Island) Explore the islands' waterways in a kayak or canoe. Look for the Boat House off Lakeshore Ave on the southern side of Centre Island, across the channel from Centreville Amusement Park (p76). Debit or credit card only.

👉 Tours

Boat
Between May and September cruise operators sail from the waterfront beside Queens Quay Terminal or York Quay Centre. Reservations are recommended for brunch and dinner cruises. Keep in mind that ferries to the Toronto Islands offer similar views for half the price.

Bus
Toronto isn't exactly London, Paris or Rome, where it's easy to ooh and ahh at endless historic marvels from the comfort of a coach. That said, taking a hop-on, hop off bus tour is a good way to get the lay of the land. If traveling on a budget, you might find better value in a TTC day pass, exploring for yourself.

★**Chariots of Fire** BUS
(Map p82; 🗹 905-877-0855; www.tourniagarafalls.com; day tours $77; ☺7am-9pm Mon-Sat, 1-9pm Sun; 🚆 King) Low-cost day tours from Toronto to Niagara Falls, including free time in the historic village of Niagara-on-the-Lake and a winery tour. A boat ride on the *Hornblower Niagara* is available as an add-on. These guys are highly organized and comfortably present the best of the Falls, from Toronto, for those who only have a day to experience it all. Highly recommended.

★**ROMBus** BUS
(Map p78; 🗹 416-586-8000; www.rom.on.ca/en/whats-on/rombus; 100 Queen's Park; full-day tours $135-145; 🚆 Museum) Toronto's Royal Ontario Museum (p81) organizes occasional special tours, with educated and enthusiastic guides, around historical, cultural and architectural themes. Full-day tours are either in town or within a couple of hours of it. Although they're pricey, the tours are well worth it if they pique your interest.

Walking & Cycling
The easiest way to experience Toronto is on foot, though cycling allows you to cover a bit more territory. If you opt for an organized tour, you'll also learn interesting facts about the city, its history, its food – even its ghosts!

★**Toronto Bicycle Tours** CYCLING
(🗹 416-477-2184; https://torontobicycletours.com; adult/child from $46/75; ☺8am-6pm) Offering year-round bike tours – even in winter (ponchos and gloves provided) – of downtown, 15 neighborhoods and the Toronto Islands. Excursions are for all levels and ages, and last 3½ to seven hours. Bike, helmet, water and snacks are provided (plus picnic lunch for longer tours). Multilingual guides or interpreters, too.

★ **Heritage Toronto**   WALKING
(Map p82; ☑ 416-338-3886; www.heritagetoronto.
org; 157 King St E; suggested donation $10; ☺ May-
Oct) A diverse offering of fascinating historical, cultural and nature walks, as well as
bus (TTC) tours, led by museum experts,
neighborhood historical-society members
and emerging historians. Tours generally
last one to three hours. Check the website
for a handful of downloadable self-guided
tours, too.

✵ Festivals & Events

January

Next Stage Festival   THEATER
(☑ 416-966-1062; http://fringetoronto.com/next-
stage-festival; 125 Bathurst St; tickets from $12;
☺ Jan; 🚌 501, 504A, 504B) From the people behind the Toronto Fringe Festival, Next Stage
showcases the work of a dozen fringe artists
at the Factory Theatre (p113), as a platform
for future success. The January event has a
heated beer tent where audiences can mingle with the cast and crew before and after
performances.

Winterlicious   FOOD & DRINK
(☑ 416-392-2489; www.toronto.ca/winterlicious;
☺ late Jan) For two weeks in January, a staggering array of restaurants lures residents
out of their living rooms for a prix-fixe extravaganza of lunches and dinners that
showcases Toronto's culinary diversity. If
you're visiting in winter, be sure to take advantage of these fantastic eats!

April

Hot Docs   FILM
(Canadian International Documentary Festival;
☑ 416-637-3123; www.hotdocs.ca; 506 Bloor St
W; from $17.50; ☺ late Apr-early May; 🚇 Bathurst)
North America's largest documentary-film
festival screens more than 200 docos from
around the globe from its home at the fantastic Hot Docs Ted Rogers Cinema (p113)
plus other venues around town, including
museums and theaters.

Seniors and students have access to free
tickets for screenings before 5pm; tickets issued same day only.

May

Doors Open Toronto   CULTURAL
(www.toronto.ca/doorsopen; ☺ late May) **FREE**
Over the fourth weekend of May, several
public and private buildings of architectural
and historical significance creak open their
doors, allowing you to sneak a free peek at

what's hot and what's not in other people's
digs. Book ahead for walking tours and big-
name buildings such as City Hall and Union
Station.

Inside Out   FILM
(Toronto LGBT Film Festival; ☑ 416-977-6847; www.
insideout.ca; 350 King St W; tickets from $48;
☺ late May-early Jun; 🚌 504) Since 1991, this
Toronto LGBTIQ+ film festival has showcased a huge range of international films
produced by and about lesbian, gay, bisexual
and trans people; screenings are at the fantastic TIFF Bell Lightbox (p113). The festival
starts the last week of May to help kick off
Pride Toronto in June.

Union Summer   FOOD & DRINK
(☑ 416-338-0889; http://torontounion.ca; Union
Station, 65 Front St W; ☺ 11am-9pm Mon-Wed, to
10pm Thu-Sat, to 6pm Sun; ♿; 🚇 Union) Union
Station's summer food market was such a hit
in 2015 that it has become a fixture, with a
daily market of gourmet food stalls, activities, free outdoor film screenings, live music
and drinks from late May to early August.

June

Dreams Festival   MUSIC
(http://dreamsfestival.ca; Ontario Place, 909 Lake
Shore Blvd W; ☺ Jun; 🚌 509) A two-day festival that draws more than 25,000 ravers
and electronic-music lovers every summer
to massive Ontario Place along Toronto's
waterfront.

Luminato   CULTURAL
(☑ 416-368-4849; www.luminatofestival.com;
☺ Jun) Luminato seeks to bring a broad selection of the world's most accomplished
musicians, dancers, artists, writers, actors
and filmmakers to venues across Toronto
in a celebration of creativity that reflects
the city's diversity. Many performances are
free. Past performers have included Aretha
Franklin, Joni Mitchell, kd lang and Rufus
Wainwright.

Pride Toronto   LGBTIQ+
(☑ 416-927-7433; www.pridetoronto.com; ☺ Jun)
Toronto's most flamboyant event celebrates
the diversity of sexuality and gender identity, with a whole month (it was a week) of
community events, workshops and gather-
ings, mostly free. The celebration climaxes
with a Trans March, Dyke March and Pride
Parade at the end of June, when the streets
around Church and Wellesley ('the Village')
heave with over a million revelers.

North by Northeast PERFORMING ARTS
(NXNE; 416-901-6963; www.nxne.com; tickets from $8, wristband $29; mid-Jun) Musos can safely write off 10 days in mid-June as they sample the plethora of indie bands and comedy acts to be had in some of Toronto's coolest venues, including nontraditional ones such as streetcars and ferries. Pay by the show or get a wristband for total access. Free shows make for a packed Yonge & Dundas Sq, the festival's epicenter.

National Indigenous Peoples Day CULTURAL
(National Aboriginal Day; www.aadnc-aandc.gc.ca; Jun 21;) Canada's heritage of First Nations, Inuit and Métis cultures is celebrated on the summer solstice, a historically significant day for several indigenous communities. Events include powwows, film screenings and workshops on the day as well as the week leading up to it.

Toronto Jazz Festival MUSIC
(416-928-2033; www.tojazz.com; late Jun) Jazz, blues and soul blaze in Toronto's streets, nightclubs and concert halls in late June. Free and ticketed shows are offered during the 10-day festival, which features more than 1500 top musicians.

Open Roof Festival FILM
(www.openrooffestival.com; $15; Jun-Aug; Dundas West) This enthusiastic bunch of film- and music-lovers puts together a season of outdoor film screenings and bands in an open lot adjacent to 158 Sterling Rd in the up-and-coming Lower Junction neighborhood. Food trucks sell a variety of tasty treats.

July

Toronto Fringe Festival CULTURAL
(416-966-1062; http://fringetoronto.com; $13; early Jul) Celebrating over 30 years in the spotlight, Toronto's largest theater and performance festival hosts more than 150 productions on three dozen stages over two weeks in early July. Ranging from offbeat to seriously emotive and including a program of kids' plays, the festival aims to make theater accessible to all. It's worth booking your trip to Toronto to coincide with it.

Beaches International
Jazz Festival MUSIC
(416-698-2152; www.beachesjazz.com; Jul) FREE This free, month-long jazz fest plays to stages at Jimmie Simpson Park, Woodbine Park and Kew Gardens and along the Beach-

es boardwalk. The highlight is the three-day Streetfest, when a 1.5km stretch of Queen St E is closed to traffic and opened to the sounds of more than 50 Canadian bands and thousands of admiring pedestrians.

Summerlicious FOOD & DRINK
(416-392-2489; www.toronto.ca/summerlicious; Jul) Be sure to book your tables in advance for this culinary extravaganza, held at almost 200 restaurants, bars and cafes across the city. Great-value prix-fixe menus in three price categories mean there's something to suit most tastes and budgets.

August
Canadian
National Exhibition AGRICULTURAL
(CNE; 416-263-3330; www.theex.com; btwn Strachan Ave & Dufferin St; adult/child $20/16; late Aug-early Sep; ; 509, 511) Dating from 1879, 'The Ex' features more than 700 exhibitors, agricultural shows, lumberjack competitions, outdoor concerts and carnivalia at **Exhibition Place** (Map p70; 416-263-3600; www.explace.on.ca;), off Lake Shore Blvd W, in the 18 days leading up to Labour Day (the first Monday of September). The air show and Labour Day fireworks take the cake.

September
Toronto International
Film Festival FILM
(TIFF; 888-599-8433; www.tiff.net; Sep; 504) Since its inception in 1976, TIFF has grown to be the crowning jewel of the Toronto festival scene and a key player in the world film circuit. Attracting over 400,000 eager cinephiles to the red-carpet celebrity frenzy of its 10-day run, the festival has become an important forum for showcasing new films.

In 1990 the festival expanded operations to include the year-round TIFF Cinematheque program, showcasing works from around the world. Two decades later, the Bell Lightbox (p113), with its five stunning cinemas, funky restaurants and bar, opened its doors as the permanent home for the festival and organization.

If you're coming to town for TIFF, be sure to book ahead: tickets for screenings and events sell fast, while already elevated room rates go through the roof closer to showtime. Celebrities and paparazzi are in town and Torontonians come from far and wide to embrace the Hollywood spirit: catch a glimpse if you can!

October

Nuit Blanche Toronto　　　　　　CULTURAL
(http://nbto.com; ⊘1st Sat Oct) One night, from
sunset to sunrise. Over 130 urban art experiences, all over town. Art installations, performance art, interactive dance pieces and
an all-night street market are part of the
(sometimes chaotic) fun.

International
Festival of Authors　　　　　　LITERATURE
(☑416-973-4000; www.readings.org; York Quay,
235 Queens Quay W; from $20; ⊘late-Oct; ⓐ;
⍟509, 510) For 11 days in late October, this
festival corrals acclaimed authors from
Canada and beyond at the Harbourfront
Centre (p72) for readings, discussions, lectures, awards and book signings. There are
kid-friendly events, too.

November

Royal Agricultural Winter Fair　AGRICULTURAL
(☑416-263-3400; www.royalfair.org; btwn Strachan Ave & Dufferin St; adult/child $27.50/16;
⊘Nov; ⍟509, 511) Since 1922 the world's largest indoor agricultural and equestrian fair
has been warming up audiences at Exhibition Place (p93), off Lake Shore Blvd W, for
10 days in November.

December

Toronto Christmas Market　CHRISTMAS MARKET
(www.torontochristmasmarket.com; 9 Trinity St;
Fri-Sun $6, Tue-Thu free; ⊘Tue-Sun mid-Nov-
late Dec; ⓐ; ⍟72, ⍟503, 504) The Distillery
District (p77) is at its festive best from
mid-November to Christmas Eve during its
European-style Christmas Market, showcasing hundreds of local handcrafted products, a carousel and photo ops with Santa.

🛏 Sleeping

Toronto has no shortage of accommodations, from high-rise hotels in the Financial District to boutique hotels in the West
End. B&Bs are in residential neighborhoods,
while hostels dot the city. Lodging can be expensive, especially in summer, when rooms
sell quickly and at a premium. It's essential
to book ahead, remembering that 13% tax
will be added to the quoted rate. An additional 3% destination tax is sometimes lev-
ied, too.

🛏 Waterfront

Hotel X Toronto　　　　　　HOTEL $$$
(Map p70; ☑647-943-9300; http://hotelxtoronto.
com; 111 Princes' Blvd; d from $399; Ⓟ⊜❄🛜🏊;

⍟509) From the incredible waterfront and
skyline views to exquisite fine-dining op-
tions, Hotel X Toronto is the ultimate urban
resort. Rooms feature floor-to-ceiling win-
dows and stylishly modern interiors. Next
door is Ten X Toronto, a 90,000-sq-ft sports-
club complex; hotel guests enjoy access to
select amenities such as indoor tennis courts
and fitness studios.

Westin Harbour Castle　　　　HOTEL $$$
(Map p82; ☑416-869-1600; www.westinharbour
castletoronto.com; 1 Harbour Sq; d from $303;
Ⓟ⊜❄🛜🏊; ⍟509, 510) If this were a ham-
burger, it'd be with the works – restaurants,
shops, gym, conference center, pool, disa-
bled-access suites etc. Staff are surprisingly
chipper for such a big hotel. Maybe the lobby keeps them amused: there's enough marble to rival any Hollywood mansion. Tasty
lake views.

🛏 Toronto Islands

Toronto Island Retreat　　　APARTMENT $$
(Map p70; ☑416-822-3454; www.torontoisland
retreat.com; 5 Third St, Ward's Island; apt $150-
175, per week $900-980; ⊘Apr-Oct; ⊜❄🛜;
🛥Ward's Island) Two impressive apartments
in a well-maintained island home have a
modern country feel, accented by throw pil-
lows and art. The larger has a sleek kitchen
and a separate sleeping area; the smaller
has a surprisingly comfortable Murphy bed
and a fully equipped kitchenette. Both have
private patios and even laundry equipment.
Picnic blankets and beach towels are nice
touches.

Smiley's B&B　　　　　　　B&B $$
(Map p70; ☑416-203-8599; www.erelda.ca; 4
Dacotah Ave, Algonquin Island; s/d with shared bath
$125/136, apt per night/week $318/1779; ⊜❄🛜;
🛥Ward's Island) Catch some zzzs in sunny little 'Eric's Room' and dine with the hosts, or
hole up in the spacious apartment (June to
September only), with its own kitchen and
bathroom. Either way, relaxation is sure to
come easy on the car-free islands. The B&B
is on the residential island of Algonquin, a
10-minute walk from the Ward's Island ferry
dock.

🛏 Entertainment & Financial Districts

Clarence Park　　　　　　HOSTEL $
(Map p82; ☑416-591-7387; www.theclarence
park.com; 7 Clarence Sq; incl breakfast dm $49-53,

TORONTO FOR CHILDREN

Toronto is a kid-friendly city with a wide range of options for children of all ages: museums and parks, sights and thrills. The TTC makes it easy – kids travel for free – and most places offer discounted admission rates.

Curious Minds

Royal Ontario Museum (p81) Towering dinosaur skeletons, mummies, suits of armor, bat caves, hands-on exhibits and more – much more – keep kiddos engaged at this remarkable museum. Trained facilitators answer questions and provide suggestions on what to do next.

LEGOLAND Discovery Centre (☐ 1-855-356-2150; www.legolanddiscoverycentre.ca/toronto; 1 Bass Pro Mills Dr, Vaughan; $28; ☉ 10am-9pm Mon-Sat, 11am-7pm Sun; P ♿; S Yorkdale) Younger kids with a penchant for Legos will be fascinated by the many building possibilities here. Master builders are on hand to help with projects big and small.

Ontario Science Centre (Map p70; ☐ 416-696-1000; www.ontariosciencecentre.ca; 770 Don Mills Rd; science center adult/child $22/13, IMAX $13/9, combined ticket $28/19; ☉ 10am-5pm Sun-Fri, to 8pm Sat; P ♿; ☐ 34, 25) Though this center is a bit dated, the hands-on science exhibits, live demonstrations and IMAX theater are hits with children, especially those with lots of questions about how the world around them works.

Thrill Seekers

CN Tower (p76) Teens can experience the ultimate thrill: the EdgeWalk, a 116-story-high walk around the outer perimeter, with nothing between them and the city below. (A tether to a metal rail keeps them safe!)

Canada's Wonderland (p89) More than 60 rides, ranging from white-knuckle roller coasters to carousels, keep children of all ages happy at this amusement park. A water park seals the deal.

Centreville Amusement Park (p76) An antique carousel, rides and a miniature train are a thrill for little ones here. A petting zoo is a great backup if the rides prove too scary!

d $110-140; P @ 🛜; S St Andrew) In a picturesque location you'll find this budget gem with cozy, clean dorms and fresh private rooms, with some overlooking a leafy park: all have en-suite bathrooms. There's free wifi, a fabulous, modern communal kitchen, and a huge rooftop deck with barbecue for those lazy summer afternoons in the city. Private rooms are next door, making them a bit quieter.

Beverley   HOTEL $$
(Map p78; ☐ 416-493-2786; www.thebeverley hotel.ca; 335 Queen St W; r from $229; ⊕ ❄ 🛜; S Osgoode, ☐ 301, 501) Tucked between shops in a trendy part of Queen St W, the Beverley is all about location. Its small, minimalist rooms are pleasant in a streamlined way, with whitewashed walls, wood floors and huge historical photos of the neighborhood. Standards only have interior-facing windows – a bummer, but that also means no street noise. The rooftop patio is fab.

★**Bisha Hotel**   BOUTIQUE HOTEL $$$
(Map p82; ☐ 416-551-2800; www.bishahotel toronto.com; 80 Blue Jays Way; d from $379; P ⊕ ❄ 🛜 ❄; ☐ 504) Upscale but decently priced Bisha is a luxury hotel and residence in the heart of the Entertainment District; it's also right off King St W, a chic neighborhood lined with popular bars and restaurants. Rooms are sleek and stylish, and there's a rooftop pool with stunning views of Toronto's famous skyline. Also on the rooftop is restaurant Kost, great for brunch.

★**Thompson Toronto**   HOTEL $$$
(Map p86; ☐ 416-640-7778; www.thompson hotels.com/toronto; 550 Wellington St W; d from $369; P ❄ 🛜 ❄ ❄; ☐ 504, 508) Many love Thompson Toronto – it's just so LA. Urban-chic rooms will be favored by those with a penchant for design and city skylines (check out the website's snaps); the rooftop bar, patio and infinity pool are easily Toronto's finest; and the on-site dining option, Thompson Diner (p100), independently deserves

mention. A brilliant location and exceptional service round things off.

Fairmont Royal York
HOTEL $$$

(Map p82; ☑416-368-2511; www.fairmont.com/royalyork; 100 Front St W; r $289-549, ste $569-799; P❋❀🐾; ⑤Union) Since 1929 Toronto icon the Royal York (a former grande dame of the Canadian Pacific Railway) has accommodated everyone from Tina Turner to Henry Kissinger – not that it shows: the 1300-plus guest rooms have undergone several renovations over the years to maintain their grandeur. Consider high tea in the Library Bar and a chance to visit the rooftop apiary.

Shangri-La Hotel
HOTEL $$$

(Map p82; ☑647-788-8888; www.shangri-la.com/toronto; 188 University Ave; r/ste from $368/475; P❀❋@🐾; ⑤St Andrew) Five-star Shangri-La's elegant guest rooms strive to synthesize Asian simplicity with Western indulgence and are among Toronto's largest. Each has separate marble bath, shower and toilet room, opening floor-to-ceiling windows, espresso machines, and smartphone docks. All have city views, too. The University Ave location is fantastic.

🛏 Old Town, Corktown & Distillery District

★ Hostelling International Toronto
HOSTEL $

(Map p82; ☑416-971-4440; www.hostelling toronto.com; 76 Church St; dm/d from $40/120; ❀❋🐾; 🚌504) This award-winning hostel doesn't look much from the outside, but it gets votes for its rooftop deck and friendly staff. Most dorms have their own bathrooms, and deluxe rooms offer good-value private accommodations. All guests receive a daily meal voucher to use at the on-site Cavern Bar & Bistro, a cool-cat hangout. Theme game nights and pub crawls help you make friends.

Cambridge Suites
HOTEL $$

(Map p78; ☑416-368-1990; www.cambridge suitestoronto.com; 15 Richmond St E; ste from $247; P❀❋🐾🐾; ⑤Queen) 🐾 An excellent midrange choice, this all-suite hotel has spacious, good-looking rooms with separate living and kitchen facilities. Cityscape suites, on upper floors, are more luxuriously appointed and their rates include continental breakfast in the on-site restaurant. Three impressive penthouses are also available.

Executive Cosmopolitan Hotel
BOUTIQUE HOTEL $$

(Map p82; ☑416-350-2000; www.cosmotoronto.com; 8 Colborne St; ste from $224; P❀❋🐾; ⑤King) This compact hotel is sleek and quiet, with only five rooms per floor. Entry-level Zen suites are on the small side. Lotus and Tranquility suites are significantly larger and have kitchens; some also have lake views. All have balconies. Both the treatment spa and the upscale steakhouse, Wildfire, add to the appeal.

🛏 Downtown Yonge

★ Anndore House
HOTEL $$

(Map p78; ☑833-745-8370; https://theanndore house.com; 15 Charles St E; r from $242; P❋🐾; ⑤Bloor-Yonge) A stylish place with 113 rooms, all with exposed-brick walls, art-deco-meets-boho bathrooms, record players and city views. A hotel app allows guests to control their room's temperature and lighting – a nice touch. Downstairs, a labyrinthine restaurant-bar and a street-side patio are great for an afternoon cocktail or snack.

Downtown Home Inn
B&B $$

(Map p78; ☑877-271-0182; www.downtownhome inn.com; 2 Monteith St; s with shared bath $71-87, d with shared bath $96-112, 1-bedroom apt $145; ❀❋🐾; ⑤Wellesley) An 1886 row house just steps from the Village's main drag, this charming little inn makes a comfortable base. Six contemporary rooms, each different in size and style (one even has a private sundeck), share two modern bathrooms. Lots of breakfast options and keyless entry make it feel homey. A neighboring one-bedroom apartment is also available.

Pantages
BOUTIQUE HOTEL $$

(Map p78; ☑416-362-1777; www.pantageshotel.com; 200 Victoria St; d incl breakfast from $243; P❋@; ⑤Queen) A good choice for longer stays, each of the urban-chic rooms in this all-suite hotel – the closest to Yonge & Dundas Sq, **Massey Hall** (Map p78; ☑416-872-4255; www.masseyhall.com; 178 Victoria St; ⊙box office from noon show days only; ⑤Queen) and the Eaton Centre (p114) – have full bathrooms, kitchen and laundry facilities. It's in a residential building sporting the same name: once you're through the main doors, turn left for the hotel lobby.

Saint James Hotel
HOTEL $$

(Map p78; ☑416-645-2200; www.thesaintjamesho tel.com; 26 Gerrard St E; r from $227; ❀❋🐾;

[S] Dundas, College) Located just off Yonge St, the Saint James offers spacious, comfortable rooms with minimal decor; each has a mini-fridge and microwave, which are great for light snacks. It's a family-run hotel, so service is personable and accommodating.

🛏 Kensington Market & Chinatown

Two Peas Pod Hostel HOSTEL $
(Map p78; ✆ 416-217-1088; www.twopeas.me; 403 Spadina Ave; incl breakfast dm $59-62, r with shared bath $159; ❉ 🛜; 🚊 306, 310, 506, 510) A labyrinthine hostel with 42 'pods': adult-size wooden boxes stacked in twos like shoeboxes. Each has privacy curtains, a memory-foam mattress, a smart TV (with headphones) and a charging station. Modern bathrooms are on the lowest level – a bummer in the middle of the night. Breakfast includes DIY waffles and fruit. A cinema room, laundry and spectacular rooftop lounge are pluses.

Baldwin Village Inn B&B $
(Map p78; ✆ 416-591-5359; www.baldwininn.com; 9 Baldwin St; d incl breakfast with shared bath $100-125; ❉ 🌐 @ 🛜; 🚊 505, 506) In the pretty enclave of Baldwin Village, just a few blocks from the Art Gallery of Ontario (p81), this yellow-painted B&B faces a leafy street filled with cheap, interesting eateries and cafes. The front courtyard is perfect for lounging and people-watching. On weekends, request a quieter garden-facing room.

Hotel Ocho HOTEL $$
(Map p78; ✆ 416-593-0885; www.hotelocho.com; 195 Spadina Ave; r from $239; ❉ 🛜; 🚊 310, 510) Dating from 1902, this heritage building was once a textile factory. Today its rooms retain an urban-industrial feel, with tall ceilings, exposed-brick walls and simple, clean lines. With just 12 rooms, service feels personalized. An upmarket restaurant and bar with floor-to-ceiling windows is a great place to start, or end, the day.

🛏 Yorkville & the Annex

★ Planet Travelers Hostel HOSTEL $
(Map p86; ✆ 647-352-8747; www.theplanettraveler.com; 357 College St; dm/d/tr incl breakfast $45/110/134; ❉ 🛜; 🚊 506) 🖋 The Planet has a long history of delighting guests with its spectacular rooftop patio bar, great rates, and commitment to being clean and green.

It still has perks like laundry facilities and in-locker chargers for your gadgets. Bike rentals, too. With 88 dorm beds, 10 private rooms and slick communal areas, you'll have everything you need to enjoy hostel life.

Annex Hotel HOTEL $$
(Map p86; ✆ 647-694-9868; https://theannex.com; 296 Brunswick Ave; d $222-271; ❉ ❉ 🛜; [S] Bathurst, Spadina) A discreet hotel with a hipster vibe, the Annex aims to make you feel as though you're home. Expect details like key-code door access (no front desk), iPads with Netflix (no TVs), a basket of snacks (just in case) and stairs (yep, no elevator). Cozy beds and huge windows, plus local art and even a record player seal the deal.

Rose Garden B&B B&B $$
(Map p86; ✆ 416-898-0746; www.rosegardenbandb.ca; 1030 Bathurst St; r with shared bath $150-160, d $170-198; P ❉ ❉ 🛜; [S] Bathurst) A little B&B in a redbrick house, the Rose Garden has four contemporary and tidy rooms with luxurious beds and fine linens. A full breakfast is served each morning – a chance to enjoy a homemade meal as well as the company of the affable owners. Common areas include a nice 2nd-story deck and a kitchen for coffee and tea.

★ Hazelton BOUTIQUE HOTEL $$$
(Map p78; ✆ 416-963-6300; www.thehazeltonhotel.com; 118 Yorkville Ave; d from $484; P ❉ 🛜 ❉ ❉; [S] Bay) Competitors in the luxury class have in recent years made it harder for the Hazelton to uphold its self-professed reputation as Toronto's most exclusive hotel: but try it will, and you'll only benefit from its efforts. Sophisticated, dramatic and sexy, this hotel is small enough (with just 62 rooms and 15 suites) to make you feel truly special.

★ Four Seasons LUXURY HOTEL $$$
(Map p78; ✆ 416-964-0411; www.fourseasons.com/toronto; 60 Yorkville Ave; d from $785; P ❉ ❉ 🛜 ❉; [S] Bay) One of Toronto's most respected high-end hotels, the Four Seasons is all about luxury, relaxation and enjoyment: crisp, light-filled rooms with stunning views, to-die-for granite bathrooms, and an exquisite lobby. A full line of treatments and wellness services (even a psychic reading!) is offered at 'spa,' where the body pampering and soul elevation are up there with heaven.

Also on-site is the Michelin-starred Café Boulud.

Kimpton St George HOTEL **$$$**
(Map p78; ☑416-968-0010; www.kimptonsaint
george.com; 280 Bloor St W; r/ste from $394/510;
P♿❄🐾🤖; Ⓢ St George, Spadina) A chic ho-
tel with a modern-meets-boho style, the St
George offers spacious and artfully appoint-
ed rooms, many with lovely city views. Su-
perb customer service is the focus, from the
doormen to the front desk. A nightly wine
hour, complimentary coffee and tea service,
and free bikes and yoga mats are a few ad-
ditional perks.

Windsor Arms BOUTIQUE HOTEL **$$$**
(Map p78; ☑416-971-9666; www.windsorarms
hotel.com; 18 St Thomas St; ste from $396; P❄🤖
❄; Ⓢ Bay) Even if you don't stay the night
at this exquisite piece of Toronto history, be
sure to drop in for afternoon tea. The 1927
neo-Gothic mansion boasts a grand entryway, stained-glass windows, polished service
and its own coat of arms. Luxurious oversize
suites have separate tub and shower, Molton
Brown amenities, butler service and buffet
breakfast.

🛏 West End

Bonnevue Manor B&B **$$**
(Map p70; ☑416-536-1455; www.bonnevuemanor.
com; 33 Beaty Ave; d incl breakfast from $135;
P♿❄🐾🤖; 🚍501, 504, 508) Tucked away
in Roncesvalles Village, this cozy place
occupies a restored 1890s redbrick
mansion with divine handcrafted ar-
chitectural details. The six guest rooms
could use a refresh – mostly the floral
motifs and mishmash of furniture –
but they're quite comfortable. Breakfast is
hearty and freshly prepared; in summer,
enjoy it on the grapevine-covered deck with
murals. Two night minimum. Adults only.

★ **Drake Hotel** BOUTIQUE HOTEL **$$$**
(Map p70; ☑416-531-5042; www.thedrakehotel.ca;
1150 Queen St W; d/ste from $312/455; P♿❄🐾🤖;
🚍501) Art is everywhere in this flophouse
turned boutique hotel. Other hotels have
rooms; the Drake has 'crash pads, dens,
salons' and a rockin' little suite, beckoning
bohemians, artists and musicians with a
little spare cash. Rooms are smallish, and
en suite bathrooms are only separated by
a curtain, but all are impeccably furnished
with a sense of fun and mid-Century Modern design.

Complimentary yoga and spinning classes are offered in neighborhood studios;

cruiser bikes are available, too. The attached
bar (p110) and band room is one of Toronto's
finest venues for live music, and in summer
the Sky Yard rooftop patio goes off to DJ
beats and icy buckets of Coronas.

★ **Gladstone Hotel** BOUTIQUE HOTEL **$$$**
(Map p70; ☑416-531-4635; www.gladstonehotel.
com; 1214 Queen St W; d/ste from $270/475;
P♿❄🐾🤖; 🚍501) The 37 artist-designed
rooms at this trendsetting hotel could have
leaped straight from a Taschen design book.
Pick a room theme, then when you arrive
take the hand-cranked birdcage elevator to
your arty boudoir on the 3rd or 4th floor.
Locally produced bathroom products and
a green roof showcase the Gladstone's eco
commitment.

Downstairs, the Melody Bar (p109) band
room and cafe are integral to the Toronto
indie scene, while the 2nd floor is dedicated
to studio space and exhibitions for renting
artists.

🛏 East Toronto & Rosedale

★ **Only Backpackers Inn** HOSTEL **$**
(Map p70; ☑416-463-3249; http://theonlyinn.com;
966 Danforth Ave; dm incl breakfast $28-33, r incl
breakfast $82; ♿❄@🤖; Ⓢ Donlands) There's
so much to love about the Only. Inspired
by the owner's globetrotting adventures, it's
everything you want a hostel to be: clean,
cozy, near the subway, and with a laid-back
traveler vibe. There are waffles for brekky
and two private patios, plus murals every-
where. The downstairs cafe has a large patio
and 24 gourmet brews on tap.

★ **Broadview Hotel** BOUTIQUE HOTEL **$$$**
(Map p90; ☑416-362-8439; www.thebroad
viewhotel.ca; 106 Broadview Ave; r from $279;
♿❄🤖; 🚍501, 502, 503) Built in 1891, this
sumptuously restored building served as a
bank, a boarding house and a strip club before becoming a boutique hotel. Rooms are
elegant and eclectic, combining hardwood
floors and heavy velvet curtains with turn-
tables and French press coffee makers. Two
eateries, a bistro and an upscale restaurant,
add to the feeling of indulgence.

🍴 Eating

Nowhere is Toronto's multiculturalism
more potent and thrilling than in its restaurants. You'll find everything from Korean walnut cakes and sweat-inducing Thai
curries to good ol' Canuck pancakes with

peameal bacon and maple syrup. Fusion food is hot: traditional Western recipes spiked with zingy Eastern ingredients. British influences also linger – fizzy lunchtime pints and formal afternoon high teas are much-loved traditions.

Waterfront

★ Boxcar Social
CAFE $

(Map p82; ☎844-726-9227; www.boxcarsocial.ca; Harbourfront Centre, 235 Queens Quay W; mains $12-18; ☺9am-5pm Mon, to 11pm Tue-Thu, to late Fri, 10am-late Sat, to 8pm Sun; ☏♨; ☒509, 510) An industrial-chic cafe/bar/coffee haven, Boxcar Social has enviable views of Lake Ontario. The menu matches the vibe, with fresh takes on salads and sandwiches (kale Caesar salad, anyone?). Mornings bring locals with coffee and computers; evenings bring drinks on the patio and twinkling lights.

Harbour 60
STEAK $$$

(Map p82; ☎416-777-2111; www.harboursixty.com; 60 Harbour St; mains $20-175; ☺11:30am-2am Mon-Fri, 5pm-2am Sat, to midnight Sun; ☒509, 510) Inside the isolated 1917 Toronto Harbour Commission building, this baroque dining room glows with brass lamps and plush booths. Indulge yourself in a variety of enormous steaks, seasonal Florida stone-crab claws and broiled Caribbean lobster tail. Side dishes are big enough for two. Reservations essential.

Toronto Islands

Island Greek Grill
GREEK $

(Map p70; Centre Island Beach, 1-5 Ave of the Island, Centre Island; mains $9-13; ☺11am-7pm May-Sep; ☝Centre Island) A beachside kiosk serving up traditional gyro sandwiches stuffed with beef, lamb, chicken or pork. Watch as the server cuts the meat right off the spit onto a fresh pita, topping it with tomatoes, onions and a tart yogurt sauce. Complete the meal with a side of fries topped with feta, of course. The next shack over has beers.

Entertainment & Financial Districts

★ Forno Cultura
BAKERY $

(Map p86; ☎416-603-8305; www.fornocultura. com; 609 King St W; items from $3; ☺7:30am-9:30pm Tue-Sat, 8am-6pm Sun; ☒☒; ☒504, 508) An Italian bakery tucked into a basement-

VEGETARIAN HAVENS

Parka Food Co (p104) Vegan comfort food in a stark, contemporary and casual setting.

Kupfert & Kim (p99) Bright and airy quick eatery serving flavorful vegetarian and gluten-free meals.

Urban Herbivore (p105) Homey cafe offering hearty salads, sandwiches and soups plus vegan baked goods.

Govinda's (p105) Hare Krishna temple serving plates brimming with vegetarian Indian food.

Fresh (p107) Popular Toronto chain specializing in organic and plant-based tacos, burgers, smoothies and more.

level shop, Forno Cultura offers a full line of bread and pastries made with ingredients imported from Italy – even the flour and butter! The bakery itself is a long room, one side lined with impossible-to-resist goods, the other with a view of bakers doing their thing. Communal tables encourage you to stay, watch and eat.

Ravi Soups
INTERNATIONAL $

(Map p82; ☎647-435-8365; www.ravisoup.com; 322 Adelaide St W; soups $11; ☺11am-10pm; ☒504, 508) This one's pretty simple: a small menu of seven soups (the likes of corn chowder with blue crab or porcini-mushroom wild-rice bisque), five wraps (curried lamb with roasted yams) and four salads (baby spinach with mango-pineapple salsa) that are done to perfection. There's a small eating area with a long shared table and a small patio with psychedelic art.

Avenue Open Kitchen
DINER $

(Map p86; ☎416-504-7131; https://aveopenkitch en.ca; 7 Camden St; mains $5-12; ☺7am-4pm Mon-Fri, 8am-3pm Sat; ☒504) This cozy, old-school diner off Spadina Ave feels as though it's been here forever, but it's spotlessly clean and great value. Go on, have a BLT with cheese and a side of fries and gravy for your lunch. Breakfasts and burgers are hearty and easy on the wallet. There's always a daily special.

Kupfert & Kim
VEGETARIAN $

(Map p86; ☎416-504-2206; www.kupfertand kim.com; 140 Spadina Ave; mains $10-12; ☺8am-10pm Mon-Fri, 9am-10pm Sat, 9am-9pm Sun;

✲ 🎇 ✐ 🎇; Ⓢ Osgoode, 🚇 501) 🍴 The Korean-Canadian couple behind these restaurants has remixed the Korean *bibimbap* into deliciously satisfying meatless and wheatless superfood bowls, using mostly organic ingredients. Pomegranate, goji, quinoa, rainbow radish and plenty of raw greens feature in the vegan dishes. A smash hit for young couples and individuals in gym gear.

SOMA Chocolatier
DESSERTS $
(Map p86; ✐416-599-7662; www.somachocolate.com; 443 King St W; chocolates from $2.50; ☺9am-8pm Mon-Thu, to 9pm Fri, noon-9pm Sat, to 6pm Sun; 🎇; 🚇304, 504) Duck into this small chocolate shop for an eyeful of handcrafted chocolate beauties, from truffles and gelato to cookies and hot cocoa. Look closely at the ingredients: chili pepper, ginger and lemongrass make appearances. A small seating area in the back enjoys a view of the kitchen and the chocolate makers doing their thing.

La Carnita
MEXICAN $
(Map p82; ✐647-348-1166; www.lacarnita.com; 106 John St; mains $10-15; ☺11:30am-11pm Sun-Tue, to midnight Wed, to 1am Thu-Sat; 🚇504) A hoppin' spot for Mexican street eats, La Carnita is the place to grab a cocktail and indulge in some of the best tacos in town. The Toronto-based chain has several locations across the city; this is the original. Tacos start at $5.

Thompson Diner
DINER $
(Map p86; ✐416-601-3533; www.thompsondiner.com; 550 Wellington St W; breakfast/mains from $11/14; ☺6am-3am; 🚇504, 511) At the sexy Thompson Toronto hotel (p95), this classic diner with a modern twist is open 21 hours a day (it serves all-day breakfast). Whenever you're there, there'll likely be good people-watching to be had: this is nightclub territory. Comfort food is also a sure thing. Will it be peameal eggs Benedict or buttermilk fried chicken with cheddar mash for breakfast?

Wvrst
EUROPEAN $
(Map p86; ✐416-703-7775; www.wvrst.com; 609 King St W; sausages from $7; ☺11:30am-11pm Mon-Wed, to midnight Thu, to 1am Fri & Sat, to 10pm Sun; 🚇504, 508) Like sausage? If Wvrst's phenomenal success is any indication, then Toronto's hipsters do, too. With more bangers and snags than you can poke a stick at, do yourself a favor and get some pork on your fork at this 'beer and sausage hall.' Will you have the duck fat or dirty fries with that?

Assembly Chef's Hall
FOOD HALL $$
(Map p78; ✐647-557-5993; www.assemblychefshall.com; 111 Richmond St E; mains $12-19; ☺7am-10pm Mon-Fri, 10am-10pm Sat; ✐; Ⓢ Osgoode) Home to a diverse set of global cuisines by some of Toronto's top chefs, this is less food court and more sprawling upscale eatery. There's everything from margherita pizza and pork *carnitas* tacos to *khao soi* beef. Weekday lunch hours are crowded with suits and professional attire (it's in the heart of the Financial District), but dinnertime is much more chill and relaxed.

Oretta
ITALIAN $$
(Map p86; ✐416-944-1932; www.oretta.to; 633 King St W; mains $16-22; ☺11:30am-10pm Mon, to 11pm Tue-Fri, 11am-11pm Sat, to 10pm Sun; 🚇504) One of Toronto's most popular Italian restaurants, known for its iconic pink art-deco interior and delicious brunch menu. It's a romantic spot perfect for date nights or catchups with friends.

Connected to the restaurant is a separate cafe, located in the alley and also coated in pink, where you'll find tasty panini, pastries and coffee.

Pai
THAI $$
(Map p82; ✐416-901-4724; www.paitoronto.com; 18 Duncan St; mains $14-18; ☺11:30am-10pm Mon-Thu, to 10:30pm Fri & Sat, 3-10pm Sun; Ⓢ St Andrew) Pai is known for its spectacular food and lively ambience, so you'll pretty much always see lines out the door no matter the time of day. The *khao soi* (curry noodle soup) is what you might see all over social media; it's definitely one of the best Thai dishes you'll find in town.

Burger's Priest
BURGERS $$
(Map p86; ✐647-748-8108; www.theburgerspriest.com; 463 Queen St W; burgers from $6; ☺10am-11pm Mon-Wed, to midnight Thu, to 2am Fri & Sat, to 8pm Sun; 🎇; 🚇501) Some say Priest's simple burgers are the best in town: fresh-ground beef, soft bun, grilled to perfection. A top choice: 'the Priest' (of course), crowned with two breaded portobello mushrooms stuffed with cheese. Check the secret menu online, if you're brave. For dessert, don't shy from the Vatican on ice: ice cream sandwiched between two grilled-cheese sandwiches...it's an experience.

Sud Forno
CAFE $$

(Map p82; ☑ 416-955-1100; www.sudforno.com; 132 Yonge St; mains cafe $8-12, restaurant $16-36; ⊘ cafe 10:30am-6pm Mon-Fri, 8:30am-6pm Sat, 9am-5pm Sun, restaurant 11:30am-10pm Mon-Fri, 5-10pm Sat; Ⓢ Queen) Part of the wildly popular Terroni brand, this downtown location houses both a casual eatery (La Mensa) and an elegant restaurant (Da Geppetto). You can enjoy lattes and pastries in the cafe on the main floor or indulge in classic southern Italian eats at the restaurant upstairs. There's also a bakery branch on Queen St W.

Khao San Road
THAI $$

(Map p82; ☑ 647-352-5773; www.khaosanroad. ca; 11 Charlotte St; mains $15-17; ⊘ 11:30am-2:30pm & 5-10pm Sun-Fri, noon-3pm & 5-10pm Sat; ☎☑; ▣ 504, 508) There's usually a line here for some of Toronto's best Thai curry and noodles. Reservations aren't accepted, but it's worth the wait. Once inside, service is like a well-oiled machine: orders are turned around fast, and the food is flavorful, spiced just right and beautifully presented.

There's a vegan menu, too.

Northern Maverick Brewing Company
PUB FOOD $$

(Map p86; ☑ 416-540-4030; https://northern maverick.ca; 115 Bathurst St; mains $16-32; ⊘ 11am-midnight Sun-Tue, to 1am Wed, to 2am Thu-Sat; ▣ 504) Northern Maverick's massive space includes a brewery, a restaurant and a retail store. From weekend brunch to $1 oysters on Sunday evenings, there's more than just craft beer going on. Restaurant dishes are farm to table or made in-house; you absolutely need to try the house-made duck prosciutto if it's offered.

Patria
SPANISH $$

(Map p86; ☑ 416-367-0505; www.patriatoronto. com; 480 King St W; small plates $5-19; ⊘ 5pm-late, plus 10:30am-2:30pm Sun; ▣ 504, 508) Everything works beautifully in this expansive, stylish and modern restaurant specializing in Spanish tapas and cuisine. Knowledgeable servers help navigate the mouthwatering menu of cheeses, meats and seafood. Tapas are meant to be shared: order plenty and don't bother coming alone. Sunday brunch is a delightful deviation from the usual suspects. Look for the entrance tucked inside of a covered parking lot.

King Taps
PUB FOOD $$

(Map p82; ☑ 647-361-2025; https://kingtaps.com; 100 King St W; mains $15-20; ⊘ 11:30am-1am; Ⓢ St Andrew) King Taps has more than 50 rotating craft beers, plus tasty cocktails, and it serves up delicious food. Pizzas are definitely a favorite, but dishes such as sushi offer quite a spin on your typical pub food.

★Buca
ITALIAN $$$

(Map p86; ☑ 416-865-1600; www.buca.ca; 604 King St W; mains $17-55; ⊘ 11am-3pm & 5-10pm Mon-Wed, 11am-3pm & 5-11pm Thu & Fri, 5-11pm Sat, 5-10pm Sun; ▣ 304, 504) A breathtaking basement-level restaurant with exposed-brick walls and a soaring ceiling, Buca serves artisanal Italian fare such as homemade pasta and nose-to-tail-style dishes such as *orecchio di maiale* (crispy pigs ears) and *cervello* (lamb's brains wrapped in prosciutto and sage).

Ease into the experience with a charcuterie board of house-cured meats, flavorful cheeses and bread knots.

★Lee
ASIAN $$$

(Map p86; ☑ 416-504-7867; www.susur.com/lee; 601 King St W; mains $16-38; ⊘ 5-10:30pm Sun-Wed, to 11pm Thu, to 11:30pm Fri & Sat; ☑; ▣ 504, 508) Truly a feast for the senses, dinner at acclaimed *cuisinier* Susur Lee's self-titled flagship is an experience best shared. Slick servers assist in navigating the artisanal selection of East-meets-West delights: you really want to get the pairings right. It's impossible to adequately convey the dance of flavors, textures and aromas one experiences in the signature Singaporean slaw, with... how many ingredients?!

Richmond Station
INTERNATIONAL $$$

(Map p78; ☑ 647-748-1444; www.richmond station.ca; 1 Richmond St W; mains $23-32; ⊘ 11:30am-10:30pm; Ⓢ Queen) Reservations are strongly advised at this busy and uncomplicated restaurant, brainchild of celebrity *Top Chef Canada* winner Carl Heinrich. Dishes are 'ingredient focused and technique driven.' Try a delicious charcuterie board and buttery lobster spaghetti. The eclectic menu is simple but gratifying, priced right and complemented by a well-paired wine list and daily chalkboard specials. Highly recommended.

Bymark
FUSION $$$

(Map p82; ☑ 416-777-1144; www.bymark.mcewan group.ca; TD Centre, 66 Wellington St W; mains $29-71; ⊘ 11:30am-3pm & 5pm-midnight Mon-Fri,

5pm-midnight Sat; ⑤St Andrew) Toronto culinary powerhouse Brooke McDougall brings his sophisticated menu of continentally hewn cuisine to this hip, bilevel downtowner. His creative kitchen crew whips ingredients like wild sockeye salmon, rabbit and soft-shell crab into sensational combinations, each with suggested wine or beer pairings. It's at street level.

✖ Old Town, Corktown & Distillery District

Patrician Grill
DINER $

(Map p82; ☑416-366-4841; http://patrician grill.com; 219 King St E; meals $5-16; ☺7am-4pm Mon-Fri, 8am-2pm Sat; ⑤King) Built in the 1950s, the Patrician has been run by the same family since 1967. Photographers will have a field day with the neon outside and the original decor inside. Food centers on burgers, BLTs, bacon and eggs (cooked to perfection) and home fries. Friday-lunch-time meat loaf is a local institution and sells out quickly.

Schnitzel Queen
EUROPEAN $

(Map p78; ☑416-504-1311; www.schnitzelqueen. ca; 211 Queen St E; schnitzels $8-12; ☺11am-9pm Wed, to 10pm Thu & Fri, noon-8pm Sat; ᵷ301, 501, 502) This poky German takeout specializes in golden-delicious breaded-schnitzel sandwiches that make great picnic fodder. These mammoth creations are excellent value and usually good for two meals – the schnitzel is double the size of the bun. Purists should nab a bar stool and stay in for the authentic dinner plates with mushroom sauce, potato salad and sauerkraut ($11 to $16).

Pearl Diver
SEAFOOD $$

(Map p82; ☑416-366-7827; https://pearldiver. to; 100 Adelaide St E; mains $16-44; ☺4pm-midnight Tue & Wed, 11am-1am Thu-Sat, to midnight Sun; ᵷ141, 143, 144, 145) A small, bustling restaurant, this place is known for its regular seafood specials. Come on Thursday for its crowning glory, the '100 for 100': $100 for 100 raw oysters, quickly and expertly shucked (no bits of sand here). On weekends, the lobster Benny is where it's at.

Terroni
ITALIAN $$

(Map p82; ☑416-203-3093; www.terroni.com; 57 Adelaide St E; mains $15-23; ☺9am-10pm Mon-Thu, to 11pm Fri & Sat, 5-10pm Sat; ᵹ; ⑤King) The Adelaide St branch of this popular Italian eatery (there are two others in Toronto, and more in LA) occupies a historic courthouse

with high vaulted ceilings and labyrinthine dining areas. It's open, cool and, despite the size, generally packed. Reasonably priced wood-fired pizzas, rich pastas and fresh panini would make the Godfather proud. Modifications to dishes are a no-no.

WORKS Gourmet Burger Bistro
BURGERS $$

(Map p82; ☑416-594-9675; https://works burger.com; 60 Wellington St E; mains $13-19; ☺11am-10pm Sun-Wed, to 11pm Thu-Sat; ⑤King) Everything and anything you could ever want in a burger. All burgers at the Works are completely customizable, including the patty, bun, toppings and sides. There are also more than 50 drool-worthy set options if you'd rather have the choice made for you. It's no wonder this chain has expanded across Ontario.

✖ The Beaches

Amma Roti House
INDIAN $

(Map p70; ☑416-944-1944; www.ammaroti.com; 2014 Queen St E; mains $10-16; ☺11:30am-9:30pm Mon-Thu, to 10pm Fri & Sat, noon-9:30pm Sun; ᵹ; ᵷ501) Across from Kew Gardens (p79) this simple eatery serves classic Indian dishes – tikka masala, vindaloo – in a eye-catchingly green room. Be sure to order the namesake roti, huge, freshly made flat bread used to scoop up and complement main dishes. A good spot to pop into for a quick, flavorful meal.

Gio Rana's Really Really Nice Restaurant
ITALIAN $

(Map p70; ☑416-469-5225; 1220 Queen St E; mains $10-23; ☺5:30-10pm Mon-Wed, to 10:30pm Thu, to 11pm Fri & Sat; ᵷ501, 502, 503) There's no signage at this quirky, fun joint, just a massive Italianate nose on the exterior of an otherwise nondescript 1950s bank building. Locals come here for the atmosphere, the good humor and the old-fashioned Italian comfort food: enormous meatballs, scallop and smoked-pancetta risotto, and veal osso buco.

Remarkable Bean
CAFE $

(Map p70; ☑416-690-2420; https://remarkable bean.com; 2242 Queen St E; items $3-10; ☺6:30am-10pm; ᵷ501) This Beaches fave serves up shepherd's pie and still-in-the-pan homemade desserts to go with your latte or *maté* (South American 'tea of life'). Fight for a window seat alongside the well-heeled.

✖ Downtown Yonge

Loblaw's
SUPERMARKET $

(Map p78; ☑ 416-593-6154; 60 Carlton St; mains from $3; ⊙ 7am-11pm; P ☑; Ⓢ College) Yeah, it's a grocery-store chain, but this flagship is a must-stop for its high-quality prepared-foods section: sushi made to order, grilled meats, thin-crust pizza, creative sandwiches and salads...and don't miss the killer patisserie and Wall of Cheese. Plenty of seating and occasional live music. Ninety minutes of free parking, too.

Okonomi House
JAPANESE $

(Map p78; ☑ 416-925-6176; 23 Charles St W; mains $9-17; ⊙ 11:30am-3pm & 4:30-10pm Mon-Fri, noon-3pm & 4:30-10pm Sat; ☑; Ⓢ Bloor-Yonge) Okonomi House is one of the only places in Toronto dishing up authentic *okonomiyaki* (savory Japanese cabbage pancakes filled with meat, seafood or vegetables). It's not fancy – just a step up from a diner – but it's a must for Japanophiles.

★ Outdoor Eateries
FOOD TRUCK $

(Map p78; 335 Yonge St; mains from $3; ⊙ 11am-10:30pm; ☑; Ⓢ Dundas, College) Food trucks, repurposed shipping containers and plywood sheds make up this outdoor food court at the heart of Yonge St. Short-order cooks prep burritos, Philly cheesesteak subs, crepes, vegan eats and more. Hungry diners (many of them students from nearby Ryerson U) fill the picnic tables in the center courtyard. Twinkling lights set the mood in the evening.

Golden Diner Family Restaurant
DINER $

(Map p78; ☑ 416-977-9898; 105 Carlton St; mains $7-16; ⊙ 6am-9pm; Ⓢ College) This good old-fashioned basement-level greasy spoon has some natty booths and one of the best-value all-day breakfasts in the city. The $6.95 breakfast includes eggs, crispy or peameal bacon, a mound of home fries and a bottomless cup of coffee. A filling choice... and you'll save some coin for dinner!

Patties Express
JAMAICAN $

(Map p78; ☑ 647-350-0111; www.pattiesexpress. ca; 4 Elm St; patties from $2; ⊙ 10:30am-11pm Mon-Fri, 11am-11pm Sat, to 9pm Sun; ☑; Ⓢ Dundas, College) A hole-in-the-wall place specializing in Jamaican patties: flaky-pastry pockets stuffed with spicy veggies, curry chicken and ground beef (non-spicy to extra spicy available). For a one-two punch to your taste buds, order your patty spicy and wrapped in coconut bread. Takeout only.

Salad King
THAI $

(Map p78; ☑ 416-593-0333; www.saladking.com; 340 Yonge St; mains $11-13; ⊙ 11am-10pm Mon-Thu, to 11pm Fri, noon-11pm Sat, to 9pm Sun; ☑; Ⓢ Dundas) An institution among students of neighboring Ryerson University, the colorful and somewhat misleadingly named Salad King dispenses large bowls of standard Thai curries, noodle soups, rice and, yes, salads, for around $12. Long stainless-steel shared tables and cozy booths are usually full of hungry patrons. You can specify your desired level of spice on a scale of one to 20!

★ Smith
CANADIAN $$

(Map p78; ☑ 416-926-2501; http://smithrestaurant. com; 553 Church St; mains $18-28; ⊙ 11am-4pm & 5-11pm Tue-Thu, to midnight Fri, 9am-4pm & 5pm-midnight Sat, 9am-4pm Sun; ☑; Ⓢ Wellesley) Come to this bohemian-chic eatery in the heart of the Village for brunch, when the classics are served with flair: eggs Benedict with leek fondue, a short stack with maple cream cheese and candied lemon, or perhaps a Bloody Mary with a bouquet of bacon on top. Is your mouth watering yet? Reservations recommended.

Hair of the Dog
PUB FOOD $$

(Map p78; ☑ 416-964-2708; www.hairofdogpub. com; 425 Church St; share plates $12-20, mains $15-24; ⊙ 11:30am-midnight Mon-Thu, to 2am Fri, 10:30am-2am Sat, to midnight Sun; Ⓢ College) At its best in the warmer months, when two levels of shaded patio spring to life with a gay and straight crowd, this chilled puppy is delightfully less mainstream than its Village neighbors a few blocks north. Equally tempting as a drinking venue, the Dog serves great sharing plates and salads, too. No nonvegetarian can possibly resist the butter-chicken grilled cheese.

Sambucas on Church
ITALIAN $$

(Map p78; ☑ 416-966-3241; www.sambucas. ca; 489 Church St; mains $12-21; ⊙ 11am-10pm Mon-Fri, 10:30am-10pm Sat & Sun; ☑; Ⓢ Wellesley) Great for weekday lunches, weekend brunches and dinner any time, Sambucas' Italian menu has some North American twists. Pastas are hearty, risottos creamy and chicken dishes noteworthy. Try the $23 prix-fixe lunch with tasty seafood linguine. If you're lucky you'll secure a window table to watch the Villagers walk by.

Senator Restaurant
DINER $$

(Map p78; ☑416-364-7517; www.thesenator.com; 249 Victoria St; mains $18-36; ⊗7:30am-2:30pm Mon, to 9pm Tue-Fri, 8am-2:30pm & 4:30-9pm Sat, 8am-2:30pm Sun; ⑤Dundas) Art deco buffs will delight in the Senator's curved glass windows, fluted aluminum counter face and original booths. Meals are refreshingly simple and home style: the fish-and-chips, meat loaf and macaroni are especially recommended. On weekends, head upstairs to its wine bar, Top O' the Senator, for drinks and live jazz until midnight.

✗ Kensington Market & Chinatown

★ Parka Food Co.
VEGAN $

(Map p86; ☑416-603-3363; www.parkafoodco.com; 424 Queen St W; ⊗11:30am-9pm Mon-Thu, to 10pm Fri, noon-10pm Sat, to 8pm Sun; ☑) A starkly white, casual restaurant serving insanely delicious vegan comfort food: burgers made from marinated portobello mushrooms and blackened cauliflower; mac 'n' (vegan) cheese with toppings like truffle mushroom and garlic and onion and thick, flavorful soups. Everything's made in-house from scratch, using locally sourced ingredients. Lots of gluten-free options, too.

★ House of Gourmet
HONG KONG $

(Map p78; ☑416-640-0103; http://houseof gourmet.blogspot.com; 484 Dundas St W; mains $8-19; ⊗8am-2am; ☑; ☐310, 510) A popular, fluorescent-bulb-lit restaurant specializing in Hong Kong–style congee, noodles, barbecue and seafood – more than 800 dishes of them! (It takes two menus in a tiny font to cover the options.) Food comes out fast and piping hot. Service is equally brisk. If in doubt, try the wonton-brisket-noodle soup, a late-night fave with chunks of tender brisket and loads of noodles.

★ Seven Lives
TACOS $

(Map p86; ☑416-803-1086; 69 Kensington Ave; tacos from $6; ⊗noon-6pm Mon-Fri, to 7pm Sat & Sun; ☐310, 510) What started as a pop-up taqueria is now a hole-in-the-wall place with lines of people snaking out the door, waiting to order Baja-style fish tacos: light and flaky mahi-mahi with pico de gallo, cabbage and a creamy sauce. Other seafood and veggie combos offered, too. Most diners eat standing or take their meal to nearby Bellevue Sq.

Dipped Donuts
BAKERY $

(Map p86; ☑647-906-3668; www.dipped donuts.ca; 161 Baldwin St; doughnuts from $3.25; ⊗10am-6pm Sun-Thu, to 7pm Fri & Sat; ☐310, 510) A *tiny* shop selling freshly made, light, moist and fluffy doughnuts with innovative toppings and glazes. Not into lemon-poppyseed glaze with blueberry-mint drizzle? How about rosewater pistachio nut or chocolate ganache with cookie crumble? Apple fritters, with big chunks of apple, are sold on weekends. Vegan doughnuts sold, too. Come early...the goodies often sell out. Cash only.

Kekou
ICE CREAM $

(Map p78; ☑416-792-8858; http://kekou.ca; 394 Queen St W; gelato/drinks from $5/6; ⊗12:30-10:30pm Sun-Thu, to 11pm Fri & Sat; ☑; ☐301, 310, 501, 510) Whiskey, black-sesame or oolong tea: no, they're not cocktails but excellent, Asian-inspired ice creams. The delicious flavors aren't overly sweet or artificial, and the ginger and dark-chocolate dairy free is the punchiest vegan gelato in Toronto. Cold tea drinks – steeped to order and served with tapioca, grass jelly or gelato – are offered, too.

Kinton Ramen
NOODLES $

(Map p78; ☑647-748-8900; www.kintonramen.com; 51 Baldwin St; noodles from $13.50; ⊗11:30am-10:30pm; ☐505, 506) Ramen noodles are practically a religion in Japan, and they're becoming increasingly popular in Toronto. The cool brains behind this clever outfit leaped on the bandwagon with their own distinct flavor: caramelized pork. There's even a version with cheese, if you can imagine. This branch oozes atmosphere – it's lively, noisy, steamy and beery, but classy. Join in the fun.

FIKA Cafe
CAFE $

(Map p86; www.fika.ca; 28 Kensington Ave; mains from $6; ⊗10am-6pm Mon-Sat; ☎☑; ☐310, 510) Meaning 'coffee break' in Swedish, FIKA is a small cafe in a turquoise Victorian house. Inside, the decor is soothing: exposed-brick walls, whitewashed wood and artful touches such as open books doubling as wallpaper. The menu's limited to fresh salads and creative sandwiches, though its coffee and homemade-pastry offerings are impressive. Try the cinnamon buns.

Jumbo Empanadas
CHILEAN $

(Map p86; ☑416-977-0056; www.jumboempa nadas.ca; 245 Augusta Ave; empanadas from $5.50;

9am-8pm Mon-Sat, 11am-6pm Sun; ⓢ 510) The chunky Chilean empanadas (toasted delights stuffed with beef, chicken, cheese or vegetables) and savory corn pie with beef, olives and eggs always sell out early here. A mini empanada will only set you back $1.50. Bread and salsas are also homemade. Take your treats to go or prepare to wait for a table.

Mother's Dumplings
CHINESE $

(Map p78; ☑ 416-217-2008; www.mothersdumplings.com; 421 Spadina Ave; 10 dumplings from $11; ⓘ 11:30am-10pm Sun-Thu, to 10:30pm Fri & Sat; ☑; ⓢ 506, 510) The cleanest and best located of Chinatown's dumpling houses prepares plump and juicy dumplings to authentic recipes passed on down for generations. However you like them – steamed or pan-fried; pork, chicken, beef, shrimp or vegetarian – these dumplings will fill your tum and delight your wallet. Always busy.

Nguyen Huong
SANDWICHES $

(Map p86; ☑ 416-599-4625; www.nguyenhuong.ca; 322 Spadina Ave; sandwiches from $3; ⓘ 8:30am-8:30pm; ⓢ 510) Cheap and delicious filled Vietnamese sandwiches are the order of the day at the original precursor to Toronto's banh mi (baguettes filled with pâté, cilantro, pork and pickled veg) phenomenon. Takeout only.

Urban Herbivore
VEGETARIAN $

(Map p86; ☑ 416-927-1231; www.herbivore.to; 64 Oxford St; mains $9-14; ⓘ 10am-7pm; ☑; ⓢ 510) This humble wholefoods joint specializes in vegetarian meals sans additives and preservatives, including salads, rice bowls, chunky soups and specialty vegan gluten-free baked goodies. Servings are hearty! There's a sister restaurant at the Eaton Centre's **Urban Eatery** (Map p78; 1 Dundas St W; mains from $5; ⓘ 10am-9pm Mon-Sat, to 7pm Sun; ⓢ☑; ⓢ Dundas), too.

Queen Mother Café
FUSION $$

(Map p78; ☑ 416-598-4719; www.queenmothercafe.ca; 208 Queen St W; mains $15-24; ⓘ 11:30am-midnight Mon-Wed, to 1am Thu-Sat, to 11pm Sun; ☑; ⓢ Osgoode) A Queen St institution, the Queen Mother is beloved for its cozy, dark wooden booths and excellent pan-Asian menu. Canadian comfort food is also on offer – try the Beefeater burger. Check out the display of old stuff they found in the walls the last time they renovated. The patio is hidden and one of the best in town.

🍴 Yorkville & the Annex

★ Aunties & Uncles
CAFE $

(Map p86; ☑ 416-324-1375; www.auntiesanduncles.ca; 74 Lippincott St; mains $8-10; ⓘ 9am-3pm; ⓢ 510) There's usually a line on the sidewalk outside the picket fence of this always-bustling brunch/lunch joint with a simple menu of cheap and cheery homemade favorites. Plop yourself down in one of the mismatched chairs and dig into dishes like grilled Brie with pear chutney and walnuts on challah, banana-oatmeal pancakes or grilled Canadian cheddar. Cash only.

Govinda's
VEGETARIAN $

(Map p70; ☑ 888-218-1040; www.govindas.ca; 243 Avenue Rd; meal platters adult/child $10/5; ⓘ noon-2:30pm & 6-9pm Mon-Sat; ☑; ⓢ Rosedale) The Hare Krishna movement has been feeding budget travelers around the globe for decades. Toronto is no exception. Politely decline any offers of religious conversion and enjoy tasty, karma-free, Indian vegetarian fare that is on the whole good for body and soul.

It's a little out of the way, at the very northern fringe of the Annex.

Trattoria Nervosa
ITALIAN $$

(Map p78; ☑ 416-961-4642; www.eatnervosa.com; 75 Yorkville Ave; mains $17-33; ⓘ 11:30am-10pm Mon-Wed, to 11pm Thu-Sat, noon-10pm Sun; ⓢ; ⓢ Bay) In the heart of fancy Yorkville, this restaurant is an attitude-free oasis. The patio is a good corner from which to people-watch well-heeled passersby while you dig into simple, excellent pasta – the *mafalde ai funghi* has incredibly deep mushroom flavors without being overly creamy.

By the Way
MIDDLE EASTERN $$

(Map p86; ☑ 416-967-4295; www.bythewaycafe.com; 400 Bloor St W; mains $10-19; ⓘ 9am-9pm Sun-Wed, to 10pm Thu, to 11pm Fri & Sat; ☑; ⓢ Spadina) An Annex fixture, this cheerful corner bistro has a fusion menu that leans toward Middle Eastern. Although there's plenty of meat on offer, vegetarians won't go hungry.

There's also an extensive and well-selected wine list.

Country Style Hungarian Restaurant
HUNGARIAN $$

(Map p86; ☑ 416-536-5966; http://countrystylehungarian.com; 450 Bloor St W; schnitzels from $15; ⓘ 11am-10pm; ⓢ Bathurst) This delightful

Hungarian diner, with its checked tablecloths and friendly family staff, hasn't changed a bit in at least a generation. The enormous breaded schnitzels, cooked to crunchy perfection, are the best in town, and the cucumber salad is a treat. Note that menu prices *include* tax!

Sassafraz
FUSION $$$

(Map p78; ☑ 416-964-2222; www.sassafraz.ca; 100 Cumberland St; mains $22-29; ⊙11:30am-11pm Mon-Thu, to 1am Fri, 11am-1pm Sat, to 11pm Sun; ⑤ Bay) Popular with visiting celebrities and a moneyed clientele, Sassafraz epitomizes Yorkville with its elegant yet breezy decor. Jazz combos serenade weekend brunchers, and sassy receptionists distribute diners between the sun-drenched patio and the leafy indoor courtyard. The food? Predictably good. Dress to impress.

✘ West End

★ Otto's Bierhalle
GERMAN $

(Map p70; ☑ 416-901-5472; www.ottosbierhalle. com; 1087 Queen St W; mains $10-16; ⊙ noon-11pm Mon & Tue, to midnight Wed & Thu, to 2am Sat, to 10pm Sun; ⑤501) Garage doors, long communal tables, a wide selection of draft beers and ciders, huge platters of brats and schnitzels – it looks like Oktoberfest pretty much year-round here (the only thing missing is the oompah band). A popular spot with an upbeat vibe, this place makes out-of-towners feel like part of the city. Reservations recommended on weekends.

Bang Bang Ice Cream
ICE CREAM $

(Map p86; ☑ 647-348-1900; http://bangbang icecream.ca; 93a Ossington Ave; scoops from $4.25; ⊙1-10pm Sun-Thu, to 10:30pm Fri & Sat; ⬛; ⑤505) From burnt toffee to banana pudding, Bang Bang has more than two dozen housemade ice-cream flavours to try. Choose regular scoops, ice-cream sandwiches or bubble waffles with ice cream. Be prepared wait in a long line, especially in summer.

Commoner
GASTROPUB $$

(Map p70; ☑ 647-351-2067; www.thecommoner restaurant.ca; 2067 Dundas St W; mains $13-27; ⊙5-11pm Mon-Thu, to midnight Fri, 11am-midnight Sat, to 11pm Sun; ⑤506) The Commoner is a swanky gastropub in Roncesvalles Village. Lush jewel tones and antique pieces fill the massive yet welcoming space, and the patio is great for sipping craft beer or cocktails

on warm summer days. Stop by for dinner during the week or brunch on the weekend. Either way, try the buffalo cauliflower.

Pizzeria Libretto
ITALIAN $$

(Map p86; ☑ 416-532-8000; http://pizzeria libretto.com; 221 Ossington Ave; mains $15-25; ⊙11:30am-10pm Mon-Wed, to 11pm Thu-Sun; ☑; ⑤505) Pizza Libretto crafts what is arguably the best pizza in town. The secret? A wood-fired oven built by a third-generation pizza-oven builder with stones shipped from Italy. Besides certified Neapolitan pizza and other Naples staples, the menu includes a prix-fixe weekday lunch (salad, pizza and gelato for $16) and an all-Italian wine list. Vegan cheese and gluten-free dough available.

Be sure to reserve a table on weekends.

Union
FUSION $$

(Map p86; ☑ 416-850-0093; www.union72.ca; 72 Ossington Ave; mains $15-38; ⊙noon-3pm & 6-10pm Mon-Wed, to 11pm Thu & Fri, 11am-3pm & 6-11pm Sat, 6-10pm Sun; ⑤501) This dandy little kitchen serves a delicious fusion of French- and Italian-inspired dishes that it touts as 'simple done right,' though you could argue that pickled swordfish with snow crab isn't simple. Fortunately, the food, decor and service are masterfully executed, using the freshest ingredients. Steak, chicken, ribs and fish are staples. There's a delightful patio out back.

✘ East Toronto & Rosedale

Bonjour Brioche
FRENCH $

(Map p90; ☑ 416-406-1250; www.bonjour brioche.com; 812 Queen St E; baked goods from $2.50, mains $8-12; ⊙8am-4pm Mon-Sat; ⑤501, 502, 503) The smell of freshly baked croissants will pull you into this little French bakery-cafe. Inside, a no-frills dining room bumps up against glass cases of picture-perfect, impossible-to-resist baked goods. Do yourself a solid: order a fresh salad, then dig into the chocolate brioche and croissants. Cash only.

★ Athens
GREEK $$

(Map p70; ☑ 416-465-4441; https://athensdan forth.ca; 707 Danforth Ave; $8-33; ⊙11am-midnight; ⑤ Donlands) As Greek as Greektown (aka The Danforth), modern and beachy Athens serves traditional dishes made with fresh, local ingredients: grilled calamari, lamb *kefte* (meatballs) and, of course, souvlaki. For a treat, try the moussaka and save room for walnut cake. Service is so friendly it feels like family...diners are even welcome in the kitchen to check out what's cooking!

Fresh VEGAN **$$**
(Map p86; ☑416-599-4442; https://freshrestau rants.ca; 894 Queen St W; mains $10-20; ⊙11:30am-10pm Mon-Fri, 10:30am-10pm Sat & Sun; ☑; ☐501) You'll find all the comfort-food faves here, from tacos to burgers, plus a range of salads, smoothies and juices – all completely plant based and organic. Fresh has five locations across the city; this is the original.

★**Ruby Watchco** CANADIAN **$$$**
(Map p90; ☑416-465-0100; http://rubywatch co.ca; 730 Queen St E; prix fixe $58; ⊙6-10pm Tue-Sat; ☐501, 502, 503) Creative farm-to-table comfort food is the game at this homey restaurant, run by two of Toronto's top chefs. (Chef Lynn even stars on the Food Network hit *Pitchin' In*.) A new menu is presented nightly, always four course, always prix fixe. Expect dishes like fried chicken with rosemary honey and maple barbecue ribs; save room for the artisanal cheeses and decadent desserts.

Reservations recommended.

Drinking & Nightlife

Toronto's drinking scene embraces everything from sticky-carpet dive bars, cookie-cutter 'Brit' pubs and Yankee-style sports bars to slick martini bars, rooftop patios, sky-high cocktail lounges and an effervescent smattering of LGBTIQ+ hangouts. Thirsty work! Strict bylaws prohibit smoking indoors in public spaces, although some patios are permissive. Taps start flowing around midday and last call hovers between 1am and 2am.

Waterfront

Against the Grain Urban Tavern PUB
(Map p82; ☑647-344-1562; http://fabrestau rants.ca/restaurant/against-the-grain-corus-quay; 25 Dockside Dr; ⊙11am-10pm Mon-Thu, to midnight Fri, 10:30am-midnight Sat, to 10pm Sun; ☐509) The best feature of this yuppyish pub is its enormous lakefront patio (seasonal), with some of the best views of the Toronto harbor front. Come with a friend to enjoy the sunshine and a couple of martinis. If you get hungry, share a plate of sesame-ginger calamari.

Entertainment & Financial Districts

Jimmy's COFFEE
(Map p86; ☑647-347-5600; www.jimmyscoffee. ca; 100 Portland St; ⊙8am-8pm Sun-Thu, to 9pm Fri & Sat; ☐) Located in a bohemian-chic row house, this hopping coffee joint serves up flavorful coffee drinks – even nitro cold brew on tap – made from beans roasted in-house. Explore and find a cozy spot: upstairs, downstairs, front patio or back, there are lots of options here.

If there's a long line, try the original Jimmy's across the street; same coffee, different vibe.

Fifth Social Club CLUB
(Map p78; ☑416-979-3000; http://fifthsocial club.thefifth.com; 225 Richmond St W; cover $20-25; ⊙9pm-2:30am Fri, 10pm-2:30am Sat; ⑤Osgoode) Known by regulars as Easy, this upscale club hosts an early- to mid-20s crowd. From the chocolate-fondue station to the life-size Jenga and the swing in the middle of the dance floor, this is not your ordinary spot for a weekend outing, but if you're looking to dress up and dance the night away, it's perfect.

Petty Cash BAR
(Map p86; ☑647-748-2274; http://pettycash toronto.com; 487 Adelaide St W; ⊙5pm-2am Mon-Fri, 4pm-2am Sat & Sun; ☐504) This King West hangout is a millennial favorite known for its killer cocktails and comfort food. Edgy murals and neon signs make it easy to prove you had a good time with an Instagram photo or two.

Old Town, Corktown & Distillery District

Dineen Coffee Company COFFEE
(Map p82; ☑416-900-0949; http://dineencoffee. com; 140 Yonge St; ⊙6:30am-7pm Mon-Fri, 8am-6pm Sat & Sun; ☎; ⑤Queen) Fancy an afternoon coffee? Dineen is perfect if you're feeling like something more lavish. This downtown location occupies a heritage building with ornate tile floors and a unique chandelier that once hung in the historic Fairmont (p96) nearby.

CRAFT BEER

Bellwoods Brewery – Award-winning beers, gourmet small plates and a hipster vibe in a two-story brewery.

Rorschach Brewing Co – Century-old house turned brewery, with two patios and an ever-changing menu of beers.

Mill Street Brewery – Distillery District brewery in a Victorian-era factory with over a dozen craft brews on tap.

C'est What – Old Town pub with an in-house brewmaster, serving a huge range of Ontario-made beers.

Mill Street Brewery   BREWERY
(Map p90; 416-681-0338; www.millstreet brewery.com; 21 Tank House Lane; 11am-1am Sun-Wed, to 2am Thu-Sat; 72, 503, 504) With 13 specialty beers made on-site in the atmospheric Distillery District (p77), these guys are a leading light in local microbrewing. Order a sample platter so you can taste all the award-winning brews, including the Tankhouse Pale Ale, Stock Ale and Organic Lager. On a sunny afternoon the courtyard is the place to be. The beer-friendly food includes burgers and wraps.

C'est What   PUB
(Map p82; 416-867-9499; www.cestwhat.com; 67 Front St E; 11:30am-1am Sun & Mon, to 2am Tue-Sat; 503, 504) More than 30 whiskeys and six dozen Canadian microbrews (mostly from Ontario) are on hand at this underground pub (look for a doorway). An in-house brewmaster tightly edits the all-natural, preservative-free beers on tap. Good bar food makes the most of fresh produce from St Lawrence Market (p77) next door.

The Beaches

Rorschach Brewing Co   BREWERY
(Map p70; 416-901-3233; www.rorschach brewing.com; 1001 Eastern Ave; 5-11pm Mon-Wed, noon-11pm Thu, to midnight Fri & Sat, to 9pm Sun; 301, 501) Come to this century-old house turned brewery to have creative craft beers, listen to live music and hang out with friends. The two patios – one in front with twinkling lights, the other on the roof with treetop views – are perfect places to partake in an ever-changing menu of IPAs,

sours, stouts and more. Good eats, including cheese pairings, also served.

Downtown Yonge

★ **O'Grady's**   PUB
(Map p78; 416-323-2822; www.ogradychurch. com; 517 Church St; 11am-2am; Wellesley) Come to this friendly Irish pub on Wednesdays for Dirty Bingo nights, when fabulous drag queens call out numbers and give winners risqué prizes from 9pm to midnight. On bingo-less nights, it's all about the patio – the Village's largest – which fills up as soon as the sun comes out. The kitchen, serving comfort food, stays open late.

Crews & Tangos   BAR
(Map p78; 647-349-7469; www.crewsand tangos.com; 508 Church St; 8pm-2am Sun-Fri, 6pm-2am Sat; Wellesley) A sprawling bar that becomes a crowded nightclub on weekends, Crews & Tangos features live drag and cabaret shows and DJs out back. Boys who like boys, girls who like girls, girlish boys and boyish girls and all their friends tend to make up the lively crowd in this welcoming space. Look for the blue brick house with the murals.

Black Eagle   GAY
(Map p78; 416-413-1219; www.blackeagleto ronto.com; 457 Church St; 3pm-3am Mon-Sat, to midnight Sun; Wellesley) Men-only Eagle lures leather-men, uniform fetishists and their admirers. The year-round rooftop patio is the perfect place to meet a Daddy: Sunday-afternoon barbecues draw a strong crowd. There's a cruising area upstairs and a renovated dance area downstairs. While it's not for the fainthearted, the folks here are generally as friendly as they come.

Kensington Market & Chinatown

★ **BarChef**   COCKTAIL BAR
(Map p86; 416-868-4800; www.barcheftoronto. com; 472 Queen St W; cocktails $16-55; 6pm-2am; Osgoode) You'll hear 'oohs' and 'aahs' coming from the tables in the intimate near-darkness of this swanky bar as cocktails emerge alongside a bonsai tree, or under a bell jar of vanilla and hickory-wood smoke. Beyond novelty, drinks show incredible, enticing complexity without overwhelming some unique flavors – truffle snow, chamomile syrup, cedar air, and soil!

Dark Horse Espresso COFFEE
(Map p78; ☑416-979-1200; www.darkhorseespresso.com; 215 Spadina Ave; coffee $3-6; ⊘7am-8pm Mon-Fri, 8am-8pm Sat & Sun; ☏; ⊞310, 510) Excellent coffee in a tall-ceilinged space, perfect for intensive writing or people-watching.

Handlebar BAR
(Map p86; ☑647-748-7433; www.thehandlebar.ca; 159 Augusta Ave; ⊘7pm-2am; ⊞505) A jolly little spot paying homage to the bicycle and its lovers, from owners with a fine pedigree. In a great spot in south Kensington Market, there's some wonderful retro styling and a nice mix of shiny happy punters. A calendar of quirky hipster events makes it an easier bar to visit if you're traveling solo.

Moonbean Coffee Company COFFEE
(Map p86; ☑416-595-0327; www.moonbeamcoffee.com; 30 St Andrew St; coffees from $3; ⊘7am-8pm; ⊞510) 'Nothing here is just ordinary,' says the dude behind the counter, and that's true. Serving the best latte west of Yonge St, Moonbean has organic and fairtrade coffees, all-day breakfasts for around $6, and 'Bite Me' vegan cookies. Grind-your-own beans from $16 per pound. Loose-leaf teas sold, too.

Yorkville & the Annex

★Oxley PUB
(Map p78; ☑647-348-1300; https://theoxley.com; 121 Yorkville Ave; ⊘11:30am-midnight Mon-Wed, to 1am Thu, to 2am Fri, 10am-2am Sat, to midnight Sun; ☏; Ⓢ Bay) A first-class British pub, the Oxley is located in a 19th-century row house in the heart of Yorkville. Two floors of leather seating, ornate wallpaper and Victorian-era decor attract business folk and the well-heeled hankering for a 20oz pour of craft beer, a glass of wine or a stiff drink. Classic English fare served, too.

Slanted Door COFFEE
(Map p86; ☑647-358-9888; https://slanteddoor.ca; 442 Bloor St W; ⊘8:30am-7:30pm Mon-Fri, 9am-6:30pm Sat, 10am-5:30pm Sun; ☏; Ⓢ Bathurst) A bright, contemporary coffee shop, the Slanted Door doubles as a gallery, showcasing work by emerging artists on its walls upstairs and down. The coffee drinks and teas are strong and flavorful, and the smoothies creative, with combos like apple-ginger-beet. Light snacks available, too. This is a popular place to catch up with friends or emails.

West End

★Bar Raval BAR
(Map p86; ☑647-344-8001; www.thisisbarraval.com; 505 College St; ⊘11am-2am Mon-Fri, 10am-2am Sat & Sun; ⊞306, 506) Standing in Bar Raval's magnificent, undulating mahogany interior, inspired by the works of Antoni Gaudí, feels like being surrounded by a set of petrified waves – it's otherworldly. The Basque-inspired *pinxtos* menu is the perfect complement to the surroundings: small sharing plates (squid in ink, smoked lamb belly, foie gras) go well with the list of layered cocktails and fine wines.

★Bellwoods Brewery BREWERY
(Map p86; www.bellwoodsbrewery.com; 124 Ossington Ave; ⊘2pm-midnight Mon-Wed, to 1am Thu & Fri, noon-1am Sat, to midnight Sun; ⊞505) Fresh, urban-chic Bellwoods pours award-winning beers, from pale ales and double IPAs to stouts and wild ales. With candles lighting up the main room and gallery, the brewery itself is decidedly cool and buzzing with locals. An elevated menu of small plates – cheese boards, chicken-liver mousse, mussels – complements the beers.

★Gladstone Hotel BAR
(Map p70; ☑416-531-4635; www.gladstonehotel.com; 1214 Queen St W; ⊘5pm-late Tue-Sat; ⊞501) This historic hotel (p98) revels in Toronto's avant-garde arts scene. The Gladstone Ballroom sustains offbeat DJs, poetry slams, jazz, book readings, alt-country and blues, and burlesque, while the Melody Bar hosts karaoke and other musical ventures. The cover varies but is usually $10 or less.

★Drake Hotel BAR
(Map p70; ☑416-531-5042; www.thedrakehotel.ca; 1150 Queen St W; ⊘11am-2am Mon-Fri, 10am-2am Sat & Sun; ⊞501) The Drake is part boutique hotel (p98), part pub, part live-music venue and part nightclub. There's a bunch of different areas to enjoy, including the chic Sky Yard rooftop bar and the hipster Drake Underground basement. Check the website for the lineup.

Henderson Brewing Company BREWERY
(Map p70; ☑416-535-1212; https://hendersonbrewing.com; 128 Sterling Rd; ⊘11am-10pm; ⊞306, 506, Ⓢ Lansdowne) A laid-back warehouse brewery in the Junction Triangle neighborhood, Henderson has a tasting

ONTARIO TORONTO

room with bar, picnic tables and huge fermentation tanks, offering views of staffers at work. Three beers (an amber, a lager and an IPA) are produced year-round; several others are created seasonally. Check the website for weekly events; there are pop-up eateries on weekends.

Snakes & Lattes   CAFE
(Map p86; ☑ 647-342-9229; www.snakesandlattes. com; 600 Bloor St W; cover $8; ⊙ 11am-midnight Sun-Thu, to 2am Fri & Sat; 🛜 ♿; ⑤ Bathurst) For a small cover fee, choose from over a thousand board games, along with local craft beers, milkshakes and shareable bites. Whether you're a Catan player or a Cards Against Humanity fan, there's a game for everyone. Snakes & Lattes has a few storefronts across the city –this Bloor St location is especially popular with University of Toronto students.

Sweaty Betty's   BAR
(Map p86; ☑ 416-535-6861; www.facebook.com/ SweatyBettysToronto; 13 Ossington Ave; ⊙ 8pm-2am Mon, 5pm-2am Tue-Thu, 3pm-2am Fri-Sun; 🚌 501) In a city of infused vodkas and creative cocktails, Betty's refuses to mix anything with more than three ingredients. This no-nonsense approach pares a night out to the essentials: having a good time and chatting people up. The tiny red-lit place is packed with hipsters on weekends, and the living room–like setup makes things feel like a college party.

🍴 East Toronto & Rosedale

★ **Rooftop**   ROOFTOP BAR
(Map p90; ☑ 416-362-8439; www.thebroadview hotel.ca; Broadview Hotel, 106 Broadview Ave; ⊙ 5pm-late Mon-Thu, 11:30am-late Fri-Sun; 🚌 501, 502, 503) This rooftop bar with floor-to-ceiling windows and a wraparound patio affords guests a 360-degree view of Toronto and a breathtaking outlook on the city skyline. Shareables and finger foods – duck-fat popcorn with sea salt, anyone? – complement the cocktail and wine lists well. Sunsets are particularly busy. Reservations highly recommended.

Comrade   COCKTAIL BAR
(Map p90; ☑ 647-340-1738; www.thecomrade restaurant.com; 1124 Queen St E; ⊙ 5:30pm-2am Mon-Thu, 5pm-2am Fri & Sat; 🚌 501, 502, 503) Reminiscent of a bygone era, the Comrade is a red-lit bar with a pressed-tin roof, mahogany accents and taxidermied animal heads

hung high. The cocktail list is long and sophisticated, the crowd mostly local. A good place to linger over a strong drink.

Jet Fuel   COFFEE
(Map p90; ☑ 416-968-9982; www.jetfuelcoffee. com; 519 Parliament St; ⊙ 6am-8pm; 🚌 506) So arty and grungy, this hangout is for east-end gentrifiers, cyclists and literati who like to jeer at the beautiful people of Yorkville. The best coffee east of Yonge St.

☆ Entertainment

As you might have guessed, there's always something going on here, from jazz to arthouse cinema, offbeat theater, opera, punk rock and hockey. In summer, free festivals and outdoor concerts are the norm, but Toronto's dance and live-music scene keeps grooving year-round. LGBTIQ+ life is also rich and open, with plenty of clubs, groups, bar nights and activities for all.

Live Music

Dust off your Iggy Pop T-shirt, don your Docs and hit the pit. Alt-rock, metal, ska, punk and funk – Toronto has a thriving live-music scene. Bebop, smoky swamp blues, classical and acoustic balladry provide some alternatives. Expect to pay anywhere from nothing to a few dollars on weeknights, up to $20 for weekend acts. The Toronto Symphony Orchestra (p112) has reduced-price tickets for anyone under 35. Megatours play the Rogers Centre (p113), Scotiabank Arena (p114) and the Budweiser Stage.

★ **Reservoir Lounge**   JAZZ
(Map p82; ☑ 416-955-0887; www.reservoirlounge. com; 52 Wellington St E; cover $5-10; ⊙ 7:30pm-2am Tue-Sat; 🚌 503, 504) Swing dancers, jazz singers and blues crooners call this cool, candlelit basement lounge home, and it's hosted its fair share of musical greats over the years. Where else can you enjoy a martini while dipping strawberries into chocolate fondue during the show? Tables are reserved for diners; prepare to drop at least $15 per person to sit down.

★ **Horseshoe Tavern**   LIVE MUSIC
(Map p78; ☑ 416-598-4226; www.horseshoe tavern.com; 370 Queen St W; ⊙ noon-2:30am; 🚌 501, 510) Well past its 70th birthday, the legendary Horseshoe still plays a crucial role in the development of local indie rock. This place oozes a history of good times and

TORONTO ISLANDS

For centuries, the Toronto Islands were not islands at all. They were joined together in an oblong peninsula, covered in ponds, marshes and millions of wildflowers, all connected to the mainland by a thin sandbar extending out from present-day Leslie Street. In 1858 a massive storm obliterated the sandbar and much of the peninsula's connective sand spits along with it, leaving the cluster of 15 islands seen today.

First Nations Ojibwe and Mississauga people long considered the area sacred, bringing the sick there to be healed. Colonizers delighted in the peninsula-turned-islands' long beaches and scenic views, and over the years numerous hotels, cottages and mansions were built there – mainly summer getaways for Toronto's well-heeled. Residential neighborhoods followed, along with shops, movie theaters and bowling alleys. A young Babe Ruth hit his first professional home run at the islands' former baseball stadium in 1914. In 1937, residents whose homes were in the way of a new airport were told they could relocate to Algonquin Island, a feat accomplished by towing whole cottages on barges.

The island's population peaked in the 1950s at around 8000. But mainlanders wanted a place to go to the beach – the hulking new Gardiner Expressway had destroyed many miles of lakeshore – and the Toronto Islands seemed just the place. The city began claiming and demolishing hundreds of homes and other structures, especially along the scenic southern shore, restoring the area to parkland. Most islanders acquiesced, but a small group did not, and a decades-long legal battle ensued. By 1980 it seemed the last 250 cottages would be torn down, but a stand-off at the Algonquin Island Bridge prevented the sheriff from serving evictions. The provincial government stepped in, and eventually granted residents 99-year leases, with strict limits on buying and selling property there. Today the Toronto Islands are home to around 600 to 800 residents. And at least one ghost. According to legend, the Gibraltar Point Lighthouse – built in 1808, it's the islands' oldest structure – is haunted by the ghost of its original lighthouse keeper, John Paul Radelmüller, whose grisly murder and dismemberment in 1815 has never been solved.

classic performances. Come for a beer and check it out.

In terms of not-so-local acts, it was here that The Police played on their first North American tour – Sting did an encore in his underwear – and Bran Van 3000 made their long-awaited comeback.

Adelaide Hall CONCERT VENUE
(Map p82; ☑ 647-344-1234; https://adelaidehallto.com; 250 Adelaide St W; ☐ 141, 143, 144, 145) One of the best small venues in town – its acoustics are tops – Adelaide Hall attracts both big-name and up-and-coming acts. On other nights, DJs and cover bands keep the place hopping. Look for the entrance tucked into an alley off Adelaide St (or just follow the line of people).

Dakota Tavern LIVE MUSIC
(Map p86; ☑ 416-850-4579; www.facebook.com/TheDakotaTavern; 249 Ossington Ave; cover $10; ⊙ 8pm-2am Tue-Sun; ☐ 63, ☐ 501) This basement tavern rocks, with wooden-barrel stools and a small stage where you can catch some twang. You'll hear mostly country and blues, plus a bit of rock. Sunday bluegrass brunches (adult/child $7/free; 10am to 2pm)

are a *big* hit – they're tasty, filling and fun, but you'll have to queue to get in.

★**Rex** JAZZ
(Map p78; ☑ 416-598-2475; www.therex.ca; 194 Queen St W; ⊙ shows 6:30pm & 9:30pm Mon-Thu, 4pm, 6:30pm & 9:45pm Fri, noon, 3:30pm, 7pm & 9:45pm Sat & Sun; ☐ 501) The Rex has risen from its pugilistic, blue-collar past to become an outstanding jazz and blues venue. Over a dozen Dixieland, experimental and other local and international acts knock over the joint each week. Cheap drinks; affordable cover.

Rivoli LIVE MUSIC
(Map p78; ☑ 416-596-1501; www.rivoli.ca; 334 Queen St W; ⊙ 11:30am-2am; ☐ 501) Songbird Feist got her start here. Nightly live music (rock, indie and solo singer-songwriters), weekly stand-up comedy and monthly hip-hop nights are all part of the lineup. There's an awesome pool hall upstairs and decent food, too.

Opera House CONCERT VENUE
(Map p90; ☑ 416-466-0313; www.theoperahousetoronto.com; 735 Queen St E; ☐ 501, 502, 503) The old Opera House is an early-1900s

vaudeville hall. Over the years, rockers like the Black Crowes, Rage Against the Machine, Eminem, Nirvana and Beck have all strutted out beneath the proscenium arch. Today it's still considered one of the best small venues in town for concerts and DJ dance parties.

Toronto
Symphony Orchestra CLASSICAL MUSIC
(TSO; Map p82; ☑ 416-593-1285; www.tso.ca; Roy Thomson Hall, 60 Simcoe St; ⊙ box office 10am-5pm Mon-Fri, noon-5pm Sat; ⑤ St Andrew) A range of classics, Cole Porter–era pops and new music from around the world is presented by the TSO at Jello-mold-like Roy Thomson Hall (sometimes also at Massey Hall and the Meridian Arts Centre). Reduced ticket prices available (from $19) for music-lovers aged 15 to 35, too.

Theater
Long winter months indoors are conducive to the creation and performance of theatrical works. This, and Toronto's relative proximity to Broadway and cosmopolitan Montréal, help sustain the city's reputation as a theater-maker's playground. Broadway and off-Broadway musicals and plays pack theaters around the Theatre Block in the Entertainment District and Yonge & Dundas Sq. There are numerous smaller venues and vibrant young production companies in the Harbourfront Centre (p72), the Distillery District (p77) and the West End (p84). Check the free street press for listings (p144). Tickets for major productions are sold through **TicketKing** (☑ 416-872-1212; www.mirvish.com/ticketking); rush tickets are occasionally sold on performance day, starting at 9am.

★ Soulpepper THEATER
(Map p90; ☑ 416-866-8666; www.soulpepper.ca; 50 Tank House Lane; ☒ 503, 504) This theater company has a repertoire ranging from new works to classics, most focused on the diversity of Canada's voices and identities. Youth-outreach initiatives and theater training programs are shining stars. Housed in the Young Centre for the Performing Arts in the heart of the Distillery District.

Young Centre for the
Performing Arts THEATER
(Map p90; ☑ 416-866-8666; www.youngcentre. ca; 50 Tank House Lane; ☒ 72, ☒ 503, 504) The $14-million Young Centre houses four performance spaces, used by theatrical tenants including Soulpepper and George Brown Theatre Co (www.georgebrown.ca/ theatre). There's an on-site bookstore and bar, too.

Young People's Theatre THEATER
(Lorraine Kimsa Theatre for Young People; Map p82; ☑ 416-862-2222; www.youngpeoplestheatre.ca; 165 Front St E; ⊙ box office 9am-5pm; ⊕; ☒ 503, 504) Catch a show at this innovative theater that has delivered enlightening children's plays and drama camps for over 50 years. Despite the common misconception, the vast majority of performances are by professional *adult* actors, not child actors.

Buddies in Bad
Times Theatre THEATER
(Map p78; ☑ 416-975-8555; http://buddiesinbad times.com; 12 Alexander St; ⑤ Wellesley) Founded in 1979, Buddies is the world's oldest queer theater company. Its mission: to develop and produce queer voices and stories on stage. Check the website for programming; pay-what-you-can tickets are available for some shows. Late night on weekends the theater opens its bar, **Tallulah's**, where proceeds from dance parties, drag shows and other events are used to support the theater.

Ed Mirvish Theatre THEATER
(Map p78; ☑ 416-872-1212; www.mirvish.com; 244 Victoria St; ⑤ Dundas) Formerly the Canon, the Ed Mirvish Theatre was renamed in 2011 in honor of the late Ed Mirvish, a well-loved Toronto businessman, philanthropist and patron of the arts. One of four Mirvish theaters, the 1920s-era vaudeville hall is a hot ticket for musical extravaganzas. Rush tickets are available for same-day performances only and are limited to two per person.

Canadian Opera Company OPERA
(Map p78; ☑ 416-363-8231; www.coc.ca; Four Seasons Centre for the Performing Arts, 145 Queen St W; ⊙ box office 11am-7pm Mon-Sat, to 3pm Sun; ⑤ Osgoode) Canada's national opera company has been warbling its phenomenal pipes for over 50 years. Tickets sell out fast, though standing-room tickets are available on performance days. Free concerts in the impressive glass-enclosed **Richard Bradshaw Amphitheatre** are held from September through May, usually at noon. Check the website for specific days.

Shakespeare in High Park
THEATER

(Map p70; ☑ 416-368-3110; www.canadianstage. com; High Park, 1873 Bloor St W; suggested donation adult/child $20/free; ⊙ 8pm Tue-Sun Jul-Sep; ⑤ High Park, ⓰ 501, 506, 508) Shakespeare in High Park (p84) is one of Canada's longest-running outdoor theater events, having started in 1982. Guests sit on grassy levels by the amphitheater or – if they pay a little extra and in advance – on a cushion in a premium area near the stage. Bring a blanket and a picnic dinner to enjoy the show like a local.

Factory Theatre
THEATER

(Map p86; ☑ 416-504-9971; www.factorytheatre. ca; 125 Bathurst St; tickets from $25; ⓰ 501, 504A, 504B) This innovative theater company – 'Home of the Canadian Playwright' – has been busy since 1970 producing exclusively Canadian plays. Stay for the talk backs ('Matt's Chats') with cast members after most shows. Sunday matinees are 'Pay What You Can.'

Students, seniors and 'arts workers' enjoy discounted tickets to all shows.

Theatre Passe Muraille
THEATER

(Theater Beyond Walls; Map p86; ☑ 416-504-7529; www.passemuraille.on.ca; 16 Ryerson Ave; ⊙ Oct-Apr; ⓰ 501) Since the 1960s the Theatre Passe Muraille, in the old Nasmith's Bakery & Stables, has focused on radical new plays with contemporary Canadian themes. Post-performance chats with the cast and producers occur often. Saturday and Sunday matinees are 'pay what you can'.

National Ballet of Canada
BALLET

(Map p78; ☑ 416-345-9595; https://national. ballet.ca; Four Seasons Centre for the Performing Arts, 145 Queen St W; ⊙ box office 11am-7:30pm Mon-Sat, to 2pm Sun; ⑤ Osgoode) The National Ballet of Canada is known for its full-length classical works and sumptuous sets, made more beautiful by the theater itself. Come early for the 'Ballet Talk,' a pre-show Q&A to learn more about the production and dancers.

Rush and standing-room tickets are available on performance days.

Cinemas

Torontonians love going to the movies – it might have something to do with the weather. Tickets cost around $14 for adults. Tuesday is discount day, when you can expect to pay around half that.

★ TIFF Bell Lightbox
CINEMA

(Map p82; ☑ 888-599-8433; www.tiff.net; 350 King St W; ⓰ 504) Headquarters of the Toronto International Film Festival (p93), this resplendent cinema complex is the hub of all the action when the festival's in town. Throughout the year it's used primarily for TIFF Cinematheque, screening world cinema, independent films, directorial retrospectives and other special events. Try to see a film here if you can.

★ Hot Docs Ted Rogers Cinema
CINEMA

(Bloor Hot Docs Cinema; Map p86; ☑ 416-637-3123; http://hotdocscinema.ca; 506 Bloor St W; ⑤ Bathurst) This art deco theater with a two-tiered balcony screens a wonderfully varied schedule of new releases, art-house flicks, shorts, documentaries and vintage films, and is home to the mind-expanding Hot Docs (p92) international documentary festival.

Sports

Many Torontonians weep with joy at the very mention of their beloved sporting teams: the Blue Jays (p114) for professional baseball and the Argonauts (p114) for football through the summer; and the Maple Leafs (p113) for hockey, the Raptors (p113) for basketball and Toronto Rock (p114) for lacrosse through the winter. Ticketmaster sells advance tickets, as do the box offices at Scotiabank Arena and the **Rogers Centre** (Map p82; ☑ 416-341-2770; 1 Blue Jays Way; 1hr tours adult/child $17/10; ⑤ Union). Ticket scalping is illegal, but that doesn't seem to stop anybody.

★ Toronto Maple Leafs
ICE HOCKEY

(Map p82; ☑ 416-815-5982; www.mapleleafs.com; 40 Bay St; ⊙ Oct-Apr; ⑤ Union) The 13-time Stanley Cup–winning Maple Leafs slap the puck around Scotiabank Arena. Every game sells out with fiery fans – hockey is intrinsic to the culture, after all – but a limited number of same-day tickets go on sale through Ticketmaster (www.ticketmaster.ca) at 10am and at the ticket window from 5pm. If you can score a ticket, it's worth the splurge.

You can also buy tickets via the website from season-ticket holders who aren't attending – expect to pay from $80.

Toronto Raptors
BASKETBALL

(Map p82; ☑ 416-815-5500; www.nba.com/raptors; 40 Bay St; ⊙ Oct-Apr; ⑤ Union) The 'Raps,' the NBA's only Canadian team, have made the playoffs 11 times since they joined the league in 1995, but they never reached the finals… until 2019, when they defeated the vaunted Golden State Warriors to become the first non-US team to win the title. Tickets are now a little harder to get; home games are at Scotiabank Arena.

Toronto Blue Jays BASEBALL
(Map p82; ☑ 416-341-1234; www.bluejays.com; 1 Blue Jays Way; ☉ Apr-Sep; ☐ 510A, 510B) Toronto's Major League Baseball team (a Toronto icon and a source of pride) plays at the Rogers Centre – it's the only MLB franchise based outside the USA. Buy tickets through Ticketmaster or at the Rogers Centre box office near Gate 9. Try for seats along the lower (pricier) level baselines: you'll have a better chance of catching a foul ball.

Toronto Argonauts FOOTBALL
(Map p70; ☑ 416-341-2746; www.argonauts.ca; ☉ Jun-Oct; ☐ 509, 511) The Toronto Argonauts crack their Canadian Football League (CFL) helmets at BMO Field at Exhibition Place (p93), off Lake Shore Blvd W. Founded in 1873, the 'Argos' have won the Grey Cup a record 17 times, most recently in 2017 against the Calgary Stampeders. Bring a jacket – BMO Field cools off at night. Get tickets through Ticketmaster or the team website.

Toronto Rock SPECTATOR SPORT
(Map p82; ☑ 416-596-3075; www.torontorock. com; 40 Bay St; ☉ Jan-Apr; ⑤ Union) Toronto's professional lacrosse team is red hot, having won the league championship six times. Games are held at Scotiabank Arena; get tickets through Ticketmaster.

Scotiabank Arena SPECTATOR SPORT
(Map p82; ☑ 416-815-5500; www.scotiabankarena. com; 40 Bay St; ⑤ Union) The Scotiabank Arena is home to the Toronto Maple Leafs and the Toronto Raptors. It also hosts countless concerts and big-ticket events.

🛍 Shopping

Shopping in Toronto is a big deal. When it's -20°C outside, you have to fill the gap between brunch and the movies with *something,* right? People like to update their wardrobes and redecorate their homes, or just walk around the sprawling **Eaton Centre** (Map p78; ☑ 416-598-8560; www.toronto

eatoncentre.com; 220 Yonge St; ☉ 10am-9:30pm Mon-Fri, 9:30am-9:30pm Sat, 10am-7pm Sun; 🛜; ⑤ Queen, Dundas). This habit continues through to summer, making boutique-hopping an excuse to hit the streets, or vice versa.

★ Arts Market ART
(Map p90; ☑ 416-778-9533; www.artsmarket. ca; 790 Queen St E; ☉ noon-5pm Mon-Thu, to 6pm Wed-Fri, 11am-6pm Sun; ☐ 501, 502, 503) A collective of local artists displays and sells work at this eclectic shop. High quality and unique, there's everything from handcrafted cards and jewelry to pottery and portraits. A few vintage finds, too.

★ Sonic Boom MUSIC
(Map p78; ☑ 416-532-0334; https://sonicboom music.com; 215 Spadina Ave; ☉ 10am-10pm; ☐ 310, 510) The largest indie record store in Canada, Sonic Boom has rows upon rows of new and used vinyl, CDs and even cassettes. Longtime staffers are deeply knowledgeable, offering direction and advice. Quirky T-shirts, irreverent souvenirs and coffee-table books (most with a musical bent) are sold at the front.

★ Courage My Love VINTAGE
(Map p86; ☑ 416-979-1992; 14 Kensington Ave; ☉ 11am-6pm Mon-Sat, 1-5pm Sun; ☐ 505, 510) Vintage-clothing stores have been around Kensington Market for decades, but Courage My Love amazes fashion mavens with its secondhand slip dresses, retro pants and white dress shirts in a cornucopia of styles. The beads, buttons, leather goods and silver jewelry are handpicked. Well stocked without being overwhelming.

★ Sunday Antique Market MARKET
(Map p82; ☑ 416-410-1310; www.facebook.com/ SundayAntiqueMarket; St Lawrence Market Complex, 125 The Esplanade; ☉ 7am-4pm Sun; ☐ 503, 504) Located in a tent-style building at the southern end of the St Lawrence Market Complex (p77), this weekly antique market brings more than 90 vendors to the neighborhood selling everything from delicate tea cups and crystal lamps to phonographs and creepy porcelain dolls. A great place to find a hidden treasure! (One person's trash…) This is a temporary location; the market is scheduled to move to the new North Market building in late 2022.

★**House of Vintage** VINTAGE
(Map p70; ☑416-535-2142; http://houseofvintage-toronto.blogspot.com; 1239 Queen St W; ☺noon-7pm Mon-Fri, 11am-7pm Sat, noon-6pm Sun; 🚌501)
Fulfill your one-of-a-kind dreams at this perfectly curated vintage boutique in Parkdale. Known as one of Toronto's hottest spots for men's and women's one-off and designer pieces, this place is bound to have something that fits the bill.

★**Glad Day** BOOKS
(Map p78; ☑416-901-6600; www.gladdaybookshop.com; 499 Church St; ☺10am-10pm Mon-Thu, to 2am Fri & Sat, 11am-7pm Sun; Ⓢwellesley) It's the oldest still-running gay bookstore in the world, making Glad Day an LGBTIQ+ landmark. The store has transformed from a place to defy censorship of LGBTIQ+ publications into an event and gathering space to promote creativity and further free speech. It's also a cafe and bar. Weekends mean Saturday-night dance parties and Sunday Drag Brunch.

★**Craft Ontario Shop** ART
(Map p70; ☑416-921-1721; www.craftontario.com; 1106 Queen St W; ☺11am-6pm Mon, 10am-6pm Tue & Wed, to 7pm Thu-Sat, 11am-5pm Sun; 🚌501) Craft Ontario has been promoting the work of artisans in its gallery boutique for over 40 years. Ceramics, jewelry, glasswork, prints and carvings make up most of the displays, but you could also catch a special exhibition of Pangnirtung weaving or Cape Dorset graphics. Staff are knowledgeable about indigenous art.

BMV BOOKS
(Map p86; ☑416-967-5757; www.bmvbooks.com; 471 Bloor St W; ☺10am-11pm Mon-Wed, to midnight Thu-Sat, noon-9pm Sun; Ⓢspadina) The biggest (and most popular) used bookstore in Toronto, with a spectacular selection of titles. Vinyls and DVDs sold, too. It has a smaller **second location** (Map p78; ☑416-482-6002; www.bmvbooks.com; Dundas Sq, 10 Edward St; ☺10am-10pm Mon-Sat, noon-10pm Sun; Ⓢdundas) on Dundas Sq.

MEC SPORTS & OUTDOORS
(Mountain Equipment Co-op; Map p78; ☑416-340-2667; www.mec.ca; 300 Queen St W; ☺10am-9pm Mon-Fri, 9am-8pm Sat, 10am-6pm Sun; 🚲; Ⓢosgoode) MEC is your mecca if you have a fetish for outdoor and adventure equipment. Multiple brands of backpacking, camping, hiking and travel gear line the walls of this

Canadian storehouse; sign up for lifetime membership ($5) on the spot to make a purchase. The helpful staff are swamped on weekends, so try midweek if you need advice.

Hoi Bo DESIGN
(Map p90; ☑647-852-5488; www.hoibo.com; 15 Trinity St; ☺11am-7pm Tue-Sat, to 6pm Sun & Mon; 🚌72, 🚌503, 504) Refined clothing and accessories, all handmade by an in-house crew and using natural materials such as organic wool, bamboo and Ontario beeswax. Items aren't cheap, but they're high quality. Think of them as investment pieces. Located in the Distillery District (p77).

Dead Dog Records MUSIC
(Map p78; ☑647-325-4575; www.deaddogrecords.ca; 568 Church St; ☺noon-8pm Tue-Thu, 11am-7pm Sat, noon-6pm Sun; Ⓢwellesley) A small used-record store with a good, well-organized selection of vinyls, CDs and even cassette tapes. Check out the merch from long-past concerts and don't leave without digging through the $2 bins – there are finds to be had! Service is friendly and knowledgeable.

Pacha Indigenous Art Collection GIFTS & SOUVENIRS
(Map p86; ☑647-525-7731; www.pachaarts.com; 614 Bloor St W; ☺10am-8pm Mon-Sat, noon-6pm Sun; Ⓢbathurst) Specializing in indigenous art from the Americas, Pacha carries one-of-a-kind creations from several Indigenous artists. Expect handmade jewelry, moccasins, leather goods, soapstone sculptures and more.

The shop occasionally hosts book talks and concerts, too.

BRIKA DESIGN
(Map p90; www.brika.com; 768 Queen St E; ☺noon-5:30pm Mon-Wed, to 6pm Thu & Fri, 11am-6pm Sat & Sun; 🚌501, 502, 503) A bright and airy boutique, BRIKA aims to inspire and create good mojo with its well-curated products, mostly home goods and beautiful accessories. What'll it be? A beautifully handcrafted messenger bag or a set of bath affirmations (test tubes filled with bath salts and daily mantras)?

A perfect place to find a special gift or memento.

Te Koop FASHION & ACCESSORIES
(Map p78; ☑416-348-9485; www.te-koop.ca; 421 Queen St W; ☺11am-8pm Mon-Sat, to 7pm

Sun; ⑤Osgoode) This backpack and luggage store champions Canadian brands such as Herschel, as well as boutique international labels. The bags aren't cheap, but they're high quality (read: they'll last forever).

Gallery Indigena
ART

(Map p90; ☑416-366-3000; www.galleryindigena.com; 46 Gristmill Lane; ⊘noon-6pm daily; ☐72, ☐503, 504) Specializing in indigenous Canadian art, this Distillery District (p77) shop sells original works by Inuit and other Aboriginal artists, along with some mass-produced artsy gifts. Prices range from museum quality to memento level, which is a plus for those on a tighter budget. Staff members are knowledgeable and ready to share background information about each piece.

Bungalow
VINTAGE

(Map p86; ☑416-598-0204; www.bungalow.to; 273 Augusta Ave; ⊘11am-6:30pm Mon-Thu, to 8pm Fri & Sat, to 6pm Sun; ☐306, 506) A vintage store selling well-curated home goods, furniture and clothing. Items change regularly, but expect mid-Century Modern tableware, teak bowls and trays, retro sunglasses and pillbox hats. New hipster clothing and accessories also sold.

ℹ Information

EMERGENCIES

Police (Map p78; ☑emergencies 911, non-emergencies 416-808-2222; www.torontopolice.on.ca; 40 College St; ⑤College)

Toronto Rape Crisis Centre (☑416-597-8808; www.trccmwar.ca; ⊘24hr)

MEDIA

Publications and news sources include the following:

Daily Xtra (www.dailyxtra.com) Online LGBTIQ+ news and entertainment source with street-press roots.

Globe & Mail (www.theglobeandmail.com) Doyen of the national daily newspapers.

Metro (www.metro360toronto.com) Free daily rag with bite-size news, sports and entertainment (often left on subway seats).

NOW (www.nowtoronto.com) Alternative weekly (good for events and concerts); free every Thursday.

Toronto Life (www.torontolife.com) An upscale monthly magazine covering lifestyle, dining, arts and entertainment.

Toronto Star (www.thestar.com) Canada's largest newspaper is a comprehensive left-leaning daily.

Toronto Sun (www.torontosun.com) Sensationalist tabloid with good sports coverage.

Where Toronto (www.where.ca/toronto) The most informative of the free glossy tourist magazines.

MEDICAL SERVICES

Toronto has several 24-hour emergency rooms, most in Downtown Yonge:

Dental Emergency Services (☑416-485-7172; www.dentalemergencyservices.ca; 1650 Yonge St; ⑤St Clair) Open 8am–midnight only.

Hospital for Sick Children (SickKids; Map p78; ☑416-813-1500; www.sickkids.ca; 555 University Ave, emergency 170 Gerrard St W; ⊘24hr; ⑤Queens Park)

Mount Sinai Hospital (Map p78; ☑416-596-4200, emergency 416-586-5054; www.mountsinai.on.ca; 600 University Ave; ⊘24hr; ⑤Queens Park)

St Michael's Hospital (Map p78; ☑416-360-4000; www.stmichaelshospital.com; 30 Bond St; ⊘24hr; ⑤Queen, Dundas)

Toronto General Hospital (Map p78; ☑emergency 416-340-3111; www.uhn.ca; 190 Elizabeth St; ⊘24hr; ⑤Queens Park)

MONEY

ATMs are widely available in Toronto, seemingly on every other corner. Look for international networks like Cirrus, Plus, Star and Maestro to ensure that your ATM, credit or debit cards will work.

Scotiabank (www.scotiabank.com) provides no-fee ATM withdrawals for members of the Global ATM Alliance, such as Westpac (Australia/NZ), the Bank of America (USA) and Barclays (UK). Your own bank, however, might still charge you a fee.

Many convenience-store ATMs charge an additional machine fee, typically $2 to $5.

POST

Toronto no longer has a main post office. There are a number of outlets in Shopper's Drug Mart stores around town. The most central full-service post offices are below.

Atrium on Bay Post Office (Map p78; ☑416-506-0911; www.canadapost.ca; 595 Bay St; ⊘9:30am-5:30pm Mon-Fri; ⑤Dundas)

Toronto's First Post Office (Map p82; ☑416-865-1833; https://townofyork.com; 31 Adelaide St E; ⊘9am-5:30pm Mon-Fri, 10am-4pm Sat, noon-4pm Sun; 🚻; ⑤Queen)

SAFE TRAVEL

By North American standards, Toronto is a safe city to live in and to visit, but be aware of the following:

➡ Yonge St can be sketchy, especially heading north toward Bloor as the strip clubs, sex shops and bars increase in density. Be aware of your surroundings and avoid walking alone at night. Alternatively, walk on University Ave, just west of Yonge.

➡ At night, Cabbagetown South – the area around Parliament and Jarvis Sts at the intersections of Carlton St, Dundas St E and Queen St E, particularly around Allan Gardens and George St – is iffy. Best take a cab or ride share.

TOURIST INFORMATION

Ontario Travel Information Centre (☎416-314-5899; www.ontariotravel.net; Union Station, 65 Front St W; ⊙9am-6pm Mon-Sat, 10am-6pm Sun; Ⓢ Union) Knowledgeable multilingual staff and overflowing racks of brochures that cover every nook and cranny of Toronto and beyond.

🛈 Getting There & Away

Toronto is well served by international and domestic flights to its main airport. There are a few more options if you're arriving from the USA, including a smaller Toronto Islands airport and a couple of Amtrak trains from Buffalo and New York. Long-distance buses also connect Toronto to towns near and far. You can make a land crossing into Ontario from the southwest at Detroit/Windsor. Flights, cars and tours can be booked online at lonelyplanet.com/bookings.

AIR

Toronto Pearson International Airport (YYZ; Lester B Pearson International Airport; Map p70; ☎Terminal 3 416-776-5100, Terminals 1 & 2 416-247-7678; http://torontopearson.com; 6301 Silver Dart Dr, Mississauga; 🚉 UP Express) Most Canadian airlines and international carriers arrive at Canada's busiest airport, 27km northwest of downtown Toronto. There is express train service to and from Union Station (p117) every 15 minutes, with stops in the Junction Triangle neighborhood and the suburb of Weston.

Billy Bishop Toronto City Airport (YTZ; Map p70; ☎416-203-6942; https://billybishop airport.com; 1 Island Airport, Centre Island; 🚉509) On the Toronto Islands, this small airport is home to the regional carrier Porter Airlines, helicopter companies and private flyers. Air Canada Jazz flights from Ottawa and Montréal land here rather than at Pearson. A free shuttle bus runs to and from Union Station every 15 minutes.

BUS

Long-distance buses operate from the art deco **Toronto Coach Terminal** (Map p78; ☎416-393-4636; 610 Bay St; Ⓢ Dundas). Megabus (https://ca.megabus.com) goes to a number of destinations. Advance tickets offer significant savings; online sales often close two hours before departure. Greyhound Canada stopped operations in mid-2021 but Greyhound USA still offers cross-border services to New York and Buffalo.

Union Station (p117) serves as the bus and train depot for GO Transit (www.gotransit.com), the commuter service of the Greater Toronto Area.

Parkbus (☎800-928-7101; www.parkbus.ca) offers limited seasonal departures to the Bruce Peninsula, Algonquin and Killarney Provincial Parks, Georgian Bay Islands and Elora Gorge. The range and frequency of services keeps expanding; check the website for the latest details. Pickup locations around downtown Toronto and its suburbs.

CAR & MOTORCYCLE

Toronto is wrapped in a mesh of multilane highways that are frequently crippled by congestion. The Gardiner Expwy runs west along the lakeshore into Queen Elizabeth Way (QEW) to Niagara Falls. At the city's western border, Hwy 427 runs north to the airport. Hwy 401 is the main east–west arterial and is regularly jammed. On the eastern side of the city, the Don Valley Pkwy connects Hwy 401 to the Gardiner Expwy. Hwys 400 and 404 run north from Toronto. A GPS is strongly recommended.

All major car-rental agencies, such as **Avis** (☎800-230-4898; www.avis.ca) and **Enterprise** (☎800-307-8009; www.enterpriserenta car.ca), have desks at Pearson airport and offices downtown and throughout the city. Book in advance for the best rates. Rates start at around $60 per day excluding taxes. On busy summer weekends prices spike and cars sell out – plan accordingly.

TRAIN

Union Station (☎416-869-3000; https://torontounion.ca; 140 Bay St; Ⓢ Union, 🚉509, 510) downtown is Toronto's main rail hub, with currency-exchange booths, the Ontario Travel Information Centre (p117) and a **Travellers' Aid Society** (Map p82; ☎416-366-7788; http://travellersaid.ca; Union Station, 140 Bay St; ⊙9am-10:30pm; Ⓢ Union) help desk. From here, VIA Rail (p71) plies the heavily trafficked

Windsor–Montréal corridor and beyond. Amtrak (www.amtrak.com) links Toronto with Buffalo, NY ($47, 4½ hours, two daily), and New York City ($131, 14 hours, two daily). GO Transit (www.gotransit.com) trains and buses also use the station, with an ever-expanding network of destinations, including Kitchener, Hamilton, Barrie and other Ontario locations, often with the cheapest rail fares.

ⓘ Getting Around

TO/FROM THE AIRPORT

UP Express The fastest way to get downtown is the **Union Pearson Express** (UP Express; www.upexpress.com; 1 way adult/child/family of 5 $12.35/free/25.70, 1 way on PRESTO card $9.25; ⊙5:30am-1am; 🛜) rail link. The comfortable trains leave every 15 minutes, have free wi-fi and power points, and take just 25 minutes to get to Union Station, stopping at Weston and Bloor stations, too. Traveling on a PRESTO card is highly recommended: the $6 rechargeable card pays for itself with a return trip to the airport and is useful for local transport in Toronto and on GO regional transit (www.gotransit.com/en).

TTC The cheapest (but not the best) way to get to the airport is on the **TTC** (TTC; ☑416-393-3030; www.ttc.ca; adult/child $3.25/free; ⊙6am-1am Mon-Sat, 8am-1am Sun). It's a pain with heavy luggage: many stairs. Catch the subway to Kipling station (you may need to change lines at Bloor-Yonge), then connect with the 900 Airport Express bus – be sure to use a transfer ticket! From the airport, the bus departs Terminals 1 and 3 every 10 to 20 minutes from 5:30am to 2am (from 7:30am Sunday). Allow *at least* an hour for the journey.

Taxi From Pearson to the city takes anywhere from 40 to 70 minutes, depending on traffic. The Greater Toronto Airports Authority (GTAA) regulates fares by drop-off zone: it's $60 to downtown, and $75 to destinations east of town. Don't pay more and remember to tip.

Airport limos often match the rate and have nicer cars and drivers.

BICYCLE

Bike-rental agencies, charging about $15/35 per hour/day, are found along the waterfront; **Wheel Excitement** (Map p82; ☑416-260-9000; www.wheelexcitement.ca; 249 Queens Quay W; bicycles per hour/day $15/35; ⊙10am-5pm; 🚌509, 510) is highly recommended.

For short rides, consider using **Bike Share Toronto** (☑855-898-2378; www.bikeshareto ronto.com), a city-wide bike-share program that rents bikes in 30-minute increments, either for a single use ($3.25) or for unlimited periods using one- and three-day passes ($7/15). These can be easy on the wallet and are a minimal hassle (no need to get back to the bike shop before it closes!). Just remember to dock your bike every 30 minutes, otherwise you'll end up paying a premium.

City buses have easily loadable bike racks; they're first come, first served. Bikes are permitted on streetcars and subway trains during off-peak hours only (before 6:30am, between 10am and 3:30pm, and after 7pm weekdays, and all weekend).

BOAT

From April to September **Toronto Islands Ferries** (Map p82; ☑416-392-8193; www.toronto.ca; 9 Queens Quay W; adult/child return $8.19/3.95; Ⓢ Union) services run from the terminal at the foot of Bay St to Centre Island (every 15 to 30 minutes from 8am to 11:15pm), Hanlan's Point (every 30 to 45 minutes from 6:30am to 10pm Monday to Friday, and 8am to 10:45pm Saturday and Sunday) and Ward's Island (every 30 to 60 minutes from 6:35am to 11:15pm). From October to March services are slashed (to roughly hourly), only running to Ward's Island and Hanlan's Point. The journey to any of the islands takes only 15 minutes.

During summer queues can be long on weekends and holidays – show up early, or book

VIA TRAIN SERVICES

DESTINATION	COST	DURATION	FREQUENCY
Kingston	$99	2½hr	frequent
London	$62	2-3hr	7 daily
Montréal	$110	5-9hr	11 daily
Niagara Falls	$22	2-3hr	seasonal, infrequent
Ottawa	$109	4½-5hr	10 daily
Sudbury Junction	$105	7hr	1 daily
Vancouver	from $498	97hr	3 weekly

online (www.toronto.ca) to skip the purchase queue.

A handful of water taxis also service the island from the ferry terminal; **Tiki Taxi** (Map p82; ☑ 647-347-8454; www.tikitaxi.ca; 441 Queens Quay W; adult/child $10/5; ☺ 9am-9pm Mon-Fri, 8am-9pm Sat & Sun; ☒ 310, 509, 510) operates from a pier just off Spadina Ave. All charge about $10 per person (pay onboard) and depart when full.

PUBLIC TRANSPORTATION

Regular city buses run every 10 minutes from 6am (8am Sunday) until 1am daily. 'Blue Night Network' buses provide service on major bus routes every 30 minutes or so from 1:30am to 5am daily (6am Saturday, 9am Sunday); transit stops are marked by reflective blue bands. Day passes are available (adult/under 12yr $13/ free).

Check the TTC's website (www.ttc.ca) for maps and timetables.

The fare is $3.25/free per adult/child, paid with exact change, ticket, token, pass or a PRESTO card. Two-hour transfers are included in the fare. Buses pick up and drop off passengers at designated stops. The only exception is between 9pm and 5am, when travelers can request to be dropped off between stops.

TAXI

Taxis are abundant and easy to hail in downtown Toronto. Often, major hotels have a line of taxis outside, too. In outer neighborhoods you'll have to call a cab. In either case, metered fares start at $4.25, plus $1.75 per kilometer, depending on traffic. A tip of 15% to 20% is customary. Credit and debit cards are typically accepted.

Diamond Taxicab (☑ 416-366-6868; www. diamondtaxi.ca)

Maple Leaf Taxi (☑ 416-465-5555; www. mapleleaftaxi.com)

Royal Taxi (☑ 416-777-9222; www.royaltaxi.ca)

NIAGARA PENINSULA

Jutting east from Hamilton and forming a natural divide between Lake Erie and Lake Ontario, the Niagara Peninsula is a legitimate tourist hot spot. Though many see only the falls and Clifton Hill on a day tour from Toronto, there's lots to explore here. Consider a several-day visit to fully experience the delights of the peninsula.

Water flows from Lake Erie, 100m higher than Lake Ontario, via two avenues: stepping down steadily through the locks along the Welland Canal, or surging over Niagara Falls in a reckless, swollen torrent. A steep limestone escarpment (p124) jags along the spine of the peninsula, generating a unique microclimate. Humid and often frost free, this is prime terrain for viticulture, a fact not lost on the award-winning wineries of Niagara-on-the-Lake.

Niagara Falls

☑ 905 / POP 88,100

An unstoppable flow of rushing water surges over the arcing fault in the riverbed with thunderous force. Great plumes of icy mist rise for hundreds of meters as the waters collide, like an ethereal veil concealing the vast rift behind the torrent. Thousands of onlookers delight in the spectacle every day, drawn by the force of the current and the hypnotic mist.

Otherwise, Niagara might not be what you expect: the town feels like a tacky, outdated amusement park. It has been a saucy honeymoon destination ever since Napoleon's brother brought his bride here – tags like 'For newlyweds and nearly deads' and 'Viagra Falls' are apt. A crass morass of casinos, sleazy motels and tourist traps lines Clifton Hill and Lundy's Lane – a Little Las Vegas! Love it or loathe it, there's nowhere quite like it.

◎ Sights

Parking access for sights and activities around the falls and Clifton Hill is expensive and limited.

◎ The Falls & Around

Niagara Falls forms a natural rift between Ontario and New York State. On the US side, **Bridal Veil Falls** (American Falls; Map p122) and the adjacent **American Falls** (Map p122) crash onto mammoth fallen rocks. On the Canadian side, the grander, more powerful **Horseshoe Falls** (Map p122) FREE plunge into the cloudy **Maid of the Mist Pool**. The prime falls-watching spot is **Table Rock** (Map p122) FREE, poised just meters from the drop. At sunset, the falls also are illuminated, in changing colors, year-round – a whimsical and beautiful sight.

Niagara is not the tallest of the world's waterfalls (it ranks a lowly 50th) but in terms of sheer volume, there's nothing like it – more than 8500 bathtubs of water

OFF THE BEATEN TRACK

BRUCE TRAIL

For 900km, the **Bruce Trail** (☑800-665-4453; www.brucetrail.org) winds along the top of the Niagara Escarpment, from the **Queenston Heights Park** (☑905-357-7808; www.niagaraparks.com; 14184 Niagara Pkwy, Queenston; ☉dawn-dusk; ℗) on the Niagara Peninsula to the Tobermory harbor on the Bruce Peninsula. This wide, well-maintained path is excellent for hiking during summer months, while those armed with cross-country skis take it through its winter paces. Day hikes along the trail are an appealing way to spend a sunny afternoon.

Opened in 1967, it's the oldest hiking trail in Canada and the longest in Ontario. The trail winds through public and private land, as well as along roadways. Wander past wineries, farmlands and forests and marvel at Georgian Bay's shimmering azure waters from the escarpment's white cliffs. A multitude of campgrounds en route have budget accommodations for those on longer trips, and trail towns offer B&Bs galore.

plummet downward every second. By day or night, regardless of the season, the falls never fail to awe: 12 million visitors annually can't be wrong. Even in winter, when the flow is partially hidden and the edges freeze solid, the watery extravaganza is undiminished. Very occasionally the falls stop altogether. This first happened on Easter Sunday morning in 1848, when ice completely jammed the flow.

Tickets for the four falls attractions listed below can be purchased separately, but the online 27% discounted **Niagara Falls Adventure Classic Pass** (www.niagaraparks.com; adult/child $65/43) is a better value. It includes a ride on Hornblower Niagara Cruises and admission to the Journey Behind the Falls, **White Water Walk** (Map p122; ☑877-642-7275; 4330 Niagara Pkwy; adult/child $14/9; ☉9am-9pm Apr-Oct) and Niagara's Fury (p123), plus two days' transportation on the WEGO bus system. If you want to go all out, upgrade to the **Niagara Falls Adventure Pass Plus** (adult/child $90/59), which includes everything on the Classic Pass plus admission to the **Floral Showhouse** (Map p122; ☑905-354-1721; www.niagaraparks.com;

7145 Niagara Pkwy; adult/child $7/4; ☉9:30am-5pm; ℗), Butterfly Conservatory, nearby historic sites, WEGO service to Niagara-on-the-Lake and unlimited rides on the Incline Railway (p127). Passes are also available from the Niagara Parks Commission at Table Rock Information Centre (p126), the Ontario Travel Information (p126) center, and most attractions.

◉ Clifton Hill

Clifton Hill is a street name, but refers to a broader area near the falls occupied by a sensory bombardment of artificial enticements. You name it – House of Frankenstein, Louis Tussaud's Waxworks, Castle Dracula – they're all here. In most cases, paying the admission will leave you feeling kinda like a sucker.

★**Skylon Tower**   VIEWPOINT
(Map p122; ☑905-356-2651; www.skylon.com; 5200 Robinson St; adult/child $16.25/10.50; ☉9am-10pm Mon-Thu, to 11pm Fri-Sun; ℗) The Skylon Tower is a 158m concrete spire with yellow pill-shaped elevators crawling up and down the tower's neck to the top. The interior itself is dated, even a little sad, but the views! They're eye-popping and simply picture perfect, with the falls to the east and, on clear days, Toronto to the north. The two observation areas – a glass-enclosed indoor deck and a wire-fenced outdoor one – give you 360-degrees views of the region. Plus, there's a revolving restaurant and a family-friendly buffet.

A great place to watch fireworks over the falls!

Niagara Falls
History Museum   MUSEUM
(Map p122; ☑905-358-5082; https://niagarafalls-museums.ca; 5810 Ferry St; adult/child $5/4, Thu 5-9pm free; ☉10am-5pm Tue-Wed & Fri-Sun, to 9pm Thu; ℗⛹) A complete change of pace from the sights near the falls, this museum uses multi-media displays and artifacts to explore the history of Niagara Falls. The focus is on the War of 1812 as well as the transformation of Niagara Falls from an indigenous settlement to one of the most touristed places in Canada. Things like colonial soldier dress-up areas and simulated tight rope walks make it fun for kids. It's inside the beautifully renovated 19th-century Town Hall.

Military history buffs will enjoy visiting **Drummond Hill Cemetery**, the site of the Battle of Lundy's Lane, known as the 'bloodiest battle' of the War of 1812. Ask for a self-guided tour pamphlet at the front desk. The cemetery is just a couple blocks from the museum.

Bird Kingdom   ZOO
(Map p122; ☑905-356-8888; www.birdkingdom.ca; 5651 River Rd; adult/child $18/14; ⊘9am-6:30pm; [P][⊕]) The jungly Bird Kingdom claims to be the world's largest indoor aviary, with 400 species of free-flying tropical birds from around the globe. You can also buddy up with a boa constrictor in the Animal Encounter Zone, and feed the birds. Discounted tickets on its website.

◉ Around Niagara Falls

Riverbrink Art Museum   MUSEUM
(☑905-262-4510; https://riverbrink.org; 116 Queenston St, Queenston; adult/child $5/free; ⊘10am-5pm Mon-Sat May-Oct, Wed-Sat Nov-Apr; [P]) A country home turned art museum, Riverbrink has well-curated exhibits of fine and decorative works of art, with a focus on Canadian historical pieces. The collection and building itself once belonged to Sam Weir, a lawyer from London, who was an avid art collector. Check the museum for lectures, art workshops and other events.

Niagara Glen
Nature Reserve   NATURE RESERVE
(☑905-354-6678; www.niagaraparks.com; 3050 Niagara Pkwy; ⊘Reserve dawn-dusk, Nature Centre 10am-5pm Apr-Nov; [P][⊕]) [FREE] About 8km north of the falls is this exceptional reserve, where you can get a sense of what the area was like pre-Europeans. There are 4km of walking trails winding down into a gorge, past huge boulders, cold caves, wildflowers and woods. Stop by the Nature Centre for trail maps and info. Park naturalists also offer daily one-hour guided nature walks ($7; 11am and 2pm) during the summer season. Bring something to drink – the water in the Niagara River is far from clean.

Botanical Gardens &
Butterfly Conservatory   GARDENS
(☑905-356-8119; www.niagaraparks.com; 2565 Niagara Pkwy; butterfly conservatory adult/child $16/10.25, gardens free; ⊘10am-4pm Mon-Fri, to 5pm Sat & Sun Sep-Jun, 10am-7pm Sun-Wed, to 8pm Thu-Sat Jul & Aug; [P][⊕]) Entry to the 40 hectares of the Botanical Gardens is free, but you'll need to pay to enter the Butterfly Conservatory, with its more than 45 species

of butterflies (some as big as birds) flitting around 130 species of flowers and plants. This is also a breeding facility where you can see young butterflies released. Parking costs $5.

Mackenzie Printery &
Newspaper Museum   MUSEUM
(☑905-262-5676; www.mackenzieprintery.org; 1 Queenston St, Queenston; adult/child $6.50/4.50; ⊘10am-5pm May-Oct; [P][⊕]) This ivy-covered museum was where the esteemed William Lyon Mackenzie once edited the hell-raising *Colonial Advocate*. Geek out over the Louis Roy Press, the oldest wooden press in Canada (there are only seven left in the world!). Or try your hand at setting a moveable type. Or better yet, make a DIY souvenir using a colonial-era printing press.

Enthusiastic young staff conduct tours every half-hour.

🏃 Activities

★ Hornblower Niagara Cruises   BOATING
(Map p122; www.niagaracruises.com; 5920 Niagara Pkwy; adult/child $26/16, fireworks cruise $40; ⊘8:30am-8:30pm May-Sep, to 5:30pm Oct) A classic Niagara Falls experience: boat tours that come so close to the spectacular Bridal Veil Falls and Horseshoe Falls that you'll be drenched (despite the rain ponchos). Hornblower offers two tours on its 700-person catamarans: a 20-minute daytime 'Voyage to the Falls'; and a 40-minute 'Fireworks Cruise,' under the fireworks on summer nights with live music and cash bar. Avoid the massive ticket lines and buy a ticket online.

Online tickets include a funicular ride to the boats ($3), a 19-story snail's-pace drop along the escarpment with a pre-recorded audio guide about the views.

★ Journey Behind the Falls   WALKING
(Map p122; ☑905-354-1551; www.niagaraparks.com; 6650 Niagara Pkwy; adult/child $22/14; ⊘9am-10pm, hours vary by season) From Table Rock Information Centre, don a very unsexy plastic poncho and take an elevator through the bedrock partway down the cliff to the Cataract- and Great Falls portals for an in-your-face view of the falls. Continue through 130-year old-tunnels to two observation decks – as close as you can get to the falls without hopping in a barrel. It's open year-round, but be prepared to queue.

In winter the lower deck is usually closed.

Niagara Falls

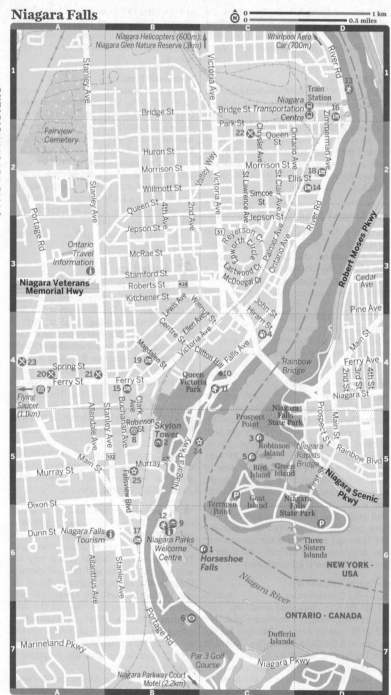

Niagara Helicopters (600m);
Niagara Glen Nature Reserve (3km)

Whirlpool Aero
Car (700m)

River Rd

Stanley Ave

Fairview
Cemetery

Bridge St

Victoria Ave

Bridge St
Park St

Train
Station

Niagara
Transportation
Centre

13

Zimmerman Ave

16

22 Queen St

Chrysler Ave

Huron St

Morrison St

Willmott St

Queen St

4th Ave

2nd Ave

Victoria Ave

Morrison St

St Clair Ave

Ellis St

18

14

Simcoe
St

Jepson St

Ontario Ave

Jepson St

Reyerson Cr
worth Circle

St Lawrence Ave

Palmer Ave

McRae St

Eastwood Cr
McDougal Cr

Ontario Ave

River Rd

Robert Moses Pkwy

Cedar
Ave

Stamford St

Roberts St

420

Pine Ave

Kitchener St

Lewis Ave

Walnut St

John St

Hiram St

Main St

Centre St

Ellen Ave

Victoria Ave

Clifton Hill

Falls Ave

4

Ferry Ave

2nd St

3rd St

4th St

Magdalen St

19

Rainbow
Bridge

Niagara Scenic Pkwy

23

20

21

Spring St

Ferry St

Ferry St

15

Clark
Ave

Buchanan Ave

Queen
Victoria
Park

10

11

Niagara Falls
State Park

Main St

Rainbow Blvd

Flying
Saucer
(1.1km)

7

Robinson
Ave

8

Skylon
Tower

2

24

Prospect
Point

3

Robinson
Island

5

Niagara
Rapids
Bridge

First St

Prospect St

Main St

Allendale Ave

Stanley Ave

102

Fallsview Blvd

Murray St

25

Bird
Island

Green
Island

Main St

Murray St

Dixon St

Niagara Pkwy

P

Goat
Island

Terrapin
Point

Niagara
Falls
State Park

P

Dunn St

Niagara Falls
Tourism

17

12

9

Niagara Parks
Welcome
Centre

1

Horseshoe
Falls

Three
Sisters
Islands

NEW YORK -
USA

Allanthus Ave

Stanley Ave

Portage Rd

6

Niagara River

ONTARIO - CANADA

Dufferin
Islands

Marineland Pkwy

Par 3 Golf
Course

Niagara Pkwy

Niagara Parkway Court
Motel (2.2km)

Portage Rd

Ontario
Travel
Information

Niagara Veterans
Memorial Hwy

Portage Rd

51

Niagara Falls

Niagara's Fury AMUSEMENT PARK
(Map p122; ☑ 905-358-3268; www.niagaraparks.
com; 6650 Niagara Pkwy; adult/child $16/10.25;
☺half-hourly 9:15am-9pm; ⊕) Inside the Table
Rock Visitor Centre, this Universal Studios–
style interactive attraction is a 360-degree
cinema-simulation of how the falls were created. Expect lots of high-tech tricks to sus-
pend disbelief, including getting splashed,
feeling snow fall and experiencing a rapid
drop in temperature. (If it's winter, taking
a stroll next to the falls might just feel the
same.) Aimed at kids.

Whirlpool Aero Car CABLE CAR
(Niagara Spanish Aero Car; ☑ 877-642-7275; 3850
Niagara Pkwy; adult/child $16/10.25; ☺9am-8pm
Apr-Nov) Dangling above the Niagara River,
4.5km north of Horseshoe Falls, the Whirlpool Aero Car was designed by Spanish engineer Leonardo Torres Quevedo and has
been operating since 1916 (but don't worry –
it's still in good shape). The gondola travels
550m between two outcrops above a dead-
ly whirlpool created by the falls – count the
logs spinning in the eddies below. No wheelchair access.

**Niagara River
Recreation Trail** WALKING
(www.niagaraparks.com) The idyllic 3m-wide
Niagara River Recreation Trail, for cycling,
jogging and walking, runs parallel to the
slow-roaming, leafy Niagara Pkwy. The
trail can easily be divided into four chunks,
each of which takes around two hours to

pedal. The parkway meanders for 56km
along the Niagara River, from Niagara-on-
the-Lake past the falls and all the way to
Fort Erie.

Along the way you'll find parks, picnic
areas, viewpoints and historical plaques. In
season, fresh-fruit stands selling cold cherry
cider adorn the side of the trail. Download
a map online, or pick one up at a visitor
center.

Namaste Niagara YOGA
(Map p122; ☑ 877-642-7275; www.niagaraparks.
com; 6650 Niagara Pkwy; $60; ☺8am Sat &
Sun Jul-Sep) During the summer, yogis can
experience Horseshoe Falls up close during an all-level class on the lower observation deck of Journey Behind the Falls
(p121). The 45-minute session is followed
by breakfast at a nearby restaurant. BYO
yoga mat and a change of clothes – you'll
be mist-soaked by the end. Parking and
meal included.

⌲ Tours

Niagara Helicopters SCENIC FLIGHTS
(☑ 905-357-5672; www.niagarahelicopters.
com; 3731 Victoria Ave; adult/child $149/92;
☺9am-sunset, weather permitting) A fantastic
12-minute falls encounter takes you on a
flight path along the Niagara River, over the
Whirlpool past the American Falls (p119)
and Bridal Veil Falls (p119) for the grand fi-
nale over Horseshoe Falls (p119). Learn facts
about the sights via clunky headphones. A

gorgeous and pricey (and not the most environmentally sensitive) way to see the falls.

Double Deck Tours BUS

(Map p122; ☏905-374-7423; www.doubledeck tours.com; cnr Falls Av & Clifton Hill; tours adult/child from $80/52; ☉10am-6pm Apr-Oct) Offers a deluxe 3½-hour tour on a red double-decker bus. The price includes admission to the Whirlpool Aero Car (p123), Journey Behind the Falls (p121) and Hornblower Niagara Cruises (p121).

★ Festivals & Events

Summer Fireworks Series FIREWORKS

(www.niagarafallstourism.com; ☉May-Oct) A magnificent fireworks show takes place over the falls during the summer months: huge, sparkling lights and multicolored puffs light up the skies and the roaring falls below. The show starts at 10pm and is held nightly from June to August and on weekends in May, September and October.

For a great view, stake out a spot near Table Rock (p119), see it from the water on a Hornblower (p121) boat tour, or head to the top of the Skylon (p120).

Winter Festival of Lights LIGHT SHOW

(☏905-374-1616; www.wfol.com; ♿) FREE A season of events from mid-November to mid-January including concerts, fireworks, more than 125 animated displays and two million tree- and ground lights. The undisputed highlight, though, is an over-the-top nocturnal light display along a 8km route, which is lit daily from 5pm to midnight.

⊨ Sleeping

There are usually more beds than heads in Niagara Falls, but the town is sometimes completely booked up. Prices spike sharply in summer, on weekends and during holidays. Cheap motels line Lundy's Lane. If you are coming from Toronto just for the falls, it really isn't necessary to stay overnight; a day trip is plenty.

**Hostelling International
Niagara Falls** HOSTEL $

(Map p122; ☏905-357-0770; www.hostelling niagara.com; 4549 Cataract Ave; dm/d incl breakfast from $39/98; ℗@⊛) Quietly adrift in the old town, this homey, multicolored hostel sleeps around 90 people. The facilities, including a sizable and well-stocked kitchen, pool table, lockers and cool basement lounge, are in good shape; staff are friendly and eco-focused. It's close to the train and bus stations, and bikes are available for rent. Rates drop a bit in the winter.

★**Cadillac Motel** MOTEL $$

(Map p122; ☏905-356-0830; www.cadillac motelniagara.com; 5342 Ferry St; r $199; ℗⊛⊛) A retro motel just west of the kitsch on Clifton Hill, rooms here are modern and chic with great beds and luxe linens. Each has an classic Caddy theme – mostly, a photo mural of vintage Cadillacs or models like the pink Fleetwood convertible made famous by Elvis. Outside, Adirondack chairs add to the throw-back feel. Reservations recommended in the summer.

★**Marriott Niagara Falls** HOTEL $$

(Map p122; ☏888-501-8916; www.niagarafalls marriott.com; 6740 Fallsview Blvd; r from $224; ℗⊜⊛@⊛⊛) This sprawling giant is so close that you could almost touch the falls... the lobby itself seems to hang over the Horseshoe Falls (p119). A variety of modern

---

JAGGED EDGES: THE NIAGARA ESCARPMENT

The Niagara Escarpment, a 725km-long land formation that creates Niagara Falls, is a designated Unesco World Biosphere Reserve. Sweeping from eastern Wisconsin and along the shore of northern Lake Michigan, down through Lake Huron and across Manitoulin Island, slicing through Ontario and then curving under Lake Ontario and ending in New York State, the escarpment is a long spine of brush-covered stone. A combination of what was originally lime bed and ancient sea floor, the dolomitic limestone that makes up the land formation is more resistant than the land around it, which has eroded and left the bulge of limestone slithering around the Great Lakes: look for the cliffs near Queenston, Hamilton, Lion's Head and Tobermory.

Great waterfalls are just one result of the escarpment. Together with Lake Ontario, the geological formation has created a microclimate perfect for viticulture. The soil (a combination of limestone and clay) and the warmth created by Lake Ontario generate growing conditions very similar to those of France's Burgundy region.

room types is available, but many love the two-level loft suites with hot tub, fireplace and spectacular views from the floor-to-ceiling windows. If you want to save some cash, opt for a city-view room.

Park Place Bed & Breakfast
B&B $$

(Map p122; ☑905-358-0279; www.parkplace niagara.ca; 4851 River Rd; r from $150; P ⊖ ✳ ☎) A gorgeous Queen Anne Revival–style house with a wraparound veranda and lush gardens is the setting for this B&B. There are just two rooms and a carriage house, each one individual in style and layout – one has a hot tub, another a working fireplace – but equally upscale. A full breakfast, prepared to order, is offered each morning. The affable owners are a font of regional information.

Always Inn Bed & Breakfast
B&B $$

(Map p122; ☑905-371-0840; www.alwaysinn.ca; 4327 Simcoe St; d incl breakfast $145-200; P ✳ @ ☎) An old Victorian house with a spick-and-span interior is a pleasant surprise in these parts. The substantial breakfast is another. Rooms are tidy and flowery. It's a pleasant 20-minute walk south along the Niagara Pkwy to the falls.

Sterling Inn & Spa
BOUTIQUE HOTEL $$

(Map p122; ☑289-292-0000; www.sterlingniagara. com; 5195 Magdalen St; r from $221; ☎) The stylish rooms of this boutique hotel (with either a *Jacuzzi* or steam shower) beckon you to relax and unwind with someone special. Expect quality furnishings, amenities and breakfast-in-bed baskets. The popular onsite AG restaurant (p126) is sleek and modern, plus there's a full-service treatment spa. Perfect for couples. No views, unfortunately.

Niagara Parkway Court Motel
MOTEL $$

(☑905-295-3331; 3708 Main St; d incl breakfast from $139; P ✳ ☎) Rooms at this quiet motel could use an update – some hearken to the '80s with a purple-and-black motif – but nevertheless are decent value for the market. Customer service is tops and the simple DIY breakfast is a nice touch. Check for last-minute deals. A great choice for lower-cost accommodations.

✖ Eating

The old downtown section of town has seen many failed revival attempts, but it's worth checking out for new restaurants, if the other options aren't appealing. Fast food (and dressed-up, overpriced fast food) is abundant in the touristy strip, but the best eats can be found a little further afield. For cuisine a cut above, head up the road to Niagara-on-the-Lake.

Queen Charlotte Tea Room
BRITISH $

(Map p122; ☑905-371-1350; www.thequeenchar lottetearoom.com; 5689 Main St; mains $8-17, high tea $25; ⊙11am-7pm Wed-Thu, Sat & Sun, to 8pm Fri) British expats craving a decent or even fancy cuppa, cucumber sandwiches, steak and kidney or fish-and-chips with mushy peas should head straight to this quaint establishment on Main St, near the intersection with Lundy's Lane, for a spot of tiffin! Reservations required for high tea; gluten-free options available.

Flying Saucer
FAST FOOD $

(☑905-356-4453; 6768 Lundy's Lane; mains $7-27; ⊙6am-1am Sun-Thu, to 2am Fri & Sat; ♿) For extraterrestrial fast food, you can't go past this iconic diner on the Lundy's Lane motel strip. Famous $3.50 early-bird breakfasts are served from 6am to 10am (eggs, fries and toast) with the purchase of a beverage. Heftier meals like steaks, seafood, fajitas, burgers and hot dogs are also on board. Takeout is in the saucer to the left.

Paris Crepes Cafe
FRENCH $$

(Map p122; ☑289-296-4218; www.pariscrepescafe. com; 4613 Queen St; mains $17-33; ⊙11am-2pm, 5-8pm Mon-Fri, 10am-2pm & 5-8:30pm Sat & Sun) In the revitalized area of Queen St you'll find this quaint creperie, a very long way from the streets of Paris: you can't miss the dark-red building. Sweet and savory crepe sensations are served among other continental delights from the wonderfully authentic Parisian menu.

Napoli Ristorante Pizzeria
ITALIAN $$

(Map p122; ☑905-356-3345; www.napoliristo rante.ca; 5545 Ferry St; mains $16-36; ⊙4:30-10pm) Head to Napoli for the best Italian in town, hands down. Delicious pizza, rich pasta, creamy risotto and veal parmigiana all feature on the familiar menu.

Koutouki Greek Cuisine
GREEK $$$

(Map p122; ☑905-354-6776; http://koutouki niagara.com; 5745 Ferry St; mains $22-42; ⊙4-10pm Tue-Sun) A local favorite with an old-world feel, Koutouki serves classic Greek cuisine with a homey but elegant touch. Meals are beautifully presented and filling. Try, if you can, to save room for the baklava, a sweet phyllo dough dessert with walnuts and honey syrup. Worth the longish walk from the falls.

AG   CANADIAN **$$$**
(Map p122; ☑ 289-292-0005; www.agcuisine.com; 5195 Magdalen St; mains $18-38; ⊙ 6-9:30pm Tue-Sun) Fine dining isn't something you find easily at the falls, which makes this fine restaurant at the Sterling Inn & Spa (p125) so refreshing. Service, decor, presentation and especially the quality of the food all rate highly. It has a seasonal menu featuring dishes like fennel-pollen pickerel, coffee-roasted venison and crispy-skinned trout, sourced locally.

☆ Entertainment

Music in the Park   LIVE MUSIC
(Map p122; Queen Victoria Park, 6345 Niagara Pkwy; ⊙ 8-10pm Thu-Sun Jun-Sep) FREE On summer weekend nights, check out local talent during free classic-rock concerts at Queen Victoria Park, facing the American Falls (p119). The music starts at 8pm and ends as the fireworks (p124) begin. A great way to spend a warm evening by the falls.

ℹ Information

Greater Niagara General Hospital (Niagara Health; ☑ 905-378-4647; www.niagarahealth. on.ca; 5546 Portage Rd; ⊙ 24hr) Emergency and urgent care services.

Niagara Falls Tourism (Map p122; ☑ 905-356-6061; www.niagarafallstourism.com; 6815 Stanley Ave; ⊙ 9am-5pm Mon-Fri) Offers information on the different neighborhoods and what's on around town. Located near the Marriott (p124).

Niagara Parks Welcome Centre (Table Rock Visitor Centre; Map p122; ☑ 877-642-7275; www.niagaraparks.com; 6650 Niagara Pkwy; ⊙ 9am-9pm, to 7pm Sep-May) Niagara Parks Commission has five welcome centers in the most touristed sections of the falls, where visitors can gather information and purchase tickets to area sights. The one at **Table Rock Visitor Centre**, in front of Horseshoe Falls (p119), is especially convenient. Other locations include near the Hornblower Niagara Cruises (p121) ticket booth and in Clifton Hill. Check the website for more details.

Ontario Travel Information (Map p122; ☑ 905-358-3221; www.ontariotravel.net; 5355 Stanley Ave; ⊙ 8:30am-5:30pm Sun-Thu, to 6pm Fri & Sat Jun-Aug, 8:30am-4:30pm Sep-May) On the western outskirts of town; offers free tourist booklets containing maps and discount coupons. Discounted tickets to area sights, including Niagara Falls Adventure Passes, are sold here too.

ℹ Getting There & Away

Niagara Falls is well serviced by buses from both Canada and the USA. Parking can be a nightmare, especially in the summer: public lots aren't particularly convenient and are expensive. Consider leaving the car behind.

BUS

The **Niagara Transportation Centre** (Map p122; ☑ 905-357-2133; 4555 Erie Ave) is in the old part of town. Greyhound buses depart for Buffalo, NY ($15, 1½ hours, five daily) from this bus station. Go Transit (www.gotransit.com) also provides service to Toronto by a combination of train and bus, via Burlington.

Niagara Airbus (☑ 905-374-8111; www. niagaraairbus.com; 8626 Lundy's Lane; ⊙ 24/7) operates door-to-door shared-shuttle services to Toronto International Airport (one way $99, two hours) and Buffalo International Airport (one way $105, 1½ hours). Discounts for groups and/ or if you leave from its bus depot.

The **Fallsview Casino** (Map p122; ☑ 888-325-5788; www.fallsviewcasinoresort.com; 6380 Fallsview Blvd; ⊙ 24hr) runs the Safeway Tours bus hourly from Toronto, making stops from Gerrard St E, to Carlton St and then Spadina Ave, finally arriving at the casino. Noncasino members pay the $30 each way. No luggage is permitted and adult ID is required as it is a casino bus. Just turn up, or reserve on the website (www.safewaytours.net/casino-tours) as it can fill up.

TRAIN

Via (☑ 888-842-7245; www.viarail.ca) and GO Transit (www.gotransit.com) provide daily rail services from Niagara Falls to Toronto ($23, two to 2½ hours, two departures). Service frequency increases on summer weekends.

ℹ Getting Around

BICYCLE

The falls are perfect for cycling from site to site. If you're just looking to explore for a few hours, try **Zoom Bike Share** (☑ 905-468-3401; https://zoombikeshare.com), a self-serve bike share system. Download the app, go to a designated bike drop-off location, scan the code, and you're good to go. Rentals cost $5 per hour.

CAR & MOTORCYCLE

Driving and parking around the center is an expensive headache, sometimes costing up to $30 per day. Park at the Niagara IMAX lot for just $10 for the whole day and walk, or follow the parking district signs and stash the car for the day (around $6 per 30 minutes, or $15 per day). In the winter, the Falls Casino occasionally offers spots for $5 per day. The huge Rapidsview parking lot (also the WEGO depot) is 3km south

DAREDEVILS

Surprisingly, more than a few people who have gone over Niagara Falls have actually lived to tell the tale. The first successful leap was in 1901, by a 63-year-old schoolteacher named Annie Taylor, who did it in a skirt, no less. This prompted a rash of barrel stunters that continued into the 1920s, including Bobby Leach, who survived the drop but met his untimely death after slipping on an orange peel and developing gangrene!

In 1984 Karl Soucek revived the tradition in a bright-red barrel. He made it, only to die six months later in another barrel stunt in Houston. Also during the 1980s, two locals successfully took the plunge lying head to head in the same barrel.

A US citizen who tried to jet ski over the falls in 1995 might have made it – if his rocket-propelled parachute had opened. Another American, Kirk Jones, survived the trip over the falls unaided in 2003. After being charged by Canadian police with illegally performing a stunt, he joined the circus.

Only one accidental falls-faller has survived – a seven-year-old Tennessee boy who fell out of a boat upstream in 1960 and survived the drop without even breaking a bone.

Take the virtual plunge at the **Niagara IMAX** (Map p122; ☑ 905-358-3611; www.imax niagara.com; 6170 Fallsview Blvd; adult/child IMAX $13/9.50, Daredevil Exhibit $8/6.50, combo $15.50/13; ☺ 9am-9pm; P ♿), and check out the over-the-falls barrels folks have used at the Daredevil Exhibit.

of the falls off River Rd. See the website for all the locations: www.niagarafallstourism.com/plan/parking.

PUBLIC TRANSPORTATION

➡ Cranking up and down the steep 50m slope between Table Rock Visitor Centre and Fallsview Blvd is the quaint, gondola-like **Incline Railway** (☑ 877-642-7275; www.niagaraparks. com; 6635 Niagara Pkwy; one way $2.50, day passes $6.25). It saves you a 10- to 20-minute walk around, and is best taken uphill.

➡ **WEGO** (☑ 905-356-1179; www.wegoniagara falls.com; adult/child 24hr pass $9/6, 48hr pass $13.50/10) is an economical and efficient year-round transit system, geared to tourists. There are three lines: red, green and blue; between them, they've got all the major sights and accommodations covered. For areas further afield, use **Niagara Transit** (☑ 905-356-7521; www.niagarafalls.ca; one-way adult/student $3/1.75, day pass $7).

WALKING

Put on your sneakers and get t'steppin' – walking is the way to go! You'll only need wheels to visit outlying sights along the Niagara Pkwy or if you're staying on Lundy's Lane. There is very little shade along the falls vantage points; in the summer be sure to wear a hat.

Niagara Peninsula Wine Country

The Niagara Peninsula adheres to the 43rd parallel: a similar latitude as northern California and further south than Bordeaux, France. A primo vino location, it has the mineral-rich soils and moderate microclimate that are the perfect recipe for viticultural success. A visit to the area makes an indulgent day trip or lazy weekend, with haughty old vineyards and brash newcomers competing for your attention.

Touring the vineyards by car is the best way to go. There are two main areas to focus on: west of St Catharines around Vineland, and north of the Queen Elizabeth Way (QEW) around Niagara-on-the-Lake. Regional tourist offices stock wine-route maps and brochures, which are also available at winery tasting rooms.

🎫 Tours

Niagara Vintage Wine Tours   WINE
(☑ 866-628-5428; www.niagaravintagewinetours. com; 2205 Mewburn Rd, Niagara Falls; tours $90-170) A top-end tour operation in Niagara's Wine Country, with expert guides, some who are even sommeliers. Trips leave with as few as two people and max out at 14. Door-to-door service in luxury cars or top-of-the-line shuttle buses too.

Crush on Niagara   WINE
(☑ 905-562-3373; www.crushtours.com; 4101 King St, Beamsville; tours $99-149) Small-group morning and afternoon van tours depart from various pickup points in the Niagara region. Signature Twenty Valley and Niagara-on-the-Lake tours are offered. Customized excursions are also possible.

✤ Festivals & Events

There are three wine-related festivals throughout the year: **Niagara Home-grown Wine Festival**, celebrating Niagara's new-season vino and regional cuisine in late June; the main event, **Niagara Grape and Wine Festival**, a two-week-long event beginning in mid-September celebrating the harvest season; and **Niagara Icewine Festival**, a 16-day winter festival held throughout the Niagara region during mid-January that showcases Ontario's stickiest, sweetest ice wines. See www.niagarawinefestival.com for more information.

🛏 Sleeping

Jordan House   INN $$
(☎905-562-9591; https://jordanhouse.ca; 3751 Main St, Jordan Station; r from $122; P❄🐾🖨) A contemporary inn offering pleasant rooms with comfortable beds and mini-fridges. It's attached to a historic tavern, a popular meeting place with occasional live music – a good place for a bite or beer. On weekends, be sure to ask for a room on the far side of the building.

Bonnybank Bed & Breakfast   B&B $$
(☎905-562-3746; www.bonnybank.ca; 4119 21st St, Vineland Station; r incl breakfast $125-154; P❄🐾🖨) A stately Tudor-meets-Grimsby-sandstone house in an owl-filled wilderness setting. It's a little off the beaten track but makes for a quiet, comfortable stay. Cash only.

Inn on the Twenty   HOTEL $$$
(☎905-562-5336; https://innonthetwenty.com; 3845 Main St, Jordan; r $219, ste $249-279; P❄🐾🖨) Inn on the Twenty is an elegant hotel in the charming village of Jordan. Guests enjoy spacious, sunny rooms, each decorated in a modern colonial style with fireplaces and soaker tubs. An on-site spa and gourmet restaurant lend it a resort-like feel, but also make it easy to unwind. A perfect getaway. Look for online specials and packages.

🍴 Eating

★**Peach Country Farm Market**   MARKET $
(☎905-562-5602; www.peachcountryfarmmarket. com; 4490 Victoria Ave, Vineland Station; items from $3; ⊙9am-8pm Jun-Aug, to 6pm Sep & Oct) A country market selling fresh fruit, jams, ice cream and fruit pies, all grown, picked and baked on-site by fourth-generation farmers – a roadside gem!

Pie Plate   BAKERY $$
(☎905-468-9743; www.thepieplate.com; 1516 Niagara Stone Rd, Virgil; sandwiches $16-20; ⊙10am-8pm Wed-Thu, to 9pm Fri-Sun; 🖋) Simple, delicious lunches (it's easy to devour the pear and Brie sandwich) in a country-house setting. It wouldn't be an Ontario bakery without butter tarts, but there are also thin-crust pizzas, meat pies, salads and a few beers on tap.

A great place to fill up your belly while touring the wine country.

ICE, ICE BABY

Niagara's regional wineries burst onto the scene at Vinexpo 1991 in Bordeaux, France. In a blind taste test, judges awarded a coveted gold medal to an Ontario ice wine – international attendees' jaws hit the floor! These specialty vintages, with their arduous harvesting and sweet, multidimensional palate, continue to lure aficionados to the Niagara Peninsula.

To make ice wine, a certain percentage of grapes is left on the vines after the regular harvest is over. If birds, storms and mildew don't get to them, the grapes grow ever-more sugary and concentrated. Winemakers wait patiently until December or January when three days of consistent, low temperatures (-8°C) freeze the grapes entirely.

In the predawn darkness (so the sun doesn't melt the ice and dilute the grape juice), the grapes are carefully harvested by hand, then pressed and aged in barrels for up to a year. After decanting, the smooth ice vintages taste intensely of apples, or even more exotic fruit, and pack a serious alcoholic punch.

Why are ice wines so expensive? It takes 10 times the usual number of grapes to make just one bottle. This, combined with labor-intensive production and the high risk of crop failure, often drives the price above $50 per 375mL bottle. Late-harvest wines picked earlier in the year may be less costly (and less sweet), but just as full-flavored and aromatic.

Restaurant at Peninsula Ridge FUSION $$$
(☑ 905-563-0900; www.peninsularidge.com; 5600 King St W, Beamsville; mains $17-41; ⊙ noon-2:30pm & 5-9pm Wed-Sat, 11:30am-2:30pm Sun) Sit outside, upstairs or down in this high-Victorian 1885 manor at the winery (p131) of the same name, serving haute cuisine paired with local wines...of course.

ℹ Information

For more info on Niagara's wine country check out http://wineriesofniagaraonthelake.com, www.twentyvalley.ca and https://winecountry ontario.ca.

ℹ Getting There & Away

The 100km drive from Toronto to the central peninsula takes around 1½ hours – take Hwy 403 then the QEW east from Hamilton toward Niagara Falls. The official Wine Route is sign-posted off the QEW, on rural highways and along backcountry roads.

Niagara-on-the-Lake

☑ 905 / POP 17,500

One of the best-preserved 19th-century towns in North America, affluent N-o-t-L is an undeniably gorgeous place, with tree-lined streets, lush parks and impeccably restored houses. Originally a Neutral First Nations village, the current town was founded by Loyalists from New York State after the American Revolution, later becoming the first capital of the colony of Upper Canada. Today, lovely Queen St teems with shops of the 'ye olde' variety selling antiques, Brit-style souvenirs and homemade fudge. Tour-bus visitors take over the streets, puffing Cuban cigars and dampening the charm; the town fountain is full of coins but there are no homeless people here to plunder it. Is this a *real* town, or just gingerbread? Is there a soul beneath the surface? Yes, after 5pm.

◉ Sights

Voices of Freedom Memorial MEMORIAL
(www.vofpark.org; 244 Regent St) Celebrating and honoring the contributions of Black Canadians to Niagara-on-the-Lake, this experiential art installation integrates West African and Underground Railroad symbolism with historical city footprints of Black neighborhoods and inspirational quotes. A beautifully manicured garden surrounds it. Download the walking tour app from the website. A place to reflect and meditate.

Fort George HISTORIC SITE
(☑ 905-468-6614; www.pc.gc.ca/fortgeorge; 51 Queens Pde; adult/child $11.70/free; ⊙ 10am-5pm May-Oct, noon-4pm Sat & Sun only Nov-Apr; Ⓟ 🅰) On the town's southeastern fringe, restored Fort George dates from 1797. The fort saw some bloody battles during the War of 1812, changing hands between British and US forces a couple of times. Within the spiked battlements are officers' quarters, a working kitchen, a powder magazine and storage houses. Ghost tours, skills demonstrations, retro tank displays and battle re-enactments occur throughout the summer. Knowledgeable staff dressed in military garb and period dress serve as interpreters and give talks. Parking costs $6.

Niagara Historical Society Museum MUSEUM
(☑ 905-468-3912; www.niagarahistorical.museum; 43 Castlereagh St; adult/child $5/1; ⊙ 10am-5pm May-Oct, from 1pm Nov-Apr; Ⓟ) A vast collection relating to the town's past, ranging from First Nations artifacts to Loyalist and War of 1812 collectibles (including the prized hat of Major-General Sir Isaac Brock). There also is an exhibit chronicling the changing demographics of Niagara-on-the-Lake, from the pre-colonial Neutral Nation to modern day winemakers. Self-guided tours, including a guide to Black Canadian history, are available in several languages. It's south of Simcoe Park.

⇆ Courses

Wine Country Cooking School COOKING
(☑ 905-468-8304; www.winecountrycooking.com; 1339 Lakeshore Rd; classes from $225; ⊙ 10am-3pm or 4-9pm Sat) The Wine Country Cooking School offers five-hour classes every Saturday, which are a gastronomic delight. In the summer, five-day classes are offered for those looking for a deep-dive culinary experience. All are held at the classy restaurant at Strewn (☑ 905-468-1229; www.strewnwinery. com; 1339 Lakeshore Rd; tastings $10-15; ⊙ 10am-6pm), a winery that produces medal-winning vintages.

☞ Tours

Grape Escape Wine Tours WINE
(☑ 866-935-4445; www.tourniagarawineries.com; tours $69-149) A well-run tour company offering a range of winery tours, by bike, van or SUV. All outings include some kind of meal

(cheese platters to three-course gourmet dinners, depending on the cost of the tour) – a welcome sight after a couple tastings. A handful of breweries and cideries also feature on some tours. Free hotel pickup/drop-off too.

Niagara Wine Tours International
FOOD & DRINK

(📞905-468-1300; www.niagaraworldwinetours. com; 9 Queen St, Suite 9½; tours $65-165; ⊙9:30am-8:30pm) Organises various bicycle and gourmet food tours to local wineries, craft breweries and distilleries, including tastings. Self-guided tours are available and include maps, tastings and picnic lunches. A second location on Niagara Stone Rd is the starting point for passenger tours; see the website for details. Bike rentals start at $12 per hour.

Whirlpool Jet Boat Tours
BOATING

(📞905-468-4800; www.whirlpooljet.com; 61 Melville St; adult/child $94/61; ⊙Apr-Oct; 🔁) A wet and wild ride, full of fishtails and splashy stops on 1500-horsepower jet boats. The ride lasts about an hour, heading upriver toward the falls, through Class V rapids, and turning around right before the Whirlpool. Bring a change of clothes (and maybe underwear); water shoes are recommended. Reservations required.

🎉 Festivals & Events

★ Shaw Festival
THEATER

(📞905-468-2172; www.shawfest.com; 10 Queens Pde; ⊙Apr-Dec, box office 9am-9pm) In 1962 a lawyer and passionate dramatist, Brian Doherty, led a group of residents in eight performances of George Bernard Shaw's *Candida* and 'Don Juan in Hell' from *Man and Superman*. Doherty's passionate first season blossomed into today's much-esteemed Shaw Festival. For almost 60 years, the festival has lured global audiences, who haven't been shy about issuing praise.

Plays run from April through December, including a variety of works from Victorian drama to contemporary plays, musicals and classics from Wilde, Woolf and Coward. Specialized seminars are held throughout the season, plus informal talks and backstage tours.

Actors tread the boards in three theaters around town: the Festival, Royal George and Jackie Maxwell theaters. Rush seats go on sale at 9am on performance days (except for Saturdays). Students, under-30s and seniors receive discounts at some matinees. Preview performances are discounted too; weekday matinees are the cheapest.

The **Shaw Express** provides round-trip shuttle service for ticket holders to/from downtown Toronto for just $25. The catch? You must buy your tickets in January and it's for matinees only. A steal if you're able to plan ahead!

Fabulicious!
FOOD & DRINK

(📞905-468-1950;www.niagaraonthelake.com/fabu licious; ⊙Feb-Mar) The Fabulicious! food festival, held one week in late February or early March, highlights the region's cuisine with well-priced 2- and 3-course lunch and dinner menus. Typically more than a dozen restaurants participate. Excellent value.

🛏 Sleeping

Although there are more than 100 small inns and B&Bs in town, accommodations are expensive and often booked out. When the Shaw Festival is running, lodging is even tighter. Plan ahead.

Historic Davy House B&B Inn
B&B $$

(📞888-314-9046; www.davyhouse.com; 230 Davy St; d incl breakfast $209-229; P🐾🛜) This reasonably priced, Historically Designated home built in 1842 has been beautifully restored to maintain its colonial charm and is meticulously maintained by expert hosts who've been in the hospitality biz for over 30 years. Guests are invited to enjoy the lush, landscaped grounds and rustic guest parlor. It's an excellent choice for comfortable, restful and authentic accommodations in this B&B-saturated area.

★ Post House Inn
INN $$$

(📞905-468-9991; www.posthouseinn.com; 95 Johnson St; r/ste incl breakfast from $285/385; P♿🐾🛜🏊) Originally the town's first post office, this historic building is now a sophisticated inn with a relaxed old-world feel – think cozy couches and leather-bound books, fine art and fireplaces. Rooms are uniquely decorated but carry the same luxe feel. All-day snacks plus milk and cookies before bed make you feel pampered. A pool and hot tub seal the deal.

Charles Hotel
HOTEL $$$

(📞800-474-0632; www.niagarasfinest.com/char les; 209 Queen St; d from $295; P♿🐾🛜) This lovable, romantic little hotel (c 1832) has a sweeping verandah overlooking the golf

WINERY DRIVING TOUR

The following drive weaves through Niagara's best wineries from Twenty Valley to Niagara-on-the-Lake. Besides tastings, most offer tours and dining. Parking is free at all vineyards.

Coming from Toronto, head to take Queen Elizabeth Way (QEW) exit 68 at Durham Rd, over Regional Rd 81 and straight to photogenic **Peninsula Ridge Estates Winery** (905-563-0900; http://peninsularidge.com; 5600 King St W, Beamsville; tastings $2-5, tours $15; 10am-5pm Nov-May, to 6pm Jun-Oct). It's unmissable on a hilltop.

Head back to Regional Rd 81 and take a right. Stay on it for about 8km and turn right on Cherry Ave and the award-winning **Tawse Winery** (905-562-9500; www.tawsewinery. ca; 3955 Cherry Ave, Vineland; tastings/tours $8/15; 10am-6pm May-Oct, to 5pm Nov-Apr) will be on your left. An elegant tasting showcases its organic and biodynamically created wine.

Continue down Cherry Ave, go up the hill, and at the first intersection turn left onto Moyer Rd for the stone buildings of **Vineland Estates Winery** (905-562-7088; www. vineland.com; 3620 Moyer Rd, Vineland; tours with tastings/purchases $15/7; 10am-6pm), the elder statesperson of Niagara viticulture, known for its Riesling.

Follow Moyer Rd east, turn right onto Victoria Ave, then left onto 7th Ave for friendly **Flat Rock Cellars** (905-562-8994; www.flatrockcellars.com; 2727 7th Ave, Jordan Station; tours with tastings $10-15; 10am-6pm Sun-Fri, to 7pm Sat). The hexagonal architecture and lake views here are almost as good as the wine.

Wander back toward the lake to 4th Ave and cheery **Creekside Estate Winery** (905-562-0035; www.creeksidewine.com; 2170 4th Ave, Jordan Station; tastings from $10, tours $12; 10am-6pm May-Nov, 11am-5pm Dec-Apr, tours at 2pm May-Oct), where you can tour the crush pad and underground cellars.

Leaving Creekside, take a right on 4th Ave for about 2km until you hit 7th St. Take a left, and 2.8km later scoot back onto the QEW, heading east toward the Niagara-on-the-Lake region. Take exit 38B and head north onto Regional Rd 90, which deadends at Niagara Stone Rd. Turn right and in 4km you'll find a beloved hockey star's winery: **Wayne Gretzky Estates Winery & Distillery** (844-643-7799; www.gretzkyestate-swines.com; 1219 Niagara Stone Rd, Virgil; wine tasting $8-15, whisky tasting $10, distillery tours $35; 10am-9pm Sun-Thu, to 10pm Fri-Sat). Opt for a whisky tasting here for a change of pace.

To the north, superiority emanates from elite **Konzelmann Estate Winery** (905-935-2866; www.konzelmann.ca; 1096 Lakeshore Rd; tours $10-35; 10am-6pm, tours May-Sep), the only winery in the region right on Lake Ontario, which allows it to take full advantage of the lakeside microclimate. Late-harvest vidal and ice wines are superb.

A short dash east is Strewn, producing medal-winning vintages and home to a classy restaurant, and Wine Country Cooking School, where one-day and week-long classes are a gastronomic delight.

Closer to Niagara-on-the-Lake, **Sunnybrook Farm Estate Winery** (905-468-1122; www.sunnybrookwine.com; 1425 Lakeshore Rd; tastings $2-5; 10am-6pm May-Oct, 11am-5pm Nov-Apr) specializes in unique Niagara fruit and berry wines, and brews a mean 'hard' cider.

Back on Niagara Stone Rd, **Stratus** (905-468-1806; www.stratuswines.com; 2059 Niagara Stone Rd; tastings $15; 11am-5pm) is a sleek modern affair, the first building in Canada to earn LEED (Leadership in Energy and Environmental Design) certification.

Head southeast to Niagara Pkwy and you'll find **Reif Estate Winery** (905-468-7738; www.reifwinery.com; 15608 Niagara Pkwy; tastings $5-10, tours $10-25; 10am-6pm Apr-Oct, to 5pm Nov-Mar), pronounced 'Rife,' a well-established winery, acclaimed for its ice wines.

Complete your tour at **Inniskillin** (905-468-2187; www.inniskillin.com; 1499 Line 3, cnr Niagara Pkwy; tastings $3-10, tours $20-35; 10am-6pm May-Oct, to 5pm Nov-Apr), the first vineyard in Niagara to get a winery license since Prohibition and another master of the ice-wine craft.

course and Lake Ontario. Rooms of varying sizes are sumptuously decorated in a diverse range of styles. Each is wonderfully comfortable – there's even a pillow menu.

Prince of Wales Hotel
HOTEL $$$

(☑ 905-468-3246; www.vintage-hotels.com; 6 Picton St; d/ste from $370/510; P ⊕ ✻ ☎ 🐾) Prince of N-o-t-L, an elegant Victorian hotel, was knocked into shape around 1864 and retains much of its period primp: vaulted ceilings, timber-inlay floors and red-waistcoated bellhops. Frills and floral prints seem angled toward the elderly and honeymooners, but it's the perfect spot for anyone looking to splash out in a colonial British sort of way.

Also on-site are a spa, afternoon tea and its elegant restaurant, Noble. A resort fee of $15 is tacked onto the daily bill.

✕ Eating

★ Pieza Pizzeria
PIZZA $$

(☑ 289-868-9191; www.piezapizzeria.com; 188 Victoria St; pizzas $17-22; ⊙ noon-9pm Tue-Sun; ✐ 🐾) A cute turn-of-the-century house repurposed into an even cuter pizzeria with simple, streamlined decor. It's the pizza that speaks loudest here: dough made from imported Italian flour, hand-crushed tomatoes, fresh mozzarella, gourmet toppings and a *pizzaiuolu* (pizza maker) born and raised in Naples. An impressive 2200kg woodburning oven sits, like a sumo wrestler, in the open kitchen.

Irish Harp Pub
PUB FOOD $$

(☑ 905-468-4443; www.theirishharppub.com; 245 King St; mains $14-18; ⊙ 11am-1am) Loved by locals throughout the Niagara region for its hearty pub meals (think Irish hot pot and corned beef and cabbage), some come just for the Irish 'craic' (fun and conversation) and, of course, beer! There are 23 taps, including Guinness and Irish Harp lager, brewed locally from a traditional recipe. All told, plenty to wet your whistle and fill your tum.

Noble
FUSION $$$

(☑ 905-468-3246; www.vintage-hotels.com/prince ofwales/noble.php; 6 Picton St; mains $16-52; ⊙ 7-11am, noon-2:30pm & 5:30-9pm) The fine-dining room at the opulent Prince of Wales Hotel takes its food seriously. The contemporary menu offers taste inventions like a tart of locally cured prosciutto, cacciatore sausage, tomato and mascarpone, followed by grilled venison with hominy and sweet corn succotash, pine mushrooms and Bordelaise sauce. Leave room for dessert (you've been warned). Tasting menu available.

❶ Information

Chamber of Commerce Visitors Information Centre (☑ 905-468-1950; www.niagaraon thelake.com; 26 Queen St; ⊙ 10am-6pm) A brochure-filled info center in the basement of the old courthouse. Pick up the *Niagara-on-the-Lake Official Visitors' Guide* for maps and a self-guided walking tour.

❶ Getting There & Around

There are no direct buses between Toronto and Niagara-on-the-Lake, so head for St Catharines or Niagara Falls and then transfer.

Central Taxi (☑ 905-685-7343; www.central niagara.com) shunts folks between Niagara Falls and Niagara-on-the-Lake. Call for pickup locations and times. A regular one-way taxi between the two towns costs around $45.

Cycling is an ace way to explore the area. Rent a bike from (or have one delivered to you by) traveler-recommended **Zoom Leisure Bicycle Rentals** (☑ 905-468-2366; www.zoomleisure. com; 431 Mississauga St; rental per half-day/ day/2 days $20/30/50; ⊙ 8:30am-7pm May-Sep, 9am-5pm Mar, Apr & Oct, by appointment only Nov-Feb). Free delivery within 10km of shop.

SOUTHWESTERN ONTARIO

Arcing around Lake Ontario are a number of the Greater Toronto Area's 'satellite' cities. Day-trip the up-and-coming hip strip of Hamilton, or really escape Toronto's gravity in the delightful villages of Elora, Fergus and the unique Mennonite settlement of St Jacobs.

For more grit, stop in the thriving university centers of Guelph, Waterloo and London, each with their own appeal if you dig deep. Nearby Stratford, birthplace of Justin Bieber and yet a remarkably cultured country town, is home to a fabulous festival of Shakespearean theater in honor of the bard's home in Stratford-upon-Avon, England.

From here, you can head northwest until the farmlands dissolve into the sandy shores of Lake Huron, or follow the dead-flat fields of gold – wheat, corn and everything-growing regions – until you reach the north shore of Lake Erie, the bird and butterfly hub of Point Pelee National Park, and quirky Pelee Island, Canada's southernmost point. The end (or beginning) of the road is in Windsor at the US border.

❶ Getting There & Away

Public transport connects Toronto with Guelph, Hamilton, Brantford, Kitchener-Waterloo, London and Stratford on Go Transit or Via trains and buses.

For other towns, and intercity travel, your own set of wheels is recommended, though not within traffic-heavy Toronto itself.

Hamilton

📞 289, 365, 905 / POP 536,920

Something special is happening in Hamilton. Once known as Canada's steel industry hub, skimmed through en route to the Niagara Peninsula, Hamilton's revitalized downtown has rebounded with unexpected hipness. A pocket of cosmopolitan life on James St N thrives with good eateries, quirky stores and independent galleries. Yet the pace remains calm, with a lovely harborside park just a short stroll away, where you can clamber up to a mansion for some sweeping harbor views.

◉ Sights & Tours

★ **Royal Botanical Gardens** GARDENS
(📞 905-527-1158; www.rbg.ca; 680 Plains Rd W, Burlington; adult/child $18/10; ⊙ 10am-8pm May-Sep, to 5pm Oct-Apr; 🅿) Northwest of Hamilton, Canada's largest and most spectacular botanical gardens comprise more than a thousand hectares of trees, flowers and plants, including numerous rare species. There's also a rock garden, an arboretum and a wildlife sanctuary with 27km of trails traversing wetlands and wooded ravines. From June to October, thousands of delicate jewels bloom in the Centennial Rose Garden, and in spring more than 125,000 flowering bulbs awaken in an explosion of color.

The Griffin House HISTORIC SITE
(📞 905-648-8144; www.hamilton.ca; 733 Mineral Springs Rd, Dundas; ⊙ 1-4pm Sun Jul & Aug; 🅿) **FREE** This well-preserved early-19th-century home belonged to Enerals Griffin, an escaped slave from Virginia who arrived in Canada via the Underground Railroad. The property was continuously occupied by Griffin's descendants for 154 years before it became a National Historic Site. A small clapboard house with period furnishings and

Southwestern Ontario

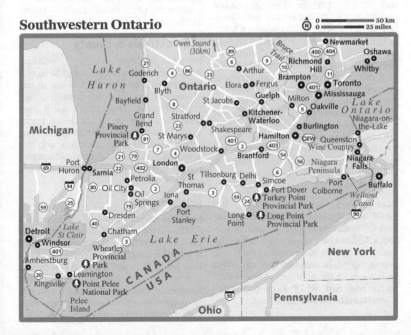

OLD FORT EIRE

East of Port Colborne and south of Niagara Falls is the town of Fort Erie, where the Niagara River leaks out of Lake Erie. Across from Buffalo, NY, it's connected to the USA by the Peace Bridge. The main draw here is the historic, star-shaped **Old Fort Erie** (☏905-871-0540; www.niagaraparks.com; 350 Lakeshore Rd; adult/child $13.25/8.40; ⊕10am-5pm May-Oct; 🅿♿), a key player in the War of 1812, and 'Canada's bloodiest battlefield.' Also known as the Old Stone Fort, it was first built in 1764. The US seized it in 1814 before retreating.

Inside there's a museum and immaculate, uniformed British soldiers performing authentic military drills. Take the worthwhile guided tour (every 30 minutes) included in the admission fee.

artifacts, it reflects not only how people lived in Griffin's time but also the sacrifices and challenges faced by the more than 40,000 African American refugees who found freedom in Canada.

Art Gallery of Hamilton MUSEUM
(AGH; ☏905-527-6610; www.artgalleryofhamilton.com; 123 King St W; special exhibitions adult/child $13.25/8.85, free first Fri of month; ⊕11am-6pm Wed & Fri, to 8pm Thu, noon-5pm Sat & Sun, to 8pm first Fri of month; 🅿) FREE The largest art museum in southern Ontario, the sleek AGH has a wide-ranging collection of 10,000 works, with a strong emphasis on modern art and 19th-century works by Canadian and European artists. Special exhibits change periodically and tend toward emerging and contemporary artists – they are often worth a look. Admission is free for the permanent collection; tickets are required for the special shows. Free docentled tours are offered on weekends and Wednesdays at 1pm.

Bayfront Park PARK
(☏905-546-2489; www.hamilton.ca; 200 Harbour Front Dr; ⊕dawn-dusk) Take a stroll to gorgeous Bayfront Park where you'll find a calm harbor with fancy yachts and a beach with people fishing. In summer, they are joined by festivals on the grass and in-line skaters on the wide path, which forms part of the 7.5km **Hamilton Waterfront Trail**.

A free shuttle (every 30 minutes, 10am to 8:30pm) runs from Gore Park in downtown Hamilton to the waterfront. Pick it up anywhere along James Street – look for the bus with a route '99' or 'Waterfront' sign. June to September only.

Dundurn Castle MUSEUM
(☏905-546-2872; www.hamilton.ca; 610 York Blvd; adult/child $12/6.50; ⊕noon-4pm Tue-Sun; 🅿) Delightful and unexpected, this columnfronted, 36-room mansion once belonged to Sir Allan Napier McNab, Canadian prime minister from 1854 to 1856. It sits on a cliff overlooking the harbor amid lovely chestnut-studded grounds and is furnished in mid-19th-century style. Castle admission includes a one-hour tour (every 30 minutes) and entry into the on-site **Hamilton Military Museum**, which focuses on the War of 1812.

Lady Hamilton Club
Walking Tours WALKING
(https://ladyhamiltonclub.com; 28 James St N; ⊕Apr-Nov) FREE A volunteer-based tourism organization, the Lady Hamilton Club leads free 1½-hour walking tours of Hamilton's historic neighborhoods. Rain or shine, tours leave from the downtown tourism information center at 2pm on the second Friday of each month (from April to November). Go to the website for tour options and to register.

⚡ Festivals & Events

Hamilton Art Crawl CULTURAL
(https://tourismhamilton.com; James St N; ⊕7-10pm, 2nd Fri of every month) Join the throng of locals at Art Crawl, when galleries and art studios on James Street North keep their doors open late on the second Friday of each month. You'll see work by emerging artists, listen to street musicians, pop into cafes and bars...basically, a night of cultured revelry. Arrive by bus or foot to avoid parking headaches.

🛏 Sleeping

Hamilton Guesthouse GUESTHOUSE $
(☏289-440-8035; http://hamiltonguesthouse.ca; 158 Mary St; dm $28, r with shared bath $50; 🛜) If you're on a tight budget and want to stay near James St N and the harbor, it may as well be in a converted 1855 mansion. The interior has mismatched furniture with spacious, quiet rooms, some with garden views. Lockers (with locks) and linens included. A

tea-filled guest kitchen adds to the homeliness and value.

C Hotel HOTEL $$
(☑ 905-381-9898; http://carmenshotel.com; 1530 Stone Church Rd E; r from $148; P ⊖ ✳ ⧠ ⛱) You may be surprised that a hotel of this caliber is both a Best Western and in Hamilton. The handsome building pays an impressive tribute to art deco; its rooms are both spacious and elegant. Add the on-site Italian restaurant and indoor pool, and it's good value. The only downer? The hotel is in the 'burbs, 12km from downtown.

✖ Eating

Hamilton Farmers' Market MARKET
(☑ 905-546-2096; https://hamiltonfarmersmarket.ca; 35 York Blvd; ⊙ 8am-6pm Tue, Thu & Fri, 7am-5pm Sat; P ☑) A sleek glass exterior belies the 180-year history of Hamilton's farmers market. Inside, two open-plan floors house 60 vendors selling produce, fresh meats, cheeses, baked goods and more. A quick-eats section on the ground floor reflects the city's diverse population: Jamaican, Mexican, Polish, Vietnamese and Hawaiian. Take your food to go or snag a table near the back.

★ Saint James CAFE $
(☑ 289-389-6565; www.saint-james.ca; 170 James St N; mains $12-17; ⊙ 8am-4pm Mon-Sat) An industrial-chic cafe in the heart of James St N serving upscale breakfast fare – lemon ricotta short stacks, avocado toast with smoked salmon, even the oatmeal has shaved coconut – along with hearty salads and sandwiches. It's a small place so come early (or late) if you don't want to wait for a table. Ah-mazing espresso-based drinks too.

ⓘ Information

Tourism Hamilton (☑ 905-546-2424; www.tourismhamilton.com; 28 James St N; ⊙ 9am-4pm Mon-Fri) This downtown tourist office is keen to assist with all things Hamilton and surrounds; or just visit their impressive and up-to-date website.

ⓘ Getting There & Away

GO Transit operates a combination of regular scheduled bus and train services between Hamilton and Toronto ($12.70, one hour) from the **Hamilton GO Centre** (☑ 416-869-3200; www.gotransit.com; 36 Hunter St E). Trains operate only during rush hour and on certain weekends

in summer. Megabus also makes stops in Hamilton. There is nowhere to eat in the GO Centre or within a couple blocks, so plan ahead.

If you're in a squeeze to find a cheap flight out of Toronto, see if Westjet flies to your destination from **John C Munro Hamilton International Airport** (☑ 905-679-1999; http://flyhamilton.ca; 9300 Airport Rd, Mount Hope), 15km southwest of town – airport taxes are cheaper here.

Brantford

☑ 519 / POP 98,200

Brantford is all about cultural sites. The Six Nations territory here has been a First Nations center for centuries, and gives you a look into the culture then and now. You can trace indigenous history, see contemporary art and visit an indigenous performance space. Captain Joseph Thayendanegea Brant led the Six Nations people here from upper New York State in 1784 and you can visit his tomb at the world's only Royal Indian Chapel. Then, for a bit more British-Canadian history, head to the former homestead of Alexander Graham Bell, who first patented the telephone.

⊙ Sights

★ Woodland Cultural Centre NOTABLE BUILDING
(☑ 519-759-2650; http://woodlandculturalcentre. ca; 184 Mohawk St; adult/child $7/5; ⊙ 9am-4pm Mon-Fri, 10am-5pm Sat; P) This well-conceived indigenous cultural center has a performance space, museum and gallery. Though dated in its presentation, the museum provides an excellent overview of the Iroquoian and Algonquian people, from prehistoric times to the present; the artifacts, some dating as far back as the 16th century, are fascinating. The gallery has rotating exhibits of contemporary art by indigenous artists. A small gift shop sells basketry and jewelry, plus books, ceramics and paintings. Check the website for upcoming events.

Woodland also oversees what was once the Mohawk Institute Residential School, one of many boarding schools set up by the Canadian government to force assimilation upon First Nation children and families. A brutal system, the Mohawk Institute was in operation from 1828 to 1970, one of the longest running in Canada. At the time of research, Woodland was in the process of repairing the building in order to re-open it as an interpretive historical site, sharing the history of the often inhumane treatment so many First Nations children endured here.

Six Nations of the Grand River
AREA

(www.sixnations.ca) Southeast of Brantford is Six Nations of the Grand River – a reserve designated for the Mohawk, Oneida, Onondaga, Cayuga, Seneca and Tuscarora – and the village of **Ohsweken**, a well-known Indigenous community. Established in the late 18th century, the territory has been reduced to just 4.9% of what was originally granted. Take a day to explore the area and get a glimpse of traditional and contemporary First Nations culture. Six Nations Tourism) is a good place to start for ideas and itineraries.

Bell Homestead National Historic Site
HISTORIC SITE

(☑519-756-6220; www.bellhomestead.ca; Tutela Heights Rd, Brantford; adult/child $7/4.75; ⊙9:30am-noon & 1-4:30pm Tue-Sun; 🅿🚼) You might know that Alexander Graham Bell, on 26 July 1874, shaped our futures by inventing the telephone (though the US Congress credits Italian Antonio Meucci). Did you know inspiration struck him at his family homestead in Brantford? Or that the first long-distance call was placed here? Bell's first North American home has been lovingly restored to its original condition; enthusiastic guides lead 60-minute tours through it, sharing details about Bell's life and invention. There's a cafe too (open April to September).

ℹ Information

Brantford Visitors & Tourism Centre (☑519-751-9900; www.discoverbrantford.com; 399 Wayne Gretzky Pkwy; ⊙9am-5pm Mon-Fri, 10am-4pm Sat) Just north of Hwy 403, the sparkling tourism center is optimistic about Brantford's future, with plenty of brochures and helpful staff.

Six Nations Tourism (☑519-758-5444; www.sixnationstourism.ca; 2498 Chiefswood Rd, Ohsweken; ⊙8:30am-4:30pm Mon-Fri, 10am-3pm Sat & Sun, closed Sat-Sun Nov-Apr) At the corner of Hwy 54, this visitors center has knowledgeable staff and lots of information on local sites, attractions and events in Six Nations of the Grand River. It's 20km southeast of Brantford.

ℹ Getting There & Away

VIA Rail operates trains from Toronto ($35, one to 1½ hours, five daily) and London ($35, one hour, five daily) to the **Brantford Train Station** (☑519-752-0867; www.viarail.ca; 5 Wadsworth St).

Guelph

☑226, 519, 548 / POP 131,800

Founded in 1827 by a Scottish novelist who planned the town's footprint in a European style, Guelph is best known for its popular university and…beer! Wellington Brewery, Canada's oldest independently owned microbrewery, and four others call Guelph home. Strong manufacturing and education sectors contribute to Guelph's low unemployment rate, which fuels a vibrant youth scene: relaxed cafes, great food, rocking pubs and hipster boutiques all await.

With a wealth of local history, a fantastic museum and lovely Victorian architecture, Guelph is worth a visit.

◉ Sights & Activities

Guelph Civic Museum
MUSEUM

(☑519-836-1221; www.guelph.ca/museum; 52 Norfolk St; $6, free 5-9pm 4th Friday of the month; ⊙10am-5pm Tue-Sun; 🅿🚼) Housed in what was originally an 1854 sandstone convent and extensively transformed in 2012, this attractive museum has attained LEED (Leadership in Energy and Environmental Design) certification. Within, the museum offers exhibitions, programs and events digging up the history of the city (named after the British royal family's ancestors, the Guelphs). Exhibits are refreshingly inclusive of First Nations' and Métis' histories. The 'Growing Up in Guelph' kids' exhibition makes a happy distraction for little ones.

Hours are extended to 9pm and admission is free on the fourth Friday of the month.

Basilica of Our Lady Immaculate
CHURCH

(☑519-824-3951; www.churchofourlady.com; 28 Norfolk St; ⊙7am-4:30pm Mon-Fri, 6-9pm Thu, to 6:30pm Sat, 8:30am-1pm Sun; 🅿) Lording over downtown Guelph is the dominant stone-faced bulk of this basilica and church in the Gothic Revival–style (think England's Houses of Parliament). It's hard to move around town without catching a glimpse of

Our Lady's twin towers and elegantly proportioned rose window – no new buildings in town are allowed to be taller than the church.

The basilica has awed parishioners since 1888, when it was a mere church. Pope Francis designated it a basilica in 2014.

Art Gallery of Guelph
GALLERY

(☑ 519-837-0010; http://artgalleryofguelph.ca; 358 Gordon St; suggested donation $5; ☉ noon-5pm Tue-Sun; ℗) More than 7000 works belong to the collection exhibited here in the Raymond Moriyama–designed galleries specializing in Inuit and Canadian art. The **Donald Forster Sculpture Park** is the largest at a public gallery in Canada and offers one hectare to explore, with gravity-defying cubes, beached boats and cell phones spiked onto agricultural sickles.

Speed River Paddling
KAYAKING

(www.fb.me/speedriverpaddling; 116 Gordon St; kayak/canoe rental per hr Mon-Fri $12/15, Sat & Sun $15/18, half-day from $30; ☉ 10am-6:30pm Tue-Sun Jun-Aug; ⛵) Get on the water then tackle the ice-cream store next door. Half-day rates (five hours) are a steal at only $30.

This is also the starting point of a self-guided **eco-heritage walk** along the banks of the Speed and Eramosa Rivers, a 6km circuit with interpretive signs.

🎊 Festivals & Events

Kazoo! Fest
MUSIC

(https://kazookazoo.ca; ☉ Apr) A five-day music and arts fest featuring unconventional and emerging artists from Canada and beyond. Expect underground punk bands, avant-jazz experimentalists and chilled-out acoustic soloists playing at venues around town. Past festival lineups have included groups like Queer Songbook Orchestra, Snotty Nose Rez Kids and Bellyrub. Art exhibits, multimedia performances, even indie video arcades are showcased too.

Hillside Festival
PERFORMING ARTS

(☑ 519-763-6396; www.hillsidefestival.ca; Guelph Lake Island, 7743 Conservation Rd; ☉ Jul) For more than 30 years, Hillside has delighted with an eclectic mix of hippie and huggy performers from seasoned pros to the up-and-coming artists of tomorrow. Feel the love and jump on board for one short weekend in July. Held on the shores of Guelph Lake. Consult the website for this year's lineup and details.

🛏 Sleeping

★ Norfolk Guest House
B&B $$

(☑ 519-767-1095; www.norfolkguesthouse.ca; 102 Eramosa Rd; r incl breakfast $139-279; ℗ ❄ �︽) A central location and sumptuously furnished, themed bedrooms, most with en suite Jacuzzi, make the Norfolk – a delightfully restored Victorian home – the logical choice for luxury B&B accommodations in downtown Guelph.

Comfort Inn
MOTEL $$

(☑ 519-763-1900; www.choicehotels.ca; 480 Silvercreek Pkwy; d incl breakfast from $130; ℗ ⊖ ❄ �︽) Tastefully renovated, this well-maintained motel offers great-value, contemporary-style rooms including a self-serve breakfast. Located about 5km north of the town center.

Delta Hotels Guelph Conference Centre
HOTEL $$

(☑ 519-780-3700; www.marriott.com; 50 Stone Rd W; d/ste from $199/219; ℗ ⊖ ❄ �︽) Conveniently located near the University of Guelph, 3km from downtown, this modern, tastefully furnished property has spacious standard rooms with dark woods and comfy beds. A variety of well-priced suites, some with fireplaces, kitchenettes and downy sofas, completes the package.

🍴 Eating

★ Crafty Ramen
RAMEN $

(☑ 519-824-8330; https://craftyramen.com; 17 Macdonell St; ramen $14-18; ☉ 11:30am-9pm Mon-Sat; ✐ ⛵) A tiny, bustling, diner-style eatery serving steaming bowls of ramen packed with ingredients like pork *chashu*, charred corn and lotus chips. Noodles are made in-house and many ingredients are locally sourced. For several years, the owners both lived, traveled and studied everything ramen in Japan before setting up shop in Guelph. Cold ramen as well as vegan 'adaptabowls' are created too.

Cadence
VEGAN $

(☑ 519-265-8225; www.withthegrain.ca; 88 Yarmouth St; mains $12-17; ☉ 11am-8pm Tue-Thu, to 9pm Fri-Sat; ✐) Plant-based meals are served at this bright and busy cafe. Dishes are hearty and made to order; expect teriyaki tempeh bowls, mac 'n' cheese (made with creamy cashew and almond sauce) and creative salads. All-day breakfast is served too. Fresh bread and desserts provided are by the cafe's sister bakery, With the Grain.

Popular with university students and baby boomers with man buns.

Miijidaa BISTRO $$

(☑ 519-821-9271; www.miijidaa.ca; 37 Quebec St; mains $13-27; ⊙ 10am-10pm Mon-Thu, to 11pm Fri & Sat, 10:30am-9pm Sun; 🛜 ☑ 🚸) This spacious cafe-bistro is a casual spot for lunch, dinner or just a drink on the patio. Mains take modern twists on cuisines that have shaped Canada – mostly French and Portuguese. Try hay-smoked duck breast with sumac fingerlings, or a 'cured' pizza of wild salmon, gravlax and capers. There are also lots of salads, vegetarian options and a kids menu.

Artisanale FRENCH $$

(☑ 519-821-3359; www.artisanale.ca; 214 Woolwich St; mains $15-36; ⊙ 11:30am-3pm & 5-9pm Wed-Fri, 5-9pm Sat, 10am-2pm Sun) With an emphasis on fresh seasonal local produce, this French country kitchen has a wonderfully simple lunch menu and is popular for its Wednesday and Thursday $35 prix-fixe dinners.

You can also create your own unfixed selection from irresistible hors d'oeuvres and sides, and hearty mains such as duck confit with crispy potatoes.

🍸 Drinking & Nightlife

Guelph Beer Bus BREWERY

(www.guelph.beer; 15 Wyndham St N; ⊙ May-Aug) Guelph's five local breweries – Brothers, Fixed Gear, Royal City, Sleeman and Wellington – have teamed up to provide free bus transportation to their tasting rooms one Saturday per month (summer only). The bus runs continuously from noon to 6pm, with visitors getting on/off as they please. An easy, tasty –and maybe a little tipsy – way to check out a wide range of beers.

Wooly PUB

(☑ 519-836-2875; www.woolwicharrow.ca; 176 Woolwich St; ⊙ 11:30am-midnight Sun-Tue, to 1am Wed-Thu & Sat, to 2am Fri) In an old redbrick house, the Wooly has a good lineup of local craft brews and ranks highly for upmarket pub grub like its pork-belly Reuben sandwich ($16) and Lake Erie fish-and-chips ($20). Saturday nights bring live music too. On warm nights, try to snag a seat on the porch.

☆ Entertainment

★ Bookshelf ARTS CENTER

(☑ 519-821-3311; www.bookshelf.ca; 41 Québec St; ⊙ bar 5pm-midnight Tue-Thu, to 2am Fri-Sat, bookstore 9:30am-9pm Mon-Sat, 11am-7pm Sun) Forty years young, Bookshelf is the pacemaker of Guelph's cultural heartbeat, a combination bookstore, cinema, bar and music venue. Swing by to read the paper, catch an arthouse flick or have a cocktail in the eBar. Regular salsa nights, poetry slams and flashback Fridays – there's something for everyone.

ℹ️ Information

The Guelph tourism website (www.visitguelph wellington.ca) is a helpful resource. There's also a self-serve tourist information kiosk in the Guelph Civic Museum (p136) with loads of brochures and maps.

ℹ️ Getting There & Away

All buses and trains depart from **Guelph Central Station** (Guelph Central GO Station; ☑ 888-842-7245; www.viarail.ca; 79 Carden St).

GO Transit (www.gotransit.com) and VIA Rail (viarail.ca) operate trains to Toronto ($17, 1½ hours, seven daily) and London ($34, 2¼ hours, twice daily).

Kitchener-Waterloo

☑ 226, 519 / POP 338,200

The sister cities of Kitchener (formerly called Berlin, due to its Germanic origins) and Waterloo are as different as they are alike. Although Kitchener is a burgeoning tech center, and the prettier 'uptown' Waterloo has some nice sandstone architecture, two universities and the largest community museum in Ontario, neither city is particularly exciting. The best time to visit is festival time, when the twins come to life – Oktoberfest here is the second-largest after Munich, Germany! Otherwise, just pass through on your way to Elora and Fergus, St Jacobs or Stratford.

⊙ Sights

Canadian Clay and Glass Gallery GALLERY

(☑ 519-746-1882; www.theclayandglass.ca; 25 Caroline St N, Waterloo; ⊙ 11am-6pm Mon-Fri, 10am-5pm Sat, 1-5pm Sun) FREE A spacious gallery displaying contemporary works of art in glass, ceramic, enamel and stained glass. It's an especially good place to see some of the Canada's best works in these art forms, though international artists also are represented. The gift shop has unique, high-quality items too.

Waterloo Region Museum MUSEUM
(☑519-748-1914; www.waterlooregionmuseum.com; 10 Huron Rd, Kitchener; adult/child $11/5; ◷9:30am-5pm Mon-Fri, 11am-5pm Sat & Sun; ℗♿) Waterloo's most modern attraction is this primary-colored local museum with exhibits on the history of Waterloo. Set on 24 hectares, it's the gateway to the **Doon Heritage Village**, a recreated 1914 settlement where costumed volunteers do their best to help you time travel to the early days of the region.

Schneider Haus
National Historic Site HISTORIC SITE
(☑519-742-7752; www.schneiderhaus.ca; 466 Queen St S, Kitchener; adult/child $6/4; ◷10am-5pm Mon-Sat, to 5pm Sun, closed Mon & Tue Oct-Jun; ℗) This National Historic Site was one of the first homes in the area, originally built for a prosperous Pennsylvanian Mennonite, Joseph Schneider. It has been restored to full 19th-century splendor – the architecture and interiors are remarkably well done, as are demonstrations of day-to-day 1800s chores and skills (everything from beadwork to making corn-husk dolls). There is a two-story washhouse and a schnitz house (a log and stucco building where an apple delicacy was made).

✴ Festivals & Events

Oktoberfest BEER
(☑519-570-4267; www.oktoberfest.ca; King St btwn Young & Queen Sts, Kitchener; ◷Oct) *Willkommen* to this nine-day beery Bavarian bash – the biggest of its kind in North America and possibly the largest outside of Germany. It's K-W's favorite event, bringing in about 500,000 people each year from early to mid-October for sauerkraut, oompah bands, *lederhosen* and *biergartens* galore. Most festivities center on King St in downtown Kitchener, though several venues host events around town.

🛏 Sleeping & Eating

Crowne Plaza
Kitchener-Waterloo HOTEL $$
(☑519-744-4141; www.kitchener-hotel.com; 105 King St E, Kitchener; d from $133; ℗❄🐕🏊) The well-located Crowne Plaza has a futuristic lobby and 201 modern, standard-issue guest rooms – all very comfortable and clean, if

somewhat lacking in character. Last-minute deals can be a steal, though.

Walper Hotel HOTEL $$
(☑519-745-4321; www.walper.com; 1 King St W, Kitchener; r from $149; ℗❄❄🐕) There's a rich sense of history at the Walper, a classy downtown player looking especially good for its age – the hotel was built in 1893 though the interior has a chic, modern style. All rooms have high ceilings and period features, flat-screen TVs and free wi-fi, but standard rooms are a tad cozy. Suites are more spacious.

Princess Cafe CAFE $
(☑519-886-0227; www.princesscafe.ca; 46 King St N, Waterloo; panini $8.50; ◷11:30am-10:30pm Mon-Thu, 9am-10:30pm Fri-Sun) This modern, minimalist cafe next to the cinema serves up coffee, toasted panini and other snacky delights. If you're a night owl, stop in for 'Cheeses Murphy': the ultimate drinking companion. Dinner and movie deals (including homemade dessert!) available for $25.

Concordia Club GERMAN $$
(☑519-745-5617; www.concordiaclub.ca; 429 Ottawa St S, Kitchener; mains $11-23; ◷11:30am-10pm Tue & Wed, to midnight Thu, to 9pm Fri, to midnight Sat, 11am-2pm Sun) Polish up your German and fill up on schnitzel at Concordia, a Teutonic fave that's been around for decades. Dark wood, low ceilings, white linen and loud conversation complement the menu. There's red-hot polka action on Saturday nights, and a summer *biergarten*.

❶ Information

City of Waterloo Visitor and Heritage Information Centre (☑519-885-2297; www.explorewaterlooregion.com; 10 Father David Bauer Dr, Waterloo; ◷9am-4pm May-Oct) Friendly staff! At the terminus of the Waterloo Central Railway.

Kitchener Welcome Centre (☑519-741-2345; www.explorewaterlooregion.com; 200 King St W, Kitchener; ◷8:30am-5pm Mon-Fri) Located inside City Hall.

❶ Getting There & Away

From **Waterloo International Airport** (☑519-648-2256; www.waterlooairport.ca; 4881 Fountain St N, Breslau), 7km east of town, there are flights to Calgary, Toronto Islands and even the Dominican Republic.

An easy walk north of downtown is **Kitchener Train Station** (☑888-842-7245; www.viarail.ca; 126 Weber St W). VIA Rail operates trains to

Toronto ($20, 1½ to two hours, seven daily) and London ($28, two hours, twice daily). GO Transit operates commuter trains to Toronto ($17, two hours, twice daily).

Elora & Fergus

No longer one of Ontario's best-kept secrets, the delightful Wellington County riverside towns of Elora and Fergus, straddling the banks of the twisty Grand River, await your visit. Both have done a magnificent job preserving their heritage facades and streetscapes. Enticing Elora, with its gorge and swimming hole, is a wonderful place to escape the summer heat, while neighboring Fergus evokes nostalgia for a lost age and a distant northern kingdom... along with the desire to sample its cozy pubs.

◉ Sights & Activities

★ **Wellington County Museum**   MUSEUM
(☑ 519-846-0916; www.wellington.ca/en/muse um-and-archives.aspx; Rte 18, 536 Wellington Rd, Elora; by donation; ⊙ 9:30am-4:30pm Mon-Fri, 1-5pm Sat & Sun; P) A National Historic Site midway between Fergus and Elora, this austere, red-roofed former 'Poor House' provided refuge for the aged and homeless for almost a century before becoming a museum in 1957. Historical and local modern-art exhibits extending through 12 galleries display an obvious pride in local history and current culture. The centerpiece is the 'If These Walls Could Speak' exhibit, which examines the lives of those who lived or worked there.

A museum trail takes visitors on a self-guided tour of the grounds, including the barn and cemetery. A worthwhile stop.

Elora Gorge Conservation Area   PARK
(www.grandriver.ca; Rte 21, 7400 Wellington County Rd, Elora; adult/child $7/3; ⊙ dawn-dusk early May–mid-Oct; P ♿) About 2km south of Elora is this photo-worthy plunging limestone canyon through which the Grand River seethes. Easy walks extend to cliff views, caves and the Cascade waterfalls – a sheet of white water spilling over a stepped cliff. For a free gorge view from downtown Elora, head to the end of James St, off Metcalfe St.

Tubing is a lazy way to spend a warm afternoon at the gorge; register and pay the tubing fee ($10) at the onsite equipment

---

THE MENNONITES OF ST JACOBS & ELMIRA

The Mennonite story harks back to a 16th-century Swiss Protestant sect who moved around Europe due to religious disagreements. They ended up in the rural setting of what is now Pennsylvania, USA, where they were promised religious freedom and prosperity. Cheaper land and their unwillingness to fight under the American flag lured many Mennonites to southern Ontario in the late 19th century, where they remain today, upholding the same basic values of family, humility, simplicity, modesty and pacifism.

For a detailed history and information see the website of the Mennonite Historical Society of Canada (www.mhsc.ca), or take a day trip to the quaint villages of St Jacobs, about 20 minutes' drive from Kitchener, and Elmira, 8km further north. In both towns, black buggies, bonnets and overalls are the norm.

The quintessential **country market** (☑ 519-747-1830; http://stjacobsmarket.com; 878 Weber St N, St Jacobs; ⊙ 7:30am-3:30pm Thu & Sat year-round, also 8am-3pm Tue Jun-Aug; P), 3km south of St Jacobs, has an earthy soul. Folks come from miles for the farm-fresh produce, smoked meats, cheese, baked treats, and arts and crafts. Pop in to the **visitors center** (☑ 519-664-1133; www.stjacobs.com; 1406 King St N, St Jacobs; ⊙ 10am-5pm Mon-Sat, from 1:30pm Sun, weekends only Jan-Mar) to see the Mennonite Story, an insightful exhibition on the Mennonites' history, culture and agricultural achievements. One of these is the production of maple syrup: learn about it at the **Maple Syrup Museum** (☑ 800-265-3353; www.stjacobs.com; 1441 King St N, St Jacobs; ⊙ 10am-6pm Mon-Sat, noon-5pm Sun; P) FREE or sample the liquid gold at the **Maple Syrup Festival** (☑ 519-669-6000; www. elmiramaplesyrup.com; ⊙ early Apr; ♿). Round out the day with fresh fruit pie and some scones for the road from the **Stone Crock Bakery** (☑ 519-664-3612; www.stonecrock.ca; 1402 King St N, St Jacobs; items from $2; ⊙ 6:30am-6pm Mon-Sat, 11am-5:30pm Sun) and be on your way.

rental building. Rentals are available here (tube/helmet/life jacket $15/10/10; complete rental package $25; open 9am to 5pm). You can also camp and zip-line here.

Elora Quarry
Conservation Area   NATURE RESERVE
(☑ 519-620-7596; www.grandriver.ca; Rte 18, 319 Wellington County Rd, Elora; adult/child $10/5; ⊙ 11am-8pm Mon-Fri, 10am-8pm Sat & Sun Jun-Sep; ℗ ♿) A short walk east of Elora, this superb swimming hole offers seemingly bottomless waters and 12m limestone cliffs. Hormone-fueled teens plummet from great heights, despite signs suggesting they don't.

A popular spot on summer weekends; come early to be sure you get in, since the site often reaches capacity (1300 people) by noon! Better yet, plan your visit mid-week to avoid the crowds.

Elora Skyrider Zipline   ADVENTURE SPORTS
(☑ 519-846-8888; https://eloraskyriderzipline.com; 29 David St W, Elora; per ride $40; ⊙ 10am-5pm Sat & Sun Jul & Aug; ♿) Test your nerves by zip-lining over the Elora Gorge on a 200-meter line – as long as you weigh at least 30lbs and are less than 7ft tall, you're good to go. Kids can ride solo or tandem with an adult. Parking is behind the Elora Community Centre.

🎊 Festivals & Events

Fergus Scottish Festival &
Highland Games   CULTURAL
(☑ 519-787-0099; www.fergusscottishfestival.com; Centre Wellington Community Sportsplex , 550 Belsyde Av E, Fergus; adult/child daily pass from $20/free; weekend pass from $60/free; ⊙ mid-Aug; ♿) If it's not Scottish, it doesn't count: tugs-of-war, caber tossing, bagpipes, Celtic dancing, kilts, haggis and Scotch nosing (aka tasting). Hoots! With more than 30,000 attendees, it is said to be the largest Highland Games held outside of Scotland. Held over three days in mid-August. Buy tickets online for a discount.

Elora Festival   MUSIC
(☑ 519-846-0331; www.elorafestival.com; Elora; ⊙ Jul) A classical, jazz, folk and arts festival held in July, with concerts at the Wellington County Museum, churches and other venues around town. Singers and musos from around the country crowd the schedule of Elora's premier event.

🛏 Sleeping

There are many B&Bs and family-run inns in the area, and even a boutique hotel in Elora.

Elora Gorge Conservation
Area Campground   CAMPGROUND $
(☑ 519-846-9742; www.grcacamping.ca; Rte 21, 7400 Wellington County Rd, Elora; campsites $40-48, reservation fee $13; ⊙ early May–mid-Oct; ℗) More than 500 campsites sit in six distinct, riverside zones. They're overflowing during summer, especially on holiday weekends – be sure to reserve in advance.

Stonehurst B&B   B&B $$
(☑ 519-843-8800; 265 St David St S, Fergus; s/d incl breakfast from $113/130; ℗ ♻ ❄ 🛜 🏊) This gorgeous country home, which belonged to one of the wealthiest families in the area from 1853 to 1933, had a brief stint as a nursing home and newspaper office before adopting its best-suited fate as a B&B in 2001. Four comfortable rooms each have en suite bathrooms. Your welcoming hosts maintain the house and common areas (including a pool and garden) magnificently. Great value.

Drew House   INN $$
(☑ 519-846-2226; www.drewhouse.com; 120 Mill St E, Elora; r incl breakfast from $150; ℗ ♻ ❄) Drew House unites the old world with the new. On spacious grounds, the inn has both renovated coach house suites (with private bathrooms) and guest rooms (with shared bathrooms) in the main house. Yard-thick stone walls whisper history as you drift into dreams before waking to a breakfast of fresh fruit, hot coffee, and bacon and eggs.

Discounts on weekdays.

★ Elora Mill Hotel & Spa   BOUTIQUE HOTEL $$$
(☑ 519-846-8464; https://eloramill.ca; 77 West Mill St, Elora; r/ste from $325/500; ℗ ♻ ❄ 🛜) Gorgeously renovated, the historic Elora Mill is the crown jewel of the region's hotels. Luxurious rooms integrate original stone walls with floor-to-ceiling windows, soaker tubs and wood-burning fireplaces. Furnishings are elegant and understated, the amenities luxe. Almost best of all, the Grand River is a constant presence, its views and sounds integrated throughout.

The on-site restaurant and spa here are treats.

✖ Eating & Drinking

Wreckless Eric CAFE $
(☑ 226-369-0261; www.wrecklesseric.ca; 90 Metcalfe St; ⊘ 6am-5pm Mon-Fri, 7:30am-5pm Sat & Sun; ☑) A small woodsy eatery specializing in bowls, burritos and salads. The scratch kitchen uses locally sourced products, so the menu changes regularly. Nevertheless, expect international flavors like Spicy Peanut (a riff on pad thai), Aloha (pulled pork and pineapple) and Sea-esta (salmon and sautéed mushroom). Coffee drinks, teas and smoothies are also offered.

★ Lost & Found Café CAFE $
(☑ 226-384-5400; www.thelostandfoundcafe.com; 45 W Mill St, Elora; mains $5-14; ⊘ 8am-6pm; ☑) A boho-chic cafe tucked between country boutiques, Lost & Found serves delicious and beautifully presented salads, sandwiches and soups. Vegetarian and gluten-free options abound. The coffee drinks are all organic. Psychic readings are sometimes offered too.

Underground Kitchen CARIBBEAN $
(☑ 226-383-7684; http://undergroundkitchen.ca; 152 St Andrew St W, Fergus; mains $6.50-8.50; ⊘ 11am-7pm Mon-Fri) A hole in the wall cooking up a variety of wrap roti: Caribbean flatbread wrapped around curried stews with vegetables, shrimp and even goat. Jerk chicken is also on deck. There's only one table, so take your meal to go – there are plenty of benches along the river. A local fave, the entrance opens onto a parking lot near the bridge.

Brewhouse PUB FOOD $$
(☑ 519-843-8871; www.brewhouseonthegrand.ca; 170 St David St S, Fergus; mains $13-24; ⊘ 11:30am-11pm Sun-Thu, to midnight Fri-Sat) Wave to the anglers on the Grand River from the shady Brewhouse patio as you weigh up the benefits of cheddar and ale soup, bangers and mash, or chicken pot pie. It sports a cozy bar, European beers on tap and live music to boot.

Shepherd's Pub PUB
(☑ 519-846-5775; http://shepherdspub.ca; 8 Mill W, Elora; ⊘ noon-11pm Mon & Tue, to midnight Wed, Fri & Sat, to 2am Thu, to 10pm Sun) Cold pints of Guinness and Ontario craft beers by the river. Trivia Nights and Open Jams plus all-day breakfast fry-ups, beer-battered fish-and-chips, and hearty beef pies will revive you if you spent too long here the night before.

☆ Entertainment

Gorge Cinema CINEMA
(☑ 519-846-0191; www.gorgecinema.ca; 43 Mill Street W, Elora) Once a 19th century hotel, today the Gorge is Canada's longest continuously operating repertory movie theater. Seats fully recline, popcorn is prepped in small batches, there's wine and beer and you can even buy Twizzlers individually. A fun night out. Cash only.

ⓘ Information

Elora Welcome Centre (☑ 877-242-6353; www.elorafergus.ca; 10 Mill St E, Elora; ⊘ 10am-5pm) The friendly staff are a great source of knowledge for all things Wellington County. Located by the bridge.

ⓘ Getting There & Away

Parkbus (p117) runs from Toronto to Elora Gorge for $49 return (including admission). Coaches make the day trip once per weekend every fortnight or so from May to October; check the website for schedules and book ahead.

Greyhound and other coaches no longer run to Elora and Fergus, so you will need your own car for longer trips than the day trip offered by Parkbus.

Stratford

☑ 226, 519, 548 / POP 31,055

Stratford is a success story: a wonderful country town that refuses to surrender to the depopulation plaguing rural centers worldwide. As the story goes, in 1952, upon hearing that the Canadian National Railways (the region's largest employer) was closing the doors of its Stratford facility, a young journalist by the name of Tom Patterson approached his council for a loan. His plan was to attract a troupe of actors to capitalize on the town's namesake: Shakespeare's birthplace. It worked. In 1953 the first performance of what has become the Stratford Festival (the largest of its kind) was born, creating a whole new industry, which continues to support the town today.

Charming, cultured and classy, with a bunch of *other* festivals to boot, Stratford packs more punch than cities twice its size: there are plenty of great places to eat and stay. Whatever the season, you'll enjoy nature, arts and architecture, and the proud local welcome.

⊙ Sights & Activities

Avon River
RIVER

Stratford's swan-filled Avon River (what else were they going to call it?) flows slowly past the town, with plenty of riverbank lawns on which to chill out. On the riverbank just west of the town center, the **Shakespearean Gardens** occupy the site of an old wool mill. Parterre gardens, manicured box hedges, herbs, roses and a bronze bust of Bill – pick up a brochure at Stratford Tourism Alliance (p145).

Further along the river is **Queen's Park**, with paths leading from the Festival Theatre along the river past Orr Dam and an 1885 stone bridge to a formal **English flower garden**.

Stratford-Perth Museum
MUSEUM

(☑ 519-393-5311; www.stratfordperthmuseum.ca; 4275 Huron Rd; adult/child $7/5; ⊙ 9am-5pm May-Oct, 10am-4pm Mon-Sat, noon-4pm Sun Nov-Apr; ℗) The diverse and significant Stratford-Perth Museum collection includes artifacts and memorabilia dating from the early 1800s to the present day, with rotating exhibits spanning everything from quilts to Justin Bieber. Outdoors, a 1km wooded trail with 15 storyboards tells the history of region.

Guided tours of the museum and historical talks (including box lunches) are offered too.

Gallery Stratford
GALLERY

(☑ 519-271-5271; www.gallerystratford.on.ca; 54 Romeo St S; ⊙ 10am-5pm Jun-Sep, to 3pm Oct-May; ℗ ⓗ) **FREE** In a wonderful renovated yellow-brick pump house (c 1880), Gallery Stratford exhibits innovative contemporary art with a Canadian emphasis. Regular art classes, movie nights and family days are also held. It's very kid friendly.

Avon Boat Tours and Rentals
CRUISE

(☑ 519-271-7739; www.avonboatrentals.ca; 30 York St; adult/child from $8.50/3.50; ⊙ 9am-dusk May-Oct) Take in the parks, swans, riverbanks and grand gardens along the Avon River on a pontoon boat (no booze or twerking). Thirty-minute tours depart from the boat house just north of the town center. Prefer DIY? Canoes ($25 per hour), kayaks ($18), paddleboats ($23) and rowboats ($35) are available for rent too.

⚑ Festivals & Events

Art in the Park
ART

(http://artintheparkstratford.ca; Lakeside Dr btwn Front St and North St; ⊙ 10am-5pm Wed, Sat & Sun May-Sep) For more than 50 years, professional artists have showcased (and sold) their works in this juried show along the banks of the Avon River. Expect everything from paintings and ceramics to leatherwork and jewelry.

Swans on Parade
CULTURAL

(www.visitstratford.ca; Lakeside Dr btwn Morenz Dr and North St; ⊙ early Apr; ⓗ) Stratford's beloved swans don't paddle around the Avon River all winter; instead, they are kept warm in winter pens. The first Sunday in April, the release of the birds to their summer home on the river is a Stratford celebration. The swans waddle down the street in parade formation, led by Stratford Police bagpipe players marching in kilts.

Stratford Summer Music
MUSIC

(☑ 519-271-2101; www.stratfordsummermusic.ca; tickets by donation to $75; ⊙ mid-Jul–mid-Aug) Four weeks of classical, jazz, gospel and theatrical music, with more than 350 acclaimed musicians from around Canada tuning up and letting loose. Concerts are held indoors and out, at various venues around town.

☰ Sleeping

There's a plethora of accommodations in Stratford, but savvy locals know how to make a buck: room rates can go through the roof during the Stratford Festival.

Stratford General Hospital Residence
HOSTEL $

(SGH Residence; ☑ 519-271-5084; www.sgh.stratford.on.ca/residence; 130 Youngs St; s/d $72/88; ℗ ⊖ ⊠) These renovated nurses' quarters are the closest thing you'll find to a youth hostel in town: 360 rooms with shared bathrooms, kitchens and a heated pool. Cheap, clean and comfy, but not party central.

Best Western Plus The Arden Park Hotel
HOTEL $$

(☑ 519-275-2936; www.ardenpark.ca; 552 Ontario St; ℗ ⊖ ❋ ⓢ ⊠) Recently updated, the rooms at this Best Western are nicer than you'd expect – spacious and modern with muted colors, some even with hardwood floors and touchscreen 'fireplaces'. There's also an indoor pool and a restaurant that serves a

DON'T MISS

THE STRATFORD FESTIVAL

Sir Alec Guinness played Richard III on opening night of the much-lauded **Stratford Festival** (☑ 519-273-1600; www.stratfordfestival.ca; 55 Queen St; ⊘ Apr-Nov), which began humbly in a tent at Queen's Park. With over 65 seasons under its belt, the festival has since achieved international acclaim. Far from its tented origins, today four theaters stage contemporary and period dramas, opera and, of course, works by the Bard, over a monster season lasting from April to November. Actors from around the world prize festival residencies.

Aside from the plays, there's a peripheral schedule of interesting programs: postperformance discussions, backstage tours, lectures, concerts and readings. Some are free.

Main-stage productions occur at the 1800-seat Festival Theatre and 1000-seat Avon Theatre. The Tom Patterson and Studio Theatres are more intimate. Tickets go on sale to the general public in early January. By showtime nearly every performance is sold out: book ahead! Deals include discounted rates for spring previews, two-for-one tickets on Sunday, Tuesday and Thursday, as well as 'Family Fun Days' with tickets starting at $41 per person.

mean Sunday brunch. Best of all, the Festival Theatre is just a short walk away.

★ The Forest Motel
MOTEL $$

(☑ 519-271-4573; www.forestmotel.on.ca; 2941 Forest Rd/RR 4; incl breakfast d $99-189, ste $159-279; P ⊖ ❋ 🕾) Friendly hosts welcome you to this wonderful woody lakeside gem, secluded yet only 10 minutes from town and close to highway amenities. Comfy renovated rooms emphasize owner Conrad's carpentry skills, feeling more like a country cottage than a motel. All rooms have microwave, refrigerator and homely touches like books and hot cocoa. Bikes and kayaks are available for exploring the property too.

Edison's Inn
INN $$

(☑ 519-305-5005; www.edisonsinn.com; 46 Ontario St; d incl breakfast $179-229; ⊖ ❋ 🕾) Edison's is a mid-century-meets-shabby-chic dream with just three rooms, all with clean lines, distressed wood elements and pops of color. Each has deluxe amenities plus unique knickknacks like turntables and chess boards that make you feel at home. The central location and relaxed atmosphere – including all-day breakfast – make it an easy place to land.

The inn is named after Thomas Edison, who lived in the building as a teenager while working as a telegrapher.

The Parlour Inn
HOTEL $$

(☑ 877-728-4036; www.theparlour.ca; 101 Wellington St; d from $169; P ⊖ ❋ @ 🕾) This handsome hotel occupies a heritage building in the center of town, near the Avon Theatre, and has been fully refitted to a high standard – most rooms are spacious and light filled. There's a pub downstairs with a lovely patio, but it doesn't get too rowdy.

Mercer Hall Hotel
BOUTIQUE HOTEL $$

(☑ 519-271-9202; www.mercerhall.ca; 104-108 Ontario St; d $159-209; P ⊖ ❋ 🕾) In the heart of downtown, Mercer Hall has more class than most: uniquely artistic rooms feature handcrafted furniture, kitchenettes and electric fireplaces. Some have Jacuzzis. The ground floor is home to an upscale restaurant and a popular beer hall; the floors are thick enough, though, that noise isn't an issue. The only downer: no elevator.

Acrylic Dreams
B&B $$

(☑ 519-271-7874; www.acrylicdreams.com; 66 Bay St; r incl breakfast $149-185; P ⊖ ❋ 🕾) Owned by a husband-and-wife team, this renovated 1879 B&B has polished wooden floorboards and spa amenities. Besides being artists (there are more than a few acrylic masterpieces on the walls) the owners also practice chair massage and reflexology, and can accommodate all diets.

★ Three Houses Bed & Breakfast Inn
B&B $$$

(☑ 519-272-0722; www.thethreehouses.com; 100 Brunswick St; ste incl breakfast $225-695; P ⊖ ❋ 🕾 ⊠) Two Edwardian town houses, a garden carriage house and an 1870s Italianate house make up this meticulous, *almost* over-the-top 18-room inn. No detail has been spared in decorating these light-filled spaces – even the luggage racks match the quirky individual room designs. A saltwater pool and secret oasis garden add relaxing touches.

✕ Eating

A local chef's school and surrounding farmland make Stratford a gourmet's delight. Reservations are recommended during festival time.

★ Sirkel Foods   CAFE $

(☑ 519-273-7084; https://sirkelfoodsstratford.com; 40 Wellington St; mains $6-13; ⊗ 8am-3pm Mon-Sat; ☑) A hopping cafe in the central square, Sirkel is a go-to for locals and visitors in the know. Breakfast is traditional and hearty, while lunch brings creative salads and sandwiches made with homemade bread and items like house-cured salmon and fancy cheeses. Arrive early to avoid a wait or just take your meal to go.

★ The Red Rabbit   BISTRO $$$

(☑ 519-305-6464; www.redrabbitresto.com; 64 Wellington St; mains $16-26, prix fixe $56-62; ⊗ 11:30am–2:30pm daily, 5-7pm Tue & Wed, 5-9pm Thu-Sat; ☑) Inventive dishes, global influences and a cool, laid-back vibe are what drive the experience at Stratford's 'it' restaurant. Order à la carte for lunch and after-theater service – the chicken and waffles dish is unreal – or double down for the prix-fixe dinner, with a seasonally changing menu that features dishes like kung pao sweetbreads, and bacon and foie-gras pâté.

Stratford Chef   GASTRONOMY $$$

(☑ 519-271-1414; https://stratfordchef.com; 136 Ontario St; from $55; ⊗ 6:30-8:30pm Tue-Sat Oct-Mar) From October to March, Stratford's renowned culinary school hosts a dinner series, when students practice their craft by prepping dinners for the general public. International guest chefs create the menu – coq au vin one night, ceviche the next – and oversee the student crew. Check out the daily menus and reserve online.

Bijou   FRENCH $$$

(☑ 519-273-5000; www.bijourestaurant.com; 74 Wellington St; prix fixe $57-63; ⊗ 4:45-10pm Tue-Sat) Classy and delightful, this French joint has a different prix-fixe menu written on the chalkboard each evening. The locally sourced meals might include duck, panzanella salad or Lake Huron whitefish ceviche. Creaky wooden floorboards and children's artwork on the walls add a personal touch.

ℹ Information

Stratford Tourism Alliance (☑ 800-561-7926, 519-271-5140; www.visitstratford.ca; 47 Downie

St; ⊗ 10am-6pm Jun-Aug, reduced hours rest of year) helps with accommodations and all things 'Festival.' The website is an excellent information source, with loads of tour options. This downtown office has one of Justin Bieber's signed guitars (an endless source of fascination for giggling teen fans from around the world) and a 'Bieber-iffic' map ($1) of JB's old haunts around town, including the site of his first date.

ℹ Getting There & Away

Stratford Direct (☑ 800-567-1600; www. stratfordfestival.ca; $19-29; ⊗ May-Nov; 🤍) is a round-trip shuttle service between Stratford's four theaters during Festival season (performance days only) and Toronto ($29, two hours) or Waterloo ($19, one hour). You must purchase your shuttle ticket by 11pm the day before you travel, but they often sell out way before then, especially on days with cheap theater tickets. Service is direct. Check the website for departure times.

Stratford Airporter (☑ 519-273-0057; www. stratfordairporter.com) runs daily shuttles to Pearson International Airport (p117), departing Stratford from 4am to 7pm, and Toronto 7:30am to 11:30pm (from $89, two hours, eight daily). It's cheaper if you're traveling with someone.

VIA Rail runs from **Stratford Train Station** (☑ 888-842-7245; www.viarail.ca; 101 Shakespeare St) to Toronto (from $58, 2¼ hours, twice daily) and London (from $34, one hour, twice daily).

Lake Huron Shoreline

Lake Huron has some of the cleanest waters of the Great Lakes and is wide enough that the sun sets on the waterline of its western shore: expect wonderful sunsets. If you've been lingering around Toronto and Lake Ontario, Lake Huron's 'blueness' will be both surprising and refreshing, as will its whitish sandy beaches.

ℹ Getting There & Away

You will need your own transport to get here. Renting a car from London is a great way to explore the Huron Coast and to avoid the stress of driving in/out of Toronto. Both Hertz and Enterprise have car-rental locations within walking distance of the London Train Station (p151).

Grand Bend

☑ 519 / POP 2685

For most of the year, Grand Bend is a sleepy, shuttered town on the southeastern shore of Lake Huron, but from late May to late October the town heaves to life with sun-hungry university students from nearby London, Kitchener and Windsor. It's hard to imagine the transformation: the handful of year-round residents' peaceful lives interrupted by a mini Florida-style Spring Break on their doorsteps.

From a vantage point on the broad, sandy shoreline of the main beach, you can see how the town got its name: the coastline arcs dramatically from this point until it becomes almost a straight line, headed north. In early spring, it's quite a surreal experience to stand on the sandy shore in the sunshine and gaze out at the frozen, snow-covered lake, its edges whipped by the wind into frozen waves.

⊙ Sights

Pinery Provincial Park   PARK
(🚗 info 519-243-2220, reservations 888-668-7275; www.ontarioparks.com; 9526 Lakeshore Rd RR #2; per car $17; ⊙8am-10pm; P🖐) South of Grand Bend is popular, picturesque Pinery Provincial Park, with 10km of wide sandy beaches, coastal dunes and lots of trails winding through wooded sections and sand dunes. The **Old Ausable Channel**, a significant wetlands area, is a favorite for those who like to explore by water. Bikes/kayaks ($50/65 per day) are available at the visitors center. For overnight stays, there are hundreds of options to choose from – campsites, cabins and yurts (from $46); book in advance as spots fill fast.

🛏 Sleeping & Eating

Whispering Pines Motel   MOTEL $$
(🚗519-238-2383; www.whisperingpinesmotel. org; 10456 Lakeshore Rd; d $129-189; P❄🕭🐾) This friendly family-run motel is located in a wooded lot just south of Grand Bend. It has comfortable rooms with grannie decor (quilts and frilly curtains), old-school aircon and gleaming bathrooms. Great value for families, the motel also has a nice pool and offers free passes to Pinery Provincial Park. An on-site restaurant is the frosting on the cake.

Bonnie Doone Manor on the Beach   INN $$
(🚗519-238-2236; www.bonniedoone.ca; 16 Government Rd; d $180-295, cottage $295; P❄@🐾) Many love this ramshackle holiday motel – the only one on the beach – that has been lovingly updated and maintained by the same family for more than 50 years. Rooms

are a time-warp with bright, colorful accents. Many face the water for unimaginably beautiful sunsets. There's also a quaint private cottage. Located a hop-skip-and-jump from Main St too.

Riverbend Pizzeria   PIZZA $
(🚗519-238-6919; www.riverbendpizzeria.ca; 26 Ontario St S; mains $12-16; ⊙3-8:45pm Mon, to 9:45pm Tue-Thu, 11:30am-9:45pm Fri & Sat, noon-8pm Sun) It may be a pizza restaurant by name, but regulars also come year-round to the Riverbend for huge portions of hot chicken wings, karaoke nights and cold beer on the patio.

Paddington Pub   INTERNATIONAL $$
(🚗519-238-5788; www.paddingtonspub.net; 18 Ontario St N; mains $15-22; ⊙11:30am-9pm Mon, to 10pm Tue-Sat, 1-9pm Sun; P) A small house repurposed as an even smaller pub, Paddington's is a local favorite with a full line of craft beers and filling, homestyle specials every night: Mexican Mondays, Tuscan Tuesdays... If in doubt, the fish-and-chips is a solid bet.

❶ Getting There & Away

There's no public transportation to Grand Bend. Rent a car from London if you want to avoid Toronto traffic.

Goderich

🚗519 / POP 7530

Once awarded the title of Canada's prettiest town, charming Goderich's most recent and tragic claim to fame is for the EF-3 tornado that tore through it at 4:03pm on August 21, 2011. It was a Sunday and the crowded market square had just emptied. The twister formed over Lake Huron and followed a direct path across the town's distinctive octagonal town square, City Hall and beyond. Of the 97 century-old trees in the square, only three remained; hundreds of buildings were damaged or destroyed, scores were injured and one life was lost.

Several years on, the restoration and reconstruction work is now complete. Though the trees are still young and sparse, visitors will be rewarded with a modern, grown-up version of a pretty town. The friendly staff at Tourism Goderich will be delighted to provide you with a self-guided heritage walking tours brochure and field any questions you have about the town, tornado-related or otherwise.

◉ Sights

Huron Historic Gaol   MUSEUM
(☑ 519-524-6971; www.huroncountymuseum.ca; 181 Victoria St N; adult/child $6/4.50; ⊙ 10am-4:30pm Mon-Sat, from 1pm Sun May-Aug, reduced hours rest of year; P ♿) Follow a creepy, prison-gray corridor into this octagonal fortress that served as courthouse and jail for almost 130 years (and was the site of Canada's last public hanging in 1869). A combined ticket with Huron County Museum is $10 for an adult, $6.50 for a child.

Huron County Museum   MUSEUM
(☑ 519-524-2686; www.huroncountymuseum.ca; 110 North St; adult/child $6/4.50; ⊙ 10am-4:30pm Mon-Sat, from 1pm Sun May-Oct, reduced hours rest of year; ♿) Walk the wooden floorboards for an informed look at local history, industry and transportation. Displays include 30,000 artifacts related to country life, from antique furniture and china to an old steam engine and a tank. It stays opens later, till 8pm, on Thursdays.

🛌 Sleeping & Eating

Samuels Hotel   HOTEL $$
(☑ 519-524-1371; www.samuelshotel.ca; 34031 Saltford Rd; d incl breakfast $149-199; P ♿❄🐾🛜) At this small hotel on the edge of town, every room has a private terrace with gorgeous views of the Maitland River and direct access to hiking trails and coveted fishing spots. Rooms themselves are spacious and modern in style with details like wood floors, fireplaces and *Jacuzzi* tubs. Service is affable and accommodating.

Colborne B&B   B&B $$
(☑ 519-524-7400; www.colbornebandb.com; 72 Colborne St; d incl breakfast $115-145; P ❄🛜) Formerly the manse for the Presbyterian Church, this handsome three-story property has four bright, smartly furnished guest bedrooms, each with en suite; two have whirlpools. Delicious gourmet breakfasts, served in the dining room, are a great way to start your day. Excellent value.

West Street Willy's   DINER $
(☑ 519-524-7777; https://weststreetwillyseatery.com; 42 West St; items $8-14; ⊙ 8am-8pm Tue-Thu, 7am-9pm Fri-Sat, to 8pm Sun; ♿) Hearty breakfasts and home-style faves await you at Willy's: pancakes, pierogi, pizza and burgers are all on the menu. For the adventurous (or very hungry), try the PB&B: peanut butter, banana and bacon stuffed between two slices of French toast. It's surprisingly delicious and so filling it'll get you through till dinner.

Culbert's Bakery   BAKERY $
(☑ 519-524-7941; www.culbertsbakery.com; 49 West St; items from $2.50; ⊙ 8:30am-5:30pm Tue-Sat) Folks come from far and wide for this old-school bakery that has served delicious and decadent cream puffs, muffins, tarts and fresh-from-the-oven loaves since the mid-1800s. The early bird catches the early calories.

❶ Information

Goderich Tourist Information Centre (☑ 519-524-6600; www.goderich.ca; 91 Hamilton St; ⊙ 9am-6pm) Grab the self-guided *4 Heritage Walking Tours* brochure or the *Visitor's Guide* to help you get your bearings.

❶ Getting There & Away

There are no longer bus links to Goderich so you will need your own transport, at least to a larger town such as London.

Southampton & Around

Southampton has happily sequestered itself from the beaten path of rowdy summer holidays. The quaint colony's sandy beach feels almost undiscovered at times, and a stroll down the main streets reveals mom-and-pop shops and the piecemeal architecture of Queen Anne–styled homes.

To the south, neighboring **Port Elgin** is the year-round home to the bulk of shopping, dining and nightlife options for the region. It also has some of the better, more accessible (free parking) and lesser known beaches on this strip of Lake Huron.

About 20km north of Southampton, **Sauble Beach** has a delicious long strip of tawny sand and warm, clear waters, but its huge popularity with holidaymakers and revelers and the high cost of car parking take some of the magic away. In winter, it's a ghost town.

◉ Sights & Activities

★ Bruce County Museum   MUSEUM
(☑ 519-797-2080; www.brucemuseum.ca; 33 Victoria St N, Southampton; adult/child $8/4; ⊙ 10am-5pm Mon-Sat, from 1pm Sun, closed Sun & Mon Nov-Apr; ♿) This two-story museum gives an excellent overview of the region's history and heritage, including the importance of the Ojibwe people and the changes (and sometimes havoc) brought by the pioneers. There's also an extensive collection

of artifacts relating to shipwrecks in the region. Kids will enjoy the hands-on exhibits.

Saugeen Rail Trail
CYCLING

(☑519-832-4176; www.saugeenrailtrail.ca) Cyclists will enjoy this 25km stretch of abandoned railway – used in the 1860s and 1870s – that starts at the corner of Adelaide and Grosvenor Sts in Southampton and ends in the small town of Paisley. There are several access points along the way; maps are available online.

Thorncrest Outfitters
KAYAKING

(☑519-797-1608; www.thorncrestoutfitters.com; 193 High St, Southampton; canoe rental from $45, tours from $60; ⏰10am-5:30pm Mon-Sat, 11am-4pm Sun) The Saugeen River, which flows into Lake Huron at Southampton, is one of the best-established routes for canoeing and kayaking in southern Ontario. Thorncrest Outfitters runs an extensive program of short self-guided and organized trips aimed at inexperienced paddlers.

🛏 Sleeping

Chantry Breezes
B&B $$

(☑519-797-1818; www.chantrybreezes.com; 107 High St, Southampton; incl breakfast r $159-219, cottage $275; 🅿😊🛜) This old Queen Anne manor, tucked gently behind gnarled evergreens, features seven rooms spread out among endearingly cluttered antiques and two garden cottages. Made-to-order breakfasts are delightful to enjoy on the porch. Two-night minimum in July and August.

🍴 Eating & Drinking

Armen's Cafe
FUSION $

(☑519-387-3864; 224 High St, Southampton; mains $7-14; ⏰11am-3pm) Forget the local greasy spoons and say hi to chatty Armen as he prepares a tasty sandwich from the ever-changing menu. A rotating summer menu highlights global cuisine; one day it's Indian, another it's Moroccan. It keeps your taste buds on their toes. Sneak upstairs and enjoy your fresh eats on the sunny rooftop deck.

Elk & Finch
CAFE $

(☑519-797-2835; www.elkandfinch.com; 54 Albert St, Southampton; mains $9-26; ⏰9am-8pm Tue-Thu, to 9pm Fri, 8am-9pm Sat, to 8pm Sun) This 'coffee pub' serves more than caffeinated and alcoholic beverages: sandwiches, salads and thin-crust pizzas will fill you up. Sip your trendy brew in the wobbly house or park yourself at a table on the breezy patio.

Outlaw Brew Co.
BREWERY

(☑519-797-1515; https://outlawbrewco.com; 196 High St, Southampton; ⏰11:30am-8pm Tue & Wed, to 9pm Thu & Fri, 9am-9pm Sat, to 3pm Sun) Stop into this local brewpub for a cold craft beer, made with Canadian barley and premium hops, and taste treats like wild blueberries. The brewery itself is in what was once the historic Southampton Hotel, a Wild West–type hotel in the mid-1800s.

❶ Information

Sauble Beach Tourism (☑519-900-0689; www.saublebeach.com; 672 Main St, Sauble Beach; ⏰10am-6pm Mon-Wed, to 3pm Fri, 12:30-4:30pm Sat) Check in for the lowdown on party town.

Saugeen Shores Chamber Office (☑519-832-2332; www.saugeenshoreschamber.ca; 559 Goderich St, Port Elgin; ⏰9am-5pm Mon-Fri) In Port Elgin, 8km down the shoreline; offers a wider array of information about the region.

Southampton Chamber of Commerce (☑519-797-2215; 201 High St, Southampton; ⏰10am-4pm Mon-Sat, noon-4pm Sun) A small office in the town hall, only open during the summer months.

❶ Getting There & Away

Passengers arriving at Pearson International Airport (p117) in Toronto can take the **Grey Bruce Airbus** (☑800-361-0393; www.greybruce airbus.com), which connects to Southampton and Port Elgin ($81, three hours, four daily). From Toronto's Union Station (p117), **Can-ar** (☑800-387-7097; www.can-arcoach.com) operates a bus service to Port Elgin ($50, 4¾ hours, one daily), arriving at Ralph's Hi-way Shoppette in the center of town.

London

☑519 / POP 383,820

Ontario's third most populous city (after the GTA and Ottawa), midway between Toronto and Detroit, is London, aka the 'forest city.' It bears little resemblance to its English namesake, short of its substantial collection of fine Victorian homes, River Thames and a plethora of leafy parks and gardens. Aside from a smattering of beautiful art deco buildings, London's downtown core is predictably turn-of-the-millennium, if not a little bit 1970s.

London is home to the University of Western Ontario in the city's north, favored by wealthy Toronto families as *the* spot to send their kids. The student population ensures a young, upbeat vibe.

There's plenty of accommodations in town, some good student-priced eateries, a handful of interesting tourist attractions and a burgeoning music scene. In fact, in 2019 London hosted the Junos, Canada's top music awards ceremony. As Toronto continues to expand, eyes will be more focused on London in years to come.

◉ Sights

Jonathon Bancroft-Snell Gallery   GALLERY
(☑ 519-434-5443; www.jonathons.ca; 258 Dundas St; ◉ 10am-6pm Mon-Fri, to 5pm Sat) Many of Canada's top ceramic artists are showcased in this labyrinthine gallery, which holds the largest collection of museum-quality ceramics in the country. Works range from mugs to large sculptures – everything is for sale, of course. Check the website for special exhibitions.

**Ska-Nah-Doht
Village & Museum**   HISTORIC SITE
(☑ 519-264-2420; www.lowerthames-conservation. on.ca/Ska-Nah-Doht; Longwoods Rd Conservation Area, 8348 Longwoods Rd, Mount Brydges; per car $4; ◉ 9am-4:30pm, closed Sat & Sun Sep-Apr; P ☗) At this re-creation of a 1000-year-old Haudenosaunee longhouse community, village structures are encircled by a protective wall and maze. Self-guided tour pamphlets are available at the visitors center, where a small museum showcases artifacts from nearby archaeological sites dating back to 800 CE. Located 27km west of London, on a 63-hectare reserve with wooded hiking trails and green expanses.

Fanshawe Pioneer Village   HISTORIC SITE
(☑ 519-457-1296; www.fanshawepioneervillage.ca; 1424 Clarke Rd; adult/child $9/7; ◉ 10am-4:30pm Tue-Sun May-Oct; P ☗) Explore London's history at this 30-building village on the eastern edge of town. Costumed blacksmiths, farmers and craftspeople carry out their duties in true 19th-century pioneer-village style. At the adjoining **Fanshawe Conservation Area** (☑ 519-451-2800; www.fanshawe conservationarea.ca; 1424 Clarke Rd; campsites $39-49, reservations $13; ◉ May-Oct; P ☳) you can swim, walk and camp.

Museum London   MUSEUM
(☑ 519-661-0333; www.museumlondon.ca; 421 Ridout St N; by donation; ◉ noon-5pm Tue, Wed & Fri-Sun, to 9pm Thu; P) Focusing on the visual arts and how they fit together with history, London's vibrant museum has 5000-plus works of art and 25,000-plus artifacts. Free tours run on Sundays at 2pm.

★☆ Festivals & Events

Londonlicious   FOOD & DRINK
(www.londonlicious.ca; ◉ Jul & Aug) A London homage to Toronto's hit Summerlicious (p93) festival brings cheap fancy eats to the peeps.

London Fringe Festival   CULTURAL
(☑ 519-434-0606; www.londonfringe.ca; $10-15; ◉ late May-early Jun) Ten days of independent theater, dance, music and visual arts around downtown. Shows are selected by non-juried lottery with no restrictions on content or style; all proceeds from ticket sales also go directly to the artists.

Sunfest   MUSIC
(☑ 519-672-1522; www.sunfest.on.ca; Victoria Park, 580 Clarence St; ◉ Jul) FREE Canada's premier jazz and world-music festival, held in Victoria Park, is a vibrant event attracting 225,000 attendees yearly. Beyond tunes, expect food carts, crafts and art from around the world.

☖ Sleeping

There's a bombardment of cheap chain motels on the Wellington Rd approach from Hwy 401, but stay downtown if you can.

Wander Inn and Hostel   HOSTEL $
(☑ 519-617-5444; https://wanderhostel.com; 252 Dundas St; dorm $39-44, r with/without bath $114/89; P ☺ ❄ ☎) This downtown hostel offers spacious rooms with wood floors and big windows that showcase the city's high-rises. Dorms have just two to three bunks; mattresses are on the thin side but are comfortable enough. There's a small guest kitchen and stylish lounge – great places to meet fellow travelers. Keyless entrance plus automated check-in/check-out make coming and going a breeze.

★ Hotel Metro   BOUTIQUE HOTEL $$
(☑ 519-518-9000; www.hotelmetro.ca; 32 Covent Market Pl; d from $169; P ❄ ☎) Rooms in this oh-so-cool boutique hotel in the heart of downtown have hardwood floors, exposed-brick walls, rainfall showers, deep soaker tubs and plenty of interesting design elements to keep you entertained. Book online for discounted rates.

Idlewyld Inn & Spa
INN $$

(☑ 519-432-5554; www.idlewyldinn.com; 36 Grand Av; d from $140; P ⊖ ❋ ❅; ☐ 1, 13) Across the River Thames, this grand Victorian mansion has 21 guestrooms with surprisingly modern decor and amenities (though some still have original fireplaces and balconies). The guest lounge and restaurant better reflect the history of the home with period furnishings, ornate woodwork and leather-like Lincrusta-Walton wallpaper. A full-service spa offers all manner of body treatments and beautification too – a treat!

Delta Hotels
London Armouries
HOTEL $$

(☑ 519-679-6111; www.marriott.com; 325 Dundas St; d from $161; P ⊖ ❋ ❅ ❆) The Armouries wing of London's premier hotel was originally a historic military training facility. Its period features remain to be enjoyed – in the bar lounge and pool area, especially – though most rooms are in the tower wing. Expect comfortable, neutrally furnished accommodations, a central location and good-value rates.

Park Hotel
HOTEL $$

(☑ 519-642-4444, 800-561-4574; www.parkhotel suites.com; 242 Pall Mall St; ste incl breakfast from $161; P ❋ @; ☐ 4, 6) Recently updated, this all-suite hotel has smart, oversized bedrooms with separate living rooms, all with microwaves and mini-fridges. Service is solid and the location near Richmond Row and Victoria Park can't be beat. Excellent value, especially considering the complimentary buffet breakfast.

✕ Eating

★ Covent Garden Market
MARKET $

(☑ 519-439-3921; www.coventmarket.com; 130 King St; items from $2; ⊕ 8am-7pm Mon-Sat, 11am-5pm Sun; P ♿) This humongous, chapel-shaped market will whet and satisfy any appetite. There's a permanent collection of delis, bakeries, chocolate shops, fresh-produce stalls and world-cuisine eateries, plus seasonal and pop-up vendors. Check out the sunny, busker-fueled buzz on the patio on Thursday and Saturday mornings (May to December only).

Zen Gardens
VEGETARIAN $

(☑ 519-433-6688; www.zengardenslondon.com; 344 Dundas St; mains $11-18; ⊕ 11:30am-2:30pm Tue-Sat, 5-9pm Tue-Sun; ♿) This Asian vegetarian restaurant downtown will impress vegetarians and their most hardened carnivorous mates alike. Tofu, mushrooms, and sauced-up soy and gluten meat feature heavily. Combinations, served in Japanese bento boxes and costing the same as a main, offer the best value.

★ The Root Cellar
CAFE $$

(☑ 519-719-7675; http://rootcellarorganic.ca; 623 Dundas St; mains $12-19; ⊕ 11am–9pm Tue-Wed, to 10pm Thu-Fri, 9am-10pm Sat; ♿; ☐ 2, 20) It's all about local and organic foods at this boho-chic cafe, with from-scratch creations like free-range water buffalo burgers, kale salad with hemp hearts and quinoa, and vegan pizza. There are lots of gluten-free options too. Located in the up-and-coming Adelaide neighborhood.

The Church Key
GASTROPUB $$

(☑ 519-936-0960; www.thechurchkey.ca; 476 Richmond St; mains $15-34; ⊕ 11:30am-10pm Sun-Tue, to 11pm Wed & Thu, to midnight Fri & Sat) An upscale pub with a casual atmosphere, dishes are heavy on meat – lamb, venison, duck, even game – beautifully prepared and presented. The sunny patio, with views of imposing St Paul's Cathedral next door, is a popular spot for happy hour and Sunday brunch.

Budapest Restaurant
HUNGARIAN $$

(☑ 519-439-3431; www.facebook.com/budapest restaurantlondon; 348 Dundas St; mains $10-31; ⊕ 11am-2pm Mon-Fri, 4-9pm daily) If you've been in business for more than 60 years, you've got to be doing something right. There is so much authenticity to this humble establishment... flower-patterned plates, Hungarian tchotchkes, even red velvet curtains separating tables. Over the years, the schnitzels, chicken paprikash and pierogi have been perfected. Yum! Lunch specials are excellent value.

Thaifoon
THAI $$

(☑ 519-850-1222; www.thaifoonrestaurant.com; 120 Dundas St; mains $13-24; ⊕ 11:30am-2pm Mon-Fri & 4:30-9pm daily; ♿) Classing Dundas St up a bit is Thaifoon. A calm, composed atmosphere and babbling water features provide relief from the mean streets, while chili-laden curries, stir-fries, soups and salads provide a kick.

🍷 Drinking & Entertainment

The vibrant student population ensures plenty of youthful, boozy entertainment. During the end of summer, before term begins, London's 'Richmond Row' (Richmond

St from Oxford to Dundas) becomes party central.

Barneys/The Ceeps PUB
(☎519-432-1425; www.facebook.com/barneyspatio; 671 Richmond St; ⏰11am-2am Mon-Sat, to midnight Sun; 🚌4,6) Don't ask about the name – we don't get it either. Hands down London's largest and most hopping patio. Come for the bands and DJs, pool tables, shuffleboard, and local beers on tap. The original Richmond Row institution.

★**TAP Centre for Creativity** ARTS CENTER
(☎519-642-2767; www.tapcreativity.org; 203 Dundas St; ⏰noon-5pm Tue-Sat) A buzzing arts center in the heart of downtown London. Programming centers on emerging and developing artists; a black box theater and gallery on the 1st floor showcase performing and visual artists, while the upper floors are home to resident artist studios and multi-use workshops. Stop in to see a show or take a drop-in class.

London Music Club LIVE MUSIC
(☎519-640-6996; www.londonmusicclub.com; 470 Colborne St; cover from $5; ⏰7pm-late Wed-Sat; 🚌1) Touring blues and folk acts fall over themselves to play here, a rockin' room out the back of a cream-brick house. Ukelele jam on Wednesday nights; acoustic open mike on Fridays.

Information

Post Office (☎866-607-6301; www.canadapost.ca; 515 Richmond St; ⏰9am-5pm Mon-Fri)

Tourism London (☎519-661-5000; www.londontourism.ca; 391 Wellington St; ⏰8:30am-4:30pm Mon-Fri, 10am-5pm Sat) Knowledgeable staff offer good advice and as many brochures as you can carry. Shares a building with the **Canadian Medical Hall of Fame** (www.cdnmedhall.org) and its interesting, sometimes gory, displays of brains, hearts and bones.

Getting There & Away

London International Airport (☎519-452-4015; https://flylondon.ca; 1750 Crumlin Rd; 🚌36) is a regional base for Air Canada, WestJet and Swoop with flights to Toronto, Montreal, and other limited Canadian and US destinations.

London Train Station (☎888-842-7245; www.viarail.ca; 205 York St; ⏰5:30am-10:15pm Mon-Fri, from 6:30am Sat & Sun) has VIA trains to Toronto (from $37, two to 3½ hours, seven daily) and Windsor (from $37, two to 3½ hours, seven daily).

Getting Around

London Transit (LTC; ☎519-451-1347; www.londontransit.ca; 150 Dundas St; ⏰7:30am-7pm Mon-Fri, 8:30am-6pm Sat) provides extensive bus services around town for $2.75 (children under 12 ride for free). If using public transportation more than a couple of times, save some money by purchasing a five-pack of bus tickets or an LTC smart card ($10 minimum) and pay just $1.90 a ride.

Windsor

☎519 / POP 287,100

At the end of the highway on the southwestern tip of Ontario (across the river from Detroit, USA) this once-booming center for trade and manufacturing has seen better days. That may change when the Gordie Howe International Bridge opens in 2024, increasing the volume of trade and speed of passage over the border.

For the moment, though, Windsor's empty facades bear the scars of decline. The upside? Cheap real estate, adjacency to the USA and proximity to Lake Erie are slowly luring city slickers looking for a change of pace.

Not a showstopper, Windsor is an interesting urban curiosity for those who want to see a small multicultural town in flux. There's great Lebanese food east of downtown, and homey Italian cuisine a little further south, making this a tasty stop before you head on to the USA.

Sights

Visitors will enjoy walking along the **Riverwalk**, a multi-use path that extends from under the Ambassador Bridge for 5km along the riverfront. The historic Walkerville neighborhood is worth a look.

★**Chimczuk Museum** MUSEUM
(☎519-253-1812; www.citywindsor.ca; 401 Riverside Dr W; adult/child $5.50/4.50, joint admission to AGW adult/child $13/7.50; ⏰10am-5pm Tue-Sat, from 11am Sun; P 👪) Sharing the building with the Art Gallery of Windsor, this remarkable museum unfolds the region's history in an inclusive and in-depth way, integrating First Nations and Métis heritage and culture; Black history and contributions in Windsor; and the experience of present-day immigrants. Exhibits are

UNCLE TOM'S CABIN

About 100km northeast of Windsor, **Uncle Tom's Cabin Historic Site** (📞519-683-2978; www.uncletomscabin.org; 29251 Uncle Tom's Rd, Dresden; adult/child $7/4.50; ⊙10am-4pm Mon-Sat, noon-4pm Sun May-Oct; 🅿) is the location of the clapboard home of Father Josiah Henson, an escaped slave who later became a conductor on the Underground Railroad (in all, he led 118 people to freedom). Henson's life was the inspiration behind Harriet Beecher Stowe's *Uncle Tom's Cabin*. The 5-hectare site has multimedia exhibits relating to Henson's life, Beecher Stowe's book and the history of enslaved people in the USA and their escape to Canada.

The site itself sits on what was once the Dawn Settlement, a Black community founded by Henson; at its peak, it had 500 inhabitants. Three historic buildings and two cemeteries can be explored. To get here, take exit 101 off Hwy 401 and follow the signs. Well worth a side trip.

multimedia and have lots of hands-on elements (even a makers space!) so everyone stays engaged.

Dieppe Gardens
GARDENS

(📞877-746-4311; www.citywindsor.ca; 78 Riverside Dr W; ⊙dawn-dusk; 🅿) These beautiful gardens, on land once used by Detroit–Windsor ferries before the 1929 bridge and 1930 tunnel put them out of business, offer the best views of the smoke-and-mirrors Detroit skyline. Dotted with monuments to the Canadian armed forces. The gardens make a good starting point for a walk along the river.

Art Gallery of Windsor
GALLERY

(AGW; 📞519-977-0013; www.agw.ca; 401 Riverside Dr W; adult/child $10/5, joint admission to Chimczuk Museum adult/child $13/7.50; ⊙11am-5pm Wed-Sun, to 9pm first Thu of month; 🅿) The jaunty glass-and-concrete prow of the AGW has an excellent permanent collection focused on Canadian visual arts, from the historical to the contemporary. On weekends, docent-led tours are included in admission. Located on the 2nd and 3rd floors of the building.

🛏 Sleeping

Stonecroft Inn
HOTEL $

(📞519-969-7600; www.stonecroftinn.com; 3032 Dougall Av; r incl breakfast from $110; 🅿❄🛜) If you don't mind staying on a busy street with strip malls and aging buildings, the Stonecroft is a solid choice. You'll find contemporary chic and squeaky-clean rooms with pillow-top beds, fridges and single-shot coffee makers. Self-serve breakfast is a good way to start the day. Located 6km from the riverfront.

Ye Olde Walkerville Bed & Breakfast
B&B $$

(📞519-254-1507; www.walkervillebb.com; 1104 Monmouth Rd; s/d incl breakfast from $109/129; ❄❄🛜) A well-maintained 1903 home with a wraparound porch. Rooms are clean and comfortable, homey and dated – it's reminiscent of staying at a favorite great aunt's home. Expect flowery wallpaper and frilly curtains alongside checkerboard sofas and homegrown art.

The owners are affable and accommodating, and make a tasty breakfast. Discounts are often available if you call to reserve. Adults only.

Caesar's Windsor Hotel and Casino
CASINO HOTEL $$

(📞800-991-7777; www.caesars.com; 377 Riverside Dr E; r from $169; 🅿❄🛜) This mammoth riverfront complex – two towers, seven eateries, spa, theater and, of course, the casino – has the best rooms in town. If you're traveling sans kids, opt for the adults-only Forum tower. Its rooms are simple yet luxurious in neutral tones, with a hint of mid-century mod. Ask for one with views of the Detroit skyline.

🍴 Eating

Squirrel Cage
CAFE $

(📞519-252-2243; www.facebook.com/TheSquirrel Cage; 1 Maiden Lane W; mains $7-14; ⊙10am-7pm Mon-Thu, to 10pm Fri, to 6pm Sat, to 3pm Sun; 🍴) Former city slickers love their new life in Windsor and bring a taste of cosmopolitan Toronto to town in this stylish, upbeat licensed cafe. Expect coffees, soups, delicious filled panini and healthy salads daily, plus weekend brunches.

Spago　　　　　　　　　　ITALIAN $$
(☑ 519-252-2233; www.spagos.ca; 690 Erie St E; mains $15-32; ⊕ 11:30am-10pm Mon-Thu, to 11pm Wed-Sat, 1-9pm Sun; 🄰) Windsor has a reputation for being the place for Italian, and Spago fits the bill. If you're not in the mood for pasta, rest assured: staff also deliver outstanding wood-fired pizzas, seafood, salad and scaloppine. Mmm...amma mia!

Cook's Shop　　　　　　　ITALIAN $$$
(☑ 519-254-3377; https://cooksshoprestaurant. wordpress.com; 683 Ouellette Ave; mains $21-33; ⊕ 5-8pm Sun & Tue-Thu, to 9:30pm Fri & Sat) This cozy, dimly lit restaurant specializes in classic Italian dishes. Pasta with your choice of 10 different sauces is the specialty; dishes are often prepared table-side, open flame and all. Appreciative locals have been coming here for almost 40 years – it could use a refresh to its aging decor. Reservations recommended.

Drinking & Nightlife

The Manchester　　　　　　　　　　PUB
(☑ 519-977-8020; www.themanchester.ca; 546 Ouellette Ave; ⊕ 11am-2am) Friendly staff, a solid lineup of draft beer and hearty British pub fare make this downtown bar a sensible choice for a coupla pints. Live music and trivia nights are regulars. Plus, there's always a Friday night fish-and-chips special. Plenty of North American munchies on the menu too.

ⓘ Information

Ontario Travel Information Centre (☑ 519-973-1338; www.ontariotravel.net; 110 Park St E; ⊕ 9am-5pm) Well stocked with brochures and helpful staff.
Tourism Windsor Essex (☑ 800-265-3633; www.visitwindsoressex.com; 333 Riverside Dr W, Suite 103; ⊕ 8:30am-4:30pm Mon-Fri) Information on Windsor and the area; best accessed from Pitt St.

ⓘ Getting There & Away

Detroit–Windsor is a major international border crossing, via either the famously expansive **Ambassador Bridge** (www.ambassadorbridge. com; Hwy 3; toll $6.25, US$5), or the **Detroit–Windsor Tunnel** (www.dwtunnel.com; Freedom Way; toll $4.75-6.25, US$4.50-5) connecting the two downtowns. **Transit Windsor** (☑ 519-944-4111; www.citywindsor.ca) runs the Tunnel Bus to Detroit ($5, 30 minutes, every 30 minutes 5:30am to 12:30am) – bring your passport.

Windsor Train Station (☑ 888-842-7245; www.viarail.ca; 298 Walker Rd), 3km east of downtown, has trains to Toronto ($70, four to 4½ hours, four daily) via London ($43, two hours).

Amherstburg
☑ 519 / POP 21,950
War of 1812 and Underground Railroad buffs will find some enthralling diversions in historic Amherstburg, a charming town south of Windsor, where the Detroit River flows into Lake Erie – although much more happened here in the past than of late.

⊙ Sights

Amherstburg Freedom Museum　　　　　　　　MUSEUM
(☑ 800-713-6336; www.amherstburgfreedom. org; 277 King St; adult/student $7.50/6.50; ⊕ noon-5pm Tue-Fri, from 1pm Sat & Sun; 🄿) This history museum explores the role of Amherstburg as the destination of many escaped slaves on the Underground Railroad, their experiences before arriving and

> ### THE UNDERGROUND RAILROAD
> ....
> Neither subterranean nor an actual railroad, the Underground Railroad refers to the secretive web of abolitionists and humanitarians – both black and white – who shepherded, sheltered, hid and transported escaped slaves north from the USA to freedom in Canada. It's estimated that before the American Civil War 40,000 brave souls made the dangerous journey. This part of southwestern Ontario, so close to the US border, is rich with historic Underground Railroad sites. Many local towns have substantial populations descended from those African Americans who found sanctuary here.
>
> Historical sights include Uncle Tom's Cabin Historic Site, Amherstburg Freedom Museum (p153), **John Freeman Walls Historic Site** (☑ 519-727-6555; www.undergroundrailroadmuseum.org; 855 Puce Rd, Emeryville; $5; ⊕ 10am-3pm Tue-Sat May-Oct; 🄿) and The Griffin House (p133). For more information visit www.blackhistorysociety.ca.

the communities they built. The highlight is the **Nazrey African Methodist Episcopal Church**, a National Historic Site, which was built by former slaves. The Taylor Log Cabin also sits on the site, an example of the modest homes many African Americans in Canada lived in during the late 1880s.

Fort Malden
National Historic Site   HISTORIC SITE
(☑519-736-5416; www.pc.gc.ca; 100 Laird Ave; adult/child $4/free; ⊙10am-5pm late May-early Oct; P🚻) This British fort was built on earthwork embankments along the river in 1840. Beginning with the arrival of the fur traders, the area saw a lot of friction between the French, First Nations and English and, later, the Americans. Here, during the War of 1812, British Major-General Brock (together with his ally, Shawnee Chief Tecumseh) conspired to take Detroit.

Knowledgeable staffers in period military garb answer questions and give musket demos.

🛏 Sleeping & Eating

Bondy House B&B   B&B $$
(☑519-736-9433; www.bondyhouse.com; 199 Dalhousie St; d from $140; P❄🛜) You can take a short stroll to the lake or just enjoy the large lily pond garden at this beautifully maintained Victorian house. The Tree Top Turret and Captain's Room are the most appealing with simple, elegant decor and polished wood floors, but all five rooms are comfortable.

The owners are warm and accommodating hosts.

Lord Amherst Pub   PUB FOOD $
(☑519-713-9165; www.lordamherst.ca; 273 Dalhousie St; mains $10-17; ⊙11:30am-9pm Sun-Thu, to 2am Fri-Sat) Fancy, delicious pub meals and top-shelf beers make this quaint, historic watering hole a lovely diversion from your heritage adventures.

Artisan Grill   CANADIAN $$
(☑519-713-9009; www.artisangrill.ca; 269 Dalhousie St; meals $12-34; ⊙11am-10pm Sun-Thu, to 11pm Fri & Sat) A casual fine restaurant serving upmarket sandwiches and salads, along with steaks and seafood. The lobster grilled cheese is heavenly. Eat in the sunny, modern dining room or on the breezy patio in back.

❶ Information

Amherstburg Visitors Information Centre
(☑519-730-1309; www.amherstburg.ca; 268 Dalhousie St; ⊙8:30am-4:30pm Mon-Fri, 9am-5pm Sat & Sun late May-Oct) This waterfront office can point you in the right direction for your historical research.

❶ Getting There & Away

You'll need your own wheels to get to Amherstburg. **Amherstburg Taxi** (☑519-736-2449; www.amherstburgtaxi.ca; ⊙24/7) can take you to Windsor, the nearest larger town, for around $55.

Leamington & Pelee Island

An agricultural center once known as the 'Tomato Capital of Ontario,' lakeside Leamington is where people typically come to catch the ferry to Pelee Island. Southeast of town, Point Pelee National Park (the southernmost point of mainland Canada) is a pit stop for thousands of migratory birds, making it a birder's paradise.

Fluttering clouds of monarch butterflies also rest here in the fall on their way to Mexico.

Canada's southernmost outpost, Pelee Island is a surprising, sleepy oasis in the middle of Lake Erie. In 1788 the Ojibwe and Ottawa Nations leased it to Thomas McKee, though it remained undeveloped until William McCormick bought it in 1823. By 1900 Pelee had 800 residents, four churches and four schools. These days there are just 235 residents and not much else. Life revolves around a very relaxed and humble form of tourism. Oh-so-green and surrounded by sandy beaches and shallow water, it's a place to get away from it all without leaving the province.

⊙ Sights

★**Point Pelee National Park**   PARK
(☑519-322-2365; www.pc.gc.ca; 1118 Point Pelee Dr, Leamington; adult/child $8/free; ⊙park dawn-dusk, visitor center 10am-6pm Mon-Fri, to 7pm Sat & Sun Jun-Aug, reduced hours rest of year; P🚻) About 13km southeast of Leamington, this well-loved national park features nature trails, a marsh boardwalk, lookout towers, forests and lovely sandy beaches. A bird-watcher's paradise, over 390 species of birds call this home, depending on the season. In the fall, the mi-

gration of monarch butterflies is a spectacle of swirling black and orange. Trekking, biking, kayaking and beachcombing are all great ways to explore the park.

Stop by the visitor centre for more info and maps.

The park boasts the title of being the southernmost tip of mainland Canada. (And a 'tip' it is! Like a pencil point.) It's also a Dark Sky Preserve; check the website for evening events or stay overnight in one of the park's tricked-out oTENTiks (tent/cabin hybrids) and see the stars all night. Kayaks and canoes can be rented at the Marsh Boardwalk.

Fish Point
Provincial Nature Reserve   PARK
(☑519-825-4659; www.ontarioparks.com/park/fishpoint; 1750 McCormick Rd, Pelee Island; ⊙dawn-dusk; ℙ) This long sandy spit is the southernmost point of *inhabited* Canada (there are some tiny rock islands – like humps of whales skimming the water – just to the south). A 3.2km-return flat forest path leads to the point, one of the island's best swimming spots. It's a bird-watcher's Eden, with black-crowned night herons and a multitude of shorebirds.

Pelee Island Heritage Centre   MUSEUM
(☑519-724-2291; www.peleeislandmuseum.ca; 1073 West Shore Rd, Pelee Island; adult/child $4/2; ⊙10am-4pm May-Oct; ℙ) Near West Dock, the small Pelee Island Heritage Centre has one of the best natural history collections in Ontario. Engrossing displays cover early indigenous to 20th-century history, geology, wildlife, industry, sailing and shipwrecks. Located across from the ferry dock, in what once was the town hall.

🛏 Sleeping & Eating

★Wandering Dog Inn   INN $$
(☑519-724-2270; https://thewanderingdoginn.com; 1060 East West Rd, Pelee Island; r with shared bath from $100, ste from $175; ℙ❄) A charming 125-year old farmhouse with seven cozy rooms, all decorated in a simple country style. All share four full bathrooms – there's rarely a wait – plus a lounge with loads of board games and books. For a bit more privacy, opt for a suite. In a separate building, rooms have private bathrooms plus screened-in porches with hammocks and grills.

Just steps from the beach.

Point Pelee National Park   TENTED CAMP $$
(☑519-322-2365; www.pc.gc.ca; 1118 Point Pelee Dr, Leamington; up to 6 people $120; ℙ) Sleep in tall forests in a comfortable oTENTik, a tented A-frame on a raised wood floor. Each sleeps six on comfy foam beds, has an eating/lounging area plus a grill (and a wildlife-proof food storage locker). Even tableware is included. And did we mention the porch with Adirondack chairs? In winter, a wood stove warms up the place by remote control.

★The Bakery   DELI $
(☑519-724-2321; www.theislandbakery.ca; 5 Northshore Dr, Pelee Island; sandwiches from $7; ⊙8:30am-7pm Mon & Thu, to 4pm Tue, to 9pm Fri-Sun May-Oct) Stop at this tiny house turned bakery/deli/pizzeria for hearty wraps and salads, pizza and all manner of baked goods (cinnamon buns, anyone?). Coffee drinks – even the fancy stuff – are sold too. Eat at one the picnic tables on the leafy lakefront property or take your eats to go. A treat!

🍷 Drinking & Nightlife

Stonehouse 1891   PUB
(☑519-724-1100; http://stonehouse1891.com; 1115 W Shore Rd, Pelee Island; ⊙11:30am-9pm Sun, Wed & Thu, to 10pm Fri-Sat, to 4pm Mon) Originally a family home, then a liquor store frequented by Al Capone's Purple Gang during Prohibition, today the Stonehouse is an upmarket bar serving craft beers and farm-to-table pub grub. Just steps from the ferry dock, it's a popular spot to wind down.

On weekends, come here for live music and general revelry.

ℹ Information

➡ For information on Leamington, go to https://visitwindsoressex.com/leamington.

➡ All there is to know about Pelee Island can be found at www.pelee.org. Book ferries and accommodations in advance. Services and amenities are limited, including internet access.

ℹ Getting There & Away

Christened in 2019, the *Pelee Islander II* is a multistoried ferry servicing its namesake island. (The original *Pelee Islander* still chugs its way across too.) The ferries depart the Leamington marina from April to December; at other times, you'll need a plane. Note: many of the island roads are unpaved.

Ontario Ferries (Pelee Island Transportation; ☑ 800-661-2220, 519-724-2154; www.ontario ferries.com; Erie St S, Leamington; ◑ Apr–early Dec) services the island from Leamington, Kingsville and Sandusky, OH. Schedules depend on the day and season; reservations are essential in the summer. The trip takes 1½ hours each way. In winter, forget it.

❶ Getting Around

Bicycles can be rented at **Comfortech Bicycle Rentals** (☑ 519-724-2828; www.peleebikeren tal.com; 1023 West Shore Rd, Pelee Island; per hour/day/week $10/25/100; ◑ Apr–Oct) near the West Dock.

Port Stanley

☑ 226, 519, 548 / POP 2150

A working fishing village in a nook of Kettle Creek, Port Stanley has a pretty downtown, pleasant beach, and an agreeable, unpretentious atmosphere: it's the kind of place where people talk to you in the streets.

The only way to get to Port Stanley is with your own transport. Parking at the beach costs $2 for 30 minutes, to a maximum of $10, and is free after 5pm. Fees are charged from May to October only.

**Port Stanley
Terminal Rail**   RAIL
(☑ 519-782-3730; www.pstr.on.ca; 309 Bridge St; adult/child $15/9; ◑ 10am-4pm Apr-Dec; ⛟) Rail buffs and the young at heart can enjoy up to 22km of the historic London–Port Stanley railroad. Rides last 60 to 90 minutes and are sometimes paired with seasonal themes like Easter or fall colors. The schedule varies: check the website for details.

Inn on the Harbour   INN $$
(☑ 519-782-7623; www.innontheharbour.net; 202 Main St; d $149-259; P◑❄🛜) Watch fishing boats come and go, offloading baskets of perch and pickerel, from this upmarket, maritime-hewn inn. A handful of themed suites – Out of Africa, French Provincial and Oriental – offer a taste (albeit a stereotypical one) of far-off places.

Port Dover & Around

Port Dover is a summer-centric beach town with a sandy, laid-back vibe. Sunburned midlifers, bikini-clad teens and ice-cream-dripping kids patrol the main drag on summer vacation. Good bird-watching and swimming make it a hot spot for outdoor types; for those who like the wind in their flowing locks, there are the massive, quirky Friday the 13th motorcycle meet-ups every Black Friday, when sleepy Port Dover turns noisy and social.

◉ Sights

Long Point Provincial Park   PARK
(☑ 519-586-2133; www.ontarioparks.com; 350 Erie Blvd, Port Rowan; admission per car $12.25, campsites from $38; ◑ May-Oct; P⛟) This excellent provincial park, 47km southwest of Port Dover, occupies a 1.5km sandy spit jagging into the lake, great for swimming, fishing and camping.

**Delhi Tobacco
Museum & Heritage Centre**   MUSEUM
(☑ 519-582-0278; www.delhimuseum.ca; 200 Talbot Rd, Delhi; by donation; ◑ 10am-4:30pm Mon-Fri, 1-4pm Sun; P) The flat, sandy soils of northern Norfolk County between Port Dover and Port Stanley provide ideal growing conditions for alternative crops – what used to be a strictly tobacco-growing area now also supports hemp and ginseng fields. For a sniff of old 'baccy, take Hwy 3 30 minutes inland, northwest from Port Dover, to this wooden-crate, leaf-filled multicultural museum with displays on local history and tobacco production.

Turkey Point Provincial Park   PARK
(☑ 519-426-3239; www.ontarioparks.com; 194 Turkey Point Rd, Turkey Point; admission per car $12.25, campsites from $38; ◑ May-Oct; P) Southwest along the coast is this provincial park with a handful of hiking trails and campsites. Its forests teem with bird nerds and nature lovers.

✲ Festivals & Events

Friday the 13th   CULTURAL
(www.pd13.com) The out-of-the-ordinary but huge Friday the 13th motorcycle festival sees hundreds of Harley Davidson lovers converge on Port Dover each Black Friday. As one of the largest meets of its kind in the world, with up to 150,000 motorcycle enthusiasts converging from across North America, it's definitely a spectacle. Book accommodations in advance and expect inflated prices.

⛺ Sleeping

Dover House B&B   B&B $$
(☑ 519-583-3654; https://doverhousebb.ca; 17 Morgan St; d with shared bath $139-149, d $149-159; P🛜) A charming country house located at

the end of a quiet cul-de-sac. Rooms are flowery and well appointed, some with fireplaces, others with bay windows. Gourmet breakfast includes fresh-baked pastries and local produce. The beach is about a 10- to 15-minute walk away – a deal breaker for some.

ℹ️ Getting There & Away

You will need a vehicle to get here as there is no public transport.

MUSKOKA LAKES

The city of Barrie marks the end of Toronto's suburban sprawl and the gateway to the Muskoka Lakes region, although pleasant, lakeside Barrie can feel like just another Toronto suburb at times.

The Muskoka Lakes (or just Muskoka) is a broader name for the region comprising Lakes Muskoka, Rosseau and Joseph, among many smaller others. Originally rich in lumber production and shipbuilding, the area is now at the heart of 'cottage country': a popular place for families to enjoy the water and, for many, to retire. Ontario's most extravagant cottages are here, many in the fabulous 'Millionaires' Row' on Lake Muskoka. Schedule a few days to explore the beauty and serenity of this forested, watery region, which is particularly delightful in the fall.

It's worth stopping at the large **Ontario Travel Information Centre** (☑705-725-7280; www.ontariotravel.net; 21 Mapleview Dr E, Barrie; ◷9am-5pm; 🛜), along Hwy 400 as you approach the lakes, to arm yourself with maps and brochures for the region.

Though there's a small airport, there's limited public transportation and no car rental agencies in the region. Instead, it is best explored by car: check out www.discover muskoka.ca/driving-tours. Note that Friday northbound traffic (from Toronto) and southbound Sunday traffic on Hwy 400 can be a nightmare from May to October.

Ontario Northland (☑800-363-7512, 705-472-4500; www.ontarionorthland.ca) Buses travel from Toronto to many towns in the Muskoka region, typically a few times per day.

Muskoka Airport (CYQA; ☑705-687-2194; www.muskoka.on.ca; Hwy 11) Two small airlines provide service to and from Toronto from May to October. Best if you're meeting someone with a set of wheels.

Orillia

☑249, 705 / POP 31,130

Orillia proudly sits at the northern end of Lake Simcoe, which pours into Lake Couchiching. Neither is technically part of the Muskoka Lakes, but both are major stops along the Trent-Severn Waterway. Triangular sails and grumbling motorboats clutter the harbor, while drivers turn off Hwy 11 for a stroll down time-warped Mississaga St, Orillia's main drag.

◎ Sights & Activities

Coldwater Canadiana Heritage Museum   MUSEUM

(☑705-955-1930; www.coldwatermuseum.com; 1474 Woodrow Rd, Coldwater; by donation; ◷10am-4pm Mon-Sat late May-Oct) Halfway between Orillia and Midland, on Hwy 12 before it connects with Hwy 400, you'll find this charming riverside folk museum with its sweet collection of colonial buildings tracing the history of village life from 1830 to 1950.

Island Princess   CRUISE

(☑705-325-2628; www.obcruise.com; 220 Mississaga St E; from $25; ◷Jun-Oct) Orillia offers a variety of sightseeing cruises on the *Island Princess*, though Penetanguishene and Parry Sound have more picturesque cruising options. There are up to four cruises daily here in July and August; most last between 1½ and 2½ hours. Lunch and dinner cruises require advance booking: check the website for cruise types, schedules and fares.

🛏️ Sleeping & Eating

Lakeside Inn Orillia   MOTEL $$

(☑705-325-2514; www.lakesideinnorillia.ca; 86 Creighton St S; d $70-130; 🅿️❄️🛜) Run by a young couple, this renovated '60s-era motel offers simple rooms with wood floors, good beds and cozy comforters. Each has a private balcony or porch with gorgeous views of Lake Simcoe. A spa was in the work at the time of research.

Stone Gate Inn   HOTEL $$

(☑705-329-2535; www.stonegateinn.com; 437 Laclie St; r incl breakfast from $145; 🅿️❄️🛜) Though the decor could use a refresh (flower patterns figure prominently), it's the extra perks that set this modern inn apart from the rest: a swimming pool, full business center and hors d'oeuvres on Friday evenings. Some rooms even have fireplaces and Jacuzzis.

Anne's Cranberry House B&B B&B $$
(📞705-326-6871; www.orillia.org/cranberryhouse; 25 Dalton Cres S; d incl breakfast from $145; P❄🛜) This B&B sits on a quiet street that feels a lot like the set for the TV show *The Wonder Years*. Every house seems tidy and welcoming, and Cranberry House is no exception. Rooms have a country cottage feel with flowered wallpaper, porcelain lamps and original landscape art.

Mariposa Market MARKET $
(📞705-325-8885; www.mariposamarket.ca; 109 Mississaga St E; items from $3; ⏱7am-6pm Mon-Sat, 8am-5:30pm Sun) This half-bakery, half-knickknack shack is a feast for the eyes and the taste buds. Try the assortment of savory pastries for a light lunch, grab a dessert, then shop for souvenirs.

ℹ️ Getting There & Away

Ontario Northland (📞705-326-4101; http://ontarionorthland.ca; 150 Front St S; $31) provides bus service between Orillia and Toronto ($31, 2¼ hours, three to four daily).

Gravenhurst

📍249, 705 / POP 12,310

While nearby Bracebridge is favored among visitors, Gravenhurst is coming into its own. Check out Muskoka Wharf, a postmillennial waterfront development including shops, restaurants, condos, a farmers bazaar and a museum.

⊙ Sights

⭐**Muskoka Steamships & Discovery Centre** MUSEUM
(📞705-687-2115; www.realmuskoka.com; 275 Steamship Bay Rd; adult/child $14/9; ⏱9am-6pm Mon-Fri, to 4pm Sat & Sun Jun-Nov, 9am-4pm Tue-Sun Dec-May; P♿) This well-conceived museum tells the region's rich history of the First Nations people who lived here, the European settlers and loggers who displaced them, and the steamships, hoteliers and 'cottage country' that followed. One room is dedicated to Muskoka's remarkable ecosystem and biodiversity. Exhibits integrate touch-screens and hands-on elements, including recreations of a steamship and lakefront hotel and experiments with mini-watersheds. Don't miss a tour of the boathouse, with North America's largest collection of antique boats.

Admission is free for visitors who take a cruise on one of the Centre's steamships: the *Segwun*, the oldest operating steamship in North America (1887), and the *Wenonah II*, a modern cruiser with an old-school design. In a past life, the *Segwun* was a mail ship serving secluded Muskoka enclaves. A variety of cruises are available; check the website for details.

🛏️ Sleeping & Eating

Four Ninety B&B B&B $$
(📞905-717-0172; www.fourninetymuskoka.com; 490 Phillip St E; r $159, with shared bath $129-149; P🚭❄🛜) Facing Gull Lake, Four Ninety offers just three rooms, all with luxurious beds and beach decor. Two rooms share a bathroom and are themselves quite small; a private deck with lake views in one, and murals that evoke the feeling of steamer ship travel in the other, make up for it. A hot tub and manicured gardens are big pluses.

Residence Inn Muskoka Wharf HOTEL $$
(📞705-687-6600; www.marriott.com; 285 Steamship Bay Rd; d/ste incl breakfast from $149/179; P❄🛜🏊) If you want to be by the water, it's hard to get closer than this hulking property in the Muskoka Wharf complex offering large, contemporary studios and suites with full kitchens, separate living and sleeping areas and generous bathrooms. Some have balconies and lake views. Rates include buffet breakfast, and spike in peak periods.

Taboo Muskoka RESORT $$$
(📞705-687-2233; www.tabooresort.com; 1209 Muskoka Beach Rd; d from $260; P❄🛜🏊) Occupying a stunning lake frontage on a compact peninsula, Taboo's rooms have clean, minimalist lines, gray and maple woods, and slick bathrooms with designer bath products. Lots of options for play – three pools, a golf course, tennis courts, nature trails, not to mention a private beach and the lake itself – make this perfect if you're bringing the kids.

Pizza Station PIZZA $
(📞705-687-3111; www.facebook.com/pizzastationcanada; 415 Bethune Dr N; small pizzas from $8; ⏱10am-10pm Mon-Thu, to 11pm Fri-Sat; ♿) Locals swear by this nondescript pizza joint for its steaming-hot cheesy goodness with just the right amount of toppings and a crispy, crunchy crust. Take out and eat by the water.

ℹ Information

Gravenhurst Chamber of Commerce (☑ 705-687-4432; www.gravenhurstchamber.com; 275 Muskoka Rd S; ⊙ 9am-5pm Mon-Fri) is located in the basement of the Services Ontario building. There's a Visitor Information Lounge with loads of brochures on the ground level, which is staffed during the summer months. Additional information can be found at www.gravenhurst.ca.

ℹ Getting There & Away

Ontario Northland (☑ 705-687-2301; www.ontarionorthland.ca; 150 Second St S) runs buses between Toronto and Gravenhurst ($41, three hours, three to four daily) on the North Bay route, which pull in to the Gravenhurst Train Station. Trains have not served the region for years.

Bracebridge

☑ 705 / POP 9,230

Woodsy Bracebridge sits on the 45th parallel, halfway between the North Pole and the equator! This enchanting town reveals its natural charms throughout the year, with towering evergreens, gushing waterfalls and brilliant maples.

◉ Sights & Activities

Bracebridge Falls　　　　WATERFALL
(off Ecclestone Dr) Near the visitor center you'll find the best known of Bracebridge's 22 waterfalls, Bracebridge Falls. Though this one is artificial – it was created as part of the town dam – some naturally made faves include **Muskoka South Falls**, about 6km south of town, and **Wilson's Falls**, 2.5km to the north.

Lady Muskoka　　　　BOATING
(☑ 705-646-2628; www.ladymuskoka.com; 300 Ecclestone Dr; cruises adult/child from $39/17; ⊙ May-Oct) Muskoka's largest cruise ship takes in the beauty of Lake Muskoka, including jaw-dropping 'Millionaires' Row', where the other half relax. A variety of sailings, including sunset dinner cruises, is available.

🍴 Sleeping & Eating

★ Tipi Adventure　　　TENTED CAMP $$
(☑ 705-706-7125; https://tipiadventure.ca; 1345 Beatrice Townline Rd; d from $110; ℗) Glamp it up in a tipi in the middle of 32 hectares of dense forest. Each is set up on a platform with bunk-style cots, murals and heaters for cold nights. There's a swimming pond and trails for exploring, plus there is a fire pit for roasting marshmallows (firewood provided).

A guest kitchen and spick-and-span bathrooms make it *almost* feel like home.

★ Griffin Gastropub　　　GASTROPUB $$
(☑ 705-646-0438; www.facebook.com/GriffinGastropub; 9 Chancery Lane; ⊙ noon-2am Wed-Sat, to 8pm Sun) Tucked into an alley just off the main drag, this small British-style pub serves up hearty, locally sourced meals – the charcuterie board is ah-mazing – and a well-chosen lineup of craft beers and cider.

Trivia nights on weekdays and live music on weekends make this a local fave.

Old Station　　　PUB FOOD $$
(☑ 705-645-9776; www.theoldstation.ca; 88 Manitoba St; mains $15-24; ⊙ 11:30am-8:30pm Mon-Thu, to 9pm Fri & Sat, to 8pm Sun) On summer evenings this is the most happening place in town. The patio overlooks the main drag – perfect for postkayak recovery sessions. Dig into a candied bacon burger and wash it back with a pint of Muskoka ale from the **brewery** (☑ 705-646-1266; www.muskokabrewery.com; 1964 Muskoka Beach Rd; ⊙ 10am-6pm Mon-Tue & Thu, to 7pm Wed & Fri-Sun) just down the road.

Riverwalk Restaurant　　MEDITERRANEAN $$$
(☑ 705-646-0711; www.riverwalkrestaurant.ca; 3 Ecclestone Dr; mains lunch $14-20, dinner $28-39; ⊙ 11:30am-2:30pm & 5:30-7:30pm Tue-Sun) Tear your eyes away from the view of the Bracebridge Falls to focus on the menu, if you can. You'll need to choose between a creative and seasonally changing menu of pork, chicken, duck, beef, lamb or seafood. Reservations recommended.

ℹ Information

Bracebridge Visitors Centre (☑ 705-645-8121; www.bracebridge.ca; 3 Ecclestone Dr; ⊙ 9am-5pm May-Oct, 10am-5pm Sat Nov-Apr, 10am-4pm Sun Sep-Oct, closed Sun Nov-Apr) Open year-round.

ℹ Getting There & Away

Ontario Northland (☑ 705-646-2239; www.ontarionorthland.ca; 300 Ecclestone Dr) buses connect Bracebridge with Toronto ($43, 3 to 3½ hours, three to four daily) on the North Bay route.

Rosseau & Port Carling

You may pass through these sleepy villages on the way elsewhere. Rosseau is a quaint town that has a small beach, a historic library, a few antique shops and one or two cafes. It's your closest village if you choose to stay in Muskoka's luxury resort, the **Rosseau** (JW Marriott Resort & Spa; ☑ 705-765-1900; www.therosseau.com; 1050 Paignton House Rd, Minett; d/ste from $319/379; P♿❄🐾📶🏊).

North of Bracebridge along Rte 118, in wealthy Port Carling, is a remarkable 33-by-14-meter **mural** of the famous RMS *Sagamo*, the 19th-century steamship still in operation in Gravenhurst. A closer glance reveals that the mural is actually a mosaic of more than 9000 vintage photographs, telling the story of the first hundred years of the town. Worth a stop.

Just a 15-minute drive south of Port Carling, **Muskoka Lakes Farm & Winery** (☑ 705-762-3203; https://cranberry.ca; 1074 Cranberry Rd, Bala; tastings/tours $7/17; ⊙ 10am-6pm Jul-Oct, to 5pm Nov-Jun) is well worth a stop. At this family-run cranberry farm, you'll learn about these hearty cold-weather berries and taste the wines they produce (who knew?).

Huntsville

☑ 249, 705 / POP 19,820

Pretty Huntsville, Muskoka's largest town, set among twisting lakes and furry pines, is the gateway to Algonquin Provincial Park in eastern Ontario. Base yourself here for day trips to the park, around Muskoka, or before setting off on an Algonquin adventure, although you'll need your own wheels.

👁 Sights

Group of Seven Outdoor Gallery PUBLIC ART
Thirty-six beautiful murals, reproductions of Ontario landscapes painted by Tom Thomson and the famous Group of Seven artists he inspired, are a highlight of a stroll through the center of town. Granted, they're copies, but ones that hopefully encourage viewers to search out the real deal. Self-guided tour information is available at the chamber of commerce.

Muskoka Heritage Place MUSEUM
(☑ 705-789-7576; www.muskokaheritageplace. org; 88 Brunel Rd; adult/child $18/12; ⊙ 10am-4pm, pioneer village & train May-Oct,; P🚉) Come here for a historical perspective of the region, which includes an authentic pioneer village with staff in period dress, a small but informative history museum and a working steam train from 1902 (departs several times per day; rides included in admission).

🎉 Festivals & Events

Festival of the Arts ART
(☑ 705-789-4975; www.huntsvillefestival.on.ca)
This arts organization brings theater and dance performances, concerts, films and art exhibits to venues around town. Art workshops are offered too. Check the website for the schedule and to buy tickets.

🛏 Sleeping

Huntsville Inn MOTEL $
(☑ 866-222-8525; http://huntsvilleinn.com; 19 King William St; d from $75; ❄📶) In a prime location by the bridge, these dated but comfortable rooms have flat-screen TVs and free wi-fi. Excellent value.

Knights Inn Motel MOTEL $
(☑ 705-789-4414; www.knightsinn.ca; 69 Main St W; d incl breakfast $75-90; P❄📶) In a nice hillside spot across the road from the lake and a short walk to downtown, this quality motel includes breakfast in a sunny common room. There is also a picnic area and in-room mini-fridges and microwaves. Ask for a room on the 2nd floor for the best views.

Echo Woods B&B B&B $$
(☑ 705-784-9800; http://echowoodsbedandbreak fast.com; 226 Echo Bay Rd; r incl breakfast $159-199; P❄📶) Three tastefully appointed rooms with luxurious bathrooms make up this welcoming and cozy B&B. Gourmet breakfast is served on the breezy deck with views of the thick Muskoka forest. The affable owners are a font of information.

Hidden Valley Resort RESORT $$
(☑ 705-789-2301; www.hvmuskoka.com; 1755 Valley Rd; d from $89; P❄📶🏊) Most of the well-proportioned, updated rooms in this '90s-style resort have a balcony with a wonderful vista of the lake and the expansive, well-tended grounds. There's a restaurant with a fabulous patio, outdoor and indoor pools and even a small ski-hill nearby. A $10-per-room resort fee is added each night.

The resort is located 8km north of Huntsville.

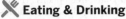 Eating & Drinking

Westside Fish & Chips
CAFE **$**

(☑ 705-789-7200; https://westsidefishandchips.com; 126 Main St W; $7-14; ⊙ 8am-8pm; 🅿) A family-run cafe serving home-style breakfast, burgers and sandwiches and a full lineup of light and crispy fish-and-chips. Take a seat in the dainty dining room or share a picnic table on the patio with fellow diners. If there's a long line, take your eats to go.

Farmer's Daughter
MARKET **$**

(☑ 705-789-5700; https://fresheverything.ca; 118 Hwy 60; items from $5; ⊙ 9am-6pm Mon-Sat, 10am-5pm Sun; 🅿🐾) Specializing in local and organic produce, this gourmet market also has an excellent prepared-foods section integrating seasonal produce as well as wild and foraged foods. Lots of vegan and gluten-free options too. A perfect place to stock up for a picnic hike or food for the road.

That Little Place by the Lights
ITALIAN **$**

(☑ 705-789-2536; www.thatlittleplacebythelights.ca; 76 Main St E; mains $8-16; ⊙ 10am-9:30pm Mon-Sat; 🐾) A local favorite, this little place by the lights is loved for its old-school pizzas, pastas and gelati. Excellent value.

Mill on Main
CANADIAN **$$**

(☑ 705-788-5150; www.themillonmain.ca; 50 Main St E; mains $13-18; ⊙ 11am-9pm Sun-Thu, to 1am Fri & Sat) With a lovely covered patio offering glimpses of the water and some classy original twists on old favorites, the Mill is a good spot for a casual meal or a few drinks. Try the wings – you won't regret it. Live music on weekends.

ℹ Information

Hunstville/Lake of Bays Chamber of Commerce (☑ 705-789-4771; www.huntsville.ca; 5 Brunel Rd; ⊙ 8:30am-4:30pm Mon-Fri) is loaded with info. An information booth (open 9am to 5pm) is also staffed during the summer months; look for the little red booth at the corner of Main and Brunel Sts.

ℹ Getting There & Away

Ontario Northland (☑ 705-789-6431; www.ontarionorthland.ca; 225 Main St W) has buses from Toronto to Huntsville ($54, 3½ to 4½ hours, three or four daily), but there is no onward public transport to the Algonquin Provincial Park.

Parkbus (p117) runs a good-value, seasonal service from Toronto to Algonquin Provincial Park ($97 return, three to four hours). It is infrequent and popular – book in advance.

GEORGIAN BAY

A vast realm of blues and greens, Georgian Bay is a land of infinite dreaming. Summer breezes blow gently along sandy shores. Maples ignite in the fall and thick pines quiver at winter's frosty kiss. These ethereal landscapes inspired Canada's best-known painters and today the bay remains home to scores of thriving artistic communities.

In the bay's southern arc sits Wasaga Beach, the longest freshwater beach in the world. Neighboring Collingwood and Blue Mountain are home to the province's most popular winter skiing.

Heading north on its western shore from Owen Sound, the magnificent Bruce Peninsula is famed for its jagged limestone outcrops, shimmering cliffs and craggy beaches. It boasts tiny but impressive Tobermory and, beyond, Manitoulin Island. Linger here for a few days if you can.

ℹ Getting There & Away

This area's long distances require a set of wheels and a strong desire for a road trip. They also make the Parkbus (p117) routes, particularly to the Bruce Peninsula, an excellent and popular summer option, so book ahead.

Parry Sound
☑ 249, 705 / POP 6400

Formerly a busy shipping port, little Parry Sound is gently tucked behind 30,000 tiny islands in Georgian Bay – the largest concentration of freshwater islands in the world. The atmosphere is laid-back and serene, despite the giant set of railroad tracks soaring overhead near the docks.

◉ Sights & Activities

Stockey Centre & Bobby Orr Hall of Fame
MUSEUM

(☑ 705-746-4466; www.bobbyorrhalloffame.com; 2 Bay St; adult/child $9/6; ⊙ 10am-6pm May-Oct, to 4pm Mon-Sat Nov-Apr; 🚹) For the uninitiated: local legend and hockey hero Bobby Orr forever changed the role of defensemen with his awesome offensive prowess. At his huge modern shrine, fans can pretend to be a sports announcer, strap on goalie gear and confront an automated puck-firing machine, or even shoot on digital NHL goalies and be heckled by the machine.

White Squall WATER SPORTS
(☑ 705-342-5324; www.whitesquall.com; 53 E Carling Bay Rd, Nobel; rentals from $29, day tours from $165; ☉ 9am-5:30pm Apr-Oct; ⊛) Explore the area's waterways with rental kayaks, canoes and stand-up paddleboards, or as part of a guided tour: friendly staff offer a range of programs. HQ is about 15km northwest of Parry Sound on Cole Lake, en route to Killbear Provincial Park.

Island Queen CRUISE
(☑ 800-506-2628; https://islandqueencruise.com; 9 Bay St; 2hr morning cruises adult/child $36/18, 3hr afternoon cruises $46/23, 2½hr Huckleberry Island tours $46/23; ☉ Jun-Oct) Cruise through the nearby 30,000 islands (that's right!) on the good ship *Island Queen*.

Alternatively, take the *Islander* speedboat to Huckleberry Island for a guided hike with a Georgian Bay Biosphere Reserve naturalist.

⚝ Festivals & Events

Festival of the Sound MUSIC
(www.festivalofthesound.ca; ☉ mid-Jul–mid-Aug) Since 1979, Parry Sound has hosted a nationally renowned festival of classical music from mid-July to mid-August. Two weekends of jazz and folk music shake things up a bit, as do Island Queen cruises with live music. Ticket prices vary.

🛏 Sleeping & Eating

Bayside Inn B&B $$
(☑ 705-746-7720; www.psbaysideinn.com; 10 Gibson St; r $153-173; P ⊕ ✳ @) Built in the 1880s as a luxurious private residence, this refurbished estate is full of pleasant surprises, including a twisting staircase behind the fireplace and 12 beautiful bedrooms with memory-foam mattresses. All rooms have en suite baths and are decorated in soothing colors.

★ The Kart FOOD TRUCK $
(☑ 705-791-2453; www.thekart.ca; 30 Pine Dr; mains $5-17; ☉ 10:30am-7pm Jun-Oct, to 3pm Apr-May; ⊿⊛) You'll find some of the region's tastiest burgers, sausages and poutine at this tidy red food truck in the parking lot of

a Canadian Tire. Ingredients are fresh and upmarket and there is a decent variety of vegetarian and gluten-free options. The remarkable number of condiments – a table's worth of bottles, jars, and shakers – is a major plus.

ⓘ Information

West Parry Sound Visitor Information Centre (☑ 705-746-4466; 2 Bay St; ☉ 10am-6pm, to 4pm Mon-Sat Nov-Apr) has loads of brochures and area maps.

ⓘ Getting There & Away

Ontario Northland (www.ontarionorthland. ca) runs buses that connect Parry Sound with Toronto ($59, three to four hours, three daily) on the Sudbury route.

Midland & Penetanguishene

The native Huron-Ouendat people first settled the region and developed a confederacy to encourage cooperation among neighboring Indigenous tribes. This alliance attracted French explorers and Jesuit missionaries eager to save their souls. Much of Midland's fascinating history focuses on the bloody altercations between the Huron and the Christian stalwarts. Midland is also known for the more than 30 vibrant murals that have transformed downtown into an outdoor art/history lesson.

Less than 6km up the road Penetanguishene (pen-uh-*tang*-wa-sheen), a small town with a big name, makes a great base for exploring the 30,000 islands that are sprinkled around Georgian Bay. Together, they make a fine day trip or easy weekend away from Toronto.

⊙ Sights

★ Huronia Museum MUSEUM
(☑ 705-526-2844; www.huroniamuseum.com; 549 Little Lake Park Rd, Midland; adult/child $12/7.25; ☉ 9am-5pm, closed Sat & Sun Oct-May; ⊛) Don't be fooled by the dated building or displays – this museum has an impressive collection of artifacts, many related to the region's maritime history as well as the Huron and Ojibwe peoples. There's also an art gallery featuring dozens of original works by members of the Group of Seven. Be sure to leave time to poke around the excellent replica 500-year-old Huron-Ouendat settlement – a fascinating peek into the 'pre-contact' past.

Georgian Bay

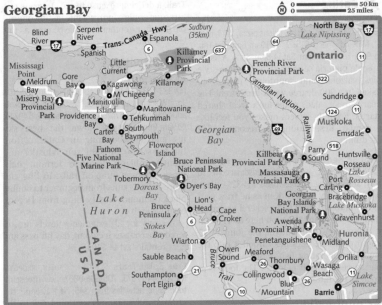

Ste-Marie among the Hurons HISTORIC SITE
(☏ 705-526-7838; www.saintemarieamongthehu
rons.on.ca; 16164 Hwy 12 East, Midland; adult/child
$12/9.25; ⊙10am-5pm May-Oct; ⊞) Costumed
staff members dote on visitors to this reconstructed 17th-century Jesuit mission, offering stories about hardship and torture with
a cheerful smile. The on-site museum offers
detailed exhibits about the site. Self-guided
audio tours also available.

A footpath connects the site to **Martyrs'
Shrine** (☏ 705-526-3788; www.martyrs-shrine.
com; 16163 Hwy 12 West, Midland; adult/child $5/
free; ⊙8am-9pm May-Oct) about 1km away.

Discovery Harbour MUSEUM
(☏ 705-549-8064; www.discoveryharbour.on.ca; 93
Jury Dr, Penetanguishene; adult/child $7/5.25;
⊙10am-5pm May-Sep; ⊞) Recommended
guided tours of this reconstructed British
naval base lead visitors through 19 buildings
and replicas of two 18th-century vessels, recounting the fort's history and the hardships
faced by sailors and officers alike.

Awenda Provincial Park PARK
(☏ 705-549-2231; www.ontarioparks.com; 670
Awenda Park Rd; day use per vehicle $11-20, camp-
ing $38-48, cottages $151; ⊙8am-10pm; ⊞)
About 15km from Penetanguishene, this picturesque park boasts four sandy swimming
beaches, 31km of easy walking trails, 17km

of backcountry ski trails and more than 200
species of birds. Cottages and camping spots
are available from May to October.

🛏 Sleeping

Midland Inn INN $$
(☏ 705-245-1166; www.midlandinn.com; 720 Pros-
pect Blvd, Midland; d from $100; P✳@🛜) A
modern two-story hotel with spacious and
squeaky-clean rooms, all with good beds,
down comforters and big flat-screen TVs.
Breakfast included. If you have lots of lug-
gage, request a room on the 1st floor (there's
no elevator).

Comfort Inn MOTEL $$
(☏ 705-526-2090; 980 King St, Midland; d from
$105; P✳@🛜🐾) Drive-up units, good dis-
counted rates and friendly staff win points
for this dated but well-maintained motel
in a leafy spot about 3km from downtown.
Breakfast included.

Georgian Terrace Guest House B&B $$
(☏ 705-549-2440; https://georgian-terrace.
business.site; 14 Water St, Penetanguishene; r incl
breakfast $150-175; P🚭✳🛜) Dramatic pil-
lars front this beautifully restored and up-
dated heritage home. Its three rooms are el-
egant without being frilly, and have en-suite
bath, wi-fi and flat-screen TVs. Two-night
minimum.

Eating

Dillon's   PIZZA $$
(☑705-245-1006; https://dillons.pizza; 244 King St, Midland; mains $15-21; ☺10am-8pm Tue-Thu, to 9pm Fri, noon-9pm Sat, 4-8pm Sun) A cozy, upscale pizzeria serving up Neapolitan-style pies, calzones and sourdough panini, all baked in a 900-degree wood-fired oven. The hearty, fresh salads make for a great shared starter. Friendly servers makes you feel like a regular. Reservations are recommended for dinner.

Captain Ken's Diner   FISH & CHIPS $$
(☑705-549-8691; www.captainkensdiner.com; 70 Main St, Penetanguishene; mains $14-32; ☺7am-9pm) Come say hello to Ken as he fries your lightly battered fresh lake pickerel to perfection. He got a part-time job here at 14 when it was a pool hall, bought the joint at 17, and over the decades has turned it into the smoothly operating fish, chips and sports-bar success story it is today. The food is as good as the tale.

❶ Information

Southern Georgian Bay Chamber of Commerce (☑705-526-7884; http://southerngeorgianbay.ca; 208 King St, Midland; ☺9am-4pm Mon-Fri) Produces the *Southern Georgian Bay Visitor Guidebook*. Download it from the website.

Tourist Office (☑705-549-2232; 2 Main St, Penetanguishene; ☺9am-6pm May-Aug, 10am-6pm Sep-Oct) You can't miss this seasonal office on Penetanguishene's dock.

❶ Getting There & Away

Linx (www.simcoe.ca) offers regular bus service from Barrie to Midland and Penetanguishene ($6, one hour, every hour 7am to 5pm Monday to Friday).

Central Taxi Midland (☑705-526-2626; www.centraltaximidland.ca) can take you between Midland and Penetanguishene (and beyond) if you don't have wheels.

Collingwood & Blue Mountain

Pretty lakeside Collingwood and neighboring Blue Mountain, a handsome ski resort and summer playground, have become a year-round mecca for those who enjoy activity with their scenery. The area is called Blue Mountains; the resort is called Blue Mountain. If outdoorsy pursuits aren't your thang, why not sink your teeth into the **Apple Pie**

Trail, a delicious excuse to see Ontario's picturesque apple country while tasting one apple pie after another and maybe even a craft cider or two.

Activities

Blue Mountain   SKIING
(☑833-583-2583; www.bluemountain.ca; 108 Jozo Weider Blvd, Blue Mountains; day lift tickets adult/child from $74/59, night lift tickets $49/44; ☺9am-9pm) Hands down the best skiing and snowboarding in Ontario, from the folks who brought you Whistler and Mont-Tremblant: freestyle terrain, half-pipes, jump-on-jump-off rails, 16 lifts and more than 43 runs from beginner to double black diamond. Night skiing from December to March.

Lessons for all experience levels are offered too; courses including day lift pass and gear rental start at $104.

Free Spirit Tours   ADVENTURE SPORTS
(☑705-446-7073, 705-606-0867; www.freespirittours.com; activities from $45; ▣) Escape the crowds and enjoy a sensational day in the Georgian Bay region rock climbing, caving, kayaking or stand-up paddleboarding in summer, or take a stab at snowshoeing in the winter. For something indoors, brewery, cidery and winery tours are offered year-round. Axe throwing, too.

🛏 Sleeping & Eating

Westin Trillium House   RESORT $$$
(☑705-443-8080; www.westinbluemountain.com; 220 Gord Canning Dr, Blue Mountain; d/ste from $369/409; ▣▣@🛜🏊🐾) Couple-friendly, pet-friendly and family-friendly, this Westin upholds its brand's reputation for excellence in service. A wide range of guest rooms and suites are all luxuriously furnished and most overlook the Blue Mountain Village, pond or outdoor pools. Experiment with your dates for the best rates and packages.

Grandma Lambe's   MARKET $
(☑519-538-2757; http://grandmalambes.com; 206570 Hwy 26, Meaford; ☺8am-6pm) You won't regret the trek to Grandma Lambe's (west on Hwy 26 just outside of Meaford). The store is a delicious jumble of maple syrup vintages, butter tarts, bushels of vegetables, and tables piled high with pies, buns and jellies.

⭐ **Tremont Cafe** EUROPEAN **$$$**

(☑ 705-293-6000; www.thetremontcafe.com; 80 Simcoe St, Collingwood; mains $16-35; ⊙ 11am-3pm & 5:30-9:30pm Wed-Mon) Come for a mouthwatering weekend brunch or classic dinner at this delightful fine-dining cafe in the historic Tremont building. Will you have the duck confit or PEI mussels after your lamb lollipops? Dinner menus change regularly.

ℹ Information

South Georgian Bay Visitor Centre (☑ 705-445-7722; www.visitsouthgeorgianbay.ca; 45 St Paul St, Collingwood; ⊙ 9am-5pm) Pop in to get inspired about the wonderful Georgian Bay region.

ℹ Getting There & Away

Colltrans (☑ 705-445-1030; www.collingwood. ca/town-services/public-transit) provides public transportation between Collingwood and Blue Mountain every 15 to 30 minutes from 7am to 9pm (adult/child $2/1.50, 20 minutes). **Ace Cabs & Kyle's Taxi** (☑ 705-445-3300; www. collingwoodtaxi.com) can drive you between Collingwood and Blue Mountain ($31, 15 minutes).

In the winter, **AUC Tours** (☑ 416-741-5200; www.auctours.com) operates a shuttle ($30, 3¼ hours) from Toronto City Hall to Blue Mountain.

Bruce Peninsula

The Bruce is a 100km limestone outcrop of craggy shorelines and green woodlands at the northern end of the Niagara Escarpment. The finger-like protrusion separates the cooler crystal waters of Georgian Bay from warmer Lake Huron. Owen Sound is the largest regional center, while delightful Tobermory is the reward at the tip of the peninsula.

Owen Sound

☑ 226, 519, 548 / POP 21,340

Owen Sound has a sordid past as a port rife with booze and prostitution. Things got so out of hand that alcohol was banned here for over 60 years – hard to believe, today. By the time the ban was lifted in 1972, the town had transformed into a thriving artists' colony and remains so today: check out the Owen Sound Artist's Co-op when you're in town.

◉ Sights

Grey Roots Museum & Archives MUSEUM

(☑ 519-376-3690; www.greyroots.com; 102599 Grey Rd 18/RR 4; adult/child $8/4; ⊙ 10am-5pm; P ♿) About 8km south of town, this interesting museum highlights the region's rich pioneering history through displays about early settlers and local heroes. Interactive presentations focus on natural resources, climate and topography. Past exhibits have explored themes as diverse as Albertan dinosaurs and the history of the toilet. Admission includes access to **Moreston Heritage Village** (May to October only), a collection of 19th century buildings – a log cabin, barn, schoolhouse, sawmill – where volunteers dressed in 19th-century garb recreate village life in pioneer days.

Owen Sound Farmers Market MARKET

(☑ 519-371-3433; www.owensoundfarmersmarket. ca; 114 8th St E; ⊙ 8am-12:30pm Sat) This co-op of vendors is one of the oldest in Ontario. Expect the freshest produce, as well as maple syrup, soaps and baked goods.

✱ Festivals & Events

Summerfolk Music Festival MUSIC

(☑ 519-371-2995; www.summerfolk.org; Kelso Beach Park, 2nd Av W; day/weekend pass from $55/125; ⊙ mid-Aug) This epic three-day folk fest in mid-August draws world-class performers and artisans from far and wide. Buy tickets in advance for a discount. Held at Kelso Beach Park, a pleasant waterfront park just north of downtown.

🛏 Sleeping & Eating

Highland Manor B&B **$$**

(☑ 519-372-2699; www.highlandmanor.ca; 867 4th Ave A W; s/d from $150/175; P ❋ @ 🛜) This magnificent Victorian mansion (c 1872) has been elegantly furnished by attentive hosts. Decadent, spacious suites all have their own bathrooms. Many have original fireplaces. Enjoy a glass of wine on the wraparound deck, or curl up by the fireplace. Highly recommended.

⭐ **Casero Kitchen Table** MEXICAN **$$**

(☑ 519-416-8226; www.caserofood.com; 946 3rd Ave E; mains $12-20; ⊙ 11:30am-3pm & 5pm-late Mon-Fri, noon-late Sat; P ✎) Set in an auto repair shop turned retro dining room, Casero offers up classic Mexican eats with a modern twist: smoked brisket tacos, crispy shrimp tortas and vegan coconut rice pudding.

Tequila and mezcal flights make a great start to a meal. *Jarritos* (flavored sodas from Mexico) are offered too.

Shorty's Grill CANADIAN $$
(☑ 519-376-0044; www.shortysonline.com; 967 3rd Ave E; mains $14-39; ⊗ 11:30am-11pm Mon-Thu, to midnight Fri & Sat) Locals love Shorty's and with good reason. Appetizers like escargots, crab cakes and calamari fail to disappoint seafood lovers, while mains range from burgers and steaks to chicken and seafood. And of course, the lively atmosphere is tough to beat.

❶ Information

The friendly localsat the **Owen Sound Visitors Information Centre** (☑ 519-371-9833; www. owensoundtourism.ca/en/explore/Visitor-Cen tre.aspx; 1155 1st Ave W; ⊗ 9am-5pm Mon-Sat Jan-Dec, 10am-4pm Sun May-Oct) can tell you about the Bruce Peninsula's hidden gems.

❶ Getting There & Away

First Student (☑ 519-376-5712; Owen Sound Transit Terminal, 1020 3rd Ave E) operates a limited bus schedule to Tobermory on Friday, Saturday and Sunday from July to early September ($34, 1½ hours, one daily).

Owen Sound to Tobermory

The 100km stretch of highway from Owen Sound to Tobermory is monotonous at best. Consider taking a side road or two to get a taste of the scenery that makes the Bruce so special.

From Owen Sound, follow Grey County Rd 1, which winds along the scenic shoreline of staggering pines between Owen Sound and the quaint village of Wiarton. Stop here to say hello to the 4-tonne limestone sculpture of **Wiarton Willie**, Canada's version of Punxsutawney Phil, then continue on Hwy 6 to the sleepy and picturesque bay at Lion's Head, a great place to stop for lunch at a mom-and-pop cafe.

Heading further north on Hwy 6 for about 25km, you'll reach Dyer's Bay Rd. Turn right and maintain your heading for another 10km to the little village of **Dyer's Bay**, reminiscent of Cape Cod with its pretty clapboard houses and shoreline scenery. From here, plow on another 11km to the remote **Cabot Head Lighthouse** (☑ 519-795-7780; www.cabothead.ca; 806 Cabot Head Rd, Miller Lake; by donation; ⊗ May-Oct), which promises stunning views from the keeper's

perch. Beware: It's a wild and wonderful drive, but the windy unpaved road is slow going and there's only one way in and out... back to Hwy 6 and then north to Tobermory.

Tobermory

☑ 226, 519, 548 / POP 1200
You've made it to the tip of the Bruce Peninsula: quite the trek from Toronto! Tiny Tobermory is a nature lover's paradise, home to some of Ontario's most stunning scenery and sunsets. The village centers on the harbor area known as Little Tub, which is bustling during ferry season (May to late October) and all but deserted in winter.

Some of the best wreck-diving in North America exists in these brilliant blue waters. Meander through 22 separate wrecks, many dating back to the 1800s, but note that the water is usually about one degree short of an ice bath. All divers must register in person at the Parks Canada Visitors Centre.

◉ Sights & Activities

★ **Bruce Peninsula National Park** NATIONAL PARK
(☑ 519-596-2233; www.pc.gc.ca/brucepeninsula; adult/child $5/free, vehicle US$12; ⊗ May-Oct; ⓟ ♿) Much of the area just south of Tobermory is protected by this national park, flaunting some of Ontario's finest assets: the Niagara Escarpment, 1000-year-old cedars, rare orchids and crystal-clear, limestone-refracted waters. Spectacular sections of the famous Bruce Trail run the park's length and include the must-see **Grotto**, **Indian Head Cove** and **Halfway Log Dump**. Don't miss **Singing Sands**, across Hwy 6. Though the park remains quiet most of the year, be prepared to share the magic with tourist busloads in July and August.

Fathom Five National Marine Park PARK
(☑ 519-596-2233; www.pc.gc.ca/fathomfive; adult/child $5/free; ♿) Established to protect the numerous shipwrecks, lighthouses and islands around Tobermory, this was the first park of its kind in Canada. Though the 22 wrecks in crystal-clear waters make for a diver's paradise, the park is best known for the much-loved **Flowerpot Island** with its top-heavy 'flowerpot' formations, eroded by waves over the centuries.

Bruce Anchor Cruises CRUISE
(☑ 519-596-2555; http://bruceanchor.com; 7468 Hwy 6; adult/child from $34/25; ⊗ May-Oct) Glass-bottom boat tours over the tops of

rusty, barnacled shipwrecks and onward to lovely Flowerpot Island depart from this private dock at the very end of Hwy 6 in Tobermory, also a brilliant spot to catch the sunset. Some sailings include shipwrecks, others go to Flowerpot direct; check online. Pay extra – the Bruce Peninsula National Park daily fee – to explore the island like Robinson Crusoe.

Diver's Den DIVING
(☑519-596-2363; www.diversden.ca; 3 Bay St; diving from $85, adult/child snorkeling from $65/45; ⊘May-Oct) In business since 1967, this reliable dive shop can hook you up with gear rentals, certification courses (open-water certification from $675) and walk-on two-tank dive trips. Snorkel excursions to one or two shipwrecks are also offered, including gear and a wetsuit (opt for the hoody).

Thorncrest Outfitters KAYAKING
(☑519-596-8908; www.thorncrestoutfitters.com; 7441 Hwy 6; rentals/courses/tours from $35/110/60; ⊘May-Sep) Choose from a variety of kayaking trips geared toward beginner and intermediate paddlers (minimum age 17). Independent paddlers can rent just about anything from this friendly outfitter.

🛏 Sleeping & Eating

Big Tub Harbour Resort MOTEL $$
(☑519-596-2219; www.bigtubresort.ca; 236 Big Tub Rd; d/cottages from $128/288; ⊘May-Oct; P✳🐾) On the other side of Big Tub Harbour, a short drive or decent walk from town, this low-key motel has spacious, updated rooms (with the clunk of footfall on the lower level) and manicured gardens with a wonderful view. A woodsy three-bedroom cottage, perfect for families, is also available. The seclusion – and stargazing – is divine. Water-sports rentals keep you occupied.

Peacock Villa MOTEL $$
(☑519-596-2242; www.peacockvilla.com; 30 Legion St; d $109-165; ⊘Apr-Oct; P🐾) Six simple, pleasantly furnished motel rooms and four cozy cabins in a peaceful, woodsy setting a hop-skip-and-jump from the harbor offer excellent value. Friendly owner Karen is a wealth of information about the town and surrounds.

Innisfree B&B $$
(☑519-596-8190; www.tobermoryaccommodations.com; 46 Bay St; r with/without bath incl breakfast $170/160; ⊘May-Oct; P🐾) Whether it's due to the scent of fresh blueberry muffins or the stunning harbor views from the sunroom and large deck, guests will adore this charming country home. Minimum two-night stay on weekends. Rates drop dramatically in the shoulder season.

Shipwreck Lee's Pirate Bistro FISH & CHIPS $
(☑705-888-5946; https://shipwrecklees.com; 2 Bay St; mains $11-17; ⊘11am-8:30pm May-Oct; 🐾) Tiki meets maritime at this colorful, quirky eatery filled with murals, pirate mannequins, and picnic tables (indoors and out). All-you-can-eat fish-and-chips is the way to go: baskets of melt-in-your-mouth whitefish with piles of fresh fries, all topped with a cocktail umbrella.

ℹ Information

Parks Canada Visitors Centre (☑519-596-2233; www.pc.gc.ca; Chi sin tib dek Rd; ⊘8am-8pm Jul & Aug, 9am-5pm May-Jun & Sep-Oct) Has a fantastic interpretive center, exhibits, a movie theater, several nearby hiking trails and a 20m viewing platform (112 steps). To get here by foot, follow the beaver signs from the Bruce Trail Monument opposite the LCBO liquor store. It's a 10-minute walk.

Tobermory Visitor Information Center (☑519-596-2452; www.tobermory.org; 7420 Hwy 6; ⊘8am-8pm Jul-Aug, 9am-5pm May-Jun & Sep-Oct, 10am-4pm Fri Nov-Apr) As you pull into town (from the south), this center is to your right; drop in for the latest updates.

ℹ Getting There & Away

Toronto The only direct public transport option from Toronto is Parkbus (p117), which offers a limited schedule of express services to Tobermory (adult/child return $99/50, five hours) with a downtown collection point. Check schedules and make bookings online. Alternatively, first make your way to Owen Sound from where First Student operates a limited bus schedule to Tobermory on Friday, Saturday, Sunday and holiday Mondays from late June to early September ($34, 1½ hours, one daily).

Manitoulin Island From Tobermory you can take the *Chi-Cheemaun* ferry from the Bruce Peninsula across the mouth of Georgian Bay. Operated by **Ontario Ferries** (☑800-265-3163; www.ontarioferries.com; adult/child/car $17/9/38; ⊘May-late Oct), the boat connects Tobermory with South Baymouth (two hours, May to October). There are four daily crossings from late June to early September, and two daily crossings during the rest of the season, with an additional voyage on Friday evenings. Reservations are highly recommended.

Manitoulin Island

Manitoulin (meaning 'Spirit Island' in the Ojibwe language) is a magical and remote place. There's a real sense of being 'away' up here. Jagged expanses of white quartzite and granite outcrops lead to breathtaking vistas and hidden runes, but you'll need patience to find them: Manitoulin is the largest freshwater island in the world and its small communities, with names like Mindemoya, Sheguiandah and Wikwemikong, are many kilometers apart. Haweaters (people born on Manitoulin) will spot you a mile away as you fumble over six-syllable words. But don't let these syllabic setbacks deter you from visiting – a few days on Manitoulin is food for the soul.

◉ Sights & Activities

Manitoulin isn't laden with historical sights as much as natural beauty. Take some time to drive around the island and explore its enclaves.

Providence Bay Beach   BEACH

(Hwy 551, Providence Bay; ♿) Set on a long curving bay facing Lake Huron, this is arguably the best beach on the island. The sand is soft and tawny, the water calm, and it's backed by sand dunes, tall grasses and a well-maintained boardwalk trail. If you're yearning for beach time, this is the place to be.

Perivale Gallery   GALLERY

(☏ 705-210-0290; www.perivalegallery.com; 1320 Perivale Rd E, Spring Bay; ⊙ 10am-5pm Jul-Sep, Fri-Sun May & Jun; ℙ) This well-respected art gallery features works by a remarkable range of Canadian fine artists, sculptors and artisans. The gallery itself, a red farmhouse, sits on a forest lot facing Lake Kagawong – a peaceful and beautiful spot. Artistic workshops are also held throughout the season; check the website for current offerings.

Ojibwe Cultural Foundation   MUSEUM

(☏ 705-377-4902; www.ojibweculture.ca; 15 Hwy 551, M'Chigeeng; by donation; ⊙ 8:30am-4pm Mon-Fri; ℙ) You're free to explore on your own, but guided tours of this insightful museum are highly recommended. Rotating exhibits reflect a rich history of legends and skilled craftwork. A small gift shop sells local art, literature and more.

★ Cup & Saucer Trail   HIKING

(6301 Bidwell Rd, Sheguiandah) From its origin near the junction of Hwy 540 and Bidwell Rd

(25km southwest of Little Current) this 9km trail on the Niagara Escarpment, with its 2km of dramatic 70m cliffs, leads to the highest point on the island (351m) with breathtaking views of the crinkled shoreline along the North Channel. Take a shortcut back on the 500m Adventure Trail, which involves descending on rickety wood ladders and clambering up, over and down massive boulders.

☞ Tours

★ Great Spirit Circle Trail   CULTURAL

(☏ 705-377-4404; www.circletrail.com; 5905 Hwy 540, M'Chigeeng; activities & tours from $40; ⊙ May-Oct; ♿) The eight local First Nation communities have collaborated to form this consortium offering a wide variety of fun activities and cross-cultural day and overnight tours throughout the year: a wonderful way to get a sense of Manitoulin and its people.

Wiikwemkoong Tourism   CULTURAL

(☏ 705-859-3477; www.wiikwemkoong.ca; 2098-G Wikwemikong Way, Wiikwemkoong; ⊙ 8am-4pm Mon-Fri Jun-Sep; ♿) Celebrating the Anishinaabek people of the Three Fires Confederacy, Wiikwemkoong Tourism helps to coordinate a wide variety of cultural tourism offerings in the community – from song and drum teachings to tours of historic sites and waterways. All excursions are in the Wiikwemkoong Unceded First Nations Reserve, the only officially recognized indigenous reserve in Canada located on territory that was never ceded to the government.

✺ Festivals & Events

★ Wiikwemkoong Powwow   CULTURAL

(Wiikwemkoong Annual Cultural Festival; ☏ 705-859-2385; www.wikwemikongheritage.org; Thunderbird Park, Wiikwemkoong; adult/child $10/2; ⊙ Aug; ♿) The unceded First Nation of Wiikwemkoong (locals say 'Wiki') hosts a huge powwow on the first weekend in August. Expect vibrant and colorful displays of dancing, drumming and traditional games. First held in 1960, this is the largest and longest-running powwow on the island.

⌖ Sleeping & Eating

★ Gordon's Park   CAMPGROUND $

(☏ 705-859-2470; www.gordonspark.com; 18777 Hwy 6, Tehkummah; campsites/tipis/cabins from $43/105/110; ⊙ May-Oct; ℙ ✷) More than 80 hectares of land makes for plenty of room for campsites, tipis, and simple cabins with psychedelic murals. Walking trails and activities like bird-watching, fishing and archery are offered, plus there's a pool. Designated a Dark Sky Preserve, Gordon's also is one of the best places in Ontario to view meteor showers and even see the northern lights.

★ My Friends Inn MOTEL $
(☏ 705-859-3115; www.myfriendsinn.com; 151 Queen St, Manitowaning; d from $85; ☐❄🐾) First-time hotelier and former nurse Maureen Friend retired to Manitoulin with her husband to be closer to their daughter; they're doing a wonderful job. Rooms in this friendly little motel outside the pretty village of Manitowaning in central Manitoulin are smart and homey with kitchenettes and patchwork bedspreads. Highly recommended.

Queen's Inn B&B $$
(☏ May-Oct 705-282-0665, Nov-Apr 416-450-4866; www.thequeensinn.ca; 19 Water St, Gore Bay; s/d from $140/180, with shared bath from $130/165; ☺May-Oct; ☐🐾) Like a pillared temple to remote elegance, this stately B&B peers over the silent cove of Gore Bay. Grab a book from the antique hutch library and idly thumb through it while relaxing on the white verandah among potted lilacs.

Lake Huron Fish and Chips FISH & CHIPS $
(☏ 705-377-4500; 20 McNevin St, Providence Bay; fish & chips from $12; ☺11am-8pm Jul & Aug, Thu-Sun May & Jun)) You're going to crave it at some point, surrounded by all this water, and this is the place to go: golden-fried fresh lake fish and crispy, crunchy fries.

★ Buoys Eatery SEAFOOD $$
(☏ 705-282-2869; www.buoyseatery.com; 1 Purvis Dr, Gore Bay; mains $12-22; ☺noon-8pm Wed-Sat, to 7pm Sun May-Oct; 🐾) This little joint on the Gore Bay marina has it all: vibe, location, and food sourced from local providers and prepared fresh. The seasoned whitefish melts in your mouth, but if you're not feeling fishy, pizza, pasta and burgers also please. When you're done, linger with a craft beer on the sunny patio and feel a million miles from home.

Garden's Gate Family Restaurant CAFE $$
(☏ 705-859-2088; www.gardensgate.ca; 316 Hwy 542, Tehkummah; mains $17-29; ☺5-8pm Tue-Sun May-Oct; ☐🐾❄) Seriously good, locally sourced food can be found here, near the junction of Hwys 6 and 542. The menu is international – from beef vindaloo to lamb tzaziki – with a creative selection of vegetar-

WORTH A TRIP

WASAGA BEACH

Wasaga Beach Provincial Park
(☏ 705-429-2516; www.ontarioparks.com/park/wasagabeach; Mosley St; day use per vehicle $20; ☐🐾) has the distinct honor of being the longest freshwater beach in the world. It's also the closest full-fledged beach resort to Toronto, attracting thousands of visitors every summer. Most of the 14km-long expanse of soft sands and crashing waves belongs to Wasaga Beach Provincial Park – the further north you head, the less crowded; no camping. The beach gets so much hype during the summer, many people forget that Wasaga's pristine sand dunes transform into awesome cross-country skiing in the winter!

ian options and simple dishes for kids too. Save room for the homemade desserts.

☆ Entertainment

Debajehmujig Creation Centre ARTS CENTER
(☏ 705-859-1820; www.debaj.ca; 43 Queen St, Manitowaning; ☺10am-5pm Mon-Fri) This art center is home to Canada's foremost aboriginal theater company, Debajehmujig Theatre Group, whose name appropriately means 'storytellers.' Its performances are original works integrating Anishnaabag/Chippewa Nation world views, culture and heritage; performances are in July and August. The center also hosts various music performances and fine-art exhibits year-round, all by local Aboriginal artists.

ℹ Information

Manitoulin Tourism Association (☏ 705-368-3021; www.manitoulintourism.com; 70 Meredith St E, Little Current; ☺9am-8pm May-Oct) Pamphlets and maps of the island can be found in the South Baymouth ferry terminal, as well as onboard the Chi-Cheemaun. If you're coming from the northern side, drop in here to get your bearings.

ℹ Getting There & Away

There are two ways on and off the island: a ferry to South Baymouth or across the swinging bridge in the north. There is no land-based public transportation to or around Manitoulin, so your own wheels are a must.

From Tobermory, take the Chi-Cheemaun vehicular ferry (two hours, two to four daily May

ST JOSEPH ISLAND

St Joseph Island, a quiet expanse of woodland about 60km southeast of Sault Ste Marie, sits alongside the US border in the northwest corner of Lake Huron. It's linked by bridge off Hwy 17. Here the 200-year-old **Fort St Joseph National Historic Site** (☑705-246-2664; www.pc.gc.ca/fortstjoseph; Hwy 548; adult/child $3.90/free; ☉10am-5pm Jul & Aug, Wed-Sun Jun & Sep) was once the most remote and westerly outpost of the British landholding in North America.

The ruins of the fort are an excellent starting point for budding archaeologists and the small visitor's center has friendly staff to answer any of your questions about the ruins of the nine historical buildings.

to October), operated by Ontario Ferries (p167), to the port of South Baymouth. Reservations highly recommended.

From here, Hwy 6 continues north for 65km to Little Current and a thin, swinging bridge that reconnects to the mainland. In summer the bridge closes for the first 15 minutes of every hour to allow shipping traffic through the channel. Crossing the bridge leads to the Trans-Canada Hwy at Espanola, 50km further up the road.

NORTHERN ONTARIO

'Big' is a theme in Northern Ontario. The area is so vast that it could fit six Englands and still have room for a Scotland or two. Industry is big here, too: most of the world's silver and nickel ore comes from local mines, while boundless forests have made the region a key timber producer. What's not so big is the local population; as of the most recent census, none of the cities has over 100,000 residents.

Two main highways weave an intersecting course across the province. Hwy 17 (the Trans-Canada) unveils the area's scenic pièce de résistance, the northern crest over Lake Superior. From Sudbury, misty fjord-like passages hide isolated beaches among dense thickets of pine, cedar and birch. Further north, Hwy 11 traverses through Cochrane – where the Polar Bear Express connects to Moosonee – to Thunder Bay, the intersection of the two highways.

Ontario Northland's (☑705-472-4500, ext 0 800-363-7512; www.ontarionorthland.ca) bus network provides connections from Toronto to North Bay and Sudbury, continuing north to Temagami and Cochrane. There is no longer any bus network north of White River, so if you are planning on heading to Thunder Bay, you will need to rent a car.

Parkbus (☑800-928-7101; www.parkbus.ca; ☉9am-5pm Mon-Fri) is a useful shuttle from Toronto to Ontario's provincial parks including Killarney. Book well ahead.

The legendary Polar Bear Express (p186) train runs north from Cochrane to the isolated outpost of Moosonee, gateway to Moose Factory island near James Bay. A VIA Rail (p174) train heads northwest from Sudbury via Chapleau to White River. Sudbury Junction station, near Sudbury, is on VIA Rail's Canadian line between Toronto and Vancouver.

There are airports with connections to Toronto and beyond, and car rental companies, in North Bay, Sudbury, Sault Ste Marie, Thunder Bay and Timmins.

Killarney Provincial Park

The 645-sq-km **Killarney Provincial Park** (☑705-287-2900; www.ontarioparks.com/park/killarney; Hwy 637; day use per vehicle $13, campsite $37-53, backcountry camping adult/child under 18yr $12.50/6, yurts/cabins $98/142; ☉year-round)covers vast expanses of Georgian Bay shoreline and is home to moose, black bears, beavers and deer, as well as over 100 bird species. The Group of Seven artists had a cabin near Hwy 6 (just west of the park) and were instrumental in its 1964 establishment; today the park is considered to be one of the finest kayaking destinations in the world.

🏃 Activities

Killarney's 80km **La Cloche Silhouette Trail** is named after Group of Seven member Franklin Carmichael's legendary painting. This rugged trek for experienced hikers twists through a mountainous realm of sapphire lakes, thirsty birches, luscious pine forests and shimmering quartzite cliffs. A network of shorter, less challenging hikes also offers glimpses of the majestic terrain, including the **Cranberry Bog Trail** (a 4km loop) and the **Granite Ridge Trail** (a 2km loop).

Killarney Kanoes (☑705-287-2197, 888-461-4446; www.killarneykanoes.com; 1611 Bell Lake Rd; canoe rental per day $27-43; ☉8am-8pm May-

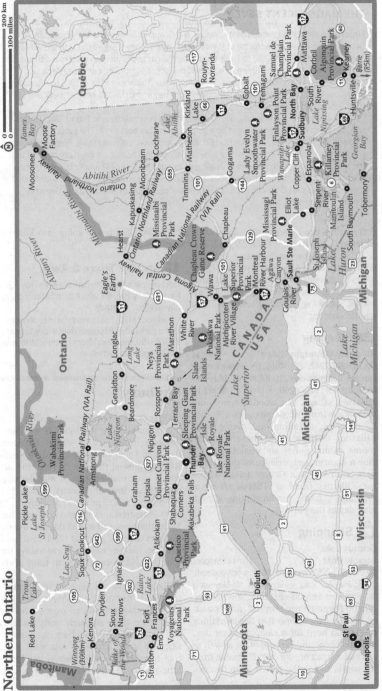

Northern Ontario

200 km
100 miles

Québec

Ontario

Manitoba

Minnesota

Michigan

Wisconsin

CANADA
USA

James Bay

Moose Factory

Moosonee

Missinaibi River

Albany River

Abitibi River

Eagle's Earth

Hearst

Kapuskasing

Moonbeam

Cochrane

Matheson

Timmins

Gogama

Chapleau

Chapleau Crown Game Reserve

Wawa

White River

Marathon

Neys Provincial Park

Longlac

Geraldton

Beardmore

Rossport

Terrace Bay

Nipigon

Thunder Bay

Isle Royale

Isle Royale National Park

Ouimet Canyon Provincial Park

Armstrong

Graham

Upsala

Shabaqua Corners

Kakabeka Falls

Quetico Provincial Park

Atikokan

Ignace

Dryden

Sioux Lookout

Pickle Lake

Red Lake

Kenora

Sioux Narrows

Fort Frances

Emo

Stratton

Voyageurs National Park

Duluth

St Paul

Minneapolis

Rouyn-Noranda

Kirkland Lake

Cobalt

Temagami

North Bay

Sudbury

Espanola

Copper Cliff

Elliot Lake

Serpent River

Sault Ste Marie

Goulais River

Michipicoten River Village

Mississagi Provincial Park

Killarney Provincial Park

Manitoulin Island

South Baymouth

Tobermory

Mattawa

Corbeil

Algonquin Provincial Park

Kearney

Huntsville

Samuel de Champlain Provincial Park

Finlayson Point Provincial Park

Lady Evelyn Smoothwater Provincial Park

Montreal River Harbour

Agawa Canyon

Lake Superior Provincial Park

Pukaskwa National Park

Michipicoten

Slate Islands

Sleeping Giant Provincial Park

Wabakimi Provincial Park

Oploskwin River

Lac Seul

Lake St Joseph

Trout Lake

Lake of the Woods

Rainy Lake

Lake Nipigon

Long Lake

Lake Superior

Lake Michigan

Lake Huron

Georgian Bay

Lake Nipissing

Wanapitei Lake

St Joseph Island

Lake Abitibi

Abitibi River

Ontario Northland Railway

Canadian National Railway

Algoma Central Railway

Canadian National Railway (VIA Rail)

Missinaibi Provincial Park

Winnipeg (200km)

Barrie (85km)

117, 66, 11, 655, 101, 144, 129, 631, 527, 599, 516, 642, 72, 502, 622, 11, 17, 105, 71, 7, 11, 61, 53, 165, 2, 61, 41, 8, 51, 45, 63, 53, 94, 35, 10, 11, 60, 23, 75, 69, 144

THE MAGNIFICENT SEVEN

Fired by an almost adolescent enthusiasm, the Group of Seven (aka the Algonquin School) were an all-male troupe of Canadian painters. They trekked through the wilds of northern Ontario from 1920 to 1933, capturing the rugged Canadian wilderness through all its seasons, their joyful energy expressed in vibrant, light-filled canvases depicting mountains, lakes, forests and towns. From Algonquin Provincial Park (p190) to Killarney Provincial Park (p170) and on up Lake Superior, they immortalised northern Ontario in their expressive landscapes.

In 1917, before the group officially formed, their fellow painter and friend, Tom Thomson, drowned in Algonquin, just as he was producing his best work. The group – AY Jackson, Arthur Lismer, JEH MacDonald, Frank Johnston, Lawren Harris, Fred Varley and Franklin Carmichael – considered him their inspiration. Thomson's deep connection to the land is evident from his works hanging in Toronto's AGO (p81) and Ottawa's National Gallery (p211). His rustic cabin has been moved onto the grounds of Toronto's McMichael Canadian Art Collection (p87). Each has magnificent examples of the Group of Seven's profound talents.

Oct) provides canoe and kayak rentals, while **Killarney Outfitters** (☑888-222-3410, 705-287-2828; www.killarneyoutfitters.com; 1076 Hwy 637, Killarney; canoe & kayak rental per day $42-64) offers equipment rentals and fully outfitted packages (just bring your toothbrush!) for hiking, canoeing, kayaking and stand-up paddleboarding.

🛌 Sleeping

Killarney Mountain Lodge   LODGE $$
(☑705-287-2242, 800-461-1117; www.killarney.com; 3 Commissioner St, Killarney; d/ste incl breakfast from $200/269; ☺May-Oct; 🛜🏊) In Killarney village, this wooden compound with waterfront accommodations is run by canoeing, kayaking and hiking buffs Killarney Outfitters. The beautiful pine rooms, cabins, suites and chalets all provide a luxurious experience of the wilderness, with views of George Island across the Killarney Channel. There's a restaurant and a sauna for unwinding after a long day in the park.

🛍 Shopping

**Grundy Lake
Supply Post**   SPORTS & OUTDOORS
(☑705-383-2251; www.grundylakesupplypostcom; 20395 Hwy 522 East; ☺9am-5pm mid-May–early Jul, 8am-9pm early Jul-early Oct) Now located 1km off Hwy 69 down Hwy 522, the renovated Grundy Lake Supply Post has everything one would need for a camping adventure, including boat and canoe rentals, as well as gas and a small on-site cafe. If coming from the south, this is the closest shop to stock up on supplies before going into Killarney Provincial Park.

ℹ Getting There & Away

Most people access the park from the Hwy 637 turnoff along Hwy 69, which terminates in the tiny village of Killarney.

Parkbus (p170) has limited summer services to the park (adult/student/child under 13 years $99/89/50, 5½ hours) from Toronto; otherwise, you'll need your own wheels.

Sudbury

☑705 / POP 88,054

Sudbury gets props for making something out of nothing. In the 1880s it was but a desolate lumber camp called Ste-Anne-des-Pins. Then, when the Canadian Pacific Railway plowed through in 1883, the discovery of a mother lode of nickel-copper ore transformed the dreary region into the biggest nickel producer worldwide. By 1920 industrial toxicity and acid rain had killed the trees and fouled the soil, leaving Sudbury a bleak place of blackened boulders. So barren was the surrounding terrain that NASA came here to train in the 1960s.

Today the story is more environmentally friendly: as part of the city's 'regreening' program, locals have planted over 9.1 million trees since 1978, although heavy industry and mining still rule. Sudbury has a university, two fantastic science museums, some cool haunts and chilled locals, but there's little reason to visit unless you're passing through, particularly in winter when a lot of tourist businesses close.

◉ Sights

If you're planning to visit both Science North and Dynamic Earth, save money with the 'Dynamic Duo Passport' (adult/child $50/41). Valid for three days, it includes admission to both attractions and their special exhibitions and movies.

★ Science North   MUSEUM

(☑705-522-3701; www.sciencenorth.ca; 100 Ramsey Lake Rd; adult/child from $27/23; ◷10am-4pm, until 5pm Sat & Sun May-Aug) After passing through a tunnel dug deep within the 2.5-billion-year-old Canadian Shield, work your way down through the spiral of exciting hands-on activities in this fantastic museum. Wander through a living butterfly garden, stargaze in the digital **planetarium** (adult/child $8/6) or fly away on a bushplane simulator. Visiting exhibits and IMAX films change regularly.

The 'Play All Day Passport,' which includes entrance to visiting exhibits, IMAX films and other extras, costs $37 (children $31). Footpaths lead along the shore of **Ramsey Lake** from here.

Dynamic Earth   MUSEUM

(☑705-522-3701; www.dynamicearth.ca; 122 Big Nickel Rd; adult/child $22/18, parking $6 in summer; ◷9am-6pm Apr-Oct) Dynamic Earth's main attraction is the underground tour with simulated dynamite blast. Visitors stand to learn lots about geology and our planet from thought-provoking interactive exhibits. In summer, tours leave roughly every 30 minutes from 10am to 3:30pm. Be sure to take a snap in front of the Big Nickel, a 9m-high stainless steel replica of a 1951 Canadian nickel.

🛏 Sleeping

Radisson Sudbury   BUSINESS HOTEL $$

(☑705-675-1123; www.radissonsudbury.com; 85 St Anne Rd; d from $116; P❄🛜❄🏋) Offering 147 comfortable rooms in a central location, Radisson's service and finish are a cut above its competitors. Facilities include a pool, hot tub, fitness center and guest laundry, while guests can wander into the adjoining Rainbow Centre mall for a food court and grocery store. The resident Italian restaurant, Pesto's, also serves breakfast, lunch and dinner.

Holiday Inn   BUSINESS HOTEL $$

(☑705-522-3000; www.holidayinn.com; 1696 Regent St; d from $119; P❄🛜❄) From the outside, this Holiday Inn looks frozen in 1972. Inside are refurbished, generic rooms of a good size. There's an indoor pool, hot tub and fitness center. A room with breakfast is an extra $10, or you can eat an à la carte breakfast in the restaurant.

🍴 Eating

Motley Kitchen   CAFE $

(☑705-222-6685; www.themotleykitchen.com; 70 Young St; mains $14; ◷11am-3pm Tue-Fri, 10am-2pm Sat & Sun) Sudbury's most popular brunch spot serves unlikely dishes such as breakfast burritos, Welsh rarebit, Croatian crepes, and French toast stuffed with bananas and Nutella or strawberries and yogurt. Plates are garnished with home fries and fresh fruit, and weekday lunches of tacos, sandwiches and salads are served. The only drawback is the popularity can mean the food arrives slowly.

★ Respect is Burning   ITALIAN $$

(☑705-675-5777; www.ribsupperclub.com; 82 Durham St; mains $19-35; ◷5-10pm Mon-Thu, to 1am Fri & Sat; 🛜) This self-proclaimed supper club's focus is on rustic Tuscan cuisine, but chefs aren't shy about getting experimental. The ever-shifting menu promises bursting flavors with every bite. Weekend evenings feature delectable sample platters and late-night drinks. It can get busy so best to make a reservation.

🍷 Drinking & Nightlife

★ Laughing Buddha   BAR

(☑705-673-2112; www.laughingbuddhasudbury. com; 194 Elgin St; ◷11am-2am Wed-Sat, to 11pm Sun-Tue, to midnight Wed) Sudbury's prime hangout for hipsters and slackers pulls off snobby sandwiches (such as the 'Brie LT'; $9) and pizzas ($13) while maintaining an uberchill vibe. In summer slip out to the crimson-brick courtyard and enjoy your casual lunch or one of the many types of craft beer.

46 North Brewing Corp   BREWERY

(☑705-586-1870; www.46north.ca; 1275 Kelly Lake rd; ◷11am-7pm Tue-Sat) Graham and Holli have set up a small taproom and brewery on the outskirts of the town, offering up a range of beers produced on-site. It's a family-run operation so children are welcome and you can also bring in food from outside to eat at the brewery. Growlers are also available to take away.

HardRock42 PUB

(☑705-586-3303; www.hardrock42.com; 117 Elm st; ⊙7am-11pm Mon-Fri, from 8am Sat & Sun, to 2pm Sun) Don't let its location inside a chain motel put you off, as HardRock42 has the largest selection of taps in Sudbury and a large enough clientele to make sure the beer is fresh. Food portions (mains from $16) are large and the bar is always full of friendly locals keen for a chat.

☆ Entertainment

Towne House Tavern LIVE MUSIC

(☎705-674-6883; www.thetownehouse.com; 206 Elgin St; ⊙11am-2am Mon-Sat, from noon Sun) This beloved grungy venue is all about Canadian indie from punk to gospel, and stages acts including local bands and big names from the south.

Adding to the musical entertainment are a games room and a bar serving pub grub with outside seating.

❶ Information

Greater Sudbury Development Corporation
(☑1-866-451-8525; www.sudburytourism.ca; Tom Davies Square, 200 Brady St; ⊙8:30am-4:30pm Mon-Fri) Help and brochures are on hand in the city hall.

❶ Getting There & Away

Greater Sudbury Airport (☑705-693-2514; www.flysudbury.ca; 5000 Air Terminal Dr) is about 25km northeast of downtown. Air Canada, Bearskin Airlines and **Porter Airlines** (☑888-619-8622; www.flyporter.com) operate services to/from Toronto, Ottawa, Sault Ste Marie, Thunder Bay, Timmins, Kapuskasing and North Bay.

Several car-rental options are available at the airport and downtown, including **Enterprise** (☑705-693-9993; www.enterpriserentacar.ca).

Ontario Northland (p170) buses connect Sudbury to Toronto ($80, 5¾ hours, three daily).

VIA Rail (☑1-888-842-7245; www.viarail. ca; 233 Elgin St) serves a small network of remote towns on its line between **Sudbury Train Station** (233 Elgin St) and White River (from $60, 8¼ hours) via Chapleau, departing Tuesday, Thursday and Saturday at 9am. **Sudbury Junction** (☑705-524-1591; 2750 Lasalle Blvd), 10km northeast of downtown, is on VIA Rail's Canadian (p868) line between Toronto and Vancouver.

Elliot Lake

The tree-lined jaunt between Sudbury and Sault Ste Marie offers little more than forest views out the car window. Elliot Lake, the largest community in the area, is popular with retirees on a tight budget and, in winter, snowmobilers. Indeed, the region is a hub for outdoor activities year-round, including hiking, fishing, canoeing and cross-country skiing.

The little town made headlines in 2012 after an accident at the town mall, when a concrete section of its roof catastrophically collapsed, without warning. The slab fell three floors, taking the lives of two women and injuring 19.

◉ Sights

Mississagi Provincial Park PARK

(☑705-865-2021, Oct-May 705-862-1203; www.ontarioparks.com/park/mississagi; Hwy 639; day use per vehicle $11.25, campsites $37; ⊙late May-early Sep) Mississagi Provincial Park, 35km north of Elliot Lake, is a secluded expanse of hemlock forests, sandy beaches, trembling aspens and chirping birds. Hiking trails range from 0.8km along Flack Lake – revealing ripple rock, a geological feature formed by a billion years of wave action – to the multiday MacKenzie (22km) through the back country. Canoes can also be rented.

Mississagi is quiet and undeveloped: none of the campsites has electricity, and the limited facilities (the gatehouse and toilets), located just off Hwy 639 between Jim Christ and Semiwite Lakes, are solar-powered. There are also toilets and a picnic area at Flack Lake. Reserve your camping spot with Ontario Parks (www.ontarioparks.com).

❶ Getting There & Away

Elliot Lake is on Hwy 108, 27km north of Hwy 17. Ontario Northland (p170) buses connect the town with Sudbury ($57, 3/½ hours, one daily) and Sault Ste Marie ($57, 2¾ hours, one daily).

Sault Ste Marie

☑705 / POP 66,313

'The Soo,' as it's commonly known, quietly governs the narrow rapids between Lakes Huron and Superior. Perched alongside the US border and the St Lawrence Seaway, the sleepy city is the unofficial gateway to the far-flung regions of northwestern Ontario. Originally known as Baawitigong ('Place of the Rapids'), it was a traditional gathering place for the Ojibwe and remains a strong First Nations area today. French fur traders changed the name to Sault Ste Marie *(soo-saynt muh-ree)* or 'St Mary's Falls,' but don't expect to see any waterfalls today: they've been tamed into a series of gargantuan locks.

Let's face it, Sault Ste Marie is not the prettiest city. Nonetheless, the Soo is a friendly place and a logical overnight stop on Trans-Canada itineraries. There's a US border crossing here too.

◉ Sights

Art Gallery of Algoma
GALLERY

(☑705-949-9067; www.artgalleryofalgoma.com; 10 East St; adult/student/child under 12yr $7/5/ free; ⊙9am-5pm Tue-Sat, to 7pm Wed & noon-5pm Sun Jun-Oct) Behind the library, this gallery has a permanent collection and seasonal exhibitions to inspire Group of Seven–themed trips along Lake Superior. Especially in summer, paintings by the group of local scenes are exhibited alongside the work of local First Nations artists.

Sault Ste Marie Canal National Historic Site
HISTORIC SITE

(☑705-941-6205; www.parkscanada.gc.ca/sault; 1 Canal Dr; ⊙visitor center 10am-4pm Mon-Fri mid-May–early Oct) FREE On the Canadian side of St Mary's River, follow the 2.2km Attikamek walking trail around South St Mary's Island to see this canal dating from 1895, once the world's longest lock and the first to operate with electrical power. It was also novel in using an emergency swing dam to protect the lock in case of an accident. The majority of freighter traffic occurs further afield in the American locks; the older Canadian lock is used for recreational vessels only.

Canadian Bushplane Heritage Centre
MUSEUM

(☑705-945-6242; www.bushplane.com; 50 Pim St; adult/child/student $13.50/3/8; ⊙9am-6pm mid-May–early Oct, 10am-4pm mid-Oct–early-May; ⊕) A visit to the Soo's most dynamic and kid-friendly museum is a great way to get a sense of how Northern Ontario works: bush planes are crucial to remote communities that are not accessible by road. Stroll among retired aircraft, housed in a former government hangar dating from 1924, to see how tiny these flyers really are. A flight simulator takes passengers on a spirited ride along sapphire lakes and towering pines.

Sault Ste Marie Museum
MUSEUM

(☑705-759-7278; www.saultmuseum.com; 690 Queen St E; adult/senior & student $8/6; ⊙9:30am-5pm Tue-Sat; ⊕) Occupying the old post office dating from 1906, this three-story museum is a tribute to the early 1900s, detailing the town's history from several perspectives. The Discovery Gallery is geared toward children and the Skylight Gallery is a must-see. An interactive timeline from prehistory to the 1960s incorporates the local historical society's unique collection of preserved fossils and relics.

☞ Tours

Agawa Canyon Tour Train
RAIL

(ACR; ☑855-768-4171, reservations 800-461-6020; www.agawatrain.com; 129 Bay St; adult/child $101/55; ⊙late Jun–mid-Oct) Constructed in 1899 to facilitate the transport of raw materials to Sault Ste Marie's industrial plants, the Algoma Central Railway is a 475km stretch of railroad from Sault Ste Marie due north to Hearst. Nowadays it transports tour guests through unspoiled wilderness along the pristine lakes and jagged granite of the Canadian Shield.

The Agawa Canyon train offers day trips north to Agawa Canyon in the rugged Lake Superior hinterland once painted by the Group of Seven, leaving Sault Ste Marie at 8am and returning at 6pm. The best time to ride is from mid-September to mid-October, as the train twists its way through jaw-dropping blazing autumn foliage for as far as the eye can see, though the price jumps to $122 per person (including children) during this time.

⌂ Sleeping

The bulk of motels are found along Great Northern Rd, near Hwy 17, lined with fast-food restaurants and malls. There are also several options scattered downtown, mostly on Bay St, where there's some scenic interest in the waterfront and the majority of attractions, but few amenities after dark.

★ Water Tower Inn
HOTEL $$

(☑705-949-8111, 888-461-7077; www.watertowerinn.com; 360 Great Northern Rd; d from $139; P❋⏼⊜) Offering a resort for the price of a room, the Water Tower continues to stand out from the rest with its indoor and outdoor pools, grill-house bar-restaurant, pizza-slinging pub and treatment spa. The variety of room types includes family rooms and suites. It's just off Hwy 17, 3.5km northeast of downtown; shuttles to town and the airport are available.

Algonquin Hotel
HISTORIC HOTEL **$$**

(☑ 705-253-2311; 864 Queen Street East; d from $75; P ☎) Built in 1888, this historical building is located close to the Soo's restaurant and shopping district. It's one of the cheaper places in town, but rooms still have comfortable, clean beds with TVs. It's worth paying a bit more for an en suite.

Sleep Inn
MOTEL **$$**

(☑ 705-253-7533; www.choicehotels.ca/cn658; 727 Bay St; d incl breakfast from $105; P ❋ ☎ 🐾) This tourist motel in a nice spot by the water has spacious and tidy rooms, an exercise room and sauna.

🍴 Eating

Muio's
DINER **$**

(☑ 705-254-7105; www.muios.com; 685 Queen St E; lunch/dinner mains $10/18; ☺ 7am-8pm Mon-Sat) In a historic building dating from 1890, among pictures of the Soo of yore, Muio's continues to bask in anachronistic glory. Started in 1961, pretty much everything is homemade, including the pasta, and locals of all ages come for cuisine from burger-joint faves to more sophisticated steaks and seafood. Muio's is famed for its breakfasts and its broasted (half broiled, half deep-fried) chicken on a bun, smothered, of course, in rich gravy.

★ Arturo's Ristorante
ITALIAN **$$$**

(☑ 705-253-0002; www.arturoristorante.com; 515 Queen St E; mains $24-45; ☺ 5-10pm Tue-Thu, to 10:30pm Fri & Sat) A shimmering jewel in a dismal downtown strip, decades-old Arturo's is the kind of place you remember after your vacation has ended. Atmospheric but unpretentious with soft lighting, starched white tablecloths and European scenes on the walls, the Italian mains such as veal marsala and chicken *piccata* (with lemon and capers) are tender and succulent, the sauces rich, and wines appropriately paired.

☆ Entertainment

LopLops
LIVE MUSIC

(☑ 705-945-0754; www.loplops.com; 651 Queen St E; ☺ 4pm-2am Wed-Sat) Grab a glass of vino or local craft beer from the glittering steel bar and enjoy an evening amid strumming guitars and the restless murmurs of tortured artists. Promoting local culture since 2003, LopLops stages live music year-round.

ℹ️ Information

Algoma Kinniwabi Travel Association

(☑ 800-263-2546; www.algomacountry.com; 334 Bay St; ☺ 8:30am-4:30pm Mon-Fri) Helpful office (and website) providing information and inspiration for travels along Lake Superior and into the hinterland.

Ontario Travel Information Centre
(☑ 705-945-6941; www.ontariotravel.net; 261 Queen St W; ☺ 8:30am-4:30pm) Sells permits for camping, fishing and hunting in the surrounding backcountry, and offers seasonal reports on where to catch the best fall colors, spring blossoms and snow. Near the International Bridge, it has a currency exchange.

Tourism Sault Ste Marie
(☑ 800-461-6020; www.saulttourism.com; Level 1, Civic Centre, 99 Foster Dr; ☺ 8:30am-4:30pm Mon-Fri) Stocks brochures and guides covering the Soo. In the Economic Development Corporation office.

ℹ️ Getting There & Away

AIR

Sault Ste Marie Airport (YAM; ☑ 705-779-3031; www.saultairport.com; 475 Airport Rd) is some 18km west of downtown. Take Second Line (Hwy 550) 13km west, then head south for 5km along Airport Rd (Hwy 565).

Flights to/from Toronto are available with Air Canada and Porter, and Bearskin Airlines offers direct services to Thunder Bay and Sudbury, with onward connections including Winnipeg, Timmins and North Bay.

BUS

Northland (www.ontarionorthland.ca) runs buses to Sudbury ($74, 4½ hours, one daily) and as far north as White River from the **bus stop** (☑ 705-541-9305; 503 Trunk Rd) outside the Howard Johnson Inn on Hwy 17, 5km east of downtown.

You can also get the **International Bridge Bus** (☑ 906-632-6882; www.saultstemarie.com/soo-area-and-great-waters-region/international-bridge; one way $2; ☺ 7am-7pm Mon-Fri, 9am-5pm Sat) over to sister Sault Ste Marie in Michigan. Buses depart the Canadian side at 20 minutes past every hour, from the bus stop near the Station Mall's front entrance on Bay St; and on the half-hour from the bus terminal on the corner of Queen St E and Dennis St, also downtown. Buses depart the US side on the hour. You must have your passport.

WINNIE THE WHO?

The little logging town of White River (www.whiteriver.ca) lays claim to being the home of the original Winnie the Pooh.

As the story goes, back in 1914, a trapper returned to White River with an orphaned baby black bear cub. A veterinarian soldier named Harry Colebourn was on a rail layover in White River when he came across the trapper and fell in love with the cub, purchasing her for $20. He named her 'Winnipeg.' She boarded the Québec-bound troop train with Harry, en route to his native Britain.

When Harry was called to serve in France, he left Winnie in the care of the London Zoo, where she became an instant hit. One of the many hearts she won over belonged to a young Christopher Robin Milne, son of AA Milne. A frequent visitor to the zoo, young Christopher's pet name for the little bear was 'Winnie-the-Pooh.' In his 1926 first edition, AA Milne noted that his stories were about his son, the bear from the London Zoo, and Christopher's stuffed animals.

Eventually, Disney purchased Milne's tales of Winnie-the-Pooh and Christopher Robin, and...the rest is history. A monument to both bears, actual and fictional, stands in the park in White River, by the visitors center.

where the Magpie meets the Michipicoten near Michipicoten River Village.

Sandy Beach   BEACH
(Sandy Beach Rd) Follow a gravel road and a path lined with dunes and fragile plants to this 1km white-sand beach on Michipicoten Bay, where Group of Seven member AY Jackson once painted. It's best accessed from Hwy 17 south of Wawa through Michipicoten and is a 5km drive north until you see the sign for Sandy Beach Rd.

★ Naturally Superior Adventures   KAYAKING
(☑ 705-856-2939, 800-203-9092; www.naturally superior.com; 10 Government Dock Rd, Lake Superior; courses/day trips from $50/137) Based 11km southwest of Wawa, the gang at Naturally Superior delight in guiding folks around the Lake Superior region by sea kayak, canoe, stand-up paddleboard and on foot. Watery trips and courses range from day-long affairs to weekend and week-long expeditions, including beach camping.

Self-guided paddle expeditions, guide-certification courses and photography workshops are also offered.

🛏 Sleeping & Eating

There's a glut of motels here from spick-and-span to the cheap and nasty. Options are found both in town and on the approaches to Wawa; those on Hwy 17 are closer to the beaches and waterfalls around Lake Superior.

Parkway Motel   MOTEL $
(☑ 800-380-7525, 705-856-7020; www.parkway motel.com; 232 Hwy 17; d from $89; 🕸) The Polish-owned Parkway's 13 appealing rooms feature microwave, fridge, coffee maker, TV with cable, and the obligatory Group of Seven repros. The rooms also have a DVD player, with a library of complimentary movies in reception, and there's a boat-shaped picnic and barbecue deck on the front lawn. It's 5km south of Wawa along the highway.

★ Rock Island Lodge   LODGE $$
(☑ 705-856-2939; www.rockislandlodge.ca; 10 Government Dock Rd, Lake Superior; d/geo-dome incl breakfast $148/60, tent/tent site $46/30; ☺ May-Oct; 🕸) Naturally Superior Adventures' lodge sits along Lake Superior between a craggy expanse of stone and smooth, sandy beach. The four basic rooms are spotless and comfortable, and those on a budget can 'glamp' in the geo-dome tents on a raised platform with a queen-size bed. There's a beautiful guest kitchen and lounge, as well as wi-fi, but no TV.

Turn off Hwy 17 around 6.5km south of Wawa, toward Michipicoten River Village, to reach the lodge.

Kinniwabi Pines   INTERNATIONAL $$
(☑ 705-856-7226; Hwy 17; mains $16-28; ☺ 9am-10pm May-Oct) What would you expect to find lurking behind the facade of a highway motel 7km south of Wawa? Food from Trinidad, mon! Add some spice to your trip and try the jerk chicken or curry wraps,

OFF THE BEATEN TRACK

CHAPLEAU

About 140km inland from Wawa, Little Chapleau (*chap*-loh) is the gateway to the world's largest crown game preserve, with nearly 1 million hectares of land; hunting is strictly prohibited. For information, check out www.chapleau. ca/en, or stop by the town's **Centennial Museum & Information Centre** (☑705-864-1122; 94 Monk Street; ☺May-Oct). Critters you might encounter include bald eagles, beavers, lynx, black bears, moose and more.

The Missinaibi River flows over 750km northeast from its source at Missinaibi Lake, 80km northwest of Chapleau, to James Bay, running through **Missinaibi Provincial Park**, a 500km-long park in Chapleau Crown Game Preserve en route. Several outfits offer canoe rental and tours along the river, including MHO Adventures.

European and Chinese dishes, and seafood including pickerel, are also available for those who don't care to dare their palate. Sit in the quaint log-cabin dining room or on the lovely rear terrace overlooking the river.

🛍 Shopping

Young's General Store　　FOOD, OUTDOORS
(☑705-856-2626; www.youngsgeneralstore.com; 111 Mission Rd; ☺8am-9pm May-Oct) Stock up for the long drive ahead at this delightfully old-fashioned store, established in 1971. Piled to the rafters and hanging from the ceiling are fresh local produce (sausage and fudge are specialties, fishing tackle, T-shirts and even the odd moose head.

❶ Information

Visitors Information Centre (☑800-367-9292, ext 260 705-856-2244; www.experiencewawa.com; 26 Mission Rd; ☺8am-8pm Jul & Aug, 9am-5pm late May, Jun, Sep & early Oct; 🖥) Drop in for info on Wawa, including an accommodations list and excellent tourist map, and the region's parks. Also here are a museum covering local history and a gallery exhibiting the town's arts and crafts.

❶ Getting There & Away

Ontario Northland (p170) buses travel to Wawa from Sault Ste Marie ($47, 2¾ hours, one daily)

and as far north as White River ($20, one hour, one daily).

Pukaskwa National Park

With only 4km of roads within the 1878-sq-km expanse of **Pukaskwa National Park** (☑807-229-0801;　www.parkscanada.gc.ca/pukaskwa; Hwy 627; day use adult/child $5.80/free, serviced campsite with hookup $30, unserviced campsite without hookup $26, backcountry tent sites $9.80; ☺May-Oct), visitors to Ontario's only wilderness national park have to explore via hiking or paddling. It's similar to Lake Superior Provincial Park but more remote; keep an eye out for moose and black bears.

Pukaskwa's frontcountry is based around its only general-use campground at **Hattie Cove**, near the park's entrance. Stop in at the **visitor center** (☑807-229-0801; Hattie Cove; ☺9am-4pm Sun-Tue & Thu, until 8pm Wed, Fri & Sat Jul-Aug; 🖥) when you arrive: guided hikes and activities depart from here most summer evenings.

Three short hiking trails begin at Hattie Cove, offering glimpses of the pristine setting. The popular **Southern Headland Trail** (2.2km) is a rocky, spear-shaped route that offers elevated photo-ops of the shoreline and craggy Canadian Shield. Look for the curious stunted trees, so formed by harsh winds blowing off the lake. The **Bimose Kinoomagewnan** (Walk of Teachings; 2.6km) loops around Halfway Lake, passing boards with stories and artwork from the Ojibwe. The **Beach Trail** (1.5km) winds along Horseshoe Bay and Lake Superior revealing sweeping vistas of crashing waves and undulating sand dunes.

The three trails can be combined for a 6.3km walk, while the **Manito Miikana** (Spirit Trail; 2km) follows a rocky ravine from the Beach Trail, to viewing decks overlooking the lake and Pic River dunes.

Pukaskwa's stunning backcountry is not for the fainthearted: the 1878 sq km of remote, untouched wilderness defines isolation. The **Coastal Hiking Trail** (60km) is the main artery for hikers, dipping along the vast shoreline. For a taste of the backcountry, many fit hikers opt to traverse the first 7.8km of this trail, culminating at the 30m-long, 25m-high **White Water Suspension Bridge**. The trek is damp and arduous, and there's only one way in and out (15km total).

Paddlers can choose from three incredible multiday routes, including the acclaimed **White River Canoe Route** (72km; four to six days), which links Hattie Cove to **White Lake Provincial Park**. Check with the visitor center; part of the route was closed when we visited due to a hydroelectric project. Gentler paddles lead around the inlets and isles of Hattie Cove and Halfway Lake.

Do not attempt any of these hiking or water voyages without proper preparation and registration. If you need a water taxi, **North Shore Adventures** (807-228-0709; www.northshoreadventures.ca; Marathon) picks up and drops off anywhere along the coast, though fickle weather can delay the pickup service.

If you're not a skilled independent hiker, Naturally Superior Adventures (p179) offers guided excursions through Pukaskwa's backcountry. It also runs multiday sea kayaking trips here.

Slate Islands

Drop by the town of **Terrace Bay** (www.terracebay.ca) and catch a boat (return from $165 each with four people) 13km to this outstanding **archipelago** (807-825-3403; www.ontarioparks.com/park/slateislands), which is possibly the remains of an ancient meteorite. The islands are home to snowshoe hare and one of the world's largest herds of woodland caribou, as well as forested inlets for kayaking explorations. Naturally Superior Adventures (p179) runs five-day kayaking expeditions here ($1950).

There are no visitor facilities on the island, and as Slate Islands is crown land, Canadian citizens and residents are allowed to camp up to 21 days free of charge. If you are not a Canadian resident, you are supposed to buy a camping permit at any ServiceOntario government office.

Sleeping Giant Provincial Park

Seen across the lake from Thunder Bay, the jagged Sleeping Giant Peninsula resembles a large reclining man. Its rugged, forested terrain has been considered a sacred realm for millennia.

The **Sleeping Giant Provincial Park** (807-977-2526; www.ontarioparks.com/park/sleepinggiant; Hwy 587; day use per vehicle $11.25, campsites $37-42, cabins from $170, camping trailers $98-142) covers much of the craggy prom-

ontory, offering unforgettable views of Lake Superior.

The park is wild enough to offer backcountry camping and over 80km of hiking trails, yet compact enough for a fulfilling day trip from Thunder Bay, around 70km west. Contact Ontario Parks (www.ontarioparks.com) for reservations. On trails such as the 40km, multiday **Kabeyun**, which follows the peninsula's dramatic coastline, you might see moose, wolf, fox or lynx in the boreal forest. There are also short trails of 1km and up, and kayak and canoe rental.

At the tip of the peninsula, you'll find the remote community of **Silver Islet**. In the mid-1880s the town exploded with the world's richest silver mine, now abandoned, and was a Hollywood location of choice in the early 20th century.

Thunder Bay

807 / POP 93,952

Thunder Bay is about as comfortably isolated as you can get – it's 706km west of Sault Ste Marie and 703km east of Winnipeg (Manitoba). If you're arriving by road, it's a welcome return to civilization: no matter how beautiful the forests and shoreline, they start to blur together after a few hundred kilometers. With a smattering of historical attractions, surrounding natural beauty, and creative restaurants and bars in its regenerated downtown Entertainment District, you might be pleasantly surprised that Thunder Bay hums along strongly, in defiance and celebration of its long, dark winters. Maybe it has something to do with the fact that 10% of the population are of Finnish descent.

If you're passing through, consider staying two nights to get a sense of the place. Otherwise, if you're looking for something different, why not watch for a seat sale and fly up from Toronto for the weekend?

Sights

Fort William Historical Park MUSEUM
(807-473-2344; www.fwhp.ca; 1350 King Rd; adult/child $14/10; 10am-5pm mid-May–mid-Sep, tours every 45min) French voyageurs, Scottish gentlemen and Ojibwe scuttle about while re-enacting life in the early 1800s at this historical park. From 1803 to 1821, Fort William was the headquarters of the North West Company. Eventually the business was absorbed

by the Hudson's Bay Company and the region's importance as a trading center declined. Today the large heritage center offers 46 reconstructed historic buildings stuffed with entertaining and antiquated props such as muskets, pelts and birch-bark canoes.

Marina Park   HARBOR

(🚗 Nov-Apr 807-625-2941, mid-May–mid-Oct 807-345-2741; www.thunderbay.ca/en/recreation/marina.aspx; Sleeping Giant Pkwy) The focus of exciting development plans, Thunder Bay's marina area is a pedestrianized haven of parkland, fountains, footpaths, a skate park and public art. Pick up the free *Public Art Walking Tour Guide,* covering the many installations along the waterfront, from the tourist offices (or download it from www.visitthunderbay.com/en/see-and-do/public-art-walking-tour.aspx). Outdoor movies, concerts and festivals take place here in summer.

The area is also known as Prince Arthur's Landing or just the plain old waterfront. Access it from downtown over the blue pedestrian bridge at the eastern end of Red River Rd, near the Pagoda Information Center.

Bay & Algoma Historical District   AREA

Thunder Bay has a population of well over 10,000 Finnish Canadians, descended from immigrants who began arriving in the late 19th century. Locals happily honor this heritage by taking saunas and eating pancakes. In this historical Finnish district around the intersection of Bay and Algoma Sts, you will see Scandinavian shops and businesses and perhaps hear older people speaking Finnish.

David Thompson
Astronomical Observatory   OBSERVATORY

(🚗 807-473-2344; www.fwhp.ca/observatory; 1350 King Rd; adult/child $10/8; ⏰ 10pm-midnight Thu-Sat May-Aug, 9-11pm Thu-Sat Sep-Oct, shorter hours rest of year) Peek at the stars through one of Canada's largest telescopes at Fort William Historical Park's (p181) fantastic, accessible observatory. Check the website for the latest viewing conditions. Even if the weather is cloudy, join a Star Walk for a virtual tour of the night sky.

Mt McKay   VIEWPOINT

(🚗 807-623-9543; www.fwfn.com; Mission Rd; per vehicle $5; ⏰ 9am-10pm mid-May–early Oct) Mt McKay rises 350m over Thunder Bay, offering sweeping views of the region's patchwork of rugged pines and swollen rock formations. The lookout is part of the Fort William First Nation reserve, and reveals its most majestic moments in the evening when the valley is but a sea of blinking lights. An easy walking trail ascends 175m from the viewing area to the top of the mountain. Watch your step while climbing – the shale rock can cause tumbles.

Terry Fox Lookout & Memorial   MONUMENT

(1000 Hwy 11/17) This memorial honors Terry Fox, a young cancer sufferer and amputee who began a trans-Canada walk on April 12, 1980 to raise money for cancer research. After traveling 5373km from St John's, Newfoundland, he arrived in Thunder Bay as his condition deteriorated. He never left. Today's memorial is erected close to where Terry ended his great 'Marathon of Hope.'

Thunder Bay Art Gallery   GALLERY

(🚗 807-577-6427; www.theag.ca; 1080 Keewatin St, Confederation College; adult/child under 12yr $5/free; ⏰ noon-8pm Tue-Thu, to 5pm Fri-Sun) Thunder Bay's premier gallery offers an eclectic assortment of contemporary art, including works by indigenous artists from northwestern Ontario and beyond. The painters' use of natural imagery, haunting masks and scorching primary colors will leave a lasting impression on visitors. A new larger venue in Marina Park is being built.

Thunder Bay Museum   MUSEUM

(🚗 807-623-0801; www.thunderbaymuseum.com; 425 Donald St E; adult/child $3/1.50; ⏰ 11am-5pm mid-Jun–early Sep, from 1pm Tue-Sun early Sep–mid-Jun) This century-old museum is engaging for adults and children alike. Displays about Ojibwe culture, fur trading, military history and recent developments incorporate well-presented artifacts to offer visitors a glimpse of the region's 10,000 years of human history.

🏃 Activities

Sail Superior   BOATING

(🚗 807-628-3333; www.sailsuperior.com; Pier 3, Sleeping Giant Pkwy) Sailboat tours on Lake Superior from Thunder Bay marina, including 1½-hour trips around the harbor (adult/child under 10 years $59/25, minimum four people).

Loch Lomond Ski Area   SKIING

(🚗 807-475-7787; www.lochlomond.ca; 1800 Loch Lomond Rd; full-/half-day lift tickets from $46/34; ⏰ Dec-Apr) With 17 runs, equally distributed between beginner, intermediate and advanced, this is a great hill to learn on and a wonderful place to ski with kids. Ski, snowboard, equipment rental and lessons are available, and there's also tubing ($15). In summer, the slopes are open to hikers and mountain bikers.

Kangas
HEALTH & FITNESS

(☑807-344-6761; www.kangassauna.ca; 379 Oliver Rd; sauna/hot tub hire from $22/20; ⊙7:30am-8pm Mon-Fri, from 8am Sat & Sun) Reflecting Thunder Bay's Finnish heritage, this local institution offers 1½-hour private rental of its saunas. Each accommodates up to six people, so go it alone or grab a 'conference room' for you and your 'associates.' There's also a hot tub, and the cafe (mains $10) is popular for breakfast.

🛏 Sleeping

Most of the big motel chains are represented south of downtown: on Memorial Ave and around the intersections of Hwy 11/17 and the Harbour Expressway, and Hwy 61 and Arthur St W (near the airport). Northeast of downtown, a few independent motels on Cumberland St N/Hodder Ave charge around $70 for a room. It is worth booking ahead, as Thunder Bay's role as a regional hub keeps the hotels busy.

Strathcona Motel
MOTEL $

(☑807-683-8136; www.strathconamotel.ca; 545 Hodder Ave; d $80; Ⓟ🛜) This tiny motel has been in the family since personable owner Ken was a kid. Dating back to 1956, the six self-catering units with separate bedrooms are a veritable time warp, but spotlessly clean and atmospheric. It's a few kilometers east of downtown, close to amenities in a lovely neighborhood with parks and bike paths.

Thunder Bay
International Hostel
HOSTEL $

(☑807-983-2042; www.thunderbayinternational hostel.ca; 1594 Lakeshore Dr; campsites $25, d per person $25; Ⓟ🛜) Colorful bric-a-brac – including antlers, a baby grand piano and an old bus – lies splayed across the shrubby lawn as though Alice in Wonderland were having a garage sale. Charismatic owner Lloyd champions the backpacking lifestyle; he's a kind-hearted, well-traveled soul who cares about his guests. The hostel is 25km east of town, close to Sleeping Giant Provincial Park.

Prince Arthur Waterfront
Hotel & Suites
HOTEL $$

(☑807-345-5411; www.princearthurwaterfront. com; 17 Cumberland St N; d with city/lake view $115/125; Ⓟ❄@🛜♨) Following a renovation, this stately, century-old building is a good option once again. Rooms are spacious, with a distinctly old-fashioned feel. Where the hotel lacks polish, it compensates with its central harborside location and pool, gym, sauna and restaurant – all for the price of a chain motel.

NorWester
MOTEL $$

(☑807-473-9123; www.bwplusnorwester.com; 2080 Hwy 61; d from $169; Ⓟ🛜♨) This fantastic Best Western hotel's location about 15km from downtown is a drawback, but its leafy setting is lovely, the staff are excellent, rooms are clean and comfortable and there's a great selection of suites.

There's also a bar-restaurant and a huge indoor pool and hot tub for those wintry nights.

★ Delta Hotel by Marriott
HOTEL $$$

(☑807-344-0777; www.marriott.com; 2240 Sleeping Giant Pkwy; d from $239; Ⓟ❄) Thunder Bay's newest and fanciest hotel, right on the waterfront, is a worthwhile splurge. The rooms are large and full of all amenities, but it's the views over the marina toward the Sleeping Giant that make it worth the price.

🍴 Eating

★ Hoito Restaurant
FINNISH $

(☑807-345-6323; www.thehoito.ca; 314 Bay St; mains $9-15; ⊙8am-3pm Sun-Thu, to 7pm Fri & Sat) You'll think you've stumbled into a staff cafeteria in Finland; indeed, that's how the Hoito started, over a century ago, providing affordable meals to Finnish workers. This Thunder Bay institution's all-day breakfast of flattened Finnish *lättyjä* pancakes is the only way to start the day here. It's in the basement of the historic Finnish Labour Temple, now a cultural center.

★ Prime Gelato
ICE CREAM $

(☑807-344-1185; www.primegelato.ca; 200 Red River Rd; cup/waffle cone from $4/5.25; ⊙2pm-9pm Wed-Fri, from noon Sat, to 4pm Sun) With ambitions to be a Ben & Jerry's of the north, Prime sells gelato and sorbet in creative flavors such as salted caramel, and sometimes alcoholic options made with Kenora's Lake of the Woods beer. The dozen or so gluten-free creations on offer frequently change, but most incorporate fresh local produce from maple syrup to strawberries.

★ **Tomlin** CANADIAN **$$**
(⌨ 807-346-4447; www.tomlinrestaurant.com; 202 Red River Rd; mains $16-28, cocktails $10-14; ⊘ 5-10pm Tue-Sat) 🍴 Locally lauded chef Steve Simpson's elevated comfort food uses seasonal local ingredients, with the regularly changing menu split between small plates (eg beef tartare and smoked cauliflower) and large (veal cavatelli, crab and scallop linguine, redfin trout). The wine list is 100% Ontarian and includes ice wine, while creative cocktails such as the smoked port Manhattan also incorporate local ingredients.

Man vs Meats BARBECUE **$$**
(⌨ 807-286-3287; www.manvsmeats.ca; 230 Leland Ave S; mains $10-35; ⊘ 11am-7pm Mon-Thu, to 9pm Fri-Sat; 🅿) It would be easy to miss or discount this unassuming place in a strip mall, but you would be wrong for doing so. Inside this sports bar-like place is probably the best barbecue available in Thunder Bay. Meat lovers will adore the carnivore cheeseburger topped with bacon and pulled pork, but we recommend the ribs.

Bight INTERNATIONAL **$$$**
(⌨ 807-622-4448; www.bightrestaurant.ca; 2201 Sleeping Giant Pkwy; mains $19-35; ⊘ 11:30am-10pm Sun-Thu, until 11pm Fri & Sat; 🅿🛜) At this understated marina restaurant, chef Allan Rebelo has created a contemporary menu including charcuterie boards, pizza, fish tacos, and shrimp and lobster pasta. Sit outside between giant teardrop sculptures, or in the black, white and metal interior.

Caribou Restaurant & Wine Bar FUSION **$$$**
(⌨ 807-628-8588; www.caribourestaurant.com; 727 Hewitson St; lunch mains $15-18, dinner mains $20-48; ⊘ 11:30am-2pm Thu & Fri, 5-9pm daily; 🅿) Between southern Thunder Bay's confusing haze of wide-set freeways and boxy mega-marts lies one of the town's best dining options. Caribou's facade is somewhat misleading, reeking of franchise banality; the inside is filled with attentive touches such as white-clothed tables and designer stemware. The menu ranges from wood-oven pizza to seafood in spicy Creole sauce and oven-baked Arctic char.

🍷 Drinking & Nightlife

Head to the Entertainment District, on and around the eastern (lake) end of Red River Rd in the regenerated downtown area, for an excellent selection of restaurants and bars offering live music. Over the pedestri-an footbridge from here, Marina Park (p182) hosts outdoor movies, concerts and festivals in summer.

Look out for the locally brewed Sleeping Giant and Dawson Trail craft beers.

★ **Sleeping Giant Brewing Co.** MICROBREWERY
(⌨ 807-344-5225; www.sleepinggiantbrewing.ca; 712 Macdonell St; ⊘ 11am-10pm Mon-Sat, from noon Sun; 🛜) Established in 2012, this microbrewery was one of the first to take the risk of making different beers in a city known as a 'lager land.' The brewery can be credited with nurturing Thunder Bay's food culture, which has grown under the mantra of local ingredients and local knowledge, something that Sleeping Giant has championed since the beginning.

★ **Red Lion Smokehouse** CRAFT BEER
(⌨ 807-286-0045; www.redlionsmokehouse.ca; 16 Cumberland St S; ⊘ noon-10pm Tue-Thu, from 5pm Mon, to midnight Fri-Sat, to 9pm Sun) Now in a new space a few doors down from its old location, Thunder Bay's favorite hangout is bigger, brighter and has 12 taps of Ontario craft beer and over 100 cans. The food (mains $13 to $20) is just as good as before and the vibe still oozes industrial cool and coziness.

Sovereign Room BAR
(⌨ 807-343-9277; www.sovereignroom.com; 220 Red River Rd; ⊘ 4pm-2am Tue-Sat, from 11am Sun) From the chandelier behind the bar to the ornate olive wallpaper, dark woody booths and upward curling staircase by the storefront window, 'the Sov' is an atmospheric spot for a beer. There's live music, and the menu (mains $12 to $20) features staples and surprises such as duck poutine, stone-baked pizza, chicken wings and nachos.

St Paul Roastery COFFEE
(⌨ 807-344-3900; 11 St Paul St; ⊘ 7:30am-5pm Mon-Fri, from 9am Sat) Get your fix of black gold at this hip temple to the bean, which doubles as a roastery and has an adjoining record shop.

The Foundry BAR
(⌨ 807-285-3188; 242 Red River Rd; ⊘ 11am-2am Mon-Sat) This long-standing local fave offers dozens of beers on tap and meals in a two-level venue. Dishes ($16 to $20) include scrumptious coconut curry soup, poutine with Thunder Bay gouda, and fish-and-chips featuring local Sleeping Giant beer in the batter. There's live music most nights.

Growing Season JUICE BAR

(☑ 807-344-6869; www.growingseason.ca; 201 Algoma St S; ⊙ 11am-8pm Mon-Sat) Healthy blended juices and shakes are the name of the game at this 'juice collective.' There are also scrumptious dishes to accompany your smoothie, with ingredients supplied by a long list of local producers.

❶ Information

Pagoda Information Center (☑ 807-684-3670; www.tourismthunderbay.com; cnr Red River Rd & Water St; ⊙ 10am-6pm Tue-Sat Jul & Aug) Canada's oldest tourist information bureau, in a distinctive building dating from 1909, remains the city's most central source of visitor information.

Tourism Thunder Bay (☑ 800-667-8386, 807-983-2041; www.tourismthunderbay.com; 1000 Hwy 11/17; ⊙ 9am-5pm) The city's largest tourist office is located 6km east of town at the Terry Fox Lookout & Memorial.

❶ Getting There & Away

Thunder Bay Airport (YQT; ☑ 807-473-2600; www.tbairport.on.ca; off Hwy 61) is on the southwest side of the city, about 10km from downtown, at the junction of Arthur St W and Hwy 61. It is served by Air Canada, WestJet, Porter, Wasaya and Bearskin airlines, with around 15 flights a day from Toronto (around $120 one way). Other connections include Sudbury, Sault Ste Marie, Ottawa and Winnipeg.

There are no longer any bus routes that travel to Thunder Bay from southern Ontario.

Cochrane to Moose Factory & Moosonee

Time has not been kind to little Cochrane, whose raison d'être is the Polar Bear Express – the whistle-stop train shuttling passengers north to the remote recesses of James Bay. Cochrane doesn't pretend to be a dainty tourist destination and, in a way, that honesty is refreshing. Evidence of harsh, long winters is conspicuous in this windswept town, but despite the inhospitable winters, the largely Francophone population is warm and accommodating.

Moosonee and Moose Factory sit near the tundra line, and are as far north as most people ever get in eastern Canada. Expeditions further north will undoubtedly involve floatplanes, canoes, snowmobiles, dogsleds or snowshoes.

The railway reached Moosonee in 1932, about 30 years after it was established by Révillon Frères as a trading post. The neighboring island of Moose Factory is a small Cree settlement and the historic site of the Hudson's Bay Company trading hub founded in 1672.

⊙ Sights & Activities

Moosonee and Moose Factory could not be more different. Moosonee has a banal industrial vibe, while Moose Factory is a spirited reservation of friendly people and scores of smoke huts. The best way to experience the region is through a tour with the local Moose Cree.

Polar Bear Habitat &
Heritage Village ZOO

(☑ 705-272-2327; www.polarbearhabitat.ca; 1 Drury Park Rd, Cochrane; adult/student/child 5-11yr $16/12/10; ⊙ 9am-5pm late May–mid-Sep, 10am-4pm mid-Sep–late May) Despite all the polar bear talk, there are no wild polar bears in the region. This center, the world's largest polar bear facility and the only one with access to a natural lake, is dedicated to the conservation, care and wellbeing of the furry giants. There are currently three resident bears: Ganuk, Inukshuk and Henry. Visitors can learn more about them at 'meet the keeper' sessions (daily in summer).

Tidewater Provincial Park PARK

(☑ 705-272-7107; www.ontarioparks.com/park/tidewater; day use/camping per person $5/10; ⊙ late Jun-early Sep) Tidewater covers five islands in the Moose River estuary, with backcountry camping offered on Charles Island between Moose Factory and Moosonee. You might glimpse a seal or the milky white back of a beluga whale from your campsite. Access the island by water taxi from Moosonee; these waterways are only for experienced canoeists. Contact Moose Cree Outdoor Discoveries & Adventures (p187) for permits.

Cree Cultural
Interpretive Centre MUSEUM

(☑ 705-658-2733; 49 Pehdabun Rd, Moose Factory; ⊙ 9am-4:30pm Sun-Fri Jun-Aug, 8:30am-5pm Mon-Fri Sep-May) Operated by Moose Cree First Nation, this center features indoor and outdoor exhibits of artifacts, including bone tools, traditional toys, reusable diapers and dwellings from the precontact era. You'll learn about *pashtamowin*, or 'what goes around, comes around' – the Cree's version of karma, if you will. It is best to explore the center with the aid of a guide, as they can relay fascinating details and personal anecdotes about the interesting displays.

THUNDER BAY TO MANITOBA

Decisions, decisions: if you're heading west from Lake Superior to Winnipeg, you have two choices. The northern route (Hwy 17) is faster and has more services along the way, but the scenic southern route (Hwy 11 and Hwy 71) offers some impressive diversions.

Leaving Thunder Bay, traffic and highway vistas thin out after Kakabeka Falls. Then, at Shabaqua Corners, the highway forks: the northern route plows straight toward Winnipeg, while the southern route takes two extra hours as it ambles through more scenic countryside. Both routes shuttle you through prime fishing country, not least the idyllic Lake of the Woods region and its unofficial capital, Kenora.

Signs mark the beginning of a new time zone (you save an hour going west).

Northern Route

Ignace and the larger town of Dryden, respectively on Agimak Lake and Wabigoon Lake (no relation to Lake Wobegon, American novelist Garrison Keillor's fictional Minnesota town), are possible stop-offs. However, the biggest and best place to pause is Kenora, the unofficial capital of the striking Lake of the Woods region and tourism hub for local summer cottages and fishing trips. Rambling across Ontario, Manitoba and Minnesota, Lake of the Woods is the local answer to Toronto's cottage country for weekending Winnipeggers.

MS Kenora (www.mskenora.com) offers daily 2¼-hour cruises around the northern section of Lake of the Woods, to see a little of the region's 100,000km of shoreline and 14,500 islands. Sunset dinner cruises are also offered.

The small Lake of the Woods Museum covers the indigenous, industrial and gold-mining history of the area, with a particular focus on the last 100 years, when Kenora changed rapidly.

Southern Route

The longer southern route from Thunder Bay to Winnipeg has some spectacular distractions. The first major stop after the northern and southern highways diverge at Shabaqua Corners is the crusty mining town of Atikokan – a good base for a day trip to the stunning and secluded Quetico Provincial Park. The endless waterlogged preserve has some of Canada's finest wilderness canoe and portage routes and hiking trails in its rugged backcountry. Canoe Canada Outfitters (http://canoecanada.com) provides both self-guided and guided adventures through this dramatic wilderness.

Further west, Fort Frances sits right on the American border, with a bridge crossing to Minnesota; Fort Frances Museum gives a historical introduction to the area. Kay-Nah-Chi-Wah-Nung, 60km west (25km past Emo), is a sacred Ojibwe site containing the largest ancient ceremonial burial grounds in Canada.

Before linking back up with Hwy 17 near Kenora, consider stopping in the serene resort towns of Nestor Falls and Sioux Narrows, both on Hwy 71.

Polar Bear Express RAIL

(☏800-265-2356, 705-472-4500; www.ontario northland.ca; 200 Railway St; round-trip adult/ child under 11yr $119/60; ☉Sun-Fri) A northern legend since 1964, this whistle-stop train remains the most popular and affordable conduit to the remote communities of Moosonee and Moose Factory. It departs Cochrane at 9am, reaches Moosonee at 2pm, then returns south at 5pm, arriving in Cochrane at around 10pm. The assortment of passengers is a sight in itself: locals, trappers, biologists, geologists, tourists, anglers and paddlers.

There is a licensed dining car, open for the whole journey with snacks and a set dinner for the trip back from Moosonee. The food is what you would expect from a train's kitchen, so it's best to bring lunch or dinner with you. It's a five-hour trip each way, so an overnight stay is recommended to avoid spending 10 hours on the train (looking at trees) just for three hours in Moosonee and Moose Factory. To guarantee your seat, book the night before at the latest, as extra cars can still be added at that stage.

While you ponder this lengthy journey, consider the following: when fur trading peaked 300 years ago, the main access to Ontario's interior was *from* the north via the Hudson and James Bays.

👉 Tours

Moose Cree Outdoor
Discoveries & Adventures   OUTDOORS
(📞705-658-4619; 22 Jonathan Cheechoo Dr, Moose Factory) 🏃 Moose Cree First Nation's tourism department offers customized trips incorporating cultural activities (storytelling and traditional foods) with, for example, canoeing in summer and snowshoeing in winter. In tailoring your adventure, friendly staff will ask you exactly what you want to experience. Prices vary depending on the number in your party, season and how long you want to visit.

🛏 Sleeping

There are a couple of lodging options in Moosonee, though we suggest staying on Moose Factory island. In addition to the eco-lodge here, Moose Cree Outdoor Discoveries & Adventures can organize accommodations and camping on Moose Factory and neighboring islands. Reserve accommodations before you arrive.

Cochrane has several options, including the **Best Western Swan Castle Inn** (📞705-272-5200; www.bestwestern.com; 189 Railway St,; s/d incl breakfast from $145/155; ❀@🛜) and Thriftlodge on the highway – and of course the inn at the station itself.

Hudson's Bay Company
Staff House   GUESTHOUSE $
(📞705-658-4619; www.facebook.com/moosecree tourism; 4 Front St, Moose Factory; d $85; 🛜) This rustic and historic building doubles as a museum, with exhibits on the ground floor covering the fur-trading era when Hudson's Bay employees lodged here and the manager stayed next door. Managed by Moose Cree First Nation, the four pastel-painted rooms share a kitchen and ablutions.

Thriftlodge   MOTEL $
(📞705-272-4281; www.travelodge.com; 50 Hwy 11 S, Cochrane; d from $90; ❀@🛜) One of the best deals in Cochrane, this chain motel offers 40 comfortable rooms with hair dryer, coffee maker and fridge, right next to the passable Terry's Steakhouse. The upstairs apartments are less pleasant and not recommended unless you are really counting the cents.

Station Inn   HOTEL $$
(📞705-272-3500, ext 3, 800-265-2356; www.ontarionorthland.ca; 200B Railway St, Cochrane; s/d $118/130; ❀🛜) Go one better than staying near the train station by staying on top of

it – you'll have no excuse to miss the Polar Bear Express. The salmon-colored hotel lobby also serves as the station's ticket office, waiting room and repository of polar bear statues, but the emphasis is on straight comfort and convenience in the boxy rooms.

🍴 Eating

Station Inn   CANADIAN $
(200 Railway St, Cochrane; mains $10-17; ⊙9am-8pm Sun-Thu, to 9pm Fri) Like the rest of the Station Inn, the restaurant is more functional than atmospheric, serving hefty meals and daily specials of steadfast Canadian food. Expect burgers, steak and wraps in large portions, served with small-town kindness.

Terry's Steakhouse   STEAK $$
(📞705-272-4770; Hwy 11 S, Cochrane; mains $17-29; ⊙11am-9pm Mon-Fri, from 4pm Sat, from 10am Sun) With its red-and-black checkered tablecloths and chintzy chandeliers, Terry's is the top choice in Cochrane for a steak. The likes of rib eye and filet mignon are charbroiled and accompanied by classic sauces such as peppercorn. Burgers, pasta, seafood, traditional favorites such as liver and onions, sandwiches and wraps ($9) are also on the menu.

ℹ Information

Cochrane Tourist Office (📞705-277-4926; www.cochraneontario.com; 4 Third Ave, Cochrane; ⊙9:30am-5pm Mon-Fri) This small office is next to the polar bear statue named Chimo (its name comes from the Cree word meaning 'be welcome'), at the intersection of Hwy 11 S (to North Bay) and Hwy 11 W (to Thunder Bay).

Cochrane Train Station The ticket desk at the train station is another useful source of northern knowledge.

Moose Cree Outdoor Discoveries & Adventures Information on accommodations and activities on Moose Factory.

ℹ Getting There & Away

Ontario Northland (p170) runs a bus between Cochrane and Timmins ($21.50, 1½ hours), to link in with the Polar Bear Express (p186) train. Timmins has an airport with regular flights to/from Toronto as well as to Moosonee with **Air Creebec** (📞705-264-9521, 800-567-6567; www.aircreebec.ca) ($440, one hour).

Ontario Northland buses also connect **Cochrane Train Station** (📞705-272-4228; 200 Railway St) to North Bay ($92.50, 6¼ hours, one daily) and Sudbury ($81.50, 6½ hours, one daily).

ℹ Getting Around

From Moosonee, water taxis shuttle passengers the 3km over to Moose Factory ($15, 15 minutes). Be sure to have cash to pay the driver. In winter the river becomes an ice bridge stable enough for cars and trucks (taxi $10). When the river is freezing in late fall and thawing in early spring, neither option is safe and you will have to take a **helicopter** (☑705-336-2725; www. moosecree.com/aviationservices/; Airport Rd, Moosonee; $40).

Taxis from Moosonee train station to the docks, about 1km east, cost $5 per person, but it's also an easy walk.

Temagami

☑705 / POP 802

While god-fearing Egyptians were commissioning wondrous pyramids, this region of majestic old-growth pines and hushed lakes was a thriving network of trading routes. Evidence of these ancient trails exists today as hidden archaeological sites strewn throughout the region's provincial parks. Temagami's reputation for canoe and portage experiences of the untrammeled Canadian wilderness has attracted adventurers such as British TV personality Ray Mears.

Check out **Obabika River Park**, or the vast **Lady Evelyn Smoothwater Provincial Park**, which has Ontario's highest point, Ishpatina Ridge (693m). There are no facilities, and campsites can only be reached by canoe. The easily accessible **White Bear Forest** has a soaring fire tower at Caribou Mountain offering a bird's-eye view of the stocky trunks below. Pick up the *White Bear Forest Old Growth Trails* map from Temagami Information Center for details of the 1km to 5km walks.

◉ Sights

Caribou Mountain Fire Tower   VIEWPOINT
(O'Connor Rd; $3; ⊙ late May–early Oct) FREE Follow the road 2km from town, then climb a short path through the trees of White Bear Forest and, finally, a vertigo-inducing spiral staircase to enjoy this tower's sweeping views. It was built in the late '50s and (don't worry) restored in 1998. If you don't fancy that staircase, there is a lookout at the base of the tower.

Finlayson Point Provincial Park   PARK
(☑705-569-3205; www.ontarioparks.com/park/finlaysonpoint; Hwy 11; day use per vehicle $14.50, campsite with/without hookup $47/41.50; ⊙late

May–Sep) This small peninsula on Lake Temagami offers canoeing, swimming and camping. Drop by the park office, just off Hwy 11 1km south of town, for information on the group of preserves surrounding Temagami.

🏃 Activities

Even by Canadian standards, Temagami is a rugged, outdoorsy place. In summer, come for canoe trips through the wilderness, and plan to spend a few days – you need at least four to reach the unpopulated outback. In winter, come for snowmobile trails.

Temagami Outfitting Co   CANOEING
(☑416-835-0963; www.temagamioutfitting.ca; 6 Lakeshore Dr) The passionate guys at Temagami Outfitting Co offer fully outfitted wilderness canoe trips (around $100 per person per day); you could turn up in a Hawaiian shirt and they would do the rest, from canoe and clothing to camping equipment. They also sell permits for parks in the region and offer shuttles to many of the lakes, starting at $100.

🛏 Sleeping

Northland Paradise Lodge   LODGE $
(☑705-569-3791; www.northland-paradise.com; 51 Stevens Rd; s/d $65/90; 🐾🖥) Right on the lake, Northland is a good old-fashioned fishing and hunting lodge with a games room, butchery and tackle-cleaning room. The motel-style rooms with kitchenette are perfect spots to crash after a day on the water, while the rustic housekeeping suites with lake-facing balconies are ideal for an outdoorsy break.

ℹ Getting There & Away

Ontario Northland (p170) buses connect Temagami with North Bay ($22, 1¼ hours, two daily), which has services to/from Toronto.

North Bay

☑705 / POP 50,396

North Bay bills itself as 'just north enough to be perfect,' which begs the question: Perfect for what? It's just north enough to make visiting Torontonians feel like adventurers, and the while lakeshore is lovely, the city is not notably attractive. That said, its real appeal lies in its access to the lake and surrounding countryside, which is slowly becoming part of cottage country (p207) as weekend home-building city slickers pioneer north from oversubscribed Muskoka. To these charms, North Bay adds plenty of decent accommodations and some great restaurants by the water.

Ontario's two major highways (11 and 17) converge as they pass through town, making North Bay a logical layover for Trans-Canada tourists. The highways don't link up again until Nipigon (just before Thunder Bay), 1000km northwest.

◎ Sights & Activities

Lake Nipissing Waterfront   PARK
A walk along the scenic Lake Nipissing shoreline reveals several enjoyable activities. Shrubs, trees and perennials line the path, maintained by the North Bay Heritage Gardeners. At the marina are the **Heritage Railway and Carousel** (☑705-495-8412; www. heritagetrainandcarousel.weebly.com; Memorial Dr; ride $2; ☺10am-dusk late Jun-early Sep, 4pm-dusk Fri, from 10am Sat-Sun May-Jun & Sep-Oct), a restaurant on the *Chief Commanda* boat, Fun Rentals kayak hire, and lake cruises on the Chief Commanda II.

Fun Rentals   KAYAKING
(☑705-471-4007; www.funrentals.ca; Memorial Dr; kayak/canoe/stand-up paddleboard 1½hr $25/35/30, 3hr $40/50/50; ☺11am-dusk Jul & Aug, from 4pm Fri, from 11am Sat & Sun May, Jun & Sep) Explore a little of Ontario's fourth-largest lake, Nipissing, in one of this outfit's kayaks, canoes or stand-up paddleboards. Take care and stay close to shore if the westerly wind is blowing, as it can be fierce. They also rent out 'unique bikes' (30 minutes/one hour from $15/20) for a family pedal along the waterfront.

Chief Commanda II   CRUISE
(☑705-494-8167; www.chiefcommanda.com; King's Landing, 200 Memorial Dr; ☺late May-early Oct) This jolly passenger liner cruises through Lake Nipissing's Manitou Islands (adult/child $30/15), along the French River ($46/25) on Sundays, and down to Callander Bay at sunset ($38/20). Dinner is available on the latter, and two-hour cruises to view the fall colors on the lake's north shore are a big hit. Book in advance.

🛏 Sleeping & Eating

Lincoln Inn   MOTEL $
(☑705-472-3231; www.thelincolninn.ca; 594 Lakeshore Dr; d/apt incl breakfast from $80/125; ❄☎) The Lincoln is a solid budget choice close to restaurants, with comfortable

rooms and self-catering apartments, the latter featuring a bedroom with two beds plus lounge with sofa bed. Discounts are often available.

★Sunset Inn   MOTEL $$
(☑800-463-8370, 705-472-8370; www.sunsetinn. ca; 641 Lakeshore Dr; d/cabins from $119/229; ❄☎) This spotless waterfront option has its own private beach in a secluded cove off Lake Nipissing, which amply compensates for the odd lapse in taste regarding the decor. Numerous room types include luxurious suites with heart-shaped Jacuzzis and large flat-screen TVs, and two- and three-bedroom chalets with full kitchens. There's a romantic beachfront cabin for two with fireplace and Jacuzzi.

White Owl Bistro   CANADIAN $$
(☑705-472-2662; www.thewhiteowlbistro.ca; 639 Lakeshore Dr; mains $25; ☺11am-9pm Mon-Sat, 10am-3pm & 5-9pm Sun; ☎☑) 🍴 Nestled among the lakefront motels, this lovely little bistro, built in 1934, serves a range of dishes including salads, pastas, venison burger, rainbow trout, pickerel and Sunday brunches, with seating inside and on the patio. The chicken and pork come from the owner-chefs' farm, Somewood. There are local beers on tap and the homemade bread comes with herb butter.

★Churchill's   STEAK $$$
(☑705-476-7777; www.churchills.ca; 631 Lakeshore Dr; mains $36-50; ☺11am-10pm Mon-Sat, from 4pm Sun; ☎) 🍴 This low-lit bistro makes up for once being the first branch of megachain Tim Hortons by serving some of Canada's finest steaks and ribs, accompanied by homegrown produce and Ontario's largest wine selection north of Toronto. Ontario lamb and Atlantic salmon are also on the menu and we highly recommend the 24-hour beef short ribs.

ℹ Information

North Bay Chamber of Commerce (☑888-249-8998, 705-472-8480; www.northbaycham ber.com; 205 Main St E; ☺9am-4pm Mon-Fri) Has brochures and the helpful staff are a font of information.
Heritage Railway and Carousel The ticket office offers brochures, maps and information.

ℹ Getting There & Away

Ontario Northland (p170) buses connect Toronto and North Bay ($80, 5½ hours, four daily).

The terminus for services is the old train station, known as the **Station** (☑705-495-4200; www.ontarionorthland.ca; 100 Station Rd).

Air Canada and Bearskin Airlines fly to the small **North Bay Jack Garland Airport** (☑705-474-3026; www.yyb.ca; 50 Terminal St), 10km northeast of town, from Toronto and Sudbury.

EASTERN ONTARIO

Eastern Ontario encompasses the countryside east of Toronto as far as the Québec border. Within weekending distance of Toronto, Prince Edward County's (p197) fertile pastures support a long farming tradition and young wine industry. Travelers journeying on the busy Hwy 401 should detour through this scenic, culinary and historic realm.

For museums, history and urban vibes, head to Kingston (p200), the first capital of modern-day Canada, and of course today's vibrant capital, Ottawa (p211). East of Kingston is the Thousand Islands (p205) region, a foggy archipelago of lonely isles along the deep St Lawrence Seaway, where the towns of Gananoque and Brockville have a genteel Victorian feel.

Eastern Ontario's natural beauty extends to the interior, which overflows with scenic parks and preserves. Algonquin Provincial Park is the area's flagship domain, offering unparalleled canoeing and wildlife spotting among towering jack pines and lakes. Similar topography extends to the Haliburton Highlands (p194), Kawarthas (p195) and Land O' Lakes (p196).

Algonquin Provincial Park

Established in 1893, Ontario's oldest and second-largest park is a sight for city-sore eyes, with over 7600 sq km of thick pine forests, jagged cliffs, trickling crystal streams, mossy bogs and thousands (thousands!) of lakes. An easily accessible outdoor gem, this rugged expanse is a must-visit for canoeists, hikers and seekers of piney fresh air.

Hwy 60 intersects a small portion of the park near its southern edge. Numerous campgrounds, lodges, attractions and short hiking trails are accessible from this well-trodden corridor. The vast, wooded interior of Algonquin is only accessible via over 2000km of charted canoe routes and strenuous hiking trails.

If you are stopping anywhere in the park, you must purchase a day permit ($18 per vehicle) at the gate. If you won't be stopping, you don't need a permit to cross Algonquin on Hwy 60.

⊙ Sights

Algonquin Visitors Centre   MUSEUM
(☑613-637-2828; www.algonquinpark.on.ca; Km 43 on Hwy 60; ⊙9am-5pm mid-May–mid-Jun & Oct, to 7pm mid-Jun–Sep, to 4pm Nov-Apr; P) At this world-class visitor center displays and dioramas illustrate the park's wildlife, history and geology. The center also has a bookstore, cafeteria, wi-fi and lookouts with spectacular views.

Algonquin Art Centre   GALLERY
(☑855-221-2278, 705-633-5555; www.algonquin artcentre.com; Km 20 on Hwy 60; by donation; ⊙10am-5pm Jun-Oct) FREE Exhibits an array of wilderness-themed art through several media including paintings, photography, carvings and sculpture. Check the website for details of summer art classes and events.

The center is located 20km from the West Gate inside the park. A valid park permit is required to visit the art center.

RIDEAU CANAL

In 2007, the **Rideau Canal** (Map p212; www.pc.gc.ca/eng/lhn-nhs/on/rideau/index.aspx) became Canada's 14th location to be named a World Heritage site, and it remains one of the country's eight cultural inclusions on the Unesco list. Opened in 1832, the 200km-long system connects Kingston with Ottawa through 47 locks, climbing 84m from Ottawa over the Canadian Shield before dropping 49m into Lake Ontario. It's a nautical paradise, lined with charming parks, lakes and towns to enjoy.

After the War of 1812, there was a fear of future skirmishes with the Americans. The Duke of Wellington decided to link Ottawa and Kingston in order to have a reliable communications and supply route between the two military centers. Construction was a brutal affair, involving as many as 4000 men battling malarial swamps and the Canadian Shield, some of the world's hardest rock. Despite their blood, sweat and tears, the canal never saw military service, although it later proved useful for shipping goods.

Eastern Ontario

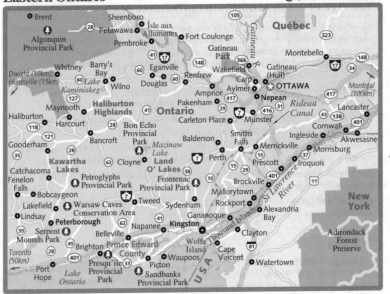

Algonquin
Logging Museum MUSEUM
(📞613-637-2828; Km 55 on Hwy 60; ⊘9am-5pm Jul-Oct) FREE This excellent museum has extensive exhibits dedicated to the park's logging heritage. The displays are spread along a 1.5km trail that remains open even when the reception area, bookstore and theater are closed.

🏃 Activities

Algonquin is famous for its wildlife-watching and scenic lookouts. During spring, you're almost certain to see moose along Hwy 60. Other creatures you may encounter include deer, beaver, otter, mink and many bird species. It's a great place to give canoeing or kayaking a whirl. Canoe Lake on Hwy 60 is a popular starting point for beginners.

★Portage Store CANOEING
(📞summer 705-633-5622, winter 705-789-3645; www.portagestore.com; Canoe Lake, Km 14 on Hwy 60; canoes per day from $34, 2-day complete outfitting packages from $100) Located 14km inside the park's West Gate on Canoe Lake at access point five, this sprawling complex has a restaurant, outfitters, grocery store and gift shop...oh, and North America's largest fleet of canoes. You can turn up in your least

rugged Hawaiian shirt and staff will dispatch you to the wilderness complete with camping, canoeing and portage essentials and know-how.

They can recommend paddle-and-portage routes, including a three-day loop with three to eight portages a day, most 300m to 800m in length. Guided half- and full-day and overnight paddling adventures, and canoe delivery to campgrounds, are also offered.

Algonquin Portage CANOEING
(📞613-735-1795; www.algonquinportage.com; 1352 Barron Canyon Rd, Pembroke; canoes per day from $30, r per adult/child under 13yr $35/25, camping per person $8; ⊘8am-4pm) Rustic accommodations (BYO sleeping bag), shuttle service, camping gear, canoes, kayaks, mountain bikes, food and gas are all available here. It's east of the park's furthest eastern extent, on Rte 28.

Canoe Algonquin CANOEING
(📞705-636-5956; www.canoealgonquin.com; 1914 Hwy 518 E, Kearney; canoes per day from $31) North of Huntsville, this outfitter is the closest to access points two (Tim River), three (Magnetawan Lake) and four (Rain Lake) on the park's western side.

TOP FIVE HIKES IN ALGONQUIN PROVINCIAL PARK

Whether you're visiting for a day or a month, sampling some of the over 140km of hiking trails, including many shorter jaunts accessible from Hwy 60, is a must. Hikes depart from various mileposts (actually kilometer-posts) along Hwy 60 between the West Gate (Km 0) and the East Gate (Km 56). You can buy a 50¢ hiking guide at the information centers and trailheads.

Mizzy Lake (moderate 11km loop) An excellent chance to see some diverse wildlife: all known species within the park have been witnessed here at some point. At Km 15.

Track & Tower (moderate 7.7km loop) A serene lakeside trail and an unusual elevated lookout point along an abandoned railway. At Km 25.

Booth's Rock (difficult 5km loop) Follow an abandoned railway for breathtaking views of the sweeping lakes and forests. To get there, follow the road 8km south from Km 40.

Centennial Ridges (difficult 10km loop) The best panoramas in the park, bar none. To get there, follow Rock Lake Road from Km 37.

Lookout Trail (moderate 2km loop) The busiest hike in Algonquin, but for good reason: a spectacular view of untouched nature awaits. At Km 40.

Tours

★ **Opeongo Outfitters** OUTDOORS
(☑613-637-5470, 800-790-1864; www.opeongo outfitters.com; 29902 Hwy 60, Whitney; canoes per day from $25) Algonquin's oldest outfitter is just outside the park's East Gate. It offers fully kitted canoeing and camping packages ($77 to $87 per person), and three- to five-day adventures (from $110 per person), which transfer you by water taxi to a ready-made campsite in a remote location for camping, canoeing, fishing and moose spotting.

Algonquin Outfitters CANOEING
(☑800-469-4948; www.algonquinoutfitters.com; canoes per day from $30, 2-day guided trips from $145) With stores in several locations, including three outlets within the Algonquin Provincial Park at Opeongo Lake, Lake of Two Rivers and Brent, these guys have got the park covered. Guided trips are available, and water taxis can be reserved to whisk you across Opeongo Lake to wilder regions ($32 per person).

Northern Edge Algonquin OUTDOORS
(☑888-383-8320; www.northernedgealgonquin. ca; 100 Ottawa Ave, South River; 3 day all-inclusive trips from $558) Offers paddling trips, women's getaways, yoga retreats, cabins and tailored programs throughout the year. The office is located in South River, while the camp is en route to access point one (Kawawaymog/Round Lake) in the northwest of Algonquin.

Voyageur Quest OUTDOORS
(☑416-486-3605, 800-794-9660; www.voyageur quest.com; Kawawaymog/Round Lake; 3-/5-day canoe trip $490/785) Based at access point one, this 25-year-old operator offers popular paddling trips and log cabins.

Algonquin North

Wilderness Outfitters CANOEING
(☑705-744-3265, 877-544-3544; www.algonquin north.com; Crooked Chute Lake, Hwy 17 & Hwy 630; canoes per day from $39) This outfitter is north of Algonquin Provincial Park at the junction of Hwy 17 and Hwy 630, about 18km west of Mattawa. From here, a paved road takes you 30km south to the Kioshkokwi Lake access point for secluded backcountry explorations. It offers both canoe rental and guided trips.

Sleeping

Algonquin is a nature preserve, which means that most noncamping accommodations are outside the park boundaries. Motels and lodges cluster outside the East Gate and West Gate, in Whitney and along Hwy 60 to Huntsville.

Ontario Parks
Campgrounds CAMPGROUND $
(☑info 705-633-5572, reservations 888-668-7275; www.ontarioparks.com/park/algonquin; campsite with/without ablutions $52-45, yurt $98, backcountry camping adult/child under 18yr $13/6) There are 11 car-accessible, developed campgrounds within the park, eight reached from Hwy 60, and some featuring yurts. Three

sites in the north (Achray, Brent and Kiosk) are accessed via minor roads, reached along Hwy 17. The backcountry camping sites are only accessible by hiking or canoeing. In all cases, book well in advance, especially in summer.

West Gate

★Wolf Den Nature Retreat   HOSTEL $

(📞705-635-9336, 866-271-9336; www.wolfden bunkhouse.com; 4568 Hwy 60, Oxtongue Lake; dm/s/d without bathroom from $31/48/69) 🏊 Located 10km outside the West Gate, this outdoorsy hostel-cum-resort offers lodging from dorms to gorgeous eco-cabins accommodating up to six. Guests can also choose between rustic '50s cabins, A-frame bunkhouses, and hostel rooms with shared bathrooms in the cozy central lodge, with its huge kitchen, stunning 2nd-floor lounge and cedar log sauna nearby.

Dwight Village Motel   MOTEL $$

(📞705-635-2400; www.dwightvillagemotel.com; 2801 Hwy 60, Dwight; r $115; ❄🛜) You'll notice this excellent motel, with its wood-fronted rooms offering all the creature comforts, from the highway. There's a lovely outdoor picnic area with fire pits and plenty of room for kids to play. It's around 25km west of the West Gate, just past the village of Dwight.

Park Interior

In addition to the camping options, there are three upscale lodges within the park, all reached along Hwy 60. Arowhon Pines, Bartlett Lodge and Killarney Lodge operate between May and October. They mostly offer American plan (full-board) or modified American plan (half-board) accommodations.

★Killarney Lodge   LODGE $$$

(📞705-633-5551, 866-473-5551; www.killarney lodge.com; Lake of Two Rivers, turnoff at Km 33 on Hwy 60; cabin per person with full board from $319; ⊘mid-May–mid-Oct; 🛜) With 27 one- and two-bedroom lakeside cabins dating from the 1930s, Killarney recalls the innocent days when rustic cabins were synonymous with family vacations. On a peninsula in the lake, it's an idyllic place to paddle or relax on your private deck with a glass of wine (BYO). The delightful, log cabin–style restaurant serves hearty and delicious meals.

Arowhon Pines   LODGE $$$

(📞705-633-5661, 866-633-5661; www.arowhon pines.ca; Arowhon Rd, turnoff at Km 16 on Hwy 60; r per person $255-428, private cabins per person $432-602; ⊘late May-early Oct; 🅿@🛜) If you've ever wondered what an adult summer camp might be like, Arowhon Pines is the answer. The largest and most luxurious of Algonquin's all-inclusive lodges has canoes, kayaks, hiking and mountain-biking trails, tennis courts, a sauna and gourmet fine dining (BYO wine). It's blissfully secluded, 8km north of Hwy 60. Rates include American-plan (full-board) accommodations.

Bartlett Lodge   LODGE $$$

(📞866-614-5355, 705-633-5543; www.bartlett lodge.com; Cache Lake, turnoff at Km 24 on Hwy 60; cabin per person $235-355, tent per person $120-170, studio per person $205-265; ⊘mid-May–Oct; 🛜) 🏊 Running completely on solar power, the two-bedroom lakeside 'Sunrise' is perhaps Bartlett's most interesting cabin, but studio suites, cabins and glamping platform tents are also available. All are accessed by boat, summoned using the telephone on the shore, from a point 24km inside the West Gate. The tents include breakfast; other accommodations also include dinner.

Couples Resort   RESORT $$$

(📞866-202-1179; www.couplesresort.ca; 139 Galeairy Lake Rd, Whitney; r incl breakfast from $964; ❄🛜🏊) Don't let the name fool you into thinking this smart resort is a naturist swingers' den; it actually caters to couples on romantic getaways. The 46 rooms benefit from a lovely position on Galeairy Lake, just outside Algonquin's border, with a park pass available on loan to guests. All accommodations have hot tub on the deck, king-size bed and fireplace.

East Gate

Algonquin East Gate Motel   MOTEL $

(📞613-637-1220; www.algonquineastgatemotel. com; Hwy 60, Whitney; r from $82; 🅿❄🛜) This cozy little motel just outside the park's East Gate has 11 comfortable rooms with small bathrooms, and friendly, helpful staff. There's also a private housekeeping cottage out back. The reservation office handles bookings for four other hotels on Hwy 60, so you're almost guaranteed to find some place to lay your head.

✖ Eating

Algonquin Lunch Bar & Restaurant   DINER $

(☑ 613-637-2670; 29553 Hwy 60, Whitney; mains $14; ☺ 8am-8pm Jun-Sep, 9am-3pm Mon-Thu, to 7pm Fri & Sat, 10am-3pm Sun Oct-May) Attached to Whitney's gas station and shop, this village hub is a good place to insulate yourself with some tea or soup before driving into the woods. Burgers, wraps and more substantial dishes are on the menu.

❶ Information

Algonquin Provincial Park is accessible year-round. Drivers can pass through the park along Hwy 60; you must pay the day-use fee ($18 per vehicle) if you plan to stop and look around. The Hwy 60 corridor has limited cell-phone coverage in the park, and for several kilometers on each side. There are payphones.

Each kilometer of Hwy 60 within the park is tagged, starting at the West Gate (known as Km 0) and terminating at the East Gate (Km 56). Outfitters and accommodations use these markers when giving directions.

The Algonquin Visitors Centre (p190) has an information desk, bookstore and wi-fi.

There are information centers at the park's **West Gate** (☑ admin 613-637-2780; info 705-633-5572; www.algonquinpark.on.ca; Km 0 on Hwy 60, West Gate; ☺ 8am-6pm May-Sep, 9am-4pm Oct-Apr) and **East Gate** (☑ admin 613-637-2780; info 705-633-5572; www.algonquinpark.on.ca; Km 56 on Hwy 60, East Gate; ☺ 8am-6pm May-Sep, 9am-4pm Oct-Apr), respectively at Km 0 and Km 56 on Hwy 60.

CRYING WOLF

Algonquin Provincial Park is active in wolf research, and public 'howls' are an incredible way to experience the presence of these furry beasts. Wolves will readily respond to human imitations of their howling, so the park's staff conducts communal howling sessions on the occasional summer evening. These events are highly organized: you could be one of 2000 people standing in the darkness waiting for the chilling wails. Wolf howls often take place on Thursdays in August and early September, but are only confirmed on the days they are actually held. Check park bulletin boards, www.algonquinpark.on.ca or phone the information line (p190) to be sure.

---

❶ Getting There & Away

Aside from the East Gate and West Gate on Hwy 60, Algonquin has 34 access points located around the periphery of the park and along the highway for access to the park's backcountry. Each kilometer of Hwy 60 within the park is tagged.

The two large Muskoka towns of Huntsville and Bracebridge are within an hour's drive of the West Gate. Other small townships include Whitney, just outside the East Gate; Maynooth and Bancroft, respectively 40km and 65km south of the East Gate; and Mattawa, north of the park on Hwy 17.

Visiting is easiest with your own wheels, but **Parkbus** (☑ 800-928-7101; www.parkbus.ca; adult/child return from Toronto $97/49, one way $70/35) offers limited summer express departures from Toronto to several Algonquin accommodations and the West Gate. Journey time is around three to four hours. Check the website for the latest schedules, and book ahead to secure a spot on this popular service. Parkbus also offers packages including transport, canoe, equipment and food.

Haliburton Highlands

This rugged expanse of needleleaf trees feels like a southern extension of Algonquin Provincial Park. Over 300 sq km of this densely forested region is part of the **Haliburton Forest** (☑ 705-754-2198, 800-631-2198; www.haliburtonforest.com; 1095 Redkenn Rd, Haliburton; day use spring, summer & fall $16, winter $49; ☺ main office 8am-5pm), a privately owned woodland reserve offering activities including hiking and mountain-biking trails. The area's main town is **Bancroft**, at the meeting of Hwy 62 and Hwy 28.

➔ Tours

South Algonquin Trails   HORSEBACK RIDING

(☑ 705-448-1751, 800-758-4801; www.southalgonquintrails.com; 4378 Elephant Lake Rd, Harcourt; 1hr ride $70; ❸) Scenic horseback trail riding in the forests of the Haliburton Highlands and southern Algonquin Provincial Park. Overnight itineraries and children's pony rides are available.

✸ Festivals & Events

Rockhound Gemboree   CULTURAL

(☑ 888-443-9999, 613-332-1513; www.rockhoundgemboree.ca; 63 Newkirk Blvd, Bancroft; ☺ Aug) Canada's largest gem festival takes place in the small town of Bancroft, nestled in the York River Valley on the southern edge of the Canadian Shield. The town is well known for its mineral-rich soils, and during the annual long weekend geologists lead tours around nearby abandoned mines to scout out stones.

🛏 Sleeping

Arlington Hotel & Pub HOSTEL $
(📞 613-338-2080; www.thearlington.ca; 32990 Hwy 62, Maynooth; HI members dm/s/d/tr/q without bathroom $25/40/63/85/108, non-members $28/45/70/95/120; ⊘ pub 7pm-1am Fri & Sat; 🛜) There's something about this towering century-old monster that makes you just want to disappear into it. In tiny Maynooth, the Arlington is a great place for artists, writers and lonely wanderers who want to escape into their craft for a while: there's nothing here but a rocking pub downstairs.

If Jack Kerouac were alive and came to Canada, well, you could just see him hanging out on the porch.

❶ Getting There & Away

You will need your own car to get here and travel around the region. Bancroft is 250km northeast of Toronto (via Peterborough) and 230km west of Ottawa (via Renfrew).

Peterborough & the Kawarthas

Peterborough, 140km northeast of Toronto in the heart of the wooded Kawarthas, is an excellent weekend getaway or launchpad for a journey through this sacred indigenous land. Offering both cultural attractions and scenic nature preserves, it's a green university town with a bustling community, surrounded by thousands of private cottages dotted around the area's many lakes. Stoney Lake, one of the largest, has some of the most lavish and beautiful private homes in the area.

If you feel like hanging around, consider staying a night in pretty Lakefield, 14km north of town at the bottom of Katchewanooka Lake. Back in Peterborough, you'll find plenty of dining and shopping options and a quaint city center. Cruises and canoes ply the waterways to the Peterborough Lift Lock on the Trent-Severn Waterway, while cycle paths lead around town and over the Otonabee River.

WORTH A TRIP

PETROGLYPHS PROVINCIAL PARK

The day use–only **Petroglyphs Provincial Park** (📞 705-877-2552; www.ontarioparks.com/park/petroglyphs; 2249 Northey's Bay Rd, Woodview; $12.25; ⊘ 10am-5pm mid-May–mid-Oct), 50km northeast of Peterborough, has Canada's largest collection of petroglyphs (ancient indigenous rock carvings), depicting turtles, snakes, birds, humans and more. Rediscovered in 1954, this important spiritual site is home to over 900 icons (although only a small percentage are discernible) carved into limestone ridges overlooking bright blue-green McGinnis Lake. There are 5km to 7km hiking trails, and visitors will be pleased to find that the site isn't overrun with other tourists.

⦿ Sights

★**Canadian Canoe Museum** MUSEUM
(📞 866-342-2663; www.canoemuseum.ca; 910 Monaghan Rd, Peterborough; adult/child $12/9.50, 5-8pm Thu free; ⊘ 10am-5pm Mon-Wed, Fri & Sat, to 8pm Thu, from noon Sun; 🚼) Displaying the world's largest collection of canoes and kayaks, this museum is a must-visit. The phenomenal display of around 150 canoes (500 are stacked in the neighboring 'canoe cathedral' warehouse) details Canada's lengthy history of water navigation, from canoes' indigenous origins through their use in exploration and fur trading to the period from 1870 to 1940, when this area was North America's canoe-building capital. After an hour at the center, you'll feel inspired to pick up a paddle.

A dynamic program of activities, tours and workshops offers more reasons to visit. A move to shiny new premises in the Lift Lock area is planned.

Whetung Ojibwa Centre GALLERY
(📞 705-657-3661; www.whetung.com; 875 Mississauga St, Curve Lake Indian Reserve; ⊘ 9am-5pm) **FREE** On a peninsula in the lakes, off Hwy 23, some 34km north of Peterborough, this gallery, shop and cultural center has a wonderful collection of indigenous crafts from around the country, including the valued work of noted artist Norval Morrisseau.

Kawartha Highlands Provincial Park PARK
(☑ ext261,613-332-3940;https://ontarioparks.com/
park/kawarthahighlands; 106 Monck Street, Bancroft; backcountry camping adult/child $13/6) Ontario's parks are by no means luxurious, but if you are craving a return to nature without running water and proper toilets, then this is the place. Most overlook this park in favor of the more established Algonquin Provincial Park (p190), but Kawartha Highlands is a rustic nature-lovers dream: 100 backcountry camping sites on 37,500 hectare of pristine nature – there are few amenities, so come prepared. You can make a booking online at the park office in Bancroft.

Warsaw Caves Conservation Area PARK
(☑ 877-816-7604,705-652-3161; www.warsawcaves.
com; 289 Caves Rd; per vehicle $17; ☉ mid-May–
mid-Oct; 🐾) Off Hwy 28, some 26km northeast of Peterborough, the Warsaw Caves Conservation Area offers hiking, swimming, camping ($47 per night), canoe rental ($12 per hour) and spelunking in eroded limestone tunnels.

🛏 Sleeping & Eating

Lake Edge Cottages RESORT $$$
(☑ 705-652-9080; www.lakeedge.com; 45 Lake Edge Rd, Lakefield; cottages from $260; 🐾🏊🐾)
This outdoorsy resort offers one- and two-bedroom rustic but well-appointed lakefront cottages with deck and kitchen, on a secluded woody property. There's a wonderful swimming pool, while the cottages have barbecues and electric or gas fireplaces and most have a private hot tub.

TRENT-SEVERN WATERWAY

The scenic **Trent-Severn Waterway** (☑ 705-750-4900; www.pc.gc.ca/en/lhn-nhs/on/trentsevern; ☉ May-Oct) cuts diagonally across eastern Ontario, linking the lakes and rivers of Simcoe County and the forested Kawarthas. The scenic hydro-highway starts at the Bay of Quinte, near Prince Edward County on Lake Ontario, and passes 45 locks before emptying into Lake Huron. A hundred years ago, this 386km-long indigenous canoe route bustled with commercial vessels. Today, it's the province of houseboats, cruise vessels and canoes.

**Peterborough
Farmers Market** MARKET $
(☑ 705-742-3276; www.peterboroughfarmersmar
ket.com; Peterborough Memorial Centre, 151 Lansdowne St W, Peterborough; ☉ 7am-1pm Sat) This community market is a great place to grab a coffee and stop at the C'est Chaud wood-fired pizza stand. It's mostly geared toward tasting and buying local produce, but stands sell bites such as vegan salads, Russian dishes and French toast. In summer, there's also a Wednesday morning outdoor market on Charlotte St between George and Aylmer Sts N.

❶ Getting There & Away

You will need your own transport to explore this area.

Land O' Lakes

South of the Haliburton Highlands and east of the Kawarthas, the majestic Land O' Lakes region links the vast inland expanse of yawning lakes and bulky evergreens to the temperate pastures of the St Lawrence Seaway. Half of the region belongs to the Unesco-designated Frontenac Arch Biosphere.

The region's crown jewel is the serene **Bon Echo Provincial Park** (☑ 613-336-2228; www.ontarioparks.com/park/bonecho; 16151 Hwy 41, Cloyne; day use per car $12.25, campsites with/without hookup $52/45, backcountry camping adult/child $10.50/5.50, yurts/cabins from $98/170; ☉ mid-May–mid-Oct), which lures artists and adventurers alike with its untainted beauty and Mazinaw Rock, a sheer cliff covered in indigenous pictographs. Closer to the St Lawrence, **Frontenac Provincial Park** (☑ 613-376-3489; www.on
tarioparks.com/park/frontenac; Salmon Lake Rd, Sydenham; day use per car $12.25, backcountry camping adult/child $12.50/6) straddles the lowlands of southern Ontario and the rugged Canadian Shield, giving it a unique menagerie of wild plants and animals. Both of the parks offer hiking and canoeing adventures.

☞ Tours

Frontenac Outfitters KAYAKING
(☑ 613-376-6220; www.frontenac-outfitters.com; 6674 Bedford Rd, Sydenham; kayak rental per day $56; ☉ 9am-5pm Apr-Oct) Canoe, kayak and stand-up paddleboard rentals near the entrance to Frontenac Provincial Park. It also

WORTH A TRIP

FRONTENAC ARCH BIOSPHERE

One of 18 Unesco-designated biosphere reserves in Canada, **Frontenac Arch Biosphere** (☑ 613-659-4824; www.frontenacarchbiosphere.ca; 19 Reynolds Rd, Lansdowne; ☺ visitor center 9am-5pm May-Oct) encompasses an ancient granite land bridge from the Canadian Shield to Upstate New York's Adirondack Mountains. A towering mountain range has been weathered down to rolling hills and rugged cliffs, still dramatic after driving through flatlands. Archaeological finds in the area indicate that it was once part of a human migration route; knives from the Yellowknife region as well as shells from the Caribbean have been found in the area.

Five forests merge in the region, which is a natural conduit for flora and fauna, creating tremendous wildlife diversity. Incorporating 70% land and 30% water (in the Thousand Islands between Gananoque and Brockville), the 2700-sq-km reserve has ample recreation opportunities, from biking and hiking to canoeing and diving. It's easily accessed from Hwy 401 and the Thousand Islands Pkwy between the aforementioned towns, and you'll find the visitor center just west of the turning for the 1000 Islands Tower. The excellent www.frontenacarchbiosphere.ca will guide you to further entry points.

offers Rideau Canal and Thousand Islands paddling tours.

❶ Getting There & Away

You will need your own transport to explore this area.

Prince Edward County

Photographers will delight in Prince Edward County's sweeping expanses, dappled branches, undulating pastoral hills, rugged bluffs and windswept shorelines. Golden fields yield bountiful harvests in this region rich in farm-to-table cuisine, peppered with providers of the finest foods, inviting accommodations and up-and-coming wineries.

Small but active **Picton** is the unofficial capital of the affluent isthmus, a favorite getaway for Torontonians. Along the shores of Lake Ontario, Sandbanks Provincial Park's sandy beaches summon old-school holidaymakers to revel in the long hot days, summer storms and balmy nights around the campfire. In winter, it's a different story entirely.

The **Loyalist Parkway** (Hwy 33) unfurls 100km from Trenton, along Lake Ontario, to Kingston, retracing the steps of the British Loyalists who settled here after fleeing the American Revolution. There's a brief interruption to the road at Glenora, beneath the mystical Lake on the Mountain, where a car ferry whisks you across to Adolphustown.

◉ Sights

Sandbanks Provincial Park PARK
(☑ 613-393-3319; www.ontarioparks.com/park/sandbanks; 3004 County Rd 12; day use per car $17; ☺ 8am-8pm late Apr-early Oct) Offering some of the best sandy swimming beaches in Ontario, popular Sandbanks Provincial Park is divided into two sections: the **Outlet**, an irresistible strip of white sandy beach – one of Ontario's cleanest; and **Sandbanks**, with its impressive undulating dunes forming the world's largest bay-mouth barrier dune formation. A short trail leads through the dunes, which are unlike anywhere else in Ontario. There are other walking trails (1km to 3.5km) and a range of campsites (p198).

Presqu'ile Provincial Park PARK
(☑ 613-475-4324; www.ontarioparks.com/park/presquile; 328 Presqu'ile Pkwy, Brighton; day use per car $14.50, campsites with/without hookup from $53/45; ☺ day visits 7am-10pm) Just west of the county proper, pop off Hwy 401 at exit 509 to find quiet Brighton and Presqu'ile Provincial Park, covering a curious, boomerang-shaped peninsula in Lake Ontario. Relax on the beach, spot migrating birds in spring, or walk short trails including the **Jobes Wood Trail**; the 1km circular path is just rural enough to glimpse the diverse woodlands and wildlife. You can also drive 6km to the lighthouse at the peninsula's tip.

The Friends of Presqu'ile (www.friendsofpresquile.on.ca) provides all there is to know about local flora and fauna. Camping reservations (late April to early October) must be made through Ontario Parks (www.ontarioparks.com).

Lake on the Mountain Provincial Park
PARK

(📞613-393-3319; www.ontarioparks.com/park/lake onthemountain; 296 County Rd 7; ⊙mid-May–mid-Oct) **FREE** Lake on the Mountain, near Glenora, is something of a mystery: 60m *above* adjacent Lake Ontario, it has a constant flow of clean, fresh water. Scientists are yet to confirm its source. The Mohawks offered gifts to its spirits and settlers thought it was bottomless. There's a delightful picnic ground with wonderful views of the Bay of Quinte on Lake Ontario.

Tours

★ Taste Trail
FOOD & DRINK

(www.tastetrail.ca) A great way to explore the wine and food producers of the county. Download a printable PDF of the self-guided tour, which takes in restaurants, farms, wineries and breweries, from the website. It's a gourmet adventure for the taste buds.

Arts Trail
TOURS

(www.artstrail.ca) The Arts Trail is a self-guided tour leading to a few dozen studios and galleries across the county. Ceramics, glassworks, photography, jewelry and painting are some of the mediums you'll encounter. You can download a PDF map from the website.

Waupoos Estates Winery
WINE

(📞613-476-8338; www.waupooswinery.com; 3016 County Rd 8; tour $20, tasting flight $6; ⊙10:30am–6pm May-Oct) White-gabled Waupoos winery, with its patio among the vines and scenic lake vistas, offers tours and tastings to discerning visitors. Tours run at 11am, 1pm and 3pm, lasting 30 to 45 minutes and include three wine samples paired with cheese. If the wine tickles your taste buds, why not stop for lunch? There's also a petting zoo for wine-indifferent kids.

Bloomfield Bicycle
CYCLING

(📞613-393-1060; www.bloomfieldbicycle.ca; 225 Bloomfield Main St, Bloomfield; half-/full-day rentals from $25/35; ⊙10am-6pm Apr-Oct) In little Bloomfield (en route to Sandbanks and Wellington from Picton), you can rent bicycles and gear to explore the surrounding countryside. In June, visitors can ride around picking luscious strawberries from the vine at numerous farms. Check out the website for a printable PDF cycling map of the area. Bikes can be delivered ($10) and picked up ($5).

🛏 Sleeping

Prince Edward County has a plethora of upscale B&Bs, boutique hotels and inns scattered among its three largest towns: Picton, Bloomfield and Wellington. Room rates are typically between $125 and $200 a night. Budget accommodations are in short supply, with more options to the north along Hwy 2 and Hwy 401, around Belleville and Trenton.

Book ahead in summer. Picton's Chamber of Tourism & Commerce (p200) office has an accommodations list.

Sandbanks Provincial Park
CAMPGROUND $

(📞613-393-3319; www.ontarioparks.com/park/sandbanks; 3004 County Rd 12; campsite without hookup from $53, cottage per week $710-2260; ⊙Apr-late Oct) Summer camping at Sandbanks is scenic and stress-free, but these lakeside sites get booked up to five months ahead. There are also two cottages, both requiring a minimum one-week stay in summer. They have two or four bedrooms, a working fireplace, satellite TV and a full kitchen. Bookings must be made through Ontario Parks.

Both electrical and nonelectrical sites are available; rates vary.

Lake on the Mountain Resort
INN $$

(📞613-476-1321; www.lakeonthemountain.com; 286 County Rd 7; cottages/r/ste from $16/130/275; ⊙late Apr-Oct; 🤳) Comprising eight homey self-catering cottages and the 'House across the Road,' a beautiful Victorian with tastefully restored rooms and stunning views, this quaint country resort is the kind of secret you'll want to keep but just can't help sharing. Check the website for a taste of what's on offer, including what's cooking at the equally noteworthy restaurants and brewery.

Newsroom Suites
GUESTHOUSE $$

(📞613-399-5182; www.newsroomsuites.ca; 269 Main St, Wellington; r $225-265; ❋🤳) Upstairs from the working offices of the *Wellington Times* you'll find these three delightful and spacious private suites, furnished to a high standard of comfort and privacy.

The Edward
B&B $$$

(📞613-661-6389; www.theedward.ca; 662 County Road 7, Picton; ste from $255; 🅿🤳) Situated on 75 acres of pristine land, this small B&B offers three well-designed suites. Even for Prince Edward County, this place is peaceful and the breakfast is one of the best you can get in the area. A minimum two-night stay is required.

Drake Devonshire Inn BOUTIQUE HOTEL $$$
(☑613-399-3338; www.drakedevonshire.ca; 24 Wharf St, Wellington; d from $349; ❋🕏) From the folks behind Toronto's legendary Drake Hotel comes the Drake Devonshire, a historic foundry-turned-inn converted to a swooningly stylish and contemporary boutique hotel, hovering on Lake Ontario. Reopened in 2015 after a three-year renovation, the inn, its restaurant and cultural programming have quickly taken the county by storm.

For a real splurge, stay in the Owner's Suite, on the top floor with a private balcony overlooking Lake Ontario ($1500).

🍴 Eating

Miller House BRASSERIE $$
(☑613-476-1321; www.lakeonthemountain.com; 246 County Rd 7; platters $18; ⊙11am-dusk) At Lake on the Mountain Resort, you can't beat the sunset views from the patio of this restaurant occupying a converted late-18th-century miller's cottage. Charcuterie and cheese platters show off the best of the county's produce. No reservations.

County Canteen FUSION $$
(☑613-476-6663; www.thecountycanteen.com; 279 Main St W, Picton; mains $18; ⊙11am-10pm; 🕏) This easygoing saloon offers a long list of craft beers and a global roster of eats, from bruschetta and quesadilla to Thai curry and Moroccan pita.

East & Main BISTRO $$
(☑613-399-5420; www.eastandmain.ca; 270 Main St, Wellington; lunch/dinner mains $15/27; ⊙11:30am-2pm Wed-Fri, to 3pm Sat & Sun, 5:30-8pm Wed-Thu & Sun, to 9pm Fri & Sat) The meals at this fine bistro taste as good as they look: farm-fresh meats, vegetables and lake-fresh seafood form the basis of this treasure of epicurean delight, which pairs local wines beautifully with the chef's creations. Dinner features dishes such as steak-frites, while lunch is a more casual affair of quiches, sandwiches, stews and burgers.

County Cider Company CAFE $$
(☑613-476-1022; www.countycider.com; 657 Bongards Crossroad, Waupoos; mains $18; ⊙11am-6pm) Served on a hilltop patio surrounded by a vineyard and overlooking the lake, lunch here consists of pizzas, burgers, salads and wraps made from local ingredients, accompanied, of course, by a range of sparkling ciders. Stop in the tasting room

to sample the products of their nearby orchards (flight $10).

**Fifth Town
Artisan Cheese Co** CHEESE $$
(☑416-984-4734; www.fifthtown.ca; 4309 County Rd 8, Picton; cheese board $18; ⊙10am-6pm) 🧀 If you're assembling a picnic, pop into this funky, solar-powered dairy to pick up its handmade, Italian-inspired goat, cow and sheep cheeses. It also offers cheese and charcuterie boards to enjoy in the on-site pavilion and, for larger groups, tutored cheese and PEC wine tastings.

The Inn INTERNATIONAL $$$
(☑613-476-1321; www.lakeonthemountain.com; 246 County Rd 7; mains $26; ⊙11am-late) At Lake on the Mountain Resort, this charming restaurant serves hearty meat and seafood dishes such as *tourtière* (a French-Canadian beef and pork pie). Meals are prepared using only the finest local ingredients, and you can accompany them with a tasting of beers from the on-site brewery.

Blümen Garden Bistro FUSION $$$
(☑613-476-6841; www.blumengardenbistro.com; 647 Hwy 49, Picton; mains $24-33; ⊙5-10pm Wed-Mon) Enjoying a reputation as Picton's best since 2008, Blümen is the work of Andreas Feller, a Swiss chef inspired by South American cuisine. With a relaxed ambience, the bistro, true to its name, features a lovely garden where stepping stones lead to private, candlelit tables surrounded by fragrant flowers.

The meat-dominated menu includes the signature braised rabbit and pan-seared pickerel. Reservations are recommended.

🍸 Drinking & Nightlife

Acoustic Grill BAR
(☑613-476-2887; www.theacousticgrill.ca; 172 Main St, Picton; ⊙11:30am-late) Acoustic folk, roots and blues acts can all be heard at this thigh-slappin' good-time bar and grill. The delicious bar menu (mains $13 to $16) is refreshingly down to earth for this foodie county, but dishes are still made fresh from local ingredients, and the music is live.

Performances kick off at 7pm every Friday and Saturday, and on summer Wednesdays, Thursdays and Sundays.

Bean Counter Cafe CAFE
(☑613-476-1718; www.beancountercafe.com; 172 Main St, Picton; ⊙7am-5pm Mon-Sat, 8am-4pm

Sun; 🐦) Picton's favorite spot for a coffee ($5), which is available in myriad forms, along with pastries, sandwiches ($9), salads, bagels and smoothies. Local art and photography adorn the walls, and the seating out front allows you to watch Picton cruise past.

☆ Entertainment

Regent Theatre
THEATER

(🖉 613-476-8416; www.theregenttheatre.org; 224 Main St, Picton; tickets $10-24) Built in 1830 and continually upgraded (including a Hollywood-style update in 1931), the funky Regent Theatre hosts a diverse series of plays, concerts and readings as well as movies from art house to mainstream.

ℹ Information

Check out Prince Edward County's inspirational tourism website at www.prince-edward-county.com.

Opposite the Scotiabank in Picton, the helpful **Chamber of Tourism & Commerce** (🖉 800-640-4717, 613-476-2421; www.pecchamber.com; 206 Main St, Picton; ⊙ 9am-4:30pm Mon-Fri) offers brochures, cycling maps, and lists of bike-rental outfits and short-term accommodations availability.

ℹ Getting There & Away

As the county's sights are spread out, you need your own wheels to appreciate the area. If you are heading along Hwy 33 to/from Kingston, a 15-minute **car ferry** (🖉 613-476-2641; www.mto.gov.on.ca/english/ontario-511/ferries.shtml#glenora; ⊙ 6am-1:15am) crossing connects Glenora with Adolphustown.

Without a car, you can catch direct VIA Rail (p71) trains from Toronto, Kingston, Brockville and Ottawa to Belleville. From Belleville, take a **Deseronto Transit** (🖉 613-396-4008; www.deseronto.ca/residents/transit; 48A Brant St, Deseronto) bus to Picton ($11, 45 minutes) via Bloomfield, with regular departures on weekdays only.

Kingston

🖉 613 / POP 117,660

Modern-day Canada's first capital, albeit only for three years, Kingston was stripped of the title when Queen Victoria worried that it was too close to the American border and could not be properly defended. Today the pretty city finds itself strategically placed as the perfect pit stop between Montréal or Ottawa and Toronto.

Often called the 'Limestone City,' Kingston is stocked with clunky halls of hand-cut stone and prim Victorian mansions. A noticeable lack of modern architecture helps to maintain the historical charm. Added to the slew of interesting museums and historical sites are the pretty waterfront location and vibrant, colorful gardens.

Founded in 1841, the same year as Kingston was proclaimed capital, Queen's University adds a dash of hot-blooded youthfulness to the mix. An assortment of great dining options, some with student-friendly prices, and a crankin' nightlife round out the package.

◉ Sights

Conveniently, most sites are found around the central, historical downtown. If you plan to spend a day or more exploring Kingston, consider buying the **K-Pass** one-to-three-day discount card (www.kpass.ca; from $94), which includes numerous sights and tours including Kingston 1000 Islands Cruises and Kingston Trolley Tours.

Kingston Public Market
MARKET

(www.kingstonpublicmarket.ca; Springer Market Sq; ⊙ 8am-6pm Tue, Thu & Sat Apr-Nov) Canada's oldest continuous market takes place in the square behind City Hall. Stalls sell food, fresh produce, handicrafts, art and, on Sundays between April and October, antiques.

Fort Henry National Historic Site
HISTORIC SITE

(🖉 613-542-7388; www.forthenry.com; Fort Henry Dr; adult/child $20/13; ⊙ 9:30am-5pm late May-early Sep, to 10pm Wed Jul & Aug) This restored British fortification, dating from 1832, overlooks Kingston from its hilltop perch. The postcard-perfect structure is brought to life by colorfully uniformed guards trained in military drills, artillery exercises and the fife-and-drum music of the 1860s. The soldiers put on displays throughout the day; don't miss the Garrison Parade (2:30pm late May to early September). Admission includes an optional guided tour of the fort's campus.

Check the website for details of the many special events throughout the year, including the ghostly Fort Fright in fall and Fort Frost in winter.

Bellevue House
MUSEUM

(☑ 888-773-8888, 613-545-8666; www.pc.gc.ca/en/lhn-nhs/on/bellevue; 35 Centre St; adult/child 6-16yr $4/free; ☺ 10am-5pm Jul & Aug, Thu-Mon late May, Jun, Sep & early Oct) In the mid-19th century, this National Historic Site was briefly home to Sir John A Macdonald, Canada's first prime minister and a notorious alcoholic. Perhaps the architect also enjoyed a drop, as the Italianate mansion is wholly asymmetrical, a pompous use of bright color abounds and balconies twist off in various directions. There are also plenty of antiques and a sun-drenched garden, with staff in period costumes adding further kooky charm and intrigue.

At the time of writing, Bellevue House was undergoing renovations but the gardens and visitor center were still open.

Penitentiary Museum
MUSEUM

(☑ 613-530-3122; www.penitentiarymuseum.ca; 555 King St W; by donation; ☺ 9am-5pm May & Jun & Sep-Oct, to 6pm Jul & Aug) The 'correctional service' is what Canadian bureaucrats call the nation's jail system, and this museum is a good way to enter that system without stealing a car. The museum, housed in the former warden's residence opposite the actual penitentiary, has a fascinating collection of weapons and tools confiscated from inmates during attempted escapes.

Visit www.kingstonpentour.com to organize a guided tour (adult/child $35/25) of the penitentiary itself, which closed in 2013.

City Hall
NOTABLE BUILDING

(☑ 613-546-4291, ext. 1389; www.cityofkingston.ca/explore/culture-history/history/city-hall; 216 Ontario St; ☺ 8:30am-4:30pm Mon-Fri, tours 10am-4pm Mon-Fri mid-May–mid-Oct, Sat & Sun late May-late Aug) **FREE** The grandiose City Hall is one of the country's finest classical buildings and a relic from the time when Kingston was capital. Friendly volunteers conduct free tours during summer, revealing colorful stained glass, dozens of portraits, dusty jail cells and an ornate council chamber. You can also download a self-guided tour brochure from the website.

Pump House Steam Museum
MUSEUM

(☑ 613-544-7867; www.kingstonpumphouse.ca; 23 Ontario St; adult/child $5/2; ☺ 10am-5pm Tue-Sun, to 8pm Thu late May-Aug; noon-4pm Thu-Fri, 10am-5pm Sat Sep-Nov; ☻) The one-of-a-kind, completely restored, steam-run pump house was used from 1849 to 1952. Today the warehouse features all things steam-related, including two full-model train sets as well as the recently restored steamboat *Phoebe*. Also here are two late-19th-century steam-powered pumps, which supplied the city with water from Lake Ontario.

☞ Tours

Haunted Walk
TOURS

(☑ 613-549-6366; www.hauntedwalk.com; 200 Ontario St; adult/child $24/20; ☺ Feb-Nov) Tours featuring stories of hangings and grave robbers leave from the ticket office in the lobby of the Prince George Hotel. Check the website for details, but the 1½-hour tour starts at 8pm most evenings. A ghoulish nocturnal walk around Fort Henry and a tamer time-travel adventure are also offered.

Kingston 1000 Islands Cruises
BOATING

(☑ 613-549-5544; www.ktic.ca; 1 Brock St, Confederation Park; cruises from $33; ☺ May-early Oct) A variety of scenic cruises departs from the dock (and ticket office) at the northeastern corner of Confederation Park. A 1½-hour Kingston Harbour cruise and three-hour Thousand Islands cruise are offered, as well as lunch and dinner jaunts. Check the website for the latest rates and sailing times.

It also operates the hop-on, hop-off Kingston Trolley Tours around the city.

Kingston Trolley Tours
TOURS

(☑ 613-549-5544; www.kingstontrolley.ca; adult/child 4-12yr/3yr & under $32/21/free; ☺ late May-early Oct) A trackless minitrain departs every 30 to 45 minutes from outside City Hall, opposite the tourist office (p205), for 1¼-hour tours with cheery historical commentary. Hop on or off at nine stops including Bellevue House. Ghost-themed evening tours also run.

★ Festivals & Events

From mid-June to early September, live music is staged in Confederation Park on Tuesday, Thursday and Saturday from 12:30pm, and at 7pm on Thursdays. There is also free music on Friday evenings by City Hall and on Saturday mornings on Sydenham St. Movies, also free, show in Springer Market Sq on Thursdays at dusk. Visit www.downtownkingston.ca for more details, and check out www.visitkingston.ca for a complete list of events throughout the year.

Kingston

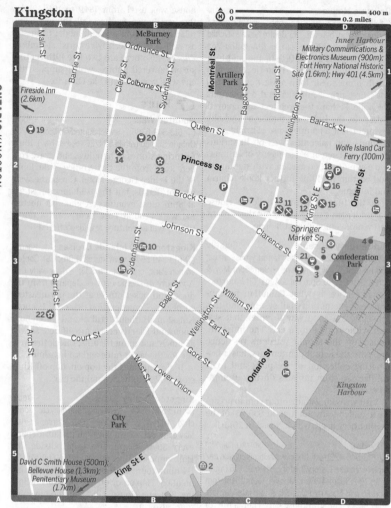

Kingston Buskers Rendezvous MUSIC
(www.downtownkingston.ca) Four days of tomfoolery in July as buskers from around the world take over downtown Kingston.

Limestone City Blues Festival MUSIC
(www.downtownkingston.ca) All-star musicians gather for a four-day jam session in August.

🛏 Sleeping

Accommodations in Kingston are top-end heavy, with a larger confluence of pricier stays than budget options. Motels are strung along Hwy 2 (aka Princess St) on either side of town. The knowledgeable staff at the tour-

ism office (p205) by Confederation Park can help you track down additional options. A few historic B&Bs are found on leafy Sydenham St; check out www.historicinnskingston.com for more.

David C Smith House HOSTEL $
(☎ 613-533-2223; http://queensu.ca/summer accommodations; 222 Stuart St; s/d $50/60; ☺ May-Aug; P ❄ @ �) Open to nonstudents when school's out for summer, these Queen's University digs offer affordable campus lodging about 20 minutes' walk from downtown. The spartan bedrooms and common rooms provide no-frills comfort and memo-

Kingston

ONTARIO KINGSTON

ries of halcyon student days. There is a basic cafe in reception and a branch of Tim Hortons coffee chain nearby.

Two-bedroom, one-bathroom units are also available ($109 to $119).

★ Rosemount Inn
B&B $$
(📞 613-480-6624; www.rosemountinn.com; 46 Sydenham St; r incl breakfast from $225; P ❇ 🐾) Enjoy a decadent stay at this former dry-goods merchant's home situated in a historic district. Built in 1850, the massive stone, Tuscan-style villa has been magnificently preserved in its 19th-century finery from the arched entrance to the ceiling roses.

A small spa offers wine-based facials and chocolate body wraps, and rates include full breakfast and afternoon tea loaded with homemade goodies.

Queen's Inn
BOUTIQUE HOTEL $$
(📞 613-546-0429; www.queensinn.ca; 125 Brock St; r incl breakfast from $140; ❇ 🐾) Constructed in 1839, the Queen's Inn is one of the oldest hotels in the country. The outside has a stately limestone facade and some rooms have stone walls, skylights and leafy views. A downstairs pub and the downtown location make this a worthy option.

Secret Garden
B&B $$
(📞 877-723-1888, 613-531-9884; www.thesecretgardeninn.com; 73 Sydenham St; r incl breakfast from $199; P ❇ @ 🐾) Whether you recline in the stately salons with chandeliers overhead, or retreat upstairs to your canopied bed, you will have a comfortable stay at this

Queen Anne–style Victorian home. Rates include breakfast; pay $10 less to 'hook the cook' and skip breakfast.

Fireside Inn
MOTEL $$
(📞 613-549-2211; www.bestwesternkingston.ca; 1217 Princess St; r incl breakfast from $199; P ❇ 🐾) The best thing about this uptown motel are the gaudy but fun fantasy suites, evoking dream worlds from a Japanese love hotel to a moon base. Standard rooms have country decor with handmade pine furniture and a fireplace. There's an outdoor pool and two restaurants.

Holiday Inn Kingston Waterfront
HOTEL $$
(📞 613-549-8400; www.hikingstonwaterfront.com; 2 Princess St; r from $180; P ❇ 🐾) You can't beat the location of this waterfront hotel. Its 197 spacious rooms have balcony, fridge, and microwave on request. Facilities include indoor and outdoor pools, and a harborside patio restaurant – Kingston's only eatery right on the water.

Residence Inn by Marriott Kingston Water's Edge
HOTEL $$$
(📞 613-544-4888; www.marriottresidenceinnkingston.com; 7 Earl St; r incl breakfast from $275; P ❇ 🐾) Geared toward longer stays, this hulking hotel offers 141 studios and apartments with king-size beds, kitchenettes and lounges with fold-out couch. It's in a prime spot on the water, near the university and a few minutes' walk from downtown. Facilities include an indoor saltwater pool and sauna.

WOLFE ISLAND

The largest island in the Thousand Islands chain, the 120-sq-km Wolfe Island divides the St Lawrence River from Lake Ontario. What was mostly undeveloped farmland is now home to hundreds of wind turbines – a little surreal. Getting to the island on the free **Wolfe Island car ferry** (☑613-548-7227; www.wolfeisland.com; ☉hourly 6:15am-2am) **FREE** from Kingston is half the fun: the 20-minute trip affords views of the city, Fort Henry and islands.

The island is cycle-friendly, with four routes marked with colored signs. Download a map at www.wolfeisland.com. Kingston Tourism can give further advice on exploring the island, and you can hire a bike from **Ahoy Rentals** (☑613-549-4277; www.ahoyrentals.com; 21 Ontario St; bike rental per hour/day $6/30, SUP $16/50, sail charter $120/500; ☉10am-8pm Mon-Fri, 9am-6pm Sat & Sun) or on the island. On the Kingston side, the ferry terminal is at the intersection of Ontario and Barrack Sts. Check the website for the complete schedule.

✖ Eating

Mlt Dwn
FAST FOOD $

(☑613-766-1881; www.mltdwn-kingston.com; 292 Princess St; sandwiches from $7; ☉11am-10pm Mon-Thu, to 11pm Fri & Sat, to 9:30pm Sun) These *fromage*-loving fast-food-meisters have already expanded from this original branch to the Canadian capital and Québec. You won't be able to resist the calorific goodness oozing from just about every conceivable twist on the humble grilled cheese sandwich – especially if you're stumbling back from the pub. The menu also features less cheesy sandwiches and snacks from pulled pork to poutine.

★ Pan Chancho
FUSION $$

(☑613-544-7790; www.panchancho.com; 44 Princess St; mains $17; ☉7am-3pm) This phenomenal bakery and cafe fuses unlikely ingredients into palate-pleasing dishes such as Vietnamese spring rolls and sesame tuna meatballs. The Moroccan-style, cumin-spiced lamb pita wrap with chickpeas is heartily recommended. The all-day breakfast menu features dishes such as curried eggs. Kingstonians crowd the rear courtyard on summer days.

Atomica
ITALIAN $$

(☑613-530-2118; www.atomica.ca; 71 Brock St; mains $21; ☉11:30am-10pm Sun-Thu, to 11pm Fri & Sat; ☑) This bustling downtown pizzeria and wine bar does all the classic pizzas with panache, as well as pastas, salads, daily specials, weekend brunches and a good dessert selection.

Gluten-free options are offered, and there's a cocktail happy hour from 2:30pm to 4:30pm.

Le Chien Noir
BISTRO $$$

(☑613-549-5635; www.lechiennoir.com; 69 Brock St; lunch/dinner mains $21/30; ☉11:30am-9pm Sun-Wed, to 10pm Thu-Sat) It's a tad pricey but locals love this little taste of Paris with a hint of Québec in the Anglophone heart of Kingston: consider the gourmet poutine. Mains include lamb, duck, and the obligatory Prince Edward Island *moules* (mussels) or steak-frites.

Chez Piggy
FUSION $$$

(☑613-549-7673; www.chezpiggy.com; 68 Princess St; lunch/dinner mains $17/35; ☉11:30am-11pm Mon-Sat, from 10am Sun) Hidden in a flowery stone courtyard, the city's best-known restaurant has earned its reputation with an innovative menu and charming ambience. Dinner mains include marinated ostrich and confit of Muscovy duck leg, while the lunch menu is more casual.

Reservations are recommended during the weekends, when Sunday brunch is popular.

🍺 Drinking & Nightlife

★ Stone City Ales
PUB FOOD

(☑613-542-4222; www.stonecityales.com; 275 Princess St; mains $15; ☉noon-midnight Mon-Thu, from 11am Fri & Sat, 11am-10pm Sun) Arguably the best beer to be found in Kingston; have a pint while the staff bustle around changing the record on the turntable, serving charcuterie boards and guiding tasters through their flight (three 6oz beers $9). Choose between mainstays and special-release beers, accompanied by a menu of ribs, wings, chips, dips, cheese platters and more.

Kingston Brewing Company
BREWERY

(☑ 613-542-4978; www.kingstonbrewing.ca; 34 Clarence St; ☺11am-2am) Chow down on burgers and sandwiches (mains $18) amid flickering Christmas lights and kitschy beer-themed paraphernalia, or grab a patio table outside. In summer they make beer using a recipe dating back to 1841, when Kingston was capital of the Province of Canada.

The local beers are good, but there is also a great selection of regional and international beers on tap. For something a little different, try their cask ale – a traditional English way to serve beer through a pump with lower carbonation, but with a lot more flavour.

Tir nan Og
PUB

(☑ 613-544-7474; www.facebook.com/kingston.tirnanog; 200 Ontario St; ☺11am-late; ☎) Set inside one of the oldest and most charming buildings along the waterfront, this Irish oasis serves up live music and overflowing pints, as well as a menu of pub grub, in its wood-lined interior. Beers come in 14oz or 18oz servings.

Red House
PUB

(☑ 613-767-2558; www.redhousedowntown.ca/index.html; 369 King St E; ☺11:30am-2am) This ranch-raunchy pub has a killer selection of beers on tap and a fantastic bar menu ranging from comfort food (poutine, house burger) to smart dining (grilled trout, steak-frites) – all in a casual pub setting. We love that there are roasted herbed potatoes cooked in duck fat as a side dish.

Coffee & Company
COFFEE

(☑ 613-547-9211; www.facebook.com/coffeeandcompanykingston; 53 Princess St; ☺7am-8pm; ☎) Get your daily dose of barista-brewed coffee here with your daily shot of free wi-fi. Why not have a Godiva chocolate or White Mountain ice cream with that?

Stages
CLUB

(☑ 613-547-5553; www.stagesnightclub.ca/; 390 Princess St; ☺10pm-3am Mon & Thu-Sat) This is where young Kingston folk get their groove on and dance till they drop. The club hosts big nights for events such as Canada Day.

☆ Entertainment

Grad Club
LIVE MUSIC

(☑ 613-546-3427; http://queensgradclub.wordpress.com; 162 Barrie St; ☺11am-late Mon-Fri) Housed in an imposing Victorian mansion, this Queen's campus mainstay is one of the hottest venues for live music. It also hosts special events such as tastings of local craft beers.

Grand Theatre
THEATER

(☑ 613-530-2050; www.kingstongrand.ca; 218 Princess St; ☺box office noon-6pm Mon-Sat) Once an opera house, then a movie theater, the Grand is now the city's premier venue for theater, concerts and comedy. It has undergone extensive renovations since 1967, including a massive overhaul in 2008. The Kingston Symphony orchestra (www.kingstonsymphony.on.ca) regularly performs here.

❶ Information

Hotel Dieu Hospital (☑ 613-544-3310; www.hoteldieu.com; 166 Brock St; ☺emergency room 8am-8pm) Yes, it's a hospital: centrally located.

Kingston Tourism (☑ 613-548-4415, 888-855-4555; http://tourism.kingstoncanada.com; 209 Ontario St; ☺10am-4pm) This useful information center has intelligent, friendly staff, well versed in the city's history. Across from City Hall, it has longer opening hours in summer.

❶ Getting There & Away

The **Kingston Bus Terminal** (☑ 613-547-4916; 1175 John Counter Blvd) is 1km south of Hwy 401, just west of Division St. **Megabus** (☑ 866-488-4452; https://ca.megabus.com) offers several daily services to Toronto (from $31, three hours) and Montréal ($26, 3¼ hours).

If you're arriving by car on Hwy 401, exits 611 to 623 will lead you downtown. Car-rental chains in town include **Enterprise** (☑ 613-547-0755; www.enterprise.ca; 2244 Princess St).

Kingston train station (☑ 888-842-7245; www.viarail.ca; 1800 John Counter Blvd) is about 300m east of where Princess St and John Counter Blvd meet. Several daily trains run to Montréal ($96, 2¾ hours), Ottawa ($87, 2¼ hours) and Toronto ($99, 2½ hours).

Thousand Islands

The 'Thousand Islands' are a constellation of over 1800 rugged islands dotting the St Lawrence River from Kingston to Brockville. The lush archipelago offers loose tufts of fog, showers of trillium petals, quaking tide pools and opulent 19th-century summer mansions, whose turrets pierce the prevailing mist.

The area has evolved from slow-paced country estates for the rich to the ultimate vacation destination, but one that many tourists still skip over in favor of the bigger cities. The growing number of craft breweries, distilleries and vineyards have followed the gastronomical boom.

Cruises leave from several harbors and visit just a handful of the islands – try renting your own canoe to explore further. If boats are not your thing, the **St Lawrence Bikeway** (www.waterfronttrail.org), part of the riverside Waterfront Trail between Niagara-on-the-Lake and Cornwall, extends the full length of the parkway and offers an alternative way to explore this under-looked part of Ontario.

◉ Sights & Activities

★ Boldt Castle   CASTLE

(✏ in season 315-482-9724, off season 315-482-2501; www.boldtcastle.com; Heart Island, Alexandria Bay, NY, USA; adult/child US$10/7; ⊘10am-6:30pm May-late Sep, 11am-5pm late Sep–mid-Oct) This lavish turn-of-the-century island castle in the middle of the St Lawrence is only around 25km from Gananoque, but technically in the USA, so you'll need your passport to visit. It was built by George C Boldt, original proprietor of New York's famous Waldorf Astoria Hotel. Many Thousand Island cruise tours stop here, or you can drive 23km from Gananoque to Alexandria Bay, NY, USA, where 10-minute shuttles cross the 1km of water to the castle.

From the Thousand Islands Pkwy, Hwy 137/81 crosses the Thousand Islands Bridge (and the border) to Alexandria Bay. Canadian cruises depart from Gananoque for a five-hour tour (including the cruise and castle visit) and from Rockport for a 3½- or five-hour tour.

★ 1000 Islands Tower   VIEWPOINT

(✏ 613-659-2335; www.1000islandstower.com; 716 Hwy 137, Hill Island; adult/child $12/7; ⊘10am-6pm May-Oct) Just east of Ivy Lea, some 20km from Gananoque, a series of soaring bridges links Ontario to New York State, USA, over several islands. Halfway across, just before crossing the international border, this 130m-high observation tower offers fantastic views of the archipelago from two open decks, plus explanatory exhibits on a glass-enclosed deck. And yes, there's an elevator.

Thousand Islands National Park   NATIONAL PARK

(✏ 613-923-5261;www.pc.gc.ca/pn-np/on/lawren/index.aspx; 2 County Rd 5, Mallorytown; parking $7, tent sites without hookup $16, oTENTik camping $100-121; ⊘visitor center 10am-4pm Sat & Sun late May-Jun, daily Jul-Sep) On the Thousand

Islands Pkwy south of Mallorytown, you'll find the Mallorytown Landing Visitors Centre for the Thousand Islands National Park, which preserves a gentle green archipelago of over 20 freckle-sized islands, scattered between Kingston and Brockville. A 2km walking trail and interpretive center allow visitors to learn more about the lush terrain and resident wildlife. Further hiking trails and canoe routes explore deeper into the park.

A dozen islands support backcountry camping (BYO boat). You can also stay in a luxurious oTENTik roofed safari tent at the visitor center or on two of the islands.

Skywood Eco Adventure   ADVENTURE SPORTS

(✏ 613-923-5120; www.parks.on.ca/attractions/skywood-eco-adventure-park; 1278 Thousand Islands Pkwy, Mallorytown; zip-line tour adult/youth 12-15yr $67/61; ⊘9am-5pm; 👪) East of Mallorytown, this fantastic center is Canada's largest aerial adventure and zip-line park, offering woodland fun from zip lines to canopy tours and a large children's tree-house play area.

Gananoque

✏ 613 / POP 5159

Little Gananoque (gan-an-*awk*-way) is the perfect place to rest your eyes after a long day of squinting at the furry green islands on the misty St Lawrence. The dainty Victorian town, deep in the heart of the Thousand Islands region, teems with cruise-hungry tourists during summer and early fall. In spring and late fall, it's quiet as a mouse.

For some historical background to a stroll around this quaint town, pick up a heritage-themed, self-guided walking tour map from the visitor center.

🏃 Activities

1000 Islands Kayaking   KAYAKING

(✏ 613-329-6265; www.1000islandskayaking.com; 110 Kate St; half-day rentals/tours from $45/85) If you're feeling energetic, paddling is a great way to tour the islands. Choose from a multitude of packages including courses, half-day, full-day and sunset trips, and canoe-and-camp weekends.

☞ Tours

Gananoque Boat Line   CRUISE

(✏ 888-717-4837; www.ganboatline.com; 280 Main St; 1hr cruise adult/child 6-12yr from $24/14; ⊘May–mid-Oct) Several trip options, including one with a two-hour stopover at Boldt Castle, make this outfit a popular choice for cruising the Thousand Islands. The castle is technically in the USA, so be sure you have your passport (and possibly visa) if you are planning to visit. Cruises depart throughout the day and for special musical evenings (Neil Diamond tribute, anyone?).

🛌 Sleeping

Gananoque Inn INN $$

(🖉 613-382-2165, 888-565-3101; www.gananoque inn.com; 550 Stone St S; r from $225; 🕾) 🖋 Signature green shutters denote this stately inn at the junction of the Gananoque River and St Lawrence Seaway. The former carriage-works first opened its doors in 1896 and has retained much of its charm; the rooms are unremarkable but the waterside location is spectacular. Packages including accommodations and activities from spa treatments to helicopter flights are offered online.

Misty Isles Lodge LODGE $$

(🖉 613-382-4232; www.mistyisles.ca; 25 River Rd, Lansdowne; r from $115, campsite with hookup $40; 🕾) Located about 5km east of Gananoque on the Thousand Islands Pkwy, you'll find this laid-back beachfront property boasting comfortable units with wicker furnishings. A variety of adventure outfitting is offered as well, including kayak rentals (half day $40) and tours (half day $80), and camping packages on some of the river's shrubby islands.

Houseboat Holidays HOUSEBOAT $$$

(🖉 613-382-2842; www.houseboatholidays.ca; 11 Clark Dr, RR3, Gananoque; weekend/midweek/

weekly rates from $600/800/1100) The only thing better than staying near the seaway is staying *on* the seaway! This experienced outfit just 4km west of Gananoque will set you up with your very own floating hotel and provides a brief instructional course for nautical newbies. It covers the whole Thousand Islands and Rideau Canal area, from Gananoque to Brockville and Kingston.

🍴 Eating

★ Stonewater Pub PUB FOOD $$

(🖉 613-382-2542; www.stonewaterpub.com; 490 Stone St S; mains $18; ⊙11am-9pm Sun-Wed, to 1am Thu-Sat) Below a B&B, this homey little waterfront Irish pub and restaurant serves up hearty and delicious fare: the 'Irish tenderloin' (grilled, bacon-wrapped ground lamb and beef) and 'porky pig' (pork loin burger) are both must-tries for self-respecting carnivores. There's a bunch of creative salads too. The vibe is straight out of *Moby Dick,* and especially delightful when there's live music.

Laverne's CAFE $$

(🖉 613-463-8800; www.laverneseatery.com; 21 King St E; mains $18; ⊙7am-4pm Mon-Thu, to 9pm Fri, 8am-6pm Sat, to 4pm Sun) Previously known as the Socialist Pig, the new restaurant still focuses on BBQ and brunch with cool decor including a counter made of old books. The food remains top notch.

Maple Leaf Restaurant CZECH $$

(Czech Schnitzel House; 🖉 613-382-7666; www. mapleleafrestaurant.ca; 65 King St E; mains $22; ⊙11am-9:30pm Wed-Sun, from 4pm Tue) As quintessentially Canadian as this old-school family diner can be, its name belies

---

COTTAGE COUNTRY

Much of Ontario, from the shores of Lake Erie to Muskoka, the Kawarthas, Haliburton Highlands and even the Thousand Islands, is cottage country – thousands of lakes dotted with rocky islands and forested shorelines offering dazzling sunsets: perfect for a weekend home. It won't be long after you arrive in Toronto that you're introduced to the slow pace and hospitality of someone's cottage, for that's what Ontario summers are all about – communing with friends, family and nature over cold beer, fine wine and good food.

Torontonians flock to the lakes as soon as the weather gets warm. Ramshackle fishing huts are prised open at the first available moment after the spring thaw, while sprawling waterfront mansions awake from their slumber. Flowerpots are replanted, freezers restocked and families begin their weekly pilgrimage from the city.

The common denominator of the cottage phenomenon is the sense of pride in one's place and the desire to be in the great outdoors. Canoes, kayaks, ski-boats and Sea-Doos all come out and the lazy days and wild nights begin, until winter, when the lakes freeze over, the snowmobiles appear and they do it all again.

the European gems found inside: golden breaded schnitzel, goulash, borscht and imported Czech beer. Burgers and poutine bring you back to terra Canadiana. There's a little patio out back, open in summer.

Ivy Restaurant CANADIAN $$$
(☑613-659-2486; www.ivyleaclub.ca; 61 Shipman's Lane, Lansdowne; mains $33; ⊙11:30am-9pm Mon-Sat, from 10:30am Sun) In a charming waterfront spot about 12km east of Gananoque, this beautifully refurbished restaurant belonging to the opulent Ivy Lea Club marina is open to the public. Casual patio lunches and Sunday brunches are more affordable ways to enjoy the stunning environment, but evening fine dining is available. If you fancy a half-chicken, go for the buttermilk-marinaded fried Cornwall hen.

Drinking & Entertainment

Gananoque Brewing Co BREWERY
(☑613-463-9131; www.ganbeer.com; 9 King St E; ⊙1-6pm Mon-Wed, to 8pm Thu, noon-late Fri & Sat, to 7pm Sun) Beneath the crisscrossing wooden beams of a converted 19th-century carriage-parts factory, try craft beers such as the Naughty Otter and the Bell Ringer IPA. Free brewery tours are also offered.

**Thousand Islands
Playhouse** THEATER
(☑866-382-7020, 613-382-7020; www.1000islandsplayhouse.com; 185 South St) This delightful waterfront theater has presented a quality lineup of mainly light summer plays and musicals since 1982.

ⓘ Information

Visitor Services Centre (☑844-382-8044, 613-382-8044; www.travel1000islands.ca; 10 King St E; ⊙9am-5pm mid-May–mid-Oct, 10am-4pm Tue-Sat mid-Oct–mid-May; ☎) The delightful staff at this immaculate visitor center are a font of information for all things Thousand Islands and beyond.

ⓘ Getting There & Away

Gananoque is a short, 2km detour off Hwy 401 about 35km east of Kingston.

Gananoque Train Station (☑888-842-7245; www.viarail.ca; North Station Rd), 6km north of town, has direct services to/from Toronto ($106, three hours, one daily) and Ottawa ($127, 1¾ hours, one daily).

Brockville & Prescott

Attractive Brockville marks the eastern edge of the Thousand Islands region. The 'City of the Thousand Islands,' as it's known, has a cache of extravagant estates. Rows of Gothic spires twisting skyward make it easy to imagine the clip-clop of carriage horses that once rang through the city. The riverfront parks and museums on the streets climbing sleepily inland make Brockville an appealing spot to while away a day.

Neighboring Prescott, 20km up the road, could be Brockville's younger brother: it's altogether smaller and scrappier, but offers accommodations and facilities. The 19th-century town is also just 6km from the International Bridge linking Johnstown, Ontario with Ogdensburg, New York State.

⊙ Sights

Fulford Place MUSEUM
(☑613-498-3003; www.heritagetrust.on.ca/en/properties/fulford-place; 287 King St E, Brockville; adult/child $6/free; ⊙10am-5pm Jun-Aug; ℗) This stunning 35-room Edwardian mansion was built in the early 1900s for quack-medicine millionaire George Taylor Fulford, the producer of the 'Pink Pills for Pale People.' Why not stop for a cup of tea on the verandah? Admission includes a guided tour, conducted hourly between 10am and 4pm.

Brockville Railway Tunnel HISTORIC SITE
(www.brockvillerailwaytunnel.com; cnr Water St E & Block House Island Pkwy, Brockville; ⊙9am-9pm) In Armagh S Price Park, diagonally opposite the tourist office, look out for the entrance to Canada's oldest railway tunnel, dating from 1860. Reopened in 2017, the new tunnel features light shows and music during the roughly 15-minute walk to Pearl St.

Aquatarium MUSEUM
(☑613-342-6789; www.aquatarium.ca; Tall Ships Landing, 6 Broad St, Brockville; adult/child $20/10; ⊙10am-5pm mid-May–Aug, 10am-5pm Wed-Sun Sep–mid-May; ⊞❀) This all-singing, all-dancing interactive center geared toward children brings to life the St Lawrence Seaway, its currents and shipwrecks.

Brockville Museum MUSEUM
(☑613-342-4397; www.brockvillemuseum.com; 5 Henry St, Brockville; by donation; ⊙10am-5pm Mon-Sat mid-May–Aug, 10am-5pm Mon-Fri Sep–mid-May) Take a look at the area's history here, where you'll find displays

on Brockville's bygone car-building and hat-making industries among other community tidbits. The museum encompasses the Isaac Beecher House, built in the mid-19th century by a tanner of the same name, and a good example of the homes built by Loyalists fleeing the USA.

Fort Wellington National Historic Site HISTORIC BUILDING
(☑613-925-2896; www.pc.gc.ca/eng/lhn-nhs/on/wellington/index.aspx; 370 Vankoughnet St, Prescott; adult/child $4/2; ☺10am-5pm Thu-Mon late May, Jun & Sep-early Oct, daily Jul & Aug; ℗) The original fort was built during the War of 1812 and was used again as a strategic locale in 1838, when an American invasion seemed imminent. Some original fortifications remain, as do the barracks, powder magazine and officers' quarters, all brought to life by costumed interpreters and exhibits.

Tours

1000 Islands Cruises BOATING
(☑800-353-3157, 613-345-7333; www.1000islandscruises.com; 30 Block House Island Pkwy, Brockville; cruises $28-50; ☺May-Oct) Offers 1½- to two-hour sightseeing tours of the Thousand Islands on two vessels: a traditional sightseeing cruiser and the high-speed *Wildcat*. The latter features views of Boldt and Singer Castles, island châteaux just over the international border. Check the website for details and schedules.

Sleeping

Brockville has plenty to satisfy, from historic B&Bs to chain motels, respectively found downtown and uptown around the junction of Hwy 401 and Stewart Blvd (Hwy 29). Prescott has some original accommodations options along the St Lawrence.

Dewar's Inn INN $$
(☑613-925-3228, 877-433-9277; www.dewarsinn.com; 1649 County Rd 2, Prescott; r $103-108, cottage $150-170; ☎) These quaint riverside cottages, efficiency units and motel rooms are pleasantly furnished and spotlessly clean. The property is built on the site of an early-19th-century brewery, and scuba dives in the backyard have revealed sunken bottles of old brew. Decks along the river's edge have views of Ogdensburg, NY. Rates include breakfast. No pets or children aged under 12.

Green Door B&B $$
(☑226-868-7345; www.greendoorbb.ca; 61 Buell St, Brockville; r incl breakfast $159; ☺May-Oct; ❄☎) On an attractive residential street, this brick tabernacle dating from 1928 has found a new calling as a B&B with four 1920s and art deco–themed bedrooms. Crisp sunlight dances through the ample common space during the day. Spend your evenings by the piano or snuggled up in an antique bed.

Eating

The Mill ITALIAN $$
(☑613-345-7098; www.themillrestaurant.ca; 123 Water St W, Brockville; mains $17-26; ☺11:30am-2pm & 5-9pm Mon-Fri, 5-9pm Sat) There's a wonderful, romantic ambience about this quaint Italian restaurant located in a restored 1852 mill, with a stream trickling past its thick stone walls. The reasonably priced menu features tapas, pasta, seafood and veal, the latter in the recommended *vitello scallopini al marsala*.

Buell Street Bistro INTERNATIONAL $$
(☑613-345-2623; www.buellstreetbistro.com; 27 Buell St, Brockville; mains $16-35; ☺11:30am-10pm Mon-Fri, from 4:30pm Sat & Sun) Three levels and a delectable patio break the space up at this local favorite. Seafood and pasta, steak-frites and surf 'n' turf mingle with curry dishes from further afield: there's enough variety to please the fussiest of palates, and there's a full gluten-free menu.

Georgian Dragon Ale House PUB FOOD $$
(☑613-865-8224; www.facebook.com/TheGeorgianDragonAleHouseAndPub; 72 King St W, Brockville; mains $16; ☺11am-late Mon-Fri, from 9am Sat & Sun) This British ale house on the main drag has a good selection of beers on tap and tasty British pub favorites such as butter chicken and cottage pie.

Entertainment

Brockville Arts Centre ARTS CENTER
(☑613-342-7122, 877-342-7122; www.brockvilleartscentre.com; 235 King St W, Brockville; ☺box office 10am-5pm Mon-Fri, to 3pm Sat) Built in 1858 as Brockville's town hall, what is now the arts center has survived one fire and several incarnations. Today the theater hosts performers from tribute bands to classical pianists, and the lobby gallery exhibits both local artists and biggish names.

EXPERIENCE AKWESASNE

Pop into this small interpretive center **Experience Akwesasne Welcome Centre** (☑ 613-575-2250; www.akwesasne.ca; Peace Tree Mall, 167 Akwesasne International Rd, Cornwall Island; ☺ 8:30am-4:30pm Mon-Fri) on Cornwall Island, between the bridge to the US border post and the bridge back to the Canadian mainland, to learn more about the Akwesasne Mohawk reservation, which sprawls across Ontario, Québec and New York. Explanatory panels, artworks and brochures are complemented by the helpful staff, who are happy to share stories from their community of over 12,000 people. The center is a hub for organizing cultural experiences and outdoor activities in the reservation.

Ask about visiting the nearby Native **North American Travelling College**, also on the island, which has exhibits on subjects such as basket making. Cars pay $3.75 to cross the bridge to Cornwall Island; in winter, phone ahead to check whether the center is open. The island is between the US and Canadian border posts; if you are returning to Cornwall afterward, you will have to cross the Canadian border, explain that you were visiting the center and show your passport.

ⓘ Information

Brockville District Tourism (☑ 613-342-4357; www.brockvilletourism.com; 10 Market St W, Brockville; ☺ 8am-6pm Mon-Sat, 10am-5pm Sun May-Oct, 9am-5pm Mon-Fri Nov-Apr) Open year-round and provides ample information about attractions all along the seaway.

ⓘ Getting There & Away

VIA Rail trains leave Brockville's **train station** (☑ 888-842-7245; www.viarail.ca; 141 Perth St), 1km north of the town center, for Toronto ($92, three hours, seven daily) and Ottawa ($76, 1¼ hours, five daily).

Megabus (☑ 866-488-4452; http://ca.mega bus.com; cnr Jefferson Dr & Steward Blvd) runs daily buses to Toronto (from $36, four hours, three daily) and Montréal ($31, 2½ hours, three daily). Buses depart from the southwest corner of Stewart Blvd (Hwy 29) and Jefferson Dr, just off Hwy 401 and about 2km inland from downtown.

Merrickville

Tiny Merrickville can thank the Canadian Railroad for never laying tracks through town. Had the wee burg become a stop on the line, it would have swapped its stone structures for industrial eyesores. Instead, today's day-tripper from Ottawa can take a canal-side stroll back in time – to when the area was a Loyalist stronghold ready to defend the Crown against the rebellious Americans. Merrickville was such a desirable locale that Colonel By, master planner of the Rideau Canal, built his summer home here, and Benedict Arnold's sons were given land nearby in return for his betrayal of the Americans.

History buffs will enjoy the grand 19th-century buildings alongside the Rideau Canal, and boutique-browsers will love the numerous artisans' workshops.

Blockhouse Museum   HISTORIC BUILDING
(☑ 613-269-2042; www.merrickvillehistory.org; cnr Main & St Lawrence Sts; ☺ noon-4pm Sat & Sun mid-May–mid-Jun & Sep–mid-Oct, 10am-6pm mid-Jun–Aug) **FREE** Explore this lockside fortification, one of the four built by the British in the early 1830s to defend the Rideau Canal. The displays inside cover the history of Merrickville and the canal, which brought the village much trade and wealth before the railways altered the picture and left Merrickville to its current slumber.

ⓘ Getting There & Away

Merrickville is 85km south of Ottawa via Hwy 416. It's easiest to come by car, but the **County Shuttle** (☑ 613-552-0432; www.thecountry shuttle.com) links the village to Ottawa Mac-Donald-Cartier International Airport (from $70, one hour).

Morrisburg

Little Morrisburg is known far and wide for its quality historic site, **Upper Canada Village** (☑ 613-543-4328; www.uppercanadavil lage.com; 13740 County Rd 2; adult/child $22/13; ☺ 9:30am-5pm May–early Sep, tours 10:30am, 1pm & 3pm early Sep–mid-Oct; ⊞). Costume-clad interpreters animate this re-created town by emulating life in the 1860s.

Around 6km east of Upper Canada Village on the riverside Hwy 2 (aka County Rd 2), the **Upper Canada Migratory Bird Sanctuary** (☑613-537-2024; www.uppercanadabird sanctuary.com; 5591 Morrison Road 2, Ingleside; campsite with/without hookup from $48/38, cabins from $96; ☺visitors center 9am-4:30pm Mon-Thu & Sun, to 9pm Fri & Sat mid-May–late Oct, hours vary late Oct–mid-May; ☑) **FREE** offers 8km of self-guided trails that meander through a variety of habitats.

❶ Getting There & Away

If you are driving to/from Cornwall, be sure to take the Long Sault Pkwy, a scenic detour from Hwy 2 along a string of beach-fringed islands in the St Lawrence.

Megabus (☑866-488-4452; https://ca.mega bus.com) will drop passengers on request at the entrance to Upper Canada Village, a 500m walk from the main site, on its run between Montréal and Toronto via Cornwall, Brockville and Kingston.

Ottawa

☑343, 613 / POP 989,567

Descriptions of Ottawa read like an appealing dating profile: dynamic, gregarious, bilingual, likes kids and long walks along the river. In person, the attractive capital fits the bill.

Canada's gargantuan Gothic parliament buildings regally anchor the downtown core, an inspiring jumble of pulsing districts around the Rideau Canal. A few days' worth of world-class museums are architecturally inspiring hosts to a variety of intriguing collections.

Parks, gardens and wide, open public spaces pay an accessible and year-round homage to all four seasons. Average temperatures are well below 0°C from December to March, but locals celebrate the city's longest-seeming season with a bunch of outdoor pursuits. Many skate to work or school on the frozen canal, while the Winterlude (p218) festival sees fantastical ice sculptures. As spring clicks to summer, auspicious tulips cheer the downtown, followed by vibrant fall leaves that line the streets with eye-popping reds and yellows.

History

Like many colonial capitals, Ottawa's birth was not an organic one. The site was chosen by Queen Victoria as a geographic compromise between Montréal and Toronto, and presto – the city was born. Canadians were initially baffled by her decision; Ottawa was far away from the main colonial strongholds. Many thought the region to be a desolate snowfield, when in fact the Ottawa area was long inhabited by Algonquin, who named the rolling river 'Kichissippi,' or 'Great River.'

For almost a century, Ottawa functioned as a quiet capital. Then, after WWII, Paris city planner Jacques Greber was tasked with giving Ottawa an urban face-lift. The master planner created a distinctive European feel, transforming the capital into the stunning cityscape of ample common and recreational spaces we see today.

◉ Sights

Most of Ottawa's numerous world-class museums are within walking distance of each other. Some offer free general admissions on Thursday evenings, and many close a day or two weekly (normally Monday) in winter. Several may let you in for free if you arrive less than an hour before closing time, smiling politely; but you won't have much time to appreciate their extensive collections. The **Museums Passport** (www.museumspassport. ca; adult $35) is a better idea. If you plan to visit both the Museum of History and the War Museum, discounted tickets are available: inquire at either.

Out of town to the west are three interesting sights: the Cold War–era nuclear shelter **Diefenbunker** (☑613-839-0007; www. diefenbunker.ca; 3929 Carp Rd, Carp; adult/ child $17.50/13; ☺10:30am-4pm Mon-Fri, 10am-4:30pm Sat & Sun May-Jun, 10:30am-4pm Jul-Apr; ☑), **Saunders Farm** (☑613-838-5440; www. saundersfarm.com; 7893 Bleeks Rd, Munster; $18; ☺10am-5pm Wed-Sun Jul-Aug; ☑) and Bonnechere Caves (p218).

★National Gallery
of Canada   MUSEUM

(Map p216; ☑800-319-2787, 613-990-1985; www. gallery.ca; 380 Sussex Dr; adult/child $16/free, 5-8pm Thu free; ☺10am-6pm daily May-Sep, 10am-5pm Tue-Sun Oct-Apr, to 8pm Thu year-round) The National Gallery is a work of art in itself: its striking ensemble of pink granite and glass spires echoes the ornate copper-topped towers of the nearby parliament buildings. Inside, vaulted galleries exhibit predominantly Canadian art, classic and contemporary, including an impressive collection of work by Inuit and other

Ottawa

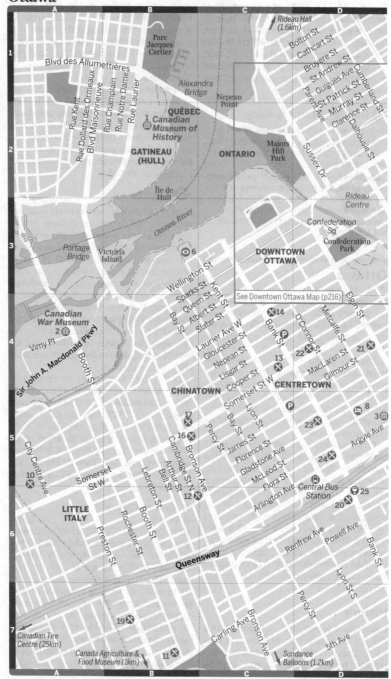

Rideau Hall
(1.6km)

Parc
Jacques
Cartier

Blvd des Allumettières

Rue Kent
Rue Dollard des Ormeaux
Blvd Maisonneuve
Rue Champlain
Rue Notre Dame
Rue Laurier

Bolton St
Cathcart St
Bruyère St
St Andrew St
Guigues Ave
St Patrick St
Cumberland St
Parent Ave
Murray St
Clarence St
Dalhousie St

Alexandra
Bridge

Nepean
Point

QUÉBEC
Canadian
Museum of
History

GATINEAU
(HULL)

ONTARIO

Majors
Hill
Park

Sussex Dr

Rideau
Centre

Île de
Hull

Ottawa River

Confederation
Sq

Confederation
Park

Portage
Bridge

Victoria
Island

6

DOWNTOWN
OTTAWA

Canadian
War Museum
2

Vimy Pl

Sir John A. Macdonald Pkwy

Booth St

Wellington St
Sparks St
Queen St
Kent St
Albert St
Slater St
Bay St

14
Bank St

O'Connor St
Metcalfe St

Elgin St

See Downtown Ottawa Map (p216)

Laurier Ave W
Gloucester St
Nepean St
Lisgar St
Cooper St

13

22
MacLaren St
Gilmour St

21

CHINATOWN

Somerset St W

CENTRETOWN

City Centre Ave

17

16

Cambridge St N
Arthur St
Bell St

Bronson Ave

Percy St

Bay St
Lyon St

James St
Florence St
Gladstone Ave
McLeod St
Flora St
Arlington Ave

8
3

23

24

Argyle Ave

25
20

10

Somerset
St W

Lebreton St

12

Central Bus
Station

LITTLE
ITALY

Preston St

Rochester St

Booth St

Queensway

Renfrew Ave
Powell Ave

Bank St

19

Carling Ave
Bronson Ave
Percy St
Lyon St S
5th Ave

Canadian Tire
Centre (25km)

Canada Agriculture &
Food Museum (1km)

11

Sundance
Balloons (1.2km)

indigenous artists. It's the world's largest Canadian collection, although additional galleries of European and American treasures include several recognizable names and masterpieces. Interpretive panels guide visitors through the nation's history and cultural development.

Deep within the gallery's interior you'll find two smooth courtyards and the remarkable **Rideau Street Convent Chapel**. Built in 1888, the stunning wooden chapel was saved from demolition and rebuilt here 100 years later – quite extraordinary.

★ **Canadian
Museum of History**   MUSEUM

(Map p212; ☑819-776-7000; www.historymu
seum.ca; 100 Rue Laurier, Gatineau; adult/child
3-12yr $20/12; ☉9am-5pm Fri-Wed, to 8pm Thu
Apr-Jun, to 6pm Jul & Aug, from 9:30am Sep-Mar;
👶) Allow plenty of time to experience this
high-tech, must-see museum across the
river, in Hull, Québec. Documenting the
history of Canada through a range of spectacular exhibits, it's an objective recounting
of the nation's timeline from the perspectives of its Indigenous peoples, its colonial
beginnings and today's rich multicultural
diversity. Entry includes admission to the
Canadian Children's Museum, based
around a theme of 'the Great Adventure':
over 30 exhibition spaces whisk kids off on
a journey around the world.

Outside, there are stunning views of Parliament Hill across the river. The building's
striking stone exterior has been sculpted
into smooth ripples, like an undulating
wave, to honor the indigenous belief that
evil dwells in angled nooks. A variety of
visiting hands-on exhibitions, events and
state-of-the-art big-screen films maintain
year-round appeal.

You can catch an **Aqua-Taxi** (Map p216;
☑819-329-2413; https://aufeeldeleau.ca; Canal
Lane; one way $7) ferry there from Ottawa
Locks.

★ **Canadian War Museum**   MUSEUM

(Map p212; ☑819-776-7000; www.warmuseum.
ca; 1 Vimy Pl; adult/child 3-12yr $17/11; ☉9:30am-
5pm Fri-Wed, to 8pm Thu Sep-Mar, from 9am May-
Aug) Fascinating displays twist through the
labyrinthine interior of this sculpture-like,
modern museum, tracing Canada's military
history with the nation's most comprehensive collection of war-related artifacts. Many
of the touching and thought-provoking exhibits are larger than life, including a replica
of a WWI trench. Take a look at the facade
in the evening, if you can: flickering lights
pulse on and off spelling 'Lest We Forget'
and 'CWM' in both English and French
Morse code.

Ottawa Locks   HISTORIC SITE

(Map p216) The series of steep, step-like locks
between the Château Laurier and Parliament Hill marks the north end of the 200km
Rideau Canal, which flows all the way down
to Kingston. Colonel By, the canal's visionary
engineer, set up headquarters here in 1826.

Parliament Hill   HISTORIC BUILDING

(Map p216; ☑613-996-0896; https://visit.parl.ca;
111 Wellington St; ☉East Block tours 8:30am-4:30pm
Jul-early Sep, West Block tours 8:30am-4:30pm)
FREE Vast, yawning archways, copper-
topped turrets and Gothic-Revival gargoyles
dominate the facade of the stunning lime-
and-sandstone parliament buildings. The
main building, known as the Centre Block,
supports the iconic Peace Tower and is
undergoing renovations until at least 2028.
Until then, visitors can still tour the House of
Commons in the West Block and the historic
East Block. The Senate is now in a new building close to Parliament Hill.

It's best to book your tour online.

Tours of the East and West block last
around 40 to 50 minutes, depending on
parliamentary activity, and may be subject
to rigorous security checks going in; it's best
to order your tickets in advance, but you can
also get them on the day from the **ticket office** (Map p216; 111 Wellington St; ☉9am-7:30pm
Mon-Fri, to 4:30pm Sat & Sun mid-May–Jun, 9am-
4:30pm Jul-early Sep, to 3:30pm Mon-Fri, to 4:30pm
Sat & Sun early Sep–mid-May).

Free tours of the grounds are also offered.
At 10am daily in summer, see the colorful
changing of the guard on the front lawns,
and at night enjoy the free bilingual sound-
and-light show on Parliament Hill. No ticket
required for either.

Visitors are welcome to watch debates
in the Senate and the House of Commons
whenever they are in session. Check the
calendars on the website to find out when
the chambers will be sitting. Again, expect
lengthy security checks.

Notre Dame Cathedral-Basilica   CHURCH

(Map p216; ☑613-241-7496; www.notredame
ottawa.com; 385 Sussex Dr; ☉9am-6pm) Built
in the 1840s, this shimmering tin-topped
house of worship is the oldest church in all
of Ottawa and the seat of the city's Roman
Catholic archbishop. Pick up the small pamphlet at the entrance outlining the church's
many idiosyncratic features, including elaborate wooden carvings and the dazzling in-
digo ceiling peppered with gleaming stars.

Canadian Museum of Nature   MUSEUM

(Map p212; ☑613-566-4700; www.nature.ca; 240
McLeod St; adult/child 3-12yr $15/11; ☉9am-5pm
Tue-Sun, to 8pm Thu Sep-May, to 6pm Jun-Aug;
🚌5, 6, 7, 14, 101, 103, 401) This imposing baronial building houses one of the world's best
natural history collections, which the vast

museum brings to life with modern and interactive exhibits. There's an impressive collection of fossils, the full skeleton of a blue whale and an excellent stock of dinosaur skeletons and models. Everyone loves the realistic mammal and bird dioramas depicting Canadian wildlife – the taxidermic creatures are so lifelike, you'll be glad they're behind a sheet of glass.

General admission is free between 5pm and 8pm on Thursdays.

Laurier House
National Historic Site   HISTORIC SITE
(Map p212; ☑ 613-992-8142; www.pc.gc.ca/en/lhn-nhs/on/laurier; 335 Laurier Ave E; adult/child $4/free; ☺10am-5pm daily Jul & Aug, Thu-Mon May & Jun) This copper-roofed Victorian home built in 1878 was the residence of two notable prime ministers: Wilfrid Laurier and the eccentric Mackenzie King. The home is elegantly furnished, displaying treasured mementos and possessions from both politicos. Don't miss the study on the top floor.

Senate of Canada   NOTABLE BUILDING
(Map p216; https://lop.parl.ca/sites/visit/default/en_CA/Senate; 2 Rideau St; ☺8:30am-4:30pm) FREE As part of the ongoing renovations on Parliament Hill, the Senate has permanently moved across the street into Ottawa's old train station. Tours last around 30 minutes and are great for history and political boffins. It's best to book in advance on the website as there are no tours when the Senate is in session.

Rideau Hall   NOTABLE BUILDING
(☑ 613-991-4422; www.gg.ca/rideauhall; 1 Sussex Dr; ☺10am-4pm Jul-early Sep, noon-4pm Sat & Sun May & Jun) FREE Home of the Governor General, Rideau Hall was built in the 1830s with grand additions made by successive governors. There are free 45-minute walking tours of the fancy residence, featuring anecdotes about the various goings-on over the years. Otherwise, from 8am to one hour before sunset, the grounds are free to be enjoyed at your leisure (as is the building between 3pm and 4:30pm in July and August).

Outside of the summer months, reservations are required for residence tours during weekdays.

At the main gate, the small changing-of-the-guard ceremony happens on the hour between 9am and 5pm from the end of June until the end of August.

Walk east along Sussex/Princess Dr to take a glance at **Rockcliffe Village**, Ottawa's swankiest neighborhood and home to prominent Canadians and most foreign diplomats.

Canada Science &
Technology Museum   MUSEUM
(☑ 613-991-3044; www.ingeniumcanada.org/scitech/index.php; 1867 St Laurent Blvd; adult/child $17/11; ☺9am-5pm May-Aug, Tue-Sun Sep-Apr) The renovated science and technology museum has educational and fun exhibits, which both adults and children will enjoy. A walk through the 'Crazy Kitchen' is a blast: the lopsided galley makes you stumble from start to finish. There are trains you can back to enlighten you on the science of coal and steam propulsion and a large display of space technology. There are daily shows during the summer months as well as various special exhibits.

RCMP Musical Ride Centre   MUSEUM
(☑ 613-993-7521; www.rcmp-grc.gc.ca/en/ride-centre; 1 Sandridge Rd; ☺9am-3:30pm May-Aug, 10am-1pm Tue & Thu Sep-Apr) FREE While the name sounds like Disney's newest attraction starring chipper red-jacketed policemen, the Musical Ride Centre is actually the stage where the Royal Canadian Mounted Police (aka the Mounties) perfect their pageant. The public are welcome to tour the stables, museum and riding school, and to meet the riders and their steeds when they are in town. They tour extensively between May and October; check their schedule on the website. It's about 7km northeast of Centretown.

Bytown Museum   MUSEUM
(Map p216; ☑ 613-234-4570; www.bytownmuseum.ca; 1 Canal Lane; adult/child $2/free; ☺10am-5pm Fri-Wed, 10am-8pm Thu Jun-Sep, 11am-4pm Thu-Mon Oct-May) Descend the stairs alongside the Ottawa Locks on Wellington St to find the Bytown Museum, sitting at the last lock before the artificial canal plunges into the waters of the Ottawa River. This well-curated collection of artifacts and documents about Ottawa's colonial past is displayed in the city's oldest stone building.

It's open until 8pm, and free after 5pm, on summer Thursdays.

Supreme Court of Canada   NOTABLE BUILDING
(Map p212; ☑ 613-995-5361; www.scc-csc.ca; 301 Wellington St; ☺9am-noon & 1-5pm daily May-Aug, Mon-Fri Sep-Apr) FREE This intimidating structure strikes an intriguing architectural balance between its modern concrete shell and its traditional copper roof. Visitors can

ONTARIO OTTAWA

Downtown Ottawa

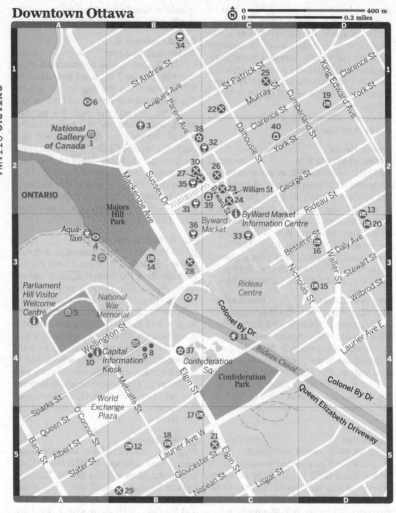

0 ———————————— 400 m
0 ———————————— 0.2 miles

34

St Andrew St

6

Guigues Ave

Parent Ave

3

National
Gallery
of Canada 1

St Patrick St
25
Murray St
Clarence St
Dalhousie St

22

38
32
30
27 26
35
31 39
24 23 William St
George St
40
York St

King Edward Ave
Clarence St
York St
19
Cumberland St
Rideau St

ONTARIO

Majors
Hill
Park

Mackenzie Ave

Sussex Dr

Aqua-
Taxi
4
2

14

36 Byward
Market
33

ByWard Market
Information Centre

Besserer St
13
20
16
Daly Ave
Waller St
Stewart St
Wilbrod St

Parliament
Hill Visitor
Welcome
Centre
5

National
War
Memorial

28

7

Rideau
Centre

Nicholas St

15

Colonel By Dr
11

Wellington St

Capital
Information
Kiosk
10

8
9

37
Confederation
Sq

Confederation
Park

Laurier Ave E

Rideau Canal

Colonel By Dr

Sparks St
Queen St
Bank St
Albert St
Slater St

World
Exchange
Plaza

Metcalfe St

O'Connor St

Elgin St

17

18
12

21

Queen Elizabeth Driveway

Laurier Ave W
Gloucester St
Nepean St
Lisgar St
Elgin St

29

stroll around the scenic grounds, grand entrance hall and dark oak-paneled courtroom. Between May and August, University of Ottawa law students conduct friendly and insightful 30-minute tours, starting on the hour. During the rest of the year, tours must be booked in advance.

Canada Aviation & Space Museum
MUSEUM

(☎613-991-3044; www.ingeniumcanada.org/aviation/index.php; 11 Aviation Pkwy; adult/child $15/10; ☺9am-5pm mid-May–Aug, from 10am Wed-Mon Sep–mid-May) With around 120 aircraft housed in this mammoth steel hang-

ar about 5km northeast of downtown, you could be forgiven for thinking you were at the airport. Wander through the warehouse, try a flight simulator and get up close and personal with colorful planes ranging from the Silver Dart of 1909 to the first turbo-powered Viscount passenger jet.

Royal Canadian Mint
NOTABLE BUILDING

(Map p216; ☎613-993-8990; www.mint.ca/tours; 320 Sussex Dr; guided tours adult/child $8/4.50; ☺10am-5pm) Although Canada's circulation-coin mint is in Winnipeg, the royal mint holds its own by striking special pieces. The imposing stone building, which looks a bit

Downtown Ottawa

like the Tower of London, has been refining gold and minting since 1908. It's an interesting tour and children will enjoy watching the sheets of metal being spun into loads of coins.

Activities

Skiing
Several nearby ski resorts offer a variety of alpine and cross-country trails. In the Gatineau Hills, about 20km from downtown, over 50 groomed slopes are available. **Camp Fortune** (⊉ext 0, 819-827-1717; www.camp fortune.com; 300 Chemin Dunlop, Chelsea) is a year-round adventure spot whose ski runs turn into a mountain-biking and ziplining paradise in summer. Popular ski resort **Mont Cascades** (⊉819-827-0301; www.mont cascades.ca; 448 Mont-des-Cascades Rd, Cantley) also flips its tricks in the summer, operating an expansive waterpark. **Mount Pakenham** (⊉613-624-5290; www.mount pakenham.com; 577 Ski Hill Rd, Pakenham), 65km west of Ottawa, is a strictly winter affair. Cross-country skiers will love the trails in Gatineau Park.

Skating
The **Rideau Canal** (Map p216; www.ottawa tourism.ca/ottawa-insider/rideau-canal-skateway), Ottawa's most famous outdoor attraction, doubles as one of the world's largest ice-skating rinks. The 7.8km of groomed ice is roughly the size of 90 Olympic-sized hockey rinks. Rest stops and changing stations are sprinkled throughout, but, more importantly, take note of the wooden kiosks dispensing scrumptious slabs of fried dough called beavertails. The three skate and sled rental stations are located at the steps of the National Arts Centre, Dow's Lake and 5th Ave.

Tours

The Capital Information Kiosk (p225) offers handy brochures for self-guided walking tours.

Gray Line   TOURS
(Map p216; ⊉613-562-9090; www.grayline.com/ ottawa; cnr Sparks & Elgin Sts; 24hr hop-on, hop-off tour from $29; ☺Apr-Oct) Sightseeing tours including hop-on, hop-off bus services, bus-and-bike tours and Ottawa River

WORTH A TRIP

BONNECHERE CAVES

About 130km west of Ottawa en route to Algonquin Provincial Park, these **Bonnechere Caves** (☑800-469-2283, 613-628-2283; www.bonnecherecaves. com; 1247 Fourth Chute Rd; tours adult/ child $19/13; ☉10am-4pm late May-June & Sep-early Oct, to 4:30pm Jul & Aug) are some of the world's finest examples of solutional caves (dissolved out of solid rock by acidic waters). Formed 500 million years ago from the floor of a tropical sea, the dank passages feature a haunting collection of fossils, including a prehistoric octopus. Learn about speleology (the study of caves) on the humorous tour, which details the site's quirky history.

Nimble guests will enjoy squeezing through a few extra-narrow, damp passages. The caves are signposted from Hwy 60 at Douglas and Eganville. Check their website for special events, including concerts and dinners located inside the caves.

cruises. Check the website or visit the sidewalk ticket booth for schedules and pricing. Bus tours depart from the booth, cruises from the Ottawa Locks.

Haunted Walk   WALKING
(Map p216; ☑613-232-0344; www.hauntedwalk. com; 46½ Sparks St; adult/child walks $24/20) Has several ghoulish walking tours including visits to the old county jail, now the HI hostel.

Ottawa Walking Tours   WALKING
(Map p216; ☑613-799-1774; www.ottawawalking tours.com; 90 Wellington St; adult/child under 11yr $15/free) These informative and fun two-hour tours with professional guides depart from the Terry Fox statue in front of the tourist office. Cash only unless you book online. There are free tours every day at 11am from May to August, though tips are appreciated.

Lady Dive   BUS
(Map p216; ☑613-223-6211; www.ladydive.com; cnr Sparks & Elgin Sts; adult/child 3-12yr $32.75/22.50; ☉May-early Sep; ☑) This one-hour tour on Lady Dive's 'amphibus' (half-bus half-boat) takes in Ottawa's favorite

sights before plunging into the Ottawa River. Kids love it.

Paul's Boat Line   BOATING
(Map p216; ☑613-225-6781; www.paulsboat cruises.com; Canal Lane; cruises adult/child from $27/19; ☉11am-7:30pm May-Oct) Scenic 1½-hour cruises on the Ottawa River, departing from the Ottawa Locks.

Sundance Balloons   BALLOONING
(☑613-247-8277; www.sundanceballoons.ca; per person from $250; ☉May-Oct) Hot-air ballooning has long been a popular leisure activity in the capital region. Sundance Balloons offers sunrise and sunset trips departing from Carleton University.

🎊 Festivals & Events

The capital is abuzz year-round with over 60 annual festivals and events. Visit www.otta wafestivals.ca for more information.

Canada Day   CULTURAL
(☑800-363-4465; www.canada.ca/en/canadian-heritage/campaigns/canada-day.html; ☉Jul 1) Ottawa is the best place in Canada to celebrate the nation's birthday. Huge crowds watch concerts and fireworks crackling and booming above the parliament buildings.

Canadian Tulip Festival   FAIR
(☑800-668-8547; www.tulipfestival.ca; ☉May) After the winter thaw, Ottawa explodes with color as beds of over 200 species of tulips come to life. Over 100,000 bulbs were gifted to the city in 1945 by the Dutch royal family in gratitude for Canada sheltering their princess and her daughters during the war. Festivities include parades, regattas, car rallies, dances, concerts and fireworks.

Winterlude   CULTURAL
(☑800-363-4465; www.canada.ca/en/canadian-heritage/campaigns/winterlude.html; ☉Feb) Three frosty weeks in early February celebrate Ottawa's winter, centering on the frozen canal, Confederation Park and Parc Jacques Cartier. Awe-inspiring ice sculptures abound, as well as the world's largest skating rink and snow playground.

Ottawa Bluesfest   MUSIC
(☑613-247-1188; www.ottawabluesfest.ca; ☉Jul) One of the world's biggest blues festivals brings in the big names for 10 days of memorable concerts in mid-July.

HOPE Volleyball Summerfest   SPORTS

(☑613-742-4673; www.hopehelps.com; ⊗Jul) A giant volleyball tournament and rock festival in mid-July to raise money for local charities.

Capital Pride   LGBTIQ+

(☑613-680-3033; https://capitalpride.ca; ⊗Aug) A week's worth of rainbow celebrations culminating in a rowdy parade in mid-August.

🛏 Sleeping

Ottawa has an impressive array of accommodations in all price ranges. Reservations are recommended during summer and over festival times, especially Winterlude.

Downtown and, sprawling south to Queensway (Hwy 417), Centretown offer numerous options, including boutique hotels, suite hotels, and hostels around ByWard Market. South of the market, the Sandy Hill district has pleasant B&Bs among its stately heritage homes and international embassies – all within healthy walking distance of downtown.

🛏 Centretown

★Hostelling International (HI)
Ottawa Jail   HOSTEL $

(Map p216; ☑613-235-2595; www.hihostels.ca/ottawa; 75 Nicholas St; dm members $37-41, nonmembers $43-53, jail rooms $61-141; P❀@) This quirky hostel occupies nine floors of the 155-year-old former Ottawa Jail, considered to be one of the city's most haunted buildings. Guests can lock themselves away in a room or dorm in an actual cell, or opt for a more conventional four- to eight-bed dorm or en suite room. Rates include a continental breakfast.

Check out the on-site gallows, where numerous criminals were hanged for their wretched crimes, in the 8th-floor 'death row' museum. The bar behind bars and free daily tours of the atmospheric building add to guests' experience of a night in the nick.

HI members pay 10% less. Parking is $12 per night.

★Lord Elgin Hotel   HISTORIC HOTEL $$

(Map p216; ☑613-235-3333; www.lordelginhotel. ca; 100 Elgin St; r from $140; P❀🛜🏊) In one of Ottawa's finest locations, the stately Lord Elgin was built in 1941 in a similar, but less grandiose, style to Toronto's Fairmont Royal York. The 346 spacious, bright rooms are comfortably furnished with modern amenities, including large flat-screen TVs. Many feature wonderful views over Confederation Park. Check online for frequent special rates and packages at this landmark property.

Best Western
Plus Ottawa Downtown   HOTEL $$

(Map p212; ☑613-567-7275; www.bestwesternottawa.com; 377 O'Connor St; r incl breakfast from $190; P❀@🛜) Your loonies go a long way at this 128-room property in a delightful position near the Canadian Museum of Nature. The bright, airy suites have separate bedroom and lounge at executive and deluxe levels, and all have cable TV, writing desk, and kitchenette with fridge, microwave and coffee maker. Continental breakfast and an 8th-floor gym and sauna are also offered.

Arc   BOUTIQUE HOTEL $$

(Map p216; ☑613-238-2888; www.arcthehotel. com; 140 Slater St; s/d from $119/129; P❀🛜) Arc is a savvy boutique hotel with 112 minimal yet elegant rooms and suites in a great location; call it low-key, muted and restfully hip. This mellow adult atmosphere continues through the chic lounge bar and restaurant. There's an extra charge for parking.

Metcalfe Hotel   HOTEL $$

(Map p216; ☑613-231-6155; www.ottawadowntownhotel.com; 123 Metcalfe St; r from $150; P❀@🛜🏊🎾) This stylish hotel offers a great location, iPad docking stations, and a selection of rooms for different budgets. Pets are welcome for an extra $75 per night.

★Fairmont
Château Laurier   HISTORIC HOTEL $$$

(Map p216; ☑866-540-4410, 613-241-1414; www. fairmont.com/laurier; 1 Rideau St; d from $278; P❀@🛜🏊) By the Ottawa Locks, the city's best-known hotel is a landmark in its own right. Built in 1912 to resemble a 16th-century French château, its 426 rooms and suites are predictably large and luxurious. Walking the opulent marble hallways, admiring the art and reclining on overstuffed chaises, guests and happy interlopers alike feel like the toast of the town. Valet parking is $49 per night.

🛏 ByWard Market & Sandy Hill

Ottawa Backpackers Inn   HOSTEL $

(Map p216; ☑613-241-3402; www.ottawahostel.com; 203 York St; dm/s/d/tr/q from $28/65/80/100/140, apt from $140; P@🛜)

ONTARIO OTTAWA

This laid-back hostel occupies a converted late-19th-century house boasting fresh-faced bathrooms, sun-drenched dorms and handy power outlets at every bed. Dorms are mixed or female-only with four to 10 beds and en suite bathrooms in the larger options. There's a lounge and a rear terrace, and an apartment accommodating five. Parking ($9) is available.

Barefoot Hostel HOSTEL **$**
(Map p216; ☎613-237-0336; www.barefoothostel.com; 455 Cumberland St; dm $48; P ❄ @ ☏) With just four mixed and single-sex four-bed dorms, Barefoot is a veritable 'boutique hostel' with a comfy lounge, small self-catering kitchen, two modern bathrooms and an outdoor patio.

★**Swiss Hotel** BOUTIQUE HOTEL **$$**
(Map p216; ☎888-663-0000, 613-237-0335; www.swisshotel.ca; 89 Daly Ave; r from $155; P ❄ @ ☏) Owner Sabina's Swiss heritage is reflected in everything from the luxuriant buffet breakfast ($15) to the rooms' design-savvy stencil decor. The 22 stylish rooms all have appliances such as espresso machines and iPads; those featuring a queen-size bed with fireplace are a good option, while the Jacuzzi suite has real wow factor.

McGee's Inn B&B **$$**
(Map p212; ☎800-262-4337, 613-237-6089; www.mcgeesinn.com; 185 Daly Ave; r incl breakfast $119-198; P ❄ ☏) Floral prints, embroidered chair caning, plush button-eyed teddy bears, varnished sewing machines and antique cuckoo clocks: this vast Victorian mansion has all the period trappings. A dozen rooms and suites take you back in time, including the elegant and atmospheric John McGee room. An excellent choice for those who love history and charm. Parking is $10.

Australis Guest House B&B **$$**
(Map p212; ☎613-235-8461; www.australisguesthouse.com; 89 Goulburn Ave; d with/without bath $139/119; P ☏) Hosts Brian and Carol create a friendly atmosphere at this homey guesthouse in the green Sandy Hill neighborhood, between the Rideau River and the University of Ottawa. A good option for solo travelers and those wishing to get a local perspective on the capital.

Eating

Ottawa's cultural diversity is reflected in its culinary prowess: its smorgasbord of gastronomic goodness rivals Toronto and Montréal, but is more accessible. The capital's compact footprint makes finding great food simple, with a plethora of excellent dining options catering to most tastes and budgets.

Look forward to a dynamic mix of flavors and aromas from around the globe, prepared using fresh, local ingredients.

Centretown & Chinatown

Saigon Boy Noodle House VIETNAMESE **$**
(Map p212; ☎613-230-8080; 648 Somerset St W; mains $13; ⊙11am-9pm) Locals rate Saigon Boy as the city's best choice for *pho,* a Vietnamese soup containing rice noodles with beef or chicken. Other dishes, such as grilled pork and rice, are also available.

Art Is In Bakery BAKERY **$**
(Map p212; ☎613-695-1226; www.artisinbakery.com; 250 City Centre Ave; sandwiches $9-15; ⊙8am-9:30pm Mon-Fri, to 4pm Sat, to 3pm Sun; P ☏) Start the day with a breakfast sandwich or croissant and an excellent cappuccino at this buzzy bakery cafe, occupying a warehouse space on an industrial estate. The gourmet sandwiches have fillings such as pickle melt and Thai chicken, with gluten-free options and salads available.

Blue Nile ETHIOPIAN **$**
(Map p212; ☎613-321-0774; www.blueniIeottawa.com; 707 Gladstone Ave; mains $12; ⊙11am-10pm Tue-Sat, noon-9pm Sun-Mon) Undoubtedly the best place to satisfy any *injera* (flat, spongy bread) cravings, this small restaurant in Chinatown also offers homemade *tej* (honey wine) and a large selection of authentic Ethiopian dishes.

★**El Camino** MEXICAN **$$**
(Map p212; ☎613-422-2800; http://eatelcamino.com; 380 Elgin St; mains/tacos $15/7; ⊙5:30pm-late Tue-Sun, takeout noon-2:30pm Tue-Fri) With a hip industrial aesthetic underscored by Day of the Dead references, El Camino is either praised as Ottawa's taco joint of the hour or derided as overpriced. Come for chorizo and crispy fish tacos, eaten at benches or taken out, and cocktails ($13) such as the sweet and spicy El Fuego – and book ahead.

★**Wilf & Ada's** DINER **$$**
(Map p212; ☎613-231-7959; www.facebook.com/wilfandadasascratchdiner; 510 Bank St; mains $16; ⊙7am-3pm Mon-Fri, from 8am Sat & Sun) This 'scratch diner' is one of Ottawa's hippest

OTTAWA FOR CHILDREN

Nope, the **Canada Agriculture and Food Museum** (☑613-991-3044; www.ingenium canada.org/agriculture/index.php; 901 Prince of Wales Dr; adult/child $12/10; ☺9am-5pm late Feb-Oct, Wed-Sun Nov-Feb) isn't about the history of the pitchfork – it's a fascinating experimental farm. The government-owned property, southwest of downtown, includes about 500 hectares of gardens and ranches. Kids will love the livestock as they hoot and snort around the barn. The affable farmhands will even let the tots help out during feeding time. The rolling farmland is the perfect place for a scenic summer picnic, and in winter the grounds become a prime tobogganing locale. The farm can be reached on the city's network of cycling routes.

Just as farm-like, but without the animals, the hedge mazes and labyrinths at Saunders Farm (p211) will keep the kids going in circles for ages, so you can put your feet up! About 45 minutes' drive southwest of Ottawa, the farm also offers a waterpark, pedal carts, hay-wagon rides and much more seasonal fun.

Otherwise, most of Ottawa's museums have been designed with families in mind; several have entire wings devoted to child's play, like the Canadian Museum of Nature (p214), the Canada Science & Technology Museum (p215), and of course the Canadian Museum of History's (p214) interactive Canadian Children's Museum.

Family-friendly accommodations include **Les Suites** (Map p216; ☑613-232-2000, 866-682-0879; www.les-suites.com; 130 Besserer St; ste from $180; P✱☎🖥🐾) and **Courtyard Ottawa East** (☑613-741-9862; www.marriott.com; 200 Coventry Rd; r from $149; P✱☎🖥).

---

breakfast and lunch spots, with its retro art and everything made from scratch. Breakfast is all home-cured bacon, buttermilk French toast, 'homies' (home fries) and maple syrup, while chunky sandwiches, soup, salads and poutine are served for lunch. If it's full, head round the back to the affiliated cafe Arlington Five.

★ Town
ITALIAN $$
(Map p212; ☑613-695-8696; www.townlovesyou. ca; 296 Elgin St; mains $23; ☺5-10pm Mon-Sat) Slick, smart and ineffably cool, this joint is always packed: arty-farty hipsters bump elbows with wealthy coiffured housewives. Ottawa foodies appreciate the use of local produce and northern Italian recipes, resulting in a short and seasonal menu of small and large plates, such as the mainstay ricotta-stuffed meatballs, with an abundance of Niagara wines to accompany them.

Shanghai
CHINESE $$
(Map p212; ☑613-233-4001; www.theshang.word press.com; 651 Somerset St W; mains $15; ☺4:30-10pm Wed-Fri, to 2am Sat, karaoke from 9pm Sat; ☝) The first restaurant in Ottawa's Chinatown, Shanghai is now run by the artistic children of the original owners. The food is great – modern Chinese cuisine with lots of veggie options – but the real draw is the trendy decor, rotating art exhibits and fabulous weekend events (think 'Disco Bingo'

and karaoke) hosted by the local diva tranny goddess China-Doll.

Ceylonta
SRI LANKAN $$
(Map p212; ☑613-237-7812; www.ceylonta.com; 403 Somerset St W; mains $18; ☺11:30am-2pm Mon-Fri, from noon Sun, 5-9pm daily) Locals recommend this friendly neighborhood Sri Lankan restaurant, serving fresh and zingy dishes. Go for the fish *thali* or the chicken or mutton *kothu rotti*. Dinner only on Saturday.

Eggspectation
BREAKFAST $$
(Map p212; ☑613-569-6505; www.eggspectation. ca; 171 Bank St; mains $10-25; ☺6am-3pm Mon-Fri, 7am-4pm Sat & Sun) The downtown location of this breakfast (and more) franchise is so handy and the menu so *egg-citing* that we couldn't resist sharing. It's cheap, cheery and full of sunshine from its bright open windows. As the day wears on, *eggs-ecutive* burgers, *eggs-traordinary* pasta and more keep the puns coming and the punters happy.

The Works
BURGERS $$
(Map p212; ☑613-235-0406; www.worksburger. com; 580 Bank St; burgers $18; ☺11am-10pm) In a little over a decade this clever burger joint has flourished into a successful franchise with restaurants across southern Ontario. Build on your Canadian beef patty with myriad house and customized toppings,

from fried eggs to Brie cheese and peanut butter.

Lapointe SEAFOOD $$
(Map p216; ☑613-241-6221; www.lapointefish.ca; 55 York St; mains $19; ⊙11:30am-9:30pm) This fish market has served the community since 1867, offering a versatile array of dishes from cod tacos to old-school fish-and-chips. Sit on the front patio or inside at a ground floor or basement table.

★**Union Local 613** MODERN AMERICAN $$$
(Map p212; ☑613-231-1010; www.union613.ca; 315 Somerset St W; mains $28; ⊙food served 11:30am-2pm Wed-Fri, from 10am Sat & Sun, 5:30pm-late Mon-Sat; ☜) Sit among the low-lit decor of hummingbirds and hot-air balloons, and drink house beers and other local craft brews from screw-top jars. It's food with attitude, including southern-fried chicken and cornmeal-crusted catfish, and there's a 'speakeasy' behind a bookshelf in the basement (open 10:30pm to 2am Wednesday to Saturday).

★**Beckta Dining & Wine Bar** CANADIAN $$$
(Map p216; ☑613-238-7063; www.beckta.com; 150 Elgin St; mains $32-45; ⊙5:30-10pm Mon-Sat, to 9pm Sun) ✿ Book in advance for one of the hottest tables in the capital, if not the whole country. Beckta offers an upmarket dining experience with an original spin on regional cuisine.

You can choose between à la carte dining or a five-course pairing with wine ($98, plus $54 with wine pairing).

Whalesbone Oyster House SEAFOOD $$$
(Map p212; ☑613-231-8569; www.thewhalesbone.com; 430 Bank St; mains $27-41; ⊙11:30am-2pm Mon-Fri, 5-10pm daily) ✿ If the local chefs are purchasing their fish from Whalesbone's wholesale wing (or should we say 'fin'), then there's really no doubt that it's the best place in town for seafood.

The on-site restaurant offers up a short list of fresh faves such as oysters, lobster and scallops ceviche on small plates. Book ahead.

Métropolitain Brasserie FRENCH $$$
(Map p216; ☑613-562-1160; www.metropolitainbrasserie.com; 700 Sussex Dr; mains $25-31; ⊙11am-midnight Tue-Fri, to 11pm Mon, 9am-midnight Sat, 9am-11pm Sun) Métropolitain puts a modern spin on the typical brasserie with its swirling zinc countertop, flamboyant fixtures and Gallic soundtrack: you'll feel like

you're dining on the set of *Moulin Rouge*. 'Hill Hour' (4pm to 7pm on weekdays and from 9:30pm daily) buzzes with the spirited chatter of hot-blooded politicos as they down *plats du jour*.

LUXE Bistro & Steakhouse STEAK $$$
(Map p216; ☑613-241-8805; www.luxebistro.com; 47 York St; mains $19-49; ⊙11:30am-9:30pm Mon-Fri, 9am-2:30pm & 5-9:30pm Sat & Sun) If you like your steak a little French with a twist of New York, this smart By-Ward Market bistro is bound to appeal. The decor is slick and the outdoor patio is a hit in the warmer months. Dress smart. Burgers, *moules-frites* and stroganoff are also on the menu, as is brunch at weekends (mains $18).

Tosca ITALIAN $$$
(Map p216; ☑613-565-3933; www.tosca-ristorante.ca; 144 O'Connor St; mains $21-40; ⊙11:30am-10pm Mon-Wed, to 11pm Thu-Fri, from 4pm Sat & Sun) In the heart of the downtown core, this upscale but accessible Italian *ristorante's* delicious, authentic food, extensive wine list and excellent service attract both business people on important meetings and parents on shopping expeditions. The evening atmosphere is candlelit and serene, perfect for romancing or long conversations with old friends.

✖ ByWard Market & Sandy Hill

★**ByWard Market Square** MARKET $
(Map p216; ☑613-244-4410; www.bywardmarketsquare.com; ByWard Market Sq; ⊙10am-8pm) Anchoring the market district, this sturdy brick building is the perfect place to stop when hunger strikes. Aside from the fresh produce and cheese, an array of international takeaway joints offers falafel, spicy curries, flaky pastries, sushi... the list goes on.

Look for the stand selling beavertails, Ottawa's signature sizzling flat-dough dish. Between William, Byward, George and York Sts.

Boulangerie Moulin de Provence BAKERY $
(Map p216; ☑613-241-9152; www.moulindeprovence.com; 55 ByWard Market Sq; items from $3, mains $14; ⊙7am-10pm) Still riding on the buzz left by a visit from former US President Barack Obama, this bakery is packed to the hilt with sugary and savory goodness. The 'Obama Cookies' are a big hit, while others swear by the flaky croissants. With sand-

wiches, salads and ready-made meals in bains-marie, it's a good stop for a quick and affordable lunch.

Zak's Diner
DINER $

(Map p216; ☑613-241-2401; www.zaksdiner.com; 14 ByWard Market Sq; mains $10-15; ⊗24hr) Shoo-bop along to the pop music that supplements the *Grease*-like atmosphere at this kitschy diner. The ByWard Market stalwart hosts families by day, but is at its best in the middle of the night, when the joint fills up for post-party munchies. Wraps, poutine and nachos are on offer, so it's not just a *Back to the Future* theme park.

Chez Lucien
BISTRO $$

(Map p216; ☑613-241-3533; http://chezlucien. ca; 137 Murray St; mains $19; ⊗11am-2am) Exposed burgundy brick and classics on the free jukebox make this Gallic-accented gastropub one of Ottawa's favorite places to kick back in style. Numerous burgers, Dijon chicken and nachos are on the menu. Come for live jazz on Sunday from 4pm to 7pm.

Fraser Cafe
CAFE $$$

(☑613-749-1444; www.frasercafe.ca; 7 Springfield Rd; mains brunch $11-20, lunch $14-21, dinner $29-34; ⊗11:30am-2pm Tue-Fri, from 10am Sat & Sun, 5:30-10pm daily) Take a little trek over to this smart cafe/restaurant across the Rideau River, northeast of ByWard Market, especially if you're in the mood for brunch (weekends only). True to its 'seasonal kitchen' subtitle, healthy, tasty, creative meals are prepared from the freshest ingredients. The atmosphere is lively and casual and the service, despite the bustle, is excellent. Reservations recommended.

Signatures Restaurant
FRENCH $$$

(Map p212; ☑613-236-2499; www.signaturesres taurant.com; 453 Laurier Ave E; lunch mains/menu $29/39, dinner menu $95; ⊗11:30am-1:30pm Tue-Fri, 5:30-9pm Tue-Sat) Housed in the historic Tudor-style Munross Mansion, this restaurant affiliated with the prestigious Le Cordon Bleu culinary school focuses on modern French cuisine, under French executive chef Yannick Anton. The lengthy wine list looks more like an encyclopedia, and the regularly changing three-course lunch and dinner menus are rich seasonal banquets of dishes such as slow-cooked lamb's thigh.

✖ Further Afield

White Horse Restaurant
DINER $

(☑613-746-7767; www.thewhitehorserestaurant. com; 294 Tremblay Rd; mains $7; ⊗5:30am-7pm Mon-Fri, to 3pm Sat, 7am-4pm Sun) This wonderful little greasy spoon is the nearest place to the Ottawa train station to get a meal, and boasts good old-fashioned home cooking and the cheapest breakfast in town.

Stoneface Dolly's
FUSION $$

(Map p212; ☑613-564-2222; www.stonefaced ollys.com; 416 Preston St; lunch mains $15-19; ⊗7:30am-2:30pm Mon-Fri, from 8:30am Sat & Sun) Named for the owner's mother, who perfected the art of a stone-cold poker bluff, this popular joint is a great spot to taste local craft brews such as Beau's. They are known for the brunch specials that are available at all times, and the eclectic and seasonal dishes range from South African cuisine to crab and porchetta fettuccine.

Benny's Bistro
BISTRO $$

(Map p216; ☑613-789-7941; www.frenchbaker. ca; 119 Murray St; mains $21; ⊗11:30am-2:30pm Mon-Fri, from 10:30am Sat & Sun) The smell of freshly baked *pain au chocolat* (chocolate croissant) emanates from the French bakery at the front of this cool and arty bistro. Pastries are prepared using tried-and-true recipes from France. If you feel like lingering in the Gallic ambience, grab a table on Benny's black-and-white checkered floor and enjoy dishes such as salmon gravlax and lamb kofta.

Atelier
FUSION $$$

(Map p212; ☑613-321-3537; www.atelierrestau rant.ca; 540 Rochester St; menu $125; ⊗5:30-8:30pm Tue-Sat) ✐ The brainchild of celebrated chef and molecular gastronomy enthusiast Marc Lépine, Atelier is a white-walled laboratory dedicated to tickling the taste buds. There's no oven or stove – just Bunsen burners, liquid nitrogen and hot plates to create the unique 12-course tasting menu.

● Drinking & Nightlife

From cheap-and-crusty beery dives to cheery local pubs and plush, see-and-be-seen lounges, Ottawa has it on tap. Head south on Bank or Elgin Sts for local hangouts, and to the buzzing ByWard Market area for out-and-out revelry. For something a little different, descend the stairs to Union Local 613's (p222) underground speakeasy. Many people cross the river to party on in Hull (Québec) when Ottawa winds down around 2am.

Heart & Crown
IRISH PUB

(Map p216; ☑ 613-562-0674; https://heartand crown.pub; 67 Clarence St; ⊙ 11am-2am Mon-Fri, from 9am Sat & Sun) This ByWard Market stalwart is popular with young Ottawa folk for beers and big platters of pub grub. Several rooms and patios sprawl into each other, incorporating four other pubs along the way. Big screens show soccer matches. There's music from live bands to acoustic sets seven days a week.

Highlander Pub
PUB

(Map p216; ☑ 613-562-5678; www.thehighlander pub.com; 115 Rideau St; ⊙ 11am-2am) Kilted servers, 17 taps and 200 single malt whiskies all add to the wonderful Scottish appeal of this ByWard Market area pub. The food is good too!

Clocktower Brew Pub
BAR

(Map p212; ☑ 613-233-7849; www.clocktower. ca; 575 Bank Street; ⊙ 11:30am-late) Enjoy homemade brews such as Raspberry Wheat and Bytown Brown in the newly renovated taproom. There is also a taproom on Rideau St and three other locations around town, but nothing beats beer right from the source!

I Deal Coffee
COFFEE

(Map p216; ☑ 613-562-1775; www.idealcoffees. com; 176 Dalhousie St; coffee $4; ⊙ 7am-7pm Mon-Wed, to 10pm Thu-Fri, 8:30am-7pm Sat, 9am-6pm Sun) Ideal indeed; handcrafted blends are produced and roasted on-site. The decor is thin, with bins and sacks of 'light organic blend' and 'prince of darkness' stacked next to the roaster; it's all about rich, flavorful cups of joe (hot or iced). In the words of one happy customer, this might be Ottawa's best cappuccino.

Manx
BAR

(Map p212; ☑ 613-231-2070; www.manxpub.com; 370 Elgin St; ⊙ 11:30am-1am Mon-Thu, to 2am Fri, 10am-2am Sat & Sun) 'Ottawa's original sinkhole,' as this basement bar has called itself since Rideau St collapsed in 2016, offers a great selection of Canadian microbrews (including the beloved Creemore), served on copper-top tables. There's food, too (mains $14 to $16) – brunch here is popular at weekends.

Château Lafayette
PUB

(Map p216; ☑ 613-241-4747; www.thelaff.ca; 42 York St; ⊙ 11am-2am) Dating from 1849, 'the Laff' is Ottawa's oldest bar and it retains much quirky charm – a run-down relic that captures ByWard's laid-back attitude. Come for live music on Tuesday, Wednesday, Saturday and Sunday evenings.

Lookout Bar
GAY & LESBIAN

(Map p216; ☑ 613-789-1624; www.thelookoutbar. com; 41 York St; ⊙ 2pm-2am Tue-Fri, to 10pm Sun & Mon) Keeping the ByWard Market crowds happy for 20 years, Lookout's nights range from karaoke on Tuesday and Wednesday to Saturday's drag show.

Social
BAR

(Map p216; ☑ 613-789-7355; www.social.ca; 537 Sussex Dr; ⊙ 11:30am-late) This chic, flowing lounge with slick DJ beats, overstuffed furniture, cocktails and equally creative cuisine (lunch/dinner mains $23/34) appeals to a trendy crowd. There's live jazz on the patio on Wednesday evenings, DJs on Friday and Saturday, and brunch on weekends.

☆ Entertainment

Ottawa has a variety of publications (print and web-based) that offer the latest scoop on the various goings-on around town. *Xpress* (www.ottawaxpress.ca) is the city's free entertainment weekly, found around town in cafes, bars and bookstores. Try www. ottawaentertainment.ca for additional info and check out Thursday's *Ottawa Citizen* (ottawacitizen.com) for club and entertainment listings.

Nightlife venues generally cluster in three zones: the ByWard Market, along Bank St in the Glebe neighborhood, and down Elgin St about halfway between the Queensway and Parliament Hill.

Live Music

Irene's Pub
LIVE MUSIC

(Map p212; ☑ 613-230-4474; www.irenespub.ca; 885 Bank St; ⊙ 11:30am-2am) Friendly and funky, if a little grimy in the thick of a busy weekend, Irene's is the three-decade-old spiritual home for the Glebe neighborhood's artists and musicians. It offers live music, with a good line in Celtic, folk and blues, and other entertainment a few nights a week.

Enjoy a great selection of whiskeys and local craft beers on tap.

Rainbow Bistro
LIVE MUSIC

(Map p216; ☑613-241-5123; www.therainbow.ca; 76 Murray St) An oldie but a goodie: the best place in town to catch live blues. See live music here nightly in summer, with some sets starting as early as 3pm.

Theaters & Cinemas

National Arts Centre
THEATER

(NAC; Map p216; ☑613-947-7000; www.nac-cna. ca; 1 Elgin St) The capital's premier performing arts complex delivers opera, drama, Broadway shows, and performances by its resident symphony orchestra. The grand building stretches along the canal in Confederation Sq.

ByTowne Cinema
CINEMA

(Map p212; ☑613-789-3456; www.bytowne.ca; 325 Rideau St; tickets adult/child $12/6) Ottawa's indie heart has been screening independent and international movies for 70 years.

Sport

TD Place Arena
SPECTATOR SPORT

(Map p212; ☑613-232-6767; www.tdplace.ca; 1015 Bank St) You can watch the Ottawa 67's (www.ottawa67s.com), a minor-league hockey team, at their home ground, the TD Place Arena. You can also catch concerts, Ottawa Fury soccer club and the Ottawa Redblacks Canadian football team here.

Canadian Tire Centre
SPECTATOR SPORT

(☑613-599-0100; www.canadiantirecentre.com; 1000 Palladium Dr, Kanata) Ottawa is a hardcore hockey town. It's worth getting tickets to a game even if you're not into hockey – the ballistic fans put on a show of their own. NHL team the Ottawa Senators (www.senators.com) play here, at their home ground, about 25km southwest of the center in Ottawa's west end. Big-ticket concerts also take place here.

🛍 Shopping

ByWard Market is the best place in town for one-stop shopping. Dalhousie St, a block east of the market, has been rising in popularity with a smattering of hipster boutiques and fashion houses.

The Glebe, a colorful neighborhood just south of the Queensway, bustles with quirky antique shops and charismatic cafes. Most of the action crowds along Bank St.

ByWard Market
MARKET

(Map p216; ☑613-562-3325; www.byward-market. com; cnr York & ByWard Sts; ⊗6am-6pm) The best place in town for one-stop shopping. Outdoor vendors cluster around the grand maroon-brick ByWard Market Square (p222) building, which dates from 1926. Many merchants operate booths year-round, but the winter weather drastically reduces the number of businesses. In summer, over 260 stalls fill the streets, selling fresh produce from local farms, flowers, seafood, cheese, baked goods, souvenirs and more.

Fire & Flower
DISPENSARY

(Map p216; ☑613-562-4647; https://yorkstreet cannabisco.com; 129 York St; 1g from $15; ⊗10am-10pm Mon-Sat, 11am-7pm Sun) With extremely helpful and knowledgeable staff, this dispensary is a great resource for novices as well as experienced smokers. Anyone over the age of 19 is allowed to purchase marijuana as well as a range of products made from THC and CBD. You will need to have ID to prove your age if you plan on visiting.

🛈 Information

ByWard Market Information Centre (Map p216; ☑613-244-4410; www.byward-market. com; ByWard & George Sts; ⊗7:30am-6pm Jul & Aug, 8am-5pm Sep-Jun) Covers the whole city.

Calforex Currency Exchange (☑613-569-4075; www.calforex.com; 50 Rideau St, store 322, Rideau Centre; ⊗8:30am-9pm Mon-Fri, from 9:30am Sat, 11am-6pm Sun) Accommodates currency exchange and wire transfers.

Capital Information Kiosk (Map p216; ☑844-878-8333; 90 Wellington St; ⊗9am-5pm) This helpful office is the city's hub for information and bookings.

Central Post Office (Map p216; ☑866-607-6301; www.canadapost.ca; 59 Sparks St; ⊗8:30am-5pm Mon-Fri) The main post office, occupying a historic building.

Ottawa Hospital (☑613-722-7000; www.otta wahospital.on.ca; 501 Smyth Rd; ⊗emergency 24hr) Southeast of downtown in Alta Vista; has an emergency department.

Ottawa Tourism (www.ottawatourism.ca) Offers a comprehensive online look at the nation's capital, and can assist with planning itineraries and booking accommodations.

🛈 Getting There & Away

AIR

The state-of-the-art Ottawa MacDonald-Cartier International Airport (p71) is 15km south of the city and, perhaps surprisingly, is very small.

Almost all international flights require a transfer before arriving in the capital (normally in Toronto's Lester B Pearson International Airport). Nonetheless, numerous North American carriers serve the airport, including Air Canada, WestJet, Porter Airlines, United Airlines, Delta and American Airlines.

BUS

The **central bus station** (Map p212; ☑ 613-238-6668; www.ottawacentralstation.com; 265 Catherine St) is just off Queensway (Hwy 417), near Kent St. Several companies operate bus services from the station.

CAR & MOTORCYCLE

Major car-rental chains are represented at the airport and offer several locations downtown, on Catherine St and at the train station (both just off Hwy 417). You will likely get a better deal hiring a car in Toronto.

TRAIN

The **VIA Rail Station** (☑ 888-842-7245; www.viarail.ca; 200 Tremblay Rd) is 7km east of downtown, near the Hwy 19/Riverside Dr exit of Hwy 417. Trains run to Toronto ($109, 4½ hours, 10 daily) via Brockville and Kingston, and to Québec City via Montréal ($114, two hours, four daily).

ⓘ Getting Around

TO/FROM THE AIRPORT

The cheapest way to get to the airport is by city bus. Take bus 97 from Slater St between Elgin St and Bronson Ave (make sure you are heading in the 'South Keys & Airport' direction). The ride takes 40 minutes and costs $3.50.

Ottawa Shuttle Service (☑ 613-680-3313; www.ottawashuttleservice.com; 1 or 2 passengers within Ottawa $59; ⊙ office 10am-10pm, shuttles 24hr) offers private and shared shuttles from downtown hotels.

Blue Line Taxi (☑ 613-238-1111; www.blueline taxi.com) and **Capital Taxi** (☑ 613-744-3333; www.capitaltaxi.com) offer cab services; the fare to/from downtown is around $30. During the week, if you're having a hard time snagging

a cab, there's always a cluster on Metcalfe St between Sparks and Queen Sts.

BICYCLE

Right on the Rideau Canal bike path, the friendly staff at **Rent-A-Bike** (☑ 613-241-4140; www.rentabike.ca; East Arch Plaza Bridge, 2 Rideau St; rentals per hour from $9; ⊙ 9am-5pm) will set you up with a bike and offer tips about scenic trails. The Capital Information Kiosk (p225) has bike maps.

CAR & MOTORCYCLE

There is free parking in World Exchange Plaza on Albert St on weekends. Hourly metered parking can be found throughout downtown and in parking lots charging around $20 a day. There are lots charging around $10 a day dotted around Centretown, including on Somerset St W east of Lyon St N.

During winter, overnight on-street parking is prohibited if there has been (or is likely to be) more than 7cm of snow – to allow the snowplows to come through. Contact the **City of Ottawa** (☑ 613-580-2400; https://ottawa.ca) with additional parking queries.

PUBLIC TRANSPORTATION

OC Transpo (☑ 613-741-4390; www.octranspo.com) operates Ottawa's useful bus network and a light-rail system known as the O-train. Bus rides cost $3.50 ($1.80 for children under 13) and you can pay on the bus. Make sure you have the exact change on you. You can also purchase a day pass ($10.50) from the driver. Be sure to take your ticket when boarding and paying; it allows you to transfer to other buses for a period of 90 minutes. The Capital Information Kiosk (p225) has bus maps.

The O-train's Confederation Line runs downtown via Parliament and the University of Ottawa and was finalising operations at the time of writing. The fare will be the same as the bus and riders will be able to transfer from the bus to train and vice versa for free.

Ottawa and Hull/Gatineau operate separate bus systems. A transfer is valid from one system to the other, but may require an extra payment.

Québec

Best Places to Eat

➡ Joe Beef (p248)

➡ Barroco (p245)

➡ Au Petit Poucet (p260)

➡ Chez Boulay (p282)

➡ Le Diapason (p292)

Best Places to Sleep

➡ Auberge St-Antoine (p281)

➡ Hôtel Gault (p244)

➡ Maison Historique James Thompson (p279)

➡ Hôtel Le Germain (p244)

➡ Auberge Festive Sea Shack (p310)

Why Go?

Québec truly feels like a country within a country, an island of Francophone linguistic and cultural identity within the greater Canadian sea. Of course, this *is* Canada, with its interplay of vast wilderness and cosmopolitanism, but Québec's embrace of *terroir*, its language, its passion for everything from winter snow to wine to gastronomy, is something else, an 'else' that encompasses identities both distinctly North American and European.

Montréal and Québec City are bustling metropolises with a perfect mixture of sophistication and playfulness, and history-soaked preserved quarters tucked away around town. The rustic allurements of old Québec are scattered among the Eastern Townships, and produce from bucolic Charlevoix graces the tables of the region's stellar restaurants. Past these creature comforts is the raw outdoors: the jagged coasts of the unblemished Gaspé Peninsula, the vast taiga and tundra of the North Shore, and the windswept isolation of the Îles de la Madeleine.

When to Go
Montréal, QC

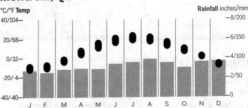

Dec & Jan Head to Mont-Tremblant – one of North America's best ski hills.

Feb Bundle up and join in the frigid festivities in Québec City's fete of the year, Carnaval.

Jul Montréal's summer-long party gets under way with the Festival International de Jazz.

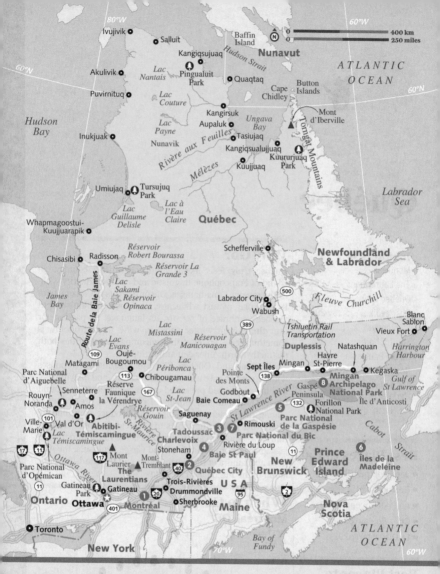

Québec Highlights

1 Montréal (p231) Drinking up the dynamic nightlife in this happening city.

2 Québec City (p272) Savoring the unparalleled culture, history and charm of this walled city.

3 Tadoussac (p296) Being sprayed by whales in the Saguenay Fjord.

4 Baie St Paul (p290) Soaking up the artsy vibe and sampling local delicacies in this most attractive little town.

5 Parc National de la Gaspésie (p311) Hiking the stunning peaks above the tree line in this pretty national park.

6 Îles de la Madeleine (p323) Enjoying Acadian music and steaming fish pie in this lovely archipelago.

7 Parc National du Bic (p306) Getting back to nature in this spectacular St Lawrence park.

8 Mingan Archipelago National Park (p321) Sea kayaking amid these remote, sculpted islands.

History

Québec has had a tumultuous history and, by Canadian standards, a very long and complicated one.

At the time of European exploration, the entire region was fully settled and controlled by various Indigenous groups, all of whom are resident today, including the Mohawks along the St Lawrence River, the Cree to the northwest, the Innu still further north and east, and the Inuit in the remote far north. Relations between the Europeans and indigenous groups were tense at times but generally amicable, and the two groups forged a relationship based on commerce (specifically the fur trade), not politics.

French explorer Jacques Cartier landed in what is now Québec City and Montréal in 1535. Samuel de Champlain, also of France, first heard and recorded the word 'kebec' (an Algonquian word meaning 'where the river narrows') when he founded a settlement at Québec City some 70 years later, in 1608.

Throughout the rest of the 17th century, the French and English skirmished over control of Canada, but where the British began settling large colonies across what would become the USA, the French Canadian population remained largely sparse. In 1759 the English, with a victory on the Plains of Abraham at Québec City, assumed a leadership role in the new colony of Canada. From that point onward, French political influence in the New World waned.

When thousands of British Loyalists fled the American Revolution in the 1770s, the new colony divided into Upper (today's Ontario) and Lower (now Québec) Canada; almost all the French settled in the latter region. Power struggles between the two groups continued through the 1800s, with Lower Canada joining the Canadian confederation as Québec in 1867.

The 20th century saw Québec change from a rural, agricultural society to an urban, industrialized one, but it continued to be educationally and culturally based upon the Catholic Church, which wielded immense power and still does (more than 75% of the population today is Roman Catholic).

The tumultuous 1960s brought the so-called 'Quiet Revolution,' during which time all aspects of Francophone society were scrutinized and overhauled. Political systems were reorganized, massive secularization and unionization took place, and a welfare state was created. Intellectuals and extremists alike debated the prospect of independence from Canada, as Québécois began to assert their sense of nationhood.

Formed in 1968, the pro-independence Parti Québécois came to power in 1976, headed by the charismatic René Lévesque. Since then, two referendums have returned 'No' votes on the question of separating from Canada. In the current century, the notion of an independent Québec is less attractive to a younger generation with more global concerns.

QUÉBEC

Land & Climate

There's a trope that the eastern seaboard of North America is tame and gentle when compared to the rugged West Coast. But Québec dispels this cliché. The Laurentians form a jagged, pine-clad arc of rugged highlands giving way to the windswept shores and forest-and-tundra vastness of the North Shore. Sheer cliffs plunge into the blue ocean off the Gaspé Peninsula, while in Charlevoix a patchwork of farms overlooks sweeping bays on the St Lawrence River. Then there is the Far North – wild, barely populated, a land of taiga, peat bogs, lichen-studded tundra and wind-carved mountains.

In terms of temperature, the province is saddled with extremes. Montréal and Québec City can go from 40°C to -40°C in six months, and May could see a dump of snow. Generally, the summers are comfortably warm, although high humidity can make Montréal pretty steamy. Winters are very snowy, but usually bright, sunny and dry.

Parks

The province's protected areas are a highlight of any trip to Québec. In addition to preserving regions of remarkable beauty, they offer a host of invigorating activities, including canoeing, kayaking, rafting, hiking, cycling and camping in the wild. Forillon National Park and Saguenay, Bic, Mont-Tremblant and Gaspésie provincial parks are especially recommended.

Parks Canada (p313) administers three national parks, 28 national historic sites and one National Marine Conservation Area in Québec. The historic sites, such as forts and lighthouses, are mostly day-use areas and reveal fascinating bits of history.

The **Société des Établissements de Plein Air du Québec** (Sépaq; ☑ 800-665-6527; www.sepaq.com) oversees Québec's 24 provincial parks and 13 wildlife reserves – confusingly, it refers to many provincial parks as 'national.' The parks, which range from beaches and bird sanctuaries to rugged gorges, provide some outstanding camping, wildlife-viewing, eco-adventures and other outdoor recreation. If there is no one staffing a provincial park entrance (often the case outside of summer), you are expected to pay the entrance fee and leave half of the receipt in a provided envelope. You retain the other half as proof of admission.

Réserve fauniques (wildlife reserves) conserve and protect the environment but also make these spaces publicly accessible. Hunters and fishers use the reserves (permits required), but more and more visitors are discovering them as less crowded alternatives to national and provincial parks.

In the Nunavik region, in the province's Far North, **Nunavik Parks** (☑ 819-964-2961; www.nunavikparks.ca) administers four more protected areas. Because of the complexity of travel to these remote parklands, this park service arranges small group tours and self-guided trips for visitors wanting to explore these northern destinations.

ℹ Getting There & Around

Québec is easily accessible by air, bus, car and train. It shares borders with the US states of New York, Vermont, New Hampshire and Maine.

AIR

Québec's main airport is Montréal-Pierre Elliot Trudeau International Airport (p257), with a smaller airport, Aéroport International Jean-Lesage de Québec (p287), in Québec City. Carriers serving the province include Air Canada, Air Canada Express, Air France, Porter Airlines, PAL Airlines, Pascan, WestJet and discount airline Air Transat. Traveling to the Far North are **First Air** (☑ 800-267-1247; www.firstair.ca), **Air Inuit** (☑ 800-361-2965; www.airinuit.com) and **Air Creebec** (☑ 800-567-6567; www.aircreebec.ca). **Air Canada Express** (☑ 888-247-2262; www.aircanada.com) covers the North Shore and Îles de la Madeleine from Québec City and Montréal.

BOAT

There are numerous ferry services across the St Lawrence River, as well as to islands in the Gulf, such as the Îles de la Madeleine, and along the remote Lower North Shore toward Labrador.

BUS

Maritime Bus connects the province with Atlantic Canada. Megabus links Montréal with Ontario. From the USA, Greyhound operates multiple daily buses between Montréal and New York City. The province is particularly well served by bus lines.

Autobus Maheux (☑ 819-762-2200; https://autobusmaheux.com)

Galland (☑ 450-687-8666; www.galland-bus.com)

QUÉBEC ITINERARIES

One Day
Start with brunch in Montréal at L'Express (p249) and work the calories off on a hike up Parc du Mont-Royal (p241). Descend through Mile End (p236) or the Plateau Mont-Royal (p236), where you'll be spoiled for choice for dinner and drinks.

Three Days
Limit your time savoring Montréal's chilled-out vibe to one day, and then drive through the Laurentians to Mont-Tremblant (p260). Leave a day to stroll within Québec City's walls (p273) in the Old Upper Town, before searching for the ultimate *table d'hôte* in the Old Lower Town.

One Week
Follow the three-day itinerary, then ramble through Charlevoix (p290) en route to the Saguenay Fjord for two days. Stop for lunch in Baie St Paul (p290) or La Malbaie (p293). Spend the last two nights in welcoming Tadoussac (p296), whale-watching or cruising the fjord.

Intercar (☑800-806-2167; www.intercar.qc.ca)

Limocar (☑866-692-8899; www.limocar.ca)

Maritime Bus (☑800-575-1807; www.maritimebus.com)

Megabus (☑866-488-4452; https://ca.megabus.com)

Orléans Express (☑833-449-6444; www.orleansexpress.com)

CAR & MOTORCYCLE

Continental US highways link directly with their Canadian counterparts at numerous border crossings. These roads connect to the Trans-Canada Hwy (Hwy 20 within Québec).

If you're visiting either Montréal or Québec City, consider leaving the car at home. Unlike many other North American cities, Québec's metropolises are European in design – easily navigated on foot, with bustling sidewalks lined with outdoor cafes.

TRAIN

VIA Rail (☑888-842-7245; www.viarail.ca) has fast and frequent services along the Québec City–Windsor corridor, via Montréal, including four-to-six daily trains between Montréal's Gare Centrale and Québec City's Gare du Palais. VIA trains also travel from Montréal and the Québec City region along the South Shore and Gaspésie en route to New Brunswick and Nova Scotia. From the USA, **Amtrak** (☑800-872-7245; www.amtrak.com) trains run once daily between Montréal and New York City.

MONTRÉAL

POP 4.1 MILLION

Historically, Montréal – the only de facto bilingual city on the continent – has been torn right in half, the 'Main' (Blvd St-Laurent) being the dividing line between the east-end Francophones and the west-side Anglos. Today French pockets dot both sides of the map, a new wave of English-speaking Canadians have taken up residence in some formerly French enclaves and, thanks to constant waves of immigration, it's not uncommon for Montréalers to speak not one, or two, but three languages in their daily life. With the new generation concerned more with global issues (namely the environment), language battles have become so passé.

One thing not up for debate is what makes Montréal so irresistible. It's a secret blend of French-inspired joie de vivre and cosmopolitan dynamism that has come together to foster a flourishing arts scene,

> ### ⓘ MONTRÉAL MUSEUM PASS
> Custom-made for culture buffs, this handy **pass** (www.museesmontreal.org; 3-day pass $80) is the most cost-effective way to access 41 of Montréal's museums over a three-day period – the price includes unlimited public transportation during this time.

an indie rock explosion, a medley of world-renowned boutique hotels, the Plateau's extraordinary cache of swank eateries and a cool Parisian vibe that pervades every *terrasse* (patio) in the Quartier Latin. It's easy to imagine you've been transported to a distant locale, where hedonism is the national mandate. Only the stunning vista of a stereotypical North American skyline from Parc du Mont-Royal's Kondiaronk Lookout will ground you.

History

In May 1642, a small fleet of boats sailed up the St Lawrence River. The few dozen missionaries aboard had survived a cold winter crossing the fierce Atlantic Ocean from their native France. Finally they had reached the spot their fellow countryman, explorer Jacques Cartier, had stumbled across over a century earlier. Led by Paul de Chomedey de Maisonneuve, the pioneers went ashore and began building a small settlement they called Ville-Marie, the birthplace of Montréal.

Ville-Marie soon blossomed into a major fur-trading center and exploration base, despite fierce resistance from the local Iroquois. Skirmishes continued until the signing of a peace treaty in 1701. The city remained French until the 1763 Treaty of Paris, which saw France cede Canada to Great Britain. In 1775, American revolutionaries briefly occupied the city, but left after failing to convince the Québécois to join forces with them against the British.

Despite surrendering its pole position in the fur trade to Hudson Bay in the 1820s, Montréal boomed throughout the 19th century. Industrialization got seriously under way after the construction of the railway and the Canal de Lachine, which in turn attracted masses of immigrants.

After WWI the city sashayed through a period as 'Sin City' as hordes of Americans seeking fun flooded across the border to

QUÉBEC MONTRÉAL

Montréal

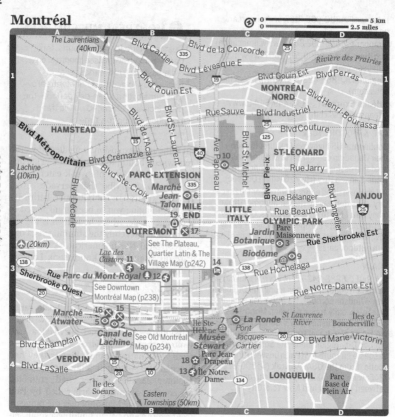

escape Prohibition. By the time mayor Jean Drapeau took the reins, Montréal was ripe for an extreme makeover. During his long tenure (1954–57 and 1960–86), the city gained the métro system, many of downtown's high-rise offices, the underground city and the Place des Arts. Drapeau also twice managed to firmly train the world's spotlight on Montréal: in 1967 for the World Expo and in 1976 for the Olympic Games.

Montréal has been enjoying a consistently positive growth rate for the past two decades, faring extremely well during the global economic recession thanks to a boom in the high-tech sector.

⊙ Sights

First on most itineraries is Old Montréal, where the heart of the city's history and grandeur can be chased through a labyrinth of winding lanes. Waterfront attractions in the Old Port have benefited immensely from continued rejuvenation, and across

the water the attractions and trails of **Parc Jean-Drapeau** (Map p232; www.parcjeandra peau.com; ℗ 🐾; ⓂJean-Drapeau) 🍃 make a great summer escape from the urban jungle. Downtown encompasses stellar museums and universities, while the bohemian Mile End and Plateau Mont-Royal districts are perfect for meandering and sipping artisanal drinks come evening. The Village and Quartier Latin jolt awake at nighttime. Just outside the city, the Olympic Park, Jardin Botanique and Lachine hold sightseeing appeal. From the panorama at Mont-Royal it's possible to take it all in at once.

⊙ Old Montréal

The oldest section of the city is a warren of crooked cobblestone lanes flanked by colonial and Victorian stone houses filled with intimate restaurants, galleries and boutiques. A stroll around here will delight romantics and architecture fans, especially at night when

Montréal

QUÉBEC MONTRÉAL

the most beautiful facades are illuminated. And the waterfront is never far away.

Old Montréal is anchored by lively Place Jacques Cartier and dignified Place d'Armes, which are linked by busy Rue Notre-Dame. The southern end of Place Jacques-Cartier gives way to Rue St-Paul, the district's prettiest and oldest street.

★**Basilique Notre-Dame** CHURCH
(Map p234; ☑846-842-2925; www.basiliquenotre
dame.ca; 110 Rue Notre-Dame Ouest; adult/child $8/5; ☺8am-4:30pm Mon-Fri, to 4pm Sat, 12:30-4pm Sun; ⓂPlace-d'Armes) Montréal's famous landmark, Notre Dame Basilica, is a visually pleasing if slightly gaudy symphony of carved wood, paintings, gilded sculptures and stained-glass windows. Built in 1829 on the site of an older and smaller church, it also sports a famous Casavant Frères **organ** and the **Gros Bourdon**, said to be the biggest bell in North America. Admission includes an optional 20-minute guided tour in English.

★**Place d'Armes** HISTORIC SITE
(Map p234; ⓂPlace-d'Armes) This open square is framed by some of the finest buildings in Old Montréal, including its oldest bank, first skyscraper and Basilique Notre-Dame. The square's name references the bloody battles that took place here as religious settlers and indigenous groups clashed over control of

what would become Montréal. At its center stands the **Monument Maisonneuve**, dedicated to city founder Paul de Chomedey, *sieur* de Maisonneuve.

★**Pointe-à-Callière Cité d'archéologie et d'histoire de Montréal** MUSEUM
(Museum of Archaeology & History; Map p234; ☑514-872-9150; www.pacmuseum.qc.ca; 350 Pl Royale; adult/child $22/8; ☺10am-5pm Tue-Fri, from 11am Sat & Sun; ⓱; ⓂPlace-d'Armes) One of Montréal's most fascinating sites, this museum takes visitors on a historical journey through the centuries, beginning with the early days of Montréal. Visitors should start with *Yours Truly, Montréal,* an 18-minute multimedia show that covers the arrival of the Amerindians, the founding of Montréal and other key moments. Afterward, head to the **archaeological crypt** where you can explore the remains of the city's ancient sewage and river system, and the foundations of its first buildings and public square.

Place Jacques-Cartier SQUARE
(Map p234; ⓂChamp-de-Mars) FREE The liveliest spot in Old Montréal, this gently inclined square hums with performance artists, street musicians and the animated chatter from terrace restaurants lining its borders. A public market was set up here after a château burned down in 1803. At its top end stands the **Colonne Nelson**, a monument erected

Old Montréal

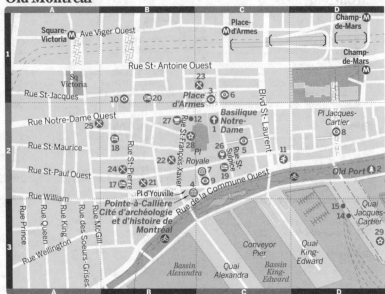

to Admiral Lord Nelson after his defeat of Napoleon's fleet at Trafalgar.

★ Old Port
PARK

(Vieux-Port de Montréal; Map p234; 🖐) Montréal's Old Port has morphed into a park and fun zone paralleling the mighty St Lawrence River for 2.5km and punctuated by four grand *quais* (quays). Locals and visitors alike come here for strolling, cycling and in-line skating. Cruise boats, ferries, jet boats and speedboats all depart for tours from various docks. In winter you can cut a fine figure on an outdoor **ice-skating rink** (Map p234; Parc du Bassin Bonsecours; adult/child $6/4, skate rental $7; ☉10am-9pm Mon-Wed, to 10pm Thu-Sun; ☐14, Ⓜ Champ-de-Mars).

Chinatown
AREA

(Map p238) Although this neighborhood, perfectly packed into a few easily navigable streets, has no sites per se, it's a nice area for lunch or for shopping for quirky knick-knacks. The main thoroughfare, Rue de la Gauchetière, between Blvd St-Laurent and Rue Jeanne-Mance, is enlivened with Taiwanese bubble-tea parlors, Hong Kong–style bakeries and Vietnamese soup restaurants. The public square, **Place Sun-Yat-Sen** (Map p238; cnr Rue de la Gauchetière & Rue Clark; Ⓜ Place-d'Armes), attracts teens, crowds of elderly Chinese and the occasional gaggle of Falun Gong practitioners.

◉ Downtown

Montréal's modern downtown has a North American look, with wide thoroughfares chopping a forest of skyscrapers into a grid pattern. At street level you'll find some of the city's most beautiful churches, striking buildings, museums, green spaces and major shopping areas. An almost Latin spirit pervades the cafes, restaurants and bars, especially along Rue Crescent.

★ Musée des Beaux-Arts de Montréal
MUSEUM

(Museum of Fine Arts; Map p238; www.mbam.qc.ca; 1380 Rue Sherbrooke Ouest; all exhibitions & pavilions adult over 30yr/21-30yr/under 20yr $24/16/free, after 5pm Wed special exhibition $12; ☉10am-5pm Tue-Sun, to 9pm Wed special exhibitions only; Ⓜ Guy-Concordia) A must for art-lovers, the Museum of Fine Arts has amassed centuries' worth of paintings, sculpture, decorative arts, furniture, prints, drawings and photographs. European heavyweights include Rembrandt, Picasso and Monet, but the museum really shines when it comes to Canadian art. Highlights include works by Prudence Heward and Paul Kane, landscapes

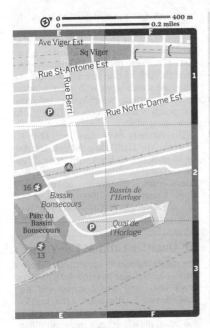

Old Montréal

by the Group of Seven and abstractions by Martha Townsend and Jean-Paul Riopelle. Temporary exhibits are often exceptional and have included a showcase on French fashion designer Thierry Mugler.

Musée d'Art Contemporain MUSEUM
(Map p242; ☎514-847-6226; www.macm.org; 185 Rue Ste-Catherine Ouest; adult/child $17/6, 5-9pm Wed half price; ⊗11am-6pm Tue, to 9pm Wed-Fri, 10am-6pm Sat & Sun; ⓂPlace-des-Arts) This showcase of modern Canadian and international art has eight galleries divided between past greats (since 1939) and exciting current developments. A weighty collection of 7600 permanent works includes Québécois legends Jean-Paul Riopelle, Paul-Émile Borduas and Geneviève Cadieux, but also temporary exhibitions of the latest trends in current art from Canadian and international artists. Forms range from traditional to new media, from painting, sculpture and prints to installation art, photography and video.

★Musée McCord MUSEUM
(McCord Museum of Canadian History; Map p238; ☎514-861-6701; www.mccord-museum.qc.ca; 690 Rue Sherbrooke Ouest; adult/student/child $20/14/ free, special exhibitions extra $5, after 5pm Wed free; ⊗10am-6pm Tue, Thu & Fri, to 9pm Wed, to 5pm Sat & Sun; ⓂMcGill) With hardly an inch to spare in its cramped but welcoming galleries, the McCord Museum of Canadian History houses thousands of artifacts and documents illustrating Canada's social, cultural and archaeological history from the 18th century to the present day, with a small-but-excellent First Nations permanent collection displaying Indigenous dress and artifacts.

McGill University UNIVERSITY
(Map p238; ☎514-398-4455; www.mcgill.ca; 845 Rue Sherbrooke Ouest; ⓂMcGill) Founded in

1828 by James McGill, a rich Scottish fur trader, McGill University is one of Canada's most prestigious learning institutions, with 40,000 students. The university's medical and engineering faculties have a fine reputation and many campus buildings are showcases of Victorian architecture. The campus, at the foot of Mont Royal, is rather nice for a stroll and also incorporates the **Musée Redpath** (Map p238; ☑514-398-4086; www.mcgill.ca/redpath/; 859 Rue Sherbrooke Ouest; suggested donation adult/child $10/free; ⊙9am-2pm Jun-Aug, 9am-5pm Mon-Fri, 11am-5pm Sat & Sun Sep-May; Ⓜ McGill) **FREE**.

★ **Marché Atwater**   MARKET
(Map p232; ☑514-937-7754; www.marchespublics-mtl.com; 138 Ave Atwater; ⊙7am-6pm Mon-Wed, to 7pm Thu, to 8pm Fri, to 5pm Sat & Sun; Ⓜ Atwater) ◢ Just off the Canal de Lachine (p240), this fantastic market has a mouth-watering assortment of fresh produce from local farms (some promoting sustainability), excellent wines, crusty breads, fine cheeses and other delectable fare. The market's specialty shops operate year-round, while outdoor eatery stalls open from March to October. It's all housed in a 1933 brick hall, topped with a clock tower, and little bouts of live music pop off with pleasing regularity. The grassy banks overlooking the canal are great for a picnic.

◉ Plateau Mont-Royal

East of Parc du Mont-Royal, the Plateau is Montréal's youngest, liveliest and artiest neighborhood. Originally a working-class district, it changed its stripes in the 1960s and '70s when writers, singers and other creative folk moved in. Among them was playwright Michel Tremblay, whose unvarnished look (check out his six-novel series *Chroniques du plateau de Mont-Royal*) at some of the neighborhood's more colorful

---

QUÉBEC CREATIONS
....
➡ Birthplace of: Trivial Pursuit, AM radio, Ski-Doo snowmobile, Plexiglas, Leonard Cohen

➡ Home of: Norm MacDonald, William Shatner, Jacques Villeneuve, Rufus Wainwright

➡ Kitschiest souvenir: cow-shaped maple syrup lollipops

---

characters put the Plateau firmly on the path to hipdom.

These days, the Plateau is more gentrified than bohemian, but it's gentrified in a way that still *seems* pretty bohemian. As you stroll through its side streets, admiring the signature streetscapes with their winding staircases, ornate wrought-iron balconies and pointy Victorian roofs, you'll begin to understand why.

The Plateau's main drags are Blvd St-Laurent ('The Main'), Rue St-Denis and Ave du Mont-Royal, all lined with sidewalk cafes, restaurants, clubs and boutiques. Rue Prince-Arthur, Montréal's quintessential hippie hangout in the 1960s, and Rue Duluth are alive with BYOW (bring your own wine) eateries.

◉ Quartier Latin & The Village

The streets themselves are attractions here – student-hotbed Rue St-Denis with its pubs, music clubs and record shops; and Rue Ste-Catherine Est, the heart of the (gay) Village, which has a small open-air art gallery and an LGBTIQ+-related museum, library and church. It sees thousands of international visitors gather to celebrate the major annual Montréal Pride parade (p243). Starting from one street and strolling to the other is a good way to cover it all.

◉ Little Italy & Mile End

The zest and flavor of the old country find their way into the lively Little Italy district, north of the Plateau, where the espresso seems stiffer, the pasta sauce thicker and the chefs plumper. Italian football games are practically broadcast straight onto Blvd St-Laurent, where the green-white-red flag is proudly displayed. Soak up the atmosphere on a stroll, and don't miss **Marché Jean-Talon** (Map p232; ☑514-937-7754; www.marchespublics-mtl.com; 7075 Ave Casgrain; ⊙7am-6pm Mon-Wed & Sat, to 8pm Thu & Fri, to 5pm Sun; ℗ ♿; Ⓜ Jean-Talon) ◢, which always hums with activity.

Dubbed the 'new Plateau' by the exodus of students and artists seeking a more affordable, less polished hangout, the Mile End district has all the coolness of its predecessor as well as two phenomenal bagel shops, upscale dining along Ave Laurier and tonnes of increasingly trendy hangouts at its epicenter: Rue St-Viateur and Blvd St-Laurent. The flavor here is multicultural:

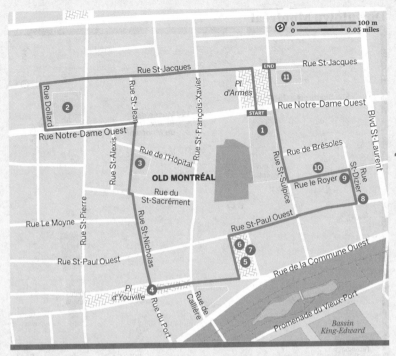

QUÉBEC MONTRÉAL

City Walk
Art & Architecture in Old Montréal

START BASILIQUE NOTRE-DAME
END PLACE D'ARMES
LENGTH 2KM; TWO HOURS

On the southeast side of Place d'Armes is the city's most celebrated cathedral, magnificent **1 Basilique Notre-Dame** (p233). Inside are a spectacularly carved pulpit and richly hued stained-glass windows.

Cross the Place and head left along Rue St-Jacques, once known as Canada's Wall St. Stop at the grand **2 Royal Bank Tower** (Royal Bank Building; Map p234; 360 Rue St-Jacques; ⊙8am-8pm; M Square-Victoria) , Montréal's tallest edifice in 1928, to see its palatial interior, with the glorious Crew Cafe at the rear. Loop back onto Rue Notre-Dame then right down Rue St-Jean. On the corner of Rue de l'Hôpital, the **3 Lewis Building** has dragons and mischievous gargoyles on the facade.

A few blocks further is **4 Place d'Youville**, one of Old Montréal's prettiest squares. Some of the first Europeans settled here in 1642 and an obelisk commemorates the city's founding.

Nearby is fascinating **5 Pointe-à-Callière Cité d'archéologie et d'histoire de Montréal** (p233). Inside see the city's ancient foundations, or go to the top floor for fine views over the Old Port.

Across the road is the Palladian-style 1836 **6 Old Customs House** (Vieille Douane; Map p234; Pl Royale). It's in front of **7 Place Royale** (Map p234; M Place-d'Armes), the early settlement's marketplace in the 17th and 18th centuries. Gaze up at the pediment to see the restored bas-relief figure of Albion, representing Britain.

Walk right down Rue St-Paul to see the 2006 bronze sculpture **8 Les Chuchoteuses** (the Whisperers), tucked in a corner near Rue St-Dizier. Head up St-Dizier and turn left onto lovely **9 Cours Le Royer** (Map p234; M Place-d'Armes), a tranquil pedestrian mall with a stained-glass window of **10 Jérôme Le Royer**, one of Montréal's founders.

Turn right on St-Sulpice and return to Place d'Armes. Note the **11 New York Life Building** (Map p234; 511 Pl d'Armes), Montréal's first skyscraper (1888), eight stories tall.

Downtown Montréal

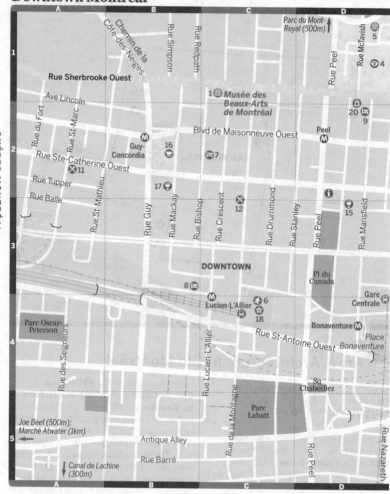

Hasidic Jews live side by side with immigrants from all over Europe – visible in the Greek restaurants along Ave du Parc, and Rue St-Urbain's neo-Byzantine Polish church, Église St-Michel.

Many of celebrated Canadian novelist Mordecai Richler's novels are set in the Mile End, including *The Apprenticeship of Duddy Kravitz.*

⊙ Olympic Park & Around

Montréal hosted the 1976 Olympic summer games, which brought a host of attractions, including a beautiful botanical garden, to the area east of central Montréal, accessible from Rue Sherbrooke.

★ Jardin Botanique   GARDENS

(Map p232; ☎ 514-872-1400; www.espacepourlavie. ca/jardin-botanique; 4101 Rue Sherbrooke Est; adult/child $21/10; ⊙9am-6pm mid-May–early Sep, 9am-5pm Tue-Sun early Sep–mid-May; 🐾; ⊠Pie-IX) 🍃 Montréal's Jardin Botanique is the third-largest botanical garden in the world, after London's Kew Gardens and Berlin's Botanischer Garten. Since its 1931 opening, the 75-hectare garden has grown to include tens of thousands of species in more than 20 thematic gardens, and its wealth

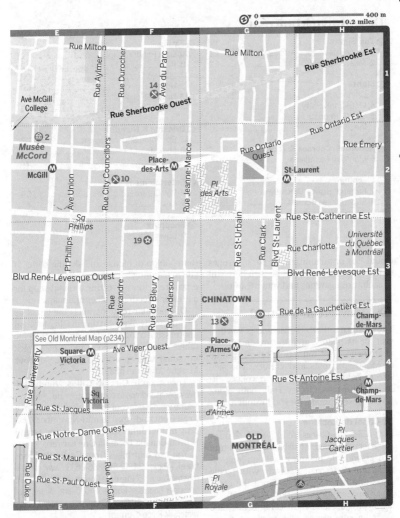

See Old Montréal Map (p234)

QUÉBEC MONTREAL

of flowering plants is carefully managed to bloom in stages. The rose beds are a sight to behold in summertime. Climate-controlled greenhouses house cacti, banana trees and 1500 species of orchid. Bird-watchers should bring their binoculars.

★ **Biodôme**   MUSEUM
(Map p232; ☑ 514-868-3000; www.espacepourlavie. ca; 4777 Ave du Pierre-De Coubertin; adult/child $20/10; ⊙ 9am-6pm late Jun-Sep, 9am-5pm Tue-Sun rest of year; ⛟; Ⓜ Viau) At this captivating exhibit you can amble through a rainforest, explore Antarctic islands, view rolling woodlands, take in aquatic life in the Gulf of St

Lawrence, or wander along the raw Atlantic oceanfront – all without ever leaving the building. The five ecosystems house many thousands of animal and plant species; follow the self-guided circuit and you will see everything. Be sure to dress in layers for the temperature swings. You can borrow free strollers; and interactive exhibits are at small-child height.

◉ **Parc Jean-Drapeau**

The two islands, Île Ste-Hélène and Île Notre-Dame, focus on nature, though most will visit for summer fun – music festivals, the

Downtown Montréal

Grand Prix or an amusement park. Vestiges of the World Expo '67 can be seen here still in sculptures, gardens and water features.

◎ Elsewhere in Montréal

The western suburb of Lachine is worth a visit for its history, architecture and general ambience. Not touristy, it reveals a little of Montréal's roots and culture. The side streets behind the impressive college St-Anne nunnery and City Hall, both along Blvd St-Joseph, make for good wandering.

★ **Canal de Lachine** CANAL
(Map p232; Rue Charles-Biddle; 👶🚲) 🚶 FREE
A perfect marriage of urban infrastructure and green civic planning: a 14km-long cycling and pedestrian pathway, with picnic areas and outdoor spaces. Since the canal was reopened for navigation in 2002, flotillas of pleasure and sightseeing boats glide along its calm waters. Old warehouses converted into luxury condos line the canal near Atwater market (p236). The Lachine Canal was originally built in 1825 as a means of bypassing the treacherous Lachine Rapids on the St Lawrence River.

🏃 Activities

Cycling & In-Line Skating
Montréal is a cyclist's haven. With **Bixi** (☎514-789-2494; http://montreal.bixi.com; per 30min $2.95; ⊙24hr mid-Apr–Oct) 🚲, a popular self-service, solar-powered bicycle rental system with over 600 stations, it's easy for anyone to reap the benefits of Montréal's more

than 500km of bicycle and skating paths. If you're planning a longer cycling trip, however, you're better off visiting a rental shop for a greater selection of bikes and maps.

One popular route parallels the Canal de Lachine for 14.5km, starting in Old Montréal and passing a lot of history en route. Picnic tables are scattered along the way, so pick up some tasty provisions at the fabulous Marché Atwater (p236).

The smooth **Circuit Gilles Villeneuve** (www.parcjeandrapeau.com) on Île Notre-Dame is another cool track. It's open and free to all from mid-April to mid-November – except in mid-June when it hosts the Grand Prix du Canada Formula One car race.

You can rent bikes from **Ça Roule Montréal** (Map p234; ☎514-866-0633; www.caroulemontreal.com; 27 Rue de la Commune Est, Old Port; bikes per hour/day from $9/40, in-line skates 1st/additional hour $9/4; ⊙9am-7pm, reduced hours winter; ⓂPlace-d'Armes).

Other Activities
Bota Bota SPA
(☎514-284-0333; www.botabota.ca; 358 Rue de la Commune Ouest, Old Port; ⊙10am-10pm, from 9am Fri-Sun; ⓂSquare-Victoria) This unique floating spa is actually a 1950s ferry that's been repurposed as an oasis on the water. It's permanently docked by the Old Port with great city views, offering a range of treatments on its five beautifully redesigned decks. The Water Circuit admission (from $40) gives you access to saunas, hot tubs and the outdoor terraces.

PARC DU MONT-ROYAL

Montréalers are proud of their 'mountain,' the work of New York Central Park designer Frederick Law Olmsted. **Parc du Mont-Royal** (Map p232; ☑514-843-8240; www.lemontroyal.qc.ca; 1260 Chemin Remembrance; ⊕; Ⓜ Mont-Royal, then bus 11) 🅿 **FREE** is a sprawling, leafy playground that's perfect for cycling, jogging, picnicking and, in winter, cross-country skiing, tobogganing and ice skating on the **Lac Aux Castors** (Map p232; ☑514-843-8240; www.lemontroyal.qc.ca; Parc du Mont-Royal; free, ice-skate rentals per 2hr $9; ⊗9am-9pm Sun-Thu, to 10pm Fri & Sat, weather permitting; 🔲11). In fine weather, enjoy panoramic views from **Kondiaronk Lookout** near **Chalet du Mont-Royal**, a grand old stone villa that hosts big-band concerts in summer, or from **Observatoire de l'Est**, a favorite rendezvous for lovebirds.

It takes about 30 minutes to walk between the two. En route you'll spot the landmark 40m-high **Cross of Montréal** (1924), which is illuminated at night. It's there to commemorate city founder Maisonneuve, who single-handedly carried a wooden cross up the mountain in 1643 to give thanks to God for sparing his fledgling village from flooding.

MTL Zipline — ADVENTURE SPORTS
(Map p234; ☑514-947-5463; http://mtlzipline.com; 363 Rue de la Commune Est; adult/child from $20/17; ⊗11am-9pm May-Oct) This urban zipline complex lets you soar over the Old Port – or see it rush toward your face at death-defying speeds via a 'Quick Jump' (basically, a bungee jump). You must be 12 or older.

Plage Jean-Doré — BEACH
(Plage des Îles; Map p232; ☑514-872-0199; www.parcjeandrapeau.com; Île Notre-Dame; adult/child $9/4.50; ⊗10am-7pm daily mid-Jun–late Aug, noon-7pm Sat-Mon late Aug-early Sep; ⊕; Ⓜ Jean-Drapeau, then bus 767) On warm summer days this artificial sandy beach on Île Notre-Dame can accommodate up to 5000 sunning and splashing souls. It's safe, clean and ideal for kids; picnic facilities and snack bars serving beer are on-site. There are also paddleboats, canoes and kayaks for rent.

🚶 Tours

Le Petit Navire — BOATING
(Map p234; ☑514-602-1000; www.lepetitnavire.ca; Quai Jacques-Cartier; adult/child 45min tour $20/10, 90min tour $27/20; ⊗10am-7pm mid-May–mid-Oct; Ⓜ Champ-de-Mars) Aside from rowing a boat yourself, this outfit offers the most ecologically friendly boat tours in Montréal. The silent, electric-powered Le Petit Navire takes passengers on 45-minute tours departing hourly around the Old Port area. Equally intriguing are the 1½-hour cruises up the Canal de Lachine, departing Friday, Saturday and Sunday at 11:30am from Quai Jacques-Cartier and 2pm from Marché Atwater.

Le Bateau Mouche — BOATING
(Map p234; ☑514-849-9952; www.bateaumouche.ca; ticket office Quai Jacques-Cartier; 1hr tour adult/child $26/13, 90min tour $30/16; ⊗1hr tour 11am, 2:30pm, 4pm, 5:30pm May-Oct, 90min tour 12:30pm May-Oct; Ⓜ Champ-de-Mars) This comfortable, climate-controlled sightseeing boat with a glass roof offers narrated cruises of the Old Port and Parc Jean-Drapeau. Dinner cruises are also available. Phone ahead for reservations and make sure you board the vessel 15 minutes before departure.

Guidatour — WALKING
(Map p234; ☑514-844-4021; www.guidatour.qc.ca; ticket office 360 Rue St-François-Xavier; adult/child $30/17; ⊗scheduled tours Fri-Sun May & daily Jun-Oct, private tours year-round) In business for more than three decades, the experienced bilingual guides of Guidatour paint a picture of Old Montréal's eventful history with anecdotes and legends. They also offer culinary tours, plus a 'Christmas Secrets of Old Montréal' tour in December.

✨ Festivals & Events

Fête des Neiges — CULTURAL
(☑514-872-6120; www.parcjeandrapeau.com; Parc Jean-Drapeau; ⊗10am-5pm Sat & Sun late Jan-early Feb; ⊕) **FREE** Montréal's family-friendly Snow Festival features ice-sculpting contests, dogsled races (MAPAQ humane regulated), snow games and costumed characters such as mascot polar bear Boule de Neige. It's held over four consecutive weekends in Parc Jean-Drapeau. A great place for sledding, ice skating, zip-lining, curling and skiing. Access and most activities are free.

The Plateau, Quartier Latin & The Village

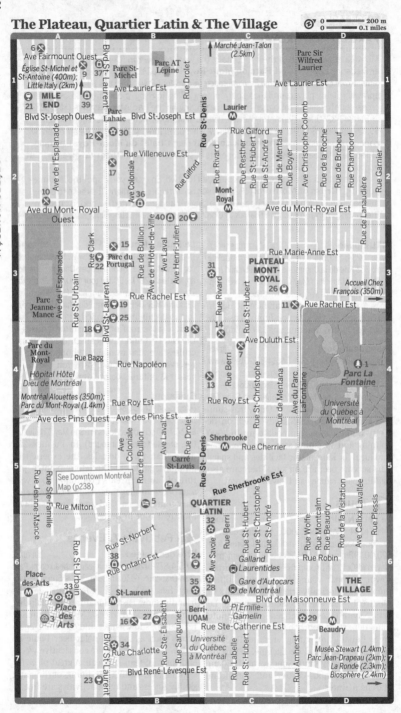

0 — 200 m
0 — 0.1 miles

QUÉBEC MONTRÉAL

Ave Fairmount Ouest
Église St-Michel et
St-Antoine (400m);
Little Italy (2km)

MILE
END

Blvd St-Laurent

Parc St-
Michel

Parc AT
Lépine

Rue Drolet

Marché Jean-Talon
(2.5km)

Parc Sir
Wilfred
Laurier

Ave Laurier Est

Ave Laurier Est

Rue St-Denis

Blvd St-Joseph Ouest

Parc
Lahaie

Blvd St-Joseph Est

Laurier

Rue Gilford

Rue Resther
Rue St-Hubert
Rue St-André
Rue de Mentana
Rue Boyer
Ave Christophe Colomb
Rue de la Roche
Rue de Brébeuf
Rue Chambord
Rue Garnier

Rue Villeneuve Est

Ave Colonial

Rue Gilford

Mont-
Royal

Ave de l'Esplanade

Ave du Mont-Royal
Ouest

Ave du Mont-Royal Est

Rue Clark

Rue de Bullion
Rue de l'Hôtel-de-Ville
Ave Laval
Ave Henri-Julien

Rue Marie-Anne Est

PLATEAU
MONT-
ROYAL

Parc du
Portugal

Rue Rivard
Rue St-Hubert

Parc
Jeanne-
Mance

Ave de l'Esplanade
Rue St-Urbain

Blvd St-Laurent

Rue Rachel Est

Rue Rachel Est

Parc du
Mont-
Royal

Rue Bagg

Rue Napoléon

Ave Duluth Est

Hôpital Hôtel
Dieu de Montréal

Rue Berri
Rue St-Christophe
Rue de Mentana
Ave du Parc
LaFontaine

Parc La
Fontaine

Montréal Alouettes (350m);
Parc du Mont-Royal (1.4km)

Rue Roy Est

Rue Roy Est

Ave des Pins Ouest

Ave des Pins Est

Ave Colonial
Ave Laval
Rue Drolet
Rue St-Denis

Sherbrooke

Rue Cherrier

Université
du Québec à
Montréal

See Downtown Montréal
Map (p238)

Carré
St-Louis

Rue Sherbrooke Est

Rue Jeanne-Mance

Rue Ste-Famille

Rue Milton

QUARTIER
LATIN

Rue St-Hubert
Rue St-Christophe
Rue St-André
Rue Wolfe
Rue Montcalm
Rue Beaudry
Rue de la Visitation
Ave Calixa Lavallée
Rue Plessis

Rue St-Norbert

Ave Savoie
Rue Berri

Galland
Laurentides

Rue Robin

Rue St-Urbain

Rue Ontario Est

Gare d'Autocars
de Montréal

THE
VILLAGE

Place-
des-Arts

St-Laurent

Blvd de Maisonneuve Est

Place
des
Arts

Berri-
UQAM

Pl Émilie-
Gamelin

Beaudry

Rue Ste-Élisabeth
Rue Sanguinet

Rue Ste-Catherine Est

Université
du Québec
à Montréal

Rue Labelle
Rue St-Hubert

Rue Amherst

Musée Stewart (1.4km);
Parc Jean-Drapeau (2km);
La Ronde (2.3km);
Biosphère (2.4km)

Rue Charlotte

Blvd St-Laurent

Blvd René-Lévesque Est

The Plateau, Quartier Latin & The Village

Montréal en Lumière   CULTURAL

(www.montrealenlumiere.com; ☺ late Feb/early Mar) Created to help shake off the late-winter doldrums, Montréal en Lumière is a kind of wintry Mardi Gras with concerts, exhibitions and fireworks. Place des Arts becomes an illuminated fairground with a Ferris wheel and zip line. Most events happen downtown.

★ **Festival International
de Jazz de Montréal**   MUSIC

(www.montrealjazzfest.com; ☺ late Jun-early Jul) For 11 days the heart of downtown explodes in jazz and blues during 1000 concerts, most of them outdoors and free. This is the world's largest jazz festival, but there's also world music, rock and some pop music.

★ **Just for Laughs Festival**   COMEDY

(www.hahaha.com; ☺ mid-Jul) Everyone gets giddy for two weeks at this international comedy festival, the world's largest, with hundreds of standup shows, including free ones in the Quartier Latin. Past performers include Tina Fey, Trevor Noah, Laverne Cox and John Mulaney. If you don't know who to see, try a themed multi-comic night, such as 'The Ethnic Show'. Book ahead.

Montréal Pride   LGBTIQ+

(Fierté Montréal; ☑ 514-903-6193; http://fiertemtl. com; ☺ Aug) Montréal's Pride Week (the largest in Canada and the Francophone world) promotes diverse local LGBTIQ+ communities every August, culminating in the annual Montréal Pride Parade on René-Lévesque Boulevard, attracting around 300,000 spectators.

🛏 Sleeping

Montréal's accommodation scene is blessed with a tremendous variety of rooms and styles. Though rates aren't particularly cheap, they are reasonable by international standards – or even compared with other Canadian cities such as Toronto or Vancouver. Reserve at least a month in advance, especially from June to September, for budget accommodations, or to snap up any discounts. French- and Victorian-style inns and independent hotels cater to a variety of budgets.

🛏 Old Montréal

Auberge Alternative   HOSTEL $

(Map p234; ☑ 514-282-8069; www.auberge-alter native.qc.ca; 358 Rue St-Pierre; dm incl tax $21-30, r $80-105; @ 🛜; M Square-Victoria) This laid-back hostel near the Old Port has a bohemian vibe with an inviting cafe-restaurant where you can mingle with other travelers or enjoy an organic breakfast ($5 extra). Guests bunk in trim, colorfully painted dorms that accommodate anywhere from four to 20 people. There's a laundry and no curfew.

★L Hotel BOUTIQUE HOTEL $$

(Map p234; ☑ 514-985-0019; www.lhotelmontreal. com; 262 Rue St-Jacques Ouest; d $219-379; P ❄ 🛜; M Square-Victoria) Inside a grand 1870 building, L Hotel is a major draw for art-lovers. Georges Marciano, founder of Guess jeans, opened the hotel in 2010, showering great artworks throughout the rooms and common areas. You might sleep in a room with an original piece by Andy Warhol, Roy Lichtenstein or Frank Stella, or one of scores of other famed artists.

★Hôtel Nelligan BOUTIQUE HOTEL $$$

(Map p234; ☑ 514-788-2040, 877-788-2040; www. hotelnelligan.com; 106 Rue St-Paul Ouest; d/ste from $225/360; P ❄ @ 🛜; M Place-d'Armes) Housed in two restored buildings and named in honor of Québec's famous and tragic poet, Émile Nelligan, this Old Montréal beauty has original details (such as exposed brick or stone) and luxurious fittings (down comforters, high-quality bath products, and Jacuzzis in some rooms). Verses, a plush bar and restaurant, is next door, with a magnificent roof patio, Terrasse Nelligan.

★Hôtel Gault BOUTIQUE HOTEL $$$

(Map p234; ☑ 866-904-1616, 514-904-1616; www. hotelgault.com; 449 Rue Ste-Hélène; r from $245; P ❄ @ 🛜; M Square-Victoria) The Gault delivers beauty and comfort in its 30 spacious rooms. Lovely 19th-century architectural details figure in some rooms, with exposed brick or stone walls, though for the most part it boasts a fashion-forward, contemporary design. Rooms have extremely comfortable beds, ergonomic chairs, high ceilings, huge windows and spotless bathrooms (some with two-person bathtubs) with heated tile floors.

🛏 Downtown

Auberge Bishop Downtown HOSTEL $

(Map p238; ☑ 514-508-8870; https://auberge bishop.ca; 1447 Rue Bishop; dm $23-30; 😊 🛜; M Guy-Concordia) You might never guess that this is a hostel, seeing the winding wooden staircase, stained-glass windows and old French fireplaces in this 1800s brick manor house. Metal beds are comfortable and quiet, though it's worth upgrading for fewer people in the room; it can get cramped in the triple-stacked bunks. There's a modern white bathroom and shared kitchen.

Auberge Les Bons Matins BOUTIQUE HOTEL $$

(Map p238; ☑ 514-931-9167; www.bonsmatins.com; 1401 Ave Argyle; d/ste from $110/160; ❄ 🛜; M Lucien-L'Allier) The Bons Matins has spacious rooms with gorgeous art, hardwood floors, brick walls and delicious breakfasts. The walk-up rooms are spread out over stately traditional town houses, and the entire affair is conveniently located at the edge of downtown.

Hotel Manoir Sherbrooke HOTEL $$

(Map p242; ☑ 514-845-0915; http://manoirsher brooke.ca; 157 Rue Sherbrooke Est; d $129-149; 🛜; M Sherbrooke) This engaging conversion of two fine Victorian houses is replete with atmosphere. Its 30 rooms range from small standards to spacious deluxes. The budget rooms are small but cozy with a warm color scheme and attractive furnishings. The best rooms have oversized gilded mirrors, decorative fireplaces and Jacuzzis. Staff are friendly.

★Hôtel Le Germain BOUTIQUE HOTEL $$$

(Map p238; ☑ 514-849-2050, 877-333-2050; www. germainmontreal.com; 2050 Rue Mansfield; r from $255; P ❄ 🛜; M Peel) This stylish hotel boasts luxurious rooms with dark wood details (headboard, wood blinds), cream-colored walls, sheer curtains and artful lighting. You'll find all the creature comforts, such as goose-down duvets, gadget docks and rain-fall showers; the bathrooms have a touch of the eccentric with one big window into the room. (Superior rooms have only a shower.) Service is friendly and professional.

🛏 Plateau Mont-Royal

★Accueil Chez François B&B $$

(Map p232; ☑ 514-239-4638; www.chezfrancois.ca; 4031 Ave Papineau; s/d from $135/160, with shared bath $115/135; P ❄ ❄; M Sherbrooke, then bus 24) Overlooking Parc La Fontaine, François indeed gives a warm *accueil* (welcome) to his pleasant and excellent-value five-room guest-house in the Plateau east. Many guests are repeat visitors, drawn by the spotless and attractive rooms, the delicious breakfasts and the great location (free parking is a bonus).

Gingerbread Manor
B&B $$

(Map p242; ☑ 514-597-2804; www.gingerbread manor.com; 3445 Ave Laval; with/without bath from $120/89; P ⊚; M Sherbrooke) The hosts give a warm welcome at this charming B&B near leafy Carré St-Louis. The house itself is a stately three-story town house built in 1885 with bay windows, ornamental details and an attached carriage house. The elegant rooms – five in all – are uniquely furnished (only one has a private bath, the others share).

✖ Eating

Montréal is one of the great foodie destinations of the North. Here you'll find an outstanding assortment of classic French cuisine, hearty Québécois fare and countless ethnic restaurants from 80-odd nationalities. Today's *haute cuisine* is as likely to be conjured by talented young African, Japanese or Indian chefs as graduates from the Académie Culinaire du Québec.

✖ Old Montréal

Noodle Factory
CHINESE $

(Map p238; www.restonoodlefactory.com; 1018 Rue St-Urbain; mains $8-12; ⊙ 11am-10pm Tue-Sun; M Place-d'Armes) Noodle fanatics roll up to this bustling hole-in-the-wall place for chef Lin Kwong Cheung's famed homemade noodles. You can watch him in the open kitchen whacking and kneading the dough into fine strips before devouring it yourself. Cash only.

★ Olive + Gourmando
CAFE $$

(Map p234; ☑ 514-350-1083; www.oliveetgour mando.com; 351 Rue St-Paul Ouest; mains $11-18; ⊙ 8am-5pm Wed-Sun; ☑; M Square-Victoria) Named after the owners' two cats, this bakery-cafe is legendary in town for its hot panini, generous salads and flaky baked goods. Excellent choices include the melted goat's-cheese panini with caramelized onions, decadent mac 'n' cheese, and 'the Cubain' (a ham, roast pork and Gruyère sandwich). Try to avoid the busy lunch rush (11:30am to 1:30pm).

★ Orange Rouge
ASIAN $$

(Map p238; ☑ 514-861-1116; www.orangerouge. ca; 106 de la Gauchetière Ouest; mains $15-20; ⊙ 11:30am-2:30pm Tue-Fri & 5:30-10:30pm Tue-Sat; M Place-d'Armes) Hidden down a narrow lane of Chinatown, Orange Rouge has a quaint, low-lit interior that's rather nondescript save for the bright open kitchen at one end and a neon-lit crab sculpture on the wall. Grab a seat at the dark lacquered bar or on one of the banquettes for a feast of Asian fusion.

Invitation V
VEGAN $$

(Map p234; ☑ 514-271-8111; 201 Rue St-Jacques; mains $15-24; ⊙ 10:30am-3pm Tue-Sun, 5:30-10pm Tue, Wed & Sat, to midnight Thu & Fri; ☑; M Place-d'Armes) 🍴 A game-changer in the world of vegan cuisine, Invitation V serves up creative, beautifully presented dishes in an elegant dining room of white brick and light woods. Start with butternut squash and roasted-red-pepper soup and a round of mushroom satay with peanut sauce, before moving onto curry stew with jasmine rice or a tempeh burger with sweet-potato fries.

★ Barroco
INTERNATIONAL $$$

(Map p234; ☑ 514-544-5800; www.barroco.ca; 312 Rue St-Paul Ouest; mains $27-41; ⊙ 5-10:30pm Sun-Wed, to 11pm Thu, to midnight Fri & Sat; M Square-Victoria) Small, cozy Barroco has stone walls, flickering candles and beautifully presented plates of roast guinea fowl, paella, braised short ribs and grilled fish. The selection is small (just six or so mains and an equal number of appetizers), but you can't go wrong here – particularly if you opt for the outstanding seafood and chorizo paella.

Garde-Manger
INTERNATIONAL $$$

(Map p234; ☑ 514-678-5044; www.crownsalts. com/gardemanger; 408 Rue St-François-Xavier; mains $34-40; ⊙ 5:30-11pm Tue-Sun; M Place-d'Armes) The buzz surrounding Garde-Manger has barely let up since its opening back in 2006. This small, candlelit restaurant attracts a mix of local scenesters and *haute cuisine*–loving out-of-towners who come for lobster risotto, short ribs, Cornish hen stuffed with foie gras and other changing chalkboard specials. The stage is set with stone walls, great cocktails and a decidedly not-stuffy vibe.

Tapas 24
SPANISH $$$

(Map p234; 420 Notre-Dame Ouest; tapas $6-20, mains $25-48; ⊙ 5-11pm Tue-Sat, also 11:30am-2:30pm Thu & Fri; M Square-Victoria) Celebrated Catalan chef Carles Abellan brings a bit of Barcelona magic to the New World with this outstanding addition to Old Montréal – his first foray outside of Spain. Mouthwatering dishes include razor clams, garlic shrimp, Galician-style octopus and Iberian ham, as well as heartier plates of *fideua* (Catalan-style paella).

QUÉBEC MONTRÉAL

1. Marché Atwater (p236) 2. Cheese stall at Marché Atwater (p236) 3. Marché de Lachine 4. Berry stall, Marché Jean-Talon (p236)

MARC BRUXELLE/SHUTTERSTOCK ©

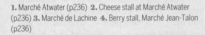

CAGKAN SAYIN/SHUTTERSTOCK ©

Montréal's Markets

Montréal is famed for its impressive year-round food markets, where you can sample the great bounty of the north. The biggest and best are Marché Jean-Talon in Little Italy and Marché Atwater just west of downtown near the Canal de Lachine. For more visit Marchés Publics de Montréal (www.marchespublics-mtl.com).

Marché Jean-Talon

The city's largest **market** (p236) has several hundred market stalls selling all manner of produce, plus food counters where you can get juices, crepes, baguette sandwiches and more. Don't miss the Québécois specialty store Le Marché des Saveurs.

Marché Atwater

This **market** (p236) is located right on the banks of the Canal de Lachine, with scores of vendors outside, and high-class delicatessens and specialty food shops inside the tiled, vaulted hall under the art deco clock tower.

Marché de Maisonneuve

About 20 farm **stalls** (www.fb.me/marchemaisonneuve; 4445 Rue Ontario Est, Montréal; ⊘7am-6pm, to 8pm Thu & Fri, to 5pm Sun; MPie-IX, then bus 139), and inside, a dozen vendors sell meat, cheese, fresh vegetables, tasty pastries and pastas in a beautiful beaux-arts building (1912–14) in Maisonneuve, girded by pretty gardens.

Marché de Lachine

In the neighborhood of Lachine in the far west of Montréal, this lively **market** (https://www.marchespublics-mtl.com/en/marches/lachine-market; 1875 Rue Notre-Dame; ⊘7am-6pm Mon-Wed & Sat, to 8pm Thu & Fri, to 5pm Sun) opens year-round, and has a loyal local following. The market has been going strong since the late 19th century.

The prix-fixe three-course lunch ($22) menu is a great way to sample the goods.

The two-level dining room boasts an artful, modernist aesthetic, with blond woods, delicate wrought-iron details and tube-like chandeliers.

✖ Downtown

Kazu
JAPANESE $

(Map p238; ☑ 514-937-2333; www.kazumontreal. com; 1862 Rue Ste-Catherine Ouest; mains $10-17; ⊙ noon-3pm Sun, Mon, Thu & Fri, also 5:30-9:30pm Thu-Mon; Ⓜ Guy-Concordia) Kazuo Akutsu's frenetic hole-in-the-wall in the Concordia Chinatown draws long lines of people waiting for *gyoza* (dumplings), ramen-noodle soup and awesome creations such as the 48-hour pork. Its popularity is well earned, but be warned: it gets cramped inside.

Satay Brothers
MALAYSIAN $

(Map p232; ☑ 514-933-3507; www.sataybrothers. com; 3721 Rue Notre-Dame Ouest; mains $9-15; ⊙ 11am-11pm Wed-Sun; Ⓜ Lionel-Groulx) Amid red walls, hanging lamps and mismatched thrift-store furnishings, this lively and Malaysia-chic bar-bistro serves some of the best 'street food' in Montréal. Crowds flock here to gorge on delicious chicken-satay sandwiches with peanut sauce served on grilled bread, tangy green papaya salad, braised pork (or tofu) buns, and *laksa lemak*, a rich and spicy coconut soup. It has great cocktails, too.

Ong Ca Can
VIETNAMESE $

(Map p242; ☑ 514-844-7817; 79 Rue Ste-Catherine Est; mains $10-19; ⊙ 11:30am-2:30pm Mon-Fri, 5-9:30pm daily; ☑; Ⓜ St-Laurent) Despite its crisp white linens and intricate artwork, this bustling Vietnamese restaurant is only slightly pricier than average but with quality ingredients. The lemongrass rolls and anything involving beef get especially high marks from loyal patrons.

LOV
VEGETARIAN $

(Map p238; ☑ 514-287-1155; www.lov.com; 1232 Rue de la Montagne; mains $14-18; ☏ ☑; Ⓜ Peel) The gold floral stylings and large marble tables of LOV might read boutique hotel, but the surprise is that this stylish vegetarian restaurant is well priced and good for both romancing somebody else, or yourself. For a starter, try the mushroom dumplings served with almond butter, or vegan poutine. Then move on to the pasta-free, cashew-cream lasagna or tofu banh-mi burgers.

★ Café Parvis
BISTRO $$

(Map p238; ☑ 514-764-3589; www.cafeparvis.com; 433 Rue Mayor; small plates $6-9; ⊙ 7am-11pm Mon-Wed, to midnight Thu & Fri, 10am-midnight Sat, to 10pm Sun; ☑; Ⓜ Place-des-Arts) Hidden on a quiet downtown lane, Café Parvis is set with oversized windows, hanging plants, old wooden floorboards and vintage fixtures. Once part of the fur district, this cleverly repurposed room serves up delicious pizzas ($10 at lunch; about $20 at night) in inventive combinations (such as duck, fennel and squid, ham and eggplant, or roasted vegetables with Gruyère).

Foodlab
INTERNATIONAL $$

(Map p242; ☑ 514-844-2033; http://sat.qc.ca/ fr/restaurant-labo-culinaire; 3rd fl, 1201 Blvd St-Laurent; mains $14-26; ⊙ 5-10pm Tue-Sat; Ⓜ St-Laurent) On the upper floor of the arts center SAT (Société des Arts Technologiques; Map p242; ☑ 514-844-2033; www.sat.qc.ca; 1195 Blvd St-Laurent; Ⓜ St-Laurent), Foodlab is a creative culinary space where the small menu changes every two weeks, and ranges around the globe. It's a casual but handsomely designed space, where patrons perch on bar stools, sipping cocktails and watching fast-moving chefs in the open kitchen.

Le Vin Papillon
INTERNATIONAL $$

(Map p232; www.vinpapillon.com; 2519 Rue Notre-Dame Ouest; small plates $7-17; ⊙ 3pm-midnight Tue-Sat; ☑; Ⓜ Lionel-Groulx) The folks behind Joe Beef continue the hit parade with this delightful wine bar and small-plate eatery next door to Liverpool House (Map p232; ☑ 514-313-6049; www.joebeef.ca; 2501 Rue Notre-Dame Ouest; mains $24-50; ⊙ 5-11pm Tue-Sat; ☑) – another Joe Beef success. Creative, mouthwatering veggie dishes take top billing with favorites such as tomato-and-chickpea salad, sautéed chanterelles and smoked-eggplant caviar, along with roasted cauliflower with chicken skin, guinea-fowl confit, and charcuterie and cheese platters.

Joe Beef
QUÉBÉCOIS $$$

(Map p232; ☑ 514-935-6504; www.joebeef.ca; 2491 Rue Notre-Dame Ouest; mains $30-55; ⊙ 6pm-late Tue-Sat; Ⓜ Lionel-Groulx) In the heart of the Little Burgundy neighborhood, Joe Beef remains a darling of food critics for its unfussy, market-fresh fare. The rustic, country-kitsch setting is a great spot to linger over fresh oysters, braised rabbit, roasted scallops with smoked onions and a changing selection of

MONTRÉAL'S THIRD WAVE

Montréal has an array of cafes where you can linger over artisanal, beautifully made coffees. To fuel a long day of wandering and sightseeing and experience *haute* cafe culture at its finest, consider one of the following cafes:

Le Falco (Map p232; ✆514-272-7766; www.cafefalco.ca; 5605 Ave de Gaspé; mains $7-13; ⊗8am-5pm Mon-Thu, to 4pm Fri; Ⓜ Beaubien)

Crew Café (Map p234; http://crewcollectivecafe.com; 360 Rue St-Jacques; ⊗8am-8pm; ☎; Ⓜ Square-Victoria)

Tommy (Map p234; www.tommymontreal.com; 200 Rue Notre-Dame Oest; ⊗8am-8pm; ☎; Ⓜ Place-d'Armes)

Myriade (Map p238; ✆514-939-1717; www.cafemyriade.com; 1432 Rue Mackay; ⊗7:30am-8pm Mon-Fri, 9am-7pm Sat & Sun; ☎; Ⓜ Guy-Concordia)

Pikolo Espresso Bar (Map p238; ✆514-508-6800; http://pikoloespresso.com; 3418b Ave du Parc; snacks $2-7; ⊗7:30am-7pm Mon-Fri, from 9am Sat & Sun; ☎; Ⓜ Place-des-Arts)

hearty Québécois dishes – all served with good humor and low pretension.

✖ Plateau Mont-Royal

Omnivore   MEDITERRANEAN **$**
(Map p242; www.omnivoregrill.com; 4351 Blvd St-Laurent; mains $6-14; ⊗noon-9pm; ✔; Ⓜ Mont-Royal) Amid rustic wood tables and potted plants, the friendly staff at little Omnivore whip up delicious Middle-Eastern mezze plates of hummus, tabbouleh, baba ghanoush, meat skewers and other Lebanese classics. There are also grilled pita sandwiches. Everything is fresh, generous and delicious and can be made vegetarian.

La Banquise   QUÉBÉCOIS **$**
(Map p242; ✆514-525-2415; www.labanquise.com; 994 Rue Rachel Est; mains $8-15; ⊗24hr; ✚; Ⓜ Mont-Royal) A Montréal legend since 1968, La Banquise is probably the best place in town to sample poutine. More than 30 varieties are available, including a vegan poutine, the boogalou (with pulled pork) and straight-up classic poutine. There's an outdoor terrace, a full breakfast menu and a selection of microbrews, plus the kitchen never closes. Expect long lines on weekends.

L'Gros Luxe   BISTRO **$$**
(Map p242; ✆514-447-2227; www.lgrosluxe.com; 451 Ave Duluth Est; small plates $5-10; ⊗5-11:30pm Mon-Fri, from 11am Sat & Sun; ✔; Ⓜ Sherbrooke) With classy vintage decor, booths or tables and inexpensive comfort fare, L'Gros Luxe has obvious appeal. The small dining room is always packed with young Plateau residents who come for pork tacos, veg-

gie burgers, and fish-and-chips. Plates are small, but nothing costs more than $10, and there's an extensive drinks menu (with much higher prices than the food).

★ L'Express   FRENCH **$$**
(Map p242; ✆514-845-5333; www.restaurantl-express.com; 3927 Rue St-Denis; mains $19-29; ⊗8am-2am Mon-Fri, from 10am Sat & Sun; Ⓜ Sherbrooke) L'Express has all the hallmarks of a Parisian bistro – black-and-white checkered floor, art-deco globe lights, papered tables and mirrored walls. High-end bistro fare completes the picture, with excellent dishes such as grilled salmon, bone marrow with sea salt, roast duck with salad, and beef tartare. The waiters can advise on the extensive wine list. Reservations are essential.

La Sala Rosa   SPANISH **$$**
(Map p242; ✆514-844-4227; www.facebook.com/lasalarosa; 4848 Blvd St-Laurent; mains $13-17; ⊗5-11pm Tue & Wed, to 2am Thu-Sat, to 10pm Sun; ✔; Ⓜ Laurier) A festive, local and often Spanish-speaking crowd comes to this little Iberian gem. La Sala Rosa is best known for its five tasty varieties of paella (including vegetarian) as well as numerous tapas dishes and a changing lineup of Spanish specials. On Thursday nights (from 8:45pm) there's a live flamenco show and the place gets packed.

Hà   VIETNAMESE **$$**
(Map p242; ✆514-848-0336; http://restaurantha.com; 243 Ave du Mont-Royal Ouest; mains $14-28; ⊗noon-3pm & 5:30-10pm Tue-Fri, 5:30-10pm Sat & Sun; ✔; Ⓜ Mont-Royal) Inspired by the street food (and beer) of Vietnam, this neighborhood charmer showcases simple but delectable recipes, near the foot of Mont-Royal.

QUÉBEC'S COMFORT FOODS

Poutine French fries, gravy and squeaky cheese curds – what's not to like?

Café au lait Dark French-roast coffee served with steamed milk, usually in a bowl-shaped mug. A perfect accompaniment to a flaky, buttery croissant.

Bagel The quintessential Montréal bagel is smaller, denser and sweeter than its New York counterpart. The secret is that it's hand-rolled and boiled in honey water before being baked in a wood-fired oven.

Maple syrup Hit a sugar shack in February or March and try this staple slathered over sausages or drizzled on pancakes.

Fèves au lard Slow-cooked baked beans, often sweetened with maple syrup, are a traditional side dish for a bacon-and-eggs breakfast.

Tourtière This hearty meat pie with a flaky crust is typically filled with ground pork, beef or veal, or sometimes wild game.

The menu is small, with highlights such as grilled beef with watercress salad, lemongrass pork ribs and spicy papaya salad.

ChuChai THAI $$
(Map p242; ☑ 514-843-4194; www.chuchai.com; 4088 Rue St-Denis; mains $16-23; ☺ 11am-2pm & 5-10pm Tue-Thu, to 11pm Fri & Sat; ✐) In Montréal's first vegetarian upscale eatery, zippy Thai-inspired stir-fries and coconut soups explore the potential of fragrant kaffir lime, lemongrass and sweet basil. The fake duck could fool even the most discerning carnivore.

Robin des Bois FUSION $$
(Map p242; ☑ 514-288-1010; www.robindesbois.ca; 4653 Blvd St-Laurent; mains $15-25; ☺ 11:30am-10pm Mon-Sat; ☎🚹; Ⓜ St-Laurent, then bus 55) 🌿 Montréal's own 'Robin Hood,' restaurateur Judy Servay donates all profits and tips from this reliable favorite to local charities. The relaxed, spacious diner vibe and varied menu are inviting to all, solo or in groups. Customizable dishes include brown rice, mashed potato, noodles or soup topped with grilled salmon or vegan tempeh. Sandwiches and salads keep everybody happy.

Au Pied de Cochon QUÉBÉCOIS $$$
(Map p242; ☑ 514-281-1114; www.aupieddecochon. ca; 536 Ave Duluth Est; mains $28-48; ☺ 5pm-midnight Wed-Sun; Ⓜ Mont-Royal) One of Montréal's most respected restaurants features extravagant pork, duck and steak dishes, along with its signature foie gras plates. Irreverent, award-winning chef Martin Picard takes simple ingredients and transforms them into works of art. Dishes are rich and portions are large, so bring an appetite. Reservations are essential.

🍴 Little Italy & Mile End

Fairmount Bagel BAKERY $
(Map p242; ☑ 514-272-0667; http://fairmount-bagel.com; 74 Ave Fairmount Ouest; bagels $1; ☺ 24hr; Ⓜ Laurier) One of Montréal's famed bagel bakeries – people flood in here around the clock to scoop them up the minute they come out of the oven. Classic sesame- or poppy-seed varieties are hits, though everything from cinnamon to all-dressed is here, too. If you want an immediate fix of these honey-water boiled bagels, there is public seating outside.

Arts Cafe INTERNATIONAL $
(Map p242; ☑ 514-274-0919; http://artscafemontreal.com; 201 Ave Fairmount Ouest; mains $13-16; ☺ 9am-6pm Mon-Fri, 10am-4pm Sat & Sun; ✐; Ⓜ Laurier) The Arts Cafe has instant appeal with its plank floors, white clapboard walls and sculptural knickknacks (a frenzy of light bulbs above the windows, vintage farmhouse relics). But it's the all-day brunches/breakfasts that warrant the most attention – excellent *fattoush*, falafel, *shakshuka* and cod cakes. Most dishes have a vegetarian option.

Caffè Italia CAFE $
(Map p232; ☑ 514-495-0059; 6840 Blvd St-Laurent; sandwiches $8, coffees $2-3; ☺ 6am-11pm; Ⓜ De Castelnau) Calling this place old school is like calling the Sahara dry. 'Old school' isn't just a descriptor, but the essence of this little Italian espresso bar – graybeards and guys unironically wearing flat caps seemingly step out of a time warp for a quick coffee at the Formica counter. Grab a panettone and an espresso, and live that *dolce vita*.

Sparrow INTERNATIONAL $$
(Map p232; ☑ 514-507-1642; http://lesparrowbar. com; 5322 Blvd St-Laurent; mains $10-16; ☺ 6pm-3am daily & 10am-3pm Sat & Sun; ✐; Ⓜ Laurier)

In a vintage chic dining room, Mile Enders feast on mussels with white wine and fries, pan-roasted trout, butter chicken and other unfussy but tasty bistro classics. For the price, it's hard to find a better meal in this city. Food aside, Sparrow serves up excellent cocktails, and the festive vibe continues until late into the night.

Impasto ITALIAN $$$
(Map p232; ☑ 514-508-6508; www.impastomtl. ca; 48 Rue Dante; mains $19-36; ⊙ 11:30am-2pm Thu & Fri, 5-11pm Tue-Sat; Ⓜ De Castelnau) There's much buzz surrounding this polished Italian eatery – largely owing to the heavy-hitting foodies behind it: best-selling cookbook author Stefano Faita and celebrated chef Michele Forgione. Both have deep connections to Italian cooking, obvious in brilliant dishes such as braised beef cheeks with Savoy-style potatoes, Arctic char with cauliflower puree and lentils, and housemade pastas like *busiate* with lobster.

 Drinking & Nightlife

Montréalers love a good drink. Maybe it's the European influence: this is a town where it's perfectly acceptable, even expected, to begin cocktail hour after work and continue well into the night. Montréal nightlife is the stuff of legend: from underground dance clubs to French hip-hop, dub reggae to breakbeat, comedy shows to supper clubs and Anglo indie rock.

★**Canal Lounge** COCKTAIL BAR
(Map p232; ☑ 514-451-2665; www.canallounge. com; 22 Ave Atwater; ⊙ 3-11pm Tue-Sat, to 10pm Sun late May-early Oct; Ⓜ Lionel Groulx) This permanently docked boat-bar nestles along the canal in front of a lovely pedestrian bridge. The over-45-year-old vessel has been converted into an upscale cocktail lounge. Sit on the rooftop for some fresh air or inside for maritime ambience. The friendly owners moonlight as bartenders and whip up finely crafted cocktails.

★**Big in Japan** COCKTAIL BAR
(Map p242; ☑ 438-380-5658; 4175 Blvd St-Laurent; ⊙ 5pm-3am; Ⓜ St-Laurent, then bus 55) Completely concealed from the street, Big in Japan always amazes first-timers. There you are walking along bustling St-Laurent, you find the unmarked door (looking for its small window) by the address, walk down a rather unpromising corridor and emerge into a room lit with a thousand candles (or so it seems). Everything is Japanese-inspired – cocktails, whiskey, beer and bar food.

★**Barfly** BAR
(Map p242; ☑ 514-284-6665; www.facebook.com/ BarflyMtl; 4062 Blvd St-Laurent; ⊙ 4pm-3am; Ⓜ St-Laurent, then bus 55) Cheap, gritty, loud, fun and a little bit out of control – just the way we like our dive bars. Live bluegrass and rockabilly bands and bedraggled hipsters hold court alongside aging rockers at this St-Laurent hole-in-the-wall.

★**La Buvette Chez Simone** WINE BAR
(Map p242; ☑ 514-750-6577; www.buvettechezsimone.com; 4869 Ave du Parc; ⊙ 4pm-3am; Ⓜ Laurier) An artsy-chic crowd of (mostly) Francophone bons vivants and professionals loves this cozy wine bar. The staff know their vino and the extensive list is complemented by a gourmet tapas menu. Weekends, the place is jammed from *cinq à sept* (5pm to 7pm 'happy hour') into the wee hours.

Bily Kun BAR
(Map p242; ☑ 514-845-5392; www.bilykun. com; 354 Ave du Mont-Royal Est; ⊙ 3pm-3am; Ⓜ Mont-Royal) One of the pioneers of 'tavern chic,' Bily Kun is a favorite local hangout for a chilled evening among friends. First-time visitors usually gawp at the ostrich heads that overlook the bar but soon settle into the music groove of live jazz (from 6pm to 8pm) and DJs (10pm onward). Absinthe cocktails, herbaceous liqueurs and organic beers rule.

Le Mal Necessaire COCKTAIL BAR
(Map p242; www.lemalnecessaire.com; 1106 Blvd St-Laurent; ⊙ 4:30pm-2am Sun-Wed, to 3am Thu-Sat; Ⓜ St-Laurent) For some of the tastiest cocktails in Montréal, look for the neon-lit green pineapple and descend the stairs to this vaguely tiki-inspired bar hidden along pedestrian-filled St Laurent. Fruity elixirs are tops here – especially the Abacaxi mai tai, served in a pineapple – whipped up by friendly, chatty bartenders.

Le Darling COCKTAIL BAR
(Map p242; www.facebook.com/RestoBarDarling; 4328 Blvd St-Laurent; ⊙ 8am-3am; Ⓜ Laurier) A mix of cafe, cocktail bar and bistro, Le Darling is a one-stop spot for top-notch drinks and bistro-quality eats. Straddling a corner on Blvd St-Laurent, just a few blocks from

QUÉBEC MONTRÉAL

Mont-Royal, this vibrant hybrid has lush tropical plants hanging from the ceiling and a seemingly endless collage of vintage decor. Come day or night.

Majestique
BAR

(Map p242; ☑514-439-1850; www.restobar majestique.com; 4105 Blvd St-Laurent; ⊙4pm-3am daily, also 11am-3pm Sun; Ⓜ St-Laurent, then bus 55) The Majestique manages to be both kitschy and classy at the same time, with wood-paneled walls, warm lighting and a buck's head presiding over the tables. The bartenders whip up some beautiful concoctions here, and the food menu is equally creative: try the *bourgots* (snails), the *tartare de cheval* (raw horse meat) or, for something simple, the *huîtres* (oysters) or *frites* (fries).

Dominion Square Tavern
TAVERNA

(Map p238; ☑514-564-5056; www.tavernedom inion.com; 1243 Rue Metcalfe; ⊙11:30am-midnight Mon-Fri, 4:30pm-midnight Sat & Sun; Ⓜ Peel) Once a down-and-out watering hole dating from the 1920s, this beautifully renovated tavern recalls a classic French bistro but with a long bar, English pub–style. Executive chef Éric Dupuis puts his own spin on pub grub, with mussels cooked with bacon, and smoked trout salad with curry dressing.

Le Saint Sulpice
PUB

(Map p242; ☑514-844-9458; www.lesaintsulpice. ca; 1680 Rue St-Denis; ⊙3:30pm-3:30am Tue-Sun; Ⓜ Berri-UQAM) This student evergreen is spread over four levels in an old Victorian stone house – a cafe, several terraces, a disco, karaoke and a sprawling back garden for drinks and chats.

The music changes with the DJ's mood, from hip-hop and ambient to mainstream rock and jazz.

Pub Pit Caribou
MICROBREWERY

(Map p242; ☑514-522-9773; www.pitcaribou.com; 951 Rue Rachel Est; ⊙2pm-1am Sun-Wed, to 3am Thu-Sat; Ⓜ Mont-Royal) There are some awesome microbreweries in this province, and Pit Caribou is one of the greats. It has an outpost here in Montréal that serves its full line of hearty, sudsy goodness, often accompanied by live music.

Upstairs
BAR

(Map p238; ☑514-931-6808; www.upstairsjazz. com; 1254 Rue Mackay; ⊙11:30am-1am Mon-Thu, to 2am Fri, 5:30pm-2am Sat, 6:30pm-1am Sun;

Ⓜ Guy-Concordia) This slick downtown bar hosts quality jazz and blues acts nightly, featuring both local and touring talent. The walled terrace behind the bar is enchanting at sunset, and the dinner menu features inventive salads and meals such as the Cajun bacon burger.

Pub Ste-Élisabeth
PUB

(Map p242; ☑514-286-4302; www.ste-elisabeth. com; 1412 Rue Ste-Élisabeth; ⊙4pm-3am; Ⓜ Berri-UQAM) Tucked off a side street, this handsome little pub is frequented by many for its heavenly vine-covered courtyard and drinks menu with a great selection of beers, whiskeys and ports. It has a respectable lineup of beers on tap, including imports and microbrewery fare such as Boréale Noire and Cidre Mystique.

Terrasse Nelligan
BAR

(Map p234; ☑514-788-4021; www.terrassenel-ligan.com; 106 Rue St-Paul Ouest; ⊙11:30am-11:30pm Jun-Sep; Ⓜ Place-d'Armes) Above heritage Hôtel Nelligan (p244), this delightful patio is the perfect spot to down a mojito while the sun sinks in summer. There's a full menu for lunch and dinner, and splendid views over the St Lawrence River and the Old Port.

Philémon
CLUB

(Map p234; ☑514-289-3777; www.philemonbar. com; 111 Rue St-Paul Ouest; ⊙5pm-3am Mon-Wed, from 4pm Thu & Fri, from 6pm Sat & Sun; Ⓜ Place-d'Armes) A major stop for local scenesters rotating between watering holes in the old city, Philémon is carved out of stone, brick and wood with large windows looking out over Rue St-Paul. Twenty-somethings fill the space around a huge central bar sipping basic cocktails and nibbling on light fare (oysters, charcuterie plates, smoked-meat sandwiches), while a DJ spins house and hip-hop.

Burgundy Lion
PUB

(Map p232; ☑514-934-0888; www.burgundylion. com; 2496 Rue Notre-Dame Ouest; ⊙11:30am-3am Mon-Fri, 9am-3am Sat & Sun; Ⓜ Lionel-Groulx) This trendy take on the English pub features British pub fare, beers and whiskeys galore, and an attitude-free vibe where everyone (and their parents) feels welcome to drink, eat and be merry. Things get the good kind of crazy on late-night weekends. Tip your cap to Queen Elizabeth, whose portrait adorns the bathroom door.

⭐ Entertainment

Montréal is Canada's unofficial arts capital, with both French and English theater, stand-up comedy, dance, classical and jazz music, and all sorts of interesting blends of the above on stage virtually every night of the week.

The city's bilingualism makes it creatively unique and encourages creative collaborations and cross-pollinations that light up the performing-arts scene.

Live Music

⭐ Casa del Popolo   LIVE MUSIC
(Map p242; ☑514-284-0122; www.casadelpopolo.com; 4873 Blvd St-Laurent; $5-20; ☺noon-3am; Ⓜ Laurier) One of Montréal's most charming live venues, the 'House of the People' has talented DJs and is a venue for art-house films and spoken-word performances. It's is also known for its vegetarian sandwiches and salads, and is associated with the tapas bar La Sala Rosa (p249) and its concert venue La Sala Rossa.

Gesù   JAZZ
(Map p238; ☑514-861-4378; www.legesu.com; 1200 Rue de Bleury; shows $18-57; ☺box office noon-6:30pm Tue-Sat) This small live-music and events venue in the basement of a church is blessed with character. Its Greek-theater acoustics means you can see and hear well from any seat. The religious setting has no bearing on performances, which include stand-up comedy, jazz, kids' shows, and even the Montréal Gay Men's Chorus.

Le 4e Mur   LIVE MUSIC
(Map p242; http://le4emur.com; 2021 Rue St-Denis; ☺5pm-3am, from 7pm Sun; Ⓜ Sherbrooke) This bar is literally behind an unmarked door – look for a big intimidating bouncer or the beautiful folks walking past him. Follow on, into a basement bar of low lighting and wicker chairs where the cocktails are expertly mixed, live music pops off regularly, and burlesque is a regular fixture.

Bistro à Jojo   BLUES
(Map p242; ☑514-843-5015; www.bistroajojo.com; 1627 Rue St-Denis; ☺noon-3am; Ⓜ Berri-UQAM) This brash venue on lively Rue St-Denis has been going strong since 1975. It's the nightly place for down 'n' dirty French- and English-language blues and rock groups. Sit close enough to see the band members sweat.

Dièse Onze   LIVE MUSIC
(Map p242; ☑514-223-3543; www.dieseonze.com; 4115 Rue St-Denis; $10; ☺6pm-late; Ⓜ Mont-Royal) This downstairs jazz club has just the right vibe – with an intimate small stage so you can get close to the musicians. There are shows most nights, with an eclectic lineup of artists. You can have a bite while the band plays, with good tapas options as well as a few heartier mains (goat's-cheese burger, mushroom risotto). Call for reservations.

Foufounes Électriques   LIVE MUSIC
(Map p242; ☑514-844-5539; www.foufounes electriques.com; 87 Rue Ste-Catherine Est; cover $4-6; ☺4pm-3am; Ⓜ St-Laurent) A one-time bastion of the alternafreak, this cavernous quintessential punk venue still stages some wild music nights (retro Tuesdays, hip-hop Thursdays, rockabilly/metal/punk Saturdays), plus the odd one-off (a night of pro-wrestling or an indoor skateboarding contest). The graffiti-covered walls and industrial charm should tip you off that 'Electric Buttocks' isn't exactly a mainstream kinda place.

Theater & Dance

⭐ Cirque du Soleil   THEATER
(Map p234; www.cirquedusoleil.com; Quai Jacques-Cartier; tickets from $67; Ⓜ Champ-de-Mars) Globally famous Cirque du Soleil, one of the city's most famous exports, puts on a new production of acrobats and music in this marvelous tent complex roughly once every two years in summer. These shows rarely disappoint, so don't pass up a chance to see one on its home turf.

⭐ Cabaret Mado   CABARET
(Map p242; ☑514-525-7566; www.mado.qc.ca; 1115 Rue Ste-Catherine Est; tickets $5-15; ☺4pm-3am Tue-Sun; Ⓜ Beaudry) Mado is a flamboyant celebrity who has been featured in *Fugues,* the gay entertainment mag. Her cabaret is a local institution, with drag shows featuring an assortment of hilariously sarcastic performers in eye-popping costumes.

Shows take place on Tuesday, Thursday and weekend nights; check the website for details.

Théâtre St-Denis   PERFORMING ARTS
(Map p242; ☑514-849-4211; www.theatrestdenis.com; 1594 Rue St-Denis; ☺box office noon-6pm Mon-Sat; Ⓜ Berri-UQAM) This Montréal landmark and historic movie house hosts

QUÉBEC MONTRÉAL

MONTRÉAL FOR CHILDREN

Montréal has many sights for young visitors. Depending on the season, you can go boating, cycling and ice-skating, or get some amusement park or skydiving thrills. On warm days, Parc Mont-Royal and neighborhood parks are great places for picnics and free-spirited outdoor activity.

Kid-Friendly Museums

➡ Kids will love Biodôme (p239), a giant indoor zoo with forest, river and marine habitats.

➡ Scheduled to reopen in late 2021, the **Insectarium** (Map p232; www.espacepourlavie. ca; 4101 Rue Sherbrooke Est; adult/child $29.50/15; ⊙9am-6pm; M Pie-IX) will have 250,000 specimens creeping, crawling or otherwise on display.

➡ Enjoy the **Planétarium** (Map p232; ☑514-868-3000; www.espacepourlavie.ca; 4801 Ave du Pierre-De Coubertin; adult/child $20/10; ⊙9am-5pm Sun, Tue & Wed, to 8pm Thu-Sat; ♿; M Viau), with domed theaters and interactive exhibits on outer space.

➡ Take your tots on a virtual mission to Mars at **Cosmodôme** (☑450-978-3600; www. cosmodome.org; 2150 Autoroute des Laurentides; exhibition & 1 mission adult/family/student/child under 7yr $16.50/45/13/free; ⊙9am-5pm late Jun-early Sep, 10am-5pm rest of year; ♿; 🚌61 or 70, M Montmorency), an engaging Québec space center.

➡ At greater Québec's **Musée Ferroviaire Canadien** (Exporail; ☑450-632-2410; www. exporail.org; 110 Rue St-Pierre/Rte 209, St-Constant; adult/family/child $20.80/54.10/10.40; ⊙10am-6pm late Jul–early Sep, hours vary other times; ♿) there are trains of every kind – stationary, moving, new and old – that will thrill adults as much as children.

touring Broadway productions, rock concerts and various theatrical and musical performances. Its two halls (933 and 2218 seats) are equipped with the latest sound and lighting gizmos and figure prominently in the Just for Laughs Festival (p243).

Centaur Theatre THEATER
(Map p234; ☑514-288-3161; www.centaurtheatre. com; 453 Rue St-François-Xavier; M Place-d'Armes) Montréal's chief English-language theater presents everything from Shakespearean classics to works by experimental Canadian playwrights. It occupies Montréal's former stock exchange (1903), a striking building with classical columns.

Sports

Bell Centre STADIUM
(Map p238; ☑877-668-8269, 514-790-2525; www. centrebell.ca; 1909 Ave des Canadiens-de-Montréal) When it's not hosting matches with the city's beloved **Montréal Canadiens** (Map p238; ☑514-932-2582; www.canadiens.com; 1909 Ave des Canadiens-de-Montréal, Bell Centre; tickets $54-277; M Bonaventure) hockey team, this 21,000-seat arena in downtown hosts all the big concerts. The likes of U2 and Céline Dion usually end up here when they're in town.

Montréal Alouettes FOOTBALL
(MontréALS; Map p232; ☑514-871-2255; www. montrealalouettes.com; Ave des Pins Ouest, Molson Stadium; tickets from $20; M McGill) The Montréal Alouettes, a star franchise of the Canadian Football League, folded several times before going on to win the league's Grey Cup trophy several times over the years. Rules are a bit different from American football: the field is bigger and there are only three downs. Games are held at McGill University's Molson Stadium and sometimes at the **Olympic Stadium** (Stade Olympique; Map p232; ☑514-252-4141; http://parcolympique.qc. ca; 4141 Ave Pierre-De Coubertin; tower adult/child $24/12; ⊙1-6pm Mon, 9am-6pm Tue-Sun mid-Jun– early Sep, 9am-5pm rest of year; M Viau).

🔒 Shopping

Style is synonymous with Montréal living. The city itself is beautiful and locals live up to the standard it sets. Maybe it's that much-touted European influence, but most Montréalers seem to instinctively lead stylish lives regardless of income level, enjoying aesthetic pleasures such as food, art and, of course, fashion. Head downtown for budget fashion, to the Plateau and Mile End for cute gift stores and vintage clothing, and the markets for foodie gifts.

➡ See oversized cannons, military parades and guides in period costumes inside an old British garrison at **Musée Stewart** (Map p232; ☑514-861-6701; www.stewart-museum.org; 20 Chemin du Tour de l'Île; adult/child $15/free; ⊗10am-5pm Tue-Sun Jul-Sep, Wed-Sun Oct-Jun) 🖋.

Outdoor Fun

➡ At Québec's largest amusement park, **La Ronde** (Map p232; ☑514-397-2000; www.laronde. com; 22 Chemin Macdonald; season pass $42; ⊗hours vary May-Oct; Ⓟ🚻; ⓜJean-Drapeau), kids will experience chills and thrills galore – plus fireworks on some summer nights.

➡ Enormous Parc du Mont-Royal (p241) in the heart of the city is especially fun for kids in winter, with tobogganing, skiing, snowshoeing and ice skating. There is more sledding, curling and snow fun at the Fête des Neiges (p241) at Parc Jean-Drapeau on some weekends. **Parc La Fontaine** (Map p242; cnr Rue Sherbrooke Est & Ave du Parc La Fontaine; ⊗6am-midnight; 🚻🎠; ⓜSherbrooke) 🖋 is perfect for a casual, outdoor stroll, and sits at the edge of the bustling Plateau. Or try **Parc Nature du Cap-St-Jacques** (☑514-280-6871; 20099 Blvd Gouin Ouest, Pierrefonds; parking $9; ⊗10am-6pm, to 5pm Sep-May; Ⓟ🚻; 🚌69, ⓜHenri-Bourassa) 🖋, a verdant park with trails, a beach, a sugar shack and a working farm.

Live Performances

➡ World-renowned Cirque du Soleil (p253) combines dance, theater and circus in powerpacked summertime shows. It will thrill the kids, but is truly for all ages.

➡ For entertaining shows year-round, head to **TOHU** (Map p232; ☑514-376-8648, 888-376-8648; www.tohu.ca; 2345 Rue Jarry Est, St-Michel; parking $8; ⊗9am-5pm; ⓜd'Iberville, then bus 94), a circular theater in the St-Michel district.

Music, Books & Stationery

⭐ **Drawn & Quarterly** BOOKS

(Map p232; ☑514-279-2224; http://mtl.drawnand-quarterly.com; 211 Rue Bernard Ouest; ⊗10am-8pm; ⓜOutremont) The flagship store of this cult independent comic-book and graph-ic-novel publisher has become something of a local literary haven. Cool book launches take place here, and the quaint little shop sells all sorts of reading matter, including children's books, vintage Tintin comics, recent fiction and art books.

Cheap Thrills MUSIC

(Map p238; ☑514-844-8988; www.cheapthrills.ca; 2044 Rue Metcalfe; ⊗11am-6pm Mon-Wed & Sat, to 9pm Thu & Fri, noon-5pm Sun) It's easy to lose track of time as you browse through this big selection of used books and music (CDs and some vinyl), both with a mainstream and offbeat bent and sold at bargain prices.

Le Port de Tête BOOKS

(Map p242; ☑514-678-9566; www.leportdete.com; 262 Ave du Mont-Royal Est; ⊗10am-10pm Mon-Sat, to 8pm Sun; ⓜMont-Royal) This is a wonderfully curated bookstore that often showcases up-and-coming work from dynamic small publishers. The French and English selection is eclectic as hell: thousands of philosophy titles share space with plays, poetry, graphic novels and kids' books. Nonfiction is across the street.

Arts & Crafts

⭐ **Monastiraki** VINTAGE

(Map p232; ☑514-278-4879; www.monastiraki. blogspot.ca; 5478 Blvd St-Laurent; ⊗noon-6pm Wed, to 8pm Thu & Fri, to 5pm Sat & Sun; ⓜLaurier) This unclassifiable store named after a flea-market neighborhood in Athens calls itself a 'hybrid curiosity shop/art space,' but that doesn't do justice to what illustrator Billy Mavreas sells: 1960s comic books, contemporary zines, silk-screen posters, and myriad antique and collectible knickknacks, as well as recent works mainly by local graphic artists.

Artpop ARTS & CRAFTS

(Map p242; ☑514-843-3443; 129 Ave du Mont-Royal Est; ⊗10am-7pm Mon-Wed & Sat, to 9pm Thu & Fri, 11am-7pm Sun; ⓜMont-Royal) Though tiny in size, Artpop is full of unique Montréal-themed gift ideas. You'll find graphic T-shirts, bags, pillowcases, iPhone covers, postcards and prints with iconic city signage (Farine Five Roses, the big Orange Julep). Other standouts include pendants, earrings and dolls by local designers.

PLACE DES ARTS

Montréal's performing-arts center is the nexus for artistic and cultural events. Several renowned musical companies call **Place des Arts** (Map p242; ☑ box office 514-842-2112; www.placedesarts.com; 175 Rue Ste-Catherine Ouest; Ⓜ Place-des-Arts) home, including **Opéra de Montréal** (Map p242; ☑ 514-985-2258; www.operademontreal.com; Pl des Arts; Ⓜ Place-des-Arts) and the **Montréal Symphony Orchestra** (OSM; Map p242; ☑ 514-840-7400; www.osm.ca; 1600 Rue St-Urbain, Maison Symphonique, Pl des Arts; ☺ box office 9am-5pm Mon-Fri & 90mins before shows; Ⓜ Place-des-Arts), based in the acoustically brilliant 2100-seat Maison Symphonique. It's also center stage for Festival International de Jazz de Montréal. A key part of the Quartier des Spectacles, the complex embraces an outdoor plaza with fountains and an ornamental pool and is attached to the Complexe Desjardins shopping center via an underground tunnel.

Au Papier Japonais ARTS & CRAFTS
(Map p242; ☑ 514-276-6863; www.aupapierjaponais.com; 24 Ave Fairmount Ouest; ☺ 10am-6pm Mon-Sat, noon-4pm Sun; Ⓜ Laurier) You might never guess how many guises Japanese paper can come in until you visit this gorgeous little shop, which stocks more than 800 varieties. Origami kits and art books make great gifts, as do the elegant teapots, pottery and Buddha boards (where you can 'paint' ephemeral works with water).

Food

Le Marché des Saveurs du Québec FOOD & DRINKS
(Map p232; ☑ 514-271-3811; www.lemarchedessaveurs.com; 280 Pl du Marché-du-Nord; ☺ 9am-6pm Sat-Wed, to 8pm Thu & Fri; Ⓜ Jean-Talon) Everything here is Québécois, from the food to the handmade soaps to one of the best collections of artisanal local beer, maple products, jams and cheeses in the city. The store was established so local producers could gain wider exposure for their regional products, and it's a joy to browse.

Clothing & Accessories

Eva B VINTAGE
(Map p242; ☑ 514-849-8246; www.eva-b.ca; 2015 Blvd St-Laurent; ☺ 11am-7pm Mon-Sat, noon-6pm Sun; Ⓜ St-Laurent) Stepping into this graffiti-smeared building on St-Laurent is like entering a theater's backstage, with a riot of vintage coats, bowling shirts, cowboy boots, leather jackets, wigs, suede handbags, summer dresses, wildly patterned sweaters and denim of all shapes and sizes. There's lots of junk, but prices are low, and you can probably unearth a few treasures if you have the time.

Jet-Setter SPORTS & OUTDOORS
(Map p242; ☑ 514-271-5058; www.jet-setter.ca; 66 Ave Laurier Ouest; ☺ 10am-6pm Mon-Wed, to 9pm Thu & Fri, to 5pm Sat, noon-5pm Sun; Ⓜ Laurier) A plethora of state-of-the-art luggage and clever travel gadgetry, Jet-Setter has inflatable sacks for wine bottles, pocket-sized T-shirts, 'dry-in-an-instant' underwear, silk sleep sacks, mini-irons and hairdryers, waterproof hats and loads of other items you might find handy when you hit the road.

ⓘ Information

EMERGENCY

Montréal Police Station (emergencies 911, nonemergencies 514-280-2222)

MEDIA

Newspapers The *Montréal Gazette* (www.montrealgazette.com) is the main English-language daily newspaper with solid coverage of national affairs, politics and arts. The Saturday edition has useful what's-on listings.

Magazines The online alternative magazines *Cult* (www.cultmtl.com) and *Hour Community* (www.hour.ca) are even better sources of what's-on listings.

Blogs *MTL Blog* (www.mtlblog.com) is great for up-to-date listings and lots of listicles.

MEDICAL SERVICES

CLSC Métro (Centre Local de Services Communautaires; ☑ 514-934-0354; www.santemontreal.qc.ca/en; 1801 Blvd de Maisonneuve Ouest; ☺ 8am-8pm Mon-Fri, 8:30am-4:30pm Sat & Sun; Ⓜ Guy-Concordia) Walk-in community health center for minor ailments.

Health Hotline (☑ 811) Call for non-urgent health services.

Montréal General Hospital (☑ 514-934-1934; www.muhc.ca/mgh; 1650 Ave Cedar, emergency entrance cnr Ave des Pins & Rue Chemin de la Côte-des-Neiges; ☺ 24hr; Ⓜ Guy-Concordia)

Pharmaprix Pharmacy (www.pharmaprix.ca; 1500 Rue Ste-Catherine Ouest; ☺ 8am-midnight; Ⓜ Guy-Concordia) This 'megachemist' also has a 24-hour branch (☑ 514-738-8464; 5122 Chemin de la Côte-des-Neiges; ☺ 24hr; Ⓜ Côte-des-Neiges) near Mont Royal.

Sexual Assault Center (☑ in Montréal 514-398-8500; www.sacomss.org/wp; 680 Rue Sherbrooke Ouest, Downtown) The phone service and drop-in center provide referrals to hospitals that have sexual-assault care centers.

POST

Canada Post (Postes Canada; ☑ 416-979-3033; www.canadapost.ca) Canada's national postal system.

TOURIST INFORMATION

Centre Infotouriste Montréal (Map p238; ☑ 514-844-5400; www.mtl.org; 1255 Rue Peel; ☺ 9am-6pm May-Sep, to 5pm Oct-Apr; Ⓜ Peel) Information about Montréal and all of Québec. Free hotel, tour and car reservations, plus currency exchange.

❶ Getting There & Away

AIR

Montréal is served by **Montréal-Pierre Elliott Trudeau International Airport** (Trudeau, YUL; www.admtl.com; Dorval), known in French as Aéroport Montréal-Trudeau, or simply as Trudeau Airport. It's about 21km west of downtown and is the hub of most domestic, US and overseas flights. Trudeau Airport (still sometimes known by its old name, Dorval Airport) has decent connections to the city by car and shuttle bus.

BUS

Limocar (www.limocar.ca) Offers bus service from Montréal to the Eastern Townships.
Moose Travel Network (www.moosenetwork.com) Popular with backpackers, this network operates several circuits around Canada, allowing travelers to jump on and off along the way. Pickup points are in Montréal, Québec City, Ottawa and Toronto, among other places. Destinations within Québec include Mont-Tremblant and the Gaspé Peninsula.
Orléans Express (www.orleansexpress.com) Makes the three-hour run between Montréal and Québec City.

CAR & MOTORCYCLE

All the major international car-rental companies have branches at the airport, main train station and elsewhere around town. **Auto Plateau** (☑ 514-281-5000; www.autoplateau.com; 3585 Rue Berri; Ⓜ Sherbrooke) is a reputable local company. **Rent-a-Wreck** (☑ 514-484-3871; www.rentawreck.ca; 6340 Rue St-Jacques; Ⓜ Vendôme) in the southwest often has the best rates.
Kangaride (☑ 855-526-4274; www.kangaride.com) is a reliable online ride-share agency that connects you with drivers with spare seats

in their car. A sample fare is around $15 to Québec City.

TRAIN

Canada's trains are arguably the most enjoyable and romantic way to travel the country. Long-distance trips are quite a bit more expensive than those by bus, however, and reservations are crucial for weekend and holiday travel. A few days' notice can cut fares a lot.

Gare Centrale (Central Train Station; ☑ arrivals & departures 888-842-7245, info & reservations 514-989-2626; www.viarail.ca; 895 Rue de la Gauchetière Ouest; Ⓜ Bonaventure) is the local hub of **VIA Rail**, Canada's vast rail network, which links Montréal with cities all across the country.

Amtrak (www.amtrak.com) provides service between New York City and Montréal on its Adirondack line. The trip, though slow (11 hours), passes through lovely scenery along Lake Champlain and the Hudson River.

❶ Getting Around

TO/FROM THE AIRPORT
Bus

Bus 747 (www.stm.info), the cheapest way to get into town, takes 25 to 60 minutes. Buses run round the clock, leaving from just outside the arrivals hall and dropping passengers downtown, first at Lionel-Groulx metro station, then on to Berri-UQAM metro station in the Quartier Latin. The $10 fare can be paid by Visa, MasterCard or cash at vending machines in the international arrivals area, or tickets may be bought on board (coins only, no change given). Your ticket gives you unlimited travel on Montréal's bus and metro network for 24 hours. Multiday tickets loaded onto the Opus transport card also provide free use of bus 747.

Taxi

It takes at least 20 minutes to get downtown from the airport and the fixed fare is $40. Limousine services ($55 and up) are also available.

PUBLIC TRANSPORTATION

STM (Société de Transport de Montréal; ☑ 514-786-4636; www.stm.info) STM is the city's bus and metro (subway) operator. Schedules vary depending on the line, but trains generally run from 5:30am to midnight from Sunday to Friday, slightly later on Saturday night (to 1:30am at the latest).

A single bus or metro ticket costs $3.25. If you're sticking around Montréal for longer, you'll save money by buying a rechargeable Opus card; the card costs $6 up front, but can be recharged at a discounted rate for 10 rides ($26.50), one day of unlimited rides ($10), three days ($18), a week ($25.50, Monday to Sunday) or a calendar month ($82).

Buses take tickets or cash but drivers won't give change. If transferring from the metro to a bus, use your original metro ticket as a free bus transfer. If you're switching between buses, or between bus and the metro, ask the driver for a free transfer slip (*correspondance* in French).

TAXI & RIDE SHARING

Flag fall is a standard $3.45, plus another $1.70 per kilometer and 63¢ per minute spent waiting in traffic. Prices are posted on the windows inside taxis.

Uber and Lyft are available in Montréal, as is Téo Taxi, a local app-driven ride-sharing service that uses electric taxis.

THE LAURENTIANS

The Laurentians (Les Laurentides in French) make for an excellent day trip from Montréal, being just an hour's drive from the city. Here you'll find gentle rolling mountains, crystal-blue lakes and meandering rivers bordered by towns and villages too cute for words. A visit to this natural paradise is like putting your feet up after a long day.

Although sometimes criticized for being overcommercialized, Mont-Tremblant offers outstanding skiing, rivaled only by Whistler in the whole of Canada. Speckling the Laurentians are many lower-profile resort villages, whose miniature town centers deliver an air of the Alps, with breezy patios and independent designer-clothing shops.

Expect higher prices and heavy crowds during high season, which includes the summer months and Christmas holidays. Check ahead for opening hours in winter, which are often curtailed severely.

❶ Information

Tourisme Laurentides (✆ 450-224-7007; www.laurentides.com; La Porte-du-Nord, Hwy 15, exit 51; ⊙ 8:30am-6:30pm Mon-Sat, to 5:30pm Sun late Jun-early Sep, to 5pm rest of year) This very helpful regional tourist office can answer questions in person or on the phone, make room bookings and mail out information. It operates a free room-reservation service, which specializes in lodgings along the **Parc Linéaire du P'tit Train du Nord** (Little Train of the North Linear Park; ✆ 450-745-0185; www.laurentides.com/parclineaire; cross-country skiing/cycling $14/free; ♿) trail.

❶ Getting There & Around

Galland Laurentides (Map p242; ✆ 450-687-8666, 877-806-8666; www.galland-bus.com;

1717 Rue Berri; Montréal-Mont-Tremblant one-way/round trip $32/57) runs buses from Montréal's Central Bus Station to the Laurentians two to three times a day. Stops along the way include St-Jérôme, St-Sauveur-des-Monts, Ste-Adèle, Val-David, Ste-Agathe-des-Monts and Mont-Tremblant.

Many of the towns in the Laurentians can be accessed via Hwy 15, the Autoroute des Laurentides. It peters out beyond Ste-Agathe-des-Monts, however, and joins the old Rte 117, which is slower but more scenic.

L'Inter des Laurentides (✆ 877-604-3377, 819-774-0485; www.transportlaurentides.ca; adult/child $6/free) has frequent buses linking St-Jérôme and Mont-Tremblant daily, calling at St-Sauveur-des-Monts, Ste-Adèle, Val-David, Ste-Agathe-des-Monts and St-Faustin-Lac-Carré along the way. Buses depart nine or 10 times a day on weekdays and four times a day on Saturday and Sunday. The adult fare is a flat $6.

From mid-May to mid-October, **Autobus Le Petit Train du Nord** (✆ 450-569-5596; www.autobuslepetittraindunord.com; rental bike per day/week $25/126; ⊙ mid-May–mid-Oct) runs two buses daily between St-Jérôme and Mont Laurier (tickets $28 to $75), stopping as needed. Bicycles are transported at no charge.

St-Jérôme

Some 43km north of Montréal, St-Jérôme is the official gateway to the Laurentians. Despite its administrative and industrial demeanor, it's worth a stop for the Roman-Byzantine-style **cathedral** (✆ 450-432-9741; https://paroissestj.ca/paroisse-saint-jerome; 355 Pl du Curé-Labelle; ⊙ 7:30am-3pm Mon-Fri, from 8am Sat, 8:30am-6pm Sun; ℗) FREE. It's also the southern terminus of the Parc Linéaire le P'tit Train du Nord, a trail system built on top of old railway tracks. Less than an hour from Montréal, the nearby **Musée d'Art Contemporain des Laurentides** (✆ 450-432-7171; www.museelaurentides.ca; 101 Pl du Curé-Labelle; by donation; ⊙ noon-5pm Tue-Fri & Sun, from 10am Sat), a contemporary-art museum, has small but superb exhibitions of work by regional artists.

St-Sauveur-des-Monts

St-Sauveur-des-Monts (usually just called St-Sauveur) is the busiest village in the Laurentians and is often deluged with day-trippers due to its proximity to central Montréal (70km). A pretty church anchors Rue Principale, the attractive main street, which is lined with restaurants, cafes and stylish boutiques.

With about 100 runs for all levels of expertise crisscrossing five major ski hills (collectively called **Les Sommets**), the downhill skiing is excellent in the region surrounding St-Sauveur. The biggest hill, Sommet St-Sauveur, is famous for its night skiing. Thrill-seekers might also enjoy other attractions here like: **Le Dragon**, a double zip line; the **Viking**, a scenic, dry 1.5km-long toboggan ride through rugged mountain terrain; and, in summer, Parc Aquatique. Cross-country skiers flock to the over 150km of interconnecting trails at **Morin Heights**, 8km to the west.

St-Sauveur's Festival des Arts takes place in late July/early August.

Activities

Parc Aquatique
WATER SPORTS

(Water Park; ☑ 514-871-0101, 450-227-4671; www.sommets.com/en/water-park-saint-sauveur; 350 Rue St-Denis; adult/youth/child per day $40/32/20; ⊙10am-5pm Jun, to 7pm Jul-late Aug, to 6pm late Aug-early Sep; ⊕) In summer, Sommet St-Sauveur is transformed into a large water park called Parc Aquatique. Kids of all ages love getting wet in the wave pool, plunging down slides (some accessible by ski chairlift, which is fantastically intimidating) or being pummeled on rafting rides.

Sommet St-Sauveur
SKIING

(☑ 450-227-4671, 514-871-0101; www.montsaintsauveur.com; 350 Ave St-Denis; all-day lift ticket adult/youth/child $62/53/40, night skiing $47/36/31; ⊙9am-10pm Mon-Fri, 8:30am-10pm Sat & Sun Nov-Mar; ⊕) Sommet St-Sauveur is one of the area's main ski centers. Hills are a bit tame, but there's night skiing from 3pm, a huge variety of runs and 100% snow coverage in season, thanks to snow blowers built right into the slopes.

Festivals & Events

Festival des Arts
de St-Sauveur
PERFORMING ARTS

(☑ 450-227-0427; http://festivaldesarts.ca/en; ⊙late Jul/early Aug) For 11 days usually starting in late July, St-Sauveur's Festival des Arts brings dozens of international dance troupes to town. Many performances are free.

Sleeping & Eating

★Le Petit Clocher
B&B $$

(☑ 450-227-7576; www.lepetitclocher.com; 216 Rue de l'Église; s $165-215, d $185-235; P❋🛜) A gorgeous inn occupying a converted Do-

minican monastery on a little hillside above town, Le Petit Clocher has seven rooms decorated in French Country style, many of which have extraordinary views. Our favorite room was once a chapel and has beautiful old wood-paneled walls.

Auberge Sous L'Édredon
B&B $$

(☑ 450-227-3131; www.aubergesousledredon.com; 777 Rue Principale; r $169-249; P❋🛜🏊) This pretty inn with the cozy-sounding name (Under the Quilt) is overflowing with character. Some of the seven delightfully decorated rooms, named after gems and a lot more modern than the exterior suggests, have fireplaces and Jacuzzis. The inn is about 2km from the village center, close to a little lake and in full view of the ski slopes.

La Brûlerie des Monts
CAFE $

(☑ 450-227-6157; www.bruleriedesmonts.com; 197 Rue Principale; soups & sandwiches $6-14; ⊙6am-7pm Mon-Thu, to 9pm Fri & Sat, 6:30am-7pm Sun; ✏) *The* place in town for breakfast, soups and sandwiches, this cafe-diner has a great terrace. Coffee beans are roasted on-site.

Orange & Pamplemousse
FUSION $$

(☑ 450-227-4330; www.orangepamplemousse.com; 120 Rue Principale; 3-course set meals $28-40; ⊙8am-2:30pm daily, 5-9pm Wed, Thu & Sun, to 9:30pm Fri & Sat) Billing itself as a *bistro actualisé* (up-to-date bistro), this restaurant is a great place to devour complex pasta dishes and extraordinary grilled fish to the relaxing gurgling of a Japanese bamboo water fountain. The breakfasts ($11 to $18) are also divine. Set meals are a snip at just $25 Wednesday and Thursday nights.

Val-David

Tiny Val-David is the sort of village where, after a few hours enjoying great food, lovely wooded trails, strong coffee and views of the narrow Rivière du Nord running through the heart of town, you might start checking out real-estate listings. Its charms have made it a magnet for artists, whose studios and galleries line the main street, Rue de l'Église.

This was a major hippie mecca in the 1960s, and there's more than a little New Age energy remaining today. This is balanced (and enhanced) by artisanal bakeries, jazz music in cafes on summer weekends and more than a few arts-and-crafts people. The town's tourist office, in a cute old train station, is conveniently located alongside the Parc Linéaire du P'tit Train du Nord recreation trail. Check out the Val-David farmers market if you're in town on a Saturday morning.

Activities

The great outdoors is one of Val-David's main attractions. **Roc & Ride** (☑819-322-7978; https://rocnride.com; 2444 Rue de l'Église; ⊙9am-5pm Sat-Wed, to 6pm Thu & Fri) rents cross-country skis, snowshoes, skates and, in summer, bicycles. **À l'Abordage** (☑819-322-1234; http://alabordage.ca; 2268 Rue de l'Église; 3hr kayak tours adult/child from $35/26; ⊙9am-4:30pm late Jun-early Sep, 10am-3:30pm Sat & Sun May-late Jun & early Sep-Oct) rents bicycles, kayaks and canoes, and offers cycle-canoe packages and guided tours on the Rivière du Nord.

Rock climbing is to Val-David what skiing is to other Laurentian villages, with more than 500 routes – from easy walls to challenging cliffs.

A particularly beautiful stretch of the Parc Linéaire du P'tit Train du Nord (p258) runs by Val-David.

A pedestrian and cycling path runs alongside **Chemin de la Rivière** (🚹🚲) 🌿, which in turn hugs the Rivière du Nord and winds through much of town. The well-maintained greenway offers lovely views onto the water, especially around **La Maison de Bavière** (☑866-322-3528, 819-322-3528; www.maisondebaviere.com; 1470 Chemin de la Rivière; r $120-185; 🅿@🛜), where a picturesque stone bridge crosses a rushing waterfall before linking up with a short footpath that leads to Chemin de l'Île.

🎊 Festivals & Events

1001 Pots Festival   ART
(www.1001pots.com; ⊙early Jul–mid-Aug) This huge ceramic exhibit and sale with workshops – now in its fourth decade – brings around 100,000 people to town for five weeks every summer.

🛏 Sleeping & Eating

★Auberge Le Baril Roulant   HOSTEL **$**
(☑819-322-2280; www.barilroulant.com/auberge; 1430 Rue de l'Académie; dm s $26-29, d $42-45, r $80-110, ste $110-130; 🅿❄🛜🐾) This wonderful inn and hostel on the river north of town is a welcome arrival in Val-David. There's a dorm with solid wooden bunk beds sleeping 14 people in 10 singles and two doubles, six

rooms with bathroom named after winds (think Sirocco and Mistral) and a suite with a Jacuzzi.

Le Mouton Noir   FUSION **$**
(☑819-322-1571; www.bistromoutonnoir.com; 2301 Rue de l'Église; mains $7.50-14.50; ⊙8am-10:30pm Mon-Thu, to 1am Fri, 10am-10:30pm Sat & Sun, closed Mon & Tue winter) This artsy spot attracts a very Val-Davidian crowd of beards – some hippie-esque, some hipster-esque, some lumberjack-y. Everyone enjoys the funky Canadian fusion on old LP menus; you gotta love a place that serves bibimbap alongside poutine. Open mike on Friday and live music on Saturday keep the 'Black Sheep' baaing till late on weekends.

★Au Petit Poucet   QUÉBÉCOIS **$$**
(☑819-322-2246, 888-334-2246; https://aupetit-poucet.ca; 1030 Hwy 117; mains $9-21; ⊙6:30am-4pm) For the ultimate Québécois dining experience, head for this rustic cabin a couple of kilometers south of the village. In place since 1945, it's every local's go-to place for huge breakfasts and such specialties as *tourtière* (meat pie), ham-hock ragout and cassoulet with smoked ham.

🍺 Drinking & Nightlife

Pub Le Baril Roulant   MICROBREWERY
(☑819-320-0069; www.barilroulant.com; 2434 Rue de l'Église; ⊙3pm-midnight Mon-Thu, to 1am Fri, noon-1am Sat, to midnight Sun) Laid-back and brimming with local color, this microbrewery complements its own creations with a plethora of other brews from the surrounding area. Chill on the deck in summer or get cozy on multicolored seating in the brightly painted interior. Live bands and DJs provide entertainment, from jazz to psychedelia to electro-pop, on Sundays a couple of times a month.

ⓘ Information

Tourist Information Office (☑ext 4235 888-322-7030, ext 4235 819-324-5678; www.valdavid.com; 2525 Rue de l'Église; ⊙9am-5pm daily mid-Jun–mid-Oct, Fri-Sun mid-May–mid-Jun, Thu-Sun mid-Oct–mid-May) This very helpful tourist office is located just off the town green, itself cut through by the Parc Linéaire du P'tit Train du Nord.

Ville de Mont-Tremblant

The Mont-Tremblant area is the crown jewel of the Laurentians, lorded over by the

875m-high eponymous peak and dotted with pristine lakes and traversed by rivers. It's a hugely popular four-season playground, drawing ski bums from late October to mid-April, and hikers, cyclists, golfers, watersports fans and other outdoor enthusiasts the rest of the year.

The area of Ville de Mont-Tremblant is divided into three sections: Station Tremblant, the ski hill and pedestrianized tourist resort at the foot of the mountain; Mont-Tremblant Village, a tiny cluster of homes and businesses about 4km southwest of here; and Mont-Tremblant Centre Ville, formerly the neighborhood of St-Jovite, the main town and commercial center off Rte 117, about 12km south of the mountain.

◉ Sights

The southern mountain base spills over into a sparkling pedestrianized ski resort, with big hotels, shops, restaurants, blaring music and an amusement-park atmosphere. The cookie-cutter architecture doesn't quite exude the rustic European charm its planners sought to emulate, but this seems of little concern to the 3.5 million annual visitors milling along its cobbled lanes year after year.

🏃 Activities

Mont-Tremblant Ski Resort (☑514-764-7546; www.tremblant.ca; 1000 Chemin des Voyageurs, Station Tremblant; lift ticket adult/youth/child $99/88/66; ☺8:30am-4pm late Nov–mid-Apr; ♿), founded in 1938, is among the top-ranked international ski resorts in eastern North America according to *Ski* magazine and has legions of loyal fans. The mountain has a vertical drop of 645m and is laced with 102 trails and four mountain faces served by 14 lifts, including an express gondola. Renting skis and poles starts at $52/43 per day per adult/youth.

Numerous kiosks in the Station Tremblant pedestrian village can arrange a variety of outdoor pursuits operated by the ski resort. These range from fishing to canoeing to horseback riding; ask for more information about the Scandinavian-style spa, dune-buggy trails, zip lines, hiking trails and literally dozens of other activities. During the summer you'll also see a **luge track** (☑819-681-3000; www.skyineluge.com/luge-canada/skyline-luge -mont-tremblant; 1000 Chemin des Voyageurs, Station Tremblant; 1/3/5 rides $17/23/32; ☺May-Oct; ♿) at the top of the incline on which the pe-

destrian village is set; the track snakes down the mountain for 1.4km.

🎉 Festivals & Events

Festival International du Blues MUSIC
(http://blues.tremblant.ca/en; ☺early Jul) For 10 days every July, the Station Tremblant resort is abuzz with music during the country's biggest blues festival.

Ironman SPORTS
(http://eu.ironman.com/triathlon/events/americas/ironman/mont-tremblant.aspx; ☺late Aug) Late August sees the annual Ironman North American Championship, which includes a 3.8km swim in Lac Tremblant, a 180km bike ride through surrounding forests and mountains, and a 42.2km run along the Parc Linéaire du P'tit Train du Nord (p258) trail, ending in the Station Tremblant pedestrian village. A shorter, less grueling Ironman 70.3 competition takes place here in late June.

🛏 Sleeping

Auberge Manitonga Hostel HOSTEL $
(☑819-425-6008; www.manitongahostel.com; 2213 Chemin du Village, Mont-Tremblant Village; dm $30-42, r $74-120; ⓟ@☞) This attractive hostel just in front of Lac Moore has a big kitchen and large party room with bar, pool table, fireplace and live music at weekends. The nine dorms (with four and eight beds) and 10 rooms with shared baths are clean and spacious; they often fill to capacity, especially in the ski season.

Homewood Suites HOTEL $$
(☑819-681-0808; www.homewoodsuites.com; 3035 Chemin de la Chapelle, Station Tremblant; ste $129-200; ❄@☞♨) Smack dab in the middle of the Station Tremblant pedestrian village, at the heart of all the action in both summer and winter (the ski gondola is 500m away), this rather sterile chain hotel (part of the Hilton group) has 101 great-value suites with stunning mountain views, spiffy decor and basic hot breakfasts. There's a 24-hour convenience store on-site.

★ Auberge Le Lupin B&B $$
(☑819-425-5474; www.lelupin.com; 127 Rue Pinoteau, Mont-Tremblant Village; s $27-157, d $143-173; ⓟ@☞) Our favorite place to stay in Mont-Tremblant, this log house built in 1945 offers snug digs just 1km from the ski station, with private beach access to sparkling Lac Tremblant. The nine themed rooms are spacious and intelligently organized. The

tasty breakfasts whipped up by hosts Pierre and Sylvie in the homey kitchen are a perfect start to the day.

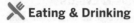 Eating & Drinking

sEb CANADIAN $$$

(☏819-429-6991; www.seblartisanculinaire.com; 444 Rue St-Georges, Mont-Tremblant Centre Ville; mains $32-55, 4-/7-course set menu $49/85; ⏱6-11pm Thu-Mon) 🍴 Escape the mediocre and get a little taste of what culinary artisans can create with seasonal, sustainable local ingredients. A flexible, eager-to-please kitchen, an unforgettable menu and a never-ending wine list enhance the jovial atmosphere. sEb is best described as alpine chalet meets globetrotter (think African masks) meets Hollywood chic (Michael Douglas is a regular). Reservations essential.

Microbrasserie La Diable MICROBREWERY

(☏819-681-4546; www.microladiable.com; 117 Chemin Kandahar, Station Tremblant; ⏱11:30am-2am) After a day of tearing down the mountain, the highlight at this lively Station Tremblant tavern is the fine lineup of microbrews: blonde, red and Belgian Trappist ales, wheat beer, double-black stout and rotating monthly specials. Filling the belly nicely are the accompanying sausages, burgers and pasta dishes (mains $14 to $19).

ⓘ Information

Centre Médical de St-Jovite (☏819-425-2728; 992 Rue de St-Jovite, Mont-Tremblant Centre Ville; ⏱7am-7pm Mon-Thu, 8am-5pm Fri May-Sep, 8am-5pm Mon-Thu, to 1pm Fri Oct-Apr) The local medical clinic.

Mont-Tremblant Tourism (☏877-425-2434; https://mont-tremblant.ca/en; 5080 Montée Ryan, cnr Rte 327; ⏱9am-6pm Sun-Fri, to 7pm Sat late Jun-early Sep, to 5pm daily early Sep-late Jun) This regional tourism office might be able to help with national park and ski resort planning.

ⓘ Getting There & Around

Galland Laurentides (p258) buses stop at 231 Rue de St-Jovite in Mont-Tremblant Centre Ville. L'Inter des Laurentides (p258) buses stop along the same road.

A shuttle bus ($3) connects Station Tremblant, Mont-Tremblant Village and Mont-Tremblant Centre Ville from 6am to 8pm Sunday to Thursday and 6am to 11pm on Friday and Saturday. The shuttle buses from the various parking lots (P2, P3, P4 etc) to the ski slopes are free.

Parc National du Mont-Tremblant

Nature puts on a terrific show at the Parc National du Mont-Tremblant, Québec province's oldest park – it opened in 1895. Covering 1510 sq km of gorgeous Laurentian lakes, rivers, hills and woods, the park has rare vegetation (including silver maple and red oak), hiking and cycling trails, and canoe routes. It is home to fox, deer, moose and wolves, and is a habitat for almost 200 bird species, including a huge blue heron colony.

The park is divided into four sectors. The most developed area is the **Diable sector**, home to beautiful Lac Monroe. The main entrance is 28km northeast of Station Tremblant. The **Discovery Center**, which closes only from mid-November to mid-December, is another 11km from the entrance. It has equipment rentals.

Diable's incredible trails range from an easy 20-minute stroll past waterfalls to daylong hikes that take in stunning views of majestic valleys. You can also take your bike out on some trails or rent canoes to travel down the serpentine Rivière du Diable. The gentle section between Lac Chat and La Vache Noire is perfect for families.

Further east, the **Pimbina sector** is 11km from St-Donat. Here you'll find an information center, canoe and kayak rentals, and campgrounds with some amenities. Activities include swimming at Lac Provost, and hiking and cycling trails nearby. A highlight is the **Carcan Trail**, a 15km-long route to the top of the park's second-highest peak (883m), which passes waterfalls and lush scenery on the way.

East of the Pimbina sector is **L'Assomption sector**, accessible via the town of St-Côme. It is the most untamed part of the park, with more trails, secluded cottages and remote camping options. In winter, you can't access this sector by car, as snow covers the roads.

At the extreme western edge of the park is the **La Cachée sector**. From Hwy 117 Nord, turn off at exit 143 toward Labelle. Its visitor center is open only from late June to early September.

The wilder interior and eastern sections are accessible by dirt roads, some of which are old logging routes. The off-the-beaten-track areas abound in wildlife. With some effort, it's possible to have whole lakes to yourself, except for the wolves, whose howls you'll hear at night.

By late August, nights start getting cold and a couple of months later a blanket of snow adds a magic touch. That's when cross-country skiing and snowshoeing are popular activities, especially in the Diable and Pimbina sectors.

🏃 Activities

Via Ferrata au Diable   CLIMBING
(☑ 800-665-6527; www.sepaq.com/pq/mot/index. dot; adult/child from $49/37; ☺ mid-Jun–mid-Oct) 🪂 A popular half-day guided climbing tour, the so-called 'Excursion' along the Via Ferrata scales the rock face of La Vache Noire to take in a stunning vista of Rivière du Diable with the Laurentians behind. No rock-climbing experience is needed, as guides cover the basics and supply the equipment. Reservations can be made through the park.

🛌 Sleeping

Campgrounds   CAMPGROUND $
(☑ 800-665-6527; www.sepaq.com/pq/mot/tarifs. dot; campsites from $30.50, 4-person tent/yurt $92/117) Camping ranges from rustic tent sites to four-person yurts and ready-to-camp Huttopia tent-cabin hybrids.

Cabins & Huts   CABIN $$
(☑ 800-665-6527; www.sepaq.com/reservation/ chalet.dot; cabins $144-250) 🪂 Two- to 10-person cabin accommodations in Parc National du Mont-Tremblant. Huts are available in summer and cost adult/child $29.50/22.

ℹ️ Information

Information Center (☑ 819-688-2281; www. sepaq.com/pq/mot/information.dot; ☺ hours vary mid-May–mid-Nov & mid-Dec–mid-May)

MONTRÉAL TO QUÉBEC CITY

There's so much charm packed into the idyllic stretch of pastoral patchwork between Québec's two metropolises that it's bursting at the borders. Kick back and stay awhile to enjoy the picture-postcard scenery of the Eastern Townships and take in the unique bilingual atmosphere that constant American tourist traffic to this area has fostered. Alternatively, the Mauricie region – from Trois-Rivières north to Lac St Jean and following the flow of the mighty Rivière St-Maurice – has been known to enchant unsuspecting visitors in search of wild, unadulterated natural beauty.

The Trans-Canada Hwy (Hwy 20) cuts a straight path to Québec City from Montréal. The Eastern Townships are nestled between here and the Vermont border, mainly along Hwy 10; Mauricie falls to the north of Hwy 20 along Hwy 40.

Eastern Townships

Lush rolling hills, crystal-clear lakes and checkerboard farms fill the Eastern Townships, or the Cantons-des-l'Est as they're known by French-speaking inhabitants. The region begins 80km southeast of Montréal and is squished between the labyrinth of minor highways that stretch all the way to the Vermont and New Hampshire borders. New Englanders will feel right at home: covered bridges and round barns dot the bumpy landscape, which is sculpted by the tail end of the US Appalachian mountain range.

A visit during spring is rewarding, as it's the season for 'sugaring off' – the tapping, boiling and preparation of maple syrup. In fall the foliage puts on a kaleidoscopic show of colors, to be toasted with freshly brewed apple cider, served in local pubs. The district is also home to a fast-growing wine region that produces some respectable whites and an excellent ice wine – a dessert wine made from frozen grapes.

👁 Sights & Activities

Summer brings fishing and swimming in the region's numerous lakes, and cycling is also extremely popular in the warmer months, with nearly 500km of trails taking in sumptuous landscapes. Winter means excellent downhill skiing at the three main ski hills: Bromont, Mont Orford and Sutton.

The tourist office (p265) produces an excellent cycle-routes map, describing more than a dozen cycling itineraries.

Frelighsburg   VILLAGE
(Rte 237, cnr Rte 213) A few kilometers from the Vermont border, this village makes a pleasant stop along the Eastern Townships Route des Vins (Wine Route). A cluster of stone and wood homes straddles the banks of the brook that runs through town, and the surrounding area is filled with apple orchards. Local eateries specialize in smoked fish and maple products; if you have a sweet tooth,

Montréal to Québec City & Around

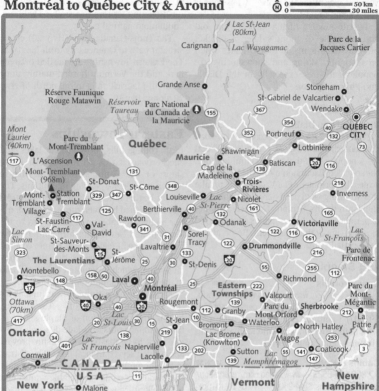

don't miss the famous maple tarts at the old general store-cafe in the center of town.

Parc de la Gorge de Coaticook PARK
(☏ 819-849-2331; www.gorgedecoaticook.qc.ca; 400 Rue St-Marc, Coaticook; adult/child $7.50/4.50; ⊗ information desk 9am-5pm; 🚻) Straddling a lovely forested gorge outside the town of Coaticook, this scenic park is famous for having the world's longest pedestrian suspension bridge. Visitors come for hiking, mountain biking and horseback riding in summer, and snow-tubing and snowshoeing in winter. You can also camp or stay in one of the park's cabins. The surrounding area boasts some of the Eastern Townships' prettiest scenery, not to mention some wonderful cheesemakers (get the cheese-route brochure from the Coaticook tourist office).

Route des Sommets SCENIC DRIVE
(Summit Drive; ☏ 800-363-5515; www.routedessommets.com) The Route des Sommets starts northeast of Sherbrooke at Parc Régional du Mont-Ham and winds 193km along the high mountain slopes north of the New Hampshire border, passing a series of villages and scenic lookouts between La Patrie and St-Adrien. This is a great option for viewing the spectacular fall colors of the Eastern Townships.

🛏 Sleeping & Eating

Au Chant de l'Onde B&B $$
(☏ 450-298-5676; www.auchantdelonde.ca; 6 Rue de l'Église, Frelighsburg; r incl breakfast from $135; 🅿🌐) This peaceful three-room B&B enjoys a prime location along the banks of the Rivière aux Brochets in the heart of pretty Frelighsburg village. Guests have access to a lovely terrace and a spacious backyard within earshot of the river, as well as a library for relaxing, reading or playing board games.

Cabane du Pic-Bois QUÉBÉCOIS $$
(☏ 450-263-6060; www.cabanedupicbois.com; 1468 Chemin Gaspé, Brigham; adult/child $32/18;

by reservation Fri Mar & Apr;) If you want to really gorge yourself, you can't do better than the all-you-can-eat spread at this traditional sugar shack. You get all the classics – omeletes, pork jowls, ham, maple sausage, beans and potatoes – plus cabbage salad dressed with Pic-Bois' famous maple vinegar. We'll gladly come back, even though they had to roll us out the door.

Information

Eastern Townships Tourist Office (Maison du Tourisme des Cantons-de-l'Est; 450-375-8774; www.easterntownships.org; 100 Rue du Tourisme, Hwy 10, exit 68, St-Alphonse-de-Granby; 8:30am-6pm Jun-Aug, reduced hours May, Sep & Oct) Just off Hwy 10, this is the most convenient branch of the Eastern Townships Tourist Office for travelers arriving by car from Montréal.

Getting There & Away

BUS

Limocar (514-842-2281; http://limocar.ca) operates bus services between Montréal's **Gare d'Autocars** (Map p242; 514-842-2281; www.gamtl.com; 1717 Rue Berri; Berri-UQAM) and Bromont ($26, 1 to 2½ hours, 8:25am and 5:40pm), Lac Brome ($25, 1¾ hours, 8am – call ahead, as this service is subject to passenger demand), Sutton ($25, 2¼ hours, 4:15pm weekdays, 8am and 12:30pm weekends), Magog ($32, 1½ hours, frequent) and Sherbrooke ($36, two to 2½ hours, frequent).

Orléans Express (p231) goes to Trois-Rivières in the Mauricie region.

CAR

Coming from Montréal, Hwy 10 will take you straight to the Eastern Townships to just east of Sherbrooke, where it continues as Rte 112. Coming from Québec City via Hwy 20, the fastest route is via Hwy 55, which you pick up near Drummondville.

Bromont

This town revolves around **Ski Bromont** (450-534-2200; www.skibromont.com; 150 Rue Champlain; half-/full day $34/42;), a year-round resort on the slopes of 533m-high Mt Brome. The mountain and its sister peaks dominate the surrounding landscape, which shifts from snowy pine woods in winter to green peaks in spring and summer to a riot of colors in the fall. Bromont is, in essence, beautiful all four seasons of the year.

On weekends from May to October, Bromont's major attraction (other than its ski resort) is its giant **flea market** (Marché Aux Puces Bromont; 450-534-0440; www.mapbromont.com; 16 Rue Lafontaine; 9am-5pm Sat & Sun May-Oct;) **FREE**, just off Hwy 10. Pop into the **Musée du Chocolat de la Confiserie Bromont** (450-534-3893; www.lemuseeduchocolatdelaconfiseriebromont.com; 679 Rue Shefford; meals from $13.25; 8am-5pm) for a mini-museum dedicated to chocolate.

In town, there's also an outstanding vegan restaurant, **Gaïa Resto Végan** (450-534-2074; www.legaia.ca; 840 Rue Shefford; mains $9-15; 8am-3pm Thu-Mon, also 5-8pm Fri & Sat;).

Lac Brome

A stroll around the cute downtown of Lac Brome, which teems with quality boutiques, art galleries, cafes and restaurants, is a fun way to spend an hour or two. Lac Brome is the name given to what is in fact seven amalgamated villages orbiting the eponymous lake, with Knowlton on the southern shore being the largest, most attractive village and considered its 'downtown'. Although there is evidence of early habitation by Abenaki peoples, the area was first formally settled by Loyalists in 1802 and the town still retains an upmarket British flair and numerous 19th-century buildings.

Musée Historique du Comté de Brome MUSEUM
(450-243-6782; www.bromemuseum.com; 130 Rue Lakeside, Knowlton; adult/child $8/2; 10am-5pm;) The exhibits at this museum include a recreated general store and courthouse (Sunday only) and, incongruously, a WWI Fokker D-VII plane. An on-site, heavily interactive children's museum is nice for young kids.

Auberge Knowlton HISTORIC HOTEL $$
(450-242-6886; www.aubergeknowlton.ca; 286 Chemin Knowlton, Knowlton; d incl breakfast from $168;) Set in a landmark 1849 inn, this place features comfortable country-themed rooms and a sprinkling of antiques throughout. The pleasant on-site restaurant Le Relais serves regional specialties. Breakfast is à la carte.

Le Relais FRENCH $$
(450-242-2232; www.aubergeknowlton.ca/relais; 286 Chemin Knowlton, Knowlton; lunch $12-21, dinner $14-35; 11am-3pm & 5-10pm Mon-Fri, 8am-10pm Sat;) At Auberge Knowlton, this

restaurant features juicy Lac Brome duck served many ways, such as duck ravioli in mushroom sauce, duck confit in orange sauce and duck livers with blackened butter. The many other options include pork tenderloin with calvados, veal piccata and garlic scampi, along with burgers, salads, soups and pasta. Guests of the hotel get a 10% discount.

ℹ️ Information

At **Lac Brome Welcome Centre** (☑️450-243-1221; http://tourismelacbrome.com; 696 Chemin Lakeside; ⏰9am-5pm mid-Jun–Aug, 10am-6pm Sat & Sun only Sep, Oct & mid-May–mid-Jun) helpful bilingual staff can set you up with accommodations and maps.

Sutton

Sutton is a little Loyalist town with a pretty main street where you can shop to your heart's content or let your hair down during après-ski partying – the ski area **Mont Sutton** (☑️450-538-2545; www.montsutton.com; 671 Rue Maple; day tickets adult/child $68/38; ⏰9am-4pm; 🐾) is nearby. One of southern Québec's most attractive villages, Sutton is popular with artsy types, who come to appreciate the scenic beauty of the surrounding landscape, dominated by the northern Green Mountains. The downtown strip is filled with cafes, restaurants, inns and B&Bs, along with a helpful tourist office.

One of the province's oldest and best-known wine producers, **Vignoble l'Orpailleur** (☑️450-295-2763; http://orpailleur.ca; 1086 Rue Bruce, Dunham; ⏰10am-4:30pm) is a 30-minute drive from Sutton. Tours of the vineyards are offered, and lunch is served at **Le Tire-Bouchon** (☑️450-295-3335; www.orpailleur.ca; 1086 Rue Bruce, Dunham; mains $19-35; ⏰11:30am-4pm late Jun–mid Oct; 🐾), the great little on-site restaurant. The vineyard is a 30-minute drive from Sutton.

👁️ Sights & Activities

Parc d'Environnement Naturel
HIKING

(☑️450-538-4085; www.parcsutton.com; adult/child $6/3; ⏰Jun-Oct; 🐾) 🌿 In summer, Sutton is prime hiking territory, especially in this conservation area, where 80km of trails have been carved through the thickly forested mountains. Backpackers can unfold their tents at three primitive campgrounds (the one at Lac Spruce is the nicest).

🛏️ Sleeping & Eating

⭐ Le Pleasant Hôtel & Café
HISTORIC HOTEL $$

(☑️450-538-6188; www.lepleasant.com; 1 Rue Pleasant; r $125-259; ✳️@🛜) This luxurious inn is a great place for a weekend escape or romantic interlude. Some of the sleek and modern rooms – well balanced by a classically historical facade – have views of Mont Sutton, and the breakfasts are memorable.

Le Cafetier
CAFE $

(☑️450-538-7333; 9 Rue Principale Nord; mains $9-15; ⏰7am-7pm; 🛜🐾) Locals flock to this cute, cheery cafe in the heart of Sutton for morning coffee, croissants, smoothies, omelets and homemade muesli, but it's just as popular in the afternoon for salads, vegetarian chili, panini and croque monsieurs. Wine and beer, free wi-fi, decks of playing cards and toys for the kids encourage people of all ages to linger.

Auberge des Appalaches
CANADIAN $$$

(☑️450-538-5799; http://auberge-appalaches.com; 234 Rue Maple; mains $25-35; ⏰5-8pm Mon, 6-10pm Tue & Fri-Sun; 🐾) Local produce and intense attention to detail characterize the cuisine at this inn. The seasonal menu is tough to predict, but may include seared calf's liver one evening, and elk tartare flavored with maple the next.

ℹ️ Information

Sutton Visitor Information Center (☑️450-538-8455; https://tourismesutton.ca; 24a Rue Principale Sud; ⏰11am-4pm, from 10am Fri, to 5pm Sat & Sun) has tourism info for the Sutton area.

Magog

Sitting pretty at the north side of the largest lake in the Eastern Townships, Magog flaunts its beauty with million-dollar waterfront properties, a pretty main street and plenty of decent restaurants and hotels. Magog lies at the confluence of the Magog River, Rivière aux Cerises and Lac Memphrémagog, a banana-shaped lake that stretches south for 44km, all the way across the US border, so visitors are rewarded with sparkling water vistas at every turn.

👁️ Sights & Activities

There's a **beach** in Magog, but in summer carving out space for your towel can be a tall order. The rest of the shore is largely in private hands, so the lake is best explored

MAPLE SYRUP & THE SUGAR SHACK

Maple syrup is Canada's most famous export, with nearly three-quarters of the world's total output hailing from Québec. Indigenous peoples taught Europeans how to make the sweet nectar, and by the 19th century cultivating the sap and transforming it into syrup had become a local tradition.

Every summer, starches accumulate in sugar maple trees, which are native to North America. When the mercury dips below zero, they turn into sucrose. To tap the sugar inside the tree, inventive types have come up with a system that sucks out the sap through a series of tubes, which snake through the maple grove to machines that cook the juice into syrup. The different grades are based on how long the syrup is cooked and to what temperature (taffy, for example, is cooked to 26°C above boiling point).

Sugar shacks became part of the Québécois experience in the early 20th century and remain the best places to experience the maple tradition. *La tire d'érable* ('taffy pull') is the most fun: steaming syrup from a piping cauldron is poured onto some snow on a plate. The syrup hardens as it hits the snow and can then be twisted onto a popsicle stick. Eat and repeat!

Sugar shacks are only open for a month or so each year, generally in March. Tourist information offices can offer recommendations.

from the water with companies such as water-sports outfitter **Club de Voile** (☑819-847-3181; www.voilememphremagog.com; 155 Chemin de la Plage des Cantons; ⊙9am-6pm Jun-Aug, 9am-5pm Sat & Sun May-Sep) and **Croisières Escapades Memphrémagog** (☑819-843-7000; www.escapadesmemphrema gog.com; adult $38-108, child $17-72; ⊙Jun-Oct; 🚢), which offers narrated cruises. Watch for Memphré, the feisty yet elusive creature that lives, Nessie-style, at the bottom of the lake!

★**Abbaye**
St-Benoît-du-Lac   MONASTERY
(☑819-843-4080; www.abbaye.ca; 1 Rue Princi-pale, St-Benoît-du-Lac; ⊙church 5am-8:30pm, shop 9-10:45am & 11:45am-6pm Mon-Sat) Sitting on the western shore of Lac Memphré-magog, about 12km south of Magog, this complex is a striking blend of traditional and modern architecture, including a hallway awash in colorful tiles and a lofty church with exposed structural beams and brick walls. If you can, visit at 7:30am, 11am or 5pm, when the monks practice Gregori-an chanting, famous throughout Québec. Equally famous are the monks' apple cider and finely made cheeses, available from the abbey's shop.

🛏 Sleeping

À L'Ancestrale B&B   B&B $$
(☑819-847-5555; www.ancestrale.com; 200 Rue Abbott; r incl breakfast $109-139; @🛜) Wake up to a five-course gourmet breakfast at this intimate retreat. The five rooms are dressed

in a romantic, countrified way and outfitted with refrigerators and coffeemakers. It's central but on a quiet street.

Ô Bois Dormant   B&B $$
(☑819-843-0450, 888-843-0450; www.obois dormant.qc.ca; 205 Rue Abbott, Magog; r incl break-fast $130-145; ❄@🛜🚢) Although only a short walk from the main street, the rambling back lawn at this towering Victorian feels like a se-cluded resort (the pool helps in this regard). Rooms are cozy, if a little chintzy.

ℹ Information

Tourist Office (☑819-843-2744; www. tourisme-memphremagog.com; 2911 Chemin Milletta; ⊙9am-5pm, to 6pm late Jun–Aug) Off Rte 115.

Parc National du Mont Orford

There's probably a better summer day than one spent in golden sunshine amid lush green foothills, cool blue lakes and spectac-ular viewpoints that take in all of the above, but we haven't found it yet. In the mean-time, we'll happily show allegiance to **Parc National du Mont Orford** (☑819-843-9855; www.sepaq.com/pq/mor; 3321 Chemin du Parc, Or-ford; adult/child $8.75/free, parking $8.50; 🅿🚢), home to snapping turtles, day-tripping fam-ilies, countless bird species, and hiking, kay-aking and canoeing opportunities. It's fairly compact, and often gets busy given its prox-imity to Magog, which dwarfs the quaint Orford township.

Station de Ski Mont-Orford SKIING

(☑ 819-843-6548; www.orford.com; 4380 Chemin du Parc; lift tickets per day adult/child $64/37) Station de Ski Mont-Orford has a vertical drop of 589m and dozens of downhill ski slopes, mostly aimed at beginners and intermediate skiers. There's also a snow park with a half pipe and other fun features.

North Hatley

All of the Eastern Townships are cute, but North Hatley is the geographic equivalent of a yawning puppy. It occupies an enchanting spot at the northern tip of the crystal-clear Lac Massawippi, about 17km east of Magog. This was a popular second home for wealthy US citizens who enjoyed the scenery – and the absence of Prohibition – during the 1920s. Many historic residences have been converted into inns and B&Bs. Popular summer activities include swimming, boating, admiring the lakeshore's natural beauty, and browsing the village's galleries, and antique and craft shops.

🏃 Activities

Randonées

Jacques Robidas HORSEBACK RIDING

(☑ 819-563-0166; www.equitationjacquesrobidas.com; 32 Chemin McFarland; riding from $67, 2-day packages from $299; ⛄) A great way to explore the rolling countryside surrounding North Hatley is on horseback with this professional outfit. Among its wide slate of horse-trekking activities, there are classes for those who are new to the experience. New riders catered for.

🛏 Sleeping & Eating

There are a few B&Bs and midrange hotels in North Hatley, but a lovely mansion, **Manoir Hovey** (☑ 819-842-2421; www.manoirhovey.com; 575 Rue Hovey; d from $300, dinner & breakfast incl from $505; P⛄@🛜☺), is the cream of the accommodations crop.

Pilsen PUB FOOD $$

(☑ 819-842-2971; www.pilsen.ca; 55 Rue Main; mains $17-39, set meals from $35; ⏰11:30am-11pm; ⛄) The liveliest restaurant in North Hatley is famous for its salmon, both grilled and smoked, and upmarket pub fare. There's a nice riverside terrace and another facing the lake.

⭐ Auberge Le Coeur d'Or QUÉBÉCOIS $$$

(☑ 819-842-4363; www.aubergelecoeurdor.com; 85 Rue School; 4-course meal $47; ⏰6-9pm, closed Mon & Tue Nov-Apr) For a delightful night out, head to this charming farmhouse inn. The restaurant's four- to five-course dinners make abundant use of local ingredients, including cheeses from Sherbrooke, rabbit from Stanstead, duck from Orford and smoked trout from East Hereford. Save room for profiteroles, chocolate mousse cake or the Coeur d'Or's trademark trio of crème brûlées.

☆ Entertainment

Piggery Theatre THEATER

(☑ 819-842-2431; www.piggery.com; 215 Chemin Simard) In summer, this popular theater stages English-language dramas, concerts and comedy acts.

ℹ Information

Café North Hatley (☑ 819-842-4722; 88 Rue Main; ⏰10am-5pm; 🛜) There is a small information center, free internet access and great coffee here, on the 2nd floor above the Passerose boutique.

Sherbrooke

Sherbrooke is the commercial center of the area, a bustling city that's perfect for refueling on modern conveniences before returning to the Eastern Townships. The historic center, 'Vieux Sherbrooke,' sits at the confluence of two rivers and is bisected by Rue Wellington and Rue King, the main commercial arteries. Highlights include the city's small but well-conceived **Musée des Beaux-Arts** (☑ 619-821-2115; http://mbas.qc.ca; 241 Rue Dufferin; adult/student $10/7; ⏰10am-5pm Jul & Aug, noon-5pm Tue-Sun Sep-Jun), with works by Québécois and Canadian artists, and the 18km **Réseau Riverain** walking and cycling path along the Rivière Magog, which starts at Blanchard Park, west of downtown.

◎ Sights

Lac des Nations LAKE

(⛄) 🚲 South of all the sights, Rivière Magog flows into the pretty Lac des Nations, which is surrounded by a scenic paved trail perfect for walking, in-line skating and cycling (rentals available).

🛏 Sleeping & Eating

Hotel Le Floral HOTEL **$$**
(📞819-564-6812; www.hotellefloral.com; 1920 12e
Ave Nord; r incl breakfast from $110; P✳︎🛜🐾)
The best of a bunch of midrange options, Le
Floral has modish, sleek, urban-chic rooms
and friendly service. It's 5km northeast of
Sherbrooke.

Au Coin du Vietnam VIETNAMESE **$$**
(📞819-566-8383; www.aucoinduvietnam.com;
1530 Rue Galt Ouest; set meals from $25; ⏲11am-
2pm & 5-9pm, closed Mon lunch) If you need a
break from Canadian/Québécois cuisine,
hit up Au Coin du Vietnam, which dishes
out excellent, fresh Southeast Asian fare –
steamed rice, grilled pork, curry chicken,
crispy noodles and plump prawns.

🍺 Drinking & Nightlife

Siboire MICROBREWERY
(📞819-565-3636; www.siboire.ca; 80 Rue du
Dépôt; ⏲6am-3am Mon-Fri, from 7:30am Sat
& Sun) Sherbrooke's historic train depot
houses this atmospheric microbrewery
with nearly a dozen beers on tap, including
Siboire's own IPA, wheat beer, oatmeal stout,
Irish red ale and seasonal maple scotch
ale. High ceilings, brick walls and a flow-
er-fringed summer terrace create an inviting
atmosphere for drinking everything in and
enjoying some of the tastiest fish-and-chips
in the Townships.

ℹ️ Information

ATMs are ubiquitous across the town center.
Banque Nationale (3075 Blvd Portland;
⏲10am-3pm Mon-Wed & Sat, to 6pm Thu, to
4pm Fri) Fee free ATM for many foreign cards.
Hospital Hôtel-Dieu (📞819-346-1110; www.
santeestrie.qc.ca; 580 Rue Bowen Sud; ⏲24hr)
Local hospital offering a wide range of services.
Tourism Eastern Townships (📞819-820-2020,
800-355-5755; www.easterntownships.org; 20
Rue Don-Bosco Sud; ⏲8:30am-4:30pm Mon-Fri)
Tourist Office (Destination Sherbrooke;
📞819-821-1919; www.destinationsherbrooke.
com; 785 Rue King Ouest; ⏲9am-5pm, to 3pm
Sun)
ZAP Sherbrooke (www.zapsherbrooke.org)
Has a list of free wi-fi zones in Sherbrooke.

ℹ️ Getting There & Away

The Limocar (p265) bus terminal is at 80 Rue
du Dépôt; there are frequent bus connections to
Montréal. Sherbrooke lies along Hwy 10, about
25km northeast of Magog.

Parc National du Mont-Mégantic

Similar to many other provincial parks in
Québec, Parc National du Mont-Mégantic
is a lovely slice of preserved eastern Canadian woodlands and wilderness, an arcadi-
an escape from the civilized world. Unlike
many provincial parks, there's a heavy science component to Mont-Mégantic: this is
the site of a major **astronomy observatory**
(📞819-888-2941; http://astrolab-parc-national-
mont-megantic.org/en; 189 Rte du Parc, Notre-
Dame-des-Bois; adult/child $19.25/free, Astronomy
Evenings $25.25/free; ⏲10am-4.30pm & 8pm-late
Jun-Aug, check website for other times), and was
the world's first International Dark Sky Reserve. In scientific terms, that means the
area possesses exceptional visibility under
nocturnal conditions. In layman's terms:
damn, the stars sure are pretty here.

Mauricie

One of Québec's lesser-known regions, Mauricie has a couple of pleasant rest stops just
as you need them, located halfway between
Montréal and Québec City. Trois-Rivières is
good for a stroll along its river promenade
and things get considerably more scenic after the river reaches the Parc National de la
Mauricie. Stretching 300km from Trois-Rivières north to Lac St Jean, this region follows
the flow of the mighty Rivière St-Maurice,
which for centuries has been the backbone
of the area's industrial heritage. Logs were
being driven down the river to the pulp and
paper mills until as recently as 1996. Centuries earlier, the region had given birth to the
country's iron industry; the original forge is
now a national historic site.

Trois-Rivières

Founded in 1634, Trois-Rivières is North
America's second-oldest city north of Mexico, but you'd never know it: a roaring fire
that swept through in 1908 left little of the
city's historic looks. Still, the city center,
right on the north shore of the St Lawrence
River, is not without charms and some bona
fide tourist attractions. A riverfront promenade leads to the oldest section of town
along Rue des Ursulines.

The name, by the way, is a misnomer
as there are only two, not three, streams
here. There are, however, three branches of

the Rivière St Maurice at its mouth, where islands split its flow into three channels.

◉ Sights & Activities

La Domaine Joly de Lotbinière MUSEUM
(☑418-926-2462; www.domainejoly.com; Hwy 132, Rte de Pointe-Platon; adult/child $17/free; ☉10am-5pm late May-late Sep; P) This stately museum between Trois-Rivières and Québec City was built for Henri-Gustave Joly de Lotbinière (1849–1908), a premier of Québec. This is one of the most impressive manors built during the seignorial period of Québec and has been preserved in its late-19th-century state. The outbuildings and huge cultivated garden are a treat, and the cafe serves lunch and afternoon teas.

Musée Québécois de Culture Populaire MUSEUM
(Musée POP; ☑819-372-0406; http://museepop.ca; 200 Rue Laviolette; adult/child $13/8; ☉10am-6pm Jul & Aug, to 4pm Wed-Fri, to 5pm Sat & Sun Sep-Jun) One of the most interesting stops in the area, this museum's changing exhibits cover the gamut from folk art to pop culture, delving into the social and cultural life of the Québécois. Previous exhibits include a quirky show on the social significance of garage sales, and woodcarvings of birds commonly sighted in the area.

Vieille Prison MUSEUM
(☑819-372-0406; http://museepop.ca; 200 Rue Laviolette; adult/child $21/13; ☉10am-6pm Jul & Aug, 10am-5pm Sat & Sun Sep-Jun) Tour guides, including some former inmates, bring the harsh realities of the lockup vividly to life during 90-minute tours that include a stop at dank underground cells known as 'the pit.' English tours run between 11:30am and 3:30pm from late June to the end of August, and by reservation the rest of the year. No children under 12!

Croisières AML BOATING
(☑866-856-6668; www.croisieresaml.com; 1515 Rue du Fleuve; adult/child $30/18; ☉mid-Jun–early Sep; ⬤) These 90-minute cruises along the St Lawrence River feature historical commentary about the town. Tours depart from Port de Trois-Rivières in Parc Portuaire and run to the Laviolette Bridge, the **Sanctuaire Notre-Dame-du-Cap** (www.sanctuaire-ndc.ca/en; 626 Rue Notre-Dame Est; ☉8:30am-8pm; P) FREE, Île St-Quentin and the confluence of the St Lawrence and St Maurice Rivers. The ticket office is near the departure point, at the foot of Rue des Forges.

🛏 Sleeping & Eating

Auberge Internationale de Trois-Rivières HOSTEL $
(☑819-378-8010; www.hihostels.ca; 497 Rue Radisson; dm/d $32/70; @🖥) This wonderfully clean and friendly youth hostel is set in a two-story brick Georgian home, within easy walking distance of the bus station, the riverfront and all the city's attractions. Dorms have four to eight beds each, and there are also reasonably priced private rooms. Bicycle rentals are available.

Le Gîte Loiselle B&B $$
(☑819-375-2121; www.giteloiselle.com; 836 Rue des Ursulines; r $95-135; P ⁂ @🖥) Local artwork, magnificent woodwork and tasteful antiques greet you at this Victorian redbrick one block from the river. Basic rooms with private toilets and shared shower put you right in the heart of the historic district. Congenial hosts Lisette and Mario, both avid cyclists and former restaurateurs, serve an ample breakfast to fuel you for the day's adventures.

★ Le Poivre Noir FUSION $$$
(☑819-378-5772; www.poivrenoir.com; 1300 Rue du Fleuve; mains $25-54, 3-course menu $46; ☉11:30am-2pm Wed-Fri, also 5:30-8:30pm Tue-Sat; ☑) At this upmarket place by the riverfront, chef José Pierre Durand's inspired, often daring, blend of French, Québécois and international influences creates a memorable dining experience. Appetizers such as asparagus and blood-orange salad, or warm goat's-cheese 'snowballs' with tomatoes and pistachios are followed by main dishes such as Québécois deer with pine-nut and squash risotto and cranberry chutney. Reservations suggested.

🍷 Drinking & Nightlife

Gambrinus BREWERY
(☑819-691-3371; www.gambrinus.qc.ca; 3160 Blvd des Forges; ☉11am-1am Mon-Fri, 3pm-1am Sat) About 3km northwest of the riverfront, this decade-old brewery serves more than a dozen varieties of beer, including seasonal cranberry, raspberry and apple ales, an excellent IPA, and an unconventional hemp-and-honey blend called Miel d'Ange.

ℹ Information

Hôpital St-Joseph (Trois-Rivières CSSS; ☑819-370-2100; 731 Rue Ste-Julie) The local hospital, 1km north from the waterfront.

Trois-Rivières Tourist Office (☑ 819-375-1122; www.tourismetroisrivieres.com; 1457 Rue Notre-Dame; ◷ 9am-5pm Mon-Fri, 10am-4pm Sat & Sun mid-May–Sep, 9am-5pm Mon-Fri Oct–mid-May) Extremely helpful tourist office.

🛈 Getting There & Away

Trois-Rivières lies about 150km northeast of Montréal and 130km southwest of Québec City, and is easily accessible via Hwys 40 and 20 or Rtes 138 and 132.

The **Gare d'Autocars** (Orléans Express station; ☑ 819-374-2944; 275 Rue St-Georges) bus station is behind the Hôtel Delta, two blocks back from the waterfront. **Orléans Express** (☑ 514-395-4000; www.orleansexpress.com) buses run to Montréal and Québec City.

Parc National du Canada de la Mauricie

Moose foraging by an idyllic lake, the plaintive cry of a loon gliding across the water, bear cubs romping beneath a potpourri of birch, poplar, maple and other trees waiting to put on a spectacular show of color in the fall – these are scenes you might possibly stumble across while visiting **Parc National de la Mauricie** (Mauricie National Park; ☑ 888-773-8888, 819-538-3232; www.pc.gc.ca/mauricie; adult/child $7.80/free; 🅿 ♿) 🏊. What may well be Québec's best-run and best-organized park is also among its most frequented. The arresting beauty of the nature here, whether seen from a canoe or a walking trail, is everyone's eye candy, but particularly suits those who don't want to feel completely disconnected from 'civilization.'

🚵 Activities

The numerous **walking trails**, which can take anywhere from half an hour to five days to complete, offer glimpses of the indigenous flora and fauna, brooks and waterfalls (the **Chutes Waber** in the park's western sector are particularly worth the hike), as well as panoramic views onto delicate valleys, lakes and streams.

The longest trail, **Le Sentier Laurentien**, stretches over 75km of rugged wilderness in the park's northern reaches. Backcountry campsites are spaced out every 7km to 10km. No more than 40 people are allowed on the trail at any time, making reservations essential. There's a fee of $46 and you must arrange for your own transportation to cover the 30km from the trail's end back to Rte

Promenade. Topographic maps are for sale at the park.

The park is excellent for **canoeing**. Five canoe routes, ranging in length from 14km to 84km, can accommodate everyone from beginners to experts. Canoe and kayak rentals (per hour/day $18/50; www.locationcanot.com) are available at three sites, the most popular being **Lac Wapizagonke**, which has sandy beaches, steep rocky cliffs and waterfalls. One popular day trip has you canoeing from the Wapizagonke campground to the west end of the lake, followed by a 7.5km loop hike to the Chutes Waber and back by canoe.

The most popular winter activity is cross-country skiing (adult/child $9.80/free), with some 85km of groomed trails.

🛏 Sleeping

Camping, the only sleeping option in the park, is at designated sites costing $26 without electricity and $29 with it; camping in the wild during canoe trips costs $16 without firewood, or $25 with firewood. For day hikers, the nearest hotels are 25km southeast of the entrances, in downtown Shawinigan.

Outdoor Lodges   LODGE **$**

(☑ 819-537-4555; per person adult/child $37.5/18.5; 🅿) You can sleep in four- to 10-person dorms in one of two outdoor lodges. They are 3.5km from the nearest parking lots, so you must come in by foot, bike, canoe or skis. There is a two-night minimum stay.

oTENTik   CABIN **$$**

(☑ 877-737-3783; www.pc.gc.ca/en/voyage-travel/hebergement-accommodation/otentik; cabins $120; 🅿) 🏊 Ideal for families, couples and groups (up to five people in three beds), part-cabin, part-tent, an oTENTik puts you in a good spot in the Rivière-à-la-Pêche section in the east end of the park. Each one has a wood stove and dishes; you bring the linens, food and drinks.

🛈 Information

Information Center - St-Jean-des-Piles
(☑ 888-773-8888; Hwy 55, exit 226, via St-Jean-des-Piles; ◷ 7am-9:30pm Jun-Sep) Information and reception center for Parc National de la Mauricie at the east side of the park.

Information Center - St-Mathieu (☑ 819-538-3232; Hwy 55, exit 217, via St-Mathieu-du-Parc; ◷ 9am-7pm, to 9:30pm Fri Jun-Sep) Information and reception center at the south entrance of the park.

QUÉBEC CITY

POP 542,045

Québec, North America's only walled city north of Mexico City, is the kind of place that crops up in trivia questions. Over the centuries, the lanes and squares of the Old Town – a World Heritage site – have seen the continent's first parish church, first museum, first stone church, first Anglican cathedral, first girls' school, first business district and first French-language university. Most of these institutions remain in some form. The historical superlatives are inescapable: flick through the *Québec Chronicle-Telegraph* and you're reading North America's oldest newspaper; if you have to visit L'Hôtel-Dieu de Québec, console yourself with the thought that it's the continent's oldest hospital.

Once past Le Château Frontenac, the most photographed hotel in the world, you'll find yourself torn between the various neighborhoods' diverse charms. In Old Upper Town, the historical hub, many excellent museums and restaurants hide among the tacky fleur-de-lis T-shirt stores. Old Lower Town, at the base of the steep cliffs, is a labyrinth, where it's a pleasure to get lost among street performers and cozy inns before emerging on the north shore of the St Lawrence. Leaving the walled town near the star-shaped Citadelle, hip St-Jean-Baptiste is one of the less historical but still interesting areas, and the epicenter of a vibrant nightlife.

History

A Huron village, 'Stadacona' – the *kanata* (settlement) referred to in Canada's name – stood on the site of Québec City when French explorer Jacques Cartier landed in 1535, on his second voyage to the New World. He returned in 1541 to establish a permanent post, but the plan failed, setting back France's colonial ambitions for 50 years. Explorer Samuel de Champlain finally founded the city for the French in 1608, calling it Kebec, from the Algonquian word meaning 'the river narrows here.' It was the first North American city to be founded as a permanent settlement, rather than a trading post.

The English successfully attacked in 1629, but Québec was returned to the French under a treaty three years later and became the center of New France. Repeated English attacks followed. In 1759 General Wolfe led the British to victory over Montcalm on the Plains of Abraham. One of North America's most famous battles, it virtually ended the long-running conflict between Britain and France. In 1763 the Treaty of Paris gave Canada to Britain. In 1775 the American revolutionaries tried to capture Québec but were promptly pushed back. In 1864 meetings were held here that led to the formation of Canada in 1867. Québec became the provincial capital.

In the 19th century, the city lost its status and importance to Montréal. When the Great Depression burst Montréal's bubble in 1929, Québec regained some stature as a government center. Some business-savvy locals launched the now-famous Winter Carnival in the 1950s to incite a tourism boom. Obviously, it's still working.

In 2008 the city marked the 400th anniversary of Québec's founding.

◉ Sights

Most of Québec City's sights are found within the compact cluster of Old Town walls, or just outside them, making this a dream destination for pedestrians.

◉ Old Town & Port

★ **Le Château Frontenac** HISTORIC BUILDING
(Map p276; ☑ 418-692-3861; www.fairmont.com/frontenac-quebec; 1 Rue des Carrières, Old Upper Town) Reputedly the world's most photographed hotel, this audaciously elegant structure was opened in 1893 by the Canadian Pacific Railway as part of its chain of luxury hotels. Its fabulous turrets, winding hallways and imposing wings graciously complement its dramatic location atop Cap Diamant, a cliff that cascades into the raging St Lawrence River. Over the years, it's lured a never-ending lineup of luminaries, including Alfred Hitchcock, who chose this setting for the opening scene of his 1953 mystery *I Confess*.

★ **Le Monastère des Augustines** MUSEUM
(Map p276; ☑ 418-694-1639; https://monastere.ca; 77 Rue des Remparts, Old Upper Town; adult/youth/child $10.50/4.50/free, guided tour $15/9/free; ⊙10am-5pm late Jun-Aug, Tue-Sun Sep-late Jun) On no account should you miss this museum, which traces the history of the order of Augustinian nuns who founded Québec's first hospital, the Hôtel-Dieu, in 1644 and ran it for over 300 years. OK, it may not sound like a crowd-pleaser, but the half-dozen rooms around a central cloister are filled with remarkable displays of religious items, crafts (artificial flowers were mandatory where flowers bloom only four

Québec City

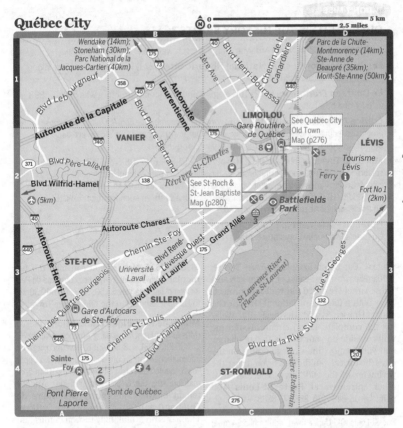

months a year), an old apothecary and an 18th-century refectory.

La Citadelle FORT
(Map p276; ☎418-694-2815; www.lacitadelle.qc.ca; Côte de la Citadelle, Old Upper Town; adult/child $16/6; ☺9am-5pm May-Oct, 10am-4pm Nov-Apr) Covering 2.3 sq km, North America's largest fort was begun by the French in the 1750s but what we see today was constructed by the British over 30 years from 1820 and meant to defend the city against an American invasion that never came. A one-hour guided tour takes in numerous historical structures, including the **King's Bastion** and the **reduit** used later as a military prison. Visit the **museum** dedicated to the Royal 22e Régiment on your own afterward.

Fortifications of Québec
National Historic Site HISTORIC SITE
(Map p280; ☎418-648-7016; www.pc.gc.ca/eng/lhn-nhs/qc/fortifications/index.aspx; 2 Rue

QUÉBEC CITY'S TOP HISTORY SIGHTS

La Citadelle (p273) North America's largest fort towers over the St Lawrence.

Fortifications of Québec National Historic Site (p273) Walk just under 5km along these largely restored old city walls.

Le Château Frontenac (p272) This elegant and now iconic structure was built in 1893 as part of a hotel chain.

Édifice Price (Price Building; Map p276; www.ivanhoecambridge.com/en/office-buildings/properties/edifice-price; 65 Rue Ste-Anne, Old Upper Town) Québec City's own art-deco 'Empire State Building' dominated the city skyline for decades.

Martello Tower 1 (Tour Martello 1; Map p273; ☑855-649-6157, 418-649-6157; www.theplainsofabraham.ca/en/history-heritage/site-history/illustrious-park/#tours; Battlefields Park, Montcalm & Colline Parlementaire; adult/youth/child incl Plains of Abraham Museum & Abraham's bus tour $15.25/11.25/5; ⊙9am-5:30pm Jul-early Sep) One of three such fortifications, this one on the Plains of Abraham can be visited.

Hôtel du Parlement (p275) This monolithic Second Empire structure is where Québec's Provincial Legislature sits.

d'Auteuil, Old Upper Town; adult/child $4/free; ⊙10am-5pm mid-May–early Oct, to 6pm Jul & Aug) These largely restored old walls are protected as both a Canadian National Historic site and a Unesco World Heritage site. Walking the complete 4.6km circuit around the walls outside on your own is free of charge, and you'll enjoy fine vantage points on the city's historical buildings as you trace the perimeter of the Old Town. There are two other entrances: at **Porte St-Louis** (Map p276; ☑418-648-7016, 888-773-8888; www.pc.gc.ca/eng/lhn-nhs/qc/fortifications/index.aspx; 100 Rue St-Louis, Old Upper Town; adult/child $4/free; ⊙10am-5pm mid-May–early Oct, to 6pm Jul & Aug) and the **Frontenac Kiosk** (Map p276; ☑888-773-8888, 418-648-7016; www.pc.gc.ca/eng/lhn-nhs/qc/fortifications/index.aspx; off Rue St-Louis, Old Upper Town; adult/child $4/free; ⊙10am-5pm mid-May–early Oct, to 6pm Jul & Aug) on the Terrasse Dufferin.

★ **Terrasse Dufferin** PARK
(Map p276; Rue des Carrières, Old Upper Town) Perched on a clifftop 60m above the St Lawrence River, this 425m-long boardwalk is a marvelous setting for a stroll, with spectacular, sweeping views. In summer it's peppered with street performers; in winter it hosts a dramatic toboggan run (p278). Near the statue of Samuel de Champlain, stairways descend to the excavations of Champlain's **second fort** (Map p276; ☑418-648-7016; www.pc.gc.ca/eng/lhn-nhs/qc/saintlouisforts/index.aspx; Terrasse Dufferin, Old Upper Town; adult/child $4/free, incl guided tour $15/10; ⊙9am-5:30pm mid-May–early Oct) 🍂, which stood here from

1620 to 1635. Nearby, you can take the **funicular** (www.funiculaire-quebec.com; Rue du Petit-Champlain; one way $3.50; ⊙7:30am-10:30pm, to 11:30pm summer) to the Old Lower Town.

Musée de l'Amérique Francophone MUSEUM
(Museum of French-Speaking America; Map p276; ☑866-710-8031, 418-643-2158; www.mcq.org/en/informations/maf; 2 Côte de la Fabrique, Old Upper Town; adult/teen/child $10/4/free; ⊙10am-5pm mid-Jun–Aug, Sat & Sun Sep–mid-Jun) Anchor tenant of the 17th-century **Séminaire de Québec** (Map p276; Côte de la Fabrique, Old Upper Town), this breathtakingly thorough museum is purported to be Canada's oldest. Enter via the awesome **Chapelle du Musée** (Museum Chapel), built in 1898 by Joseph-Ferdinand Peachy, who earlier built the Église St-Jean-Baptiste. Access the main building pavilion by underground tunnel and its three floors of exhibits exploring the diaspora of French-speaking people in North America, the early years of New France, and the work of artists and artisans here since 1930.

⊙ Old Lower Town

Sandwiched between the Old Upper Town and the waterfront, this area has the city's most intriguing museums, plus numerous plaques and statues, and plenty of outdoor cafes and restaurants along its pedestrian-friendly streets. Street performers in period costume help recapture life in distant centuries.

Teeming Rue du Petit-Champlain forms the heart of the Quartier Petit-Champlain, the continent's oldest commercial district. Look for the incredible wall paintings that feature on the 17th- and 18th-century buildings.

From the Upper Town, you can reach the Lower Town in several ways. Walk down Côte de la Canoterie from Rue des Remparts to the Vieux-Port or edge down the charming and steep Rue Côte de la Montagne. About halfway down on the right there is a shortcut, the Escalier Casse-Cou (Break-Neck Stairs), which leads down to Rue du Petit-Champlain. You can also take the funicular.

★ **Musée de la Civilisation** MUSEUM
(Museum of Civilization; Map p276; ☑ 418-643-2158; www.mcq.org/en; 85 Rue Dalhousie, Old Lower Town & Port; adult/teen/child $17/6/free, with temporary exhibitions $22/7/free; ⊙ 10am-5pm mid-Jun–early Sep, closed Mon early Sep–mid-Jun) This world-class museum wows even before you've clapped your eyes on the exhibits. It is a fascinating mix of modern design that incorporates preexisting buildings with contemporary architecture. The permanent exhibits – 'People of Québec: Then and Now' and 'This Is Our Story' on the province's Indigenous people today – are unique, sensitively curated and highly educational, with some clever interactive elements. At any given moment there's an outstanding variety of rotating shows.

⊙ **Outside the Walls**

Most visitors venture through Porte St-Louis to take a peek at Québec City's most significant attraction outside the walls: Battlefields Park, site of the famous Plains of Abraham. Unfortunately, most then scuttle back to the safety of that fairy-tale land inside the walls. Some of the sights here are certainly more interesting than taking yet another snap of the Château – notably Hôtel du Parlement and Obsérvatoire de la Capitale (p277). The St-Jean-Baptiste and St-Roch areas, which offer a taste of everyday Québec, are a depressurization chamber after the onslaught of historical tourism in the Old Town. Other up-and-coming areas include St-Sauveur northwest of St-Roch, and Limoilu north of St-Roch across the St-Charles River.

Musée National des
Beaux-Arts du Québec MUSEUM
(Québec National Museum of Fine Arts; Map p273; ☑ 418-643-2150; www.mnbaq.org; 179 Grande Allée Ouest, Plains of Abraham; adult/youth/child

$20/11/free; ⊙ 10am-6pm Jun-Aug, to 5pm Tue-Sun Sep-May, to 9pm Wed year-round) Spare at least a half-day to visit this extraordinary art museum, one of the province's best. Permanent exhibitions range from art in the early French colonies to Québec's contemporary artists, with individual halls devoted entirely to 20th-century artistic giants such as Jean-Paul Lemieux, Fernand Leduc and Jean-Paul Riopelle. Arguably the museum's highlight is the **Brousseau Collection of Inuit Art**, a selection of 100 pieces by 60 artists located at the top of the **Pavillon Pierre Lassonde**.

★ **Battlefields Park** HISTORIC SITE
(Parc des Champs-de-Bataille; Map p273; ☑ 418-649-6157; www.theplainsofabraham.ca; Ave George VI, Montcalm & Colline Parlementaire; ⊙ 9am-5:30pm; ▣) ✿ One of Québec City's must-sees, this verdant clifftop park contains the **Plains of Abraham**, site of the infamous 1759 battle between British General James Wolfe and French General Louis-Joseph Montcalm that determined the fate of the North American continent. Packed with old cannons, monuments and Martello towers, it's a favorite local spot for picnicking, running, skating, skiing and snowshoeing, along with Winter Carnival festivities and open-air summer concerts. For information and to learn more, visit the Musée des Plaines d'Abraham.

Musée des Plaines d'Abraham MUSEUM
(Plains of Abraham Museum; Map p276; ☑ 418-649-6157; www.theplainsofabraham.ca; 835 Ave Wilfrid-Laurier, Montcalm & Colline Parlementaire; adult/youth/child $12.25/10.25/4, incl Abraham's bus tour & Martello Tower 1 Jul-early Sep $15.25/11.25/5; ⊙ 9am-5:30pm) This museum spread over three levels presents a fine multimedia history show entitled *Battles: 1759–60*. Incorporating maps, scale models, interactive games, period uniforms and an overly long audiovisual presentation, the exhibit immerses visitors in the pivotal 18th-century battles that shaped Québec's destiny during the Seven Years' War between France and England. The experience is enlivened by first-hand accounts from the French, British, Canadian and Amerindian protagonists of the period.

Hôtel du Parlement HISTORIC BUILDING
(Parliament Building; Map p280; ☑ 418-643-7239; www.assnat.qc.ca/en/visiteurs; 1045 Rue des Parlementaires, enter from Grande Allée Est, Montcalm & Colline Parlementaire; ⊙ 8:30am-4:30pm Mon-Fri,

Québec City Old Town

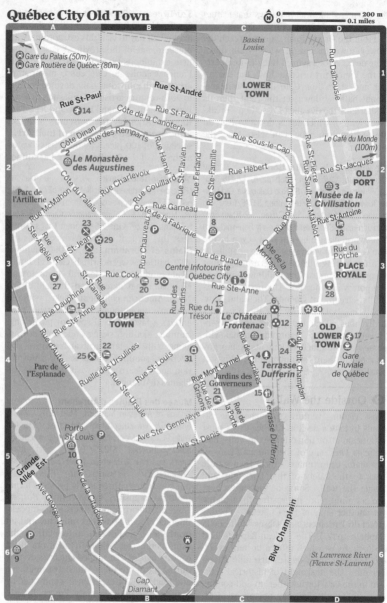

Gare du Palais (50m);
Gare Routière de Québec (80m)

Bassin Louise

LOWER TOWN

Rue Dalhousie

Rue St-André

Rue St-Paul

Rue St-Paul

14

Côte de la Canoterie

Rue Sous-le-Cap

Le Café du Monde (100m)

Côte Dinan

Rue des Remparts

Côte du Palais

Rue McMahon

Parc de l'Artillerie

Le Monastère des Augustines

Rue Charlevoix

Rue Couillard

Rue Hamel

Rue St-Flavien

Rue Ferland

Rue Ste-Famille

Rue Hébert

Rue St-Pierre

Rue Sault-au-Matelot

Rue St-Jacques

OLD PORT

Musée de la Civilisation

3

Rue St-Antoine

18

Rue du Porche

Rue Garneau

Côte de la Fabrique

11

8

Rue de Buade

Côte de la Montagne

PLACE ROYALE

28

Rue Ste-Angèle

Rue St-Jean

23

29

26

27

Rue St-Stanislas

Rue Cook

Rue Chauveau

Rue des Jardins

Centre Infotouriste Québec City

20

5

16

Rue Ste-Anne

Rue Dauphine

19

OLD UPPER TOWN

Rue Ste-Anne

Rue du Trésor

13

Le Château Frontenac

6

30

12

1

OLD LOWER TOWN

17

Gare Fluviale de Québec

Rue d'Auteuil

22

25

Ruelle des Ursulines

Rue St-Louis

31

Rue Ste-Ursule

4

24

Terrasse Dufferin

Parc de l'Esplanade

Rue Mont Carmel

Rue des Grisons

Jardins des Gouverneurs

21

15

Terrasse Dufferin

Rue de la Porte

Ave Ste-Geneviève

Ave St-Denis

Porte St-Louis

10

Côte de la Citadelle

Grande Allée Est

Ave George VI

9

7

Cap Diamant

Blvd Champlain

St Lawrence River (Fleuve St-Laurent)

9:30am-4:30pm Sat & Sun late Jun-Aug, 8am-5pm Mon-Fri Sep-late Jun) **FREE** Home to Québec's Provincial Legislature, the gargantuan Parliament building is a Second Empire structure completed in 1886. Free 30-minute tours, offered in English and French, get you into the **National Assembly Chamber**,

Legislative Council Chamber and **President's Gallery**. The facade is decorated with 26 statues, mostly of significant provincial historical figures, including explorer Samuel de Champlain (1570–1635), New France governor Louis de Buade Frontenac (1622–98), and English and French generals

Québec City Old Town

James Wolfe (1727–59) and Louis-Joseph Montcalm (1712–59).

Obsérvatoire de la Capitale VIEWPOINT
(Capital Observatory; Map p280; ☑ 888-497-4322, 418-644-9841; www.observatoirecapitale.org; 1037 Rue de la Chevrotière, Montcalm & Colline Parlementaire; adult/student/child $14.75/11.50/5; ⊙10am-5pm Feb–mid-Oct, Tue-Sun mid-Oct–Jan) Head 221m up to the 31st floor of the Édifice Marie-Guyart for great views of the Old Town, the St Lawrence River and (if it's clear) even the distant Laurentians. It all helps to get your bearings, and the information panels along the way will get you up to speed on some of the local history, city superlatives and 'fun facts.'

St-Jean-Baptiste AREA
(Map p280; St-Jean Baptiste) Strolling along Rue St-Jean is a great way to feel the pulse of this bohemian district. The first thing that strikes you, once you've recovered from crossing busy Ave Honoré Mercier, is the area's down-to-earth ambience. Good restaurants, interesting shops and hip cafes and bars, many catering to a gay clientele, line the thoroughfare as far as Ave Turnbull. Take

any side street and walk downhill (north) to the narrow residential streets like Rue d'Aiguillon, Rue Richelieu and Rue St-Olivier.

St-Roch AREA
(Map p280; St-Roch) Traditionally a working-class district for factory and navy employees, St-Roch has been slowly gentrifying over the past decade or so. On the main artery, Rue St-Joseph, spiffy restaurants and bars have sprung up among the junk shops and secondhand clothing stores. Private art galleries are also found here and along Rue St-Vallier Est.

Walking down Côte Ste-Geneviève in St-Jean-Baptiste, you will come to a steep staircase called Escalier de la Chapelle, which will take you down to St-Roch.

🕴 Activities

★**Corridor du Littoral & Promenade Samuel-de-Champlain** CYCLING, WALKING
(Map p273; 📶) 🚲 Starting southwest of Québec City at Cap-Rouge and extending northeast via the Old Lower Town to Montmorency Falls, the Corridor du Littoral is a 48km multipurpose recreation path along

QUÉBEC CITY FOR CHILDREN

Québec City is certainly about history, architecture and food. While much of the Old Town, including accommodations and restaurants, is geared toward adults, there are also good things to do with younger ones in the central core, while around the edges are sights fully designed for kids' enjoyment.

Youngsters go giddy over the ubiquitous street performers and guides in period costume, the uniformed soldiers beating the retreat at the Citadelle (p273) and the antique cannons sprinkled around Battlefields Park (p275). Walking the Fortifications (p273) or rampaging down the pedestrian-friendly Terrasse Dufferin (p274), with its river views and buskers, always delights children. Place d'Armes and Place-Royale are also good for street performers. A slow tour of the Old Town in a *calèche* (horse-drawn carriage) appeals to the whole family.

In winter, children will be mesmerized by the **Glissade de la Terrasse** (Terrace Slide; Map p276; ☑ 418-528-1884; www.au1884.ca; Terrasse Dufferin, Old Upper Town; per person 1/4 slides $3/10; ☺ 10am-5pm Sun-Thu, to 6pm Fri & Sat mid-Dec–mid-Mar; ⊞) toboggan run on Terrasse Dufferin; the ice palace, ice slides, snow tubing and dogsledding at Winter Carnival; the whimsically decorated rooms at the Ice Hotel (p283); and the outdoor ice-skating rinks at Place d'Youville and the Plains of Abraham.

The **Érico** (Map p280; ☑ 418-524-2122; www.ericochocolatier.com; 634 Rue St-Jean, St-Jean Baptiste; ☺ 10:30am-6pm Mon-Wed & Sat, to 9pm Thu & Fri, 11am-6pm Sun, to 9pm daily summer) chocolate shop in St-Jean Baptiste also has a museum devoted to all things chocolaty. Get a history lesson, see the kitchen, sample a chunk and try to resist the shop. Make sure you try the hot chocolate.

Outside the center, **Aquarium du Québec** (Map p273; ☑ 418-659-5264, 866-659-5264; www.sepaq.com/ct/paq; 1675 Ave des Hôtels, Ste-Foy; adult/child $20.50/10.25; ☺ 9am-5pm Jun–mid-Oct, 10am-4pm mid-Oct–May; ⊞) ⋒ has walrus, seals, polar bears and thousands of smaller species.

the St Lawrence River, popular with cyclists, walkers and in-line skaters. The heart of it is the Promenade Samuel-de-Champlain, an especially beautiful 2.5km section.

Patinoire de la Place d'Youville ICE SKATING (Place d'Youville Skating Rink; Map p280; ☑ 418-641-6256; www.quebec-cite.com/en/businesses/outdoor-activities/snow/skating/patinoire-de-la-place-dyouville; 995 Place d'Youville, St-Jean-Baptiste; skating free, skate rental $9.25; ☺ noon-10pm Mon-Thu, 10am-10pm Fri-Sun mid-Nov–mid-Mar; ⊞) In the shadow of the Old Town walls and the **Palais Montcalm** (Map p280; ☑ 877-641-6040, 418-641-6040; www.palaismontcalm.ca; 995 Place d'Youville, St-Jean Baptiste; ☺ box office noon-6pm Mon-Fri, to 5pm Sat), this improvised outdoor rink is one of the most scenic and popular places for ice skating once winter rolls around. It's a great place to mingle with locals, and you can also rent skates at the nearby Pavillon des Services.

⛵ Tours

Hugely popular are bus tours that allow you to sit back and watch the sights go by. Another option is to jump on a horse-driven coach.

Calèches (Map p276; ☑ 418-683-9222, 418-520-1555; www.calecheduvieuxquebec.com; Place d'Armes, Old Upper Town; 35/80/120min rides $90/180/270)

Les Tours de Vieux Québec (Map p276; ☑ 800-267-8687, 418-664-0460; www.toursvieux quebec.com; 12 Rue Ste-Anne, Old Upper Town)

★ **Lévis Ferry** BOATING (Map p276; ☑ 877-787-7483; www.traversiers.com; 10 Rue des Traversiers, Gare Fluviale de Québec, Old Lower Town & Port; car & driver/adult/child one way $8.65/3.65/2.45) For city views, you can't beat the 12-minute ferry ride to Lévis; boats operate from 6am to 2am, departing every 30 to 60 minutes depending on the time, day and season. If you purchase a round-trip ticket, you must disembark for security reasons. There's usually a 20-minute layover in Lévis.

Cyclo Services CYCLING (Map p276; ☑ 418-692-4052, 877-692-4050; www.cycloservices.net; 289 Rue St-Paul, Old Lower Town & Port; rental per 2/24hr city bike $17/38, electric bike $34/76; ☺ 9am-5:30pm Mon-Fri, 10am-5pm Sat & Sun, variable hours Nov-Apr; ⊞) This outfit rents a variety of bikes (city, tandem, road, electric, kids') and organizes excellent cycling tours of the city and outskirts to places such as Wendake (half-day $95) and La Chute Montmorency (four hours $77). The knowledgeable and fun guides frequently give tours in English. In winter it rents snowshoes only ($15), and hours are limited; call ahead.

Les Tours Voir Québec WALKING
(Map p276; ☑418-694-2001, 866-694-2001; www.toursvoirquebec.com; 12 Rue Ste-Anne, Old Upper Town; walking tour adult/student/child $23/19.50/11) This group offers excellent tours on the history, architecture and food of Québec City. The popular two-hour 'grand tour,' probably the city's best walking tour, takes in the Old City's highlights, while the food tour includes tastings of wines, cheeses, crepes and chocolate at a variety of shops and restaurants. Buy tickets at and depart from Centre Infotouriste Québec City (p286).

Festivals & Events

Carnaval de Québec CARNIVAL
(Québec Winter Carnival; ☑866-422-7628, 418-626-3716; www.carnaval.qc.ca; ☉Feb) This annual event is unique to Québec City. It bills itself as the biggest winter carnival in the world, with parades, ice sculptures, a snow slide, boat races, dances, music and lots of drinking over 17 days. Activities take place all over town and the iconic slide is on the Terrasse Dufferin (p274) behind the Château Frontenac.

Fête Nationale du Québec CULTURAL
(Québec National Day; ☑514-527-9891; www.fete-nationale.quebec; ☉Jun 23 & 24) Two-day party honoring Québec's national day (June 24). As well as being the feast day of the province's patron, St John the Baptist, this day has evolved into a quasi-political event celebrating Québec's distinct culture. Major festivities on the Plains of Abraham start around 8pm on June 23 and the city parties hard all night.

Festival d'Été de Québec MUSIC
(Québec Summer Festival; ☑418-529-5200; www.infofestival.com; ☉Jul) With 300 shows on 10 stages, this 11-day festival in July attracts musicians and top new talent from all over the world.

Sleeping

From old-fashioned B&Bs to stylish boutique hotels, Québec City has some fantastic overnight options. The best choices are the numerous small European-style hotels and Victorian B&Bs scattered around the Old Town.

Old Upper Town

HI Auberge Internationale de Québec HOSTEL $
(Map p276; ☑418-694-0755, 866-694-0950; www.aubergeinternationaledequebec.com; 19 Rue Ste-Ursule, Old Upper Town; dm $26-34, r without bath $69-84, with bath $89-125, all incl breakfast; ❇@☎) The frustrating labyrinth of corridors in three contiguous buildings goes on forever, but this lively, well-located place heaves with energy year-round. It attracts a mix of independent travelers, families and groups. Staff are friendly but often harried just trying to keep up with all the comings and goings. It's usually full in summer, despite having almost 300 beds; book ahead.

★**Le Monastère des Augustines** HISTORIC HOTEL $$
(Map p276; ☑418-694-1639, 844-694-1639; https://monastere.ca/fr/hebergement; 77 Rue des Remparts; r $184-230, with shared bath $130-160; P❇☎) Attached to the convent museum (p272), this fabulous hostelry is the most atmospheric place to stay in Québec City. Choose among 32 'authentic' rooms (shared bath) – former cells inhabited by the nuns when it was a much larger working convent – or 33 'modern' rooms in a new wing with all the usual commodities. There's an attached restaurant serving multicourse set meals ($24) at 6pm and 7pm Thursday to Saturday. The monastery is a nonprofit organization and all proceeds go to the Augustinian Sisters Heritage Fund.

★**Maison Historique James Thompson** B&B $$
(Map p276; ☑418-694-9042; www.bedandbreakfastquebec.com; 47 Rue Ste-Ursule; r $75-135; P❇☎) History buffs will get a real kick out of staying in the 18th-century former residence of James Thompson, a veteran of the Battle of the Plains of Abraham. The beautifully restored house comes complete with the original murder hole next to the front door. The three rooms are spacious – check out the High Priestess.

★**La Marquise de Bassano** B&B $$
(Map p276; ☑877-692-0316, 418-692-0316; www.marquisedebassano.com; 15 Rue des Grisons; r $129-279; ❇@☎) The congenial owners have done a beautiful job with this

QUÉBEC QUÉBEC CITY

St-Roch & St-Jean Baptiste

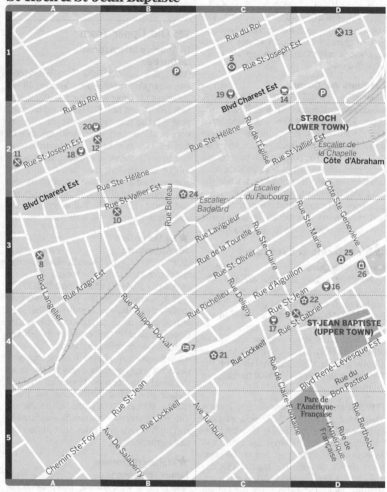

welcoming family home dating from 1888, outfitting its five rooms with thoughtful touches, whether it's a canopy bed or a claw-foot bathtub. It's peacefully placed on a low-traffic street surrounded by period homes, minutes from the important sights. Only two rooms – including the delightful Library – have private baths.

★Hôtel Marie-Rollet
INN $$

(Map p276; ☎800-275-0338, 418-694-9271; www. otelmarierollet.com; 81 Rue Ste-Anne; r from $129; ❋🛜) This lovely inn overlooking the Hôtel de Ville was once owned by the Ursuline nuns at the nearby convent, which is why you'll spot tell-tale signs like ecclesiastical stained glass in some of the public areas. The 13 rooms are on the smallish side and there's no elevator, but the warmth of the place and lovely furnishings excuse all that.

★Fairmont
Le Château Frontenac
HOTEL $$$

(Map p276; ☎866-540-4460, 418-692-3861; www. fairmont.com/frontenac; 1 Rue des Carrières; r $229-700, ste $408-2700; 🅿❋🛜🐾) More than a hotel, the iconic Frontenac is Québec City's most enduring symbol. Its 611 rooms come in a dozen-plus categories. The coveted river-view rooms – beg, borrow or steal room

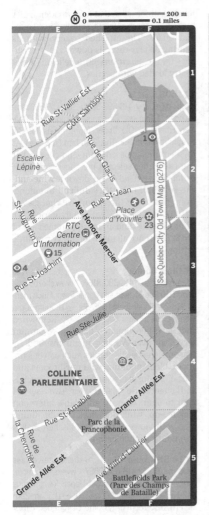

1001 – range in price from Deluxe units tucked under the 18th-floor eaves to the 60 ultraspacious Fairmont Gold rooms, with concierge service, curved turret windows and vintage architectural details.

⌂ Old Lower Town

★ **Auberge St-Antoine**　DESIGN HOTEL $$$
(Map p276; ☎888-692-2211, 418-692-2211; www.saint-antoine.com; 8 Rue St-Antoine; r $259-429, ste $720-1450; ⓟ❊@⌘) Auberge St-Antoine is probably Québec's finest smaller hotel, with phenomenal service and endless amen-

ities. The 95 plush and spacious rooms come with high-end mattresses, goose-down duvets, luxury linens and atmospheric lighting, while the halls resemble an art gallery, filled with French-colonial artifacts from the 18th and 19th centuries uncovered during excavations to expand the hotel.

⌂ Outside the Walls

Prices are drastically lower and rooms bigger outside the walls, and for drivers, parking suddenly becomes a less complicated affair. Many lodgings are within a 15-minute walk from the Old Town.

Centre de Plein Air de Beauport
CAMPGROUND $

(☑ 877-641-6113, 418-641-6112; www.centrepleinair beauport.ca; 95 Rue de la Sérénité, Beauport; campsites & RV sites $38-48; ☺ Jun-early Sep; P 🐾) This excellent campground near Montmorency Falls is green, peaceful and just a 15-minute drive from the Old Town. To get there, take Hwy 40 toward Montmorency, get off at exit 321 and turn north.

★ Auberge JA Moisan
B&B $$

(Map p280; ☑ 418-529-9764; www.jamoisan.com; 695 Rue St-Jean, St-Jean-Baptiste; s $110-170, d $120-180; P ❉ 🛜) This lovely B&B above the historical JA Moisan (p286) grocery store has four relatively small bedrooms tucked under the eaves and gorgeously furnished in period style. The floor below holds common areas, including a parlor, tearoom, solarium, terrace and computer room. Gregarious host Clément St-Laurent makes guests feel right at home. Rates include breakfast, afternoon tea and valet parking.

Château des Tourelles
B&B $$

(Map p280; ☑ 418-647-9136, 866-346-9136; www. chateaudestourelles.qc.ca; 212 Rue St-Jean, St-Jean-Baptiste; r $99-183, ste $129-245; P ❉ @ 🛜) You'll recognize this B&B by its soaring turret, which mirrors the steeple of the Church of St-Jean-Baptiste to the east. The affable Breton owner has completely refurbished this old house, equipping the 11 rooms with wood floors, triple-paned windows, hi-def TV and new bath; other perks include the bright-orange-hued breakfast area and lounge, and rooftop terrace with great views.

✕ Eating

Québec City's restaurant scene has never been better. While the capital has always excelled at classic French food, a number of new arrivals have put a trendy modern spin on bistros. Better places can get a bit pricey, but remember: a carefully chosen *table d'hôte* (fixed-price menu) at lunchtime will give you exactly the same food for a more manageable price.

✕ Old Upper Town

Paillard
CAFE, BAKERY $

(Map p276; ☑ 418-692-1221; www.paillard.ca; 1097 Rue St-Jean, Old Upper Town; sandwiches $9-11; ☺ 7am-9pm Sun-Thu, to 10pm Fri & Sat) At this bright, buzzy and high-ceilinged *café-boulangerie* (cafe-bakery) crammed with tourists, diners seated at long wooden tables tuck into tasty gourmet sandwiches, soups and salads. The attached bakery, with its alluring display cases, is downright irresistible – try the *tentation* ($3), a delicious sweet pastry loaded with berries.

★ 1608
CHEESE $$

(Map p276; ☑ 418-692-3861; http://1608baravin.com; 1 Rue des Carrières, Fairmount Le Château Frontenac, Old Upper Town; mains $21-34; ☺ 4pm-midnight Sun-Thu, 2pm-1am Fri & Sat) At this Frontenac-based wine-and-cheese bar you can either select some cheeses yourself or let the staff take you down a wine-and-cheese rabbit hole that's difficult to emerge from; platters of three/four/five cheeses are $21/26/30 (five types with charcuterie $34). Wine, *fromage* and an incomparable view of the St Lawrence all make for a very romantic setting.

★ Chez Boulay
QUÉBÉCOIS $$$

(Map p276; ☑ 418-380-8166; www.chezboulay. com; 1110 Rue St-Jean, Old Upper Town; lunch menus $18-24, dinner mains $26-35; ☺ 11:30am-10pm Mon-Fri, 10am-10pm Sat & Sun) 🌿 Renowned chef Jean-Luc Boulay's flagship restaurant serves an ever-evolving menu inspired by seasonal Québécois staples such as venison, goose, blood pudding, wild mushrooms and Gaspé Peninsula seafood. Lunch specials and charcuterie platters for two (served 2pm to 5pm) offer an affordable afternoon pick-me-up, while the sleek, low-lit dining area with views of the open kitchen makes a romantic dinner setting.

★ Le St-Amour
FRENCH, QUÉBÉCOIS $$$

(Map p276; ☑ 418-694-0667; www.saint-amour. com; 48 Rue Ste-Ursule, Old Upper Town; mains $42-52, tasting menus $72 & $130; ☺ 11:30am-2pm Mon-Fri, 5:30-10pm daily) One of Québec City's top-end darlings, Le St-Amour has earned a loyal following for its beautifully prepared grills and seafood, and luxurious surrounds. The soaring greenhouse-style ceiling trimmed with hanging plants creates an inviting setting, and the midday *table d'hôte* ($18 to $33; available weekdays) offers that rarest of Upper Town experiences – a world-class meal at an extremely reasonable price.

✕ Old Lower Town

★ Le Lapin Sauté
FRENCH $$

(Map p276; ☑ 418-692-5325; www.lapinsaute.com; 52 Rue du Petit-Champlain, Old Lower Town & Port;

mains $17-29; ⊙11am-10pm Mon-Fri, 9am-10pm Sat & Sun) Naturally, *lapin* (rabbit) plays a starring role at this cozy, rustic restaurant just south of the funicular's lower terminus, in such dishes as rabbit cassoulet or rabbit poutine. Other enticements include salads, French onion soup, charcuterie platters and an excellent-value lunch menu (from $16). In good weather, sit on the flowery patio overlooking tiny Parc Félix-Leclerc.

Le Café du Monde
BISTRO $$

(Map p273; ☑418-692-4455; www.lecafedumonde. com; 84 Rue Dalhousie, Old Lower Town & Port; mains $20-33; ⊙11:30am-10pm Mon-Fri, from 9am Sat & Sun) This Paris-style bistro is the only restaurant in town directly on the St Lawrence River, although actually getting a table with a view can sometimes be a challenge. Persevere. Bright, airy and casually elegant, it swears by bistro classics like *steak-frites* (steak-and-fries) and duck confit, but there's also a great choice of other dishes, from grilled salmon to deer stew.

✖ Outside the Walls

Le Croquembouche
BAKERY $

(Map p280; ☑418-523-9009; www.lecroquem bouche.com; 225 Rue St-Joseph Est, St-Roch; pastries from $2, sandwiches from $5.25; ⊙7am-6:30pm Tue-Sat, to 5pm Sun; ⊛) Widely hailed as Québec City's finest bakery, Le Croquem-bouche draws devoted locals from dawn

to dusk. Among its seductive offerings are fluffy-as-a-cloud croissants, tantalizing cakes and éclairs, brioches brimming with raspber-ries, and gourmet sandwiches on fresh-baked bread. There's also a stellar array of *danoises* (Danish pastries), including orange and an-ise, cranberry, pistachio and chocolate.

Morena
BISTRO $

(Map p273; ☑418-529-3668; www.morena-food. com; 1038 Ave Cartier, Montcalm & Colline Parle-mentaire; mains $12-16; ⊙8am-7pm Mon-Wed, to 8pm Thu & Fri, to 6pm Sat & Sun) Tucked into a gourmet grocery-deli on chichi Ave Cartier, this Italian-themed neighborhood bistro makes a lively but low-key lunch stop. Daily chalkboard specials are beautifully present-ed, with fresh veggies on the side and a soup or salad appetizer. After 3pm there's an à la carte snack menu. After your meal it's also a fun place to browse for food-related gifts.

Poutineville
QUÉBÉCOIS $

(Map p280; ☑581-981-8188; www.poutineville. com; 735 Rue St-Joseph Est, St-Roch; mains $12-16; ⊙11am-10pm Sun-Wed, to 11pm Thu, to midnight Fri & Sat) This could be the place for poutine virgins to try what has become the Québé-cois national dish – french fries served with cheese curds and swimming in gravy. But don't stop at just the garden-variety poutine: this is *la poutine réinventée*, where you'll find such additions as hot dogs, smoked meat, feta cheese or Mexican chili.

QUÉBEC'S COOLEST HOTEL

Visiting the **Ice Hotel** (Hôtel de Glace; ☑888-384-5524, 418-844-2200; www.valcartier.com/en; 1860 Blvd Valcartier, Village Vacances Valcartier; r per person from $495, day pass adult/youth/child $21/16/free; ⊙Jan-Mar; Ⓟ❊♠) is like stepping into a wintry fairy tale. Nearly everything here is made of ice: the reception desk, the sink in your room, your bed – all ice.

Some 500 tonnes of ice and 15,000 tonnes of snow go into the five-week construc-tion of this perishable hotel every winter. First impressions are overwhelming – in the entrance hall, tall, sculpted columns of ice support a ceiling where a crystal chandelier hangs. To either side, carved sculptures, tables and chairs fill the labyrinth of corridors and guest rooms. Children will love the ice slides, while grown-ups gravitate to the ice bar, where stiff drinks are served in cocktail glasses made of ice (there's hot chocolate – in mugs – for the kids too).

The 42-room Ice Hotel usually opens from mid-January to March and offers pack-ages starting at $349 per person (promo offers can knock around $100 off that price). Sleeping here is more about the adventure, and less about getting a good night's sleep, although thick sleeping bags laid on plush deer pelts do help keep things cozier than you might expect.

A better option for most people is to buy a day pass (adult/youth/child $21/16/free), which allows you to visit the guest rooms and all of the hotel's public spaces, including the ice bar and ice slides. The hotel is in St Gabriel de Valcartier, some 35km northwest of Québec City off Rte 371.

POUTINE, BIEN SÛR

Like all fast food, Québec's beloved poutine is perfect if you have a *gueule de bois* (hangover) after a night on the Boréale Blonde. In the calorie-packing culinary Frankenstein, the province's exemplary fries (fresh-cut, never frozen or served limp and greasy) are sprinkled with cheese curds and smothered in gravy. The dish was devised in the early 1980s and spread across Québec like a grease fire.

Poutine is a staple of the oft-seen roadside diners, *cantines* or *casse croûtes*, where you can sample embellished versions such as Italienne – with spaghetti. Some eateries have their own top-secret recipe or unusual spin on the classic; for example, Le Mouton Noir (p260) in Val-David has a version with guacamole, tomatoes and sour cream. Other great spots for poutine include Poutineville (p283) in Québec City and renowned La Banquise (p249) in Montréal.

La Cuisine
DINER $

(Map p280; ☑ 418-523-3387; www.barlautrecuisine. com; 205 Rue St-Vallier Est, St-Roch; mains $11.50; ☺11am-1am Mon-Wed, 11am-3am Thu & Fri, 2pm-3am Sat, 2pm-1am Sun) Retro decor and comfort food served till the wee hours are the hallmarks of this cool, low-lit hangout between St-Jean-Baptiste and St-Roch. Formica tables, mismatched china and silverware, light fixtures made from colanders, a vintage Wurlitzer jukebox and an oversized Lifesavers roll give the place a fun, relaxed feel. On weekend nights, DJs spin everything from electronica to soul.

★ Buvette Scott
FRENCH $$

(Map p280; ☑ 581-741-4464; www.buvettescott. com; 821 Rue Scott, St-Jean-Baptiste; mains $12-18; ☺4:30-11pm Mon-Sat) At this tiny wine bistro with just eight tables and seating at the bar, enlightened French classics like breaded calf's brains, bone marrow and *brandade de morue* (Provençal puree of cod mixed with milk, olive oil and garlic, and served with croutons) dominate the menu. The chalkboard wine list is exceptional, with six reds and six whites.

★ Battuto
ITALIAN $$

(Map p280; ☑ 418-614-4414; www.battuto.ca; 527 Blvd Langelier, St-Roch; mains $21-23; ☺5:30-

10pm Tue-Sat) Considered by many Québécois to be the best Italian restaurant in town, this wonderful place on the edge of St-Roch mixes traditional dishes like *vitello tonnato* (veal topped with a tuna sauce) with more inventive pasta ones such as Sicilian *casarecce* served with sweetbreads and sherry. It's a tiny place, with a mere 24 seats, so book well ahead.

L'Affaire est Ketchup
BISTRO $$

(Map p280; ☑ 418-529-9020; www.facebook. com/laffaireest.ketchup; 46 Rue St-Joseph Est, St-Roch; mains $20-28; ☺6-10:30pm Tue-Sun) Book ahead for this quirky local favorite with only eight tables. Dressed in T-shirts and baseball caps, bantering relaxedly with one another as they cook on a pair of electric stoves, founders Olivier Lescelleur St-Cyr and François Jobin specialize in home cooking with a trendy modern twist. Good selection of wines and mixed drinks at the well-stocked bar.

🍷 Drinking & Nightlife

★ Le Sacrilège
BAR

(Map p280; ☑ 418-649-1985; www.lesacrilege. com; 447 Rue St-Jean, St-Jean-Baptiste; ☺noon-3am) With its unmistakable sign of a laughing, dancing monk saucily lifting his robes, this bar has long been the watering hole of choice for Québec's night owls. Even on Monday, it's standing-room only. There's a quite good selection of beers (including many craft varieties), live music most nights at 8pm and seating on a lovely garden terrace out back.

★ Griendel Brasserie Artisanale
MICROBREWERY

(Map p273; ☑ 591-742-2884; www.facebook.com/ Brasserie.artisanale.griendel; 195 Rue St-Vallier Ouest, St-Sauveur; ☺3pm-1am Mon-Wed, to 3am Thu & Fri, 1pm-3am Sat, to 1am Sun) Anchor tenant on Rue St-Vallier Ouest in up-and-coming St-Sauveur, Griendel occupies a huge old corner shop with lots of windows and great light. Choose from among the two-dozen *broues* (brews) on the blackboard, most of which are brewed in-house. There are burgers and poutine, but it's generally agreed they serve the best fish-and-chips ($15) in town.

★ Noctem Artisans Brasseurs
MICROBREWERY

(Map p280; ☑ 581-742-7979; www.noctem.ca; 438 Rue du Parvis, St-Roch; ☺11am-3am) One of the most interesting microbreweries in town, Noctem goes beyond the *blonde* (lager), *blanche* (white), *rousse* (red) and IPA tick list to offer a blackboard of up to 18 different beers and ales that change daily. If peckish, eschew the pizza/burger/taco choices in favor of a platter of charcuterie to share.

Le Moine Échanson   WINE BAR

(Map p280; ☑418-524-7832; www.lemoineechanson.com; 585 Rue St-Jean, St-Jean-Baptiste; ☺4-10pm Sun-Wed, to 11pm Thu-Sat) A darling of the city's wine connoisseurs, this convivial brick-walled wine bar and bistro pours an enticing and ever-changing array of wines from all over the Mediterranean, by the glass and by the bottle, accompanied by hearty and homespun snacks and main dishes such as blood sausage, cheese fondue or lentil soup. Three-/four-course set menus are $40/45.

La Revanche   CAFE

(Map p280; ☑418-263-5389; www.facebook.com/publarevanche; 585 Blvd Charest Est, St-Roch; ☺5pm-midnight Mon, 4pm-1am Tue-Thu, to 2am Fri, noon-2am Sat, to midnight Sun) This eclectic cafe-pub *ludique* (games cafe-pub) with the relevant name 'Revenge' is dedicated to table-top and board gaming. Seriously, there's a wall here that looks like it could have been plucked from a toy store. Staff are on hand to help you learn the ropes of any game. Pro tip: several pints do not, in fact, improve your Jenga performance.

Macfly Bar Arcade   BAR

(Map p280; ☑418-528-7000; www.macflybararcade.com; 422 Rue Caron, St-Roch; ☺3pm-3am) This bar's *Back to the Future*-ish name is no accident: the entire interior evokes the 1980s, or at least an idea of what the '80s were about – old-school arcade consoles, bright countertops, TV set stuck on a test pattern and pinball machines awaiting your wizardry. Not that it's easy to top your highest score after a couple of well-pulled beers...

La Barberie   MICROBREWERY

(Map p273; ☑418-522-4373; www.labarberie.com; 310 Rue St-Roch, St-Roch; ☺noon-1am) This cooperative St-Roch microbrewery, in place since 1997, is beloved for its spacious tree-shaded deck and its ever-evolving selection of some 30 home brews. Seasonal offerings range from classic pale ales to

quirkier options such as hot pepper amber or a range of sour beers. Undecided? Sample 'em all in the popular eight-beer carousel ($19.75).

Le Drague   GAY

(Map p280; ☑418-649-7212; www.ledrague.com; 815 Rue St-Augustin, St-Jean-Baptiste; ☺10am-3am) The star player on Québec City's tiny gay scene, Le Drague is a large club with an attractive outdoor terrace that gets packed in summer, a dance bar and stage on the ground floor where drag shows are held, and a more laid-back cocktail bar on the upper level called Zone 3.

Bar Ste-Angèle   BAR

(Map p276; ☑418-692-2171; www.facebook.com/BarSainteAngele; 26 Rue Ste-Angèle, Old Upper Town; ☺8pm-3am) A low-lit, intimate hipster hangout, where the genial staff will help you navigate the list of cocktail pitchers and local and European bottled craft beers. Live jazz performed by local and visiting musicians on selected nights.

L'Oncle Antoine   PUB

(Map p276; ☑418-694-9176; 29 Rue St-Pierre, Old Lower Town & Port; ☺11am-1am) Set clandestinely in the vaulted brick cellar of one of the city's oldest surviving houses (dating from 1754), this great tavern pours excellent Québec microbrews (try the Barberie Noir stout), several drafts and various European beers. Its in-house brews include #1 Blonde (lager), #21 Rousse (red) and #29 IPA. Try its famous onion soup on a cold Sunday afternoon.

Shaker   BAR

(Map p280; ☑418-781-0402; http://shakercuisineetmixologie.com; 226½ Rue St-Joseph Est, St-Jean-Baptiste; ☺11am-3am) This monstrous-sized place over two levels shakes and stirs nightly till the wee hours but especially from Thursday to Saturday when there's a DJ on hand to keep the crowds on the tables. The menu is varied, with everything from burgers ($15 to $19) to fish tatares ($15 to $27).

☆ Entertainment

The performing arts are in fine form in Québec City. Live-performance venues abound, from concert halls to open-air amphitheaters, little jazz and rock clubs, and exuberant *boîtes à chanson* (Québec folk-music clubs), where generations of locals dance and sing with uncensored glee.

French-language theater is also an interesting scene, with tons of small companies producing a variety of shows.

Pape Georges
LIVE MUSIC

(Map p276; ☑418-692-1320; https://m.facebook.com/papegeorges; 8 Rue de Cul-de-Sac, Old Lower Town & Port; ◑11am-3pm) With live music from 10pm on Friday and Saturday night at the very minimum (more in the summer), this charming bar located in a 400-year-old house also serves cheeses, meats and baguettes with a healthy dollop of Québécois culture. It always attracts a lively crowd.

Fou-Bar
LIVE MUSIC

(Map p280; ☑418-522-1987; www.foubar.ca; 525 Rue St-Jean, St-Jean-Baptiste; ◑2:30pm-1am Sun & Mon, to 2am Tue & Wed, to 3am Thu-Sat) Laidback and offering an eclectic mix of bands, this bar is one of the town's classics for good live music. It's also popular for its reasonably priced food menu and its free *pique-assiettes* (literally 'freeloaders' aka appetizers) on Thursday and Friday evenings. There can be a cover charge of up to $20 depending on the band.

Scanner Bistro
LIVE MUSIC

(Map p280; ☑418-523-1916; www.scannerbistro.com; 291 Rue St-Vallier Est, St-Roch; cover charge $5-12; ◑4pm-3am Tue-Fri, 8pm-3am Sat-Mon) Ask any local between the ages of 18 and 35 to suggest a cool place for a drink and this is where they might send you. DJs and live bands serve up a potent musical mix, from heavy metal to hard rock to punk to rockabilly. There's a terrace outside in summer, plus table football and pool inside year-round.

Bar Les Yeux Bleus
LIVE MUSIC

(Map p276; ☑418-694-9118; 1117 Rue St-Jean, Old Upper Town; ◑9pm-3am Mon, Tue & Thu, 8pm-3am Wed, 4pm-3am Fri-Sun, closed Mon-Wed winter) One of the city's better *boîtes á chanson* (live, informal singer-songwriter clubs), this is the place to catch newcomers, the occasional big-name Francophone concert and Québécois classics. It's in an old wooden house down a narrow alleyway from Rue St-Jean in the Old Upper Town.

Bateau de Nuit
LIVE MUSIC

(Map p280; ☑418-977-2626; www.facebook.com/bateaudenuit; 275 Rue St-Jean, St-Jean-Baptiste; ◑7pm-3am Mon & Tue, from 5pm Wed-Fri, from 8pm Sat & Sun) We really love it when our dive bars come with a heavy dose of live music, which is exactly the case at this sweet little upstairs venue in the heart of St-Jean-Baptiste. The in-the-know bartenders can tell you about local musicians or who's carved their initials into the wall – most likely most of the crowd here on both counts.

🛍 Shopping

Small, unique and authentic little boutiques are Québec City's claim to retail fame. The best streets for aimless window-shopping include Rue du Petit-Champlain and Rue St-Paul in the Old Lower Town, Ave Cartier in Montcalm, Rue St-Joseph in St-Roch, and Rue St-Jean (both inside and outside the walls).

★ JA Moisan Épicier
FOOD

(Map p280; ☑418-522-0685; www.jamoisan.com; 695 Rue St-Jean, St-Jean-Baptiste; ◑8:30am-7pm Mon-Wed & Sat, to 9pm Thu & Fri, 10am-7pm Sun, extended hours summer) Established in 1871, this charming store bills itself as North America's oldest grocery. It's a browser's dream come true, packed with beautifully displayed edibles and kitchen and household items alongside antique cash registers and wood shelving. You'll find items here you've never seen before, along with heaps of local goods and gift ideas.

Galerie d'Art Inuit Brousseau
ART

(Map p276; ☑418-694-1828; www.artinuit.ca; 35 Rue St-Louis, Old Upper Town; ◑9:30am-5:30pm) Devoted to Inuit soapstone, serpentine and basalt carvings and sculptures from artists all over Arctic Canada, this place is gorgeously set up and elaborately lit, with well-trained staff who knowledgeably answer questions. Works range from the small to the large and intricate. Expect high quality and steep prices. International shipping is available.

❶ Information

Clinique Proactive Santé de la Cité-Limoilou
(☑418-781-0022; www.proactivesante.com; 400 Blvd Jean Lesage, Old Lower Town & Port; ◑7:30am-9pm Mon-Fri, 8:30am-1pm Sat & Sun) This facility near the train and bus stations is the most central walk-in clinic in town.

Centre Infotouriste Québec City
(Québec Original; Map p276; ☑418-641-6290, 877-266-5687; www.quebecoriginal.com; 12 Rue Ste-Anne, Old Upper Town; ◑9am-5pm Nov-Jun, to 6pm Jul-Oct) Québec City's main tourist office, in the heart of the Old Town, opposite Château Frontenac.

Getting There & Away

AIR

Aéroport International Jean-Lesage de Québec (YQB; ☑ 877-769-2700, 418-640-3300; www.aeroportdequebec.com; 505 Rue Principal, Ste-Foy) Québec City's airport lies just under 16km southwest of the center.

BOAT

Gare Fluviale de Québec (Québec River Ferry Station; Map p276; ☑ 877-787-7483; www. traversiers.com; car & driver/adult/child one way $8.65/3.65/2.45) The car and passenger ferry (p278) between Québec City and Lévis takes 12 minutes and leaves from this ferry station.

BUS

Gare Routière de Québec (Québec Bus Station; Map p273; ☑ 418-525-3000; 320 Rue Abraham-Martin) Adjacent to the train station, with regular bus service to Montréal, Côte-de-Beaupré, Charlevoix and the Gaspé Peninsula. There are luggage lockers ($4) for daytime use only.

RTC Centre d'Information (RTC Information Center; Map p280; ☑ 418-627-2511; www. rtcquebec.ca; 884 Rue St-Joachim, St-Jean-Baptiste; ⊙10:30am-6pm Mon-Thu, to 9pm Fri, noon-5pm Sat) Information and tickets for bus service within Québec City.

Gare d'Autocars de Ste-Foy (Ste-Foy Bus Station; Map p273; ☑ 418-650-0087; 3001 Chemin des Quatre Bourgeois, Ste-Foy) Suburban long-distance bus station.

Transport Accessible du Québec (Québec Accessible Transport; ☑ 418-641-8294; www.taq. qc.ca) Wheelchair-adapted vans available. Make reservations at least 24 hours in advance.

CAR & MOTORCYCLE

Québec City lies about 260km northeast of Montréal (three hours by car). The most common routes are Autoroute 20, on the south shore of the St Lawrence River, and the slightly longer Autoroute 40 along the north shore.

TRAIN

VIA Rail (p257) has between four and six daily trains between Montréal's Gare Centrale and Québec City's **Gare du Palais** (Palace Station; ☑ 888-842-7245; www.viarail.ca; 450 Rue de la Gare du Palais, Old Lower Town & Port). Normal prices for the 3¼-hour journey start at $42/87 for a one-way/return ticket. Some trains stop at the suburban **Gare de Ste-Foy** (Ste-Foy Train Station; ☑ 888-842-7245; www.viarail.ca; 3255 Chemin de la Gare, Ste-Foy) as well.

Service is also good along the so-called Québec City–Windsor corridor that connects Québec City with Montréal, Ottawa, Kingston, Toronto and Niagara Falls.

Getting Around

TO/FROM THE AIRPORT

A taxi is your best option for travel between the airport and downtown Québec City, as there is no convenient public transportation along this route.

A taxi costs a flat fee of $34.25 to go into the city, or $15 if you're only going to the boroughs surrounding the airport. Returning to the airport, you'll pay the metered fare, which should be less than $30.

BICYCLE

Québec City has an extensive network of bike paths (more than 70km in all), including a route along the St Lawrence that connects to paths along the Rivière St-Charles. Pick up the free *Carte Vélo Officielle/Official Cycling Map* at local tourist offices or bike shops.

Just across from Québec City's train station, Cyclo Services (p278) rents a wide variety of bikes, including city, tandem, road, electric and kids' models. It also organizes cycling tours in the Québec City region.

CAR & MOTORCYCLE

Compact Old Québec lends itself better to exploration on foot than by car. If you're driving up here, plan to park your vehicle for as much of your stay as possible. Parking garages in and around the Old Town typically charge a day rate of $17.50 to $25 Monday to Friday, and $8 to $12 overnight and on weekends.

PUBLIC TRANSPORTATION

RTC's bus network has a few useful lines for travelers; the most convenient hub for catching multiple buses is on Place d'Youville, just outside the Old Town walls.

Bus 1 Links the Old Lower Town and ferry terminal with St-Roch and St-Sauveur via the Gare du Palais train and bus stations.

Bus 11 Links Montcalm and Colline Parlementaire with the Old Upper Town (the only bus running here).

Bus 807 Links Place d'Youville with St-Jean-Baptiste and Ste-Foy.

TAXI

Flag fall is a standard $3.50 plus another $1.75 per kilometer and 65¢ per minute spent waiting in traffic.

Taxis Coop (☑ 418-525-5191; www.taxis coop-quebec.com) Provides taxi service in Québec City.

AROUND QUÉBEC CITY

The area around Québec City is a patchwork quilt of rustic villages, day-tripper-friendly hamlets and suburbs that embrace the Euro-hybrid identity of the *ville*. Other than Lévis, the sights in this area are all on the northern side of the St Lawrence River: Wendake, St-Gabriel de Valcartier, Stoneham and Parc de la Jacques Cartier to the north and northwest, and the rest to the northeast of Québec City. The south side of the river is equally lovely.

Lévis

The 19th-century American poet Ralph Waldo Emerson once observed that 'Life is a journey, not a destination.' That just about sums up the town of Lévis, opposite Québec City on the right bank of the St Lawrence River. The 1km ferry crossing affords some of the best views of the capital, with the Citadelle, Château Frontenac and the Séminaire de Québec dominating the clifftop cityscape. Once you disembark, riverside Lévis is a relaxing escape from the intensity of Québec City's Old Town.

Above the ferry landing, the Terasse du Chevalier-de-Lévis offers excellent vistas of Québec and beyond from the top of a hill on Rue William-Tremblay. For more views, head south on the riverside path through Parc de l'Anse-Tibbits.

Fort No 1

FORT

(Lévis Forts National Historic Site; ☑888-773-8888, 418-835-5182; www.pc.gc.ca/en/lhn-nhs/qc/levis; 41 Chemin du Gouvernement; adult/child $3.90/free; ⊙10am-5pm late Jun-early Sep, Sat & Sun early Sep-early Oct; 🖲) Between 1865 and 1872, the British built three forts on the south shore to protect Québec against an American invasion that never materialized. One, known as Fort No 1, has been restored and operates as a national historic site with guided tours four times a day (11 am, 1pm, 2pm and 3pm). It's located amid suburban subdivisions, on the east side of Lévis, just off Rte 132 (Blvd Guillaume-Couture).

Parc des Chutes de la Chaudière

CYCLING

(☑418-838-6026; https://chaudiereappalaches.com/en/travel-quebec/levis/levis/parc-des-chutes-de-la-chaudiere/park; Hwy 73, exit 130) 🏵 This 5km trail runs along the picturesque Chaudière River and is a popular spot for walkers and cyclists in Lévis.

ℹ️ Information

Tourisme Lévis (Map p273; ☑418-838-6026; https://levis.chaudiereappalaches.com; Rue St-Laurent; ⊙8:30am-5pm mid-May–mid-Oct) Tourism office at the ferry landing in the old ferry terminal; has maps.

Wendake

Wendake, a dynamic Indigenous community, could be a town plucked from anywhere in the province, but for signs posted in the Huron-Wendat (Ouendat) language dotting the streets. In that language, the number eight is a letter, pronounced 'oua' (like the 'wh' in 'what'), which explains the curious name of the reconstructed village Onhoüa Chetek8e, the world's only Huron village.

In 1960, Wendake became the first reserve with its own bank; today, it provides employment for other Indigenous groups as well. The town is very residential, even quiet, and beyond the reconstructed village and the big hotel with its own museum, the main signs of life are day-to-day things: schools, churches and a few warehouses. If driving, the stop signs don't say '*arrêt*' here as elsewhere in Québec but '*seten*'.

The **Huron-Wendat Museum** (☑418-847-2260; http://tourismewendake.ca/en/activities/cultural-events/huron-wendat-museum; 5 Place de la Rencontre, Hôtel-Musée Premières Nations; adult/child $14.50/7.25; ⊙10am-noon & 1-4pm May-Oct, 3-6pm Mon-Fri, 10am-noon & 1-4pm Sat & Sun Nov-Apr) houses a small but impressive assortrment of tools, clothing and other artifacts (moccasins, canoes, wampum, baskets). Out back is the reconstructed 30m-long Ekionkiestha longhouse of elm bark that traditionally housed eight to 10 families (up to 70 people).

Wendake's best-known attraction is **Onhoüa Chetek8e** (☑418-842-4308; www.huron-wendat.qc.ca; 575 Rue Chef Stanislas Koska; adult/youth/child $14.75/11.75/9.75; ⊙9am-5pm mid-May–Sep, 10am-4pm Oct–mid-May; 🖲), a reconstructed Huron Village. On an excellent 45-minute tour, you'll learn about Huron history, culture and daily life.

Wendake is an easy 25-minute drive from Québec City via QC-175.

Contact Tourisme Wendake (https://tourismewendake.ca/) for information on shuttle services between Wendake and Québec City.

Île d'Orléans

Before Jacques Cartier named Île d'Orléans in honor of the Duke of Orleans, it was known as L'Île de Bacchus for its wild grapes. Today, there's no sign of Dionysian debauchery on sleepy Île d'Orléans, 15km northeast of Québec City, but there is plenty to attract visitors. The island (population 6825), still primarily a farming region, has emerged as the epicenter of Québec's agritourism movement. Foodies from all around flock to the local *économusées* (workshops) to watch culinary artisans making everything from cider to nougat.

One 60km-long road encircles the island, with two more cutting across it north–south. Their edges are dotted with strawberry fields, orchards, cider producers, windmills, workshops and galleries. Some of the villages contain wooden and stone houses that are up to 300 years old.

There are six villages on the island. They are (traveling clockwise): St-Pierre, Ste-Famille, St-François, St-Jean, St-Laurent and Ste-Pétronille.

◉ Sights & Activities

La Forge à Pique-Assaut　　　GALLERY
(☑418-828-9300; www.forge-pique-assaut.com; 2200 Chemin Royal, St-Laurent; ☺9am-5pm late Jun–early Sep, 9am-noon & 1:30-5pm Mon-Fri mid-Sep–mid-Jun) Artisan blacksmith Guy Bel makes star railings and decorative objects at this *économusée* (workshop). There's a store attached.

Maison Drouin　　　HISTORIC BUILDING
(☑418-829-0330; www.maisondrouin.com; 2958 Chemin Royal, Ste-Famille; adult/child $6/free; ☺10am-6pm mid-Jun–early Sep, noon-4pm Sat & Sun early Sep–mid-Oct) 🕭 This old house was built in 1730 and is one of the most fascinating stops on the island as it was never modernized (ie no electricity or running water) even though it was inhabited as recently as 1984. Guides in period dress give tours of the house in summer.

Québec Aventure Tours　　　CYCLING
(☑418-828-2048; https://quebecaventuretours.com; 507 Rte Prévost, St-Laurent; 5hr road bike/electric bike/tandem/scooter $50/60/60/100; ☺9:30am-6pm May-Oct) Hires out traditional bikes in addition to electric bikes, tandems and scooters. It also runs a daily shuttle ($20) departing from here for the Place d'Armes in Québec City at 9am, returning at 5:15pm.

🛏 Sleeping & Eating

Camping Orléans　　　CAMPGROUND $
(☑888-829-2953, 418-829-2953; www.camping orleans.com; 3547 Chemin Royal, St-François; campsites $38-65; ☺mid-May–mid-Oct; 🅿🛜🏊) This leafy site is at the water's edge at the far end of the island from the bridge. It's the only campsite left in the greater Québec City area. There's a swimming pool and pub on-site.

★Auberge La Goéliche　　　BOUTIQUE HOTEL $$
(☑888-511-2248, 418-828-2248; www.goeliche.ca; 22 Rue du Quai, Ste-Pétronille; r $198-228; 🅿❄🛜🏊) Probably the nicest place to stay on the island, the Victorian-style Auberge La Goéliche has 19 rooms individually decorated with antiques and wood furniture; all of them have balconies and stunning views of the river. Guests relax on the large porch, in the gardens or by the outdoor pool. The in-house **restaurant** (☑888-511-2248, 418-828-2248; www.goeliche.ca; 22 Rue du Quai, Ste-Pétronille; mains $23-29; ☺noon-2pm & 5.30-9pm May-Oct, dinner Fri & Sat, weekend brunch only winter) is top class.

La Boulange　　　BAKERY $
(☑418-829-3162; www.laboulange.ca; 4624 Chemin Royal, St-Jean; light meals $5-12; ☺7:30am-5:30pm Mon-Sat, to 5pm Sun late-Jun–early Sep, see website for times outside these months) A memorable bakery with a small irresistible store, La Boulange is the perfect spot for a light lunch of sandwiches or pizza, or to gather picnic supplies. Devour to-die-for croissants while taking in views of the St Lawrence and the 18th-century **Église St-Jean** (Church of St John; ☑418-828-2551; www.patrimoine-culturel.gouv.qc.ca/rpcq/detail.do?methode=consulter&id=92814&type=bien; 4623 Chemin Royal, St-Jean) next door.

Le Moulin de St-Laurent　　　MEDITERRANEAN $$
(☑418-829-3888; www.moulinstlaurent.qc.ca; 754 Chemin Royal, St-Laurent; mains $18-28, set menus $37-47; ☺11:30am-2:30pm & 5:30-8:30pm May-Oct) You'd be hard-pressed to find a more agreeable place to dine than the terrace at the back of this early-19th-century flour mill, with tables inches from a waterfall. The well-prepared, diverse menu is continental with regional flourishes, such as trout and veal. Cottages (from $90) are also available.

🛍 Shopping

Chocolaterie de l'Île d'Orléans　　　CHOCOLATE
(☑418-828-2252, 800-363-2252; www.chocolaterie orleans.com; 8330 Chemin Royal, Ste-Pétronille;

⊕ 9:30am-5pm Mon-Fri, to 6pm Sat & Sun) Using cocoa beans from Belgium, the *chocolatiers* above this delightful shop in a 200-year-old house churn out tasty concoctions, including almond bark and flavored truffles. The various assortments come in beautifully colored little paper bags. There's a cozy little cafe attached that serves coffee, cakes, lunch and, in summer, ice cream.

Domaine Steinbach　　　　FOOD & DRINKS
(☑418-828-0000; www.domainesteinbach.com; 2205 Chemin Royal, St-Pierre; ⊕10am-7pm May-Oct, to 5pm Nov & Dec, to 4pm Mar & Apr) This store stocks dozens of farm products, including five ciders made using apples from its organic orchard, one with maple syrup. A tasting flight of five ciders costs $4. There is a lovely *gîte* next door with four rooms ($135) and terrace overlooking the river (open May to October).

Cassis Monna & Filles　　　　FOOD & DRINKS
(☑418-828-2525; www.cassismonna.com/en; 1225 Chemin Royal, St-Pierre; ⊕10am-8pm Jun-Sep, 11:30am-5pm Oct-May) Learn all you ever wanted to know about *cassis* (blackcurrant), also known as *gadelle noire* in Québécois, and pick up some treats to go, including jam (currant-onion is popular), honey, vinaigrette, mustard, wine and, of course, *crème de cassis* liqueur. The on-site restaurant pairs the star of the show with dishes like warm goat's cheese salad or duck-leg confit.

❶ Information

Île d'Orléans Tourist Office (☑866-941-9411, 418-828-9411; http://tourisme.iledorleans.com/en; 490 Côte du Pont, St-Pierre; ⊕8:30am-6pm early Jun-early Sep, to 4:30pm rest of year) It's worth spending $1 on the *Autour de Île d'Orléans* (Around the Île d'Orléans) brochure at the helpful tourist office, which you'll come to after crossing the Pont de l'Île d'Orléans.

Ste-Anne de Beaupré

You may never fully appreciate how deep Québec's Catholic roots go in its larger cities, but here in the provinces that identity is more than evident, and *here*, in Ste-Anne de Beaupré, it's almost overwhelming. Approaching the town along Rte 138, the twin steeples of the 1920s basilica tower above the motels, *dépanneurs* (convenience stores) and souvenir shops. It's one of the few remaining mega-attractions in the

province related not to nature or artificial diversions, but to faith. Since the mid-1600s, the village has been an important Christian site; the annual pilgrimage around the feast day of St Anne (July 26) draws thousands of visitors, who crowd every open space.

PLUMobile (☑418-827-8484, 866-824-1433; www.plumobile.ca) buses run between Place d'Youville and Gare du Palais (p287) in Québec City and the basilica. The comfortable buses have free wi-fi.

CHARLEVOIX

Charlevoix is a stunning outdoor playground. In summer, the brilliant blue sky is matched by the deep azure of the St Lawrence, while the hills, lined with hiking trails, are carpeted in green. Fall brings colorful foliage, and in winter, snowcapped mountains loom above the rural valleys. For 200 years, this pastoral skein of streams and rolling hills has been a summer retreat for the wealthy and privileged. Of late, it has become Québec City's preferred retreat from the stresses of city life.

Unesco classified the entire area a World Biosphere Reserve, which resulted in worthwhile restrictions on the types of permitted developments, and a sense of pride among residents. There's also a lot to be proud of in the lovely towns such as Baie St Paul, with *ateliers* (artists' studios), galleries and boutiques lining its narrow streets.

While Charlevoix totals 6000 sq km, it's home to just 30,000 people.

A driving route to consider taking is the 'River Drive' (Rte 362) one way, through Baie St Paul, Ste Irénée and La Malbaie. On the way back you can ride the ear-popping hills of the 'Mountain Drive' (Rte 138) inland and stop in at **Parc National des Hautes Gorges de la Rivière Malbaie** (☑800-665-6527, 418-439-1227; www.sepaq.com/pq/hgo; 25 Blvd Notre-Dame, Clermont; adult/child $8.75/free; ⊕visitor center 9am-8pm mid-Jun–early Sep, see website for other months; ♿🐾) ⚑ for a hike en route.

Baie St Paul

Of all the little towns that lie within daytripping distance of Québec City, this beautiful blend of the outdoors and the bohemian – this is Cirque du Soleil's hometown – may be the most attractive. Not that we recom-

Charlevoix, Saguenay & South Shore

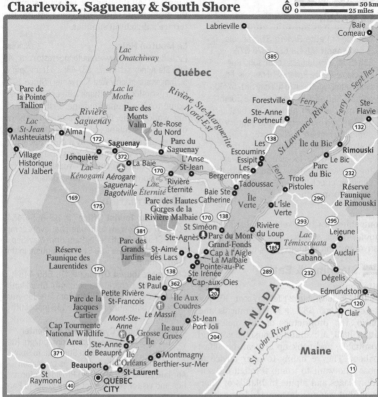

mend day-tripping: if you're coming to Baie St Paul, book a night in a historic house converted into a superb *gîte*, linger over local cuisine, have a glass of wine and set your watch to the estuarine rhythm of the St Lawrence and Gouffre Rivers.

◉ Sights

Parc National des Grands Jardins   PARK
(☑ 418-439-1227; www.sepaq.com/pq/grj; adult/child $8.75/free; ⛺) Excellent hiking and rugged topography are the lures at this provincial park, which covers 310 sq km, much of it taiga. The hills frame more than 100 small lakes, and if you're lucky, you might spot caribou. The 8.6km (round-trip) trek up **Mont du Lac-des-Cygnes** (Swan Lake Mountain) is an exceptional half-day hike. You can test your climbing prowess on the **Via Ferrata** (adult/youth from $48.50/36.25, June to mid-October), with two different guided climbing routes.

Musée d'Art Contemporain de Baie St Paul   MUSEUM
(☑ 418-435-3681; www.macbsp.com; 23 Rue Ambroise-Fafard; adult/student/child $10/7/free; ⊙ 10am-5pm mid-Jun–Aug, 11am-5pm Tue-Sun Sep–mid-Jun) ✐ This architecturally attention-grabbing gallery houses contemporary art by local artists and some photographic exhibits both from its own 3000-piece collection or on loan from the National Gallery of Canada. The museum also organizes an international contemporary art symposium in early August.

🏃 Activities

Katabatik   KAYAKING
(☑ 800-453-4850; www.katabatik.ca; 210 Rue Ste-Anne; half-day sea kayaking tours adult/youth $64/49, half-day canyoning adult/youth $94/74, paragliding $114; ⊙ 8am-6:30pm Jul & Aug, 9am-4:30pm Sun-Fri, to 6pm Sat May & Jun, 9am-4pm Tue-Sun Sep & early Oct; ⛺) ✐ One of the most well-established outdoor/adventure tour

DON'T MISS

LE MASSIF

Outside of Petite-Rivière-St-François is **Le Massif** (☑ 418-632-5876, 877-536-2774; www.lemassif.com; 1350 Rue Principale, Petite-Rivière-St-François; lift ticket adult/youth/child full day $81/57/40, half-day $60/42/29, luge $45; ⊙ 8:30am-4pm mid-Dec–Apr), perhaps the best little-known ski center in the country. It offers the highest vertical drop (770m) and most snow (600cm) east of the Rockies, and has fabulous views over the St Lawrence. Hours change with the seasons; check the website or call for more information.

companies in Charlevoix, Katabatik offers, among other services, sea-kayaking tours, canyoning and tandem paragliding.

🛏 Sleeping & Eating

Gite Fleury B&B $

(☑ 418-435-3668; http://gitefleury.com; 102 Rue St-Joseph; r from $83; P ❋ 🕾) François and Mario, the proprietors of this cute-as-a-kitten B&B, are simultaneously classy and hospitable, and cook up a mean breakfast to boot. They're happy to offer advice to those who want to tromp through the seaside villages and alpine highlands of Charlevoix, but you may be tempted to crash out in one of their four cozy, simply appointed bedrooms.

Auberge à l'Ancrage INN $$

(☑ 666-344-3264, 418-240-3264; www.auberge ancrage.com; 29 Rue Ste-Anne; r from $169) Arguably the most charming place to stay in Baie St Paul, this little inn on the Rivière du Gouffre counts but four rooms – two facing the river and two the street. There's a kind of maritime theme going on at the 'Anchorage,' with lots of antiques in public areas and a wonderful porch. The garden runs down to the river.

★ Le Diapason ALSATIAN $$

(☑ 418-435-2929; www.restolediapason.com; 1 Rue Ste-Anne; mains $19-32; ⊙ 11:30am-2pm & 5-9pm) This pleasant surprise (Alsatian in Charlevoix?) serves all our favorites from eastern France: *flammekueche* (Alsatian 'pizza'), *tartiflette* (potatoes roasted with cheese) and, of course, *choucroute garnie* (sauerkraut simmered with assorted smoked meats and

sausages). All the produce is locally sourced, the atmosphere more than convivial and the terrace a delight in summer.

Le Mouton Noir FRENCH $$$

(☑ 418-240-3030; www.moutonnoirresto.com; 43 Rue Ste-Anne; set meals $37-43; ⊙ 11am-3pm & 5-11pm, evenings only Wed-Sun winter) Since 1978 the rustic-looking 'Black Sheep' has been home to fine French cuisine. Fish – including walleye, the freshwater queen – is on offer when available, as are buffalo, caribou and steak, all enlivened by a deft touch that incorporates wild mushrooms and local produce. The outdoor terrace overlooks the Rivière du Gouffre. Reservations advised.

🛈 Information

Baie St Paul Tourist Office (☑ 418-665-4454, 800-667-2276; www.tourisme-charlevoix.com; 6 Rue St-Jean-Baptiste; ⊙ 9am-6pm May-Sep, to 4pm Oct-Apr) On Rue St-Jean-Baptiste in the town center.

Charlevoix Tourist Office (☑ 418-665-4454; www.tourisme-charlevoix.com; 444 Blvd Monseigneur de Laval; ⊙ 8:30am-7pm late Jun-Aug, 9am-4pm Sep-late Jun) On Rte 138 just south of town.

Mont du Lac-des-Cygnes Visitors Center (☑ 418-439-1227; www.sepaq.com/pq/grj; Rte 381, Km 21; ⊙ 8:30am-8pm Sun-Thu, to 9pm Fri & Sat late Jun-late Aug, varies by season Apr-late Jun & late Aug-Dec) Provides information and visitor services for those going to Parc National des Grands Jardins.

🛈 Getting There & Away

The **bus station** (☑ 418-435-0101; https://inter car.ca; 909 Blvd Monseigneur de Laval) is at a gas station along Rte 138 (Blvd Monseigneur de Laval), about a 20-minute walk from downtown. Intercar buses go to Québec City three times daily ($24, 1¼ hours), twice on Saturdays and Sundays.

Île Aux Coudres

Quiet and rural, 23-km-long Île Aux Coudres feels remarkably remote. The hills of the north shore are never far from view, but this is nonetheless a place to forget the rest of the world. A 'coudriers,' by the way, is a small hazelnut tree, and the island is blanketed in bucolic woods. In the southwest corner, Anse de l'Église is a small, postcard-perfect curve of sandy shoreline fronted by a small village and Catholic church.

CHOO-CHOO CHARLEVOIX

If you're a rail junkie, or simply a lover of a more nostalgic means of getting around, consider the train. The **Train de Charlevoix** (✔418-240-4124, 844-737-3282; http://train decharlevoix.com; Montmorency–Baie St-Paul round-trip adult/child $88/50; ⊘mid-Jun–late Oct), to be exact, which chugs along 125km, connecting Québec City to La Malbaie via seven seaside settlements, taking in much of the natural beauty of Charlevoix in the process. The trip takes about 4½ hours in total one way, but if you'd like to get off the train, explore and reboard, that's cool – you're just not guaranteed a seat when the next train comes.

There's free wi-fi on the trains, but cellular service is pretty spotty. There's no full dining cart, but snacks that are often sourced from the area's many local agricultural producers are served. It's about as relaxing a way of seeing the spectacular Charlevoix countryside as you can imagine. Plus, the rail track passes areas that are completely separate from the road system, spaces you'd never discover unless you were a particularly avid hiker.

The main admin office for the train is in Baie St Paul and the main ticket offices are in that town, Québec City and La Malbaie, but you can purchase tickets on board the train or at small inter-station platforms that can be found all along the route.

◉ Sights & Activities

Les Moulins   MUSEUM
(✔418-760-1065;   www.lesmoulinsdelisleaux coudres.com; 36 Chemin du Moulin; adult/child $10.44/5.50; ⊘10am-5pm mid-May–mid-Oct) *Économusée* Les Moulins has two restored 19th-century mills and exhibits showing how wheat and buckwheat were once ground using grindstones.

Musée Maritime de Charlevoix   MUSEUM
(✔418-635-1131; www.museemaritime.com; 305 Rue de l'Église, St-Joseph-de-la-Rive; adult/child $10/7.50; ⊘10am-6pm mid-May–mid-Oct) Before boarding the ferry on the mainland in St-Joseph-de-la-Rive, drop into Musée Maritime. It details the schooner-building history of a region where it was common to see 320 different types of commercial boat on the St Lawrence. Visitors can climb aboard some beauties in the shipyard. There's also a display on the area's famous meteorite crater.

Centre Vélo-Coudres   CYCLING
(✔418-438-2118; www.velocoudres.com; 2926 Chemin des Coudriers; bicycles per hour $12; ⊘10am-5pm May, 9am-5pm Jun & Sep, to 6pm Jul & Aug) You can use the (free) climbing wall here, or rent bikes and bike equipment such as helmets and child carriers, along with e-bikes ($20 per hour).

✗ Eating

Boulangerie Bouchard   BAKERY
(✔418-438-2454; www.boulangeriebouchard.com; 1648 Chemin des Coudriers; ⊘9am-5pm Jun-Aug,

reduced hours other seasons) Operating since 1945, this bakery on the island's west side is known for *pâté croche*, a meat pie with a 'broken' or cracked top ($5), which is served with housemade ketchup. Another favorite is a sugar pie topped with *pets de soeurs*, rolled pastries that translate as 'nuns' farts.'

❶ Information

Tourist Office (✔418-760-1066; www.tour ismeisleauxcoudres.com; 1024 Chemin des Coudriers; ⊘8am-noon & 1-4pm) Near the crossroads above the port.

❶ Getting There & Away

A free year-round car and pedestrian **ferry** (✔877-787-7483; www.traversiers.com) operates between St-Joseph-de-la-Rive to the north shore of Île Aux Coudres. The crossing takes 20 minutes.

La Malbaie

Encompassing six previously separate villages, La Malbaie was one of Canada's early holiday resorts. From the late 19th century, steamers run by the Richelieu and Ontario Navigation Company and Canada Steamship Lines docked here.

Arriving from the south on Rte 362 or the west on Rte 138, the first village is **Pointe-au-Pic**. This was a holiday destination for the wealthy at the beginning of the 20th century, drawing the elite from as far away as New York. One of its famous residents was former US president William Howard Taft, who had a summer home built here.

Ste-Agnès lies to the northwest, away from the St Lawrence. Adjoining Pointe-au-Pic (and technically merged with it) is **La Malbaie**, which begins west of the Malbaie River and continues to the other side. North of La Malbaie is **Rivière Malbaie**, while **St-Fidèle** and the ridiculously cute **Cap à l'Aigle** are east on Rte 138.

⊙ Sights

Les Jardins du Cap à l'Aigle GARDENS
(☑ 418-665-3747; 625 Rue St-Raphael, Cap à l'Aigle; adult/child $6/free; ⊙ 9am-5pm Jun-Oct) In Cap à l'Aigle, a little village 2km east of La Malbaie, are these gardens, where 800 types of lilac range up the hill between a waterfall, a footbridge and artists selling their daubs. When this spot is in full bloom it's a heavenly little detour.

Musée de Charlevoix MUSEUM
(☑ 418-665-4411; www.museedecharlevoix.qc.ca; 10 Chemin du Havre, Pointe-au-Pic; adult/child $8/6; ⊙ 9am-5pm Jun–mid-Oct, 10am-5pm Mon-Fri, 1-5pm Sat & Sun mid-Oct–May; 🖻) 𝒫 One of the most charming provincial museums in Québec, this waterfront gallery portrays the life and times of Charlevoix through a variety of media: from the impact of the meteors that created the valleys making up the town to the lives of log drivers on the river and the role of folk art in this creative region.

Observatoire de l'Astroblème
de Charlevoix OBSERVATORY
(☑ 418-324-4522; www.astroblemecharlevoix.org; 595 Côte Bellevue, Pointe-au-Pic; 1/2/3 activities adult $14/26/36, child $7/13/18; ⊙ 10am-5pm late Jun-early Sep, to 9pm when cloudy; 🖻) Quite an unusual attraction for adults and kids alike is this observatory, which, through multimedia exhibits, looks at how meteors created the valleys on which Charlevoix sits. Another activity involves stargazing, weather permitting (three hours; available by reservation only in May, June, September and October). A third activity is a geological excursion in the area (three hours).

Maison du Bootlegger HISTORIC BUILDING
(☑ 418-439-3711; www.maisondubootlegger.com; 110 Rang du Ruisseau-des-Frênes, Ste-Agnès; adult/child $10/5, meal, tour & entertainment from $45; ⊙ 10am-4:30pm & 6-11:30pm Jul–mid-Oct, Sat & Sun Jun & late Oct) This unexpected venue in a conventional-looking 19th-century farmhouse was surreptitiously modified by an American bootlegger during the Prohibition period of the 1920s. Tours reveal the marvel of secret doorways and hidden chambers intended to deter the morality squad. From 6pm, it turns into a party restaurant where meat feasts are accompanied by Al Capone beer in boot-shaped glasses.

🛏 Sleeping & Eating

Camping des Chutes Fraser CAMPGROUND $
(☑ 418-665-2151; www.campingchutesfraser.com; 500 Chemin de la Vallée, La Malbaie; tent & RV sites from $33, cottages from $115; ⊙ camping May-Oct, cottages year-round; 🕿) This campground with a waterfall, toward Mont Grand-Fonds park, is idyllic. There's a snack bar, grocery store and laundry on-site, as well as a swimming pool and mini-golf.

Auberge des Eaux Vives B&B $$
(☑ 418-665-4808; www.aubergedeseauxvives.com; 39 Rue de la Grève, Cap à l'Aigle; r $145-175) Sylvain and Johanne are the perfect hosts at this three-room B&B with breakfasts to write home about – think smoothies and a four-course extravaganza on a sunny terrace overlooking the St Lawrence. The decor is modern and chic, and there's a guest-only nook with a Nespresso machine, a full kitchen, two fireplaces and killer views.

Auberge des 3 Canards INN $$
(☑ 800-665-3761, 418-665-3761; www.auberge3canards.com; 115 Côte Bellevue, Pointe-au-Pic; r $145-225, ste $265; 🅿❄🛜🕿) A sprawling white clapboard property looking out to what people call *la mer* (the sea), the 3 Ducks has 48 rooms sporting flat-screen TVs, vintage photos of steamers, local art and balconies overlooking the tennis court (with the St Lawrence behind). The staff are attentive and the restaurant (mains $34 to $42, set dinner $42) features impeccably presented regional cuisine.

Fairmont Le Manoir
Richelieu HISTORIC HOTEL $$$
(☑ 866-540-4464, 418-665-3703; www.fairmont.com/richelieu-charlevoix; 181 Rue Richelieu, Pointe-au-Pic; r $199-399, ste from $550; 🅿❄🛜🕿) The gray-stone country cousin of Québec City's Fairmont Le Château Frontenac (p280), this palatial structure with 405 rooms can claim almost as much history and prestige: it dates back to 1899 and was the venue of the 44th G7 summit in 2018. The sprawling, copper-roofed, castle-like structure, rebuilt

PARC NATIONAL DES HAUTES GORGES DE LA RIVIÈRE MALBAIE

Work off all that Charlevoix produce with an invigorating hike in this 233-sq-km provincial park, which has several unique features, including the highest rock faces east of the Rockies. Sheer rock plummets (by as much as 800m) to the calm Rivière Malbaie, creating one of Québec's loveliest river valleys. The park is located about 40km northwest of La Malbaie.

There are trails of all levels, from ambles around the 2.5km loop of the L'Érablière (Maple Grove) to vigorous hikes of up to 11km ascending to permafrost.

A highlight is the **boat cruise** (☑800-665-6527; www.sepaq.com/pq/hgo; adult/child $36/free; ☺late May-early Oct; 🖭) 🖉 up the river, squeezed between mountains. The river can also be seen from a canoe or kayak, which are available for hire, as are mountain bikes. Boat tickets and rentals are available at the **Le Draveur Visitor Center** at the park entrance.

Many people make it a day trip from La Malbaie, but there are basic **campsites** (☑800-665-6527; www.sepaq.com/pq/hgo; campsites $24-60; 🅿) 🖉 available. Canoes can be used to reach the three riverside campgrounds. Bring all required supplies.

To reach the park from La Malbaie, head northwest on Rte 138 toward Baie St Paul, then take the turn for St-Aimé des Lacs and keep going for 30km.

after a 1927 fire, has two pools, a massive spa and five restaurants.

Pains d'Exclamation BAKERY $
(☑418-665-4000; www.painsdexclamation.com; 398 Rue St-Étienne, La Malbaie; sandwiches $7-12; ☺6:30am-5:30pm, closed Sun & Mon winter) This bakery makes a good lunchtime stop, mainly for the grilled sandwich with a Brie-like local cheese called Le Fleurmier, apples and walnuts. Soups ($6.75) are usually good, too.

Chez Truchon BISTRO $$$
(☑418-665-4622, 888-662-4622; www.auberg echeztruchon.com; 1065 Rue Richelieu, Pointe-au-Pic; mains $26-36; ☺7:30-11:30am Mon-Sat, to 12:30pm Sun, 5:30-8:30pm Mon-Thu, to 9pm Fri-Sun) Considered by some to be the best restaurant in La Malbaie, this bistro-cum-auberge serves Québécois specialties made from local produce at breakfast and dinner only. The double-roomed dining room with hardwood floors and an old fireplace is lovely; views include the St Lawrence and the open kitchen, through a wall of wine bottles. Gracious service.

ℹ Information

Charlevoix Regional Tourist Office (☑418-665-4454, 800-667-2276; www.tourisme-char levoix.com; 495 Blvd de Comporté, La Malbaie; ☺8:30am-7pm late Jun-mid-Oct, 9am-5pm May-late Jun, 9am-4pm mid-Oct–Apr) Located in the center of La Malbaie and serves as the regional tourism office for all of Charlevoix.

St Siméon

A cozy fishing town perched on the St Lawrence, St Siméon is mainly known for Parc d'Aventure Les Palissades and the **ferry** (☑418-638-5530, 418-638-2856; https://traverserdl.com; 116 Rue du Festival, St-Siméon; one way adult/child/car $19.80/13.20/47.10; 🖥🖭) to Rivière du Loup. Otherwise, the road through town – and the quay road to the ferry – offers some great views of the headlands to the north.

Parc d'Aventure Les Palissades (☑418-647-4422; http://aventurex.net/pages/palissades decharlevoix; 1000 Rte 170, St Siméon; via ferrata $45-99; ☺9am-5pm; 🖭) is an adventure sports center with multiple hiking trails, copious rock climbing (150-plus routes), a suspension bridge, rappelling and two *via ferrata* cliff walks with safety cables (no experience required). There's also a zip line. Accommodations range from camping and dorms to chalets; there's also a lakeside spa and sauna.

St Siméon is about 35km north of La Malbaie via Rte 138.

Baie Ste Catherine

A line of multicolored homes clings to the rocks and fronts the rough seas of the St Lawrence in this attractive, laid-back center for outdoor exploration.

Pointe Noire Observation Centre
MUSEUM

(☑418-237-4383, 888-773-8888; www.pc.gc.ca/eng/amnc-nmca/qc/saguenay/pointe-noire; 141 Rte 138; adult/child $5.80/free; ⊙10am-5pm daily mid-Jun–Aug, Fri-Sun Sep–mid-Oct) Up the hill from the ferry landing, this whale-study post, at the confluence of the Saguenay and St Lawrence Rivers, features an exhibit, a slide show and films, plus an observation deck with a telescope. From the boardwalk, you can often spy belugas in the Saguenay very close to shore, especially when the tide is coming in.

Pourvoirie Humanité
BOATING

(☑418-638-5151; http://pourvoiriehumanite.com/en; off Chemin des Loisirs; kayaking $35-50; ⊕) 🏊 Located about 10km outside of Baie Ste Catherine, the 'Humanity Lodge' is a pretty outdoor-activity-center-cum-cabin collection. The main draw is kayaking in four icy blue lakes, but you can also do some stand-up paddling, fishing for speckled trout, geocaching, moose observation and, in August, blueberry picking.

Croisières AML
WHALE WATCHING

(☑418-237-4274, 800-563-4643; www.croisieresaml.com/en; 159 Rte 138; adult/child $80/60; ⊙late Apr-Oct) Offers various whale-watching tours into the St Lawrence Seaway via large observation craft and smaller Zodiacs.

Gîte Entre Mer Et Monts
B&B $

(☑877-337-4391, 418-237-4391; www.entre-mer-et-monts.com; 476 Rte 138; r from $75; P🐾) This friendly little B&B whips out some mean pancakes and brioche in the mornings, and offers cozy, antique-style rooms when you're worn out in the evening.

ℹ Getting There & Away

At the northern end of town, a free 10-minute ferry (☑877-787-7483; www.traversiers.com; 119 Rte 138; ⊙year-round) to Tadoussac runs across the Saguenay River. Ferries operate 24 hours a day, year-round.

SAGUENAY

A deeply forested, craggy cleft tears into the heart of this province: the Saguenay Fjord. Overlooking its deep blue waters are wind-blown, lichen-and-pine-studded cliffs that stretch some 500m high. Formed during the last ice age, the fjord is the most southerly one in the northern hemisphere. As deep as 270m in some places, the riverbed rises to a depth of only 20m at the fjord's mouth near Tadoussac.

This makes the relatively warm, fresh waters of the Saguenay jet out atop the frigid, salt waters of the St Lawrence, leading to massive volumes of krill, which in turn attract the region's visitor highlight: whales. The marine life, and the entire waterway, now enjoy protected status.

There are three main areas of the Saguenay-Lac St Jean region. The first, to the east, is the fjord itself, with parks and scenic villages along both sides. In the center, along the Rivière Saguenay, is the more urban, industrialized section around the city of Saguenay, which is comprised of the boroughs Chicoutimi, Jonquière and La Baie. To the west of Saguenay is Lac St Jean, the third-largest lake in Québec, surrounded by parkland and small towns, many of which house cheesemakers, microbreweries and other food artisans – there's even a chocolate shop run by Trappist monks.

Tadoussac

This small community is the gateway to Québec's Côte-Nord, the North Shore of the St Lawrence River. Located on the river at the fjord's mouth, the village draws hordes of summertime visitors for its main attraction: whales.

Not only do Zodiacs zip out in search of the behemoths, but you can often glimpse smaller whales such as belugas and minkes from shore. Beyond whale-watching, Tadoussac's activities range from sea kayaking and 'surfbiking,' to exploring the fjord by boat, to simply wandering the dunes and headlands.

Tadoussac begins to emerge from its off-season slumber in May and can be packed with visitors from late June into the fall. By the end of October or early November, when the majority of the whales have migrated elsewhere, many of the town's accommodations, eateries and other businesses close for the winter.

History

Tadoussac became the first fur-trading post in European North America in 1600, eight years before the founding of Québec City. The word *tatouskak* in the Innu-aimun

(Montagnais) language means breast, and refers to the two, rounded hills by the fjord and bay. When the Hudson's Bay Company closed its doors, Tadoussac was briefly abandoned, only to be revived as a resort with the building of Hotel Tadoussac in 1864, and as an important cog in the pulp and paper wheel.

Sights

Centre d'Interprétation des Mammifères Marins   MUSEUM
(CIMM; ☑ 418-235-4701; http://gremm.org; 108 Rue de la Cale Sèche; adult/child $14/free; ⊙ noon-5pm mid-May–mid-Jun, 9am-8pm mid-Jun–mid-Sep, 11am-6pm mid-Sep–mid-Oct; ⊕) Gives excellent background information on local sea creatures through multimedia exhibits. There are beautiful views of the river and surrounding cliffs from the grounds.

🏃 Activities

Whale-Watching
Tourists flock to Tadoussac from May to October. The whale-watching is phenomenal, particularly between August and October, when blue whales can be spotted. All over town, tickets are available for boat tours, from 12-person Zodiacs to the 600-person *Grand Fleuve*; check out the options carefully. Wait for a calm day, when the view won't be marred by waves and a rocking boat, and go out in the early morning or evening, when the whales are livelier and there are fewer vessels around.

Zodiac passengers are given waterproofs; whatever trip you do, take lots of warm clothes.

Croisières AML (☑ 866-856-6668; www.croisieresaml.com; 177 Rue des Pionniers; trips adult/child from $70/40; ⊙ May-Oct; ⊕) runs whale-watching trips in boats ranging from smaller Zodiacs to large ferries.

For the adventurous, **Mer et Monde** (☑ 418-232-6779; www.meretmonde.ca; 148 Rue du Bord de l'Eau; 3-hr kayak trips from $58, whale-watching from $68) ⦿ offers whale-watching expeditions and excursions up the fjord by kayak.

Hiking
Parc National du Fjord-du-Saguenay (p301) borders the fjord on both sides of the river. The provincial park has over 100km of splendid hiking trails, views down the fjord from atop 350m-plus cliffs, plus trailside refuges where you can spend the night. There are three refuges on the 42km trail from Tadoussac to Baie Ste-Marguerite, open May to October. Side note: what everyone calls 'dunes' in the Tadoussac area are actually marine terraces – formed by waves, not wind, as dunes are.

There are also several 1km to 2km paths in and around Tadoussac, marked on the map given out by the tourist office (p298). The lovely trails around Pointe de l'Islet, by the quay and, at the other end of the beach, Pointe Rouge, are the best for spying whales from the shore.

🎊 Festivals & Events

Festival de la Chanson   MUSIC
(Song Festival; ☑ 418-235-2002; www.chansontadoussac.com; ⊙ Jun) Tadoussac's busy summer season begins with a vengeance at the annual Festival de la Chanson, a celebration of Francophone, mostly Québécois, music and a serious party, an event that got its start more than 30 years ago. Stages spring up all over town, and accommodations fill up for the long weekend.

🛏 Sleeping

Domaine des Dunes   CAMPGROUND $
(☑ 418-235-4843; www.domainedesdunes.com; 585 Chemin du Moulin à Baude; tent & RV sites $31-36, trailer or motorhome sites $45, chalets $149-177, tipi $149; ⊙ May-Oct; P ⓢ) This leafy campground is located about 3km from town. Self-catering chalets, and even a tipi, are also available; prices are highest in July and August.

Hôtel Tadoussac   HOTEL $$
(☑ 418-235-4421, 800-561-0718; www.hoteltadoussac.com; 165 Rue du Bord de l'Eau; r from $179; ⊙ May-Oct; P ⓢ ⚶) Commanding the sweep of Tadoussac's bay, this hotel is winning the location contest, hands down. There's a sense of historic heritage as well; it's been hosting guests since 1870. Functional if not flashy rooms have plush carpets, ceiling fans and river views.

Rates vary largely outside of the July-August high season.

🍴 Eating & Drinking

Café Bohème   CAFE $$
(☑ 418-235-1180; www.lecafeboheme.com; 239 Rue des Pionniers; mains lunch $15-22, dinner $21-31; ⊙ 7am-11pm Jul & Aug, 8am-10pm May, Jun & Sep-Oct; ⓢ ⦿ ⊕) This village hangout

is a prime place to sip an espresso or nitro cold brew and breakfast on fruit and yogurt or crêpes filled with duck confit. Later, choose between such dishes as a baguette stuffed with local lobster and shrimp or a smoked-salmon pancake at lunch, or venison braised with haskap berries or fresh pasta in the evening.

Chez Mathilde
CANADIAN $$$

(☑ 418-235-4443; www.chezmathildebistro.com; 227 Rue des Pionniers; mains $15-30, set meals $50-75; ☺ noon-3pm & 6-11pm Jun-Oct; ☑) The stellar chef at this colorful little house utilizes plenty of local products, from seafood to greens to cheeses, in the short but creative menu.

The innovative dishes are served up alongside a view of the port from the airy patio.

Microbrasserie Tadoussac
CRAFT BEER

(☑ 418-980-4900; www.microtadoussac.com; 145 Rue du Bord de l'Eau; ☺ 11am-11pm daily) Linger over a tasting flight at Tadoussac's microbrewery, where the beers on offer might range from the Pale (Wh)ale to a dry stout to a pilsner. A few snacks – jerky, olives, pizza – are served for when the munchies strike.

ℹ Information

Tourist Information Office (☑ 418-235-4744, 866-235-4744; www.tadoussac.com; 197 Rue des Pionniers; ☺ 9am-5pm daily Jun-Aug, reduced hours Sep-May) Located in the middle of town, with patient staff who can help with accommodations.

ℹ Getting There & Away

Tadoussac can be reached by traveling north through Charlevoix or after circling the Saguenay Fjord.

The 10-minute ferry from Baie Ste Catherine in Charlevoix is free and operates 24 hours a day. The terminal is at the end of Rue du Bateau-Passeur.

Tadoussac is off Rte 138. Intercar (p231) buses connect Tadoussac with Montréal ($114, eight hours) and Québec City ($57, four to 4½ hours) twice a day and run as far northeast as Sept Îles, with connections to Havre St Pierre.

The bus stop is at the Chantmartin Motel (414 Rue du Bateau-Passeur/Rte 138), just above the village.

Les Bergeronnes

The slow pace of the North Shore begins in Les Bergeronnes, and in the nearby community of Les Escoumins, both of which are pleasingly quiet but for a handful of attractions and an excellent campground.

◉ Sights

The Innu community of **Essipit** sits outside of Les Escoumins, 12km northeast of Les Bergeronnes on Rte 138. The Essipit Centre offers whale-watching cruises (Zodiac tours from $59, June to mid-October); blue whales are more likely to be seen in this area. It also offers guided black-bear-viewing experiences (adult/child $30/16, mid-June to mid-September).

Marine Environment Discovery Centre
SCIENCE CENTER

(☑ 418-235-4414; www.pc.gc.ca/en/amnc-nmca/qc/saguenay/Centre-Decouverte-du-Milieu-Marin; 41 Rue des Pilotes, Les Escoumins; adult/child $7.80/free; ☺ 9am-6pm mid-Jun–Aug, to 5pm Fri-Sun Sep–mid-Oct; P ♿) ✿ Sophisticated facilities with interpretive exhibits and a video link with naturalist-divers foraging on the estuary floor. Operated by Parks Canada, the center's staff help visitors observe marine mammals from the shore.

Cap de Bon Désir Interpretation Centre
SCIENCE CENTER

(☑ 418-232-6751; www.pc.gc.ca/en/amnc-nmca/qc/saguenay/Cap-de-Bon-Desir; 13 Chemin du Cap de Bon Désir; adult/child $7.80/free; ☺ 9am-6pm mid-Jun–Aug, 9am-5pm Wed-Sun Sep–mid-Oct; P ♿) ✿ Part science center, part park, this site managed by Parks Canada consists of nature trails, observation platforms that look out onto the (hopefully) whale-studded St Lawrence and a historic lighthouse. Check the website or call ahead to learn about different lectures and activities (and to confirm if they're available in English).

Centre Archéo Topo
MUSEUM

(☑ 418-232-6286; www.archeotopo.com; 498 Rue de la Mer; adult/child $8/4; ☺ 9am-5pm Jun–mid-Oct, to 8pm Jul & Aug; P ♿) This research and exhibition center is dedicated to archaeological findings along the North Shore. Outside, trails lead down to the beach and offer some fantastic views over the Côte-Nord sea cliffs.

🛏 Sleeping

Camping Paradis Marin CAMPGROUND $
(☑ 418-232-6237; www.campingparadismarin.
com; 4 Chemin Émile Boulianne; campsites/
chalets from $35/100; ☺ May-Oct; ℗) You can
hear whales breathing from your tent, rent
kayaks ($10 per day) or arrange kayak tours
($67) here. It's off Rte 138 northeast of Les
Bergeronnes.

Essipit Centre ACCOMMODATION SERVICES $$
(☑ 418-233-2266; 888-868-6666; http://vacances
essipit.com/en; 46 Rue de la Réserve, Essipit;
camping/cottages/condos from $31/149/198;
℗ ✳ 🛜) The Essipit Centre can put you
up in campgrounds, cottages and comfort-
ably appointed seaside condos near Les
Escoumins. Rates drop outside of July and
August.

L'Anse St Jean

A little village with a lot going on in its
ateliers, L'Anse St Jean is the first stop on
the south side of the fjord. There's a pleas-
ant mix here of hippie-style self-exiles and
families looking for a rustic escape, not to
mention a good infrastructure for outdoor
activities.

If you drive west along the fjord,
you'll find marvelous views at **L'Anse de
Tabatière**, where there's also an informa-
tion kiosk (mid-May to October) for Parc
National du Fjord-du-Saguenay (p301). It's
about 5km from the covered bridge off Rue
du Faubourg; follow Chemin St Thomas to
Chemin de l'Anse.

🏃 Activities

Fjord en Kayak KAYAKING
(☑ 418-272-3024, 866-725-2925; www.fjord-en-
kayak.ca; 359 Rue St-Jean-Baptiste; 3hr/1-day
tours $63/139; ☺ mid-May–mid-Oct; 🖐) 🎐 Op-
erates well-regarded paddling excursions
ranging from two-hour family outings to
multiday adventures. The outfit also rents
bikes, kayaks, and stand-up paddleboards,
and can organize sailing-kayaking combo
packages.

**Navettes Maritimes
du Fjord** BOATING
(☑ 800-363-7248, 418-543-7630; www.navettes
dufjord.com; 355 Rue St-Jean-Baptiste; fjord cruise
adult/child from $59/30; ☺ Jun–mid-Oct; 🖐)
This efficient tour company runs excellent
trips up the Saguenay Fjord. Rates vary

depending on where you're going and the
length of your excursion; for $155 you can
get a one-week 'Passe-Fjord,' which lets you
hop on and off the boats at your leisure (in
July and August). Some boats also transport
bicycles.

**Centre Équestre
des Plateaux** HORSEBACK RIDING
(Equestrian Center; ☑ 418-272-3231; www.cedp.ca;
34 Chemin des Plateaux; 3hr tours $85; 🖐) Offers
trail rides for riders from beginners and up,
and has a horse-drawn sleigh for winter fun.
It's signposted up the hill from Rue St-Jean-
Baptiste.

🛏 Sleeping & Eating

Chalets du Fjord INN $$
(☑ 800-561-8060, 418-272-3430; www.chalets-
sur-le-fjord.com; 354 Rue St-Jean-Baptiste; studios/
condos/chalets from $119/170/194; ℗ 🛜 ♨)
Accommodations ranging from studios to
condos to hillside cabins of varying sizes
and amenities. It overlooks the marina and
has its own quality restaurant, **Chez Mon-
tagner**, serving salads, pizzas and seafood
(mains $18 to $27). Book well in advance.

Auberge des Cévennes INN $$
(☑ 418-272-3180, 877-272-3180; www.auberge-
des-cevennes.qc.ca; 294 Rue St-Jean-Baptiste; r
from $85-110; ℗ 🛜) You can hear the river
gurgling across the street at this lovely
inn, overlooking the covered bridge. The
interior is old-school, even a little grand-
ma's cottage-y, but the decor fits the lo-
cation, and the owners are as friendly as
anything. A buffet breakfast is available
(adult/child $7/5); rooms have microwaves
and refrigerators if you prefer to make
your own.

Bistro de L'Anse PUB FOOD $$
(☑ 418-272-4222; www.bistrodelanse.com; 319
Rue St-Jean-Baptiste; mains $15-20; ☺ noon-
midnight late Jun-Aug, from 5pm mid-May–late Jun
& Sep–mid-Oct) Popular local hub where you
can tuck into poutines, salads and burgers
on the verandah and catch live music on
the weekends. Try a beer from the owners'
nearby nano-brewery, **Microbrasserie La
Chasse-Pinte**.

ℹ Getting There & Away

L'Anse St Jean is 75km northwest of Saint
Siméon, in the Charlevoix region, via Hwy 170.
The village is about 7km from the Hwy 170
turnoff.

Saguenay

This regional center is a pleasant-enough place to take care of errands before returning to the Saguenay wilds. The site of a 1676 fur-trading post, it was founded as late as 1842, and became a world pulp-and-paper capital in the early 20th century. It looks rather industrial from the approach roads, but downtown buzzes with students from the town's university and Cégep (pre-university college).

Saguenay is made up of the boroughs Chicoutimi (the largest), Jonquière and La Baie.

⊙ Sights

La Pulperie   MUSEUM
(☑418-698-3100; www.pulperie.com; 300 Rue Dubuc, Chicoutimi; adult/child $14.50/7; ⊙9am-6pm daily mid-Jun–Aug, 10am-4pm Wed-Sun Sep–mid-Jun; P ♿) Until the 1920s, this was Canada's biggest pulp mill. Even the paper for the *New York Times* came from Chicoutimi pulp. Exhibits and guided tours explain the mill's history and its pivotal role in the development of a town that grew from 708 people in 1899 to 4255 in 1929. Also inside the building is the **House of Arthur Villeneuve**, former residence of a barber-turned-artist, who painted the entire structure inside and out in his bright, folk style.

Musee du Fjord   MUSEUM
(☑418-697-5077; http://museedufjord.com; 3346 Blvd de la Grande-Baie Sud, La Baie; adult/child $16/9; ⊙9am-6pm mid-Jun–Aug, 9am-4:30pm Tue-Fri, 1-5pm Sat & Sun Sep–mid-Jun; P ♿) ♪ Half museum, half aquarium, the Musee du Fjord helps visitors understand the unique ecosystem of the Saguenay Fjord and the history of the region. It's a friendly, informative spot, but unless you have kids in tow, we recommend skipping the corny multimedia theater introduction.

✕ Eating

★La Parizza   PIZZA $$
(☑418-973-9732; https://lp.pizza; 337 Rue Racine E, Chicoutimi; pizzas $17-27; ⊙4pm-midnight Tue & Wed, to 3am Thu-Sat; ♪) Pizza, objectively, is awesome. The Québec obsession with *terroir* ingredients is also awesome. When these two culinary concepts collide, you get La Parizza, which features such brilliant creations as Margherita pizza served with a veritable charcuterie of lo-

cal meats; pizza topped with wild shrimp, scallops and smoked salmon; and a pie containing spinach, goat's cheese, pancetta and walnuts.

❶ Information

Tourist Office (☑418-698-3157, 800-463-6565; http://tourisme.saguenay.ca; 295 Rue Racine E, Chicoutimi; ⊙8:30am-4:30pm Mon-Thu, to 8pm Fri, 10am-4pm Sat & Sun) Offers helpful bookings in the greater fjord region.

❶ Getting There & Away

Located about 16km from downtown Chicoutimi, **Saguenay-Bagotville Airport** (YBG; ☑418-677-2651; http://aeroport.saguenay.ca; 7000 Chemin de l'Aéroport, La Baie) offers flights to Montréal and Baie Comeau on Air Canada Express and Pascan.

Intercar (☑reservations 800-806-2167, station 418-543-1403; https://intercar.ca; 55 Rue Racine E, Chicoutimi) buses connect three to four times daily to Québec City ($52, 2½ hours) and Montréal ($102, six hours) and daily to Tadoussac ($28, 1½ hours).

La Société de Transport du Saguenay (STS; ☑418-545-2487; https://sts.saguenay.ca; $3.50; ⊙6am-midnight Mon-Fri, 6:30am-7pm Sat, 7:30am-6:30pm Sun) operates bus service in the Saguenay region, primarily around Chicoutimi and between Chicoutimi, La Baie and Jonquière.

Lac St Jean

The open flats between Saguenay and Lac St Jean are not as immediately compelling as the cliff-straddled ruggedness of the nearby fjord, but upon reaching Lac St Jean's titular lake, you'll find a subtle beauty in this wide open space, where the meeting of sky and water is interrupted only by pale wooden houses and shining church spires. The area claims to be the province's blueberry and *tourtière* (meat pie) capital, as well as the heartland of Québec nationalism.

⊙ Sights & Activities

Musée Amérindien de Mashteuiatsh   MUSEUM
(☑418-275-4842; www.cultureilnu.ca; 1787 Rue Amishk, Mashteuiatsh; adult/child $13/9; ⊙9am-5pm daily mid-May–mid-Oct, closed Mon & Sun mid-Oct–mid-May; P) In an Indigenous community on the lakeshore north of Roberval,

this museum features good exhibits on the area's Pekuakamiulnuatsh group.

Village Historique Val Jalbert HISTORIC SITE
(☑ 418-275-3132; www.valjalbert.com; 95 Rue St-Georges, Chambord; adult/child $29/15; ⏱ 9am-6pm late Jun-late Aug, 10am-5pm late May-late Jun & late Aug–mid-Oct) A ghost town that was inhabited from 1901 until a few years after the pulp mill closed in 1927. There's a trolleybus with running commentary from one of the zealous, costume-wearing guides, and a pleasant restaurant (set meal adult/child $49/22) in the old mill by the dramatic waterfall. This peaceful spot also has a campground (sites $30 to $50) and cabins ($80).

Parc National de la Pointe-Taillon PARK
(☑ 418-347-5371; www.sepaq.com/pq/pta; 835 Rang 3 W, Saint-Henri-de-Taillon; adult/child $8.75/free; ⏱ Jun–mid-Oct; P ♿) ⚑ Want to get *into* the lake? On the north side of Lac St Jean, this provincial park has sandy lakeside beaches where you can swim, as well as rent canoes, kayaks and stand-up paddleboards. Cyclists can explore 45km of bike paths along the lake; bike rentals are available. You can camp (sites from $24) or stay in 'ready-to-camp' tents (from $92) or cabins (from $104) by the shore as well.

Véloroute des Bleuets CYCLING
(Blueberry Bike Trail; https://veloroutedesbleuets.com/en) The 256km of cycling trails around the lake combine to form the Blueberry Bike Trail, and nearly every town along the way has facilities to make the trip easier: rental and repair shops, B&Bs that cater to cyclists and rest areas. For maps, suggested itineraries and a list of helpful stops, visit the **Maison du Vélo** (Bicycle Tourism Information Center; ☑ 418-668-4541; https://veloroutedesbleuets.com/en; 1692 Ave du Pont N, Alma; ⏱ 8am-5:30pm mid-Jun–Aug) in Alma.

🛏 Sleeping & Eating

Auberge Île du Repos CAMPGROUND, HOSTEL $
(☑ 418-347-5649; www.iledurepos.com; 105 Chemin de l'Île du Repos, Péribonka; campsites/dm/r from $27/38/80; P) Taking up an entire little island off Péribonka, near Parc National de la Pointe Taillon, this lodging features dorms, kitchen facilities, private chalet rooms, camping, a cafe-bar, a beach with all kinds of water sports, croquet and volleyball. You're not too close to town here, so

WORTH A TRIP

PARC NATIONAL DU FJORD-DU-SAGUENAY

This **park** (www.sepaq.com/pq/sag; adult/child $8.75/free) protects a wide swath of land along the banks of the Saguenay Fjord; the water itself is within Parc Marin du Saguenay–St-Laurent. The park is divided into several sectors. The Baie-Éternité sector at Rivière Éternité, where the park's headquarters is located, has a campground, visitor center and a *via ferrata*, a guided climbing experience with several different routes for differing ability levels (adults $49 to $89).

Contact the Rivière Éternité–based park information **office** (Parc National du Fjord-du-Saguenay; ☑ 418-272-1556; www.sepaq.com/pq/sag; 91 Rue Notre Dame; ⏱ 9am-4pm Mon-Fri, from 8:30am Sat & Sun mid-May–late June, 8am-9pm daily late Jun–mid-Oct, 9am-4pm daily mid-late Oct) about trips, trails, sea kayaking, sailing, Zodiac outings and numerous guided activities.

it helps to have a car (or bicycle) to come and go.

La Bonne Cuisine de Roberval DINER $
(☑ 418-275-6605; https://labonnecuisine.ca; 562 Blvd Marcotte/Rte 169, Roberval; mains $5-15; ⏱ 4am-midnight; P) This traditional roadside diner in a little house on the highway serves local Québec classics, from breakfasts of eggs, meat and beans, to smoked meat, poutine and *tourtière* (meat pie). In the summer, there's blueberry pie. And in case you're circling the lake and need a coffee before dawn, it opens at 4am.

Ste Rose du Nord

On the Saguenay River's quieter north side, Ste Rose du Nord is a member of the Association of the Most Beautiful Villages of Québec. Wander beneath the purple cliffs to the quay, with the fjord beyond, and it's easy to see why.

You can pitch your tent on a hill at **Camping Descente des Femmes** (☑ 418-675-2581; http://campingsaguenay.com; 154 Rue de la Montagne; campsites $24-32; ⏱ Jun-Sep; P) and wake up to a breathtaking view over the village and onto the fjord.

QUÉBEC STE ROSE DU NORD

Signposted off Rte 172 between Ste-Fulgence and Ste-Anne du Rose, **Pourvoirie du Cap au Leste** (☑ 418-675-2000; www.capau leste.com; 551 Chemin du Cap à l'Est; r $120-160, ste $180-220; P❋🛜) is worth the bumpy 7km ride for its dramatic views over a large stretch of the fjord. The frugal but charming cabins have wood burners and balconies, and the restaurant (set meals from $30) serves superb regional cuisine. Hiking, canoeing, kayaking and climbing can be organized.

SOUTH SHORE

It's tempting to rush through the South Shore, which includes the Chaudière-Apalaches and Bas St-Laurent regions, en route to the Gaspé Peninsula. However, the area has a wonderfully eclectic mix of attractions, from haunting Grosse Île to cool Rivière du Loup. Other stops include a major woodcarving center, an island once used as a smugglers' stash and museums devoted to a *Titanic*-like tragedy, Basque whalers and accordions.

Throughout the region, you have spectacular views across the island-dotted St Lawrence to the undulating North Shore. Hwy 20 is fastest, but Rte 132 is more scenic and goes through the heart of numerous riverside villages.

Grosse Île

The first stop outside Québec City's urban sprawl is one of the region's most interesting. Grosse Île served as a major quarantine station for European immigrants in the 19th and early 20th centuries. A tour of the **historic site** (☑ 418-234-8841, 888-773-8888; www.pc.gc.ca/en/lhn-nhs/qc/grosseile; adult/child $17.60/free; ☉ daily Jul & Aug, Wed-Sun May-Jun & Sep-Oct) sheds light on this little-known aspect of North American history. Wear warm clothing (it can be chilly on the water) and comfortable shoes for exploring the island.

Boat tours to Grosse Île depart from Berthier-sur-Mer marina, on Rte 132 (also accessible via Hwy 20), 55km northeast of Québec City and 15km west of Montmagny.

Croisières AML (☑ 855-268-9090; www.croisieresaml.com; 110 Rue de la Marina, Berthier-sur-Mer; tours adult/child $69/30) offers a narrated return cruise to Grosse Île.

Montmagny

Montmagny, the first town of any size east of Lévis, exemplifies the laid-back, family-oriented attitude that seems to permeate the South Shore. Rue St-Jean-Baptiste E is as pretty a main street as you'll find anywhere in Québec. The town is also the departure point for **ferries** (☑ 877-562-6560; www.traversiers.com; 45 Ave du Quai; free; ☉ Apr-Dec) **FREE** to nearby Île aux Grues, a small island where you can stroll or cycle and visit a local cheesemaker.

St Jean Port Joli

This pretty town became known as a center of craftsmanship in the 1930s, a reputation it works hard to keep. Riverside Parc des Trois Berets, named after the three beret-wearing brothers, Médard, Andre and Jean-Julien Bourgault, who launched the town as a woodcarving capital, is the venue for a biennial summer **sculpture festival**.

There are scores of ateliers, boutiques and roadside pieces of art, covered by a free map available from the tourist office.

Philippe Aubert de Gaspé, author of *Les Anciens Canadiens*, is buried in the 18th-century **church**.

◎ Sights

Musée de la Mémoire Vivante   MUSEUM
(Museum of Living Memory; ☑ 418-358-0518; www.memoirevivante.org; 710 Ave de Gaspé W; adult/child $10/4; ☉ 9am-6pm Jul & Aug, 10am-5pm Jun & Sep–mid-Oct, 10am-5pm Sun-Fri Mar-May & mid-Oct–Dec, 10am-5pm Mon-Fri Jan & Feb; P) ✆ This fascinating museum explores the culture of Québec (particularly St Jean Port Joli) via exhibits sourced from thousands of community contributions and oral history interviews. It's most interesting for French-speakers, since most recordings and videos are presented only in French; you may want to call ahead to see if any English-speaking staff can assist you when you visit.

Musée Maritime du Québec   MUSEUM
(☑ 418-247-5001; www.mmq.qc.ca; 55 Chemin des Pionniers E, L'Islet; adult/child $14/8; ☉ 9am-6pm Jul & Aug, 10am-5pm Jun, 10am-4pm Tue-Sun Sep–mid-Oct, 10am-4pm Wed-Sun Mar-May & mid-Oct–mid-Dec; P👪) This large, modern facility explores the deep historical and cultural ties this area has to shipbuilding

and the sea. You can listen to interesting video interviews with river pilots and others who've made their livings on the water. There's a life-size ship to board and lots of hands-on activities that should please youngsters. It's 13km south of St Jean Port Joli.

🛏 Sleeping & Eating

Camping de la Demi-Lieue CAMPGROUND $
(☑800-463-9558, 418-598-6108; www.camping union.com/en/saint-jean-port-joli-demi; 598 Ave du Gaspé E/Rte 132 E; campsites from $34, cottages from $129; ☉May-Sep; @🐾) Huge but well-equipped and closer to town than other campgrounds.

La Maison de l'Ermitage B&B $$
(☑877-598-7553, 418-598-7553; www.maison ermitage.com; 56 Rue de l'Ermitage; r incl breakfast from $100, without bath from $80; P❄🐾) This eye-catching house with red-and-white towers hides simple, artfully decorated rooms inside. The friendly alpacas in the backyard are popular with kids, and the friendly owners are happy to suggest things to do nearby.

Café Bonté Divine CAFE $
(☑418-598-3330; http://cafebontedivine.com; 2 Chemin du Roy E; pastries $3-5; ☉7am-6pm Mon-Fri, from 8am Sat & Sun; 🐾) This coffeehouse in the town center is a laid-back locale for sipping espressos and Americanos amid furnishings that include an antique stove and old trunks. The cafe roasts its own beans and serves scones, other pastries and a few sandwiches to accompany your caffeine fix. There's a lengthy selection of teas, plus hot chocolates as well.

La Roche à Veillon QUÉBÉCOIS $$
(☑418-598-3061; www.rocheaveillon.com; 547 Ave de Gaspé E/Rte 132 E; mains $15-25; ☉8am-9pm Thu-Sun mid-late May, 8am-9pm daily Jun–mid-Oct; P🐾) Renowned for huge portions of local classics such as pork ragout, *cipâte* (meat pie) and *chiard* (an Acadain beef stew), and for its adjacent theater with productions (in French only) from late June through August.

🍷 Drinking & Nightlife

Microbrasserie Ras L'Bock MICROBREWERY
(☑418-358-0886; www.raslbock.com; 250 Rue du Quai; ☉4pm-midnight Wed, to 3am Thu & Fri, noon-3am Sat, to 10pm Sun) Live music, strong beer, an outdoor garden where the cool kids hang out and a laid-back vibe that's not afraid to throw down and party – this beloved microbrewery is a South Shore winner.

ℹ Information

Tourist Office (☑418-598-3747; 20 Ave de Gaspé W; ☉9am-7pm late Jun–mid-Oct) Provides maps of town and can connect you to local ateliers.

ℹ Getting There & Away

Orléans Express buses to/from Québec City stop at 704 Rte de l'Église, a gas station near the intersection of Autoroute 20.

Rivière du Loup

Its curious name ('the Wolf River') refers either to seals (known in French as *loups de mer*, or sea wolves), an Amerindian group or a 17th-century French ship, but one thing is certain: Rivière du Loup is a town of some distinction. Its key position on the fur and postal routes between the Maritimes and the St Lawrence made it the main town in eastern Québec during the 19th century. Formerly an English-speaking community, it was planned according to the British model, with open spaces in front of grand buildings such as the Gothic silver-roofed St Patrice church. Having declined in the early 20th century, it's booming again, with an influx of urban runaways and graduates returning to their beautiful birthplace.

◉ Sights

Parc des Chutes PARK
(Rue de la Chute; P🚻) ✎ You can take a short stroll to (or a short but steep hike above) the 30m waterfalls that power a small hydro-electric power station in the pretty Parc des Chutes, a few minutes' walk from downtown at the end of Rue Frontenac. If you're lucky, on a sunny afternoon, a photogenic rainbow may shimmer across the falls.

Parc de la Croix PARK
A short drive into the hilly part of town leads to tiny Parc de la Croix, where an illuminated cross guards a stunning view across the city and the river.

Musée du Bas-St-Laurent MUSEUM
(☑418-862-7547; www.mbsl.qc.ca; 300 Rue St-Pierre; adult/student $7/5; ☉9am-5pm daily Jun-Aug, from 1pm Tue-Sun Sep-May) The lively

WORTH A TRIP

LE TÉMIS

Le Témis is the name affectionately given to a region concentrated around its main geographical feature, the 40km-long **Lac Témiscouata**. The sleepy, little-explored area is perfect for a Sunday drive.

Busy Hwy 85 passes mills and farms cradled between the low-lying hills, giving a foretaste of New Brunswick, before you detour onto meandering lakeside secondary roads. **St Louis du Ha! Ha!** possibly owes its odd name to an archaic French word for something unexpected, or to the exclamation of wonder the area's colonizers uttered upon seeing such beauty. We favor another explanation: the name comes from a 15th-century French expression for 'dead end'.

In the town of **Cabano**, there are motels as well as some pleasant restaurants on the waterfront; you can stop for a snack at **Boulangerie Tentations Gourmandes** (755a Rue Commerciale N). **Fort Ingall** is a reconstructed 1839 British fort established to keep out Americans who had set their sights on the area. The six buildings include the blockhouse with its 'whipping horse'.

The hourly ferry ride between Notre Dame du Lac and St Juste du Lac is a fine summer diversion, and even as you drive the waterfront roads, there are good views of the slender lake through the trees.

On the northeast side of the lake in Auclair, you can taste the country's first alcoholic drinks made from a maple-sap base at *économusée* **Domaine Acer**. Made on-site, the aperitifs' name comes from *acer*, the Latin word for maple. The gift shop also sells maple jelly, which is delicious on toast. Tours take in the aging cellars and demonstrate how maple sap is turned into syrup. There are English signs throughout the facility and some guides speak a little English.

Also on the north shore of the lake is a provincial park, **Parc National du Lac-Témiscouata**, which has eight trails totaling some 35km of hiking opportunities, as well as canoe, kayak, and stand-up paddleboard rentals.

Le Témis is about a 45-minute drive from Rivière du Loup along Hwy 85. The more scenic Rte 293 will also take you to the lake from Trois Pistoles in just under an hour.

Musée du Bas-St-Laurent has a collection of contemporary Québec art, but the main event is the 200,000 vintage photos of the local area, used in thematic, interactive exhibits that explore life on the St Lawrence. At the time of research, the museum was revamping its permanent exhibits; stay tuned.

🏃 Activities

Société Duvetnor CRUISE
(☑ 418-867-1660; www.duvetnor.com; 200 Rue Hayward) 🛥 Offshore from Rivière du Loup, a series of protected islands sport bird sanctuaries and provide habitat for other wildlife. The nonprofit group Société Duvetnor offers bird-watching and nature excursions to the islands from June through September. Sighting belugas is common. There are 45km of trails on the largest island, **l'Île aux Lièvres**, and accommodations, including a campground.

Petit Témis Interprovincial Linear Park CYCLING, WALKING
(☑ 418-868-1869; www.petit-temis.ca) The first cycling path to link two Canadian provinces,

the Petit Témis Interprovincial Linear Park is a scenic bike and walking trail, mainly flat, which runs along an old train track for 135km to Edmundston, New Brunswick. The tourist office has maps and rents bikes (late June through early October).

🛏 Sleeping & Eating

Auberge Internationale HOSTEL $
(☑ 418-862-7566; www.aubergerdl.ca; 46 Rue de l'Hôtel de Ville; dm/r incl breakfast from $30/68; 🅿 @ 🛜) This central HI hostel in an old house has small dorms with attached bathrooms, as well as private rooms, some with their own showers. The long-term staff create a welcoming atmosphere, and there's a good communal vibe going on.

Auberge de la Pointe RESORT $$
(☑ 800-463-1222, 418-862-3514; www.auberge delapointe.com; 10 Blvd Cartier; r $105-205, ste from $355; ☉ May-Oct; 🅿 ❄ 🛜 🏊) This enormous complex, located a short drive from the city center, consists of several pavilions overlooking a lovely bend of the St Law-

rence. The rooms are brilliantly designed, achieving a nice balance between stripped-down-cool and warm coziness, and there's a spa, restaurant, bar and even a theater on the grounds.

★ **L'Innocent** CAFE $
(☑ 418-862-1937; 460 Rue Lafontaine; mains $10-15; ☺ 11am-4pm Tue, to 9pm Wed-Fri, 8am-9pm Sat, to 4pm Sun; ☑) The hippest cafe around serves great-value daily specials to a ska/indie/name-your-cool-music-genre-here soundtrack. It's the best place in town to meet locals or hang out over a coffee.

L'Estaminet PUB FOOD $$
(☑ 418-867-4517; www.restopubestaminet.com; 299 Rue Lafontaine; mains $15-32; ☺ 7am-11pm Mon-Wed, to midnight Thu, to 1am Fri, 8am-1am Sat, to 11pm Sun) Feast on hearty pub grub, from pizzas to burgers to pastas, in this *bistro du monde* with 150 types of beer. Give the bison burger a whirl. It also serves substantial (and delicious) breakfasts and keeps your coffee cup full when you're lingering in the morning.

Microbrasserie
Aux Fous Brassant CRAFT BEER
(☑ 418-605-1644; www.auxfousbrassant.com; 262 Rue Lafontaine; ☺ 3pm-1am Wed-Fri, from 1pm Sat & Sun) With five beers always on offer, and up to a dozen more in rotation, you always have something new to try at this microbrewery with a sidewalk terrace and occasional music events. Pâtés, cheeses and bruschetta are some of the beer-friendly snacks that can accompany your brews.

❶ Information

Tourist Office (☑ 418-862-1981, 888-825-1981; www.tourismeriviereduloup.ca; 189 Blvd de l'Hôtel de Ville; ☺ 8:30am-6pm late Jun–mid-Jul, to 7pm mid-Jul–Aug, 8:30am-4:30pm Mon-Fri, 11am-4pm Sat & Sun Sep, 8:30am-4:30pm Mon-Fri Oct-late Jun; ☎) Has internet access and a free Old Town walking map.

❶ Getting There & Away

A **ferry** (☑ 418-862-5094; www.traverserdl.com; 199 Rue Hayward; round-trip adult/child $24/16.30; ☺ mid-Apr–Dec) runs between Rivière du Loup marina and St-Siméon in Charlevoix.

Hwy 20 (exit 503), Rte 132 and Hwy 85 lead directly into Rivière du Loup.

Orléans Express buses to Québec City and Rimouski stop at the **bus station** (317 Blvd de l'Hôtel de Ville). Transfer at Rimouski for New Brunswick.

Rivière du Loup is linked by **VIA Rail** (☑ 888-842-7245; www.viarail.ca; 615 Rue Lafontaine) three times a week to Québec City and Halifax. The station is open only when the trains arrive, in the middle of the night.

Île Verte

For a quick island escape, take the 30-minute ferry to Île Verte. Primarily a summer holiday destination, the island has a permanent population of about 1200. It's popular for birding, cycling, whale-watching and, in the winter, ice-fishing.

By the lighthouse, **Les Maisons du Phare** (☑ 418-898-2730; http://phareileverte.com; 2802 Chemin du Phare; s/d incl breakfast $110/140; ☺ May-Oct; ☎) has colorful, cozy rooms.

Ferries (☑ 418-898-2843; www.traversiers.com; 1804 du Quai d'En Bas, Notre-Dame-des-Sept-Douleurs; one-way adult/car $6.90/41.45; ☺ May–mid-Nov) run between the island and Notre-Dame-des-Sept-Douleurs two to five times a day.

Trois Pistoles

You'll notice, upon entering this village, that Francophone Québec seems to have shifted to an outpost of Basque nationalism; every other business name seems to refer to local Basque heritage. The Basques arrived as whalers, who were the first Europeans after the Vikings to navigate the St Lawrence, predating Jacques Cartier. The main reason for stopping here is exploration of the St Lawrence; the folks at **Coop Kayak des Îles** (☑ 418-851-4637; www.kayaksdesiles.com; 60 Ave du Parc; 3hr tours from $55; ☺ Jun-Sep) ☞ run good-value sea-kayaking expeditions onto the water.

◉ Sights

Île-aux-Basques ISLAND
(☑ 418-851-1202; www.provancher.org; adult/child $30.50/17.25; ☺ Jun-Aug) ☞ This wooded speck of Arcadian prettiness is dotted with 16th-century Basque ovens, has 2km of trails and is home to a bird refuge. Three-hour guided tours are offered during the summer – this is the only means of accessing the island.

⌂ Sleeping

Camping & Motel des Flots
Bleus Sur Mer CAMPGROUND $
(☑ 418-851-3583; www.flotsbleus.ca; Rte 132; tent & RV sites $30, r $71-87; ☺ May–mid-Oct; ☑☎)

This small, quiet campground, 7km west of Trois Pistoles, includes a very bare-bones motel.

La Rose des Vents B&B $$
(📞 418-851-4926; www.gitelarosedesvents.com; 80 2e Rang W; r incl breakfast $115; 🅿️ @ 🛜) This lovely old place in the countryside south of town is easily recognizable by its modified roofline. There's a breakfast room with huge windows gazing at the North Shore and simple rooms with big, soft beds for those who need a break from the road.

Parc National du Bic

As you approach the Gaspé Peninsula, the cloud banks begin to roll in off the St Lawrence and percolate into a series of darkly forested inlets, islets and crescent bays. A 33-sq-km chunk of this land is protected as **Parc National du Bic** (📞 418-736-5035; www.sepaq.com/pq/bic; 3382 Rte 132; adult/child $8.75/free; ☺ year-round). There's an excellent interpretation center here, and activities on offer, most of which can be organized by the helpful staff, include hiking, mountain biking, sea kayaking, guided walks, wildlife observation, snowshoeing and Nordic skiing. The two-hour-return trail to **Champlain Peak** (346m) rewards with views across to Îlet au Flacon; the park runs a shuttle here (late June to mid-August, round-trip $9.25).

Rimouski

Although Rimouski isn't as immediately charming as some of Québec's more postcard-perfect towns, it's a prosperous, energetic regional hub, with a busy port, a growing high-tech and maritime-sciences sector, and many of the region's corporate headquarters. All this activity means good restaurants, interesting museums and a healthy number of students.

◉ Sights & Activities

Île St-Barnabé ISLAND
(📞 418-723-2280; www.ilestbarnabe.com; adult/child $25/15; ☺ departures every 30min 9am-2:30pm, returns every 30min 10:15am-6:15pm Jun-Sep) 🏄 A quiet, forested chunk of sylvan loveliness, cut through with gentle trails, surrounded by lapping, stone-and-sand beaches and inhabited by blue herons and seals, Île St-Barnabé is about 20 minutes (and a world of activity) away from Ri-

mouski. Sturdy inflatable boats depart from the Rimouski marina. The tourist office can provide more details about the island and these excursions.

Empress of Ireland Museum MUSEUM
(📞 418-724-6214; www.shmp.qc.ca; 1000 Rue du Phare; museum only adult/child $10/6.50; ☺ 9am-6pm Jun–mid-Oct, to 5pm Thu-Sun Mar-May; 🅿️ ♿) Narrates the 1914 *Empress of Ireland* tragedy, the worst disaster in maritime history after the *Titanic* – all but forgotten with the outbreak of WWI two months later. In the 14 minutes it took for the ship to disappear into the St Lawrence near Rimouski after colliding with a Norwegian collier, 1012 people lost their lives. Through a film and artifacts recovered from the vessel, the exhibition details life on the ship, backgrounds of its passengers, and the wreck itself.

Le Canyon des Portes de l'Enfer HIKING
(📞 418-735-6063; http://canyonportesenfer.qc.ca; 1280 Chemin Duchénier, St-Narcisse-de-Rimouski; adult/child $14.50/7.50; ☺ mid-May–mid-Oct; ♿) 🏄 For hiking, mountain biking and a view of a canyon and waterfalls from the province's highest suspended bridge (63m), head to Le Canyon des Portes de l'Enfer (Hell's Gate Canyon), near St-Narcisse-de-Rimouski, 30km south of town along Rte 232.

🛏️ Sleeping & Eating

Auberge de l'Évêché INN $$
(📞 866-623-5411, 418-723-5411; www.auberge deleveche.com; 37 Rue de l'Évêché W; r incl breakfast $99-120; 🅿️ 🛜) In a 1909 home near the city center, the eight rooms in this inn have TVs and are attractively decorated with vintage photos. There's a general aged-but-not-chintzy vibe.

Hôtel Rimouski HOTEL $$
(📞 418-725-5000; www.hotelrimouski.com; 225 Blvd René-Lepage E; r from $129, ste from $149; 🅿️ ❄️ @ 🛜 🏊) With a genteel elegance and a slightly faded regal demeanor, this grande dame of Rimouski has neat rooms, most with views of the boardwalk and water across the street. It's big with business travelers for the on-site convention center, and families for the super-fast, super-fun water slide and indoor pool.

★ La Brûlerie d'Ici CAFE $
(📞 418-723-3424; www.bruleriedici.com; 91 Rue St-Germain W; sandwiches $6-10; ☺ 7am-9pm Mon-Fri, from 8am Sat & Sun; 🛜 ♿) This hip hangout with complimentary wi-fi offers

Guatemalan and Ethiopian coffees and light bites from sandwiches to bagels to banana bread.

Le Crêpe Chignon CAFE $

(☑ 418-724-0400; www.crepechignonrimouski.com; 140 Ave de la Cathédrale; mains $9-15; ⊗ 7am-9pm Mon & Tue, to 10pm Wed & Thu, to 11pm Fri, 8am-10pm Sat, to 9pm Sun; 🛜 🖗) This bright light on the Rimouski dining scene serves delicious savory and sweet crêpes. You can choose your own fillings or opt for favorites like 'C'est La Mienne,' filled with cranberries, apples, cinnamon and cheddar cheese. In a cozy house downtown, decorated with local art, this *crêperie* is well-loved by both locals and visitors, so expect a wait.

Les Complices QUÉBÉCOIS $$

(☑ 418-722-0505; www.lescomplices-resto.com; 108 Rue St-Germain E; mains $19-22; ⊗ 7:30am-9pm Tue-Thu, to 10pm Fri, 9am-10pm Sat, to 2pm Sun; 🅿 🖗) The kitchen at Les Complices demonstrates lots of dedication and love for the fish, produce and livestock of the South Shore and the Gaspé Peninsula. Salmon tartare, mussels and *frites*, poutine – this is delicious local fare with a minimum of pretension.

ℹ️ Information

Tourist Office (☑ 800-746-6875, 418-723-2322; http://tourismerimouski.com; 50 Rue St-Germain W; ⊗ 8:30am-8pm Jun-Aug, 8:30am-5:30pm Mon-Fri, 11am-4pm Sat & Sun Sep & Oct, 9am-noon & 1-4:30pm Mon-Fri Nov-May) In the city center, just off Rte 132 at Rue des Marins.

ℹ️ Getting There & Away

BOAT

From May through September, a one-hour **ferry** (☑ 418-725-2725, 800-973-2725; https://traversier.com; 1 Route du Quai; one-way adult/child/car $30/17/50; ⊗ May-Sep) links Rimouski with Forestville on the North Shore.

The **Relais Nordik** (☑ 800-463-0680, 418-723-8787; www.relaisnordik.com; 17 Ave Lebrun; round-trip to Blanc Sablon from $750; ⊗ early Apr–mid-Jan) takes passengers on its weekly cargo ship to Sept Îles, Île d'Anticosti, Havre St Pierre, Natashquan and the Lower North Shore. It departs Rimouski marina on Monday evening and gets to Blanc Sablon by Friday morning. One-way fares start at $340 (fare only, without a cabin) for the full journey. Meals are available on board; mains run from $6 to $20. Round-trip fares between Rimouski and Blanc Sablon including a cabin and meals start at $750 per person. Cars can be taken, although it's extremely costly (fares are calculated according to the weight of the vehicle), and a bicycle is more convenient at the brief stopovers. Reservations are best made months in advance.

BUS

Orléans Express buses leave from the **bus station** (☑ 888-999-3977; www.orleansexpress.com; 90 Rue Léonidas) to Québec City, Rivière du Loup and Gaspé.

CAR

Ride-share agencies like Kangaride (p257) hook up drivers and passengers for locations including Québec City and Montréal.

TRAIN

The VIA Rail **train station** (☑ 888-842-7245; www.viarail.ca; 57 Rue de l'Évêché E) is open only when trains pull in, which is usually after midnight. Trains travel between Montréal and Halifax three times a week in each direction.

GASPÉ PENINSULA

There's nowhere quite like La Gaspésie, a peninsula of pine forests and looming cliffs that pokes into the chilly Gulf of St Lawrence. Somewhere on the road east of Matane, the landscape becomes wilder, the cottages more colorful and precariously positioned along rockier promontories, the winds sharper and more scented with salt, and you realize you have entered, effectively, a Francophone version of the maritime provinces.

A crazy amount of fantastic landscape is packed into this relatively small landmass. There's the famous pierced rock in Percé and endless beaches backed by glacier-patterned cliffs. The mountainous, forested hinterlands, home to the breathtaking Parc National de la Gaspésie, are crossed by few routes, among them the Matapédia Valley drive, the International Appalachian Trail and Rte 198, one of the province's quietest roads.

Outside tourist season (June to mid-September), things seriously wind down, and many attractions, accommodations and restaurants close for the winter.

History

Like the whales that can often be spotted spouting off in the distance, Normans, Bretons, Basques, Portuguese and Channel Islanders were attracted here by rich fishing grounds. English, Scottish and Irish fugitives

Gaspé Peninsula

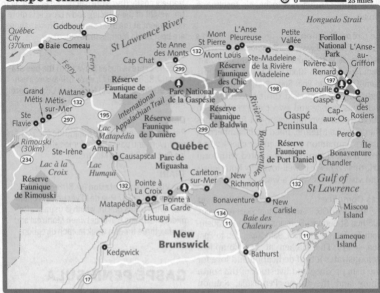

from upheavals such as the Great Famine and American independence settled on the south shore, leaving isolated Anglophone communities. The Acadian red, white and blue flag dotted with a gold star can be seen fluttering above many homes along Rte 132.

Ste Flavie

The sense you're somewhere different becomes evident in Ste Flavie, where the road hugs the coast and...a crowd of odd figures can be seen marching in from the sea? More on this in a sec – just know that this is a relaxing place to pause before tackling the rocky landscape that soon rises above Rte 132.

⊙ Sights

Centre d'Art Marcel Gagnon　　GALLERY
(☑ 866-775-2829, 418-775-2829; www.centredart.
net; 564 Rte de la Mer; ⊙7:30am-9pm May-Sep;
P) **FREE** The star of the town's art trail is the Centre d'Art Marcel Gagnon. Outside, the extraordinary sculpture *Le Grand Rassemblement* (The Great Gathering) has more than 100 stone figures filing out of the St Lawrence. Inside, the gallery displays paintings and sculptures by the eponymous artist along with works by his wife Ghislaine Carrier, his son Guillaume and daughter Is-

abelle. It's a commercial gallery, rather than a museum, a cross between an art exhibition and a souvenir shop.

Vieux Moulin　　MUSEUM
(☑ 418-775-8383; http://vieuxmoulin.qc.ca/wp; 141 Rte de la Mer; museum $2.50; ⊙8am-9pm) This 19th-century windmill offers free tastings of Shakespeare's favorite tipple, mead, and sells a variety of honeys, mustards, butters and other products made with honey. There's also a small museum containing colonial and prehistoric Indigenous artifacts.

🛏 Sleeping & Eating

**Centre d'Art Marcel
Gagnon Auberge**　　INN **$$**
(☑ 866-775-2829, 418-775-2829; www.centredart.
net/chambres; 564 Rte de la Mer; r incl breakfast $99-149; ⊙May-Sep; P🛜) The inn on the 2nd floor above the Centre d'Art Marcel Gagnon has small, understated artistic rooms, decorated with works by Gagnon, with private bathrooms. The more expensive units overlook the river.

**Centre d'Art Marcel Gagnon
Restaurant**　　PUB FOOD **$$**
(☑ 418-775-2829; 564 Rte de la Mer; mains $16-33; ⊙7:30am-9pm May-Sep; P🛗) The restaurant at Centre d'Art Marcel Gagnon dishes up salads, pasta and a plethora of seafood, all

served with a great view. In the morning, you can dig into eggs or crêpes with the same river vista.

Capitaine Homard
SEAFOOD $$$

(☑418-775-8046; http://capitainehomard.com; 180 Rte de la Mer; mains $18-40; ⊙4-10pm May, from 11am Jun-Aug; P ⊛) 'Captain Lobster' has been the area's destination for lobster and local fish since 1968. Its family-friendly dining room overlooking the river serves great seafood beneath a Davy Jones' locker–like ceiling, decorated with buoys, nets, and other nautical gewgaws, and offers internet access, camping (sites $28 to $38) and chalets (from $300 for three-night stays).

ℹ️ Information

Tourisme Gaspésie Office (☑800-463-0323, 418-775-2223; www.tourisme-gaspesie.com/en; 1020 Blvd Jacques-Cartier, Mont Joli; ⊙8am-8pm mid-Jul–mid-Aug, to 7pm late Jun–mid-Jul, 8:30am-7pm mid-Aug–early Sep, to 5:30pm early Sep–mid-Oct, 8:30am-noon & 1-4:30pm Mon-Fri, 9am-4pm Sun mid-Oct–late Jun) This Tourisme Gaspésie office in Mont Joli is the Gaspé Peninsula's main tourist office and can help with information about the region. If you're here in the off-season, pick up the pamphlet listing winter facilities.

Grand Métis

Grand Métis is a speck of a town that's primarily known for its lovingly landscaped gardens. As you drive northeast on Rte 132, the town effectively feels like an extension of Ste Flavie.

The beach towns of **Métis Beach** and **Métis sur Mer** are about 10km east. With big lawns and British names on their street signs and mailboxes, they resemble US towns along the New England seaside. Traditionally a retreat for the Anglophone bourgeoisie, the area has a predominantly English-speaking population.

One of Gaspé's most revered attractions, the **Jardins de Métis** (Reford Gardens; ☑418-775-2222; www.refordgardens.com; 200 Rte 132; adult/child $22/free; ⊙8:30am-6pm Jun, Sep & Oct, to 8pm Jul & Aug; P) 𝒫 comprises more than 90 hectares of immaculately tended gardens boasting 3000 varieties of plants.

Matane

This commercial fishing port isn't as picture-perfect as other villages on the pen-

insula, but it's good for sampling screamingly fresh local seafood, or as a base for day-tripping around the northwestern part of the Gaspé.

🏃 Activities

Sentier International des Appalaches
HIKING

(☑418-562-7885; www.sia-iat.com; 968 Ave du Phare W/Rte 132; 2-day, 1-night treks with meals from $305; ⊙office 9am-5pm Mon-Fri) 𝒫 The International Appalachian Trail extends into the Gaspé, and this office organizes advanced and beginner hikes on part of that route. Many of its treks cut through the wild, rugged Réserve Faunique de Matane. Reserve by phone or email well in advance.

Observation Center
FISHING

(Zec de la Rivière Matane; ☑418-562-0000; http://rivierematane.com; 235 Ave St-Jérôme; adult/child $5/free; ⊙8am-7:45pm Jul & Aug, to 5:45pm Jun & Sep; ⊛) What's there to observe here? Fish. Big ones. Salmon weighing up to 19kg swim up the Rivière Matane to spawn in June, and if you'd like to see them, this observation center at the dam is worth a visit. It also sells permits to fish the 100km river starting right in town.

🛏️ Sleeping & Eating

Camping Rivière
CAMPGROUND $

(☑418-562-3414; www.campingmatane.com; 150 Rte Louis Félix Dionne; tent/RV sites from $29/33; ⊙Jun–mid-Sep; 🐾) This campground southwest of downtown has 124 secluded, private sites among the trees. From town, head south toward Amqui, on Rue Henri Dunant.

Auberge La Seigneurie
INN $$

(☑418-562-0021, 877-783-4466; http://aubergela seigneurie.com; 621 Ave St-Jérôme; r incl breakfast $79-139; ⊙May-Sep) This friendly B&B occupies an impressive property dating from 1919 with attic rooms, a grand piano and a freestanding bath in the 'lovers' room.' The owners are a veritable clearinghouse of local tourism information.

La Fabrique
PUB FOOD $

(☑418-566-4020; www.publafabrique.com; 360 Ave St-Jérôme; mains $12-19; ⊙kitchen 11:30am-10pm, pub to 1:30am; P) Locally sourced, internationally inspired variations on pub grub – including a slate of creative burgers, grilled-cheese sandwiches, and *moules frites* (mussels and fries) – grace the menu at this excellent microbrewery. Pair your

QUÉBEC GRAND MÉTIS

meal with beers like the Gros Chars IPA or the Whiskey Jane scotch ale.

ℹ Information

Tourist Office (☎418-562-1065, 877-762-8263; www.tourismematane.com; 968 Ave du Phare W/Rte 132; ⊘8:30am-7:30pm Jul & Aug, 9am-6pm Jun & Sep–mid-Oct) Based in a lighthouse alongside a maritime museum.

ℹ Getting There & Away

A daily **ferry** (☎877-562-6560, 418-562-2500; www.traversiers.com; 1410 Rue Matane-sur-Mer; adult/child/car $20/12.30/48.80) runs between Matane and the North Shore communities of Baie Comeau and Godbout (adult/child/car $20/12.30/48.80). The ferry terminal is off Rte 132, about 2km west of the town center.

Buses (☎418-562-4856; www.orleansexpress.com; 521 Ave du Phare E/Rte 132) arrive at and depart from the Irving gas station, 1.5km east of the town center. Daily Orléans Express (p231) buses go to Gaspé ($42, five hours) and Rimouski ($29, 1½ hours).

Cap Chat

Cap Chat is a typical Gaspésie village...apart from those 133 windmills beating above its white houses. This major Canadian wind farm produces more than 100 megawatts of electricity. Covering 100km, the dreamlike structures perch on hilltops above the start of the St Lawrence Gulf. Dominating the gang is the world's largest vertical-axis windmill, which, alas, is no longer used.

If you'd like to take a one-hour tour of the area's windmills, contact **Éole Cap-Chat** (☎418-786-5719; 3 Rte du Cap; tours $10; ⊘9:30am-5:30pm Jun-Oct). Look for the signs on Rte 132 just west of Cap Chat. English-language tours are available.

Off Rte 132 east of the bridge at Cap Chat, **Camping au Bord de la Mer** (☎418-786-3013; http://campingauborddelamer.wix.com/campingmer; 173 Rue Notre Dame E; campsites $26-40; ⊘Jun–mid-Oct) is a simple campground that offers river views and access to some windswept, pebbly beaches.

Ste Anne des Monts

A natural stopping point before heading into Parc National de la Gaspésie, as well as a pretty riverside town, Ste Anne des Monts is an ideal location to stock up before heading inland to the wilderness or further

out along the coast. As you travel along the north coast of the peninsula, the cliffs get rockier and the drops more sheer; there are houses in this town that look as precarious on the rocks as a herd of mountain goats.

◉ Sights

Exploramer　　　　　　　　　　AQUARIUM
(☎418-763-2500; www.exploramer.qc.ca; 1 Rue du Quai; adult/child $18/12; ⊘9am-5pm Jun–early Oct; 🅿🚼) ⚓ This aquarium focuses on the marine life of the St Lawrence. There are lots of tactile exhibits – in case you've ever wanted to touch a sea cucumber – and also a maritime museum, sea excursions and a peek into the process of sea harvesting. Little ones might prefer the nautically themed playground outside.

🛏 Sleeping & Eating

★**Auberge Festive**
Sea Shack　　　　　　　　　　HOSTEL $
(☎866-963-2999, 418-763-2999; www.aubergefestive.com; 292 Blvd Perron E; campsites $20, yurts from $30, dm from $38; 🅿@🛜) With a huge common area and beach bar where bands often play, plus dorm beds in cabins, bungalows and yurts, this HI hostel – about 10km east of Ste Anne des Monts – is the sort of lodging that gets people into backpacking. Water-lovers can kayak on the river or just gaze at it from the outdoor hot tub.

Auberge Château
Lamontagne　　　　　　　　　　INN $$
(☎418-763-7666; www.chateaulamontagne.com; 170 1e Ave E; r $99-140, ste & chalets from $175; 🅿🛜) This colorful inn has an expansive river-view terrace and seven refined rooms with polished oak floors in a brick manor overlooking the St Lawrence. Also on the property are three two-room chalets facing the waterfront. The inn's upscale, romantic restaurant highlights local products from land and sea; try the seafood chowder topped with gooey melted cheese.

La Seigneurie des Monts　　　INN $$
(☎418-763-5308; www.bonjourgaspesie.com; 21 1e Ave E; r $134-184; 🅿🛜) This lovably odd inn is all vintage weird (in a good way!): creaky floorboards, 'his and hers' dressing gowns, antiquarian books and chaise lounges. The effect could feel artificial, but it doesn't, especially given the sincere and friendly owners who make it all the more appealing. Also: the breakfast buffet is on point.

EAT & DRINK LIKE A LOCAL: GASPÉSIE MICROBREWERIES

The Gaspé Peninsula is a land of rough seas, strong winds and rugged hikes, populated by people who tend to favor flannel, fleeces and sensible footwear. When that demography mixes with that geography, for some reason, really good beer seems to be the result. Here are some favorite regional microbreweries:

La Fabrique (p309) – Located in Matane, this brewpub dishes out a menu full of rich, hearty goodness, perfect for soaking up its seasonal beers.

Microbrasserie Le Malbord – A brewpub in Ste Anne des Monts that is a delicious pit stop after exploring Parc National de la Gaspésie.

Microbrasserie Cap Gaspé (p314) – This family-owned microbrewery crafts German-style beers in the town of Gaspé.

Pub Pit Caribou (p316) – Out in Percé, this dark little pub is a lovely outpost for the peninsula's most well-known microbrewery.

Le Naufrageur (p318) – In Carleton, there's a superlative amount of brewing skill working wonders at this relatively off-the-radar brewery.

Microbrasserie Le Malbord PUB FOOD $$
(📞418-764-0022; www.lemalbord.com; 178 1e Ave W; mains $8-17; ⊙11am-midnight Jul & Aug, from 3pm Tue-Sat Sep-May; 🅿) Nothing will warm you up after a long day of hiking in Parc National de la Gaspésie like a tall glass of red beer and some bacon and cheese melted over potatoes, or pizza with smoked salmon, or a hearty smoked-meat sandwich. All this – local beer, good grub – plus a busy live music schedule.

ⓘ Information

Tourist Bureau (Vacances Haute-Gaspésie; 📞418-763-0044; www.vacanceshaute-gaspesie.com; 96 Blvd Ste-Anne W/Rte 132; ⊙9am-8pm Jul & Aug, 10am-6pm Jun & Sep) Just off Rte 132, near the intersection of 28e Rue Ouest.

Parc National de la Gaspésie

You'd be forgiven for thinking you'd left the Atlantic coast and plunged into the heart of the Rocky Mountains here. Except making that comparison isn't fair when describing **Parc National de la Gaspésie** (📞418-763-7494; www.sepaq.com/pq/gas; adult/child $8.75/free; ⊙year-round; 🅿🏠🐾) 🐾, which has a raw, rugged beauty all its own, one as rooted in oceanic proximity (even in the peninsula's interior) as mountainous soul.

Be warned: even into May, there are trails and roads here that will be inaccessible due to snowfall or ice. Welcome to Canada!

🏃 Activities

The park is a prime hiking destination. The easiest trail is a 1.7km round-trip walk from the visitor center to **La Chute Ste-Anne**, an impressive waterfall. Another short hike (2.6km) takes you to **Le Lac-aux-Américains**, a dramatic glacial basin. A longer waterfall trek that ascends through some stunning alpine scenery is the 7km hike to **La Chute du Diable**.

🛏 Sleeping

Park Campgrounds CAMPGROUND $
(tent & RV sites from $31, huts/ready-to-camp tents/cabins from $31/94/115; 🅿) 🐾 The park has four campgrounds. The busiest serviced grounds are near the Interpretation Center (p312); try for a spot at the quietest – Lac Cascapédia. Two- to eight-person cabins, rustic huts and permanent tents are also available.

Gîte du Mont Albert INN $$
(📞418-763-2288, 866-727-2427; www.sepaq.com/pq/gma; 2001 Rte du Parc; r from $169; ⊙Jun-Oct & Jan-Mar; 🅿🌡@🛜🏊) A large, comfortable lodge near the Interpretation Center (p312) for those who like their nature spliced with luxury. Facilities include a pool, sauna, first-class restaurant (June to mid-October, mains $21 to $30) with mountain views through the floor-to-ceiling windows, and rooms with a surprisingly contemporary-chic aesthetic.

ℹ️ Information

Interpretation Center (🕐 8am-8pm daily Jul-Aug, reduced hours Sep-Jun; ♿) Staff here are extraordinarily helpful in planning a schedule to match your time and budget. Also rents out hiking equipment.

ℹ️ Getting There & Away

A bus (round-trip adult/child $7.50/5.75) runs from the Ste Anne des Monts' Tourist Bureau (p311) to the park's Interpretation Center. It leaves at 8am daily from late June to the end of September, returning at 5pm.

Driving to Mont St Pierre from the Interpretation Center, taking Rte 299 and the coastal Rte 132, is faster, safer and more scenic than the tree-lined track through the park.

Mont St Pierre

Mont St Pierre takes its name from a 418m mountain with a cliff that's one of the continent's best spots for hang gliding and paragliding. For several days in late July, the hang-gliding festival **Fête du Vol Libre** fills the sky with hundreds of sails. Near the eastern end of town and south of **Camping Municipal** (📞 418-797-2250; www.mont-saint-pierre.ca; 103 Rte Pierre-Godefroi-Coulombe/Rte 2; campsites/RV sites $28/44; 🕐 mid-Jun–mid-Sep; 🚐) 🏕, rough roads climb Mont St Pierre, where there are takeoff stations and excellent views. It takes about an hour to hoof it up the mountain.

The scenery on the Gaspé Peninsula becomes ever more spectacular in this region, as you travel east of Ste Anne des Monts. The North Shore, across the St Lawrence, disappears from view, and the road winds around rocky cliffs, every curve unveiling a stretch of mountains cascading to the sea.

East of Mont St Pierre

Some of the region's most dramatic scenery stretches along the north coast of La Gaspésie, extending from Mont St Pierre around the peninsula to Forillon National Park. Here the land is all towering cliffs, pebbly beaches and telegraph poles protruding from mounds of scree. Rte 132 winds along the coast, with striking views around many of the road's curves.

Forillon National Park

The official Land's End of the Gaspé Peninsula jutting into the Gulf of St Lawrence is simply gorgeous, encompassed by the boundaries of Forillon National Park. Here you'll find treks that ascend into high tree lines over fields populated by porcupines and chipmunks, and views out to the ocean that would take your breath away, were it not for the winds blowing in some fantastically fresh sea air.

👁 Sights & Activities

The can't-miss trail here – and it is truly one of the great walks in the province – is the 8km round-trip **Les Graves Trail** from L'Anse-aux-Amérindiens to **Land's End**. You'll cross an entire ecology textbook of bi-

---

CANADIAN APPALACHIAN

Crossing the peaks and valleys of the Appalachian Mountains, the 4574km International Appalachian Trail (IAT), North America's longest continuous hiking trail, stretches from Mt Springer, GA, in the United States to Forillon National Park at the tip of the Gaspé Peninsula.

The 1034km Canadian section, added to the US portion of the trail in 2001, begins on the Maine/New Brunswick border, crosses New Brunswick, including the province's highest peak, Mt Carleton, and enters Québec at Matapédia. The 650km Québec part of the trail winds up the Matapédia Valley to Amqui, where it swings northeast for the highlight of this section, Parc National de la Gaspésie and the surrounding reserves. It then descends from the mountains to Mont St Pierre and follows the coast for 248km to its final destination, Cap Gaspé.

The main hiking season runs from late June to October. The trail is clearly marked and generally well maintained, and there are shelters and campgrounds along the way. Some portions should only be attempted by experienced hikers, and everyone should seek advice about matters such as black bears. More information and maps are available at tourist offices and park information offices in locations such as Matapédia, by calling 418-562-7885 and by visiting www.sia-iat.com.

omes, from fields to forests to seaside cliffs, passing gorgeous coves scooped into the rocks along the way. At Cap-Gaspé, you'll find the terminus of the International Appalachian Trail, a solar-powered lighthouse, and some of the freshest salt air this side of the Atlantic.

The south coast (which includes the Land's End Trail) features more beaches, some sandy, with small coves. **Penouille Beach** is said to have the warmest waters. The rare maritime ringlet butterfly flourishes in the salt marshes here, and the end of the curving peninsula is a prime sunset-watching spot. There's another wonderfully secluded beach at the bottom of the steps that lead away from the heritage site (with historic homes and a restored general store) at Grande-Grave.

Another recommended hike is the **Mont-Saint-Alban Trail**, which climbs up to a lookout with a panoramic vista. You can access this moderate trail as a 7.2km loop from Petit-Gaspé Beach, or a 7.8km loop from Cap-Bon-Ami.

The park's more rugged north coast consists of steep limestone cliffs, some as high as 200m, and long pebble beaches, best seen at **Cap-Bon-Ami**. In the **North Sector**, south of Cap-des-Rosiers, you'll find a great picnic area with a small, rocky beach, and you can follow the 2km **Du Banc** trail for more cliff views.

Parks Canada (☑ 888-773-8888; www.pc.gc. ca) offers activities (at least one a day in English), including a whale-watching cruise, sea kayaking, fishing and horseback riding.

⛳ Tours

Cap Aventure   KAYAKING
(☑ 877-792-5055; www.capaventure.net; 2052 Blvd de Grande-Grève, Cap-aux-Os; half-/full-day excursions from $82/140; ⊙ May-early Oct) 🚗 A lot of the most spectacular views within Forillon National Park aren't visible from the land. You need to be at sea to see some of the park's rawest juxtapositions of land and ocean – a good reason for organizing a kayaking tour through Cap Aventure.

Croisières Baie de Gaspé   WHALE WATCHING
(Baleines Forillon; ☑ 418-892-5500; www.bale ines-forillon.com; 2448 A Blvd de Grande-Grève, Quai de Grande-Grave; adult/child $80/50; ⊙ Jun-early Oct; ⚓) Having a hard time spotting the whales from those Forillon cliffs? On board the *Narval III*, you can get up close and personal with around six different

cetacean species. The departure point, at the Grande-Grave Wharf, is 7km from the south entrance gate of the national park.

🛌 Sleeping

Forillon Campgrounds   CAMPGROUND $
(☑ North America 877-737-3783, outside North America 519-826-5391; www.pccamping.ca; campsites/cabins/oTENTiks from $25.50/90/100; ⊙ Jun-Sep; 🅿🐾❄) 🚗 The park's 350+ campsites in three campgrounds often fill to capacity. Petit-Gaspé is the most popular area, as it's protected from sea breezes and has hot showers. Cap-Bon-Ami is the smallest, with 38 tent-only sites. Permanent platform tents with beds, called 'oTENTiks,' are installed in the Petit-Gaspé and Des-Rosiers areas; the latter also has a tiny 'micrOcube' cabin for two.

**Auberge La Petite École
de Forillon**   HOSTEL $
(☑ 844-762-5451, 418-892-5451; www.auberge-ecoleforillon.com; 1826 Blvd Forillon, Cap-aux-Os; dm/s/d from $29/50/60; 🅿🛜) This well-managed year-round hostel in a brick former school building has an eight-bed dorm and 10 good-value private rooms with double-height windows and a variety of bed configurations; a few have views over the bay. The huge kitchen/dining area, with its rows of tables, feels (not surprisingly) like a school cafeteria, and there's even a playground outside for the kids.

ℹ Getting There & Around

Transportation is limited. While Orléans Express (p231) buses between Rimouski and Gaspé stop in the park daily during the summer, at locations including Cap-des-Rosiers and Cap-aux-Os, you'd still have to walk along Rte 132 to reach the hiking trails and campgrounds.

Gaspé

The most scenic aspect of the peninsula's nominal capital is its view of Forillon, across the sweep of the Baie de Gaspé. This was where Jacques Cartier first landed in July 1534. After meeting the Mi'kmaq of the region, he ignored their settlements, planted a wooden cross and claimed the land for the king of France. Today, Gaspé makes for a good refueling point or a base for day-tripping into Forillon National Park; it's not as touristy as Percé, although it's not quite as picturesque either.

QUÉBEC GASPÉ

⊙ Sights

Musée de la Gaspésie
MUSEUM

(☑418-368-1534; http://museedelagaspesie.ca; 80 Blvd Gaspé; adult/child $15.25/9.25; ☉9am-5pm Jun-Oct, from 10am Tue-Fri, from 12:30pm Sat & Sun Nov-May; Ⓟ♿) This museum evokes the peninsula's maritime heritage through traditional exhibits and more contemporary multimedia activities. You might examine artifacts such as a 17th-century hourglass or head out to sea on a fishing boat in a virtual-reality experience. You can learn more about Jacques Cartier, the former ship's boy who persuaded the French navy to back the voyages that laid the foundation for the European settlement of Québec. Outside, a bronze **monument** commemorates Cartier's landing.

Site d'Interpretation Micmac de Gespeg
MUSEUM

(☑418-368-7449; www.micmacgespeg.ca; 783 Blvd Pointe-Navarre; adult/child $11.25/8.75; ☉9am-5pm early Jun-early Oct; Ⓟ♿) This center explains the culture and history of the local Mi'kmaq group through an exhibition, English- and French-language tours, a recreated village and workshops. It's northwest of town, next to the **Notre-Dame-des-Douleurs** church, a Catholic pilgrimage site.

⊨ Sleeping

Auberge sous les Arbres
INN $$

(☑418-360-0060; www.aubergesouslesarbres. com; 146 Rue de la Reine; r $125-160; Ⓟ❀🛜) Book in advance to score a gilded room at this lovely old home, which has been converted into a stately country cottage/inn. The interior decor has an early-20th-century summer-retreat vibe, while the central location gives guests easy access to town.

✗ Eating & Drinking

Marché des Saveurs Gaspésiennes
DELI $

(☑418-368-7705; https://marche-de-saveurs-gaspesiennes.business.site; 119 Rue de la Reine; sandwiches $7-12; ☉8am-7pm Mon-Wed, to 7:30pm Thu-Fri, to 6pm Sat, 10am-6pm Sun) This small gourmet market makes sandwiches, from duck rillettes with pickles, to smoked salmon or smoked meat, and sells pastries, cheeses, jams and other products from around the region. You can eat at one of the few tables or take a picnic down to the river.

Microbrasserie Cap Gaspé
CRAFT BEER

(☑418-360-9000; 286 Blvd de York S; ☉noon-9pm Jul-Sep, Thu-Sat only Oct-Jun; 🛜) The father-daughter team that owns Gaspé's microbrewery took over a former Molson warehouse and opened a tasting room just outside downtown, where you can sample the locally made German-style beers.

ⓘ Getting There & Away

Daily **Air Canada** (☑888-247-2262; www.air-canada.com) flights connect the small **airport** (☑418-368-2104; 60 Rue de l'Aéroport) 6.5km south of town with Îles de la Madeleine and Montréal via Québec City.

Orléans Express buses (p231) stop at **Motel Adams** (☑418-368-2244, 800-463-4242; http://moteladams.com/en; 20 Rue Adams; r $93-164; Ⓟ❀🛜) and link to the rest of the peninsula and beyond.

Percé

One of Canada's best-known landmarks rears out of the sea at the tip of the Gaspé Peninsula. No matter which way you approach the town of Percé, when you glimpse its famous Rocher Percé, a massive offshore slab with a seemingly gravity-defying archway, it's always striking. The rock and the adjacent Île Bonaventure encompass North America's largest migratory bird refuge. Both are now protected as part of **Parc National de l'Île-Bonaventure-et-du-Rocher-Percé** (☑418-782-2240; www.sepaq. com/pq/bon; 4 Rue du Quai; adult/child $8.75/free; ☉8:30am-5pm mid-May–mid-Oct; Ⓟ) 🏊, sitting in a patch of gulf that, from 1784, attracted schools of European cod fishers.

On the mainland, having stained a lobster bib or gorged on a platter of fish, you can work off the seafood pounds with a hike in the hills, part of the Appalachians, that shelter the peninsula's most appealing town. Or simply stroll the boardwalk and climb up the waterside lookout tower to see Percé's offshore attractions from yet another vantage point.

⊙ Sights & Activities

Rocher Percé
LANDMARK

(Pierced Rock) The town's landmark attraction, this 88m-high, 475m-long chunk of multihued limestone has inspired descriptive entries in travel journals dating back to Samuel de Champlain's captain's log of 1603. It is accessible from the mainland only by

GANNET GATHERING

Of the hundreds of feathered species found in Québec, none is closer to the hearts of Québécois than the northern gannet *(fou de bassan)*. Île Bonaventure is home to more than 115,000 of them, one of the world's largest colonies and certainly the most accessible. But it's not their sheer numbers or the squawking din that makes seeing them so memorable. Adult gannets are strikingly beautiful, with blazing white plumage and, at the base of a handsome gray-blue bill, piercing blue eyes surrounded by a black patch. During mating season, their heads turn pale yellow, as if glowing from within.

Mature gannets have a wingspan of about 2m, evident in their graceful flight, which sometimes seems to not require a single flap. Seeing them return to their lifelong mates, apparently without a moment's confusion despite the mob, and indulge in a little friendly caressing is both touching and amusing.

And then there's the birds' dive-bomb approach to fishing. They strike from a height of about 20m, plunging straight down, and resurfacing from as deep as 5m after swallowing a mouthful of fish.

Visiting them on the island, where you can get close without disturbing them, is a highlight of any Île Bonaventure cruise.

boat, but it's dangerous to try to go ashore on this fragile natural wonder. Île Bonaventure cruises include a journey around the rock with commentary on its history and folklore.

Île Bonaventure
ISLAND

🌿 Meeting the more than 100,000 gannets on green Île Bonaventure is a highlight of any Gaspé Peninsula experience. Boat operators sell tickets for trips to the island from their offices and from booths on Rue du Quai near the Percé dock. While it's possible to choose a boat going directly to the island, most tours first circle Rocher Percé, then pull alongside Île Bonaventure to get up close to the gannet colony before docking on the island's west side.

👉 Tours

Les Croisières Julien Cloutier
BOATING
(📞 418-782-2161, 877-782-2161; http://croisieres-julien-cloutier.com; 5 Rue du Quai; adult/child $38/16; ☺ mid-May–mid-Oct) One of the established tour companies that conducts excursions to Île Bonaventure and Rocher Percé. Also does whale-watching tours (adult/child $80/40) from mid-June to September.

🛏 Sleeping

Hôtel-Motel Rocher Percé B&B
B&B $
(📞 418-782-2330, 877-467-3740; www.hotelperce.com; 111 Rte 132 W; s/d from $65/79; ☺ late May–Oct; 🅿❄🖥) A decent breakfast and a homey vibe, plus local art decorating the walls, is what you get at this warm little bed and breakfast. The owner can point you in the

direction of local hiking trails, and many rooms boast a good view of the rock.

Au Pic de l'Aurore
CHALET $$
(📞 418-782-2151, 866-882-2151; www.percechalet.com; 1 Rte 132 W; r $80-175, chalets $80-210; ☺ late May-early Oct; 🅿❄@🖥🐾) Perched high on a cliff overlooking Percé, the sprawling grounds of the 'Peak of Dawn' offer something for everyone: chalets with or without kitchenettes, motel rooms and even a whole four-bedroom house to rent. Interiors have a cozy log-cabin feel with pine furniture, and there's a bar with outstanding views.

Hôtel La Normandie
HOTEL $$
(📞 418-782-2112, 800-463-0820; www.normandieperce.com; 221 Rte 132 W; r $119-349; ☺ mid-May–mid-Oct; 🅿@🖥) The classiest spot in town, the retreat-like Normandie has serious amenities: the beach, room balconies, a dining room for seafood and expansive lawns with panoramic views of the rock.

Gîte au Presbytère
B&B $$
(📞 866-782-5557, 418-782-5557; www.perce-gite.com; 47 Rue de l'Église; s/d incl breakfast $82/139; ☺ May-Oct; 🅿@🖥) With a well-tended garden by the massive church, this sizable, bright old rectory with gleaming hardwood floors and homey rooms is a nice option. Friendly and gracious host Michel is a wealth of local knowledge.

🍴 Eating & Drinking

Boulangerie Le Fournand
CAFE $
(📞 418-782-2211; www.boulangerielefournand.com; 194 Rte 132 W; snacks $4-13; ☺ 7:30am-6:30pm

May-Oct) Try this colorful bakery for picnic breads, decent Italian coffee and mouthwatering French pastries and quiche.

La Maison du Pêcheur SEAFOOD $$
(📞418-782-5331; www.maisondupecheur.ca; 157 Rte 132 W; pizzas $15-28, mains $22-49; ⊙11:30am-3pm & 5:30-9:30pm Jun-Oct; 🅿🛜) This long-standing fish house is located in a former fishers' shack that became a commune in the 1960s, rebuilt – with a wall of windows overlooking Pierced Rock – after suffering damage in a severe storm. It serves seafood, including lobster, and at least a half-dozen types of pizza baked in a wood-heated oven. Reservations strongly recommended.

Restaurant La Maison Mathilde SEAFOOD $$$
(📞418-782-2349, 800-463-9700; www.aubergeles troissoeurs.com; 85 Rte 132 W; set meals $24-49; ⊙7-11:30am & 5:30-10pm Jun-Sep; 🅿) This cozy, down-to-earth spot in a cute cottage serves up pretty stellar local seafood. This being the Gaspé, expect lots of flounder, cod and lobster, and expect it served after getting a rich treatment of melted butter and cream. Does a fine steak as well.

Pub Pit Caribou MICROBREWERY
(📞418-782-1443; www.pitcaribou.com; 182 Rte 132 W; ⊙11am-1am Jun-Aug, 2-10pm Sun, Tue & Wed, to 11pm Thu-Sat Sep-May) With its dark interior, dusty wooden walls and a cast of characters seemingly culled from a Hemingway novel, this is an excellent spot for trying one of the Gaspé's fabled microbrews and, on some nights, enjoying live music.

❶ Information

Tourist Office (📞855-782-5448, 418-782-5448; www.perce.info; 142 Rte 132; ⊙8am-8pm Jul & Aug, to 5pm Jun, Sep & Oct) Located in the middle of town.

❶ Getting There & Away

Orléans Express (p231) buses stop at the tourist office daily en route to Gaspé ($15, one hour) and west to Rimouski ($85, eight hours).

New Carlisle

One of the main English towns on the peninsula, Loyalist-founded New Carlisle has New Brunswick–style clapboard houses and Protestant, Anglican and Presbyterian churches on grid-arranged streets. Incongruously,

René Lévesque, that icon of Québécois Francophone identity politics, grew up here, at 16 Rue Mount Sorel.

The Palladian **Hamilton Manor** (📞418-752-6498; www.manoirhamilton.com; 115 Blvd Gérard Lévesque; tours $5; ⊙tours May-Dec) was built in 1852 by the town's first mayor. It's a wonderful portrait of colonial life – from the picture of Queen Victoria to the bread oven to the maids' attic quarters. Call ahead to arrange a tour. You can also book a room here for the night.

If you need to grab a bite to eat while here, **Cafe Luna** (📞418-752-7005; 148 Blvd Gérard Lévesque; sandwiches $6-10; ⊙10am-4:30pm Mon-Wed & Sat, to 9pm Thu-Fri) has strong coffee, delicious panini, board games and a general surfeit of bohemian bonhomie.

Bonaventure

Bonaventure spreads out in skinny lines between Rte 132 and the water, eventually clustering into a small town 'center' that's the nexus of local civic activity. Founded by Acadians in 1760, the town is widely known as a major waypoint for the group during their 'Great Upheaval,' and Acadian flags remain a common sight throughout town.

◉ Sights & Activities

Grotte de St Elzéar CAVE
(📞418-534-3905, 877-524-7688; https://lagrotte. ca; 184 Rte de l'Église, Saint-Elzéar de Bonaventure; adult/child $45/35; ⊙Jun-early Sep; 🅿) 🧭 The almost 500,000-year-old Grotte de St Elzéar is one of Québec's oldest caves. You descend into the cool depths (bring warm clothes) and view the stalactites, stalagmites and moon milk (a mysterious, semi-liquid deposit found in caves). In July and August, four daily tours are offered between 8am and 3pm; check website for details and for reduced tour hours in June and September. Book English tours in advance.

Musée Acadien du Québec MUSEUM
(📞418-534-4000; www.museeacadien.com; 95 Ave de Port-Royal; adult/child $13/9; ⊙9am-5pm Jul-Oct, reduced hours Nov-Jun; 🅿) With bilingual exhibits, the small Acadian Museum showcases the history of Acadians in Québec, from daily life to religion to family structures, as well as the Acadian exile from Canada and eventual resettlement across North America.

Cime Aventure

KAYAKING

(☑800-790-2463, 418-534-2333; www.cimea
venture.com; 200 Chemin Athanase-Arse-
nault; campsites/yurts/ecolodges/chalets from
$33/100/159/239; ☺Jun-Sep; 🌲) 🏄 Leads
canoe, kayak or stand-up paddleboard trips
lasting from two hours (from $50) to a full
day ($90), mostly on the scenic, tranquil
Rivière Bonaventure. The company can
organize multiday trips with food and
equipment, too. It also runs an excellent
campground, with eight- or 12-person chalets, ecolodges reached by treetop walkways
and a rustic resto-bar.

🍴 Eating

Boulangerie Artisanale
La Pétrie

CAFE $

(☑418-534-3445; www.boulangerieartisanalela
petrie.com; 128 Ave Grand-Pré; mains $7-10;
☺7am-6pm Mon-Fri, to 4:30pm Sat, to 3pm Sun;
P🏠☑) Bracketed by an enormous, vibrant
mural, this artsy cafe serves up delicious
hot sandwiches, slices of fluffy quiche and
bowls of granola, plus some coffee that will
give you enough fuel to drive all the way to
Montréal.

Cafe Acadien

CAFE $$

(☑418-534-4276; www.cafeacadien.com; 168
Rue Beaubassin; mains $18-28; ☺7am-9pm Jun-
Sep; P🏠) On a spit of land jutting into
the bay at the marina, this boat-shed-like
cafe is great for breakfast crêpes, smoked-
salmon omeletes, and bacon and eggs. Aca-
dian dishes, with lots of seafood options,
are on the menu later in the day. There are
several small, colorful guest rooms upstairs
(single/double including breakfast $80/90).

ℹ️ Information

Tourist Office (☑418-534-4014; www.tour-
ismebonaventure.com; 93 Ave de Port-Royal;
☺9am-noon & 1-4pm Mon-Fri Jun-Sep; 🏠) Has
free wi-fi and computer access.

Carleton

A pleasant swath of mountainous coastline
hugging the Baie-des-Chaleurs, Carleton-
sur-Mer is much loved by Gaspésien
day-trippers and other travelers for its sand-
bars, bird-watching and walking trails.

👁 Sights

Boats depart from the quay for fishing or
sightseeing excursions. At the **bird obser-**
vation tower on the Banc de Carleton, be-
yond the marina, you can see herons, terns,
plovers and other shorebirds along the sand-
bar. Walking paths and Rue de la Montagne
climb to the blue, metal-roofed oratory on
top of **Mont St-Joseph** (☑418-364-3723;
www.montsaintjoseph.com; 837 Rue de la Mon-
tagne; chapel tours adult/child $8.50/free; ☺chap-
el 8am-6pm late Jun-Aug, 9am-5pm Sep–mid-Oct)
🏄 (555m), which provides fine views over
the bay to New Brunswick. You can also find
stunning mosaics, stained-glass windows
and art-deco marble finishes inside, plus an
art gallery.

For a fascinating glimpse of the past, vis-
it **Parc National de Miguasha** (☑418-794-
2475; www.sepaq.com/pq/mig; 231 Rte Miguasha
W, Nouvelle; adult/child $8.75/free; ☺9am-5pm
Jun-Oct, reduced hours Nov-May; P) 🏄, the
world's premier fossil site for illustrating the
Devonian period (a time when sea creatures
started evolving into tetrapods, which could
walk on land). The park is located on a pen-
insula 7km south of Rte 132, near Nouvelle
(20km west of Carleton).

🛏 Sleeping & Eating

Camping de Carleton

CAMPGROUND $

(☑418-364-3992; www.carletonsurmer.com; 319
Ave du Phare; campsites from $29; ☺Jun–mid-
Oct; P) This campground occupies a spit of
land between the Baie-des-Chaleurs and the
calm inner bay, with access to kilometers of
beach, where you can camp.

Manoir Belle Plage

HOTEL $$

(☑800-463-0780, 418-364-3388; www.manoirbelle
plage.com; 474 Blvd Perron; r incl breakfast from
$89; P❄@🏠) Modern rooms with luxuri-
ous linens await in this cheery hotel on the
highway. There's an upscale restaurant on-
site serving local specialties and a tasteful,
whimsical nautical theme throughout the
hotel – think strategically placed driftwood
and marine poetry.

Brûlerie du Quai

CAFE $

(☑418-364-6788; www.brulerieduquai.com; 200
Rte du Quai; coffees from $2; ☺7:30am-6pm, to
9pm Jul & Aug) Locals flock to this lively roastery, store and coffee shop for out-of-this-
world espresso drinks. There's a small patio
overlooking the quay, and you're welcome to
bring lunch or picnic supplies – the nearby
La Mie Véritable (☑418-364-6662; 578 Blvd
Perron; baked goods $2-6; ☺7am-5:30pm Tue-Sat;
P🏠☑) can help with that.

🍷 Drinking & Nightlife

Le Naufrageur   MICROBREWERY
(✆418-364-5440; www.lenaufrageur.com; 586 Blvd
Perron; ⊙3-10pm) With all due respect to the
Irish, the St-Barnabé stout the folks at Naufrageur are putting out gives any black beer from
the Emerald Isle a run for its money. Honestly,
you can't go wrong with anything produced
by the talented staff at this microbrewery.

❶ Information

Tourist Office (✆418-364-3544; www.carle
tonsurmer.com; 774 Blvd Perron; ⊙8am-8pm
Jul-Aug, 9am-5pm Jun & Sep) In Quai des Arts,
Carleton's arts and performance center.

❶ Getting There & Away

Orléans Express (p231) buses stop at 561 Blvd
Perron; get tickets inside Restaurant Le Héron.
Buses go to Rimouski ($57, 3½ hours) and
Gaspé ($37, four hours).

Matapédia Valley

Driving through the Matapédia Valley, you'll
get a taste of the terrain that challenges
walkers on the International Appalachian
Trail. The trees covering the hillsides only
stop for rivers, cliffs and lines of huge py-
lons charging through the wilderness. If it's
raining, the mist-swathed pines look like
they could have been plucked from a fantasy
novel. The Rivière Matapédia, famous for its
salmon fishing, attracted former US presi-
dents Nixon and Carter.

Matapédia

Nature-Aventure (✆418-865-3554; www.
matapediaaventure.com; Parc Adams, 20 Rue de
l'Église, Matapédia; 2-/4-hour tours $50/70, 1-/2-
/3-/4-/5-day excursions $115/335/445/555/665;
⊙mid-May–Sep) runs rugged paddles of varying difficulty along local rivers, including
the Matapédia. It also rents canoes, wet suits
and camping gear, and leads several different hiking excursions into the mountains.
Camping can be arranged (sites from $20).

Causapscal

As its monolithic statue of 'the king of our
rivers' suggests, Causapscal is crazy about
salmon. The largest salmon caught here
weighed over 16kg. Other outdoor activities
on the town's doorstep include hiking, with
trails meandering through the surrounding

hills. The town itself has a beautiful stone
church and many old houses with typical
Québécois silver roofs, though odors from
nearby sawmills sometimes spoil the picturesque scene.

Rivière Matapédia is the healthiest river
for salmon fishing; 13kg beauties are regularly netted there at the beginning of the
season. Anglers cast their lines where the
Matapédia and Causapscal meet.

Rivière Matapédia is the healthiest river for salmon; 13kg beauties are regularly
netted there at the beginning of the season.
There are covered bridges south of town
and, in the center, a pedestrian-only **suspension bridge** across the Matapédia. Anglers go there to cast their lines where the
Matapédia and Causapscal meet.

Appealingly old-fashioned **Auberge La
Coulée Douce** (✆418-756-5720, 888-756-
5270; www.lacouleedouce.com; 21 Rue Boudreau;
r/chalets from $102/143; [P ✸ 🛜]) is perfect for
fishers, and for those who simply want to
sit in the comfortable dining room listening to ripping fishing yarns. The on-site
restaurant is the best (well, OK, practically
the only) spot in town for a home-cooked
meal.

CGRMP (Corporation de Gestion des Rivières
Matapédia et Patapédia; ✆418-756-6174; www.
cgrmp.com; 462 Rue St-Jacques N; ⊙Jun-Sep)
can arrange (expensive) fishing permits.

The **tourist office** (✆418-756-6048; www.
causapscal.net; 5 Rue St-Jacques S; ⊙8am-8pm
Jul & Aug) provides information on lodging,
fishing and treks in the Matapédia Valley.

NORTH SHORE

As you drive (and drive, and drive) into
the heart of the Côte-Nord (North Shore),
the feeling of frontier becomes ever more
pronounced. The patchwork of agriculture
gradually evolves into endless kilometers
of taiga, wide swaths of dark forest, and
past that, the steel-gray St Lawrence River,
stretching to the Gulf of St Lawrence and
the Atlantic beyond. There's just one way in
and out – Rte 138 – evoking an eerie sense
of isolation.

This enormous area comprises two regions – Manicouagan (from Tadoussac to
Godbout) and Duplessis (east to the Labrador border) – with statistics as overwhelming as the distances you have to drive to
cross them.

The two regions encompass an awesome 328,693 sq km (the size of New Zealand, Belgium and Switzerland combined). In this vast expanse live just over 100,000 hardy souls, mostly on the 1250km of coastline, making the area's population density just 0.3 persons per sq km.

Baie Comeau

Modern-day Baie Comeau is the sort of industrial town that has decided things like locavore food and microbreweries should not solely be the province of places like Montréal, which makes it a pleasant enough place to stop for a break from the highway.

The town owes its existence to Robert McCormick, former owner of the *Chicago Tribune*, who in 1936 decided to build a colossal pulp-and-paper factory here. This enterprise necessitated harnessing the hydroelectric power of the Manicouagan and Outardes Rivers, which in turn begat other hydro-dependent industries such as aluminum processing.

◉ Sights

Baie Comeau is at the beginning of Rte 389, which runs north past the Manicouagan Reservoir, the fifth-largest meteorite crater in the world, to Labrador City and Wabush. Along the way is a fascinating landscape of lake-filled barrens, tundra and, about 120km north of the hydroelectric complex Manic Cinq, the Groulx Mountains, where the peaks reach as high as 1000m.

🛏 Sleeping & Eating

L'Hôtel Le Manoir   HOTEL $$
(🗷 418-296-3391; www.manoirbc.com/en; 8 Ave Cabot; r from $130; P ❄ 🛜) This stately hotel lives up to its name, at least externally: it resembles a riverside château. The interior is a little more modest, but the rooms are perfectly comfortable and well appointed for those who need a soft night's sleep.

Manoir du Café   CAFE $
(🗷 418-294-6652; 5 Pl La Salle; mains $10-14; ⊙7am-10pm Mon-Fri, from 7:30am Sat & Sun; 🛜 🗷) The spectrum of coffee offered here is pretty fantastic, and the staff brew it strong and tasty, served alongside a colorful menu of fresh sandwiches and homemade pizzas.

All in all, an unexpectedly lovely spot for wi-fi and a filling meal.

Café Vieille France   FRENCH $$$
(🗷 418-295-1234; 1050 Rue de Bretagne; set menu $26-38; ⊙11:30am-8pm Tue-Fri, 5:30-9pm Sat) *Whoa.* Where did this place come from? It's a nondescript building set across from a nondescript housing complex, but inside? Incredible French cuisine: rabbit draped in bacon cooked in local maple syrup, fresh cod in a rich butter sauce, and desserts to die for. Call ahead.

🍷 Drinking

Microbrasserie St-Pancrace   MICROBREWERY
(🗷 418-296-0099; www.stpancrace.com; 55 Pl La Salle; ⊙3-11pm Mon & Tue, to midnight Wed, to 1am Thu, 1pm-1am Fri & Sat, 1-11pm Sun) If you're going to sink a beer in this town, let it be a local brew from this friendly microbrewery. Also serves up some decent midrange (mains $11 to $16) pub grub for soaking up said suds.

ℹ Getting There & Away

A year-round ferry (🗷 877-562-6560, 418-562-2500; www.traversiers.com; 14 Rte Maritime; one-way adult/child/car $20/12.30/48.80) makes the 2½-hour journey to Matane daily, providing the easternmost water link to the Gaspé Peninsula. It's essential to make a reservation for vehicles and advisable to reserve at least a day ahead for foot passengers.

Intercar (p231) buses stop at 675 Blvd Laflèche.

Godbout

The principal activity in this sleepy village, which occupies a nicely dramatic bay, is the arrival of the ferry (🗷877-562-6560; www.traversiers.com; 117 Rue Pascal-Comeau; one-way adult/child/car $20/12.30/48.80). If you feel like swimming, hit the beach below the Amérindien museum.

Musée Amérindien et Inuit (🗷418-568-7306; 134 Rue Pascal-Comeau; adult/child $5/2; ⊙9am-7pm Jul-Sep; P) is more a gallery of Native American art and indigenous crafts – as you may guess from the name, there's a focus on Inuit objets d'art. The on-site boutique is a good spot for souvenirs.

The ferry links Godbout with Matane. Intercar (p231) bus services run to the ferry terminal, arriving from the south around 6pm and from Sept Îles at 10:30am.

Pointe des Monts

This little promontory, buffeted by storms and sea breezes, marks the point where the coast veers north and the St Lawrence graduates from river to gulf.

Pointe des Monts Lighthouse (☎418-939-2400; http://pharedepointedesmonts.com; 1830 Chemin du Vieux Phare; adult/child $12/6; ◷9am-5pm mid-Jun–early Sep; P) is a circa 1830 lighthouse, and one of Québec's oldest. Sitting on a picturesque spit of land, it has been converted into a museum explaining the lives of the keepers and their families.

There are also four guestrooms in the former lighthouse-keeper's quarters ($125).

Located next to the lighthouse, **Le Gîte du Phare de Pointe-des-Monts** (☎418-939-2332, 866-369-4083; www.pointe-des-monts.com; 1937 Chemin du Vieux Phare; campsites $25-25, chalets per day/week from $88/580; ◷May-Oct; P) is a collection of chalets that are all comfortably decked out and boast nice views.

Sept Îles

Sept Îles feels a bit like the last city before civilization ends, which is not an entirely inaccurate impression, with all due respect to Havre St Pierre. So one would be forgiven for not expecting this busy port town to

be as cool as it is. Exploring local museums, having a good meal and hitting up a neighborhood bar are perfect cures for the fatigue of long-distance driving.

◉ Sights

Île Grande Basque
ISLAND

(◷Jun-Sep) The largest island of the small archipelago off Sept Îles is a pretty spot to spend a day, walking on the 12km of trails or picnicking on the coast. During the summer (June to September), Les Croisières du Capitaine runs regular ferry tours (adult/child from $25/15), traveling between the island and Sept Îles port, as well as archipelago cruises. Tickets are available at the port, in the Parc du Vieux Quai (Old Docks).

Musée Régional de la Côte-Nord
MUSEUM

(☎418-968-2070; http://museeregionalcotenord.ca; 500 Blvd Laure; adult/child $7/free; ◷9am-5pm daily Jul & Aug, 10am-noon & 1-5pm Tue-Thu, 10am-5pm Fri, 1-5pm Sat & Sun Sep-Jun; P⌕) This modern museum conveys the history of the North Shore and its 8000 years of human habitation through a mix of multimedia displays and artifacts such as a canoe, a dogsled and an 1890s harmonium that once sat in a Sept Îles church. Temporary exhibits often feature artists from the region.

Musée Shaputuan
MUSEUM

(☎418-962-4000; 290 Blvd des Montagnais; adult/child $5/free; ◷8am-noon & 1-4:30pm Mon-Fri, plus 1:30-4pm Sat & Sun Jul & Aug) This is one of the North Shore's best museums on Indigenous culture. The atmospheric circular exhibition hall, divided into four sections symbolizing the seasons, follows the Innu (Montagnais) people as they hunt caribou or navigate the treacherous spring rivers. Photography, traditional clothes, sculptures and mythological tales are incorporated.

⌲ Tours

Les Croisières du Capitaine BOATING
(☎418-968-2173; http://lescroisieresducapitaine.com; Vieux Quai, Ave Arnaud; adult/child from $25/15) Offers boat tours to Île Grande Basque.

⌂ Sleeping & Eating

Auberge Le Tangon HOSTEL $
(☎418-962-8180; www.aubergeletangon.com; 555 Ave Cartier; dm/s/d $27/42/65; P@⌖) The

WORTH A TRIP

RIDING THE TSHIUETIN RAILS

Indigenous-owned **Tshiuetin Rail Transportation** (☎866-962-0988, 418-962-5530; www.tshiuetin.net; 1 Rue Retty) operates a twice-weekly service between Sept Îles and Schefferville, 568km north, one of the province's most remote spots, though once a thriving mining town. The scenery en route is phenomenal. Cutting through forests, the tracks pass over gorges, dip inside valleys, curve around waterfalls and rapids, slice through a section of mountain and jut along stretches of lakes, rivers and hills as far as the eye can see. The train crosses a 900m-long bridge, 50m over Rivière Moisie and past the 60m-high Tonkas Falls. You can stop in the wilderness to camp and fish, then catch the next service back.

wooden balcony here is an uplifting sight after kilometers of Rte 138. Inside, this well-managed hostel has friendly faces in reception, power showers, small dorms and private rooms clustered into mini-suites around a sitting area or kitchenette. On the main floor, there's a homey lounge, large communal kitchen and laundry facilities.

Hôtel le Voyageur HOTEL $$

(📞 418-962-2228; www.hotellevoyageur.com; 1415 Blvd Laure; r $110-251; 🅿🌐📶) Cozy rooms with modern furniture contrast with the kitschy retro sign out front at this solidly midrange choice on the west end of the city. The more expensive units have been updated more recently.

Chez Sophie BISTRO $$

(📞418-968-1616; www.restaurantchezsophie.ca; 495 Ave Brochu; mains $15-28; ⊙4-11pm Tue-Sat; 📶) This welcoming bistro-bar with original art on the walls is a lively spot for a meal-size salad topped with grilled salmon, a duck confit pizza or a plate of pasta with a glass of wine.

Les Terrasses du Capitaine SEAFOOD $$$

(📞418-961-2535; 295 Ave Arnaud; set meals from $28; ⊙11am-1:30pm Mon-Fri & 4-9pm daily; 🅿) This unapologetically old-school eatery is famous across the North Shore for local seafood. You won't walk away hungry after sampling the fish-and-chips, seafood pizza or pasta with shrimp. If *guédille au crabe* (fresh crab salad on a grilled bun) is on the menu, it's an excellent choice. Find it behind the fish market at the port.

🍷 Drinking & Nightlife

Edgar Cafe Bar BAR

(📞418-968-6789; 490 Ave Arnaud; ⊙4pm-midnight) The beautiful people flock to this bar for a deep beer selection and a decent sampling of spirits.

❶ Information

Tourist Office (📞418-962-1238, 888-880-1238; www.tourismeseptiles.ca; 1401 Blvd Laure W; ⊙8am-noon & 1-4:30pm Mon-Fri) On the highway west of town.

❶ Getting There & Away

Sept Îles airport is 10km east of town; a taxi will cost about $20 to the city center. **PAL Airlines** (📞800-563-2800, 709-576-1666; www.palairlines.ca) serves the Lower North Shore, Labrador, Newfoundland, Québec City and Montréal.

The **Relais Nordik** (📞418-968-4707, 800-463-0680; www.relaisnordik.com) ferry travels to Île d'Anticosti and along the Lower North Shore (from Rimouski).

Intercar (📞418-962-9736; https://intercar.ca; 27 Rue Comeau) runs a daily bus to/from Baie Comeau ($43.30, 3¾ hours) and, Monday to Friday, another to/from Havre St Pierre ($41.50, 2¾ hours).

Mingan Archipelago National Park

The landscape becomes primeval and sparse beyond Sept Îles, with lichen-laced black bog stretching to a gray horizon, dotted by a few copses of wet pine trees huddled against the wind. The region's main attraction is **Mingan Archipelago National Park Reserve** (📞418-949-2126, 418-538-3285; www.pc.gc.ca/en/pn-np/qc/mingan; adult/child $5.80/free; ⊙Jun-Sep; 🅿) 🌿, a slice of Canadian wilderness that encompasses 20 main islands and nearly 1,000 smaller isles. You came a long way to get here; now add a boat to your itinerary and engage in some North Shore island-hopping.

The park has two visitor centers where you can get information and organize your visit: the **Reception & Interpretation Center** (📞418-949-2126; www.pc.gc.ca/en/pn-np/qc/mingan; 625 Rue du Centre, Longue-Pointe-de-Mingan; ⊙8am-6:30pm mid-Jun–Aug) in the small town of Longue-Pointe-de-Mingan, and the Tourist Information Office (p322) in Havre St Pierre, 45km further east.

◉ Sights & Activities

Park staff offer a number of interpretive activities on the islands, from a 'boreal flavors' hike to explore edible berries and plants, to experiences that let you learn more about the region's Innu culture. Many activities are offered in French only, but check with staff at one of the visitor centers about the availability of English-language programs.

Mingan Island Cetacean Interpretation Center MUSEUM

(📞418-949-2845; www.rorqual.com; 378 Rue du Bord de la Mer, Longue-Pointe-de-Mingan; adult/child $10/5; ⊙9am-5pm mid-Jun–early Sep; 🅿♿) 🌿 Built by the researchers at Mingan Island Cetacean Study, this museum gives as many insights into the science of studying whales as it does into the mysterious mammals themselves.

Les Entreprises
Touristiques Loiselle BOATING
(☑ 418-949-2307, 866-949-2307; www.tourisme-loiselle.com; 207 Rue du Bord de la Mer, Longue-Pointe-de-Mingan; tours from $65; ☺ Jun-Sep; 🚻)
Offers 3½-hour tours to several of the Mingan islands in 12-passenger boats, departing from Longue-Pointe-de-Mingan.

🛏 Sleeping

Camping CAMPGROUND $
(☑ 877-737-3783;https://reservation.pc.gc.ca/parks canada; campsites from $15.70, permanent tents $120) Camping is allowed on several of the islands, but you must register (for an additional $5.80 fee) at the Reception & Interpretation Center or the Havre St Pierre tourist information office. Mingan has permanent 'oTENTik' platform tents on Quarry Island, which are good for families or those seeking a little more comfort.

Île aux Perroquets HERITAGE HOTEL $$$
(☑ 418-949-0005; www.ileauxperroquets.ca; per person from $250; ☺ Jun-Sep; 🐾) Fancy a little historical heritage and quilted luxury during your visit to the Mingans? The lighthouse and lighthouse-keeper's compound on Île aux Perroquets have been converted into a cozy, comfortable retreat. Rooms are decked out in art and crafts created on the North Shore, and packages include stays aimed at food-lovers and bird-watchers. The rates here include transportation to the island.

🅾 Getting There & Away

The park encompasses a huge swath of Hwy 138. Intercar runs buses between the park and Sept Îles or Havre St Pierre.

If you're going to Île d'Anticosti, you can catch the **Croisières Anticosti** (☑ 418-949-2095, 418-538-0911; www.croisieresanticosti.com; one-way/round-trip from $130/200; ☺ Jun-Sep) ferry (50 minutes) from Rivière-St-Jean, 10km west of Longue-Pointe-de-Mingan.

Havre St Pierre

This fishing town is a main departure point for tour boats to Mingan Archipelago National Park Reserve (p321), and it's a lovely spot for a stroll along the riverfront beaches. If you're traveling north, it also has the last gas station for 124km.

The Havre St Pierre harbor is a nice spot to watch the boats come in; during the summer, dockside operators run tours out to the **Mingan islands** (around $65 for a three-hour tour). Be on the lookout for red, white and blue flags embellished with a gold star dotted around town – that's the symbol of the Acadians.

Auberge Boréale (☑ 418-538-3912; www.aubergeboreale.com; 1288 Rue Boréale; r $60-75; ☺ May-Oct; 🅿❄🐾) has nine cool, blue-and-white rooms and a pretty sea view.

Gîte Chez Françoise (☑ 418-538-3778; www.gitechezfrancoise.ca; 1122 Rue Boréale; r $68-95; 🅿❄@🐾) is a friendly place that boasts five artistically decorated rooms.

The **tourist information office** (☑ 418-538-2512, 418-538-3285; 1010 Promenade des Anciens; ☺ 8am-8pm Jul–mid-Aug, to 5pm Jun & mid-Aug–Sep; 🐾) and **Variété Jomphe et Les Confections Minganie** (☑ 418-538-2035; 843 Rue de l'Escale; ☺ 9am-9pm) are great hubs for information on tours.

Intercar (p231) buses pick up at 843 Rue de L'Escale daily at 5:30pm going to Sept Îles ($40, 2½ hours).

Natashquan

Wild, windswept and lonely, Natashquan feels like the end of the road. Well, OK, Kegashka, 50km east, is the actual end of Rte 138, but you get the picture.

What's here? A sweep of coast, some cottages huddled against the tundra breeze, damp taiga forest, scads of mist and views onto the stormy St Lawrence. Aside from enjoying the beaches, you can hike inland trails through isolated, peaceful woods full of waterfalls and lookouts.

🅾 Sights

Les Galets HISTORIC SITE
🏴 A cluster of white huts with bright-red roofs, Les Galets huddle together on a wind-blown peninsula; from a distance, they look like a textbook illustration for the concept of lonely isolation. No longer occupied, the buildings were constructed in the late 1800s, when fishers salted and dried their catch here. To get here, follow Allée Les Galets off Rte 138.

Vieille École MUSEUM
(Old School; Allée des Pères Eudistes; adult/child $5/2; ☺ 10:30am-noon & 1:30-4:30pm mid-Jun–early Sep) This little one-room schoolhouse once educated Gilles Vigneault, the Natashquan native who would go on to be-

come, effectively, Québec's national songwriter. Today the schoolhouse has been converted into a museum that explores both Vigneault's music and the history of Natashquan.

Sleeping

Auberge La Cache HOTEL $$
(☑ 418-726-3347; www.aubergelacache.com; 183 Chemin d'en Haut; r from $150; P ☎) This two-story inn on the main road at the east end of town offers simple rooms with quilt-topped beds and dishes out a hearty breakfast. The friendly owner is happy to share all sorts of Natashquan stories.

❶ Information

Tourist Information Office (☑ 418-726-3054; www.copactenatashquan.net; 24 Chemin d'en Haut; ⊗ 8:30am-5:30pm Jun-Aug) Doubles as an interpretive center.

ÎLES DE LA MADELEINE

Salt-swept red-dirt islands crusted with fuzzy tufts of grass lie scattered in the Gulf of St Lawrence, and they're a sight to behold. The Îles de la Madeleine (Magdalen Islands), a stringy archipelago that resembles a Mandelbrot set on maps, are 105km north of Prince Edward Island. Between the islands' 350km of beach are iron-rich red cliffs, molded by wind and sea into coves and caves that cry out to be explored by kayak.

As you circle above the crescent beaches on one of the tiny airplanes that fly here, you may wonder how anyone could traverse this windswept chain; in fact, the six largest islands are connected by the 200km-long, classically named Rte 199. It takes a little over an hour to drive from one end of the archipelago to the other, assuming you don't stop to gawp at the views. Which you will.

❶ Getting There & Away

AIR

The airport is on the northwestern corner of Île du Havre aux Maisons. Air Canada Express (p230) offers daily flights from Montréal, Québec City and Gaspé; **Pascan** (☑ 888-313-8777; www.pascan.com) flies from Toronto (Billy Bishop), St-Hubert, Québec City, Mont-Joli and Bonaventure.

In March 2016, former federal cabinet minister and journalist Jean Lapierre and six others, including his wife, his sister and his two brothers, were killed when their private plane crashed while approaching the islands. Since that tragedy, air-traffic-control officials have seemed particularly cautious with Îles de la Madeleine-bound flights, and delays and cancellations occur regularly when there is low visibility – which is quite often the case, even in summer.

BOAT

The cheapest and most common arrival method is by ferry from Souris, Prince Edward Island, to Île du Cap aux Meules. **CTMA Ferries** (☑ 418-986-3278, 888-986-3278; www.ctma.ca; adult/child/bicycle/car $54.30/27.35/15.60/101.25) makes the five-hour cruise throughout the year.

The large ferry, which can operate in most inclement weather, departs daily from July to early September; every day but Monday in May, June and September; and three to four times a week from October to April. In midsummer, reservations are strongly recommended if you're traveling by car (and are a good idea even if you're on foot). Fares are substantially discounted between mid-September and mid-June.

Between June and October, CTMA also operates a seven-day cruise from Montréal (from $1019 with cabin), which stops in Chandler, on the Gaspé Peninsula. It's a great way of seeing the St Lawrence River, and you could always take your car ($305) and return by road.

❶ Getting Around

Le Pédalier (☑ 418-986-2965; www.lepedalier.com; 545 Chemin Principal; 1hr/4hr/day/1-week rental $6/18/24/85; ⊗ 9:30am-5:30pm Mon-Wed, 9am-9pm Thu & Fri, 9am-5pm Sat, noon-5pm Sun), in Cap aux Meules, rents bicycles. Hertz and local companies have airport car-rental outlets; book as far ahead as possible.

RéGÎM (☑ 418-986-6050, 877-521-0841; www.regim.info; one-way fare $4, 10-ticket carnets $30; ⊗ Mon-Fri) connects the islands via several bus routes, but bizarrely it doesn't operate on weekends. Check the website for schedules and be at the bus stop five minutes before the stated arrival time; note that drivers do not carry change, so you'll need the exact money. There are bike racks on most vehicles.

Île du Cap aux Meules

As the arrival point for the ferry, Île du Cap aux Meules is most people's first impression of the Madelinot archipelago, and at first sight it's a little deceiving. More than half the islands' population lives on this wind-swept islet, so it feels relatively developed compared with its neighbors – you'll actual-ly find shops here (including a Tim Hortons and a Subway), as well as a cinema, and the islands' main hospital and high school. With a decent range of accommodations and res-taurants, it's probably the most practical base for exploring.

◉ Sights

The island is split into three districts: the main town of Cap-aux-Meules, the western area of L'Étang-du-Nord, and Fatima in the north.

On the island's western side are the red cliffs in all their glory. Their erosion patterns can be glimpsed from the clifftop path be-tween La Belle Anse and Fatima.

Southwest, the lighthouse at **Cap du Phare** (Cap Hérissé) is a popular sunset-watching spot, and a cluster of bright bou-tiques and cafes overlooks a shipwreck at **Anse de l'Étang du Nord**.

In the middle of the island, **Butte du Vent** offers views along the sandbanks run-ning north and south.

⌖ Tours

Aerosport Carrefour
d'Aventures   KAYAKING
(☑ 418-986-6677; www.aerosport.ca; 1390 Chemin La Vernière, L'Étang-du-Nord; 3hr sea-kayak tour $59; ⊙9am-6pm Jul-Sep) ⚐ Young, enthusi-astic thrill-seekers run this company, which offers kayaking expeditions and cave visits that bring you face to face (well, paddle to water) with dramatic island scenery that is simply inaccessible from the shore. Wind-blown 'kite buggies' are also a blast. It rents bikes and SUPs, too.

⌂ Sleeping & Eating

Blue Paradise   HOSTEL $
(☑ 418-986-1392; www.blueparadisehostel.com; 156 Rte 199, Fatima; dm/s/d $39/75/87) Well-traveled young Madelinots Lisa and Mitchell have crafted a delightful hostel in this modern A-frame building, which is filled with fun things such as table football, a pool table, darts, and hammocks to lounge around in. There are lots of cool design touches – bare-brick walls, reclaimed street-lights – kayaks and bikes to borrow, plus a free pancake breakfast.

Parc de Gros-Cap   HOSTEL, CAMPGROUND $
(☑ 418-986-4505, 800-986-4505; www.parcdegros cap.ca; 74 Chemin du Camping, L'Étang-du-Nord; campsites from $26, dm/r from $34/72, cabins from $95; ⊙Jun-Sep; ℗@☎) Situated on the Gros-Cap peninsula overlooking a bay dotted with fishers in waders, this could be the HI network's most tranquil retreat. It's got accommodations to suit pretty much all comers: lots of camping pitches, plus dorms and private rooms in the inn and pavilion, self-contained cabins, and retro 1930s-inspired 'mini-trailers'.

Restaurant la Côte   CAFE $$
(☑ 418-986-6412; www.restaurantlacote.com; 499 Chemin Boisville W, L'Étang-du-Nord; mains $12-25; ⊙11:30am-9pm Jun-Sep) There's a chilled, beach-hut vibe to this attractive bistro, on the western side of the island near the fish-ers statue in L'Etang-du-Nord. The menu is mouthwatering: *incontournables* include lobster arancini, island lamb burger, crab grilled cheese and seafood risotto. The ad-joining *boîte à chanson* puts on outdoor Acadian music shows on summer evenings.

La Pêcherie   SEAFOOD $$
(La Renaissance des Îles; ☑ 418-986-2710; www. lrdi.ca; 521 Chemin du Gros-Cap; mains $8-20; ⊙11am-6pm) Stock up on seafood straight from the tanks here, from live crab and lob-ster to mussels and whelks (if you prefer, you can order cooked lobster from 3:30pm). There's also a little cafe, La Cantine, which serves the tastiest lobster poutine this side of Prince Edward Island.

La Table des Roy   CANADIAN $$$
(☑ 418-986-3004; www.restaurantlatabledesroy. com; 1188 Chemin La Vernière; mains $39; ⊙6-10pm) Serious French-inspired fine dining is on offer at Roy's upscale restaurant, where you can feast on wild boar, turbot with seaweed, and platters of lobster, oysters and clams. It's one of the islands' longest-running gourmet restaurants, and still the place for a slap-up (if rather formal) supper.

❶ Information

Main Tourist Office (☑ 877-624-4437, 418-986-2245; www.tourismeilesdelamadeleine. com; 128 Chemin Principal, Cap-aux-Meules; ⊙7am-8pm Jul & Aug, 9am-5pm Jun & Sep, 9am-noon & 1-5pm Oct-May) The principal source of information on the islands is located near the ferry terminal. Accommodations bookings, activities, local tips – these guys have it covered.

❶ Getting There & Around

Cap aux Meules is the most centrally located of the islands, and provides easy access to both the airport and the **ferry terminal** (☑ 418-986-3278; www.traversierctma.ca; 70 Chemin du Débarcadère, Cap-aux-Meules).

Île du Havre Aubert

The original Acadian settlers put down roots on Havre Aubert, at the southern end of the archipelago. The largest of the islands, it's reached via a breezy drive south from Cap aux Meules along Rte 199, flanked by the electric-blue Atlantic. Unlike several of the other islands, it's retained some tree cover, but it still feels pretty windswept when the Atlantic gales get up.

The liveliest area of Havre-Aubert town is **La Grave**, which, with its small cottages, craft shops, beached boats and laundry lines, exemplifies the rustic charm of a quintessential (or maybe clichéd) Madelinot fishing community. It takes about half an hour to drive a beautiful loop around the island via Chemin du Bassin.

◉ Sights

Sandy Hook   BEACH
(Plage de Havre-Aubert; Havre Aubert; ⓟ🐾) This huge, 12km stretch of windswept sand, accessible via Chemin du Sable, pretty much feels like the edge of the world. Be careful if you swim here, as there are no lifeguards. It stages a **sandcastle-building contest** every August.

Le Site d'Autrefois   NOTABLE BUILDING
(☑ 418-937-5733; www.sitedautrefois.com; 3106 Chemin de la Montagne, Havre Aubert; adult/child $10/5; ⊙ 9am-5pm Mon-Sat, 11am-5pm Sun mid-Jun–Aug, 10am-4pm Sep; ⓟ) Places such as the Îles de la Madeleine tend to attract eccentric folks, and they don't get much more interesting than flamboyant fisher Claude F Bourgeois, who preserves Madelinot traditions through storytelling and singing at this self-built model village.

🛏 Sleeping & Eating

★**Chez Denis à François**   INN **$$**
(☑ 418-937-2371; www.aubergechezdenis.ca; 404 Chemin d'en Haut, Havre Aubert; d incl breakfast $150-180; ⓟ🌸🛜) This handsome yellow inn strikes quite a pose as you drive past – according to the owners, parts of the building were built from shipwreck lumber. Inside,

the spacious rooms are prettily decorated; some have sofas or rattan chairs to lounge on, all have ceiling fans, and everything feels crisp, clean and modern. Breakfast is a treat.

Café de la Grave   CAFE **$$**
(☑ 418-937-5765; www.cafedelagrave.com; 969 Rte 199, Havre Aubert; mains $9-29; ⊙ 11am-10pm Mon-Sat, from 9am Sun) Located in a historic general store, this restaurant is more than a local institution: it's one of the islands' vital organs. *Pot-en-pot* (fish pie), wild-boar stew, scallop carbonara and bread-bowl clams feed a loyal and lively crowd. There's live music several nights a week.

★**Vent du Large**   QUÉBÉCOIS **$$$**
(☑ 514-919-9662; www.ventdularge.ca; 1009 Chemin de la Grave, Havre Aubert; tapas $8-22; ⊙ 11am-11pm Mon-Fri, from 9am Sat & Sun; ⓟ🏠) Owners Isabelle and François host a nightly *souper-spectacle* (dinner concert) at their much-loved restaurant in La Grave, featuring musicians from the islands and from further afield (often accompanied by François himself on violin). Tapas-style plates are on hand to share while you listen.

❶ Information

Île du Havre Aubert is the southernmost island in the archipelago, and is about a 20-minute drive from Cap aux Meules.

Île du Havre aux Maisons

In the middle of the archipelago, Île du Havre aux Maisons is an elongated green island fringed by red cliffs and dunes, and notable for its near-total lack of trees – practically every one was chopped down for lumber by the end of the 19th century. If you fly into the islands you'll land here, but even if you don't arrive this way, it's worth exploring: the pretty area around Havre-aux-Maisons town is dotted with colorful clapboard houses, and there are sweeping coastal views as you drive along Rte 199. Look out for mussel farms offshore.

A short climb from the car park on Chemin des Échoueries near Cap Alright, the cross-topped **Butte Ronde** has wonderful views of the lumpy coastline.

Le Fumoir d'Antan   FACTORY
(☑ 418-969-4907; www.fumoirdantan.com; 27 Chemin de Quai; guided tour mid-Jun–Aug $5, rest of year $4.50; ⊙ 9am-5pm Mon-Sat) Three generations of the Arseneau family have

smoked herring at this traditional smoke-house, where you can learn about the process and taste the goods. Tours take place daily at 3:30pm from mid-June, and three times daily (at 11am, 1pm and 3pm) in September; at other times of year you can show yourself around.

Fromagerie du Pied-de-Vent FARM
(☑418-969-9307; 149 Chemin de la Pointe-Basse; ⊙8am-6pm Jun-Sep) Here you can taste island-made cheeses produced according to traditional methods or take a guided tour of the dairy farm (adult/child $15/5). You'll see Pied-de-Vent cheeses on restaurant menus all over the islands.

La Butte Ronde B&B $$
(☑418-969-2047, 866-969-2047; www.labutteronde. com; 70 Chemin des Buttes, Havre-aux-Maisons; r incl breakfast $120-165) With ticking clocks, classical music, beautiful rooms decorated with photos of Tuareg nomads, and a sea-facing conservatory, this grand home in a former schoolhouse has a calming, library-like air.

Grosse Île

This island is home to most of the archipelago's English-speaking minority, their Newfoundland-like accents telling of their Scottish roots. The older Anglophone community long had an uneasy relationship with their Francophone neighbors; bar brawls and the like were not unheard of. Even today, many Anglophones cannot speak French, but intermarriage and bilingualism are becoming more common, and much of the tourism infrastructure on Grosse Île is run by Francophones.

Seacow Rd in Old Harry leads to the site where walrus were landed and slaughtered for their oil. Nearby, **St Peter's by the Sea**, built in 1916 using wood from shipwrecks, is bounded by the graves of Clarkes and Clarks. The surname evolved as it was misspelt on formal documents.

Between Pointe de la Grosse Île and Old Harry, the wetlands of the 684-hectare East Point National Wildlife Reserve have the archipelago's most impressive beach, **Plage de la Grande Échouerie** (☎) ✦. The 10km sweep of pale sand extends northeast from Pointe Old Harry; there are car parks there and en route to Old Harry from East Cape.

The island is 40km north of Cap aux Meules, separated from the rest of the archipelago by a causeway buttressed by gently humping dunes.

FAR NORTH

This area represents Québec's final frontier, where the province extends northward and eventually disappears into the depths of the Arctic Ocean. Here in the great Far North, remote villages, a strong Indigenous presence and stunning geography entice those wanting to drop off the tourist radar, learn more about Indigenous cultures, or arrange epic outdoor adventures.

The North is an immense region, the most northerly sections of which are dotted with tiny Inuit and First Nations settlements accessible only by plane. The developed areas largely owe their existence to massive industrial operations – mining for silver, gold and copper, forestry and hydroelectricity. While accessing the really Far North (the Inuit communities in Nunavik) requires expensive flights, other areas of the Abitibi-Témiscamingue and Eeyou Istchee Baie-James (James Bay) regions can, with time, be reached by car or bus, and will provide a taste of Canada's true North, Québec style.

Abitibi-Témiscamingue

The people barely outnumber the lakes in the over 65,140 sq km here. But despite the shortage of humans, this area occupies a special place in the Québécois imagination. The last area to be settled and developed on a major scale, it stands as a symbol of dreams and hardships.

The traditional land of the Algonquins, Abitibi-Témiscamingue is an amalgamation of two distinct areas, each named after different indigenous groups. Témiscamingue, accessible via Northern Ontario or Rte 117 west from Val d'Or, is beginning to draw more visitors who circle the grand Lac Témiscamingue and explore Parc National d'Opémican, a scenic preserve of forests, lakes and historic buildings. Further north, Abitibi mixes small industrial communities where mining is still a major industry with remote wilderness regions, like the stunning valleys and cliffs of Parc National d'Aiguebelle.

This vast region of Québec retains an exotic air, partially due to its remoteness. Generally, visitors are seeking solitude in its parks or are en route to still more epic northern destinations.

Réserve Faunique la Vérendrye

If you think there's nothing better than breaking up kilometers of driving with a bit of paddling, Réserve Faunique la Vérendrye, which encompasses a gorgeous series of lakes (4000 of them!), is practically perfect.

Camping, fishing, hunting and canoeing are the main attractions at the **park** (☑819-438-2017; www.sepaq.com/rf/lvy; Hwy 117; adult/child $8.75/free; ☉mid-May–early Sep; **P**) ✦. Even in a heat wave in midsummer, you may well have entire lakes virtually to yourself.

The southern entryway to the park is via Hwy 117, at Km 276. **Southern Registration Center** (☑819-435-2216; www.sepaq. com/rf/lvy; Hwy 117; ☉7am-7pm Sat-Wed, to 9pm Thu, to 10pm Fri mid-May–early Sep) has more information.

Val d'Or

Born in the 1930s around the Sigma gold mine, Val d'Or today looks like a mining boomtown of yesterday, with wide avenues and a main street (3e Ave) that retains its traditional rough edge – you can easily imagine how frenzied it would have been in the gold-rush days. The Sigma mine still operates, though it's no longer the city's economic engine, with forestry, health care and education providing a growing number of jobs.

La Cité de l'Or   MUSEUM
(The City of Gold; ☑855-825-1274, 819-825-1274; www.citedelor.com; 90 Ave Perreault; 2-/4hr tours adult $26/39, child $13/19; ☉tours 8am-5:30pm Jul & Aug, 8:30am-5pm Wed-Sun Jun & Sep, 8:30am-3pm Thu-Sun Oct, by appointment Nov-May; **P**) You don mining gear to go underground in this restored gold mine, which operated from 1935 to 1985 – cool! Actually, it's more than cool – it can get downright chilly down there, as you're getting a sampling of a miner's life. Above ground, there's an interpretive center about the region's mining history. Nearby, you can wander through **Village Minier de Bourlamaque**, a restored miners' village with 80 log houses, which are now private homes.

Hôtel Forestel   HOTEL $$
(☑819-825-5660; www.forestel.ca; 1001 3e Ave Est; r from $150; **P**❄@☎) With its big glass windows, smooth stone floors, industrial-design chic and geometric accents, this modern two-story motel provides sleek and chic accommodations out here in the hinterlands.

**Microbrasserie
Le Prospecteur**   PUB FOOD $$
(☑819-874-3377; www.microleprospecteur.ca; 585 3e Ave; mains $14-27; ☉11am-3am Mon-Fri, from 4pm Sat; ✦) Poutine with beer gravy, duck confit pizza, burgers and tartares all make an appearance alongside a nice hearty rack of home-brewed beers in Val d'Or's lively microbrewery.

ℹ Information

Tourist Office (☑819-824-9646; http://tourismevaldor.com; 1070 3e Ave Est; ☉8:30am-6:30pm mid-May–Aug, 8:30am-4:30pm Mon-Fri, 9am-3pm Sat, noon-3pm Sun Sep & Oct, 8:30am-4:30pm Mon-Fri, 9am-3pm Sat Nov–mid-May) On Hwy 117 at the eastern end of town.

ℹ Getting There & Away

Air Canada Express (p230), Air Creebec (p230) and Pascan (p323) all fly into Val d'Or from Montréal. **Autobus Maheux** (☑819-874-2200; www.autobusmaheux.com; 1420 4e Ave) buses go to Montréal ($95, seven hours, three daily), Rouyn-Noranda ($26, 1½ hours, three daily), Matagami ($58, 3½ hours, daily except Saturday) and Chibougamau ($81, six hours, daily).

Parc d'Aiguebelle

With cliffs and canyons, gorges and gorgeous woods, **Parc National d'Aiguebelle** (☑819-637-7322; www.sepaq.com/pq/aig; 12373 Rte d'Aiguebelle; adult/child $8.75/free; ☉year-round; **P**) ✦ offers up some stunning scenery. Within day-tripping distance of either Rouyn-Noranda or Val d'Or, the park is known for its hiking (and in winter, snowshoeing), with trails that lead you across its lakes and through its forests. A popular route is **La Traverse**, a 3km loop that takes you across a suspension bridge, 22m above Lac La Haie. You can also head out on the lakes by canoe, kayak or stand-up paddleboard; gear is available to rent at several locations in the park.

Permanent Huttopia tents are available at the **campgrounds** (☑819-637-7322; www.sepaq.com/pq/aig; sites from $26, cabins from $132, ready-to-camp tents from $94; ☉Jun-Nov; **P**) ✦ from summer through fall.

James Bay

Here in Québec's hinterland, a seemingly endless forest of boreal spruces sprouts from the earth. On many evenings, the sky turns a kaleidoscope of pinks and blues, which give way to blazing orange sunsets, and later, to swirls of the northern lights. Only 42,000 people live in this area roughly the size of Germany. Almost half are Cree residing in nine communities separated by hundreds of kilometers.

The near mythic Route de la Baie James ends at Radisson, 1400km north of Montréal. A 100km extension branches westward to Chisasibi, a Cree community near James Bay. The immense James Bay hydroelectric project, a series of hydroelectric stations that produces half of Québec's energy, defines the region. Many visitors trek north just to glimpse these massive developments.

Chibougamau and Oujé-Bougoumou are the region's most accessible destinations, offering experiences that introduce you to the North's outdoor activities and Indigenous Cree culture.

Matagami

After a lot of boreal forest, Matagami kind of pops out of nowhere and feels surprisingly busy. Since 1963, when the town was founded, it has been the site of a copper and zinc mine, as well as an active forestry industry. Both of these industries are still going strong here, and shift workers are always coming and going. Plus, almost everyone driving through on Rte 109 on the way to Radisson stops here for the night.

Hôtel-Motel Matagami (☑ 819-739-2501, 877-739-2501; www.hotelmatagami.com; 99 Blvd Matagami; r from $110; ❋ @ ☎) is considered the top place in town. It's decent enough and always seems to be crowded – mainly because of the restaurant (open 5am to 10pm).

Route de la Baie James

This road, an extension of Rte 109 to the James Bay hydroelectric projects, is paved, wide and in good shape. At 620km, it's the longest unserviced road in Canada.

Traveling along the Route de la Baie James (James Bay Rd), you'll see trees, and lots of them. You'll also pass loads of bogs, the occasional moose, ravens, foxes and, in the summer, the collected biomass of the world's flying insects.

As you're heading north (or returning south), it's possible to detour west to several Cree communities along James Bay: Waskaganish, at Km 237; Eastmain, at Km 350; Wemindji, at Km 518; and Chisasibi, at Km 600. Each of these communities is roughly 100km west of the James Bay Rd; except for the road to Chisasibi, the roads are unpaved. Note: there are no roads connecting these communities, so to visit more than one, you have to return to the highway.

At Km 6, the **tourist office** (☑ 819-739-4473; Km 6; ⊗ 24hr) operates 24 hours a day throughout the year. It's highly recommended that you stop; for safety reasons, everyone traveling north should register here.

Radisson

Named after explorer Pierre-Esprit Radisson, this village was set up in 1973 to house the workers on the James Bay hydroelectric project. It looks and feels larger than its population of less than 500 would suggest – partly because it was built to accommodate fluctuating numbers of workers (who work for eight days, then fly home for six) and partly because some families have decided to settle permanently here and create a real village.

The scenery around Radisson is spectacular, with views of the majestic Rivière La Grande from the built-up area around the larger-than-life LG2 hydroelectric power station – officially called the Robert-Bourassa Generating Facility – just outside town.

Everyone who makes it here takes a free, guided tour of the **power station** (☑ 800-291-8486; www.hydroquebec.com/visit/baie-james/bourassa.html; 66 Rue des Groseilliers, Complexe Pierre-Radisson; ⊗ English-language tours 1pm Mon & Fri mid-Jun–Aug, by appointment Sep–mid-Jun) **FREE** – the world's largest underground power-generating facility.

After driving until your fingers fall off, **Auberge Radisson** (☑ 819-638-7201, 888-638-7201; www.aubergeradisson.com; 66 Rue des Groseilliers; r from $150; P ❋ ☎) is actually quite a nice little hotel. It's even got a lounge where you can have a beer and a hot meal!

The **tourist office** (☑ 819-638-8687; www.localiteradisson.com; 198 Rue Jolliet; ⊗ 8am-8pm mid-Jun–early Sep) has Radisson travel information and can help arrange tours at the power plant.

Chisasibi

Near the point where Rivière La Grande meets James Bay, 100km west of Radisson, Chisasibi is a Cree village well worth visiting. The surrounding environment, windswept taiga doused by the Arctic breezes from James Bay, is haunting.

The town as it looks now has existed only since 1981. Before this, the residents lived on the island of Fort George, 10km from town, where the Hudson's Bay Company had set up a fur-trading post in 1837. Due to the James Bay Project, a massive hydroelectric project implemented in northern Québec in the 1970s, more than 200 houses were relocated from the island to the mainland. A vestige of the old-fashioned way of life survives in the many tipis seen in backyards, mainly used for smoking fish.

Contact **Cree Nation of Chisasibi** (☑ 819-855-3311, 819-855-2878; www.chisasibi. org; ☺ 9am-noon & 1-5pm Mon-Fri) for information on things to do and potential tours in and around Chisasibi.

Nunavik

This is Québec's northern limits, a land larger than Spain, yet populated by only around 13,000 people living in 14 villages. Hundreds of kilometers of tundra separate them from one another, and no roads join them. Almost 90% of the population is Inuit; the remainder includes Cree, Naskapis and white Québécois. This surreal territory stretches from the 55th to the 62nd parallel, bordered by Hudson Bay to the west, the Hudson Strait to the north, and Ungava Bay and the Labrador border to the east.

Because Nunavik can only be accessed by plane, few casual tourists make the trip. Yet those willing to make their own local con-

tacts can travel independently. Be prepared for high prices for goods and services. On average, food prices are close to double what they are in Québec City.

Land & Climate

There is great geographic diversity here. Even the tundra has many rich shades of beauty, and the region is far from a desolate plain of snow and ice. In the southwest, beaches and sand dunes stretch as far as the eye can see. In the northeast, the formidable Torngat Mountains extend in a series of bare, rocky peaks and untamed valleys 300km along the border of Labrador. The province's highest peak, Mont d'Iberville (1652m), is here.

There are also three meteorite-formed craters in Nunavik (of the 144 known on earth). The largest – indeed one of the largest on earth – is called Pingualuit, a 1.4-million-year-old cavity with a diameter of 3.4km and a depth of 433m (the height of a 145-story building) in parts. The lake that's formed inside the crater contains water considered among the purest in the world. In terms of transparency, it's second only to Japan's Lake Masyuko. Pingualuit lies 88km southwest of Kangiqsujuaq.

Floating above this unusual terrain are the magical northern lights (aurora borealis), which can be seen an average of 243 nights each year.

ⓘ Getting There & Away

First Air (p230) provides service between Montréal and Kuujjuaq. Air Inuit (p230) flies between Montréal and Kuujjuarapik, with connections to Kuujjuaq; it also flies between Québec City and Kuujjuaq.

These flights from Montréal or Québec City to Nunavik will typically run over $1000 each way; getting up here isn't cheap.

Nova Scotia

📞 902 / POP 923,598

Best Places to Eat

➡ Edna (p343)
➡ Canteen (p349)
➡ Lincoln Street Food (p357)
➡ Le Caveau (p370)

Best Places to Stay

➡ Prince George Hotel (p342)
➡ Alicion B&B (p356)
➡ Quarterdeck (p358)
➡ Oceanstone Seaside Resort (p350)

Why Go?

Facing the restless swells of the Atlantic, Nova Scotia is a place that's steeped in the sea. With its candy-striped lighthouses, salty fishing towns and towering red cliffs, this Maritime province feels thrillingly rugged and wild, especially in winter, when storms thrash the coastline and the ocean freezes. But come summer it's a different picture: Nova Scotians emerge to hike the trails, lounge on the beaches, tuck into gigantic lobster suppers and celebrate their Celtic roots with lively ceilidhs (parties with music and dancing). Life here has always been tough, but the locals' warm-hearted humor can't fail to make you feel welcome.

Most adventures begin in seaside Halifax, followed by postcard-perfect Peggy's Cove and Unesco-listed Lunenburg. Further afield, the vineyards of the Annapolis Valley beckon, along with the wild coastline of Cape Breton, the lakes and forests of Kejimkujik National Park and the incredible tides of the Bay of Fundy.

When to Go

Halifax

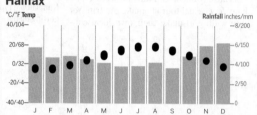

May & Jun You'll beat the summer crowds and prices – but some things may be closed.

Jul & Aug Peak summer season means long, warm days and events galore.

Sep & Oct Locals make the most of stunning fall foliage before the long winter comes.

History

From time immemorial the Mi'kmaq First Nation has lived throughout present-day Nova Scotia. When the French established the first European settlement at Port Royal (today's Annapolis Royal) in 1605, Grand Chief Membertou offered them hospitality and became a frequent guest of Samuel de Champlain.

That close relationship with the French led to considerable suspicion by the British after they gained control of Nova Scotia, and rewards were offered for Mi'kmaw scalps. Starting in 1755, most French-speaking Acadians were deported to Louisiana (where they became known as Cajuns) and elsewhere for refusing to swear allegiance to the British Crown.

Nova Scotia was repopulated by some 35,000 United Empire Loyalists retreating from the American Revolution, including a small number of African slaves owned by Loyalists as well as freed Black Loyalists. New England planters settled other communities, and from 1773 waves of Highland Scots arrived in northern Nova Scotia and Cape Breton Island.

Most Nova Scotians trace their ancestry to the British Isles, as a look at the lengthy 'Mac' and 'Mc' sections of the phone book easily confirms. Acadians who managed to return from Louisiana after 1764 found their lands in the Annapolis Valley occupied. They settled instead along the French Shore between Yarmouth and Digby, on Cape Breton Island around Chéticamp, and on Isle Madame. Today Acadians make up some 12% of the population, although not as many still identify French as their first language. African Nova Scotians make up about 5% of the population. Nova Scotia has close to 34,000 people of Indigenous identity, of which around 22,000 are First Nations people, predominantly from 18 Mi'kmaq communities.

ⓘ Information

Tourism Nova Scotia (☑ 902-425-5781, 800-565-0000; www.novascotia.com) operates visitor centers in Halifax and other locations within Nova Scotia province, plus a free accommodation-booking service, which is useful when rooms are scarce in midsummer. It publishes the *Doers & Dreamers Guide*, which lists places to stay, attractions and tour operators.

ⓘ Getting There & Away

AIR

The province's main air hub is Halifax Stanfield International Airport (p348), which has year-round daily flights to Canadian cities including Toronto, Montréal, Ottawa, Calgary, Fredericton, Saint John, Charlottetown and Moncton, as well as US cities including New York, Boston, Chicago, Philadelphia and Orlando.

In summer and fall there are also regular flights (some direct, some via a Canadian hub) to London, Paris and Frankfurt. Air Canada and Westjet cover nearly all the Canadian flights, with United and Delta handling most US flights.

In addition to the main airport at Halifax, Nova Scotia has two smaller airports: **JA Douglas McCurdy Sydney Airport** (www.sydneyairport.ca), which has regular flights to Halifax, Toronto and Montréal, and Yarmouth International Airport (www.yarmouthairport.ca/), which generally only handles charter and private flights.

PAL Airlines (PB; ☑ 800-563-2800; www.palairlines.ca) can be useful for getting to Nova Scotia from regional locations in Québec, New Brunswick and Newfoundland.

Air St-Pierre (☑ 877-277-7765; www.airsaintpierre.com) offers flights between Sydney and the French territory of St Pierre and Miquelon.

BOAT

The **Bay Ferries** (☑ 877-762-7245; www.ferries.ca) service from Yarmouth to Portland, Maine, is planned to resume in spring 2022; check the website for updates.

Prince Edward Island

Bay Ferries (www.ferries.ca; adult/car $20/79; ☺ May-Dec) operates the ferry between Caribou, near Pictou, and Wood Islands on Prince Edward Island (PEI) up to nine times daily. No reservations are required, but it's wise to show up half an hour before departure. Vehicle fees include all passengers for the 1¼-hour trip.

The ferry is free if you're traveling from Nova Scotia to PEI, but it's worth making a reservation anyway to guarantee a space. Note that there is no ferry service from January through April.

New Brunswick

Bay Ferries operates boats from Digby to Saint John, NB (adult/child from $39/23, 2¼ to 2¾

NOVA SCOTIA FAST FACTS

➡ Population: 923,598

➡ Area: 55,284 sq km

➡ Capital: Halifax

➡ Quirky fact: Has the only tidal power plant in the western hemisphere

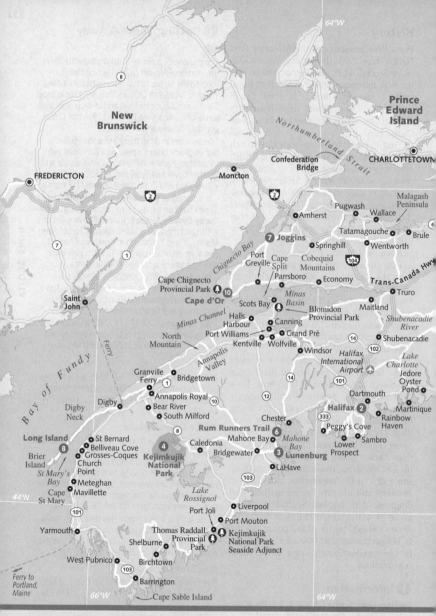

Nova Scotia Highlights

1 **Cabot Trail** (p379) Driving Cape Breton's snaking coastal road.

2 **Canadian Museum of Immigration at Pier 21** (p335) Learning about the immigrant experience.

3 **Lunenburg** (p353) Wandering the orderly streets of this model colonial town.

4 **Kejimkujik National Park** (p358) Hiking this wonderfully preserved wilderness.

5 **Louisbourg National Historic Site** (p388) Exploring Nova Scotia's colonial past at this fascinating fortress.

6 **Rum Runners Trail** (p349) Cycling along the beautiful South Shore.

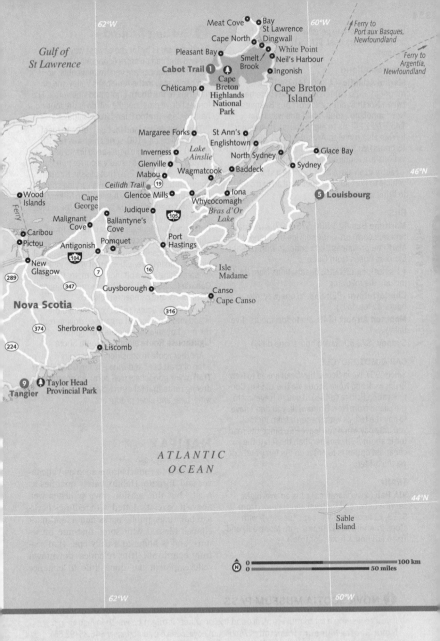

Gulf of St Lawrence

Meat Cove
Bay
St Lawrence
Cape North
Dingwall
Pleasant Bay
White Point
Neil's Harbour
Smelt Brook
Chéticamp
Cabot Trail ❶
Cape Breton Highlands National Park
Ingonish
Cape Breton Island

Margaree Forks
St Ann's
Inverness
Englishtown
Lake Ainslie
North Sydney
Glace Bay
Glenville
Sydney
Mabou
Wagmatcook
Baddeck
Ceilidh Trail
Glencoe Mills
Iona
Whycocomagh
Wood Islands
Cape George
Judique
Bras d'Or Lake
❺ Louisbourg
Malignant Cove
Ballantyne's Cove
Caribou
Pomquet
Port Hastings
Pictou
Antigonish
New Glasgow
Isle Madame
Nova Scotia
Guysborough
Canso
Cape Canso
Sherbrooke
Liscomb
❾ Tangier
Taylor Head Provincial Park

ATLANTIC OCEAN

Sable Island

0 — 100 km
0 — 50 miles

Ferry to Port aux Basques, Newfoundland
Ferry to Argentia, Newfoundland

❼ **Joggins Fossil Cliffs** (p372) Viewing 300-million-year-old fossils.

❽ **Whale watching** (p366) Getting up astonishingly close to cetaceans on an expedition

from Long Island into the Bay of Fundy.

❾ **Sea kayaking** (p389) Paddling into the spectacular 100 Wild Islands.

❿ **Cape d'Or Lighthouse** (p373) Gawking at the view from this lighthouse near Advocate Harbour.

hours); it's more expensive if you don't book ahead. Vehicles cost $113/119 in low/peak season.

Newfoundland

Marine Atlantic (☑ 800-341-7981; www.marineatlantic.ca) ferries ply the route between North Sydney and Port aux Basques, Newfoundland (adult/child one way from $45.57/21.24, six to eight hours). In summer, ferries also travel to Argentia ($121.26/58.88, 16 hours) on Newfoundland's east coast. Reservations are required for either trip.

Factor in an extra $114 to bring a standard-size vehicle to Port aux Basques, and an extra $203 to bring one to Argentia.

BUS

Maritime Bus (☑ 1-800-575-1807; www.maritimebus.com) provides service throughout the Maritime provinces and connects with Orléans Express buses from Québec.

Useful long-distance destinations from Halifax include the following:

Charlottetown (PEI; $58.25 one way, 4½ hours, twice daily)

Moncton Airport ($49, 3½ to four hours, five daily)

Sydney ($72.50, seven hours, one daily)

CAR & MOTORCYCLE

Since 1997, Nova Scotia has been linked to New Brunswick and Nova Scotia via the 12.9km Confederation Bridge (p438). If you're traveling to the island from New Brunswick, you don't have to pay the toll; as with the ferry from Pictou, you only pay when you leave PEI. Since the road toll is about $30 cheaper than the ferry, the cheapest option is to enter on the ferry and exit via the bridge.

TRAIN

VIA Rail (www.viarail.ca) runs an overnight service between Montréal and Halifax (from $223, 21 hours, daily except Tuesday), with stops in Amherst (17 hours from Montréal) and Truro (18 hours from Montréal).

🛈 Getting Around

Renting a car is by far the easiest way to get around and can be more economical than taking the bus. Distances are very manageable; you can easily stay in the Annapolis Valley and do day trips to the South Shore and vice versa. The longest drive most people will do is the four-hour haul to Cape Breton Island from Halifax.

The most direct (and fastest) route to most places will be on a 100-series highway (eg 101, 102, 103); these have high speed limits and limited exits. There's usually a corresponding older highway (eg 1, 2, 3) that passes through communities; these roads have varying speed limits, but they're rarely higher than 80km/h. The older roads might be slower, but the scenery along the way is much, much better, so take these routes whenever you can for the most enjoyable experience.

Ubiquitous car-rental agencies can be found at airports and in larger cities, but if you're looking for something with a bit more room, try **Cruise Canada** (☑ 800-671-8042; www.cruisecanada.com) for RV and camper rentals.

Tourism Nova Scotia (p331) has divided the island into a number of organised driving routes, the most popular of which is the signposted **Lighthouse Route** along the South Shore.

Another route to consider – especially if you're a fan of craft beer and wine – is the **Good Cheer Trail** (www.goodcheertrail.com), an organised driving route that takes in Nova Scotia's top wine, beer and cider producers.

HALIFAX

☑ 902 / POP 403,390

Compared to conurbations such as Vancouver and Toronto, Halifax barely qualifies as a city, but this seaside town punches well above its size: it's dotted with redbrick heritage buildings, public parks and a landmark citadel; blessed with some first-rate museums; and is home to a truly epic 4km seafront boardwalk. True, relentless downtown redevelopment has done little to enhance

---

🛈 NOVA SCOTIA MUSEUM PASS

If you're visiting a lot of museums around the province, it might be worth investing in a **Nova Scotia Museum Pass** (https://museum.novascotia.ca; adult/family $46.85/92.65), which grants unlimited admission to 28 museums for 12 months.

Museums covered by the pass include the Museum of Natural History (p339) and Maritime Museum of the Atlantic (p338) in Halifax, the Fisheries Museum (p355) in Lunenburg, the Dory Shop (p360) in Shelburne, the Acadian Village (p361) in Yarmouth, the Fundy Geological Museum (p371) in Parrsboro and loads more.

You can buy the pass online or at the first participating museum you visit.

the city's charm: boxy office blocks and uninspiring concrete carbuncles are rising where handsome ironstones and Victorian town houses once stood, although some exceptions (notably the new Central Library) show what can be achieved when planners exercise a little more quality control.

Above all, Halifax is a livable city: its small size, fresh air and easygoing lifestyle mean it scores high in quality-of-life tables. The nightlife and dining scene has come on in leaps and bounds in recent years: there are craft breweries and locavore bistros galore, especially around the trendy North End.

History

Pirates, warring colonialists and exploding ships make the history of Halifax read like an adventure story. From 1749, when Edward Cornwallis founded Halifax along what is today Barrington St, the British settlement expanded and flourished. The destruction of the French fortress at Louisbourg in 1760 increased British dominance and sealed Halifax's place as Nova Scotia's most important city.

Despite being home to two universities from the early 1800s, Halifax remained a rough-and-ready sailors' nest that, during the War of 1812, became a center for privateer black-market trade. As piracy lost its government endorsement, Halifax sailed smoothly into a mercantile era, and the city streets, particularly Market and Brunswick Sts, became home to countless taverns and brothels.

On April 14, 1912, three Halifax ships were sent in response to a distress call: the 'unsinkable' RMS *Titanic* had hit an iceberg. Over 1500 people were killed in the tragedy and many were buried at Fairview Cemetery, next to the Fairview Overpass on the Bedford Hwy.

A lesser-known piece of tragic local history occurred in 1917, during WWI, when the SS *Mont-Blanc,* a French munitions ship carrying TNT and highly flammable benzol, collided in the Halifax Narrows with a Norwegian vessel, the SS *Imo,* causing a fire. The French ship burned for 20 minutes before the fire reached its toxic cargo. The subsequent blast that ripped through the city became known as the Halifax Explosion and was the world's most powerful detonation prior to the testing of the atomic bomb. More than 1900 people were killed, and 9000 were injured. The entire suburb of

Richmond was leveled by the blast and First Nations Mi'kmaq communities along the shoreline were inundated by the resultant tsunami. The event remains the most significant disaster in Haligonian history.

◉ Sights

The downtown area, three universities and the older residential neighborhoods are contained on a compact peninsula cut off from mainland Halifax by an inlet called the North West Arm. Almost all sights of interest to visitors are concentrated in this area, making walking the best way to get around.

Point Pleasant Park is at the extreme South End of the peninsula, and the lively and multicultural North End neighborhood – home to African Nova Scotians, art-school students and plenty of hipsters – stretches from the midpoint to the northern extreme.

Two bridges span the harbor, connecting Halifax to Dartmouth and leading to highways north (for the airport) and east. The MacDonald Bridge at the eastern end of North St is closest to downtown.

The North End has been a distinct neighborhood for almost as long as Halifax has existed. In the early 1750s the 'North Suburbs' area became popular and subsequently grew thanks to its larger building lots. It's now the city's hippest district.

★**Canadian Museum of Immigration at Pier 21**   MUSEUM
(🖉902-425-7770; www.pier21.ca; 1055 Marginal Rd; adult/child $12/8; ⊗9:30am-5:30pm May-Nov, reduced hours Dec-Apr) There's an argument that this dockside museum is Canada's most important institution. Between 1928 and 1971, Pier 21 was the Canadian version of the USA's Ellis Island, where all prospective immigrants arrived. More than a million people passed through these redbrick halls, and it's an emotional experience to walk through the very same doorways where refugees from across the globe began new lives. A mix of audiovisual exhibits, poignant artifacts and personal testimonies make for a powerful and moving museum.

★**Citadel Hill National Historic Site**   HISTORIC SITE
(🖉902-426-5080; www.pc.gc.ca/en/lhn-nhs/ns/halifax; 5425 Sackville St; adult/child Jun–mid-Sep $11.70/free, May & mid-Sep–Oct $7.80/free, other times free; ⊗9am-6pm Jul & Aug, to 5pm rest of year) Perched atop the grassy hillock looming over town, this star-shaped fort played

Halifax

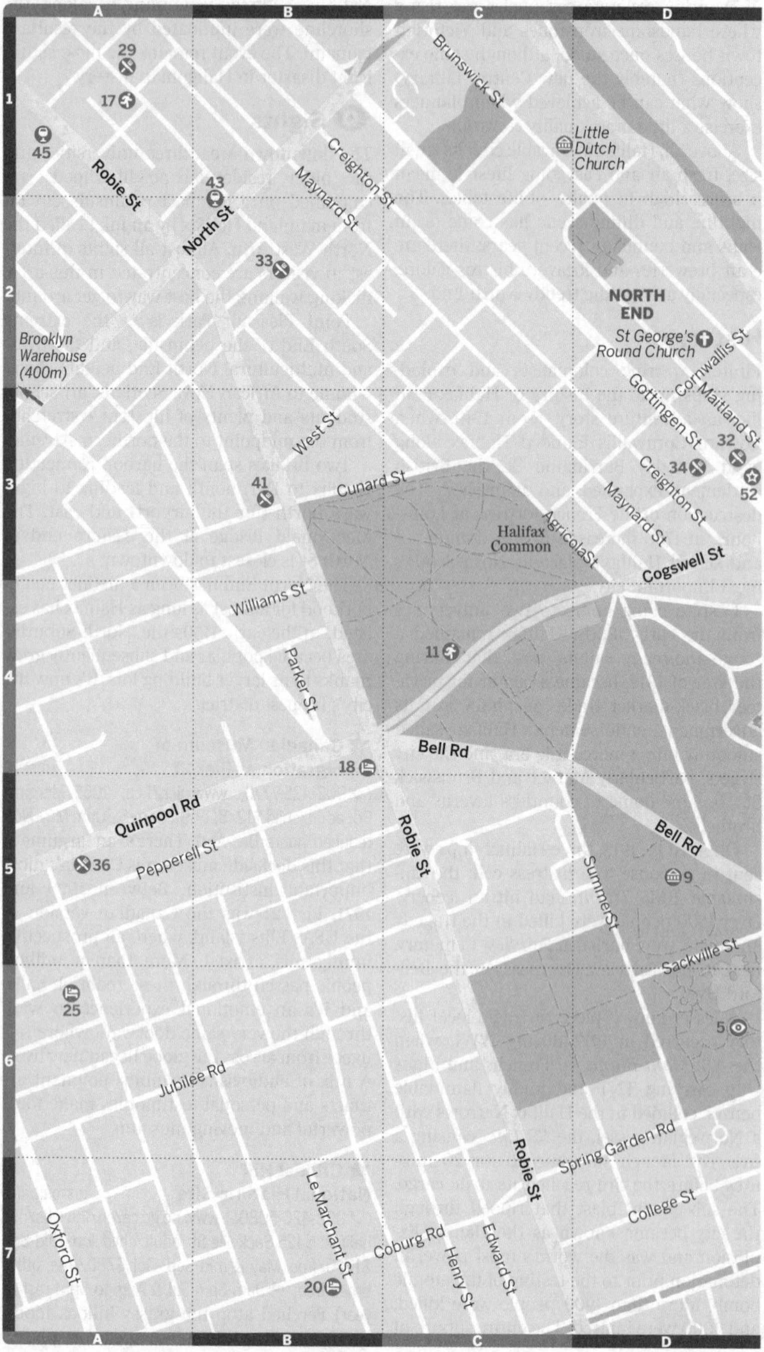

A **B** **C** **D**

29

17

45

Robie St

Creighton St

Brunswick St

Little
Dutch
Church

43

North St

Maynard St

33

NORTH
END

St George's
Round Church

Gottingen St

Cornwallis St

Maitland St

32

Brooklyn
Warehouse
(400m)

West St

Cunard St

41

Creighton St

Maynard St

34

52

Halifax
Common

Agricola St

Cogswell St

Williams St

11

Parker St

18

Bell Rd

Bell Rd

Quinpool Rd

36

Pepperell St

Robie St

Summer St

9

Sackville St

25

5

Jubilee Rd

Oxford St

Le Marchant St

Coburg Rd

Henry St

Edward St

Robie St

Spring Garden Rd

College St

20

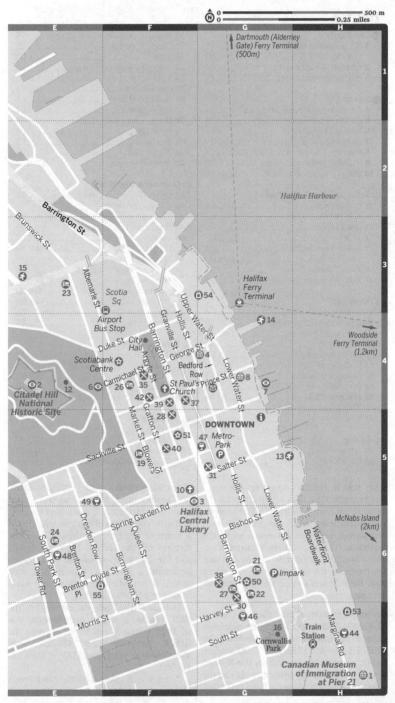

0   500 m
0   0.25 miles

Dartmouth (Alderney Gate) Ferry Terminal (500m)

Halifax Harbour

Brunswick St

Barrington St

15

23

Albemarle St

Scotia Sq

Airport Bus Stop

Granville St

Hollis St

Upper Water St

54

Halifax Ferry Terminal

14

Woodside Ferry Terminal (1.2km)

Duke St

City Hall

George St

4

Scotiabank Centre

Barrington St

Bedford Row

Lower Water St

8

6

Carmichael St

Argyle St

26

35

St Paul's Church

Prince St

7

2

Citadel Hill National Historic Site

12

42

39

37

28

DOWNTOWN

Market St

Grafton St

51

47

Metro-Park

Sackville St

40

Blowers St

19

31

Salter St

Hollis St

13

10

3

Halifax Central Library

49

Bishop St

Lower Water St

McNabs Island (2km)

Waterfront Boardwalk

24

Dresden Row

Spring Garden Rd

Queen St

Birmingham St

South Park St

48

Brenton St

Barrington St

21

Impark

Tower Rd

Brenton Pl

Clyde St

55

38

50

27

22

30

46

Morris St

Harvey St

16

Cornwallis Park

Train Station

53

44

South St

Marginal Rd

Canadian Museum of Immigration at Pier 21

1

Halifax

a key role in Halifax's founding. Construction began in 1749; the current citadel is the fourth, built from 1818 to 1861. The grounds and battlements inside the fort are open year-round, with free admission when the exhibits are closed, but it's better to come between May and October, when you can visit the barracks, the guards' room, the signal post, the engineer's store and the gunpowder magazines.

Maritime Museum of the Atlantic   MUSEUM
(☏ 902-424-7490; http://maritimemuseum.nova scotia.ca; 1675 Lower Water St; adult/child May-Oct $9.55/5.15, Nov-Apr $5.15/3.10; ⊙9:30am-5pm May-Oct, closed to 1pm Sun & all day Mon Nov-Apr) Sea dogs will love this briny museum on the waterfront, which houses a huge collection of maritime memorabilia relating to Atlantic Canada's many nautical activities, from merchant shipping and small-boat building to the days of the world-war convoys. There's a range of permanent exhibits, including displays on the Halifax Explosion (p335) and the *Titanic* (you can sit in a replica deckchair), a collection of small boats, scale models of important steamships, and a recreation of a 1900s chandlery.

Outside at the dock you can explore the **CSS Acadia**, a retired hydrographic vessel from England, and WWII corvette the **HMCS Sackville** (☏902-429-2132; www. hmcssackville.ca; adult/child $3/2; ⊙10am-5pm Jun-Oct).

Admission is covered by the Nova Scotia Museum Pass (p334).

Art Gallery of Nova Scotia   GALLERY

(☑902-424-5280; www.artgalleryofnovascotia.
ca; 1723 Hollis St; adult/child $12/5, 5-9pm Thu
free; ⊘10am-5pm Sat-Wed, to 9pm Thu & Fri) The
province's premier art institution is a must-
see. It has a strong collection of local art,
particularly the work of folk artist Maud
Lewis, including the original tiny house
(measuring 3m by 4m) where she lived most
of her life, and which she turned into a living canvas. The main exhibit in the lower
hall changes regularly and features anything
from ancient art to the avant-garde.

Halifax Public Gardens   GARDENS

(www.halifaxpublicgardens.ca; 5665 Spring Garden
Rd; ⊘sunrise-sunset) `FREE` Established in
1867 to mark Confederation, but formally
opened to the public in 1875, Halifax's delightful 6.5-hectare public gardens are a fine
example of Victorian horticultural planning.
Stocked with lakes, statues, fountains, bridges, ponds and a huge variety of trees and
formal flower beds, the gardens also have a
bandstand where old-time tunes parp away
on Sunday afternoons.

★Halifax Central Library   LIBRARY

(☑902-490-5700; www.halifaxpubliclibraries.ca;
5440 Spring Garden Rd; ⊘9am-9pm Mon-Thu, to
6pm Fri & Sat, noon-6pm Sun) `FREE` Built on a
former parking lot, this stunning modern
library, composed of glass boxes stacked
artfully on top of each other, was opened in
2014 and has become a much-loved meeting
spot for Haligonians. Inside, concrete staircases ascend Escher-like through the central
atrium, leading toward a rooftop where
there's an excellent cafe and viewing garden.

Halifax Town Clock   NOTABLE BUILDING

(Old Town Clock; Brunswick St) Atop Citadel Hill,
Halifax's Palladian-style town clock looks as
though it would be more at home in a Vene-
tian lane, but it has been faithfully keeping
time here for over 200 years. The inner
workings arrived in Halifax from London in
1803, after being ordered by Prince Edward,
the Duke of Kent.

Museum of Natural History   MUSEUM

(☑902-424-7353; http://naturalhistory.novasco
tia.ca; 1747 Summer St; adult/child $6.30/4.05;
⊘9am-5pm; ▣) Natural history with a Nova
Scotian bent is the modus operandi of this
interesting museum, where informative exhibits cover everything from the gold rush to
Mi'kmaw culture, whaling and Nova Scotian
woodlands. A perennial favorite is Gus the

Gopher Tortoise, who's been a resident here
for more than 70 years.

St Mary's Cathedral Basilica   CHURCH

(☑902-429-9800; www.halifaxyarmouth.org/
cathedral; 1508 Barrington St) You can't miss
Halifax's most ornate cathedral, which has
the largest freestanding granite spire in
North America.

Fairview Lawn Cemetery   HISTORIC SITE

(☑902-490-4883; 3720 Windsor St) When the
RMS *Titanic* sank, the bodies of those not
lost at sea were brought to Halifax. Among
other sites, there are 19 graves at **Mt Olivet
Catholic Cemetery** (7076 Mumford Rd) and
121 here at the Fairview Lawn Cemetery.
Frequently visited graves include the touching Celtic Cross and Unknown Child monuments, and one belonging to J Dawson, a
possible namesake of Leonardo DiCaprio's
character in the film *Titanic* – although
according to director James Cameron, the
name echo is simply an eerie coincidence.

🏃 Activities

I Heart Bikes   CYCLING

(☑902-406-7774; www.iheartbikeshfx.com; 1507
Lower Water St; rentals per hour from $12; ⊘10am-
6pm May, 9am-8pm Jun-Aug) If you prefer two
wheels to two legs, you'll heart these folks,
too. Centrally located near the Halifax waterfront, it's a great spot to pick up a chariot
and start pedaling. It offers a range of city
bikes and e-bikes, and also runs city tours.

Timber Lounge   ADVENTURE SPORTS

(☑902-453-8627; www.timberlounge.ca; 2712 Agricola St; per person $30; ⊘4:30-10:30pm Tue-Thu
& Sun, noon-10:30pm Fri & Sat) Always harbored
lumberjack fantasies? Head here and learn

AFRICAN HALIFAX

The **Africville Heritage Trust
Museum** (www.africvillemuseum.org;
5795 Africville Rd; adult/child $5.75/free;
⊘10am-4pm Tue-Sat) tells the story of
Halifax's predominantly African suburb,
the residents of which were evicted and
their homes razed in what became the
local scandal of the 1960s. In 2010 Halifax's mayor issued a formal apology to
the community. Poignantly, the museum is housed in a replica of the Seaview
United Baptist Church that was once
the center of the neighborhood.

how to chuck an ax like a pro. The aim is to hit a target using a double-headed ax; staff are on hand to show you the ropes. For a confirmed booking, you'll need a minimum of six, although walk-in spots are often available on the day.

If not, you can always just turn up, have a beer and enjoy the ax-tion.

Seven Bays Bouldering
CLIMBING

(☑902-407-9656; www.sevenbaysbouldering. com; 2019 Gottingen St; bouldering day passes $16; ⏰8am-11pm Mon-Sat, to 9pm Sun, boulder wall closed 8am-1pm Tue) Now this is something you'd only see in Canada: a coffee shop with its own bouldering wall and gym next door. Kick yourself into gear with a cortado and buckle up, or just sit back and watch the show. There's an early-bird discount of $3 before 2pm.

McNabs Island
HIKING

(https://mcnabsisland.ca) Fine sand and cobblestone shorelines, salt marshes, forests and abandoned military fortifications paint the landscape of this 400-hectare island in Halifax Harbour. The website has a list of local boat operators who can shuttle you over (from $20 per person). It's a popular hiking and bird-spotting location, and in summer there are guided tours once a week.

Point Pleasant Park
HIKING

(☑902-490-4700; 5718 Point Pleasant Dr; ⏰sunrise-sunset; 🚌9) Some 39km of nature trails, picnic spots and the beautiful 18th-century Martello Tower are all found within this 75-hectare sanctuary, just 1.5km south of the city center. Trails around the perimeter of the park offer views of McNabs Island, the open ocean and the North West Arm.

Emera Oval
SKATING

(☑902-490-2347; www.halifax.ca/skatehrm; 5775 Cogswell St; ⏰7am-7pm) FREE This fabulous municipal facility features in-line skating in summer and ice-skating in winter, including free winter skate rentals. Photo ID is required.

🧭 Tours

Halifax Free Tours
WALKING

(www.halifaxfreetours.wixsite.com/halifaxfreetours; ⏰10am & 3pm Jun-Sep) FREE You can't beat the price of these free 1½-hour walking tours of downtown Halifax, led by friendly local guides. Send an email to reserve a spot, and please remember to tip! All tours leave from the viewing platform next to Halifax Citadel.

Local Tasting Tours
FOOD & DRINK

(☑902-818-9055; www.localtastingtours.com; tours from $44) Eat and drink your way around Halifax's burgeoning restaurant scene on these fun foodie-themed tours. A variety of itineraries is available, covering downtown, SoMo (South of Morris St) and a night out on the town.

Ambassatours
CRUISE

(☑1-800-565-9662; www.ambassatours.com; 6575 Bayne St) This operator runs Halifax Harbour tours, including popular family-oriented trips on the Harbour Hopper amphibious bus (adult/child $37/21, 55 minutes) and the Theodore Tugboat ($21/16, 30 minutes).

It also runs cruises on the **Tall Ship Silva** (www.tallshipsilva.com; 1751 Lower Water St; 1½hr cruises adult/child $33/21.50) and the yacht **J Farwell** (adult/child $80/70), as well as hop-on, hop-off bus tours.

All trips run from one of the piers along the waterfront, but head office is way out of town in the Hydrostone district.

Tattle Tours
WALKING

(☑902-494-0525; www.tattletours.ca; $25; ⏰10am & 2pm mid-Jul–mid-Oct) Lively two-hour tours filled with local gossip, pirate tales and ghost stories depart from Cornwallis Park, opposite the Westin Nova Scotian Hotel.

⭐ Festivals & Events

TD Halifax Jazz Festival
MUSIC

(www.halifaxjazzfestival.ca; tickets from $28; ⏰Jul) Now in its fourth decade, Halifax's beloved jazz festival boasts free outdoor jazz concerts and evening performances ranging from world music to classic jazz trios.

Nova Scotia Tattoo
CULTURAL

(www.nstattoo.ca; ⏰Jul) Honoring Nova Scotia's Celtic heritage, this military-style musical tattoo features an array of marching bands.

Halifax Pride Week
LGBTIQ+

(www.halifaxpride.com; ⏰Jul) The largest LGBTIQ+ Pride festival east of Montréal paints the town pink and every other shade of the rainbow.

Halifax International
Busker Festival
PERFORMING ARTS

(www.buskers.ca; ⊙Aug) The oldest and largest festival of its kind in Canada draws comics, mimes, daredevils and musicians from around the world to the Halifax waterfront.

Halifax Seaport
Cider & Beerfest
FOOD & DRINK

(www.seaportbeerfest.com; ⊙Aug) Brewers from across the Maritimes and other beer-loving areas around the world congregate on Halifax for this summertime celebration of craft beer and cider.

Atlantic International Film Festival
FILM

(www.finfestival.ca; ⊙Sep) Halifax's week-long film fest showcases quality flicks from the Atlantic region, Canada and beyond.

Atlantic Fringe Festival
THEATER

(www.atlanticfringe.ca; ⊙Sep) The theater comes to town for 10 days in September, showcasing offbeat and experimental works by emerging and established artists.

Halifax Pop Explosion
MUSIC

(www.halifaxpopexplosion.com; passes from $80; ⊙Oct) Venues across the city host established and emerging acts over four heady days in October.

🛏 Sleeping

Halifax has plenty of hotels, from heritage properties through to modern aparthotels and the usual chain suspects. Unlike in the rest of the province, there isn't a huge selection of B&Bs, nor are there any luxury hotels that could be considered truly world-class. Be sure to book ahead during the peak months of June to September, when beds fill fast and prices are at their highest.

HI Halifax
HOSTEL $

(📞902-422-3863; www.hihostels.ca; 1253 Barrington St; dm members/nonmembers $26/30; 🎧) In a rambling, wood-clad Victorian house, this hostel is a cheery place to stay, even if the building does look as though it's about to fall down. Rooms are shabby: basic steel bunk beds, minimal frills. The common areas, including a good kitchen and a small back garden, are the best part. Several pubs and venues are a walk away.

Marigold B&B
B&B $

(📞902-423-4798; www.marigoldbedandbreakfast.com; 6318 Norwood St; s/d $75/85; 🅿️🚭🎧) Feel at home in this welcoming artist's nest full of bright floral paintings and fluffy cats.

CRYSTAL CRESCENT BEACH

Eighteen kilometers south of Halifax, near the village of Sambro, this gorgeous **provincial park** (http://parks.novascotia.ca/content/crystal-crescent-beach; 223 Sambro Creek Rd) boasts three distinct beaches in separate coves; the third one out, toward the southwest, is clothing optional and gay friendly. An 8.5km hiking trail begins just inland and heads through barrens, bogs and boulders to Pennant Point.

Marigold is located in a tree-lined residential area in the North End, with easy public-transport access.

Dalhousie University
HOSTEL $

(📞902-494-8840; www.dal.ca/dept/summer-accommodations.html; 6230 Coburg Rd; s/d from $45/69; ⊙May-Aug; 🅿️🎧♿) The single and twin dorm rooms with shared bathrooms here are clean but bland. Most are adjacent to all the included university amenities, a short walk from the Spring Garden Rd area.

★Cambridge Suites Halifax
HOTEL $$

(📞902-420-0555; www.cambridgesuiteshalifax.com; 1583 Brunswick St; d $159-209, ste $169-299; 🅿️🚭❄️🎧) It's not the prettiest from the outside, but this large, well-run hotel offers perhaps the most practical rooms in the city, with modern studio-style spaces that include kitchenettes, sofas and desks. Best value are the one-bedroom suites. Free continental breakfast is served in the dining room downstairs.

Halliburton
INN $$

(📞902-420-0658; www.thehalliburton.com; 5184 Morris St; d $169-229, ste $299-350; 🅿️❄️@🎧) Smart, refined and with a dash of Haligonian history that's getting increasingly hard to find, the Halliburton occupies a classic redbrick Victorian edifice in the middle of downtown. It offers 29 traditionally decorated rooms with varying layouts, and a very pleasant hidden garden out the back.

Lord Nelson Hotel & Suites
HOTEL $$

(📞902-423-5130; www.lordnelsonhotel.ca; 1515 S Park St; d $169-239, ste $289-399; 🅿️🚭@🎧) Opened in 1928 opposite Halifax's Public Gardens (p339), this heritage beauty is the choice for those who like their hotels with a touch of class (the chandelier-lit, wood-paneled, painting-lined lobby alone makes a stay here worthwhile). After the grand entrance, the rooms feel a tad generic, but spoils like Nespresso machines and Aveda spa products don't go amiss.

Homewood Suites by Hilton Halifax-Downtown
HOTEL $$

(☑ 855-605-0320; www.hilton.com; 1960 Brunswick St; r $226-473; P ⊜ ❋ 🛜 ≋) Tapping into the Airbnb trend, these multiroom studios and suites are ideal for families or long stays, with fully kitted-out kitchens and space to spare. Admittedly, they're fairly bland, but rates include daily breakfast, use of the pool and occasional guest socials. The location on the corner of a busy intersection isn't ideal.

Atlantica Hotel
HOTEL $$

(☑ 902-423-1161; www.atlanticahotelhalifax.com; 1980 Robie St; d $129-214; P ⊜ ❋ 🛜 ≋) This North End hotel feels old school, mostly in a good way. The office-block facade is downright ugly, but inside it's spruced up and modern, with big pluses such as a restaurant and an attic-style indoor pool. Rooms fall into three tiers (silver, gold and platinum), plus there are suites and family studios; go gold or higher for any kind of view.

Waverley Inn
INN $$

(☑ 902-423-9346; www.waverleyinn.com; 1266 Barrington St; d $135-245; P ❋ 🛜) In business since 1876, this lemon-yellow inn has rooms with their own little quirks, from bold antiques to luxurious linens, swagged curtains and Turkish rugs. It feels rather theatrical, and fittingly the guest book includes both Oscar Wilde and PT Barnum. The period building means that, apart from the suites, rooms are small, and some are only accessible by stairs.

★ Prince George Hotel
HOTEL $$$

(☑ 902-425-1986; www.princegeorgehotel.com; 1725 Market St; d $229-367; P ❋ @ ≋ ≋) This suave city hotel is as slick as Halifax gets: every inch looks as though it's been designed for an Instagram post, from the arch-windowed interior pool to the landscaped patio and the LevelBar cocktail corner. Rooms are equally stylish (Crown-floor rooms have their own private lounge), and the Gio restaurant is really good.

Pebble Bed & Breakfast
B&B $$$

(☑ 902-423-3369; www.thepebble.ca; 1839 Armview Tce; r $245-345; ⊜ 🛜 ❋) The two suites of this luxurious B&B, in a posh, waterfront residential area, feature plush, high beds, gorgeous bathrooms and modern-meets-antique decor. Irish owner Elizabeth grew up in a pub-owning family and brings lively, joyous energy from the Emerald Isle to her delightful home. It's a stone's throw from downtown. There's a two-night minimum stay from June to October.

🍴 Eating

If you're going to splurge on eating out anywhere in Nova Scotia, Halifax is the place to do it. The city has some fantastic restaurants, with a particular concentration in the trendy North End. Bars and pubs nearly always serve food, too.

The free quarterly *Curated* (www.curatedmagazine.ca) keeps track of the city's hot dining tips and publishes a popular annual guide. It's available at restaurants and bars around the city.

Board Room Game Cafe
CAFE $

(☑ 902-423-7545; www.boardroomgames.ca; 1256 Barrington St; wraps $8.50-9.50, pizzas $6-8; ⊙ 11am-midnight Mon-Thu & Sun, to 2am Fri & Sat) There's a choice of 500 board games, from classic to contemporary, at this fun hangout, with wraps, pizzas, good coffee and craft beers to guzzle as you play. Don't worry if you're a beginner: the staff's encyclopaedic knowledge will match you up with something fun.

It seems a *lot* busier since Nova Scotia relaxed its pot laws...

Heartwood Bakery
VEGETARIAN $

(☑ 902-425-2808; www.iloveheartwood.ca; 6250 Quinpool Rd; mains $11-16; ⊙ 11am-8pm; 🍴) Everything feels as though it's doing you good at this fantastic veggie-vegan restaurant, which became so popular it now has a second location (at 3061 Gottingen St), plus a seasonal spot on the harbor. Delicious salads, kamut-crust pizzas, buddha bowls, veggie burgers – Heartwood really nails it. In fact, for non-carnivores there's nowhere better to eat in Halifax.

★ Bar Kismet
BISTRO $$

(☑ 902-487-4319; www.barkismet.com; 2733 Agricola St; small plates $12-15, large plates $25-27; ⊙ 5pm-midnight Tue-Sun) Impeccable small plates of seafood have made this tiny bar-bistro a favorite among foodie North Enders, and deservedly so: dishes zing with surprising combinations and flavors, such as bass with morel mushrooms and artichokes, or raw scallop with lemongrass and turnip. The decor's stripped right back – bare wood, mirrors, pendant lights – putting the focus firmly on the food.

★**Edna** CANADIAN **$$**
(☑902-431-5683; www.ednarestaurant.com; 2053 Gottingen St; brunch $12-20, mains $24-36; ☺5-11pm Fri & Sat, 5-10pm Tue-Thu & Sun) At the edge of the North End, this hipster diner has strong competition but is still many people's first choice. It's bare bones as far as decor goes: a long wooden table for communal dining, a tiled bar, metal stools and tables for two. Food is modern bistro: risotto, seared scallops, classic steaks, all lovingly prepared. Edna equals excellence.

★**Field Guide** BISTRO **$$**
(☑902-405-4506; www.fieldguidehfx.com; 2076 Gottingen St; mains $12-24; ☺5pm-midnight Tue-Sat, 10am-2pm & 5pm-midnight Sun) At this hipster diner you order according to hunger level (from 'Sorta Hungry' starters to 'Still Hungry' desserts). It's a gimmick, but the food is first rate: fresh, surprising and modern, from cured salmon on seed bread with ricotta to fried chicken on a biscuit. The decor is minimal: brushed-concrete floors, a long bar, and big windows onto the street.

★**Brooklyn Warehouse** CANADIAN **$$**
(☑902-446-8181; www.brooklynwarehouse.ca; 2795 Windsor St; mains lunch $12-18, dinner $23-30; ☺11:30am-10pm Mon-Sat; ☑) It's aptly named: there's definitely a New York flavor to this neighborhood eatery, with its worn wood, tobacco-yellow walls and chalkboard menus. The food selection changes fast, but it's strong on rich, hearty bistro fare; hopefully the Dragon's Breath (a take on the classic Caesar salad) will be on when you visit.

Antojo Tacos MEXICAN **$$**
(☑902-405-2790; www.antojo.ca; 1667 Argyle St; tacos $4.50-6, mains $12-22; ☺4-10pm Sun & Mon, 11:30am-10pm Tue-Thu, 11:30am-midnight Fri & Sat) This downtown taco joint is equally popular for a midday lunch or a late-night mescal-fueled feria. Tacos are the star, of course: zingy chipotle chicken, spicy battered Baja fish or crispy

cauliflower, accompanied by barbecued corn and a bewildering tequila selection. Day of the Dead decor adds to the Mex-themed fun. It's popular: reserve or queue – your call.

Highwayman SPANISH **$$**
(☑902-407-5260; www.highwaymanhfx.com; 1673 Barrington St; small plates $5-12; ☺4pm-midnight Sun & Tue-Fri, 2pm-midnight Sat) You could be in a backstreet of Barcelona at this moody tapas joint, which specializes in Spanish-inspired small plates and Basque-style *pintxos:* manchego and jamon, quail egg and chorizo, Arctic char. There's a great cheese and charcuterie selection, and a fantastic cocktail bar. It looks lovely, too, with its tall windows, dark tones and intimate nooks. No reservations.

Studio East ASIAN **$$**
(☑902-422-8096; www.studioeastfood.ca; 6021 Cunard St; mains $13-22; ☺5-10pm or 11pm Tue-Sat) Asian fusion of the first order: sticky hoisin-braised ribs, pork- and fish-curry ramen, Thai salads and Japanese 'Karaage' chicken dinners, with pickles, fried rice and spicy gochujang mayo. It's good for non meat-eaters, too: most dishes can be made with tofu. Order a tiki cocktail, an event in itself.

enVie: A Vegan Kitchen VEGETARIAN **$$**
(☑902-492-4077; www.enviehalifax.com; 5775 Charles St; mains $11-18; ☺11am-9pm Tue-Thu, to 10pm Fri, 10am-10pm Sat, to 9pm Sun; ☑) Halifax's roster of vegan restaurants is growing fast, but enVie is one of the first and best. It serves exactly the kind of food you'd want: delicious homemade soups, crunchy pear and arugula salads, loaded flatbreads, and imaginative non-meat versions of cheeseburgers, wings, tacos and pad thai (thanks to the miracles of tofu, seitan and oyster mushrooms).

Stubborn Goat PUB FOOD **$$**
(☑902-405-4554; www.stubborngoat.ca; 1579 Grafton St; small plates $9-19, mains $14-28; ☺11:30am-2am) Belly-filling pub grub, from generous burgers to fish-and-chips, is what's on offer at the Goat. The beer selection is good, and it also has a seasonal beer garden down on the waterfront.

Morris East ITALIAN **$$**
(☑902-444-7663; www.morriseast.com; 5212 Morris St; pizzas $15-20; ☺11:30am-9pm, to 10pm Fri & Sat) Halifax has some good pizza joints,

344

BRIGITTE SMITH/GETTY IMAGES ©

BENEDEK/GETTY IMAGES ©

MOLLIEGPHOTO/SHUTTERSTOCK ©

1. Cape Breton Highlands National Park (p379)

The best known of Nova Scotia's two national parks.

2. Lunenburg (p353)

A perfect example of a Nova Scotian fishing town, Lunenberg's architecture has earned it Unesco World Heritage status.

3. Joggins Fossil Cliffs (p372)

One of the most complete fossil records anywhere in Canada.

4. Fortress of Louisbourg (p388)

Built by the French but battled over countless times before being burned to the ground in 1760, the current site recreates the 1744 fortress.

but this is the pick. Pies are available in your choice of white, whole-wheat or gluten-free dough, and there are some really left-field options: try the peach, rosemary aioli, goat's cheese and prosciutto.

It's proved so popular that there are three other outlets dotted around the city.

Wooden Monkey CANADIAN $$
(📞 902-444-3844; www.thewoodenmonkey.ca; 1707 Grafton St; mains $15-30; ⏱ 11am-10pm; 🅿) 🍴 A cross between a neighborhood diner and a city pub, the Monkey is a good stop if you're just looking for a simple supper and pint of something local and cold. It looks convincingly worn in, with a Victorian facade and lots of dark wood. Pasta, seafood, burgers, steaks – the menu covers it all.

Chives Canadian Bistro CANADIAN $$$
(📞 902-420-9626; www.chives.ca; 1537 Barrington St; mains $25-35; ⏱ 5-9:30pm) Proper, formal Canadian fine dining in the heart of downtown is on offer at Chives, one of the city's longest-running restaurants. Seasonally driven, artfully presented dishes are the stock-in-trade of chef Craig Flinn, and the food tastes as lovely as it looks.

The venue features dark wood, bluevelour benches and antique-mirrored walls.

Press Gang SEAFOOD $$$
(📞 902-423-8816; www.thepressgang.ca; 5218 Prince St; single oysters $3.25, mains $35-46; ⏱ 5-10pm) This is one of the city's old-school supper spots, in more ways than one. The building (erected in 1759) is one of the oldest stone structures in downtown Halifax, and the walls give it a cellar-like atmosphere very different from that of most of the city's restaurants. Oysters are the specialty, plus indulgent 'from the sea' and 'from the land' mains.

Five Fishermen SEAFOOD $$$
(📞 902-422-4421; www.fivefishermen.com; 1740 Argyle St; mains $29-49; ⏱ 5-9pm Sun-Thu, to 10pm Fri & Sat) As the name suggests, this upscale place focuses on the fruits of the fisher's art: oysters, lobsters, halibut, Arctic char, swordfish and plenty more, alongside premium steaks and classic lobster dinners. There are booth seats and tasteful lighting in the formal main restaurant, plus a more relaxed oyster bar next door.

🍷 Drinking & Nightlife

Halifax rivals St John's, NL, for the most drinking holes per capita. The biggest concentration of bars is on Argyle St, where temporary street-side patios expand the sidewalk each summer (it can get a little boisterous on weekends). Pubs and bars close at 2am (a few hours earlier on Sunday).

★ **Stilwell** CRAFT BEER
(📞 902-421-1672; www.barstillwell.com; 1672 Barrington St; ⏱ noon-2am Thu-Sat, 4pm-2am Sun-Wed) A massive, wall-size chalkboard of brews from across Canada and beyond (all with a handwritten description and each delivered through a brass tap) gives this downtown bar probably the best beer selection in the city. Staff are incredibly knowledgeable and will help guide your choice. There's a menu of delicious small plates for late-night snacking.

It also runs a summer **beer garden** (5688 Spring Garden Rd; ⏱ noon-late in fine weather).

★ **Good Robot** CRAFT BEER
(📞 902-446-1692; www.goodrobotbrewing.ca; 2736 Robie St; ⏱ noon-2am Mon-Fri, 10am-2am Sat & Sun) This North End microbrewery has become known for its wild beers: you might taste a watermelon-and-kiwi fruit Pink Flamingo, a coffee-and-cherry-pie ale or a jalapeño-spiked lager (the names are equally wild). It's in a warehouse-style space with a pleasant beer garden; the pub snacks are delicious, too.

★ **Lot Six** COCKTAIL BAR
(📞 902-428-7428; www.lotsix.ca; 1685 Argyle St; cocktails $12-15; ⏱ 4pm-2am, plus brunch 11am-2pm Sat & Sun) The soaring glass atrium that floods the room with light adds an extra touch of class to this slinky cocktail joint, which mostly crafts its own mixes but also offers a few shaken-up classics. Try the Springtime Smash, with tequila, Aperol, lemon, grapefruit and mint. It also serves fantastic food (mains $14 to $24).

Chain Yard Urban Cidery PUB
(📞 902-407-2244; www.chainyardcider.com; 2606 Agricola St; ⏱ 11:30am-11pm or 11:30pm) Craving a change from the craft-beer tsunami in Halifax? No sweat: head for the city's only craft cidery, with wares made from 100% Nova Scotia apples. Try a dry Pippin Russet, a super-tart Farmhouse Sour or a Polar Perry (made with pears), or really offbeat brews

laced with kombucha, grape skins and rose petals. There's a patio for outdoor drinking.

Propeller Brewing Company   MICROBREWERY
(☑ 902-468-1026; www.drinkpropeller.ca; 2015 Gottingen St; ⊙ 10am-8pm Mon & Tue, to 10pm Wed & Thu, to midnight Fri & Sat, noon-10pm Sun) In the first wave of Halifax microbreweries, Propeller is still leading the way with its consistently good beers: the core range includes a pilsner, a lager, a porter and several pale ales, with seasonals based on pumpkin, coffee, dark berries and stone fruit.

Even better, there's a vintage arcade in the basement: let the Asteroids tournament commence!

Tom's Little Havana   BAR
(☑ 902-423-8667; www.tomslittlehavana.wix.com/cafe; 1540 Birmingham St; ⊙ 11:30am-2am) Craft beers, game nights, Scotch nights and a daily happy hour (5pm to 8pm) make Tom's feel like an extension of the living room at your best mate's place.

Garrison Brewing Company   BREWERY
(☑ 902-453-5343; www.garrisonbrewing.com; 1149 Marginal Rd; ⊙ 10am-8pm Sun-Thu, to 9pm Fri, 8am-9pm Sat) A grandaddy of the Halifax brewing scene, Garrison is down by the waterfront in an impressive warehouse space full of upturned beer barrels and scuffed wood. There's a huge range of brews: if you're not sure which to pick, order a tasting flight of five (or 16, if you're really indecisive). There's a small patio out the front.

Henry House   PUB
(☑ 902-423-5660; www.henryhouse.ca; 1222 Barrington St; ⊙ 11:30am-12:45am) Solid as a brick, this National Historic Site is one of the city's best surviving examples of the Halifax House, a 19th-century stone style developed by Scottish masons. These days it's a cozy pub downstairs and a stylish drawing-room bar upstairs. There are plenty of wines, beers and classic pub dishes to choose from.

Middle Spoon
Desserterie & Bar   COCKTAIL BAR
(☑ 902-407-4002; www.themiddlespoon.ca; 1559 Barrington St; ⊙ 4-11pm Mon-Wed, to midnight Thu, to 1pm Fri & Sat) One for those late-night sweet cravings: a cocktail bar that also serves ice-cream sundaes and sinful desserts such as lemon pavlova, peanut-butter pie and chocolate lava cake.

☆ Entertainment

Check out the *Coast* (www.thecoast.ca) to see what's on. This free weekly publication, available around town, is the essential guide for music, theater, film and events.

Halifax loves its music, with folk, hip-hop, alternative, country and rock gigs around town every weekend. Cover charges depend on the band.

Seahorse Tavern   LIVE MUSIC
(☑ 902-423-7200; www.theseahorsetavern.ca; 2037 Gottingen St) Indie acts and local bands are the mainstay at the rough-and-ready Seahorse. It also hosts a monthly dance party, plus retro nights devoted to the '80s and '90s. It's worth a visit just to see the giant seahorses on the bar.

Carleton   LIVE MUSIC
(☑ 902-422-6335; www.thecarleton.ca; 1685 Argyle St; ⊙ noon-2am) The Carleton's lineup is famously eclectic: folk, indie, jazz, rock and Celtic all regularly feature. There's a good dinner menu, too, served till late if you want a post-gig supper.

Neptune Theatre   THEATER
(☑ 902-429-7070; www.neptunetheatre.com; 1593 Argyle St) This downtown theater presents musicals and well-known plays on its main stage and edgier stuff in the studio.

Bearly's House of Blues & Ribs   LIVE MUSIC
(☑ 902-423-2526; www.bearlys.ca; 1269 Barrington St; ⊙ 5pm-midnight) Some of the best blues musicians in Atlantic Canada play here, often at very low cover charges.

🛍 Shopping

★ Halifax Seaport
Farmers Market   MARKET
(☑ 902-492-4043; www.halifaxfarmersmarket.com; 1209 Marginal Rd; ⊙ 10am-5pm Mon-Fri, 7am-3pm Sat, 9am-3pm Sun) Although it has operated in several locations since its inception in 1750, what's now known as the Halifax Seaport Farmers Market (in its present location since 2010) is North America's longest continuously operating market. With more than 250 local vendors from a province that prides itself on strong farm-to-table and maritime traditions, it's well worth a visit.

NSLC Clyde St   DISPENSARY
(☑ 902-423-6716; www.mynslc.com; 5540 Clyde St; ⊙ 10am-10pm Mon-Sat, noon-5pm Sun) This is the flagship NSLC cannabis store in Halifax;

the staff are well informed, so head here if you're after advice, equipment or supplies.

Historic Properties
SHOPPING CENTRE

(www.historicproperties.ca; 1869 Upper Water St; ☺ store hours vary) The Historic Properties are a group of restored warehouse buildings on Upper Water St, built between 1800 and 1905, that have been converted into boutiques, restaurants and bars connected by waterfront boardwalks. The 1814 **Privateers Warehouse** was the former storehouse of government-sanctioned pirates and is the area's oldest stone building.

ℹ Information

Useful websites include Discover Halifax (https://discoverhalifaxns.com) and the Halifax Regional Municipality (www.halifax.ca).

Family Focus (☑ 902-420-2038; www.the familyfocus.ca; 5991 Spring Garden Rd; ☺ 8:30am-9pm Mon-Fri, 11am-5pm Sat & Sun) Walk-in or same-day medical appointments.

Halifax Airport Visitor Information Centre (VIC; ☑ 902-873-1223; www.novascotia.com; Halifax International Airport; ☺ 10am-9pm Jun-Oct, 9am-4:30pm Mon-Fri Nov-May) The official province-run welcome center at Halifax airport.

Halifax Infirmary (Charles V Keating Emergency and Trauma Centre; ☑ 902-473-3383, 902-473-7605; www.cdha.nshealth.ca; 1796 Summer St; ☺ 24hr) For emergencies.

Halifax Waterfront Visitor Information Centre (VIC; ☑ 902-424-4248; www.novascotia.com; 1655 Lower Water St; ☺ 9am-7pm Jul & Aug, to 5pm mid-May–Jun, Sep & Oct) On the Halifax waterfront, this official province-run center will load you up with maps and friendly advice.

Main Post Office (☑ 902-494-4670; www. canadapost.ca; 1660 Bedford Row; ☺ 9am-5pm Mon-Fri)

ℹ Getting There & Away

AIR

Halifax Stanfield International Airport (YHZ; ☑ 902-873-4422; www.hiaa.ca; 1 Bell Blvd) is 32km northeast of town on Hwy 102, toward Truro.

BOAT

Catch the Alderney (to downtown Dartmouth) and Woodside ferries from Halifax's central **terminal** (www.halifax.ca/transit/ferries.php).

BUS

Maritime Bus (p334) runs services from Halifax to various points around Nova Scotia, as well as Prince Edward Island (PEI) and New Brunswick. Some services require you to book at least three hours ahead.

A few useful destinations from Halifax:
Charlottetown (PEI; $58.25 one way, 4½ hours, two daily)
Lunenburg ($25.50, 1¾ hours, two daily)
Mahone Bay ($20.25, 70 minutes, one daily) Three-hour advance booking required.
Moncton Airport ($49, 3½ to four hours, five daily)
Truro ($25.50, 1¾ hours, five daily)
Wolfville ($20.25, 1½ hours, two daily)
For journeys along the South Shore, **Cloud Nine Shuttle** (☑ 902-742-3992; www.thecloud nineshuttle.com) can drop you at any point as far as Yarmouth for a flat $75 fare. It also offers airport transfers for $80.

TRAIN

One of the few examples of monumental Canadian train-station architecture left in the Maritimes is found at 1161 Hollis St. VIA Rail (www.viarail.ca) operates an overnight service to Montréal (from $223, 21 hours, daily except Tuesday).

ℹ Getting Around

TO/FROM THE AIRPORT

By far the cheapest way to get to/from the airport is by public bus 320 ($3.50), which runs half-hourly to hourly between 5am and midnight to/from the **bus stop** on Albemarle St between Duke and Cogswell Sts.

If you arrive in the middle of the night, as many flights do, your only choice is a taxi, which costs $56 to downtown Halifax. There are often not enough taxis, so it's prudent to reserve one in advance. Try **Halifax Airport Taxi** (☑ 902-999-2434; www.halifaxairportlimotaxi.com), which has 24-hour airport service. The journey shouldn't take much longer than 30 minutes.

Maritime Bus (www.maritimebus.com) operates an hourly airport shuttle ($22, 30 to 45 minutes) between May and October. You'll need the exact fare; buy tickets in advance online or at the airport's Ground Transportation Booth. The shuttle picks up and drops off at most city-center hotels, as well as the main bus station. From the airport, buses run from 8am to 7pm; from downtown they run from 7am to 6pm.

CAR

Pedestrians almost always have the right of way in Halifax, so watch out for cars stopping suddenly.

Outside the downtown core you can usually find free on-street parking for up to two hours. Halifax's parking meters are enforced from 8am to 6pm Monday to Friday.

All the major national car-rental chains are represented at the airport and in downtown Halifax. Most will let you pick up in town and drop off at the airport free of charge.

PUBLIC TRANSPORTATION

Halifax Transit (☑ 902-480-8000; www.
halifax.ca/transit; single ride $2.50-3.50) runs
the city bus system and the ferries to Dartmouth. Maps and schedules are available at the
ferry terminals and at the information booth in
Scotia Sq mall.

Bus 7 cuts through downtown Halifax and the
North End via Robie and Gottingen Sts, passing
both of Halifax's hostels. Bus 1 travels along
Spring Garden Rd, Barrington St and the southern part of Gottingen St before crossing the
bridge to Dartmouth.

AROUND HALIFAX

Dartmouth

☑ 902 / POP 92,301

Founded in 1750, just a year after its counterpart across the harbor, working-class
Dartmouth was long regarded as Halifax's
grubby little brother – but as the cost of living spirals in the capital, many young people
and commuters are finding more space to
breathe on the other side of the water, turning formerly down-at-heel Dartmouth into
a rather trendy little town in its own right.

Dartmouth's compact, historic downtown is a pleasant place for a stroll and a
pint: getting here on the ferry from Halifax
– the oldest saltwater ferry system in North
America – is half the fun, especially at sunset. Before you return, head west on Alderney Dr to climb the bluffs of **Dartmouth
Commons** for excellent views across the
harbor. Exercise the usual caution in the
park after dark.

✖ Eating & Drinking

Cafe Good Luck   CAFE $
(☑ 902-469-9658; www.manualfoodanddrink
co.com/goodluck; 145 Portland St; mains $6-14;
⊙ 8am-3pm Tue & Wed, 8am-9pm Thu & Fri, 10am-
9pm Sat, 10am-3pm Sun) Dartmouth's latest
brunch-spot love affair, the Good Luck is
the place for a comforting croque monsieur,
a freshly baked muffin or a hangover-fixing
breakfast sandwich. It's a fresh, friendly
place, with the requisite retro-meets-mod-
ern decor, reclaimed furniture and, of
course, plenty of potted plants.

Portland Street Creperie   CRÊPES $
(☑ 902-466-7686; www.portlandstreetcreperie.
com; 55 Portland St; crepes $6-9; ⊙ 8:30am-5pm

DON'T MISS

RUM RUNNERS TRAIL

This 119km bike route runs from Halifax to Lunenburg via most of the main
South Shore towns, including St Margaret's Bay, Chester and Mahone Bay. The
website and route maps handily split the
route into seven subsections that can
each easily be done in a day. The 10km
Mahone Bay to Lunenburg section is
particularly popular.

Train Station Bike & Bean (☑ 902-
820-3400; www.bikeandbean.ca; 5401
St Margaret's Bay Rd; ⊙ cafe 8am-5pm,
bike shop 10am-5pm) in Tantallon, about
25km west of Halifax, is a handy place
to hire a bike for a quick day trip.

Mon-Thu & Sat, to 7pm Fri, 10am-2:30pm Sun) A
beloved snack stop for locals, this hip creperie corners the market in all things pan-
cakey: go savory with a mushroom melt or
ham and Swiss, or indulge that sweet tooth
with an Oreo-cheesecake, honeycomb or
chocolate-covered-berry crepe.

Two If By Sea   BAKERY $
(☑ 902-469-0721; www.twoifbyseacafe.ca; 66 Och-
terloney St; pastries $3-5; ⊙ 7am-6pm Mon-Fri,
8am-5pm Sat & Sun) Be warned: if you want
to gorge on the massive, buttery chocolate
croissants that TIBS is famous for, get in
quick as they're often sold out by 1pm.

★Canteen   BISTRO $$
(☑ 902-425-9272; www.thecanteen.ca; mains
lunch $10-18, dinner $18-24; ⊙ 11am-2:30am &
5-11pm Tue-Fri, 10am-2pm & 5-11pm Sat) This
pared-back bistro has become Dartmouth's
dining hot spot for its fresh, flavoursome
dishes: big bowls of mussels, panzanella sal-
ad, lobster tagliatelle and scallop risotto, all
driven by the seasons and served in a light,
minimal space. It's very popular, so bookings
are advised. If you miss out, its sandwich
takeout, **Little C**, is next door.

**★Battery Park
Beerbar & Eatery**   MICROBREWERY
(☑ 902-446-2337; www.batterypark.ca; 62 Och-
terloney St; ⊙ 11:30am-midnight Sun-Thu, to 1am
Fri & Sat) The best place for a brew in Dart-
mouth, this industrially styled beer bar has
20 taps, plus a super menu of snacky food
such as burgers, chicken skewers, tacos and
calamari. Drinkers make the pilgrimage

from Halifax just to come here – it's that good.

❶ Getting There & Away

BOAT

Halifax Transit (www.halifax.ca/transit) operates an extensive, easy-to-use network of buses and ferries. You can catch the ferry to Halifax ($2.50, 12 minutes) from the **Dartmouth Ferry Terminal** (complete with public-use piano) at Alderney Gate.

CAR

The Macdonald Bridge (built 1955) and the Mackay Bridge (built 1970) provide 24-hour links between Halifax and Dartmouth. The toll for each is $1.

A sidewalk on the Macdonald Bridge allows cyclists and pedestrians to cross (for free); the Mackay Bridge is for cars only.

Peggy's Cove

📞 902 / POP 640

With its red-and-white-striped lighthouse, colorful clapboard cottages and boulder-strewn shoreline, this tiny fishing cove presents the classic Nova Scotia picture that every visitor wants to snap. And it is undeniably pretty – especially on a calm summer's day when the sea shines china blue, seagulls wheel overhead and you can watch the lobster boats chugging out to sea. Unfortunately, the hordes of tourist buses that descend on the cove somewhat shatter the illusion, so visit early or late in the day (before 10am or after 6pm) if you don't want to be caught in the crush, or save your visit for any time but summer.

If you're looking for the same vibe without the mass of visitors, albeit without the iconic lighthouse as well, cute-as-a-button **Lower Prospect** is 30km east via Terence Bay.

◉ Sights & Activities

Peggy's Point Lighthouse
LIGHTHOUSE
(185 Peggys Point Rd; ⊙9:30am-5:30pm May-Oct) The highlight of the cove is this picture-perfect lighthouse, built in 1914. It's supposedly the most photographed lighthouse in Canada, and for many years served as a post office.

You can wander freely around the granite landscape that undulates much like the icy sea beyond, but take care: several people have been swept away by freak swells here.

William E deGarthe Gallery
& Monument
GALLERY
(📞902-823-2256; 109 Peggy's Point Rd; $2; ⊙gallery 10am-4pm May-Oct) Finnish-born local artist William deGarthe (1907–83) carved the magnificent *Lasting Monument to Nova Scotian Fishermen* into a 30m granite outcrop behind his home. The sculpture depicts 32 fishermen, their wives and children, St Elmo with wings spread, and the legendary Peggy of her eponymous cove. The homestead is now a gallery showcasing 65 of deGarthe's other works.

Swissair 111 Memorial
MEMORIAL
(8250 Hwy 333) This moving memorial commemorates the 229 people who lost their lives on September 2, 1998, when Swissair Flight 111, bound for Geneva, Switzerland, plunged into the ocean 8km off the coast of Peggy's Cove not long after taking off from New York's JFK airport.

Peggy's Cove Boat Tours
BOATING
(📞902-541-9177; www.peggyscoveboattours. com; Government Wharf; tours adult/child from $35/21.50) Get a different perspective on the cove and the lighthouse with this experienced local guide. The standard sightseeing tour runs several times daily in summer; there are also seal- and puffin-watching trips, lobster dinner cruises, and special sunset trips on Tuesday, Thursday and Friday.

🛏 Sleeping

Wayside Camping Park
CAMPGROUND $
(📞902-823-2271; www.waysidecampground. com; 10295 Hwy 333, Glen Margaret; tent/RV sites $30/40; ⊙May-Oct; 🛜🐾) About 10km north of Peggy's Cove and 36km from Halifax, this camping park has lots of shady, wooded sites but gets crowded in midsummer. Firewood is available by the armload ($5).

★Oceanstone Seaside Resort
RESORT $$
(📞902-823-2160; www.oceanstoneresort.com; 8650 Peggy's Cove Rd, Indian Harbour; r $170-235, ste $270-315, cottages $410-570; 🅿🐾❄@🛜🐾) Smart rooms and lovely sea-view cottages are on offer at this large complex just a short drive from Peggy's Cove. The decor is very stylish, with lots of distressed wood, maritime detailing and big windows that make the most of the briny scenery. **Rhubarb** (mains $15 to $17), the inn's dining room, is considered one of the region's best seafood restaurants.

Peggy's Cove Bed & Breakfast B&B $$
(☎902-823-2265; www.peggyscovebb.com; 17 Church Rd; d $159; ☺Apr-Oct; 🖥) If you want to stay in Peggy's Cove proper, this B&B has an enviable position with one of the best views in Nova Scotia, overlooking the fishing docks and the lighthouse; it was once owned by artist William deGarthe. You'll definitely need advance reservations.

ⓘ Information

Visitor Information Centre (VIC; ☎902-823-2253; 109 Peggy's Point Rd; ☺9am-7pm Jul & Aug, to 5pm mid-May–Jun & Sep–Oct) There's a free parking area with washrooms and a tourist office as you enter the village. Free 45-minute walking tours leave from the tourist office daily from mid-June through August.

ⓘ Getting There & Away

Peggy's Cove is 43km southwest of Halifax on Hwy 333.

SOUTH SHORE

This is Nova Scotia's most visited coastline (for good reason) and it's here you'll find all those quintessential lighthouses, protected forested coves with white beaches, and quaint fishing villages turned tourist towns. The area from Halifax to Lunenburg is cottage country for the capital's elite and ever-popular with day-tripping tourists and locals.

A great way to explore the area on two wheels is along the excellent Rum Runners Trail (p349), which runs for 119km from Halifax to Lunenburg.

ⓘ Getting There & Away

Hwy 3 from Halifax – labeled the 'Lighthouse Route' by tourism officials – can be busy and slow. Take this scenic route if you're not pressed for time and want to check out antique shops or artisans' wares along the way. Travel times can be halved by taking Hwy 103 directly to the closest exit for your destination. You'll need your own vehicle to get down here.

Chester

☎902 / POP 1200
The clapboard seaside village of Chester is one of the prettiest stops along the South Shore. Established in 1759, it's had a colorful history as the haunt of pirates and Prohibition-era bathtub-gin smugglers, and it keeps its color today via the many artists' studios about town. It's also a popular place for well-to-do Haligonians to buy a summer home.

Many visitors to Chester also take a day trip out to Big Tancook Island, the largest of the islets in Mahone Bay. It offers some great walking and interesting settlement history. The one-way trip takes about 50 minutes.

◉ Sights & Activities

Big Tancook Island ISLAND
(www.tancookcommunitynews.com; adult/child round-trip $7/free) Big Tancook Island (population 120) is a 50-minute ferry ride from Chester's government wharf. Settled by Germans and French Huguenots in the early 19th century, the island is famous for its sauerkraut, and is crisscrossed with **walking trails**. It also has some pleasant beaches at Southeast Cove and Gravel Cove. The best way to get around is by bike; rentals are available as you step off the ferry. Ferries sail at least twice daily.

The **Tancook Ferry** (☎902-275-7885) runs four times daily Monday to Friday (first sailing from Chester at 6am, last sailing from Tancook at 5pm), with two extra sailings on Friday evening, at 6:30pm and 9:30pm (returning at 8:30pm and 11pm). The ferry runs twice daily on weekends (first sailing from Chester at 9am; last sailing from Tancook at 6pm on Saturday and 5pm on Sunday). The ferry stops en route at Little Tancook.

Kayak Shack KAYAKING
(☎902-221-2298; www.kayakshack.ca; 89 Water St; kayaks & SUPs per 2hr $30; ☺8am-7pm mid-May–mid-Oct) Single and double kayaks and stand-up paddleboards are available here for you to explore the bay under your own paddle power.

🛏 Sleeping & Eating

**Graves Island
Provincial Park** CAMPGROUND $
(☎902-275-4425; https://parks.novascotia.ca/content/graves-island; campsites $26.70-35.60; ☺mid-May–mid-Oct) An island in Mahone Bay connected by a causeway to the mainland has 95 wooded campsites, 33 of which are serviced. RVs usually park in the middle of the area, but some shady, isolated tent sites are tucked away on the flanks of the central plateau. It's 3km northeast of Chester, off Hwy 3.

Mecklenburgh Inn B&B
B&B $$

(✍902-275-4638; www.mecklenburghinn.ca; 78 Queen St; r $149-169; ☺May-Dec; 🐾) Known as 'The Meck', this 1902 house is the only B&B in central Chester, with four heritage-style rooms featuring upscale touches such as clawfoot tubs, wooden floors, Frette linens and Lindt-chocolate pillow treats. Owner Suzi is a Cordon Bleu–trained chef, so expect a breakfast treat.

Kiwi Café
CAFE $

(✍902-275-1492; www.kiwicafechester.com; 19 Pleasant St; mains $9-16; ☺8am-4pm Sun-Wed, to 8pm Thu-Sat; 🐾✍) Friendly as anything and serving comforting food cooked with love by an NZ-born chef, this is exactly the kind of community cafe you'd hope to find in a place like Chester. Choose from lobster rolls, fish cakes, burgers, superfood salads and an entire page of all-day breakfasts. Leave room for dessert: the cookies and cakes are divine.

★White Gate inn
CANADIAN $$$

(✍902-275-4400; www.whitegate.ca; 28 Pleasant St; mains $26-38; ☺5-8pm, 8:30pm or 9pm Wed-Sun) This beautiful heritage inn is by far Chester's swishest place to eat. The sophisticated menu features the likes of rack of lamb, lobster pie and chicken ballotine, served in the elegant surroundings of a gabled, white-weatherboard building right in the town center. Upstairs there are delightful rooms, decked out in pale blues and tasteful creams.

🍸 Drinking & Entertainment

Fo'c'sle
PUB

(✍902-275-1408; www.focslechester.com; 42 Queen St; ☺11am-11pm) Dubbing itself 'Chester's Living Room', this ramshackle pub is a lively place to rub shoulders with the locals. There's been a pub of some sort on this site since 1764.

Chester Playhouse
THEATER

(✍902-275-3933; www.chesterplayhouse.ca; 22 Pleasant St; tickets around $25) This quaint theater space has great acoustics for live performances. Plays or dinner theater are presented most nights in July and August, with occasional concerts during spring and fall.

❶ Information

Since the closure of the visitor center, Tourism Chester (www.tourismchester.ca) is the best resource for things to see and do around town.

❶ Getting There & Away

Chester is 67km southwest of Halifax via Hwy 103.

Mahone Bay
📶902 / POP 950

The sun shines more often in Mahone Bay than anywhere else along the coast, apparently. With more than 100 islands in its bay, and a location less than 100km from Halifax, it's a great base for exploring this section of the South Shore. Take out a kayak or a bike or simply stroll down Main St, which skirts the harbor and is scattered with shops selling antiques, quilts, pottery and works by local painters.

◉ Sights & Activities

Mahone Bay Settlers' Museum
MUSEUM

(✍902-624-6263; www.mahonebaymuseum.com; 578 Main St; ☺10am-4pm late May–mid-Oct) ⓕ⓻⓮⓮ This modest little local-history museum is worth a visit to understand the development of Mahone Bay, particularly the 1754 settlement, the building of the three churches and the long tradition of shipbuilding.

Sweet Ride Cycling
CYCLING

(✍902-531-3026; www.sweetridecycling.com; 523 Main St; half-/full-day rentals $25/35; ☺10am-5pm Mon-Sat, noon-5pm Sun) This friendly bike shop rents out a good range of bikes, including fat-wheeled cruisers. It's devised some good local routes, and can also help you out with the Rum Runners Trail (p349).

🛏 Sleeping

Heart's Desire B&B
B&B $$

(✍902-624-8470; www.heartsdesirebb.com; 686 Main St; cottages $116, r $126-130; 🐾) John and Denise Perry's house, originally built for a local schoolteacher, is a quintessential example of a Victorian 'Foursquare', and it retains lots of its original fixtures. The three rooms have hardwood floors and are prettily decorated with cheery quilts, and there's also a separate cottage in the lovingly tended garden.

🍴 Eating & Drinking

LaHave Bakery
DELI $

(✍902-624-1420; www.lahavebakery.com; 3 Edgewater St; sandwiches $5-9.50; ☺8:30am-5:30pm; ✍) This bakery is famous for its hearty bread. Sandwiches are made on thick slabs of it.

★ **Biscuit Eater** CAFE $$
(☑902-624-2665; https://thebiscuiteater.com; 16 Orchard St; mains $14-21; ☺9am-4pm Mon-Fri, to 7pm Sat, 10am-3pm Sun; 🕿) This is many people's dream come true: a vintage bookstore that doubles as a cafe, serving homemade soups, burgers and all-day breakfasts, not to mention absolutely knockout cakes. The house special is the 'biscuit bowl': roast chicken, barbecue brisket, lobster or veggies served on a bed of greens and a homemade biscuit.

Oh My Cod! SEAFOOD $$
(☑902-531-2600; www.oh-my-cod.ca; 567 Main St; mains $14-18.50; ☺11am-8pm) For quick and easy eating, this friendly seafood diner is hard to beat: enjoy clams, scallops, battered haddock and fish tacos, along with hand-cut chips, a cold beer and a great view over Mahone Bay. What's not to like?

★ **Mateus Bistro** CANADIAN $$$
(☑902-531-3711; www.mateusbistro.ca; 533 Main St; mains $23-35; ☺5-9pm Tue-Thu, 11:30am-9pm Fri-Mon) The Bratislavan-born chef has made this little restaurant into a real destination address: people drive to Mahone Bay just to eat here. The food is really fresh and tasty, with lots of herbs and garnishes, running the gamut from Moroccan lamb shank to panko-crusted haddock.

Saltbox Brewing Company MICROBREWERY
(☑902-624-0653; www.saltboxbrewingcompany. ca; 363 Main St; ☺11am-9pm Mon & Tue, 10am-10pm Wed-Sat, 11am-7pm Sun) Mahone Bay's very own small-batch craft brewery has a taproom where you can try all the latest brews.

ℹ Information

Mahone Bay Visitor Information Centre
(☑902-624-6151; www.mahonebay.com; 165 Edgewater St; ☺9am-6pm May-Oct) Lots of info on the town, plus self-guided walking-tour brochures.

ℹ Getting There & Away

Mahone Bay is 86km southwest of Halifax on Hwy 103 and 11km northwest of Lunenburg. Maritime Bus (p334) has services to Halifax ($20.25, 70 minutes, one daily). Three-hour advance booking required.

Lunenburg

☑902 / POP 2263
After Peggy's Cove, lovely Lunenburg is the place that everyone stops off to see on their trip along the South Shore. And no wonder: with its brightly painted weatherboard houses, lawned squares and slate-topped churches, it's such a perfect example of a Nova Scotian fishing town that it almost looks like a model. And in some ways that's exactly what it is: it was

NOVA SCOTIA LUNENBURG

THE TREASURE OF OAK ISLAND

Oak Island, near Mahone Bay, is home to a so-called 'money pit' that has cost over $2 million in excavation expenses – and six lives. Few facts are known about what the pit is or what might be buried there, but if you're keen to find out more, *The Curse of Oak Island*, an ongoing reality-TV series, documents the efforts of a team of treasure hunters.

The mystery began in 1795, when three inhabitants of the island came across a depression in the ground. Knowing that pirates (including the legendary Captain Kidd) had once frequented the area, they decided to dig and see what they could find. Just over half a meter down, they hit a layer of neatly placed flagstone; another 2.5m turned up one oak platform, then another. After digging to 9m, the men temporarily gave up, but they returned eight years later with the Onslow Company, a professional crew.

The Onslow excavation made it 27.5m down; when the crew returned the next morning, the shaft had flooded and they were forced to halt the digging. A year later, the company returned to dig 33.5m down in a parallel shaft, which also flooded. It was confirmed in 1850 that the pit was booby trapped via five box drains at Smith Cove, 150m from the pit. The beach was found to be artificial.

Ever since, people have come from far and wide to seek their fortune at the 'money pit', including Rick and Marty Lagina, stars of *The Curse of Oak Island*. They've made progress – recent finds include coins, a lead cross and a garnet brooch – but so far they're yet to strike it really rich.

Lunenburg

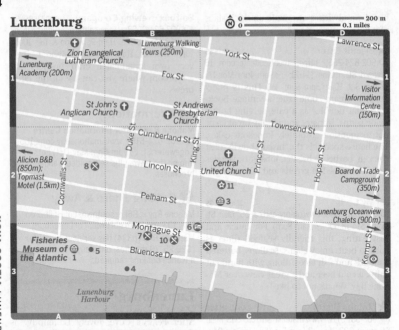

Lunenburg

◎ Top Sights

◎ Sights

☺ Activities, Courses & Tours

⊜ Sleeping

⊗ Eating

☺ Entertainment

designed according to the standard British blueprint for colonial settlements in the 18th century, and it seems barely to have changed since it was built. The old town's beautifully preserved architecture has earned it Unesco World Heritage status, and deservedly so, but it gets very busy in summer – visit in May or September to see it at its pastel-tinted best.

History

The Mi'kmaq lived for many centuries along this area of the South Shore prior to the first European arrivals, the Acadians, who founded the small farming community of Mirliguèche in the mid-1600s.

A century later the area was claimed by the British, who established one of their earliest Nova Scotian settlements here, naming it in honor of the Duke of Braunschweig-Lüneburg (later George II). The town was populated by 'Foreign Protestants' (mostly Germans, Swiss and Protestant French), who gradually switched from farming to fishing for their livelihood.

Lunenburg subsequently established itself as an important fishing and shipbuilding port, and during Prohibition in the 1920s it became a major rum-running center.

The town remains a working fishing town, although dwindling stocks have made many fishers give up the trade in search of a more secure income.

The town was listed as a World Heritage site by Unesco in 1995.

⊙ Sights & Activities

Look out around town for the distinctive 'Lunenburg Bump', a distinctive architectural feature of older buildings whereby a five-sided dormer window on the 2nd floor overhangs the 1st floor.

There are four handsome 18th- and 19th-century churches in the old town (each of the different religious denominations – Anglican, Presbyterian, Lutheran and Methodist – built its own, in an astonishing show of ecclesiastical one-upmanship). Look out for the weathervane atop **St Andrews Presbyterian Church** on Townsend St; it's cod shaped. Only in Lunenburg!

★**Fisheries Museum of the Atlantic**　　　MUSEUM
(☑902-634-4794; http://fisheriesmuseum.nova scotia.ca; 68 Bluenose Dr; adult/child $13/3.50; ☉9:30am-5pm or 5:30pm mid-May–Oct) You simply can't understand Lunenburg unless you've visited this maritime museum, which traces the history of fishing from the days of the Mi'kmaq through to the present time. Fascinating exhibits explore fishing grounds, vessels and techniques, and film screenings and talks are scheduled throughout the day. The museum also has two vintage vessels: the *Theresa E Connor*, the oldest saltbank dory schooner in Canada, built in 1938; and the *Cape Sable*, a steel-hulled side trawler built in 1962.

There's a large parking lot opposite the museum. Admission is covered by the Nova Scotia Museum Pass (p334).

Ironworks Distillery　　　DISTILLERY
(☑902-640-2424; www.ironworksdistillery.com; 2 Kempt St; ☉4 tours daily mid-Jun–mid-Sep, contact for other times) Lunenburg's renowned brewery crafts a selection of fruity liqueurs, a strong apple brandy, a pear eau-de-vie, an apple vodka and – fittingly for a maritime

town – several rums. You can follow the distilling process on a guided tour.

The name comes from the distillery's location in Lunenburg's former blacksmith's shop, which produced ironworks for the shipbuilding industry.

Knaut-Rhuland House　　　MUSEUM
(☑902-634-3498; www.lunenburgheritagesociety. ca/museum; 125 Pelham St; ☉11am-5pm Mon-Sat, noon-4pm Sun Jun-Sep) **FREE** This 2½-story house – named after its first owners, merchants Benjamin Knaut and Conrad Rhuland – is considered the finest example of Georgian architecture in the province. It's an intriguing insight into how a wealthy Lunenburg home would have looked to early settlers, although some of the rooms are quite spartan.

Pleasant Paddling　　　KAYAKING
(☑902-541-9233; www.pleasantpaddling.com; 245 The Point Rd, Blue Rocks; kayak rentals from $38, tours from $60; ☉May-Oct) The knowledgeable folks at this beautiful place to paddle offer rentals and tours in single or double kayaks. They're based at Blue Rocks, about 9km east of Lunenburg.

⊂ Tours

Lunenburg Walking Tours　　　WALKING
(☑902-521-6867; www.lunenburgwalkingtours. com; tours adult/child from $25/15) The enthusiastic and very experienced Sheila Allen and her team lead informative history tours during the day and spooky lantern-lit ones at night. Tours begin outside the impressive edifice of the Lunenburg Academy, built in 1895 and currently undergoing restoration.

Trot in Time　　　TOURS
(☑902-634-8917; www.trotintime.ca; adult/child $30/15; ☉Jun–mid-Oct) For that old-timey photo op, take a half-hour tour of town in a

NOVA SCOTIA LUNENBURG

THE BLUENOSE

Designed by renowned boat maker William J Roué, the original *Bluenose* was built right here in Lunenburg in 1921. She was the largest schooner ever built: 25 tonnes. She served as a fishing vessel and an award-winning racing yacht under local captain Angus Walters before being wrecked in a storm near Haiti in 1946. You might well have seen her without ever being aware of it: the boat features on one side of the Canadian dime.

The **Bluenose II** (☑902-634-1963; https://bluenose.novascotia.ca; 2hr cruises adult/child $65/36), a replica of the original vessel launched in 1963, runs unforgettable trips along the South Shore during summer; depending on the day, it might be moored in Lunenburg or Halifax. Check the website to see when it's next in town.

If you're just after a souvenir, there's a Bluenose Company Store at 121 Bluenose Dr.

LUNENBURG, THE MODEL TOWN

Lunenburg was laid out as a colonial 'planned settlement' along a geometric grid pattern drawn up by British planners: eight blocks, each divided into 14 lots measuring from 12m to 18m, with a four-block area in the center (including a parade ground) designated as public space. Each settler family received a 'town lot', and a 'garden lot' where they could grow vegetables and keep animals; most of the town's houses have small or no gardens as a result. Unfortunately, the off-the-shelf design made no allowance for topography, which explains why some of Lunenburg's streets are so ludicrously steep. Originally the town would have been protected by forts, blockhouses and palisades, but these are now mostly gone (although one still houses the town's visitor center).

horse-drawn cart. It leaves from outside the Fisheries Museum of the Atlantic (p355).

🎨 Festivals & Events

Nova Scotia Folk Art Festival ART
(www.nsfolkartfestival.com; ⊙ Aug) Buffet dinner, artist talks and then a big art show and sale on the first Sunday in August.

Boxwood Festival MUSIC
(www.boxwood.org; festival pass $50; ⊙ Jul) Flautists and pipers from around the world put on stellar public concerts.

Lunenburg Folk Harbour Festival MUSIC
(☑ 902-634-3180; www.folkharbour.com; ⊙ Aug) Singer-songwriters from Canada and beyond, plus traditional music and gospel.

🛏 Sleeping

Board of Trade Campground CAMPGROUND $
(☑ 902-634-8100; www.lunenburgns.com/camp ground; 11 Blockhouse Hill Rd; sites from $36.80; ⊙ late May–early Oct; 🛜) Perched on Blockhouse Hill, high above Lunenburg (the site of the old fort), this campground guarantees you a pitch with a view, although the sites are pretty packed together and there's not much shade.

★ Alicion B&B B&B $$
(☑ 902-634-9358; www.alicionbb.com; 66 McDonald St; r $159-179; 🅿 ⊕ ❄ 🛜) 🅿 Wow, what a beauty: a 1911 former senator's home, built on a hilltop, with a wraparound veranda that radiates Revival elegance. There are four beautiful nature-themed rooms: tranquil Kingfisher, garden-view Periwinkle, south-facing Tamarack and double-aspect Dragonfly, all stuffed with antiques and thoughtful touches. Owners Christopher and Joe do everything with class (there's even a sweet treat in the afternoon).

★ Sail Inn B&B B&B $$
(☑ 902-634-3537; www.sailinn.ca; 99 Montague St; r $120-180; 🅿 ⊕ 🛜) If you want to be down by the harbor, this smart B&B is a really lovely choice. It's housed in a heritage building, but the rooms are bright, airy and modern, and all have harbor views. Look out for the old well on the ground floor that's been turned into a fishpond!

Lunenburg Oceanview Chalets COTTAGE $$
(☑ 902-640-3344; www.lunenburgoceanview.com; 78 Old Blue Rocks Rd; cottages $149-179; 🅿 ⊕ 🛜) For something a little different, these rustic log cabins with private decks atop a hill on Lunenburg's outskirts might be just what the doctor ordered. They're fully self-contained, and have wi-fi, log fires, ocean views (at a distance) and the refreshing sound of horses neighing in the meadows. Basic, but rather romantic and reasonably priced. Two-night minimum stay June to September.

Topmast Motel MOTEL $$
(☑ 902-634-4661; www.topmastmotel.ca; 76 Masons Beach Rd; d $139-154) Arguably the best prospect in Lunenburg is the main selling point at this simple, friendly and spotlessly clean motel. Yes, the rooms are no-frills – but the views more than make up for any shortcomings.

🍴 Eating

There are plenty of great restaurants here. Lunenburg's offbeat dining specialties include Solomon Gundy (pickled herring with onions) and Lunenburg pudding (pork and spices cooked in the intestines of a pig), which goes well with whiskey and water.

★ South Shore Fish Shack SEAFOOD $$
(☑ 902-634-3232; www.southshorefishshack.com; 108 Montague St; mains $12-20; ⊙ 11am-8pm

Sun-Wed, to 9pm Thu-Sat) There are two main reasons to swing by this place: to eat the best fish-and-chips in Lunenburg and to enjoy the view from the deck. Chuck in great lobster buns, panko-crusted scallops and a fun sea-shack vibe, and you really can't go wrong.

Salt Shaker Deli   DELI **$$**
(☑902-640-3434; www.saltshakerdeli.com; 124 Montague St; mains $12-20; ⊙11am-9pm) This friendly downtown diner is where everyone, local or tourist, heads for a meal in Lunenburg: crispy-crust pizzas, piles of mussels, salmon cakes and fisherman's stew keep the punters packed in, and there's a great selection of craft beers and Nova Scotian wines. Try for a spot on the deck on summer nights.

It's recently added upstairs **rooms** (from $130), several of which have water views, but inevitably there's spillover noise from the restaurant.

Half Shell Oyster Bar   SEAFOOD **$$**
(☑902-634-8503; www.halfshelloysterbar.com; 108 Montague St; oysters from $3.25, mains $12-22; ⊙noon-midnight Jul & Aug, to 9pm Jun & Sep) A long ice bar loaded with such seafood goodies as snow-crab claws, chilled lobsters, littleneck clams and, of course, freshly shucked oysters is the main feature at this newly opened restaurant, run by the team behind the Salt Shaker Deli and the South Shore Fish Shack. The idea is hands-on seafood – yes, you'll get messy, but what fun!

★Lincoln Street Food   CANADIAN **$$$**
(☑902-640-3002; www.lincolnstreetfood.ca; 200 Lincoln St; mains $26, 3-course prix fixe $47; ⊙5-9pm Tue-Sat; ☑) This smart, contemporary bistro is a sign of the town's changing times: stripped back in style, with exciting dishes such as halibut with charred-cucumber salsa verde and summer panzanella salad that feel unusually urban for olde-worlde Lunenburg. Unsurprisingly, it's popular: bookings are essential.

☆ Entertainment

Lunenburg Opera House   THEATER
(☑902-634-4010; www.lunenburgoperahouse. com; 290 Lincoln St; tickets $5-25) This recently refurbished 400-seat theater is rumored to have a resident ghost. Built as an Odd Fellows Hall in 1907, it's now a favorite venue for rock and folk musicians. Check the posters in the window for what's coming up.

ℹ Information

Visitor Information Centre (VIC; ☑902-634-8100; www.lunenburgns.com; 11 Blockhouse Hill Rd; ⊙7:30am-7pm Jul & Aug, 9am-5pm May, Jun, Sep & Oct) Perched high above town, this helpful center has loads of information on old Lunenburg, and can help find the last available rooms around town if you're stuck in summer.

ℹ Getting There & Away

Lunenburg is just shy of 100km from Halifax on Hwy 103.

Maritime Bus (p334) runs a regular bus along the South Shore to Halifax ($25.50, 1¾ hours, two daily).

Liverpool
☑902 / POP 2549

Like that of other South Shore settlements, Liverpool's history takes in fishing, privateering, shipbuilding, rum running and pretty much every other maritime trade you could mention. Despite this, Liverpool has never managed to reinvent itself as a tourist center as many of the other towns have. As such, it looks a little run-down, but it's worth a stop for its attractive beaches and the distinctive lighthouse at Fort Point.

It makes a particularly handy base for exploring Kejimkujik National Park's Seaside Adjunct.

Every June, the town celebrates its piratical history during the **Privateer Days** (www.privateerdays.ca).

◎ Sights

★Rossignol Cultural Centre   MUSEUM
(☑902-354-3067; www.rossignolculturalcentre. com; 205 Church St; adult/child $5/3; ⊙10am-5pm Tue-Sat) This brilliantly oddball museum explores the eclectic fascinations of local photographer Sherman Hines, born in Liverpool in 1941. There are halls of taxidermy animals, cases of gorgeous indigenous beadwork, walls of Hines' beautiful photography (including some from his Mongolian adventures), the interior of a Halifax apothecary and – most bizarre of all – a room dedicated to outhouses around the world.

Hank Snow Home Town Museum   MUSEUM
(☑902-354-4675; www.hanksnow.com; 148 Bristol Ave; $5; ⊙9am-5pm Mon-Sat, 1-5pm Sun) Country-music star Clarence Eugene 'Hank' Snow was born on May 9, 1914, in the village of

Brooklyn, not far from Liverpool. Housed in the old train station, this little museum explores his life, along with that of Wilf Carter and fellow crooners and yodelers.

Fort Point
Lighthouse   LIGHTHOUSE
(☑902-354-5260; 21 Fort Lane; ⊘cafe 10am-6pm May-Oct) FREE Built in 1885, this lighthouse at the end of the spit of land overlooking Liverpool harbor stands on the place where Frenchmen Pierre Dugua and Samuel de Champlain landed in 1604. Before the lighthouse was built, a privateer fort stood on the site to guard the harbor, hence the name.

There's now a pleasant seasonal cafe here, operated by the owners of Lane's Privateer Inn, and some small displays on the lighthouse's history.

🛏 Sleeping & Eating

Lane's Privateer Inn   INN $$
(☑902-354-3456; www.lanesprivateerinn.com; 27 Bristol Ave; d $125-175; P🐾) Liverpool's main place to stay, this rambling, old-school inn on the main road through town was once the residence of a Liverpudlian privateer. Rooms are large; the best have wooden floors and attractive artwork, but the budget ones look very dated. Downstairs are a **coffee shop and restaurant** (mains $18 to $25). There's lots of parking next to the inn.

★ **Quarterdeck**   BOUTIQUE HOTEL $$$
(☑1-800-565-1119; www.quarterdeck.ca; 7499 Hwy 3, Summerville; villas $299-429) Like a contemporary take on a family-friendly resort, Quarterdeck has modern, luxurious weatherboard villas on Summerville Beach and offers digs ranging from one-roomers to swanky multiroom lofts. There's an on-site **grill** (mains $24 to $30) and a rec center with its own movie screen. Style galore on the South Shore.

Five Girls Baking   CAFE $
(☑902-354-5551; 181 Main St; sandwiches $4-8; ⊘8am-5pm Tue-Fri, 9:30am-4pm Sat, 10am-4pm Sun) Sandwiches, muffins, cookies and freshly baked buns, plus lots of local foodie treats, are reason enough to check out this attractive little cafe on Main St.

❶ Getting There & Away

Liverpool is 67km southwest of Mahone Bay on Hwy 103, and 64km northeast of Shelburne.

Kejimkujik National Park

Some of Nova Scotia's most unique, magnificent and unspoiled terrain is found within the boundaries of Kejimkujik National Park (shortened to 'Keji' by locals). Generations of Mi'kmaw people paddled, camped and hunted here, and the area is dotted with ancient camping sites, many marked by rock engravings known as petroglyphs. In summer you can join a fascinating guided hike led by Mi'kmaw guides.

These days Keji remains popular for hiking, backcountry camping, bird-watching and kayaking. The main park occupies 381 sq km in the center of the mainland, while its smaller **Seaside Adjunct**, protecting an important coastal habitat of dunes, beaches and creeks between Port Joli and Port Mouton, is 107km south.

Incredibly, even today less than 20% of Keji's wilderness is accessible by car; the rest can only be reached on foot or by canoe.

🏃 Activities

Petroglyph Tour   HIKING
(⊘10:30am daily Jul & Aug, 10:30am Sat & Sun Sep) FREE Hike into restricted areas of the park to see some of the 500 ancient petroglyphs left behind by Mi'kmaw people. Located mainly around Kejimkujik's lakes, the carvings depict figures, symbols, animals, sailing ships and clothing. There are only 20 places, so bookings should be made well ahead through the visitor center. Tours leave from the Merrymakedge parking lot.

Whynot Adventure   OUTDOORS
(Keji Outfitters; ☑902-682-2282; www.whynot adventure.ca; 1507 Main Pkwy; canoe rental per hour/day/week from $15/40/165; ⊘8am-8pm Jun-Sep) This company rents out kayaks, canoes, bikes and paddleboards for adventures around Keji. It offers 'Quickie Adventure' guided trips (from $50/80 for a two-/four-hour expedition), plus multiday trips including overnight camping. Its shuttle service is useful, and it also rents out camping gear.

Mi'kmaw Encampment   CULTURAL
(Wejisqalia'ti'k; ⊘2pm Tue-Sat Jul & Aug) FREE Hear local tales and legends from Mi'kmaw guides while sipping a cup of bush tea at these fascinating storytelling sessions (in Mi'kmaw, *wejisqulia'ti'k* roughly translates as 'tell us that we grew from the earth'). They also offer stories around a campfire at

10pm on Saturdays in July and 9:30pm in August.

Birch Bark Canoe
Carving Demonstration CULTURAL
(⊙2-4pm Thu-Sun Jul-early Sep) Seventh-generation Mi'kmaw and master craftsman Todd Labrador demonstrates the art of birch-bark-canoe carving. If you'd like to have a go yourself, he also holds workshops from 10am to 12:30pm on Sunday morning ($65).

Demonstrations take place at the Merrymakedge car park on the shore of Kejimkujik Lake.

Sleeping

★ **Jeremy's Bay**
Campground CAMPGROUND $
(☎877-737-3783; www.pc.gc.cax; campsites $25.50-29.40, cabins & yurts $70, oTENTiks $100; ⊙May-Oct) This excellent campground is one of the best places in the park to sleep under the stars. There's a wide choice of campsites (both serviced and unserviced), plus rustic wooden cabins, yurts and pre-pitched tents (called oTENTiks) that come with mattresses, furniture, a private deck, a firebox and a picnic area. It's in a great lakeside location near Jake's Landing.

Thomas Raddall
Provincial Park CAMPGROUND $
(☎902-683-2664; http://parks.novascotia.ca/content/thomas-raddall; campsites $25.60-35.70; ⊙May-Oct) Thomas Raddall Provincial Park, across Port Joli Harbour from Kejimkujik's Seaside Adjunct, has large, private campsites, eight of which are walk-in. The forested campground extends onto awesome beaches.

★ **Mersey River**
Chalets CABIN $$
(☎902-682-2447; www.merseyriverchalets.ns.ca; 315 Mersey River Chalets Rd E, Caledonia; tipis $90-120, cabins $185-208; ⊙☎) Get back to nature at this cabin complex, deep in the woods beside Harry's Lake. There's a choice of pine chalets, a spacious log house, a four-room lodge and (best of all) tipis. Cabins have wood-burning stoves and private porches with barbecues; rooms in the lodge have private decks with lake views; and the cozy tipis have fully equipped kitchens.

Canoes and kayaks are available for guests.

ⓘ Information

There are black bears in the park: campers should take the usual precautions when hiking and backcountry camping.

Biting insects, including some seriously large mosquitoes, are rampant in summer. Also watch out for eel-like leeches in the lakes.

Kejimkujik National Park Visitor Centre
(☎902-682-2772; www.parkscanada.gc.ca/keji; 3005 Main Pkwy, Maitland Bridge; park entry adult/child $6/3; ⊙8:30am-7pm or 8pm mid-Jun–Aug, to 4:30pm mid-May–mid-Jun & Oct) Get an entry permit and park maps and reserve backcountry campsites here. It also reserves places on various activities and tours around the park. It's off the main road through the park, Hwy 8.

ⓘ Getting There & Away

Entry to Kejimkujik National Park is through the visitor center (on Hwy 8), which can be approached from Annapolis Royal, 49km northwest. From the east, the park is 68km from Liverpool, from where it's another 19km to Lunenburg.

The only access into Kejimkujik National Park's Seaside Adjunct is via Hwy 103 and then along a 6.5km gravel road. The adjunct is 47km east of Shelburne and 32km west of Liverpool. For GPS navigation systems, search for 1188 St Catherine's River Rd, Port Joli.

Shelburne
☎902 / POP 1690
Shelburne's historic waterfront area bobs with sailboats and has 17 homes that were built before 1800 – it feels like a historical recreation, but it's real. The wonderfully maintained, low-in-the-earth buildings once housed Loyalists who retreated here from the American Revolution. In 1783 Shelburne was the largest community in British North America, with 16,000 residents, many from the New York aristocracy, who exploited the labor of Black Loyalists living in nearby Birchtown. Shelburne's history is celebrated with **Founders' Days** over the last weekend of July.

⊙ Sights

Black Loyalist Heritage Centre MUSEUM
(☎902-875-1310; https://blackloyalist.novascotia.ca; 119 Old Birchtown Rd; adult/child $9.20/5.75; ⊙10am-5pm) In 2015 Birchtown's Black Loyalist Heritage Centre and museum was moved to its shiny new facility 7km outside town, on the site of what was Canada's

WORTH A TRIP

TROUT POINT LODGE

Situated at the edge of the Tobeatic Wilderness Area, this fabulously luxurious **forest lodge** (📞 902-761-2142; www.troutpoint.com; 189 Trout Point Rd, East Kemptville; r from $358; 🅿) offers a taste of the wild blended with old-fashioned country comfort. Built from giant eastern-spruce logs, the three-story lodge is the epitome of rustic chic, with beamed ceilings, stone fireplaces, handmade log furniture, a mezzanine library and an excellent Atlantic Acadian restaurant.

Guides offer a range of backcountry experiences, including stargazing, forest bathing and geological excursions. You're way, way off the map here – cell-phone coverage is nonexistent – so switch off for a few days and feel the call of the wild.

largest free African settlement in the 1780s. The museum offers an insight into this largely untold Canadian story.

Dory Shop Museum MUSEUM
(📞 902-875-3219; https://doryshop.novascotia.ca; 11 Dock St; adult/child $4/free; ⊙ 9:30am-5:30pm Jun–mid-Oct) Shelburne dories (small wooden open boats used for fishing from a mother schooner) were the staple craft for Nova Scotian fishermen on the Grand Banks fishery, thanks to their lightweight construction, shallow draft, durability and maneuverability. This fascinating workshop is one of the only places in the world that still makes them to order, and it has a collection of vintage craft.

Ross-Thomson House MUSEUM
(📞 902-875-3141; https://rossthomson.novascotia.ca; 9 Charlotte Lane; adult/child $4/free; ⊙ 9:30am-5:30pm Jun–mid-Oct) Go shopping, 1780s style, at this merchant's house, once owned by traders George and Robert Ross, who supplied Shelburne's residents with staple goods and luxury items. There's a replica of the original store counter, and you can also see around the sparsely furnished house and the pleasant gardens.

🛏 Sleeping & Eating

Cooper's Inn B&B B&B $$
(📞 902-875-4656; www.thecoopersinn.com; 36 Dock St; r $140-230; 🛜) Part of this waterfront

building dates from 1784 and was brought here from Boston. Now it's a relatively modern but still charmingly heritage-style inn with eight rooms. There's also a flower-filled garden.

Bean Dock CAFE $
(📞 902-875-1302; Dock St; sandwiches $3.50-7; ⊙ 8:30am-4pm Mon-Fri, 9am-3pm Sat & Sun) A chilled coffee shop overlooking the waterfront, serving grilled cheese sandwiches, muffins and paninis. There's also a gift shop selling souvenir tees, candles and kitchen items – although the giant Adirondack chair isn't up for sale, so don't ask.

★ Charlotte Lane Cafe CANADIAN $$$
(📞 902-875-3314; www.charlottelane.ca; 13 Charlotte Lane; mains lunch $11.50-22, dinner $20-42; ⊙ 11:30am-2:30pm & 5-8pm Tue-Sat) This colorful cafe is everyone's top tip; evening reservations are highly recommended. Swiss chef Roland Glauser serves a varied menu of seafood, meat and pasta dishes, featuring dashes of spice and exotic ingredients picked up on his travels.

ℹ Information

Visitor Information Centre (VIC; 📞 902-875-4547; www.shelburneandlockeport.com; 43 Dock St; ⊙ 9am-4pm May-Sep) In a dinky little building at the end of the harbor, the town's tourist office has a few historical walking trails to try.

ℹ Getting There & Away

Shelburne is 64km southwest of Liverpool on Hwy 103, and 97km east of Yarmouth.

ACADIAN SHORES

Acadian culture has left a strong influence on the history of this part of Nova Scotia: you'll often spy the Stella Maris, the single-starred, tricolored Acadian flag, and you'll still hear the Acadian dialect spoken in many areas. The area's main town is Yarmouth, an important lobster port and – theoretically – the transit point for ferries to Portland, Maine.

The Acadian Shores cover roughly 120km of coast between Digby to the north and the city of Yarmouth and the communities of the Pubnicos to the south. This area is a lot less prettified than the coastal communities of the South Shore and the Annapolis Valley: this is hardworking country, and proud of it.

Yarmouth

📞 902 / POP 7217

Founded in 1761 by New Englanders from Massachusetts, Yarmouth reached the peak of its prosperity in the 1870s. It's still the biggest town in southern Nova Scotia, and one of the province's largest centers for lobster fishing.

It's very much a working town, but there are a few compelling reasons to stop on your way through, including an outpost of the Art Gallery of Nova Scotia and a landmark lighthouse at Cape Fourchu.

◎ Sights

★ Cape Forchu Lightstation   LIGHTHOUSE

(Yarmouth Light; 📞902-742-4522; www.cape forchu.com; Hwy 304; ⊙9am-5pm Jun-Sep) FREE Instantly recognisable thanks to its strange 'apple core' shape (designed to deflect winds around the structure), the present-day lighthouse on the lonely headland of Cape Forchu was built in 1962, but there's been a beacon here since 1839. It's a wild location with epic views: even on clear days, rogue waves have been known to crash over the parking lot. There's a small seasonal cafe, the **Keeper's Kitchen**, and a couple of walking trails to explore.

Art Gallery of Nova Scotia   GALLERY

(📞902-749-2248; www.artgalleryofnovascotia.ca/ visit-yarmouth; 341 Main St; adult/child $6/2.50, from 5pm Thu free; ⊙10am-5pm, to 8pm Thu) The work of Maritime artists provides the backbone of the collection at this impressive outpost of the main Halifax gallery (p339), spread over three floors. If you save your ticket you'll get 50% off admission to the gallery in Halifax.

Yarmouth County Museum   MUSEUM

(📞902-742-5539; www.yarmouthcountymuseum. ca; 22 Collins St; adult/student $5/3; ⊙9am-5pm Mon-Sat Jun-Sep, 2-5pm Tue-Sat Oct-May) This museum in a former church has a typically eclectic collection of artifacts: look out for a Victorian funeral hearse and stagecoach, an original Fresnel lamp from the Cape Forchu Lightstation, and a mysterious 'runic stone' that some people claim was left by Viking explorers.

Your ticket includes admission to **Pelton-Fuller House** (20 Collins St) next door, which is filled with period artwork, glassware and furniture.

Le Village historique acadien de la Nouvelle-Écosse   HISTORIC SITE

(Historical Acadian Village of Nova Scotia; 📞902-762-2530; http://levillage.novascotia.ca; 91 Old Church Rd, Lower West Pubnico; adult/child $8/3; ⊙9am-5pm Jun-Oct) This 17-acre site overlooking Pubnico Harbour recreates an Acadian village, with vintage Acadian buildings and a cemetery. The village is located in West Pubnico, one of Nova Scotia's original Acadian communities (and not to be confused with all the other nearby Pubnicos), about a 40-minute drive southeast of Yarmouth.

🛏 Sleeping

★ Ye Olde Argyler Lodge   HOTEL $$

(📞902-643-2500; www.argyler.com; 52 Ye Old Argyle Rd; r $140-260) Situated 34km from central Yarmouth, the Argyler has nothing olde worlde about it: it's a modern, veranda-encircled lodge built in a truly glorious spot overlooking a creek. Set along a central corridor, the smart rooms have comfy beds, feather-down pillows and lovely bathrooms (ask if you want a water view). There's great food, too, including lobster parties and Acadian dishes.

NOVA SCOTIA YARMOUTH

DUMPING DAY

If you happen to be in Yarmouth around the end of November, you might be lucky enough to see one of the area's most exciting events: Dumping Day. This long-standing tradition is held to mark the beginning of the main lobster-fishing season: scores of boats head out from the harbors at the crack of dawn, watched by hundreds of locals cheering them on from the dockside. It's a lucrative business: after months of not being fished, the best lobster grounds can yield huge hauls, with experienced boats pulling in thousands of pounds of lobsters on each trip. The first week of the season is the richest of all, and many skippers will stay out as long as possible, only heading back to shore to land their catch. But it's a dangerous business, too: sinkings are not unknown, and the first day of the fishery is usually watched over by search-and-rescue teams from the Canadian Coast Guard.

Lakelawn B&B Motel
MOTEL **$$**

(☑902-742-3588; www.lakelawnmotel.com; 641 Main St; r $129-179; 🐾❄) This place is as cute and service-oriented as motels come. Rooms are clean and basic, and some of the better meals in town are available in the country-style dining area. Go even classier in the four B&B-style rooms in the central Victorian house.

MacKinnon-Cann
House Historic Inn
INN **$$**

(☑866-698-3142; www.mackinnoncanninn.com; 27 Willow St; r $149-289; 🐾) Each of the six rooms here represents a decade, from the Victorian 1900s to the groovy 1960s, and depicts the era at its most stylish while managing to stay calming and comfortable. Two rooms can be joined to create a family suite.

✕ Eating & Drinking

Shanty Cafe
CAFE **$**

(☑902-742-5918; www.shantycafe.ca; 6b Central St; items $4-9; ⊙7am-7pm Mon-Sat; 🖋) Fishers and shoppers alike head for the all-day breakfast at this simple town cafe, which dabbles in Indian and Mexican flavors alongside burgers, salads and steaks.

★ Gaia Global Kitchen
FUSION **$$**

(☑902-881-2627; www.gaiaglobalkitchen.com; 222 Main St; mains $14-19; ⊙11am-8pm Tue-Sun, to 9pm Fri & Sat) This little restaurant takes a surprisingly pan-global trip on its menu, which includes everything from Jamaican jerk chicken to dhaba curry, Lebanese meze, drunken noodles and even Korean barbecue-pork poutine. It has a whole-food, eco-conscious ethos. They mix a pretty mean cocktail, too, and the desserts are divine.

Rudder's Brew Pub
PUB FOOD **$$**

(☑902-742-7311; www.ruddersbrewpub.com; 96 Water St; mains $13-30; ⊙11am-late) Join a local crowd tucking into no-nonsense Maritime classics such as bar clams and fries and Acadian *rappie* pie (meat pie topped with grated potato) at this waterfront pub, which also brews its own ales, including an English-style brown, a raspberry-red wheat beer and a malty Scottish-style 'wee heavy.'

Heritage Brewing Co
MICROBREWERY

(☑902-881-2777; www.heritagebrewing.beer; 250 Main St; ⊙noon-11pm Sun-Wed, 11am-11pm Thu-Sat) Founded in 2017, this brewery has fast become Yarmouth's drinking venue of choice, with a range of core ales supplemented by guest ales from around Nova Sco-

tia. The taproom is a cool warehouse-style space; you can see the vats at work through little windows off the bar.

Perky Owl Coffee
CAFE

(☑902-881-2140; www.perkyowlcoffee.com; 255 Main St; ⊙7:30am-5:30pm Mon-Fri, 8:30am-4:30pm Sat, 10am-3pm Sun) Pop into the Perky Owl for a caffeine pick-me-up or something sweet and sticky for the road.

❶ Information

Visitors Information Centre (VIC; ☑902-742-5033; 228 Main St; ⊙9am-5pm Jun & Sep–mid-Oct, to 7pm Jul & Aug) Has maps and a couple of walking tours.

❶ Getting There & Away

Yarmouth is 300km southwest of Halifax on Hwy 103 and 104km south of Digby on Hwy 101.

There are no scheduled bus services from Yarmouth to Halifax and beyond, but if you're unable to rent your own wheels, Cloud Nine Shuttle (p348) can get you to the capital or to Halifax International Airport for a flat $75 fare.

Since 2016 Yarmouth has been served by a regular catamaran to Portland, Maine, but at the time of writing the service had been suspended due to construction work. See www.ferries.ca/thecat for the latest updates.

French Shore

The villages of Church Point, Grosses-Coques, Belliveau Cove and St Bernard, on the mainland directly across St Mary's Bay from Digby Neck, make up the heart of the French Shore. This is where Acadians settled when, after trekking back to Nova Scotia following deportation, they found their homesteads in the Annapolis Valley already occupied. Now linked by Hwy 1 – pretty much the only road in each town – these are small fishing communities.

The best way to explore this fading but unique part of the province is to follow Hwy 1 as it hugs the shoreline from Belliveau Cove as far south as Mavillette Beach. It can also be approached in the reverse direction.

◎ Sights & Activities

★ Gilbert's Cove Lighthouse
LIGHTHOUSE

(☑902-837-5584; www.gilbertscovelighthouse.com; 244 Lighthouse Rd, Gilbert's Cove; ⊙10am-4pm Mon-Sat, noon-4pm Sun mid-Jun–Sep) FREE Built in 1904, this gorgeous little lighthouse had only two light keepers throughout its

BEAR RIVER

Bear River is a delightful riverside enclave popular with artists and those who moved here from larger centers for a tree change. There's a strong Mi'kmaq presence here: the **Bear River First Nation Reservation** (☑902-467-0301; www.bearriverfirstnation.ca; 194 Reservation Rd) FREE is spread out on the hills above town. Some buildings near the river are on stilts, while other historic homes nestle on the steep hills of the valley.

A few wineries are starting to pop up just out of town, including the excellent **Bear River Winery** (☑902-467-4156; www.wine.travel; 133 Chute Rd; ⊘11am-6pm May-Thanksgiving) 🍷, which makes award-winning using solar energy, biodiesel, wind power and the natural slope of the property. Stop by for a free tour and tasting (July to September) or stay at the one-room B&B (from $90 per night) to enjoy wine-making workshops and retreats.

Bear River is 16km from Digby, off Hwy 101. There's no public transport.

years of service: William Melanson and his daughter Louise. It was rescued in 1982 from vandalism and decay by the local historical society, who have turned it into a charming museum. There's a scenic picnic area and a great spot for beachcombing and swimming.

Mavillette Beach Provincial Park
BEACH

This huge, dune-backed beach sprawls for 1.5km overlooking Cape St Mary and can be accessed by boardwalks from the parking lots. The receding tide reveals huge areas of sand flats, and in summer the shallow water heats up fast, making for great paddling. The beach is only supervised on Saturday and Sunday in July and August.

Smuggler's Cove Provincial Park
STATE PARK

(http://parks.novascotia.ca; 7651 Hwy 1, Meteghan; ⊘mid-May–mid-Oct) Named for its popularity with 19th-century pirates, this park is today frequented by picnickers. A hundred wooden stairs take you down to a rocky beach and a good cave for treasure hunting. There are picnic sites containing barbecue pits at the top of the stairs, with a view across St Mary's Bay to Brier Island.

Rendez-Vous de la Baie
CULTURAL CENTER

(www.rendezvousdelabaie.com; 23 Lighthouse Rd, Church Point; ⊘8am-6pm Mon-Fri, 9am-5pm Sat & Sun) FREE This interpretive center on the grounds of Université Sainte-Anne in Church Point is a really useful stop as you drive along the coastal road. You can acquire background about Acadian culture at the small museum, then get tourist tips at the information center. There is also a theater and a few walking trails to explore.

Église Ste-Marie
CHURCH

(St Mary's Church; ☑902-769-2808; 1713 Hwy 1, Church Point; incl guide $2; ⊘9am-5pm May-Oct) The town of Church Point, also commonly known as Pointe de l'Église, takes its name from Église Ste-Marie, which towers over the town. Built between 1903 and 1905, the church is said to be the tallest wooden church in North America. An informative guide will show you around. Adjacent is the **Université Ste-Anne**, the only French university in the province and a center for Acadian culture.

🍴 Eating

Roadside Grill
ACADIAN $

(☑902-837-5047; 3334 Hwy 1, Belliveau Cove; mains $9-18; ⊘8am-9pm) Try the steamed clams or the *rappie* pie at this pleasantly old-fashioned and long-running local restaurant. There's live Acadian music Tuesday night from 5:30pm to 7:30pm June through August.

La Cuisine Robicheau
ACADIAN $$

(☑902-769-2121; www.lacuisinerobicheau.ca; 9651 Hwy 1, Saulnierville; mains $12-25; ⊘8am-7pm Tue-Sun Apr-Oct) This is the most elevated Acadian cuisine on the French Shore. The *rappie* pie, seafood lasagna and chocolate pie are so good and affordable they may make you exclaim *'sacre bleu!'* It's family-run and always busy, and there's often live music at suppertime during summer.

ℹ Getting There & Away

The French Shore begins in Belliveau Cove, 43km south of Digby, and hugs Hwy 1 south as far as Mavillette Beach, 35km from Yarmouth.

ANNAPOLIS VALLEY

Historically, the fertile and sparsely populated Annapolis Valley was known as the breadbasket of colonial Canada. Today the region still produces much of Nova Scotia's fresh produce, especially apples, but the real excitement surrounds the growth of the valley's wine industry. The valley's vineyards, which boast a similar latitude to that of Bordeaux, France, have taken advantage of the sandy soil and reconnected with the area's French roots.

Regional highlights include the **Annapolis Valley Apple Blossom Festival** (www. appleblossom.com; ⊙ late May), the Fundy coast at Annapolis Royal for tidal vistas over patchwork farmland, the vibrant and spirited town of Wolfville, and taking a moment to contemplate the past while gazing upon the World Heritage landscape of Grand Pré.

❶ Getting There & Away

Hwy 101, which begins on the outskirts of Halifax, continues for 74km to Wolfville at the northern edge of the Annapolis Valley, then runs straight down to Digby in the south. Because of the distance between towns and the many side trips to discover, self-driving is the most practical and enjoyable way to explore the region.

Maritime Bus (www.maritimebus.com) runs a direct service from Halifax to Wolfville.

Bay Ferries (www.ferries.ca) links Digby to Saint John, New Brunswick, via car ferry. The journey takes approximately 2¼ hours in peak season and 2¾ hours in low season.

❶ Getting Around

Kings Transit (www.kingstransit.ns.ca) runs a bus every other hour from 6am to around 7pm from Weymouth (just north of Church Point) to Bridgetown (just north of Annapolis Royal) and then as far as Wolfville, stopping in every little town along the way. The fare is $3.50.

Kentville-based **Valley Stove & Cycle** (☑ 902-542-7280; www.valleystoveandcycle.com; 353 Main St; bike rental half/full day from $25/35; ⊙ 9am-5:30pm Mon-Thu, to 7pm Fri, to 5pm Sat) rents out trail bikes, fat bikes, tandems and e-bikes.

Digby

☑ 902 / POP 2060

Nestled in a protected inlet off the Bay of Fundy, Digby is known across Nova Scotia for one thing: scallops. These sought-after shellfish grow in great numbers on scallop beds just offshore and command a premium price – you'll find them at most of the town's restaurants. Digby is now home to the largest fleet of scallop boats in the world, and hosts its own scallop-themed festival, **Digby Scallop Days** (www.digbyscallopdays.com; ⊙ Aug), in honor of its most prized export.

The town may lack the quaint charm of the other Annapolis Valley settlements, but it's an honest, down-to-earth base for exploring the valley and nearby Digby Neck.

If you're here only briefly, the best things to do are to stroll the waterfront, watch the scallop draggers come and go, eat as much of their catch as you can, and then squeeze in a sunset at **Point Prim**.

🛏 Sleeping & Eating

Digby Backpackers Inn   HOSTEL $
(☑ 902-245-4573; www.digbyhostel.com; 168 Queen St; dm/r $30/65; 🛜) Saskia and Claude keep their solid four-bed dorms spotless and often spontaneously host barbecues or take the whole hostel out to see the sunset. The heritage house has plenty of communal areas, including a deck, and there's a lively, welcoming vibe. Internet access, a light breakfast and towels are included in the price. Cash only.

Hillside Landing   B&B $$
(☑ 902-247-5781; www.hillsidelanding.com; 152 Queen St; d $150-180) Originally from Ontario, owners Henry and Linda have renovated this wonderful mansion with real love and care. The three rooms are spankingly stylish: one looks over the street, while Vye and Rutherford both have panoramic aspects over the harbor. Throw in posh jet showers, a magnificent veranda and a copious breakfast, and you have Digby's top B&B.

Shoreline Restaurant   SEAFOOD $$
(☑ 902-245-6667; 88 Water St; mains $12-30; ⊙ 11am-9pm) This is *the* spot in Digby for top-notch scallops – and clams, crab, lobster, haddock and pretty much every other fish you care to mention – along with salads and steaks. Grab a booth or head out to the waterfront deck and dig in. It's easy to miss, located at the back of a gift shop.

Sydney St   PUB $$
(☑ 902-245-1066; www.sydneystreetpub.ca; 14 Sydney St; mains $14-26; ⊙ noon-9pm Sun-Thu, to 11pm Fri & Sat) In a turreted, decked building just off the main drag, this lively pub is where everyone heads for a pint of some-

CAPE BLOMIDON

The **North Mountain**, which ends at dramatic Cape Blomidon, defines one edge of the Annapolis Valley. On the other side of the mountain are the fishing communities of the Bay of Fundy. The valley floor is crisscrossed with small highways lined with farms and orchards. It's a great place to get out your road map – or throw it away – and explore.

Around 3km from the village of **Port Williams**, the 1814 **Prescott House Museum** (☑902-542-3984; http://prescotthouse.novascotia.ca; 1633 Starr's Point Rd; adult/student $3.90/2.80; ⊙10am-5pm Mon-Sat, 1-5pm Sun Jun-Sep) – considered one of the finest examples of Georgian architecture in Nova Scotia – is the former home of the horticulturalist who introduced many of the apple varieties grown in the Annapolis Valley.

In the quaint, historic town of **Canning**, stop for a fair-trade coffee (or an art class) at **ArtCan Gallery & Café** (☑902-582-7071; https://artcan.com; 9850 Main St; mains $10-14; ⊙9am-5pm; 🐾) or head just out of town to sample wines at **Blomidon Estate Winery** (☑902-582-7565; www.blomidonwine.ca; 10318 Hwy 221; ⊙10am-6pm Mon-Fri, to 7pm Sat, 11am-6pm Sun Jun-Sep).

North of Canning, along Hwy 358, stop at the well-signposted **Look-Off**. About 200m above the Annapolis Valley, it's the perfect spot to view the farmlands below and, if you're lucky, bald eagles above: from November to March they number in the hundreds, attracted by local chicken farms.

Hwy 358 ends in **Scots Bay**, where the dramatic 13km **Cape Split hiking trail** (https://parks.novascotia.ca/content/cape-split) leads to views of the Minas Basin and the Bay of Fundy. If you're not up for the hike, nearby **Blomidon Provincial Park** (☑902-582-7319; https://parks.novascotia.ca/content/blomidon; 3138 Pereau Rd; campsites $26.70-35.60; ⊙mid-May–mid-Oct) has a picnic area and plenty of easier walks.

If you need some lunch after all that fresh air, head to **Halls Harbour Lobster Pound** (☑902-679-5299; www.hallsharbourlobster.com; 1157 W Halls Harbour Rd, Centreville; mains $15-24; ⊙noon-7pm mid-May–Jun, Sep & Oct, 11:30am-9pm Jul & Aug) and gorge yourself on ocean delicacies straight from the source.

Round out your afternoon with a visit to **Kentville**, the county seat for the area, where you can rent a bike at Valley Stove & Cycle to admire the town's stately old homes, or check out the region's apple-farming history at **Blair House Museum** (Kentville Agricultural Centre; ☑902-678-1093; www.nsapples.com/museumb.htm; 32 Main St; ⊙8:30am-4:30pm Mon-Fri Jun-Sep) FREE or other local history and art at **Kings County Museum** (☑902-678-6237; www.kingscountymuseum.ca; 37 Cornwallis Ave; ⊙9am-4pm Mon-Sat Jun–mid-Aug, 9am-4pm Mon-Fri Apr, May & mid-Aug–mid-Dec) FREE.

thing cold and local. It also does decent grub, including (of course) pan-fried Digby scallops.

❶ Getting There & Away

Digby is 32km southwest of Annapolis Royal, just off Hwy 1. From Yarmouth, it's 104km along Hwy 101 heading northeast.

Kings Transit (☑902-628-7310; www.kbus.ca; 1 way adult/child $4/2.25) operates a local bus service that runs as far north as Wolfville, via Annapolis Royal.

Bay Ferries (www.ferries.ca) operates a daily car-ferry service to Saint John, NB, on the *Fundy Rose* (adult/child from $39/23, 2¼ to 2¾ hours). Rates are about $10 more expensive in peak season, and much pricier if you don't pre-book. Vehicles cost $113 in low season and $119 in peak season.

Long Island & Brier Island

The long, narrow strip of land that resembles a giraffe's neck craning out to take a peek into the Bay of Fundy is known as **Digby Neck**. At the far western end of this appendage are two islands: Long Island and Brier Island, connected by ferry with the rest of the peninsula. The entire area is a haven for whale and seabird watchers.

Long Island is easier to get to and has a few more residents. The main towns are **Tiverton** at the northeastern end and **Freeport** at the southwestern end, connected via Hwy 217.

Brier Island is best known as the one-time home of sailor Joshua Slocum who, in 1895, became the first man to sail solo around the world. These days it's also famous as a whale-watching spot. The only town is **Westport**, a quaint fishing village and a good base for exploring the island's numerous excellent, if rugged and windy, hiking trails.

◉ Sights & Activities

★ Ocean Explorations
Whale Cruises WHALE WATCHING
(☑ 902-839-2417; www.oceanexplorations.ca; Tiverton; adult/child $85/60; ☺ Jun-Oct) One of the best whale-watching tours in the province is led by biologist Tom Goodwin and has the adventurous approach of getting you down to whale-breaching level in a Zodiac. Shimmy into a coastguard-approved orange flotation suit and hold on tight! Times depend on weather, whale sightings and demand. It's based in a white-gabled building 100m from the ferry wharf.

Brier Island Whale
& Seabird Cruises WHALE WATCHING
(☑ 902-839-2995; www.brierislandwhalewatch. com; 223 Water St, Westport; adult/child from $50/28; ☺ mid-May–Oct) You can book excellent whale-watching tours (2½ to five hours, depending on where the whales are) with this eco-conscious company. Tours are very popular, so it's worth booking as far ahead as possible.

Brier Island Lighthouse LIGHTHOUSE
(Western Light; 720 Lighthouse Rd) Originally built in 1809, this rugged outpost has seen many incarnations over the years. Its present form, a striking red-and-white-striped concrete tower standing 18.3m tall, was built in 1944 and has been automated since 1987.

Islands Historical Society Museum MUSEUM
(☑ 902-839-2034; www.islandshistoricalsociety. com; 243 Hwy 217, Freeport; by donation; ☺ 9:30am-4:30pm Jun-Sep) Island life is explored at this little museum, which has lots of boat models, vintage fishing gear, sepia-tinted photos and a small exhibit on one-time Brier Island resident Joshua Slocum.

🛏 Sleeping

Brier Island Lodge LODGE $$
(☑ 902-839-2300; www.brierisland.com; 557 Water St, Westport; r $109-169; ☺ May-Oct; ☻ 🕸 🐾) Atop cliffs 1km east of Westport, Brier Island Lodge has 37 rooms, many with ocean views. Its pine-paneled **restaurant** (mains $10 to $30) has views on two sides, friendly service

and fabulously fresh seafood. Boxed lunches are available.

Hooking by the Sea B&B $$
(☑ 902-308-2107; www.hookingbythesea.com; Church St, Westport; r $80-125; 🅿 🕸) Centered on Westport's first schoolhouse, this working farm also has cozy B&B rooms inside the traditional tin-roofed farmhouse. There's a barbecue and fire pit for guests' use, and you can try your hand at the old craft of rug hooking with the owners, should you so desire.

❶ Getting There & Away

Long Island is connected to Digby Neck by ferry from East Ferry to Tiverton, departing on the half-hour and returning on the hour. From Tiverton, it's another 18km along Hwy 217 to Freeport, where you can catch a second ferry over to Westport on Brier Island.

Both ferries run hourly (after midnight they're on an 'on-call' basis); each costs $7, payable only for travel toward Brier Island (the trip back to Digby is free). There's more information in the 'Important Details – Getting Here' section of www.brierisland.org.

Annapolis Royal
☑ 902 / POP 491
The epitome of a homey Nova Scotian town, with a lovely main street lined by cafes and B&Bs, Annapolis Royal also has historical significance: the area was the location of Canada's first permanent European settlement and was the capital of Nova Scotia until the founding of Halifax in 1749.

Named in honor of the English Queen Anne, the town's main sight is its dramatic 17th-century fort. Its ramparts are now covered in grass, but the fort once commanded control of the nearby Annapolis River.

◉ Sights & Activities

★ Fort Anne
National Historic Site HISTORIC SITE
(☑ 902-532-2397; www.parkscanada.gc.ca/fort anne; Upper St George St; adult/child $3.90/free; ☺ 9am-5:30pm daily mid-Jun–Aug, Tue-Sat only mid-May–mid-Jun & Sep–mid-Oct) The strategic importance of Annapolis Royal, particularly its access to the Annapolis River, led to decades of conflict, mostly centered on this impressive fort. The first redoubt was built by the French in the 1630s; the current structure was designed by French military architect Vauban in 1702. You can wander

the bulwarks and battlements (now mostly grassed over), and there's an interesting **museum** in the old officers' quarters with exhibits including a four-panel tapestry depicting 400 years of the fort's history.

Port Royal National
Historic Site
HISTORIC SITE

(☑902-532-2898; www.pc.gc.ca/en/lhn-nhs/ns/portroyal; 53 Historic Lane; adult/child $3.90/free; ☺9am-5:30pm daily mid-Jun–Aug, Tue-Sat mid-May–mid-Jun & Sep–mid-Oct) Some 14km northwest of Annapolis Royal, Port Royal National Historic Site is the location of one of the earliest permanent European settlements in North America, established by French colonist and explorer Samuel de Champlain as a fur-trading outpost. A replica of the settlement, complete with wooden stockades and timber buildings, has been created here. Brought to life by guides in period costume, it gives a surprisingly convincing insight into early colonial times.

Annapolis Royal
Historic Gardens
GARDENS

(☑902-532-7018; www.historicgardens.com; 441 St George St; adult/child 12-18yr/child 6-11yr $14.50/6/3; ☺9am-8pm Jul & Aug, to 5pm May, Jun, Sep & Oct) These gorgeous gardens cover a rambling 6.5 hectares and have various themed areas, such as an Acadian kitchen garden one might have seen in the late 1600s and an innovative modern one. Munch blueberries, ogle the vegetables and look for frogs. The **Secret Garden Café** offers lunches and German-style baked goods.

Delap's Cove Wilderness Trail
HIKING

Over the North Mountain from Annapolis Royal, the Delap's Cove Wilderness Trail lets you get out on the Bay of Fundy shore. It consists of two loop trails connected by an old inland road that used to serve a Black Loyalist community. Today only foundation relics and apple trees remain in the woods. Each loop trail is a 9km round-trip.

★ Tour Annapolis
Royal Graveyard Tour
WALKING

(☑902-532-3034; www.tourannapolisroyal.com; adult/child 13-18yr/under 12yr $10/5/3; ☺Jun–mid-Oct) This company runs several local history walks. The best is where a guide in undertaker's garb leads a creepy tour of the Fort Anne graveyard. Everyone carries a lantern and winds through the headstones to discover the town's history through stories

of those who've passed. Hour-long tours run nightly at 9:30pm.

There's also a regular historical tour of Annapolis Royal at 2pm every Monday and Wednesday, departing from the lighthouse. Proceeds go to the Annapolis Royal Historical Society.

🛏 Sleeping

Annapolis Royal has some glorious Victorian architecture, including several fine Queen Anne–style mansions that have been turned into heritage B&Bs.

Dunromin Campground
CAMPGROUND $

(☑902-532-2808; www.dunromincampground.ca; 4618 Hwy 1, Granville Ferry; sites $33-47, cabins from $65; ☺May-Oct; P🐾🛜🐕) This popular, offbeat campground has some secluded riverside sites as well as nifty options such as waterfront 'camping cabins' and a rustic caravan.

★ Queen Anne Inn
INN $$

(☑902-532-7850; www.queenanneinn.ns.ca; 494 Upper St George St; r $129-209; ☺May-Oct; P🌸🛜) The most elegant property in Annapolis Royal, this eye-popping B&B looks as though it's blown straight off the *Gone with the Wind* set. Built in 1865 as a private home for local notables William Ritchie and Fanny Foster, it's a real museum piece: sweeping staircases, carriage clocks, four-poster beds, Tiffany-lamp replicas and a glorious central turret.

Bailey House B&B
B&B $$

(☑902-532-1285; www.baileyhouse.ca; 150 Lower St George St; r $145-175; P🛜) The only B&B on the waterfront, Bailey House is also the oldest inn (built around 1770) and one of the best in town. The friendly owners have managed to keep the vintage charm (anyone over 6ft might hit their head on the doorways!), while adding all the necessary modern comforts.

🍴 Eating & Drinking

★ Restaurant Compose
EUROPEAN $$

(☑902-532-1251; www.restaurantcompose.com; 235 St George St; mains lunch $11-18, dinner $16-34; ☺11:30am-2pm & 5-8:30pm; 🛜) This waterfront bistro is the place for dining with a view: there's a wonderful outlook over the Bay of Fundy. It majors in classy seafood, steaks and schnitzels, and there's a greenhouse-covered patio for sunny days.

Bistro East

BISTRO $$

(☑ 902-532-7992; www.bistroeast.com; 274 St George St; mains $16-28; ⊙ 11am-10pm) Annapolis Royal's down-home downtown diner serves pretty much every kind of food you could fancy: quesadillas, chicken Alfredo, Cajun haddock and great pizza. It's in an attractive redbrick corner building on the main street.

German Bakery Sachsen Cafe

GERMAN $$

(☑ 902-532-1990; www.germanbakery.ca; 358 St George St; sandwiches $9.25-10.95, mains $19.45-23.95; ⊙ 9am-7pm) The owners of this Teutonic-themed cafe hail from Saxony in Germany, and specialize in goodies such as schnitzel, sausages and *belegte brötchen* (sandwiches on Kaiser bread). Baking has been in the family for three generations.

Annapolis Brewing

MICROBREWERY

(☑ 902-286-2080; www.annapolisbrewing.com; 302 St George St; ⊙ noon-8pm Sun-Tue, to 10pm Wed & Thu, to 11pm Fri, 10am-11pm Sat) With a cannon-themed logo commemorating the historic 40th Regiment of Foot, this great brewery and taproom has become a firm town favorite: all its beers have names relating to the town's history, from King George to Acadian Honey.

Sissiboo Coffee Roaster

CAFE

(☑ 902-286-3010; www.sissiboocoffee.com; 262 St George St; ⊙ 7:30am-4pm Mon-Fri, 9am-4pm Sat & Sun) Great home-roasted coffee and delicious homemade biscotti keep this cafe busy throughout the day.

🛍 Shopping

Farmers & Traders Market

MARKET

(www.annapolisroyalfarmersmarket.com; cnr St George & Church Sts; ⊙ 8am-1pm Sat May-Oct, plus 10am-2pm Wed Jul & Aug) Annapolis Royal's thriving community of artists and artisans offer their wares alongside local farm produce at this popular market. There's live entertainment most Saturday mornings.

ℹ Information

Tourist Information Centre (☑ 902-532-5769; www.annapolisroyal.com; 236 Prince Albert Rd; ⊙ 10am-5pm Jun–mid-Oct) Located at the tidal-power station in summer and at the town hall in winter.

ℹ Getting There & Away

Annapolis Royal is 108km southwest of Wolfville on Hwy 101. Continuing a further 32km on Hwy 101, you'll come to Digby, from where you can catch the ferry to Saint John, NB.

Kings Transit (www.kbus.ca) shuttles along the valley between Wolfville and Digby for a flat $3.50 fare.

Wolfville & Grand Pré

☑ 902 / POP 4195

Wolfville has a perfect blend of old-college-town culture, small-town homeyness and a culinary scene that has developed in concert with the surrounding wine industry. When added to the town's permanent residents, the students and faculty of the local Acadia University bump the population to more than 7000, injecting youthful vigor into this otherwise quiet district and making Wolfville one of the most livable and ethnically diverse towns in the province.

Essentially just down the road is the small bilingual community of Grand Pré, Wolfville's bucolic neighbor. In the 1750s, however, it was the site of one of the most tragic but compelling stories in eastern Can-

DON'T MISS

BRAVE THE BORE

Tiny Maitland is the place to brave the Shubenacadie River's legendary **tidal bore**, a mass of churning white water caused by the river's outflow meeting the blasting force of the incoming Fundy tide. Depending on the phase of the moon, the tidal bore can create wave heights of up to 3m, a wild washing machine of water that has to be experienced to be believed.

There are plenty of rafting companies in the area, including **Shubenacadie River Runners** (☑ 902-261-2770, 800-856-5061; http://riverrunnersns.com; 8681 Hwy 215; 2/3hr tour $65/85; ⊙ Jun-Sep) and **Shubenacadie River Adventures** (☑ 902-261-2222; www.shubie.com; 10061 Hwy 215; tours from $85; ⊙ Jun-Sep); check their websites for tour times and bore conditions. Outboard-powered Zodiacs plunge right through the white water for the two to three hours that the rapids exist. Prepare to get very, very wet indeed.

ada's history: the Acadian deportation. In 2012 the marshland and polder farmland of Grand Pré were given Unesco World Heritage status.

Beyond the two towns you'll find Acadian dikes, scenic drives and some of the best hiking along the Bay of Fundy.

◎ Sights

★ Grand Pré
National Historic Site · HISTORIC SITE
(📞902-542-3631; www.pc.gc.ca/en/lhn-nhs/ns/grandpre; 2205 Grand Pré Rd, Grand Pré; adult/child $7.80/free; ⊙9am-5pm May-Oct) This interpretive center explains the historical context for the deportation of the French-Acadian people from Acadian, Mi'kmaw and British perspectives, and traces the many routes Acadians took from, and back to, the Maritimes. Beside the center, a serene park contains gardens, an Acadian-style stone church, and a bust of American poet Henry Wadsworth Longfellow, who chronicled the Acadian saga in *Evangeline: A Tale of Acadie,* and a statue of his fictional Evangeline, now a romantic symbol of her people.

★ Tangled Garden · GARDENS
(📞902-542-9811; www.tangledgarden.com; 11827 Hwy 1, Grand Pré; $8; ⊙10am-6pm May-Oct) A one-woman passion project, these glorious terraced gardens are a must-see for horticulturalists. Split into a series of 'rooms' by hedges of beech, box and yew, and stocked with a wonderful array of flowers, trees and herbs, this is a lovely place to wander. At the delightful **tearoom** (open 11am to 4:30pm Wednesday to Sunday) all the jams and chutneys are made with garden goodies.

The gift shop is probably the best-smelling shopping experience in Nova Scotia; there's a huge selection of herb jellies, vinaigrettes, cordials, liqueurs and chutneys to try and buy.

The gardens are 5.5km from Wolfville along Hwy 1.

✲ Festivals & Events

Canadian Deep Roots Festival · MUSIC
(www.deeprootsmusic.ca; ⊙late Sep) If you're in Wolfville in early fall, rock out to modern roots music at this annual festival.

⌷ Sleeping

★ Olde Lantern Inn & Vineyard · INN $$
(📞902-542-1389; www.oldlanterninn.com; 11575 Hwy 1, Grand Pré; r $137-157; ☎) Among the

world-famous Grand Pré vines, this little vineyard has a pleasant guesthouse with four attractive, clutter-free rooms, all with whirlpool bath. Two are in the timber-framed main house, while another two are in a modern wing. There are wonderful views over the Bay of Fundy and the Grand Pré landscape.

★ Roselawn Lodging · MOTEL $$
(📞902-542-3420; www.roselawnlodging.ca; 32 Main St, Wolfville; d $95-185; 🅿⊕@✖) This fun 1960s-style complex features a variety of motel-like rooms and freshly updated, cute-as-a-button cottages with full kitchens. It makes a welcome alternative to Wolfville's sedate B&Bs. With a pool, a tennis court and spacious grounds, it's easy to make this place your home away from home.

Victoria's
Historic Inn · INN $$
(📞902-542-5744; www.victoriashistoricinn.com; 600 Main St, Wolfville; r $149-229) This elegant inn is directly opposite Acadia University. The luxuriously appointed rooms vary in style, but all are decorated with sumptuous taste: four-poster beds, period furnishings, antiques, fine linens. The Chase suite is hard to top for old-world grandeur. Ask for the main inn; the carriage-house rooms are underwhelming.

Blomidon Inn · INN $$
(📞800-565-2291; www.blomidon.ns.ca; 195 Main St, Wolfville; d $149-169, ste $189-219; ✲@☎) Old-fashioned elegance is on offer in this imposing house set amid 2.5 hectares of lawned grounds. This isn't one for minimalists: expect dark wooden furniture, four-poster beds and ornate Victoriana. There's no elevator.

✕ Eating

★ Noodle Guy · PASTA $
(📞902-697-3906; https://thenoodleguy.wordpress.com; 964 NS 358, Port Williams; small/large plates $7/11; ⊙10am-7pm Mon-Thu, to 8pm Fri & Sat, 11am-7pm Sun) Owner Ross Patterson perfected his art running a noodle stall, and diners now travel from far and wide to his laid-back pasta place in the village of Port Williams, 4km from Wolfville. Every day there's a ravioli, tagliatelle, spaghetti and conchiglie dish, plus a Japanese-style soba-noodle bowl. The pasta's 100% handmade and tastes like it.

LOCAL KNOWLEDGE

WOLFVILLE WINERIES

Most of Nova Scotia's best wineries and vineyards are found in the rolling hills and valleys around Wolfville and Grand Pré. If you want to dodge the problem of deciding on a designated driver, hop on the vintage double-decker **Magic Winery Bus** (☑902-542-4093; www.magicwinerybus.ca; hop-on/hop-off pass $50; ☻Thu-Sun Jun-Oct).

Lightfoot & Wolfville (☑902-542-7774; www.lightfootandwolfville.com; 11143 Evangeline Trail; ☻10am-6pm Mon-Wed, to 9pm Thu-Sun mid-Jun–mid-Oct, shorter hours rest of year) This organic, biodynamic winery produces vintages from a bubbly rosé and blanc de blancs to a crisp chardonnay and an ice wine. It has a great bistro.

Domaine de Grand Pré (☑902-542-1753; www.grandprewines.com; 11611 Hwy 1, Grand Pré; tours $9; ☻10am-6pm Mon-Wed, to 7pm Thu-Sat, 11am-6pm Sun Jul & Aug, shorter hours rest of year) A great destination winery and one of the best known in the province, Grand Pré features a delicious spicy muscat and a nice sparkling Champlain Brut.

Luckett Vineyards (☑902-542-2600; www.luckettvineyards.com; 1293 Grand Pré Rd, Wolfville; tastings from $5; ☻10am-5pm May-Oct, tours 11am & 3pm) Palatial views over the vines and hillsides down to the Bay of Fundy cliffs are on offer here. Sample the red, white, fruit and dessert wines, and the particularly good ice wine, then stay for lunch on the patio.

Gaspereau Vineyards (☑902-542-1455; www.gaspereauwine.com; 2239 White Rock Rd, Gaspereau; ☻10am-6pm Jun-Sep, to 5pm rest of year) One of the province's best-known wineries, Gaspereau has award-winning ice wine and an elegant estate Riesling.

L'Acadie Vineyards (☑902-542-8463; www.lacadievineyards.ca; 310 Slayter Rd, Wolfville; ☻11am-5pm May–mid-Oct, by appointment other times) ⬤ Overlooking the Gaspereau Valley, this geothermally powered winery grows certified-organic grapes to make traditional-method sparkling and dried-grape wines.

Naked Crepe CRÊPES $
(☑902-542-0653; www.thenakedcrepebistro.ca; 402 Main St, Wolfville; crepes $3-12; ☻9am-11pm) Who doesn't enjoy a flaky, wafer-thin crepe filled with delicious sweet or savory goodness? Hardly anyone, it seems, judging by this newcomer's rise to become one of Wolfville's best-loved eateries. Catering to the breakfast crowd *and* the late-nighters, Naked Crepe boasts a huge range of inventive fillings.

★**Troy** MEDITERRANEAN $$
(☑902-542-4425; www.troyrestaurant.ca; 12 Elm Ave, Wolfville; mains $18-32; ☻11am-9pm Mon-Sat, noon-9pm Sun; ☑) Zingy meze dishes, kebabs, falafel and stuffed vine leaves bring the flavours of the Mediterranean and the Middle East to well-to-do Wolfville. Order a selection of items and eat tapas style. There are loads of veggie options.

★**Le Caveau** EUROPEAN $$$
(☑902-542-1753; https://grandprewines.com/pages/le-caveau; 11611 Hwy 1, Grand Pré; mains lunch $14-21, dinner $28-38; ☻11:30am-2pm & 5-9pm May-Oct) Overseen by head chef Jason Lynch, this upscale bistro at the Domaine de Grand Pré winery has become a destination

in its own right. The ethos is rich, indulgent dining with a taste for game and seafood; as much produce as possible comes from surrounding farms. The beautiful patio is paved with fieldstones and shaded with grapevines.

🍷 Drinking & Nightlife

Annapolis Cider Company BAR
(☑902-697-2707; www.drinkannapolis.ca; 388 Main St, Wolfville; ☻10am-7pm) Red-and-white-striped awnings and a swanky tasting room provide an impressive introduction to this craft cidery, which makes all its brews from local apples, with a particular penchant for heirloom and heritage varieties. Occasionally it produces a 'Something Different' brew: a cherry-and-cilantro cider has featured in the past.

Library Pub & Wine Tavern PUB
(☑902-542-4315; www.thelibrarypub.ca; 472 Main St, Wolfville; ☻11am-midnight Mon-Sat, 11:30am-8pm Sun) This friendly pub, with a wood-lined interior and plenty of wines by the glass, makes a great place to sink a pint or three. Downstairs has more of a wine-bar feel; upstairs it's more like a pub.

⭐ Entertainment

Acadia Cinema's
Al Whittle Theatre   THEATER
(☑902-542-3344; www.acadiacinema.coop; 450 Main St, Wolfville) Operated by the volunteer-run Acadia Cinema Co-op, this fabulous historic building, a Wolfville cultural icon, functions as a multipurpose cinema, theater and performance space. Check the website for regular event listings and screening times and to learn a little about the theater's history.

ℹ Information

Wolfville Visitor Information Centre (☑902-542-7000; www.wolfville.ca; 11 Willow Ave, Wolfville; ⊘10am-6pm May-Oct) A well-run center with lots of info on local vineyards and the wider valley.

ℹ Getting There & Away

Wolfville is linked to Halifax by Hwy 101; the journey takes an hour in good traffic.
Maritime Bus (www.maritimebus.com) services from Halifax stop at Acadia University in front of Wheelock Hall off Highland Ave (Wolfville; $20.25, 1½ hours, two daily).
Kings Transit (www.kingstransit.ns.ca) buses run between Cornwallis (southwest of Annapolis Royal) and Wolfville, stopping at 209 Main St. The fare is a flat $3.50.

CENTRAL NOVA SCOTIA

Hiking, rafting and rock-hounding are the activities of choice around this pleasant and often overlooked region. For those traveling overland from the rest of Canada, the town of **Amherst**, geographic center of the Maritimes and a crossroads between New Brunswick, Prince Edward Island and Nova Scotia, will be your first taste of the province if you swing off the Trans-Canada Hwy (Hwy 104 at this point).

From Amherst you can follow the 'Glooscap Trail' – named for the figure in Mi'kmaw legend who created the unique geography of the Bay of Fundy – as far as Wolfville in the Annapolis Valley, or take the road less traveled and hug the shoreline, visiting the World Heritage–listed Joggins Fossil Cliffs, the delightful hamlet of Advocate Harbour and the village of Parrsboro.

This is the part of Nova Scotia famed for the legendary Fundy tides and tidal-bore rafting.

ℹ Information

Amherst Visitor Information Centre (VIC; ☑902-667-8429; ⊘9am-7pm Jul & Aug, to 5pm mid-May–Jun, Sep & Oct, to 4:30pm Nov-May) This massive visitor center is at exit 1 off Hwy 104, just as you cross the border from New Brunswick.

ℹ Getting There & Away

Amherst is the gateway to Nova Scotia for visitors arriving overland, although the town is largely bypassed by the Trans-Canada Hwy (Hwy 104).

Maritime Bus (www.maritimebus.com) connects Amherst with Moncton, NB ($14, one hour, three daily) and Halifax ($41.75, three hours, three daily), and Truro with Halifax ($25.50, 1¾ hours, five daily).

Parrsboro
☑902 / POP 1205

Rock hounds come from far and wide to forage on the shores of Parrsboro, the largest of the settlements along the Minas Basin. The town's Fundy Geological Museum has wonderful exhibits and good programs that take you to the beach areas known as Nova Scotia's 'Jurassic Park.'

⦿ Sights

⭐**Fundy Geological Museum**   MUSEUM
(☑902-254-3814; http://fundygeological.novascotia.ca; 162 Two Islands Rd; adult/child $6/4; ⊘10am-5pm mid-May–mid-Oct) If you want to understand the geological history of the Bay

---

WORTH A TRIP

SHUBENACADIE PROVINCIAL WILDLIFE PARK

Shubenacadie, or simply 'Shube', 35km south of Truro off Hwy 2, is best known for this **wildlife park** (☑902-758-2040; https://wildlifepark.novascotia.ca; 149 Creighton Rd; adult/child $4.75/2; ⊘9am-6:30pm mid-May–mid-Oct, to 3pm Sat & Sun mid-Oct–mid-May). It's the place to commune with Nova Scotia's native fauna: moose, porcupines, timber wolves, lynx, bobcats, cougars, black bears and bald eagles. Contained within large enclosures, the animals were mostly born in captivity, but a few have been rescued from private ownership as 'pets' and thus cannot be released into the wild.

of Fundy this excellent museum should be your first port of call. It has a wide range of interactive exhibits, but inevitably the highlights are the fossils and dinosaur skeletons unearthed around the Fundy coastline – perhaps the most famous are the tiny dinosaur footprints found in 1984 by Eldon George. You can also peer into a working lab where new specimens are being processed.

Fun beach tours ($15 to $25) allow you to try out your newly acquired knowledge in the wild.

Age of Sail Museum MUSEUM

(☑902-348-2030; www.ageofsailmuseum.ca; 8334 Hwy 209, Port Greville; $4; ⊙9:30am-5pm daily Jul & Aug, Thu-Mon Apr-Jun, Sep & Oct) This museum on the banks of the tidal Greville River, about 20km west of Parrsboro, memorializes the age of sail and the area's shipbuilding past. A restored church and a working blacksmith shop are also on-site.

🛏 Sleeping

★Gillespie House Inn B&B $$

(☑902-254-3196; www.gillespiehouseinn.com; 358 Main St; d $129-149; P🐾) The pick of Parrsboro's B&Bs, this lovingly restored sea captain's mansion has heritage-themed rooms stocked with burnished sleigh beds, clawfoot tubs, antique settees and wingback chairs. There's a fabulous staircase and veranda, a yoga studio and a blueberry field where you can pick your own berries in summer. A real stunner.

Maple Inn B&B $$

(☑902-254-3735; www.mapleinn.ca; 2358 Western Ave; d $99-169; ⊙May-Oct; P🐾❄🐾) There's a room to suit every taste and budget at this huge heritage house, from a basic buttercup-colored twin to two grand bay-windowed suites (there's also a Freemasons-themed room and one that served as a delivery ward when the house was still a hospital). Standards are very high throughout, and there's a daily special for breakfast.

Sunshine Inn MOTEL $$

(☑877-706-6835; www.thesunshineinn.net; 4487 Hwy 2; r $117-122, cottages $139-149; ⊙May-Nov; P🐾🐾) Practical, no-frills motel rooms are what to expect from the Sunshine, out on the Glooscap Trail 3km north of Parrsboro. In addition to the motel units there are self-contained cottages on the grassy grounds (some have views of the motel's own lake).

🍴 Eating & Drinking

Black Rock Bistro BISTRO $$

(☑902-728-3006; www.blackrockbistro.ca; 151 Main St; mains $14-20; ⊙7am-8pm; P) New owners have brought fresh flavors to this downtown bistro, pretty much the pick of Parrsboro's eating places. Steak-frites, hand-made burgers, slow-roasted ribs, and the odd pasta and risotto dish will make sure you don't leave hungry, and there are on-tap brews from Two Islands Brewing down the road.

DON'T MISS

JOGGINS FOSSIL CLIFFS

Buried deep in the cliffs along the edge of the Bay of Fundy is one of the most complete fossil records anywhere in Canada. Laid down during the Carboniferous period – sometimes known as the 'Coal Age', when much of the surrounding landscape was covered in swampy forest – the life-forms preserved in these ancient cliffs predate the dinosaurs by about 100 million years.

Start at the impressive **Joggins Fossil Cliffs Visitor Centre** (www.jogginsfossilcliffs. net; 100 Main St, Joggins; tours from $10.50; ⊙9:30am-5:30pm Jun-Aug, 10am-4pm late Apr–May, Sep & Oct), which explains the geological context through audiovisual displays and exhibits before you take a guided tour down to the cliffs. Hidden in the rocks here lies an entire ecosystem, including fossilized lycopsid trees, root systems known as stigmaria and ancient shrimp-like creatures called pygocephalus. Tours range in duration and difficulty from an easy half-hour trip to two- and four-hour expeditions that visit more remote sections of the cliffs.

The best time to visit is at low tide, when all of the beaches can be accessed; at other times you'll be cut off from some of the more interesting sites by high water. Note that tours leave on an irregular schedule that depends on the tides. It's a good idea to reserve ahead.

Harbour View Restaurant   CANADIAN $$
(☑ 902-254-3507; 476 Pier Rd; mains $12-24; ☺ 7am-8pm) If it's fish-and-chips, homemade chowder, delicious pies and supersize club sandwiches you want, this homey diner down by the water will definitely fit the bill. Zero pretension, checked tablecloths, bottomless coffee and a warm welcome.

Two Islands Brewing   MICROBREWERY
(☑ 902-728-2221; www.twoislandsbeer.ca; 169 Main St; ☺ 10am-8pm Sun-Wed, to 11pm Thu-Sat) This newly opened microbrewery has four core ales: a blonde, an Irish red, a porter and an American pale ale. It also runs a small cafe next door.

☆ Entertainment & Shopping

Ship's Company Theatre   THEATER
(☑ 902-254-3000; www.shipscompanytheatre. com; 18 Lower Main St; tickets from $15; ☺ Jul-Sep) Surely the most unusual theater space in Nova Scotia, this place is built around the MV *Kipawo*, the last of the Minas Basin ferries. There's a summer season of plays, plus kids' shows, comedy, readings and music gigs.

Tysons' Fine Minerals   GIFTS & SOUVENIRS
(☑ 902-728-8364; www.tysonsfineminerals.com; 114 Lamb's Hill Rd; ☺ 10am-4pm) This place is more like a museum than a shop, displaying some of the most sparkling, massive and colorful minerals you're likely to see anywhere.

❶ Getting There & Away

Parrsboro is closer to New Brunswick's largest city (Moncton, 120km away) than it is to Nova Scotia's (Halifax, 180km). There are no scheduled bus services to the area.

Advocate Harbour

Advocate Harbour is a breathtaking little cove with a 5km-long beach, piled high with driftwood, that changes dramatically with the tides. Behind the beach, salt marshes – reclaimed with dikes by the Acadians – are now replete with birds. The town's best-known sight is the dramatic Cape d'Or lighthouse, and nearby is the hikers' paradise of Cape Chignecto.

Otherwise, most visitors pass through here on the scenic route to Amherst or on the way to the famous Unesco World Heritage–listed fossil cliffs in Joggins, 32km south of Amherst.

◉ Sights & Activities

★ Cape d'Or Lighthouse   LIGHTHOUSE
(☑ 902-670-0534; www.capedor.ca; 1 Cape d'Or Rd, Diligent River) This spectacular cape of sheer cliffs was misnamed Cape d'Or (Cape of Gold) by Samuel de Champlain in 1604 – the glittering veins he saw were actually copper. Mining from 1897 to 1905 removed the sparkle. The present lighthouse was added in 1922. Access is via a partly unsealed road off Hwy 209 to Cape d'Or; you must then hike down a dirt trail. If you can't bear to leave, the former keeper's residence is now a seasonal **guesthouse and restaurant** (r $135, houses $490; ☺ May-Oct; 🛜 🍽).

★ Cape Chignecto Provincial Park   STATE PARK
(☑ 902-392-2085; http://parks.novascotia.ca/ content/cape-chignecto; Red Rocks Entrance, W Advocate Rd; campsites $26.70-35.60; ☺ mid-May–mid-Oct) This isolated wilderness on the Bay of Fundy offers some of the best coastal hiking in Nova Scotia. The 55km **coastal loop** usually takes three days to complete, encompassing dramatic coastline, isolated bays and lofty sea cliffs, but there are plenty of options for easier hikes. The tides are dangerous, so stick to the trail. All hikers must register at the visitor center, where you can discuss itineraries and make backcountry-campground reservations.

NovaShores Sea Kayaking   KAYAKING
(☑ 866-638-4118; www.novashores.com; 3838 Hwy 209, Advocate Harbour; day tours $129) See the Bay of Fundy from a different perspective – on a sea-kayaking trip with this excellent outfit. There are regular day trips to see the Three Sisters sea stacks and the lovely beach at Horseshoe Cove, plus two- and three-day camping tours. You're pretty much guaranteed to see seals and seabirds; if you're really fortunate you'll see bears and whales.

🛏 Sleeping & Eating

★ Wild Caraway Restaurant & Cafe   CANADIAN $$
(☑ 902-392-2889; www.wildcaraway.com; 3721 Hwy 209; mains lunch $8-16, dinner $22-38; ☺ 11am-3:30pm & 5-7:30pm Thu-Mon mid-May-Oct; 🛜) Local products and seasonal cooking underpin the menu at this superb coastal cafe, in a little house with a view of the driftwood-strewn beach of Advocate Harbour. The food is as good as you'll find in this part of Nova Scotia: crumbed fishcakes, mackerel

bento bowls, pan-seared scallops, and cheeses from That Dutchman's Cheese Farm.

There are also two upstairs **rooms** ($100), with wi-fi, breakfast and shared bathrooms.

❶ Getting There & Away

Advocate Harbour is 46km west of Parrsboro on Hwy 209 and 90km south of Amherst.

SUNRISE TRAIL

It's claimed that the Northumberland Strait between Nova Scotia's north shore and Prince Edward Island has some of the warmest waters north of the US Carolinas, with sea temperatures averaging slightly over 20°C in summer. The Sunrise Trail is a prime area for beach-hopping, cycling and exploring friendly countryside towns.

The Sunrise Trail runs 227km from Amherst in the west to Antigonish in the east. You'll need your own wheels to get around.

Tatamagouche

📷 902 / POP 2037

The Malagash Peninsula, which juts into protected Tatamagouche Bay, is a low-key, bucolic loop for a drive or bike ride. Taste local wines, go beachcombing or visit some interesting museums found just inland. Tatamagouche is the largest town on the Northumberland Shore coast west of Pictou and makes a great base for exploring the region.

◉ Sights

Jost Winery WINERY
(📷 902-257-2636; www.jostwine.ca; 48 Vintage Lane, Malagash; tours $5; ☉ wine store 10am-5pm Mar-Dec, tours noon & 3pm Mon-Fri, 11am Sat Jun-Sep) Among Nova Scotia's best-known wineries, Jost offers informative guided tours including two tastings, and you can pick up vintages in the shop. It produces well-regarded whites, rosés and reds (including the rather brilliantly named Great Big Friggin' Red), as well as unusual skin-fermented wines, ice wines and maple wines.

Signs direct you about 5km off Hwy 6; it's about 17km from Tatamagouche.

Balmoral Grist Mill HISTORIC SITE
(📷 902-657-3016; http://balmoralgristmill.nova scotia.ca; 660 Matheson Brook Rd, Balmoral Mills; adult/child $3.90/2.80; ☉ 10am-5pm Jun-Oct) In a gorgeous setting on the stream that once provided it with power, the Balmoral Grist Mill still grinds wheat in summer. From Tatamagouche, turn south on Hwy 311 (at the eastern edge of town) and then east on Hwy 256. It's about a 14km drive south of Tatamagouche.

Sutherland Steam Mill HISTORIC SITE
(📷 902-657-3365; http://sutherlandsteammill. novascotia.ca; 3169 Denmark Station Rd, Denmark; adult/child $3.90/2.80; ☉ 10am-5pm Wed-Sat Jun-Oct) During the 19th century wood was the wonder material that underpinned nearly every aspect of construction. Built in 1894, this steam-powered sawmill produced an incredible range of products, including furniture, windows, shingles, decorations known as 'Gingerbread Trim', and even bathtubs. It's 15km east of Tatamagouche.

To get here from Tatamagouche, follow Hwy 6 for about 10km until the junction with Hwy 326, then drive south for 5km.

Wallace Bay National Wildlife Area BIRD SANCTUARY
(📷 800-668-6767; www.ec.gc.ca) About 30km northwest of Tatamagouche, this vast sanctuary protects 585 hectares, including tidal and freshwater wetlands. A 4km loop trail winds through the reserve; it's great for bird-watching, especially for waterfowl and, if you're lucky, bald eagles.

🛏 Sleeping

★ Train Station Inn INN $$
(📷 902-657-3222; www.tatatrainstation.com; 21 Station Rd; carriages $129.50-189.50; ☉ May-Nov; 🛜🐾) Top prize for Nova Scotia's quirkiest accommodations has to go to this train-spotters' paradise, where several railway cabooses have been converted into cozy accommodations, decorated with period posters, toy trains and locomotive books. There's also a railway dining car for dinner.

The dreamer behind the inn, James Le-Fresne, grew up across the tracks and saved the train station from demolition when he was just 18.

🍴 Eating & Drinking

Sugar Moon Farm CANADIAN $$
(📷 902-657-3348; www.sugarmoon.ca; 221 Alex MacDonald Rd, Earltown; mains $12-30; ☉ 9am-4pm Jul & Aug, reduced hours Sep-Jun) The food – simple, delicious pancakes and locally made sausages served with maple syrup – is the highlight of this working maple farm and woodlot. To reach the farm from Tatama-

gouche, take Hwy 311 south for 25km, then follow the signs on Alex MacDonald Rd.

★ **Tatamagouche Brewing Co** MICROBREWERY
(📞902-657-4000; www.tatabrew.com; 235 Main St; ⊙10am-6pm Sun-Thu, to 9pm Fri, to 8pm Sat) Tata's beloved brewery now has a Nova Scotia–wide reputation, and for good reason: its beers are world-class. The lagers and session ales in particular are worth trying, and look out for 'weird' beers such as a chocolatey breakfast porter and a wild-yeast plum beer.

Pictou

📞902 / POP 3186

Many people stop in Pictou for a side trip or as a stopover via the ferry from Prince Edward Island, but it's also an enjoyable base for exploring Northumberland Strait. Water St, the main street, is lined with interesting shops and beautiful old stone buildings. Unfortunately, the views are blighted by a giant, smoking pulp mill on the opposite side of the estuary; the mill has long been slated for closure due to environmental concerns.

The town is sometimes known as the Birthplace of New Scotland because the first Scottish immigrants to Nova Scotia landed here in 1773.

◉ Sights

Hector SHIP
(📞902-485-4371; www.shiphector.ca; 33 Caladh Ave; adult/child $8/3; ⊙10am-4pm Jun-Oct) A replica of the ship *Hector,* which carried the first 200 Highland Scots to Nova Scotia, is tied up for viewing on Pictou's waterfront. You can descend into the bunk-crammed hull to get a sense of how challenging the crossing would have been. The historical context is explored in the heritage center nearby.

Northumberland Fisheries Museum MUSEUM
(📞902-485-8925; www.northumberlandfisheries museum.ca; 21 Caladh Ave; adult/child $8/3; ⊙10am-6pm Mon-Sat) In the old train station, this museum explores the area's fishing heritage. Exhibits include a replica of a fishermen's bunkhouse and the spiffy *Silver Bullet,* an early-1930s lobster boat. You can also visit the nearby lobster hatchery, where baby lobsters are reared before being released into the wild, and a small lighthouse research center just along the front.

✴️ Festivals & Events

Pictou Landing First Nation Powwow CULTURAL
(📞902-752-4912; www.plfn.ca; ⊙Jun) Across Pictou Harbour (a 25-minute drive through New Glasgow), this annual powwow on the first weekend in June features sunrise ceremonies, drumming and craft demonstrations. Camping and food are available on-site; it's strictly alcohol and drug free.

Lobster Carnival FOOD & DRINK
(📞902-485-5150; www.pictoulobstercarnival.ca; ⊙Jul) Started in 1934 as the Carnival of the Fisherfolk, this four-day event now offers free entertainment, boat races and lots of chances to feast on lobster.

🛏️ Sleeping

Caribou-Munroes Island Provincial Park CAMPGROUND $
(📞902-485-6134; https://parks.novascotia.ca/ content/caribou-munroes-island; 2119 Three Brooks Rd; campsites $26.70-35.60) Less than 10km from Pictou, this park is set on a gorgeous beach. Sites 1 to 22 abut the day-use area and are less private; sites 78 to 95 are gravel and suited for RVs. The rest are wooded and private.

★ **Pictou Lodge** RESORT $$
(📞902-485-4322; www.pictoulodge.com; 172 Lodge Rd; r $199-239, cottages $215-445; 🛜🍴♿) In business since the 1920s, this complex feels rather quaint, with cedar-log cabins, paddleboats and family-friendly 60-hectare grounds (including a private beach). Cabins range in size from one to three bedrooms, or you can book lodge-style rooms; most have been attractively renovated. The restaurant (mains $25 to $30) is the best place for dinner in town.

Customs House Inn INN $$
(📞902-485-4546; www.customshouseinn.ca; 38 Depot St; d $95-125; 🛜) Probably the grandest building in Pictou, this imposing brick building looms over the waterfront and offers eight spacious, rather old-fashioned rooms with hardwood floors and antique furniture. Rarely full, it can feel a little spooky if you're the only guest.

Willow House Inn B&B $$
(📞902-485-5740; www.willowhouseinn.com; 11 Willow St; r $105-140; 🅿🛜) A blue-slatted house dating from around 1840, Willow

House has pleasant rooms, all named after trees and accessed via an unusual double flight of staircases. Owners Brenda and George are really friendly, and serve an extremely good breakfast.

ⓘ Information

Eastern and Northumberland Shores Visitor Information Centre (☑ 902-485-8540; Pictou Rotary; ⊘ 9am-6:30pm Jun-Thanksgiving) is a large info center situated northwest of town to meet travelers arriving on the Prince Edward Island ferry.

Town of Pictou (www.townofpictou.ca) has links to sights and festivals.

ⓘ Getting There & Away

Pictou is familiar to most Nova Scotians as the departure point for ferries to Prince Edward Island. Bay Ferries (p331) operates the service from May to December, with around five sailings a day in spring and autumn, up to nine per day in summer.

The terminal is a few kilometers north of Pictou.

Antigonish

☑ 902 / POP 4364

The pleasant student town of Antigonish is best known for its well-regarded seat of learning, St Francis Xavier University, and for its Celtic roots: since 1861 the town has hosted its own **Highland Games** (www.antigonishhighlandgames.ca; ⊘ Jul), and the event continues to attract thousands of visitors.

A 4km hiking and cycling trail to the nature reserve at **Antigonish Landing** begins just across the train tracks from the Antigonish Heritage Museum, then 400m down Adam St. The landing's estuary is a good bird-watching area where you might see eagles, ducks and ospreys.

Another popular destination for beach walks and swimming is Crystal Cliffs Beach, about 15km northeast of Antigonish.

🛏 Sleeping & Eating

Antigonish Victorian Inn   B&B $$
(☑ 902-863-1103; www.antigonishvictorianinn.ca; 149 Main St; d $140-210; P ❄ 🕸) As its name suggests, this turreted B&B is solidly Victorian throughout, in terms of both architecture and decor. The rooms are all different in style; it's worth bumping up to a Queen

for space. There are also apartments on the ground floor. Breakfast is very generous.

Antigonish Evergreen Inn   MOTEL $$
(☑ 902-863-0830; www.antigonishevergreeninn.ca; 295 Hawthorne St; d $159-179; P @ 🕸) A really homey motel about five minutes' drive from Main St, with side-by-side rooms offering big beds, work desks, armchairs, and views over the lawned grounds. Rates include breakfast in the little dining room in the office, and there are often fresh muffins and cakes.

Gabrieau's Bistro   CANADIAN $$
(☑ 902-863-1925; www.gabrieaus.com; 350 Main St; mains lunch $8-16, dinner $18-30; ⊘ 10am-9pm Tue-Fri, 4-9pm Sat & Mon; 🕸) Fine dining inspired by classic French and Italian cuisine is chef Mark Garibeau's stock-in-trade, and his restaurant is far and away Antigonish's top table.

Brownstone Restaurant   CAFE $$
(☑ 902-735-3225; www.brownstonecafe.ca; 244 Main St; mains $8-20; ⊘ 11am-9pm Mon-Sat) This attractive little cafe on Main St has some surprises inside, including Italianate murals, brick-effect wallpaper and a bizarre copper-effect stucco ceiling. It's the town's any-time-of-day choice for something to eat, with generous breakfasts; big salads and flatbread pizzas for lunch; and stir-fries, steaks and pasta for dinner.

Antigonish Townhouse   PUB FOOD $$
(☑ 902-863-2248; www.antigonishtownhouse.com; 76 College St; mains $15-25; ⊘ 4pm-midnight Tue-Sat, 10am-11pm Sun, 4-11pm Mon) Swing by this popular town pub for a pint of something local or a plate of chicken-confit poutine or moules frites. It's a favorite hangout for students and locals, especially at Sunday brunch.

ⓘ Information

Antigonish Visitor Information Centre (☑ 902-863-4921; www.visitantigonish.ca; 145 Church St; ⊘ 8am-8pm Mon-Sat, 1-6pm Sun Jun-Sep; 🕸) Brochures, free local calls and free internet access. Located in the Antigonish Mall parking lot at the junction of Hwys 104 and 7.

ⓘ Getting There & Away

Antigonish is at the northern end of Hwy 7, 62km from Sherbrooke. New Glasgow is 57km to the west on the Trans-Canada Hwy (Hwy 104).

CAPE GEORGE

The eastern arm of the Sunrise Trail, from New Glasgow to Antigonish, has some gorgeous diversions – it's perfect for a half-day excursion when the weather's fine. Be sure to pack some snacks and remember your beach towel.

Perhaps start your day with a hands-on visit to the **Museum of Industry** (☑902-755-5425; http://museumofindustry.novascotia.ca; 147 N Foord St, Stellarton; adult/child $8.90/3.90; ☺9am-5pm Mon-Sat, 10am-5pm Sun Jul-Oct, shorter hours rest of year; ⓐ), especially if you have kids in tow, then head along the coast to pretty **Arisaig Provincial Park** (☑902-863-4513; https://parks.novascotia.ca/content/arisaig; 5704 Hwy 245), where you can take a dip or search for fossils. Continue to **Malignant Cove**; from here the 55km coastal stretch of Hwy 245 has been compared in beauty to parts of the Cabot Trail, although it's less mountainous and more accessible.

After a short drive east you'll reach **Cape George Point Lighthouse** (www.parl.ns.ca/lighthouse), the handsome jewel in the day's crown, where you can look out over the calm waters of St Georges Bay. If it's nearing lunchtime, head just around the cape to the fish-and-chip truck near the **Ballantyne's Cove Tuna Interpretive Centre** (☑902-863-8162; 57 Ballantyne's Cove Wharf Rd; ☺10am-5:30pm Jul-Sep) FREE, then enjoy a dip or a stroll at **Crystal Cliffs Beach** (Crystal Cliffs Farm Rd).

Just 15 minutes south, there's plenty to see and do in Antigonish, or keep to the outdoorsy theme and round out the day with a roar, high above the trees at **Anchors Above Zipline Adventure** (☑902-922-3265; www.anchorsabovezipline.ca; 464 McGrath Mountain Rd, French River; 1 ride $30; ☺10am-5pm), about 40km from Antigonish – watch for the signs on the Trans-Canada Hwy (Hwy 104).

Maritime Bus (www.maritimebus.com) has various services from Antigonish. Most stop at the Bloomfield Centre at St Francis Xavier University. Useful destinations include the following:

➡ Halifax ($41.75, 3½ hours, two daily)

➡ Sydney ($46, 3¼ hours, one daily)

➡ Truro ($25.50, 1½ hours, two daily)

CAPE BRETON ISLAND

Rugged, wooded and genuinely wild, the northwestern region of Nova Scotia almost feels like a province apart. Famous for its circuitous coastal road, the 297km-long Cabot Trail, which dips and dives round the edge of Cape Breton Highlands National Park, it's a dream destination for road-trippers, and figures pretty high on everyone's must-see list – so expect traffic jams aplenty in summer.

The best time to visit is in fall, when the area's roads are quieter and the forests light up with color.

Beyond the borders of the national park, Cape Breton has a rich Celtic and Acadian heritage, so you'll almost certainly hear live music wafting out from many pubs and bars, especially during the **Celtic Col**ours (www.celtic-colours.com; ☺Oct) festival. Also well worth visiting is the historic fort at Louisbourg, arguably the most evocative fort in all of Nova Scotia.

❶ Getting There & Away

Cape Breton Island is linked to mainland Nova Scotia by the Canso Causeway. The Trans-Canada Hwy (Hwy 105) runs straight into the middle of the island to Sydney, which has air and ferry links to other Canadian centers.

The Cabot Trail forms a massive loop around the island's northwestern corner.

Maritime Bus (p334) operates limited services from Halifax into the region, but by far the best way to explore the dramatic scenery at your own pace is by renting a car. From Halifax, Hwy 102 meets the Trans-Canada Hwy heading north through the middle of Nova Scotia to the Canso Causeway. For a more scenic route, consider taking some smaller roads up the Eastern Shore (p388).

Ceilidh Trail

The snaking road along the western coast of Cape Breton Island from Port Hastings (Hwy 19) has been dubbed the Ceilidh Trail thanks to its history of Scottish settlement and a regular program of ceilidhs (parties with music and dancing), Celtic gigs and square dances in summer – not to mention a renowned whisky distillery.

The small town of **Mabou** makes the most logical base. From here, the trail continues to the former coal-mining town of **Inverness**, with its sandy beach and 1km-long boardwalk, and then twists north to **Margaree Forks**, where you can pick up the Cabot Trail.

◉ Sights & Activities

★ **Glenora Inn & Distillery** DISTILLERY
(☑ 902-258-2662; www.glenoradistillery.com; 13727 Hwy 19, Glenville; guided tours incl tasting $7; ☉ tours hourly 9am-5pm Jun-Oct) The first distillery in North America (and the only one in Canada) to make single-malt whisky, this renowned producer claims to take its secrets straight from the old country. Guided tours explore the process and include an all-important tasting.

The distillery also has its own **pub** (mains $12 to $17) and a fine-dining warehouse **restaurant** (mains $32 to $47). From June to October you can catch a ceilidh at lunch or dinner. There are also attractive **rooms** ($189 to $319), either in the original inn or in a separate lodge, as well as a selection of self-contained timber **chalets** (from $359).

Celtic Music
Interpretive Centre MUSEUM
(☑ 902-787-2708; www.celticmusiccentre.com; 5473 Hwy 19, Judique; exhibit room from $8; ☉ 10am-5pm Mon-Fri Jun-Aug) This well-run center is one of the region's best places to experience Celtic music. The main exhibit room explores the origins and styles of the local musical culture, and there are often fiddling sessions and step-dancing workshops during summer, as well as 1½-hour walking tours with one of the center's instrument-playing guides. The restaurant hosts regular lunchtime ceilidhs (parties with music and dancing).

Cape Mabou Highlands HIKING
(www.capemabouhiking.com) Within the Cape Mabou Highlands an extensive network of hiking trails extends between Mabou and Inverness toward the coast west of Hwy 19. The trails are sometimes closed when the fire danger is high; otherwise, hikes ranging from 4km to 12km start from three trailheads.

The most-used trailhead is at Mabou Mines, about 12km from Mabou; the other two are at Cape Mabou and Sight Point Rd, near Inverness.

Maps are posted at the trailheads.

🛏 Sleeping & Eating

★ **MacLeods Inn** INN $$
(☑ 902-253-3360; www.macleodinn.com; 30 Broad Cove Marsh Rd, Inverness; r $180-199; ☉ Jun-Oct; 🅿🌫🛜) There are Macs galore at this plush B&B near Inverness: four rooms are named after a Scottish clan, from oceanview MacLeod and MacKinnon to elegant MacDonald and MacLellan (the last, Gillis, is the smallest and cheapest). Stylish taupe-and-blue color schemes, smart furnishings, a peaceful garden and a fine veranda make this B&B hard to beat – especially with its copious breakfasts.

The owners also offer **coastal cottages** (☑ 902-258-2653; www.macleods.com; $140 to $220) and a beachside **campsite** (☑ 902-258-2433; unserviced sites $40, serviced sites $45 to $59).

Duncreigan Country Inn INN $$
(☑ 902-945-2207; www.duncreigan.ca; 11411 Hwy 19, Mabou; r $165-210; 🛜) A pleasant inn set among oak trees, the Duncreigan feels rather dated, but its rooms offer plenty of space, and some have terraces and water views. There's a licensed **dining room** (mains $12 to $25) that serves breakfast to guests or dinner by reservation.

★ **Red Shoe Pub** PUB FOOD $$
(☑ 902-945-2996; www.redshoepub.com; 11533 Hwy 19, Mabou; mains $13-25; ☉ noon-11pm Sun-Wed, to 2am Thu-Sat) The Red Shoe is *the* place to catch a bit of Celtic music as you mosey down the Ceilidh Trail. The homey, ramshackle pub hosts at least one gig seven nights a week, from country crooners to folky fiddlers, and you can tuck into a menu of hot wings, fish-and-chips and homemade gingerbread as you listen.

The pub is run by the renowned Rankin Sisters, who hail from Mabou and whose Celtic-tinged music has scooped them numerous national awards; they often join in with the show.

Getting There & Away

The Ceilidh Trail begins near the Port Hastings visitor center and runs north through the towns of Mabou and Inverness for 107km until it links up with the Cabot Trail in Margaree Forks.

Cabot Trail

This is the big one: the incomparable Cabot Trail is a looping, diving, dipping roller coaster of a road that snakes for 297km around the northern tip of Cape Breton, with epic views of rolling seas, mountain passes and thick forests, and – if you're lucky – perhaps the sight of a moose, an eagle or even a whale along the way.

From Englishtown to St Ann's Bay, artists' workshops dot the southeastern flank of the trail like Easter eggs: there are pottery, leather, glass and pewter workers, plus painters and sculptors, and you can also discover living remnants of Mi'kmaw and Acadian culture.

This is not a road to rush. Many people race through in a day, but the real pleasure of the trail is taking your time, stopping at the roadside lookouts, hiking the hidden trails and really getting the most out of the scenery.

Cape Breton Highlands National Park

The better known of Nova Scotia's two national parks, **Cape Breton Highlands** (☑902-224-2306; www.pc.gc.ca/en/pn-np/ns/ cbreton; adult/child day pass $7.80/free, summer season pass adult/family $39.20/78.50) offers visitors some of Maritime Canada's most dramatic scenery.

Most people visit it as they follow the Cabot Trail, a third of which runs along the park edge. Established in 1936 and encompassing 20% of Cape Breton's landmass, it's the fancy feather in Nova Scotia's island cap, with mountain scenery that early visitors thought was powerfully reminiscent of the Scottish highlands: deep glens, high heaths, dark forests and snowy mountains aplenty.

Entry is free if you already hold a **Parks Canada Discovery Pass** (adult/family $67.70/136.40). If you're visiting outside the July–October summer season, you can purchase an 'early bird' park pass for $19.60/49 per adult/family.

There are two entrances, one at Chéticamp and one at Ingonish Beach; park permits can be purchased at either one. A one-day pass remains valid until noon the next day.

It's a drive of about 104km between the two entrances, but due to the winding, twist-ing road and seasonal traffic, you should allow a minimum of 2½ hours to cover the distance, plus extra for stops.

Activities

Hiking

Aside from the stunning scenery, the other reason many people come to Cape Breton Highlands is for the hiking. Plenty of trails crisscross the park, the most famous of which is the **Skyline Trail**, an 8.2km loop that runs along a ridge to an impressive cliff with amazing views of the Cape Breton coast. The trailhead is near the top of French Mountain, about 22km north of Chéticamp and 20km south of Pleasant Bay; it's very well known, so don't expect to be alone in summer.

Two other notable routes are the **Coastal Trail**, an 11km round-trip along the eastern coast of the park, just south of Neil's Harbour. On the west coast, **Fishing Cove Trail** descends 330m over 8km to the mouth of rugged Fishing Cove River; a steeper, shorter hike of 2.8km runs from a second trailhead about 5km north of the first. Round-trip distances are double; the park's only back-country campsite is located at the bottom if you feel like overnighting.

A good alternative to the popular Skyline Trail is **Broad Cove Mountain**, a 1.6km hike with 168m of ascent to the top of the eponymous mountain: the view of the coast, Middle Head and Cape Smokey is superb, and you may see eagles soaring over the summit.

The Cabot Trail website (www.cabot trail.com) has loads more suggestions for hikes. Parks Canada runs a program of guided hikes and interpretive events during summer; contact the park offices for more details.

Wheelchair-accessible trails are indicated on the free park map available at either entrance.

Cycling

Don't make this your inaugural trip: the riding is tough, there are no shoulders in many sections and you must be comfortable sharing the incredible scenery with RVs. Alternatively, you can mountain bike on four inland trails in the park; only **Branch Pond Lookoff Trail** offers ocean views.

ⓘ DRIVING THE CABOT TRAIL

The best way to enjoy the trail, with the freedom of starting and stopping as you choose, is by self-driving. Most folks rent a car in Sydney or Halifax and drive across, although it's worth noting that car-rental agencies charge high one-way fees for returning the vehicle in a different town, so it's a good idea to plot your route in a loop.

The next decision is which way round you're going to follow the trail. The majority of drivers drive from west to east, starting in Chéticamp and ending in Ingonish, but there's a good case for doing it in the opposite direction: there's less traffic and you get to drive coast-side the whole way, making for better views and easier stops. It also means that, if you do the trail in a day, you'll hit the west coast for sunset: cue photo ops aplenty. Note that there are very few gas stations along the way: make sure you fill up in Chéticamp or Ingonish before you set out.

Accommodations along the way are limited. If you intend to drive the trail in one or two days, base yourself at Baddeck or Ingonish on its eastern flank, or Chéticamp or Pleasant Bay in the west. In the peak times of July and August, book well ahead.

The official Cabot Trail website (www.cabottrail.travel) has loads of information on accommodations, activities and stops along the way, as well as useful planning tools.

🛏 Sleeping

Cape Breton Highlands National Park Campgrounds
CAMPGROUND (☑1-877-737-3783; https://reservation.pc.gc.ca; unserviced tent sites $17.60-27.40, serviced RV sites $29.40-38.30, oTENTiks $100; ⊙mid-May–late Oct) The park operates six campgrounds; from west to east, they are: Chéticamp, Corney Brook, MacIntosh Brook, Big Intervale, Broad Cove and Ingonish Beach. You can reserve online or at park visitor centers (essential in summer).

The largest campgrounds are at Chéticamp and Broad Cove, with 122 and 202 sites, respectively; smaller campgrounds away from the main entrances are usually quieter.

Chéticamp, Ingonish and Broad Cove all have ready-pitched cabin-tents called oTENTiks, which are very handy if you don't have gear. Discounts are available for stays of seven nights or more.

There's also one backcountry campground at Fishing Cove; with just eight sites, booking is mandatory here.

ⓘ Information

Chéticamp Information Centre (☑902-224-2306; 16646 Cabot Trail; ⊙8:30am-7pm Jun-Sep, 9am-5pm Oct-May) Has displays and a relief map of the park, plus a bookstore, Le Nique. Plans are afoot to redevelop the center.

Ingonish Beach Information Centre (☑902-285-2535; 37677 Cabot Trail; ⊙8am-8pm May-Oct) At the park's eastern edge, with displays,

maps and friendly bilingual staff. A short trail nearby leads to a lookout over Freshwater Lake.

Chéticamp

☑902 / POP 3039

Chéticamp is not only the western gateway to Cape Breton Highlands National Park; more importantly, it's Nova Scotia's most vibrant and thriving Acadian community, owing much of its cultural preservation to its geographical isolation – the road didn't make it this far until 1949.

Strung out along the coastal road, it's a busy little summer town with a working fishing fleet, a couple of interesting museums and a few craft shops (Chéticamp is famed for its hooked rugs), but if you're visiting outside the warmer months it's extremely quiet.

◉ Sights

Les Trois Pignons MUSEUM (☑902-224-2642; www.lestroispignons.com; 15584 Cabot Trail; adult/child $5/4; ⊙8:30am-6pm Jul & Aug, to 5pm mid-May–Jun & Sep–mid-Oct) This excellent museum explains how rug hooking went from home-based activity to international business. Artifacts illustrate early life and artisanship in Chéticamp. Almost everything – from bottles to rugs – was collected by one eccentric local resident, Marguerite Gallant.

Among the amazing array of hooked rugs, look out for portraits of Jacqueline Kennedy Onassis, the Queen, and Christ attended by angels.

Le Centre de la Mi-Carême
MUSEUM
(☎902-224-1016; www.micareme.ca; 51 Old Cabot Trail Rd, Grand Étang; adult/child $5/free; ◷10am-5pm Jun-Aug, to 4pm Mon-Fri Sep & Oct) Mi-Carême, celebrated in the middle of Lent, is Chéticamp's answer to Mardi Gras. Locals wear masks and disguises, and visit houses in a bid to get people to guess who they are. This museum covers the history of the celebration and displays traditional masks.

SLEEPING

Albert's Motel
MOTEL $
(☎902-224-2077; www.albertsmotelcheticamp. com; 15086 Cabot Trail; d $75-120; ◷May-Oct; ℗♿📶) Colorful patchwork quilts really liven up the decor at this simple but homey motel, where the rooms also have mini-fridges, microwaves and large flat-screen TVs, plus there's a communal deck overlooking the harbor.

★Maison Fiset House
B&B $$
(☎902-224-1794; www.maisonfisethouse.com; 15050 Cabot Trail; d $159-179, ste $169-229; ℗♿📶) A little luxury in Chéticamp is found in this grand old 1895 home, once owned by the town's first doctor. All the rooms are nicely appointed in a heritage style; if you're in a suite, lounge in your hot tub and enjoy the ocean views.

Unusually for Chéticamp, it's open all year-round.

Chéticamp Outback Inn
MOTEL $$
(☎902-224-8025; cheticampoutbackinn@bella liant.com; 909 Chéticamp Back Rd; r $155-225; ℗♿📶) Inland from Chéticamp, this backroad country motel looks standard, but the rooms are a bit of a surprise: they have wood-effect walls, enormous TVs, comfy beds with scatter cushions, and a work desk with coffee machine. Each room has a small deck area for mountain contemplation. There's no breakfast, but sometimes the owner supplies pastries from La Boulangerie Aucoin.

Cornerstone Motel
MOTEL $$
(☎902-224-3232; www.cornerstonemotel. com; 16537 Cabot Trail; d $99-169; ◷May-Oct; ℗♿📶) Last stop before the national-park gates, this endearingly retro motel is located about 7km from town. It offers pretty much what you'd expect in terms of accommodations; the rural location, communal fire pit and gray-clapboard exterior are nice touches.

✕ Eating & Drinking

La Boulangerie Aucoin
BAKERY $
(☎902-224-3220; www.aucoinbakery.com; 14 Lapointe Rd; items $3.50-9; ◷7am-5pm Mon-Sat; 📶) If you've never tried an Acadian meat pie, this fine little bakery, founded in 1959, will happily oblige. It also has fresh homestyle breads (including baguettes), cinnamon rolls, molasses cookies, scones and sandwiches for the trail.

Harbour Restaurant
SEAFOOD $$
(☎902-224-1144; www.baywindsuites.com; 15299 Cabot Trail; mains $13-39; ◷11am-9pm) A reliable stalwart in central Chéticamp, with windows looking onto the strait and a slightly alarming slope in the floors at low tide. Seafood's the specialty: chow down on a snow-crab or lobster dinner, or go for the 'best of both' if you can't decide.

Le Gabriel
DINER $$
(☎902-224-3685; www.legabriel.com; 15424 Cabot Trail; mains $15-24; ◷11am-10pm) This big pub-diner is buzzing on the weekend: locals come for the generous plates of fish, steak and seafood (all served with potato or rice, vegetables and a baguette), and to play free billiards. It's not fancy, but it'll definitely fill your belly.

Go for the gargantuan Captain's Platter if you're absurdly hungry.

ℹ Information

Tourist Information Centre (☎902-224-2642; www.lestroispignons.com/visitor-information; 15584 Cabot Trail; ◷8:30am-6pm Jul & Aug, to 5pm mid-May–Jun & Sep–mid-Oct) In the same building as Les Trois Pignons museum.

ℹ Getting There & Away

Chéticamp is 104km from Ingonish, 56km northeast of Inverness on Hwy 219, and 88km from Baddeck via the Cabot Trail. There's no public transport.

Pleasant Bay

Situated 43km north of Chéticamp, aptly named Pleasant Bay is cradled in a sheltered cove framed by brooding, forested mountains. It makes a useful break as you drive the Cabot Trail, especially at sunset, and it's also a good place for whale-watching.

Somewhat unexpectedly, there's a **Tibetan monastery** (☎902-224-2752; www.gampo abbey.org; 1533 Pleasant Bay Rd; ◷tours 1:30-3:30pm Mon-Fri Jun-Sep) 8km north of town.

⊙ Sights & Activities

Whale Interpretive Centre   MUSEUM
(☑902-224-1411; 104 Harbour Rd; adult/child $5/4; ⊙9am-5pm Jun-Oct) Get some background on cetaceans at this modest visitor center, which has illustrations of 16 whale species, and a life-size model of a pilot whale suspended from the ceiling.

**Captain Mark's Whale
& Seal Cruise**   WHALE WATCHING
(☑902-224-1316; www.whaleandsealcruise.com; adult/child $60/40; ⊙May-Sep) The best of the whale-watching operators in Pleasant Bay, Captain Mark and his team pilot fast Zodiacs into the bay in search of cetacean visitors; as always, sightings aren't guaranteed, so it's worth asking about recent activity before you book.

Tours leave from the wharf next to the Whale Interpretive Centre.

🛏 Sleeping & Eating

Pleasant Bay has a few motels strung along the main street, but Chéticamp and Ingonish have better options.

HI-Cabot Trail Hostel   HOSTEL $
(☑902-224-1976; www.cabottrailhostel.com; 23349 Cabot Trail; dm/r $25/65; @🛜) This basic but friendly hostel has a 10-bed bunkhouse, three bathrooms and three private rooms, as well as a couple of kitchens for guests' use (you can help yourself to herbs in the garden). There's also a fire pit for summer barbecues.

Rusty Anchor   DINER $$
(☑902-224-1313; 23197 Cabot Trail; mains $10-28; ⊙11am-9pm) Pit stops are few and far between on the Cabot Trail, which makes this waterfront diner a boon if you've run out of picnic snacks. The food's mostly good; pan-fried fish, scallops and lobster rolls are all on offer. You can't miss it – look out for the fiberglass fisherman in the yellow sou'wester brandishing a lobster.

❶ Getting There & Away

Pleasant Bay is 43km north of Chéticamp and 61km west of Ingonish.

Ingonish

☑902 / POP 1250

At the eastern entrance to Cape Breton Highlands National Park are **Ingonish** and **Ingonish Beach**, small settlements sheltering in a large bay under the headland of **Cape Smokey**, where there's a community-run ski area in winter. The region is a sensible base for beginning or ending a jaunt along the Cabot Trail, but there's not a huge amount to see or do, so one night is likely to be as much as you'll want to spend here.

As you drive north over Cape Smokey you'll first come to Ingonish Beach, set above a large inland lagoon. Ingonish itself is 10km further north; you'll pass into the national park as you drive there.

🛏 Sleeping

Driftwood Lodge   INN $
(☑902-285-2558; www.driftwoodlodge.ca; 36139 Cabot Trail, Ingonish; d/ste from $55/100; ⊙May-Nov; P🐾🐕) It's hard to find wallet-friendly accommodations along the Cabot Trail, but this rustic beside-the-beach inn definitely fits the bill; it's been going since 1973, and is still run by the same family. The main building has pine-paneled rooms and apartments, and there's an old housekeeper's cottage in the grounds: a little dated, maybe, but quite comfortable.

Seascape Coastal Retreat   CABIN $$
(☑902-285-3003; www.seascapecoastalretreat.com; 36086 Cabot Trail, Ingonish; cottages $139-279; P❄🛜) Seascape's pleasant cottages are set in pretty landscaped gardens only a five-minute drive from central Ingonish. Each cottage has a separate sitting room and bedroom, a private bathroom with whirlpool tub, a deck with barbecue and a cracking ocean view. Free kayaks and mountain bikes are available for guests' use.

Maven Gypsy B&B & Cottages   B&B $$
(☑902-929-2246; www.themavengypsy.com; 41682 Cabot Trail, Wreck Cove; r $120-141, cottages $148-158; ⊙Jun-Nov; 🛜🐕) On the other side of Cape Smokey from Ingonish Beach (a drive of about 20km), this 19th-century lemon-yellow farmhouse is a peaceful refuge, with generously sized rooms in the main house and pretty cottages overlooking the surrounding woodland. It's only three minutes' walk to a pebbly cove.

Lantern Hill & Hollow   COTTAGE $$$
(☑902-285-2010; www.lanternhillandhollow.ca; 36845 Cabot Trail, Ingonish; r $250-260, cottages $225-335; ⊙May–mid-Oct; P🛜) For a proper spoil, head to this fancy cottage complex

that sits in a dreamy beachfront location and offers extremely stylish rooms, decorated in soothing grays and blues, with modern furniture and top-notch fixtures. There's a choice of one- or two-bed cottages, plus enormous suites in the main house. If you fancy a twilight cookout on the beach, they'll supply you with firewood.

✗ Eating

Dancing Moose Cafe CAFE $
(☑902-929-2523; www.thedancingmoosecafe.com; 42691 Cabot Trail, Birch Plain; pancakes $5-10; ⊘7:30am-4pm Jun-Oct) Stop in here for Dutch *pannenkoeken* (pancakes), either savory (loaded with green onions and Gouda cheese) or sweet (whipped cream, honey, fruit, nuts – the works). There are some fun souvenirs to browse, and it also has a cottage and a few camping cabins for rent.

Clucking Hen Deli & Bakery CAFE $
(☑902-929-2501; 45073 Cabot Trail; mains $7-18; ⊘7am-7pm May-Oct) This fun cafe and bakery makes an ideal stop at the start or end of your Cabot Trail drive. The decor centers on chickens and hen-based puns, while the menu serves a solid choice of sandwiches, soups and salads, along with made-on-the-day cakes.

★**Main Street
Restaurant & Bakery** CANADIAN $$
(☑902-285-2225; 37764 Cabot Trail, Ingonish Beach; mains $10-24; ⊘8am-8pm) Come breakfast, brunch, lunch or dinner, Ingonish's friendly diner is the place most people head for when they're feeling hungry. Chunky BLT sandwiches, homemade waffles, big plates of chicken, pasta and seafood, and yummy cakes – what's not to like?

❶ Getting There & Away

Ingonish and Ingonish Beach are at the eastern entrance to Cape Breton Highlands National Park. From here it's 93km to Baddeck via the Cabot Trail and 134km to Sydney via the Cabot Trail and the Trans-Canada Hwy (Hwy 105).

The Far North

Heading north of Ingonish, the Cabot Trail (p379) skirts the coastline as far as the little fishing settlement of **Neil's Harbour**, where you can take a scenic detour away from the main trail and travel through small coves, including picturesque **White Point**, where fishing boats outnumber houses. From here

you can follow winding White Point Rd before rejoining the main trail near South Harbour. Shortly afterward, another turnoff leads to the village of **Dingwall**.

If you're determined to reach the top of Nova Scotia you'll need to turn off at **Cape North** and follow Bay St Lawrence Rd along a beautiful valley; you'll eventually reach the eponymous fishing village after about 18km. From here the road gets rougher and the scenery wilder as you head toward unedifyingly named **Meat Cove**; the last 7km of road is bone-jarring gravel.

◉ Sights & Activities

★**Captain Cox's
Whale Watch** WHALE WATCHING
(☑902-383-2981; www.whalewatching-novascotia.com; 578 Meat Cove Rd, St Margaret Village; adult/child $45/25; ⊘mid-Jun-Oct) One of the first three whale-watching operations in Nova Scotia, Captain Cox's tours leave from the fishing harbor at Bay St Lawrence and have a very good rate of whale sightings (around 96%). Trips run at 10:30am, 1:30pm and 4:30pm in July and August, with afternoon-only sailings in late June and late September.

★**White Point** HIKING
This little-known 2km trail follows a single-track path along the coast out to a headland with fine views of several offshore islands. The area was once a notorious ships' graveyard, and locals claim that many sailors were buried here in unmarked graves. On a sunny evening it's one of the best short walks anywhere along the Cabot Trail.

Cabots Landing Provincial Park STATE PARK
(☑902-662-3030; https://parks.novascotia.ca/content/cabots-landing) Stop in this wonderful provincial park, 10km north of the Cabot Trail en route to Bay St Lawrence, to enjoy Aspy Bay and its spectacular beach.

The area is supposedly the site of the historic 1497 landing of John Cabot, the first European to set foot in North America; a cairn marks the spot, although some historians still dispute the claim that Cabot actually landed here.

Grassy Point HIKING
You can't beat the views over the coast from Grassy Point, accessible via a small trail (about 40 minutes round-trip) that starts just past the Meat Cove Campground. Sit for

a while at the point to look for whales and nesting bald eagles.

Dixon's Zodiac Safari
WHALE WATCHING

(☑1-855-259-4122; www.dixonszodiacseafari.com; 36 Lighthouse Rd, Neil's Harbour; adult/child $49/25; ⊙May-Sep) Four daily whale-watching tours leave from little Neil's Harbour; your vessel is the 25ft *Highland Hurricane*, a fast Zodiac designed for maximum maneuverability.

Cabot Trail Adventures
CYCLING

(☑902-383-2552; www.cabottrailoutdooradventures.com; 299 Shore Rd, Dingwall; bike rental per day/week $45/225, kayak tours $65; ⊙9am-5pm Jun-Oct) Sea-kayaking tours, guided hikes and bike rental are all offered by this outdoors company near the Cape North turnoff.

🛏 Sleeping & Eating

Meat Cove Campground
CAMPGROUND $

(☑902-383-2379; www.meatcovecampground.ca; 2475 Meat Cove Rd, Capstick; tent sites/cabins from $35/80; ⊙Jun-Nov; P🐾) This is the place if you enjoy camping in the middle of nowhere. The campground sits on a grassy bluff with incredible ocean views: gorgeous on a sunny day, spooky as anything when the fog rolls in. There are basic cabins, plus ample space for camping, with a shared toilet and shower block. You'll need your own gear and bedding.

The **Chowder Hut** (mains $8 to $15) serves simple meals, and there's also a small store.

Blue Bayou Resort
TENTED CAMP $$

(☑647-995-1633; www.bluebayouresort.com; 25 Old Road Loop, South Harbour; domes $180-200, tipis $120; P) Sleep under the stars in a geodesic dome or traditional tipi at this wooded campground. Domes are set on a wooden base, feature proper beds and private bathrooms, and have a skylight to see the stars; tipis are set around a central fire pit, but you'll be in sleeping bags and will have to use the communal toilet block.

Chowder House
SEAFOOD $$

(☑902-336-2463; 90 Lighthouse Rd, Neil's Harbour; chowder $7-12, mains $14-24; ⊙noon-6:45pm Tue-Sun May-Oct) This establishment, out beyond the lighthouse at Neil's Harbour, is famous for its chowder, but it also serves great-value suppers of snow crab, lobster, mussels and more. There are plenty of dining locals, who like to chat with folks from

far away while they splatter themselves with seafood juice.

ℹ Getting There & Away

Neil's Harbour and White Point are 16km and 23km from Ingonish, respectively, via the Cabot Trail, New Haven Rd and White Point Rd.

Meat Cove is at the northernmost tip of Nova Scotia, 60km from Ingonish. The road is steep, winding, and in poor condition in parts, with the last 7km rough gravel. It's not advised to come here in a compact rental car; a 4WD or SUV is highly recommended.

Baddeck
☑902 / POP 769

The small resort town of Baddeck sits beside mighty Bras d'Or Lake, the largest lake in Nova Scotia – at 1099 sq km, it's more like an inland sea. The town makes a useful staging post before you head up to the highlands. Its main claim to fame is its link with inventor Alexander Graham Bell: he built himself a grand country estate across the water from Baddeck in the late 19th century, and the town now has an interesting museum (and National Historic Site) dedicated to the great man.

◉ Sights & Activities

★Alexander Graham Bell National Historic Site
MUSEUM

(☑902-295-2069; www.pc.gc.ca/en/lhn-nhs/ns/grahambell; 559 Chebucto St; adult/child $7.80/free; ⊙9am-5pm May-Oct) Telecommunications pioneer and inventor Alexander Graham Bell fell in love with Bras d'Or during a family holiday – apparently the hilly scenery reminded him of his Scottish homeland. In the late 1880s he built a lavish summer estate, **Beinn Bhreagh** (Gaelic for beautiful mountain), on a peninsula across the bay from Baddeck. This fascinating museum at the edge of town houses full-scale replicas of Bell's groundbreaking Silver Dart aircraft, along with electrical devices, telegraphs, telephones, kites and medical inventions.

Amoeba
CRUISE

(☑902-295-7780; www.amoebasailingtours.com; 2hr tour adult/child $30/15; ⊙Jun-Oct) Climb aboard this handsome schooner for tours around Bras d'Or Lake. Trips include fine views of Alexander Graham Bell's estate Beinn Bhreagh, the site of the first flight of the Silver Dart, and the chance to spot local wildlife, including bald eagles and seals.

Donelda's Puffin Boat Tours
BIRDWATCHING

(✆902-929-2563; www.puffinboattours.com; 1099 Hwy 312, Englishtown; adult/child $52/22) Boats head to a bird sanctuary off Cape Dauphin where puffin sightings are guaranteed. You may well see gray seals lounging on the rocks, too. There's a discount of $4/3 per adult/child if you pay in cash.

Highland Village Museum
MUSEUM

(✆902-725-2272; http://highlandvillage.nova scotia.ca; 4119 Hwy 223, Iona; adult/child $11/5; ⊙10am-5pm Jun-Oct) Perched on a hilltop overlooking the Bras d'Or Lake, this living-history museum explores the region's Gaelic heritage. Costumed Scots demonstrate the day-to-day activities of early settlers' lives, from storytelling to weaving, cooking, music and daily chores. There are Celtic-inspired workshops from spring through fall.

🛏 Sleeping

⭐Silver Dart Lodge
LODGE $$

(✆902-295-2340; www.silverdartlodge.com; 257 Shore Rd; r/chalets from $165/195; 🅿😊❄ 🛜💺) Cracking views over Bras d'Or Lake are the main selling point here. There's a wide choice of accommodations, with rooms divided between the original main house, three motel-style lodges and several cute clapboard chalets, and you can eat with a lake view in McCurdy's Dining Room (mains $15 to $26).

⭐Broadwater Inn & Cottages
INN $$

(✆902-295-1101; www.broadwaterinn.com; 975 Bay Rd; r & cottages $129-169; ⊙May-Nov; 🅿🛜💺) Situated 2km northeast of Baddeck, this 1830s home belonged to JD McCurdy, who worked with Alexander Graham Bell on early aircraft designs. The rooms in the main house are full of character; the best is the A-frame library room, but they're all spacious and most have a lake view. For even more space, ask for one of the self-contained cottages.

Telegraph House
HOTEL $$

(✆902-295-1100; www.baddeckhotel.com; 479 Chebucto St; r $110-155; 🅿🛜) This hotel-motel has Alexander Graham Bell connections: opened in 1861, it served as the town's telegraph office for many years, and the inventor himself stayed in room 1. There are 18

rooms in the main lodge – some old-fashioned and frilly, others modern – supplemented by 13 bland rooms in the motel alongside.

Dunlop Inn
B&B $$

(✆902-295-1100; www.dunlopinn.com; 552 Chebucto St; d $175-270; 🅿❄🛜) A great B&B choice in downtown Baddeck, this modern gabled house has fabulous lake frontage – most of the tasteful rooms have a water outlook. There's a self-serve breakfast in the swish modern kitchen.

🍴 Eating & Drinking

Highwheeler Cafe
CAFE $

(✆902-295-3006; www.visitbaddeck.com/high wheeler-cafe; 486 Chebucto St; sandwiches $9; ⊙7am-6pm Tue-Sun May-Oct; 🛜) Everyone's choice for lunch, this Baddeck cafe ticks all the boxes: grilled sandwiches, delicious quesadillas, homemade soups, and delicious muffins and blueberry-raspberry scones, plus a pleasant deck. You can phone ahead and ask for a packed lunch if you're hiking or hitting the Cabot Trail.

Herring Choker Deli
DELI $

(✆902-295-2275; www.herringchokerdeli.com; 1958 Hwy 105; items $6-17; ⊙9am-5pm Tue-Sun May-Oct; 🛜) Swing by this roadside diner-deli, 12km southwest of Baddeck, for a pit stop. It serves up soups, sandwiches, wraps and salads, plus breads, pastries and cakes cooked on-site.

⭐Baddeck
Lobster Suppers
SEAFOOD $$$

(✆902-925-3307; www.baddecklobstersuppers. ca; 17 Ross St; mains $24-36; ⊙4-9pm Jun-Oct) In Baddeck's former legion hall, this local institution offers your choice of lobster, salmon, snow crab or strip loin with all-you-can-eat mussels, chowder and dessert for an all-in $50. It's no-frills dining: you're encouraged to just get stuck in.

Big Spruce Brewing
MICROBREWERY

(✆902-295-2537; www.bigspruce.ca; 64 Yankee Line Rd, Nyanza; ⊙noon-7pm) Pop into this farmyard brewery, about 14km southwest of Baddeck, to grab a growler of unfiltered, unpasteurized, 'unbelievably good', locally brewed beer.

Baddeck Gathering Ceilidhs
LIVE MUSIC

(✆902-295-0971; www.baddeckgathering.com; St Michael's Parish Hall, 8 Old Margaree Rd; adult/child from $10/5; ⊙7:30pm Jul & Aug) Proper community ceilidhs (parties with music and dancing) with plenty of fiddling, twirling and Celtic atmosphere are held in Baddeck's parish hall, opposite the tourist-information center.

Tickets are only available on the night, and it's cash only.

ⓘ Information

Baddeck Tourist Information Centre (☑902-295-1911; www.visitbaddeck.com; 454 Chebucto St; ⊙10am-5pm Jun-Oct) A small visitor center offering useful info on the Bras d'Or area and the Cabot Trail.

ⓘ Getting There & Away

Baddeck is located on the Trans-Canada Hwy (Hwy 105), 78km southwest of Sydney.

Maritime Bus (www.maritimebus.com) services from Sydney to Halifax stop in town once or sometimes twice a day.

Sydney & North Sydney

☑902

The second-biggest settlement in Nova Scotia and the only real city on Cape Breton Island, Sydney is the embattled core of the island's collapsed industrial belt. The steel mill and coal mines – once the region's largest employers – have all closed down, and as a result the city feels a bit empty, but there are some lovely older houses, especially in the North End residential areas where most of the B&Bs are found. Overall, the city is well serviced and you get more bang for your buck making this your base for exploring Louisbourg and the Cabot Trail than you would in more scenic areas.

Industrial North Sydney is a small and friendly town, although there's not much to see or do. The main reason you'll be passing through is if you're heading to the Cabot Trail from Sydney, or traveling to or from Newfoundland on the ferry.

◉ Sights

★**Cape Breton Miners' Museum**   MUSEUM
(☑902-849-4522; www.minersmuseum.com; 42 Birkley St, Glace Bay; museum adult/child $6.95/5.65, tour & mine visit $16/8; ⊙10am-6pm mid-May–Oct) Coal mining played a central role in the development of this part of Nova Scotia, so you shouldn't pass up the chance to venture into a disused mine in the company of a former miner. It's fascinating, a little spooky, and not for the claustrophobic. The

museum has interesting exhibits on this aspect of Cape Breton's past. It's at Glace Bay, 22km east of Sydney.

Membertou Heritage Park   CULTURAL CENTER
(☑902-567-5333; www.membertouheritagepark. com; 35 Su'n Awti, Membertou; adult/child $8/5; ⊙9am-4:30pm) This First Nations reserve has an interesting visitor center where you can learn about Mi'kmaw culture, and workshops (from $25) where you can try your hand at making a traditional tribal basket, drum or dream catcher. There's also a good restaurant, Kiju's, where you can sample Mi'kmaw dishes, and a shop selling indigenous crafts and petroglyph engravings.

Old Sydney Society Ghost Tour   TOURS
(☑902-539-1572; www.oldsydneysociety.org; 173 Charlotte St; $13; ⊙7pm Thu Jul & Aug) In the town's old Bank of Montreal building, this local-history society offers a weekly ghost tour in July and August, leaving from St Patrick's Church Museum (☑902-562-8237; 87 Esplanade; $2; ⊙9am-5pm Mon-Sat Jun-Oct).

It maintains a few heritage museums around town, including Cossit House (☑902-539-7973; http://cossithouse.novascotia. ca; 75 Charlotte St; adult/concession $2/free; ⊙9am-4pm Tue-Sat), Jost Heritage House (☑902-539-0366; 54 Charlotte St; $3; ⊙9am-5pm Mon-Sat Jun-Aug, 10am-4pm Sep-Oct) and St Patrick's.

⏟ Sleeping

★**Colby House**   B&B $$
(☑902-539-4095; www.colbyhousebb.com; 10 Park St; r $100-130; ☎) This 1904 house makes a grand spot to stay in Sydney, with three handsome rooms tricked out in turn-of-the-century style. It's been beautifully maintained, from the central staircase to the elegant veranda, and the tree-lined location is surprisingly peaceful. A real delight.

Cambridge Suites Sydney   HOTEL $$
(☑902-562-6500; www.cambridgesuitessydney. com; 380 Esplanade; d $160-200; P❋☎) This smart hotel in a hard-to-beat downtown location has comfortable, nicely renovated rooms in a variety of configurations, many with water views (although some still smell a bit from pre-nonsmoking days). Rates include a decent serve-yourself breakfast spread and free wi-fi. The **Trio Restaurant**

NOVA SCOTIA SYDNEY & NORTH SYDNEY

GOAT ISLAND

Lying 40km southwest of Sydney, in Bras d'Or Lake, Goat Island is home to one of Nova Scotia's largest Mi'kmaq communities. **Eskasoni Cultural Journeys** (☑ 902-322-2279; www.eskasoniculturaljourneys.ca; 1 Goat Island Trail; adult/child $40/20; ⊙ 9am-5pm Mon-Fri May-Oct) offer enthralling tours that provide an introduction to Mi'kmaw culture and allow you to participate in a smudging ceremony (a smoke bath used for purification). This is one of the best cultural experiences in Nova Scotia; book ahead.

You'll also have the opportunity to weave baskets, try traditional dances, learn about hunting and cooking techniques, and hear tribal stories. Along the way you'll get to sample some bush tea and luskinigan: a bannock-style bread (sometimes known as 'four-cent bread' because it's so cheap to make) cooked over an open fire. The 2.4km trail winds along the lake and offers lovely views.

(mains $22 to $35) is high quality, if a little overpriced. Parking costs $7 a night.

A Boat to Sea   B&B **$$**
(☑ 902-794-8326; www.aboattosea.com; 61 Queen St, North Sydney; r $120-140; P ⊜ ☎ ☎) Right on the water and surrounded by beautiful gardens, this grand home is accented by stained glass and has a quirky antique collection. Relax on the waterfront patio and enjoy hearty breakfasts. There are only three rooms, so book ahead in high season, when there's a two-night minimum stay. There's a dock if you're arriving by yacht.

✗ Eating

Governors Pub & Eatery   PUB FOOD **$$**
(☑ 902-562-7646; www.governorseatery.com; 233 Esplanade; mains $9-22; ⊙ 11am-11pm) Governors is easily the most popular place in Sydney. Stop by to mingle with the after-work crowd for drinks, dine on gourmet pub grub or just sink a beer on the 1st-floor deck. There are regular live-music jams.

Flavor on the Water   BISTRO **$$**
(☑ 902-567-1043; www.cbflavor.com/flavor; 60 Esplanade; mains $11-28; ⊙ 11am-9pm; ☑) Sydney's swankiest restaurant, this high-ceilinged bistro in a large waterfront complex serves upscale plates of salmon, blackened cod, strip loin and halibut. Go for the monster sharing platters ($99), loaded with East Coast goodies, if you're feeling flush. There's a second branch downtown.

Flavor Downtown   BISTRO **$$**
(☑ 902-562-6611; www.cbflavor.com; 16 Pitt St; mains lunch $8-12, dinner $15-20; ⊙ 8am-8pm Mon-Sat, 10am-3pm Sun) If you can't make it to the main Flavor on the waterfront, this downtown diner is the next best thing: an urban-style cafe serving sandwiches, soups and salads, along with more substantial mains like Thai curries and panko-crusted haddock after 4pm.

★ Black Spoon   CANADIAN **$$**
(☑ 902-241-3300; www.blackspoon.ca; 320 Commercial St; mains $12-19; ⊙ 11am-9pm Mon-Thu, to 10pm Fri & Sat) If you ask a local where to eat in North Sydney, they'll point you straight to the Spoon. It's a small space that goes big on flavours – hazelnut-crusted salmon, scallop carbonara, bacon-bourbon ribs – washed down with a good selection of Nova Scotian wines. Sometimes there'll be a band playing while you dine.

Kiju's   NATIVE AMERICAN **$$$**
(☑ 902-562-6220; www.kijus.com; 50 Maillard St, Membertou; mains $22-46, 3-course menu $40; ⊙ 11am-9pm Sun-Thu, to 10pm Fri & Sat) Based at Membertou Heritage Park, this restaurant provides the rare opportunity to try Mi'kmaw-inspired dishes, such as four-cent bread, cedar-plank salmon, barbecued duck and a foraged-fruit-and-berry salad.

🍷 Drinking & Entertainment

★ Breton Brewing   MICROBREWERY
(☑ 902-270-4677; www.bretonbrewing.ca; 364 Keltic Dr; ⊙ 10am-8pm Mon-Wed, to 11pm Thu-Sat, noon-5pm Sun) The top place around Sydney for a beer is the taproom of this up-and-coming brewery, jointly run by Welsh and BC beer masters. You can watch the brewing process while you drink, and maybe have a food-truck snack on weekend nights. Look out for seasonal beers, such as the rhubarb kettle sour and the maple lager.

LOUISBOURG

The fortunes of the province that became Nova Scotia are inextricably bound up with the mighty **Fortress of Louisbourg** (☑902-733-3552; www.fortressoflouisbourg.ca; 58 Wolfe St; adult/child $17.60/free; ⊘9:30am-5pm mid-May–mid-Oct, to 4pm Mon-Fri mid-Oct–mid-May), built by the French but battled over countless times before finally being burned to the ground in 1760. The current site recreates the fortress as it was in 1744, right down to the people – costumed soldiers, cooks, orderlies, musicians, gardeners and artisans create a real sense of time travel, and bring the place to life with stories and free guided tours.

Built to protect French interests in the region, Louisbourg was the area's administrative capital. It developed from around 1713 to 1745, when the British captured it after a gruelling 46-day siege. The fortress then changed hands twice more until 1760: that year, when British troops under the command of General James Wolfe took Québec City, the walls of Louisbourg were destroyed and the city was put to the torch.

In 1961 the federal government funded the largest historical reconstruction in Canadian history. Fifty buildings are now open to visitors, although three-quarters of Louisbourg remains in ruins. The 2.5km **Ruins Walk** guides you through the untouched terrain and out to the Atlantic coast.

Louisbourg is 35km from Sydney on Hwy 22.

Highland Arts Theatre ARTS CENTER
(☑902-565-3637; www.highlandartstheatre.com; 40 Bentinck St) Housed in the old St Andrew's Church, the HAT has become the town's top venue for live performance, music and dance. There are often Celtic music nights in summer.

❶ Getting There & Away

AIR

Air Canada and Westjet offer direct services to Halifax, Toronto and Montréal from Sydney's compact JA Douglas McCurdy Airport (p331), 13km from downtown.

BUS

Maritime Bus (p334) travels from Sydney to Halifax ($72.50, seven hours) and Truro ($63.50, five hours), from where you can connect to services bound for New Brunswick and Prince Edward Island.

It's faster and slightly cheaper to book the **Cape Shuttle Service** (☑855-673-8083; www.capeshuttleservice.com), which runs a private shuttle direct to Halifax (one way $70). The pickup in Sydney starts around 7am; you should be in Halifax sometime between noon and 1pm, when the shuttle runs in the opposite direction. It also runs shuttles to Truro and Baddeck ($65 one way), New Glasgow ($60), Antigonish ($55) and a few other local destinations.

CAR & MOTORCYCLE

Sydney is 403km by road from Halifax via Hwy 104, a journey of four to 4½ hours depending on traffic.

EASTERN SHORE

If you want to escape into the fog, away from summer crowds, this pristine region is the place to explore. Running from the outskirts of Dartmouth, across the harbor from Halifax, to Cape Canso at the extreme eastern tip of the mainland, the Eastern Shore has no large towns and the main road is almost as convoluted as the rugged shoreline it follows. For those seeking wildlife and barely touched wilderness, and opportunities to enjoy hiking, kayaking or fishing, this is your heaven.

Historically, villages in the region were linked only by boat, then by rail, which was later taken away. Spirited and resilient, these close-knit communities have upheld and maintained their family histories and traditions for decade upon decade.

◉ Sights

★ **Memory Lane Heritage Village** MUSEUM
(☑877-287-0697; https://heritagevillage.ca; 5435 Clam Harbour Rd, Lake Charlotte; adult/child $8/3; ⊘9:30am-4pm Jun-Sep) A 20-minute drive from Tangier, this place is an outstanding example of how a community can work together to preserve its history. It recreates a 1940s Eastern Shore village in a series of lovingly relocated and restored buildings, chock-full of hands-on antiques, as if frozen in time. You'll find vintage cars, a farmstead with animals (great for kids), a schoolhouse, a church, a miner's hut, a blacksmithery,

shipbuilding shops and so much more. A must for history buffs of any kind.

From 11:30am to 3pm, 1940s-style chow is served in the cookhouse.

★**Sherbrooke Village**   MUSEUM
(☑902-522-2400; http://sherbrookevillage.nova scotia.ca; 42 Main St, Sherbrooke; adult/child $15.95/4.95; ⊙9:30am-5:30pm Jun-Oct) This living-history village offers a chance to really step back in time: you can chat with people in period costume as you wander the streets of a typical Nova Scotian village as it might have looked before WWI. Among the 80 buildings, 25 of which you can step inside, are a blacksmith's shop, a printery, a woodworkers' workshop, a weaving house and a traditional tearoom.

Fisherman's Life Museum   MUSEUM
(☑902-889-2053; http://fishermanslife.nova scotia.ca; 58 Navy Pool Loop, Jeddore Oyster Pond; adult/child $4/3; ⊙9am-4pm Wed-Sun Jun, Tue-Sun Jul-Sep) The tiny Fisherman's Life Museum, 35km west of Tangier, paints a convincing picture of the tough lives of the people – particularly the women – who lived along the Eastern Shore at the turn of the 20th century. The museum is dotted with family memorabilia, and costumed guides offer tea, tales and hospitality.

Musquodoboit Harbour
Railway Museum   MUSEUM
(☑902-889-2689; www.mhrailwaymuseum.com; 7895 Hwy 7, Musquodoboit Harbour; by donation; ⊙9am-5pm Jun-Sep) This wonderful little railway museum, loved by train buffs and kids alike, looks a little incongruous in its surroundings: it's hard to believe there was once a passenger service through here. Housed in the 1918 station, the museum has train memorabilia inside and rolling stock outside. There are also some picnic tables on the grounds.

🏃 Activities

There are beautiful, long, white-sand beaches all along the Eastern Shore and, although the water never gets very warm, brave souls venture in for a swim or a surf, particularly if the fog stays offshore.

The busiest of the Eastern Shore beaches, 1km-long **Rainbow Haven** has washrooms, showers, a canteen and a boardwalk with wheelchair access to the beach.

The most popular destination for surfers, cobblestone **Lawrencetown Beach** faces directly south and often gets big waves, compliments of hurricanes or tropical storms hundreds of kilometers away. It boasts a supervised swimming area, washrooms and a canteen.

The longest swimming beach in Nova Scotia and the prettiest in the area, with more than 3km of grass-backed white sand, is **Martinique Beach**. Even if you find the water too cold for a swim, it's a beautiful place to walk, watch birds or play Frisbee.

About 10km southwest of Taylor Head Provincial Park, Tangier is one of the best settings for kayaking in the Maritimes.

★**Coastal Adventures**
Sea Kayaking   KAYAKING
(☑902-772-2774; www.coastaladventures.com; half/full-day tour $85/125; ⊙Jun-Sep) Based at Mason's Cove, off Hwy 7, this hugely experienced sea-kayaking company (in business since 1980) offers some of the best day trips in Nova Scotia, exploring the isolated '100 Wild Islands' along the east coast. It also has a simple lodge, the **Paddlers' Retreat** (rooms $65 to $100).

East Coast Surf School   SURFING
(☑902-449-9488; www.ecsurfschool.com; 4348 Lawrencetown Rd, East Lawrencetown; lessons from $75) Daily surfing lessons are conducted on Lawrencetown Beach by Nova Scotia's first

NOVA SCOTIA EASTERN SHORE

WORTH A TRIP

TAYLOR HEAD PROVINCIAL PARK

A little-known scenic highlight of Nova Scotia, this spectacular **park** (☑902-772-2218; http://parks.novascotia.ca/content/taylor-head; 20140 Hwy 7, Spry Bay) encompasses a peninsula jutting 6.5km into the Atlantic. On one side is a long, very fine, sandy beach fronting a protected bay. Some 17km of hiking trails cut through the spruce and fir forests. The **Headland Trail** is the longest at 8km round-trip and follows the rugged coastline to scenic views at Taylor Head. The shorter **Bob Bluff Trail** is a 3km round-trip hike to a bluff with good views.

In spring you'll see colorful wildflowers, and this is a great bird-watching area. Pack a picnic and plan to spend a full day hiking, lounging and – if you can brave the cool water – swimming.

and only professional surfer, Nico Manos, and his team. Board and wetsuit rentals are also available.

🎉 Festivals

Stan Rogers Folk Festival
MUSIC
(www.stanfest.com; ⊙ Jul) Most people who come to Canso come for the Stan Rogers Folk Festival, the biggest event in Nova Scotia. It quadruples the town's population, with six stages showcasing folk, blues and traditional musicians from around the world.

🛏 Sleeping & Eating

Murphy's Camping
on the Ocean
CAMPGROUND $
(☑ 902-772-2700; www.murphyscamping.ca; 291 Murphy's Rd; tent/RV sites $30/40; ⊙ May-Oct; P 🐕 🛜) This is oceanside camping at its finest, with plenty of secluded sites (serviced and unserviced) spread out under the trees with views over the 100 Wild Islands. Tuck into a bowl of freshly steamed mussels by the communal campfire. The owners also run boat trips.

Liscombe Lodge Resort
RESORT $$
(☑ 902-779-2307; www.liscombelodge.ca; 2884 Hwy 7, Liscomb; r/chalets from $155/189; ⊙ May-Oct; P 🐕) A nature-lover's dream, this rambling country lodge comprises 30 spacious, nicely decorated riverside rooms in the main lodge, five rustic four-room cottages, and 17 sweeter-than-sweet chalets with fireplaces as well as decks overlooking the woodsy

grounds and river. There's loads to keep kids occupied, including an indoor pool, a tennis court, free bikes and kayaking.

Dobbit Bakehouse
BAKERY $
(☑ 902-889-2919; 7896 Hwy 7, Musquodoboit Harbour; baked goods $2-6; ⊙ 7am-5pm Mon-Fri, 8am-5pm Sat; 🐕) Come chat with the friendly baker, a font of local knowledge, at this wonderful country bakery, which boasts rustic fresh breads and baked goods free from preservatives and using only seasonal local ingredients wherever possible. The selection changes daily. Make sure you try the fair-trade coffee and grab a pie to take with you on your journey.

Rare Bird
MICROBREWERY
(☑ 902-533-2128; www.rarebirdbeer.com; 80 Main St; ⊙ 10am-5pm mid-Jun–Oct) The first man to set up a brewery in Guysborough was Nicolas Denys, way back in 1659, and the beer-heads at Rare Bird are proud to continue that legacy with their brews. Check out the seasonal beers, made with spruce, maple and pumpkin.

❶ Getting There & Away

The Eastern Shore runs from Eastern Passage, south of Dartmouth, to Canso at the eastern tip of the mainland. It is serviced by a veiny network of ancient roads (you'll need your own wheels) that vary in condition depending on the time of year – some communities are cut off during winter storms. Hwy 7 forms the spine of the Eastern Shore but heads inland, due north, at Liscomb.

New Brunswick

Best Places to Eat

➡ Fresco (p430)

➡ La Terrasse à Steve (p427)

➡ 11th Mile (p397)

➡ Tipsy Tails Restaurant (p419)

➡ The Chandler Room (p404)

Best Places to Stay

➡ Cielo (p427)

➡ Compass Rose (p411)

➡ Earle of Leinster Inn (p414)

➡ Château Albert (p428)

➡ Evandale Resort (p397)

Why Go?

Once the favored stomping grounds of millionaires and celebrities who journeyed here for silver, salmon-filled rivers and rustic lodges deep in primeval forests, New Brunswick's beauty and abundance has slipped off most bucket lists in recent decades. Living in the shadows of its more fashionable neighbors, Prince Edward Island (PEI) and Nova Scotia, New Brunswick is regularly referred to as the 'forgotten' or 'drive-through' province. Those who do explore its majestic, brown-sugar beaches, culturally rich Acadian villages, quaint coastal islands and vast tracks of forests brimming with wildlife are richly rewarded. Whether you're kayaking through the world's highest tides, wandering through world-class museums, or bibbing up for a lobster feast, it'll often just be you and the locals. Visit before the secret gets out.

When to Go
Fredericton

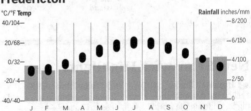

Jul–Sep St Andrews By-The-Sea bustles with crowds of whale-watchers.

Aug Acadians unleash their Franco-Canadian spirit for the Festival Acadien in Caraquet.

Nov–Mar Cross-country skiers hit the groomed trails of Fundy National Park.

New Brunswick Highlights

1 Hopewell Rocks (p418) Feeling the power of the highest tides in the world.

2 St Andrews By-The-Sea (p402) Exploring the history and bustling streets of this picturesque seaside town.

3 Grand Manan Island (p410) Breathing in the fresh sea air on this peaceful island.

4 Fredericton (p393) Soaking up culture in a world-class art gallery.

5 Kouchibouguac National Park (p426) Setting up camp in this award-winning, beach- and lagoon-laden park.

6 Kings Landing (p394) Living Acadian history at this reconstructed scene.

7 Moncton (p419) Enjoying the hopping music scene in the province's biggest small city.

8 Saint John (p412) Buying food and artisans' wares at the spirited morning market.

9 Acadian Peninsula (p427) Soaking up Acadian culture and sunshine on this string of stunning islands.

History

What is now New Brunswick was originally the land of the Mi'kmaq and, in the western and southern areas, the Maliseet First Nations. Many places still bear their indigenous names, although the First Nation people (who today number around 17,000) are now mainly concentrated in small communities.

Following in the wake of explorer Samuel de Champlain, French colonists arrived in the 1600s. The Acadians, as they came to be known, farmed the area around the Bay of Fundy. In 1755 they were expelled by the English, many returning to settle along the Bay of Chaleur. In the years following, the outbreak of the American Revolution brought an influx of British Loyalists from Boston and New York seeking refuge in the wilds of New Brunswick. These refugees settled the valleys of the Saint John and St Croix Rivers, established the city of Saint John and bolstered the garrison town at Fredericton.

Through the 1800s, lumbering and shipbuilding boomed, and by the start of the 20th century, other industries, including fishing, had developed. That era of prosperity ended with the Great Depression. Today pulp and paper, oil refining and potato farming are the major industries.

Language

New Brunswick is Canada's only officially bilingual province; one-third speak French as their first language. Many of these are concentrated around Edmundston, the Acadian Peninsula, along the East Coast, and Moncton. You will rarely have a problem being understood in English or French.

ℹ️ Information

There are tourist information centers at most border crossings and in many towns. Opening times vary, but these are open from June to October only. **Tourism New Brunswick** (☑ 800-561-0123; www.tourismnewbrunswick.ca) publishes useful information on its excellent website.

ℹ️ Getting There & Away

AIR

Air Canada has several daily flights from cities across Canada into Moncton, Saint John, Fredericton and Bathurst. WestJet serves Moncton and Fredericton.

BOAT

The **Bay Ferries** (☑ 877-762-7245; www.bayferries.com; adult/child/senior $49/34/39, car/

➡ Population: 747,100

➡ Area: 73,400 sq km

➡ Capital: Fredericton

➡ Quirky fact: Home to the world's biggest fake lobster (Shediac), axe (Nackawic) and fiddlehead (Plaster Rock).

bicycle $118/10) sails between Saint John and Digby, Nova Scotia, year-round. The three-hour crossing is pricey but can save a lot of driving.

Free government ferries service Deer Island and White Head Island; East Coast Ferries (p406) runs between Campobello Island and Deer Island. Another private ferry company also serves Grand Manan Island. Reserve ahead.

BUS

Maritime Bus (☑ 800-575-1807; www.maritimebus.com) services the major transportation routes in New Brunswick, with service to Nova Scotia, PEI and into Québec as far as Rivière-du-Loup, where buses connect with **Orléans Express** (☑ 833-449-6444; www.orleansexpress.com) services to points west.

CAR & MOTORCYCLE

For drivers, the main access points into New Brunswick are the cities of Edmundston from Québec and Houlton or Calais from Maine. Many enter the province from Nova Scotia or over the bridge from PEI. If you're going to PEI, there's no charge to use the Confederation Bridge eastbound from Cape Jourmain – you pay on the way back. Traffic is generally light, although crossing the Maine borders sometimes means a delay at customs.

TRAIN

VIA Rail (☑ 888-842-7245; www.viarail.ca) operates passenger services between Montréal and Halifax, with stops in Campbellton, Bathurst, Miramichi and Moncton.

FREDERICTON

POP 58,200

The Saint John River curves lazily alongside the provincial capital, watched over by stately historic buildings, tree-lined banks and walking paths. On warm weekends, 'The Green,' as it's known, looks like something out of a watercolor – families strolling, kids kicking soccer balls and couples picnicking.

The small downtown commercial district is a neat grid of redbrick storefronts set on a flat, broad curve in the riverbank. Surrounding it are residential streets lined with tall, graceful elms shading beautifully maintained Georgian and Victorian houses and abundant flower beds.

◉ Sights

The two-block strip along Queen St between York and Regent Sts is known as the Historic Garrison District. It comprises **Barracks Square** (497 Queen St; ◷ Guard House 9:30am-5pm Fri-Wed, to 8pm Thu May-Oct) FREE and **Officers' Square** (www.historicgarrisondistrict.ca; btwn Carleton & Regent Sts; ◷ ceremonies 11am & 4pm daily, plus 7pm Tue & Thu Jul & Aug). In 1875 Fredericton became the capital of the newly formed province of New Brunswick, and the garrison housed British soldiers for much of the late 18th and early 19th centuries. It's now a lively multiuse area with impressive stone architecture.

★ **Kings Landing**　　　HISTORIC SITE
(☑ 506-363-4999; www.kingslanding.nb.ca; 5804 Rte 102, Prince William; adult/youth/family $31/22/72; ◷ 10am-5pm mid-Jun–Oct) A visit to Kings Landing, 36km west of Fredericton, is a somewhat surreal step back in time. The majority of the early-19th-century buildings are original, moved here and beautifully restored to create a Loyalist village with homes, churches, a schoolhouse, general store, sawmill and print shop. Staff role-play actual people who lived and worked here and are busy with everyday 19th-century life, chatting about the village's goings on. Don't be shy – ask lots of questions to learn and experience the most.

★ **Beaverbrook Art Gallery**　　　MUSEUM
(www.beaverbrookartgallery.org; 703 Queen St; adult/student/child $10/5/free; ◷ 10am-5pm Mon-Wed, Fri & Sat, to 9pm Thu, noon-5pm Sun) This excellent gallery was a gift to the town from Lord Beaverbrook. The exceptional collection includes works by international heavyweights and is well worth an hour or so. Among others you will see Dalí, Freud, Gainsborough and Turner, Canadian artists Tom Thompson, Emily Carr and Cornelius Krieghoff, as well as changing contemporary exhibits of Atlantic art.

New Brunswick
Sports Hall of Fame　　　MUSEUM
(www.nbsportshalloffame.com; 503 Queen St; adult/student/family $3/2/8; ◷ noon-5pm Tue-Fri, 10am-5pm Sat mid-Jun–Aug) Housed in the 19th-century customs office, this museum and gallery celebrates the province's star teams and athletic achievements. Learn about local athletes including hockey player Gordie Drillon, tennis player Ethel Babbitt and baseballer Jason Dickson. Test out the sports simulator, peek inside the virtual locker room and explore momentum and center of gravity in the hands-on biomechanics exhibit.

Fredericton Region Museum　　　MUSEUM
(☑ 506-455-6041; www.frederictonregionmuseum.com; Officers' Sq; adult/student $6/4; ◷ 10am-4pm Apr-Jun & Sep-Nov, to 5pm Jul & Aug, by appointment Dec-Mar) What this museum lacks in gloss, it makes up for in care and some serious creativity. Housed in the 19th-century officers' quarters on the western side of Officers' Sq, the artifact-filled displays take you through the city's past with stories of merchants, military, Acadians and Loyalists. Don't miss the Coleman Frog, a 42lb creature of Fredericton legend. Real or plaster? Decide for yourself.

Government House　　　HISTORIC BUILDING
(www.gnb.ca/lg/ogh; 51 Woodstock Rd; ◷ 10am-4pm Mon-Sat, noon-4pm Sun) FREE This magnificent sandstone palace was erected for the British governor in 1826. The representative of the queen moved out in 1893 after the province refused to continue paying his expenses, and during most of the 20th century the complex was a Royal Canadian Mounted Police (RCMP) headquarters. It now evocatively captures a moment in time with tours led by staff in period costume.

New Brunswick
Legislative Building　　　HISTORIC BUILDING
(☑ 506-453-2506; www.gnb.ca/legis; 706 Queen St; ◷ 10am-5pm, last tour 4:30pm Jul & Aug, 9am-4pm Sep-Jun by appointment) Following a fire that destroyed the original Provincial Hall, the impressive stone Legislative Building opened its doors to New Brunswick's Provincial Government in 1882. Join a half-hour tour to check out the 41m central domed tower and the dramatic spiral staircase in the entrance hall. Next door is the Education Building, built in 1816 and Fredericton's oldest surviving public building; it now houses the Opposition Offices.

☆ Activities

Fredericton is blessed with parkland. Lovely **Wilmot Park** is popular with families, of-

Fredericton

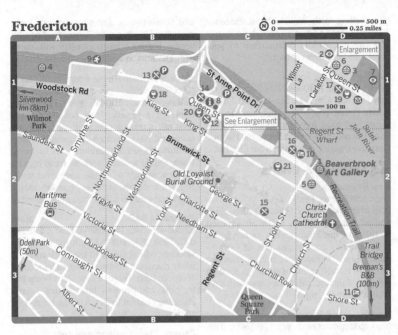

Fredericton

Top Sights
1 Beaverbrook Art Gallery D2

Sights
2 Barracks Square D1
3 Fredericton Region Museum D1
4 Government House A1
5 New Brunswick Legislative
  Building D2
6 New Brunswick Sports Hall of
  Fame D1
7 Officers' Square D1

Activities, Courses & Tours
8 Heritage Walking Tours C1
9 Second Nature Outdoors A1

Sleeping
10 Crowne Plaza Fredericton-
   Lord Beaverbrook D2
11 Quartermain House B&B D3

Eating
12 11th Mile C1
   540 Kitchen & Bar .... (see 17)
13 Byblos B1
14 Chess Piece Patisserie & Cafe C1
15 Fredericton Boyce Farmers
   Market C2
16 Isaac's Way C2
17 The Abbey D1

Drinking & Nightlife
18 Graystone Brewing B1
19 Red Rover Craft Cider D1
20 The Capital Complex B1
21 The Muse C2

fering shade, lots of lawn for picnics, playgrounds and a water park. In the southwest of town, massive **Odell Park** has botanical gardens, an arboretum and and a huge wooded expanse of trails to explore. Parking is off Prospect Rd or Cameron Court.

For trail maps visit the information center or www.frederictontrailscoalition.com.

Second Nature Outdoors BOATING
(www.secondnatureoutdoors.com; off Woodstock Rd; kayak/paddle board/canoe per hr $17/17/22, half-day bike rental $15; ⊙May-Sep) Operating out of the Small Craft Aquatic Centre, on the Saint John River beside Government House, Second Nature Outdoors rents out canoes, double and single kayaks, paddleboards and

bikes, along with children's attachments. They will drop you at Heart Island Resort and you can paddle downstream to your heart's and muscle's content.

Heritage Walking Tours WALKING
(☑ 506-457-1975; 796 Queen St; ⊙ 10am & 2:30pm daily Jul & Aug, 4pm Jun & Sep–mid-Oct) Enthusiastic young people wearing historic costumes lead good, free hour-long tours of the river, the government district or the Historic Garrison District, departing from City Hall.

🎉 Festivals & Events

New Brunswick

Highland Games Festival CULTURAL
(http://highlandgames.ca; ⊙ late Jul) Kilts, clans and all things positively Celtic are exposed at this fun highlands games extravaganza held annually on the grounds of Government House. Competitors and visitors are drawn to its celebration of all things Scottish culture: dancing, caber-toss competitions, whiskey tastings, piped music and more.

Harvest Jazz & Blues Festival MUSIC
(www.harvestjazzandblues.com; ⊙ Sep) This weeklong event transforms the downtown area into the 'New Orleans of the North.' Jazz, blues and Dixieland performers arrive from across North America to fill three stages with more than 100 performances.

Silver Wave Film Festival FILM
(www.swfilmfest.com; ⊙ early Nov) Three days of New Brunswick, Canadian and international films and lectures organized by the NB Filmmakers' Cooperative.

🛏 Sleeping

Silverwood Inn MOTEL $
(☑ 506-458-8676; www.silverwoodinn.ca; 3136 Woodstock Rd; r from $90; 🐾🏊) A 10-minute drive towards Kings Landing, this friendly motel is a bit of a steal with clean, spacious rooms, some with kitchenettes, and a small, well-kept outdoor pool. Don't worry – the trippy night lighting can be turned off.

University of New Brunswick UNIVERSITY ACCOMMODATIONS $
(☑ 506-447-3227; http://stay.unb.ca; 20 Bailey Dr; s/d with bath $41/65, ste $85-115; ⊙ 7am-11pm May–mid-Aug; P🐾) Fredericton's only budget accommodations is located at the university. It's a great deal, but rooms are available in summer only. Traditional rooms have shared bathrooms and include a light continental breakfast and pass to the university pool and fitness rooms. Suites have private bathrooms and kitchenettes. Rooms may be a bit sparse, but it's a lovely campus with views over Fredericton and the Saint John River.

★Quartermain House B&B B&B $$
(☑ 506-206-5255; www.quartermainhouse.com; 92 Waterloo Row; r $110-145; P🐾) The former home of a premier, this beautiful 1840s B&B offers three rooms that epitomize old-fashioned class. Located on enviable Waterloo Row, it's just a 10-minute walk to downtown. Subtle touches, such as fresh cookies and tea, push way up the uber-great scale. Breakfast dishes such as braised maple pears and soufflés will set you up for the day.

Brennan's B&B B&B $$
(☑ 506-455-7346; 146 Waterloo Row; s $115-195, d $125-210; P🐾✴@🐾) Built for a wealthy wood-merchant family in 1885, this turreted white riverfront mansion is now a handsome six-room B&B. Three of the rooms boast water views and two have kitchenettes. There's stunning original fretwork throughout. It's a 10-minute stroll to downtown.

Crowne Plaza Fredericton-Lord Beaverbrook HOTEL $$$
(☑ 506-455-3371; www.cpfredericton.com; 659 Queen St; r $180-220; P✴🐾🏊) Looking rather lacklustre from its beaver-mosaiced exterior, this 1948 vintage hotel is all vintage glamour once you step inside. Wrought-iron railings and a sweeping staircase are leftovers from when Lord Beaverbrook owned the place. Spacious rooms are renovated and modern if a little lacking in character. Ever-popular, it pays to book ahead.

🍴 Eating

Fredericton Boyce Farmers Market MARKET $
(www.frederictonfarmersmarket.ca; 665 George St; ⊙ 6am-1pm Sat) This Fredericton institution is great for picking up fresh fruit, vegetables, meat, cheese and dessert. Many of the 150 or so stalls recall the city's European heritage, with everything from German-style sausages to French duck pâtés to British marmalade. There is also an eatery where Frederictonians queue to chat and people-watch. Pick up souvenirs from the many artisan stalls.

The Abbey VEGETARIAN $
(www.facebook.com/abbeycafegallery; 546 Queen St; $9-11; ⊙ 9am-9pm Mon-Fri, 11am-9pm Sat, noon-6pm Sun; 🐾) If you're vegan, this place will get your stomach giddy. Burritos with cashew

cheese, pulled pork that's actually jackfruit, and hot and cold bowls of veggie goodness will fill you up. You'll find it in the back of the Red Rover ciderhouse. Regular events such as comedy nights and music are held in the basement. Check the website for listings.

Chess Piece Patisserie & Cafe CAFE $
(☑506-459-1969; www.chesspiece.ca; 361 Queen St; snacks $3-8; ⊙7am-9pm Mon-Fri, 8am-9pm Sat, 10am-4pm Sun) This tiny cafe has an in-house patisserie bakery creating to-die-for macaroons, mini cheesecakes and pastries. There's also soup, quiche and sausage rolls but they're hard to notice amid all of that caramel and chocolate. The coffee here is top-notch, too.

★11th Mile CANADIAN $$
(☑506-443-1187; www.11thmile.ca; 79 York St; small plates $12-18) All class, the muted colors of this chef-owned restaurant belie the bright flavors of its food. An ever-changing menu of small plates goes the distance with dishes such as roasted broccoli with walnut crema, seared coulotte steak and salmon with salsa verde. Bespoke cocktails are exceptional. The secret is well and truly out; book ahead.

540 Kitchen & Bar CANADIAN $$
(☑506-449-5400; http://540kitchenandbar.com; 540 Queen St; mains $16-25; ⊙11:30am-9pm Mon & Tue, to 10pm Wed & Thu, to 11pm Fri & Sat; ☑) Fashionable and just classy enough to not feel like a pub, this place has a stellar, seasonal menu with locally sourced produce and nearly everything made from scratch. Wash down the likes of pork-belly gnocchi, wild-mushroom risotto or panko and lemon haddock with one of 10 local beers on tap. Get here early or reserve ahead; it's popular.

Isaac's Way CANADIAN $$
(☑506-474-7222; www.isaacsway.ca; 649 Queen St; mains $15-22; ⊙11am-10pm Mon-Fri, 10am-10pm Sat & Sun; ☑) Using local products, Isaac's has quickly become a favorite of locals, especially in summer for its patio with river views. Big portions of burgers, seafood and pasta keep families happy, and while the menu isn't unique, dishes are created with care and a real knack for flavor. There are plenty of options for vegetarians and weekend breakfasts are a hit.

Byblos LEBANESE $$
(☑506-454-5552; 215 Queen St; meals $15-19; ⊙11:30am-8pm Mon-Fri, 5-9pm Sat) Crazy popular, this elegant Lebanese restaurant has

EVANDALE

A century ago, tiny **Evandale** was bustling, where a dance band would entertain passengers stopping off here for the night. These days, you can stop for an outdoor swim, patio drink – and maybe a night – at **Evandale Resort** (☑506-468-2222; www.evandaleresort.com; 3500 Rte 124, Evandale; r $100-170; ⊙May-Oct; ❋☎⊠), restored to its grandeur as an 1889 riverboat hotel. Even if you're not a guest, you can swim ($5) and enjoy pub meals on the patio overlooking the dock.

The cable ferry at Evandale Ferry Landing takes you across the short, rapid St John river to Rte 124 and the Belleisle Ferry to rural Kingston Peninsula.

a bustling atmosphere. Linger over garlic-laced dishes, marinated meats and homemade pita bread.

🍷 Drinking & Nightlife

In the evening the bars, pubs and rooftop patios of King and Queen Sts come alive. There's a prerequisite brewery and a great ciderhouse here. Younger things hit the multi-venue Capital Complex.

★The Muse COCKTAIL BAR
(www.facebook.com/musecafefredericton; 86 Regent St; ⊙8:30am-6pm Mon & Tue, to 10pm Wed-Sun) If you're feeling drinky in the afternoon, come here for cool cocktails or coffee alongside bagels and gourmet cream cheese with muddled raspberry or vermouth and oregano. Beer, cider, prosecco and kombucha are all on tap. Most evenings there's live music by touring or local musicians. See the website for listings.

Graystone Brewing BREWERY
(www.graystonebrewing.com; 221 King St; ⊙11am-11pm Mon-Thu, to midnight Fri & Sat, noon-9pm Sun) Somewhat industrial with a hopping street patio, the cool cats hang out here to sip on Graystone and other local brews. Although still in its infancy, the brewery is already expanding. A food truck outside serves fancy hearty naanwiches, rice bowls, lettuce wraps and poutine.

Red Rover Craft Cider BAR
(www.redrovercider.com; 546 Queen St; ⊙5-9pm Mon, noon-9pm Tue-Thu, noon-10pm Fri & Sat) This convivial ciderhouse serves craft brews made by New Brunswick's original (and very

FLORENCEVILLE-BRISTOL

The tidy, green riverside village of **Florenceville-Bristol** is ground zero of the global french-fry industry. It's home to the McCain Foods frozen-foods empire, which is sustained by the thousands of hectares of potato farms that surround it in every direction. Started by the McCain brothers in 1957, the company produces one-third of the world's french-fry supply at its Florenceville factory. That adds up to 453,600kg of chips churned out every hour and $5.8 billion in annual net sales. To get your head around the spud industry, head to **Potato World** (www.potatoworld.ca; Rte 110; tours adult/family $5/16, experiential tours $10/32; ⊙9am-6pm Mon-Fri, to 5pm Sat & Sun Jun-Aug, 9am-5pm Mon-Fri Sep—mid-Oct), an interactive exposition of the history of the humble potato in these parts.

Twenty kilometers further south, the tiny country hamlet of **Hartland** is home to the granddaddy of New Brunswick's many wooden covered bridges. The photogenic and functioning 390m-long **Hartland Bridge** over the Saint John River was erected in 1897 and is the world's longest.

passionate) cider producers. Try all four on tap with a short flight ($10), sit back with a glass or a pint, or buy a few tall tins to take with you.

The Capital Complex
CLUB

(www.thecapitalcomplex.com; 362 Queen St; ⊙4pm-midnight Mon, to 2am Tue-Fri, 6pm-2am Sat) A series of balconies, floors, clubs, bars and venues, this complex is where it's at on summer nights. Whether you're into beer, cocktails, live comedy or owning the dance floor, the Capital Complex doesn't disappoint. Enter down Piper's Lane off Queen St, or through the Tannery shopping complex on King St.

❶ Information

The entire CBD is wired for free internet access.
Main post office (☑506-444-8602; 570 Queen St; ⊙8am-5pm Mon-Fri)
Visitor Information Centre (☑506-460-2129; www.tourismfredericton.ca; City Hall, 397 Queen St; ⊙10am-8pm Jul & Aug, to 5pm Jun & Sep, to 4:30pm May & Oct) Fredericton's main tourist office provides free three-day city parking passes to visitors. A secondary office opens in summer at **Kings Landing** (42 Prince William Rd, Prince William; ⊙10:30am-5:30pm Jun-Oct).

❶ Getting There & Away

AIR
Fredericton International Airport (YFC; ☑506-460-0920; www.frederictonairport.ca) is located on Hwy 102, 14km southeast of town. Air Canada has flights between Fredericton and the US, including New York City and Orlando (via other Canadian cities), as well flights to London, UK. Fredericton is also part of a good network of domestic flights.

BUS
The **Maritime Bus** (☑506-455-2049; www.maritimebus.com; 105 Dundonald St; ⊙8am-8pm Mon-Fri, 10am-8pm Sat & Sun) terminal is a few kilometers southwest of downtown. Some useful destinations include Moncton ($42, 2¼ hours, three daily), Charlottetown, PEI ($69, 5½ hours, two daily) and Saint John ($26, 1½ hours, three daily).

CAR & MOTORCYCLE
Cars with out-of-province license plates are eligible for a free three-day parking pass for downtown Fredericton from May to October; pick one up from the visitor center at City Hall. In-province visitors can get a one-day pass.

Major car-rental agencies all have desks at the airport.

❶ Getting Around

A taxi to the airport costs $18 to $22.

The city has a decent bus system; tickets cost $3 and include free transfers. Service runs Monday through Saturday from 6:15am to 11pm. Most city bus routes begin at King's Place Mall, on King St between York and Carleton.

Bicycle rentals are available at **Radical Edge** (☑506-459-3478; www.radicaledge.ca; 386 Queen St; rental per day $25).

UPPER ST JOHN RIVER VALLEY

The St John River winds along the western border of the province past forests and lush farmland. It drifts through Fredericton between tree-lined banks and around flat islands between rolling hills before emptying into the Bay of Fundy 700km later. The river is the province's dominant feature and for centuries has been its major thoroughfare.

The valley's eye-pleasing landscape along the Trans Canada Trail (TCT) follows the river for most of its length.

Two automobile routes carve through the valley: the quicker Trans-Canada Hwy (Hwy 2), mostly on the western side of the river, and the more scenic old Hwy 105 on the eastern side, which meanders through many villages. Branching off from the valley are Hwy 17 (at St-Léonard) and Rte 385 (at Perth-Andover), which cut northeast through the Appalachian highlands and lead to rugged Mt Carleton Provincial Park.

Mt Carleton Provincial Park & the Tobique Valley

The 17,427-hectare provincial park is one of the region's best-kept secrets. It offers visitors a wilderness of mountains, valleys, rivers and wildlife including moose, deer and bear. The park's main feature is a series of rounded glaciated peaks and ridges, including Mt Carleton (820m), the Maritimes' highest. This range is an extension of the Appalachian Mountains, which begin in Georgia, USA, and end in Québec.

The park is open from mid-May to October. All roads are gravel-surfaced. The nearest towns are Riley Brook, 40km to the south, and St Quentin, 42km to the west, so bring all food and a full tank of gas.

 Activities

Canoeing

The Mt Carleton area boasts superb wilderness canoeing. In the park itself, the Nictau and Nepisiguit chains of lakes offer easy day-tripping through a landscape of tree-clad mountains. For experienced canoeists, the shallow and swift Little Tobique River rises at Big Nictau Lake, winding in tight curls through dense woods until it joins the Tobique itself at Nictau. The more remote Nepisiguit River flows out of the Nepisiguit Lakes through the wilderness until it empties into the Bay of Chaleur at Bathurst, more than 100km away.

The lower reaches of the Tobique, from Nictau, through minute Riley Brook and down to Plaster Rock is a straight, easy paddle through forest and meadow that gives way to farmland as the valley broadens, with a couple of waterfront campgrounds along the way. The easy 10km between Nictau and the Bear's Lair landing in Riley Brook make for a relaxing afternoon paddle.

Guildo Martel WATER SPORTS
(☑ 506-235-0286; 8162 Rte 385; kayak & canoe rental per day $40, plus transport $15, tubing adult/child $20/15; ◷ Jun-Sep) Guildo Martel rents canoes and kayaks for the day and will deliver them where required. He's located 4km from the park toward St Quentin. He will guide for a total of $100 on top of rental prices (for up to six people).

Bill Miller CANOEING
(☑ 506-356-2409; www.millercanoes.com; 4160 Rte 385, Nictau) Bill Miller welcomes visitors to his cluttered canoe-making workshop in Nictau (population roughly eight), on the forested banks of the Tobique River, where he and his father and grandfather before him have handcrafted wooden canoes since 1922.

Bear's Lair KAYAKING
(☑ 506-356-8351; www.bearslairhunting.com; 3349 Rte 385, Riley Brook; kayak/canoe rental per day $35/45) Owners will drop you off upriver so you can paddle and float your way downstream and back to home base, Bear's Lair (p400), the cozy lodge.

Hiking

The way to explore Mt Carleton is on foot. The park has a network of nearly 70km of trails: most of them are loops winding to the handful of rocky knobs that are the peaks. The International Appalachian Trail (IAT) passes through here.

The easiest peak to climb is **Mt Bailey**; a 7.5km loop trail to the 564m hillock begins near the day-use area. Most hikers can walk this route in three hours. The highest peak is reached via the **Mt Carleton Trail**, a 10km route that scales rocks to reach the 820m knob, where there's a fire tower. Plan on five hours for the trek, wear good footwear and pack your parka; the wind above the tree line can be brutal.

TOBIQUE SALMON BARRIER

Each spring, the government-funded **Tobique Salmon Barrier** (4320 Rte 385; ◷ May-Sep) FREE holds back salmon from swimming upstream, protecting them from low water levels and poachers. From the viewing platform, you can see the barrier as well as flashes of 30lb Atlantic salmon that return every two years to spawn. At the end of September, the barrier is removed and the salmon swim free.

WORTH A TRIP

NEW BRUNSWICK BOTANICAL GARDEN

Working-class Edmundston has a large paper mill, a utilitarian town center and a mainly bilingual French citizenry. Much of the downtown seems to be for sale or closed down but there are some nearby sights that are worthy of your time – especially the **New Brunswick Botanical Garden** (☎506-737-4444; www.jardinnbgarden.com; off Rte 2, St-Jacques; adult/student/child/family $18/15/8/40; ⏲9am-5pm May, Jun & Sep, to 8pm Jul & Aug). Located in the small community of St-Jacques, this 7-hectare garden has peaceful paths, an unusual Celestial Garden, more than 80,000 plants and a team of artists-in-residence at work in small pavilions. The cafe here is a popular lunch spot for locals.

The most challenging hike (and the most rewarding for the views) is the **Sagamook Trail**, a 6km loop to a 777m peak with superlative vistas of Nictau Lake and the highlands area to the north of it; allow four hours for this trek. The **Mountain Head Trail** connects the Mt Carleton and Sagamook Trails (the latter being part of the Appalachian Trail), making a long transit of the range possible.

All hikers intending to follow any long trails must register at the visitor center before hitting the trail. Outside the camping season (mid-May to mid-September), you should call ahead to make sure the main gate will be open, as the Mt Carleton trailhead is 13.5km from the park entrance.

Festivals & Events

World Pond Hockey Tournament SPORTS
(http://worldpondhockey.ca; Rte 109, Plaster Rock; admission free; ⏲Feb) Every February, the forest town of Plaster Rock (population 1200), 84km from Mt Carleton, hosts the World Pond Hockey Tournament. More than 20 rinks are plowed on Roulston Lake, which is ringed by tall evergreens, hot-chocolate stands and straw-bale seating for the thousands of spectators drawn to the four-day event. More than 120 amateur four-person teams come from around the world.

Fiddles on the Tobique MUSIC
(☎506-356-2409; ⏲late Jun/early Jul) Fiddles on the Tobique is a weekend festival held annually in Nictau and Riley Brook. It is a magical idea: a round of community-hall suppers, jam sessions and concerts culminating in a Sunday-afternoon floating concert down the Tobique River from Nictau to Riley Brook. Upward of 800 canoes and kayaks join the flotilla each year – some stocked with musicians, some just with paddlers – and 8000 spectators line the riverbanks to watch.

Sleeping

Heritage Cottages COTTAGE $
(☎506-235-0793; https://parcsnbparks.ca; Mt Carleton Provincial Park; d $60-90) These damn cute log cabins dating from the late 1800s sit on Bathurst Lakes and at Little Nictau right within the park. You must bring everything, including bedding, pots and pans. Some share facilities; others have their own kitchens and bathrooms.

Armstrong Brook Campground CAMPGROUND $
(☎506-235-0793; https://parcsnbparks.ca; campsites $28; ⏲May-Oct) The park's largest campground has 88 sites nestled among the spruce on the northern side of Nictau Lake, 3km from the entrance. It has toilets, showers and a kitchen shelter, but no sites with hookups. RV drivers often have their noisy generators running, so tenters should check out the eight tent-only sites on the northern side of the campground.

Bear's Lair INN $
(☎506-356-8351; www.bearslairhunting.com; 3349 Rte 385, Riley Brook; r from $80, 4-/8-person cabin $150/175; ⏲May-Sep; P) Even if you aren't planning to hunt, you need to be fine with taxidermy to feel comfortable here. Moose and his friends festoon the walls of this log hunting lodge on the banks of the Tobique River. Rooms are very basic but spick-and-span and right on the river.

The lodge's friendly owners offer meals and canoe and kayak rentals. Be aware that since this is predominantly a hunting lodge, you might be sharing with those who partake in this activity.

Information

A **visitor center** (☎506-235-0793; www.nbparks.ca; off Rte 385; per vehicle $10; ⏲8am-8pm May-Sep, to 6pm Oct) at the park entrance has maps and information. Park entry is paid here; cash only. At the time of research, an interpretive center was also being built inside the park.

WESTERN FUNDY SHORE

Almost the entire southern edge of New Brunswick is presided over by the constantly rising and falling waters of the Bay of Fundy.

The resort town of St Andrews By-The-Sea, the serene Fundy Isles, fine seaside scenery and rich history make this easily one of the most appealing regions of the province. Whale-watching is a thrilling activity here with fin, humpback and minke commonly seen along with the occasional but increasingly rare right whale. Porpoises and dolphins are plentiful. And let's not overlook the seafood – it's bountiful and delicious.

St Stephen

POP 4420

Right on the US border across the river from Calais, ME, St Stephen is a busy entry point with small-town charm. Elegant historic homes line the residential streets and the tidy downtown has a handful of shops, cafes and an honest-to-goodness chocolate factory that you can tour.

The Ganong family has been making chocolate since 1873, sending its products across Canada and the world. Long-standing treats include the once 5¢ Pal-o-Mine (a fudge and peanut bar) and 'chicken bones' (cinnamon-flavored candy filled with chocolate). They are also credited with the heart-shaped box of chocolates seen everywhere on Valentine's Day. Today their factory is on the edge of town with the original location now a museum (✆506-466-7848; www.chocolatemuseum.ca; 73 Milltown Blvd; adult/student/family $10/8.50/30; ⊙10am-6pm Jul & Aug, 10am-4pm Mon-Sat Apr-Jun & Sep-Nov, shop 9am-7pm Mon-Fri, to 6pm Sat, 11am-5pm Sun) with taste-testing-filled tours and the chance to see chocolate hand-dippers at work.

The town celebrates its love of chocolate during the Chocolate Fest (www.chocolate-fest.ca; ⊙early Aug), which features a parade, tours of the local Ganong factory and unlimited sampling of the goods (yes, really!).

🛏 Sleeping & Eating

Winsome Inn MOTEL $$
(✆506-466-2130; www.winsomeinn.com; 198 King St; d/q $112/125; ❋ 🛜) Located on the edge of town, this motel is super-clean, friendly and – some might even say – winsome. Standard rooms are smartened up with some modern furnishings. It's a drive into town but a short walk to Carmen's Diner. This is the

WORTH A TRIP

GRAND FALLS

Grand Falls lives up to its name. Dropping 25m into a narrow gorge with walls towering 80m, the falls are the focal point of the town. The Grand Falls are best when the dam gates are open, often after rain. During spring freshet, 6 million litres of water cascade over the falls every second – nine-tenths the volume of Niagara Falls. In summer much of the water is diverted for generating hydroelectricity – yet the gorge is pretty at any time.

To see the falls, follow the boardwalk trails from the tourist center (www.grandfallsnb.com/malabeam) on the western side of the bridge, Lovers' Lane is a garden trail with fabulous views.

Maritime Bus services (www.maritimebus.com) stop at the Esso station, just west of downtown, with departures to Fredericton ($42, two hours 40 minutes, one or two daily), Moncton ($73, 5½ hours, daily) and Quebec City ($86, four hours, twice daily) via Riviere Du Loup.

best (read: only) deal in town. Watch for the colorful, giant lawn chairs.

Blair House INN $$
(✆506-466-2233; www.blairhouseheritageinn.com; 38 Prince William St; r incl breakfast $105-140; ⊙mid-Apr–Dec; P 🐾 ❋ 🛜) Three rather beautiful and extremely comfortable rooms are complemented by a quiet garden at this fabulous Victorian home. A generous cooked breakfast is served at the large dining table and tea, lemonade and cookies are available in the evening in the living room. It's an easy walk from here to downtown.

Carman's Diner DINER $
(✆506-466-3528; 164 King St; mains $5-15; ⊙7am-9pm) Home cooking is served up at this 1960s throwback with counter stools and your own mini (and working) jukeboxes at the tables. There's everything from burgers to sandwiches, but the homemade pies are the things to go for. It's only really convenient if you have a car, as it's not in the center of town.

ℹ Getting There & Away

Across the border in Calais, **West's Coastal Connection** (✆800-596-2823; www.westbusservice.com; 189 Main St, Calais, Maine) buses

NEW BRUNSWICK ST STEPHEN

head to Bangor (one-way ticket $27, four hours, one daily), connecting with Bangor airport.

There are no transport options from here to other provincial destinations. You'll need your own wheels.

St Andrews By-The-Sea

POP 1790

St Andrews is a genteel summer resort town. Blessed with a fine climate and picturesque beauty, it also has a colorful history and feels much like a living museum. Founded by Loyalists in 1783, it's one of the oldest towns in the province, with plaques of the original owners next to many of the stately Georgian homes. It's extremely busy with holidaymakers and summer residents in July and August, but the rest of the year there are more seagulls than people.

The town sits on a peninsula pointing southward into the Bay of Fundy. Its main drag, Water St, is lined with quaint buildings, restaurants and boutiques.

◉ Sights

Ministers Island ISLAND
(☑ 506-529-5081; www.ministersisland.ca; adult/student/child under 8yr $15/13/free; ☉ May-Oct) This picturesque tidal island was once used as a retreat by William Cornelius Van Horne, builder of the Canadian Pacific Railway and one of Canada's wealthiest men. As well as touring the island on foot along 20km of marked trails, you can visit Covenhoven, his splendid 50-room Edwardian cottage, plus the towerlike stone bathhouse, tidal swimming pool and stunning, château-like barn (the largest freestanding wooden structure in Canada).

Important: the island can only be visited at low tide, when you can drive (or walk, or bike) on the hard-packed sea floor. At high tide, it's 3m under water but staff will kick you off in plenty of time. To get to Ministers Island from downtown St Andrews, follow Rte 127 northeast for about 1km and then turn right on Bar Rd. If you walk over, take Cedar Lane just past the toll booth, which was planted in the 1800s as a dust-free path to Covenhaven.

Ross Memorial Museum HISTORIC BUILDING
(☑ 506-529-5124; www.rossmemorialmuseum.ca; 188 Montague St; ☉ 10am-4:30pm Tue-Sat Jun-Sep, plus Mon Jul & Aug) Hark back to a time when beds were so high, you needed an ornate step stool to climb in. This 1820s home was bought by the wealthy Ross couple who

traveled the world and filled their eclectic home with souvenirs. Fine furnishings and artifacts successfully turn back the clock to the early 1900s. Knowledgeable staff will give you a tour or you can wander independently.

Fundy Discovery Aquarium AQUARIUM
(www.huntsmanmarine.ca; 1 Lower Campus Rd; adult/child $14.25/10; ☉ 10am-7pm Jun-Sep) Linked to a nonprofit research center, this impressive aquatic center has a 20,000-sq-ft aquarium containing most specimens found in Bay of Fundy waters. In addition to the exhibits, try to see the seal, seahorse and salmon feedings; arrive at 10am or 3pm to get a chance to take it all in. Brave the touch pool reserved just for slippery skates and join a behind-the-scenes tour ($10, ages eight and up).

St Andrews Blockhouse HISTORIC BUILDING
(Joe's Point Rd; by donation; ☉ 10am-6pm Jun-Aug) Built in 1812 by town folk anticipating an attack by the USA, this wooden blockhouse was run by local militia. Restored and set up to look like 1812 inside, it is one of the few surviving blockhouses in Canada. At low tide, there's a path extending from the blockhouse across a great stretch of beach and the tidal flats.

Kingsbrae Garden GARDENS
(☑ 506-529-3335; www.kingsbraegarden.com; 220 King St; adult/student/family $16/12/38, tours per person $3; ☉ 9am-7pm May-Oct) Extensive, multihued Kingsbrae Garden is considered one of the most beautiful horticultural displays in Canada. Check out the wollemi pine, one

St Andrews By-The-Sea

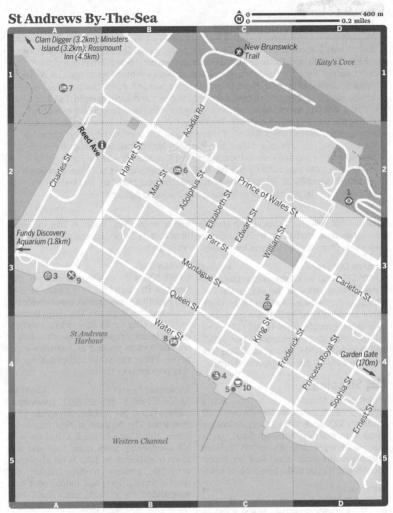

Clam Digger (3.2km); Ministers
Island (3.2km); Rossmount
Inn (4.5km)

New Brunswick
Trail

Katy's Cove

Reed Ave

Acadia Rd

Charles St

Harriet St

Mary St

Adolphus St

Elizabeth St

Prince of Wales St

Edward St

William St

Parr St

Montague St

Queen St

Carleton St

King St

Water St

Frederick St

Princess Royal St

Garden Gate
(170m)

Sophia St

Ernest St

St Andrews
Harbour

Western Channel

Fundy Discovery
Aquarium (1.8km)

of the world's oldest and rarest trees, and the functioning Dutch windmill. In summer, try to time your visit for the daily 12:30pm alpaca walk on the lawn or the 2pm ladybug release in the rose garden.

Activities

Numerous companies offering boat trips and whale-watching cruises have offices by the wharf at the foot of King St. They're open from mid-June to early September. The cruises (around $60) take in the lovely coast with its seabirds and whales. The ideal waters for whale-watching are further out in

the bay, so if you're heading for the Fundy Isles, do your trip there.

Jolly Breeze BOATING
(506-529-8116; www.jollybreeze.com; Quoddy Link Marine; adult/child $67/45; tours 9am, 12:45pm & 4:30pm Jun-Oct) This antique-style tall ship sails around Passamaquoddy Bay looking for seals and whales as well as porpoises and eagles. Trips are 3½ hours long, with a 95% success rate of whale encounters.

Quoddy Link Marine BOATING
(506-529-2600; http://quoddylinkmarine.com; adult/youth/child $69/49/39; mid-Jun–Oct)

WORTH A TRIP

NEW RIVER PROVINCIAL PARK

Just off Hwy 1, about 35km west of Saint John on the way to St Stephen, this large **park** (☎506-755-4046; www.tourismnnewbrunswick.ca; Jun-Sep per vehicle $10) has one of the best beaches along the Fundy shore, a wide stretch of sand bordered on one side by the rugged coastline of Barnaby Head. During camping season the park charges a fee per vehicle for day use, which includes parking at the beach and Barnaby Head trailhead.

You can spend an enjoyable few hours hiking Barnaby Head along a 5km network of nature trails. The **Chittick's Beach Trail** leads through coastal forest and past four coves, where you can check the catch in a herring weir or examine tidal pools for marine life. Extending from this loop is the 2.5km **Barnaby Head Trail**, which hugs the shoreline most of the way and rises to the edge of a cliff 15m above the Bay of Fundy.

The park's **campground** (☎506-755-4046; https://parcsnbparks.ca; 78 New River Beach Rd; tent/RV sites $28/31; ☺May-Sep) is across the road from the beach and features 100 secluded sites, both rustic and with hookups, in a wooded setting.

Serious whale-watchers should hop aboard this catamaran, staffed by trained marine biologists. There are one to three tours daily.

Eastern Outdoors KAYAKING
(☎506-529-4662; www.easternoutdoors.com; 165 Water St; kayak rental per day $65; ☺May-Oct) This St Andrews–based outfitter offers a variety of kayaking trips, including a three-hour tour around nearby Navy Island ($79), and full-day trips to Passamaquody Bay ($155) and Deer Island ($159). Mountain bikes (per hour/day $20/30) can also be rented here.

🛏 Sleeping

Picket Fence Motel MOTEL $
(☎506-529-8985; www.picketfencenb.com; 102 Reed Ave; r $90-110; P❄🛜) This retro-looking motel is the real deal. Although dated, rooms are neat-as-a-pin and it's within walking distance of the main drag. Staff are super-friendly and it's one of the best deals in town.

Rossmount Inn INN $$
(☎506-529-3351; www.rossmountinn.com; 4599 Rte 127; r $140-150; ☺Apr-Dec; P❄🛜≋) Flags flap in the breeze in front of this stately yellow summer cottage, perched atop a manicured slope overlooking Passamaquoddy Bay. Inside the 17 elegant rooms have hand-carved wooden furniture and white linens. The feather overlays on the beds make for a cloud-like sleep. Dinner is available in the classy dining room by reservation only, as is breakfast.

Treadwell Inn B&B $$
(☎888-529-1011, 506-529-1011; www.treadwellinn. com; 129 Water St; r $140-210; ☺mid-Jun–Oct; ☺❄🛜) You will feel very at home in these big, handsome rooms in an 1820 ship chandler's house. The pricier rooms have private decks and ocean views. With wooden beams

and a sleigh bed, Room 6 has the edge. Breakfast is buffet continental. Minimum two nights.

Garden Gate B&B $$
(☎506-529-4453; www.bbgardengate.com; 364 Montague St; r from $150; P🛜) Built in 1910, this beautiful house has six comfortable but small and simple rooms. The Tilley Room is worth nabbing for its Jacuzzi tub. Excellent cooked breakfasts and small touches such as tea and cookies make it an enjoyable experience. Prices are on the higher side but it's very popular nonetheless.

Algonquin Resort HOTEL $$$
(☎506-529-8823, 855-529-8693; www.algonquinresort.com; 184 Adolphus St; r from $230; P❄🛜≋) The doyenne of New Brunswick hotels, this 'Castle-by-the-Sea' has sat on a hill overlooking town since 1889 and was given a makeover in 2015. With its elegant verandah, gardens, rooftop terrace, golf course, tennis courts and indoor pool with waterslides, it's a world unto itself. Prices vary according to seasons and demand; check the website for deals.

🍴 Eating & Drinking

Clam Digger SEAFOOD $
(4468 Hwy 127, Chamcook; mains $6-15; ☺11:30am-3pm & 5-9pm Apr-Sep) Cars park three-deep outside this teeny red-and-white seafood shack, a summertime tradition in these parts. Order your clams, burger, scallops, poutine and milkshakes at the window and claim one of the red-painted picnic tables. It's 3.5km north of the visitor center.

⭐**The Chandler Room** CANADIAN $$
(www.treadwellinn.com/the-chandler-room; 129 Water St; share plates $10-18; ☺4-10pm Wed-Sun)

Polished yet comfortable, this tapas-style restaurant is yards above the competition. Simple-sounding dishes such as beef carpaccio, spicy cauliflower and local seafood are elegantly presented and bursting with flavor. Expect a carefully chosen wine and whiskey list and bespoke cocktails. Inside it's candlelit and intimate; outside the deck views are substantial.

Rossmount Inn Restaurant   CANADIAN **$$**
(☑506-529-3351; www.rossmountinn.com; 4599 Rte 127; mains $18-30; ☺5-9:30pm) The Swiss chef-owner makes wonderful use of local bounty in this warm, art-filled dining room. The ever-changing menu might include local ingredients such as wild mushrooms, periwinkles or New Brunswick lobster turned into exquisite dishes such as lobster with nasturtium-flower dumplings and vanilla bisque. By reservation only. The restaurant is 3km north of town.

Niger Reef Tea House   CANADIAN **$$**
(☑506-529-8005; https://niger-reef-tea-house. business.site; 1 Joes Point Rd; mains lunch $14-21, dinner $22-30; ☺11am-3pm & 5-8pm May-Oct) Built in 1926 and used as a teahouse to raise money for charity until WWII, this tiny, atmospheric place is a popular spot for well-prepared meals such as loaded seafood sandwiches and homemade soup. Next to the St Andrews Blockhouse, it has an enviable location overlooking the water. The impressive and unmissable murals on the walls were discovered during restoration in the 1990s. The teahouse is named after the reef on the outer approaches of St Andrews.

Something's Brewing   CAFE
(☑506-529-4702; www.facebook.com/some thingsbrewingcfe; 209 Water St; bistro $10-15; ☺7:30am-5pm Mon-Wed, to 8pm Thu-Sun, bistro Thu-Sun only) Down by the water, this tiny cafe-bar is dynamite. Grab a spot on the big deck for morning coffee or afternoon cocktails, wine and New Brunswick beer. The bistro menu will wow you with shareable and main dishes. Everything is local and homemade, from the cheeses to the smoked salmon and the blueberry-ale ice-cream sandwich.

ⓘ Information

Tourist Office (www.townofstandrews.ca; 46 Reed Ave; ☺9am-7pm Jul & Aug, to 5pm May, Jun, Sep & Oct; ☜)

FUNDY ISLES

The thinly populated, unspoiled Fundy Isles are ideal for a tranquil, nature-based escape. With grand scenery, colorful fishing wharves tucked into coves, supreme whale-watching, uncluttered walking trails and steaming dishes of seafood, the islands will make your everyday stresses fade away. The three main islands each have a distinct personality. Outside the summer season, all are nearly devoid of visitors and most services are shut.

Deer Island

Deer Island, the closest of the three main Fundy Isles to the mainland, is an unassuming fishing settlement with a lived-in look. Just 16km-by-5km, the island has been inhabited since 1770. Around 1000 people live here year-round, kept company by the many deer that reside in the island's dense forests. Lobster is the main catch with wharves and lobster pounds dotted around the island.

Deer Island can be easily explored on a day trip. Narrow, winding roads run south down each side toward Campobello Island and the ferry.

⊙ Sights & Activities

Whales usually arrive in mid-June and stay until October. You can be lucky enough to spot these offshore; for a closer look, head out on a kayak tour with Seascape Kayak Tours.

Old Sow Whirlpool   WATERFRONT
(Deer Island Point Park) From the shores of the pretty, community-run 16-hectare Deer Island Point Park, Old Sow, the world's second-largest natural tidal whirlpool, is seen offshore a few hours before high tide. Check at the tourist information center (p406) for tide times. Whales pass occasionally, too.

Seascape Kayak Tours   KAYAKING
(☑506-747-1884; www.seascapekayaktours.com; 40 NW Harbour Branch Rd, Richardson; half-/full-day trips $85/150, sunset trips $65; ☺mid-May–mid-Sep) Fabulous guided paddling excursions around Deer Island and Passamaquoddy Bay with experienced guides. Multiday island-jumping camping trips also available.

🛏 Sleeping & Eating

Deer Island Inn   GUESTHOUSE **$**
(☑506-747-1998; www.deerislandinn.com; 272 Rte 772, Lords Cove; r incl breakfast $95-105;

Fundy Isles

yourself at a gingham-checked table and fill up on good home cooking. Family-run for more than 50 years, this diner-style restaurant serves up local seafood and burgers. Big pancake breakfasts are for motel guests only, who also enjoy clean, basic rooms (single/double/twin $50/60/70), an outdoor pool, firepit and tremendous hospitality.

ℹ Information

Tourist information (☑506-747-0119; www.deerisland.nb.ca; 193 Rte 772, Lords Cove; ◷10am-5pm Jul-Sep) Based in Lord's Bay community with helpful staff.

ℹ Getting There & Away

A free government-run ferry (25 minutes) carries vehicles and passengers to the northern end of Deer Island from Letete, which is 14.5km south of St George on Hwy 172 via Back Bay. The ferry runs year-round every half-hour from 6am to 7pm, and hourly from 7pm to 10pm. Get in line early on a busy day.

In summer **East Coast Ferries** (☑506-747-2159; www.eastcoastferries.nb.ca; car & driver $22, additional passenger $5; ◷9am-7pm) services Campobello Island.

Campobello Island

POP 800

The wealthy have long been enjoying Campobello as a summer retreat, with private estates that aren't much in tune with the rustic feel of the rest of the island. Like many moneyed families, the Roosevelts bought property here at the end of the 1800s and the house and its surrounding park is now the island's main attraction. With a bridge to Maine, it feels as much a part of the USA as of Canada, and most of the tourists here are day-tripping Americans.

Once billed as unspoiled and ideal, Campobello's residents are dealing with a lack of garbage disposal, few medical services and limited groceries. With the ferry running only during summer months, residents must travel through US customs to reach mainland Canada, and many are feeling exiled.

◎ Sights & Activities

★**Roosevelt Campobello International Park**   PARK
(www.fdr.net; Hwy 774; ◷Roosevelt Cottage 10am-6pm mid-May–mid-Oct) **FREE** Southernmost Campobello Island is home to this 1133-hectare park. Its star attraction is **Roo-**

◷May–mid-Oct) If island stays are your thing, this excellent-value home brings a touch of Deer Island heritage with its five pleasantly appointed rooms. Excellent full breakfasts set you up for taking on the local sights. The inn is conveniently located along the main road in Lords Cove, close to a shop and the information center.

Deer Island Point Park   CAMPGROUND $
(☑506-747-2423; www.deerislandpointpark.com; 195 Deer Island Point Rd; tent sites $25-30; ◷Jun-Sep) Set up your tent on the high bluff and spend an evening watching the Old Sow whirlpool. The campground is directly above the Campobello ferry landing with a rocky beach and a few wilderness sites. There is no swimming here due to the dangerous pull of Old Sow.

45th Parallel Restaurant & Motel   DINER $
(www.45thparallel.ca; 941 Rte 772; mains; ◷restaurant 11am-7:30pm, shorter hours Oct-May, motel Jul & Aug; 🖳) Slide into a wooden booth or park

sevelt Cottage, the 34-room lodge where Franklin D Roosevelt came with his family between 1905 and 1921 and visited periodically throughout his US presidency (1933–45). The surprisingly rustic structure is furnished with original Roosevelt furniture and artifacts; well-versed tour guides give insight into the Roosevelts' personal lives. Adjacent **Hubbard House**, built in 1891 and home to an insurance broker and concert pianist, is far more glamorous.

Head Harbour Lighthouse LIGHTHOUSE
(210 Lighthouse Rd; $5) The oldest surviving lighthouse in New Brunswick, and one of the most photographed, this 51ft structure was built in 1829 and decorated with a distinctive St George red cross. Also called East Quoddy Lighthouse, you can visit and climb it at low tide only; tide water comes in here at 5ft per hour and can leave you stranded. Whales are regular visitors offshore and many people sit along the rocky coast with binoculars enjoying the sea breezes.

Mulholland Park Lighthouse LIGHTHOUSE
(81 Narrows Rd; ⊘10am-6pm) A favorite spot for seal-watching, the diminutive Mulholland Lighthouse was built in 1884 to guide ships through Lubec Narrows. Next door the Marine Interpretive Centre displays info on local marine life and the work of the Whale Emergency Network that operates off the island.

Herring Cove Provincial Park PARK
FREE On the southeastern side of the island, Herring Cove Provincial Park has 10km of walking trails and a rocky-sandy beach arching for 1.5km. A century ago, this was the stomping ground of the wealthy who would follow the 1.9km **Gibraltar Trail** to Glenseven Lake, which separates the forest from the sea and was once the site of a teahouse. There is also a golf-course restaurant, campground and picnic tables here.

Island Cruises Whale Watch CRUISE
(☑506-752-1107; www.bayoffundywhales.com; 62 Harbour Head Rd, Wilson's Beach; adult/child $58/48; ⊘mid-Jun–Oct) Offers daily 2½-hour whale-watching cruises with guaranteed sightings.

🛏 Sleeping & Eating

Herring Cove Provincial Park CAMPGROUND $
(☑506-752-7010; www.campobello.com/cmpgrdfe.html; 136 Herring Cove Rd; tent/RV sites $28/31, rustic shelter $43; ⊘Jun-Sep) This 76-site park on the eastern side of the island, 3km from

the Deer Island ferry, has some nice secluded sites in a forest setting, plus there's a sandy beach and ample hiking.

Owen House B&B B&B $$
(☑506-752-2977; www.owenhouse.ca; 11 Welshpool St, Welshpool; d private/shared bath from $115/105; 🅿) This large, wooden manor on the water hales from yesteryear, complete with antique spool beds made up with quilts, cozy reading nooks and lots of windows looking out to the ocean.

The Pier CANADIAN $
(☑506-752-2200; www.facebook.com/thepierwaterfront; 6 Pollac Cove Rd; mains $9-18; ⊘11:30am-9pm) It's a difficult choice whether to eat inside the nautically themed dining room with big windows and regular live music, or outside on the killer patio alongside the ocean. Filling burgers and smoked or baked seafood dinners are strong contenders on the menu and local craft beers are on tap. There's a kids' menu, too.

The Prince Cafe CAFE $
(459 Rte 774, Roosevelt Campobello National Park; meals $10-14; ⊘10am-4pm mid-May–mid-Oct) Next to Roosevelt's Cottage, get your lunch canteen-style. On a nice day, sit on the verandah for a sea view. Soups, salads, sandwiches and baking is all freshly prepared and scrumptious. We can't help but think that even Franklin would approve.

Family Fisheries Restaurant SEAFOOD $$
(1977 Rte 774, Wilson's Beach; mains $6-18; ⊘11:30am-9pm Apr-Sep) Part of a fresh-fish market, this ultra-casual seafood shack specializes in fish-and-chips (all the seafood is caught by family members), plus lip-smacking chowders and lobster grilled cheese.

ℹ Information

Visitor Center (☑506-752-2922; www.fdr.net; Hwy 774; ⊘10am-5pm) Co-billed as an Adventure Centre, this is principally an information center for the Roosevelt Campobello International Park with maps and information on local flora and wildlife. Nevertheless, they also carry information on activities and accommodation elsewhere on the island.

ℹ Getting There & Away

East Coast Ferries (p406) connects Deer Island to Welshpool (25 minutes, half-hourly) on Campobello Island. In reality, it's a tugboat pulling and pushing a barge across the open sea. The island has no gas station; arrive prepared.

NEW BRUNSWICK CAMPOBELLO ISLAND

MADSCI/GETTY IMAGES ©

1. Old City Market (p415)
One of New Brunswick's top markets is located in Saint John and is home to produce, artisan and souvenir stalls.

2. Hopewell Rocks (p418)
Sandstone erosion formations rising from the ocean floor, the Rocks resemble giant arches, stone mushrooms and animals.

3. St Andrews By-The-Sea (p402)
A genteel summer resort town on the Bay of Fundy, it has a colorful history and feels much like a living museum.

4. Kings Landing (p394)
A surreal step back in time, this recreated village has staff role-playing people who lived and worked here.

Grand Manan Island

Grand Manan is a peaceful, unspoiled place. There are no fast-food restaurants, no night-clubs, no traffic lights and no traffic. Just a ruggedly beautiful coastline of high cliffs and sandy coves, spruce forests and fields of long grass. Wonderful lighthouses, including the famous Swallowtail Lighthouse, stand guard above cliffs, looking out over the fishing weirs. Along the eastern shore and joined by a meandering coastal road sit a string of pretty and prosperous fishing villages. There is plenty of fresh sea air, amazing beaches and that rare and precious commodity in the modern world: silence, broken only by the rhythmic ocean surf. Some people make it a day trip, but lingering is recommended.

◉ Sights

★ **Swallowtail Lighthouse**　　　LIGHTHOUSE
(www.swallowtaillighthouse.com; 50 Lighthouse Rd; adult/under 12yr $5/free; ◷ 10am-6pm Jul & Aug) Clinging to the clifftop about 1km north of the ferry wharf, atmospheric Swallowtail Lighthouse (1860) is the island's signature vista. Climb down 53 stairs and across a wooden footbridge to enter. Inside you'll find tales of shipwrecks and survivors, artifacts left by lighthouse keepers' families, and fascinating equipment from yesteryear. Climb four flights of curved stairs plus a ladder to the light at the tippy top. If you want to visit a lighthouse, here's the one.

Fishing Weirs　　　LANDMARK
Those round contraptions of wooden posts that you see dotting the waters around Grand Manan are based on the design of ancient fishing traps; some of those you see date back to the 19th century. They were formerly labeled with names such as 'Ruin,' 'Winner,' 'Outside Chance' and 'Spite,' evoking the heartbreak of relying on an indifferent sea for a living.

Grand Manan Art Gallery　　　GALLERY
(☑ 506-662-3662; www.grandmananartgallery. com; 21 Cedar St, Castalia; adult/child $2/free; ◷ noon-6pm Mon-Sat, 1pm-5pm Sun mid-Jun–late Sep) Housed in what looks like a 1970s church, this lovely, nonprofit local gallery showcases local and regional artists, as well as well-known historic and emerging figures. Exhibits change regularly. Watch for a sign off the main highway, just south of North Head.

Grand Manan Historical Museum　　　MUSEUM
(☑ 506-662-3524; www.grandmananmuseum.ca; 1141 Rte 776, Grand Harbour; adult/student & senior $5/3; ◷ 9am-5pm Mon-Fri Jun-Sep, plus 9am-5pm Sat, 1-5pm Sun Jul & Aug) This museum makes a good destination on a foggy day. Its diverse collection of local artifacts provides a quick primer on island history. You can see a display on shipwreck lore and the original kerosene lamp from nearby Gannet Rock lighthouse (1904). There is also a room stuffed with 200-plus taxidermied birds (including the now-extinct passenger pigeon).

Seal Cove　　　HISTORIC SITE
For a century, smoked herring was king on Grand Manan. A thousand men and women worked splitting, stringing and drying fish in 300 smokehouses up and down the island. The last smokehouse shut down in 1996 but you can still see many clustered around the tidal creek mouth at tiny Seal Cove village.

☞ Tours

Sea Watch Tours　　　BIRDWATCHING
(☑ 877-662-8552, 506-662-8552; www.seawatch tours.com; Seal Cove Fisherman's Wharf; Machias Seal Island per person $150, whale-watching adult/ child $75/55; ◷ Mon-Sat late Jun-late Sep) From late June until the end of July, make the pilgrimage out to isolated **Machias Seal Island** to see the Atlantic puffins waddle and play on their home turf. Access is limited to 15 visitors a day, so reserve well in advance. Getting onto the island can be tricky, as the waves are high and the rocks slippery. Wear sturdy shoes. Tours to see humpback, finback and Atlantic right whales run from July until the end of September.

Adventure High　　　KAYAKING
(☑ 506-662-3563; www.adventurehigh.com; 83 Rte 776, North Head; half-/full-day tours $65/110, evening tours $45, bicycles per half-day/day/week $18/25/125; ◷ May-Oct) This outfitter offers tours of the Grand Manan coastline ranging from lovely two-hour sunset paddles to multiday Bay of Fundy adventures. In addition to high-quality mountain bikes, they also rent double bikes and bike trailers.

⮕ Sleeping

Anchorage Camping　　　CAMPGROUND $
(☑ 506-662-7022; https://parcsnbparks.ca; 136 Anchorage Rd, Anchorage; tent/RV sites $24/26; ◷ May-Sep) Family-friendly camping in a large field surrounded by the tall evergreens of Anchorage Provincial Park. Located be-

tween Grand Harbour and Seal Cove, the campground has a kitchen shelter, playground, laundry and a long pebbly beach. The area adjoins marshes, which comprise a migratory bird sanctuary, and there are several short hiking trails and bird hides.

★ **Compass Rose** B&B $$
(📞506-662-3563; www.compassroseinn.com; 65 Rte 776, North Head; r $100-165; 🅿 ❄ 🖥) It's hard to go wrong at this quaint little spot, which has seven airy rooms with wrought-iron beds, sea views and access to the beach. It's within walking distance of the ferry dock, and has one of the island's most tasteful restaurants (mains $20 to $25) with big windows, daily fresh menus and sumptuous desserts.

Island Home B&B B&B $$
(📞506-662-8777; http://islandhomebnb.ca; 22 Rte 776, North Head; r $125; 🕙year-round; ❄ 🖥) Directly across from the ferry and set in a tranquil yard, this six-bedroom guesthouse is like stepping into the pages of a gorgeous magazine layout. Beautiful linens, furnishings and bathrooms will make you want to stay in all day. There's also a lovely patio, sitting room and dining room where equally beautiful breakfasts are served. It shouldn't be surprising that a professional decorator lives here.

Inn at Whale Cove INN $$
(📞506-662-3181; www.whalecovecottages.ca; Whistle Rd, North Head; s/d incl breakfast $145/155; 🕙May-Oct; ❄ 🖥) 'Serving rusticators since 1910,' including writer Willa Cather, who wrote several of her novels here in the 1920s and '30s. The main lodge (built in 1816) and six shingled cottages (two with fully equipped kitchens) retain the charm of that earlier era. They are fitted with polished pine floors and stone fireplaces, antiques, chintz curtains and well-stocked bookshelves.

🍴 Eating

The island's dining options are decent if not plentiful in summer but nearly nonexistent in the off-season. The majority are found around North Head or south in Grand Harbour. Be sure to try dulse, a dark-purple seaweed harvested locally and eaten like crisps (chips) by locals. Chefs use it as a seasoning. You might even see a 'DLT sandwich' on the menu (yep, that's dulse instead of bacon).

Old Well House Cafe CAFE $
(📞506-662-3232; www.facebook.com/theoldwellhousecafe; 56 Rte 776, North Head; meals $9-15;

🕙8am-4pm) This shingled cottage from 1832 is a local meeting place. Get comfy on a couch, perch at a wooden table or relax outside at a picnic table. Order excellent coffees, homemade soups, grilled wraps and some of the best baking you'll find in New Brunswick (try the flourless peanut butter cookies). The bagels are shipped from Montréal.

Sunrise Seafoods SEAFOOD $
(📞506-660-0156; Woodwards Cove Breakwater Rd; $8-18; 🕙11am-9pm) Right down by the fisheries, with a smokehouse pluming into the air, this place is the real deal. Get your chowders, chips, scallops and clams, lobster roll and fish, all as fresh as fresh can be. There are a few picnic tables or take it to go. Cash only.

Trapped SEAFOOD $$
(📞506-662-3696; 7 Norman Rd, Grand Harbour; meals $18-24; 🕙noon-7pm Mon-Sat Jul & Aug) A family-owned fishery since 1969, these guys know their lobster. Chill out on the deck with a beer or a smoothie and hot lobster or spinach dip to share. The 'Trapped' clothing in the attached store makes for great souvenirs.

Inn at Whale Cove CANADIAN $$$
(📞506-662-3181; www.whalecovecottages.ca; Whistle Rd; mains $22-28; 🕙5-7pm) Wonderful food in a relaxed country setting on Whale Cove. The menu changes daily, but includes mouthwatering upscale meals such as pulled pork and tagliatelle, seafood bouillabaisse and a to-die-for hazelnut crème caramel for dessert. Come early and have a cocktail by the fire in the cozy, old-fashioned parlor.

Roland's Sea Vegetables MARKET
(📞506-662-3468; 174 Hill Rd; per pound $11.50; 🕙9am-5pm year-round) Grand Manan is one of the few remaining producers of dulse, a type of seaweed that is used as a snack food or seasoning. Dulse gatherers wade among the rocks at low tide to pick the seaweed, then lay it out on beds of rocks to dry, just as they've been doing for hundreds of years. For three generations, Roland's has been producing dulse and shipping it as far as Japan and Hawaii. Buy it here by the bag full.

ℹ Information

Visitor Information Centre (📞506-662-3442; www.grandmannb.com; 130 Rte 776, North Head; 🕙mid-Jun–late Aug) Locally run tourist organization that has maps, brochures and ferry schedules.

❶ Getting There & Away

The only way to get from Blacks Harbour on the mainland to North Head on Grand Manan is by a private ferry company, **Coastal Transport** (☑506-662-3724; http://grandmanan.coastaltransport.ca; adult/child/car/bicycle $12/6/36/4.10). The crossing takes 1½ hours, and there are around three to four daily departures from each port in summer. Reserve and pay in advance as it gets busy. It's best to pay for a return trip, rather than one way, so you don't get stuck on the island. Watch for harbor porpoises and whales en route.

The ferry dock is within walking distance of several hotels, restaurants, shops and tour operators. To explore the whole of the island, bring your own car, as there is no rental company on Grand Manan.

❶ Getting Around

The ferry disembarks at the village of North Head at the northern end of the island. The main road, Rte 776, runs 28.5km down the length of the island along the eastern shore. You can drive from end to end in about 45 minutes. The western side of Grand Manan is uninhabited and more or less impenetrable: a sheer rock wall rising out of the sea, backed by dense forest and bog, broken only at Dark Harbour where a steep road drops down to the water's edge. Hiking trails provides access to this wilderness.

Adventure High (p410) rents out bicycles. The roads are winding and keen cyclists will enjoy the undulating routes.

SAINT JOHN

POP 67,600

Saint John has long been a force to be reckoned with. Once a gritty port city, and the original economic engine of the province, it has since cleaned up its act. Its lively historic core is home to one of New Brunswick's top markets and there's a dynamic restaurant and pub scene worth exploring. Wander past beautifully preserved redbrick and sandstone 19th-century architecture, down narrow side streets that offer glimpses of the sea, or along the harbor where the mighty Saint John and Kennebecasis Rivers empty into the Bay of Fundy. Check out the city's unique museums and zip-line over the Reversing Falls. Sure, some of the surrounding natural beauty is diminished by pulp mill smokestacks and an oil refinery but Saint John will welcome you with open arms and knows how to show you a good time.

◉ Sights

★ New Brunswick Museum   MUSEUM
(www.nbm-mnb.ca; 1 Market Sq; adult/student/family $10/6/22; ◷9am-5pm Mon-Wed & Fri, to 9pm Thu, 10am-5pm Sat, noon-5pm Sun) The New Brunswick Museum has a varied and interesting collection. There's a surprisingly captivating section on industrial history with 1908 figurines by Acadian Alfred Morneault and an outstanding section on marine life, including a life-size specimen of a whale. There are also hands-on exhibits, models of old sailing ships and a stunning collection of Canadian and international artwork on the top floor. This is the province's top museum and worth a visit.

Reversing Rapids   NATURAL FEATURE
The Bay of Fundy's phenomenal tides are a defining characteristic along this coast. Here, where the Saint John River nears this tidal bay, one of the province's best-known sights occurs. Known as the Reversing Rapids, the real action is happening underwater, where a 61m waterfall drops into a plunge pool. What you see from above is the high tides of the Bay of Fundy colliding with the strong river current, causing rapids, standing waves and the water to flow upstream.

Irving Nature Park   PARK
(www.facebook.com/IrvingNaturePark; Sand Cove Rd; ◷8am-dusk May-Oct) For those with a vehicle and who like nature, Irving Nature Park, 9km southwest of Saint John, has rugged, unspoiled coastal topography. It's also a remarkable place for bird-watching, with hundreds of species regularly spotted, while seals sometimes gather on the rocks offshore. Seven trails lead around beaches, cliffs, woods, mudflats, marsh and rocks. Wear sturdy footwear.

Loyalist House   HISTORIC BUILDING
(☑506-652-3590; www.loyalisthouse.com; 120 Union St; adult/child/family $5/2/7; ◷10am-5pm late May-Oct) Dating from 1810, this Georgian-style Loyalist House was maintained with minimal changes for five generations until the family moved out in 1959. As one of the city's oldest unchanged buildings and a survivor of the 1877 fire, it's now a museum, depicting the Loyalist period. Tours led by guides in period dress take 30 to 45 minutes.

🏃 Activities & Tours

Saint John Adventures   ADVENTURE SPORTS
(☑506-634-9477; www.saintjohnadventures.ca; Fallsview Park; per person $65) Five lines are strung between six towers allowing you to

Saint John

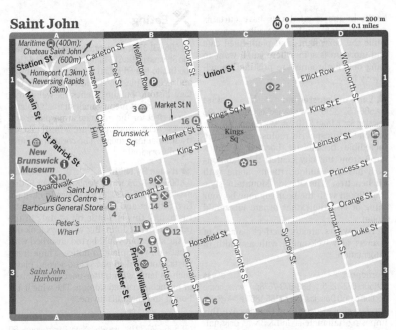

Saint John

◎ Top Sights

◎ Sights

◎ Sleeping

◎ Eating

◎ Drinking & Nightlife

◎ Entertainment

◎ Shopping

zip over the Reversing Rapids on Saint John River. The zip-line course takes one to two hours.

Walks 'n' Talks with David Goss WALKING
(☑506-672-8601; walks free-$5; ⏱7pm Tue & Fri Jun-Sep) Local storyteller David Goss leads themed walks throughout the city and natural environments. The walks have so much flair that locals as well as visitors frequent the fun. Departure locations and hours vary; check with the visitor center. Friday-night ghost walks leave from New River Beach.

🛏 Sleeping

Saint John motels sit primarily along Manawagonish Rd, 7km west of uptown. There are also a couple of upscale chain hotels uptown, some great B&Bs and a fabulous hostel.

⭐ **BunkHaus Hostel** HOSTEL $
(☑506-646-9895; www.bunkhaushostel.com; 36 Water St; dm/private $40/90; ⏱year-round; ❋🛜) Super-hip BunkHaus is just what this city needed: clean, budget accommodation in the heart of downtown. Solid wooden

bunks in the co-ed dorms have curtains and individual outlets for ultra privacy, while the cozy, light- and plant-filled cafe and taproom is somewhere you'll want to hang out. Bathrooms are pristine but relatively few.

★ **Earle of Leinster Inn** B&B $$
(☎506-652-3275; www.earleofleinster.com; 96 Leinster St; r from $110; 🅿🏧🛜) Come for the original, atmospheric rooms; stay for the incredible breakfasts. Located a quick stroll from the city center, this fabulous B&B has nine unique rooms, some with kitchenettes. The Rocky Mountain–style Pine Room with the bear rug may be your thing or else the rather ornate Fitzgerald Room.

The owners are the perfect balance of discreet and welcoming with a wealth of information.

Homeport B&B $$
(☎506-672-7255, 888-678-7678; www.homeportinn.ca; 60 Douglas Ave; r $135-180; 🅿🛜🏧🛜) Perched above once-grand Douglas Ave, this imposing Italianate-style B&B was originally two separate mansions belonging to shipbuilder brothers. It has a boutique-hotel vibe, with a stately parlor, a full bar and 10 elegant old-world guest rooms (try to snag the lovely Veranda Queen). It's about 1km west of the uptown peninsula, en route to the Reversing Rapids.

Mahogany Manor B&B $$
(☎506-636-8000; http://mahoganymanor.ca; 220 Germain St; d from $125; 🅿🛜🛜) Tucked into the heart of Uptown, this beautiful Victorian B&B is a wonderful place to call home. Rooms are fairly standard but comfortable, and there are antique sitting rooms and sun porches to relax in. The upbeat owners know more about the city than you'll be able to absorb.

Chateau Saint John BUSINESS HOTEL $$
(☎506-644-4444; www.chateausaintjohn.ca; 369 Rockland Rd; r from $185; 🅿🏧🛜) Situated on a main road on the edge of the CBD, behemoth Chateau Saint John has large, spacious rooms and city views. Professional service and the price-to-quality ratio make it a good choice. It's a 15-minute walk into town and there's ample parking on-site. It's popular with groups and business people.

 Eating

★ **Port City Royal** INTERNATIONAL $$
(☎506-631-3714; www.portcityroyal.com; 45 Grannan St; small plates $12-18, mains $23-29; ⏲4-11pm Tue-Thu, to late Fri & Sat) With exposed brick and peeling plaster, the interior of this vintage historic building defies its well-cared-for and elegant menu. Small shareable plates are perfect for the intimate atmosphere and the ever-changing mains are a fresh take on traditional ingredients. The cocktail menu is equally original.

★ **Italian By Night** ITALIAN $$
(☎506-214-8259; www.italianbynight.com; 97 Germain St; mains $15-30; ⏲5-9pm Mon-Thu, to 10pm Fri & Sat) Big and open, and with a slightly rustic feel, this is a little bit of Italy in the center of Saint John. Big windows look out to the street but you'll be too absorbed with what's on your plate to notice. Think fresh pasta, stone-baked pizzas and second plates such as lamb with butter-poached potatoes or pistachio-crusted salmon. The wine list is honed and cocktails divine.

East Coast Bistro FRENCH $$
(☎506-696-3278; www.eastcoastbistro.com; 60 Prince William St; mains $24-30; ⏲11am-9pm Tue-Thu, to 10pm Fri, 10am-10pm Sat) Combining French flair with local ingredients, this chic, brick-walled bistro is all about flavor. Watch elegant dishes featuring seafood, duck or steak being created in the open kitchen.

Billy's Seafood Company SEAFOOD $$$
(www.billysseafood.com; 49 Charlotte St; mains lunch $15-30, dinner $24-36; ⏲11am-10pm Mon-Thu, to 11pm Fri & Sat, 4-10pm Sun, closed Sun Jan-Mar, raw bar 6-9pm Mon-Sat) Next to the City Market, locals and visitors alike come here to dine on satisfying seafood dishes. Try bayou seafood stew, white-wine garlic mussels or lobster with warm butter. Oysters at the raw bar are $2.50 a pop. In summer, the polished restaurant opens up onto a sidewalk patio.

Saint John Ale House MODERN AMERICAN $$$
(www.sjah.ca; 1 Market Sq; mains $18-40; ⏲11am-late Mon-Fri, 10:30am-late Sat & Sun) On summer evenings this place is popular for its big, wharfside patio and long list of beers on tap. Head upstairs for a menu of locally sourced dishes such as bacon maple scallops, market chowder or giant lobster roll. It's also a favorite spot for weekend brunch.

🍸 Drinking & Nightlife

⭐ **Rouge** COFFEE

(📞506-639-6011; 36 Grannan Lane; ⊙7am-6pm Mon-Fri, 8am-5pm Sat & Sun) Hands down the best coffee in town, if not the province. If your curiosity peaks, you can also try elder-flower mimosa, pink lemonade or a variety of cold brews. The funky interior is entire-ly welcoming or the flower-bedecked patio has outdoor seating. You'll find it tucked off Grannan Lane.

Picaroons BREWERY

(📞506-648-9834; http://picaroons.ca; 32 Canterbury St; ⊙10am-10pm Mon & Tue, to 11pm Wed-Sat, noon-8pm Sun) With a mothership in Fredericton, this cool brewery creates six beers on-site. With a long wooden table wound around the room and additional barrel ta-bles next to big, often open windows, it a great place to chill out. If you like it a lot, grab a growler to go.

Happinez Wine Bar BAR

(www.happinezwinebar.com; 42 Princess St; ⊙4pm-midnight Wed & Thu, to 1am Fri, 5pm-1am Sat) If you want a break from beer, duck into this intimate little wine bar. The list is main-ly international, and while cellar wines by the bottle come with a hefty price tag, there's a good selection available by the glass.

Big Tide Brewing Company BREWERY

(www.bigtidebrew.com; 47 Princess St; ⊙11am-midnight Mon-Sat, 3-9pm Sun) This subterrane-an brewpub is a local hangout and a cozy spot for a pint (try the Confederation Cream Ale or the Whistlepig Stout). They have five beers on tap that are brewed right here.

Imperial Theatre THEATER

(📞506-674-4100; www.imperialtheatre.nb.ca; 24 Kings Sq S) Now restored to its original 1913 splendor, this is the city's premier venue for performances ranging from classical music to live theater.

🛍 Shopping

⭐ **Old City Market** MARKET

(📞658 2820; 47 Charlotte St; ⊙7:30am-6pm Mon-Fri, to 5pm Sat) Wedged between North and South Market Sts, this sense-stunning food hall has been home to wheeling and dealing since 1876. The impressive brick in-terior is packed with produce stalls, baker-ies, fishmongers and butcher shops, as well as numerous counters selling the full meal deal. There are also plenty of skilled artisans with stalls, making this a top place to pick up unique souvenirs.

ℹ Information

MEDICAL SERVICES

Saint John Regional Hospital (📞506-648-6000; 400 University Ave; ⊙24hr) Located northwest of the town center.

POST

Main Post Office (126 Prince William St)

TOURIST INFORMATION

Saint John Visitors Centre – Barbours Gen-eral Store (St Andrew's Bicentennial Green; ⊙10am-6pm mid-May–Sep) Conveniently located in the old-fashioned Barbours General Store, at the central St Andrew's Bicentennial Green.

Saint John Visitors Centre – Reversing Rap-ids (450 Bridge Rd; ⊙9am-6pm mid-May–Sep, to 7pm Jul & Aug)

Visitor & Convention Bureau (📞506-658-2990; www.discoversaintjohn.com; City Hall, 15 Market Sq; ⊙9am-6pm mid-May–mid-Oct, to 7pm Jul & Aug) Knowledgeable, friendly staff. Ask for the self-guided walking-tour pamphlets.

ℹ Getting There & Away

AIR

The airport is 5km east of town on Loch Lomond Rd toward St Martins. Air Canada runs daily flights to Toronto, Montréal and Halifax.

BOAT

The Bay Ferries (p393) sails daily between Saint John and Digby, Nova Scotia, year-round. The three-hour crossing can save a lot of driving.

Arrive early or call ahead for vehicle reser-vations, as the ferry is very busy in July and August. Even with a reservation, arrive an hour before departure. Walk-ons and cyclists should be OK at any time. There's a restaurant and a bar on board.

BUS

Long-haul bus services are operated by **Mari-time Bus** (📞506-672-2055; www.maritimebus. com; 125 Station St; ⊙8am-8pm Mon-Fri, 9am-8pm Sat & Sun). Routes include Fredericton ($25.50, 1½ hours) and Moncton ($34, two to four hours).

ℹ Getting Around

Downtown (known as Uptown) Saint John sits on a square, hilly peninsula between the mouth of the Saint John River and Courtenay Bay. Kings Sq marks the nucleus of town, and its pathways duplicate the pattern of the Union Jack.

West over the Harbour Bridge is Saint John West. Many of the street names in this section of the city are identical to those of Saint John proper, and to avoid confusion, they end in a west designation, such as Charlotte St W. Saint John West has the ferries to Digby, Nova Scotia.

EASTERN FUNDY SHORE

Much of the rugged, unspoiled Eastern Fundy Shore from Saint John to Hopewell Cape has been incorporated into the Fundy Trail Parkway, a 30km-long road with sweeping coastal views and countless trails to explore by foot or bike. Nature-lovers will be enchanted by this marvelous coast, edged by dramatic cliffs and tides.

The plan to link the parkway to Fundy National Park has been delayed due to the discovery of traditional Mi'kmaq hunting grounds; rerouting is underway with hopes the link will happen in late 2021. Until then, an inland detour by Sussex is necessary.

St Martins

POP 276

A 40km drive east of Saint John, St Martins is a winsome seaside hamlet surrounded by steep cliffs and flower-studded pastureland. Once a major wooden shipbuilding center, this relaxed community springs to life in summer. Hikers, bikers and scenic-drivers flock to the 30km Fundy Trail Parkway, which starts just 10km east of the village and winds along a jaw-dropping stretch of coastline. In town, check out the impressive red sandstone sea caves at Mac's Beach, accessible by foot when the tide is low. The village's twin covered bridges are also a popular photo op.

🏃 Activities

Red Rock Adventure OUTDOORS
(📞 506-833-2231; www.bayoffundyadventures. com; 415 Main St; walking tours per person $25-130, kayaking/boat trips $65; ⊙ 9am-5pm) Located opposite the St Martins Wharf, Red Rock Adventures offers walking tours, including multiday treks in the parkway, kayaking adventures and scenic boat trips.

River Bay Adventures KAYAKING
(📞 506-663-9530; www.riverbayadventures.com; tours from $80) Runs two- to three-hour guided sea-kayaking trips from St Martins Harbour to the sea caves at nearby Mac's Beach, under the bridges, along the coast and to nearby islands.

🛏 Sleeping & Eating

Fundy Woods Campground & Cottages CAMPGROUND $
(www.fundywoods.com; 2644 Rte 111; tent sites $30, RV sites $40-50, cottages $120; ⊙ mid-May– Sep; 🐾🐕) Just a few minutes from Main Street, this wooded campground offers friendly services and fully kitted-out cottages that sleep four.

Salmon River B&B B&B $$
(📞 506-833-1110; www.salmonriverbandb.com; 4 Snows Lane; r $115-125; ⊙ mid-May–mid-Oct; 🐾🐕) Eight plain but pleasant rooms named after local personalities. It's in a handy location bang in the middle of town, above Fiori's restaurant.

Octopus Ice Cream ICE CREAM $
(www.octopusicecream.com; 404 Main St; $3-8; ⊙ 10am-7pm May-Oct) Come to this place right on the harbor to be spoiled by choice. Black cherry, pistachio, chocolate peanut butter and countless other flavors come as cones, milkshakes, banana splits and sundaes. And then there's the toppings. Be sure to try the homemade fish-shaped waffle cones.

The Caves SEAFOOD $
(www.cavesrestaurant.com; 82 Big Salmon River Rd; mains $10-27; ⊙ 11am-7pm May, Jun, Sep & Oct, to 8:30pm Jul & Aug) One of two seaside spots known for their creamy chowder sitting side by side on Mac's Beach. Get your fill of seafood with toasted lobster tail or seafood casserole, or grab a salad or burger, all served next to the gorgeous sand with views of the caves.

Seaside Restaurant & Take Out SEAFOOD $$
(80 Big Salmon River Rd; mains $10-20; ⊙ 11am-8pm Mar-Nov) Right on Mac's Beach, the simple but spacious Seaside Restaurant serves fish-and-chips, scallops, chowder and more next to the sand and with views of the caves. Now you know you are on holiday.

Fundy National Park

Fundy National Park (www.pc.gc.ca/eng/pn-np/nb/fundy; daily permit adult/under 17yr/family $7.80/free/15.70; ⊙ May-Oct) is understandably the region's most popular sight. Highlights include the world's highest tides, the irregularly eroded sandstone cliffs and the wide beach at low tide that makes exploring the shore for small marine life and debris such a treat. The park is delightfully wooded

DON'T MISS

FUNDY TRAIL PARKWAY

Stretching east from St Martins for 30 glorious kilometers, this magnificent **parkway** (www.fundytrailparkway.com; adult/youth $9.50/5.50; ⊘ 9am-5pm mid-May–Jun & Sep, 8am-8pm Jul–mid-Aug, 9am-7pm late Aug) provides big ocean views and access to a large network of trails and footpaths along the Bay of Fundy coast. The parkway offers numerous viewpoints, picnic areas and beach access points while trails lead to waterfalls, suspension bridges and more sandy beaches. There are hopes to extend the parkway to Fundy National Park by late 2021.

At Big Salmon River visit the **Big Salmon River Interpretive Center** (Fundy Trail Pkwy; ⊘ 9am-5pm mid-May–Jun & Sep, 8am-8pm Jul–mid-Aug, 9am-7pm late Aug), which has exhibits from when a logging community lived here, plus lots of information on hikes. Nearby, a suspension bridge crosses over the crystal-clear river, leading to the 61km Fundy Footpath, a solid five-day trek from Big Salmon River to Goose River in Fundy National Park for which you must register at either end.

If you're looking for something a little less giant, try the 4.4km **Long Beach Footpath** or the beautiful and non-strenuous 2.3km trail to **Walton Glen Gorge** beginning at the end of the parkway. Running parallel to the parkway is an accessible 10km-long multiuse trail for walkers and cyclists. In the off-season, the main gate is closed, but you can park at the entrance and hike or pedal in. On weekends, a shuttle runs within the parkway to various trail heads.

and lush, and features an extensive network of impressive hiking trails and lakes. Unusual for a national park, you'll also find a motel, a golf course and an outdoor saltwater swimming pool.

🏃 Activities

Hiking

Fundy features 120km of walking trails, where it's possible to enjoy anything from a short stroll to a three-day trek. Several trails require hikers to ford rivers, so be prepared.

The most popular backpacking route is the **Fundy Circuit**, a three-day trek of 45km through the heart of the park. Hikers generally spend their first night at Tracy Lake and their second at Bruin Lake, returning via the Upper Salmon River. You must reserve your wilderness campsites online (https://reservation.pc.gc.ca; $20 per night).

Enjoyable day hikes in Fundy National Park include the **Matthews Head Loop**, a 4.5km stretch with the nicest coastal views of the park (ranked moderate to difficult); and the **Third Vault Falls Trail**, a challenging one-way hike of 3.7km to the park's tallest falls. Alternatively, a short and pleasant stroll along a boardwalk takes you to **Dickson Falls**.

For serious, experienced hikers, the most popular one-night backcountry trek is the **Goose River Trail**. It joins the **Fundy Footpath** (not to be confused with Fundy Circuit). The Fundy Footpath is an undeveloped five-day wilderness trek and one of the most difficult in the province. While you can cycle to Goose River, the trail beyond can only be done on foot.

Pick up maps and trail condition information at Headquarters Visitors Centre (p418). In summer rangers lead a variety of family-friendly educational programs, including night hikes.

Mountain Biking

Mountain biking is permitted on 10 trails, including both easy routes suitable for beginners and moderate trails for those after a challenge. Park maps detail where bikes are permitted; on all trails, you share the path with hikers. Adult and child mountain bikes can be rented at Chignecto South (half/full day $30/50).

Swimming

The ocean is pretty bracing here. A solar-heated saltwater **swimming pool** (off Wolfe Point Rd; ⊘ 11am-6:30pm Jul & Aug), located near the park's southern entrance, was recently renovated and is the perfect place to cool off.

🛏 Sleeping

Chignecto North CAMPGROUND $
(☎ 877-737-3783; http://reservation.pc.gc.ca; tent/RV sites $26/36) This beautifully wooded campground (with 251 sites in total) is popular with families as it has playgrounds and

HOPEWELL ROCKS

The **Hopewell Rocks** (www.thehope wellrocks.ca; off Hwy 114; adult/child/ family $10/8/25.50, shuttle per person $2; ⊙9am-5pm May-Oct, longer hours in summer; ⓘ) are bizarre sandstone erosion formations known as 'flowerpots,' rising from the ocean floor. They resemble giant arches, stone mushrooms and animals. Many come to marvel at their Dr Seussian look, making the rocks New Brunswick's top attraction and certainly one of its most crowded. You can only walk amid the rocks at low tide; at high tide, the rock towers are still visible from the well-trafficked trails that wind through the woods above, or you can join a kayaking tour to bob around them.

Check the tide tables at any tourist office or area hotel. From the interpretive center at the entrance to the rocks, you can walk 20 minutes or take a shuttle that stops steps away from the main viewing deck. It is free for those with a disability and anyone accompanying them. Hopewell Rocks is located 38km southwest of Moncton.

good facilities. Sites are secluded and private, despite its generous size, and it's just a 4km drive from the beach. There are also yurts and Otentiks (both $100).

Point Wolfe Campground   CAMPGROUND $
(☑877-737-3783; http://reservation.pc.gc.ca; tent sites $26, RV sites $33-35, Otentiks $100) This lovely campground (with 146 sites and 10 Otentiks), 8km southwest of the Headquarters Visitor Center, is a little more secluded than the park's other main campgrounds and it's the closest of all the campgrounds to the water. Twelve sites have water and electricity for RVs.

Headquarters Campground   CAMPGROUND $
(☑877-737-3783; http://reservation.pc.gc.ca; tent/ RV sites $26/35, Otentiks/yurts $100/115) Of all the campsites in Fundy National Park, this is the most mainstream, and the only one close to both the beach and Alma village. It has 101 sites and offers yurts and Otentiks for those who don't have their own camping gear. It's not entirely wooded but the tent sites are grassy and a couple have excellent bay views.

Fundy Highlands Motel & Chalets   CABIN, MOTEL $$
(☑506-887-2930, 888-883-8639; www.fundyhigh lands.com; 8714 Hwy 114; d $110, cabins $125-135; ⊙May-Oct) The only private accommodations in Fundy National Park, this spot has charming little cabins, all with decks, kitchenettes and superlative views. On the same premises is a small, well-kept motel that offers big rooms with kitchenettes that open onto a lovely lawn. While it's not luxurious, it's spotless and has friendly owners and an appealing touch of retro 1950s.

✖ Eating

Be prepared to bring your own supplies. The village of Alma does a good job at servicing the park; while there aren't supermarkets, it has many restaurants, a couple of decent takeouts and a good bakery.

❶ Information

Headquarters Visitors Centre (☑506-887-6000; Rte 114 & Wolfe Point Rd; ⊙10am-6pm May & Aug-Oct, to 8pm Jun & Jul) Just inside the park's southern entrance, the park rangers at this center have information on trail conditions, dole out maps and info and can take reservations for campsites.

❶ Getting There & Away

If heading east, it's not yet possible to drive directly along the coastline from St Martins to Fundy National Park; instead, a detour inland by Sussex is necessary. There's no public transport in the area.

Alma

POP 213

The tiny, cheerful fishing village of Alma is bustling in the summertime. A worthwhile stop in its own right, it also serves as a supply center for Fundy National Park, with accommodation, restaurants, a grocery store and laundry. Most facilities close in winter when the only one left standing is Molly Kool (OK, statue of), the first female sea captain on the continent. The beach on the edge of town offers a sandy stretch at low tide and views of the colorful fishing fleet.

Fresh Air Adventure (☑506-887-2249, 800-545-0020; www.freshairadventure.com; 16 Fundy View Dr; 2-/3hr tours from $50/62; ⊙Jun-Sep) offers myriad kayaking tours, from two-hour trips to multiday excursions, in and around Fundy. For experienced paddlers

CAPE ENRAGE

Perched at the top of a suitably windblown and rocky precipice since 1840, **Cape Enrage Lighthouse** (www.capeenrage.ca; 650 Cape Enrage Rd; adult/child $6/5; ⊙10am-6pm mid-May–Oct, to 8pm Jul & Aug) is one of the oldest in the province. The 150-year-old clifftop lightstation, with its lighthouse, former lighthouse-keeper's house (now a restaurant) and a small gallery, provides dramatic views. The more adventurous can do on-site rappelling ($90 per person for two hours) and zip-lining ($45 per person for three runs). Or you can simply wander the beach looking for fossils (low tide only).

At Mary's Point, 22km east of Cape Enrage, is the **Shepody Bay Shorebird Reserve** (Mary's Point Rd, off Hwy 915) FREE, where hundreds of thousands of shorebirds, primarily sandpipers, gather from mid-July to mid-August to fuel up before their southern migration. The interpretive center is open from late June to early September, but you can use the 6.5km of trails any time. The only way to reach the cape is with your own wheels or on a tour; there is no public transport to the cape.

and serious adventurers, they offer surf-ski wave-riding tours.

🛏 Sleeping & Eating

Alpine Motor Inn　　　MOTEL $$
(☑866-87-2052; www.alpinemotorinn.ca; 8591 Main St; r $105-160; ⊙May–mid-Oct; 🖥) This busy, renovated motel has clean, standard rooms, the majority of which have bay views. Colorful lawn chairs next to the sea are a relaxing place to be, and the staff is both helpful and welcoming.

Parkland Village Inn　　　INN $$
(☑506-887-2313; www.parklandvillageinn.com; 8601 Main St; r $125-165; ⊙May–mid-Oct; 🖥) Originally a garrison moved from Sussex in 1949, Parkland Village Inn has standard, renovated rooms, some with balconies and killer Bay of Fundy views. Breakfast is only included out of high season.

★Tipsy Tails Restaurant　　　CANADIAN $$
(☑506-887-2190; www.facebook.com/tipsytails; 8607 Main St; mains $13-30; ⊙11am-9:30pm May–mid-Oct) With a patio looking out over the marina and a chef who winters as a fisherman, this restaurant serves top-quality grub. Local seafood, PEI beef ribs and pulled pork with house-made kimchi all grace the menu. There's nothing standard about this place. Be sure to try the loaded corn on the cob.

Alma Lobster Shop　　　SEAFOOD $$
(☑506-887-1987; www.thankfultoo.com; 36 Shore Lane; mains $16-25; ⊙11am-9pm) Get your seafood straight from the source – this is where local fishing boats unload. Dine on the beach or buy it to take away, but either way check out the touch tank with its 14lb lobsters and ask to peek in the back room to see the hundreds of incoming lobsters being sorted into size.

Holy Whale Brewery　　　BREWERY
(☑506-887-1999; 8576 Main St; ⊙noon-10pm Mon-Fri, 10am-10pm Sat & Sun) Housed in a converted church, this lively brewery is making a name for itself across the Maritimes. The punchy Devil's Half Acre IPA and creamy Medusa Milk Stout are often accompanied by sessionals such as the Creamsicle Pale. You'll also find Buddha Bear Coffee Roaster here, a summertime menu and regular live music.

SOUTHEASTERN NEW BRUNSWICK

The southeastern corner of New Brunswick province is a flat coastal plain sliced by tidal rivers and salt marshes. Moncton, known as 'Hub City,' is a major crossroads with two well-known attractions where nature appears to defy gravity. Southeast, toward Nova Scotia, are significant historical and birdlife attractions.

Moncton
POP 71,900
Once a major wooden shipbuilding port and then in a slump, Moncton is now the fastest-growing city in the Maritime provinces with the motto: 'I will rise again.' And thanks to a new economy built on transportation and call centers drawn here by the bilingual workforce, it is rising quickly. Its small, red-brick downtown along the glistening banks

FORT BEAUSÉJOUR

Sitting atop a hill overlooking green fields rolling down to the Bay of Fundy and across to Nova Scotia, this **historical site** (☑506-364-5080; www.pc.gc.ca/fortbeausejour; 111 Fort Beauséjour Rd, Aulac; adult/child $3.90/free; ☉interpretive center 9am-5pm late Jun-early Sep) is well worth a visit. Built in 1751 to hold back the British and later reinforced by the British invaders, it was used as a stronghold during the American Revolution and War of 1812. The fort's unique star-shaped design, with angles and corners, made it trickier to hit. Exploring underground barracks and casement rooms makes for an atmospheric adventure.

of the Petitcodiac River has a lively pub and restaurant scene. There is also a bustling Acadian farmers market, a couple of worthwhile museums and popular nearby sights including Hopewell Rocks and Magnetic Hill. To top it off, Moncton's event calendar is full in summer.

⊙ Sights

Resurgo Place & Moncton Museum   MUSEUM

(☑506-856-4383; www.resurgo.ca; 20 Mountain Rd; adult/youth/child/family $10/7/5/24; ☉10am-5pm Mon-Sat, noon-5pm Sun, closed Mon Sep-May) This modern, engaging museum inside Resurgo Place follows the story of Moncton. Steer a car-cart over a giant floor map to see video footage and learn the history of landmarks and check out impressive artifacts such as a French Bible from 1747. The transportation exhibit is kid-tastic; drive a train, build a truck and a boat, pilot a sub and launch a rocket. Stop by the traveling exhibitions as well.

Magnetic Hill   AMUSEMENT PARK

(☑506-877-7720; Mountain Rd; per car $6; ☉8am-8pm May-Sep) There is a hint of nostalgia about Magnet Hill, one of Canada's earliest tourist attractions. It continues to draw crowds and is worth visiting purely for the novelty. Since the 1930s, motorists noticed that they had to accelerate to go downhill and coasted uphill – that gravity appeared to work in reverse. During the summer, expect a half-hour wait for your turn. There is

also a colorful boardwalk nearby with restaurants and shops, a covered bridge, water park and zoo.

Magnetic Hill is about 10km northwest of downtown off Mountain Rd.

Thomas Williams House   HISTORIC BUILDING

(☑506-857-0590; 103 Park St; entrance by donation, high tea $15; ☉house 10am-5pm, tea 11am-5pm Wed-Sun Jun-Sep) Williams arrived in Canada from England in 1864 when he was just 18. He went on to become the treasurer of the Canadian Railway. Built in 1883, the house has been restored to its former glory of the late 1800s when he lived here with his wife and 11 children. Enjoy tea or lemonade and some homemade sweets in the dining room or patio.

Acadian Museum   MUSEUM

(☑506-858-4088; Pavillon Clément-Cormier, 405 University Ave, University of Moncton; adult/student/child/family $5/3/2/10; ☉9am-5pm Mon-Fri, 1-5pm Sat & Sun Jun-Sep, 1-4:30pm Tue-Fri, 1-4pm Sat & Sun Oct-May) Follow the engaging, bilingual exhibits along the story of the Acadians from when the first French pioneers arrived in 1524, through their expulsion by the British to present day. A generous number of artifacts, interesting side tales and examples of the cultural Acadian renaissance keep it interesting.

Tidal Bore   NATURAL FEATURE

(Main St; ☉high tide, times vary) Witnessing the tidal bore is something of a right of passage for tourists. As the giant tide rises in the Bay of Fundy, it pushes upstream against the flow of the chocolate-colored Petitcodiac River. The result is a solid wave unfurling like a carpet down the riverbed in one dramatic gesture. The height of this oncoming rush can vary from just a few centimeters to over 1m; it's usually somewhere in between.

Tide times are posted everywhere, including on the digital billboard outside Tidal Bore Park – the place to see the action. You may see locals surfing the wave; in 2013 they broke a world record by riding it for 29km. Unless you're an experienced surfer with knowledge of the river, don't try it.

Blue Roof Distillers   DISTILLERY

(☑506-538-7767; www.blueroofdistillers.com; 4144 Rte 16, Malden; tours $5; ☉9am-5pm Mon, 10am-5pm Tue-Sat, noon-4pm Sun) This isn't your average potato farm. Just 10km west of Cape Jourimain, en route to Moncton, this sixth-generation farmstead has decided to

Moncton

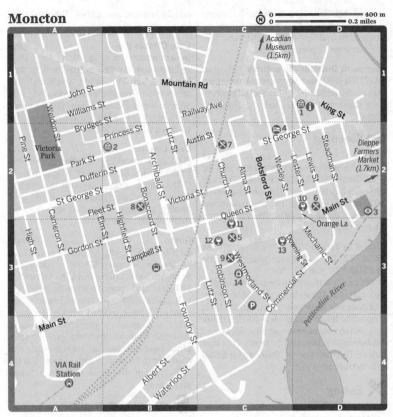

Moncton

⊙ Sights
1	Resurgo Place & Moncton Museum D1
2	Thomas Williams House B2
3	Tidal Bore D2

🛏 Sleeping
4	Glory Inn C2
	L'Hotel St James .... (see 11)

🍴 Eating
5	Cafe C'est la Vie C3
6	Café Cognito D2
7	Calactus C2
8	Co Pain Bread Company B2
9	Gusto C3

🍷 Drinking & Nightlife
10	Pump House D2
11	Saint James' Gate C3
12	The Furnace Room C3
13	Tide & Boar C3

🛍 Shopping
14	Moncton Market C3

try something new. Taking the province's prized possession, skin and all, it works its magic on them using a unique process of cooking, mashing, fermenting and distilling with custom fabricated machinery to create premium vodka. See the process and have a taste test on a tour of the micro-distillery.

☞ Tours

Roads to Sea   BUS
(☎506-850-7623; www.roadstosea.com; per person $174; ☉May-Oct) Roads to Sea offers nine-hour bus tours to Hopewell Rocks and the Bay of Fundy (including the Fundy National Park and Cape Enrage, plus lighthouses and

covered bridges). The company's unique marketing pitch is that you get to see extreme high and low tides in the same day. The bus seats 12 people.

Baymount Outdoor Adventures KAYAKING (☑877-601-2660; www.baymountadventures.com; tours adult/child $69/59; ⊙Jun-Sep) Offers two-hour kayaking tours around the Hopewell Rocks.

🛏 Sleeping

Glory Inn INN $
(☑506-858-9888; www.bbcanada.com/gloryinn; 89 St George St; r $75-115; [P][❄][🗢]) Friendly and well-located, this tidy inn has rooms with a few antiques, private bathrooms and lots of home comforts. There's a shared kitchen too.

L'Hotel St James BOUTIQUE HOTEL $$$
(☑888-782-1414; www.st-jamesgate.ca; 14 Church St; r $180-290; [P][❄][🗢]) This downtown boutique hotel has 10 sleek rooms that wouldn't look a bit out of place in a style magazine. Expect gorgeous tiled bathrooms, sunken tubs, crisp white linens and golden wooden floors plus all the conveniences of iPod docks and flat-screen TVs. Downstairs there's a popular **pub** (⊙11am-2am Mon-Fri, 10am-2am Sat & Sun) and restaurant.

🍴 Eating

Two excellent markets, the **Dieppe Farmers Market** (www.marchedieppemarket.com; cnr Acadie Ave & Gauvin Rd, Dieppe; ⊙7am-1:30pm Sat, express market 11:30am-6:30pm Wed & Fri) and **Moncton Market** (www.marchemoncton-market.ca; 120 Westmoreland St; ⊙7am-2pm Sat), are the places to buy fresh produce, baked goods and all kinds of food from many of Moncton's diverse cultures.

Co Pain Bread Company BAKERY $
(http://copainbread.ca; 98 Bonaccord St; snacks $3-6; ⊙7am-7pm Tue-Sat) Follow your nose to this amazing bakery for fresh bread, scones, raisin rolls and almond croissants. Cheese and sliced meat is also available for a full picnic.

Calactus VEGETARIAN $
(☑506-388-4833; www.calactus.ca; 125 Church St; mains $12-18; ⊙11am-10pm; [🍴]) Busy, bright and welcoming with a bit of a hippy vibe, this vegetarian restaurant excels with unexpected dishes such as lasagna and burgers. You'll also find filling salads, falafel plates

and Indian-inspired dishes. Fabulous local beer makes it all the better.

Cafe C'est la Vie CAFE $
(www.cafecestlavie.ca; 75 Main St; $8-14; ⊙7:30am-6pm Mon-Wed, to 8pm Thu & Fri, 9am-6pm Sat & Sun) This bright, well-loved spot serves panini, risottos and salads along with organic soups and *bibimbap* (Korean mixed rice dish). The bulletin board here is weighted down with local info.

Café Cognito CAFE $
(581 Main St; snacks $3-8; ⊙7:30am-5:30pm Mon-Fri, 8:30am-3pm Sat) Get your morning joe at Café Cognito, a tiny cafe with sandwiches, soups and all-day breakfasts served at a handful of bistro tables that spill onto the sidewalk.

Gusto ITALIAN $$
(☑506-204-7177; http://gustoitaliangrill.ca; 130 Westmorland St; mains $18-30; ⊙11am-2pm & 4-9pm Sun & Mon, to 10pm Wed & Thu, to 11pm Fri & Sat) Handmade pasta in all of its variations, rich sauces and the option to add some butter-poached lobster, roasted chicken breast or other scrumptiously prepared morsels to your dish all make this multi-leveled restaurant a busy spot. Downstairs is intimate and classy; upstairs is open and brighter. But the eight types of cheesecake taste divine wherever you sit.

🍷 Drinking & Nightlife

Main St, between Lester and Robinson, and the blocks spilling north along here offer a good choice of pubs and bars including some great microbreweries.

The Furnace Room PUB
(☑506-229-5559; www.facebook.com/the furnaceroommoncton; 191 Robinson St; ⊙2pm-2am Jun-Sep, 4pm-2am Oct-May) In an alley behind the Capitol Theatre, this leafy patio with big wooden barrel tables and strings of lights is a lovely place to while away an evening. Inside the pub has a comfortable rustic look with a glossy wooden bar and a long list of provincial beers. This intimate place is where locals escape the crowds. Shhhh...

Tide & Boar PUB
(☑506-857-9118; www.tideandboar.com; 700 Main St; mains $15-30; ⊙11am-midnight Mon-Wed, to 2am Thu-Sat, noon-midnight Sun) A classy gastropub that serves it's own and other local beer, plus wines and fancy cocktails. When

its smoker is going, order brisket, ribs, pulled pork or smoked wings with corn on the cob. Other mains include fried-chicken sandwiches, beer-battered cod or boar poutine. This place is hopping and there's often live music on weekends. It's shaded patio is an oasis in summer.

Pump House BREWERY
(www.pumphousebrewery.ca; 5 Orange Lane; mains $12-15; ☺11am-late Mon-Sat, noon-midnight Sun) At the laid-back Pump House, duck into a booth and devour a good burger, fish-and-chips or wood-fired pizza. Beers brewed here are understandably popular; try the Blueberry Ale or Muddy River Stout. This is where locals gather; above the bar hangs 400-plus steins with names on the bottoms, many of them used daily.

ⓘ Information

Visitors Information Centre (20 Mountain Rd, Resurgo Palace; ☺10am-5pm Mon-Sat, noon-5pm Sun) A well-stocked and helpful center in the lobby of the Moncton Museum. There is a second visitor center in Tidal Bore Park.

ⓘ Getting There & Away

AIR

Greater Moncton International Airport (YQM; ☑506-856-5444; www.gmia.ca) is about 6km east of Champlain Place Shopping Centre via Champlain St. Air Canada runs daily flights to Toronto and Montréal.

BUS

Maritime Bus (☑506-854-2023; www.maritimebus.com; 1240 Main St) has multiple daily services to Fredericton ($41.75, 2½ hours), Saint John ($33.75, two hours), Charlottetown, PEI ($41.75, three hours) and Halifax ($53.25, four hours).

CAR & MOTORCYCLE

There are six municipal parking lots around town, plus several private lots. Public parking meters cost $1 to $2.50 per hour. The municipal parking lot at Moncton Market on Westmorland St is free on Saturday, Sunday and evenings after 6pm. The city uses HotSpot Parking, a mobile payment service where you can pay for parking (and top up your metered space parking time) with your cell phone. Rates and maps can be found at www.moncton.ca.

TRAIN

Services depart **VIA Rail Station** (☑506-857-9830; www.viarail.ca; 1240 Main St) on the Ocean line (Montreal–Halifax), passing through northern New Brunswick, including Miramichi

OFF THE BEATEN TRACK

CAPE JOURIMAIN

Set on the Northumberland Strait, this 675-hectare **nature center** (☑506-538-2220; www.capejourimain.ca; Rte 16; $5; ☺8am-7pm May-Oct) has 13km of walking trails. A four-storey tower affords great views of the Confederation Bridge that crosses to Prince Edward Island, and the Cape Jourimain Lighthouse that was built in 1869. It's a twitcher's favorite for the migratory birds, with tours available upon request. The red, sandy beach is long and beautiful.

($37, two hours) and Campbellton ($77, 5½ hours), and into Québec, on its way to Montréal ($167, 17½ hours). The train to Halifax (from $61, four hours) departs three days a week.

ⓘ Getting Around

The airport is served by bus 20 from Champlain Pl nine times a day on weekdays. A taxi to the town center costs about $20.

While downtown is very walkable, if you want to go further afield, Codiac Transit (www.codiactranspo.ca) is the local bus system, with 40 wi-fi-equipped buses going all over town.

If you need wheels, there are car-rental desks at the airport, or try **Discount Car Rentals** (☑506-857-2309; www.discountcar.com; 470 Mountain Rd, cnr High St; ☺7:30am-5:30pm Mon-Fri, 8am-noon Sat) in town.

Sackville
POP 5300

Sackville is a small university town with big green spaces and flanked by grand old homes. The **Sackville Waterfowl Park** (☺24hr) FREE is on a major bird migration route with more than 180 species sighted and 35 breeding within the grounds. From May to August is the best time to visit.

The **Black Duck Cafe** (www.theblackduck.ca; 19 Bridge St; meals $5-12; ☺7am-9pm, brunch 9am-3pm) is the most popular hangout in town, serving up yummy lunches such as kimchi grilled cheese or strawberry and Brie panini, plus brunches of eggs Benny, buttermilk biscuits and the drool-worthy Quack Madam – an egg-battered sandwich with bacon, old cheddar, maple and spinach.

ℹ️ Information

Sackville Visitor Centre (https://sackville.com/explore-sackville/visitor-information; 34 Mallard Dr; ⊙ 9am-5pm May-Oct, to 8pm Jul & Aug)

ℹ️ Getting There & Away

Buses run between Sackville and Moncton ($14.25, 45 minutes, three daily).

NORTHUMBERLAND SHORE

New Brunswick's Northumberland Shore stretches from the Confederation Bridge in the south to Kouchibouguac National Park and is dotted with fishing villages and summer cottages. Shediac, on all lobster-lovers' itineraries, is a popular resort town in a strip of summer seaside and beach playgrounds. A good part of the population along this coast is French-speaking, and Bouctouche is an Acadian stronghold. Further north, Kouchibouguac National Park protects a large swath of scenic coastal ecosystems.

Shediac

POP 6700

Shediac, a self-proclaimed lobster capital, is a busy summer beach town and home of the annual Lobster Festival in July. Nearby are plenty of sandy beaches, including Canada's golden child, **Parlee Beach** (per vehicle $9), which has the country's warmest sea water.

After dinner at one of the town's relaxed seafood restaurants, catch a flick at the wonderfully retro **Neptune Drive-In** (www.neptunedrivein.ca; 691 Main St; adult/child/couple/carload $10/5/18/25; ⊙ box office 8pm, movie starts 9pm Jun-Sep).

◉ Sights & Activities

Homarus Eco-Centre AQUARIUM
(☎ 506-878-9315; www.ecocentrehomarus.org; Pointe-du-Chêne Wharf; adult/child $7/4; ⊙ 10am-6pm Mon-Sat Jun-Aug, plus noon-5pm Sun Jul & Aug) Focusing on the local bay's marine life with particular attention to it's star, the lobster, 20-minute tours of the eco-centre begin in the hatchery and include the chance to get up close with the rare blue and albino lobsters. The impetus behind nonprofit Homarus was to increase the local lobster population. You can adopt a baby lobster and, with the certificate number, follow its release. Since 2002, more than five million baby lobsters have been delivered to the sea.

Shediac Paddle Shack ADVENTURE SPORTS
(☎ 506-532-8914; www.shediacpaddleshack.com; 229 Main St; paddleboard or kayak 1-/3hr $25/47, party board/tandem kayak 1hr $55/35; ⊙ Jun-Sep) Next to the information center, this shack will meet all of your paddling needs. Party boards fit up to six people. They also run regular lesson including SUP yoga and paddle-with-your-dog.

Shediac Bay Cruises CRUISE
(☎ 506-532-2175, 888-894-2002; www.lobstertales.ca; 60 Pointe-du-Chêne Wharf; lobster tales adult/child/family $79/56/245, bay tour adult/child/family $24/19/75) The popular Lobster Tales cruise takes passengers out on the water, pulls up lobster traps, then prepares a feast complete with Acadian music. The Bay Cruise is a 75-minute scenic boat ride around the bay.

🛏️ Sleeping & Eating

Maison Tait INN $$
(☎ 506-532-4233; www.maisontaithouse.com; 293 Main St; r incl breakfast from $100; 🛜) Lodgings at Maison Tait, a luxurious 1911 mansion, consist of nine classy, sun-drenched rooms, some with four-poster beds and zen bathtubs. There's a steakhouse and bar on-site. Excellent hot breakfast served.

Shediac Lobster Shop SEAFOOD $
(☎ 506-533-1437; www.shediaclobster.ca; 261 Main St; whole cooked lobster $10; ⊙ 10am-7pm) Just before the bridge at the northern end of town, get your lobster wholesale, ready to eat, with crackers and all. There are also scallops and clams along with canned goods to take home. If you're feeling flush, you can have a lobster shipped anywhere in Canada.

Paturel's Shore House SEAFOOD $$
(☎ 506-532-4774; www.paturelrestaurant.ca; 2 Blvd Cap Bimet, Grand-Barachois; mains $17-33; ⊙ 4-10pm Tue-Sun Jun–mid-Sep) Locals have been hauling themselves out to this seafood restaurant located on the seashore, 7km east of Shediac, for years. It's hard to know if it's the lobster chowder or bacon-wrapped scallops that keep drawing them back, but to join them, turn off Main St and head north on Blvd Cap Bimet.

MIRAMICHI RIVER VALLEY

The 217km-long Southwest Miramichi River flows from near Hartland through forest to Miramichi where it meets the Northwest Miramichi. This area holds potent cultural significance for the Mi'kmaq Nation who have lived on the river's banks for 3000 years. Forty kilometers northwest of Miramichi, on the Esk River, the **Metepenagiag Heritage Park** (☑506-836-6118; www.metpark.ca; 2156 Micmac Rd, Red Bank; adult/child $8/6; tipis 2/4 people $85/150; ☺10am-5pm May-Oct, to 3pm Nov-Apr) has interpretive tours of Mi'kmaq culture and history on a 3000-year-old archaeological site.

Throughout the region is a web of rivers and tributaries draining much of central New Brunswick. These waterways have inspired reverent awe for their tranquil beauty and incredible Atlantic salmon fly-fishing. Famous business tycoons, international politicians, sports and entertainment stars along with Prince Charles have all wet lines here. Even Marilyn Monroe is said to have dipped her toes in the water.

You can learn about the valley's storied fishing history at the **Atlantic Salmon Museum** (www.atlanticsalmonmuseum.com; 263 Main St, Doaktown; adult/child $8/5; ☺9am-5pm Mon-Sat, noon-5pm Sun Jun-Oct) in Doaktown, 90km southwest of Miramichi, then swing by **WW Doak & Sons** (www.doak.com; 331 Main St, Doaktown; ☺8am-5pm Mon-Sat), one of Canada's finest fly-fishing shops.

There are no tours to the Miramichi River Valley Area. Having your own vehicle is useful, especially to explore some off-piste roads and river areas.

❶ Information

Visitors Information Centre (☑506-533-7925; www.shediac.ca; 229 Main St; ☺9am-5pm May-Sep, to 9pm Jul & Aug) On the northern edge of town, this center provides excellent information on New Brunswick and maps of Shediac and surrounds. It's next to the world's largest lobster. (No, really...)

❶ Getting There & Away

Maritime Bus (www.maritimebus.com; 167 Main St) runs from Shediac to Moncton ($12.25, 30 minutes, one daily) and Fredericton ($46, three hours, one daily); you must reserve three hours in advance. Buses also run from Shediac to Halifax, Nova Scotia.

Bouctouche

POP 2360

This small, surprisingly busy waterside town is an Acadian cultural focal point. The visitor center at the town's southern entrance features an impressive boardwalk that extends over the salt marsh, across the bridge and along the waterfront.

◉ Sights

★**Irving Eco Centre** PARK
(www.irvingecocentre.com; 1932 Rte 475, St-Édouard-de-Kent; ☺interpretive center 10am-6pm late May-late Sep) Just 9km northeast of Bouctouche, Irving Eco Centre makes accessible 'La Dune de Bouctouche,' a gor-

geous, powder-soft sandspit jutting into the strait. The interpretive center has worthwhile displays, but the highlight is the 800m boardwalk that weaves above the sea grass along the dunes.

The peninsula itself is 12km long, taking more than four hours to hike over the loose sand and back. If you're short on time, walk the boardwalk and return along the beautiful beach, stopping to take a dip along the way.

There's a 12km hiking and cycling trail through mixed forest to Bouctouche town, which begins at the Eco Centre parking lot.

Le Pays de la Sagouine PARK
(☑506-743-1400; www.sagouine.com; 57 Acadie St; adult/student/family $22/17/55; ☺10am-5:30pm Jul & Aug) Sitting on a small island in the Bouctouche River, this Acadian village is constructed to bring to life the setting from La Sagouine, a play by writer Antonine Maillet. Monologues from the play are acted out throughout the village, sometimes over the soup pot or local handicrafts and often accompanied by music.

Several cafes serve old-fashioned Acadian cuisine, and in July and August there are regular supper theater performances (tickets from $63; French only).

Olivier Soapery MUSEUM
(www.oliviersoaps.com; 831 Rte 505, Ste-Anne-de-Kent; ☺10am-6pm Jun-Aug, 8:30am-4:30pm

Mon-Fri Sep-May) If you're a market-goer, you've likely already seen Olivier Soap around New Brunswick. In their old-fashioned soap factory, you can sit on a wooden bench and see a batch of soap being made while learning about its history. The attached shop sells beautiful and often delicious-smelling wares. Check out the lobster-shaped butter soap, sage and clay or carrot soap.

🛏 Sleeping & Eating

Gite de la Sagouine   B&B **$**
(www.sagouinerestaurant.com; 43 Irving Blvd; d $85-100, q $125; P ✱ 🐾 🛜) Conveniently located on the edge of the town center, this six-room inn has clean, comfortable accommodation. Check the website for deals that include a night's stay and dinner in the attached restaurant.

Chez les Maury   CAMPGROUND **$**
(✆ 506-743-5347; 2021 Rte 475, St-Édouard-de-Kent; campsites with/without hookups $25-30; ⊙ May-early Oct) On the grounds of a family-run vineyard, 200m from the Irving Eco Centre, this sweet campground is set in the field next to the farmhouse. The welcoming owner rings a bell at 6:30pm for the 7pm free sampling of wares such as elderberry and strawberry wine. Facilities are clean and there's a private beach across the way.

SCKS Société culturelle Kent-Sud   CAFE **$**
(www.sckentsud.com; 5 Irving Blvd; snacks $9-11; ⊙ 8am-4pm Tue-Sat Sep-May, to 5pm daily Jun-Aug) Full of local art, baked goods, salads and soups, this little nonprofit cafe is a pleasant place to stop for coffee and simple French-style snack lunches using, where possible, local produce.

Restaurant La Sagouine   ACADIAN **$**
(www.sagouine.nb.ca; 43 Irving Blvd; mains $8-18; ⊙ 6am-10pm) With seafood in its various presentations alongside fried chicken and crepes for good measure, this old-fashioned spot has a summer patio for great sidewalk gazing.

ℹ Information

The **Visitors Information Center** (✆ 506-743-8811; www.tourismnewbrunswick.ca; 14 Acadie St; ⊙ 10am-3pm late May-late Sep, longer hours in summer) has lots of info on the surrounding area.

ℹ Getting There & Away

No public transport services Bouctouche; you'll need your own wheels.

Kouchibouguac National Park

Beaches, lagoons and offshore sand dunes stretch for a gorgeous 25km, inviting strolling, bird-watching and clam-digging. The **park** (www.pc.gc.ca; Rte 117; adult/youth $7.80/free; ⊙ 8am-dusk year-round) encompasses hectares of forest and salt marshes, crisscrossed or skirted by bike paths, hiking trails and groomed cross-country ski tracks. Kouchibouguac (*koosh*-e-boo-gwack), a Mi'kmaq word meaning 'River of Long Tides,' is home to moose, deer and sometimes black bear.

🏃 Activities

Hiking

The calm, shallow water between the shore and the dunes, which run for 25km north and south, makes for a serene morning paddle. For a real adventure, head out to the sandy barrier islands in a **Voyageur Canoe** (✆ 506-876-2443; per person $30) to see hundreds of seals and birds and learn about the Mi'kmaq way of life along the way.

Kayaking

The park has 10 trails, mostly short and flat. The excellent **Bog Trail** (1.9km) is a boardwalk beyond the observation tower, and only the first few hundred meters are crushed gravel. The **Cedars Trail** (1.3km) is a lovely boardwalk trail with interpretation boards. The **Osprey Trail** (5.1km) is a loop trail through the forest. **Kelly's Beach Boardwalk** (600m one way) floats above the grass-covered dunes. When you reach the beach, turn right and hike around 6km to the end of the dune (the limits vary according to the location of the piping plover's nesting grounds). Take drinking water.

🛏 Sleeping

Kouchibouguac has two drive-in campgrounds and three primitive camping areas totalling 360 sites. The camping season is from mid-May to mid-October, and the park is very busy throughout July and August, especially on weekends. Camping reservations are necessary for the majority of sites. Park entry costs extra.

THE ACADIAN PENINSULA

The northeastern tip of the province is breathtaking. A chain of low-lying islands pointing across the Gulf of St Lawrence to Labrador, it offers a surprising slew of fantastic sights, plenty of opportunities to unwind by the sea and cheerful Acadian culture. Rte 113 cuts across salt marsh, arriving first in **Shippagan**, home of the province's largest fishing fleet. Get up close to life under the Atlantic, touch blue lobsters and feed the seals at the worthwhile **New Brunswick Aquarium** (☑506-336-3013; www.aquariumnb.ca; 100 Aquarium Rd, Shippagan; adult/child $9.50/6; ⊗9am-6pm Jun-Sep).

Hop the bridge to **Lamèque**, with its modern windmills and tidy fishing village that has hosted the **Lamèque International Baroque Festival** (☑506-344-5846; www.festivalbaroque.com; ⊗late Jul) for more than 30 years. Nearby, the **Ecological Park** (☑506-344-3223; 65 Ruisseau St, Lamèque; ⊗9:30am-5:30pm Jun-Sep) **FREE** offers a boardwalk to a bird-filled 2.6km forested loop trail. Watch for the endangered piping plover, kingfishers and great blue herons. Definitely stop at the unbelievable **Sainte Cécile Church** (8166 Rte 313, Petite-Rivière-de-l'Ile; ⊗8am-5pm, shorter hours in winter) **FREE**. Built in 1913 and unremarkable from the outside, the inside was repainted in the 1960s by one psychedelic reverend who opted for a kaleidoscope of color. Grab a light lunch at the **Aloha Café-Boutique** (41 Principale St, Lamèque; mains $7-9; ⊗7am-4pm Mon-Thu, to 9pm Fri, 8:30am-4pm Sat & Sun; 🖘) then continue north over the arched bridge to **Miscou Island**.

Stretch your legs over at the peaceful **Cheniere Lake Boardwalk** and learn about the local peat industry. The road dead-ends at a **Miscou Lighthouse** (☑506-344-7203; Rte 113, Miscou Island; adult/child $6/4; ⊗9am-5pm Jun-Sep), built in 1856 and one of New Brunswick's most impressive. Climb 100ft to the top for killer views and then relax in the cafe next door. On your way south down the island, stop at **Miscou Beach** for sugar-like sand and great swimming. Just before you cross the bridge, gorge yourself on stuffed, steamed or oven-baked lobster and seafood at **La Terrasse à Steve** (9650 Rte 113, Quai de Miscou, Miscou Island; mains from $20; ⊗noon-8pm May-Sep). Near here, at very low tide, you can see the ruins of New Brunswick's first church, built in 1634 by Catholic missionaries.

Back on Lamèque, you can spend the night at the homey **Aux Peupliers B&B** (☑506-344-5145; https://aux-peupliers.business.site; 66 North Pêcheur Rd, Lamèque; ⊗d $95; ❄🖘). Otherwise, continue on to Shippagan where the ultra-cool **Cielo** (☑501-601-8005; www.glampingcielo.com; 232 Haut-Shippagan Dr; 2/4 people $180/240, min 2 nights; ⊗bar 10am-8pm Sun-Wed, to 11pm Thu-Sat; ❄🖘) has otherworldly domes to stay in, complete with stargazing lofts, hand-built hot tubs and green-egg barbecues. Even if you can't stay, hit their bar for a local brew and a look-see. Dinner can be had at **Pinokkio** (☑506-336-0051; 121 16e St, Shippagan; mains $13-25; ⊗4:30-8pm daily, from 11:30am Wed-Fri Jun-Sep) with its fresh pasta and seafood. All three of the islands also have campgrounds and information centers with local maps.

The three primitive campgrounds cost $16 per person per night; they have only vault (pump) toilets and you must take your own water.

Cote-a-Fabien
CAMPGROUND $

(☑877-737-3783; www.pccamping.ca; Kouchibouguac National Park; campsites Otentiks/walk-in $120/16) On the northern side of Kouchibouguac River, Cote-a-Fabien is the best choice for those seeking a bit of peace and privacy. There is water and vault toilets, but no showers. Some sites are on the shore, others nestled among the trees, with a dozen walk-in sites (100m; wheelbarrows are provided for luggage) for those who want a car-free environment.

South Kouchibouguac
CAMPGROUND $

(☑877-737-3783; www.pccamping.ca; Kouchibouguac National Park; campsites with/without hookup $27/38, equipped camping/Otentiks $70/100) South Kouchibouguac is the largest campground. It's 13km inside the park near the beaches in a large open field ringed by trees, with oTENTiks (a type of yurt) and equipped tents sites, plus showers and a kitchen shelter. You can also rent bikes and all kinds of water toys here, including kayaks, paddleboards and pedal boats.

ℹ Information

Visitor Center (☑506-876-2443; www.pc.gc.ca/kouchibouguac; 186 Rte 117; ⊗8am-4:30pm

Oct-May, to 8pm Jul-Sep) Has maps and helpful staff with good information. If the center is closed, visit the administration office opposite, which is open year-round.

NORTHEASTERN NEW BRUNSWICK

The North Shore, as it is known to New Brunswickers, is the heartland of Acadian culture in the province. The region was settled 250 years ago by French farmers and fishers, starting from scratch again after the upheaval of the Expulsion, frequently marrying the original Mi'kmaq inhabitants. The coastal road north from Miramichi, around the Acadian Peninsula and along Chaleurs Bay to Campbellton, passes through small fishing settlements with peaceful ocean vistas and soft, sandy beaches. At Sugarloaf Provincial Park, the Appalachian Mountain Range comes down to the edge of the sea. Behind it, stretching hundreds of kilometers into the interior of the province, is a vast, trackless wilderness of rivers and dense forest, rarely explored.

Caraquet

POP 4250

The oldest of the Acadian villages, Caraquet was founded in 1757 by refugees from forcibly abandoned homesteads further south. It's now the commercial center of the peninsula's French community. Caraquet's colorful, bustling wharf on Ave du Carrefour has shops, bars, restaurants and sea breezes. Downtown is spread along Rte 145, divided into East and West Blvd St-Pierre.

Caraquet is the self-proclaimed 'cultural capital of Acadia.' Each August the town is the proud host of the massive Festival Acadien, a historic occasion that celebrates their survival. It's also the closest town to the popular Acadian Historic Village.

◉ Sights

★ **Acadian Historic Village** PARK
(www.villagehistoriqueacadien.com; 14311 Rte 11; adult/student/family mid-Jun–Sep $20/16/45, early Jun & Oct $9.50/8/21.50; ◷10am-6pm mid-Jun–Sep, to 5pm early Jun & Oct) Just 15km west of Caraquet, this village of old is 33 original buildings relocated to this historical site. Staff in period costumes reflect life from 1780 to 1880. Several hours are required to have a good look, then head for a traditional

meal at La Table des Ancêtres. Join Madame Savoie in her 1860s kitchen for a lesson in Acadian cooking ($75, twice daily) or get your kids kitted with costumes and a day full of historical activities ($35).

Founding Cultures Museum MUSEUM
(☑506-732-3003; 184 Rte 11, Grande-Anse; by donation; ◷9am-5pm Jun-Sep) If you're traveling down Rte 11 and feel the need to be wowed, stop in at the Founding Cultures Museum in Grande-Anse. Sure, there are detailed displays on Scottish, English, Irish, First Nation and Acadian cultures, but the real wowzer is an unlikely and very intricate scale model of the St Peter's Basilica in Rome. Crafted by European artisans in the 1890s, it's precise down to the final statue on the colonnades. If you need a place to unwind afterwards, there is a popular beach around the corner with a popular canteen.

✦ Festivals & Events

Festival Acadien CULTURAL
(www.festivalacadien.ca; ◷Aug) The largest annual Acadian cultural festival, Festival Acadien, is held here the first two weeks of August. It draws 100,000 visitors, and more than 200 performers including singers, musicians, actors, dancers from Acadia and other French regions (some from overseas).

⌂ Sleeping

Motel Bel Air MOTEL $
(☑506-727-3488; www.motelbelair.ca; 655 W St-Pierre Blvd; r from $90; ❉🐾) The stylish and extremely comfortable rooms at this motel are a true bargain. But word is out – book ahead.

Maison Touristique Dugas INN $
(☑506-727-3195; www.maisontouristiquedugas.ca; 683 Blvd St-Pierre W; campsites serviced/unserviced $23/30, r/cabins from $70/100) Five generations of the ultra-friendly Dugas family have run this rambling, something-for-everyone property, 8km west of Caraquet. The homey, antique-filled 1926 house has 11 rooms, four with shared bathrooms. There are also five clean, cozy cabins with private bathrooms and cooking facilities, a guesthouse with private and family rooms, and a quiet, tree-shaded campground.

★ **Château Albert** INN $$
(☑506-726-2600; https://villagehistoriqueacadi en.com/en/hotel; Acadian Historic Village; d incl dinner & site visit $100-150; 🅿🐾) For complete

immersion in Acadian culture, spend the night in a Historical Village – no TV and no phone, just 15 quiet rooms restored to their original 1909 splendor, complete with claw-foot tubs. The hotel bar pours local brews and Acadian cocktails. The original Albert stood on the main street in Caraquet until it was destroyed by fire in 1955.

Hotel Paulin   HOTEL **$$$**
(☑ 866-727-9981, 506-727-9981; www.hotelpaulin. com; 143 Blvd St-Pierre W; r incl breakfast $195-315; P 🐾) The somewhat shabby outside of Hotel Paulin is not a reflection of what's inside. This vintage seaside hotel overlooking the bay was built in 1891 and has been run by the Paulin family since 1905. Good old-fashioned service remains and the rooms are sunny and polished, done up in crisp white linens, lace and quality antiques. But there's no denying that it's pricey.

The hotel has earned a reputation for fine cuisine, so make a reservation to sample the fiddlehead fern soup followed by Acadian chicken fricot with herb dumplings (three-course meal $48).

✕ Eating

Pro-Mer   SEAFOOD **$$**
(☑ 506-727-7931; 9 Quai St; meals $15-23; ⊗ 11am-9pm Sun-Thu, to 10pm Fri & Sat) The is *the* place to eat seafood in town. Next to the bobbing boats in the marina, get your fill of breaded clam poutine, seafood lasagna or whole lobster in a relaxed restaurant setting or on the patio. In the attached shop, you can buy oysters on ice or jars of your favorite crustaceans to take home.

Origines   ACADIAN **$$$**
(☑ 506-727-2717; www.originescuisinemaritime. com; 49a W St-Pierre Blvd; 5-course meal $68; ⊗ 5-9pm Thu-Sat) While the seaside restaurant may be relatively new on the scene, the chef isn't. This culinary artist has returned to his hometown to create five-course meals from local, seasonal producte. In summer, it's largely seafood based. Flavor-filled and polished, it's as much an experience as a meal.

ⓘ Information

Visitor Centre (☑ 202-726-2676; www.cara quet.ca/en/tourism/discover-caraquet; 39 W Blvd St-Pierre; ⊗ 9am-5pm Jun-Sep) Information on all things local, and the Acadian Historic Village.

Bathurst
POP 11,900

Set on a pretty harbor and sheltered by Carron and Alston Point, tiny Bathurst is a former mining town that's morphed into a relaxed seaside destination. The town itself is joined by a bridge that spans the harbor, with most things of interest for the tourist on the southern side.

Join locals in stretching your legs on the boardwalk at the revamped harborfront, home to the tourist office and a couple of restaurants. There are no less than three local microbreweries to sample and plenty of fresh seafood. Not far from town is the gorgeous Youghall Beach and Pabineau Falls.

Bathurst's original name was Nepisiguit, a Mi'qmaq word meaning 'Rough Waters.'

◎ Sights

Pabineau Falls   WATERFALL
(Pabineau Falls Rd, Pabineau First Nation) On the territory of the Mi'kmaq Pabineau Nation, this pretty waterfall tumbles down the Nepisiguit River, about 14km south of Bathurst. The drive here is scenic and many people picnic on the banks. Check with locals about conditions before swimming.

Note: ask the tourist office (p430) for directions, as there is limited signage. It's on property owned by a former paper mill (you enter at own risk etc).

Point Daly Reserve   NATURE RESERVE
(Carron Dr) Stop in at the interpretive center before heading out on one of this nature reserves' nine marked trails, all courtesy of a former mining company. Just 5km from Bathurst, come here to see Canada geese on their migratory voyage, along with eagles, osprey and the rare maritime ringlet butterfly that appears at the end of July.

🛏 Sleeping & Eating

Auberge & Bistro l'Anjou   B&B **$$**
(http://aubergedanjou.com; 587 Principale St, Petit-Rocher; r $90-110; P ✳ 🐾) About 20 minutes northwest of Bathurst in the village of Petit-Rocher, this lovely B&B with very comfortable rooms is a home away from home – and you're just minutes away from the local beach. The on-site bistro is a favorite with locals and visitors; don't miss the Acadian sugar pie.

BON AMI ICE CREAM

From Campbellton, take the coastal Rte 134 27km east to Dalhousie, where Bon Ami Ice Cream serves 24 flavors of ice cream and 20 flavors of frozen yoghurt. Locals have been coming here for more than 20 years – and with lactose-free, sugar-free and tofu options, there's a cone for everyone.

L'Étoile du Havre B&B
B&B $$

(☑506-545-6238; www.etoileduhavre.com; 405 Youghall Dr; r $125; 🅿 ❄ 🛜) Situated in a tranquil location opposite a golf course, and en route to Youghall Beach, this designer-sleek, open-plan, ultra-contemporary B&B with six rooms looks like it's out of the pages of an LA showroom magazine. Cooked breakfasts are served in the massive open-plan kitchen-lounge room.

★ Fresco
CANADIAN $$$

(☑506-546-1061; 224 King St; $25-40; ⊙5-9pm Tue, to 10pm Wed-Sat) Following on from a successful food truck and an appearance on Canada's *Top Chef*, Joel Aubie is working his culinary magic in his own open-kitchen restaurant. The well-honed menu uses local ingredients and everything is made from scratch, from hand-rolled pasta to pâté and stocks. These gourmet dishes are so good, you'll want to lick your plate. Make reservations if you can.

❶ Information

Tourist office (☑506-548-0412; www.bathurst.ca; 86 Douglas Ave, Bathurst Harbor; ⊙9am-4pm Mon-Fri Sep-Apr, to 5pm May, to 8pm Jun-Aug) This helpful office will direct you to nature-based activities around Bathurst and rents bikes (half/full day $25/40).

❶ Getting There & Away

Maritime Bus (☑506-544-9892; www.maritimebus.com; 896 Main St) services Bathurst. Handy links include Fredericton ($68.50, six hours, one daily), Campbellton ($25.50, 1½ hours, one daily), Saint John ($63.50, 6¼

hours, one daily) and Moncton ($46, 3¼ hours, one daily). Note: for Shediac ($41.75, 2¾ hours, one daily) you must book 24 hours ahead. See the website for services to Sydney, Nova Scotia.

Campbellton

POP 6900

Campbellton is a pleasant humdrum mill town on the Québec border. The lengthy Restigouche River, which winds through northern New Brunswick and then forms the border with Québec, empties to the sea here. The Bay of Chaleur is on one side and dramatic rolling hills surround the town on the remaining sides. Across the bridge to Québec lies Pointe-à-la-Croix and Hwy 132 leading west to Mont Joli and east to Gaspé.

The last naval engagement of the Seven Years' War was fought in the waters off this coast in 1760. The Battle of Restigouche marked the conclusion of the long struggle for Canada by Britain and France.

The town is dominated by Sugarloaf Mountain, which rises nearly 400m above sea level and looks vaguely like one of its other namesakes in Rio. **Sugarloaf Provincial Park** (www.parcsugarloafpark.ca; 596 Val d'Amours Rd, Atholville; Downhill Bike Park full/half-day/single ride $30/25/5; ⊙8am-dusk late May-late Sep) is located off Hwy 11 at exit 415. From the base, it's just a half-hour walk to the top – well worth it for the extensive views of the town and part of the Restigouche River. The park also has 76 lovely **campsites** (☑506-789-2366; www.parcsugarloafpark.ca; 596 Val d'Amours Rd; tent sites $28, RV sites with hookup $36, yurts $43; ⊙late May-late Sep; 🛜).

❶ Getting There & Away

Maritime Bus (☑506-753-6714; www.maritimebus.com; 157 Roseberry St; ⊙6am-9pm) services stop at the Pik-Quik convenience store, near Prince William St. Buses departs daily for Fredericton ($82, 7½ hours) and Moncton ($59, five hours).

The **VIA Rail station** (www.viarail.ca; 99c Roseberry St) is conveniently central. Trains depart three times weekly to Montréal ($243, 12 hours).

Prince Edward Island

Best Places to Eat

➡ FireWorks (p445)

➡ Terre Rouge (p439)

➡ Blue Mussel Cafe (p450)

➡ Dunes Studio Gallery & Cafe (p447)

Best Places to Stay

➡ Fairholm National Historic Inn (p438)

➡ Great George (p438)

➡ Barachois Inn (p450)

➡ Johnson Shore Inn (p444)

Why Go?

Fringed by grassy bluffs, flat pastures and miles of rust-red sand, Prince Edward Island (PEI) presents a postcard-worthy picture of pastoral Canada. Every summer, thousands of tourists descend on the island to visit its beaches and seaside villages, many of which lie within the boundaries of Prince Edward Island National Park. Famed for its shellfish, lobsters and oysters, the island excels in farm-to-table dining, and it's a great place to experience modern Canadian cuisine at its finest.

But for many visitors, it's the adventures of a red-headed, straw-hatted little girl that will forever define PEI in their imaginations. Published in the early 1900s, Lucy Maud Montgomery's *Anne of Green Gables* tales are as popular as ever. The astonishing thing is how little the island's landscape has changed since then: farmhouses, fields, creeks and dunes straight out of a children's storybook. Cycling the 435km-long Confederation Trail makes a fine way to explore.

When to Go
Charlottetown

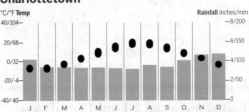

Jun Enjoy the spring calm and blooming wildflowers before the crowds hit.

Jul & Aug The entire island is in festival mode with live music and lobster suppers nightly.

Sep Traditional music and a bevy of food events mark PEI's Fall Flavours Festival.

North Cape
Seacow Pond
64°30'W
64°00'W
63°30'W
47°00'N
Tignish R
Tignish
Skinners Pond
Cape Kildare
Mimenegash
152
2
14
Campbellton
150
Bloomfield
Cascumpec Bay
Cape Wolfe
St Anthony
O'Leary
147
Woodstock
142
12
12
14
West Point
Cedar Dunes Provincial Park
Green Park Provincial Park
East Bideford
Lennox Island
Hog Island
Gulf of St Lawrence
Egmont Bay
Mount Pleasant
Tyne Valley
Malpeque Bay
Malpeque
Park Corner
Prince County
2
Grand River
104
20
New London
Cavendish
2
Prince Edward Island
46°30'N
Wellington
12
Indian River
Margate
North Rustico
Rusticoville
Miscouche
177
Confederation Trail
Kensington
8
St Ann
Brackley Beach
Rustico
Cape Egmont
11
Mont Carmel
Summerside
Wilmot River
New Glasgow
Bedeque Bay
1A
Dunk River
225
Springton
2
7
15
Seven Mile Bay
Borden-Carleton
13
Queens County
1
New Brunswick
15
Cape Jourimain
Confederation Bridge
10
Victoria
19
Murray Corner
Cape Tormentine
933
15
16
St Peters Island
Port Elgin
940
16
Northumberland Strait
Nova Scotia
366
63°30'W
Perival R

Prince Edward Island Highlights

1 Charlottetown (p435) Wandering the elegant streets of PEI's compact capital.

2 Cavendish (p454) Following in Anne of Green Gables' fictional footsteps around the home of author LM Montgomery.

3 Basin Head Provincial Park (p445) Stepping on the strange squeaking sands of this far-easterly beach.

4 Lennox Island (p458) Learning Mi'kmaq lore on a guided walk of this forested isle.

5 FireWorks (p445) Devouring the barbecue-of-a-lifetime at celeb chef Michael

Map Labels

63°00'W · 62°30'W · 62°00'W

47°00'N

46°30'N

46°00'N

0 — 20 km
0 — 10 miles

– – – – Confederation Trail

Ferry to Îles de la Madeleine

North Lake · East Point
Naufrage
Greenwich
St Peter's Bay
Fortune Bay
Souris R.
Elmira · South Lake
Harmony Junction
National Park
Dalvay by the Sea
Mt Stewart
Midgell
Kings County
Souris
Basin Head Provincial Park
Red Point Provincial Park
Hillsborough River
Morell River
Midgell River
Bay Fortune
Albion Cross
Rollo Bay
Howe Bay
Colville Bay
Charlottetown
Prince Edward Island
Cardigan
Newport
Brudenell River Provincial Park
Boughton Bay
Governors Island
Vernon Bridge
Montague
Georgetown
Cardigan Bay
St Mary's Bay
Panmure Island
Orwell
Hillsborough Bay
Eldon
Gaspereaux
Point Prim
Caledonia
Murray River
Murray Islands
Cape Bear
Murray Harbour
Wood Islands
Northumberland Provincial Park
Little Sands
High Bank
Ferry to Caribou, Nova Scotia

Smith's culinary HQ in Bay Fortune.

6 New Glasgow Lobster Supper (p451) Cracking your way through the island's original lobster extravaganza.

7 Greenwich Dunes (p446) Walking the floating boardwalk into a world of dunes.

8 East Point Lighthouse (p443) Climbing up the tower of this historic lighthouse.

9 Confederation Trail (p439) Spinning along a section of this fabulous railway-turned-bike-trail.

History

Its Indigenous inhabitants, the Mi'kmaq, knew the island as Abegeit (Land Cradled on the Waves). Although Jacques Cartier of France first recorded PEI's existence in 1534, European settlement didn't begin until 1603. Initially small, the French colony grew only after Britain's expulsion of the Acadians from Nova Scotia in the 1750s. In 1758 the British took the island, known then as Île St Jean, and expelled the 3000 Acadians. Britain was officially granted the island in the Treaty of Paris of 1763.

To encourage settlement, the British divided the island into 67 parcels and held a lottery to give away the land. Unfortunately, most of the 'Great Giveaway' winners were speculators and did nothing to settle or develop the island. The questionable actions of these absentee landlords hindered population growth and caused incredible unrest among islanders.

One of the major reasons PEI did not become part of Canada in 1867 was because union did not offer a solution to the land problem. In 1873 the Compulsory Land Purchase Act forced the sale of absentee landlords' land and cleared the way for PEI to join Canada later that year. Foreign land ownership, however, is still a sensitive issue in the province. The population has remained stable, at around 140,000, since the 1930s.

In 1997, after much debate, PEI was linked to New Brunswick and the mainland by the Confederation Bridge.

ℹ Getting There & Away

AIR

Charlottetown Airport (p441) Located 8km from town, it serves all flights entering and leaving the province.

Air Canada (AC; ☑ 888-247-2262; www.aircanada.com) Has daily flights to Charlottetown from Halifax, Montréal and Toronto, plus seasonal flights to Ottawa.

WestJet (WS; ☑ 888-937-8538; www.westjet.com) Direct flights to Toronto.

PEI FAST FACTS

➡ Population: 142,907

➡ Area: 5700 sq km

➡ Capital: Charlottetown

➡ Quirky fact: 1.3 billion kilograms of potatoes produced per year

---

BOAT

Bay Ferries (☑ 877-762-7245; www.bayferries.com) operates the ferry service that links Wood Islands, in PEI's southeast, to Caribou, Nova Scotia. There are up to nine daily sailings in each direction during summer, and five in the fall and spring. Vehicle fees include all passengers for the 1¼-hour trip. Note that there is no ferry service from January through April.

The ferry is free if you're traveling from Nova Scotia to PEI, but it's worth making a reservation anyway to guarantee a space. Traveling in the other direction, the standard fare applies, making the ferry about $30 more expensive than the bridge.

BUS

Maritime Bus (☑ 800-575-1807; www.maritimebus.com) operates two buses a day to/from Halifax (one way $58.25, 4½ hours). There are also three buses from Moncton, New Brunswick (one way $41.75, three hours), with stops at Borden-Carleton and Summerside en route. Both services require a transfer in Amherst, Nova Scotia.

T3 Transit (p441) operates a County Line Express service between Charlottetown and Summerside (one way $9, 80 minutes, two daily).

CAR, BICYCLE & MOTORCYCLE

The 12.9km **Confederation Bridge** (☑ 902-437-7300; www.confederationbridge.com; car/motorcycle $47.75/19; ⊙ 24hr), the longest bridge in the world over ice-bound waters, is the quickest way to travel between PEI and New Brunswick, and on to Nova Scotia. Opened in 1997, it's an impressive sight and a major engineering achievement, but unfortunately the 1.1m-high guardrails rob you of any hoped-for view.

The standard toll covers travel to and from the island, and includes one car and all passengers. It's only charged on departure from PEI, so it works out around $30 cheaper than the ferry.

If you're planning on traveling one way on the bridge and the other way by ferry, since you only pay on exit, it's cheaper to take the ferry to PEI and return via the bridge ($47.75 versus $79).

Cyclists and pedestrians are banned from the Confederation Bridge and must use the 24-hour, demand-driven shuttle service (bicycle/pedestrian $9/4.50). On the PEI side, go to the bridge operations building at Gateway Village in Borden-Carleton; on the New Brunswick side, the pickup is at the Cape Jourimain Nature Centre at exit 51 on Rte 16.

ℹ Getting Around

Bus services are fairly limited on the island; what services there are are provided by Maritime Bus and T3 Transit (p441).

While your easiest option to get around the island is by car, bicycle is also a fine choice. The flat and well-maintained Confederation Trail runs the length of the island through some beautiful countryside and small towns. For details, check out www.tourismpei.com/pei-confederation-trail.

CHARLOTTETOWN

📞 902 / POP 44,739

If there's a prettier provincial capital in Canada than Charlottetown, we're yet to find it (even its name sounds quaint). Eschewing the headlong rush for concrete and glass that characterizes many big Canadian cities, Charlottetown has stayed true to its small-town roots, with a low-rise downtown that retains many of the redbrick facades and Victorian buildings of its late-19th-century heyday. Covering just a few blocks inland from the harbor, the old part of town was designed to be walkable, and it pays to wander and soak up the sights – including its impressive mock-Gothic cathedral and a surfeit of heritage homes, browsable shops and colorful clapboard buildings. The town's fast-growing food and craft-beer scene is boosted by the presence of the Culinary Institute of Canada downtown.

History

Charlottetown is named after the consort of King George III. Her African roots, dating back to Margarita de Castro Y Sousa and the Portuguese royal house, are as legendary as they are controversial.

While many believe the city's splendid harbor was the reason Charlottetown became the capital, the reality was less glamorous. In 1765 the surveyor-general decided on Charlottetown because he thought it prudent to bestow the poor side of the island with some privileges.

As every Canadian schoolkid knows, Charlottetown's main historical event of note was its role as host of the 1864 Confederation Conference – the event that led to the founding of modern Canada.

◉ Sights

In terms of 'attractions,' Charlottetown isn't top-heavy on sights. That said, think of the whole of the downtown area (known as Old Charlottetown), with its beautifully preserved, quaint and colorful colonial buildings, and the wealth of boutiques, bistros and bars they contain, as the main event.

The significant sights are all in this downtown area.

★ Victoria Park   PARK

(www.discovercharlottetown.com/listings/victoria-park) Dedicated in 1873, Charlottetown's most popular and beautiful waterfront green space has 16 hectares of lush loveliness for you to enjoy on a fine day. A boardwalk runs along the park's southern edge.

St Dunstan's Basilica   NOTABLE BUILDING

(📞 902-894-3486; www.stdunstanspei.com; 45 Great George St; ⊙ 9am-5pm) **FREE** Rising from the ashes of a 1913 fire, the three towering stone spires of this Catholic, neo-Gothic basilica are now a Charlottetown landmark. The marble floors, Italianate carvings and decoratively embossed ribbed ceiling are surprisingly ornate.

Beaconsfield
Historic House   NOTABLE BUILDING

(📞 902-368-6603; www.peimuseum.ca; 2 Kent St; adult/student/family $5/4/14; ⊙ 10am-4pm daily Jul & Aug, Mon-Fri May, Jun, Sep & Oct, from noon Mon-Fri Nov-Apr) Charlottetown has its fair share of impressive period buildings, but this handsome mansion is the finest. Designed and built by the prominent PEI architect WC Harris in 1877 for James Peake, a wealthy shipowner, and his wife Edith, it sports all the fashionable features of the day: elegant 19th-century furnishings, gingerbread trim, a grand verandah and a crowning belvedere.

COWS Creamery   FACTORY

(📞 902-566-5558; www.cowscreamery.ca/tours; 397 Capital Dr; ⊙ 10am-6pm) **FREE** Apart from the potato, the ice cream produced here is arguably PEI's best-known export (there's even a COWS in Beijing these days). So it would be a crime not to sample some – you can take a self-guided tour of the factory, step into a cheese cave, try some Avonlea Clothbound Cheddar and, of course, eat enough ice cream to make yourself ill.

⌖ Tours

★ Confederation
Players Walking Tours   WALKING

(📞 800-565-0278; www.confederationcentre.com/heritage/confederation-players; 6 Prince St; adult/child $17/12; ⊙ Jul & Aug) There is no better way to tour Charlottetown. Playing the fathers and ladies of Confederation, actors garbed in 19th-century dress educate and

PRINCE EDWARD ISLAND CHARLOTTETOWN

Charlottetown

400 m
0.2 miles

East (Hillsborough) River

Peake's Wharf

Maritime Bus (900m); T3 Transit (900m)

Charlottetown Farmers Market (2km)

Victoria Park

Government House

Charlottetown

entertain visitors as they walk through the town's historic streets. Tours leave from the Visitor Information Centre (p441) at Founders' Hall, with a variety of themes and itineraries to choose from.

Peake's Wharf
Boat Cruises CRUISE
(☎ 902-566-4458; www.charlottetownboattours.com; 1 Great George St; tours from $40; ☺ Jun-Sep) Observe sea life, hear interesting stories and witness a wonderfully different perspective of Charlottetown from the waters of its harbor aboard the 45ft good ship *Fairview*. Assorted itineraries of varying durations are available.

🎊 Festivals & Events

Fall Flavours FOOD & DRINK
(☎ 866-960-9912; www.fallflavours.ca; ☺ Sep) Now one of the island's largest festivals, this massive, month-long kitchen party merges traditional music with incredible cuisine. Don't miss the oyster-shucking championships or the chowder challenge.

Farm Day in
the City FOOD & DRINK
(www.discovercharlottetown.com/events/farm-day-in-the-city; ☺ Oct) PEI farmers get their big day out in early October, when 150 producers and food stalls, a beer garden and tasting events take over the center of Charlottetown.

PEI International
Shellfish Festival FOOD & DRINK
(www.peishellfish.com; ☺ mid-Sep) Crustaceans and shellfish take center stage at this high-profile seafood fest.

PEI Burger Love FOOD & DRINK
(www.peiburgerlove.ca; ☺ Mar) Although a province-wide event, this month-long celebration of the humble burger has gained cult-like status in the restaurants of Charlottetown, which try to outdo each other for the title of PEI's most-loved burger.

Festival of Small Halls MUSIC
(www.smallhalls.com; ☺ mid-Jun) Island musicians, dancers and storytellers who have 'made it' out of the province return to their homeland to perform in rural community halls around PEI during this popular festival.

Charlottetown Festival PERFORMING ARTS
(☎ 800-565-0278; www.confederationcentre.com; ☺ Jun-Sep) This long-running festival organized by the Confederation Centre of the Arts (p440) features free outdoor performances, a children's theater and dance programs.

🛏 Sleeping

Charlottetown Backpackers Inn HOSTEL $
(☎ 902-367-5749; www.charlottetownbackpackers.com; 60 Hillsborough St; dm/r incl breakfast $34/95; ☺) Impossible to miss with its bright red-and-white paint job and happy

hostellers milling about on the lawn, this superbly happening backpackers has single-sex or mixed dorms, a good kitchen and a quirky common room with a turntable and a rather epic vinyl collection. Be prepared for spontaneous barbecues and pub outings.

★ Great George
BOUTIQUE HOTEL $$

(☑902-892-0606; www.thegreatgeorge.com; 58 Great George St; d/ste from $199/259; ✿☎) This colorful collage of celebrated buildings along Charlottetown's most famous street has rooms ranging from plush and historic to bold and contemporary. Its room designs cover all bases – from multiroom layouts (ideal for families) to self-contained suites.

Hotel on Pownal
HOTEL $$

(☑902-892-1217; www.thehotelonpownal. com; 146 Pownal St; d from $189; P☎) Charlottetown can be pricey, which makes this motel-conversion hotel a handy find. Rooms are boxy but well appointed, and rates include parking and a complimentary breakfast – and they stay reasonable even in the height of summer. Ask for an upper-floor room, as the ground-floor ones can feel a bit dingy. Soundproofing isn't the best; bring earplugs.

Holman Grand Hotel
HOTEL $$

(☑877-455-4726; www.theholmangrand.com; 123 Grafton St; d/ste from $209/299) Rising rather incongruously above Charlottetown's redbrick facades, this central and practical hotel is an excellent base. Rooms are modern and rather functional, but some have added bonuses like outside terraces and floor-to-ceiling windows.

Charlotte's Rose Inn
INN $$

(☑902-892-3699; www.charlottesrose.com; 11 Grafton St; apt/d from $150/165; ✿☎) Frilly as a pair of lace curtains, this feminine B&B has attractive, antique-filled rooms, mostly named after PEI notables (LM Montgomery, Jacques Cartier and John A Macdonald), as well as a spacious loft suite with its own private deck. Creaky hallways and vintage decor add to the charm – as do the complimentary tea and cakes.

Fitzroy Hall B&B
B&B $$

(☑866-627-9766; www.fitzroyhall.com; 45 Fitzroy St; d/ste from $199/249; ☎) Built for a banker in 1872, this Victorian house brims with antiques: original fireplaces, mahogany beds, wing-back chairs, secretary desks and period styling to match. It's definitely not one for minimalists, though.

★ Fairholm National Historic Inn
INN $$$

(☑902-892-5022; www.fairholminn.com; 230 Prince St; d $179-309; ☎) Always hankered to stay in a museum? Well, the Fairholm can oblige, with a gorgeous selection of rooms inside a stunning, bay-windowed period inn dating from 1838, plus self-catering rooms and apartments in several other period properties just along the street. It feels seriously luxurious – it's well worth bumping up to the king rooms for architectural bragging rights.

Sydney Boutique Inn & Suites
BOUTIQUE HOTEL $$$

(☑902-367-5888; www.sydneyinn.com; 55 Weymouth St; d/ste from $199/349; P✿☎) You won't find a more imposing facade in Charlottetown than the Sydney's – converted from the town's old Notre Dame Convent (built 1857), it's a redbrick eye-catcher. Rooms are smart, in shades of cream and pale yellow, ranging from 'micro' doubles to roomy self-catering suites. It's worth bumping up the price bracket for more space and views.

Delta Prince Edward
HOTEL $$$

(☑902-566-2222; www.marriott.com; 18 Queen St; d/ste from $211/321; P⊖✿☎▣) The town's traditional choice for delegates and overnighting business travelers (it's linked to the Convention Centre), the Marriott-owned Delta might belong to a big chain, but you can't beat its waterfront location. Rooms are mostly fresh and modern, and there are the usual upscale amenities like a fitness room and spa.

Eating

Sugar Skull Cantina
MEXICAN $

(☑902-367-5141; www.sugarskullcantina.ca; 83 Water St; mains $9-13; ⊙noon-8pm) *Arriba!* This on-trend Mexican joint is one of the funnest places to eat in town, with its zingy Mexicano decor, outside deck and pitchers of pink lemonade, sangria and blueberry mojitos.

There's a choice of dining styles – you can go classic with fish tacos, spit-roasted chicken or a burrito bowl, or pick a 'share-and-compare' platter of taquito fingers or street corn.

THE CONFEDERATION TRAIL

Following the course of the railway that once cut right across PEI but was finally abandoned for good in 1989, the Confederation Trail (www.tourismpei.com/pei-confederation-trail) is one of the best cycling routes in Canada. Winding through a varied landscape of fields, forests, rivers, valleys and coastline, it's a pleasure to cycle – not least because it's almost entirely flat. Some sections of the trail are completely canopied; in late June and the early weeks of July the trail is lined with bright, flowering lupines, and in fall the changing colors of the foliage are a wonder.

The tip-to-tip distance from Tignish in the northwest to Elmira in the northeast is 273km, but branch trails bring the total possible distance to 435km. You don't necessarily have to do the trail in one go: it's easily done in sections, since the main trail passes through major towns including Summerside, Kensington and Mt Stewart, with branches to other towns including Charlottetown, Souris and Montague.

Distance is measured from west to east (Tignish is at 0km, Elmira at 273km); since prevailing winds on PEI blow from the west and southwest, cycling in this direction is easier.

You can download a trail map and route guide from the Tourism PEI website, and information centers can help with route guidance, accommodations and bike rental.

Receiver Coffee DINER $

(www.receivercoffee.com; 128 Richmond St; coffee $2-5; ⊙7am-7pm Sun-Thu, to 8pm Fri & Sat) Receiver is the coffee connoisseurs' choice in Charlottetown. Come here for the perfect flat white made with ethically sourced Ethiopian single-origin beans. And don't miss the muffins. It's on the attractive pedestrianized part of Richmond St known as Victoria Row (look out for the wrought-iron sign).

Charlottetown Farmers Market MARKET

(☑902-626-3373; www.charlottetownfarmersmarket.com; 100 Belvedere Ave; ⊙9am-2pm Sat) Enjoy some prepared island foods or peruse the cornucopia of fresh organic fruit and vegetables. The market is north of the town center, off University Ave.

Kettle Black CAFE $

(☑902-370-0776; www.kettleblackpei.com; 45 Queen St; light lunches $9; ⊙7am-7pm) Every town needs its coffee corner, and this place is Charlottetown's, with hand-written menus and sofas to lounge around on while indulging in your flat white and home-baked muffin. The brunch menu and lunchtime falafels are good too.

Leonhard's CAFE $

(☑902-367-3621; www.leonhards.ca; 142 Great George St; mains from $10; ⊙9am-5pm) A little slice of PEI countryside comes to downtown Charlottetown with this friendly, frilly spot serving generous sandwiches, German pastries, all-day breakfasts and country-style dishes. Get in early around lunchtime.

★ Terre Rouge CANADIAN $$

(☑902-892-4032; www.terrerougepei.ca; 72 Queen St; mains $15-28; ⊙11am-10pm) For our money, the top table in Charlottetown, known for its creative use of island ingredients: a seasonal island veggie platter, brined local lamb chops, a PEI beef burger infused with pork belly, or a deconstructed lobster picnic for two. The space is lovely, with potted plants, colorful furniture, big windows onto the street and a showpiece bar.

★ Water Prince Corner Shop & Lobster Pound SEAFOOD $$

(☑902-368-3212; http://waterprincelobster.ca; 141 Water St; mains $12-36; ⊙9:30am-8pm) When locals want seafood they head to this inconspicuous, sea-blue eatery near the wharf. It is deservedly famous for its scallop burgers, but it's also the best place in town for fresh lobster. You'll probably have to line up for a seat; otherwise order take-out lobster, which gets you a significant discount.

Brickhouse Kitchen & Bar CANADIAN $$

(☑902-566-4620; http://brickhousepei.com; 125 Sydney St; mains $16-30; ⊙11am-10pm) An upscale-grub pub that's crammed with rough-bricked, industrial chic, from the trendy booth seats and open-view kitchen to the pop-art prints on the walls. Dishes take their cue from PEI ingredients – chef Seth's seafood chowder is a favorite, as is the tandoori-spiced roasted hen.

WORTH A TRIP

THE ROAD TO POINT PRIM

If you're looking for a sweet, kid-friendly, half-day trip from Charlottetown and have had your fill of *Anne of Green Gables* action, head east on Rte 1. After about 30km, you'll come to **Orwell Corner Historic Village** (☑902-651-8510; www.orwellcornervillage.ca; Resource Rd 2, Vernon Bridge; adult/child $10.30/5.18; ⊙8:30am-4:30pm daily Jul & Aug, Mon-Fri Jun), a recreation of a rustic 19th-century farming community with animals, antiques and costumed locals. Further down the road, the **Sir Andrew MacPhail Homestead** (☑902-651-2789; www.macphailhomestead.ca; 271 MacPhail Park Rd, Vernon Bridge; ⊙9:30am-4:30pm Tue-Fri Jun-Sep) is open for tea on summer afternoons.

The real delight of the excursion is found continuing south on Rte 1 for a further 11km, where you'll come to signs for Point Prim. This skinny spit of land is covered in wild rose, Queen Anne's lace and wheat fields through summer and has views of red-sand shores on either side. At the tip is the **Point Prim Lighthouse** (☑902-659-2768; www.pointprim lighthouse.com; 2147 Point Prim Rd, Belfast; adult/child $5/3.50; ⊙10am-6pm mid-Jun–mid-Sep): the province's oldest and, we think, prettiest. If you're lucky, you'll be able to climb to the top to pump the foghorn.

Round out your day with a cup of chowder by the ocean at **Point Prim Chowder House** (☑902-659-2187; www.chowderhousepei.com; 2150 Point Prim Rd, Belfast; mains $9-46; ⊙11am-3pm & 4:30-8pm mid-Jun–Sep), then head back to Charlottetown, or continue south to Wood Islands (30km) for your ferry to Nova Scotia.

Pilot House CANADIAN $$$
(☑902-894-4800; www.thepilothouse.ca; 70 Grafton St; mains $25-33; ⊙11am-10pm Mon-Sat) The old Roger's Hardware building has now become this smart gastropub, but the old wood beams, brick columns and etched windows have been left in situ for character.

There's a choice of pub classics or upscale dining, washed down with a generous supply of beers, wines and whiskies.

Drinking & Nightlife

★**Hopyard** BAR
(☑902-367-2599; 131 Kent St; ⊙11am-midnight) It's almost too-cool-for-school, this place – with craft beer on tap, racks of vinyl to browse and a regularly changing menu of small plates to snack on. It's a big hit locally, and has since spawned a sister establishment over in Halifax.

Craft Beer Corner BREWERY
(Upstreet Craft Brewing; ☑902-894-0543; www.upstreetcraftbrewing.com; 156 Great George St; ⊙noon-midnight) Charlottetown's premier craft brewer now has a downtown location for its trendy taproom, where you can sip brews like the Commons Pilsner, White Noize IPA and unusual strawberry-rhubarb Rhuby Social. The brewery serves sharing plates too.

Charlottetown Beer Garden BEER GARDEN
(☑902-367-6070; www.beergardenpei.com; 190-192 Kent St; ⊙4pm-1am or 1:30am Mon-Fri, from 2pm Sat & Sun) This building on Hunter's Corner has been many things – house, tearoom, bike shop, tattoo parlor – but its current incarnation as a beer garden seems to be the most popular. Pan-Canadian brews on tap, with a special focus on beers from Nova Scotia, New Brunswick and PEI.

Merchantman BAR
(☑902-892-9150; www.merchantman.ca; 23 Queen St; ⊙11am-9pm) Merchantman wears many hats; it's a bar, it's a restaurant, it's a takeout. In summer months, the patio tables are a great place to soak up the sun and enjoy a drink while you work up your appetite for fresh PEI oysters, seafood or all manner of upscale pub grub.

Entertainment

★**Confederation Centre of the Arts** THEATER
(☑902-566-1267; www.confederationcentre.com; 145 Richmond St) This modern complex's large theater and outdoor amphitheater host concerts, comedic performances and elaborate musicals. *Anne of Green Gables – The Musical* has been entertaining audiences here as part of the Charlottetown Festival since 1964, making it Canada's longest-running

musical. You'll enjoy it, and your friends will never have to know.

Mack THEATER
(☑902-566-1267; www.confederationcentre.com/venues/the-mack; 128 Great George St) An intimate venue where guests sit at round tables for (mainly) comedy gigs. Bookings are handled through the Confederation Centre Box Office.

Baba's Lounge LIVE MUSIC
(☑902-892-7377; 181 Great George St; ⊙11am–midnight) Known to locals just as Baba's, this small upstairs venue is the place to go for local bands.

Benevolent Irish Society LIVE MUSIC
(☑902-963-3156; 582 North River Rd; $10; ⊙8pm Fri) On the north side of town, this is a great place to catch a ceilidh. Come early, as seating is limited.

❶ Information

MEDICAL SERVICES
Queen Elizabeth Hospital (☑902-894-2111; 60 Riverside Dr; ⊙24hr) Emergency room.
Polyclinic Professional Centre (☑902-629-8810; www.polycliniconline.com; 199 Grafton St; ⊙5:30-8pm Mon-Fri, 9:30am-noon Sat) Charlottetown's after-hours, walk-in medical clinic.

POST
Main Post Office (☑902-628-4400; 101 Kent St; ⊙9am-5pm Mon-Fri) Central post office.

TOURIST INFORMATION
Charlottetown Visitor Information Centre (☑902-368-4444; vicharlottetown@gov.pe.ca; 6 Prince St; ⊙9am-5pm) The island's main tourist office at Founder's Hall has all the lowdown you need on Charlottetown and the wider island, plus a plethora of brochures and maps, and free wi-fi.

❶ Getting There & Away

AIR
Charlottetown Airport (YYG; ☑902-566-7997; www.flypei.com; 250 Maple Hills Ave) is 8km north of the city center. A taxi to/from town costs $16, plus $5 for each additional person.

BUS
T3 Transit County Line Express (T3 Transit; ☑902-566-9962; www.t3transit.ca; 7 Mt Edward Rd) runs between Charlottetown and Summerside ($9, 1½ hours, Monday to Friday only).

Maritime Bus (p334) also runs a bus service to/from Halifax ($58.25 one way, 4½ hours, two daily).

CAR & MOTORCYCLE
Rental cars, available from a variety of providers with city and airport depots, are the preferred method of transportation to/from Charlottetown. Cars are in short supply during summer, so be sure to book ahead.

❶ Getting Around

BICYCLE
MacQueen's Bicycles (☑902-368-2453; www.macqueens.com; 430 Queen St; rental per day/week $40/210) Rental bikes for getting around town and the Confederation Trail.

BUS
Limited public transportation is provided by T3 Transit, but walking or renting a bike are both great ways to get around this compact city.

TAXI
City Taxi (☑902-892-6567; www.citytaxipei.com; 195 Kent St)
Yellow Cab PEI (☑902-566-6666; www.yellowcabpei.com; 1-14 MacAleer Dr)

EASTERN PRINCE EDWARD ISLAND

Outside the summer beach season, few folk make the trek out to explore the eastern part of PEI, and that's a real shame – it's every bit as pretty as the middle of the island, and arguably offers a truer picture of the island's rural character. From stretches of neatly tended homesteads to the sinuous eastern shore with its sheltered harbors, country inns, historic lighthouses and white, sandy beaches, it's well worth the road trip – and easily doable in a day from Charlottetown.

The 338km Points East Coastal Drive (www.pointseastcoastaldrive.com) makes a full circuit around the eastern headland of PEI. Planning tools and maps are available on the website.

Wood Islands
☑902 / POP 470

The strung-out coastal settlement of Wood Islands is principally of interest if you're planning on catching a ferry to Nova Scotia – boats chug across the channel at least once a day. If you have time to spare, it's worth detouring via the artsy little fishing community of Murray River, and the historic lighthouses at Cape Bear and Wood Islands, which can be reached along the coastal Rte 18.

◉ Sights

Cape Bear Lighthouse & Marconi Station
LIGHTHOUSE

(www.capebearlighthouse.com) This three-story lighthouse looks like many others in PEI, but it has its own unique place in history. Built in 1881, it was chosen in 1905 as the site of a Marconi Wireless Telegraph Station. Seven years later, on the night of April 14, 1912, operator Thomas Bartlett was the first person to receive a distress call from a passenger vessel that was sinking somewhere off the coast of Newfoundland. That vessel's name? The *Titanic*.

Wood Islands Lighthouse
LIGHTHOUSE

(www.woodislands.ca; ☉ 9:30am-5:30pm Jun-Sep) If you'll be waiting a while at the ferry terminal, it's worth visiting this 1876 lighthouse, which has a good gift shop, a small shipbuilding gallery and fabulous views from its tower. Tours run from June to September.

Newman Estate Winery
WINERY

(☑902-962-4223; www.newmanestatewinery.com; 9404 Gladstone Rd, Gladstone; ☉by appointment) Head toward the coast from Murray River along Rte 348 (Gladstone Rd) to find Newman Estate Winery. This lovely place specializes in blueberry wines, but has recently begun making white wine from its grapes, too.

Rossignol Estate Winery
WINERY

(☑902-962-4193; www.rossignolwinery.com; 11147 Shore Rd, Murray River; ☉10am-5pm Mon-Sat, from noon Sun May-Oct) For wine tasting on a grand scale, cruise over to Little Sands, 9km from the Wood Islands Ferry, where Rossignol Estate Winery has free tastings and specializes in fruit wines. The blackberry mead has won a string of gold medals and the wild rose liqueur made from rose hips is also well worth a try; call ahead for winter hours.

❶ Information

Wood Islands Visitor Information Centre (☑ 902-962-7411; 13054 Shore Rd; ☉10:30am-5pm mid-May–mid-Oct) Right on the Confederation Trail, this is the main visitor center for those arriving on PEI by ferry.

❶ Getting There & Away

Wood Islands is 51km southeast of Charlottetown and the boarding point for Bay Ferries (p331) services to Caribou, Nova Scotia (adult/child $20/free, 1¼ hours). A standard vehicle costs $79, bicycles $20.

Montague & Georgetown

The fact that Montague isn't flat gives it a unique, inland feel. Perched on either side of the Montague River, the busy little town is the service center for Kings County; its streets lead from the breezy, heritage marina area to modern shopping malls, supermarkets and fast-food outlets.

Around the peninsula, the many historic buildings in Georgetown are testament to the town's importance as a shipbuilding center in the Victorian era. Today it's a mix of sleepy village and tourist spot thanks to its great places to eat and its waterfront setting.

The **Panmure island Powwow** (☑902-892-5314; ☉mid-Aug) is held in mid-August with drumming, crafts and a sweat tent – attracts around 5000 visitors, so don't expect to find any secluded beaches around here during that time.

◉ Sights & Activities

Panmure Head Lighthouse
LIGHTHOUSE

(www.panmureislandlighthouse.ca; 62 Lighthouse Rd, Panmure Island; tours $5; ☉10am-6pm mid-Jun–mid-Sep) Completely restored by community volunteers in 2015, this 1853 lighthouse was constructed to guide shipping vessels into Georgetown Harbour. It has an unusual octagonal design, shingled in wood and laid out over four stories, measuring 17.5m from base to vane. Tours of the lighthouse are available in the summer season.

Garden of the Gulf Museum
MUSEUM

(☑902-838-2467; www.montaguemuseumpei.com; 564 Main St, Montague; adult/child under 12yr $5/free; ☉9am-5pm Tue-Sat Jul & Aug, Mon-Fri Sep) On the southern side of the river, the statuesque former post office and customs house (1888) overlooks the marina, and since 1958 has been home to this small community museum (the oldest on PEI, apparently). The displays are strictly local-interest: historic photos of the town, Mi'kmaq artifacts and a recreation of an old general store.

Tranquility Cove Adventures
FISHING

(☑902-969-7184; www.tcapei.com; Fisherman's Wharf, 1 Kent St, Georgetown; half-day tours from $45) Starfish hunting, deep-sea fishing and a giant bar clam dig are just a few of the activities offered by this adventure company based at the Georgetown wharf. In winter, it arranges snowmobile tours.

🛏 Sleeping

Brudenell River
Provincial Park   CAMPGROUND $
(✑902-652-8966; www.tourismpei.com/provin
cial-park/brudenell-river; off Rte 3, Cardigan; tent
sites $28-30, RV sites $32-37; ⊙May-Oct; ℗) Development meets nature at Brudenell River
Provincial Park, a park and resort complex
just north of town. Tent and RV sites are
available, as well as cottages and motel-style
accommodations. Activities range from kayaking to nature walks and golf on two championship courses.

Georgetown Inn & Dining Room   INN $$
(✑902-652-2511; www.peigeorgetownhistoricinn.
com; 62 Richmond St, Georgetown; d from $120;
🛜) Eight island-themed rooms are on offer
at this fine old Georgetown house, includ-
ing a spacious captain's room with jet tub
and a shared outside deck, a bay-windowed
harbor room and (of course) a Green Gables
suite. The restaurant is good too (mains
from $15).

🍴 Eating & Drinking

Clam Diggers   SEAFOOD $$
(✑902-583-3111; www.clamdiggerspei.com; 6864
Water St, Georgetown; mains $12-35; ⊙11:30am-
9pm) Recently relocated to a creekside spot,
this popular seafood diner is a brilliant
place for brunch, lunch or dinner, with local
specialties such as breaded clams, old-fashioned shanty bake (basically fish pie) and
hot scallop caesar.

Wheelhouse Inn   DINER $$
(✑902-652-2474; www.wheelhouseingeorgetown.
com; 7 West St, Georgetown; mains $15-36;
⊙11:30am-9pm) This waterside pub has the
best dinner views in Georgetown, looking
clear across the harbor. The menu is di-
vided into 'lower deck' (casual dishes like
fish-and-chips and lobster melt), 'upper
deck' (mains of fish, meat and steaks) or big
'shareables' platters of mussels, seafood and
snow crab. There's a fun cocktail menu – try
the Terry's berries blueberry lemonade.

★Cardigan Lobster Suppers   SEAFOOD $$$
(✑902-583-2020; www.peicardiganlobstersup
pers.com; 4557 Wharf Rd, Cardigan; seafood
mains $25-35; ⊙5-9pm Jun-Oct) In tiny Car-
digan, enjoy a five-course lobster supper in
a heritage building on the harbor. There's
also good-quality pub grub – fish cakes,
Irish stew, steak sandwiches – on offer in

1888, housed in a separate building next
door.

★Copper Bottom Brewing   BREWERY
(✑902-361-2337; www.copperbottombrewing.
com; 567 Main St, Montague; ⊙11am-10pm Mon-
Wed, to 11pm Thu-Sat, noon-8pm Sun) The first
craft brewery and taproom to open in King's
County, this lively establishment serves up
a range of ales to its Montague clientele,
including an intriguing Blueberry Sour and
an extra-hoppy double IPA, Parkman Ave.
Founder Ken Spears learned his craft at Propeller (p347) in Halifax, so he really knows
his beers, as does his equally ale-crazy wife,
Ashley Condon.

ℹ Getting There & Away

Georgetown is 52km east of Charlottetown.
Montague is 16km west of Georgetown.

Souris & Around

✑902 / POP 1173
Wrapped around the waters of Colville Bay
is the bustling fishing community of Souris
(*sur*-rey). It owes its name to the French
Acadians and the gluttonous mice (*souris* in
French) who repeatedly ravaged their crops.
It's now known more for its joyous annual
music festival than for the hungry field ro-
dents of old.

This is a working town that's a friendly
jumping-off point for cycling the coastal
road (Rte 16) and the Confederation Trail,
which comes into town. Souris is also the
launching point for ferries to the Îles de la
Madeleine in Québec.

The wooded coast and lilting accents
along this stretch of coastline offer some
welcome variety from the patchwork of
farms found inland. Giant white windmills
march across the landscape. North Lake
and Naufrage harbors are intriguing places
to stop and, if you feel so inclined, join a
charter boat in search of a monster 450kg
tuna.

◉ Sights

★East Point Lighthouse   LIGHTHOUSE
(✑902-357-2106; www.eastpointlighthouse.ca;
adult/child $6/3.50; ⊙10am-6pm Jun-Aug) Built
in 1867 (the same year as Confederation),
the East Point Lighthouse still guards PEI's
northeastern shore. As you climb the 67
steps to the top, you'll see a collection of
old lenses, a gallery of former lighthouse

keepers and the original lantern machinery, before topping out on the 5th floor for wrap-around views of East Point.

The lighthouse has been moved twice. After its original location inland was blamed for the 1882 wreck of the British *Phoenix*, the lighthouse was moved a half-mile closer to shore in 1885 using a system of weighs, capstan and horses. The lighthouse was moved again in 1908 due to coastal erosion, and to accommodate the expansion of the foghorn building, which now houses a pleasant craft shop (open 9am to 7pm in summer).

Elmira Railway Museum
MUSEUM

(☑902-357-7234; Rte 16A; adult/student/family $5/4/10; ⊙9:30am-4pm daily Jul & Aug, Mon-Fri Jun & Sep) Once upon a time, the station at Elmira represented the end of the line for PEI's railway; it now marks the eastern end of the Confederation Trail. This little museum explores the railway's history, and is home to the largest model railway collection in Canada. There's also a miniature train (adult/student/family $6/4/15) that winds through the surrounding forest.

✲✲ Festivals & Events

PEI Bluegrass &
Old Time Music Festival
MUSIC

(☑902-569-3153; http://peibluegrass.tripod.com; ⊙early Jul) The PEI Bluegrass & Old Time Music Festival draws acts from as far away as Nashville. Come for just a day, or camp out for all three.

🛏 Sleeping & Eating

Johnson Shore Inn
INN $$

(☑902-687-1340; www.jsipei.com; 9984 North-side Rd, Hermanville; r from $120; ⊙May-Jan; 🛜) Coastal luxury and stunning views of St Lawrence Bay are the calling cards at this lovely seaside inn, clad in white clapboard and full of Atlantic Canadian character. Rooms are priced according to the quality of the sea view, but they're all extremely elegant.

★ Inn at Bay Fortune
INN $$$

(☑902-687-3745; https://innatbayfortune.com; 758 Rte 310, Bay Fortune; r from $225; P✳🛜) Without doubt the plushest place to stay (and dine) on the whole of PEI, this swanky inn is the domain of celebrity chef Michael Smith. Built in 1913 as a 20-hectare summer residence for Broadway playwright Elmer Harris and family, it's been renovated with serious style. There's a choice of palatial rooms in the main inn or the attached towers.

21 Breakwater
CANADIAN $$

(☑902-687-2556; 21 Breakwater St; mains $12-28; ⊙11:30am-8pm or 9pm Mon-Sat) Owners Pedro and Betty have made their little restaurant in Souris a destination for casual fine dining. Yes, you'll find mussels and fish chowder on the menu, but also poached haddock, Portuguese fish-and-chips and brined pork steak.

It's in a handsome mansion overlooking the waterfront.

WORTH A TRIP

PEI DISTILLERIES

Two distinctly different distilleries operate on PEI, echoing the province's fame for boot-legging during Prohibition. Even today many families distill their own moonshine (which is technically illegal) and this is what is often mixed in punch and cocktails at country weddings and parties.

Prince Edward Distillery (☑902-687-2586; www.princeedwarddistillery.com; Rte 16, Hermanville; ⊙11am-6pm) has two varieties on its list: the original potato vodka (this is PEI, after all!), and a more recent one that's made from wild blueberries. You can take a tour of the distillery and try your hand at mixology with a cocktail-making masterclass.

Myriad View Distillery (☑902-687-1281; www.straitshine.com; 1336 Rte 2, Rollo Bay; ⊙10am-6pm Mon-Sat, 11am-5pm Sun) produces Canada's first and only legal moonshine. The hard-core, double-distilled Straight Lightning Shine is 75% alcohol and so potent it feels like liquid heat before it evaporates on your tongue. Take our advice and start with a micro-sip. A gulp could knock the wind out of you. The 50% alcohol Straight Shine lets you enjoy the flavor a bit more. Myriad View also brews a brandy, pastis, gin, whiskey, rum, vodka and even a unique dandelion 'shine. Tours and tastings are free.

It's about 17km along Rte 307 between the two distilleries.

★ **FireWorks** CANADIAN $$$

(☑902-687-3745; https://innatbayfortune.com/fireworks; 758 Rte 310, Bay Fortune; per person $155; ⊙from 5pm) Since taking over the Inn at Bay Fortune in 2015, Food Network star Michael Smith has created one of PEI's most unique dining experiences: the 'Fire-Works feast,' based around a monstrous 7.5m brick-lined, wood-burning oven. It features a smorgasbord of oysters, hot-smoked fish, flame-grilled steaks, seafood chowder and fire-oven bread, served at long butcher-block tables: a truly epic barbecue banquet.

Guests staying at the Inn automatically receive a reservation at the feast. The event also includes a tour of the kitchen garden and farm.

❶ Getting There & Away

Souris is 72km east of Charlottetown and located in the northeast corner of the island. Souris is also the boarding point for the **CTMA Ferry** (☑ 902-687-2181; www.traversierctma.ca/en) to Québec's Îles de la Madeleine (one way from $54.30 in high season, $101.25 with car, five hours).

St Peter's Bay to Mt Stewart

The area between the villages of St Peter's Bay and Mt Stewart is a hotbed for cycling. The section of the Confederation Trail closest to St Peter's Bay flirts with the shoreline and rewards riders with an eyeful of coastal views.

In Mt Stewart, three riverside sections of the Confederation Trail converge, giving riders and hikers plenty of attractive options within a relatively compact area.

★ **Trailside Cafe & Inn** CAFE $$

(☑902-628-7833; www.trailside.ca; 109 Main St, Mt Stewart; mains $12-17) This stomping venue is one of the best places in eastern PEI to catch some live music – owners Pat and Meghann are passionate music lovers, and they attract top artists to their night-time performances. The shingled building, dating from 1897, makes an intimate space, and you can dine on pizzas, cheese and charcuterie platters while you enjoy the show.

There are also four rooms upstairs. If you can't make a dinner show, try and catch the Hillsborough River Gospel Brunch

---

DON'T MISS

BASIN HEAD PROVINCIAL PARK

The star attraction of **Basin Head Provincial Park** (www.tourismpei.com/provincial-park/basin-head) is the sweeping sand of golden **Basin Head Beach**. Many islanders rank this as their favorite beach and we have to agree. The sand is also famous for its singing – well, squeaking – when you walk on it. Unfortunately, the sand only performs when dry, so if it's been raining, it's no show. Five minutes of joyous 'musical' footsteps south from the park's fisheries museum and you have secluded bliss – enjoy!

($22), held on summer Sundays in July and August.

CENTRAL PRINCE EDWARD ISLAND

Central PEI contains a bit of all that's best about the island: verdant fields, quaint villages and forests undulating north to the dramatic sand-dune-backed beaches of Prince Edward Island National Park.

The main attraction for many people is Cavendish, the fictional home of Anne of Green Gables, the engaging heroine of Lucy Maud Montgomery's 1908 novel – but in truth, the town has changed a bit since Lucy's day (unless we missed the passages filled with parking lots, gift shops and chain hotels). It's still worth visiting for die-hard fans, but everyone else will be much better rewarded by taking a leaf out of PEI-ers' books and heading straight to the beach.

❶ Information

For those entering central PEI via the Confederation Bridge, it's worth stopping at the **Borden-Carleton Visitor Information Centre** (☑902-437-8570; Hwy 1; ⊙8:30am-8pm), just off the bridge on the PEI side, for its free maps, brochures and restrooms.

Victoria

☑902 / POP 100

A place to wander and experience more than 'see,' this lovely little fishing village has

GREENWICH DUNES

Massive, dramatic and ever-shifting sand dunes epitomize the amazing area west of Greenwich. These rare parabolic giants are fronted by an awesome, often empty beach. Preserved by Parks Canada in 1998, this 6km section of shore is now part of Prince Edward Island National Park. Learn about it all in the **Greenwich Interpretation Centre** (🖉902-961-2514; Rte 13; ⊘9:30am-7pm Jul & Aug, to 4:30pm May, Jun, Sep & Oct).

shaded, tree-laden lanes that scream character and charm. The entire village still fits neatly in the four blocks laid out when the town was formed in 1819. Colorful clapboard and shingled houses are home to more than one visitor who was so enthralled by the place they decided to stay. There's a profusion of art, cafes and eateries, as well as an excellent summer theater festival.

By the Sea Kayaking (🖉902-658-2572; www.bytheseakayaking.ca; 1 Water St; kayak rentals per hour/day from $25/50) rents kayaks or stand-up paddleboards by the hour, or you could sign up for a guided expedition to the local sea colony at Granville Island or to the Confederation Bridge. They also offer kayak-and-clamming expeditions ($90), where you get to learn to dig like a true PEI-er on the Tryon Shoal.

🛏 Sleeping & Eating

Treetop Haven   TREEHOUSE $$
(🖉902-439-0267; www.treetophaven.ca; 1210 Mount Tryon Rd; pods from $200) And now for something a little different: five geodesic 'tree-pods,' hidden away in woodland about 19km from Victoria. The pods range in size, but all have proper beds, kitchen, wooden deck and private hot tub, and you can listen to the sounds of nature as you nod to sleep. Glamping's not for everyone, but it's a change from boring B&Bs.

★ Landmark Oyster House   CAFE $$
(🖉902-658-2286; www.landmarkcafe.ca; 12 Main St; mains lunch $13-22, dinner $19-34; ⊘11am-9pm or 10pm daily May-Oct, 9am-2pm Sat-Sun only Nov & Dec) Despite the name, there's a lot more on offer at this super-friendly cafe-diner than oysters (although you can certainly sample the holy bivalves if you want, choosing 'em raw, deep-fried or baked). The menu

is a catch-all treat of island flavors: pot pies, fish cakes, surf and turf, as well as a selection of sumptuous platters.

Lobster Barn Pub and Eatery   PUB
(🖉902-658-2722; 19 Main St; ⊘noon-10pm) This gorgeous little pub in an old barn is a great place for a beer, but the food's good too – and yes, there's lobsterr.

ⓘ Getting There & Away

Victoria is midway between Summerside (37km) and Charlottetown (36km) on the Trans-Canada Hwy.

Prince Edward Island National Park

For most Canadians, if you mention PEI, the image that comes immediately to mind is the sprawling, dune-backed beaches of the north shore – nearly all of which are encompassed within the borders of Prince Edward Island National Park. Established in 1937, the park runs in a narrow strip for 42km along the island's north coast, ranging in width from a few kilometers to just a few hundred meters.

Beaches lined with marram grasses and wild rose span almost the entire length of the park's 42km coastline: from west to east, the main ones are Cavendish (the largest and busiest), MacNeills Brook, North Rustico, Brackley, Stanhope and Dalvay. Greenwich Beach, on the west side of Tracadie Bay, is also inside the national park. The beaches further east tend to be quieter.

In summer, it's sunbathing central – finding a free patch of sand (or a parking space) can be a challenge. But outside July and August, the beaches are much quieter – and in winter, the park's pretty much deserted.

A beautiful bike lane runs all the way along the coast.

PEI National Park Campgrounds   CAMPGROUND $
(🖉800-414-6765; www.pc.gc.ca/eng/pn-np/pe/pei-ipe/visit.aspx; campsites $27.40-35.30; ⊘Jun-Aug) Parks Canada operates three campgrounds: at Cavendish, Robinsons Island and Stanhope, spread along the park's length. You can request a campground, but not a specific campsite. Booking online is the most sensible option: 80% of sites can be booked in advance; the remaining sites are first-come, first-served, so it's wise to arrive early.

❶ Getting There & Away

The park's western entrance is in Cavendish, 37km from Charlottetown. Its eastern gate in North Rustico is 25km from Charlottetown.

Brackley Beach

At the eastern end of Prince Edward Island National Park, Brackley Beach isn't so much a town as a rural area, with a few hotels, restaurants and cafes dotted on or around the coastline. The main attraction here is, of course, the eponymous beach.

A few miles east along the coast, Stanhope is a tranquil corner of the national park, popular with beachgoers and golfers, as well as *Green Gables* tourists wanting afternoon tea at the historic hotel Dalvay by the Sea, a frequent location used back in the 1980s miniseries. It's also of interest to historians: Stanhope was the site of one of the first communities of British settlers in PEI, who arrived in the late 18th century.

🛏 Sleeping & Eating

Brackley Beach Hostel　　　HOSTEL **$**
(☑902-672-1900; www.brackleybeachhostel. com; 37 Britain Shore Rd; dm/d/tr/f from $39.10/79.35/108.10/143.75; 🅿🛜) For near-the-beach budget digs you won't find better than this clean and super-friendly hostel housed in a big barn about 2km from the shoreline. There are several eight-bed dorm rooms, plus a few private doubles and family-size rooms, as well as plenty of showers, a game room and an equipped kitchen.

Shaw's Hotel & Cottages　　　COTTAGE **$$**
(☑902-672-2022; www.shawshotel.ca; 99 Apple Tree Rd; d/cottages from $135/175; ✳🛜) With its red roof, geranium-filled window boxes and stripy awnings, Shaw's offers a cheery welcome – as befits Canada's oldest family-operated inn (founded 1860!). Unsurprisingly, rooms feel old-fashioned – flock wallpaper, dated furnishings – but have a certain homey charm. Self-catering chalets offer more comfort (although older cottages don't have kitchens), and the beach is just a 600m walk away.

The dining room is open to outside guests (mains $18 to $30); reservations are recommended for the popular Sunday-evening buffet (held in July and August).

★**Dalvay by the Sea**　　　HISTORIC HOTEL **$$$**
(☑902-672-2048; www.dalvaybythesea.com; 16 Cottage Cres, Dalvay; d/cottages from $189/389; ⊙May-Oct; ✳🛜♨) Built in 1895 by businessman Alexander MacDonald, this gabled mansion will be immediately familiar to *Anne of Green Gables* fans – it featured in the TV series as the White Sands Hotel. It's a sprawling, old-fashioned affair: Adirondack armchairs, huge fireplaces, an enormous dining room and a choice of fusty rooms or self-contained two-room cabins on the hotel's lavishly lawned grounds.

Richard's Seafood　　　SEAFOOD **$**
(☑902-672-3030; www.richardsfreshseafood. com; 9 Wharf Rd, Covehead; mains $8-15; ⊙noon-8:30pm Jun-Sep) Lobster rolls, fish sandwiches, sea-scallop burgers – when it comes to seafood on the north shore, Richard's long-standing shack is the place to go to try it. But it's the crispy haddock and Burbank fries that keep the customers flocking back.

★**Dunes Studio Gallery & Cafe**　　　FUSION **$$**
(☑902-672-2586; www.dunesgallery.com; 3622 Brackley Point Rd; dinner mains $11-30; ⊙cafe 11:30am-9pm Jun-Aug, gallery 9am-6pm or later May-Sep) Wow – this place is worth the trip. Buddha statues, gleaming glass, island artworks and Canadian crafts aplenty in the gallery; a lovely garden filled with exotic plants and blooms; and a great cafe serving sophisticated dishes like Thai mussels, pan-seared scallops and a PEI ploughman's board. Chef Norman Day scooped up the coveted 'Taste Our Island' award in 2018.

Rustico & North Rustico

☑902 / POP 583

Acadian culture lives on in these two seafront settlements, separated by around 5km

---

DON'T MISS

BRACKLEY DRIVE-IN THEATRE
. . . .
Generations of PEI-ers have grown up catching the features at this drive-in **movie theater** (☑902-672-3333; www. drivein.ca; 3164 Brackley Point Rd; adult/child from $12/7.50; ⊙May-Sep). Screening since the 1950s, the drive-in was restored in 1992 – making this a real island experience that's not to be missed. Check the website for forthcoming attractions. Adult prices include a soft drink.

Around PEI National Park

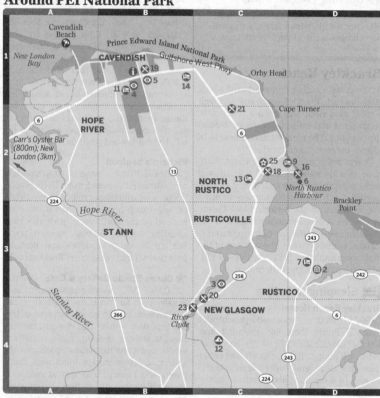

Around PEI National Park

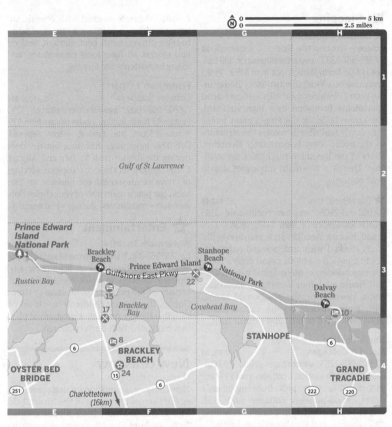

along Rte 6. The first Acadians put down roots here in the 1700s: you can still see several fine historic buildings, and visit the old farmer's bank, now an intriguing museum.

Of the two, North Rustico is the more attractive, with rickety, boxy fisher's houses painted in navies, brick reds and beiges. Taking a walk east from the pier along the boardwalk is a great way to take in the sights, sounds and smells of this atmospheric little village and its busy harbor packed with fishing boats.

Sights & Activities

Farmer's Bank of Rustico & Doucet House   MUSEUM
(☑902-963-2194; www.farmersbank.ca; Church Rd, Rustico; adult/student $6/3.50; ◎9:30am-5:30pm Mon-Sat, 1-5pm Sun Jun-Sep) The solid red-stone Farmer's Bank of Rustico operated here between 1864 and 1894, and served an important role in providing funds for local Acadian communities. It's now a museum

describing the settlement and the importance of the bank's role in local history.

Beside the bank is Doucet House, a wooden-clad Acadian dwelling that's believed to be one of the oldest such structures in the province. It's been carefully restored and contains some interesting Acadian items and 19th-century artifacts.

Outside Expeditions   OUTDOORS
(☑902-963-3366; www.getoutside.com; 374 Harbourview Dr, North Rustico; tours from $45; ◎May-Oct) Situated at the far end of the harbor in a bright-yellow fishing shed, this outdoors company runs regular guided kayak tours, and rents canoes (from $30 per hour), stand-up paddleboards (from $25 per hour) and bikes. Beginners can go for the 1½-hour introductory 'Beginner Bay' tour, but the three-hour 'Harbour Passage' ($65) and two-hour evening 'Cavendish Coves' ($55) tours offer more coastal scenery.

🛏 Sleeping

★ Canada's Rotating
House – Around the Sea APARTMENT $$
(☑ 866-557-8383; www.aroundthesea.ca; 130 Lantern Hill Dr, North Rustico; apt from $169; P 🛜) Truly one of a kind, this two-story home 'in-the-round' features four fully self-contained apartments furnished to a high standard. The entire building sits atop a giant motor that slowly and silently rotates the structure so the ocean view is constantly changing. Tours of the basement mechanics are available. There's a two-night minimum stay in peak season.

★ Barachois Inn B&B $$
(☑ 902-963-2906; www.barachoisinn.com; 2193 Church Rd, Rustico; r from $140; ❄🛜) This grand, historic Acadian-style mansion is liberally stocked with antiques and paintings, not to mention an 1890s grand piano. There are two buildings: the original gabled Gallant House, with four Victorian-style rooms; and a newer copy, the MacDonald House, with more modern rooms and a fitness suite. Both are a refined and elegant treat.

North Rustico
Motel & Cottages MOTEL $$
(☑ 902-963-2253; www.cottages-pei.ca; 7103 Cavendish Rd, North Rustico; r/cottages from $99/135; P 🛜🏊) Take your pick from motel-style suites, wood-paneled cottages and B&B rooms in the original house: all are simple and pleasant, and the grounds are lovely.

🍴 Eating

★ Blue Mussel Cafe SEAFOOD $$
(☑ 902-963-2152; www.bluemusselcafe.com; 312 Harbourview Dr, North Rustico; mains $15-30; ⊙ 11:30am-8pm or 9pm mid-May–Oct) Simple seafood fresh off the boats is the order of the day at this stylish harborside cafe: Daisy Bay oysters, seared halibut, seafood bubbly bake and a banquet-worthy lobster dinner. The space is light and modern, with glass doors and a wooden-decked interior that seems to bring the outside in. Nothing pretentious here: just great grub. No reservations.

★ Pearl Eatery CANADIAN $$$
(☑ 902-963-2111; http://pearleatery.com; 7792 Cavendish Rd, North Rustico; mains $18-35, 3-course menu $60; ⊙ 5-9pm Tue-Sat mid-Jun–Sep) Local sourcing and seasonal ingredients are key to the ethos at this refined restaurant, overseen by chef Steven Wilson. Set in

a shingled house stocked with eclectic antiques and bric-a-brac, it's a model of farm-to-table dining: lamb, beef, chicken, seafood and oysters all have local provenance, and many ingredients are foraged.

Fisherman's Wharf
Lobster Suppers SEAFOOD $$$
(☑ 902-963-2669; www.fishermanswharf.ca; 7230 Rustico Rd, North Rustico; lobster dinners from $35; ⊙ noon-8:30pm late Jun-Aug, 4-8pm Sep–mid-Oct) This huge place has lines out the door during the dinner rush in July and August. Come hungry, as there are copious servings of chowder, all-you-can-eat mussels, an 18m salad bar plus a main dish of your choice (lobster, snow crab, jumbo shrimp – you name it).

☆ Entertainment

Watermark Theatre THEATER
(☑ 902-963-3963; www.watermarktheatre.com; 57 Church Hill Ave, North Rustico; ticket prices vary) Opened in 2008 to mark the 100th anniversary of the publication of *Anne of Green Gables,* the popular children's novels set on PEI, this theater presents a program of plays in a renovated 19th-century church.

New Glasgow

☑ 902 / POP 1240

New Glasgow is a quiet town that spreads elegantly across the shores of the River Clyde. This is the favorite lobster-supper getaway for folks from Charlottetown, although it's becoming equally respected for its luscious preserves.

⊙ Sights

Glasgow Glen Farm FARM
(☑ 902-963-2496; http://glasgowglenfarm.ca; 190 Lower New Glasgow Rd; ⊙ 10am-5pm Mon-Sat May-Oct) Blessed are the cheesemakers, or so they say. This one produces numerous variants of Gouda, which makes the perfect addition to any picnic hamper. Otherwise, the cheesy goodness is liberally applied to the island's most delicious pizzas.

🛏 Sleeping & Eating

★ New Glasgow Highlands
Camping & Cabins CAMPGROUND $
(☑ 902-964-3232; www.newglasgowhighlands.com; 2499 New Glasgow Rd, Hunter River; tent/RV sites from $38/48, cabins from $65; ⊙ Apr-Nov; 🛜🏊) This lovely wooded campground with well-spaced sites, each with a fire pit, is lo-

cated in Hunter River, 7km south of New Glasgow. For rainy days there are simple cooking facilities in the lodge. There are also bright cabins, each with two bunks, a double bed, a sofa and a picnic table, but no linens or pillows; bathrooms are shared.

★ **The Mill in New Glasgow** CANADIAN $$

(☑902-964-3313; www.themillinnewglasgow.com; 5592 Rte 13; mains $18-35; ☺noon-3pm & 5-9pm Wed-Sun) Chef Emily Wells has turned this lakeside restaurant into a destination address since winning the 'Taste Our Island' competition in 2015. The ethos is comfort food with an upscale twist, often with an Asian-inspired or Provençal flair (fish cakes with sriracha lime mayo, or chicken stuffed with arborio rice, feta, parmesan, almonds and dried cranberries).

Prince Edward Island Preserve Company CAFE $$

(☑902-964-4300; www.preservecompany.com; 2841 New Glasgow Rd; mains $12-26; ☺9am-8pm; ☑) This place carries on the old island tradition of making preserves, chutneys, marmalades, jellies and curds, many from local fruit. There's a cafe too, serving island dishes like hodgepodge haddock, seafood bubbly pie and maritime fish cakes – not to mention a bakeshop and a gift store.

★ **New Glasgow Lobster Supper** SEAFOOD $$$

(☑902-964-2870; www.peilobstersuppers.com; 604 Rte 258; lobster dinners from $37.95; ☺4-8pm Jun–mid-Oct) There are plenty of places to get a lobster supper these days, but this spot claims to be the original – in any event, it's been serving these shellfish feasts since 1958. Getting messy while you crack your crustacean is part of the fun – but leave room for chowder, mussels, salads, breads and a mile-high lemon pie.

New London

The patchwork of fields and dune-fringed coastline around New London is quintessential *Anne of Green Gables* country: author Lucy Maud Montgomery was born nearby, and drew much of the inspiration for her novels from the island scenery. Gift shops and antique boutiques give it a quaint heritage feel, but the tiny village gets pretty overrun in summer.

◉ Sights

Anne of Green Gables Museum MUSEUM

(☑902-886-2884; www.annemuseum.com; 4542 Rte 20; adult/child $6/2; ☺9am-5pm Jul & Aug, 10am-4pm Jun & Sep, 11am-4pm May & Oct) This homestead is an important part of the *Anne of Green Gables* mythos. Set in 110 hectares of fields and woodland, the house was built by author Lucy Maud Montgomery's uncle and aunt; she called the house the 'wonder castle of my childhood' and used it as the inspiration for Silver Bush. It's full of memorabilia, including Lucy Maud's writing desk, the original 'enchanted bookcase,' a patchwork quilt made by her, autographed 1st editions and a gallery of hand-tinted photos.

The house was so dear to Lucy Maud, she chose it as the venue for her own wedding: in 1911 she was married to Presbyterian minister Ewan Macdonald in the parlor. Visitors here can also take a horse carriage down to Campbell's Pond, the real-life 'Lake of Shining Waters.'

Lucy Maud Montgomery Birthplace MUSEUM

(☑902-886-2099; www.lmmontgomerybirthplace.ca; cnr Rtes 6 & 20; $5; ☺9am-5pm mid-May–Thanksgiving) Author Lucy Maud Montgomery was born in this humble little white-and-green clapboard house on November 30, 1874. Fans of *Anne of Green Gables* will thrill at the prospect of visiting the writer's childhood bedroom, and seeing her wedding books and scrapbooks; everyone else might feel a little underwhelmed.

✗ Eating & Drinking

★ **The Table Culinary Studio** COOKING

(☑902-314-9666; www.thetablepei.com; 4295 Graham's Rd; dinner $75-80, courses from $70; ☺dinner around 7pm mid-May–Sep) Under the stained glass and wooden beams of the old New London United Church, this place is part cooking school, part fine-dining restaurant. Chef Derrick Hoare provides custom culinary courses exploring everything from bread-making to PEI potatoes, and every evening there's a slap-up island-themed supper served on platters at the central harvest table.

Blue Winds Tea Room BRITISH $

(☑902-886-2860; http://bluewindstearoom.blogspot.com; 10746 Rte 6; meals $10-14; ☺2-5pm Mon-Thu, from 11:30am Fri-Sun) A most charming place to stop for a bite and a cup of tea, surrounded by English gardens. Of course,

BRYTTA/GETTY IMAGES ©

V J MATTHEW/SHUTTERSTOCK ©

1. Charlottetown (p435)
Provincial capital of Prince Edward Island, Charlottetown is named after the consort of King George III.

2. East Point Lighthouse (p443)
Built in 1867, the East Point Lighthouse has been moved twice and still guards PEI's northeastern shore.

3. Confederation Trail (p439)
See beautiful coastline, forests and farmland along the course of PEI's decommissioned railway.

4. Greenwich Dunes (p446)
These dramatic and ever-shifting sand dunes are part of the Prince Edward Island National Park.

EMILIE NGUYEN/SHUTTERSTOCK ©

like everything else in this region, the fare can be very *Anne of Green Gables*–centric and perhaps too twee for some. Order a raspberry cordial or 'new moon pudding' – both recipes have been taken from author Lucy Maud Montgomery's journals.

Sou'West
BAR

(☑902-886-3000; www.souwest.ca; 6457 Rte 20; ☺noon-11pm May-Oct) Dining on the waterview deck or quaffing some sundowner beers: that's what you come to Sou'West for. There's an oyster bar plus a standard range of seafood-y mains and a good selection of beers on tap. There might be some live music too.

🔒 Shopping

★ Village Pottery
CERAMICS

(☑902-886-2473; www.villagepottery.ca; 10567 Rte 6; ☺10am-5pm) PEI's longest-running pottery studio is a family affair and a labor of love – it's been operated by the same clan since opening in 1973. The colorful pots, cups and ceramics make great souvenirs, and if you're lucky you might meet current owner Suzanne Scott. There's also a lovely little ice-cream parlor and cafe next door.

Kensington

☑902 / POP 1619

Kensington is a busy market town about halfway between Cavendish and Summerside. It's a good place to replenish supplies and the closest service center for those attending the popular **Indian River Festival** (www.indianriverfestival.com; ☺Jul-Sep).

Malpeque Bay Kayak Tour Ltd (☑902-836-3784, 902-266-5706; www.peikayak.ca; Princetown Point; 2½hr kayak tour $55) offers guided kayak tours out to Ram Island, an important migratory stop-off for birds including eagles, cliff swallows, osprey, geese and blue herons. This outfit can also arrange one-on-one stand-up paddleboard and kayak lessons, plus private rentals. It's about a 15km drive from Kensington.

Home Place Inn
INN $$

(☑902-836-5686; www.thehomeplace.ca; 21 Victoria St E; d from $99; ☺May-Oct; 🅿🛜) Constructed in 1915 by a local merchant (the brilliantly named Parmenius Orr), this fine, verandah-encircled house exudes period elegance. It's still decorated with vintage furnishings, photographs and paintings, and each of the five rooms is named after a different family member. Breakfast is a home-cooked treat.

★ Malpeque Oyster Barn
SEAFOOD $$

(☑902-836-3999; www.facebook.com/malpequeoysterbarn; 10 Malpeque Wharf Rd; 6 oysters from $14; ☺11am-9pm Jun-Sep) If you want to sample Malpeque's legendary bivalves, this harborside fisherman's barn in Kensington is the place to do it. Experienced eaters take them straight-up raw, fresh-shucked with maybe a twist of lemon; first-timers might perhaps prefer pan-fried with a sauce. If oysters aren't your thing, there are other dishes like fish tacos, lobster rolls and fried haddock, too.

Cavendish

☑902 / POP 266

Cavendish is famous across Canada as the hometown of Lucy Maud Montgomery (1874–1942), author of the beloved *Anne of Green Gables* stories (around here she's known simply as Lucy Maud or LM). While it provided the model for the fictional town of Avonlea, fans of the stories might be in for a bit of a shock on arrival in Cavendish. Far from a quaint country village filled with clapboard houses and clip-clopping horses, these days the town has become a full-on tourist mecca, crisscrossed by busy roads, swallowed up by parking lots and populated with a mishmash of attractions of questionable value.

👁 Sights

Lucy Maud Montgomery's Cavendish Homestead
HISTORIC SITE

(☑902-963-2231; www.lmmontgomerycavendishhome.com; 8523 Cavendish Rd; adult/child $6/free; ☺9:30am-5:30pm Jul & Aug, 10am-5pm May, Jun & Oct) This restored homestead arguably offers a more authentic picture of author Lucy Maud Montgomery's life and times than the more heavily marketed Green Gables Heritage Place. Lucy Maud lived here from 1876 to 1911 with her maternal grandparents Alexander and Lucy Macneill, after her mother Clara died of tuberculosis. It's here that she wrote books including *Anne of Green Gables* and *Anne of Avonlea*. There's a small museum and an Anne-themed bookstore.

Green Gables Heritage Place
HISTORIC SITE

(☑902-672-7874; www.pc.gc.ca/en/lhn-nhs/pe/greengables; 8619 Hwy 6; adult/child $7.80/free; ☺10am-5pm May-Oct) Owned by author LM Montgomery's grandfather's cousins, the now-famous House of Green Gables and its Victorian surrounds inspired the setting for *Anne of Green Gables* and other stories. Now a National Historic Site, the house has been carefully restored to reflect how it would have appeared in Anne's day, including the furniture, furnishings and decor. Tour guides and audiovisual displays are on hand to provide context – you might even spy Anne herself wandering about.

Outside, you can explore the grounds and woodlands, including the original Lover's Lane. A 1.1km trail leads through the 'Haunted Wood' to Lucy Maud Montgomery's Cavendish Homestead.

🛏 Sleeping & Eating

Parkview Farms
Tourist Home & Cottages   GUESTHOUSE $
(☏ 902-963-2027;   www.parkviewfarms.com;
8214 Cavendish Rd; r/cottages from $70/180;
🛜🐾) Simple tourist-home rooms and self-contained cottages are both on offer at this working dairy farm, 2km east of Cavendish: expect plenty of frills and floral wallpaper.

Kindred Spirits Inn & Cottages   INN $$
(☏ 902-963-2434; www.kindredspirits.ca; 46 Memory Lane; r from $165; 🅿❄🛜🐾) This prim, spread-out complex goes big on the storybook style. Rooms are every *Anne of Green Gables* fan's dream, with dotty floral prints, glossy wood floors and fluffy, comfy beds: they're split between the main inn and a separate gatehouse.

Lost Anchor Pub   PUB $$
(☏ 902-388-0118; www.lostanchorpei.com;   8572 Cavendish Rd; mains $14-29; ⊘noon-9pm) If all the talk of Cavendish's favorite fictional orphan Anne of Green Gables is driving you to drink, here's where to come. Simple but hearty pub meals are available: lobster mac 'n' cheese, fish-and-chips and pork-belly tacos.

Carr's Oyster Bar   SEAFOOD $$
(☏ 902-886-3355; www.carrspei.ca; 32 Campbellton Rd, Stanley Bridge; mains $16-40; ⊘11am-8pm) Dine on oysters straight from Malpeque Bay, or lobster, mussels and seafood you've never even heard of, like quahogs from Carr's own saltwater tanks (the menu helpfully divides dishes up into raw, steamed, fried or baked). There is also plenty of fish on offer.

❶ Information

Cavendish Visitor Information Centre
(☏ 902-963-7830; cnr Rte 6 & Hwy 13; ⊘9am-5pm) *Anne of Green Gables* fans will want to chat with the happy, friendly staff here; they really know their stuff about all things Lucy Maud Montgomery, the series' author.

❶ Getting There & Away

Cavendish is 37km northwest of Charlottetown via Rtes 224 and 13. The junction of Rtes 6 and 13 is the tourist center and the area's commercial hub.

WESTERN PRINCE EDWARD ISLAND

Separated from the central part of PEI by a narrow stretch of land, bordered to north and south by Malpeque and Bedeque Bays, the western third of the island is a picture of pastoral peace and quiet. Inland, you'll find arable and potato farms, sleepy villages, and tractors chugging down country roads; along the coast, quiet beaches, fishing towns and pockets of rugged shore. Apart from the area's main town, Summerside, and the lonely headland at North Cape, there are no major sights to speak of, but that doesn't mean it's an area not worth exploring: this is quintessential rural PEI, ideal for a day's road-tripping.

There's culture too: Lennox Island has a lively Mi'kmaq community, while Egmont and Bedeque Bays have clung on to their French Acadian roots.

The 350km-long North Cape Drive (www.northcapedrive.com) is an organized route that hits all the area's major sights.

Summerside
☏ 902 / POP 13,814
PEI's second-largest city, Summerside lacks the cosmopolitan cachet of Charlottetown, but it makes a more practical base for exploring the western side of the island. Recessed deep within Bedeque Bay, this tiny seaside town possesses a modern waterfront and quiet streets lined with leafy trees and grand old homes, although sadly many of the old farmsteads have been swallowed up by a tangle of roads and sprawling development. The town's most attractive parts are along, or near to, Water St, which runs parallel to the waterfront.

⦿ Sights

★ **Maisons de Bouteilles**   ARCHITECTURE
(Bottle Houses;   ☏ 902-854-2987;   www.bottlehouses.com;   Rte 11, Cape Egmont;   adult/child

PRINCE EDWARD ISLAND SUMMERSIDE

Summerside

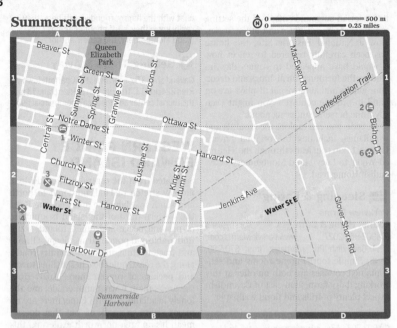

◉ 0 ——— 500 m
0 ——— 0.25 miles

Summerside

🛏 Sleeping
1 Summerside Bed &
   Breakfast.............................A2
2 Willowgreen Farm D1

✴ Eating
3 Holman's Ice Cream Parlour A2
4 Samuel's Coffee House.....................A2

🍷 Drinking & Nightlife
5 Evermore Brewing Company A3

✴ Entertainment
6 College of Piping & Celtic
   Performing Arts.................................D2

$8/3; ⊙9am-8pm July & Aug, to 6pm May, Jun, Sep & Oct) This amazing place brings a new meaning to recycling. The three buildings here are constructed entirely from reclaimed bottles, collected from the local community by fisherman, carpenter and lighthouse keeper Edouard Arsenault. The first, six-gabled house was built in 1980 from 12,000 bottles; a second, hexagonal 'tavern' was added in 1982 from 8000 bottles, followed by a chapel (10,000 bottles) in 1983, complete with altar. The light refracted through the bottles creates a unique effect: come at sunset for maximum impact.

★**West Point Lighthouse**   LIGHTHOUSE
(☎902-859-3605; www.westpointlighthouse.ca; West Point; ⊙9am-8:30pm mid-May–mid-Oct) Built in 1875, this striking lighthouse is immediately recognizable thanks to its black-and-white paint job. At 21m high, it's the tallest lighthouse in PEI, and is now home to a small museum exploring the structure's history (it was manned until 1963), as well as a craft shop and inn.

Near the lighthouse, the **Cedar Dunes Provincial Park** (☎902-859-8785; www.tourismpei.com/provincial-park/cedar-dunes; tent sites $28-30, RV sites $32-37) offers some lovely stretches of sand, although it can be a little windy out this way.

Acadian Museum   MUSEUM
(☎902-432-2880; http://museeacadien.org/an; 23 Maine Dr E, Miscouche; $4.50; ⊙9:30am-5pm Jul & Aug, 9:30am-5pm Mon-Fri & 1-4pm Sun Sep-Jun) The very worthwhile Acadian Museum, in Miscouche, uses 18th-century Acadian artifacts, texts, visuals and music to enlighten visitors about the tragic and compelling history of the Acadians on PEI since 1720. An introspective video introduces a fascinating theory that the brutal treatment of the Acadians by the British may have backhandedly helped preserve a vestige of Acadian culture on PEI.

🛏 Sleeping

West Point Lighthouse
B&B $$

(☏902-859-3605; www.westpointlighthouse.ca; d from $169; P❄🛜) This lighthouse toward West Point ranks as one of PEI's quirkiest places to stay. Located on the lighthouse's 2nd floor, the tower room commands breathtaking views over the Northumberland Strait. Less impressive (but probably more practical) is the adjacent 11-room inn, which has simple modern rooms, all with private balconies.

You can also sleep in the former lighthouse-keeper's quarters.

Summerside Bed & Breakfast
B&B $$

(☏902-620-4993; www.summersideinnbandb. com; 98 Summer St; r from $125; ❄🛜) The pick of Sumerside's B&Bs, in a handsome Queen Anne Revival house on the corner of Summer and Winter Sts. The winter room is the prettiest, with a four-poster bed and clawfoot tub; the spring room is even more spacious, with a twinset of original window seats, while the blue room offers arguably the best value.

Willowgreen Farm
B&B $$

(☏902-436-4420; www.willowgreenfarm.com; 117 Bishop Dr; r from $100; 🛜) A slice of homespun Summerside here, on one of the town's oldest farmsteads. Rambling rooms filled with antiques, homemade textiles, creaky floorboards and wooden furniture make for a really cozy stay, and a generous breakfast is served communally in the downstairs dining room. It feels surprisingly rural, even though you're just moments from downtown Summerside.

✗ Eating & Drinking

Holman's Ice Cream Parlour
ICE CREAM $

(☏1-800-350-1367; www.facebook.com/Holmans icecream; ice creams from $3.50; ☉noon-10pm Mon-Sat) This ice-cream emporium is where everyone in Summerside comes for their fix: 100% homemade, served in a cake cone or waffle cone, and with delicious flavors like peanut butter fudge swirl, sticky bun and maple walnut. Holman's also has an 80-year-old soda fountain for that extra retro cred.

Samuel's Coffee House
CAFE $

(☏902-724-2300; https://samuelscoffeehouse. ca; 4 Queen St; mains $8-14; ☉7:30am-6pm Mon-Thu, to 9pm Fri, 8am-5pm Sat & Sun) A perennially popular hangout for morning coffee, lunchtime wraps and afternoon muffins, this stylish cafe is enclosed in a redbrick building in downtown Summerside. With its arched windows and wooden floors, it feels a bit Brooklyn-esque: try the grilled-cheese sandwich with your choice of PEI cheeses.

★ Evermore Brewing Company
CRAFT BEER

(www.facebook.com/evermoorebrewing; 192 Water St; ☉noon-8:30pm Mon-Wed, to 11pm Thu-Sat, 11am-5pm Sun) This on-trend brewery serves up a choice of ales, sours, seasonal brews and punchy stouts (you can see the stainless-steel vats from the bar). Located in Summerside's former railway station since 2018, the building's original architecture is still in evidence: look out for the original station telephone. Bar snacks and regular bands complete the craft-beer package.

☆ Entertainment

College of Piping & Celtic Performing Arts
LIVE MUSIC

(☏902-436-5377; www.collegeofpiping.com; 619 Water St E) Schooling students in the traditional instruments of Celtic music since the 1980s – from bagpipes to fiddles – this highly regarded music college also stages an impressive Celtic concert called 'Highland Storm' (adult tickets $46) in summer. Expect plenty of step dancing, stirring drums and haunting pipes.

In July and August, there are also hourly mini-concerts ($7) between 11am and 3pm Monday to Friday.

❶ Information

Visitor Information Centre (☏902-888-8364; www.exploresummerside.com; 124 Heather Moyse Dr; ☉9am-7pm Jul & Aug, reduced hours May, Jun, Sep & Oct; 🛜) Summerside's information center has plenty of local listings, information on the Confederation Trail and self-guided tours. There's also free wi-fi.

❶ Getting There & Away

Summerside is 61km west of Charlottetown on Rte 2.

T3 Transit (p441) operates a twice-daily service between Summerside and Charlottetown ($9, 1½ hours, Monday to Friday only).

Maritime Bus (p334) services from Halifax to Charlottetown stop in Summerside en route.

TIGNISH & NORTH CAPE

Tignish is a quiet town tucked up near the North Cape; it sees only a fraction of PEI's visitors. The main reason to make the journey is simply to say you've been to PEI's northern point; it's an impressively remote (and windblown) spot, home to the Wind Energy Institute of Canada and the longest natural rock reef on the continent. At low tide, it's possible to walk out 800m, exploring tide pools and searching for seals.

The **North Cape Interpretive Centre** (902-882-2991; www.north cape.ca; Rte 12, North Cape; $6; 9am-8pm Jul & Aug, 10am-6pm May, Jun, Sep & Oct) provides displays dedicated to wind energy, local history and wildlife, as well as a small aquarium. The Black Marsh Nature Trail (2.7km) leaves the interpretive center and takes you to the west side of the cape – at sunset these crimson cliffs glow against the deep-blue waters. There's also a restaurant.

Tyne Valley

This area, famous for its Malpeque oysters, is one of the most scenic in the province. The village, with its cluster of ornate houses, gentle river and art studios, is definitely worth a visit.

Set in the mouth of Malpeque Bay, sheltered behind Hog Island, is Lennox Island and its 250 Mi'kmaq people. The island is connected by a causeway, making it accessible from the town of East Bideford off Rte 12.

◎ Sights

★ Lennox Island
Cultural Centre   CULTURAL CENTRE
(866-831-2702; www.lennoxisland.com; 2 Eagle Feather Trail, Lennox Island; by donation; 10am-6pm Jun-Aug, to 5pm Sep) Mi'kmaq culture remains strong on the little 535-hectare wooded islet known as Lennox Island, and this cultural center provides a decent primer on understanding the history, beliefs and traditions of this ancient First Nations people. It's also the starting point for the Path of Our Forefathers, a **nature trail** that winds through the island's forests and along the coastline.

There's a choice of two trails, one 3km and the other 10km; in July and August, you can follow them in the company of a Mi'kmaq guide, who can tell you all about the local plants, wildlife and traditional medicines.

Canadian Potato Museum   MUSEUM
(902-859-2039; www.canadianpotatomuseum. info; 1 Dewar Lane, O'Leary; $10; 9:30am-5pm mid-May–mid-Oct) It had to happen: a museum dedicated to the humble spud, and where better than in potato-capital-of-Canada PEI? Admittedly it's a niche affair, with displays exploring the history of potato farming alongside antique farm machinery and period photos, but it's worth visiting for the **Potato Country Kitchen** (mains $5-12; 11am-5pm mid-May–mid-Oct), where you can try numerous spud-based dishes.

Green Park Shipbuilding Museum & Yeo House   MUSEUM
(902-831-7947; www.peimuseum.ca; 360 Green Park Rd; adult $5.75; 9am-4:30pm daily Jul & Aug, Mon-Fri Jun) This museum tells the story of the booming shipbuilding industry in the 19th century. It's located in a painstakingly restored Victorian-era home known as the Yeo House, once home to a prominent local shipbuilder, James Yeo.

✲ Festivals & Events

Tyne Valley Oyster Festival   FOOD & DRINK
(www.tvoysterfest.ca; Aug) Four days of shucking and slurping slimy oysters.

⌸ Sleeping & Eating

Green Park Campsites   CAMPGROUND $
(902-831-7912; www.greenparkcampground. com; 364 Green Park Rd; tent sites $25, with hookups $30, cabins without bath $50; Jun-Sep) The park has 58 campsites spread within a mixed forest. The dozen cabins are a steal.

★ Tyne Valley Teas Cafe   CAFE $
(902-831-3069; www.teastynevalley.com; 6980a Rte 12; mains $7.50-11; 9am-3:30pm Mon-Fri, 10am-3pm Sat & Sun) This cute village cafe is the top place for lunch in Tyne Valley. There's a great selection of food, from teahouse crepes to Montréal bagels, but it's the cakes and puddings that will have you drooling – served on tradition English bone-china plates, and accompanied by a bewildering choice of teas.

Newfoundland & Labrador

Best Places to Eat

➡ Boreal Diner (p484)

➡ Merchant Tavern (p471)

➡ Bonavista Social Club (p484)

➡ Norseman Restaurant (p499)

➡ Piatto (p471)

Best Places to Stay

➡ Fogo Island Inn (p492)

➡ Artisan Inn (p482)

➡ Skerwink Hostel (p482)

➡ Green Point Campground (p496)

➡ Blue on Water (p467)

Why Go?

They call Newfoundland 'the Rock', a fitting name, as this is an island of thoroughly elemental attractions and aesthetics. The muskeg and cliffs are barren and salt-drenched. The trees give off the smell of spruce like the air is spiced. The ocean roils, flecked with icebergs and spouting whales. The wind roars, and at any time, a storm may scream across the bights and coves.

If you enjoy the rugged and the rough, there are few more beautiful places. Yet ever contrasting the harsh geography is a culture that is, simply, magic. Bright houses painted like rainbows spill over the cliffs; menus advertise cod tongue and crowberries; at night, fiddles compete with the howling wind; and the ever-present chill is countered by the warmest locals you'll ever meet. This, then, is Canada's easternmost, most idiosyncratic province, a marriage of land and salt and storm all its own.

When to Go
St John's

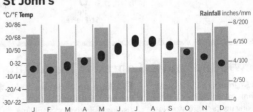

Jun Icebergs glisten offshore, though the weather can be wet and foggy.

Jul & Aug Whales cavort, festivals rock the weekends, and the province is at its sunniest.

Dec & Jan Skiers hit the slopes as Marble Mountain receives most of its 5m of snow.

510
Port Hope Simpson

Labrador

Mary's Harbour

Belle Isle

Strait of Belle Isle

Red Bay

L'Anse aux Meadows National Historic Site

Quirpon Island

Québec

Pinware

Cape Onion

4

St Lunaire-Griquet

Old Fort Bay

Blanc Sablon

Forteau

430

St Anthony

St Barbe

Hare Bay

Main Brook

Plum Point

432

Conche

Roddickton

Grey Islands

ATLANTIC OCEAN

Port au Choix

430

Northern Peninsula

Hawke's Bay

Fleur de Lys

Gulf of St Lawrence

The Arches

Cow Head

Baie Verte

La Scie

Change Islands

Sally's Cove

5 **Gros Morne National Park**

Baie Verte Peninsula

Notre **Twillingate Island**

Fogo Island

Rocky Harbour

Norris Point

410 Springdale

Dame Bay

7

Moreton's Harbour

Farewell

Trout River

Woody Point

Boyd's Cove

Glenburnie

1

340

York Harbour

Deer Lake

Grand Lake

Lewisporte

330

450

Corner Brook

Marble Mountain

Grand Falls-Windsor

Gander

320

Port au Port Peninsula

Red Indian Lake

Newfoundland

Burnside

Bonavista Bay

Salvage

Bonavista 6

Lourdes

Stephenville

Skerwink Trail

Elliston

Port au Port West

Barachois Pond Provincial Park

Maelpaeg Lake

Terra Nova National Park

2 Port Rexton

Trinity

Bay de Verde Peninsula

480

360

Bonavista Peninsula

St George's Bay

Head of Bay d'Espoir

Bay du Nord Wilderness Reserve

Clarenville

70 *Conception Bay*

Cape Anguille

Isle aux Morts

Rose Blanche

St Alban's

McCallum

Heart's Content

Harbour Grace

St John's 1

Cape Ray

Burgeo

Grey River

François

Pool's Cove

Heart's Delight

Cupids

Brigus

Petty Harbour

Port aux Basques

Sandbanks Provincial Park

Ramea

Hermitage

Harbour Breton

Dildo

Avalon Peninsula

Witless Bay Ecological Reserve

3

South Coast Outports Ferry

Fortune Bay

Burin Peninsula

210

Argentia

91 Placentia

La Manche PP

Ferryland

Cabot Strait

Île de Miquelon

St-Pierre & Miquelon (FRANCE)

Fortune

Grand Bank

Marystown

Burin

St Lawrence

Cape St Mary's

100

St Mary's

Avalon Wilderness Reserve

Chance Cove PP

Argentia–North Sydney (NS) Ferry

8 **Île St-Pierre**

St Mary's Ecological Reserve

St Vincent's

Mistaken Point Ecological Reserve

0 ——— 100 km
0 ——— 50 miles

Newfoundland & Labrador Highlights

1 **St John's** (p462) Hoisting a drink, taking a ghost tour and soaking up the history of North America's oldest city.

2 **Skerwink Trail** (p482) Trekking through magnificent coastal scenery.

3 **Witless Bay Ecological Reserve** (p476) Sharing the waves with whales and puffins.

4 **L'Anse aux Meadows National Historic Site** (p498) Visiting Leif Eriksson's sublime 1000-year-old Viking pad.

5 **Gros Morne National Park** (p494) Hiking the ridges and kayaking the fjord-like lakes.

6 **Bonavista** (p483) Exploring a synthesis of modern Canada and old outport.

7 **Twillingate Island** (p488) Ogling icebergs, hiking and seeing whales every morning.

8 **St-Pierre** (p486) Getting your French fix – wine, chocolate éclairs and baguettes.

History

The Paleo-Indians walked into Labrador 9000 years ago. They hunted seals, fished for salmon and tried to stay warm. The Vikings, led by Leif Eriksson, washed ashore further south at L'Anse aux Meadows in Newfoundland in 1000 CE and established North America's first European settlement.

John Cabot (Italian-born Giovanni Caboto) sailed around the shores of Newfoundland next. It was 1497, and he was employed by England's Henry VII. Cabot's stories of cod stocks so prolific that one could nearly walk on water spread quickly throughout Europe. Soon the French, Portuguese, Spanish and Basques were also fishing off Newfoundland's coast.

The 1713 Treaty of Utrecht ceded all of Newfoundland to England. The land remained a British colony for most of the next two centuries, with life revolving around the booming fishing industry. Newfoundland's Indigenous people, the Beothuk, did not fare well after settlement began. Diseases and land conflicts contributed to their demise by 1829.

Ever true to its independent spirit, Newfoundland was the last province to join Canada, doing so in 1949. While Labrador was always part of the package, it wasn't until 2001 that it became part of the provincial name.

Language & People

Two hundred years ago, coastal fishing families from Ireland and England made up almost the entire population. Since then, as a result of living in isolated outposts, their language has evolved into almost 60 different dialects. Strong, lilting inflections, unique slang and colorful idioms pepper the language, sometimes confounding even residents.

The authoritative source is the *Dictionary of Newfoundland English* (www.heritage.nf.ca/dictionary).

Inuit and Innu have occupied Labrador for thousands of years. Until the 1960s they were the sole inhabitants, alongside a few longtime European descendants known as 'liveyers,' who eked out an existence by fishing and hunting from tiny villages that freckled the coast. The interior was virgin wilderness.

While populations of both groups can be found in Labrador, remember that 'Inuit' and 'Innu' are not interchangeable terms, but rather two distinct peoples. The Inuit are an Arctic people who inhabit a broad swath of the globe stretching from Greenland through Canada (mainly Nunavut) to

the USA (Alaska). The Innu can be found throughout Labrador and eastern Québec; they refer to this homeland as Nitassinan.

Land & Climate

They don't call it the Rock for nothing. Glaciers tore through here, leaving behind a rugged landscape of boulders, lakes and bogs. Newfoundland's interior remains barren, while the island's cities and towns congregate at its edges near the sea.

Labrador is sparser than Newfoundland, puddled and tundra-like, with mountains thrown in for good measure.

Temperatures peak in July and August, when daytime highs average 20°C (68°F). These are also the driest months; it rains or snows about 15 out of every 30 days. Wintertime temperatures hover at 0°C (32°F). Fog and wind plague the coast much of the year (which makes for a lot of canceled flights).

Parks & Wildlife

Whales, moose and puffins are Newfoundland's wildlife stars, and most visitors see them all. Whale-watching tours depart from all around the province and will take you close to the sea mammals (usually humpback and minke). Puffins – the funny-looking love child of the penguin and parrot – flap around Witless Bay and Elliston. Moose nibble shrubs near roadsides throughout the province, so keep an eye out while driving. Some visitors also glimpse caribou near the Avalon Wilderness Reserve, which is special because usually these beasts can only be seen in the High Arctic. Caribou herds also roam in Labrador, though their numbers have been declining sharply in recent years.

ℹ Getting There & Away

AIR

St John's International Airport (p474) is the main hub for the region, though **Deer Lake Airport** (YDF; ☎709-635-3601; www.deerlakeairport. com; 1 Airport Rd; ☎) is an excellent option for

---

NEWFOUNDLAND & LABRADOR

NEWFOUNDLAND ITINERARIES

Five Days

Start in St John's by visiting Signal Hill (p463) and Cape Spear (p474). Both are historical sites, but they also offer walking trails and views where you just may see an iceberg, a whale or both. At night sample St John's eateries, funky shops and music-filled pubs.

After a couple of days of 'big city' life, move onward through the Avalon Peninsula. Cruise to see whales and puffins at Witless Bay Ecological Reserve (p476), plan a picnic in Ferryland (p477) or visit the birds at Cape St Mary's Ecological Reserve (p480).

Spend the last day or two soaking up the historical eastern communities of Trinity (p481) and Bonavista (p483), and the cliffside hikes in between.

Ten Days

Do the five-day itinerary and then go west, possibly via a quick flight to Deer Lake (p461), and reap the reward of viewing the mighty fjords of Gros Morne National Park (p494) and the monumental Viking history at L'Anse aux Meadows National Historic Site (p498). With a few extra days you could sail across the Strait of Belle Isle and slow waaay down among the wee towns and bold granite cliffs of the Labrador Straits (p506).

visitors focusing on the Northern Peninsula. Airlines flying in include **Air Canada** (☑ 888-247-2262; www.aircanada.com), PAL Airlines (p474), Porter (p474) and United (p474).

BOAT

Marine Atlantic (☑ 800-341-7981; www.marineatlantic.ca) operates two massive car/passenger ferries between North Sydney (NS) and Newfoundland. There's a daily six-hour crossing to Port aux Basques (western Newfoundland) year-round, and a thrice-weekly 14-hour crossing to Argentia (on the Avalon Peninsula) in summer. Reservations are recommended, especially to Argentia.

Provincial Ferry Service (www.gov.nl.ca/ferryservices) runs the smaller boats that travel within the province to various islands and coastal towns. Each service has its own phone number with up-to-the-minute information; it's wise to call before embarking.

BUS

DRL (p474) sends one bus daily each way between St John's and Port aux Basques (13½ hours), making dozens of stops en route. Other than DRL, public transportation consists of small, regional shuttle vans that connect with one or more major towns. Although not extensive, the system works pretty well and will get most people where they want to go.

CAR & MOTORCYCLE

The Trans-Canada Hwy (Hwy 1) is the main cross-island roadway. Driving distances are deceptive, as travel is often slow going on heavily contorted, single-lane roads. Watch out for moose, especially at dusk.

Be warned: rental-car fleets are small (thanks to the island's remoteness and short tourist season), which means loads of visitors vie for limited vehicles in midsummer. Costs can rack up to $100 per day (including taxes and mileage fees). Reserve well in advance – April or May is recommended if you're traveling during the mid-July-to-early-August peak – and confirm the booking before you arrive.

St John's to Port aux Basques 905km
St John's to Gros Morne 708km
Gros Morne to St Anthony 372km

ST JOHN'S

POP 114,000

Newfoundland is an island of austere, washed-out beauty and vast unpopulated wilderness. Yet here, in its capital and largest city, one finds scads of homes colored like tropical fruit, plus bustling street life and a dim urban (yet small-town friendly) buzz. For all that, North America's oldest city doesn't just contrast the province it dominates. St John's exudes wry wit, stoicism and lust for life, and to this end embodies some of Newfoundland's best values.

The town paints the steep slopes of a harbor that shelters hectares of green space, winding paths, rainbow row houses, artists, technocrats and engineers – St John's is by far the most economically dynamic corner of Newfoundland; not coincidentally, it's also where you'll find the province's only university and ethnic enclaves. Signal Hill dominates the topography, while new restaurants, an active outdoors scene, and nights on the town dominate the social life.

◉ Sights

Most sights are downtown or within a few kilometers, though be prepared for some serious uphill walking.

★Signal Hill
National Historic Site HISTORIC SITE
(☑709-772-5367; www.pc.gc.ca/signalhill; 230 Signal Hill Rd; ⊙grounds 24hr, visitor center 10am-6pm; P) The city's most famous landmark is worth it for the glorious view alone, though there's much more to see. The tiny castle atop the hill is **Cabot Tower** (⊙8:30am-5pm Apr-Nov) FREE, built in 1898 to honor both John Cabot's arrival in 1497 and Queen Victoria's Diamond Jubilee. In midsummer, soldiers dressed as the 19th-century Royal Newfoundland Company perform a tattoo (p473) and fire cannons.

The **Signal Hill Visitor Centre** (adult/child $3.90/1.90; ⊙10am-6pm May-Oct) features interactive displays on the site's history. The last North American battle of the Seven Years' War took place here in 1762, and Britain's victory ended France's renewed aspirations for control of eastern North America. The tattoo takes place next to the center at O'Flaherty Field.

You can see cannons and the remains of the late-18th-century British battery at **Queen's Battery & Barracks** further up the hill. Inside Cabot Tower, educational displays relay how Italian inventor Guglielmo Marconi received the first wireless transatlantic message from Cornwall, England, at the site in 1901. An amateur radio society operates a station in the tower in July and August.

Various activities and events kick off throughout the year, including guided walks, ghost tours ($15) and beer tastings ($39.50). Call ahead or check the website for details.

An awesome way to return to downtown is along the 1.7km North Head Trail (p466). The trailhead isn't marked; look for it right before you enter the lot. It's the path leading furthest to the right. Because much of the trail runs along the bluff's sheer edge, this walk is not something to attempt in icy, foggy or dark conditions. Free maps are available at Cabot Tower. If you're looking for an easier walk, take the 710m hike to the Ladies Lookout (p466). The site sits 1.5km from downtown, up Signal Hill Rd.

★The Rooms MUSEUM
(☑709-757-8000; www.therooms.ca; 9 Bonaventure Ave; adult/child $10/5, 6-9pm Wed free; ⊙10am-5pm Mon, Tue, Thu & Sat, to 9pm Wed, to 10pm Fri, noon-5pm Sun, closed Mon Oct-Apr; ♿) Not many museums offer the chance to see a giant squid, hear avant-garde sound sculptures and peruse ancient weaponry all under one roof. But that's The Rooms, the province's all-in-one historical museum, art gallery and archives. The building itself, a massive stone-and-glass complex, is impressive to look at, with views that lord it over the city. Has an on-site cafe and excellent restaurant.

Quidi Vidi VILLAGE
Over Signal Hill, away from town, is the tiny picturesque village of Quidi Vidi. Check out the 18th-century battery and the lakeside regatta museum, but make your first stop Quidi Vidi Brewery (p473), which whips up Newfoundland's most popular microbrews. Located in an old fish-processing plant on the small wharf, it's a scenic place to slake your thirst.

Nearby there's one of the oldest cottages in North America, the 1750s-era Mallard Cottage (p471), a restaurant that serves Newfoundland comfort food. Nearby is the Inn of Olde Pub (p471), a dive bar located in what is not the oldest cottage in North America, but sure feels like it. Also in this vicinity is the **Quidi Vidi Village Plantation** (☑709-570-2038; http://qvvplantation.com; 10 Maple View Pl; ⊙10am-4pm Wed-Sat, 11am-4pm Sun), an arts center that hosts a rotating collection of local creatives.

The 1762 **Quidi Vidi Battery**, atop the hill end of Cuckold's Cove Rd, was built by the French after they took St John's. The British quickly claimed it, and it remained in military service into the 1800s.

Inland from the village, **Quidi Vidi Lake** is the site of the St John's Regatta (p466). The **Royal St John's Regatta Museum** (☑709-576-8921; cnr Lakeview Ave & Clancy Dr, off Forest Rd; ⊙by appointment May-Aug 15) FREE is on the 2nd floor of the boathouse. A popular walking trail leads around the lake.

Quidi Vidi is about 2km from the northeast edge of downtown. Take Plymouth Rd, go left on Quidi Vidi Rd, then right on Forest Rd (which becomes Quidi Vidi Village Rd). For the brewery, bear right onto Barrows Rd. For the battery, veer off on Cuckold's Cove Rd. For the regatta museum, take a left off Forest Rd onto Lakeview Ave. You can also

St John's

walk from Signal Hill via the Cuckold's Cove Trail, which takes about 30 minutes.

CA Pippy Park

PARK

(www.pippypark.com; 👫 🎿) The feature-filled 13-sq-km CA Pippy Park coats downtown's northwestern edge. Recreational facilities include walking trails, picnic areas, playgrounds, a golf course and a campground. **Memorial University**, the province's only university, is here too. The university's botanical garden is at Oxen Pond, at the park's western edge off Mt Scio Rd.

St John's

NEWFOUNDLAND & LABRADOR ST JOHN'S

Cultivated areas and a nature reserve fill the botanical landscape. Together, these and the park's **Long Pond** marsh give visitors an excellent introduction to Newfoundland's flora, habitats (including boreal forest and bogs) and animals (look for birds at Long Pond and the occasional moose). Take the 3km **Long Pond Walk** for the full effect.

The **Fluvarium** (☑709-754-3474; www.fluvarium.ca; 5 Nagle's Pl; adult/child/family $8/6/25; ☺9am-5pm Mon-Fri, from 10am Sat & Sun Jul & Aug, reduced hours Sep-Jun; P ♿), a glass-sided cross-section of a 'living' river, is located across the street from the campground.

To get here from downtown, take Bonaventure Ave north to Allandale Rd and follow the signs; it's about 2km.

Memorial University Botanical Garden
GARDENS

(☑709-737-8590; www.mun.ca/botgarden; 306 Mt Scio Rd, CA Pippy Park; adult/child $9/6; ☺10am-5pm May-Aug, reduced hours Sep-Apr) The premier botanical garden of the province, with nature trails, a large cultivated garden and a greenhouse within a 100-acre nature reserve.

Johnson Geo Centre
MUSEUM

(☑709-737-7880; www.geocentre.ca; 175 Signal Hill Rd; adult/child $12/6; ☺9:30am-5pm) Nowhere in the world can geo-history, going back to the birth of the earth, be accessed so easily as in Newfoundland. The Geo Centre does a grand job of making snore-worthy geological information perk up with appeal via its underground, interactive displays.

Anglican Cathedral of St John the Baptist
CHURCH

(☑709-726-5677; www.stjohnsanglicancathedral.org; 16 Church Hill; ☺10am-4pm Mon-Sat) Serving Canada's oldest parish (1699), this Anglican cathedral is one of the finest examples of ecclesiastical Gothic architecture in North America. Although originally built in the 1830s, all but its exterior walls were reduced to ashes by the Great Fire of 1892. Rebuilt in 1905, its Gothic ribbed ceiling, graceful stone arches and long stained-glass windows are timeless marvels. High tea (adult/child $10/6) is offered in the crypt on weekday afternoons in July and August.

✦ Activities

★ Rennie's River Trail
WALKING

(access at Carpasian Rd) **FREE** It takes a city as understated as St John's to not make a big deal about this trail, which must be one of the most pleasant urban walks anywhere. Right in the middle of the city is a 2.9-mile (5km) trail, much of which runs alongside the rushing Rennie's River, which forms natural waterfalls and is flanked by grassy banks.

★ North Head Trail
WALKING

(Signal Hill) You only have to go to Signal Hill (p463) to get a taste of Newfoundland's majestic, rugged beauty. The North Head Trail (1.7km) connects Cabot Tower (p463) with the harborfront Battery neighborhood, and is a beloved local gem. The walk departs from the tower's parking lot and traces the cliffs, imparting tremendous sea views and sometimes whale spouts.

Ladies Lookout
HIKING

(Signal Hill) The North Head Trail is justifiably the most famous walk in St John's, but it's demanding. The nearby Ladies Lookout (710m) is much easier, and still yields superlative views. The walk was so named because sailors' wives would supposedly head here watching for their husbands (the trail also gives a view of Cuckold's Cove; make of that what you will).

Grand Concourse
WALKING

(☑709-737-1077; www.grandconcourse.ca) The Grand Concourse is an ambitious 160km-long network of trails all over town and linking St John's with nearby Mt Pearl and Paradise via downtown sidewalks, trails, river corridors and old railway beds.

☞ Tours

★ St John's Haunted Hike
WALKING

(www.hauntedhike.com; adult/child $10/5; ⊙9:30pm Sun-Thu Jun-Sep) As you may expect, the oldest city on the continent has generated its share of ghost stories, and you can explore this phantasmal heritage on these popular adventures. Departure is from the Anglican Cathedral's west entrance. On midsummer Fridays and Saturdays, the action moves to Signal Hill (p463) for a seated, indoor show of ghost stories (8pm, tickets $15).

Outfitters
KAYAKING

(☑800-966-9658, 709-579-4453; www.the-outfitters.nf.ca; 220 Water St; half-/full-day tour

$89/189; ⊙10am-6pm Mon-Wed & Sat, to 9pm Thu & Fri, noon-5pm Sun) Popular kayak tours at Bay Bulls, with shuttle service (round-trip $60 for up to two people) from the Outfitters (p473) store downtown.

Fairy Door Tours
WALKING

(☑709-682-9724; http://fairydoortours.com; $9; ⊙Sat 11am & 1pm; ☻) If there are faeries in North America, there must be a few in Newfoundland, one of the most magical islands anywhere. On these tours you'll be on the lookout for hand-painted miniature doors set in trees and the like, leading to other worlds and lots of excitement if you've got kids (or kids at heart).

The tour kicks off near the Fluvarium (p465); the hosts will give you an exact location. You won't be walking more than a kilometer, and the tour lasts around 75 minutes.

McCarthy's Party
BUS

(☑888-660-6060, 709-579-4444; www.mccarthysparty.com; 566 Water St; 3hr tour adult/child from $60/35) A seasoned tour company with wonderful guides that will give you a true sense of local culture.

Offerings range from half-day tours of St John's and Cape Spear to 12-day trips around the island ($3470).

Iceberg Quest
BOATING

(☑709-722-1888; www.icebergquest.com; Pier 6; 2hr tour adult/child $70/30) Departs from St John's Harbour and makes a run down to Cape Spear in search of icebergs in June and whales in July and August. There are multiple departures daily.

✲ Festivals & Events

Royal St John's Regatta
SPORTS

(http://stjohnsregatta.ca; ⊙1st Wed Aug) The streets are empty, the stores are closed and everyone migrates to the shores of Quidi Vidi Lake. This rowing regatta officially began in 1825 and is now the oldest continuously held sporting event in North America. Postponed if the rowing conditions are poor.

Shakespeare by the Sea Festival
THEATER

(☑709-722-7287; www.shakespearebytheseafestival.com; tickets $20-25; ⊙early Jul–mid-Aug) Live outdoor productions are presented at Signal Hill, local parks and other venues. Buy all tickets on-site; cash only. Some performances are free.

Downtown Busker Festival
CARNIVAL

(www.downtownstjohns.com; ⊙early Aug) Jugglers, magicians, acrobats, comedians and more take their performances to the streets for a long weekend. Performances are centered on Water St.

Newfoundland & Labrador Folk Festival
MUSIC

(www.nlfolk.com; Bannerman Park; ⊙early Aug) This three-day event celebrates traditional Newfoundland music, dancing and storytelling. It's held the weekend after the regatta.

George Street Festival
MUSIC

(www.georgestreetlive.ca; daily/weekly tickets from $30/199; ⊙late Jul/early Aug) The mighty George St becomes one big nightclub for a fabulous week of daytime and nighttime musical performances.

🛏 Sleeping

Scores of B&Bs offer a place to rest your head in the heart of St John's; they're usually better value than the hotels and motels. They fill fast, so book ahead. Many have a two-night minimum-stay requirement. The ones listed here all serve a hot breakfast. The city's 17% tax is not included in prices listed here. Parking is available at or near all accommodations.

Memorial University Rooms
ACCOMMODATION SERVICES $

(☎877-730-7657; www.mun.ca/stay; r with shared bath $69; ⊙late Jun-Aug; 🅿🛜🏊) One of the best deals in town, the local university offers summer accommodations in its dormitory housing with shared washroom facilities. There's the option of twin or double beds in modern, pleasant rooms. Guests have access to kitchen facilities, a pool and fitness center. There are no TVs.

HI St John's
HOSTEL $

(☎709-754-4789; www.hihostels.ca; 8 Gower St; dm/r $38/79; ⊗@🛜) It's everything a good hostel should be: well located near the action, with spick-and-span facilities, not too big (16 beds in all), and helpful. A whiteboard lists everything of interest happening in town each day. The hostel also books reasonably priced tours.

★ Blue on Water
BOUTIQUE HOTEL $$

(☎709-754-2583; www.blueonwater.com; 319 Water St; r $199-249; 🖩@🛜) One of the more stylish hotels in the St John's lineup, Blue on Water has all the fresh, modern dressings the hip hotel-hopper desires: crisp white sheets, exposed brick, distressed accents, and a downstairs bar that attracts the attractive. The central location on Water St (imagine that) is a serious draw.

JAG
BOUTIQUE HOTEL $$

(☎844-564-1524; www.steelehotels.com; 115 George St W; r $216-286, ste $366; 🖩🛜) What's not to like about a hotel that blasts the Stones or Dylan in the lobby? This rock-and-roll-themed boutique hotel occupies a tall multistory building with harbor views. Spacious rooms have a sleek look of muted colors with pleated leather headboards and oversize windows (double-paned with blackout curtains specially made for rock stars).

Cabot House
B&B $$

(☎709-754-0058; www.abbainn.com; 26 Monkstown Rd; r/ste $209/259; 🅿🛜) A stunning 1904 Queen Anne-revival mansion, this sprawling house full of antiques and stained-glass windows makes for a subdued stay. Gorgeous, spacious rooms are mostly restored to their original layout, with the addition of bathrooms and a Jacuzzi suite. With no on-site host, the experience is more hotel-like.

ⓘ PLANNING YOUR TRIP

➡ Book ahead for rental cars and accommodations. If you're arriving during the mid-July to early August peak, secure a car by April or May and don't wait much longer to book a room. **Newfoundland & Labrador Tourism** (☎800-563-6353; www. newfoundlandlabrador.com) has listings.

➡ Driving distances are lengthy, so have realistic expectations of what you can cover. For instance, it's 708km between St John's and Gros Morne National Park, and a lot of those kilometers are curving and twisty. The Road Distance Database (www.stats.gov.nl.ca/DataTools/RoadDB/Distance) is a good reference.

➡ Know your seasons for puffins (May to August), icebergs (June to early July) and whales (July to August). Icebergs, in particular, can be tricky to predict. Check Iceberg Finder (www.icebergfinder.com) to get the drift.

GAIL SHORTLANDER/GETTY IMAGES ©

1. Twillingate Island (p488)
A good place for spotting whales and icebergs, Twillingate is located at the top of the Central Coast.

2. Witless Bay Ecological Reserve (p476)
Four islands off Witless Bay, and southward, represent one of the top seabird breeding areas in eastern North America.

3. St John's (p462)
North America's oldest city, and Newfoundland's capital, has a bustling streetlife and a friendly buzz.

4. Skerwink Trail (p482)
This 5km-long trail near Trinity offers dramatic coastal vistas of sea stacks, early-summer icebergs and a lighthouse.

WINDCOAST/SHUTTERSTOCK ©

Leaside Manor B&B $$
(☑709-722-0387; www.leasidemanor.com; 39 Topsail Rd; r $229; ☻❀@✿) The rooms in this old merchant's home have been updated with boutique-hotel contemporary flourishes, including big tubs, plush beds (some with canopies), fireplaces, sitting areas and Jacuzzis, which explains why the *Globe and Mail* designated Leaside one of Canada's 'most romantic destinations.' Each room has its own individual vibe, but they're all plush and comfortable.

The Roses B&B $$
(☑877-767-3722; www.therosesnl.com; 9 Military Rd; r $99-169; ✿) The Roses boasts a dozen nicely appointed guest rooms spread out over two Victorian properties located near the heart of the St John's action. Breakfasts vary by day, and can include Newfoundland berry pancakes, a breakfast sandwich and hash browns. Rooms have en suite bathrooms, and duvets filled with Canadian goose down.

At Wit's Inn B&B $$
(☑709-739-7420; www.atwitsinn.ca; 3 Gower St; r $170; ☻❀@✿) Polished floorboards, plasterwork ceilings, ornate fireplaces, brightly colored walls, and beds you'll have trouble leaving make this B&B memorable. The living and dining rooms are as swank as they are comfy. It's also in a convenient location.

Abba Inn B&B $$
(☑709-754-0058; www.abbainn.com; 36 Queen's Rd; r $135; ☻❀@✿) The Abba shares a building with **Balmoral House** (☑709-754-5721; www.balmoralhouse.com; 38 Queen's Rd; r $129-159; ☻❀@), and both B&Bs have similar amenities and ambience. Rooms are surprisingly large and absolutely comfortable, and the townhouse setting is attractive. If Abba is full, the owner also has nearby **Gower House** (☑709-754-0058; www.abbainn.com; 180 Gower St; r $129; ❀✿) and Cabot House (p467), which are comparable. There's often no on-site host; guests let themselves in with a lock code.

★**Luxus** BOUTIQUE HOTEL $$$
(☑844-722-8899; www.theluxus.ca; 128 Water St; r $439-599; ❀✿) Opened by a businessman originally from the area, the Luxus' amenities read like a wish list of those who travel for a living. Bose speakers, check. Dual-jet shower and freestanding tub, check. Electronic Japanese toilet, check. All the luxurious rooms boast harbor views, minibar and a whopping 70-inch (178cm) flat-screen TV. Don't miss happy hour at the ambient cocktail bar.

🍴 Eating

★**Adelaide Oyster House** INTERNATIONAL $
(☑709-722-7222; www.facebook.com/theadelaide oysterhouse; 334 Water St; small plates $8-17; ☺5-11pm Mon-Wed, to midnight Thu, to 1am Fri, 11am-3pm & 5pm-1am Sat, 11am-3pm & 5pm-midnight Sun) The Adelaide is a stylish sliver of a bar and restaurant where the specialty is small plates such as fish tacos, Kobe beef lettuce wraps topped with spicy kimchi, and, of course, fresh oysters from both coasts, plus some brick-strong cocktails to get the party started.

★**Georgestown Cafe and Bookshelf** CAFE $
(☑709-579-7134; https://georgestowncafe.word press.com; 73 Hayward Ave; mains $5-10; ☺8am-5pm Mon-Sat, from 10am Sun; 🎨) If you've got younger kids and you need to kill time before heading to The Rooms (p463), Georgestown Cafe is here to answer your every prayer. It's a cafe, sure, serving fair-trade coffee and yummy treats such as granola, bagels, scones and muffins, but there's also a bookstore on-site, and a play area stacked with kids' books and toys.

Rocket Bakery BAKERY $
(☑709-738-2011; www.rocketfood.ca; 272 Water St; mains $3-10; ☺7:30am-9pm Mon-Sat, to 6pm Sun; ✿) Cheery Rocket is the perfect spot for a cup o' joe, a groovy sandwich or a sweet treat. Try the hummus on crusty homemade multigrain bread, or maybe a croissant with lemon curd. The fish cakes also win raves. Order at the counter, then take your goodies to the tables in the adjoining room.

Hungry Heart CAFE $
(☑709-738-6164; www.hungryheartcafe.ca; 142 Military Rd; mains $13-16; ☺8am-3pm Tue-Sat) Eat in this warm-toned cafe and you're helping abused women and others in need to train in food service. Try the curry mango chicken or pulled-pork sandwiches. Saturday brunch brings out the cheese scones with crisp, house-cured bacon and cherry bread pudding. Lots of baked goodies too.

Sprout VEGETARIAN $
(☑709-579-5485; www.thesproutrestaurant.com; 364 Duckworth St; mains $10-15; ☺11:30am-

8:30pm Mon-Wed, to 9:30pm Thu-Sat; 🍴) Full-on vegetarian food is almost unheard of in rural Newfoundland, but Sprout almost makes up for the difference in St John's. Take a seat and savor your marinated tofu burger, walnut-pesto-melt sandwich and brown rice poutine (fries served under miso gravy) before leaving town. Sandwiches feature thick slices of homemade bread. Cash and debit only.

★ **Piatto** PIZZA $$

(☑709-726-0709; www.piattopizzeria.com; 377 Duckworth St; mains $12-19; ⊘11:30am-10pm Mon-Thu, to 11pm Fri & Sat, to 9pm Sun; 🚻) Offering a great night out without breaking the bank, cozy brick Piatto wood-fires pizza like nobody's business. Go trad or try a thin-crust pie topped with prosciutto, figs and balsamic. It's all good. There are nice fresh salads, wine and Italian cocktails. Children's plates plus pizza and ice-cream specials for kids make this a good option for families.

Bagel Cafe CANADIAN $$

(☑709-739-4470; http://thebagelcafe.ca; 246 Duckworth St; mains $10-28; ⊘7am-9pm) For a moment, disregard the name of this spot and note the crowds, which absolutely pack this downtown eatery, especially on weekend mornings. Now back to the name: of course the Bagel Cafe has many variations of its eponymous circle of doughy delight, but you'll also find poutine hash browns, burgers, toutons (pancakes) with baked beans and bologna, and strong coffee.

Get Stuffed CANADIAN $$

(☑709-757-2480; www.facebook.com/getstuffed-sj; 190 Duckworth St; mains $15-26; ⊘noon-3pm & 5:30-10pm Tue-Sat, to 9pm Sun) Contemporary Canadian and home-cooking kicked up a notch, served in a comfortably laid-back atmosphere, is the name of the game at Get Stuffed, where the food will get you – well – stuffed. Fancy cheese 'n' doo (mac 'n' cheese) is cooked with Gruyère and sharp cheddar, while a lovely meat-loaf comes with a nice scoop of mushroom demi-cream.

★ **Merchant Tavern** CANADIAN $$$

(☑709-722-5050; http://themerchanttavern.ca; 291 Water St; mains $21-40; ⊘11:30am-10pm Tue-Fri, from 10:30am Sat, 10:30am-2:30pm Sun) An elegant tavern housed in a former bank building, this restaurant is a fine choice for

a splurge. Gorgeous seafood stews, duck and lentils, and cod with parsnip make for near culinary perfection – just bear in mind this is a seasonal, changing menu (but always solid). Some seating faces the open-view kitchen – good for chatting with the cooks.

Chinched CANADIAN $$$

(☑709-722-3100; www.chinchedbistro.com; 7 Queen St; mains $14-35; ⊘5:30-9:30pm Mon-Sat) Quality dishes without the white-tablecloth pretense – think octopus tacos or Newfoundland wild mushroom risotto served in a warm, dark-wood room. On an ever-changing menu, meat figures prominently – don't skip the charcuterie boards or homemade pickles. The young chefs' creativity extends to the singular desserts (say, wild-nettle ice cream) and spirits (partridgeberry vodka) made in-house. If you don't want to commit to a full meal, the bar menu lets you sample dishes for $6 to $10.

Mallard Cottage CANADIAN $$$

(☑709-237-7314; www.mallardcottage.ca; 2 Barrows Rd; mains $19-35; ⊘10am-9pm Wed-Sat, to 6:30pm Sun, to 5pm Mon & Tue) A lot of restaurants give lip service to 'local and sustainable,' but this one is spot-on and devilishly good. The blackboard menu changes daily. Think turnips with yogurt and crispy shallots or brined duck with spaetzle and fried rosemary. The adorable Mallard Cottage, which dates from the 1750s, is a historical site in and of itself.

🍷 Drinking & Nightlife

★ **Inn of Olde Pub** BAR

(☑709-576-2223; 67 Quidi Vidi Village Rd; ⊘noon-2am) Step inside the Inn of Olde and you'll feel like you've walked into the collective attic of the city, with a jumble of laminate tables, dusty hockey gear, black-and-white photos, framed newspaper clippings and faded NHL jerseys. Presiding over everything is Linda, who has been tending bar and bending ears for as long as anyone can remember.

★ **Geeks Public House** BAR

(☑709-746-8469; www.facebook.com/geeks publichouse; 288 Duckworth St; ⊘6pm-midnight Wed, Thu, Sun & Mon, to 1am Fri & Sat; 🛜) This bar serves its own butterbeer and scores a +5 bonus for getting customers happily buzzed while they peruse all five editions of

LOCAL KNOWLEDGE

GEORGE STREET: PUB CRAWL LIKE A PRO

Tell a Canadian you've been to St John's, and almost inevitably someone will say, 'So you went to George Street' with a knowing smile. Though only two blocks long, this thoroughfare is known nationally as one of Canada's prime party promenades.

You'd never pick up on this vibe during the day. Under the harsh, sober glare of the sun, George St emanates the stale smell of dried booze and sick, set adjacent to shuttered bars and clubs. Throughout the day a lonely truck will drop off kegs and bar supplies, but there's little movement otherwise. By early evening, confused tourists wander by businesses that have opened their doors but are still largely empty.

But show up at midnight and you'll find a weird cross between a fraternity rager, a Newfoundland house party and a karaoke concert. For all of the diversity of those nightlife genres, the bars here are more or less interchangeable. Folks come here to get smashed and sing, and the local landlords have catered their businesses to provide this opportunity. The crowd is largely students, tourists, and folks from the province hitting the town for a big night. If you're after a quiet spot for some craft cocktails or a hard-to-find Riesling, you may want to drink elsewhere.

A few rules of thumb:

➡ George St does not get going until 11pm. Show up beforehand and you'll be wondering what all the fuss is about.

➡ Bring some identification with you, especially if you're under 30. The doormen at George St bars all seem to err on the side of checking ID.

➡ St John's does not have ride-sharing services, but if you need a taxi, they tend to queue all around George St.

➡ You can find food – greasy mystery meat on a bun – at almost any hour of the night. We assume these sausage vendors are vampires, because they seem to vanish into the foggy air as the sun cracks the horizon.

the *Dungeons & Dragons Player's Handbook*. If that last sentence got you excited, you'll love this place. If it made you scratch your head, you'll likely still love this spot, dedicated to nerdy pursuits and affectations.

★**Battery Cafe**　　　　　　CAFE
(☑709-722-9167; www.batterycafe.ca; 1 Duckworth St; ⊘7:30am-5:30pm Mon, Tue & Thu, to 9pm Wed, 7am-5:30pm Fri, 8am-9pm Sat, 8am-5:30pm Sun) This bright, cozy espresso bar and cafe brews some of the finest caffeine jolts in town; there are also good sandwiches and baked goods. Has outdoor picnic-table seating in good weather.

★**Duke of Duckworth**　　　　　　PUB
(☑709-739-6344; www.dukeofduckworth.com; McMurdo's Lane, 325 Duckworth St; ⊘noon-2am; 🕾) 'The Duke,' as it's known, is an unpretentious English-style pub that represents all that's great about Newfoundland and Newfoundlanders. Stop in on a Friday night and you'll see a mix of blue-collar and white-collar workers, young and old, and perhaps even band members from Great

Big Sea plunked down on the well-worn red-velour bar stools.

Newfoundland Chocolate Company　　　　　　CAFE
(☑709-579-0099; www.newfoundlandchocolate company.com; 166 Duckworth St; ⊘10am-6pm Mon-Wed & Sat, to 8pm Thu & Fri, noon-5pm Sun) This small local chain dishes out bonkers-good artisan chocolates, including cups of hot chocolate ($5 to $7) with flavors including sea salt, caramel, and local berries that will make your head spin. Look for a big Newfoundland-as-chocolate-paradise mural near this flagship location. There's another branch in the Signal Hill Visitor Centre (p463) that's open from 9am to 8pm daily.

Yellow Belly Brewery　　　　　　PUB
(☑709-757-3780; www.yellowbellybrewery. com; 288 Water St; ⊘11am-1am Sun & Mon, 11:30am-2am Tue-Thu, to 3am Fri, 11am-3am Sat) Refreshing brews crafted on-site are front and center at this casual meeting spot, a brick behemoth dating back to 1725. Everyone's having a good time and there's

decent pub grub to soak up the brews. For extra ambience descend to the underbelly – a dark basement bar with a speakeasy feel.

Quidi Vidi Brewery
BREWERY

(☑ 709-738-4040; www.quidividibrewery.ca; 35 Barrows Rd; tasting or tour $10; ⊗ tastings 11am, taproom noon-10pm Sun-Wed, to midnight Thu-Sat) This microbrewery is located in an old fish-processing plant on the tiny wharf. It's a swell place to enjoy a drink. Call ahead to book a tasting, which lasts around 45 minutes. Locals prefer you to park on the outskirts of town and walk in.

☆ Entertainment

Check out www.musicnl.ca for updated listings. Perhaps because this is such an intimate city, word of mouth and flyers slapped on light poles are also major vehicles for entertainment information. Venues are close together – have a wander and enjoy.

Ship Pub
LIVE MUSIC

(☑ 709-753-3870; www.facebook.com/The ShipPubKitchen; 265 Duckworth St; ⊗ noon-late) Attitudes and ages are checked at the door of this little pub, tucked down Solomon's Lane. You'll hear everything from jazz to indie, and even the odd poetry reading. The pub closes when things slow down, but tends to stay open until 3am on weekends.

Resource Centre for the Arts
PERFORMING ARTS

(☑ 709-753-4531; www.rca.nf.ca; 3 Victoria St) Sponsors indie theater, dance and film by Newfoundland artists, all of which play downtown in the former longshoremen's union hall (aka LSPU Hall).

Shamrock City
LIVE MUSIC

(☑ 709-758-5483; www.shamrockcity.ca; 340 Water St; ⊗ noon-2am) Bands playing everything from Newfoundland folk to '80s hair ballads take the stage nightly at this all-ages pub.

Signal Hill Tattoo
LIVE MUSIC

(☑ 709-772-5367; www.signalhilltattoo.org; Signal Hill National Historic Site; $10; ⊗ 11am & 3pm Wed & Thu, Sat & Sun Jul & Aug) This award-winning historical reenactment program recreates 19th-century British military drills with cannon fire, mortars and muskets, all backed by a fife and drum band.

🔒 Shopping

Outfitters
SPORTS & OUTDOORS

(☑ 709-579-4453; www.theoutfitters.nf.ca; 220 Water St; ⊗ 10am-6pm Mon-Wed & Sat, to 9pm Thu & Fri, noon-5pm Sun) At this camping and gear shop you can get the local outdoorsy lowdown (check the bulletin board) and good rentals. Hikers should note this spot sells East Coast Trail (p476) maps and butane canisters.

Fred's
MUSIC

(☑ 709-753-9191; www.fredsrecords.com; 198 Duckworth St; ⊗ 9:30am-9pm Mon-Fri, to 6pm Sat, noon-5pm Sun) This is the premier music shop in St John's. It features local music from blue-chip provincial artists such as Hey Rosetta, Buddy Wasisname, Ron Hynes, Amelia Curran, The Navigators and Great Big Sea.

Invasion
ART

(☑ 709-746-8469; www.facebook.com/invasionnl; 114 Duckworth St; ⊗ 11am-6pm Mon & Wed-Fri, from 10am Sat, noon-5pm Sun) Pop art, comic books, science fiction and geek culture gets mashed up with St John's cityscapes and Newfoundland photography at this oddball art gallery. Think pictures of Godzilla rampaging through Quidi Vidi, or sketches of Marvel Comics villains kissing the cod.

Living Planet
GIFTS & SOUVENIRS

(☑ 709-739-6811; www.livingplanetstudio.com; 181 Water St; ⊗ 9am-3pm Mon-Thu, 8am-4pm Fri) Head here for quirky tourist T-shirts and buttons with Newfoundland slang even locals are proud to wear.

ℹ Information

MEDICAL SERVICES

Health Sciences Complex (☑ 709-777-6300; 300 Prince Phillip Dr; ⊗ 24hr) A 24-hour emergency room.

MONEY

Banks stack up near the Water St and Ayre's Cove intersection.

CIBC (☑ 709-576-8800; 215 Water St; ⊗ 9:30am-5pm Mon-Fri)

Scotia Bank (☑ 709-576-6000; 245 Water St; ⊗ 10am-5pm Mon-Fri)

POST

Central Post Office (☑ 709-758-1003; 354 Water St; ⊗ 8am-4pm Mon-Fri)

CAPE SPEAR

A 15km drive southeast of St John's leads you to the most easterly point in North America, with spectacular coastal scenery and whale-watching during much of the summer.

In a stunning windswept setting, **Cape Spear National Historic Site** (☎709-772-2191; www.pc.gc.ca/en/lhn-nhs/nl/spear; Blackhead Rd; adult/child $3.90/free; ⊘10am-6pm) includes an interpretive center, a refurbished 1835 lighthouse, and the heavy gun batteries and magazines built in 1941 to protect the harbor during WWII. The remains of the concrete bunkers are particularly atmospheric, and under the right light, pretty darn spooky. Hikers can join up with the East Coast Trail here.

Heed all signs warning visitors off the coastal rocks, as rogue waves have knocked people into the water.

TOURIST INFORMATION

Visitors Center (☎709-576-8106; www.stjohns.ca; 348 Water St; ⊘9am-4:30pm Mon-Fri May-early Oct) Excellent resource with free provincial and city road maps, and staff to answer questions and help with bookings. There's another outlet at the Quidi Vidi Village Plantation (p463) open from 10am to 4pm Tuesday to Saturday, and noon to 4pm Sunday. The **Airport Visitors Center** (☎709-758-8515; St John's International Airport; ⊘10am-5pm) is the only St John's visitor center that's open year-round.

Some useful websites:

City of St John's (www.stjohns.ca) The 'Visiting Our City' category has descriptions of and links to attractions, accommodations, eateries and events.

Downhome (www.downhomelife.com) A folksy, *Reader's Digest*–style monthly for the region.

St John's Telegram (www.thetelegram.com) The city's daily newspaper.

ⓘ Getting There & Away

AIR

St John's International Airport (YYT; ☎709-758-8500; www.stjohnsairport.com; 100 World Pkwy; ☜)

Air Canada offers a daily direct flight to and from London; WestJet goes direct to Dublin and Gatwick. **United Airlines** (☎800-864-8331; www.united.com) flies to the USA. The main carriers:

Air Canada (p462)

PAL Airlines (☎800-563-2800; www.palairlines.ca)

Porter Airlines (☎888-619-8622; www.flyporter.com)

WestJet (☎888-937-8538; www.westjet.com)

BUS

DRL (☎709-263-2171; www.drl-lr.com) sends one bus daily each way between St John's and Port aux Basques ($126, cash only, 13½ hours) via the 905km-long Hwy 1, making 25 stops en route. It leaves at 7:30am from Memorial University's Student Centre, in CA Pippy Park (p464).

CAR & MOTORCYCLE

Avis, Budget, Enterprise, Hertz, National and Thrifty have offices at the airport or adjacent to it (in the latter case, they'll pick you up in a free shuttle).

SHARE TAXIS

These large vans typically seat 15 and allow you to jump on or off at any point along their routes. You must call in advance to reserve. They pick up and drop off at your hotel. Cash only.

Newhook's Transportation (☎709-682-4877; griffinevlynn@hotmail.com) Travels down the southwestern Avalon Peninsula to Placentia ($35, two hours), in sync with the Argentia ferry schedule.

Shirran's Taxi (☎709-468-7741) Plies the Bonavista Peninsula daily, making stops at Trinity ($50, 3½ hours) and Bonavista ($40, four hours), among others.

ⓘ Getting Around

BUS

The **Metrobus** (☎709-570-2020; www.metrobus.com) system covers most of the city (fare $2.50). Maps and schedules are online and in the Visitors Center. Bus 3 is useful; it circles town via Military Rd and Water St before heading to the university.

The Link loops around the main tourist sights, including Signal Hill, between 10am and 5:30pm Wednesday to Sunday from late June to September. Hop-on/hop-off fare is $10.

CAR & MOTORCYCLE

The city's one-way streets and unique intersections can be confounding. Thankfully, citizens are incredibly patient. The parking meters that line Water and Duckworth Sts cost $1.50 per hour.

Sonco Parking Garage (☎709-754-1489; cnr Baird's Cove & Harbour Dr; ⊘6:30am-11pm) is central, but there are several others; most charge around $2 per hour.

TAXI

Except for the trip from the airport, all taxis operate on meters. A trip within town should cost around $8 to $10. **Jiffy Cabs** (☑709-722-2222; www.facebook.com/jiffycabs) provides dependable service. As of this writing, there were no ride-sharing services (ie Uber or Lyft) in St John's.

AVALON PENINSULA

The landscape along the coastline's twisting roads is vintage fishing-village Newfoundland. Many visitors make day trips to the peninsula's sights from St John's, which is easily doable, but there's something to be said for burrowing under the quilt at night, with the sea sparkling outside your window, in Cupids or Branch. Four of the province's six seabird ecological reserves are in the region, as are 28 of its 41 national historical sites.

Much of the East Coast Trail (p476) runs through the area; keep an eye out for free guided hikes. The ferry to Nova Scotia leaves from Argentia.

Southeastern Avalon Peninsula

This area, sometimes called the South Shore, is known for its wildlife, archaeology, boat and kayak tours, and unrelenting fog. Scenic Rtes 10 and 90, aka the **Irish Loop** (www.irishloop.nf.ca), lasso the region. For a quick taste, visit the **Cape Spear Lighthouse** (☑709-772-2191; www.pc.gc.ca/en/lhn-nhs/nl/spear; Blackhead Rd, Cape Spear; entry incl with Cape Spear National Historic Site; ⊘10am-6pm Jun-Aug, reduced hours May, Sep & Oct) and the fishing village of Petty Harbour, though sites further south are well worth exploring. Highlights include watching the puffins and whales in Witless Bay, exploring La Manche Provincial Park (p477) and hiking the East Coast Trail (p476).

Goulds & Petty Harbour

Backed against steep slopes, beautiful, pocket-sized Petty Harbour sits like an opal embedded into the coast. While you'll spot many tourists experiencing what may be their first settlement outside of St John's, it's worth noting the weathered boats in the active port are the real deal – this is a true fishing village. Check out the harbor, learn to fish, and pet some aquatic creatures at the

DON'T MISS

RUNNING THE GOAT

The active printing press **Running the Goat** (☑709-334-3239; http://runningthegoat.com; Cove Rd, Tors Cove; ⊘10:30am-5:30pm Thu-Tue mid-May–Oct), south of St John's, is a bibliophile's dream. Owner Marnie Parsons gives tours of her presses, one from 1830s London. In addition to handmade poetry chapbooks and manifestos, there's a wonderful selection of local artists' prints, and good adult and children's books authored by Newfoundlanders.

aquarium. Nearby Goulds is a useful stop for groceries.

⊙ Sights & Activities

★**Fishing for Success** FISHING
(☑709-740-3474; www.islandrooms.org; 10d Main Rd, Petty Harbour; adult/child $99/50) 🖋 Run by Kimberly and Leo, a local fishing family, this nonprofit organization seeks to rescue the local fishing traditions by teaching them to local kids and visitors. Dory trips include rowing lessons in a traditional wood dory (boat) and cod jigging. There's also a full-day option that includes net-knitting, rope work and a historical wharf tour.

Harbour Lookout VIEWPOINT
(Main Rd, Petty Harbour) Drive or hike up to this outcrop, popular with local road-trippers, find a spot to sit (or stand), then enjoy the stellar views of icebergs and fishing ships returning home (or setting out).

North Atlantic Zip Lines ADVENTURE
(☑709-368-8681; www.zipthenorthatlantic.com; 32 Main Rd, Petty Harbour; adult/child $130/95) Canada's longest zip-line course has 10 ziplines ranging from 300ft to 2200ft in length. Tours run at 11am, 3pm and 6pm.

✗ Eating & Drinking

Tinkers Ice Cream Shop ICE CREAM $
(☑709-747-1629; www.facebook.com/tinkersicecream; 20 Main Rd, Petty Harbour; ice cream $3-6; ⊘11am-9pm Jun-Sep) Every summer holiday escape deserves a great ice-cream place, and Tinker's is the spot in Petty Harbour. The house specialty is an iceberg – of course – a scoop of vanilla placed on a flavored slushie. You can also get floats,

milkshakes and ice-cream tacos (the shell is a waffle cone).

Chafe's Landing
SEAFOOD $$

(☏709-747-0802; www.chafeslanding.com; 11 Main Rd, Petty Harbour; mains $9-19; ⊘11am-9pm) A lot of folks here day-trip from St John's specifically for the fish-and-chips, which are quite good (if not particularly mind-blowing). Lines get long and parking might be impossible, but it's worth it. Chafe's also serves locally made moose sausage, beer-steamed mussels, and salads.

WaterShed
CAFE

(☏709-747-0500; 24a Main Rd, Petty Harbour; ⊘10am-5pm Jun-Sep; 🛜) Joy is here: real espresso drinks at a refurbished waterfront shed. Owner Karen loves talking local lore; she also makes a mean hiker cookie, packed with seeds. There's also great baked treats and sandwiches. If you have an extra few hours to chill out, spend them on the deck.

Witless Bay Ecological Reserve & Around

This is a prime area for whale-, iceberg- and puffin-watching. Several boat tours will take you to see them from the towns of Bay Bulls (35km south of St John's) and Mobile (10km south of Bay Bulls). Midway between the towns, there's lodging in Witless Bay.

Four islands off Witless Bay and southward are preserved as the Witless Bay Ecological Reserve (www.flr.gov.nl.ca/natural_areas/wer/r_wbe) and represent one of the top seabird breeding areas in eastern North America.

The best months for trips are late June and July, when the humpback and minke whales arrive to join the birds' capelin (a type of fish) feeding frenzy. If you really hit the jackpot, in early summer an iceberg might be thrown in too.

👉 Tours

Tours from Bay Bulls visit Gull Island, which has the highest concentration of birds in the Witless Bay Ecological Reserve. Tours that depart to the south around Bauline East head to nearby Great Island, home to the largest puffin colony. Bauline East is closer to the reserve, so less time is spent en route, but you see the same types of wildlife on all of the tours.

Also popular, kayaking provides a special perspective on wildlife. After all, you don't just see a whale while paddling, you feel its presence.

You can't miss the boat operators – just look for signs off Rte 10. Sometimes the smaller companies cancel tours if there aren't enough passengers; it's best to call ahead to reserve and avoid such surprises. They operate from mid-May through mid-September. Most depart several times daily between 9:30am and 5pm.

Captain Wayne's
BOATING

(☏709-763-8687; www.captwaynes.com; Northside Rd, Bay Bulls; tour $80) Descended from generations of Newfoundland fishermen, Captain Wayne really knows his coast and his enthusiasm proves contagious. Best of all, he only does small, 12-person tours in his custom boat. The three-hour tour includes puffin-

---

THE EAST COAST TRAIL

Skirting gaping cliffs, fairy-tale forests and fields of edible berries, the world-class East Coast Trail (☏709-738-4453; www.eastcoasttrail.ca) is a through-hiker's delight. It stretches 265km from Cape St Francis (north of St John's) south to Cappahayden, with an additional 275km still under way.

Its 26 sections range in difficulty from easy to challenging, but most make good day hikes. For a sample, try the scenic 9.3km path between Cape Spear and Maddox Cove (near Petty Harbour); it should take between four and six hours.

For seasoned hikers, the ECT can also be walked as a through-hike, combining camping with lodging in villages along the way. Campsites generally feature pit toilets and a good water source nearby. Fires are prohibited. A local taxi service operates at the trailheads and can bring you to nearby lodging or your vehicle.

Topographical maps are available in St John's at Outfitters (p473) or Downhome (☏709-722-2970; http://shopdownhome.com; 303 Water St; ⊘10am-5:30pm Mon-Wed & Sat, to 8:30pm Thu & Fri, noon-5pm Sun). Check out the ECT trail website for detailed 'how to' information and the lowdown on guided hikes.

and whale-watching. There are several departures daily, but photographers should go at 5pm for best light.

Molly Bawn Tours
BOATING

(☑709-334-2621; www.mollybawn.com; Rte 10, Mobile; adult/child/child under 5yr $50/45/free; 🐾) These popular tours cruise over the waves on a small, 10m boat. Mobile is half-way between Bay Bulls and Bauline East.

Outfitters
KAYAKING

(☑800-966-9658, 709-579-4453; www.theoutfit ters.nf.ca; 18 Southside Rd, Bay Bulls; half-/full-day tour $89/189) Popular half-day kayak tours leave at 9am and 2pm; full-day tours depart at 9:30am and travel beyond the inner bay of Bay Bulls to the top of the eco-reserve. There is a shuttle service from St John's that leaves from Outfitters (p473) at 220 Water St; rates are $30 per person.

Gatherall's
BOATING

(☑800-419-4253; www.gatheralls.com; Northside Rd, Bay Bulls; tour adult/child $62/29, family (2 adults & 2 children) $155; 🐾) This large, fast catamaran is a good choice for people prone to seasickness.

🛏 Sleeping & Eating

Armstrong's Suites
MOTEL $

(☑709-334-2201; 236 Main Hwy, Witless Bay; r $80; 🐾) Though this is just your run-of-the-mill roadside motel, it's unlikely that even your own grandmother could better receive your visit. The kind owner thinks nothing of going the extra mile, providing extra cots and towels and breakfast fixings to East Coast Trail through-hikers.

Bears Cove Inn
B&B $$

(☑866-634-1171; https://thebearscoveinn.ca; 15 Bears Cove Rd, Witless Bay; r $135-165; 🐾) A pleasant place to stay, this seven-room B&B has all the amenities you could want, including water views and a lovely garden and barbecue area. Rooms feature country decor and flat-screen TVs. The helpful owners also run a local pub and speak French.

Bread & Cheese
B&B $$

(☑709-334-3994; www.breadandcheeseinn.com; 22a Bread & Cheese Rd, Bay Bulls; r $155-175; 🐾) This gorgeous country house with a wraparound porch and sprawling lawn is a sight for sore feet, located a short stroll from the East Coast Trail. Rooms are smart and modern, and there is one wheelchair-

AVALON WILDERNESS RESERVE

Dominating the interior of the region is the 1070-sq-km **Avalon Wilderness Reserve** (☑709-637-2081; www.flr.gov.nl.ca/natural_areas/wer/r_aw; free permit required). Illegal hunting dropped the region's caribou population to around 100 in the 1980s; 30 years later, a couple of thousand roam the area. Permits for hiking, canoeing and bird-watching in the reserve are available at La Manche Provincial Park.

Even if you don't trek into the wilds, you still might see caribou along Rte 10 between Chance Cove Provincial Park and St Stevens.

accessible option. Our only wish is for a cheerier welcome.

La Manche Provincial Park

Diverse birdlife, along with beaver, moose and snowshoe hare, can be seen in this lush park (www.tcii.gov.nl.ca/parks/p_lm; NL 10, Tors Cove) FREE only 53km south of St John's. A highlight is the 1.25km trail to the remains of La Manche, a fishing village that was destroyed in 1966 by a fierce winter storm. Upon arrival, you'll see a beautiful suspension bridge dangling over the narrows – it's part of the East Coast Trail. Find the trail-head at the park's fire-exit road, past the main entrance.

There is excellent camping, with many sites overlooking large La Manche Pond, which is good for swimming. There is also a drive-through entry kiosk with information and fee collection for camping.

Ferryland

POP 414

Ferryland, one of North America's earliest settlements, dates to 1621, when Sir George Calvert established the Colony of Avalon and figured the winters here weren't too bad. A few Newfoundland seasons of ice and snow later and he was scurrying for Maryland, where he eventually became the first Lord Baltimore. Other English families arrived later and maintained the colony despite it being razed by the Dutch in 1673 and the French in 1696. These days, Ferryland and

MISTAKEN POINT ECOLOGICAL RESERVE

Designated a World Heritage site in 2016, the **Mistaken Point Ecological Reserve** (☑709-438-1011; www.flr.gov. nl.ca/natural_areas/wer/r_mpe; Portugal Cove South) FREE protects 575-million-year-old multicelled marine fossils – the oldest in the world. The only way to reach it is via a free ranger-guided hike from the **Edge of Avalon Interpretive Centre** (☑709-438-1100; www.edge ofavalon.ca; Rte 10, Portugal Cove; adult/child $8/5; ☉10am-6pm mid-May–Oct) in Portugal Cove South.

You can also drive the bumpy gravel road between here and Cape Race. At the end, a lighthouse rises up beside an artifact-filled replica 1904 Marconi wireless station. It was the folks here who received the fateful last message from the *Titanic*.

The 'Mistaken Point' name, by the way, comes from the blinding fog that blankets the area and has caused many ships to lose their way over the years.

surrounding communities make the most of showcasing both the history and arts of the region.

For gorgeous windswept panoramas, don't miss the 2km walk out to the lighthouse.

☉ Sights

Colony of Avalon   ARCHAEOLOGICAL SITE
(☑709-432-3200; www.colonyofavalon.ca; Rte 10; adult/child $15/11.50; ☉10am-6pm Jun-Sep; P⛟🐾) The seaside surrounds of the Colony of Avalon archaeological site only add to the rich historical atmosphere that permeates Ferryland. Join a tour and you'll see archaeologists unearthing everything from axes to bowls. The worthwhile interpretation center is very kid friendly and houses beautiful displays of the artifacts that have been recovered. Guided 45-minute tours are offered upon request. Leashed dogs are allowed on the site (but probably shouldn't do their own digging).

Historic Ferryland Museum   MUSEUM
(☑709-432-2711; www.manl.nf.ca/ferrylandmuse um; Baltimore Dr; adult/child $3/2; ☉10am-4pm Mon-Sat, 1-4pm Sun Jun-Aug) The village's for-

mer courthouse is now the small Historic Ferryland Museum. The towering hill behind the museum was where settlers climbed to watch for approaching warships, or to escape the Dutch and French incursions. After seeing the view, you'll understand why the settlers named the hill 'the Gaze.'

✖ Eating

★**Lighthouse Picnics**   SANDWICHES $$
(☑709-363-7456; www.lighthousepicnics.ca; Lighthouse Rd; per person $26; ☉11:30am-4:30pm Wed-Sun Jun-Sep; 🐾) Lighthouse Picnics has hit upon a winning concept: it provides a blanket and organic picnic meal (say, a curried chicken sandwich, mixed-green salad and lemonade from a Mason jar) that visitors wolf down while sitting in a field overlooking explosive ocean views. Reserve in advance.

It's at Ferryland's old lighthouse, off Rte 10; you have to park and hike 2km to reach it, but oh it's worth it.

Southern Shore Folk Arts Council Dinner Theatre   THEATRE
(☑709-432-2052; www.ssfac.com; The Pool; adult/child $54/38; ☉7pm Tue, Thu & Fri Jul & Aug) Get a taste of local cuisine and Irish–Newfoundland sketch humor and folk songs at this well-regarded dinner-theater production. Expect the entire show to wrap up around 10pm. A lunch production also runs on select days while the theater operates; the cold-plate meal kicks off at noon and runs $40. Note 'The Pool' is the name for an actual road.

Along Route 90

The western arm of the Irish Loop (p475) doesn't receive as much attention as the east-coast stretch, partly because tourism infrastructure is simply not as developed. That said, this is still an area rife with dramatic scenery, and when it comes to the road between St Vincent's to St Mary's, potential wildlife spotting. This stretch of the loop is great for seeing whales, particularly humpbacks, which feed close to shore. Otherwise, even as rural Newfoundland goes, this a quiet area of little villages clinging to rocks and a sense of time gone by.

The stony beach at **St Vincent's** (Rt 90, St Vincent's; P) FREE is raw even by Newfoundland standards. It's also a brilliant spot to engage in a bit of whale-watching (your best bet is throughout summer), and all without having to board a boat. The paved path means that whale-watching here is wheelchair accessible. Even if there aren't whales around, this is a beautiful cove that's photogenic on its own merits.

Baccalieu Trail

The Bay de Verde Peninsula sticks out like a hitchhiker's thumb just west of St John's, marking what is for many visitors their first Newfoundland peninsular road trip. The scenic route here is known as the Baccalieu Trail. Fishing villages and pirate haunts stretch endlessly along Conception Bay's scenic western shore, and make for a wonderful day trip a mere 80km from the provincial capital.

Highlights include Brigus, in all its Englishy, rock-walled glory combined with North Pole history, and Cupids, a 1610 settlement complete with an archaeological dig to explore. To the west, thick forest and serenity define Trinity Bay.

Brigus

POP 720

If you took an English countryside village, scooped it out of the green hills of that rainy island, and then dumped it on the rocky shores of *this* rainy island, you'd get Brigus. Walk around postcard-perfect stone-walled streams and watch them meander slowly past old buildings and colorful gardens before emptying into the serene Harbour Pond. Seriously, if this place was any more idyllic it would vanish into the mists every 100 years.

Back in its heyday as a busy port, Captain Abram Bartlett needed a new deepwater berth. Brigus was ideal, but the surrounding cliffs made docking tricky. His solution? Blast a hole through the rock with the help of Cornish miner John Hoskins. Four months, some drill bits and a lot of gunpowder later, their efforts yielded the **Brigus Tunnel** (The Walk): about 24m long, and tall enough for a horse and carriage to traverse. It's now a cool, damp landmark.

The town's most famous son, Captain Robert Bartlett, made more than 20 Arctic expeditions, and in 1909 cleared a trail in the ice that enabled US commander Robert Peary to make his celebrated dash to the North Pole. Bartlett's old home, **Hawthorne**

Cottage (☑709-528-4004; www.pc.gc.ca/en/lhn-nhs/nl/hawthorne; 1 South St, cnr Irishtown Rd & South St; adult/child $3.90/free; ⊙10am-6pm Jun-Aug), is an ornate example of a wealthy Newfoundland mariner's mansion, and is today managed as a national historical site and museum.

Cupids

POP 740

This atmospheric village is imbued with rich history and surrounded by towering sea cliffs. Those rock formations didn't ward off merchant John Guy, who sailed here in 1610 and staked out England's first colony in Canada.

The first English colony, **Cupids Cove Plantation Provincial Historic Site** (☑709-528-3500; www.seethesites.ca/the-sites/cupids-cove-plantation.aspx; Seaforest Dr; adult/child $6/free; ⊙9:30am-5pm May-Oct; ℙ) features an ongoing archaeological dig that's worth touring. A stone's throw down the road is the **Cupids Legacy Centre** (☑709-528-1610; www.cupidslegacycentre.ca; Seaforest Dr; adult/child $8/4; ⊙9:30am-5pm Jun-Oct; ℙ), with fascinating exhibits.

There are a couple of local trails to tackle: the 2.5km **Burnt Head Trail**, with good views, forests, picnic areas and a sea arch; and the **Spectacle Head Trail**, a bumpy 100m climb that ends at the 'American Man,' a cairn that has overlooked Conception Bay for generations.

Afterwards, you can warm up at the **Cupid's Haven Tea Room** (☑709-528-1555; www.cupidshaven.ca; Burnt Head Loop; r $119-169; 🐾) or treat yourself to a tipple at the **Newfoundland Distillery Company** (☑709-786-0234; www.thenewfoundlanddistillery.com; 97 Conception Bay Hwy; ⊙noon-9pm Mon-Wed, to 10:30pm Thu-Sat, 1-6pm Sun).

Harbour Grace & Around

Notable historic figures have paraded through Harbour Grace over the past 500 years, including the pirate Peter Easton and aviator Amelia Earhart. Their stories are told at **Conception Bay Museum** (☑709-596-5465; www.conceptionbaymuseum.com; 1 Water St; adult/child $3/2; ⊙10am-4pm Jun, to 5pm Jul & Aug).

Nearby **Harbour Grace Airfield** (www.hrgrace.ca/site/tourism-heritage/attractions/airstrip; Earhart Rd; ⊙sunrise-sunset) is the site where

CAPE ST MARY'S ECOLOGICAL RESERVE & AROUND

Tucked away amidst the sea and cliffs and incessant winds that braid around the south-western tip of the peninsula, you'll find the **Cape St Mary's Ecological Reserve** (☑ 709-277-1666; www.flr.gov.nl.ca/natural_areas/wer/r_csme) **FREE**, one of the most accessible large-bird colonies in North America. You will smell before you see some 70,000 birds, including gannets, kittiwakes, murres and razorbills, but when you do spy all of those winged beasts, your heart won't soon forget the sight. The nearest town is little St Bride's, but services here are limited.

The best-known viewpoint is **Bird Rock**, reached via an easy footpath through fields of sheep and blue irises; suddenly you're at the cliff's edge facing a massive, near-vertical rock swarmed by squawking birds.

A small **Interpretive Centre** (☑ 709-277-1666; ☺ 9am-5pm May-Oct; ℗) offers info on nesting seabirds and the local ecology.

Placentia is 45km to the north, while St John's is 180km to the northeast.

Earhart launched her historic solo Atlantic flight.

It's hard to miss the large ship beached at the mouth of the harbor. This is the **SS Kyle** (1913), wrecked during a 1967 storm. Locals liked the look of it so much they paid to have it restored instead of removed.

Clinging to cliffs at the northern end of the peninsula are the remote and striking villages of Bay de Verde and Grates Cove. Hundreds of 500-year-old **rock walls** line the hills around Grates Cove and have been declared a national historical site.

Further offshore, in the distance, is the inaccessible **Baccalieu Island Ecological Reserve**, which is host to three million pairs of Leach's storm petrel, making it the largest such colony in the world.

Dildo

POP 1200

Oh, go on – take the obligatory sign photo. For the record, no one knows definitively how the name came about; some say it's from the phallic shape of the bay, others think it's named for an oar pin. Nevertheless, proud and stalwart locals have denied several campaigns to change the town name, which makes sense: tourists flock here to say they've had a romantic evening on Dildo Harbour. All jokes aside, Dildo is a lovely village and its shore is a good spot for whale-watching.

The **Dildo Interpretation Centre** (☑ 709-582-3339; Front Rd; adult/child $2/1; ☺ 10am-4:30pm Jun-Sep) has a whale skeleton and exhibits on the ongoing Dorset Eskimo archaeological dig on Dildo Island. It's not terribly exciting, but outside you can snap a picture with a fisherman in a yellow rain slicker dubbed Captain Dildo, and a giant squid, and really, how many times do you get to say that happened?

Cape Shore

The ferry to Nova Scotia, French history and lots of birds fly forth from the Avalon Peninsula's southwesterly leg.

ⓘ Information

A provincial **Visitors Center** (☑ 709-227-5272; Rte 100; ☺ hours vary) is 3km from the ferry on Rte 100. Its opening hours vary to coincide with ferry sailings.

ⓘ Getting There & Away

Newhook's Transportation (p474) runs a taxi service that connects the towns of Argentia and Placentia to St John's. The 14-hour Argentia **ferry** (☑ 800-341-7981; www.marineatlantic. ca; Charter Ave; adult/child $121/59, per car/motorcycle $244/122; ☺ mid-Jun–late Sep) links Newfoundland to Nova Scotia.

Placentia

POP 3500

In the 17th century, Placentia – then Plaisance – was the French capital of Newfoundland, a place where French fishermen laid out their cod catches and French militia plotted raids against the English, including the 1696 Avalon Peninsula Campaign, when Pierre Le Moyne d'Iberville effectively annihilated English Newfoundland – for a year.

Today Placentia is more of a working town than a tourism hub, although tourists do come here. That said, they're almost always passing through on their way to or from Nova Scotia via the ferry, which sails out of nearby Argentia. Still, there are a few historical sites around that are worth some exploration.

⊙ Sights & Activities

Castle Hill National Historic Site   HISTORIC SITE
(☑709-227-2401; www.pc.gc.ca/en/lhn-nhs/nl/castlehill; Old Castle Hill Rd; adult/child $3.90/free; ⊙10am-6pm Jun-Aug) French and British forces spent almost a decade fighting over this land, all in the name of expanding their fisheries and seizing control of the North American continent. This historical site commemorates that conflict; the rubble of an old stone fort can be seen here.

Great Beach Boardwalk   WALKING
(Beach Rd) You'll find nice views of Placentia Bay on this 1.4km-long boardwalk. It's a simple, easy walkway, and it's worth noting it's one of the few wheelchair-accessible means of enjoying the province's natural beauty. There are multiple access points along Beach Rd.

🛏 Sleeping & Eating

Rosedale Manor B&B   B&B $$
(☑877-999-3613; www.rosedalemanor.ca; 40 Orcan Dr; r $120-150; ☺🛜) This beautiful heritage B&B has flower gardens, romantic rooms with claw-foot tubs, and waterfront views that will make you sigh with happiness.

Philip's Cafe   CAFE $
(☑709-227-6596; 170 Jerseyside Hill; mains $5-12; ⊙7:30am-3:30pm Wed-Mon; 🛜) A must pre- or post-ferry stop for yummy baked goods and creative sandwiches such as apple and sharp cheddar on molasses-raisin bread. The breakfasts are the stuff of legend around here; come early to skip the wait. Note that this spot may be closed or have reduced hours outside of summer.

Three Sisters   PUB FOOD $$
(☑709-227-0124; www.facebook.com/thethreesisterspub; 2 Orcan Dr; mains $8-30; ⊙11am-9pm daily, bar closes 11pm Sun-Tue, midnight Wed, Thu & Sat, 1am Fri) Lovely pub grub and chilly pints of beer are served in this atmospheric Placentia house. It's often busy, and come evening, it's the best nightlife going in town.

❶ Getting There & Away
It's a 10-minute drive from the Argentia ferry, and about 14km from here to St John's.

EASTERN NEWFOUNDLAND

Two peninsulas, webbing like a pair of amoeba arms into the Atlantic, comprise eastern Newfoundland. The beloved, well-touristed Bonavista Peninsula projects northward. Historic fishing villages freckle its shores, and windblown walking trails swipe its coast. Clarenville (www.clarenville.net) is the Bonavista Peninsula's access point and service center, though there's not much for sightseers.

To the south juts the massive but less-traveled Burin Peninsula, with fishing villages struggling to find their way in the post-cod world. You will need your passport to hop the ferry from Fortune to the nearby French islands of St-Pierre and Miquelon, a regional highlight complete with wine, éclairs and Brie.

❶ Getting There & Away
The region is a half-day drive from St John's, and you really need your own wheels to properly explore. From Fortune you can take a fast ferry to St-Pierre and Miquelon, from where you can fly to St John's.

Trinity
POP 170

Before we wax on about how ridiculously picturesque and scenic Trinity is, let's set the record straight: Trinity is the Bonavista Peninsula's most popular stop, a historic town of crooked seaside lanes, storybook heritage houses, and gardens with white picket fences. Trinity Bight, on the other hand, is the name given to the 12 communities in the vicinity, including Trinity, Port Rexton and New Bonaventure.

If it all looks familiar, it may be because *The Shipping News* was partly filmed here. While the excitement has faded, there are still historic buildings, stunning hiking and theater along with whale-watching.

First visited by Portuguese explorer Miguel Corte-Real in 1500 and established as a town in 1580, Trinity is one of the oldest settlements on the continent.

Sights & Activities

One admission ticket (adult/child $20/free) lets you gorge on seven buildings scattered throughout the village of Trinity. They are run by both the **Trinity Historical Society** ($709-464-3599; www.trinityhistoricalsociety.com; 41 West St) and the provincial government (www.seethesites.ca), and are open from 9:30am to 5pm, May to mid-October.

Trinity Museum   MUSEUM
($709-464-3599; www.trinityhistoricalsociety.com; Church Rd; 7-site admission adult/child $20/free; 9:30am-5pm mid-May–mid-Oct) This creaking collection of bric-a-brac displays more than 2000 pieces of historical relics, including North America's second-oldest fire wagon. It's got that whole 'attic of fascinating stuff' vibe.

Random Passage Site   FILM LOCATION
($709-464-2233; www.randompassagesite.com; Main Rd, New Bonaventure; adult/child $10/3.50; 9:30am-5:30pm) Back in 2002, the CBC and Ireland's RTÉ made a miniseries out of Bernice Morgan's 1992 novel *Random Passage*. The show was partially filmed at a pretty cove a little south of Trinity, and the set, a painstakingly recreated 19th-century Newfoundland outport (small fishing village), is open to the public for guided tours.

You'll learn a lot about the miniseries and a bit about historical Newfoundland – we'd appreciate more of the latter than the former, but this is still a good detour.

★ Skerwink Trail   HIKING
(www.theskerwinktrail.com) This 5km loop is well worth the effort, with dramatic coastal vistas of sea stacks, early summer icebergs and a lighthouse. Be on guard for moose. The trailhead is near the church in Trinity East, off Rte 230.

Trinity Eco-Tours   BOATING
($709-464-3712; www.trinityecotours.com; Zodiac/kayaking tours $90/109) Head out on the water, either in an inflatable Zodiac or a sea kayak, and spot whales, icebergs and the rest while enjoying the crazy beautiful coast of this corner of Newfoundland.

Rugged Beauty Tours   WILDLIFE
($709-464-3856; www.ruggedbeautyboattours.net; 3hr tour adult/child $90/60; 10am & 2pm May-Oct) Unique trips with Captain Bruce, who takes you to abandoned outports and makes their history come alive. You might even see an eagle along the way.

Sleeping

★ Skerwink Hostel   HOSTEL $
($709-436-3033; www.skerwinkhostel.com; Rocky Hill Rd; campsite $5-15, dm $34, r $85-120; May-Oct; P☢) Travelers of all ages stay at homey, community-oriented Skerwink. With two six-bed dorms (with squishy, plastic-coated mattresses) and two private rooms, it's part of Hostelling International. Many locals drop by to chat and play guitar with the staff. Fresh bread and weak coffee are included for breakfast, and the fabulous Skerwink Trail is across the street. Located off Rte 230.

★ Artisan Inn & Campbell House   INN $$
($709-464-3377; www.trinityvacations.com; 57 High St; r incl breakfast $159-235; mid-May–Oct; ☢) A fantasy coastal getaway, these gorgeous properties are adjacent to each other and managed by the same group. Both have ocean vistas. The three-room inn hovers over the sea on stilts; set further back, Campbell House has lush gardens.

Fishers' Loft   INN $$
($709-464-3240; http://fishersloft.com; Rocky Hill Rd, Port Rexton; r incl breakfast $160-309; ☢) Featuring traditional 19th-century local architecture, this colonial is a favorite of return travelers. Rooms and suites are bright and spacious with fluffy duvets and down pillows; the treetop rooms offer stunning views of the bay. It's kitted out perfectly, with iPod docks, hiking poles and binoculars.

Eriksen Premises   B&B $$
($709-464-3698; www.mytrinityexperience.com/eriksen-premises; 8 West St; r $119-190; mid-May–mid-Oct; ☢) This 19th-century merchant home offers elegance in accommodations and dining (mains $20 to $30, open lunch and dinner). It also manages four other properties, ranging from small B&Bs to furnished apartment rentals, in the village.

Eating & Drinking

Skipper Bob's   CANADIAN $
(50 Church Rd; mains $8-16; 7am-8pm) This simple spot has friendly service and a juicy

moose burger that's as good as much fancier versions plied at much more expensive restaurants. Also serves a basic, tasty menu of soups and sandwiches.

★ **Twine Loft**   CANADIAN **$$$**
(☑709-464-3377; www.trinityvacations.com/our-restaurant; 57 High St; prix fixe $55) The up-scale restaurant of the Artisan Inn serves a three-course, prix-fixe meal of local specialties, with wonderful seafood and wine selections guided by an in-house sommelier. Reservations are necessary, but you can also stop by for a sunset drink on the deck. Check the daily menu posted out front.

Two Whales Cafe   COFFEE
(☑709-464-3928; http://twowhales.com; 99 Main Rd, Port Rexton; ☺10am-6pm) An adorable coffee shop serving the full-octane variety and lemon blueberry cake that's off the charts. It also does good vegetarian fare and organic salads.

☆ Entertainment

Trinity Pageant   THEATER
(adult/child $20/15; ☺2pm Wed & Sat) One of the mainstays of the Rising Tide theater company is this outdoor dramedy, a heartfelt (and at times hilarious) theatrical exploration of Trinity's identity and history, held at the **Rising Tide Theatre** (☑888-464-3377; www.risingtidetheatre.com; 40 West St; ☺Jun-Sep).

❶ Information

The town website (www.townoftrinity.com) has lots of tourism information. Make sure to pop into the **Trinity Visitor Centre** (☑709-464-2042; www.seethesites.ca; West St; ☺9:30am-5pm mid-May–mid-Oct).

❶ Getting There & Away

Trinity is 259km from St John's and is reached via Rte 230 off Hwy 1. **Shirran's Taxi** (☑709-468-7741) offers a daily taxi service to St John's.

Bonavista

POP 3450

The town of Bonavista is one of the highlights of the peninsula that bears the same name. It has a lashing of historic sites, plus creative restaurants, businesses and accommodations that have worked in concert to effect a small, innovative downtown revival. Visitors should understand Bonavista is a working town. This is no assemblage of painstakingly elegant historical homes à la Trinity, and the village does not spill down a raw rock face like settlements on the Irish Loop. Rather, Bonavista remains something of a fishing village, all cottages starting to peel and sag, plus modern convenience stores. But peel back a layer and you'll find a living, functioning community, where the warmth and friendliness is vital and sincere, even compared to other Newfoundland towns, and raw natural beauty is a quick hike away.

⊙ Sights & Activities

Dungeon Park   PARK
(Cape Shore Rd, off Rte 230; **P**) **FREE** The sheer power of the ocean is more than evident at the Dungeon, a deep chasm 90m in circumference that was created by the collapse of two sea caves. The thunderous waves that shattered the caves now slam the coast, and are often shrouded in pea-soup fogs.

Cape Bonavista Lighthouse   LIGHTHOUSE
(☑709-468-7444; www.seethesites.ca; Rte 230; adult/child $6/free; ☺9:30am-5pm late May–mid-Oct) This brilliant red-and-white-striped lighthouse dates from 1843. The interior has been restored to the 1870s, and includes the original lead-weight pulley device that kept the lighthouse lights turning automatically, as well as period costumes curious tourists can try on. A puffin colony lives just offshore; the birds put on quite a show around sunset.

Ye Matthew Legacy   HISTORIC SITE
(☑709-468-1493; www.matthewlegacy.com; Roper St; adult/child $7.25/3; ☺9:30am-5pm Jun-Sep) Enter this structure and discover a wonderful replica of John Cabot's 15th-century ship *Matthew*, which Cabot sailed into Bonavista. Travelers who love history, especially those of a nautical bent, will love the attention to detail that's been put into this reconstruction. While the *Matthew* is smaller than many contemporary sailing yachts, it sailed halfway around the world.

Ryan Premises National Historic Site   HISTORIC SITE
(☑709-468-1600; www.pc.gc.ca/en/lhn-nhs/nl/ryan; Ryans Hill Rd; adult/child $3.90/free; ☺10am-6pm Jun-Sep) Explore a restored 19th-century saltfish mercantile complex at this National Historic Site, which consists of a slew of white clapboard buildings. The exhibits honor five centuries of fishing in Newfoundland via multimedia displays and interpretive programs.

ELLISTON

The Root Cellar Capital of the World, aka Elliston, lies 6km south of Bonavista on Rte 238. The teeny town was struggling until it hit upon the idea to market its 135 subterranean veggie storage vaults, and then presto – visitors came a knockin'. Actually, what's most impressive is the **puffin colony** just offshore and swarming with thousands of chubby-cheeked, orange-billed birds from mid-May to mid-August. A quick and easy path over the cliffside brings you quite close to them and also provides whale and iceberg views.

Stop at the Elliston Visitors Center as you enter town, and the kindly folks will give you directions to the site along with a map of the cellars (which you're welcome to peek inside). If you're interested in the local practice of sealing, make sure to stop by the **Sealers Interpretation Centre** (John C. Crosbie Sealers Interpretation Centre; ☎ 709-476-3003; www.homefromthesea.ca; Elliston; $7; ☺ 9am-5:30pm May-Oct; P), which provides a careful examination of this hunting tradition.

Work up an appetite while you're here, because **Nanny's Root Cellar Kitchen** (☎ 709-468-5050; 177 Main St, Elliston; mains $8-16; ☺ 8am-8pm; P) in historic Orange Hall cooks a mighty fine lobster, Jiggs dinner (roast meat with boiled potatoes, carrots, cabbage, salted beef and pea-and-bread pudding) and other traditional foods, plus it's licensed.

In September, the **Roots, Rants & Roars Festival** (www.rootsrantsandroars.ca; Elliston; ☺ mid-Sep) celebrates the province's top chefs, who prepare outdoor feasts in a dramatic setting.

From the adjoining hamlet of **Maberly**, a gorgeous 17km **coastal hiking trail** winds over the landscape to Little Catalina.

Seas the Day Boat Tours
BOATING

(☎ 709-468-8810; www.seasthedayboattours.com; Station Rd; adult/child $60/35; ☺ tours depart 10am, 1pm, 4pm & 7pm May-Sep) Come for the punny name, stay for the boat tours all along the nearby coast. Spot whales, puffins and icebergs – plus, if you're lucky, the staff might show you how to gut a codfish. Memories!

Sleeping

HI Bonavista
HOSTEL $

(☎ 709-468-7741; www.hihostels.ca; 40 Cabot Dr; dm $35, r $79; @ 🛜) This tidy white-clapboard hostel offers four private rooms, two shared dorm rooms, free bike use, and kitchen and laundry facilities. It's a short walk from the center of town.

Russelltown Inn & Vacation Homes
INN $$

(www.russelltowninn.com; 134 Coster St; r $140-193, pods $80, cottages $275-350) This property manages several accommodations throughout town: a main inn with clean, understated but attractive rooms; several guest cottages (minimum two-night stay); and 'glamping' in eco pods – effectively, nicely renovated studio shacks – with solar lighting. All of the options are well executed and comfortable.

Harbourview B&B
B&B $$

(☎ 709-468-2572; www.harbourviewgetaway.com; 21 Ryans Hill Rd; r $139; ☺ Jun-Sep; 🛜) The name doesn't lie: you get a sweet view and pretty historical accents at this simple, four-room B&B, plus an evening snack (crab legs) with owners Florence and Albert. Breakfast has a gluten-free option.

Eating & Drinking

★ Boreal Diner
CANADIAN $$

(☎ 709-476-2330; www.theborealdiner.com; 61 Church St; mains $13-19; ☺ noon-9pm Mon-Thu, to 10pm Fri & Sat, 5-9pm Sun; ✔) In a bright-red colonial house, this innovative restaurant manages what many others aspire to: creative, international takes on local Newfoundland ingredients. Thus crab pot stickers, cod in tarragon sauce, and polenta with wild mushroom stew are all potential options on the ever-shifting menu. It also does vegan and gluten free. Real espresso drinks keep you wired.

Bonavista Social Club
CANADIAN $$

(☎ 709-445-5556; www.bonavistasocialclub.com; Upper Amherst Cove; mains $12-26; ☺ 11am-8pm Tue-Sun) 🍃 Social Club's innovative meals are sourced on-site and served with a view to die for. From incredible wood-fired breads and pizzas to rhubarb lemonade and moose burgers with partridgeberry ketchup, the kitchen is on fire (literally; there's a wood-burning oven for those pizzas). The goats roaming the grounds provide milk for cheese, while the chickens lay the eggs. Reserve ahead.

The rustic restaurant is about 15 minutes from Bonavista via Rte 235 (turn left when you see the sign for Upper Amherst Cove). The chef's dad carved all the beautiful wood decor in his workshop next door.

Quintal Cafe CAFE
(☑709-476-2191; www.facebook.com/TheQuintalCafe; 63 Church St; ◷8am-6pm Mon-Thu, to 8pm Fri-Sun) The folks at the Boreal Diner also operate this friendly little coffee shop, which has strong caffeinated goodness and a bunch of board games if you just feel like passing the time.

☆ Entertainment

Garrick Theatre THEATER
(☑709-468-5777; www.garricktheatre.ca; 18 Church St) The artfully restored Garrick is an anchor for downtown Bonavista. The theater screens mainstream and indie films, and hosts live-music performances that often showcase a rich tableau of local talent.

🛍 Shopping

Newfoundland Salt Company FOOD
(☑709-770-7412; https://newfoundlandsaltcompany.com; 45 Church St; ◷11am-5pm Tue-Fri, from 10am Sat, from noon Sun) As creative gifts go, it doesn't get much more unique than the locally sourced sea salt sold at this little storefront. We're particularly enamored of its flavored salts, including a green alder sea salt that makes your food taste as though it's been seasoned with a forest (in a good way).

ℹ Information

The town website (www.townofbonavista.com) has tourism information.

ℹ Getting There & Away

Bonavista is a scenic 50km drive north of Trinity along Rte 230. **Shirran's** (☑709-468-7741; www.facebook.com/ShirransTransportation) offers a daily shuttle service from St John's ($40 one way).

Burin Peninsula

This is a foggy, isolated peninsula, a place where the towns have been depressed by the loss of fishing and the spruce-furred cliffs are wet and massive. But as with anywhere in Newfoundland, locals are over-the-top welcoming, and you can easily lose a day or two wandering down coastal walks before embarking toward the baguettes of France (aka St-Pierre).

Marystown is the peninsula's largest town; it's jammed with big-box retailers but not much else. **Burin** is the area's most attractive town, with a gorgeous elevated boardwalk over the waters of its rocky shoreline. **St Lawrence** is known for fluorite mining and scenic coastal hikes. In **Grand Bank**, there's an interesting self-guided walk past historic buildings and along the waterfront. Just south is fossil-rich **Fortune**, the jumping-off point for ferries to St-Pierre.

👁 Sights

Fortune Head Geology Centre MUSEUM
(☑709-832-3569; www.fortunehead.com; Bunker Hill Rd, Fortune; adult/child $7.50/5; ◷9am-5pm Thu-Tue, 8am-7pm Wed Jun-Aug) Exhibits examine the geology of the Burin Peninsula, minerals and rocks, the 1929 Grand Banks tsunami and prehistoric animals. Kids will appreciate this interactive center with fossils to touch from Fortune Head Ecological Reserve; it's in town by the St-Pierre ferry dock. It also offers a children's day camp with a daily rate. Daily tours go to the reserve (adult/child $20/10).

Fortune Head Ecological Reserve PARK
(☑709-637-2081; www.flr.gov.nl.ca/natural_areas/wer/r_fhe; off Rte 220; ◷24hr) The reserve protects fossils dating from the planet's most important period of evolution, when life on earth progressed from simple organisms to complex animals some 550 million years ago. The reserve is about 3km west of Rte 220, by the Fortune Head Lighthouse.

🛏 Sleeping & Eating

Thorndyke B&B B&B $$
(☑709-832-0820; www.thethorndyke.ca; 33 Water St, Grand Bank; r $165; ◷May-Oct; ☺) This handsome old captain's home overlooks the harbor. Antique wood furnishings fill the four light and airy rooms (each with private bathroom). The hosts will provide dinner with advance notice.

Sharon's Nook & the Tea Room CAFE $
(☑709-832-0618; 12 Water St, Grand Bank; mains $7-12; ◷8:30am-6pm Mon, Tue & Sat, to 9pm Wed-Fri, 11am-7pm Sun) This kitschy and countrified eatery serves up lasagna, chili, sandwiches and over a dozen varieties of heavenly cheesecake.

❶ Getting There & Away

The Burin Peninsula is accessed via Rte 210 off Hwy 1. The drive from St John's to Grand Bank is 359km and takes just over four hours; this is a narrow road, and in heavy rains you'll want to pace yourself. **Matthew's Taxi** (☑709-832-0491) runs from St John's down the peninsula as far as Fortune.

ST-PIERRE & MIQUELON

POP 6100

Twenty-five kilometers offshore from the Burin Peninsula lies a little piece of France. The islands of St-Pierre and Miquelon aren't just French-like with their berets, baguettes and Bordeaux – they *are* France, governed and financed by the *tricolore*. Locals kiss their hellos and pay in euros, sweet smells waft from myriad pastry shops, and French cars crowd the tiny one-way streets. It's a world away from Newfoundland.

St-Pierre is the more populated and developed island, with most of its 5500 residents living in the town of St-Pierre. Miquelon is larger geographically but has only 600 residents overall.

Jacques Cartier claimed the islands for France in 1536, after they were discovered by the Portuguese in 1520. At the end of the Seven Years' War in 1763, the islands were turned over to Britain, only to be given back to France in 1816. And French they've remained ever since.

◉ Sights & Activities

When Prohibition dried out the USA's kegs in the 1920s, Al Capone decided to slake his thirst – and that of the nation – by setting up shop in St-Pierre.

He and his mates transformed the sleepy fishing harbor into a booming port crowded with warehouses filled with imported booze. Bottles were removed from their crates, placed in smaller carrying sacks and taken secretly to the US coast by rum runners. The piles of Cutty Sark whiskey crates were so high on the docks that clever locals used the wood both to build and heat houses. At least one house remains today and is known as the 'Cutty Sark cottage'; most bus tours drive by.

The tourist information center offers a special two-hour Prohibition tour (adult/child €20/10) that covers sites related to the theme. If nothing else, drop by the Hotel Robert near the tourist information center

and check out Al Capone's hat; it hangs in the gift shop.

Miquelon & Langlade   ISLAND
(☑508-416-187; mne@ct975.fr; adult/child 3hr tour €45/35; ☉Jun-Sep) The island of Miquelon is less visited and far less developed than St-Pierre. The village of Miquelon, centered on the church, is at the northern tip of the island. From nearby l'Étang de Mirande a walking trail leads to a lookout and waterfall. From the bridge in town, a scenic 25km road leads across the isthmus to the wild and uninhabited island of Langlade. There are some wild horses, and around the rocky coast you'll see seals and birds.

Tours are operated by the Comite Regional de Tourisme.

Île aux Marins   VILLAGE
(☑508-410-435; 3hr tour adult/child €30/25; ☉9am & 1:30pm May-Sep) The magical Île aux Marins ('Sailor Island'; often translated as 'Pioneer Island') is a beautiful abandoned village on an island out in the St-Pierre harbor. A bilingual guide will walk you through colorful homes, a small schoolhouse museum, lonely cemeteries and a grand church, built in 1874. Book tours at **L'Arche Museum** (☑508-410-435; www.arche-musee-et-archives. net; Rue du 11 Novembre; adult/child €7/5; ☉9am-5pm Jul & Aug, 9:30am-noon & 1:30-4:30pm May, Jun & Sep). You can also go over on a ferry (€6; 10 to 15 minutes) sans guide during July and August; boats run roughly every two hours.

Zodiac Tours   BOATING
(☑508-414-736; adult/child €41/35; ☉Jun-Sep) Full-day bilingual tours by Zodiac cover both Miquelon and Langlade. Book at the visitor center. Rates include snacks.

✨ Festivals & Events

Bastille Day   CULTURAL
(☉Jul 14) The largest holiday of the year, both in this part of France and that other bit of France across the Atlantic.

Basque Festival   CULTURAL
(☉mid-Aug) A weeklong festival with music, marching and invigorating street fun.

🛏 Sleeping

★ **Auberge St Pierre**   B&B $$
(☑508-414-086; www.aubergesaintpierre.fr; 16 Rue Georges Daguerre; d €88-179; ☜) Guests rave about the warm service and lovely atmosphere of this family-run island B&B.

Arrive to chilled wine and cheese. Remodeled rooms feature flat-screen TVs and hydromassage showers; they're also stocked with robes and extra towels. Transportation to and from the ferry and island tours included.

Nuits St-Pierre
B&B $$

(☑ 508-412-027; www.nuitssaintpierre.com; 10 Rue du Général Leclerc; r €140-200; ☺ 🛜) An upscale lodging aimed at the honeymoon crowd. The five rooms, each with private bath and blissful, downy beds, are named after famous French authors. There's free pickup from the airport or ferry. The attached tea salon is open every afternoon from 2pm to 6pm; it's a must for a restorative beverage and slice of cake.

Hotel Robert
HOTEL $$

(☑ 508-412-419; www.hotelrobert.com; 2 Rue du 11 Novembre; r €80-133, ste $105-165; 🛜) Most visitors end up in this decent-value hotel, the largest on the island. Rooms are pleasant, with crisp white sheets and powerful showers. Some are dated. A downstairs restaurant serves breakfast (not included). It's within close walking distance of the ferry.

✖ Eating

★ Guillard Gourmandises
BAKERY $

(☑ 508-413-140; 31 Rue Boursaint; pastries €2-5; ☺ 7am-noon & 2-5:30pm Tue-Sat, 7:30am-12:30pm Sun) It's worth memorizing the complicated schedule to make good on this slice of *la belle* France. After all, these cream-plumped chocolate éclairs, macarons, piping-hot pastries and gateaux are the reason you came, right?

Tiffin
ASIAN $$

(☑ 508-552-531; www.facebook.com/pg/tiffin.spm; 9 Rue Saveaur Ladret; mains €12-18, multicourse set meals from €40; ☺ noon-1pm & 6-8pm Wed, Fri & Sat) At this creative pan-Asian restaurant, there isn't a restaurant. Rather, you order set meals served in Indian-style tiffins – stackable metal lunchboxes – that you eat on the go. The meals span the Asian continent, ranging from garlic cauliflower and Indonesian *gado gado* (vegetable salad) to Vietnamese *banh mi* (baguette) laced with mint and coriander to coconut chicken and basmati rice.

Le Feu de Braise
FRENCH $$

(☑ 508-419-160; www.feudebraise.com; 14 Rue Albert Briand; mains €12-23; ☺ noon-1:30pm & 7-9:30pm) As French restaurants go, this one is wonderfully old-school, serving a master class in stick-to-your-ribs rural classic cuisine: steak in Roquefort sauce, duck breast, and grilled sausage in mustard sauce. Everything is delicious, and you'll have to roll yourself through the narrow streets after polishing off *crème brûlée* for dessert.

Crêperie Restaurant du Vieux Port
FRENCH $$

(☑ 508-412-700; www.facebook.com/creperies taurantduvieuxport; 10 Rue du 11 Novembre; €8-25; ☺ 7am-10pm Jul & Aug, noon-1:30pm & 7-9:30pm Sep-Jun) This *crêperie* boasts a fantastic location overlooking St-Pierre's old port, and a kitchen to match the view: dine out on crepes stuffed with cod and chorizo, beef in a shallot and wine sauce, or just enjoy some excellent scallops. Should you have some good wine to wash everything down? You really should.

🛈 Information

Americans, EU citizens and all visitors except Canadians need a passport for entry. Those staying longer than 30 days also need a visa. Other nationalities should confirm with their French embassy if a visa is needed prior to arrival. Canadians can enter with a driver's license.

To merit the duty-free waiver on alcohol, you must stay on the islands at least 48 hours.

MONEY

Most vendors accept credit cards. Some accept the loonie, though they return change in euros. If you're staying more than an afternoon, it's probably easiest to get euros from the local ATMs.

OPENING HOURS

Most shops and businesses close between noon and 1:30pm. Some stores also close on Saturday afternoons, and most are closed on Sunday.

TELEPHONE

Calling the islands is an international call, meaning you must dial 011 in front of the local number. Phone service links to the French system, so beware of roaming charges on your mobile.

TIME

The islands are half an hour ahead of Newfoundland Time.

TOURIST INFORMATION

Office de Tourisme (Tourist Information; ☑ 508-410-200; www.spm-tourisme.fr; Place du Général de Gaulle; ☺ 8:30am-8pm; 🛜) The visitors center, near the ferry dock, provides a map showing all the banks, restaurants etc. Staff also provide information on the islands' hotels and tours, and make bookings for free. The same organization operates conventional tours, boat tours and guided hikes.

❶ Getting There & Away

AIR

Air St-Pierre (☎ 508-410-000, 877-277-7765; www.airsaintpierre.com; round-trip from St John's $360) flies to St John's, Montréal and Halifax. There are two to three flights weekly to each city. Taxis to/from the airport cost around €5.

BOAT

From Fortune on Newfoundland, the **St-Pierre Ferry** (☎ 508-410-875; www.spm-ferries.fr; 14 Bayview St, Fortune; adult/child return from Fortune €74/50) makes the hour-long trip to and from the island once daily (twice on Wednesdays) in July and August. It runs less often the rest of the year. Departure times vary, so check the website. Boats carry foot passengers only, though plans are in the works for two car ferries. Ferry staff coordinate Fortune parking in lots near the dock (per day $10). Buy tickets in advance and arrive 30 minutes early (or one hour before departure if you need to leave a car).

❶ Getting Around

Much can be seen on foot. Roads are steep, so prepare to huff and puff. Car-rental agencies are resistant to renting to tourists, who admittedly have difficulty navigating the unsignposted, narrow one-way streets.

The visitor center (p487) rents bicycles (per day €13) as well as motorized bicycles. Local ferries head to Miquelon (adult/child return €24/13) and Langlade (adult/child return €17/8); check the tourist office for departure times.

CENTRAL NEWFOUNDLAND

Central Newfoundland elicits fewer wows per square kilometer than the rest of the province, but that's because huge chunks of the region are virtually inaccessible hinterlands of bogland and trees. Still, this area is in every way as beautiful as the rest of Newfoundland, as evidenced by the misty islands of Notre Dame Bay – particularly Twillingate, which is whale-and-iceberg central – and the long, forested vistas of Terra Nova National Park.

Gander

POP 11,700

Gander sprawls across the juncture of Hwy 1 and Rte 330, which leads to Notre Dame Bay. It's a convenient stopping point and offers a couple of sights for aviation buffs; it's also the site of a major Canadian Forces air base. This is the region's main town – it may not feel quintessentially 'Newfoundland' with its glut of big-box retailers and lack of anything resembling scenery, but this is one of the few places in the province that isn't experiencing population loss. If you need to stock up on anything, do it here.

The **Gander Airport** (YQX; ☎ 709-256-6677; www.ganderairport.com) gets a fair bit of traffic. **DRL** (☎ 709-263-2171; www.drl-lr.com) buses stop at the airport en route to St John's (four hours) and Port aux Basques (nine hours).

Twillingate Island & New World Island

Pastel houses, the rock-ribbed coast, the steel-gray ocean, a breaching whale, a turquoise iceberg: all in a day's sightseeing here at the top of the central coast. Twillingate (comprised of two barely separated islands, North and South Twillingate) is one of Newfoundland's most popular tourism towns, and with good reason. The area is connected to 'mainland' Newfoundland by narrow causeways, and between local trails, endless views and friendly locals, it's a tough place to tear yourself away from.

◉ Sights

★ **Prime Berth Fishing Museum**   MUSEUM
(☎ 709-884-2485; www.primeberth.com; Main Tickle Causeway; $5, tour $8; ⊙ 10am-5pm Jul & Aug) Run by an engaging fisherman, this private museum, with its imaginative and deceptively simple concepts (a cod-splitting show!), is brilliant, and fun for mature scholars and schoolkids alike. It's one of the first places you see as you cross to Twillingate.

Long Point Lighthouse   LIGHTHOUSE
(☎ 709-884-2247; ⊙ 10am-6pm) **FREE** Long Point provides dramatic views of the coastal cliffs. Travel up the winding steps, worn from lighthouse-keepers' footsteps since 1876, and gawk at the 360-degree view. Located at the tip of the north island, it's an ideal vantage point for spotting icebergs in May and June.

Isles Wooden Boat Museum   MUSEUM
(☎ 709-884-5841; www.isleswoodenboatbuilders. com; 4 St Peters Church Lane; $10; ⊙ 9am-5pm mid-May–Sep; ℙ) Wooden boats were once as common as cod in Newfoundland, but

WORTH A TRIP

TERRA NOVA NATIONAL PARK

In the popular imagination, Newfoundland's beauty, to say nothing of her population, is constantly associated with the coast. But there is a magic to the island's interior, a strange, alluring blanket of bogs, boreal forest and cloud-cloaked hills. **Terra Nova National Park** (709-533-2801; www.pc.gc.ca/terranova; adult/child/family per day $5.80/ free/11.75) is the province's best showcase of this sort of inner-island scenery. You can lose days here hiking amidst moss-floored and spruce forest, mere physical meters and an entire wilderness world away from the nearby Trans-Canada Hwy.

All that said, this area does include oceanside real estate – the park is fronted by the salty waters of Clode and Newman Sounds.

Terra Nova's 14 hiking trails total almost 100km; pick up maps at the **Visitors Center** (709-533-2942; Hwy 1; ⊙10am-6pm Jul & Aug, to 4pm May, Jun & Sep). The epic **Outport Trail** (48km) provides access to backcountry campgrounds and abandoned settlements along Newman Sound. The loop in its entirety is rewarding, but be warned: parts are unmarked, not to mention mucky. A compass, a topographical map and ranger advice are prerequisites for this serious route.

Camping is the only option within the park itself. Those with aspirations of a bed should head to Eastport; it's near the park's north end on Rte 310, about 16km from Hwy 1. For camping reservations (recommended on summer weekends), call **Parks Canada** (877-737-3783; www.pccamping.ca; reservation fee $10.80) or go online.

The park is 259km northwest of St John's. While buses on the Trans-Canada Hwy can drop you near the east and west entrances of the park, the interior is best accessed by private vehicle.

---

these classic craft have since been largely replaced by fiberglass vessels. This museum, staffed by both passionate youngsters and old timers committed to the craft of their forefathers, keeps the wooden boatbuilding tradition alive. In many ways it's as much boatbuilding studio as learning institution; every few months, the museum creates a new wooden boat, and you can see the process unfold in real time.

Auk Island Winery　　　　　WINERY
(709-884-2707; www.aukislandwinery.com; 29 Durrell St; tastings $3, with tour $5; ⊙10am-6:30pm Jul & Aug, reduced hours Sep-Jun) Visit the grounds that produce Moose Joose (blueberry-partridgeberry), Funky Puffin (blueberry-rhubarb) and other fruity flavors using iceberg water and local berries. There's also ice cream made from iceberg water.

Twillingate Museum　　　　　MUSEUM
(709-884-2825; www.tmacs.ca; 1 St Peters Church Rd; admission by donation; ⊙9am-5pm May-Sep) Housed in a former Anglican rectory off Main St, this museum tells the island's history since the first British settlers arrived in the mid-1700s. The exhibits feel a bit dated, but the docents are kind and you'll likely learn a little something. There's a historical **church** next door.

Activities

Fun two-hour tours to view icebergs and whales depart daily from mid-May to early September.

★**Lower Little Harbour Trail**　　HIKING
(Lower Little Harbour Rd) This 4.8km loop, rated moderate-difficult, takes in just about everything that makes Newfoundland special: big root cellars, a 9m natural sea arch, cliffs, coast, forests and the remains of a community, since resettled. The abandoned houses you'll wander by give parts of this trail the whole icy-fingers-on-the-neck vibe.

Rock Adventures　　　　　KAYAKING
(709-884-9801; www.rockadventures.ca; 185 Main St; 2hr tour $75) The frigid waters off Twillingate may seem foreboding when all that's between you and you is a little bit of kayak hull. But paddling around this area with Rock Adventures is an exercise in repeatedly having your mind blown by nature's sheer beauty and Newfoundland's deep reserve of this quality.

Iceberg Man Tours　　　　　BOATING
(800-611-2374; www.icebergtours.ca; 50 Main St; adult/child $50/25) Captain Cecil's popular two-hour tours depart at 9:30am, 1pm and 4pm. Guests rave about the service.

Twillingate Adventure Tours   BOATING

(📞 888-447-8687; http://twillingateadventuretours.com; Wharf; adult/child $60/40) Whale-watching and iceberg-spotting tours depart from Twillingate's wharf off Main St at 10am, 1pm and 4pm (and sometimes 7pm).

🛏 Sleeping

Despite a glut of lodging options, Twillingate gets very busy in the summer. Book early.

HI Tides Hostel   HOSTEL $

(📞 709-884-8477; www.twillingateandbeyond.com; 94 Main St; dm/d/q $35/75-80/99; 🛜) This hostel occupies a saltbox home built way back in 1885. It must have been built pretty well, because this is a warm, welcoming spot, although that probably partly comes down to the budget-traveler vibe. Berry pancakes, coffee and tea are on the house.

Anchor Inn Hotel   HOTEL $$

(📞 709-884-2777; www.anchorinntwillingate.com; 3 Path End; r $150-190; ⊘ Mar-Dec; 🅿🛜) The waterfront Anchor has attractive rooms with deliciously soft beds and heart-melting scenic vistas. Amenities include the hotel's view-worthy deck and the barbecue grill for do-it-yourself types.

Captain's Legacy B&B   B&B $$

(📞 709-884-5648; www.captainslegacy.com; Hart's Cove; r $115-160; ⊘ May-Oct; 🅿🛜) A real captain named Peter Troake once owned this historical 'outport mansion,' now a gracious four-room B&B overlooking the harbor.

🍴 Eating

★ Doyle Sansome & Sons   SEAFOOD $$

(📞 709-628-7421; www.sansomeslobsterpool.com; 25 Sansome's Place, Hillgrade; mains $8-24; ⊘ 11am-9pm; 🅿) Head out of your way for this classic cash-only seafood spot, serving crisp cod, fish cakes with rhubarb relish, and fresh lobster. If it's a nice day, the dock seating provides a fine view. Don't be fooled by the name – a slew of friendly women cook here. The village of Hillgrade is about 17km from Twillingate.

Annie's Harbour Restaurant   SEAFOOD $$

(📞 709-884-5999; www.anniesrestaurant.ca; 128 Main St; mains $11-22; ⊘ 8:30am-9pm) Annie's is a solid choice if you want to eat all of the denizens of the ocean you've been admiring from Twillingate's shores (speaking of which, this spot has some nice waterfront views). Fish-and-chips are firm and flavorful, and the cod melt burger is a standout.

Georgie's Restaurant   CANADIAN $$

(📞 709-884-2777; www.georgiesrestaurant.com; 3 Path End; mains $17-29; ⊘ 8am-10am & 5-8pm) Upscale your Twillingate dining experience at this pretty waterfront spot, a romantic setting for dining on sesame-crusted scallops, shrimp penne and root-cellar bisque.

🍷 Drinking & Nightlife

★ Crow's Nest Café   CAFE

(📞 709-893-2029; www.facebook.com/CrowsNestCafe; Main St, Crow Head; ⊘ 10am-5pm Tue-Sat & 8-10pm Wed, Fri & Sat, 11am-4pm Sun) True to its name, the Crow's Nest occupies a high hill overlooking Twillingate. Even better than the views are the coffee, scones, cakes and other baked goods ($3 to $6) – all superlatively delicious and made with care. There's a bohemian vibe and plenty of local art on the walls.

The main cafe is in Crow Head, about 5km north of Twillingate, but there's a takeout stand at 127 Main St near 'downtown.'

Stage Head Pub   BREWERY

(📞 709-893-2228; www.splitrockbrewing.ca; 119 Main St; ⊘ noon-midnight) This pub, which exudes contemporary stylized charm, is attached to the local brewmasters at Split Rock Brewing. The minimalist drinking hall is a good spot to meet someone from around, enjoy the occasional live-music performance or just sink a local beer. Note that the bar closes when it wants to.

ℹ Information

For tourist information, travelers should visit the websites for the town (www.townoftwillingate.ca) and the island (www.visittwillingate.com).

ℹ Getting There & Away

From the mainland, Rte 340's causeways almost imperceptibly connect Chapel Island, tiny Strong's Island, New World Island and Twillingate Island.

Fogo Island & Change Islands

POP 2400

All across Newfoundland, you'll find fishing villages that have struggled to sustain themselves off the tourism trade. This rugged island chain seems to have figured out the formula, which is partly down to creating an ambitious, arts-oriented tourism infrastructure, and partly down to anchoring said infrastructure with an internationally renowned hotel.

Founded in the 1680s, Fogo is both an outport and a (by and large) well-heeled artists' colony. It's a unique and beautiful place, cut through by lovely trails and art studios, a slice of 21st-century cosmopolitan chic in the middle of a salt-battered province at the edge of the world.

◎ Sights

On Fogo, the village of **Joe Batt's Arm**, backed by rocky hills, is a flashback to centuries past – though it now has a mod twist thanks to the luxe Fogo Island Inn (p492). A **farmers market** takes place at the ice rink on Saturday mornings.

Nearby **Tilting** is perhaps the most engaging village on the island. Irish roots run deep here and so do the accents. The inland harbor is surrounded by picturesque fishing stages and flakes, held above the incoming tides by weary stilts.

The **Newfoundland Pony Sanctuary** (☑709-884-6953, 709-621-6381; www.nlpony sanctuary.com; 12 Bowns Rd, Change Islands; admission by donation; ☺by appointment) maintains the world's largest herd of endangered Newfoundland ponies. The small creatures are renowned as hardy workers (especially in winter) with gentle temperaments. Pony rides may be available. Call first to make sure someone is on-site before visiting.

✈ Activities

Turpin's Trail   HIKING
(NL 334, Tilting) Set aside the better part of a day for this roughly 8km trail, which crosses a tableau of sea barrens, coastal views and windy heath that is simply jaw dropping. While this is a longer hike than most on the island, the elevation changes aren't too terrible. The trail begins at **Lane House**, a historical saltbox home.

Brimstone Head   HIKING
(off Sargents Rd, Fogo) Near the village of Fogo, the indomitable Brimstone Head rises from the sea like a rocky knob. This is a short (2km there and back) but steep hike; the rewards are an almost mystical view of the ocean. To begin the hike, look for signs for Brimstone Head Park.

Lion's Den Trail   HIKING
The Lion's Den Trail (4.2km) forms a loop that begins at a Marconi radio site (an early long-distance radio transmitter), where there is a small interpretation center. The route passes tons of gorgeous scenery; hikers should keep an eye out for the caribou and fox that roam the area.

⛏ Sleeping

★Tilting Harbour B&B   B&B $
(☑709-658-7244; www.tiltingharbourbnb.ca; 10a Kelley's Island Rd, Tilting; r $98-110; ☻☏) Outstanding in hospitality, this traditional 100-year-old home has four spotless rooms with renovated bathrooms. While angles are sharp, it's comfortable and cozy. Best of all, the owner Tom is an accomplished chef who offers wonderful, social dinners ($35)

THE ART STUDIOS OF FOGO ISLAND

Newfoundland is an ancient place, geologically but even spiritually – this is an island with an old soul. Yet on Fogo Island you may notice buildings that appear to have been plucked from a science fiction film. Iconic art studios dot local walking trails, serving as a work space for painters, filmmakers, authors and photographers from around the world.

The studios were designed by Newfoundland native Todd Saunders, who also designed the Fogo Island Inn. They're sleek assemblages of clean, sharp angles, almost jarring in their modernity. But they are also encased in spruce shells and stand on stilts, a nod to Newfoundland. The intended effect is of a minimalist, futuristic take on the local fishing shed.

The studios serve as residencies for visiting artists, so you can't just peek your head in, but you're free to walk by and take a picture that will inevitably provoke a reaction on your preferred social media platform. Check out http://saunders.no/work for more information on these structures.

featuring fresh local seafood. Breakfast scones are also a big hit.

If you're lucky, Phil Foley's shed will be open next door. It's a very improvised speakeasy with local musicians and merriment.

★ **Old Salt Box Co** ACCOMMODATION SERVICES **$$**
(☑709-658-7392; www.theoldsaltboxco.com; home rental $180; ✳🛜) The Old Salt Box Co operates heritage-home rentals across the province, and three of their best properties are here. These may be historical homes, but their interiors are exercises in contemporary minimalist design, with sleek staircases, fresh furnishings, lots of natural light and gorgeous views. Warning: these book up fast. Your booking will be for a whole home rental.

★ **Fogo Island Inn** INN **$$$**
(☑709-658-3444; www.fogoislandinn.ca; Joe Batt's Arm; 2-night stay incl meals $1975-2875; 🅿🛜) 🏊 The Fogo Island Inn is a groundbreaking exploration of the concept of local sourcing. *Everything* in this place comes from at least as close as Newfoundland, including the community guides every visiting party is paired with. Architecturally, the Inn is a jaw-dropper, starkly minimalist yet growing organically from the rugged island landscape.

🍴 Eating

Growler's ICE CREAM **$**
(☑709-658-7015; www.facebook.com/Growlers IceCream; 125 Main Rd, Joe Batt's Arm; cones $5; ⏱noon-8pm) It would be a pity to miss this seaside stop, serving homemade partridgeberry-pie ice cream flecked with cinnamon and salty crumbs of crust.

Scoff Restaurant CANADIAN **$$**
(☑709-658-3663; www.scoffrestaurant.com; 159 Main Rd, Joe Batt's Arm; mains $12-26; ⏱11am-3pm & 5-10pm) Scoff – Newfoundland slang for a good meal – serves fancy takes on local cuisine in a cozy yet upscale setting. Salt beef comes with split pea 'fries,' smoked herring is served with marmalade, fresh toast and onion-and-fennel salad, and salt cod pierogies pair with fried onions and scruncheons (fried pork fat). A beautiful setting for original eats.

Fogo Island Inn Restaurant CANADIAN **$$$**
(☑709-658-3444; www.fogoislandinn.ca; Joe Batt's Arm; lunch mains $20-48, prix-fixe dinner $115; ⏱7-10am, noon-3pm & 6-9pm, by reservation only) 🏊 With sparkling sea views, this tiny gourmet eatery dishes up innovative three-course dinners sourced as locally as possible. The menu changes daily. Think delicate preparations of snow crab with sea salt, Prince Edward Island grass-fed beef, and rye ice cream with nettles. Nonguests should reserve at least three days ahead and park roadside, a five-minute walk from the inn.

ℹ Information

Valuable sources of local information are www. changeislands.ca and www.townoffogoisland.ca.

ℹ Getting There & Away

Rte 335 takes you to the town of Farewell, where the ferry sails to the Change Islands (20 minutes) and then onward to Fogo (45 minutes). Demand is heavy in summer – it is worth arriving two hours before your departure to ensure a spot for your vehicle. Note that bad weather can cause ferries to be cancelled, so you want to leave a day's grace period when traveling here to account for unforeseen climatic conditions.

Five boats leave between 7:45am and 8:30pm. Schedules vary, so check with **Provincial Ferry Services** (☑709-627-3492; www.gov.nl.ca/ferryservices; round-trip Fogo vehicle/passenger $25.50/8.50). Note it is about 25km from Fogo's ferry terminal to Joe Batt's Arm.

Central South Coast

If you're looking to get far away from just about everything, hop on Rte 360. This windy road runs 130km through the center of the province to the south coast, another land of long vistas, little towns and isolated coves. It's a long way down to the first settlements at the end of **Bay d'Espoir**, a gentle fjord. **St Alban's** is on the west side of the fjord. You'll find a few motels with dining rooms and lounges around the end of the bay.

Further south is a concentration of small fishing villages. The scenery along Rte 364 to **Hermitage** is particularly impressive, as are the landscapes around **Harbour Breton**. The largest town (population 1700) in the region, it huddles around the ridge of a gentle inland bay.

To access this remote area it's best to go by private vehicle. **Provincial Ferry Services** (☑709-729-3835; www.tw.gov.nl.ca/ferryservices) serve Hermitage, making the western south-coast outports accessible from here.

Assuming you do drive, gas up often, as service stations are spaced pretty far apart.

New-Wes-Valley

Tell someone in St John's you've been to New-Wes-Valley and they might ask, 'Where?' This is a little-known detour off the main Newfoundland tourism trail, but no less beautiful than the rest of the island. It's a land of foggy coves and rocky shorelines and great friendliness. Here you'll also find a living history museum and one of the province's more appealing offshore islands.

New-Wes-Valley is the name of a small town; it takes its name as a portmanteau of several other nearby towns – Newtown, Wesleyville and Valleyfield.

◉ Sights

★ Greenspond   ISLAND

(Greenspond Rd) This windy island, which seems to dangle somewhere between the Atlantic and the end of the world, is one of Newfoundland's oldest continuously inhabited outports. While connected to the mainland by bridge, Greenspond (and its population of roughly 270 souls) still has the feel of existing somewhere out of time. Walking trails thread over this 2.85-sq-km island, some winding through cemeteries, others dipping past rocky coves and bays. It's a 30km drive from New-Wes-Valley.

Barbour Living
Heritage Village   HISTORIC SITE

(☑709-536-3220; www.barbour-site.com; Newtown; adult/child $10/5; ⊙10am-4pm mid-Jun–early Sep; ℗) Get a taste of the life of the Barbours, a prosperous merchant family, at this village consisting of 19 homes (two of which are historically registered). The exhibits and staff provide insight on multiple generations of family history, spanning 1873 to 1960. Visit is by guided tour. Frequent live-music performances kick off around the village on many summer evenings. From Tuesday to Thursday you can buy an 'inside-out' ticket ($25), which adds a guided kayaking excursion to your visit.

Pool's Island   ISLAND

(Quay Rd) Drive allllll the way to the end of the road and you'll get to Pool's Island, an outcrop of smoothed boulders and pebbly beach often cloaked in a thick pea-soup fog. There's not a ton to do but soak up the lonely ambience and walk along several informal trails, all of which lead to somewhere haunted and beautiful.

🛏 Sleeping & Eating

★ Aunt Christi's   B&B $$

(☑709-658-7392; www.theoldsaltboxco.com/aunt-christis-greenspond; whole home (sleeps four) $180; ℗❋🤖) This lovely B&B is located by the ocean in Greenspond, within walking distance of some convenience stores and stark, wind-lashed stretches of moorland and coast. Despite the old-school exterior of the building, the interior drips with hanging lanterns and other contemporary design features.

Audrey's Tickle Bliss   B&B $$

(☑709-536-3220; www.barbour-site.com/accommodations; Barbour Living Heritage Village, Newtown; r $110; ℗🤖) This place sounds like one of those naughty tricks they recommend in men's and women's magazines, but in fact it's a really cute B&B with quilted bedspreads and, yes, blissful views of a nearby tickle (Newfoundland English for a narrow strait). Audrey's is located at the Barbour Living Heritage Village, and was formerly the Director's residence.

Norton's Cove Cafe   CANADIAN $$

(☑709-536-2633; www.nortonscove.com/pages/cafe; 114 Main St, Brookfield; mains $8-22; ⊙10am-8pm Thu-Tue; ℗) This gorgeous cafe boasts a light, airy interior, brilliant waterfront views, and a menu that takes enjoyable license with local cuisine; try cod with basmati rice and vegetables, or local squid stir-fried Korean style. On-site coffee and baked goods are excellent.

❶ Getting There & Away

NL 320 is the main road through this area, and connects to Gander on one side via NL 330, and the Trans-Canada Hwy near Gambo. You need your own car to explore the area.

NORTHERN PENINSULA

The Northern Peninsula points upward from the body of Newfoundland like an extended index finger, and you almost get the feeling it's wagging at you saying, 'Don't you dare leave this province without coming up here.'

Heed the advice. Two of the province's World Heritage–listed sites are here: Gros Morne National Park (p494), with its fjord-like lakes and geological oddities, rests at the peninsula's base, while the sublime, 1000-year-old Viking settlement (p498) at

ROW, ROW, ROW YER BOAT

There are oodles of boat tour companies in Newfoundland; what sets **Hare Bay Adventures** (☑709-537-2028; www.harebayadventures.com; Rogers Lane, Hare Bay; rowboat tour $95) apart is their use of wooden boats to explore the region. Three-hour rowboat trips allow visitors an uncommon, quiet and gentle communion with the rugged landscape. Hiking treks, birding trips and fishing trips can also be arranged.

Hare Bay is about 67km east of Gander, and 55km south of New-Wes-Valley.

L'Anse aux Meadows stares out from the peninsula's tip. Connecting these two famous sites is the **Viking Trail** (www.vikingtrail.org), aka Rte 430, an attraction in its own right that holds close to the sea as it heads resolutely north past the ancient burial grounds (p497) of Port au Choix and the ferry jump-off point to big, brooding Labrador.

The region continues to gain in tourism, yet the crowds are nowhere near what you'd get at Yellowstone or Banff, for example.

❶ Getting There & Away

Visitors to Gros Morne National Park usually fly into the Deer Lake Airport (p461). Long-distance **DRL** (☑709-263-2171; www.drl-lr.com) buses transit the Trans-Canada Hwy.

It's a five- to six-hour drive from Deer Lake at the peninsula's southern edge to L'Anse aux Meadows at its northern apex. Towns and amenities are few and far between, so don't wait to fuel up.

Gros Morne National Park

The stunning flat-top mountains and deeply incised waterways of this **national park** (☑709-458-2417; www.pc.gc.ca/grosmorne; per day adult/child/family $9.80/free/19.60) are simply supernatural playgrounds. Designated a World Heritage site in 1987, the park offers special significance to geologists as a blueprint for the planet. The bronze-colored Tablelands feature rock from deep within the earth's crust, supplying evidence for theories such as plate tectonics. Nowhere else in the world is such material as easily accessed as it is in Gros Morne.

Several small fishing villages dot the shoreline and provide amenities. Bonne Bay swings in and divides the area: to the south is Rte 431 and the towns of **Glenburnie**, **Woody Point** and **Trout River**; to the north is Rte 430 and **Norris Point**, **Rocky Harbour**, **Sally's Cove** and **Cow Head**. Centrally located Rocky Harbour is the largest village and most popular place to stay. Nearby Norris Point and further-flung Woody Point also make good bases.

◉ Sights

The park is quite widespread – it's 133km from Trout River at the south end to Cow Head in the north – so it takes a while to get from sight to sight; you could easily spend an hour on the road driving between two of the visitor centers (which have interpretive programs and guided walks).

Tablelands NATURAL FEATURE
(Rte 431) Dominating the southwest corner of the park, near Trout River, are the unconquerable and eerie Tablelands. This huge flat-topped massif was part of the earth's mantle before tectonics raised it from the depths and planted it squarely on the continent. Its rock is so unusual that plants can't even grow on it. You can view the barren golden phenomenon up close on Rte 431, or catch it from a distance at the stunning **photography lookout** above Norris Point.

Bonne Bay Marine Station AQUARIUM
(☑709-458-2550; www.bonnebay.ca; Rte 430, Norris Point; adult/child/family $6.25/5/15; ☺9am-5pm Jun-Aug; 🖑) At the wharf in Norris Point is this small research facility, which is part of Memorial University. Every half-hour there are interactive tours, and the aquariums display the marine ecological habitats in Bonne Bay. For children, there are touch tanks, whale bones and an activity room.

Gros Morne Wildlife Museum MUSEUM
(☑709-458-3396; https://grosmornewildlife museum.ca; 76 Main St N, Rocky Harbour; adult/child $8/5; ☺10am-6pm Jun, 9am-9pm Jul & Aug) While this spot falls into the kitschy-but-fun attraction-cum-gift-shop category, we want to stress: it *is* fun. Several rooms, each themed around a Gros Morne ecosystem, are filled with the taxidermied bodies of some of the park's most iconic animals. Kids love this spot, especially seeing as the owners give guests a scavenger hunt activity to complete.

Lobster Cove Head Lighthouse
LIGHTHOUSE

(☑709-453-2127; Rocky Harbour; included in park admission; ⊙10am-5:30pm mid-May–mid-Oct; P ♿) Overlooking the Gulf of St Lawrence, this lighthouse is picturesque enough to grace the cover of a nautically inclined calendar. Inside you'll find parks staff and exhibits dedicated to the cultural history of this part of Newfoundland; outside are trails winding through the tuckamore to a rocky coast studded with tide pools. Kids can play dress-ups with period clothes, and locals come here to whale-watch and fly kites. Sunsets over the St Lawrence defy hyperbolic description.

During summers the lighthouse hosts a slew of events, including guided walks, drum and fire circles, and evening music and storytelling ($14.70; call to reserve a spot).

Shallow Bay
BEACH

The gentle, safe, sand-duned beach at Shallow Bay seems out of place, as if transported from the Caribbean by some bizarre current. The water, though, provides a chilling dose of reality, as it rarely gets above 15°C (59°F).

Arches Provincial Park
PARK

(off Rt 430, Portland Creek; ⊙8am-11pm; P) **FREE**
The relentless force of the ocean has carved out these scenic arched rocks on Rte 430, north of Parsons Pond. The area is nice for a picnic assuming the wind isn't howling (which it usually is).

SS Ethie
SHIPWRECK

(Rte 430, past Sally's Cove) Follow the sign off the highway to a parking lot, and from here take a short path to where the waves batter the rusty and tangled remains of the SS *Ethie*. The story of this 1919 wreck, and the subsequent rescue, was the inspiration for the folk song 'Wreck of the Steamship *Ethie*'.

Broom Point Fishing Camp
HISTORIC SITE

(Rte 430, Broom Point; ⊙10am-5:30pm May-Oct)
FREE This restored fishing camp sits a short distance north of Western Brook Pond. The three Mudge brothers and their families fished here from 1941 until 1975, when they sold the entire camp, including boats, lobster traps and nets, to the national park. Everything has been restored; it's staffed by guides.

 Activities

Hiking

Twenty maintained trails of varying difficulty snake through 100km of the park's most scenic landscapes. The gem is the 16km **Gros Morne Mountain Trail** (www.pc.gc.ca/en/pn-np/nl/grosmorne) to the peak of Gros Morne, the highest point at 806m. The 16km **Green Gardens Trail** is almost as scenic and challenging, and has the added advantage of stunning views over water.

Shorter scenic hikes are **Tablelands Trail** (4km), which extends to Winterhouse Brook Canyon; **Lookout Trail** (5km), which starts behind the Discovery Centre (p497) and loops to the site of an old fire tower above the tree line; **Lobster Cove Head Trail** (2km), which loops through tidal pools; and **Western Brook Pond Trail** (Rte 430), the most popular path.

The granddaddies of the trails are the **Long Range Traverse** (35km) and **North Rim Traverse** (27km), serious multiday treks over the mountains. Permits and advice from park rangers are required.

If you plan to do several trails, invest in a copy of the *Gros Morne National Park Trail Guide,* a waterproof map with trail descriptions on the back, which is usually available at the visitor centers.

Kayaking/Boating

Kayaking in the shadow of the Tablelands and through the spray of whales is truly something to be experienced. Companies such as **Gros Morne Adventures** (☑709-458-2722; www.grosmorneadventures.com; Norris Point Wharf; 2hr kayak tour adult/child $59/49) can help get you on the water.

Bon Tours (☑709-458-2016; www.bontours.ca; Norris Point Wharf) will get you cod jigging ($40) or, during July and August, take you on a sunset cruise ($47). If you haven't purchased a park pass, you must do so before embarking. Reserve tickets well in advance. Bon also runs the phenomenal **Western Brook Pond boat tour** (105 Pond Rd, Rocky Harbour; 2hr trip per adult $58-65, child $26-30) every hour between 10am and 5pm.

★ Festivals & Events

Trails Tales Tunes Festival
MUSIC

(www.facebook.com/trailstalestunes; Norris Point; ⊙late May) This 10-day festival blends all of the things that make Newfoundland great: walks into the rugged landscape, folk music

NEWFOUNDLAND & LABRADOR GROS MORNE NATIONAL PARK

on small stages, and kitchen parties with screech. Lots of screech.

Writers at Woody Point Festival
LITERATURE

(☑709-453-2900; www.writersatwoodypoint.com; Woody Point; tickets from $20; ☺mid-Aug) Authors from across Newfoundland, Canada and the world converge at the Woody Point Heritage Theatre to do readings. There are also live-music events.

🛌 Sleeping

Sometimes it feels like every house in the region turns into a B&B or short-term rental come summer. However, places fill fast in July and August. Rocky Harbour has the most options; Woody Point and Norris Point are also good bets.

For backcountry campsites reachable by hiking, inquire at the Main Visitor Centre. Five developed campgrounds (☑877-737-3783; www.pccamping.ca; campsites $25.50-32.50, oTENTik & cabins per night $120; ☺Jun-Sep; P) lie within the park: Berry Hill, Lomond, Trout River, Green Point and Shallow Bay.

Aunt Jane's Place
B&B $

(☑709-453-2485; www.grosmorneescapes.com; Water St, Woody Point; d $75-95; ☺May-Oct; ☺) This welcoming B&B is an excellent spot to post up in Woody Point. Your lodging is a classic historical home with authentic accents (including bureaus and shelving made by the original owner). Rooms are smallish, but clean, comfy and good value. The owners manage local whole-home rentals as well.

Bonne Bay Inn
BOUTIQUE HOTEL $$

(☑709-453-2223, 709-400-6583; www.woodypointmagic.com; 145 Main Rd, Bonne Bay; r $199-219, ste 249-299; ❋🛜) There's a nice spread of options at this spot, from a main hillside hotel with nicely sized rooms that afford great views out to the fjords, to more plush suites on the Bonne Bay main drag with small outdoor seating areas.

Gros Morne Cabins
CABIN $$

(☑709-458-2020; www.grosmornecabins.ca; 72 Main St S, Rocky Harbour; cabins $149-209; 🛜) While backed by tarmac, most of these beautiful log cabins are fronted by nothing but ocean (ask when booking to ensure a view). Each has a full kitchen, TV and pullout sofa for children. Bookings can be made next door at Endicott's variety store.

Wildflower Country Inn
INN $$

(☑709-458-3000; www.wildflowerscountryinn.ca; 108 Main Street N, Rocky Harbour; r $109-119, cabin $129; P🛜) This 90-year-old home boasts four warm, wood-accented rooms with en suite bathrooms, plus two more spacious cabins (only available during the summer) if you need a little more room to stretch out after your hike. Located near the heart of Rocky Harbour's main drag. Rates drop by about $10 between October and May.

🍴 Eating & Drinking

Earle's
CANADIAN $

(☑709-458-2577; 111 Main St S, Rocky Harbour; mains $8-14; ☺11am-9pm; 🍴) Earle is an institution in Rocky Harbour. This spot gets packed with tourists and locals, from pensioners to families, and has great ice cream, decent moose burgers, plenty of pizzas and traditional Newfoundland fare that you can chomp on the patio.

Java Jack's
CAFE $$

(☑May-Sep 709-458-2710; https://javajacks.ca; 88 Main St, Rocky Harbour; mains $12-28; ☺7:30am-8:30pm Wed-Mon May-Sep, closed Oct-Apr; P🌿) 🍃 Escape the tyranny of fried food and head to Jack's, the outpost for an artsy crowd into locally sourced fare. There's a vintage-but-hip vibe, and Gros Morne's best coffees, wraps and soups by day. At night, the upstairs dining room fills hungry post-hike bellies with fine seafood, caribou and vegetarian dishes. Greens come fresh from the property's organic garden.

Black Spruce
CANADIAN $$$

(☑709-458-3089; www.theblackspruce.ca; 7 Beach Rd, Norris Point; mains $26-40; ☺5-9pm) Named for the province's most iconic tree, the Black Spruce has brought fine dining to Norris Point. It's got a luxury-lodge ambience and an atmosphere underlined by dishes such as cider-brined chicken and parsnip puree, or lobster and squid ink fettuccine. Scrub the trail dirt off your boots and treat yourself.

★Galliott Studios
CAFE

(☑709-453-2328; www.galliottstudios.blogspot.com; 10 Water St, Bonne Bay; ☺8am-7pm Jun-Sep) Part espresso house, part cheesemonger, part beer bar, part artists' gallery, all awesome: Galliott is a highlight of any visit to the Woody Point side of Gros Morne. Make sure to enjoy the phenomenal view from the back porch. It's a favorite hangout for those attending the Writers at Woody Point Festival.

🔒 Shopping

⭐ The Hunky Dory   ARTS & CRAFTS
(☑ 709-453-2304; 60 Main Rd, Woody Point; ⊙ hours vary) Besides the great punny name, this is a brilliant spot to pick up local folk arts and crafts, including stuff you genuinely can't find in other shops. The owners live next door, so knock on their door at a reasonable hour and they'll be happy to show you around.

ℹ️ Information

Park admission includes the trails, the Discovery Centre and all day-use areas.

Discovery Centre (☑ 709-453-2490; Rte 431, Woody Point; ⊙ 9am-6pm May-Oct) Has interactive exhibits and a multimedia theater explaining the area's ecology and geology. There's also an information desk with maps, daily interpretive activities and a small cafe.

Main Visitor Centre (☑ 709-458-2066; Rte 430; ⊙ 8am-8pm May-Oct) As well as issuing day and backcountry permits, it has maps, books, Viking Trail (p494) materials and an impressive interpretive area.

Park Entrance Kiosk (Rte 430, Wiltondale; ⊙ 9am-5pm May-Oct) Near Wiltondale.

Rocky Harbour (www.rockyharbour.ca) Online information about lodging, restaurants and attractions in Rocky Harbour.

Western Newfoundland Tourism (www. gowesternnewfoundland.com)

ℹ️ Getting There & Away

Deer Lake Airport (p461) is 71km south of Rocky Harbour. There are shuttle-bus services (p502) from the airport to Rocky Harbour, Woody Point and Trout River.

Port au Choix

POP 790

Dangling on a stark peninsula 13km off the Viking Trail (p494), Port au Choix houses a large fishing fleet, a quirky art gallery , and a worthy archaeological site that delves into ancient burial grounds.

👁️ Sights

**Port au Choix National
Historic Site**   HISTORIC SITE
(☑ 709-861-3522; www.pc.gc.ca/portauchoix; Point Riche Rd; adult/child $3.90/1.90; ⊙ 9am-6pm Jun-Sep; ℗) This site is dedicated to the ancient burial grounds of three different Indigenous groups that date back 5500 years. The modern **visitors center** tells of creative survival

in this rough area and of one group's unexplained disappearance 3200 years ago. Several good trails around the park let you explore further. Reached by walking, **Phillip's Garden**, a site with vestiges of Paleo-Eskimo houses, is a highlight.

Ben's Studio   GALLERY
(☑ 709-861-3280; 24 Fisher St; ⊙ hours vary) 🆓 At the edge of town is Ben Ploughman's capricious studio of folk art. Pieces such as *Crucifixion of the Cod* are classic and the artist himself is happy to bend your ear for a while. Ben lives next door, so just knock if it's a decent hour and he'll open the studio for you if he's not already working there.

🛏️ Sleeping & Eating

Jeannie's Sunrise B&B   B&B $
(☑ 709-861-2254; www.jeanniessunrisebb.com; Fisher St; r $99-119; ℗ 🤝) Jeannie radiates hospitality through her spacious rooms, bright reading nook and demeanor as sweet as her muffins. Guests rave about the big breakfasts with homemade jam. Rooms at the lower end of the price spectrum share a bathroom.

⭐ Anchor Cafe   SEAFOOD $$
(☑ 709-861-3665; Fisher St; mains $12-18; ⊙ 11am-8pm; ℗ 🙌) You can't miss this place – the front half is the bow of a boat – and don't, because it has great service and some of the best seafood on the Northern Peninsula. Perfect fries and cod, rich moose stew and original salads are served in cozy leather booths with *lots* of nautical-themed decorations. There's a kids' menu for the little ones.

ℹ️ Getting There & Away

Port au Choix sits in the middle of the Viking Trail (p494) on Rte 430. Most travelers come on a day trip by car.

L'Anse aux Meadows & Around

As the Viking Trail (p494) winds ever north, the land gets more, well, Viking-esque. Muskeg and hills framed by snow-capped mountains edge onto the bays, themselves peppered with sailing icebergs. At St Barbe, the waters of the gulf quickly narrow, so ferries can ply the desolate shores of Labrador. Further on, at Eddies Cove, the road leaves the coast and heads inland.

THE FRENCH SHORE

From 1783 until 1904, the eastern coast of the Northern Peninsula was visited by seasonal fishermen from Brittany, France. These men arrived thanks to 18th-century treaties, all part of the colonial chess game that characterized so much of early North American history.

The French Shore of the Northern Peninsula has thus always been a land apart, even from Newfoundland, itself a bit of a place apart from the rest of Canada. While the area is hardly Francophone, its unique history is captured in the stunning *French Shore Tapestry*, a 66m-long work of art that tells the story of this strand of woods, cliffs and sea from prehistoric days to the modern era. The tapestry draws clear influence from the 11th-century *Bayeux Tapestry*, and was created by women from the tiny outport of Conche.

The tapestry really has to be seen to be appreciated. One panel might show a Newfoundland dog shaking hands with a Canadian beaver, representing the Confederation debate. Another may show battles between Native Americans and Vikings, while another depicts diplomatic missives between the kings and queens of England and France.

To take in this stunning work of folk art, head to Conche itself, where the tapestry is displayed at the **French Shore Interpretation Centre** (☑ 709-622-3500; www. frenchshoretapestry.com; Rt 434, Conche; adult/child $8/free; ⊙ 9am-5pm Mon-Fri, from 1pm Sat & Sun May-Sep; P). Conche is a good 150km (two hours) south of St Anthony, and part of the road is unpaved (hard-packed gravel) – strap in for a bumpy ride.

So what else awaits on the French Shore? Keep an eye out for the turnoff to the **Tuckamore Lodge** (☑ 709-865-6361; www.tuckamorelodge.com; Main Brook; r incl breakfast $155-180; P @ 🛜), an assemblage of chalet-style lodgings in the middle of the woods that comes with excellent home-cooked meals and, if you're into it, fishing, hunting or birding classes.

As you approach the northern tip of the peninsula, Rte 430 veers off toward St Anthony, and two new roads wind through foggy passes and scraggly woods to L'Anse aux Meadows National Historic Site. Rte 436 hugs the eastern shore and passes through a series of tiny fishing villages, including (from south to north) St Lunaire-Griquet, Gunners Cove, Straitsview and L'Anse aux Meadows village, which has a stunning end-of-the-road ambience.

⊙ Sights

★ L'Anse aux Meadows National Historic Site
HISTORIC SITE

(☑ 709-623-2608; www.pc.gc.ca/lanseauxmeadows; Rte 436; adult/child $11.70/free; ⊙ 9am-6pm Jun-Sep; P) Leif Eriksson and his Viking friends lived here circa 1000 CE. Visitors can see the remains of their waterside settlement: eight wood-and-sod buildings, now just vague outlines left in the spongy ground, plus three replica buildings inhabited by costumed docents. The latter have names such as 'Thora' and 'Bjorn' and simulate Viking chores such as spinning fleece and forging nails. Allow two or three hours to walk around and absorb the ambience.

The premise may seem dull – visiting a bog in the middle of nowhere and staring at the spot where a couple of old sod houses once stood – but somehow this site, lying in a forlorn sweep of land, turns out to be one of Newfoundland's most stirring attractions.

Be sure to browse the interpretive center and watch the introductory film, which tells the captivating story of Norwegian explorer Helge Ingstad and his wife, archaeologist Anne Stine, who rediscovered the site in 1960. Also worthwhile is the 3km trail that winds through the barren terrain and along the coast surrounding the interpretive center.

Whale Point
HILL

(Ship Cove) Phew, that view. This windswept hill overlooks the cold ocean, drifting icebergs and breaching whales. It's located at the end of the road in the 'town' of Ship Cove, adjacent to a series of fantastically atmospheric geographic nomenclature, including Cape Onion, Diable Cove and Savage Cove. The lonely, end-of-the-world atmosphere is underlined by a nearby cemetery.

Norstead HISTORIC SITE

(☎709-623-2828; www.norstead.com; Rte 436; adult/child/family $10/6.50/30; ☺9:30am-5:30pm Jun-Sep) Can't get enough of the long-bearded Viking lifestyle? Stop by Norstead, just beyond the turnoff to the national historic site. This recreated Viking village features costumed interpreters smelting, weaving, baking and telling stories around real fires throughout four buildings. Sounds cheesy, but they pull it off with class. There's also a large-scale replica of a Viking ship on hand.

🏃 Activities

⭐**Quirpon Lighthouse Inn** ADVENTURE SPORTS

(☎709-634-2285; www.linkumtours.com; Main Rd, Quirpon; 2-person package incl boat transfer $425-450, Zodiac tour only $55; ☺May-Sep) Whales and icebergs skim by this island located 9km west of L'Anse aux Meadows. As remote getaways go, it would be hard to beat the on-site 10-room inn, close by a working lighthouse. Package stays include hiking, Zodiac tours and guided kayaking; if you don't want to shell out big bucks, you can just book a Zodiac iceberg/whale-watching tour.

Cape Raven HIKING

(Off Hwy 436) This wonderful, moderately difficult trail takes you up a fairly steep incline to the spot where James Cook supposedly surveyed Noddy Bay. On the way up you'll pass through spruce woods, over fast streams, before reaching a terminus that overlooks a spectacular vista of cliffs, gray ocean, fishing villages and speckled icebergs.

Dark Tickle Expeditions WILDLIFE

(☎844-999-2374; www.darktickle.com; 75 Main St, St Lunaire-Griquet; tours adult/child $65/40) The Dark Tickle complex offers its own Zodiac tours to connect visitors to marine life and icebergs. It's a wild tour that guests rave about.

🎉 Festivals & Events

Iceberg Festival CULTURAL

(☎877-778-4546; www.theicebergfestival.ca; ☺early Jun) Well, that settles it: there's a festival for everything. We joke: it makes sense that Northern Peninsula folks celebrate the iceberg, given how crucial these frozen chunks are to tourism, and how iconic they are to the seascape. This party, lasting a week at least, includes music, lectures, food demonstrations and more at locations near L'Anse aux Meadows.

🍴 Sleeping & Eating

Valhalla Lodge B&B B&B $$

(☎709-754-3105; www.valhalla-lodge.com; Rte 436, St Lunaire-Griquet; r $120-175, cottage $175-270; ☺May-Sep; P🐾) Sea views from this hilltop location inspired Pulitzer Prize–winning author Annie Proulx, who penned *The Shipping News* here. Sleep in a cottage (the more expensive ones can sleep up to four people) or in the more modern main lodge with a cozy living-room fireplace and a deck to watch icebergs in comfort. It's only 8km from the Viking site.

Burnt Cape Cabins CABIN $$

(☎709-452-3521; www.burntcape.com; 4 Main St, Raleigh; cabins $129-189; P🐾) The lonely town of Raleigh sits west of L'Anse aux Meadows, and makes for a less touristed base for exploring the region. These rustic wood cabins are located near the Raleigh harbor and include satellite TVs and comfortable beds. The owners run **Burnt Cape Tours** (☎709-452-3521; www.burntcape.com; $75; ☺9am late-Jun-early Sep). There's a convenience store and gas station next door.

⭐**Daily Catch** SEAFOOD $$

(☎709-623-2295; 112 Main St, St Lunaire-Griquet; mains $10-26; ☺11am-9pm) A stylish little restaurant serving finely prepared seafood and wine. The basil-buttered salmon gets kudos. Fish cakes, crab au gratin and cod burgers also please the palate. There's live music on Wednesday nights during the summer.

⭐**Norseman Restaurant & Art Gallery** SEAFOOD $$$

(☎709-754-3105; www.valhalla-lodge.com; Rte 436, L'Anse aux Meadows village; mains $20-38; ☺noon-9pm May-Sep; P) This lovely waterfront outpost ranks among Newfoundland's best. Emphasizing local products and creative preparations, the menu will have you wavering between options such as perfectly grilled lamb chops, kale Caesar salad with Arctic char, seared scallops or tender Labrador caribou tenderloin. Espresso drinks are served and cocktails come chilled with iceberg ice.

🛍 Shopping

Dark Tickle FOOD

(www.darktickle.com; 75 Main St, St Lunaire-Griquet; ☺9am-9pm) Dark Tickle is a shop in the grand tradition of the Québécois *économusée:* a place that showcases a particular

THE VIKINGS

Christopher Columbus gets the credit for 'discovering' North America, but the Vikings were actually the first Europeans to walk upon the continent. Led by Leif Eriksson, they sailed over from Scandinavia and Greenland some 500 years before Columbus and landed at L'Anse aux Meadows. They settled, constructed houses, fed themselves and even smelted iron out of the bog to forge nails, attesting to their ingenuity and fortitude. That it was all accomplished by a group of young-pup twenty-somethings is even more impressive.

Norse folklore had mentioned a site called 'Vinland' for centuries. But no one could ever prove its existence – until 1968, when archaeologists found a small cloak pin on the ground at L'Anse aux Meadows. Archaeologists now believe the site was a base camp, and that the Vikings ranged much further along the coast.

kind of heritage craft. In this case, it's the jam-making of Newfoundland and Labrador. You'll learn how the people of this province take northern fruit – bakeapple, crowberries, partridgeberries and more – and create preserves that would make an angel sigh.

On-site, you'll also find loads of gifts, souvenirs and artwork. The owners speak French, and the excellent **Cafe Nymphe** (☑709-623-2354; www.darktickle.com/content/18-cafe-nymphe; 75 Main St, St Lunaire-Griquet; mains $7-15; ☺9am-9pm) is located upstairs.

❶ Getting There & Away

The road to the Northern Peninsula is narrow and often potholed. Travel extra slow in the rain. You'll need your own wheels to explore the area.

A ferry travels between St Barbe and Blanc Sablon, Québec (near the Labrador border), daily. The 1¾-hour trip across the Strait of Belle Isle is run by **Labrador Marine** (☑866-535-2567; www.tw.gov.nl.ca/ferryservices/schedules/j_pollo.html; adult/child/vehicle $11.75/9.50/25.25); see the website for schedules. You'll want to show up at least an hour ahead of time to reserve your spot in the car line, even if you've already purchased tickets (which is a good idea).

St Anthony

Congratulations. You've made it to the end of the road, your windshield has culled the insect population and you have seen two World Heritage sites. After such grandeur, St Anthony may be a little anticlimactic. Though not pretty, it possesses a rough-hewn charm, and inspiring hiking and whale- and iceberg-watching.

Grenfell is a big name around here. Sir Wilfred Grenfell was a local legend and, by all accounts, quite a man. This English-born and educated doctor first came to Newfoundland in 1892 and, for the next 40 years, traveling by dogsled and boat, built hospitals and nursing stations and organized much-needed fishing cooperatives along the coast of Labrador and around St Anthony. A number of local sites pertaining to the pioneering doctor can be visited round town, including the doctor's own house, now an intriguing **museum** (☑709-454-4010; www.grenfell-properties.com; multisite admission adult/child/family $10/3/22; ☺8am-5pm Jun-Sep).

The main road through town ends at **Fishing Point Park**, where a lighthouse and towering headland cliffs overlook the sea. The Iceberg Alley Trail and Whale Watchers Trail both lead to cliff-top observation platforms – the names say it all.

If you want to get closer, **Northland Discovery Tours** (☑709-454-3092, 877-632-3747; www.discovernorthland.com; 2½hr tour adult/child $63/27; ☺9am, 1pm & 4pm Jun-Sep) offers highly recommended cruises for whale- or iceberg-viewing that leave from the dock behind the Grenfell Interpretation Centre on West St. This far north, the chances of spotting either icebergs or whales are excellent, so this tour is great value for money.

The St Anthony Airport is 35km (22 miles) northwest of town. **PAL Airlines** (☑800-563-2800; www.provincialairlines.ca; St Anthony Airport) makes the trip from St John's daily.

If you're leaving St Anthony by car, you have two options: backtrack entirely along Rte 430, or take the long way via Rte 432 along the east coast and Hare Bay. This will meet up with Rte 430 near Plum Point, between St Barbe and Port au Choix.

WESTERN NEWFOUNDLAND

Western Newfoundland presents many visitors with their first view of the Rock, thanks to the ferry landing at Port aux Basques. It's big, cliffy, even a bit forbidding with all those wood houses clinging to the jagged shoreline against the roaring wind. From Port aux Basques, poky fishing villages cast lines to the east, while Newfoundland's second-largest town, Corner Brook, raises its wintry head (via its ski mountain) to the northeast.

Corner Brook

POP 19,800

Where St John's is a Newfoundland city on the cusp of globalization, Corner Brook, the province's number-two town, is local to the core. This is a city for mill workers and fisher folk, as well as tour outfitters who work in Gros Morne. While Newfoundland attracts visitors from all over, Corner Brook attracts many from Newfoundland itself, specifically skiers who love the handsome Humber Valley, about 10km east. The valley offers adventure-sport junkies places to play, while the city itself sprawls with big-box retailers and a smoke-belching pulp-and-paper mill.

◉ Sights

Captain James Cook Monument   MONUMENT

(Crow Hill Rd) While this cliff-top monument is admirable – a tribute to James Cook for his work in surveying the region in the mid-1760s – it's the panoramic view over the Bay of Islands that is the real payoff. Cook's names for many of the islands, ports and waterways you'll see, such as the Humber Arm and Hawke's Bay, remain today.

Railway Society of Newfoundland   MUSEUM

(☑709-634-2720; Station Rd, off Humber Rd; admission $3; ⊘9am-8pm Jun-Aug) Within historical Humbermouth Station, the Railway Society of Newfoundland has a good-looking steam locomotive and some narrow-gauge rolling stock that chugged across the province from 1921 to 1939.

🏃 Activities

Cycle Solutions   CYCLING

(☑709-634-7100; www.cyclesolutions.ca; 35 West St; ⊘9am-6pm Mon-Wed & Sat, to 8:30pm Thu & Fri) This sweet bike shop runs local cycling

and caving tours; it's attached to the Brewed Awakening (p502) coffee shop.

Marble Zip Tours   ADVENTURE SPORTS

(☑709-632-5463; www.marbleziptours.com; Thistle Dr; 2hr tour adult/child $99/89) The highest zip line in eastern Canada. Strap in near the mountaintop, and zigzag platform to platform down a gorge traversing Steady Brook Falls. It'll take your breath away. Tours depart four to five times daily. The office is past Marble Mountain's lodge, behind the Tim Hortons.

Marble Mountain   SKIING

(☑709-637-7616; www.skimarble.com; Hwy 1; day pass adult/child $60/35; ⊘10am-4:30pm Sat-Thu, 9am-9:30pm Fri Dec-Apr) Marble Mountain is the lofty reason most visitors come to Corner Brook. With 35 trails, four lifts, a 488m vertical drop and annual snowfall of 5m, it offers Atlantic Canada's best skiing. There are snowboarding and tubing parks, as well as night skiing on Friday, plus Oh My Jesus (you'll say it when you see the slope).

🍴 Sleeping & Eating

Brookfield Inn   B&B $

(☑709-639-3111; brookfieldinn@gmail.com; 2 Brookfield Ave; r $70-90; 🛜) A cool couple runs this B&B. The white-frame house has homey rooms with hardwood floors and plump beds. In the morning make your own breakfast from the eggs, bacon, cheeses and breads in the well-stocked kitchen. In the evening watch the sunset from the deck. The house dogs will amble up for a scratch if you want.

Glynmill Inn   HOTEL $$

(☑709-634-5181; www.steelehotels.com; 1 Cobb Lane; r incl breakfast $125-165; ❄@🛜) Lawns and gardens surround the gracious Tudor-style Glynmill. It was built originally for the engineers supervising the pulp mill's construction in the 1920s, at that time the largest project in the history of papermaking. The property retains an elegant if somewhat faded ambience.

★Harbour Grounds   CAFE $

(☑709-639-1677; 9 Humber Rd; mains $7-12; ⊘7:30am-6pm Mon-Fri, from 9am Sat, 9am-5pm Sun) This excellent breakfast and lunch spot boasts great views and one of the most consistently good menus in Corner Brook. Garden-pesto paninis, Irish stew, omeletes and steak-and-Guinness pie are all complemented by friendly service and some very fine coffee.

Corner Brook

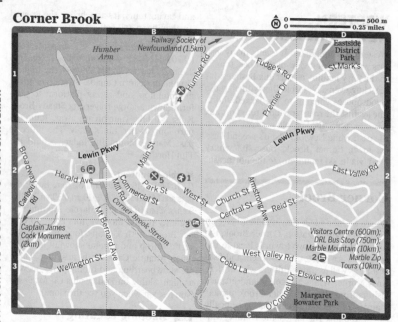

Brewed Awakening   COFFEE
(☑709-634-7100; www.brewedawakening.ca; 35 West St; ☺7am-6pm Mon-Fri, from 8am Sat, from 9am Sun; 🛜) This small, funky, art-on-the-wall coffee shop pours fair-trade organic java done right. It's attached to the groovy bike shop Cycle Solutions (p501). Baked goods $3 to $7.

ⓘ Information

Visitors Center (☑709-639-9792; www.cornerbrook.com; 15 Confederation Dr; ☺9am-5pm) Just off Hwy 1 at exit 5. Has a craft shop.

ⓘ Getting There & Away

Corner Brook is a major hub for bus services in Newfoundland. **DRL** (☑709-263-2171; www.drl-lr.com; Confederation Dr) stops on the outskirts of town at the Irving Gas Station, just off Hwy 1 at exit 5 across from the Visitors Center.

All other operators use the bus station in the Millbrook Mall building. Prices listed for the following shuttle vans are one way; you must make your own reservations.

Burgeo Bus (☑709-886-7777; bus station, Millbrook Mall) Runs to Burgeo ($40 cash only, two hours) departing at 3pm Monday through Friday. Leaves Burgeo between 8am and 9am.

Deer Lake Airport Shuttle (☑709-634-4343) Picks up from various hotels en route to Deer Lake Airport ($22, 45 minutes) three to five times daily.

Gateway (☑709-695-9700; bus station, Millbrook Mall) Runs to Port aux Basques ($40, three hours) on weekdays at 3:45pm. Departs Port aux Basques at 7:45am.

Martin's (☑709-634-7777; martins.transportation@nf.sympatico.ca; bus station, Millbrook Mall) Operates weekdays, departing for Woody Point ($18, 1½ hours) and Trout River ($20, two hours) at 4:30pm. Returns from Trout River at 9am.

Pittman's (☑709-458-2486; bus station, Millbrook Mall) Runs to Rocky Harbour ($35, two hours) via Deer Lake on weekdays at 4:30pm. Departs Rocky Harbour at noon.

Blomidon Mountains

The Blomidon Mountains (aka Blow Me Down Mountains) – heaved skyward from a collision with Europe around 500 million years ago – run along the south side of the Humber Arm, west of Corner Brook. They're tantalizing for hikers, providing many sea vistas and glimpses of the resident caribou population. Some of the trails, especially those up on the barrens, are not well marked; topographical maps and a compass are essential for all hikers.

Corner Brook

Further on, Blow Me Down Provincial Park has beaches and scenery.

The only accommodations option is a provincial-park **campground** (📞709-681-2430; www.nlcamping.ca; Rte 450; campsites $18, per vehicle $5; ⊗ Jun-Aug).

🏃 Activities

Copper Mine Trail HIKING
(York Harbour) This moderately difficult 7km trail by York Harbour provides awesome views of the Bay of Islands and also links to the International Appalachian Trail (IAT).

Blow Me Down Brook Trail HIKING
(Frenchman's Cove) One of the easiest and most popular trails in the Blomidon range, this 5km trail begins west of Frenchman's Cove at a parking lot. The trail can be followed for an hour or so; for more avid hikers it continues well into the mountains, where it becomes part of the International Appalachian Trail (IAT).

Port au Port Peninsula

Jutting into the Gulf of St Lawrence like a nose bitten raw by the chilly ocean winds is the Port au Port Peninsula, the only officially bilingual corner of Newfoundland. While everyone here speaks English, Francophones may find many residents engaging them in a distinctive French dialect that is neither of Québec or France itself.

The peninsula is simply stunning, all jaw-dropping sea cliffs and wild views, and there is a lot to be said for taking a long, lazy day to drive NL 460 and 463, which tie a loop around the entire landmass.

◉ Sights

Boutte du Cap VIEWPOINT
(Cape St George; P) The southwestern tip of the peninsula is one of those Newfoundland places where the wind blows and the ocean rumbles and you generally feel as if you're about to fall off the face of the Earth. The loneliness is underlined by a memorial to the Acadians – French Canadians who were expelled from the region after the British conquest of Canada – and their exile.

The Gravels LANDMARK
The spit of land that connects Port au Port to the mainland looks as if it could be snipped away with a pair of dull scissors. In fact, this isthmus is great for bird-watching, and a parking lot allows access to about 3.5km of lovely walking trails.

🛏 Sleeping & Eating

Inn at the Cape INN $$
(📞888-484-4740; www.innatthecape.com; 1250 Oceanview Dr, Cape St George; s/d incl breakfast $99/129; P📶) At this nicely run inn, you'll find nine comfortable rooms, decks with excellent views, and a buffet supper along with a full breakfast.

Oliver's Restaurant CANADIAN $
(📞709-642-5178; 42 NL 463; mains $8-16; ⊗11am-8pm) Head to this friendly roadside restaurant for great-quality fish-and-chips and some of the meanest poutine you'll ever devour outside of Québec.

Secret Cove Brewing BREWERY
(📞709-648-2683; www.secretcovebrewing.com; 92-96 Main St, Port au Port; ⊗1-9pm Mon-Thu, noon-midnight Fri & Sat, 1-6pm Sun) It's not enough that this isolated peninsula has great natural beauty and one of the world's rarest dialects of French; thanks to Secret Cove, there's a very fine brewery, complete with beer garden, here as well. Pop in for a craft beer, some live music, good camaraderie and other reminders of the joys of life.

◉ Getting There & Away

Access the peninsula via private vehicle. Stephenville is the closest large town. It's about 91km to Corner Brook. Fair warning: the roads here are twisty, even by Newfoundland standards, and a distance of a few kilometers will take longer to drive than you may initially think.

Port aux Basques

POP 4070

Traditional wood houses painted aqua, scarlet and sea-green clasp the stony hills, but it's all about the ferry in Port aux Basques. Most visitors come here to jump onto the Rock from Nova Scotia, or jump off for the return trip. That doesn't mean the town isn't a perfectly decent place to spend a day or night. Laundry blows on the clotheslines, boats moor in backyard inlets and locals never fail to wave hello to newcomers.

Port aux Basques (occasionally called Channel-Port aux Basques) was named in the early 16th century by Basque fishers and whalers who came to work the waters of the Strait of Belle Isle.

The town is a convenient place to stock up on food, fuel and money before journeying onward.

Hotel Port aux Basques   HOTEL $$

([phone] 709-695-2171; www.hotelpab.com; 1 Grand Bay Rd; r $109-189; [icons]) This is an older hotel, but it's clean, comfortable and has a lot of character. An executive suite features a Jacuzzi tub. Kids stay for free, and the hotel has an autism-friendly sensory room.

St Christopher's Hotel   HOTEL $$

([phone] 800-563-4779, 709-695-3500; www.stchris hotel.com; Caribou Rd; r $140; [icons]) This is the most professional hotel in town, with a small fitness room and a seafood restaurant called the **Captain's Room** ([phone] 709-695-3500; 146 Caribou Rd; mains $10-19; [clock] 7am-1:30pm & 5-10pm). Odd-numbered rooms have harbor views.

Alma's   CANADIAN $

([phone] 709-695-3813; www.facebook.com/almasfamily restaurant; Grand Bay Mall, Grand Bay Rd; mains $7-15; [clock] 7:30am-8pm Mon-Wed, to 9pm Thu & Fri, to 7pm Sat, 9:30am-7pm Sun) Follow the locals

Port aux Basques

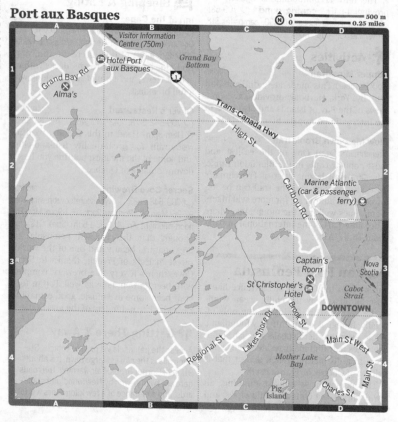

into this no-frills family diner for heaping portions of cod, scallops, fish cakes and berry pies. Your best bet for a good meal in town, it serves breakfasts, burgers and sandwiches too.

❶ Information

Visitors Center (🕿 709-695-2262; www.portauxbasques.ca; Hwy 1; ☺ 9am-5pm Mon-Fri May-Oct) Information on all parts of the province; sometimes open later to accommodate ferry traffic.

❶ Getting There & Away

The car and passenger **ferry** (🕿 800-341-7981; www.marineatlantic.ca; adult/child/car $45/21/119) goes to Nova Scotia. Buses (p474) go on to St John's and Corner Brook. If you exhaust stuff to do around here, Corner Brook is the nearest large town, 'only' 220km to the north.

Cape Ray

Adjacent to **John T Cheeseman Provincial Park** (🕿 709-637-2040; www.tcii.gov.nl.ca/parks/p_jtc; Rte 408; ☺ sunrise-sunset) **FREE** and 19km north of Port aux Basques is Cape Ray. The coastal scenery is engaging, and the road leads up to the windblown **Cape Ray Lighthouse** (Cape Ray; 🅿) **FREE**. This area is the southernmost-known Dorset Paleo-Eskimo site, dating from 400 BCE to 400 CE. Thousands of artifacts have been found here and some dwelling sites can be seen.

There's camping at **John T Cheeseman Provincial Park** (🕿 877-214-2267; www.nlcamping.ca; Rte 408; campsites $18-28, per vehicle $5; ☺ Jun-Sep).

South Coast

Visitors often ignore Rte 470, and that's a shame because it's a beauty. Heading east out of Port aux Basques for 45km and edging along the shore, the road rises and falls over the eroded, windswept terrain, looking as though it's following a glacier that plowed through yesterday.

Isle aux Morts (Island of the Dead) got its name from the many shipwrecks that occurred just offshore over some 400 years. Named after a family famous for daring shipwreck rescues, the **Harvey Trail** (7km) twists along the rugged shore and makes a stirring walk. Look for the signs in town.

OFF THE BEATEN TRACK

CAPE ANGUILLE

The westernmost point of Newfoundland is Cape Anguille, located 58km north of Port aux Basques. Drive out to explore the windswept lighthouse, where you can watch blue whales and stay in an adjoining lightkeeper's **cottage** (🕿 709-634-2285; www.linkumtours.com; 1 Lighthouse Rd; r incl breakfast $130-160; ☺ May-Sep). Don't expect phones or TVs – the idea is to get away here. Spring $10 extra for an ocean view. Dinner with locally sourced fish and berries is available ($30).

It's 45 minutes north of Port aux Basques in moose country; pay particular attention if driving at dusk or at night.

Another highlight is the last settlement along the road, **Rose Blanche**, an absolutely splendid, traditional-looking village nestled in a cove with a fine natural harbor – a perfect example of the classic Newfoundland fishing community. From here follow the signs to the restored **Rose Blanche Lighthouse** (🕿 709-956-2052; www.roseblanchelighthouse.ca; Rose Blanche; admission $6; ☺ 9am-9pm May-Oct).

KILLICK COAST

The peninsula just north and west of St John's is known as the Killick Coast, a 55km one-way journey that makes a good day trip. The main things to see out here are some quiet beaches (that can get not quite so quiet during summer weekends), a kid-friendly aquarium, and a mine where it gets so dark, you can't actually see anything at all.

To reach Bell Island (p506), go 14km northwest from St John's to Portugal Cove and the ferry.

Ocean Sciences Centre AQUARIUM (🕿 709-864-2459; www.mun.ca/osc; Marine Lab Rd; ☺ 10am-5pm Jun-Aug; 🆔) **FREE** Right out of *20,000 Leagues Under the Sea,* this university center examines the salmon life cycle, seal navigation, ocean currents and life in cold oceanic regions. The outdoor visitors area consists of local sea life in touch tanks. It's about 8km north of St John's, just before Logy Bay.

From the city, take Logy Bay Rd (Rte 30), then follow Marine Dr to Marine Lab Rd and take it to the end.

Bell Island
Community Museum   MUSEUM

(☑709-488-2880; www.bellislandminetour.com; Compressor Hill; museum & mine tour adult/child $12/5; ☉11am-6pm Jun-Sep) Miners here used to work in shafts under the sea at the world's largest submarine iron mine. Conditions were grim: the museum tells tales of adolescents working 10-hour days by candlelight. Visitors can also go underground; dress warmly.

Bell Island   ISLAND

(www.tourismbellisland.com) The largest of Conception Bay's little landmasses makes an interesting day trip from St John's. It was the only place on the continent hit by German forces in WWII. U-boats torpedoed the pier and 80,000 tonnes of iron ore in 1942. At low tide, you can still see the aftermath. The island sports a pleasant mélange of beaches, coastal vistas, lighthouses and trails.

❶ Getting There & Away

Visitors will need a car to explore the Killick Coast. The **Bell Island Ferry** (☑709-895-6931; www.tw.gov.nl.ca; per passenger/car $4/10; ☉hourly 6am-10:30pm) provides quick transit between Portugal Cove and the island.

LABRADOR

POP 27,000

Welcome to the 'Big Land': an undulating expanse of spruce woods, muskeg, bog and tundra that stretches from St Lawrence to the Arctic Circle and back again. The vast landscape contains military bases, little towns, Inuit and Innu villages, and some of the world's oldest geologic formations, the latter a most fitting addition to this most primeval of landscapes.

The simplest means of access is the Labrador Straits region, which connects to Newfoundland via a daily ferry. From there, a solitary road – the stark, rough Trans-Labrador Hwy – connects the interior's main towns. The Indigenous-influenced northern coast is accessible only by plane or supply ferry. Here, Torngat Mountains National Park offers a privileged glimpse into ultra-remote wilderness.

Labrador is cold, wet and windy, and its bugs are murderous. Facilities are few and far between throughout the behemoth region, so planning ahead is essential.

❶ Getting There & Away

Wabush and Goose Bay have flight connections to Newfoundland, Nova Scotia and Québec. **Air Borealis** (☑800-563-2800; www.palairlines.ca) flies to small communities in far north Labrador.

Overland visitors enter Labrador via Québec at Labrador West or the Labrador Straits village of L'Anse au Clair.

Those taking the ferry from Newfoundland to Labrador arrive in Blanc Sablon, 6km from L'Anse au Clair.

Labrador Straits

And you thought the Northern Peninsula was commanding? Sail the 28km across the Strait of Belle Isle and behold a landscape even more windswept and black-rocked. Clouds rip across aqua-and-gray skies, and the water that slaps the shore is so cold it's purplish. Unlike the rest of remote Labrador, the Straits region is easy to reach and exalted with sights such as Red Bay and a slew of great walking trails that meander past shipwreck fragments and old whale bones.

'Labrador Straits' is the colloquial name for the communities that make up the southern coastal region of Labrador.

❶ Information

The Straits' excellent **Gateway to Labrador Visitors Center** (☑709-931-2013; www.labradorcoastaldrive.com; Rte 510, L'Anse au Clair; ☉9am-5pm Jun-Oct) is in an old church that doubles as a small museum. Be sure to pick up hiking trail information for the region.

❶ Getting There & Away

Labrador Marine (☑709-535-0811, 866-535-2567; www.labradormarine.com; adult/child/vehicle $11.75/9.50/35.25; ☉May-early Jan) sails the two hours between St Barbe in Newfoundland and Blanc Sablon from May to early January. The boat runs one to three times daily between 8am and 6pm. Schedules vary from day to day. In July and August, it's not a bad idea to reserve in advance. Note that the ferry terminal in Blanc Sablon operates on Newfoundland Time and not Eastern Time (as in the rest of Québec).

PAL Airlines (☑800-563-2800; www.palairlines.ca) has flights to Blanc Sablon from St John's and St Anthony. Just to confuse you,

SOUTH COAST OUTPORTS

If you have the time and patience, a trip across the south coast with its wee fishing villages – called outports – is the best way to witness Newfoundland's unique culture. They're some of the most remote settlements in North America, reachable only by boat as they cling to the convoluted shore. **Burgeo** (population 1460) is accessible by an easy road trip, while **Ramea** (population 525) is an island just offshore from Burgeo.

In Burgeo, you could climb the stairs to **Maiden Tea Hill**, or head for the 7km of white-sand beaches at **Sandbanks Provincial Park**, possibly the best in the entire province. Author Farley Mowat lived in Burgeo for several years, until he penned *A Whale for the Killing*, which tells the story of how Burgeo's townsfolk treated an 80-tonne fin whale trapped in a nearby lagoon. Let's just say the outcome was not a happy one for the whale. Locals can point out the lagoon and Mowat's old house, though expect to get an earful about it.

The other outports are great areas for remote camping, hiking and fishing; ask locals or at the visitor center in Port aux Basques about arranging a guide. Tiny **François**, surrounded by towering walls of rock, is particularly gorgeous.

A good base is **Ramea Retreat** (Island View Lodge; ☑709-625-2522; www.easternoutdoors.com; 2 Main St, Ramea; dm/r/house $39/89/195; ☺May-Nov; ☎), an adventure lodge with 10 hostel beds and options for kayaking, bird-watching, hiking and fishing tours. The lodge owners also rent rooms in various vintage clapboard houses scattered around Ramea.

departure times from the airport are on Eastern Time versus Labrador Straits (ie Newfoundland) Time.

Rental cars are available at the airport from **Eagle River Rent-a-Car** (☑709-931-2292, 709-931-3300; Forteau).

Blanc Sablon to Pinware

After arriving by ferry or plane in Blanc Sablon, Québec, and driving 6km northeast on Rte 510 you come to Labrador and the gateway town of L'Anse au Clair.

The town makes a good pre-ferry base, with sleeping and basic dining options and a useful visitor center.

Heading northeast on Rte 510 you'll pass a glut of blink-and-miss-it towns: Forteau, L'Anse Amour, L'Anse au Loup, West St Modeste and Pinware. Scattered among these settlements are fascinating historical sites, pretty walks and a few other interesting detours as you make your way to Red Bay.

◉ Sights & Activities

Point Amour Lighthouse   LIGHTHOUSE
(☑709-927-5825; www.pointamourlighthouse.ca; L'Anse Amour Rd; adult/child $6/4; ☺9:30am-5pm May-Oct) At 109ft, this is the tallest lighthouse in Atlantic Canada, with 127 steps to climb. When you reach the top, you will be rewarded with a spectacular 360-degree view of the coastline. The HMS *Raleigh* went aground here in 1922 and was destroyed in 1926.

L'Anse Amour Burial Mound   HISTORIC SITE
(L'Anse Amour Rd) A pile of stones, placed here by the Maritime Archaic Indigenous people, is the oldest burial monument in North America. A small roadside plaque marks the 7500-year-old site.

Labrador Adventures   TOURS
(☑709-931-2840; www.tourlabrador.ca) Provides knowledgeable guides for Straits-oriented day tours by SUV ($450). It also arranges all-inclusive overnight packages. This is a good way to see the area if you're without a car.

🛏 Sleeping & Eating

Grenfell Louie A Hall B&B   B&B $$
(☑709-931-2916; www.grenfellbandb.ca; Willow Ave, Forteau; r $110-125, cottages $165; ☺May-Oct; P☎) This charming B&B is in the old nursing station where generations of Labrador Straits folk were born – there's also rumor of a few ghosts floating around. With quilts and country decor, the five simple rooms share two bathrooms. Some have sea views.

Max's House   HISTORIC HOTEL $$$
(Point Amour Lighthouse; ☑709-931-2840; www.tourlabrador.ca; Point Amour Lighthouse; cottage $325; ☺Jun-early Oct; ☎) On the grounds of the Point Amour Lighthouse, this historic building was the residence of lighthouse keeper Max Sheppard. The house features

Labrador

N

| 0 | | 200 km |
| 0 | | 100 miles |

65°W 60°W 55°W

Nunavut

Akpatok Island

Button Islands

Cape Chidley

60°N 60°N

Ungava Bay

Pointe Hubbard

Torngat Mountains National Park

Kangiqsualujjuaq

Hebron

Kaumajet Mountains

Québec

Labrador Sea

Fraser River

Nain

Cabot Lake

Voisey's Bay

Mistastin Lake

Natuashish

Harp Lake

Hopedale

Nain–Cartwright Passenger Only Ferry

55°N

Makkovik

Postville

Scefferville

Nipishish Lake

Cape Harrison

Rigolet

Hamilton Inlet

Happy Valley–Goose Bay–Cartwright Ferry

Esker

Smallwood Reservoir

Labrador

Cartwright

Wapusakatto Mountains

Churchill Falls

(500)

North West River

International Military Base

Lake Melville

Mealy Mountains National Park Reserve

Paradise River

Grand Hermine Park

Labrador City

Lake Joseph

Churchill River

Happy Valley-Goose Bay

(510)

Wabush

(510)

Port Hope Simpson

Battle Harbour

Atikonak Lake

Mary's Harbour

Red Bay

Pinware

Forteau

Strait of Belle Isle

Vieux Fort

Blanc Sablon

L'Anse au Clair

St Barbe

Québec

Newfoundland

Aylmer

Pointe Parent

(138)

Sept Îles

St Lawrence River

Port Menier

Vauréal

Sépaq Anticosti Île d'Anticosti

Gulf of St Lawrence

50°N

(132)

(430)

Deer Lake

(1)

60°W

five guest rooms with quilted bedcovers, a well-stocked kitchen and two bathrooms, accommodating 10. Dinner is served in the lighthouse; there's also whale- and iceberg-viewing. No phones on-site.

Seaview Restaurant   CANADIAN $$
(Rte 510, Forteau; mains $10-25; ⊘ 11am-9pm) Enjoy some fresh seafood or chow down on the famous fried chicken and tender caribou. A grocery store and jam factory are also on-site.

Red Bay

Spread between two venues, **Red Bay National Historic Site** (☑ 709-920-2051, 709-458-2417; www.pc.gc.ca/en/lhn-nhs/nl/redbay; W Harbour Dr; adult/child $7.80/free; ⊘ 9am-5pm Jun-Sep) – declared a Unesco World Heritage site in 2013 – uses different media to chronicle the discovery of three 16th-century Basque whaling galleons on the seabed here. Well-preserved in the ice-cold waters, the vestiges of the ships tell a remarkable story of what life was like here some four centuries ago. For many visitors, this is as far as they travel in Labrador, and if you're going to terminate your trip to the Big Land, this harbour – lined with icebergs and creaking salt box shacks – is a scenic place to do so.

Rarely does a walking trail live up to its atmospheric name like Red Bay's **Boney Shore Trail** (Tracey Rd). This is where Basque whalers tossed bits of skeleton from the whales they killed, and even today, discarded vertebrae still litter the shore. This 1km out-and-back route also skirts windswept fields of lichen and muskeg, and affords some great views of Red Bay.

Whaler's Station   INN $$
(☑ 709-920-2156; www.redbaywhalers.ca; 72-76 West Harbour Dr; r $125-150) Divided between several buildings, these rustic but comfortable lodgings provide a central base for visits to the historic site. Some rooms offer water views. They all have private bathrooms, TV, a microwave and refrigerator. There's also an on-site restaurant.

Whaler's   SEAFOOD $$
(☑ 709-920-2156; www.redbaywhalers.ca; W Harbour Dr; mains $9-20; ⊘ 8am-8pm) For fish-and-chips with partridgeberry pie, look no further than this friendly restaurant, a focal point for visitors to the bay. It also serves substantial breakfasts, and picnickers can order boxed lunches.

❶ Getting There & Away

Red Bay is about 80km northeast of the ferry landing at Blanc Sablon. Past here, the road is paved, but it is...lonely, to say the least. It's another 90km northeast to Mary's Harbour.

Battle Harbour

Sitting on an island in the Labrador Sea is the elaborately restored village and saltfish premises of Battle Harbour. Now a national historic district, it used to be the unofficial 'capital' of Labrador during the early 19th century, when fishing schooners lined its docks. Another claim to fame: Robert E Peary gave his first news conference here after reaching the North Pole in 1909.

★**Battle Harbour**
Heritage Properties   INN $$
(☑ 709-921-6325;   http://battleharbour.com; dm $50, r $195-335, cottages $245-800; ⊘ Jun-Sep; ☏) In addition to a classic inn, there are adorable heritage homes and cottages throughout the settlement. Think decks with sea views and little distraction: there are no cars, cell signal or TVs on the island. Instead you will find hiking trails with good berry-picking prospects and boat rides.

Battle Harbour Dining Room   CANADIAN $$
(Battle Harbour Inn; meals incl with lodgings; ⊘ 8am-6pm) If you're staying on the island, you get a package deal that includes gourmet dining at this fine restaurant.

❶ Getting There & Away

Battle Harbour is accessed by boat from Mary's Harbour (departure at 11am, one hour). The passenger ferry is included with accommodations. The return ferry leaves Battle Harbour daily at 9am.

Central Labrador

Making up the territorial bulk of Labrador, the central portion is an immense, sparsely populated and ancient wilderness. Paradoxically, it also has the largest town in Labrador, Happy Valley-Goose Bay, home to a military base. The town (population 7600) has all the usual services, but unless you're an angler or hunter, there isn't much to see or do.

Goose Bay was established during WWII as a staging point for planes on their way to Europe, and has remained an aviation center. The airport is also an official NASA alternate landing site for the space shuttle.

TORNGAT MOUNTAINS NATIONAL PARK

Named from the Inuktitut word *torngait* (place of spirits), the **Torngat Mountains National Park** (☑709-922-1290; www.pc.gc.ca/torngat) is the ancestral home of Inuit and their predecessors. Its spectacular wilderness features herds of caribou, polar bears and even seals in a freshwater habitat. The park comprises 9700 sq km, extending from Saglek Fjord in the south, including all islands and islets, to the very northern tip of Labrador.

Visitation is difficult since there is only plane and boat access. The **Torngat Mountains Base Camp and Research Station** (☑709-635-4336; www.thetorngats.com; Torngat Mountains National Park; 4-night all-inclusive packages from $6212; ☉Jul & Aug) offers package tours with four-night and seven-night options, including air transportation from Happy Valley-Goose Bay. You sleep in comfortable yurts or more luxuriant dome tents with heat and electricity, and spend your days hiking, boating and heli-touring (if you wish, you can spend just a few nights at base camp and the rest of the time in the wilderness with Inuit guides). Meals are provided, and an electrified fence keeps out polar bears.

No superlatives can do the beauty of this place justice.

⊙ Sights & Activities

Labrador Interpretation Centre   MUSEUM
(☑709-497-8566; www.therooms.ca/labrador-interpretation-centre; 2 Portage Rd, North West River; ☉9am-4:30pm Mon-Sat, 1-4:30pm Sun) FREE Officially opened by Queen Elizabeth II in 1997, the Labrador Interpretation Centre is the provincial museum, which holds some of Labrador's finest works of art and a fine slew of historical exhibits. It's in North West River, via Rte 520.

Northern Lights Building   DEPARTMENT STORE
(☑709-896-5939; 170 Hamilton River Rd, Happy Valley-Goose Bay; ☉10am-5:30pm Tue-Sat) The Northern Lights Building is a one-stop shop for a good range of winter, fishing and hunting gear, and a ton of souvenirs and random gifts – because you didn't come all the way to Labrador to not get the refrigerator magnet. The sheer massive everything-and-the-kitchen-sink nature of the place makes it worth a visit.

🛏 Sleeping & Eating

Emma's Suites   B&B $$
(☑709-896-8694; www.emmassuites.ca; 214 Kelland Dr, Happy Valley-Goose Bay; r from $149; 🛜🐾) This pet-friendly spot has clean rooms, decent wi-fi, a gym and satellite TVs – in other words, it has all the comforts of home way up in Labrador. As creature comforts go, this is one of the better options in town.

Royal Inn & Suites   HOTEL $$
(☑709-896-2456; www.royalinnandsuites.ca; 5 Royal St, Happy Valley-Goose Bay; s/d/ste from $120/130/150; ❄🛜) The good-looking Royal has a variety of well-lit, blue-and-white rooms to choose from; many of them have kitchens. The inn also loans out satellite phones to drivers through the region-wide safety program.

Mariner's Galley   SEAFOOD $$
(☑709-896-9301; 25 Loring Dr, Happy Valley-Goose Bay; mains $7-24; ☉6am-9pm) Come here for fried cod tongues with scruncheons (pork rind) or crab cocktail. Visitors rave about the friendly service and buffet options.

ℹ Information

Visitor Information Centre (☑709-896-8787; www.tourismlabrador.com; 6 Hillcrest Rd, Happy Valley-Goose Bay; ☉8:30am-8pm Mon-Fri, 9am-5pm Sat & Sun; 🖥) Provides information on Central Labrador, plus brochures and maps. Events are announced on its Facebook page.

There's also a useful town website (www.happyvalley-goosebay.com).

ℹ Getting There & Away

AIR

Daily flights are available to Happy Valley-Goose Bay from St John's via Deer Lake and Halifax. Montréal has daily flights to Wabush. The following also offer services:

Air Canada (☑888-247-2262; www.aircanada.com)

PAL Airlines (Provincial Airlines; ☑800-563-2800; www.palairlines.ca)

Air Inuit (☑800-361-2965; www.airinuit.com)

BOAT

You can reach Happy Valley-Goose Bay by a seasonal, passenger-only ferry via **Nunatsiavut Marine** (☑855-896-2262; www.labradorferry.

ca; Main Dock, Happy Valley-Goose Bay; adult/child to Nain $99/70; ⊘ Jul-Aug).

CAR & MOTORCYCLE

From Happy Valley-Goose Bay you can take the mostly gravel Rte 500 west to Churchill Falls and then on to Labrador City. The drive to Labrador City takes about seven hours. There are no services until Churchill Falls, so stock up. The Royal Inn & Suites has free satellite phones you can take on the road (part of a region-wide safety program).

The partially paved Rte 510 heads southeast toward Cartwright (383km) and L'Anse au Clair (623km).

Before leaving, contact the Department of Transportation & Works (www.roads.gov.nl.ca) for the latest conditions. Many rental-car agreements prohibit driving on the Trans-Labrador Hwy or will not provide insurance; some have vehicles specifically designated for the route. You can hire cars from **National** (📞709-896-5575; www.nationalcar.com), among others.

Labrador West

Just 5km apart and 15km from Québec, the twin mining towns of Labrador City (population 8600) and Wabush (population 1900) are referred to collectively as Labrador West. This is where the province's western population is concentrated. The largest open-pit iron ore mine in the world is in Labrador City, a place that is mining town and wilderness outpost all at once. Out here the landscape is massive, and the celestial polychromatic artwork can expand throughout the entire night sky.

From Wabush, 39km east on Rte 500 is **Grande Hermine Park** (📞709-282-5369; ⊘ Jun-Sep), which has a beach and some fine scenery. The Menihek hiking trail (15km) goes through wooded areas with waterfalls and open tundra.

🛏 Sleeping & Eating

Wabush Hotel   HOTEL **$$**
(📞709-282-3221; www.wabushhotel.com; 9 Grenville Dr, Wabush; r $165-175; ❋🅐) Centrally located in Wabush, this chalet-style, 68-room hotel has spacious and comfortable rooms and an old-world ski lodge vibe. The dining room has a popular dinner buffet.

Sushi Lab   SUSHI **$**
(📞709-944-4179; www.facebook.com/sushilabrador; 118 Humphrey Rd, Labrador City; mains $6-16; ⊘ noon-2pm & 5-10pm Mon-Fri, 5-10pm Sat & Sun) The dining experience here is nouveau-Labrador all the way. Order from a selection of dozens of sushi rolls, then expect a bit of a long wait, although the food does tend to be worth it once it arrives. For less adventurous diners, there's also Chinese food or pizza.

Baba Q's   CANADIAN **$$**
(📞709-944-2355; www.facebook.com/BabaQs; 211 Drake Ave, Labrador City; mains $8-23; ⊘6:30am-11pm Sun-Thu, to midnight Fri) After a day in the woods, a nice slab of grilled or smoked pure meaty goodness goes down a treat. At this smokehouse you can wolf down rib eyes, burgers and similar carnivore friendly fare; the on-site bar can get pretty busy too.

ℹ Information

Destination Labrador (www.destinationlabrador.com) is a comprehensive tourism website with special events, services and tips, and there's a **visitors center** (📞709-944-5399; www.labradorwest.com; 1365 Rte 500) just west of Labrador City, in the Gateway Labrador building.

ℹ Getting There & Away

AIR

Air Canada (📞888-247-2262; www.aircanada.com), **PAL Airlines** (Provincial Airlines; 📞800-563-2800; www.palairlines.ca), and **Air Inuit** (📞800-361-2965; www.airinuit.com) fly into Happy Valley-Goose Bay and Wabush, with some other destinations.

CAR & MOTORCYCLE

Fifteen kilometers west from Labrador City along Rte 500 is Fermont, Québec. From there, Rte 389 is mainly paved (with some fine gravel sections) and continues south 581km to Baie Comeau.

Happy Valley-Goose Bay is a seven-hour drive east on Rte 500, considered a good gravel road. **Budget** (📞709-282-1234; www.budget.ca; 1 Airport Rd) has an office at the airport; rental cars may not be driven on Rte 500.

Manitoba

Includes ➡

Best Places to Eat

- ➡ Close Company (p523)
- ➡ Lazy Bear Cafe (p533)
- ➡ Forks Market (p522)
- ➡ Kevin's Bistro (p522)

Best Places to Stay

- ➡ Beechmount B&B (p519)
- ➡ Blue Sky Bed & Sled (p532)
- ➡ Lazy Bear Lodge (p532)
- ➡ Inn at the Forks (p519)
- ➡ Mere Hotel (p519)

Why Go?

The two prominent stars of Manitoba are Winnipeg, with its big-city sophistication, and Churchill, with its profusion of natural wonders. But it's what lies between that truly defines this often misunderstood prairie province. Open spaces seem to stretch forever – gently rolling fields of grain punctuated by silos reach all the way north to the boreal forest and the Arctic tundra beyond.

The magnitude of this land can only be fully appreciated while standing on the edge of a vivid yellow canola field, watching a lightning storm on the horizon, or on the edge of Hudson Bay's rugged coastline counting polar bears while belugas play in the water. Drive its empty roads, stop in its evocative little towns, find the subtle dramas in the land and expect surprises, whether it's a moose looming in front of you on the road or a local blues legend performing in a characterful Winnipeg joint.

When to Go
Winnipeg, MB

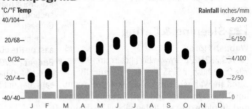

May Wildflowers spring up along the roads and signal the end of a long winter.

Jun–Aug Balmy days and cool nights are perfect for hiking, camping and canoeing.

Oct & Nov The best time to see polar bears around Churchill.

History

Tired of being labeled soft, early European explorers shunned the more hospitable south and braved the cold, rugged north coast of Hudson Bay. Indigenous Dene got involved in the fur trade soon after the Hudson's Bay Company (HBC) established trading posts here in the 17th century.

British agricultural settlers moved to the future site of Winnipeg in 1811, creating constant friction with existing Métis over land rights. When the HBC sold part of the land to the federal government, Métis leader Louis Riel launched a rebellion and formed a provisional government. Negotiations between Riel and the federal government resulted in Manitoba joining the federation as Canada's fifth province in 1870, though Riel himself was executed for treason.

Land & Climate

Manitoba's geography is as wide-ranging as you'll find anywhere in the country. Southern agricultural flatlands blend into green woodlands embracing Canada's largest lakes. Glacial footprints of potholed lakes, stubby vegetation and scraped-bare lands of the Canadian Shield characterize the north. Everywhere you go, the skies are massive.

The climate is just as variable and totally unpredictable. Average northern temperatures range from -50°C to summer highs of 20°C. Southern summers average 25°C dropping to -15°C during winter. Notoriously strong winds all year create summer dust storms, even the occasional tornado, and winter blizzards where wind chills make it feel 30 degrees colder than it is. Spring flooding is common in southern areas, and there is nothing like an intense prairie summertime thunderstorm.

❶ Getting There & Away

Major airlines connect Winnipeg with the main Canadian cities and US Midwest hubs. Calm Air (p533) serves northern communities in Nunavut as well as Churchill.

Manitoba shares more than a dozen US–Canada vehicle border crossings with North Dakota and Minnesota. There are several routes into Saskatchewan, but only the Trans-Canada Hwy (Hwy 1) leads into Ontario. Southern Manitoba's extensive road network disappears heading north, where Hwy 10 or Hwy 6 are the only options and services are few (watch your gas gauge).

VIA Rail's *Canadian* passes through Winnipeg and southern communities two or three times a week. Also out of Winnipeg, there is a service to subarctic Churchill two or three times a week.

WINNIPEG

📞 204 / POP 749,540

Winnipeg surprises. Rising above the prairie, it's a metropolis where you least expect it. Cultured, confident and captivating, it's more than just a pit stop on the Trans-Canada haul, but rather a destination in its own right, with a couple of world-class museums and a wonderfully diverse dining scene. Explore its boom of craft beer breweries and specialty coffee shops, wander its historic neighborhoods and lap up a vibe that both enjoys being the butt of a *Simpsons* joke ('That's it! Back to Winnipeg!') and revels in one of the world's best fringe theater festivals (p519).

History

A First Nations hub for 6000 years and center of the 19th-century fur-trade rivalry between the HBC and North West Company, the settlement at the confluence of the Assiniboine and Red Rivers took its name from the Europeanized version of *win nipee* (Cree for 'muddy waters').

French settlers established the neighborhood of St-Boniface, birthplace of the controversial Métis leader Louis Riel.

The railroad's arrival in 1886 solidified Winnipeg's commercial importance, but this was later rendered moot by the opening of the Panama Canal. The town subsequently stagnated, although a landmark general strike in 1919 helped raise union recognition across Canada. Today it has a diverse economy and modest growth. Its most notable brand will be familiar to anyone with the munchies: Old Dutch, the potato-chip maker.

◉ Sights

Winnipeg is mostly concentrated around the walkable downtown area; other sights are reached most easily by vehicle.

'Portage and Main' marks the center of downtown and is famous for incredibly strong winds and frigid temperatures – Randy Bachman and Neil Young wrote a song

---

MANITOBA FAST FACTS

➡ Population: 1,352,000

➡ Area: 647,797 sq km

➡ Capital: Winnipeg

➡ Quirky fact: Manitobans are the highest per-capita consumers of 7-Eleven slurpees in the world.

Churchill
Cape Churchill
Fort Prince of Wales
National Historic Site
Wapusk
National
Park
Hudson
Bay

Seal River

Reindeer
Lake

Saskatchewan

Southern
Indian
Lake

Lynn
Lake

South
Indian
Lake

Manitoba

Churchill River

Owl River

Nelson River

York Factory
National Historic Site

Leaf
Rapids
391

Pukatawagan

280

Gillam

Thompson

VIA Rail

Hayes River

Burntwood R

Pisew Falls
Provincial Park

Snow Lake

Gods
Lake

Flin
Flon
106

Ponton
373

Clearwater Lake
Provincial Park
The Pas
9

Norway
House

Cedar
Lake
6

Ontario

3

77
10

60

Grand Rapids

Lake
Winnipegosis

Lake
Winnipeg

Saskatoon
(170km)

Pigeon River

Bloodvein R

Regina
(40km)
5
16

Dauphin

Lake
Dauphin

Grahamdale

Hecla/Grindstone
Provincial Park

Lac
Seul

Inglis
5

Riding Mountain
National Park

Gimli

Victoria Beach

Grand Beach Provincial Park

1

16
10

Minnedosa

Lake
Manitoba

Winnipeg
Beach

Grand Beach

Whiteshell
Provincial Park

Dryden

Lake
Nipigon

Neepawa

Stonewall

Brandon
83

2

Spruce Woods
23 Provincial Park

13
3

Winnipeg
1

Steinbach

Lake
of the
Woods

17

Turtle Mountain
Provincial Park

75

59

12

Rainy
Lake

74
11

Atikokan

Thunder
Bay
11

85

North
Dakota
281

USA
29

59

11

Minnesota

Manitoba Highlights

1 Churchill (p529) Reveling in polar bears, beluga whales and an ancient fort in this surprising subarctic town.

2 Winnipeg (p513) Exploring the world-class dining scene, and an explosion of microbreweries.

3 Riding Mountain National Park (p528) Hiking and paddling in Manitoba's best natural setting.

4 Canadian Museum for Human Rights (p515) Delving deep into Canada's past with interactive exhibits and cutting-edge architecture.

5 Inglis Grain Elevators National Historic Site (p528) Seeking out the monumental

sentinels of the prairie from bygone days.

6 Hecla/Grindstone Provincial Park (p527) Contemplating nature virtually surrounded by Lake Winnipeg.

7 Pisew Falls Provincial Park (p528) Driving lonely roads and stopping for waterfall-gazing.

about it, 'Prairie Town,' with the chorus repeating the line 'Portage and Main, 50 below.'

To the north, 1900s limestone architecture marks the warehouse-and-arts Exchange District. South of downtown is the Forks and across the Red River is the French neighborhood of St-Boniface; west of there is the very strollable Osborne Village and Corydon Ave. A short drive west of the city center is Assiniboine Park (p517) with its terrific zoo (p518). Other attractions are found on the outskirts of the city in all directions.

⊙ Downtown

★ Winnipeg Art Gallery GALLERY
(WAG; ☑204-786-6641; www.wag.ca; 300 Memorial Blvd; adult/child $12/6; ⊙11am-5pm Tue, Wed & Fri-Sun, to 9pm Thu) This ship-shaped gallery displays contemporary Manitoban and Canadian artists and has the world's largest collection of Inuit carvings housed in the custom-built Qaumajuq, which opened in 2021, alongside a permanent collection of European Renaissance art. Temporary exhibits have included artworks by Eugène Boudin, Canadian artist and potter Robert W Archambeau, and printmaker and painter David Blackwood. There's also a rooftop sculpture garden and a terrific gift shop.

Upper Fort Garry
Heritage Provincial Park HISTORIC SITE
(Map p520; www.upperfortgarry.com; 130 Main St; ⊙24hr) FREE Original 1830s oak, stone and mortar walls stand where four different forts have stood since 1738. The entire site – known as Winnipeg's birthplace and formerly a trading center for a chunk of Canada larger than Eastern Europe – has had a drastic revamp and reopened in 2015 as a rather lavish urban park, complete with trellises showing the course of some of the old walls and a sound-and-light show (every 10 minutes from 8am to 10pm).

Manitoba
Legislative Building NOTABLE BUILDING
(Map p520; ☑204-945-5813; 450 Broadway Ave; ⊙9am-8pm, tours hourly 9am-4pm Jul & Aug) FREE Designed during Winnipeg's optimistic boom of the early 20th century, this 1920 building flaunts neoclassical beaux-arts design, limestone construction and governmental importance above the Red River. Surrounded by impeccable lawns and gardens, ancient gods and contemporary heroes are immortalized, including the Louis Riel mon-

---

WORTH A TRIP

OAK HAMMOCK MARSH

Smack in the middle of southern Manitoba's wetlands, **Oak Hammock Marsh** (☑204-467-3300; www.oakhammockmarsh.ca; Rte 200, at Hwy 67; adult/3-17yr $9/7; ⊙10am-4:30pm), a watery home and migratory stopping point for hundreds of thousands of birds, is one of the best sanctuaries around. Springtime has diversity and autumn sees up to 400,000 geese. The admission fee is for the visitor center and floating boardwalk only; access to the network of short trails is free. Leave your car keys at reception in exchange for a pair of binoculars.

---

ument facing St-Boniface. *Eternal Youth and the Spirit of Enterprise* – aka Golden Boy – shines his 23½-carat-gold-covered splendor atop the oxidized copper dome.

⊙ The Forks

Strategically important and historically significant, the Forks – the meeting place of the muddy and small Assiniboine River and the muddy and large Red River – has been drawing people for millennia.

It's the focus for many visitors and combines several distinct areas. Parks Canada runs a historic site (p516) amid beautifully landscaped parks. Nearby, old railway shops have been converted into the Forks Market, (p522) a touristy collection of shops, cafes and restaurants in renovated old buildings.

★ Canadian Museum
for Human Rights MUSEUM
(Map p520; ☑204-289-2000; www.humanrights.ca; Waterfront Dr & Provencher Blvd; adult/student/7-17yr/$18/14/9; ⊙10am-5pm Thu-Tue, to 9pm Wed; ℙ) Housed in a stunning contemporary building designed by American architect Antoine Predock, this terrific museum explores human rights issues as they relate to Canada, its culture and the rest of the world through striking interactive displays, videos, art and more. Exhibits don't shy away from sensitive subjects, such as the internment of Canadian-Japanese people during WWII and Indigenous children forced into residential schools as recently as the 1990s, and the Holocaust and

Holodomor (Ukrainian famine of 1932–33) are treated sensitively.

On a high-profile site near Provencher Bridge, this is the first national museum outside of Ottawa. Symbolism abounds, with an enormous glass cloud wrapping around the northern facade, modeled in the image of five dove wings wrapping one over the other. Head up the Israel Asper Tower of Hope in the elevator for an excellent view of Winnipeg. Exhibits also cover the plight of the Rohingya in Myanmar and the disproportionate mortality by homicide of First Nations and Inuit women.

Winnipeg Railway Museum MUSEUM
(Map p520; ☑204-942-4632; www.wpgrailwaymuseum.com; 123 Main St; adult/child $7/4; ☺10am-4pm Apr-Oct, 9am-1pm Mon & Thu, 11am-4pm Sat & Sun Nov-Mar; ▣) Winnipeg's imposing and underused Union Station (opened in 1911 and designed by the same firm that did New York's Grand Central Terminal) houses a thorough museum on the history of Canadian railways. Highlights include impressive model railways, striking railway art, the *Countess of Dufferin* locomotive and a collection of historic Canadian railway cars that you can climb inside.

Forks National Historic Site HISTORIC SITE
(Map p520; ☑204-957-7618; www.theforks.com; ☺24hr; ▣▣) In a beautiful riverside setting, modern amenities for performances and interpretive exhibits in this park outline the area's history as the meeting place of First Nations people for centuries.

The rivers routinely overflow during spring runoff and flooded pathways are not uncommon, which is as exciting as it is dangerous. Follow the waterways with a canoe from **Splash Dash** (Map p520; ☑204-783-6633; www.splashdash.ca; 1 Forks Market Rd; adult/child $11.50/10; ☺10am-sunset May-Oct). Kids can go nuts in the heritage-themed playground, the **Variety Heritage Adventure Park.**

◉ Exchange District

Restored century-old brick buildings are the backdrop to the Exchange District, Winnipeg's most vibrant neighborhood downtown. Hipsters, tourists and vagrants congregate amid heritage buildings housing restaurants, clubs, boutiques and art galleries. It's been declared a national historic site; walking tours provide context.

The grassy haven of **Old Market Square** is the neighborhood focal point. There's regular live music in summer at the controversially modern **Cube** (Map p520; Old Market Sq).

★Manitoba Museum MUSEUM
(Map p520; ☑204-956-2830; www.manitobamuseum.ca; 190 Rupert Ave; adult/3-12yr from $19.50/11.50; ☺10am-5pm Fri-Wed, to 9pm Thu; ▣) Nature trips through the subarctic, history trips into 1920s Winnipeg, cultural journeys covering the past 12,000 years – if it happened in Manitoba, it's here. Amid the superb displays are a planetarium and an engaging science gallery. One exhibit shows what Churchill was like as a tropical jungle, a mere 450 million years ago, while a replica of the *Nonsuch,* the 17th-century ship that opened up the Canadian west to trade, is another highlight.

◉ St-Boniface

Canada's oldest French community outside of Québec sits just across the Red River from the Forks. Visitor information centers have an excellent historical self-guided walking map. **Taché Promenade** follows the Red River along Ave Taché, past many of St-Boniface's historical sites.

★St-Boniface Museum MUSEUM
(Map p520; ☑204-237-4500; www.msbm.mb.ca; 494 Ave Taché; adult/under 12yr $7/free; ☺10am-4pm Mon-Wed, Fri & Sat, 9am-9pm Thu) A mid-19th-century convent is Winnipeg's oldest building and the largest oak-log construction on the continent. The museum inside focuses on the establishment of St Boniface, the birth of the Métis nation, and the 3000km journey of the first Grey Nuns, who arrived here by canoe from Montréal. Artifacts include pioneer furniture and tools, First Nations beadwork and weaponry, Louis Riel's execution hood and the coffin used to transport his body afterward.

Fort Gibraltar PARK
(Map p520; ☑204-237-7692; www.fortgibraltar.com; 866 Rue St Joseph; adult/6-17yr $10/6; ☺10am-6pm Wed & Thu, to 4pm Fri & Sat) Behind wooden walls sits this recreated fur-trade fort. Along with inspired interpreters, the genuine clothes, tools, furs, bunks, and bannock and blacksmith shops give a sense of 1810-era life at the Forks, the fort's original location.

Greater Winnipeg

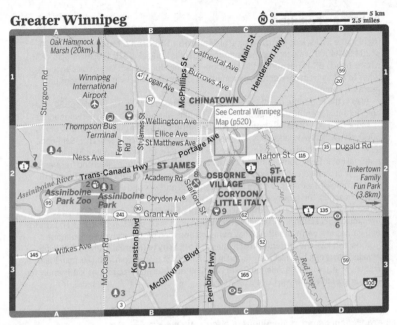

See Central Winnipeg Map (p520)

St-Boniface Basilica HISTORIC SITE

(Map p520; 151 Ave de la Cathédrale; ☺hours vary; P) Though the basilica was mostly destroyed by fire in 1968, the original white-stone facade still stands as a 100-year, imposing reminder of the building that once stood here. A new structure was rebuilt on the ruins and Manitoba founder Louis Riel rests in a modest grave in the cemetery.

⊙ Greater Winnipeg

★ **Assiniboine Park** PARK

(Map p517; www.assiniboinepark.ca; Corydon Ave; ☺24hr; P🚼) FREE Winnipeg's emerald jewel, this 4.5-sq-km urban park is easily worth at least a half-day's frolic. Besides the top-notch zoo (p518), there are playgrounds, gardens, a conservatory and the Leo Mol sculpture garden full of bronzes.

Royal Canadian Mint NOTABLE BUILDING

(Map p517; ☎800-267-1871; www.mint.ca; 520 Blvd Lagimodière; tours adult/under 17yr $7/4; ☺8am-7pm Mon-Fri; P) Producing loonies to the tune of billions of dollars, this high-tech mint produces money for Canada and 60 other nations. Tour the pyramid-shaped glass facility to see how money is made. It lies 9km southeast of the city center.

Greater Winnipeg

Living Prairie Museum PARK

(Map p517; ☎204-832-0167; www.friendsofliving prairie.org; 2795 Ness Ave; ☺10am-5pm Jul & Aug, Sun only May, Jun, Sep & Oct; P🚼) FREE This park protects 12 hectares of original, unplowed and now-scarce, tall prairie grass. A self-guided walk from the nature center showcases the prairie wildflowers in late

MANITOBA WINNIPEG

WINNIPEG FOR KIDS

Right in the Forks, kids learn by doing at **Manitoba Children's Museum** (Map p520; ☑204-924-4000; www.childrensmuseum.com; 45 Forks Market Rd; $11; ◷9:30am-6pm; ℗♿), where 'hands off' is not part of the program. The colorful, interactive exhibits encourage tykes to act as train conductors, astronauts and empire builders. It has outdoor programs in summer.

Also in the Forks, the much-heralded Manitoba Theatre for Young People (p524) uses colorful sets for enthusiastic performances for kids without being too treacly for adults.

More than 2000 animals populate **Assiniboine Park Zoo** (Map p517; ☑204-927-6000; www.assiniboineparkzoo.ca; 460 Assiniboine Park Dr; adult/child $20/11; ◷9am-6pm; ℗♿), which specializes in animals that are indigenous to harsh climates. The International Polar Bear Conservation Centre has exhibits on its namesakes and frequently cares for orphaned cubs. It's part of the zoo's huge, excellent **Journey to Churchill**, which combines exhibits and live animals, such as muskox and wolves. From bogs to Arctic beaches, the province's ecology is covered.

For old-fashioned thrills, **Tinkertown Family Fun Park** (☑204-257-8095; www.tinkertown.mb.ca; 621 Murdock Rd; unlimited ride ticket $19; ◷noon-6pm May-Sep; ℗♿) has rides and games in a carnival setting. Play mini-golf and then have a miniature doughnut.

Kids also love the critters and activities at **Fort Whyte** (Map p517; ☑204-989-8355; www.fortwhyte.org; 1961 McCreary Rd; adult/3-17yr $10/8; ◷9am-5pm Mon-Thu, from 10am Fri-Sun; ℗♿), while the Science Gallery at Manitoba Museum (p516) has kid-friendly fun including a lab where you build a race car.

spring. This ocean of color across the prairie provinces once supported millions of bison. Hands-on exhibits for kids include animal pelts; Thursday is family activity day.

Riel House National Historic Site
HISTORIC SITE

(Map p517; ☑204-257-1783; www.parkscanada.ca/riel; 330 River Rd; adult/child $4/free; ◷10am-5pm Fri-Wed, 1-8pm Thu; ℗) After Louis Riel's 1885 execution for treason, his body was brought to his family home before being buried in St-Boniface Basilica. Riel grew up on this farm in a cabin by the river; the 1880s house now on display housed his descendants as recently as the 1960s. Now surrounded by subdivisions, the house is 9km south of the city center.

☞ Tours

★ Winnipeg Trolley Company
CULTURAL

(Map p520; ☑204-226-8687; www.winnipeg.tours; 1 Forks Market Rd) Entertaining, engaging tours departing from just outside the Forks Market. The Ale Trail on Wednesdays and Fridays ($40 to $80) takes in three of Winnipeg's finest craft beer breweries, while the Trolley of Terror ($40 to $50, Thursdays from August to October) introduces you to Winnipeg's ghosts, UFO sightings and a Nazi invasion. Class tours of the city, as well (daily except Monday from mid-June to September).

★ Historic Exchange District Walking Tours
WALKING

(Map p520; ☑204-942-6716; www.exchangedistrict.org/tours/historic-walking-tours; Old Market Sq; adult/child $10/free; ◷9am-4:30pm Mon-Sat May-Sep) Entertaining themed and history tours departing from Old Market Sq. Book in advance.

Heartland International
WALKING

(Map p517; ☑866-890-3377; www.heartlandtravel.ca; 3111 Portage Ave) Highly recommended operator running entertaining themed tours of Winnipeg, from the Magical Musical History Tour ($48) and Ghost Tour ($46) to an in-depth walking tour that reveals the secret of the Manitoba Legislative Building. Various meeting points.

SquarePeg Tours
WALKING

(Map p520; ☑204-898-4678; www.squarepegtours.ca; Union Station; adult/child from $13/8) Entertaining and historically themed walking tours – including the popular 'Murder, Mystery & Mayhem' and 'Pestilence, Shamans & Doctors' – depart on regular schedules all summer, with much audience participation. 'Symbols, Secrets & Sacrifices Under the Golden Boy' is an acclaimed look at the hidden meanings in the capital, while the 'Naughty Bawdy Tour' of the Exchange District is for over-18s only.

✨ Festivals & Events

★ **Winnipeg Fringe**
Theatre Festival PERFORMING ARTS
(☑204-943-7464; www.winnipegfringe.com; 174
Market Ave; ⊙mid-Jul) North America's
second-largest fringe fest; the comedy, drama, music and cabaret are often wildly creative, raw and great fun. Held over 12 days in
the Exchange District.

★ **Manito Ahbee** CULTURAL
(☑204-956-1849; www.manitoahbee.com; ⊙mid-
May) A huge celebration of First Nations' and
Métis culture, involving music, arts, crafts
and dance, that draws participants from
across the globe.

★ **Winnipeg Folk Festival** MUSIC
(☑204-231-0096; www.winnipegfolkfestival.ca; ⊙
early Jul) More than 100 concerts on seven
stages over four days in Birds Hill Provincial
Park.

Festival du Voyageur CULTURAL
(www.festivalvoyageur.mb.ca; Fort Gibraltar; ⊙mid-
Feb) Winnipeg's signature event. Everyone
gets involved in the 10-day winter festival
celebrating fur traders and French voyageurs. It's centered around Fort Gibraltar;
enjoy concerts, dogsled races, a torchlit procession and joie de vivre.

Folklorama CULTURAL
(☑204-982-6230; www.folklorama.ca; ⊙early
Aug) Longest-running multicultural event of
its kind in the world. Performances, storytelling and more in pavilions representing
various cultures, all across town.

🛏 Sleeping

You'll find plenty of chain motels on main
routes around Winnipeg and near the airport. Downtown hotels are the city's prici-
est options but convenient for exploring on
foot. There's a proliferation of guesthouses
and room-sharing options in quieter residential areas within easy walking distance
of downtown.

Hansen Inn GUESTHOUSE $
(☑204-960-6516; www.hanseninn.com; 150 Sher-
brook St; s/d from $58/70; ❄🕾) This quiet res-
idential house comprises several spacious
fan-cooled rooms (most of them en suite)
and studios, all with kitchen access, fridge
and fast wi-fi. Within easy reach of downtown and the airport, and with a couple of
good eateries just steps away.

Malborough Hotel HOTEL $
(Map p520; ☑204-942-6411; www.themarlbor
ough.ca; 331 Smith St; r from $94; ❄🕾🏊) This
grand old Goth-Renaissance dame has been
resting on her laurels since her 1920s heyday. Some rooms have been renovated since
Sir Winston Churchill stayed here, while
others are in need of some TLC. The staff
are friendly and helpful, public spaces are
grand, but wi-fi is patchy and the hotel attracts a colorful clientele. Great location.

★ **Mere Hotel** BOUTIQUE HOTEL $$
(Map p520; ☑204-594-0333; www.merehotel.
com; 333 Waterfront Dr; r $116-254; P❄🕾) It's
being too modest, we say. It's not a 'mere'
hotel: it's a bold architectural statement on
the banks of the Red River in the Exchange,
with an eye-catching, distinctive facade and
spacious, minimalist rooms with custom
feature walls and bold splashes of color.
Creature comforts abound – king-sized beds,
rain showers, Nespresso machines – and the
service is efficient and friendly.

★ **Beechmount B&B** B&B $$
(☑866-797-0905; www.beechmount.ca; 134 W
Gate; d $108-130, f $216; 🕾🏊) The rich history of this beautifully restored 19th-century
heritage home is intertwined with that of
Winnipeg. Its three sumptuous rooms are
presided over by the affable Christine and
Giovanni, and the excellent cooked breakfast comes with Italian touches. Your hosts
are happy to share their local knowledge.
Four-night minimum.

★ **Inn at the Forks** BOUTIQUE HOTEL $$
(Map p520; ☑204-942-6555; www.innforks.com;
75 Forks Market Rd; r/ste from $234/289; P❄🕾)
🕗 This funky boutique hotel has a lot going
for it: a quiet, green location in the Forks,
eco-credentials, supermodern bathrooms,
splashes of contemporary art and solid
colors in 117 spacious rooms, and a great
restaurant that makes the most of locally
sourced ingredients... Enjoy river views and
the services of a high-end spa, too.

Alt Hotel Winnipeg BUSINESS HOTEL $$
(Map p520; ☑431-800-4279; www.althotels.
com; 310 Donald St; r from $124; P❄🕾🏊) 🕗
Sleek, shiny and right in the middle of the
Exchange District, this is a favorite with the
visiting business set. Rooms are stylish, with
particular attention given to creature comforts (fantastic beds, rain showers, goose-
down comforters). Minimalist decor is all

Central Winnipeg

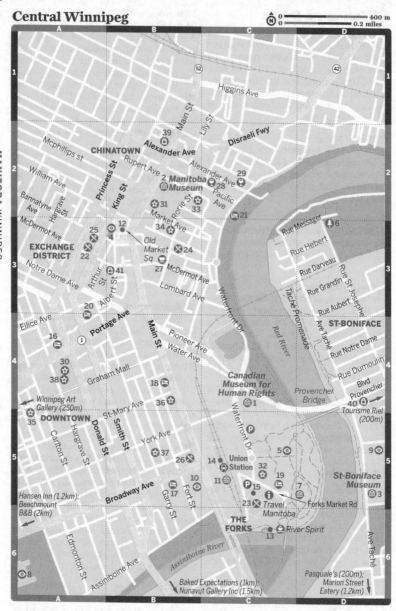

N 0 —————— 400 m
0 —————— 0.2 miles

whites and charcoals, with the exception of some eye-bending color in the gym. Climate control only; windows don't open.

Humphry Inn   HOTEL **$$**
(Map p520; ☎204-942-4222; www.humphryinn. com; 260 Main St; r $129-169; P ❋ @ ☎ ☀)

This modern, six-story hotel is well located downtown. Rooms are large and nicely appointed with fridges and microwaves; get one facing east for good views. There's free continental breakfast, but on-site parking costs $10.

Central Winnipeg

Fort Garry Hotel   HOTEL **$$**
(Map p520; ☑204-942-8251; www.fortgarryhotel.
com; 222 Broadway Ave; r/ste from $159/359;
P❄@🛜🐾) Winnipeg history radiates
from this locally owned 1913 limestone
grande dame of a hotel, built as one of Can-
ada's château-style railway stopovers. The
grand foyer embodies the hotel's spirit: look
for historical photographs lining the walls.
There's an extensive breakfast and an excel-
lent spa, too, and the faux-fur throws on the
rooms' high beds hark back to Winnipeg's
trapper heritage.

✖ Eating

Winnipeg's dining scene is ever evolving,
with a diverse range of cuisines spanning
the globe. The Exchange District, Osborne
Village and the Corydon Ave strip are par-
ticularly good for ethnic eats, solid Canadian
comfort food and cutting-edge fusion.

✖ Downtown

VJ's Drive-In   FAST FOOD **$**
(Map p520; ☑204-943-2655; 170 Main St; burg-
ers $7-11; ☺10am-midnight) Across from Un-
ion Station, VJ's is a fave for takeout fixes.
There may be a line at lunchtime, but the
overstuffed chili dogs, greasy cheeseburgers
and bronze-hued fries – consistently voted
among the best in Winnipeg – won't dis-
appoint. Seating is limited to outdoor pic-
nic tables. Staff won't win any congeniality
awards.

✖ The Forks

The commercial area of the Forks has a
number of indifferent restaurants aimed at
tourists, but the Forks Market offers great
redemption, with a plethora of terrific lunch
spots in one building.

★ Forks Market   MARKET $

(Map p520; www.theforks.com; 1 Forks Market Rd; mains $6-20; ⊙9:30am-6pm Mon-Thu & Sat, to 9pm Fri; [P]🅿️♿) Where else in Manitoba can you find gourmet burgers, artisan pizza, sushi, Caribbean dishes, a specialist **coffee roaster** (Map p520; ☑204-415-3902; www.foolsandhorses.ca; 1 Forks Market Rd; ⊙8am-9pm Sun-Thu, to 11pm Fri & Sat), craft beer and select wines, and an award-winning bakery all under one roof? Enjoy the bounty at the bustling communal dining area inside or picnic by the river outside.

★ Tall Grass Prairie   BAKERY $

(Map p520; ☑204-957-5097; www.tallgrassbakery. ca; 1 Forks Market Rd; mains from $4; ⊙7am-9pm Mon-Sat, to 6:30pm Sun; [P]) 🥐 Spread over two stalls in the Forks Market, this local legend uses organic Manitoba fare to create lovely baked goods (try the wild rice bannock!), sandwiches and prepared meals.

★ Red Ember   PIZZA $$

(Map p520; ☑204-504-8998; www.redembercommon.com; 1 Forks Market Rd; pizza $14-20; ⊙11am-8pm Mon-Thu, to 10pm Fri & Sat, to 9pm Sun; [P]🅿️) Award-winning pizza with bold combinations of toppings. Our favorite? The Fig Lambowski, with fresh figs, tender lamb and curry sauce.

Passero/Corto   FUSION $$

(Map p520; ☑204-219-7300; www.passerowinnipeg.com; 1 Forks Market Rd; dishes $16-25; ⊙11am-4pm & 5-10pm; [P]🅿️) With the austerity of the decor standing out against the hustle and bustle outside, this is the Forks Market take on fine dining, with small plates ideal for sharing. The gossamer-thin beef tartare is all lusciousness and indulgence, the ricotta gnocchi with black garlic is clearly prepared by someone who truly loves both, and the wine list is smashing.

✖️ Exchange District

On a summer evening, sitting outside at a funky place on the lively, historic streets of the Exchange District is a treat. Some of Winnipeg's most imaginative restaurants are found here, along with the flavors of Winnipeg's small Chinatown.

★ Kevin's Bistro   CANADIAN $

(Map p520; ☑204-221-5028; www.kevinsbistro. ca; 141 Bannatyne Ave; mains $13-17; ⊙11am-9pm Tue-Thu & Sun, to 11pm Fri & Sat; 🛜🅿️) This brightly lit industrial space is a temple to mac 'n' cheese. If you thought that involved macaroni and, erm, cheese, prepare to be amazed by NOLA (okra, blackened chicken and andouille sausage), el Mejor (chicharrón and poblano peppers), Hops & Blue (hops, blue cheese, caramelized onions) and more. Short and sweet wine and craft beer menu, too.

★ King + Bannatyne   SANDWICHES $

(Map p520; ☑204-691-9757; www.kingandbannatyne.com; 100 King St; sandwiches $10-15; ⊙7:30-10am & 11am-8pm Mon-Sat; 🛜) The hand-cut meat sandwiches at this brisk, casual spot verge on the sublime. There are only five to choose from: brisket, smoked chicken, BLT, braised beef and one sole delicious concession to the noncarnivorous: the jalapeño pineapple barbecue jackfruit. They've branched out into heaped breakfast specials, too.

Deer + Almond   FUSION $$

(Map p520; ☑204-504-8562; www.deerandalmond.com; 85 Princess St; dishes $14-26; ⊙11am-3pm & 5-11pm Mon-Sat; 🛜) This stylish yet informal small-plate restaurant in the Exchange District has an ever-evolving menu, with chef Mandel pairing unusual combinations of ingredients either to spectacular or merely good effect. Sweetbreads with lime tartare and Manitoba pickerel with bacon, dashi grits, roasted pumpkin and jalapeño feta stand out. There's a carefully curated wine and craft beer list, too.

✖️ St-Boniface

The charming old neighborhood of St-Boniface has some fine little restaurants, which, not surprisingly, reflect the local French accent and specialize in comfort food. None are more than a 20-minute walk over the river from the city center.

★ Marion Street Eatery   CANADIAN $

(☑204-233-2843; www.marionstreeteatery.com; 393 Marion St; mains $13-16; ⊙7am-3pm Mon-Fri, to 4pm Sat, 9am-2pm Sun; 🛜🅿️) With its industrial-chic decor and plenty of room around the horseshoe bar for solo diners, this bustling spot is all about eating well. It specializes in comfort food, from apple whiskey pancake stack for breakfast to the chunky extreme BLT and some of the best mac 'n' cheese in town. Sundays offer a brunch menu only.

Pasquale's   ITALIAN $$

(☑204-231-1403; www.pasqualesrest.com; 109 Marion St; pizza $17-26; ☺11am-10pm Mon-Fri, from 4pm Sat; ☑) Classic red-sauce Italian fare keeps this family-run eatery packed. The mussels and the thin-crust pizza are standouts, although the cannelloni is a quiet contender. The portions here are bounteous.

When weather allows, head straight to a table on the rooftop patio and bathe in the twinkle of the prairie's stars.

✖ Osborne Village

Some of Winnipeg's trendiest restaurants are in Osborne Village, close to the city center; a number double as excellent drinking venues.

All manner of places line genteel Corydon Ave, which runs through one of Winnipeg's oldest and nicest neighborhoods. Near the middle is a string of cafes that comprise Little Italy, most with terraces perfect for having a cup of strong coffee.

Baked Expectations   CAFE $

(☑204-452-5176; www.bakedexpectations.ca; 161 Osborne St; mains $9-19; ☺noon-midnight Sun-Thu, to 1am Fri & Sat; ☑☑) A delightful cafe specializing in all sorts of decadent baked goodies and light meals.

✖   GREATER WINNIPEG

★Close Company   FUSION $$

(☑204-691-7788; www.close.company; 256 Stafford St; dishes $16-20; ☺5-11pm Sun-Thu, to midnight Fri & Sat; ☎) With only 12 seats, this on-trend little restaurant is aptly named. The 10 small-plate dishes change at the chef's whim, but you might be treated to tuna with black garlic or scallop ceviche singing with the high notes of passion fruit. The short and sweet cocktail menu also mostly changes with the seasons, though Oui Chef is a keeper.

Máquè   FUSION $$

(☑204-284-3385; www.maque.ca; 909 Dorchester Ave; dishes $7-24; ☺5pm-midnight Tue-Sun; ☑) The setting at this small-plate bistro is minimalist and the focus is squarely on the food. Bring company (or a date) and share fluffy *bao* buns stuffed with smoked duck, crab-fried rice, beef tartare with Oriental touches, beets with beet kimchi and shaved fennel, and other imaginative, nicely presented plates.

★529 Wellington Steakhouse   STEAK $$$

(☑204-487-8325; www.529wellington.ca; 529 Wellington Cr; steak $38-62; ☺11:30am-2pm & 5-11pm Mon-Fri, 5-11pm Sat, 5-9pm Sun; ℗✳) A historic 1920s mansion provides a refined setting for some of Winnipeg's best steak, smoky and seared in all the right places – perfect for wooing your carnivorously inclined sweetie. The wine list is as thick as an Old Testament Bible and one of the best in town. Service is exemplary.

🍷 Drinking & Nightlife

★Torque Brewing   MICROBREWERY

(Map p517; ☑204-410-2124; www.torquebrewing. beer; 330-830 King Edward St; ☺noon-9pm Tue & Wed, to 11pm Thu-Sat; ☎) The winner of the 2019 Canadian Brewing Awards, Torque is an offbeat brewery decked out with a vintage motorbike, foosball and sports on TV. Their four core beers are equally no-nonsense – the most popular being Witty Belgian – and they keep experimenting with tea beers and more. Live music Fridays 4pm to 7pm, and a great food truck parked outside.

★Trans-Canada Brewing Co   BREWERY

(Map p517; ☑204-666-2337; www.tcbbeer; 1290 Kenaston Blvd #1; ☺11am-11pm Mon & Wed-Sat, noon-7pm Sun; ☑) Buzzing with pizza-munching families and raucous groups of friends, this busy beer hall also serves a bewildering array of interesting beers. Winners include Bluebeary Ale, Saskatoon Berry Radler and a Czech-style dark lager. Sample the Country Sour series and take a growler away with you.

★Common   CRAFT BEER

(Map p520; ☑204-942-6216; www.facebook.com/thecommonwpg; 1 Forks Market Rd; ☺11:30am-9pm Sun-Thu, to 11pm Fri & Sat) There's 16 rotating craft beers on tap from all over Canada and beyond, plus carefully selected wines, courtesy of Véronique Rivest, one of the world's best sommeliers with awards to prove it.

★Brazen Hall Kitchen & Brewery   BREWERY

(Map p517; ☑204-453-7980; www.brazenhall.ca; 800 Pembina Hwy; ☺11:30am-1am Mon-Sat, to 11pm Sun) This loosely Viking-themed brewpub has been riding high since it opened in 2017, brewing experimental small batches of beer every Thursday, running brewery tours, earning praise from local beer connoisseurs for their Søsken stout, plus their

IPA, blonde ale, red ale and braggot (barley and honey beer), and serving a wonderfully balanced pint of a hardcore IPA (IBU 104).

★ **Forth**   COFFEE
(Map p520; ☑ 204-505-7073; www.forth.ca; 171 McDermot Ave; ⊗ 9am-4pm Mon & Tue, to 9pm Fri & Sat) This is the epitome of a 21st-century hipster specialty coffee joint. It roasts its own beans (Dogwood) on-site, serves epic breakfasts, sells a range of fun merchandise, skater wear and grooming cream for men with beards, has a Bitcoin ATM and is spread across a split-level, industrial-chic space, with upstairs for socialising and a quieter nook downstairs.

★ **Nonsuch Brewing Co**   MICROBREWERY
(Map p520; ☑ 204-666-7824; www.nonsuch. beer; 125 Pacific Ave; ⊗ 4-11pm Tue-Thu & Sat, from noon Fri) As you enter, you're greeted by myriad gold umbrellas, making you feel as if you've walked in on a model photo shoot. The models in question are the beautiful Belgian-style beers, from the refreshing Blonde and the popular Tripel to the sultry Baltic Porter and fruity Saison. Quality charcuterie platters, too.

Patent 5   DISTILLERY
(Map p520; ☑ 204-808-8614; www.facebook.com/ patent5spirits; 108 Alexander Ave; ⊗ 4-11pm Tue-Sat) Combining a homemade copper still and a heritage tasting room with stained glass dating back to the early 1900s, this whiskey distillery is happy to show visitors around and to introduce them to the range of whiskies – served either on the rocks or as part of a cocktail.

☆ Entertainment

After hockey, Winnipeg's impressive arts and cultural scene earns well-deserved applause – as is only fitting for the town that produced Neil Young.

Live Music

★ **Times Change(d) High & Lonesome Club**   LIVE MUSIC
(Map p520; ☑ 204-957-0982; www.highandlone someclub.ca; 234 Main St; ⊗ 8pm-late) Honky-tonk/country/rock/blues weekend bands jam while beer and whiskey flows at this small, rough, raunchy and real throwback. Don't miss the Sunday-night jam, led by the legendary bluesman Big Dave McLean, recent recipient of the Order of Canada.

Windsor Hotel   LIVE MUSIC
(Map p520; ☑ 204-942-7528; www.facebook.com/ the.windsor.blues; 187 Garry St; ⊗ 11am-2am Mon-Sat) The well-worn Windsor is Winnipeg's definitive live blues bar. There's open stage some nights; bands perform at weekends. The local color that hangs out here is either a boon or a bane, depending on what you're into.

Performing Arts

Royal Manitoba Theatre Centre   THEATER
(Map p520; ☑ 204-942-6537; www.royalmtc.ca; 174 Market Ave) This company produces popular shows on the main stage and more daring works at the MTC Warehouse.

Winnipeg Symphony Orchestra   CLASSICAL MUSIC
(Map p520; ☑ 204-949-3999; www.wso.ca; Centennial Concert Hall, 555 Main St; tickets $30-105; ⊗ Sep-May) Classical music performances, as well as appearances from the likes of Jann Arden and Sheena Easton.

Manitoba Opera   OPERA
(Map p520; ☑ 204-942-7479; www.mbopera.ca; Centennial Concert Hall, 555 Main St; tickets $35-115; ⊗ Nov-Apr) From classics such as *The Marriage of Figaro* to premieres such as *Massenet Werther*.

Royal Winnipeg Ballet   BALLET
(Map p520; ☑ 204-956-0183; www.rwb.org; 380 Graham Ave) An excellent international reputation means performances at **Centennial Concert Hall** (Map p520; ☑ 204-956-1360; www.centennialconcerthall.com; 555 Main St) are popular.

MTC Warehouse   THEATER
(Map p520; ☑ 204-956-1340; www.mtc.mb.ca; 140 Rupert Ave) Cutting-edge drama performances.

Manitoba Theatre for Young People   THEATER
(Map p520; ☑ 204-942-8898; www.mtyp.ca; 2 Forks Market Rd; tickets from $20; ⊗ Oct-Apr; ⊕) The much-heralded Manitoba Theatre for Young People uses colorful sets for enthusiastic performances for kids without being too yawn-inducing for adults.

Sports

★ **Winnipeg Jets**   ICE HOCKEY
(Map p520; ☑ 204-987-7825; www.nhl.com/ jets; Bell MTS Place, 345 Graham Av; ⊗ Sep-May) There's Manitoba mania for the Jets who play at the Bell MTS Place. The ice-hockey

games are raucous and often sold out; ask around for tickets.

Bell MTS Place STADIUM
(Map p520; ☑204-987-7825; www.bellmtsplace. ca; 260 Hargrave St) Modern downtown arena that hosts concerts and sports.

Shopping

The Exchange District groans with art galleries and funky stores. Osborne Village and Corydon Ave are excellent places to browse (especially around Lilac St along the latter). Academy Rd has top-end boutiques, and Canadian Museum for Human Rights (p515) has a terrific gift shop.

★**Nunavut Gallery Inc** ART
(☑204-478-7233; www.nunavutgallery.com; 603 Corydon Ave; ☺10am-5pm Mon-Sat) Second to none when it comes to its selection of Inuit prints and carvings, this place is both for serious collectors and people simply looking to explore the works of Kenojuak Ashevak, Andrew Qappik, Ningiukulu Tivi, Toonoo Sharky, Jessie Oonark and other prominent printmakers and carvers. Richard is happy to show true enthusiasts around.

★**CreeAtions & Artist Showcase** ARTS & CRAFTS
(Map p520; ☑204-219-7428; creeationscanada@ gmail.com; 586 Main St; ☺9:30am-6pm Mon-Fri, from noon Sun) Run by friendly Métis proprietress Bobbie Lee Proulx and her extended family, this is half-workshop, half-gallery. You can get made-to-measure mukluks and custom beadwork moccasins, artwork and stone carvings by Cree and other First Nations artists from across Manitoba, jewelry and more.

Tara Davis Studio Boutique GIFTS & SOUVENIRS
(Map p520; ☑204-504-8272; www.taradavis. ca; 246 McDermot Ave; ☺11am-5pm Mon, Tue & Thu-Sat) 🎔 Is it a studio? Is it a fashion boutique? Is it a gallery? Whatever it is, we love it. Here you can pick up unique gifts 'made with love' in Canada, from ceramics and baby items to clothing and jewelery. The owner is a firm believer in giving back to the community and is partnered with numerous local organizations.

Foxy Shoppe FASHION & ACCESSORIES
(Map p520; www.facebook.com/thefoxyshoppe; 140 Provencher Blvd; ☺10:30am-6pm Tue-Sat) Retro and rockabilly fashion, burlesque

workshops, and pinup photography sessions. Girly fun!

❶ Information

St-Boniface Hospital (☑204-233-8563; www. sbgh.mb.ca; 409 Taché Ave) General hospital with 24-hour emergency services.

Tourisme Riel (☑204-233-8343; www. tourismeriel.com; 219 Blvd Provencher; ☺8:30am-4:30pm Mon-Fri) St-Boniface visitor information center, specializing in francophone attractions.

Travel Manitoba (Map p520; ☑204-945-3777; www.travelmanitoba.com; 25 Forks Market Rd; ☺9am-5pm) Provincial information center at the Forks, with plenty of info on Winnipeg and the rest of Manitoba.

❶ Getting There & Away

AIR

Winnipeg International Airport (YWG; Map p517; www.waa.ca; 2000 Wellington Ave) has a flash terminal a convenient 10km west of downtown. It has service to cities across Canada, such as Toronto, Montréal, Calgary and Vancouver, and to major hubs in the USA. Regional carriers handle remote destinations, including Churchill.

BUS

There were six weekly buses up to Thompson ($100, 9¼ hours) at research time with **Thompson Bus** (Map p517; ☑204-939-3991; www. thompsonbus.com; 2015 Wellington Ave).

TRAIN

VIA Rail's transcontinental *Canadian* departs **Union Station** (☑204-691-7611; 123 Main St) three times weekly in each direction.

The painfully slow *Hudson Bay* service to Churchill runs twice a week via Thompson.

❶ Getting Around

Downtown Winnipeg is walkable, and neighborhoods further out are reachable by public bus, but to reach attractions out of town you'll need your own wheels.

BUS

Winnipeg Transit (☑204-986-5700; www. winnipegtransit.com; adult/child $2.95/2.45) runs extensive bus routes around the area, most converging on Fort St. Get a transfer and use exact change. Alternatively, buy a reloadable Peggo card if you're in Winnipeg for a while.

Free *Downtown Spirit* buses run on three daily routes, connecting the Forks with Portage Ave, the Exchange District and Chinatown.

WATER TAXI

See the city from a new perspective on the water bus run by **River Spirit** (Map p520; ☑ 204-783-6633; www.splashdash.ca; The Forks; one way/day pass $4/20; ☺ noon-9pm Sun-Thu, to 11pm Fri & Sat Jul & Aug) between the Forks, the Legislature Building, Osborne Village, St-Boniface and the Exchange District.

LAKE WINNIPEG

The southern end of Canada's fifth-largest lake has been a resort destination since the 1920s. Sandy white beaches, constant sunshine and the ocean-like size of the lake made a visit like 'going to the coast' for all Winnipeggers. It's a tremendously popular summer destination; in winter, when snowy white beaches line the frozen lake, it's virtually deserted.

The most appealing of the southern beach towns found here is Gimli, while nearby Hecla is a living example of 1920s Icelandic heritage.

There is good birding and animal-watching at the Hecla/Grindstone Provincial Park, and decent hiking in **Grand Beach Provincial Park** (☑ 204-754-2212; Hwy 12).

❶ Getting There & Away

The south end of Lake Winnipeg is around an hour's drive north of the city.

Gimli

☑ 204 / POP 2250

On the surface it could be another clichéd little tourist town, but beneath the kitsch and tackiness is historic Gimli (Icelandic for 'Home of the Gods'). Settled by around 1000 emigrants from Iceland as part of 'New Iceland' in 1875, this neat small town has retained its fascinating heritage.

The New Iceland Heritage Museum is packed with history and artifacts telling the story of an unlikely people settling an unlikelier part of Canada. Look for the huge **Viking statue** by the lake – a symbol of Gimli's Icelandic heritage.

The general store, **HP Tergesen & Sons** (☑ 204-642-5958; 82 1st Ave; ☺ 10am-6pm Mon-Sat), has been around since 1899 and the building offers visitors here a hefty slice of local history.

◎ Sights

New Iceland Heritage Museum MUSEUM
(☑ 204-642-4001; www.nihm.ca; 94 1st Ave; adult/under 6yr $7/free; ☺ 10am-4pm Jun-Aug) This small, lovingly put together museum tells the story of intrepid Icelanders who settled an unlikely part of Canada in 1875 after fleeing hardships in their native land. Farming implements, formal family portraits and household objects set the scene. There's tourist information, too.

✦ Festivals & Events

Islendingadagurinn CULTURAL
(www.icelandicfestival.com; ☺ early Aug) It's all Iceland during Islendingadagurinn, a provincially popular fest including Islendingadance (Icelanders Dance), Icelandic games, live music (no Björk), Viking battles, fireworks and, of course, an Iceland-themed parade with a lot of blond people.

⬛ Sleeping

Lakeview Resort HOTEL $$
(☑ 204-642-8565; www.lakeviewhotels.com; 10 Centre St; r $190-210; ✳ ☎ ☒) Its balconies catching the lake breeze, this large hotel offers spacious, if impersonal, rooms with satellite TV and coffee makers. Not likely to make your social media posts, but comfortable and right by the lake.

✗ Eating & Drinking

Ship and Plough PUB FOOD $$
(☑ 204-642-5276; www.shipandplough.ca; 42 Centre St; mains $16-30; ☺ noon-11pm Mon-Thu, to 2am Fri & Sat; ☎) This cozy pub offers the likes of house-made meat loaf, fish-and-chips, ribs and fish tacos to the accompaniment of live music on weekends. There's no drinks list but it serves reliable classic cocktails, as well as beergaritas and a few local brews.

★ **Flatland Coffee Roasters** COFFEE
(☑ 204-651-0169; www.flatlandcoffee.com; 40 Centre St; coffee from $2.80; ☺ 7am-5pm) Almost too cool for tiny Gimli, this cafe has a sign stating: 'We are the coffee shop.' And they are, though they're a roastery first. Whether you're craving an espresso, latte or frappuccino, they'll do it perfectly, with Ethiopia Worka, Colombia Nodier Andrade or other exotic beans. One for connoisseurs.

Hecla & Grindstone Provincial Park

On an island away from the hustle of Lake Winnipeg's beaches sits a natural oasis featuring Manitoba the way it's meant to be seen. The islands, marshes and forests are full of deer, moose, beavers and bears. The **park office** (www.manitobaparks.com; Village Rd, Hecla School; ⊙ 2-4pm Sat, 11am-3pm Sun Jul & Aug) provides information for visitors.

Hecla Village (Village Rd; driving permit $5) is an Icelandic settlement dating back to 1876 and the whole place has historic heritage status. In addition to visiting a reconstructed 1920s Icelandic immigrant house, you can poke around the old lakefront buildings.

SOUTHEASTERN MANITOBA

Heading east from Winnipeg, the flat expanse typical of the prairies blends with forests and lakes typical of the Great Lakes region. While most visitors speed through toward Kenora and beyond, the eastern region of Manitoba has the same rugged woodland terrain as neighboring Ontario.

Whiteshell Provincial Park

Foreshadowing the green forests, clear lakes and Canadian Shield of northern Ontario, pine-covered hills erupt from the plains immediately inside this **park** (www.manitobaparks.com; Provincial Rd 307).

The park is fairly commercialized: resorts and stores are found every few kilometers and larger centers have park offices. However, there is still a sense of spirituality and you can get away via hiking trails of varying lengths – the longest being the six-day, 60km **Mantario** – and canoe routes, the most popular being the tunnels of **Caddy Lake**.

🛏 Sleeping

Falcon Lakeshore Campground CAMPGROUND $
(☑ 204-948-3333; www.gov.mb.ca; Hwy 1; tent sites $12-24, RV sites $16-29) The large, well-equipped and tree-lined Falcon Lakeshore Campground is only a short walk from the eponymous lake's beaches.

❶ Getting There & Away

Whiteshell Provincial Park is around 1½ hours' drive from Winnipeg along Hwy 44 E.

WESTERN MANITOBA

Between Winnipeg and Saskatchewan, Manitoba is a seemingly endless sea of agriculture until you decide to make a few detours here and there to often-overlooked natural delights, such as unexpected sand dunes and the atmospheric early-20th-century train elevators found in Inglis and along Hwy 16.

The dense woodland and lakes of Riding Mountain National Park make it an ideal summer destination for hiking, biking and canoeing, and there are bison to be spotted, too.

❶ Getting There & Away

Brandon is 214km (2½ hours) west of Winnipeg, while Riding Mountain National Park is 244km (2¾ hours) northwest of Winnipeg and 97km (one hour) north of Brandon. There were no bus services in western Manitoba at research time.

Brandon

☑ 204 / POP 48,860

Manitoba's second-largest center is a reasonably attractive residential city with a historic downtown bisected by the Assiniboine River – worth a stop if passing through but not worth a detour. Start your riverside walks from the **Riverbank Discovery Centre** (☑ 204-729-2141; www.brandontourism.com; 545 Conservation Dr; ⊙ 8:30am-5pm Mon-Fri, from noon Sat & Sun), which is also a good source of visitor information.

The **Royal Canadian Artillery Museum** (☑ 204-765-3000; www.rcamuseum.com; Hwy 340, Shilo; adult/student $6/4; ⊙ 10am-5pm), a 15-minute drive to the east of Brandon, is worth seeking out for its displays of weaponry through the centuries.

Toward the west end of Brandon, the unpretentious **Chilli Chutney** (☑ 204-573-9310; www.thechillichutney.ca; 555 34th St; mains $12-17.50; ⊙ 11:30am-9pm Mon-Fri, noon-9:30pm Sat, 4-9:30pm Sun; P ❄ 🛜 🖋) restaurant makes up for what it lacks in atmosphere with authentic East Indian flavours. The Goan prawn curry is a wonderful balance

GRAIN ELEVATORS

Barn-red, brilliant white, midnight-black or tractor-green; striking yet simple; displaying both function and form; and characterizing prairie landscapes like the wheat they hold, grain elevators were once flagships of prairie architecture.

Introduced in 1880, more than 7000 of the vertical wooden warehouses lined Canadian train tracks by 1930. Their importance was invaluable, as the prairies became 'the breadbasket of the world,' and they were built next to the railway lines, which revolutionized the loading and sorting of grain. Also, their stoic simplicity inspired Canadian painters, photographers and writers, who gave them life.

Today's concrete replacements are as generic as their fast-food-chain neighbors. For a glimpse of the vanishing past, make the detour to **Inglis Grain Elevators National Historic Site** (☑204-564-2243; www.ingliselevators.com; Railway Ave, Inglis; ☺10am-6pm Mon-Sat, from noon Sun Jun-Sep) **FREE**, where a stunning row of five 1920s elevators is in the process of being restored to its original splendor. Inside the creaky interior of the Paterson elevator, exhibits capture the thin lives of farmers where success or failure rested upon the whims of commodity brokers.

Inglis is 20km north of the Yellowhead Hwy (Hwy 16) near the Saskatchewan border.

---

of flavours with kick, the naan bread is perfect and the buffet ($16) is excellent value.

Riding Mountain National Park

Rising like a vision above the plains, **Riding Mountain National Park** (☑204-848-7275; www.parkscanada.ca/riding; adult/child $8/free) comprises more than 3000 sq km of boreal forest, deep valleys, lofty hills and alpine lakes. It rewards vistors who have an hour or a week. The unpaved Rte 354 runs west from Onandole (30 minutes) to the **Bison Enclosure**, where you can spot these giants from the road or lookout point. Elsewhere, you might even see a bear or a moose.

Along Hwy 10, which cuts through the park, there are various short hiking trails and pristine lakes for paddling.

Most of the park is wilderness; **Wasagaming**, on the south shore of aptly named Clear Lake, is almost a cliché in its perfection as a little lakeside town.

The beautiful 1930s **visitor center** (☑204-848-7275; Wasagaming Dr, Wasagaming; ☺9:30am-8pm Jul & Aug, to 5pm May, Jun, Sep & Oct) contains impressive dioramas, and offers the invaluable *Visitor Guide* and backcountry permits.

🛏 Sleeping & Eating

Idylwylde Cabins   LODGE $$
(☑204-848-2383; www.idylwylde.ca; 136 Wasagaming Dr, Wasagaming; cabins $197-269 off-season; weekly rates only Jul & Aug; 🐾) These cute,

self-contained cabins range from compact and rustic to lavish and Jacuzzi-endowed.

Whitehouse Bakery   BAKERY $
(☑204-848-7700; www.whitehousebakeryclear lake.ca; 104 Buffalo Dr, Wasagaming; mains $11-15; ☺8am-4pm May-Sep) From sticky cinnamon buns to wraps, panini, bison burgers, club sandwiches and salads, this is the place to stock up on picnic supplies.

NORTHERN MANITOBA

'North of 53' (the 53rd parallel), convenience takes a backseat to rugged beauty as lake-filled timberland dissolves into the treeless tundra of the far north. The ample wildlife around Churchill is justifiably the big draw and reason enough to make the journey north, with Thompson now playing 'Wolf Capital' to Churchill's 'Polar Bear Capital.' Around 80km southwest of Thompson along Hwy 6, **Pisew Falls Provincial Park** (www.manitobaparks.com; Hwy 6) **FREE** is a great place to stop and get drenched by the spray from the waterfall that roars through a gorge.

The Pas

☑204 / POP 5370

A traditional meeting place of First Nations and European fur traders, The Pas (pronounced 'pah') is a useful stop for services on northern trips.

Clearwater Lake Provincial Park (☑204-624-5525; www.gov.mb.ca), near the airport, is a pelican haven and there's a picturesque walking trail. While The Pas itself is not big on charm, it's particularly worth visiting during the **Northern Manitoba Trappers' Festival** (www.trappersfestival.ca; ⊗ mid-Feb) that honors local heritage in raucous winter celebrations. Look out for First Nations crafts around town, including decent moccasins.

🛏 Sleeping & Eating

Andersen Inn & Suites MOTEL **$$**
(📞 204-623-1888; www.anderseninn.com; 1717 Gordon Ave; r from $159; 🛜 ⛧ 🐾) This motel may not make your social media posts, and soundproofing between rooms could be improved, but it's clean, comfortable and comes with an indoor pool and waterslide, making it a family and corporate favorite.

Good Thymes INTERNATIONAL **$$**
(📞 204-623-2412; www.goodthymes.ca; 1607 Gordon Ave; mains $13-23; ⊗ 11am-11pm Mon-Thu, to 1am Fri & Sat) Convivial sports bar and busy diner all in one, Good Thymes dishes up such crowd-pleasers as Caesar salad, burgers, nachos, ribs and pizza just south of the main town.

❶ Getting There & Away

VIA Rail's sluggish **train** (380 Hazelwood Ave) passes through The Pas three times weekly on its way south to Winnipeg and north to Churchill via Thompson.

Calm Air (p533) connects The Pas to Winnipeg several times weekly from the **airport** (📞 20 4-624-5233; 81 Edwards Ave).

The Pas is 140km from Flin Flon and 392km from Thompson.

Thompson

📞 204 / POP 12,500
Carved out of the boreal forest by mining interests in the 1950s, Thompson is the 'Wolf Capital of the World,' which makes it a worthwhile stop (mostly for travelers on their way to Churchill), in spite of its relative lack of charm as a town. A **Spirit Way** (www.thompsonspiritway.ca; Princeton Dr) connects the town's important landmarks, from the **Heritage North Museum** (📞 204-677-2216; www.heritagenorthmuseum.ca; 162 Princeton Dr; ⊗ 10am-5pm Mon-Fri) FREE to the immense wolf mural, **wolf statues** (www.thompsonspiritway.ca) and a restored Norseman floatplane. In the coming years, the **Boreal**

Discovery Centre (📞 204-677-5919; www.borealdiscoverycentre.org; 110 UCN Dr) will allow visitors to learn all about the local wolves, common in the wilderness around town, as well as other denizens of the boreal forest.

🛏 Sleeping

Best Western Thompson Hotel & Suites HOTEL **$$**
(📞 204-778-8887; www.bestwestern.com; 205 Mystery Lake Rd; r $160; ❋ 🛜) The brown and beige color scheme of Thompson's best accommodations is not the most original, but the Best Western is spotless, centrally located (a stone's throw from two malls), and makes for a decent overnighter.

❶ Getting There & Away

Calm Air (www.calmair.com) connects Thompson with Winnipeg (from $374 one way) via **Thompson Airport** (YTH; 📞 204-778-5212; www.thompsonairport.ca; Airport Rd), 10km north of town.

From the **bus station** (📞 204-939-3991; www.thompsonbus.com; 725 Thompson Dr), Thompson Bus runs overnight services to Winnipeg from Sunday to Friday ($100, 9¼ hours).

Thompson marks the end of paved roads; the lethargic VIA Rail train runs north to Churchill (5pm Monday, Wednesday and Friday, 16 hours) and south to Winnipeg (2pm Wednesday, Friday, Sunday, 24 hours) via The Pas (the Wednesday train terminates at The Pas). Trains are frequently late. The **train station** (📞 204-677-2241; 1310 Station Rd), in an industrial area 1km from town, is not a safe spot to leave your vehicle. **McCreedy Campground** (📞 204-679-6315; 114 Manasan Dr; tent & RV sites from $22; ⊗ May-Sep) offers vehicle storage and shuttles to the train (per night/week $8/40).

Churchill

📞 204 / POP 900
The 'Polar Bear Capital of the World,' Churchill lures people to the shores of Hudson Bay for its majestic predators, beluga whales, a huge old stone fort and endless subarctic majesty. But while the highly accessible wildlife is enough for Churchill to be on any itinerary, there's something less tangible that makes people stay longer and keeps them coming back: a hearty seductive spirit that makes the rest of the world seem – thankfully – even further away than it really is.

Prime times to visit are July and August and then again during the peak polar-bear-viewing period of mid-October to mid-November. In winter Churchill is frozen and desolate, which has its own appeal for chasers of the sky's eerie light show.

History

Permafrost springs upwards about 2.5cm per millennia, chronicling old shorelines and leaving nearby evidence of aboriginal settlements up to 3000 years old. In terms of European exploration, Churchill is one of the oldest places in Canada. The first outpost of the HBC (said to stand for 'Here Before Christ') was built here in 1717, and explorers such as Samuel Hearne and Lord Churchill, former HBC governor and the town's namesake, stopped here on their attempts to find the fabled Northwest Passage.

Churchill's strategic location ensured a military presence over centuries. The railway's arrival and opening of the huge port in 1929 have made the town a vital international grain-shipping point for the prairie provinces.

⊙ Sights

The town itself is an assemblage of tattered Northern structures. Wander the streets, stop and peruse the beach (though not in polar bear season!) and its *inukshuk* (Inuit stone monument), visit the excellent museum, and then get out onto the surrounding land and water to see nature at its most magnificent.

★ **Itsanitaq Museum** MUSEUM
(🖉 204-675-2030; 242 La Verendrye Ave; by donation; ⊙ 1-5pm Mon, 9am-noon & 1-5pm Tue-Sat) This one-room museum showcases an exceptional collection of Inuit carvings made of whalebone, soapstone and caribou antler, as well as millennia-old harpoon heads and bone carvings of shamans and bears left over from the pre-Inuit Thule and Dorset cultures of the Igloolik region. The place really sucks you in and you can spend hours here.

The obvious standouts – stuffed polar bear and musk ox, narwhal horns and original sealskin-covered *qayaq* – are immediate attention grabbers, but closer inspection reveals items such as loon-skin shoes, a pickled polar bear fetus, snow goggles made of caribou antler, and miniature carvings showing intricate scenes of Inuit life (look for *Bear Hunt* and *First Airplane*). An extensive range of Northern books and Inuit carvings is for sale.

★ **Cape Merry** HISTORIC SITE
A lone cannon behind a crumbling wall is all that's left of the battery built at Cape Merry, 2km northwest of town. It's an incredibly beautiful location in its own right and, during summer, belugas can be seen from the shore. It's included in cultural tours of Churchill.

Polar Bear Jail NOTABLE BUILDING
(Button St) Located in a former aircraft hangar near the airport, this secure facility serves as holding center for problem polar bears who repeatedly turn up in Churchill and pose a danger to its residents. With the exception of family groups, bears are held for at least 30 days before being released. Repeat offenders may be relocated by helicopter.

Fort Prince of Wales
National Historic Site HISTORIC SITE
(www.pc.gc.ca/en/lhn-nhs/mb/prince) It took 40 years to build and its cannons were never used, but the star-shaped, stone Fort Prince of Wales has been standing prominently on rocky Eskimo Point across the Churchill River since the 1770s. As English-French tensions mounted in the 1720s, the HBC selected the site for strategic purposes, but surrendered during the first French attack in 1782, making it an Anglo Maginot Line forerunner. The fort can only be visited on wildlife-watching boat tours (entry fee included).

A 15-minute boat trip away from Churchill, the fort is one of three sites in the area documenting Churchill's varied history, administered by Parks Canada (p533). It's a lonely, buggy place, and gives a real sense that duty here was best avoided.

Four kilometers south of the fort, **Sloop's Cove** was a harbor for European vessels during Churchill's harsh winters. The only evidence of early explorers is simple yet profound: names such as Samuel Hearne, local 18th-century governor and first to make an overland trip to the Arctic Ocean, are carved into the seaside rocks.

Wapusk National Park PARK
(🖉 204-675-8863; www.parkscanada.ca/wapusk) Established primarily to protect polar bear maternity denning sites (*wapusk* is Cree for 'white bear') and critical habitats for waterfowl and shore birds, this remote park

extends along Hudson Bay's shores 45km southeast of Churchill. Its location between boreal forests and Arctic tundra makes it important when monitoring the effects of climate change. Visits center on polar bears and are only possible through licensed operators.

York Factory National Historic Site
HISTORIC SITE

(www.parkscanada.ca/yorkfactory; ☉ Jul-Sep) Around 250km southeast of Churchill and impossibly remote, this HBC trading post, near Hayes River, was an important gateway to the interior and active for 273 years until 1957. The stark-white buildings are an amazing sight contrasting with their barren setting. It's accessible only by air or boat.

Parks Canada Museum
MUSEUM

(☎204-675-8863; Hendry St; ☉8am-noon & 1-4pm Mon-Fri) There's a small museum and nature center in the train station along with the Parks Canada (p533) info desk. It has a good model of the fort and excellent nature dioramas and information on the many creatures you've come far to see. Check for any scheduled lectures.

🦫 Courses

Churchill Northern Studies Centre
WILDLIFE WATCHING

(CNSC; ☎204-675-2307; www.churchillscience.ca; Launch Rd; courses $1995-3485) Located at Fort Churchill, 23km east of town, CNSC is an active base for researchers. Learning vacations feature all-inclusive (dorms, meals and local transportation) multiday courses with scientists working on projects involving belugas, wildflowers, birds and polar bears. There are also courses in winter survival, northern lights and astronomy.

☞ Tours

Independent exploration is not encouraged in Churchill, not just for reasons of safety but primarily due to expertise. Local guides have a wealth of knowledge that guide you to wildlife and provide vital context for exploring the area.

Polar Bear Tours

Polar bears overshadow Churchill's other draws. In summer you may see them while on other land tours and even swimming in the river and Hudson Bay. Later in the year, however, is the main event. Special light-

weight vehicles riding high on huge tires to protect the tundra venture out on day trips (about $499 per person during polar bear season, September to early November). Heated cabins and open-air porches allow you to get good views of the marauding bears.

★ Lazy Bear Lodge Tours
WILDLIFE

(☎204-663-9377; www.lazybearlodge.com; 313 Kelsey Blvd; 2-night summer tour from $595) Has liveaboard tundra coaches and also runs multiday beluga- and polar-bear-spotting adventures in the summer, based out of its lodge (p532). Excellent day outings include kayaking and aquaplaning (floating on a giant foam mat) with belugas ($249), tundra vehicle ventures, half-/full-day whale-watching boat tours on Hudson Bay, and cultural tours of Churchill and its environs.

Tundra Buggy Adventure /58° North
WILDLIFE

(☎204-949-2050; www.tundrabuggy.com; 124 Kelsey Blvd; tours $299-499; ☉Feb, Mar & Jun-Nov) The pioneers of tundra-buggy polar-bear-viewing run six-hour tundra tours in summer and all-day tours in search of polar bears and other wildlife in October and November. In February and March the tundra buggies are used for aurora-viewing.

The attached store (9am to 5pm) sells Canada Goose jackets, art by Yellowknife artist Robbie Craig and more.

Great White Bear Tours
WILDLIFE

(☎204-487-7633; www.greatwhitebeartours.com; 266 Kelsey Blvd; per day from $473; ☉mid-Oct to mid-Nov) Uses tundra coaches but only operates day tours; guests sleep in town. Daily bear-spotting outings in October and November; multiday wildlife-viewing package tours in July and August (from $6495 for seven days).

Land & Sea Tours

Several outfits offer land tours of the area in summer. These typically take in Cape Merry, Churchill Northern Studies Centre (CNSC) and the disused missile site, plus novelties such as a crashed plane and a grounded ship. The cost averages $100 for several hours and you may well see a bear or two.

Sea tours typically center around whale-watching combined with visits to the Fort Prince of Wales, plus aquaplaning (floating on a giant foam mat) and kayaking with belugas.

There are short dogsledding outings available in summer and winter, as well as scenic flights.

★ **Nature 1st** WALKING
(☑204-675-2147; www.nature1sttours.ca; half-/full-day tours from $105/180; ◔ Jun-Aug) Hiking, trekking and birding are combined in half- and full-day nature tours that explore the four distinct ecosystems around Churchill.

★ **Sea North Tours** ADVENTURE
(☑204-675-2195; www.seanorthtours.com; Polar Inn & Suites, Kelsey Blvd; tours $117-170; ◔ Jul & Aug) Summer beluga-whale tours use a custom viewing boat and Zodiac inflatables; visits to Fort Prince of Wales (p530) are often included. Floe-ice tours in early June present terrific bird-watching opportunities, while kayaking and paddleboarding with the curious belugas in July is another terrific tour option.

Bluesky Expeditions DOG SLEDDING
(☑204-675-2001; www.blueskymush.com; per person $140) Entertaining, safety-conscious dogsledding in winter and dog-carting in summer around a forested loop, courtesy of Gerald and Jenafor. Outings end with a slide show and freshly baked bannock. Pickup from your hotel.

Churchill Wild ADVENTURE
(☑204-377-5090; www.churchillwild.com; multiday tours from $11,450; ◔ Jul-Oct) 🖉 This outfit has three remote lodges you reach from Churchill by floatplane and boat. The highlight is its photography and wildlife-watching safaris that get close to bears and other wildlife, and the remote locations, ideal for uninterrupted viewing of the northern lights.

Wapusk Adventures DOG SLEDDING
(☑204-675-2887; www.wapuskadventures.com; Kelsey Blvd; per person $95; ◔ 9am-5pm) Métis dog whisperer Dave lets you meet his exuberant huskies, explains the workings of a dog team, and takes you for a ride in a dogsled or dog-cart along the 'Iditamile' loop track in the forest. Snowshoeing and northern lights tours also available in winter.

🛏 Sleeping

Rates rise dramatically in polar-bear season and people book up to a year in advance. There's a good selection of motel-style hotels, a lodge, several guesthouses/B&Bs and a couple of cheapies. All are walkable and central. Camping is not possible as there are rules against feeding yourself to the bears. Most places close between December and June.

★ **Blue Sky Bed & Sled** B&B $$
(☑204-675-2001; www.blueskymush.com; 100 Button St; r $150, 3-night package for 2 incl dog-sled ride $400; 🖝) Right on the edge of the tundra, Churchill's loveliest B&B is run by Gerald, who takes his guests husky-sledding, and his indefatigable wife, Jenafor, who cooks up the best breakfast in town and whose cookies are the stuff of local legend. The four snug rooms are decorated with north-themed prints and there is a friendly husky underfoot.

Polar Bear B&B B&B $$
(☑204-675-2819; www.polarbearbandb.com; 87 Hearne St; s/d $90/160; ◔ closed Dec-Apr; 🖝) This is the closest the town has to a hostel. There are snug, basic twin rooms, a kitchen for guest use and free bicycles for guests. Helpful owner Don can arrange ultralight flights.

Polar Inn & Suites MOTEL $$
(☑204-675-8878; www.polarinn.com; 153 Kelsey Blvd; s/d/apt $205/245/300; 🖝) Spacious motel-style units come with fridges inside an appealing log-cabin setting. There are also studios with small kitchens, and full apartments, which tend to get booked up first. Owned by Sea North and popular with tour groups.

★ **Lazy Bear Lodge** LODGE $$$
(☑866-687-2327; www.lazybearlodge.com; 313 Kelsey Blvd; 2-night package incl tours per person from $575; 🖝) Making great use of a natural disaster, Churchill's coziest lodge is built entirely from reclaimed forest-fire-singed tree trunks. The common spaces are welcoming, particularly the dining room with its massive stone fireplace. Guest rooms are compact and wood-paneled, the bathrooms come with tubs, and the service is friendly and helpful. Group packages take precedence, but independent travelers are also welcomed.

🍴 Eating

Look out for wild items on menus, such as elk and bison. Seek out Arctic char, a delicious local fish that is like a cross between salmon and trout. Out of a handful of places to eat in town, two restaurants are particularly good. There's a reasonably well-stocked supermarket.

★ Lazy Bear Cafe
CANADIAN $$

(☏204-675-2969; www.lazybearlodge.com; 313 Kelsey Blvd; mains $15-30; ⊙7am-9pm; 🛜🅿) Serving elk, Arctic char and bison, augmented with local berries and mushrooms, this restaurant acquaints you with Manitoba's wild ingredients. Lunchtime mains include epic burgers. Creative vegetarian specials make a daily appearance and this is the only place in town with an espresso machine. On a cold day, pick a spot by the stone fireplace.

Tundra Inn Lounge
CANADIAN $$

(☏204-675-8831; www.tundrainn.com; 32 Franklin St; mains $15-25; ⊙4pm-late Tue-Sat; 🛜🅿) Combining innovative dishes with the town's most popular watering hole, Tundra Inn Lounge is on to a winner. The wild rice/bean/vegetable Borealis Burger and vegetable curry are veggie-pleasers, while carnivorous diners can tuck into elk meatloaf, ribs, wings and fish tacos. Tuesday is open mike night at the adjoining bar, with local beers and spirits fueling local talent.

🛍 Shopping

Arctic Trading Company
ARTS & CRAFTS

(☏204-675-8804; www.arctictradingco.com; 141 Kelsey Blvd; ⊙10am-5pm Mon-Fri, from 11am Sat) Stocks antler carvings, some Inuit stone sculpture, psychedelic paintings by local Cree artist Allan Chapman, bone jewelry, caribou hair-tufting art, appliqué and felt art from around Baffin Island and locally made beaded moccasins and mukluks.

ℹ Information

In summer it's war with the swarms of mosquitoes and large biting flies ('bulldogs'). Pack bug repellent with *at least* 30% DEET. Always have warm clothing handy as it can get cold fast in summer. Heed all polar-bear warnings.

Royal Bank (La Verendrye Ave, Bayport Plaza; ⊙24hr) One of several local ATMs.

Parks Canada (☏204-675-8863; www.pc.gc.ca; Hendry St; ⊙8am-noon & 1-4pm Mon-Fri)

An essential first stop, but opening hours are variable. Located inside the train station.

ℹ Getting There & Away

There is no road to Churchill; access is by plane or train only. A popular option is to explore Manitoba up to Thompson and then to catch a train or plane from there.

AIR

Calm Air (☏800-839-2256; www.calmair.com; Airport Rd, Churchill Airport) and **First Air** (☏800-267-1247; www.firstair.ca) both serve Winnipeg (one to two daily), as well as Nunavut destinations north of Churchill. Airfares can feel as savage as the bite of a polar bear: a one-way from Winnipeg averages $760; a return around $1600.

TRAIN

Via Rail's **Churchill train** is back in operation after the rails were washed out in May 2017 and Churchill was cut off from the rest of Manitoba for a year and a half. The train runs from the station on Hendry St to Winnipeg (seat/berth/private cabin from $233/742/1121, 45¼ hours) at 7:30pm on Thursdays and Saturdays via Thompson (seat/berth/private cabin $67/367/553, 15½ hours) and The Pas (seat/berth/private cabin $116/541/813, 28 hours); Tuesday departures via Thompson terminate at The Pas.

There is a mesmerizing quality to the slow and ponderous journey, as you fall asleep amid boreal forest and wake up to an endless vista of muskeg and stunted trees, or vice versa. Bring food with you as well as something warm; temperatures drop at night.

ℹ Getting Around

Most locals walk or cycle around the compact town but you should be bear aware. **Polar Inn** (☏204-675-8878; 15 Franklin St; per day $20) rents out bicycles, while the Polar Bear B&B has free bicycles for guest use. **Tamarack Rentals** (☏204-675-2192; www.tamarackrentals.ca; 299 Kelsey Blvd; ⊙8:30am-noon & 1-5:30pm Mon-Fri, to 5pm Sat) rents battered pickup trucks and SUVs, and can meet you at the airport. Prices are $150 to $200 per day.

Taxis (☏204-675-2517) will cost you $25 to/from the airport and $10 to destinations around town.

Saskatchewan

Best Places to Eat

➡ Oda Coffee & Wine Bar (p549)

➡ Drift Sidewalk Cafe & Vista Lounge (p553)

➡ Willow on Wascana (p540)

Best Places to Stay

➡ Hotel Senator (p552)

➡ Keyhole Castle B&B (p556)

➡ Hotel Saskatchewan (p539)

➡ Ghostown Blues B&B (p547)

➡ Lakeside Country Inn (p549)

Why Go?

To paraphrase an old line, there are no boring parts of Saskatchewan, just boring visitors. Yes, the terrain lacks drama, there's not a lot of people here, the two major towns define the vaguely complimentary 'nice,' and so on. But that simply means that the savvy visitor can dig deep to discover the province's inherent appeal.

Start with all that flat: those rippling oceans of grain have a mesmerizing poetry to their movement, the songbirds and crickets providing accents to the endlessly rustling wind. If you're ready for the sheer tranquility of solitude, pick any unpaved road and set off across the country – and delight when you find water-dappled coulees and tree-covered hills.

And don't forget the province's people. Not just the plain-spoken residents of today, but also the people who populate Saskatchewan's story, whether eking out a living off the land, fomenting revolution or taming a frontier.

When to Go
Saskatoon

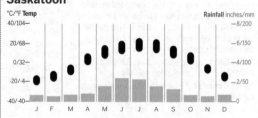

May Spring wildflowers paint the landscape and birdsong fills the air as life, post-winter, returns.

Jun–Aug Long sunny days draw happy locals to lakes, parks and patios.

Sep Crisp air, endless skies and dramatic fall colors herald the year's final harvests.

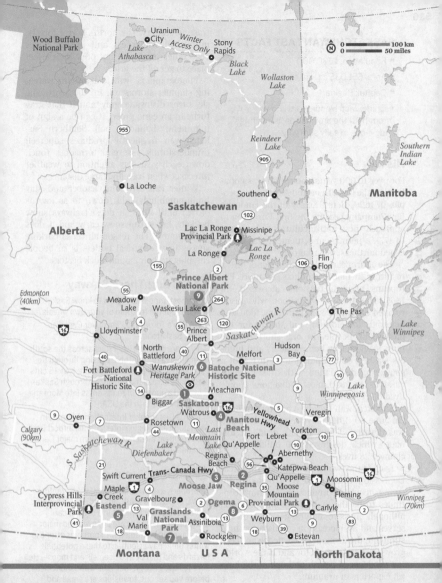

Saskatchewan Highlights

1 Saskatoon (p549)
Enjoying the urban pleasures of the Paris of the Prairies.

2 Regina (p540) Donning a watermelon hat at a Roughriders game.

3 Moose Jaw (p541)
Digging deep to experience the town's underground past.

4 Manitou Beach (p549)
Swimming in Dead Sea–like Lake Manitou.

5 Eastend (p547) Visiting Scotty at the T-rex Discovery Centre.

6 Batoche National Historic Site (p556)
Remembering the Métis revolutionaries.

7 Grasslands National Park (p546) Hearing the rustling of the long grass and the thunder of the bison.

8 Ogema (p544) Boarding the Southern Prairie Railway.

9 Prince Albert National Park (p556) Hiking or canoeing in the wilderness park.

History

For over 10,000 years, the region was populated by the Cree, Dene and Assiniboine people. In 1690, Henry Kelsey of the Hudson's Bay Company became the first European to approach these native cultures to buy furs. In 1774, a permanent settlement was established northeast of Saskatoon.

The Europeans demanded land, often resulting in bloody conflicts. As more Europeans arrived, tensions increased. In 1865, an estimated 60 million wild bison roamed Saskatchewan, providing food and materials for clothing and shelter for the indigenous people. In one short decade, mass slaughter by homesteaders and hunters slashed that population to just 500: a staggering decimation with drastic repercussions. By 1890, most indigenous people lived on reserves.

Saskatchewan became a province in 1905. On June 30, 1912, its young capital Regina was devastated by Canada's deadliest tornado, which destroyed 500 buildings and claimed 28 lives.

Each of the two world wars and the Great Depression contributed to a meteoric increase in wheat production. Farming continues to be the lifeblood of the province, although massive natural-gas and oil reserves and an increase in immigration help stimulate the economy. Saskatchewan has a growing petroleum sector and is the world's top producer of potash and one of the largest exporters of uranium.

Land & Climate

Short, warm summers are ideal for traveling: days are long and nights are cool. Don't be fooled into thinking Saskatchewan's scenic beauty is limited to the mesmerizing tableau of grain and sky you whiz past on Hwy 1. If you're coming from other parts of Canada, you'll be interested in exploring the south, with its unique and con-trasting scenery. The north's boreal forests, untouched wilderness and pristine lakes echo other provinces, but offer the perfect place to get off the grid.

Photographers will delight in watching summer storms roll in: the azure-blue sky turns dishwater gray, and if that gray turns to an eerie green, it can be a sign of imminent, significant hail. Southern Saskatchewan frequently produces supercell thunderstorms – several tornadoes touch down each year. Pay attention to weather forecasts when traveling large distances.

Winter can arrive in October and stay brain-numbingly cold (down to as low as -40°C) until April; it doesn't always snow buckets, but it can snow early and it does stick around. The reason all those parking spaces have electrical outlets is so people can plug in their engine-block heaters.

❶ Getting There & Away

It's almost impossible to get to know Saskatchewan without the freedom of your own wheels.

VIA Rail's Toronto to Vancouver *Canadian* serves Saskatoon.

If you are driving, Hwy 1 runs across the south from Alberta to Manitoba, passing through Regina, Moose Jaw and Swift Current; Hwy 16 cuts diagonally across the province, through Saskatoon; and a number of roads cross into Montana and North Dakota in the USA.

John G Diefenbaker International Airport in Saskatoon and Regina International airport both have frequent air services to/from major Canadian destinations.

❶ Getting Around

To properly explore the deepest wilds, renting a 4WD or SUV is useful, although you can still traverse rural backwaters in a regular car. Many provincial roads are unpaved and major highways can be riddled with potholes after the winter melt; pay attention to these potential hazards and that of wild deer, elk and moose. Be sure to have enough fuel, music and munchies before you set out; townships are small and separated by significant distances.

REGINA

On the Trans-Canada Hwy, the provincial capital is by default the primary destination of visitors to Saskatchewan. There's heady rivalry with Saskatoon, the attractive city 230km to the north, ever since it was a hunting ground for the Cree, who called Regina Wascana (Pile of Bones).

Leafy parks make the capital a pleasant place to be: the Wascana Centre and Victoria Park are great spots to sit and ponder. Other highlights include the gentrified Cathedral Village and the up-and-coming Regina Warehouse District, although on game days, the town's sole focus is on the Roughriders football team.

Regina has good restaurants, bars and comfortable accommodations. These, combined with its location, make it a good base from which to explore southern Saskatchewan, and an appropriate place for a sojourn as you cross the Canadian interior.

⊙ Sights

★ Royal Saskatchewan Museum

MUSEUM

(☑ 306-787-2815; www.royalsaskmuseum.ca; 2445 Albert St; by donation; ⊙ 9:30am-5pm; P) The Royal provides a great insight into the people and geography that make up Saskatchewan. Galleries focus on earth and life sciences and indigenous history. Prairie dioramas tell the story of the native flora, fauna and cultures that lived off the harsh land. See Scotty, the biggest T.rex ever discovered – this skeleton replicates that in the Museum's T-rex Discovery Centre (p547) in Eastend.

★ Provincial Legislature

NOTABLE BUILDING

(☑ 306-787-2376; www.legassembly.sk.ca; Legislative Dr; ⊙ 8am-9pm Jun-Aug, to 5pm Sep-May; P) FREE Escaping significant damage from the devastating tornado in its year of completion (1912), the arresting 'Leg,' nestled in Wascana Centre's leafy embrace, stands as a proud symbol to the people of Regina. Ponder the rich marble and ornate carvings of this lavish example of beaux-arts architecture on free half-hourly tours or just play Frisbee out front on the Great Lawn.

Wascana Centre

PARK

(P) The geographic and cultural center of Regina, this sprawling public nature haven has miles of lakeside walking trails and is home to the Royal Saskatchewan Museum, Saskatchewan War Memorial and Saskatchewan Science Centre. Public events and celebrations are held by Wascana Lake's clear waters, which mirror such vistas as the stunning Provincial Legislature building and the Spruce Island bird sanctuary. Park residents include mink, hare, beavers and countless geese.

RCMP Heritage Centre

MUSEUM

(☑ 306-522-7333; www.rcmphc.com; 5907 Dewdney Ave W; adult/child $10/6; ⊙ 11am-5pm; P) Exhibits chart the past, present and future of the iconic Canadian Mounties (you even get to dress up like one). This is also part of the Royal Canadian Mounted Police (RCMP) training center: check out the jutting jaws at the Sergeant Major's Parade.

Saskatchewan Science Centre

MUSEUM

(☑ 306-791-7914; www.sasksciencecentre.com; 903 Powerhouse Dr; adult/child $15/12, incl IMAX feature $20/18; ⊙ 10am-6pm Mon-Fri, 11am-6pm Sat & Sun; P🚼) Science class was never this much fun! Try your hand at scoring a goal against a virtual goalkeeper, blow bubbles the size of a car or discover the secret to burping. With over 180 hands-on exhibits, it's a hit with kids; the center also has an IMAX theater and an observatory.

MacKenzie Art Gallery

GALLERY

(☑ 306-584-4250; www.mackenzieartgallery.ca; 3475 Albert St; by donation; ⊙ 10am-5:30pm Mon & Wed-Sat, noon-5:30pm Sun; P) This gallery features a permanent outdoor sculpture garden, grazed by Joe Fafard's famed bronzed cows, and keeps things fresh with rotating and special exhibitions primarily concerned with historical and contemporary Canadian art.

🏃 Activities

Wascana Canoe Kayak Rentals

WATER SPORTS

(Marina Rentals; ☑ 306-757-2628; www.facebook.com/wascancanoekayakarentals; 3000 Wascana Dr; canoe/kayak/paddleboard per hr $20/15/20; ⊙ 10am-7pm May-Sep) In the grounds of Wascana Centre at the Wascana Marina, you'll find this seasonal provider of canoes, kayaks and paddleboards for use on Wascana Lake.

🎆 Festivals & Events

Queen City Ex

FIESTA

(☑ 306-781-9200; www.evrazplace.com/events/queen-city-ex; 1700 Elphinstone St; ⊙ Jul-early Aug) Saskatchewan's favorite festival; people dress up in pioneer garb for six days

Regina

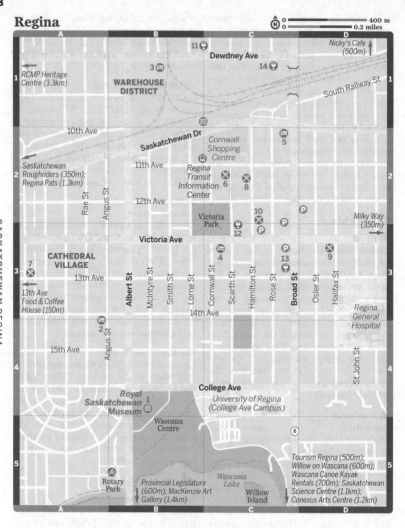

Regina

⊙ Top Sights
1 Royal Saskatchewan Museum.............B4

🛏 Sleeping
2 Dragon's Nest B&B.............................A4
3 Four Points by Sheraton Regina.........B1
4 Hotel Saskatchewan..........................C3
5 Wingate by Wyndham........................C2

⊗ Eating
6 Beer Bros. Gastropub C2

7 Dessart Sweets Ice Cream
   & Candy Store.................................A3
8 Green Spot Cafe...............................C2
9 Italian Star Deli...............................D3
10 Victoria's Tavern C2

🍷 Drinking & Nightlife
11 Bushwakker Brewing B1
12 O'Hanlon's Irish Pub.........................C3
13 Q Nightclub and Lounge....................C3
14 Rebellion Brewing............................C1

of concerts, pancake breakfasts, amusement-park rides, a beard-growing contest and parades. Dates vary year to year.

**First Nations University
of Canada Pow Wow**   CULTURAL

(www.fnuniv.ca/powwow; ☺Apr) Held over a weekend in spring, dancers from around North America converge for this, the largest and longest running celebration of First Nations' culture in the province.

🛏 Sleeping

There is plenty of decent accommodations in Regina. Victoria Ave (Hwy 1) east of town has no shortage of chain motels.

★Hotel Saskatchewan   HISTORIC HOTEL $$

(☑306-522-7691; www.marriott.com; 2125 Victoria Ave; r from $160; P☺✳🛜) Overlooking Victoria Park, this 1927 former grand dame of the Canadian National Railroad maintains a lofty presence. There's a degree of wow-factor upon entry. The 224 rooms come in sizes from compact to grand and feature luxe, period decor. It's affiliated with Marriott.

**Four Points by
Sheraton Regina**   HOTEL $$

(☑306-789-8008; www.marriott.com; 2415 Dewdney Ave; r from $110; P☺✳🛜⛱) Just north across the tracks from downtown, this hotel is in walking distance for Roughriders games and the nightlife of the Warehouse District. The 127 rooms are large and have fridges and microwaves. The pool is indoors.

Homesuites by d3h   MOTEL $$

(☑306-522-4434; www.homesuites.ca; 3841 Eastgate Dr; r incl breakfast from $100; P☺✳🛜) Practicality and good design are the hallmarks of this above-average property on the Hwy 1 motel strip outside town. The 60 roomy suites include kitchenettes and have access to a spa.

Wingate by Wyndham   HOTEL $$

(☑306-992-6929; www.wingatebywyndhamregina. com; 1700 Broad St; r from $109; P☺✳🛜) The central Wingate offers 118 good-value, large and comfortable guest rooms in a modern seven-story building. Rooms have fridges and microwaves.

Dragon's Nest B&B   B&B $$

(☑306-525-2109; www.dragonsnestbb.com; 2200 Angus St; s/d incl breakfast from $100/115, without

bath $70/90; ☺✳🛜) This stylish six-room B&B is run by a feng shui consultant, so it's all lined up for optimum comfort. Included breakfasts are country fresh and hearty. The house dates to 1912.

🍴 Eating

Regina has a good share of interesting and inventive restaurants in the center and in nearby neighborhoods.

**★13th Ave Food
& Coffee House**   CAFE $

(☑306-522-3111; www.13thavecoffee.com; 3136 13th Ave; mains from $8; ☺7:30am-8pm Mon-Fri, 8:30am-8pm Sat, 10am-7pm Sun; 🍴) 'Healthy, fresh and local' is the mantra of this Cathedral Village anchor. Come for your fix of locally roasted, fair-trade java and get your daily dose of quinoa, antioxidants and vitamins as well. Carnivores aren't excluded, but vegetarians will feel right at home.

Milky Way   ICE CREAM $

(☑306-352-7920; www.milkywayicecream.com; 910 Victoria Ave; snacks from $2; ☺11am-10pm Mar-Oct) Regina's taste of summer is flavored by fun. Six types of soft-serve ice cream are the basis for shakes, sundaes, cones and myriad treats.

Italian Star Deli   DELI $

(☑306-757-6733; www.italianstardeli.com; 1611 Victoria Ave; sandwiches from $6; ☺9am-5:30pm Tue-Sat) Since 1966, this authentic Italian deli has brought the flavors of Europe to the prairies. Folks flock for the delicious panini and you're well advised to follow suit – they're great value and bursting with freshness. Perfect for your picnic basket.

**Dessart Sweets
Ice Cream & Candy Store**   ICE CREAM $

(☑306-522-2663; www.dessartsweets.com; 3036 13th Ave; ice cream from $3.75; ☺11am-9pm Mon-Fri, to 6pm Sat & Sun) A top spot on warm summer days. Order an ice cream or banana split at the outside hole-in-the-wall and enjoy the outside seating, or head inside for a huge selection of candy and sweets.

Nicky's Cafe   CANADIAN $

(☑306-757-3222; www.nickys.ca; 1005 8th Av; mains from $8; ☺5:30am-8pm; 👶) Comfort food doesn't get more comfy – or tasty – than this. Breakfasts feature famous hash browns, superb omelets and winter-insulating pancakes. Later in the day, burgers come in a dozen variations or you can go for seafood or ribs. Portions are large and quality is high.

Green Spot Cafe
VEGETARIAN **$**

(☑ 306-757-7899; www.greenspotcafe.ca; 1812 Hamilton St; snacks from $4; ⏱ 7am-5pm Mon-Fri, 8am-3pm Sat; ✈) This 100% vegetarian cafe features a downtown location and a menu of healthy treats chock-full of good karma.

★ Victoria's Tavern
GASTROPUB **$$**

(☑ 306-352-8427; www.victoriastavern.ca; 1965 Hamilton St; mains from $15; ⏱ 10am-2am) This loud and lively downtown pub is popular all day long, with local craft beers on tap and a solid food menu with favorites such as fish-and-chips, cajun tacos and sandwiches, plus tasty options such as Southwest Bowl and Korean Bowl. There's a popular weekend brunch.

★ Willow on Wascana
CANADIAN **$$**

(☑ 306-585-3663; www.barwillow.ca; 3000 Wascana Dr; mains lunch from $12, dinner from $15; ⏱ 11:30am-11pm Mon-Thu, to 1am Fri-Sun) Views over Wascana Lake are one of Regina's upscale pleasures. The menu here changes seasonally and is a classic example of farm-to-table creativity. Dishes are kept simple to let the flavors come through. Sample the kitchen's best with a four-course tasting menu. Long wine list.

Beer Bros. Gastropub
PUB FOOD **$$**

(☑ 306-586-2337; www.beerbros.ca; 1821 Scarth St; mains from $12; ⏱ 11:30am-11pm Sun-Thu, to 1am Fri & Sat) It's hard not to love this downtown pub in the heritage Northern Bank building. Think hearty – sandwiches, burgers, cheese plates – but with a gourmet twist. As you'd expect from the name, the beer list is long and has an excellent range of Canadian microbrews. Sidewalk seating available.

Drinking & Nightlife

There are good bars and breweries in and around downtown and the nearby Warehouse District (www.warehousedistrict.ca). In summer, people flock to the many patios.

★ Rebellion Brewing
MICROBREWERY

(☑ 306-522-4666; www.rebellionbrewing.ca; 1901 Dewdney Ave; ⏱ 11:30am-10pm Mon-Sat, to 5pm Sun) Hard by the old train tracks, Saskatchewan's best microbrewery has a taproom with excellent burgers and pizza. There's

a modern corrugated-metal aesthetic and hop-shaped fixtures. The beer list is long and changing, but don't miss the Sour Rye.

Bushwakker Brewing
PUB

(☑ 306-359-7276; www.bushwakker.com; 2206 Dewdney Ave; ⏱ 11am-late Mon-Sat, noon-9pm Sun) In a 1913 warehouse, Bushwakker is reason enough to cross the tracks to the Warehouse District. There's live music many nights, but the real draw is the beer: over a dozen house brews on rotating taps. Try the Chinook ESB, a British-style extra-special bitter.

Q Nightclub and Lounge
GAY

(☑ 306-569-1995; 2070 Broad St; ⏱ 5pm-late Mon-Sat) Occupying a former church building, this gay bar and club is a welcoming, straight-friendly affair, run by a members co-op. The awesome rough-around-the-edges, multilevel space has an outdoor patio. There are DJs many nights.

O'Hanlon's Irish Pub
PUB

(☑ 306-566-4094; www.ohanlons.ca; 1947 Scarth St; ⏱ 11am-2am) O'Hanlon's has a grungy Irish pub feel and sidewalk tables overlooking Victoria Park and the Hotel Saskatchewan. It's the kind of place where you can find yourself eating, drinking and babbling on until the wee hours. Great beer list.

☆ Entertainment

★ Trial of Louis Riel
THEATER

(☑ 306-728-5728; www.rielcoproductions.com; 2272 Pasqua St; adult/child $25/15) Actual transcripts from Riel's 1885 trial – which resulted in his hanging – are the basis of this, Canada's second-longest-running play, first performed in 1967. Check for dates on the website.

Saskatchewan Roughriders
FOOTBALL

(☑ 306-525-2181; www.riderville.com; Mosaic Stadium, Elphinstone St; ⏱ Jun-Nov) The Green Riders, as they're known to legions of rabid locals, have achieved cult status within the Canadian Football League (CFL). Don't underestimate how crazy things get in this town, for this team. The new home venue, Mosaic Stadium opened in 2017 and seats 33,000, which is more than one-quarter of the local population!

Regina Pats
HOCKEY

(☑ 306-543-7800; www.reginapats.com; Brandt Centre, 1700 Elphinstone St; from $15; ⏱ Sep-Mar)

The younger, tougher, more eager players of the Western Hockey League (WHL) make for an exciting brand of hockey. The stadium is about 3km west of the center.

Conexus Arts Centre THEATER
(✆306-565-4500; www.conexusartscentre.ca; 200a Lakeshore Dr) Home of the symphony orchestra and venue of choice for touring musicians and shows, the Arts Centre vaguely resembles vintage Saskatchewan grain elevators.

❶ Information

Main Post Office (✆866-607-6301; 2200 Saskatchewan Dr; ⊙9am-5pm Mon-Fri)
Prairie Dog (www.prairiedogmag.com) Feisty and free biweekly newspaper with good entertainment and restaurant listings.
Regina General Hospital (✆306-766-4444; www.rqhealth.ca; 1440 14th Ave; ⊙24hr) Emergency room.
Tourism Regina (www.tourismregina.com; 2900 Wascana Dr; ⊙9am-5:30pm Fri-Wed, 9am-9pm Thu) A good collection of local guides and maps at the Wascana Center in the park.

❶ Getting There & Away

Regina International Airport (YQR; ✆306-761-7555; www.yqr.ca; 5200 Regina Ave), 5km west of downtown, has services to major Canadian destinations.

❶ Getting Around

The airport is a 10-minute cab ride ($15) from downtown; there is no public transit service.
Regina Transit (✆306-777-7433; www.regina.ca; 2124 11th Ave; adult/child $3.25/2.75; ⊙8am-6pm Mon-Fri, 9am-4:30pm Sat) operates city buses, most of which converge on 11th St downtown.
Regina Cabs (✆306-543-3333; www.reginacabs.com) comes when you call.

SOUTHERN SASKATCHEWAN

Along the Trans-Canada Hwy (Hwy 1) is iconic Saskatchewan, the sort of wide open prairie that country songs are written about. As you explore the rabbit warren of unpaved, lonely back roads, it's easy to feel divorced from modern life. It's not hard to imagine thousands of bison charging over a nearby hill, indigenous villages in the valley or the North-West Mounted Police (NWMP)

patrolling the prairie on horseback. There is diversity among this immensity, though, with rolling grasslands, short sharp hills and badlands befitting a classic Western.

❶ Getting There & Away

Southern Saskatchewan is the place to have your own vehicle.

Moose Jaw

The province's fourth-largest city, Moose Jaw is a welcome island in a prairie sea, a rough diamond with surprising charm. From grassroots beginnings as a Canadian Pacific Railway outpost, the town grew steadily in size and infamy, earning a reputation for rebellion, corruption, brushes with the Ku Klux Klan and even slavery. In the days of US Prohibition, it was a haven for Al Capone and his gang, who used it as a base for smuggling whiskey across the border on Soo Line trains to Chicago.

Today's Moose Jaw bears little resemblance to its wild past, though an intriguing battle is going on. Moose Jaw is competing with Stor-Elvdal, Norway, over who has the biggest moose in the world. Mac the Moose, outside the Visitor Centre, held the title for 31 years before losing it to Norway in 2015. A new set of bigger antlers in 2019 saw Canada proudly reclaim the title.

◉ Sights & Activities

Main St and the historic downtown should be your focus. Expect to spend a couple of hours wandering about. More than 45 **murals** capturing tamer moments in Moose Jaw's history adorn walls around town. A few seedy motels in the center provide an edge.

★ **Tunnels of Moose Jaw** TUNNEL
(✆306-693-5261; www.tunnelsofmoosejaw.com; 18 Main St; tours adult/child from $16/9; ⊙hours vary) Buried deep under the town's streets is a series of passages that have a tragic and fascinating history. Take a tour and learn about the hardship and discrimination heaped upon Chinese workers on their 'Passage to Fortune.' Fast-forward a few decades to make the 'Chicago Connection.' Al Capone is rumored to have visited Moose Jaw in the 1920s to oversee his bootlegging operation, masterminded in these very tunnels.

1. Moose Jaw (p541)
Mac the Moose, outside the Visitor Centre in Moose Jaw, holds the title of biggest moose in the world.

2. Saskatoon (p549)
The majestic South Saskatchewan River winds through downtown, offering beautiful, natural diversions.

3. Batoche National Historic Site (p556)
A virtual civil war was fought here in what is known as the Northwest Resistance of 1885.

4. Grasslands National Park (p546)
A sprawling place of isolation and beauty, Grasslands NP is home to wild bison.

Western Development Museum

MUSEUM

(WDM; ☑ 306-693-5989; www.wdm.ca; 50 Diefen-baker Dr; adult/child $10/4; ◷ 9am-5pm; P) If you can drive it, fly it, pedal it or paddle it, odds are you'll find an example of it at this branch of the WDM. Dedicated to transport within Saskatchewan, it has planes, trains, automobiles and even the odd wagon. It's by the bypass, north of the center.

Yvette Moore Gallery

GALLERY

(☑ 306-693-7600; www.yvettemoore.com; 76 Fair-ford St W; ◷ 10am-5pm Mon-Sat) FREE Just west of Main St in a proud heritage building built in 1910, this renowned local artist displays her evocative and hyper-realistic works por-traying Saskatchewan and its people. It has a simple but good cafe serving lunch.

Temple Gardens Mineral Spa

SPA

(☑ 306-694-5055; www.templegardens.sk.ca; 24 Fairford St E; adult/child Mon-Thu $10.25/8.75, Fri-Sun $17/14.50; ◷ 10am-late) This modern complex houses the locally famous indoor-outdoor pool filled with steaming mineral water from deep below the prairie. A long list of treatments are available. The annexed resort accommodations are less inspiring.

👉 Tours

Moose Jaw Trolley Company

BUS

(☑ 306-693-8537;www.tourismmoosejaw.ca;adult/child $14.50/8; ◷ Jun-Aug) Enjoy a tour of the town's murals and historic buildings aboard a fake trolley. Departures from the Visitors Centre.

🛏 Sleeping

Grant Hall Hotel

HISTORIC HOTEL $$

(☑ 844-885-4255; www.granthall.ca; 401 Main St N; r from $90; P 🅿 ❄ 🛜) Small-town luxe describes this vintage (1928) hotel in the center. Opulently restored, the hotel's public spaces are grand. The 28 rooms offer tradi-tional comforts. The terrace is a good place to relax in the sun and enjoy park views.

Wakamow Heights Bed & Breakfast

B&B $$

(☑ 306-693-9963; www.wakamowheights.com; 690 Aldersgate St; r incl breakfast from $99; P 🅿 🛜) In an elevated spot on the out-skirts of town, this historical B&B, built in 1902, has lush gardens and a variety of de-liciously furnished rooms of differing color schemes.

🍴 Eating

Déjà Vu Cafe

DINER $

(☑ 306-692-6066; www.dejavucafe.ca; 23 High St E; mains from $9; ◷ 11am-9pm) Plethora – that's the theme at this legendary diner located downtown. Milkshakes come in 80 flavors, and there are dozens of dipping sauces for the various fried treats (chicken tenders, fries, onion rings) on offer. Yes, it's a simple menu, but everything on it is superb.

Bobby's Place

PUB FOOD $

(☑ 306-692-3058; www.bobbysplace.food-24h. com; 63 High St E; mains from $10; ◷ 11am-late Mon-Sat) Bobby's place is always busy and has been for years. Come for a beer on the patio or, as everyone else does, for the fabu-lous home-cooked meals. The home-breaded chicken fingers are tender, juicy and always popular.

ℹ Information

Visitors Centre (☑ 866-693-8097; www. tourismmoosejaw.ca; Hwy 1; ◷ 9am-5pm mid-May–Aug, 9:30am-noon & 1-4:30pm Sep–mid-May) Look for Mac the Moose near the bypass.

ℹ Getting There & Away

Moose Jaw is 74km west of Regina and 175km east of Swift Current on Hwy 1.

Ogema

In this desolate part of the province's deep south, two extraordinary attractions are worthy draws to this tiny hamlet with a huge community spirit. Be sure to ride the Southern Prairie Railway and visit the Deep South Pioneer Museum. Also of interest, in the main street check out the 1915 Fire Hall (complete with jail cell), built in response to a fire that devastated the east side of Ogema's main street. Town councilors did more than build a Fire Hall though; they erected a mammoth brick firewall halfway down the street so that only half the build-ings in the street would burn in the event of another fire. The costly firewall stands today.

👁 Sights

Deep South Pioneer Museum

MUSEUM

(☑ 306-459-7909; www.ogema.ca; 510 Govern-ment Rd; adult/child $5/3; ◷ 10am-5pm Sat &

Sun May-Sep) Formed as early as 1977 from a desire to preserve the memories, stories and possessions of Ogema's forefathers, the un-expected Deep South Pioneer Museum is an astounding collection of over 30 preserved buildings, along with farming equipment, scores of vehicles and a huge volume of historic artifacts. Townsfolk young and old have contributed to the creation and main-tenance of this unique memorial site. The authenticity of its lovingly preserved build-ings and the openness with which they are presented is extraordinary.

Tours

★ Southern Prairie Railway   RAIL
(306-459-7808; www.southernprairierailway. com; 401 Railway Ave; tours adult/child from $49/32; Sat & Sun Jun-Sep) Ogema's South-ern Prairie Railway has been turning heads since its maiden voyage for the town's centenary in 2012. The informative 2½- to 3½-hour tours chug across the prairie to ex-plore an abandoned grain elevator among other sights. Special tours are held through-out the year, including the occasional star-gazing expedition.

Gravelbourg

About 190km southwest of Regina, delight-ful Gravelbourg is one of the last places you'd expect to find a taste of France, adrift on a vast sea of prairie. Lavish buildings designed to lure French settlers date to the early 1900s. Palatial buildings and houses are scattered along 1st Ave, including the tiny community's elementary school, École Élémentaire de Gravelbourg.

Sights

The best way to explore this surprising des-tination is to do the Heritage Walking Tour found at www.gravelbourg.ca.

Our Lady of the
Assumption Co-Cathedral   CHURCH
(La Co-Cathédrale Notre Dame de l'Assomption; 306-648-3322; www.gravelbourgcocathedral. com; 1st Ave; P) FREE The undisputed cen-terpiece of this *très jolie* little town is the disproportionately large and beautiful Our Lady of the Assumption Co-Cathedral, built in 1919 in a Romanesque and Italianate style. It was designated a National Historic Site in 1995. Enter if it's open and crane your

neck to marvel at the Sistine Chapel–esque frescoes. Monsignor Maillard, who not only designed the chapel's interior and presided over the parish, painted the frescoes himself, from 1921 to 1931 – an astonishing feat.

Gravelbourg &
District Museum   MUSEUM
(306-648-2332; www.southcentralmuseums.ca; 300 Main St; $5; 9am-6pm Mon-Sat, noon-6pm Sun) Learn about Gravelbourg's rich cultural traditions at this museum, two blocks south of the cathedral. Entrance to the museum plus a guided tour of the Cathedral is avail-able for $10.

Sleeping & Eating

★ Bishop's Residence   B&B $
(888-648-2321; www.bishopsresidencebandb. com; 112 1st Ave W; r incl breakfast from $70; P) The handsome yellow-brick former bishop's residence has been turned into a unique B&B with nine rooms, some with private bathrooms and balconies. Take a look at individual rooms online before you book them.

Café de Paris   CAFE $
(306-648-2223; www.facebook.com/CafeParis Gravelbourg; 306 Main St; mains from $8; 8am-7pm Mon-Fri, 9am-5pm Sat) Pop in to see the friendly folks at the Café de Paris for a light lunch and a delicious milkshake. It's right downtown; vintage details include a pressed-tin ceiling.

Swift Current

Swift Current's main claim to fame is as a travelers' oasis on Hwy 1. The downtown area is about 3km south of the highway strip – follow the signs. With a population of 16,600, Swift Current is the province's fifth-largest city; one of the main reasons lo-cals turn up is the Living Sky Casino.

Sights

Swift Current Museum   MUSEUM
(306-778-2775; www.tourismswiftcurrent.ca; 44 Robert St W; 9am-5pm Mon-Fri, from 1pm Sat & Sun) FREE You'll want to make a stop to check out the massive woolly bison in this little museum in the same building as Tour-ism Swift Current. It has good information on the link between the people and the land in this part of southern Saskatchewan.

Mennonite Heritage Village
MUSEUM

(☑306-778-2364; www.mennoniteheritagevillage.ca; 17th Ave SE; by donation; ☺1-5pm Fri-Sun Jul & Aug) This 1900s heritage village depicts a way of life unfamiliar to most. Many Mennonite and Hutterite communities still exist in the area. There's an annual summer watermelon festival.

🛏 Sleeping

Safari Inn Motel
MOTEL $

(☑306-773-4608; www.tourismswiftcurrent.ca; 810 S Service Rd E; r from $60; P☺☺☎) A non-chain alternative on the motel strip, the Safari beckons with a throwback neon sign. The owners can't do enough to please, and the rooms have all the amenities: fridges and microwaves. It's far from flashy, but it compensates with spirit.

Home Inn & Suites
MOTEL $$

(☑306-778-7788; www.homeinnswiftcurrent.ca; 1411 Battleford Trail E; r incl breakfast from $130; P☺✳☎☒) Modern, tastefully decorated suites in this chain motel have kitchenettes, comfortable beds and room to move. There's an indoor pool with a waterslide and a little day spa so you can relieve those tired driving muscles.

🍴 Eating

Akropol Family Restaurant
GREEK $

(☑306-773-5454; www.akropol.ca; 133 Central Ave N; mains from $10; ☺11am-9pm Mon-Sat) This Greek restaurant serves up traditional favorites such as gyros, calamari and spanakopita. There's a lovely outdoor patio and it has locally brewed Black Bridge beers. The lounge is popular and there is often live music.

Miso House
ASIAN $

(☑306-778-4411; 285 N Service Rd W; mains from $9; ☺11am-9pm Tue-Sun) Miso House has done a great job of bringing tasty sushi, Korean delights and Japanese bento boxes to the prairies. Take a look at the Facebook page for details.

Val Marie & Grasslands National Park

Val Marie, at the gateway to Grasslands National Park, is tiny, rough around the edges and endearing. Val Marie (Valley of Mary) was founded in 1910 with most of the early settlers being ranchers and farmers from Québec and France. The village remained ethnically French and by the 1950s had 450 people, though the population declined significantly with low grain commodity prices and droughts in the 1980s. Of late, Grasslands National Park has attracted new people into the area.

◎ Sights & Activities

★ Prairie Wind & Silver Sage
MUSEUM

(☑306-298-4910; www.pwss.org; Centre St; ☺9am-midday & 1-5pm) **FREE** In what was the brick Val Marie schoolhouse (1927–85), the Friends of Grasslands have set up a museum, gallery, bookstore, gift shop and cafe. It's beautifully done, with courtesy wi-fi, brewed coffees and daily homemade treats such as cinnamon buns and brownies. Don't miss this place!

Grasslands National Park
NATIONAL PARK

(☑877-345-2257; www.parkscanada.ca/grasslands) Grasslands National Park is a sprawling place of isolation and beauty, where treeless hills meet the endless sky. The visitor center is an essential port of call for advice on where to camp and how best to experience the full majesty of the park. Prepare well for expeditions and BYO shade – Grasslands is wild and lonely; there's the potential for rattlesnake encounters. If you're lucky, you might catch a glimpse of the resident herd of bison. Park accommodations include campsites ($30) and tipis ($45).

Grasslands Ecotour Scenic Drive
SCENIC DRIVE

(www.parkscanada.ca/grasslands) This self-guided drive is a well-signposted course through the West Block, starting 15km east of Val Marie. Pick up a map and advice at the visitors center. There are seven points of interest and two short walks. Do the full 80km drive in a couple of hours or drive in to Frenchman Valley campground and back (34km).

🛏 Sleeping

★ Convent Inn
B&B $

(☑306-298-4515; www.convent.ca; Hwy 4; r incl breakfast from $85; P☺☎) For a holier-than-thou sleeping experience, the Convent offers beds amid classic brickwork and beautiful hardwood floors. Built in 1939, this former residential school has nine beautifully restored rooms, a labyrinth of staircases and even a confessional (in case you break a vow or two during the night). It has lovely patios for chilling with a view.

Eastend

Isolated in southwest Saskatchewan, Eastend would be tumbleweed quiet if not for the discovery of Scotty, the biggest T-rex ever to be found. Scotty was unearthed nearby in 1991 and the Royal Saskatchewan Museum's T-rex Discovery Centre has put Eastend on the tourist map.

Eastend in not without charm. The town began as the most eastern detachment from Fort Walsh and as it was at the eastern end of their patrol, received its rather dreary name. It sits in a small valley, with the town's few streets lined with older buildings dating from its founding in 1914.

◉ Sights

★ **T-Rex Discovery Centre**   MUSEUM

(☏306-295-4009;   www.royalsaskmuseum.ca/trex; T-Rex Dr; by donation; ⊙10am-6pm Jun-Aug; ℗) Eastend's claim to fame is the 1991 discovery of the biggest, most complete Tyrannosaurus rex skeleton ever found. Known as Scotty, the mammoth T.rex is 13m long. The T-Rex Discovery Centre is a glitzy working lab carved into the hillside. There is a variety of tours available, along with dinosaur dig options if you feel the need to, er, bone up.

Eastend Historical Museum   MUSEUM

(☏306-295-3375; www.eastendhistoricalmuseum.com; 306 Red Coat Dr; adult/child $5/free; ⊙10am-5:30pm May-Sep) FREE The Eastend Historical Museum has fossils and bones on display, plus a 1909 log cabin next door. The Machine Shed features a 1903 Case steam engine, a 1927 Federal Truck, stage coaches, a miniature steam engine and a firefighting water pumper.

🛏 Sleeping & Eating

Cypress Hotel   HOTEL $

(☏306-295-3505; www.dinocountry.com; 343 Red Coat Dr; r from $60; ⊛🐾) The Cypress Hotel could well be your one-stop shop in Eastend as it includes functional rooms, a cafe (The Loft) and bar. Built in 1914, it is hard to miss – it's the brick cube on the town's main street.

Jack's Cafe   CANADIAN $

(☏306-295-3313;   www.facebook.com/jackscafe 326; 326 Red Coat Dr; mains from $10; ⊙9am-8:30pm) A local favorite serving up steaks, pizza and pasta on the main street.

Maple Creek

Founded in 1883, this small town right on the railroad main line has an attractive center and makes a good stop, 8km off the Trans-Canada Hwy (Hwy 1). Jasper St, one of the town's main shopping strips, makes for a nice stroll. The town is a gateway to Cypress Hills Interprovincial Park and has activities and services.

🛏 Sleeping & Eating

★ **Ghostown Blues B&B**   B&B $$

(☏306-661-8481; www.ghostownblues.com; Box 744, Maple Creek; cabin from $145; ℗⊛🐾) Stay in historic cabins for a fun experience just west of Maple Creek. This is a full service bed and breakfast, though with shared bathroom facilities. Cabins have fireplaces with firewood provided and Ghostown Blues regularly hosts concerts. Check the website for availability and pricing for each individual cabin. You can even sleep in a sheep wagon.

★ **Shop Bakery & Deli**   BAKERY $

(☏306-662-2253;   www.theshopmc.com;   113 Harder St; bread from $4.50; ⊙6am-6pm Mon-Fri) Lovingly run by Chef Jordyn, this place will meet all your bread, bakery, pastry and coffee needs during the day in the middle of Maple Creek. The cheese platter bento box with French baguette ($14.99) makes a filling lunch. Good outdoor seating.

Cypress Hills Interprovincial Park

The contrasts within this isolated interprovincial park (www.cypresshills.com; ℗) straddling the Alberta–Saskatchewan border are arresting: endless prairies turn to undulating hills forested with cypress, harboring inland lakes. Elk, deer, moose and birdlife flourish in this fertile sanctuary. Each of the two sections has a distinctly different feel. We recommend exploring both to get the full perspective.

The small town of Maple Creek is a gateway to the park. It has a historic main street and good cafes, plus activities and services.

◉ Sights & Activities

★ Fort Walsh
National Historic Site
HISTORIC SITE

(☎306-662-3590; www.parkscanada.ca/fortwalsh; off Hwy 271, Cypress Hills Interprovincial Park; adult/child $10/5; ⊙9:30am-5:30pm daily Jul & Aug, 9:30am-5:30pm Tue-Sat Jun & Sep; P) Amid rolling prairies at the eastern edge of the Western Block is this interesting historic site. Established in 1875 and operational for eight years, this outpost had a small yet significant role in the history of the west. After the battle of Custer's Last Stand, Chief Sitting Bull and 5000 of his followers arrived in the area. The local mounties moved their headquarters to Fort Walsh and maintained peaceful relations with the Sioux while they remained in Canada.

Treeosix Adventure Parks
ADVENTURE SPORTS

(☎306-663-1221; www.treeosix.com; off Hwy 21 S; adventures from $65; ⊙10am-6pm) The friendly outdoorsy folks at Treehills will have you whizzing above the forest floor on Saskatchewan's only zip-line canopy tour in next to no time. A bunch of other adrenaline-fueled activities including slacklining, rock-wall climbing, axe-throwing and, our fave, the treetop free fall, are available. Reservations recommended.

🛌 Sleeping

Cypress Hills Campgrounds
CAMPGROUND $

(☎Centre Block reservations 855-737-7275; www.cypresshills.com; tent & RV sites $16-36; P) The popular Cypress Hills Centre Block campgrounds fill up over weekends and on holidays: five campgrounds accommodate more than 600 campsites with a range of services and hookups. It's best to reserve ahead in summer at www.saskparks.net. The Western Block has more than 350 sites near Elkwater.

Resort at Cypress Hills
RESORT $$

(☎306-662-4477; www.resortatcypresshills.ca; 5 Pine Ave; r from $125; P⊖🕸🌊🎧) Surrounded by a dense thicket of cypress, this sprawling woody resort has a bunch of comfortable motel rooms, cabins (great value) and town houses. There's an on-site restaurant and a plethora of fun activities to enjoy within the park.

Elkwater Lake
Lodge & Resort
RESORT $$

(☎403-893-3811; www.elkwaterlakelodge.com; 401 4th St, Elkwater, Alberta; r from $150, cabins from $190; P⊖🕸🎧🌊) Occupying a lakeside spot on the Alberta side of Cypress Hills Interprovincial Park, at the picturesque township of Elkwater Lake, this quiet resort offers a wide variety of comfortable, modern rooms and suites, some with Jacuzzis and fireplaces. All are decorated in a style befitting the woodsy location.

ℹ️ Information

Cypress Hills Interprovincial Park Visitors
Centre
(☎306-662-5411; www.cypresshills.com; off Hwy 221, Centre Block; ⊙hours vary) Near the main entrance to the park's Centre Block, this is an essential stop.

Qu'Appelle Valley

The Qu'Appelle Valley's wide river and gently rolling hills highlight Saskatchewan's remarkable contrasts.

Heading northeast from Regina on Hwy 10, don't be afraid to get off the main road and explore. After 70km, pass through **Fort Qu'Appelle** and turn right on Hwy 56 toward the village of **Lebret** and the beautiful fieldstone **Sacred Heart Church**, completed in 1925. Spin around and ponder the ominous **Stations of the Cross** and **Chapel on the Hill**. You can walk up there if you feel inspired.

Take Hwy 22 off Hwy 10 for the tiny village of **Abernethy** and the nearby historic park.

Katepwa Beach is a small waterfront village on scenic Hwy 56. There's a lovely grassy campground and swimming spot with walking trails, picnic areas and shady trees.

◉ Sights

Motherwell Homestead
National Historic Site
HISTORIC SITE

(www.pc.gc.ca; Hwy 22, Abernethy; adult/child $4/2; ⊙10am-4pm daily Jul & Aug, 10am-4pm Mon-Fri Jun; P) Some 3km south of Abernethy, Motherwell Homestead National Historic Site is a fascinating early Saskatchewan farm where you can make hay with huge draft horses and meet characters dressed up in period costume. A small cafe serves homemade lunches.

🛌 Sleeping & Eating

Sunday's Log Cabins
CABIN $$

(☎306-621-3900; www.sundayslogcabins.com; off Hwy 56, Katepwa Beach; cabins from $129;

VEREGIN & THE DOUKHOBORS

A century ago in mother Russia lived a group of people called the Doukhobors. Oppressed because of their pacifist leanings and opposition to the Orthodox church, 7500 Doukhobors immigrated to Canada in 1899. Their benefactor? Leo 'War and Peace' Tolstoy. Today, this tiny hamlet is a withering outpost from that era.

Learn the story of Veregin's Russian roots at the **National Doukhobor Heritage Village** (☑306-542-4441; www.ndhv.ca; Hwy 5; adult/child $5/3; ☉10am-6pm mid-May–mid-Sep), a living artifact of provincial life in the early 1900s. Against a backdrop of historic grain elevators, a compound of buildings furnished in period style are open to the public. If you're lucky, there'll be bread baking.

Veregin is about 70km northeast of Yorkton via Hwys 9 and 5.

☉May-Oct; P ☎) These four handsome, well-maintained log cabins offer all the comforts of home in an almost beachfront setting. Follow Hwy 56 until you come to Katepwa Point Provincial Park, and turn south to get to the park beach; the cabins are across the street, next to the store.

Main Beach Bar and Grill PUB FOOD $
(☑306-332-4696; www.katepwahotel.com; Hwy 56, Katepwa Beach; mains from $9; ☉11am-8:30pm) If it's a sunny day, linger a while here. It's open year-round, serving cold beer and the best (and only) pub grub in town. There's a fantastic large patio overlooking the park and the lake.

Manitou Beach

Near the town of Watrous, Manitou Lake is a hidden gem. The lake is one of only three places in the world with Dead Sea–like waters full of minerals and salt, meaning that you can't sink! The others are Karlovy Vary in the Czech Republic and the Dead Sea itself. If the cool waters of the lake don't appeal, there's an indoor heated pool in town.

Right on the water, the village feels like a throwback to a simpler time. In the 1920s and '30s it was extremely popular, with thousands coming to enjoy the mineral waters and beach during summer. There were three large dance halls, two indoor bathhouses, restaurants, cafes and apparently bootleggers and a brothel too. Things went downhill during the Great Depression, but today there's a new energy in Manitou Beach to return to the glory days.

🍴 Sleeping & Eating

⭐**Lakeside Country Inn** INN $$
(☑306-946-3456; www.lakesidemanitou.com; 504 MacLachlan Ave; r from $109; P ☉ ❊ ☎) This

lovely spot just back from the lake offers excellent, super-clean rooms, a complimentary breakfast and lots of enthusiasm. There are hydrobikes, paddleboards, funboat and canoe for rent, and a private pontoon.

⭐**Oda Coffee & Wine Bar** CANADIAN $$
(☑306-952-5493; 305 MacLachlan Ave; mains from $15; ☉4-9pm Mon-Wed, from 11am Thu & Fri, from 9am Sat & Sun) The top spot to eat and chill out is on the waterfront with both indoor and outdoor seating. The food is excellent and there's a good, reasonably priced wine selection. Sit outside and enjoy the beach and lake if you get the chance. Check out the Facebook page.

SASKATOON

Saskatoon is full of hidden treasures. Head into the downtown core and inner neighborhoods to get a sense of this vibrant city. The majestic South Saskatchewan River winds through downtown, offering beautiful, natural diversions. Leafy parks and rambling riverside walks help you make the most of long, sunny summer days, and there are plenty of great spots to stop for a refreshing drink and a chat with locals.

Saskatoon knows how to heat up cold winter days and short summer nights, with a proud heritage of local rock and country music and a vibrant live-music scene. Local girl Joni Mitchell made good and there are plenty hoping to follow. If you only have time for one Saskatchewan stop, make it Saskatoon.

👁 Sights

The river is crossed by a gaggle of attractive bridges including the rickety 1907 **Victoria Bridge** and the soaring 1908 **Canadian**

Pacific Railway Bridge. The banks are lined with walking and cycling paths that link serene parks throughout the center, including **Kiwanis Memorial Park** and **River Landing**.

Just west of the center, **Riversdale** is an old and gentrifying neighborhood with creative boutiques and eateries. South of the river, **Nutana**, especially the **Broadway** area, is a great place to wander for a day of food, drinks and music.

★**Meewasin Valley**   NATURE RESERVE
(www.meewasin.com) The Meewasin Valley, formed by the South Saskatchewan's wide swath through the center of town, is named for the Cree word for 'beautiful'. Mature trees populate the riverbanks, while sections of the 60km **Meewasin Trail**, extend from downtown paths, winding through forests and along the riverbank. It is popular with walkers, cyclists and wandering travelers, and picnic areas line the trails. Further north, **Mendel Island** is home to abundant wildlife. The website has downloadable maps and info.

★**Remai Modern**   GALLERY
(✆306-975-7610; www.remaimodern.org; 102 Spadina Cres E; adult/child $12/10; ◷10am-5pm Tue-Sun) A huge attraction that anchors River Landing, Remai Modern is a museum of modern and contemporary art for Saskatoon. It has 11 gallery spaces over three floors, learning studios, a theater, restaurant, store, lounges and play areas. There are changing exhibitions, so check the website for what's coming up.

Western Development Museum   MUSEUM
(WDM; ✆306-931-1910; www.wdm.ca/saskatoon; 2610 Lorne Ave S; adult/child $12/5; ◷9am-5pm; P) The flagship Saskatoon branch of the province's Western Development Museum is a faithful re-creation of Saskatoon the boom town, c 1910. Inside Canada's longest indoor street, you can roam through the town's many buildings, from a dentist's office straight out of a horror film to the pharmacy, the walls of which are lined with hundreds of vintage concoctions. There are trains, tractors, buggies, sleighs and a jail. It's about 4km south of downtown.

Wanuskewin Heritage Park   PARK
(✆306-931-6767; www.wanuskewin.com; Penner Rd, off Hwy 11; adult/child $10/7; ◷9am-4:30pm; P) Devoted to the history of the province's first inhabitants, this riverside heritage park 17km northeast of Saskatoon interprets a 7000-year history. At Wanuskewin (wah-nus-*kay*-win; Cree for 'seeking peace of mind') you can wander interpretive trails through the 116 hectares of grassy hills and valley meadows, discovering some of the 19 pre-contact sites. Invisible from the surrounding prairie, the untouched Opamihaw Valley is a spiritual and sacred place. Cultural dance performances take place on summer afternoons.

Children's Discovery Museum   MUSEUM
(✆306-249-3574; www.wonderhub.ca; 950 Spadina Cres E; $8; ◷9am-6pm Tue-Sun; ♠) Saskatoon's children's museum, also known as Wonderhub, is making the most of its location down by the river with three floors of fun for kids. Parks Canada is in there with a glimpse into Saskatchewan's national parks and experiences (such as touch-and-feel animal footprints), while there are play areas and all sorts of learning experiences.

Saskatchewan Railway Museum   MUSEUM
(✆306-382-9855; www.saskrailmuseum.org; off Hwy 60; adult/child $6/4; ◷10am-5pm Fri-Sun May-Sep; P) The railroad opened up Saskatchewan to settlers and was a vital lifeline for getting grain to market. This museum shows how things were when rails, not roads, were the most important links in the province. It's west of the center on Hwy 7, then 2km south on Hwy 60.

Ukrainian Museum of Canada   MUSEUM
(✆306-244-3800; www.umc.sk.ca; 910 Spadina Cres E; adult/child $8/6; ◷10am-5pm Tue-Sat, 1-5pm Sun; P) This museum tells the story of Ukrainian immigration to Canada. With an emphasis on traditional clothing and contemporary artwork, it provides a good insight into the world of Ukrainian Canadians. Check out the gift shop for *pysanka* (decorated Easter eggs).

 Activities

Prairie Lily   CRUISE
(✆306-955-5459; www.theprairielily.com; 950 Spadina Cres E; adult/child from $25/16; ◷hours vary) The Prairie Lily riverboat runs popular sightseeing, dinner and specialty cruises, such as Sunday brunch cruises, on the South Saskatchewan River from its dock beside the

Saskatoon

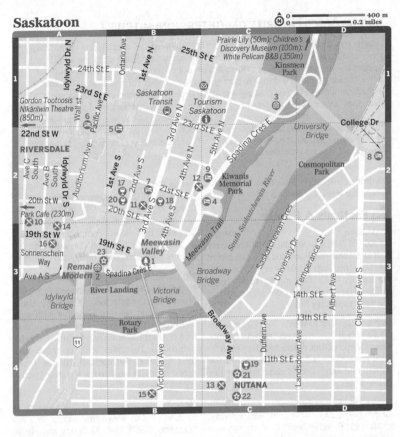

N 0 _____ 400 m
0 _____ 0.2 miles

SASKATOON'S FAVORITE DAUGHTER: JONI MITCHELL

Legendary Canadian singer-songwriter Joni Mitchell lived in Saskatchewan towns Maidstone and North Battleford before her family moved to Saskatoon when she was 11. Apparently she wasn't the best of students when it came to formal education, but had a free-thinking outlook and took to poetry, taught herself guitar and sang with friends around campfires. Her first paid gig was at the Louis Riel coffeehouse in Saskatoon's Broadway area in 1962 in order to earn 'smoking money.' What happened after that is history, with Joni Mitchell winning nine Grammy awards as a singer-songwriter and receiving countless prestigious honors. Saskatoon has honored her with plaques on Broadway, outside what was the Louis Riel coffeehouse, at River Landing and by naming a road Joni Mitchell Promenade.

Children's Discovery Museum. Check the website for weekly schedules.

🎪 Festivals & Events

Saskatoon Ex CARNIVAL
(☑ 306-931-7149; www.saskatoonexhibition.ca; cnr Ruth St & Lorne Ave, Prairieland Park; adult/child $16/12; ☺ mid-Aug) Saskatoon comes alive for the Ex, with live music, racing pigs, chuck-wagon races and rides to reacquaint you with your fairy floss.

Taste of Saskatchewan FOOD & DRINK
(☑ 306-975-3175; www.tasteofsaskatchewan.ca; Kiwanis Memorial Park; ☺ mid-Jul) More than 30 local restaurants sell various treats over five days in mid-July; there is also a full schedule of live music.

Saskatoon Fringe Festival THEATER
(☑ 306-664-2239; www.25thstreettheatre.org; ☺ Jul/Aug) Rough-edged acts, music and avant-garde theater quirk up the streets and performance halls in late July or early August.

Sasktel Saskatchewan Jazz Festival MUSIC
(☑ 306-652-1421; www.saskjazz.com; ☺ Jun) Come show your soul patch at this jazzy festival, Saskatchewan's largest, at venues throughout town from late June. Some events are free.

🛏 Sleeping

White Pelican B&B B&B $
(☑ 306-249-2645; www.whitepelican.ca; 912 Queen St; s/d from $80/105; ☺ ✷ 🛜) This three-room B&B is in a comfy 100-year-old house close to the river and the downtown parks. Two rooms share a bathroom. Prices include a choice of continental, hot or vegetarian breakfast. Promisingly, the owners have written a breakfast cookbook.

Inn on College GUESTHOUSE $
(☑ 306-665-9111; www.innoncollege.com; 1020 College Dr; s/d from $65/72; P ☺ ✷ 🛜) Saskatoon's best-value digs, this home-style property has clean, compact rooms and a communal kitchen. It's a satisfying 15-minute walk across the bridge to the center.

★ James Hotel BOUTIQUE HOTEL $$
(☑ 306-244-6446; www.thejameshotel.ca; 620 Spadina Cres E; r from $160; P ☺ ✷ 🛜) Attentive service at the James begins with your welcome to the property. From the minimalist yet sumptuous rooms featuring marble bathrooms, balconies and top-notch bedding to the stylish cocktail bar, the James gets it right. It's close to the riverfront parks; try for a room with a view.

★ Hotel Senator HISTORIC HOTEL $$
(☑ 306-244-6141; www.hotelsenator.ca; 243 21st St E; r from $99; P ☺ ✷ 🛜) Dating from 1908, this well-maintained and updated hotel is creaky but cool. You can get a sense of the ornate past in the lobby. The pub is a good place to while away the night, and you can't beat the location – everything is a short walk away.

★ Delta Bessborough HERITAGE HOTEL $$
(☑ 306-244-5521; www.marriott.com; 601 Spadina Cres E; r from $150; P ☺ ✷ 🛜 ☷) In the grand tradition of the famed Canadian railway hotels, the Bessborough, opened in 1935, lives up to the castle standard; it is the architectural exclamation point on the Saskatoon skyline. The refurbished interior blends modern pastel styling with grand post-deco architecture. Rooms and suites come in many shapes and sizes. Relax in the lush public gardens.

Hilton Garden Inn HOTEL $$
(☑ 306-244-2311; www.hiltongardeninn3.hilton. com; 90 22nd St E; r from $120; P ☺ ✷ 🛜 ☷)

There are great views from this high-rise hotel downtown. Rooms are large and blandly corporate; you can't beat the location.

Holiday Inn
Saskatoon Downtown HOTEL **$$**
(☑ 306-986-5000; www.ihg.com; 101 Pacific Ave; r from $120; P ☻ ✳ ☎ ☒) A vision in grey, this modern, high-rise Holiday Inn is right in the center. Rooms are bright, airy and stylish. Splurge for the fantastic penthouse suite with a grand piano and pool table.

✖ Eating

A rich tradition of farm-to-table cuisine is evident in Saskatoon's many restaurants. Graze your way around downtown, Riversdale and Broadway.

★ Drift Sidewalk
Cafe & Vista Lounge CAFE **$**
(☑ 306-653-2256; www.driftcafe.ca; 339 Ave A S; lunch mains from $8; ⊙ 8am-10pm Mon-Thu, 8am-11pm Fri & Sat, 10am-3pm Sun) Split personalities mark this hip Riversdale spot. The cafe serves crepes, sandwiches and a long list of varied snacks through the day; enjoy a coffee at a table outside. The lounge is sleeker and has a fun cocktail list, many with housemade libations. It also serves mid-priced international dishes.

Homestead Ice Cream ICE CREAM **$**
(☑ 306-653-5588; www.homesteadicecream.ca; 822 Victoria Ave; treats from $2.50; ⊙ noon-10pm) A red-and-white vision of fun, this old-style ice-cream parlor is in a residential neighborhood close to Nutana. The list of flavors is endless; enjoy them outside under a pine tree.

Asian Hut ASIAN **$**
(☑ 306-954-0188; www.facebook.com/asianhutres taurant; 320 Ave C S; mains from $8; ⊙ 11am-2pm & 5-9pm Tue-Fri, 11am-9pm Sat & Sun) There's a down-at-the-heels hipster vibe at this Riversdale outpost for cheap and cheerful Asian food. People line up for the fresh and tasty Chinese, Vietnamese and Thai fare.

Saskatoon Farmers Market MARKET **$**
(☑ 306-384-6262; www.saskatoonfarmersmarket. com; 414 Ave B S; ⊙ market 10am-3pm Wed & Sun, 8am-2pm Sat, cafes 10am-3pm Tue-Sun) In the River Landing area, this market has an indoor area with cafes and stalls open through the year, but the main action is outside on market days in summer, especially Saturdays.

Park Cafe CAFE **$**
(☑ 306-652-6781; www.parkcafe.ca; 515 20th St W; mains from $8; ⊙ 8am-4pm) For breakfasts to fuel your adventures, this unassuming Riversdale joint serves up legendary morning platters: the hash browns are works of art, as are the onion rings.

★ Cathedral Social Hall PUB FOOD **$$**
(☑ 306-668-1011; www.cathedralsocialhall.com; 608 Spadina Cres E; mains from $14; ⊙ 11am-midnight) CSH focuses on local Saskatchewan fare and beer, including gluten-free and vegetarian options. Try the Beer Soup ($8) or the Social Hall Burger ($15) out on the front terrace, along with your choice from the 30 taps.

Berry Barn CAFE **$$**
(☑ 306-978-9797; www.berrybarn.ca; 830 Valley Rd; lunch mains from $13; ⊙ 11am-8pm Mon-Fri, from 9am Sat & Sun) The highly commercial Berry Barn, 15km south of town, has the expected over-cluttered gift shop as well as a popular cafe. Enjoy the riverside setting, and in summer pick some juicy Saskatoon berries – plump dark blue numbers that are like sweet boysenberries. Feast on hearty fare and all manner of berry-laced drinks, mains and desserts.

Calories Restaurant CANADIAN **$$**
(☑ 306-665-7991; www.caloriesrestaurant.ca; 721 Broadway Ave; lunch mains from $12; ⊙ 11am-10pm Mon-Thu, to 11pm Fri & Sat) Menus change regularly at this classy yet casual affair on Broadway that is proud of its commitment to using local, organic ingredients in its creative cuisine. With an extensive wine list, a Sunday brunch menu to look forward to, and a dessert counter that will make you drool, you can't go wrong. Outside tables, too.

Christie's Il Secondo CAFE **$$**
(☑ 306-384-0506; www.christiesbakery.com; 802c Broadway Ave; mains from $15; ⊙ 8am-8pm Tue-Sat) Fresh pizzas, daily-baked bread specials and delicious Italian-style filled sandwiches are popular at this Nutana institution. Tables inside and out are always busy.

★ Ayden Kitchen and Bar CANADIAN **$$$**
(☑ 306-954-2590; www.aydenkitchenandbar.com; 265 3rd Ave S; mains from $22; ⊙ 5:30-9pm Mon-Sat) ✐ Saskatoon's restaurant-of-the-moment works magic with local produce and other seasonal specialties. Chef Dale MacKay is a star on the Canadian food

scene. You never know what surprises he has in store at this unpretentious downtown bistro. Book ahead.

 Drinking & Nightlife

★**Shelter Brewing Co** MICROBREWERY
(☑ 306-979-9249; www.shelterbrewing.ca; 255 2nd Ave S; ⊘4-11pm Tue-Thu, from 3pm Fri & Sat) Shelter Brewing goes off with locals, with some extremely tasty brews and tacos options. The core brews are solid with a great New England IPA and a classic Brown Ale.

★**Hose & Hydrant Brew Pub** PUB
(☑ 306-477-3473; www.hoseandhydrant.com; 612 11th St E; ⊘11am-late) A fun pub in the Broadway area in what was Firehall No 3, built in 1911 and now a heritage-listed building. Enjoy tables on a patio and deck with mellow side-street outlooks.

Congress Beer House PUB
(☑ 306-974-6717; www.congressbeerhouse.com; 215 2nd Ave S; ⊘11am-late) This huge pub has a bit of a ski-lodge vibe. Seating is at tables and in comfy leather booths. As you'd surmise, the beer list is one of the best around, with numerous choices of craft brews. The food options are excellent, with creative takes on burgers and other pub faves (mains $10 to $20).

Winston's English Pub & Grill PUB
(☑ 306-374-7468; www.hotelsenator.ca/winstons-pub; 243 21st St E; ⊘11am-2am) A huge and popular pub with 72 taps. Besides a predictable domestic and imported lineup, the beer list includes a rotating array of excellent local microbrews. The food is solid: fish-and-chips, burgers and the like (mains from $12). Lots of big screens for sports.

Diva's Nightclub GAY & LESBIAN
(☑ 306-665-0100; www.divasnightclub.com; 220 3rd Ave S; ⊘9pm-late Wed-Sat) Gay or straight, you don't have to be a diva to get your groove on at this straight-friendly gay bar. Enter through the alley.

☆ **Entertainment**

Persephone Theatre THEATER
(☑ 306-384-7727; www.persephonetheatre.org; 100 Spadina Cres E) This perennial theatrical standout has excellent quarters in the Remai Arts Centre at River Landing. Comedy, drama and musicals are all regulars.

Gordon Tootoosis Nīkānīwin Theatre THEATER
(GTNT; ☑ 306-933-2262; www.gtnt.ca; 808 20th St W) Contemporary stage productions by Canadian First Nations, Métis and Inuit artists highlight cultural issues through comedy and drama.

Broadway Theatre CINEMA
(☑ 306-652-6556; www.broadwaytheatre.ca; 715 Broadway Ave) This historic cinema on Broadway shows cult classics and art-house films, and has live performances and other events.

Saskatoon Blades HOCKEY
(☑ 306-975-8844; www.saskatoonblades.com; 3535 Thatcher Ave, SaskTel Centre; adult/child from $25/15; ⊘Sep-Mar) This WHL team plays a fast, rough and sharp style of hockey.

Buds on Broadway LIVE MUSIC
(☑ 306-244-4155; http://buds.dudaone.com; 817 Broadway Ave; ⊘4pm-late) Classic blues and old-time rock and roll are the standards here in this beer-swilling joint. Check the website for upcoming live music and jam nights.

🔒 **Shopping**

Wanuskewin Gift Store GIFTS & SOUVENIRS
(☑ 306-931-9933; 810 Broadway Ave; ⊘10am-5:30pm Mon-Sat) Lovely store on Broadway selling authentic, handmade items made by local First Nation artisans. Pieces are unique and beautifully handcrafted using traditional techniques.

ⓘ **Information**

Main Post Office (☑ 800-267-1177; www.canadapost.ca; 309 4th Ave N; ⊘8am-5pm Mon-Fri)
Planet S (www.planetsmag.com) Irreverent and free biweekly newspaper with good entertainment listings.
Saskatoon City Hospital (☑ 306-655-8000; www.saskatoonhealthregion.ca; 701 Queen St; ⊘24hr)
Tourism Saskatoon (☑ 306-242-1206, 800-567-2444; www.tourismsaskatoon.com; 202 4th Ave N; ⊘8:30am-5pm Mon-Fri) Has local and regional info.

ⓘ **Getting There & Away**

AIR

John G Diefenbaker International Airport
(YXE; ☑ 306-975-8900; www.skyxe.ca; 2625 Airport Dr) is 5km northeast of the city, off Idylwyld Dr and Hwy 16. Westjet and Air Canada have services to major Canadian cities.

LA RONGE & THE FAR NORTH

La Ronge is the southern hub of the far north – your last chance for supplies before heading off the grid. It's a rough, basic town, popular with anglers, hunters and folks on the run.

It's hard to believe that almost half of Saskatchewan still lies further north. This is frontier territory, the end of the paved road. If you're not skittish about extreme isolation and you're outfitted appropriately, then this is it! You'll discover tiny burgs such as **Southend**, and pass the vast **Reindeer Lake**, before arriving at the winter-only section at **Stony Rapids**, some 12 hours north of La Ronge. Self-sufficiency here is key: make sure you maintain your vehicle, have plenty of fuel, gear and supplies, and keep your head together.

TRAIN

Saskatoon's **train station** (Chappell Dr) is 8km southwest from downtown; the thrice-weekly VIA Rail *Canadian* stops here on its Vancouver–Toronto run.

ⓘ Getting Around

A taxi to the airport or train station costs about $20. **Blueline Taxi** (☎0191-262-6666; www.unitedgroup.ca) is easily reached.

Bike Doctor (☎306-664-8555; www.bikedoctor.ca; 623 Main St; per day from $60) rents bikes.

Saskatoon Transit (☎360-975-7500; www.transit.saskatoon.ca; 226 23 St E; adult/child $3/2.25) runs city buses, which converge on the transit hub of 23rd St E (between 2nd and 3rd Aves N).

NORTHERN SASKATCHEWAN

North of Saskatoon, driving options funnel into one northern route as the scenery changes around you. Gone are the vast wheat fields of the south, replaced by rugged boreal forests and myriad lakes. There is a cultural shift up here too: an independent spirit that carved a life out of the rugged landscape.

ⓘ Getting There & Away

To discover this region, you'll want your own wheels.

The Battlefords

Linked by bridge across the North Saskatchewan River, Battleford and its larger sibling North Battleford seem only slightly removed from a century ago, when they embodied the hardscrabble existence of early prairie settlers.

◉ Sights

Western Development Museum MUSEUM
(WDM; ☎306-445-8083; www.wdm.ca; Hwy 16, at Hwy 40, North Battleford; adult/child $10/4; ☉9am-5pm daily Apr-Dec, 9am-5pm Tue-Sun Jan-Mar) The re-created town at North Battleford's branch of the WDM is an insight into the immense amount of labor required by the pioneers to convert prairie to farmland. Walking along the boardwalk-covered streets and through the preserved houses, it's easy to imagine how hard life would have been.

Allen Sapp Gallery GALLERY
(☎306-445-1760; www.allensapp.com; 1 Railway Ave E, North Battleford; by donation; ☉11am-5pm daily Jun-Sep, noon-4pm Wed-Sun Oct-May) Art lovers will be enthralled by this gallery right on Hwy 4 in North Battleford. Sapp's work, depicting his Cree heritage, is a breathtaking mix of landscapes and portraits.

Fort Battleford
National Historic Site HISTORIC SITE
(☎306-937-2621; www.pc.gc.ca/en/lhn-nhs/sk/battleford; off Hwy 4, Battleford; adult/child $4/2; ☉10am-4pm daily Jul & Aug, 10am-4pm Mon-Fri Jun) At this historic site, costumed guides and cannon firings give life to the North-West Mounted Police (NWMP) fort, built in 1876.

Prince Albert

Prince Albert (PA) has a dilapidated yet evocative old brick downtown in a pretty location beside the North Saskatchewan River.

WORTH A TRIP

BATOCHE NATIONAL HISTORIC SITE

A virtual civil war was fought at the **Batoche National Historic Site** (☎306-423-6227; www.pc.gc.ca/en/lhn-nhs/sk/batoche; Rte 225; adult/child $7.80/free; ⊙9am-5pm daily Jul & Aug, 9am-5pm Mon-Fri Jun & Sep) in what is known as the Northwest Resistance of 1885, when Louis Riel led the Métis in defending their land from the government. Once-prosperous Batoche was devastated and within a few years almost nothing was left except for the church you see today. This historic site is an auspicious place to contemplate the events of 1885, as silent waves of prairie grass bend in the wind. Batoche is 70km north of Saskatoon, east of Hwy 11.

The children of French fur traders and indigenous mothers, the Métis were forced from Manitoba in the mid-1800s and many made their home in Batoche. Frustrated by the government's continual betrayal of treaties, the Métis and a number of Cree declared their independence from Canada: an announcement met by military force, led by Major General Frederick Middleton. Although outnumbered by 800 to 200, the Métis fought for four days and almost won, but Riel was captured (and later hanged for treason).

Established in 1776 as a fur-trading post, PA was later named after Queen Victoria's husband, Prince Albert of Saxe-Coburg-Gotha, who died in 1861. Prince Albert became the capital of the District of Saskatchewan, a regional administrative division of what then constituted the Northwest Territories, and there were hopes for a great future. This ended in 1905 when Saskatchewan became a full province and Regina became the new provincial capital. PA's plans for growth at the time were based on the hope that the Transcontinental Railroad would pass through the city, but the Canadian Pacific Railway chose a more southerly route.

These days, PA is the gear-up spot for trips to the forested and lake-riddled north and Prince Albert National Park.

Sleeping

★Keyhole Castle B&B B&B $$
(☎306-763-3321; www.keyholecastle.com; 1925 1 Ave E; r from $159; P ⊖ ❄ ⊜) This is an opportunity to stay in an extraordinary 'castle', built during Prince Albert's boom times in the early 1900s, when it was believed that the Transcontinental Railroad would be going through town. In the East Hill neighborhood, it's a designated National Historic Site, and has two stunning B&B rooms, and even a ballroom on the top floor.

Prince Albert National Park

Prince Albert National Park is a jewel in the wild. Just when you thought the vast prairie would never end, the trees begin, signaling the start of the vast boreal forest. This national park is one of those special places that will give you the feeling that you are truly on the edge of the known world. The quaint little resort village of Waskesiu Lake is your base for exploration within the park.

Sights & Activities

Prince Albert National Park PARK
(☎306-663-4522; www.parkscanada.ca/princealbert; adult/child $8/4) A forested sanctuary of lakes, untouched land and wildlife, this park puts the 'wild' back into 'wilderness.' Outdoor activities such as canoeing, hiking and camping are at their shining best here. Indeed, there is a multitude of potential adventures to be had here, whether it be the unforgettable 20km trek to **Grey Owl's Cabin**, a canoe trip or even just chilling out on a beach.

Waskesiu Marina BOATING
(☎306-663-1999; www.waskesiumarina.com; Waskesiu Lake; kayaks per hr from $20) Waskesiu Marina rents canoes, kayaks and motorboats. It has guided boat trips to Grey Owl's Cabin ($500 for up to six people) or you can rent a boat (from $370) for a self-guided tour.

Sleeping & Eating

★Hawood Inn LODGE $$
(☎306-663-5911; www.hawood.com; 188 Waskesiu Lake, Waskesiu Lake; r from $140; P ⊖ ❄ ⊜) This family-run place right on the waterfront in the little resort village of Waskesiu Lake is a good spot to relax. There's a good dining

room and lounge, rooftop hot tubs, and nearby shops, restaurants and activities. Chill out in the fireside lobby.

Patio Cafe
CAFE $

(☑306-663-5233; 929 Waskesiu Dr, Waskesiu Lake; pastries from $3; ☺8am-10:30pm) The spot to come for cafe eats and coffees in Waskesiu, with a solid menu including burgers, salads, pizzas and Mexican, along with muffins and baked goods. Enjoy the sun out on the patio.

❶ Information

Prince Albert National Park Visitor Center (☑306-663-4522; www.pc.gc.ca; 969 Lakeview Dr, Waskesiu Lake; ☺7am-8pm Jun-Aug) Has park information.

Waskesiu Chamber of Commerce (☑306-663-5410; www.waskesiulake.ca; 35 Montreal Dr, Waskesiu Lake; ☺9am-5pm Jul & Aug, reduced hours Sep-Jun) For regional information.

Alberta

POP 4,067,000

Best Places to Eat

➜ Corso 32 (p568)

➜ Market (p579)

➜ 49° North Pizza (p620)

➜ Trough (p591)

Best Places to Stay

➜ Deer Lodge (p606)

➜ Tekarra Lodge (p612)

➜ Mt Engadine
Lodge (p588)

➜ Varscona (p566)

Why Go?

Alberta does lakes and mountains like Rome does cathedrals and chapels, but without the penance. For proof head west to Jasper and Banff, two of the world's oldest national parks; despite their wild and rugged terrain, they remain untrammeled and easily accessible. They're majestic, breathtaking, awesome. No one should leave without first laying eyes on Peyto Lake and the Columbia Icefield, nor before traveling east to the fossil-encrusted badlands around Drumheller, south to the Crypt Lake trail in Waterton Lakes National Park, and north to spot bison in the vast, empty northern parklands.

In the center of the province, the wheat blows and the cattle and pronghorn roam; here you'll find historic ranches, sacred native sights and the eerie, martian landscape of the hoodoos. Calgary has become unexpectedly cool, with top museums and cocktail bars, while Edmonton's fringe theater festival is the world's second largest.

When to Go
Edmonton

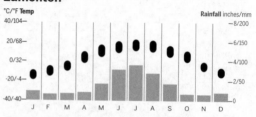

Jul Prime time for festivals, with Edmonton's Street Performers and the Calgary Stampede.

Jul–Sep Banff and Jasper's trails are snow-free, making a full range of hikes available.

Dec–Feb Winter-sports season in the Rocky Mountains.

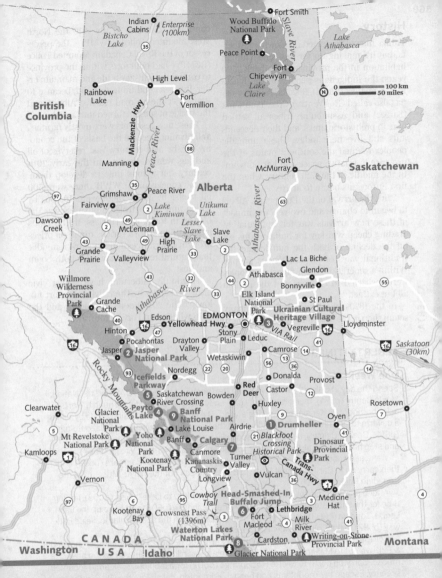

Alberta Highlights

1 **Royal Tyrrell Museum of Palaeontology** (p614) Exploring Jurassic remnants.

2 **Miette Hot Springs** (p607) Soaking amidst spectacular mountain peaks.

3 **Ukrainian Cultural Heritage Village** (p567) Stepping back in time to the days of new immigrants.

4 **Peyto Lake** (p593) Taking in its otherworldly emerald waters.

5 **Icefields Parkway** (p592) Driving between towering mountains and stunning vistas.

6 **Head-Smashed-In Buffalo Jump** (p617) Delving into the fascinating history of First Nations culture.

7 **National Music Centre** (p574) Learning about music at Calgary's newest museum.

8 **Waterton Lakes National Park** (p619) Exploring fairy-tale scenery by kayak.

9 **Lake Agnes Teahouse** (p606) Enjoying glacial-water tea high above bluer-than-blue Lake Louise. in Banff NP.

History

Things may have started off slowly in Alberta, but it's making up for lost time. Human habitation in the province dates back 7500 years: the indigenous peoples of the Blackfoot, Kainaiwa (Blood), Siksika, Peigan, Atsina (also called Gros Ventre), Cree, Tsuu T'ina (Sarcee) and Assiniboine tribes all settled here in prehistoric times, and their descendants still live here today. These nomadic peoples roamed the southern plains of the province in relative peace and harmony until the middle of the 17th century, when the first Europeans began to arrive.

With the arrival of the Europeans, Alberta began to change and evolve – the impact of these new arrivals was felt immediately. Trading cheap whiskey for buffalo skins set off the decline of both the buffalo and the traditional ways of the indigenous people. Within a generation, the indigenous peoples were restricted to reserves and the buffalo all but extinct.

In the 1820s, the Hudson's Bay Company set up shop in the area, and European settlers continued to trickle in. By 1870 the North West Mounted Police (NWMP) – the predecessor of the Royal Canadian Mounted Police (RCMP) – had built forts within the province to control the whiskey trade and maintain order. It was a good thing they did, because 10 years later the railroad reached Alberta and the trickle of settlers turned into a gush.

These new residents were mostly farmers, and farming became the basis of the economy for the next century. Vast reserves of oil and gas were discovered in the early 20th century, but it took time to develop them. At the conclusion of WWII there were 500 oil wells; by 1960, there were 10,000, by which time the petroleum business was the biggest in town. Nevertheless, in the 1980s and again in 2016, a serious dip in oil prices brought heavy recession – a stark reminder that natural resources can offer both boom and bust.

Thankfully, Albertans have strong civic pride, as shown by the rallying support following the 2013 floods in Calgary and the 2016 wildfires in Fort McMurray.

ALBERTA ITINERARIES

One Week

Spend the day in Calgary (p571) exploring the Glenbow Museum (p574) and the National Music Centre (p574), then grab a meal on trendy 17th Ave or wander through the artsy neighborhoods of Kensington and Inglewood. The next day, get into dino mode by taking a day trip to Drumheller (p614) and visiting the Royal Tyrrell Museum of Palaeontology (p614). Back in Calgary, head east to spot wild bison at Elk Island National Park (p570) and step back in time at the authentic Ukrainian Cultural Heritage Village (p567).

Wake early and head west. Have fresh bagels for breakfast in Canmore (p589) and then carry on to Banff National Park (p585) and check out the Whyte Museum of the Canadian Rockies (p595).

After a stay in Banff, follow the scenic Bow Valley Pkwy to Lake Louise (p603), finding time for the short, steep hike to the Lake Agnes Teahouse (p606) and a trip up the Lake Louise Gondola (p603) to spot grizzly bears. Head out on the spectacular Icefields Parkway (p592) to the Columbia Icefield (p593).

Roll into Jasper (p607) and check into Tekarra Lodge (p612) for some much-needed R & R. Drive out to Maligne Lake (p607), where a short hike might let you spot a bear or a moose. Carry on north to Miette Hot Springs (p607) for a fabulous soak amid mountain scenery. Escape the mountains and head to Edmonton, diving into the Old Strathcona neighborhood, and finishing your Alberta adventure with a gourmet meal at Corso 32 (p568).

The Complete Rockies

Follow the One Week itinerary, but before reaching Canmore, head south down Hwy 5, known as the Cowboy Trail (p584), to take in Bar U Ranch (☑403-395-3044; www.parkscanada.gc.ca/baru; Hwy 22, Longview; adult $7.80; ☺10am-5pm mid-May–Sep). Continue south, detouring a bit to see Head-Smashed-In Buffalo Jump (p617) and then continuing to Waterton Lakes National Park (p619), experiencing this less-visited mountain paradise. Return north through Kananaskis Country (p585), stopping for tea or an overnight stay at Mt Engadine Lodge (p588). Then carry on north to Canmore (p589).

Land & Climate

The prairies that cover the eastern and southern parts of Alberta give way to the towering Rocky Mountains that form the western edge of the province. That mountainous spine forms the iconic scenery for which Alberta is known.

Alberta is a sunny sort of place; any time of year you can expect the sun to be out. Winters can be cold, when the temperature can plummet to a bone-chilling -20°C (-4°F). Climate change has started to influence snowfall, with the cities receiving less and less every year.

Chinook winds often kick up in the winter months. These warm westerly winds blow in from the coast, deposit their moisture on the mountains and give Albertans a reprieve from the winter chill, sometimes increasing temperatures by as much as 20°C (36°F) in one day!

Summers tend to be hot and dry; the warmest months are July and August, when the temperature sits at a comfortable 25°C (77°F). The 'June Monsoon' is often rain-filled, while the cooler temperatures and fall colors of September are spectacular.

ℹ Information

Travel Alberta (☑ 800-252-3782; www.travel alberta.com) Links to info on parks and visitor centers across the province.

ℹ Getting There & Away

AIR

The two major airports are in Edmonton and Calgary, and there are daily flights to both from major hubs across the world. Carriers serving the province include Air Canada, American Airlines, British Airways, Delta, Horizon Air, KLM, United Airlines and WestJet.

BUS

There is service via Red Arrow (https://red arrow.ca) to much of the province.

Moose Bus Adventures (☑ 604-297-0255; https://moosebus.travel) runs a variety of trips in western Canada. Tours start in Vancouver or Banff and along the way hit the highlights of the mountain parks and other Alberta must-sees. In winter it operates ski-focused tours that are a great option for car-less ski bums. Trips depart daily during the summer months and a few times per week in the winter season.

CAR & MOTORCYCLE

Alberta was designed with the automobile (and an unlimited supply of gas) in mind. There are high-quality, well-maintained highways and a

➡ Population: 4,067,175

➡ Area: 642,317 sq km

➡ Capital: Edmonton

➡ Quirky fact: A relative of the T-rex, the Albertosaurus was first discovered in the Horseshoe Canyon in 1884.

network of back roads to explore. Towns will for the most part have services, regardless of the population.

Be aware that in more remote areas, especially in the north, those services could be a large distance apart, and often you will be hours between cell service areas. Fill up your gas tank wherever possible and be prepared for possible emergencies with things like warm clothes and water.

TRAIN

Despite years of hard labor, countless work-related deaths and a reputation for being one of the great feats of 19th-century engineering, Alberta's contemporary rail network has been whittled down to just two regular passenger train services. **VIA Rail** (☑ 888-842-7245; www. viarail.ca) runs from Vancouver to Toronto two or three times per week, passing through Jasper and Edmonton in both directions. Edmonton to Vancouver costs $225 and takes 27 hours; Edmonton to Toronto costs $405 and takes 55 hours. The Toronto-bound train stops in Saskatoon, Saskatchewan; Winnipeg, Manitoba; and Sudbury Junction, Ontario. VIA Rail also operates the train from Jasper to Prince Rupert, BC ($117, 32 hours, three weekly).

Rocky Mountaineer (☑ 604-606-7200; www. rockymountaineer.com; 2/5/14/21 days from $1250/2010/4660/7580; ⊘ May-Oct) tours chug east from Vancouver through the Rockies via Kamloops to Jasper or Banff, or north from Vancouver to Jasper via Whistler and northern BC. These luxury trains have been transporting tourists on multiday journeys for a quarter century.

EDMONTON

☑ 780 / POP 932,000

Modern, spread out and frigidly cold for much of the year, Alberta's second-largest city and capital is a government town that you're more likely to read about in the business pages than the travel supplements. Edmonton is often a stopover en route to Jasper National Park, four hours' drive west, or explorations into the vast and empty landscape to the north.

Downtown has changed a lot in the past few years since Roger's Place was completed. Chic upscale shops and eateries sit in stark

Edmonton

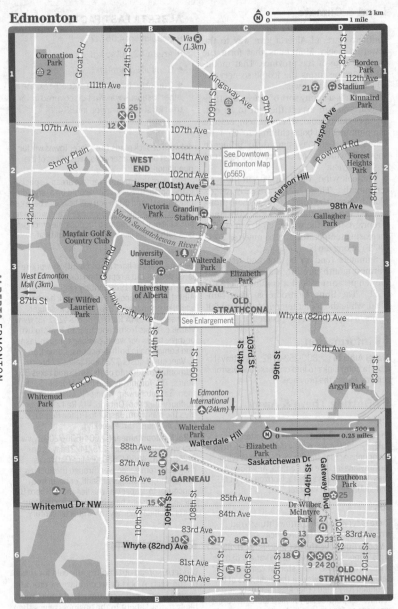

See Downtown Edmonton Map (p565)

See Enlargement

contrast to the homeless people outside. For the soul of the city, head south of the river to the university district and Whyte Ave, home to small theaters, diners and a spirited Friday-night mood. Edmonton also has a few decent museums, an annual fringe festival second only to Edinburgh's, and some top

nearby sights like the Ukrainian Cultural Village and Elk Island National Park.

History

The Cree and Blackfoot tribes can trace their ancestry in the Edmonton area for 5000

Edmonton

years. It wasn't until the late 18th century that Europeans first arrived in the area. A trade outpost was built by the Hudson's Bay Company in 1795, which was dubbed Fort Edmonton.

Trappers, traders and adventurers frequented the fort, but it wasn't until 1870, when the government purchased Fort Ed and opened up the area to pioneers, that Edmonton saw its first real growth in population. When the railway arrived in Calgary in 1891, growth really started to speed up.

Meanwhile, the indigenous tribes had been severely weakened by disease and the near extinction of their primary food source, the bison. Increasingly vulnerable, they signed away most of their land rights to the Canadian government in a series of treaties between 1871 and 1921 in return for money, reservation lands and hunting rights.

In the 1940s, WWII precipitated the construction of the Alaska Hwy, and the influx of workers further increased the population. Ukrainians and other Eastern European immigrants came to Edmonton in search of work and enriched the city.

Edmonton is again the hub for those looking to earn their fortune in the north. But it isn't gold or roads this time – it's oil.

In 2016, a terrifying forest fire raced through the Fort McMurray area, claiming no fatalities but burning hundreds of homes and thousands of acres. Edmonton was the main city to help out, offering temporary shelters and relocation, as well as food and supplies. That fire is history, but the threat remains, and tourists should heed fire warnings carefully.

◎ Sights

★ **Art Gallery of Alberta** GALLERY
(Map p565; ☑780-422-6223; www.youraga.ca; 2 Sir Winston Churchill Sq; adult/child $13.13/8.93; ◎11am-5pm Tue-Sun, to 8pm Thu) With the opening of this maverick art gallery in 2010, Edmonton at last gained a modern signature building to counter the ubiquitous boxy skyscrapers with its giant glass-and-metal space helmet. Its collection comprises 6000 pieces of historical and contemporary art, many of which have a strong Canadian bias, that rotate through eight galleries. Numerous worthwhile temporary shows also pass through, and you'll find a shop, cafe and restaurant on-site.

Telus World of Science MUSEUM
(Map p562; ☑780-451-3344; www.telusworldofscience.com; 11211 142nd St; adult/child $26/18; ◎9am-5pm Oct-Apr, to 6pm May-Sep; ⊞) With an emphasis on interactive displays, this science museum has a million things to do, all under one roof, including a planetarium. Fight crime with the latest technology, see what living on a spacecraft is all about, go on a dinosaur dig and explore what makes the human body tick. The center also includes an IMAX theater (extra cost) and an observatory with telescopes (no extra cost).

Ukrainian Museum of Canada MUSEUM
(Map p562; www.umcalberta.org; 10611 110th Ave; by donation; ◎9:30am-4:30pm Mon-Fri May-Aug)

Given Edmonton's huge Ukrainian population and long history of immigration, this museum is surprisingly small. While it continues to search for bigger digs, it shows a tiny collection of traditional costumes, toys and artwork. The cultural center in the same building hosts pierogi suppers on the last Friday of each month (adult/child $17/6). Check its website (www.uocc-stjohn.ca) for details.

North Saskatchewan River Valley PARK
(Map p562) Edmonton has more designated urban parkland than any other city in North America, most of it contained within an interconnected riverside green belt that effectively cuts the metropolis in half. The green zone is flecked with lakes, bridges, wild areas, golf courses, ravines, and approximately 160km worth of cycling and walking trails. It is easily accessed from downtown.

Royal Alberta Museum MUSEUM
(Map p565; ☑780-453-9100; www.royalalberta museum.ca; 103A Ave; adult/child $19/10; ☺10am-5pm Sep–mid-May, 10am-6pm mid-May–Sep, to 8pm Thu & Fri) Since getting its 'royal' prefix in 2005 when Queen Liz II dropped by, Edmonton's leading museum has a new downtown home, which opened in 2018. The museum is the largest in western Canada, with an enormous collection of Alberta's natural and cultural history, featuring interactive exhibits and live animals.

Alberta Railway Museum MUSEUM
(☑780-472-6229; www.albertarailwaymuseum. com; 24215 34th St; adult/child $10/5; ☺10am-5pm Sat & Sun mid-May–Aug) This museum, on the northeast edge of the city, has a collection of more than 75 railcars, including steam and diesel locomotives and rolling stock, built and used between 1900 and 1950. On weekends, volunteers fire up some of the old engines, and you can hop on the diesel locomotives or the 1913 steam locomotive on holiday weekends.

👉 Tours

Quirky free walking tours of downtown are offered in the summer months by students on vacation and employed by the Downtown Business Association. They leave weekdays at 1pm from the corner of 104th St and 101st Ave.

⭐**Cobblestone Freeway** CULTURAL
(☑780-436-7482; http://cobblestonefreeway.ca; day tours from $89) These tours have knowledgeable guides with strong links to the local Ukrainian community. You can experience traditional dance performances, authentic Ukrainian food and heritage sights, and neighboring Ukrainian communities. The tours can also get you to the city's must-see sights or as far afield as Jasper. Especially great at tailoring tours to travelers' interests; service is both personable and professional.

Edmonton Ghost Tours WALKING
(www.edmontonghosttours.com; per person $15; ☺9pm Mon-Thu Jul & Aug) Spooky walking tours led by storytellers recounting the ghostly history of Edmonton. Tours cover various neighborhoods; check the website to see where to meet. No booking is required; just turn up 15 minutes early.

🎭 Festivals & Events

Edmonton International Fringe Festival THEATER
(www.fringetheatre.ca; tickets $13-16; ☺mid-Aug) The ultimate Edmonton experience is an 11-day program of live alternative theater on outdoor stages, in the parks, and in small theaters and venues. It's second in size only to the Edinburgh Fringe Festival. Many shows are free and no ticket costs more than $16. There's no booking – you choose a theater and stand in line.

International Street Performers Festival THEATER
(www.edmontonstreetfest.com; ☺2nd week Jul) Sometimes the best theater is outside. International performers perform alfresco in this busker bonanza. Performers are curated and most strut their stuff in Sir Winston Churchill Sq. Shows are by donation in the pass-the-hat fashion.

K-Days CARNIVAL
(www.k-days.com; ☺late Jul) For years, Capital Ex (Klondike Days) was the big summer festival in Edmonton. Since 2012, it has been known as K-Days, with less focus on goldrush history and more on contemporary fun. Big names in music grace two stages, the midway has adrenaline-charged rides and you'll still find a nugget's worth of olden-days fun.

🛏️ Sleeping

While many hotels in the city bank on visitors traveling on an expense account, Edmonton has a decent range of independent accommodations, including some with some

Downtown Edmonton

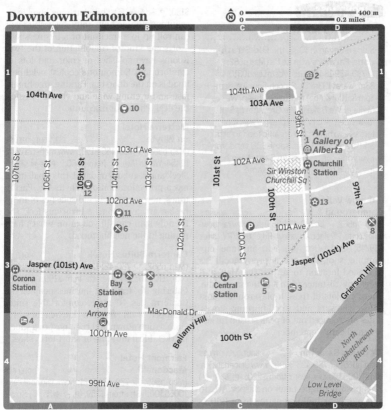

N 0 ————————— 400 m
   0 ————————— 0.2 miles

ALBERTA EDMONTON

Downtown Edmonton

character. If you are in town mainly to visit the West Edmonton Mall, then staying in or near it is feasible, but the digs there are definitely leaning toward the touristy side of the spectrum.

HI Edmonton Hostel   HOSTEL **$**
(Map p562; ☑780-988-6836; www.hihostels.ca; 10647 81st Ave; dm/d with shared bath $42/94,

d $109; ℗@☎) In the heart of Old Strathcona, this busy hostel is a safe bet. Many of the rooms are a bit jam-packed with bunks and it feels somewhat like a converted old people's home (it used to be a convent), but renovations have brightened things up and produced a fantastic outdoor patio. The location and price are hard to beat.

FARMERS MARKET

Since it began in 1983, the **Old Strath-cona Farmers Market's** (Map p562; ☑780-439-1844; https://osfm.ca; 10310 83rd Ave, at 103rd St; ⊙noon-5pm Tue, 8am-3pm Sat Jul & Aug) motto has been 'We Make it! We Bake it! We Grow it! We Sell it!' Inside the city's old bus garage, it offers everything from organic food to arts and crafts, and hosts some 130 vendors. Everyone comes here on Saturday morning. You'd be wise to do the same.

Rainbow Valley

Campground & RV Park   CAMPGROUND $
(Map p562; ☑780-434-5531; www.rainbow-valley.com; Rainbow Valley Rd; tent/RV sites $39/45; ⊙May-Oct; P) For an inner-city camping spot, this one is pretty good. It's in a good location to get to 'The Mall' and keep some distance from it at the same time. There are lots of trees, a playground, cookhouse, showers and wood-burning stoves. Rates are reduced out of peak season (ie late May and early September).

★Union Bank Inn   BOUTIQUE HOTEL $$
(Map p565; ☑780-423-3600; www.unionbankinn. com; 10053 Jasper Ave; r from $220; P❄@🛜) This posh boutique hotel on Jasper Ave, in a former bank building dating from 1910, is an upscale masterpiece. With just 40 rooms, the staff will be at your beck and call, and the in-room fireplaces make even Edmonton's frigid winters almost bearable. There's an equally fancy restaurant – Madison's Grill (p568) – on the ground floor.

★Matrix   BOUTIQUE HOTEL $$
(Map p565; ☑780-429-2861; www.matrixed monton.com; 10640 100th Ave; r from $170; P⊖ ❄@🛜) Modern and slick, the lobby here could be James Bond's living room, complete with brushed aluminum panels, low leather furniture, and a large glassed-in fireplace. Rooms are similarly stylish with plenty of up-to-date gadgets. Service is stellar and genuine, breakfasts are mammoth, there's free wine and cheese in the evening, and a shuttle downtown. What more could you want?

★Varscona   BOUTIQUE HOTEL $$
(Map p562; ☑780-434-6111; www.varscona.com; 8208 106th St, cnr Whyte Ave; r incl breakfast from

$180; P⊖❄@🛜) This charming hotel is elegant but not too hoity-toity, suggesting you can roll up in a tracksuit or a business suit – or some kind of combination of the two. Rooms have splashes of color and lots of comfort, and Edmonton's coolest neighborhood is on the doorstep. Parking, free breakfast, and evening wine and cheese sweeten the deal. Phone for discounts.

Metterra Hotel

on Whyte   BOUTIQUE HOTEL $$
(Map p562; ☑780-465-8150; www.metterra.com; 10454 Whyte Ave; r from $160; P⊖❄@🛜) Sleek and regularly updated, this small hotel has a prime location on Whyte Ave. Earthy tones, new mattresses and splashes of Indonesian art give rooms a luxurious feel. The friendly staff can fill you in on what's happening in the neighborhood.

Canterra Suites Hotel   HOTEL $$
(Map p562; ☑780-421-1212; www.canterrasuites. com; 11010 Jasper Ave; ste from $199; ⊖❄🛜) Catering to traveling businesspeople, the Canterra has 40 large, comfortable suites equipped with modern kitchenettes. It's close to downtown and right next to a supermarket. Ideal for long- or short-term stays.

Fairmont Hotel

Macdonald   HOTEL $$$
(Map p565; ☑780-424-5181; www.fairmont.com; 10065 100th St; r from $259; P⊖❄🛜▨) Stealing the best nook in town (as Fairmont always does), Edmonton's historic Fairmont Hotel exhibits the usual array of intricate stucco, Italian marble, ornate chandeliers and lush carpets. In the early 20th century it was one in a luxurious chain of railway hotels that dotted the cross-continental line from east to west. The top two floors were remodeled in 2019.

🍴 Eating

Edmonton's food scene reflects its multiculturalism and if you're willing to hunt around, you can get a quality meal at any price. The most varied and economical place to eat is on or around Whyte Ave, while the best downtown nexus is Jasper Ave or the rejuvenated warehouse district north of Jasper Ave on 104th St.

★Duchess Bake Shop   BAKERY, CAFE $
(Map p562; ☑780-488-4999; www.duchessbake shop.com; 10720 124th St; baked goods from $2, breakfast & lunch $8-13; ⊙9am-7pm Tue-Fri, 10am-6pm Sat, to 5pm Sun) Duchess is a destination.

You'd cross town to eat here – barefoot in snow if necessary. Feeling like it dropped straight from France, complete with Louis XV–style chairs, the Duchess' French-press coffee and huge array of fresh baking leave you spoiled for choice. Mocha meringues, cream-cheese-and-leek croissants, and cherry basil eclairs are just the tip of the iceberg.

Duchess is also famous for its macarons. Try the salted caramel and you'll know why. Arrive early, before the queuing locals have stripped the cases bare. There's an affiliated provisions shop next door where you can pick up the cookbook, coffee and kits for baking at home.

★ **Block 1912** CAFE $
(Map p562; 780-433-6575; www.block1912. com; 10361 Whyte Ave; snacks $6.50-15; ⊙9am-11pm Sat-Thu, to midnight Fri) A regal attempt at a genuine Torinese coffee bar, this inviting place allows you to recline on European-style sofas and armchairs and enjoy your coffee, beer or wine beneath twinkly lights. Grab a snack or something more substantial like coffee-crusted steak or Thai chicken. Gelato comes in fab flavors like green apple or white-chocolate mousse and desserts are drool-worthy.

Remedy Cafe INDIAN $
(Map p565; 780-757-7720; http://remedycafe.ca; 10279 Jasper Ave; coffee & chai $3-5, mains $8-10; ⊙7:30-midnight Mon-Fri, from 8am Sat & Sun;) The 'remedy' here is cheap, authentic Indian food served in an ultra-casual cafe – meaning you can use wi-fi with one hand and dip your naan in curry sauce with the other. Everyone raves about the chai and butter chicken, but there are also good cakes (vegans catered for) and excellent masala dosas (curried vegetables in a crisp pancake).

The larger, original **branch** (Map p562; 780-433-3096; 8631 109th St; coffee & chai $3-5, mains $8-17; ⊙7:30am-midnight Mon-Fri, from 8am Sat & Sun;) is in Garneau on the south side of the river.

Café Mosaics VEGETARIAN $
(Map p562; 780-433-9702; www.cafemosaics. com; 10844 Whyte Ave; mains $7-18; ⊙11am-9pm Mon-Thu, 10am-10pm Fri & Sat, 10am-9pm Sun;) A Strathcona institution, this artsy, cool vegetarian-vegan haunt is a meat-free zone that has taken a page out of San Francisco's book: it makes vegetable dishes both interesting and tasty. Think earthy and clean, rather than hippy and crusty. As a litmus test, check the number of carnivores who take a day off meat to come here.

ALBERTA EDMONTON

LOCAL KNOWLEDGE

EDMONTON'S UKRAINIAN COMMUNITIES

If you've been in Edmonton for any length of time, you may well be wondering, 'Why all the pierogies?'. Between the 19th and early 20th century, around 250,000 Ukrainians immigrated to Canada, settling in farming communities on the prairies where the landscape reminded them of the snowy steppes of home. Today the Ukrainian population in Canada is second only to that in Russia and Ukraine itself, and many famous Canadians trace their roots back to Ukraine, including Wayne Gretzky and Randy Bachman. The largest number of Ukrainian-Canadians live in and around Edmonton and, with nearly 11% of the city's population claiming Ukrainian heritage, the cultural influence extends far beyond pierogies.

It is difficult not to feel the presence of Ukrainians in Edmonton. There are stores and restaurants, dance groups and choirs, and domes decorating the skyline. The culture is very alive and very present. One of the most interesting ways to experience it is to explore the **Ukrainian Cultural Heritage Village** (780-662-3640; https://ukrainianvillage.ca; adult/child/family $15/10/40; ⊙10am-5pm May-Sep) with its character role players acting out what life in a rural Ukrainian-Canadian community would have been like. You can also check out other towns near the city, including **Vegreville**, with the world's largest Easter egg; **Mundare**, with a giant Ukrainian sausage; and **Glendon**, with the biggest – you guessed it – pierogi.

But today's Ukrainian-Canadian culture isn't just grandmas pushing pierogies; many young Edmontonians are full of Ukrainian pride. There are many Ukrainian specialty restaurants, and the churches often have special pierogi nights and sell bulk pierogies to take home for emergencies. To experience Ukrainian culture firsthand, check out Cobblestone Freeway (p564), which runs both city and regional tours.

Meat
RIBS **$$**

(Map p562; ☏587-520-6338; www.meatford inner.com; 8216 104th St; mains $16-28; ⊙5-10pm Mon-Thu, to 11pm Fri, 11am-11pm Sat, to 10pm Sun) Spicy fried chicken, pulled pork by the pound and beef brisket are why people pack into this tasty restaurant night after night. It's got decent beers on draft and a nice cocktail selection, but more than anything people come here for the (wait for it)...meat.

Tiramisu Bistro
ITALIAN **$$**

(Map p562; ☏780-452-3393; http://tiramisu bistro.ca; 10750 124th St; pastas $17-24; ⊙8am-9pm Mon-Thu, to 10pm Fri, 9am-10pm Sat, to 4pm Sun; 🖖) This bistro serves fresh salads, wraps, panini and pasta, but its risottos are the coup. Mornings bring breakfast pizzas and crepes with fillings like elk cherry sausage. It also has a kids' menu that assumes children like food beyond chicken strips. If you're ordering takeout, opt for the 'spaghetti cone,' which, like it sounds, is spaghetti you can hold in your hand.

Three Boars Eatery
TAPAS **$$**

(Map p562; ☏780-757-2600; www.threeboars.ca; 8424 109th St; small plates $16-24; ⊙5pm-midnight Tue-Thu, to 2am Fri & Sat, to 1am Sun) 🌱 Three Boars is part of the burgeoning farm-to-table food movement, using local suppliers to create gourmet food. It specializes in small plates, fine Edmonton microbrews on draft and divinely crafted cocktails. If you have an appetite for a large Alberta steak, this isn't your bag. If you're up for tasting a liver 'bomb' or smoked quail, it definitely is.

Blue Plate Diner
CAFE **$$**

(Map p565; ☏780-429-0740; www.blueplate diner.ca; 10145 104th St; mains $9-18; ⊙7:30am-9pm Mon-Thu, to 10pm Fri, 9am-10pm Sat, to 9pm Sun; 🖖) 🌱 In a redbrick building in Edmonton's warehouse district, this diner serves healthy food in hearty portions with vegetarian options. And there's style, too. Cool colored lighting and exposed brickwork mean you can eat locally grown veggies without feeling as if you've joined a hippie commune. The creative menu is well executed, there's an excellent kids' menu, and the desserts? Mmm...

Try the tofu stir-fry or steak sandwich and enjoy larger-than-average plates of crisp, locally grown vegetables. Alternatively, go for the enormous sticky buns, available weekends only, which the menu claims are 'larger than your head' (not quite, but they're big, trust us!).

Da-De-O
CAJUN **$$**

(Map p562; ☏780-433-0930; www.dadeo.ca; 10548a Whyte Ave; mains $15-30; ⊙11:30am-10pm Mon, Tue & Thu, to 11pm Fri & Sat, noon-9pm Sun) An unexpected summoning up of the Big Easy in the frozen north, this retro diner – complete with red vinyl chairs, chrome kitchen tables and a jukebox – whips up Cajun calamari, oysters, jambalaya and southern fried chicken. Plucked straight out of Louisiana legend are the spice-dusted sweet-potato fries and the ginormous po'boys (especially the blackened catfish). No minors allowed.

Tokyo Noodle Shop
JAPANESE **$$**

(Map p562; ☏780-430-0838; www.tokyonoodle shop.com; 10736 Whyte Ave; mains $11-27; ⊙11:30am-9:30pm Mon-Wed, to 10pm Thu, to 10:30pm Fri & Sat, 11:30am-9pm Sun) Great sushi and noodles by the gallon, plus bento boxes, rice bowls and all the tasty appetizers you'd expect in an authentic Japanese restaurant. Nothing fancy, but that's the point.

★ Corso 32
ITALIAN **$$$**

(Map p565; ☏780-421-4622; www.corso32.com; 10345 Jasper Ave; mains $31-36; ⊙5-10pm Sun-Thu, to 11pm Fri & Sat) Chef and owner, Daniel Costa, delivers the best of Italy. Classy, small and candlelit, with a narrow interior and minimalist decor, Corso 32's evolving menu features dishes with ingredients like homemade goat ricotta, rabbit and pancetta ragu or black truffle honey. The pasta is all handmade and the wine list is the best in Edmonton (if you're into Italian tipples).

Madison's Grill
FUSION **$$$**

(Map p565; ☏780-401-2222; www.unionbank inn.com/madisons-grill; 10053 Jasper Ave; mains $36-51; ⊙7am-10pm Mon-Fri, 8-11am & 5-10pm Sat, 8-11am & 5-9pm Sun) Located in the posh Union Bank Inn (p566), Madison's has no problem keeping up with the hotel's high standards of service and quality. Its delicate dishes are beautifully presented; try pork-cheek pierogi with Saskatoon berries, seared halibut with basil gnocchi, or fig- and brie-stuffed chicken roulade wrapped in prosciutto. The three-course meal with wine pairing for $105 is well worth it.

Hardware Grill
STEAK **$$$**

(Map p565; ☏780-423-0969; www.hardwaregrill. com; 9698 Jasper Ave; mains $32-50; ⊙5-9:30pm Mon-Thu, to 10pm Fri & Sat) A plush oasis in a converted brick building downtown, this restaurant is a comfortable, bustling place where you'll want to linger over the amazing wine list and original menu. Try crabcrusted salmon, crispy duck and waffle or bacon-wrapped elk, all with a side of mac 'n' cheese.

 Drinking & Nightlife

The best nightlife scene has traditionally centered on or around Whyte Ave in Old Strathcona. Clubs open and close in a blink; bars tend to stay longer. Some bars host music and/or DJs.

★**Baijiu**   COCKTAIL BAR
(Map p565; 📞780-421-7060; www.baijiuyeg.com; 10359 104 St NW; ⊘5pm-midnight Tue-Thu, to 1am Fri & Sat) Baijiu is where anyone wanting great cocktails goes, but it's tough to describe the place exactly. First one thinks tiki, but it's not quite that. Then one thinks dance club, but it's not that either. The long bar, dim lights and talented bartenders are what make it great for drinks, but the food's good, too.

Yellowhead Brewery   GAY & LESBIAN
(Map p565; 📞780-423-3333; www.yellowhead brewery.com; 10229 105th St NW; ⊘11am-9pm Thu-Sat, 10am & 1pm Sun brunch seatings) First things first. This isn't a pub per se. Nor is it gay per se. It's an all-welcome tasting room next door to a brewery where you can sup on Yellowhead's tasty offerings, which range from its flagship lager to a tasty and refreshing pale ale. It also serves small plates and offers brewery tours if you book in advance.

Cavern   WINE BAR
(Map p565; 📞780-455-1336; www.thecavern.ca; 10169 104th St NW; ⊘11am-8pm Mon-Thu, to 11pm Fri & Sat) 🍴 This industrial and candlelit small cafe is an underground bastion of good taste on in-vogue 104th St, particularly in the deli department (plates $6 to $22). You can browse the glass cabinet filled with divine cheese before you choose, and wash it down with a glass of wine. There are even instructions on how to make a great cheese board.

Transcend Coffee   COFFEE
(Map p562; 📞780-756-8882; www.transcend coffee.ca/garneau; 8708 109th St; coffee $4-6.50; ⊘7am-9pm Mon-Fri, 8am-9pm Sat, 8am-6pm Sun; 📶) 🍴 In a city where cafes producing their own micro-roasted coffee beans are few, Transcend should be treated like gold dust. Expert baristas on first-name terms with their Guatemalan farmer-producers concoct cups of their own roasted coffee with

enough precision to satisfy a severely decaffeinated Seattleite. In a renovated theater, this spot is hip but not remotely pretentious.

Black Dog Freehouse   PUB
(Map p562; 📞780-439-1089; www.blackdog.ca; 10425 Whyte Ave; ⊘2pm-2am) Insanely popular with all types, the Black Dog is essentially a pub with some hidden extras: a rooftop patio, known as the 'wooftop patio,' a traditional ground-floor bar (normally packed cheek by jowl on weekday nights), and a basement that features live music, DJs and occasional parties. The sum of the three parts has become a rollicking Edmonton institution.

☆ **Entertainment**

Theater! Don't leave Edmonton without trying some. *See* and *Vue* are free local alternative weekly papers with extensive arts and entertainment listings. For daily listings, see the entertainment section of the *Edmonton Journal* newspaper.

Garneau Theatre   CINEMA
(Map p562; 📞780-425-9212; www.metrocinema. org; 8712 109th St NW; adult/child $13/8) Edmonton's only surviving art deco–era cinema has operated under various guises since 1940, changing hands most recently in 2011. It's

ELK ISLAND NATIONAL PARK

In case you hadn't noticed, there are five national parks in Alberta, and three of them *aren't* Jasper or Banff. Overshadowed by the Gothic Rockies, tiny **Elk Island National Park** (☑780-922-5790; www.parkscanada.gc.ca/elkisland; adult/child/senior $7.80/free/6.80, campsites & RV sites $25.50, campfire permits $8.80; ☺visitor center 8:30am-5:30pm, gates 24hr) attracts just 5% of Banff's annual visitor count despite its location only 50km east of Edmonton. Not that this detracts from its attractions. The park – the only one in Canada that is entirely fenced – contains the highest density of wild hoofed animals in the world after the Serengeti. If you come here, plan on seeing the 'big six' – plains bison, wood bison, mule deer, white-tailed deer, elk and the more elusive moose. It's also an official Dark Sky preserve, offering great night views for skywatchers.

The wood bison live entirely in the quieter southern portion of the park (which is cut in two by Hwy 16), while the plains bison inhabit the north. Most of the infrastructure lies in the north, too, around **Astotin Lake**. Here you'll find a campground, a nine-hole golf course (with a clubhouse containing a restaurant), a beach and a boat launch. Four of the park's 11 trails lead out from the lakeshore through trademark northern Albertan aspen parkland – a kind of natural intermingling of the prairies and the boreal forests.

Public transportation to the park is nonexistent. Car hire or a private tour are the best options.

filled with vintage decor, some original and some not, but who cares when you roll in for a *Trainspotting* matinee and the concession stand is selling beer?

Roxy Theatre
THEATER
(Map p562; ☑780-453-2440; www.theatre network.ca; 8529 Gateway Blvd) This theater opened after Theatre Network's beloved 1940s Roxy theater burned down. Nevertheless, it keeps things eclectic, showing burlesque, live bands and comedy.

New Varscona Theatre
THEATER
(Map p562; ☑780-433-3399; www.varscona theatre.com; 10329 83rd Ave; tickets from $15) There are only 176 precious seats at the Varscona, a cornerstone of the Old Strathcona theater district that puts on 350 performances annually of edgy plays, late-night comedy and morning kids' shows.

Blues on Whyte
LIVE MUSIC
(Map p562; ☑780-439-9381; www.bluesonwhyte. com; 10329 Whyte Ave) This is the sort of place your mother warned you about: dirty, rough, but still somehow cool. It's a great place to check out some live music; blues and rock are the standards. The dance floor is small but hopping. There are also pool tables and a games room.

Princess Theatre
CINEMA
(Map p562; ☑780-433-0728; www.princess theatre.ca; 10337 Whyte Ave; tickets adult/student & child $11/8) The Princess is a grand old theater that defiantly sticks her middle finger up at the multiplexes that are dominant elsewhere. Dating from the pre-talkie days (1914), it screens mainstream, first-run, arthouse and classic films. Tickets for Mondays and weekend matinees are reduced ($6).

Citadel Theatre
THEATER
(Map p565; ☑780-425-1820; www.citadeltheatre. com; 9828 101A Ave; tickets $35-115; ☺Sep-May) Edmonton's foremost theater company, with a large indoor garden and multiple stages, is based right in downtown's Winston Churchill Sq. Expect glowing performances of Shakespeare and Stoppard, Dickens adaptations and the odd Sondheim musical.

Edmonton Oilers
SPECTATOR SPORT
(Map p565; www.edmontonoilers.com; tickets from $41) To avoid any embarrassing situations, wise up on the Oilers before you arrive in Edmonton. The local National Hockey League (NHL) team dominated the game in the 1980s thanks to a certain player named Wayne Gretzky – aka 'The Great One' – but hasn't won much since. The season runs from October to April at the Roger's Place arena.

Edmonton Eskimos
SPECTATOR SPORT
(Map p562; ☑780-448-3757; www.esks.com; tickets from $45) The Eskimos take part in the Canadian Football League (CFL) from July to October at **Commonwealth Stadium** (11000 Stadium Rd).

ℹ Information

Edmonton Tourism (☏780-401-7696; https://exploreedmonton.com) A website with lots of useful links and info.

International Currency Exchange (☏780-425-5426; www.ice-canada.ca; 101 St Pedway, Edmonton City Centre West, 2nd level; ☏10am-5:25pm Mon-Fri, to 3:55pm Sat) Can exchange currencies and provide other tourist-related banking needs.

Royal Alexandra Hospital (☏780-477-4111; 10240 Kingsway Ave; ☏24hr) Has a 24-hour trauma center. Located 1km north of the downtown core.

ℹ Getting There & Away

Edmonton International Airport (YEG; ☏780-890-8382; www.flyeia.com) is about 30km south of the city along the Calgary Trail, approximately a 45-minute drive from downtown.

Red Arrow (Map p565; www.redarrow.ca; 10014 104th St; ☏5:30am-10pm Mon-Fri, from 7:30am Sat, from 8am Sun) buses stop downtown at the Holiday Inn Express and serve Calgary ($73, 3½ hours, six daily) and Fort McMurray ($90, six hours, three daily). The buses are well equipped, with wi-fi, sockets for your laptop, single or double seats, a free minibar and hot coffee.

All the major car-rental firms have offices at the airport and around town. **Driving Force** (www.thedrivingforce.com; 11025 184th St) will rent, lease or sell you a car. Check the website; it often has some good deals.

The **VIA Rail Station** (www.viarail.ca; 12360 121st St) is rather inconveniently situated 5km northwest of the city center near Edmonton City Centre Airport. The Canadian travels three times a week east to Saskatoon ($204, 10 hours), Winnipeg ($432, 25 hours) and Toronto ($937, 56 hours), and west to Jasper ($115, 6½ hours), Kamloops ($147, 19½ hours) and Vancouver ($313, 32 hours). At Jasper, you can connect to Prince George and Prince Rupert.

ℹ Getting Around

TO/FROM THE AIRPORT

Bus 747 leaves from outside the arrivals hall every 30 to 60 minutes and goes to Century Park ($5), the southernmost stop on Edmonton's Light Rail. From here regular trains connect to Strathcona and downtown.

Sky Shuttle Airport Service (☏780-465-8515; www.edmontonskyshuttle.com; adult/child $18/10) runs three different routes that service hotels in most areas of town, including downtown and the Strathcona area. The office is by carousel 12. Journey time is approximately 45 minutes. If you're looking for a lift to the airport, reserve at least 24 hours in advance.

Cab fare from the airport to downtown is about $50.

CAR & MOTORCYCLE

There is metered parking throughout the city, which is often free after 6pm. Most hotels in Old Strathcona offer complimentary parking to guests. Visitors can park their car for the day and explore the neighborhood easily on foot. Edmonton also has public parking lots, which cost about $17 per day or $1.50 per half-hour; after 6pm you can park for a flat fee.

PUBLIC TRANSPORTATION

City buses and a 16-stop Light Rail Transit (LRT) system cover most of the city. The fare is $3.50. Buses operate at 30-minute intervals between 5:30am and 1:30am. Check out the excellent transit planning resources at www.edmonton.ca. Daytime travel between Churchill and Grandin stations on the LRT is free.

Between mid-May and early September you can cross the High Level Bridge on a streetcar ($5 round-trip, every 30 minutes between 11am and 10pm). The vintage streetcars are a great way to travel to the Old Strathcona Market (103rd St at 94th Ave), where the line stops. Or go from Old Strathcona to the downtown stop, next to the Grandin LRT Station (109th St between 98th and 99th Aves).

TAXI

Two of the many taxi companies are **Yellow Cab** (☏780-462-3456; http://edmtaxi.com) and **Alberta Co-Op Taxi** (☏780-425-2525; http://co-optaxi.com). The fare from downtown to the West Edmonton Mall is about $25. Flag fall is $3.60, then it's 20¢ for every 150m. Most cab companies offer a flat rate to the airport calculated from your destination.

CALGARY

☏403 / POP 1,240,000

Calgary will surprise you with its beauty, cool eateries, nightlife beyond honky-tonk, and long, worthwhile to-do list. Calgarians aren't known for their modesty; it's their self-love and can-do attitude that got them through disastrous flooding in 2013 and, in 2016, saw them helping residents of wildfire-stricken Fort McMurray with unquestioning generosity. We mustn't forget – Calgary also hosted the highly successful 1988 Winter Olympics, elected North America's first Muslim mayor, and throws one of Canada's biggest festivals, the Calgary Stampede.

Calgary

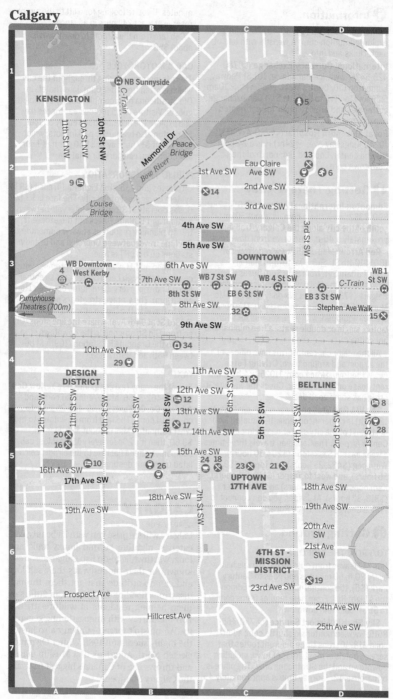

Map labels:

KENSINGTON

NB Sunnyside

C-Train

11th St NW

10A St NW

10th St NW

Memorial Dr

Bow River

Peace Bridge

5

9

Louise Bridge

1st Ave SW

Eau Claire Ave SW

14

2nd Ave SW

13

25

6

3rd Ave SW

4th Ave SW

5th Ave SW

DOWNTOWN

3rd St SW

WB Downtown - West Kerby

4

6th Ave SW

7th Ave SW

WB 7 St SW

8th St SW

EB 6 St SW

WB 4 St SW

WB 1 St SW

C-Train

Pumphouse Theatres (700m)

8th Ave SW

32

EB 3 St SW

Stephen Ave Walk

15

9th Ave SW

10th Ave SW

34

29

11th Ave SW

31

BELTLINE

DESIGN DISTRICT

12th Ave SW

12

6th St SW

5th St SW

4th St SW

2nd St SW

1st St SW

8

13th Ave SW

17

14th Ave SW

28

12th St SW

11th St SW

10th St SW

9th St SW

8th St SW

20

16

15th Ave SW

27

26

24

18

23

21

10

16th Ave SW

17th Ave SW

UPTOWN 17TH AVE

18th Ave SW

18th Ave SW

7th St SW

19th Ave SW

19th Ave SW

20th Ave SW

21st Ave SW

4TH ST - MISSION DISTRICT

19

23rd Ave SW

24th Ave SW

Prospect Ave

Hillcrest Ave

25th Ave SW

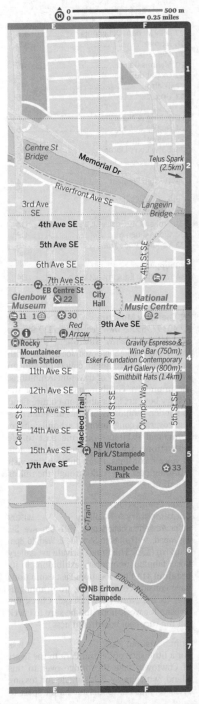

The city is waking up and smelling the single-origin home-roasted coffee, too, with top-notch craft bars, boutique shops, restaurants and entertainment venues exhibiting more color and experimentation. Long stretches of riverside jogging and even a lone surfing spot make for outdoor activities that other cities can't hold a candle to. The longer you stay, the more there is to surprise you.

History

From humble and relatively recent beginnings, Calgary has been transformed into a cosmopolitan modern city that has hosted an Olympics and continues to wield huge economic clout. Before the growth explosion, the Blackfoot people had called the area home for centuries. Eventually they were joined by the Sarcee and Stoney tribes on the banks of the Bow and Elbow Rivers.

In 1875 the North West Mounted Police (NWMP) built a fort and called it Fort Calgary after Calgary Bay on Scotland's Isle of Mull. The railroad followed a few years later and, buoyed by the promise of free land, settlers started the trek west to make Calgary their home. The Blackfoot, Sarcee and Stoney indigenous groups signed Treaty 7 with the British Crown in 1877, which ushered them into designated reservations and took away their wider land rights.

Long a center for ranching, the cowboy culture was set to become forever intertwined with the city. In the early 20th century, Calgary simmered along, growing slowly. Then, in the 1960s, everything changed. Overnight, ranching was seen as a thing of the past, and oil was the new favorite child. With the 'black gold' seeming to bubble up from the ground nearly everywhere in Alberta, Calgary became the natural choice of place to set up headquarters.

The population exploded, and the city began to grow at an alarming rate. As the price of oil continued to skyrocket, it was good times for the people of Cowtown. The 1970s boom stopped dead at the '80s bust. Things slowed and the city diversified.

The 21st century began with an even bigger boom. House prices have gone through the roof, there is almost zero unemployment and the economy is growing 40% faster than the rest of Canada. Not bad for a bunch of cowboys.

ALBERTA CALGARY

Calgary

⊙ Sights

Calgary's downtown has the Glenbow Museum and the National Music Centre, but it's the surrounding neighborhoods that hold more allure. **Uptown 17th Avenue** has some of the top restaurants and bars and is a hive of activity in the evening. **Inglewood**, just east of downtown, is the city's hippest neighborhood, with antique shops, indie boutiques and some esoteric eating options. **Kensington**, north of the Bow River, has some good coffee bars and a tangible community spirit.

★National Music Centre   MUSEUM
(☑403-543-5115; http://nmc.ca; 850 4th St SE; adult/child $18/11; ☉10am-5pm May-Aug, Wed-Sun Sep-Apr) Looking like a whimsical copper castle, this fabulous museum is entirely entertaining, taking you on a ride through Canada's musical history with rotating exhibits, cool artifacts (like the guitar Guess Who used to record 'American Woman') and interactive displays. Test your skill at the drums, electric guitar or in a sound-recording room and even create your own instruments. Don't miss the Body Phonic room or the solar-powered Skywalk with its repurposed pianos destroyed in the 2013 flood.

★Glenbow Museum   MUSEUM
(☑403-777-5506; www.glenbow.org; 130 9th Ave SE; adult/child/family $18/11/45; ☉9am-5pm Mon-Sat, noon-5pm Sun, closed Mon Oct-Jun) With an extensive permanent collection and an ever-changing array of traveling exhibitions, the impressive Glenbow has plenty for the history buff, art lover and pop-culture fiend to ponder. Temporary exhibits are often daring, covering contemporary art and culture. Permanent exhibits bring the past to life with strong historic personalities and lots of voice recordings. Hang out in a tipi, visit a trading post and walk through the railcar of a train.

Esker Foundation Contemporary Art Gallery   MUSEUM
(https://eskerfoundation.com; 1011 9th Ave SE, Inglewood; ☉11am-6pm Sun, Tue & Wed, to 8pm Thu & Fri) **FREE** This small, private art gallery hosts fabulous temporary exhibitions in its beautiful 4th-floor location. Past exhibitions have considered everything from immigration to the Northwest Passage. Check the website for workshops and be sure to check out the very cool boardroom nest.

Prince's Island Park   PARK
For a little slice of Central Park in the heart of Cowtown, take the bridge over to this island, with grassy fields made for tossing Frisbees, plus bike paths and ample space to

stretch out. During the summer months, you can catch a Shakespeare production in the park's natural grass amphitheater or check out the Folk Music Festival (p577) in July. You'll also find the upscale **River Island** restaurant here.

Watch yourself around the river. The water is cold and the current is strong and not suitable for swimming. The bridge to the island from downtown is at the north end of 3rd St SW, near the Eau Claire Market shopping area.

Heritage Park
Historical Village   HISTORIC SITE
(☑ 403-268-8500; www.heritagepark.ca; 1900 Heritage Dr SW, at 14th St SW; adult/child $26.25/13.65; ⊙ 10am-5pm daily May-Aug, Sat & Sun Sep & Oct; ⊕) Want to see what Calgary used to look like? Head down to this historical park (the largest in Canada!) where all the buildings are from 1915 or earlier. There are 10 hectares of recreated town to explore, with a fort, grain mill, church and school. Go for a hay ride, visit the antique midway or hop on a train. Costumed interpreters are on hand to answer any questions.

You can ride on the steam train, catch a trolley and even go for a spin on the SS *Moyie*, the resident stern-wheeler, as it churns around the Glenmore Reservoir. Heritage Park has always been a big hit with the kiddies and is a great place to soak up Western culture. To get there, take the C-Train to Heritage station, then bus 502. The park is 10km south of Calgary's downtown. It is a registered charity, so your money is going to a good cause.

Calgary Zoo   ZOO
(☑ 403-232-9300; www.calgaryzoo.com; 1300 Zoo Rd NE; adult/child $37/27; ⊙ 9am-5pm; ⊕) More than 1000 animals from around the world, many in enclosures simulating their natural habitats, make Calgary's zoo one of the top rated in North America. The zoo's well-regarded conservation team study, reintroduce and protect endangered animals in Canada.

Besides the animals, the zoo has a **Botanical Garden**, with changing garden displays, a **tropical rainforest**, a good **butterfly enclosure** and the 6½-hectare **Prehistoric Park**, featuring fossil displays and life-size dinosaur replicas in natural settings. There's also a captive breeding program for whooping cranes. Picnic areas, concessions and cafes dot the zoo. During winter, when neither

you nor the animals will care to linger outdoors, the admission price is reduced. To get here, take the C-Train east to the Zoo stop.

Calgary Tower   NOTABLE BUILDING
(☑ 403-266-7171; www.calgarytower.com; 101 9th Ave SW; adult/youth $18/9; ⊙ observation gallery 9am-9pm Sep-Jun, to 10pm Jul & Aug) This 1968 landmark tower is an iconic feature of the Calgary skyline, though it has now been usurped by numerous taller buildings and is in danger of being lost in a forest of skyscrapers. There is little doubt that the aesthetics of this once-proud concrete structure have passed into the realm of kitsch, but, love it or hate it, the slightly phallic 191m structure is a fixture of the downtown area.

Telus Spark   MUSEUM
(☑ 403-817-6800; www.sparkscience.ca; 220 St George's Dr NE; adult/child $26/19, plus $10 parking; ⊙ 10am-5pm; ⊕) You'll wish science class was as fun as the Telus Spark. Kids get a big bang out of this user-friendly and very interactive science center. There is a giant dome, where light shows depicting the cosmos are projected, and a whole raft of other things to discover. Adults Only Nights (random Thursdays) let the 18-plus crowd experience the place without kids.

Contemporary Calgary   GALLERY
(☑ 403-770-1350; www.contemporarycalgary.com; 701 11th St SW; ⊙ noon-6pm Wed-Sun) **FREE** This inspiring modern-art gallery has three floors of temporary exhibits that change every four months. The gallery is now in the former Centennial Planetarium in the southwest of Calgary, with displays of modern and contemporary art. The building itself is famous for its brutalist-style architecture.

Inglewood Bird Sanctuary   NATURE RESERVE
(☑ 311; 2425 9th Ave SE; ⊙ grounds dawn-dusk, interpretive center 10am-4pm May-Sep, 10am-4pm Mon-Fri, noon-4pm Sat Oct-Apr) **FREE** Get the flock over here. With more than 260 bird species calling the sanctuary home, you're assured of meeting some feathered friends. It's a peaceful place, with walking paths and benches to observe the residents. Twenty-one species of mammal live here too, along with 347 plant species. The center has renovations in the works.

Fish Creek Provincial Park   PARK
(☑ 403-297-5293; www.albertaparks.ca; ⊙ 8am-dusk) Cradling the southwest edge of Calgary, this huge park is a sanctuary of wilderness

hidden within the city limits. Countless trails intertwine to form a labyrinth, to the delight of walkers, mountain bikers and the many animals who call the park home.

Calaway Park   AMUSEMENT PARK

(☎ 403-240-3822; www.calawaypark.com; adult/family $42/130; ⏰ 10am-7pm Jul-early Sep, 11am-6pm Sat & Sun early Sep-early Oct, 10am-7pm Sat & Sun late May-Jun; 🖰) Children of all ages will enjoy Calaway Park, western Canada's largest outdoor family amusement park. It features 30 rides from wild to mild, live stage entertainment, 22 food vendors, 28 different carnival games, a trout-fishing pond and an interactive maze. Youngsters will love the fact that you can camp (☎ 403-249-7372; Hwy 1; tent/RV sites from $29/41; ⏰ mid-May–late Sep; P🛜) at the amusement park.

Activities & Tours

Eau Claire Rapid Rent   CYCLING

(☎ 403-444-5845; Barclay Pde SW; bikes/rollerblades/helmet per day from $40/25/7; ⏰ 10am-6pm May-Sep) Rents out bikes, junior bikes, tandem bikes, child trailers and rollerblades. And rafts, if you happen to have a car and trailer.

Olympic Oval   ICE SKATING

(☎ 403-220-7954; www.ucalgary.ca/oval; 288 Collegiate Blvd NW, University of Calgary; adult/child/family $7/5/18.50; ⏰ Aug–mid-Mar) Get the Olympic spirit at the University of Calgary, where you can go for a skate on Olympic Oval. Used for the speed-skating events at the Olympics, it offers public skating on the long track and has skates available to rent, as well as mandatory helmets. See the website for current schedules.

Canada Olympic Park   ADVENTURE SPORTS

(☎ 403-247-5452; www.winsport.ca; 88 Canada Olympic Rd SW; mountain biking hill tickets/lessons $30/150; ⏰ 9am-9pm Mon-Fri, 10am-5pm Sat & Sun) In 1988 the Winter Olympics came to Canada for the first time. Calgary played host, and many of the events were contested at Canada Olympic Park. It's near the western edge of town along Hwy 1 – you can't miss the distinctive 70m and 90m ski jumps crowning the skyline.

Check out the Sports Hall of Fame (admission $12) and learn about some great Canadian athletes and the story of the Calgary games. If you're feeling more daring, go for a 60-second bobsled ride ($135) with a professional driver on a 120km/h

Olympic course. It could be the most exhilarating and expensive minute of your life. Alternatively, you can take a trip along a zip line ($69) from the top of the ski jump. In winter you can go for a ski, or strap on a snowboard and hit the superpipe. Summer is for mountain biking, when you can ride the lift-serviced trails till your brakes wear out.

Calgary Walking Tours   CULTURAL

(☎ 855-620-6520; www.calgarywalks.com; adult/under 3yr/youth $28/free/18) Join the two-hour Downtown City tour to learn about the architecture, history and culture of various buildings, sculptures, gardens and hidden nooks.

🎇 Festivals & Events

Calgary Stampede   RODEO

(☎ ticket office 403-269-9822; www.calgarystampede.com; adult/child $18/9; ⏰ 2nd week Jul) Billed as the greatest outdoor show on earth, rodeos don't come much bigger than the Calgary Stampede. Daily shows feature bucking broncos, steer wrestling, chuckwagon races, a midway and a sensational grandstand show. Civic spirits soar, with free pancake breakfasts and a cowboy hat on every head in the city. All of this is strongly tempered by animal rights issues.

Each year, numerous animals are injured and several are put down. Humane societies and animal rights activists strongly oppose endangering animals for entertainment and money-making, and spotlight calf roping and chuckwagon races as two of the most dangerous activities at the Stampede. In 2019 three horses died.

Countering that grim reality is the fact that these same chuckwagon races often allow thoroughbred horses that would have been euthanized immediately after suffering injuries on the horse track to live on for years, even decades, doing what they love most: racing. The owners don't always like the term 'rescue' horse, but it's often true. So the Stampede is a complex, multifaceted issue and a personal one. If you do decide to go to the rodeo, be prepared for the possibility of an injury to happen before your very eyes. There are lots of other entertainment options: rides, amusements and games. But the tradition has always been the rodeo.

If you do decide to visit Calgary during Stampede, book ahead for accommodations and prepare to pay premium prices: nearly

CAR-LESS IN CALGARY

As the main operations center for Canada's oil industry, Calgary has a reputation for big, unsubtle automobiles plying endless low-rise suburbs on a network of busy highways. But, hidden from the ubiquitous petrol heads is a parallel universe of urban parkways (712km of 'em!) dedicated to walkers, cyclists and skaters, and many of them hug the banks of the city's two mighty rivers, the Bow and the Elbow. Even better, this non-car-traffic network is propped up by a cheap, efficient light-rail system: the C-Train carries a number of daily riders comparable to the Amsterdam metro. Yes, dear reader, Calgary without a car is not an impossible – or even unpleasant – experience.

Not surprisingly, the best trails hug the riverbanks. The Bow River through downtown and over into Prince's Island is eternally popular, with the pedestrian-only Peace Bridge providing a vital link. If you're feeling strong, you can follow the river path 20km south to Fish Creek Provincial Park and plenty more roadless action. Nose Creek Parkway is the main pedestrian artery to and from the north of the city, while the leafy Elbow River Pathway runs from Inglewood to Mission in the south.

Abutting the downtown Bow River Pathway is Eau Claire Rapid Rent, located next to the Eau Claire shopping center.

The city publishes an official *Calgary Pathways and Bikeways* map available from any local leisure center or downloadable from the City of Calgary website (www.calgary.ca). There's also a mobile app at www.calgary.ca/mobileapps.

every hotel will be full, and rates go through the roof.

Calgary Folk
Music Festival　　　　　　　MUSIC
(www.calgaryfolkfest.com; ☉ late Jul) Grassroots folk is celebrated at this annual four-day event featuring great live music on Prince's Island. Top-quality acts from around the globe make the trek to Cowtown. It's a mellow scene hanging out on the grass listening to the sounds of summer with what seems like 12,000 close friends. Tickets per day are around $85 or it's $195 for all four days.

Carifest
　　　　　　　　　　　　　　CARNIVAL
(☑ 403-836-1266; www.carifestcalgary.com; Shaw Millennium Park; ☉ mid-Aug) The Caribbean comes alive right here in Calgary for two days in August. There's live music, food stalls and a parade full of Carnival-style outfits and merry-making.

🛏 Sleeping

★ HI Calgary City Centre　　　　HOSTEL $
(☑ 403-269-8239; www.hihostels.ca/calgary; 520 7th Ave SE; dm/d from $61/162; @ 🕾) Clean, comfortable and pleasant, this helpful hostel is one of the only options for budget-minded travelers downtown, with fairly standard bunk rooms and a few doubles. It has a kitchen, laundry, pool table and internet facilities, as well as a patio with a barbecue.

It's a popular crossroads for travelers and a good place to organize rides and share recommendations.

Compared to other hostels in the area, this is a tight ship, with little leeway for those who want to smoke (whatever herb that may be!), drink or be wild and crazy until 4am. It's open 24 hours, but quiet time is from 11pm to 7am, which means you'll actually be able to sleep. God forbid you're here trying to get work done, but if so, you'll find the days are almost library quiet and the common areas have lots of places to plug in sans distractions.

Calgary West
Campground　　　　　　CAMPGROUND $
(☑ 403-288-0411; www.calgarycampground.com; Hwy 1; tent/RV sites for 2 people $42/61, extra person $5; ☉ mid-Apr–mid-Oct; 🅿 @ 🕾 ⛟) Featuring terraced grounds with views across the city, this campground has sites with great facilities, including a heated outdoor pool, nature trails, mini-golf and free wi-fi. Situated west of downtown Calgary on the Trans-Canada Hwy (Hwy 1), it's a quick trip into the city.

★ Hotel Elan　　　　　BOUTIQUE HOTEL $$
(☑ 403-229-2040; www.hotelelan.ca; 1122 16th Ave SW; r weekday/weekend from $189/149; 🅿 ⊖ ❄ 🕾) Stylish and modern, Hotel Elan is popular with business travelers. The 62 rooms are a splendid surprise, with heated

bathroom floors and luxury linens among the creature comforts, along with rain shower heads and gourmet coffee pods. Away from downtown, it's an easy walk to the happening scene on 17th Ave.

★ **Hotel Arts Kensington** BOUTIQUE HOTEL $$
(☑403-228-4442; www.hotelartskensington. com; 1126 Memorial Dr NW; r from $223; P⊖☎) This small inn is a great spot across the river. Impeccable service and rooms to match, plus soaker tubs, fireplaces, balconies, French doors and fine linens are all to be found. It's a short trip over the bridge to downtown and the hotel restaurant is top-notch.

Nuvo Hotel Suites HOTEL $$
(☑403-452-6789; www.nuvohotel.com; 827 12th Ave SW; ste from $150; P⊖❄☎☎) Your hip home away from home, the Nuvo has large, stylish studio apartments with full kitchens, including washing machines, all for an excellent price in the Beltline neighborhood. Handy for downtown and Uptown 17th action. If you've got Fido or Rover along, this spot is pet friendly as well.

Centro Motel MOTEL $$
(☑403-288-6658; www.centromotel.com; 4540 16th Ave NW; r incl breakfast from $114; P❄@☎) A 'boutique motel' sounds like an oxymoron until you descend on the misleadingly named Centro (not in the center at all!), an old motel building that has been transformed with modern features. Rooms are comfy, almost chic, and come with bathrobes and walk-in spa showers. You'll find it 7km northwest of downtown on the Trans-Canada Hwy (Hwy 1, aka 16th Ave).

Hotel Alma BOUTIQUE HOTEL $$
(☑403-220-3203; www.hotelalma.ca; 169 University Gate NW; r from $120, ste $180; ⊖☎) Cleverly tucked away on the university campus, this fashionable boutique establishment has a definite hip vibe. Super-modern Euro-style rooms are small but cozy rather than cramped. The city suites have one bedroom and are lovely.

Guests have a free breakfast, as well as access to on-campus facilities, including a fitness center and pool.

Hotel Arts BOUTIQUE HOTEL $$
(☑403-266-4611; www.hotelarts.ca; 119 12th Ave SW; d $188-380; P⊖❄☎☎) This boutique hotel plays hard on the fact that it's not part of an international chain. Aimed at travelers

with an aesthetic eye, there are hardwood floors, thread counts Egyptians would be envious of, and art on the walls that could be in a gallery. Standard king rooms are small but well designed with rain shower heads and blackout curtains.

★ **Hotel Le Germain** BOUTIQUE HOTEL $$$
(☑403-264-8990; www.germaincalgary.com; 899 Centre St SW; d from $299; P⊖❄@☎) 🖉 A posh boutique hotel to counteract the bland assortment of franchise inns that service downtown Calgary. Part of a small French-Canadian chain, the style verges on opulent. Rooms are elegant, while the 24-hour gym, in-room massage, complimentary newspapers and stylish lounge add luxury touches.

✕ Eating

In Calgary, the restaurant scene is blossoming, with lots of options for great eats in all price ranges. Where solitary cows once roamed, vegetables and herbs now prosper, meaning that trusty old stalwart, Alberta beef, is no longer the only thing on the menu.

You'll find good eat streets in Kensington, Inglewood, Uptown 17th Ave and downtown on Stephen St.

★ **Alforno Cafe & Bakery** CAFE $
(☑403-454-0308; www.alforno.ca; 222 7th St SW; mains $9-21; ⊘7am-9pm Mon-Fri, 8am-9pm Sat, 8am-5pm Sun) This ultra-modern, super-comfortable cafe is the kind of place you'll want to hang out all day. Bellinis, beer on tap, carafes of wine and excellent coffee won't discourage you from lingering, nor will magazines, comfy sofas or window seats. With pastas, flatbreads, salads, soups and panini, all homemade, it's difficult to leave room for the amazing cakes, tarts and biscuits.

The sweets category includes espresso shortbread with caramelized sugar and chocolate cream puffs. Breakfasts tempt with eggs Bennie, smashed avocado toast and a bacon breakfast sandwich.

★ **1886 Buffalo Cafe** BREAKFAST $
(☑403-269-9255; www.1886buffalocafe.com; 187 Barclay Pde SW; breakfast mains $9-19; ⊘6am-3pm Mon-Fri, from 7am Sat & Sun) This is a true salt-of-the-earth diner in the high-rise-dominated city center. Built in 1911 and the only surviving building from the lumber yard once here, the exterior's peeling clap-

boards sure make it look authentic. This is a ketchup on the table, unlimited coffee refills kind of place famous for its brunches, especially its huevos rancheros.

Myhre's Deli
DELI **$**

(☑ 403-244-6602; 1411 11th St SW; mains $11-14; ⊙ 11am-4pm, to 8pm Thu-Sun) Satisfying meat cravings for 15 years, this deli's mahogany interior and vintage signs are from the Palace of Eats, a Stephen Ave institution from 1918 to 1964. Well-filled smoked Montreal meat sandwiches are made fresh, and all-beef hot dogs, including the steamed Reuben dog with sauerkraut, are embellished with your choice of seven mustards. Everything is topped with a pickle.

Jelly Modern Doughnuts
BAKERY **$**

(☑ 403-453-2053; www.jellymoderndoughnuts. com; 1414 8th St SW; doughnuts $2.50-3; ⊙ 7am-6pm Mon-Fri, 9am-6pm Sat, to 5pm Sun) Bright pink and sugary-smelling, Jelly Modern has grabbed the initiative on weird doughnut flavors. The maple and bacon or bourbon vanilla varieties won't help ward off any impending heart attacks, but they'll make every other doughnut you've ever tasted seem positively bland by comparison.

Gravity Espresso & Wine Bar
CAFE **$**

(☑ 403-457-0697; www.cafegravity.com; 909 10th St SE; light lunches $7-12; ⊙ 8am-5pm Sun & Mon, to 10pm Tue-Thu, to midnight Fri & Sat) 🍴 This hybrid cafe-bar, which alters its personality depending on the clientele and the time of day, is a thoughtful, community-led business. The crux of the operation is the locally roasted Phil & Sebastian coffee beans, but that's just an overture for loads of other stuff, including live acoustic music, curry nights, home-baked snacks and fund-raisers.

Galaxie Diner
DINER **$**

(☑ 403-228-0001; www.galaxiediner.ca; 1413 11th St SW; mains $12-18; ⊙ 7am-3pm Mon-Fri, to 4pm Sat & Sun) Looking more authentic than themed, this classic, no-nonsense 1950s diner serves all-day breakfasts, burgers and milkshakes. Squeeze into a booth, grab a seat at the bar or (more likely) join the queue at the door. The Calgary Sandwich, a scrumptious mix of just about everything under the sun, is a popular favorite, as are the extra-thick, ample-sized, made-to-order milkshakes.

Without Papers
PIZZA **$$**

(☑ 403-457-1154; https://wopizza.ca; 1216 9th Ave SE, Inglewood; pizzas $17-22; ⊙ 11am-10pm Mon-Thu, to midnight Fri & Sat, noon-9pm Sun) These authentic pizzas are baked in an Italian pizza oven that was lowered through the ceiling (you can still see the hole!). The busy pizzeria's name is a nod to early Italian immigrants, while its pizzas and calzones are fresh and creative. The walls are covered in old movie posters and the tables are filled with happy pizza eaters.

Una
PIZZA **$$**

(☑ 403-453-1183; www.unapizzeria.com; 618 17th Ave SW; pizzas $17-24; ⊙ 11:30am-1am) There's often a line out the door but nobody seems to mind waiting – that's how good these thin-crust pizzas are. There's plenty of good house wine, too.

Ox Bar de Tapas
TAPAS **$$**

(☑ 403-457-1432; www.oxtapas.com; 528 17th Ave SW; tapas $5-18; ⊙ 5-11pm Sun, 4-10pm Tue-Thu, to midnight Fri & Sat) Recreating Spain in modern Calgary isn't an obvious go-to, but Ox Bar de Tapas has somehow managed it with colorful tiles and delicious tapas. Order piecemeal from a menu of Manchego cheese, tortilla (Spanish omelet) and cured *jamón serrano*.

★ Market
CANADIAN **$$$**

(☑ 403-474-4414; www.marketcalgary.ca; 718 17th Ave SW; mains lunch $19-26, dinner $18-42; ⊙ 11:30am-11pm) With an earthy yet futuristic feel, award-winning Market has gone a step further in the fresh-local trend. Not only does it bake its own bread, but it also butchers and cures meat, makes cheese and grows 16 varieties of heirloom seeds year-round. As if that weren't enough, it's then all whipped into meals that are scrumptious and entirely satisfying.

★ Teatro
ITALIAN **$$$**

(☑ 403-290-1012; www.teatro.ca; 200 8th Ave SE; mains lunch $19-40, dinner $30-60; ⊙ 11:30am-3pm Mon-Fri, 5-10pm Sun-Thu, to 11pm Fri & Sat) In a regal bank building next to the Epcor Centre for the Performing Arts, Teatro has an art nouveau touch with its marble bar top, swirling metalwork and high-backed curved sofas. Dishes are works of art and fuse Italian influences, French nouvelle cuisine and a bit of traditional Alberta. Service is friendly and impeccable.

PENG GE/500PX ©

CHRIS BABCOCK/GETTY IMAGES ©

1. Ukrainian Cultural Heritage Village (p567)

Watching role-players acting out what life in a rural Ukrainian-Canadian community was like is an interesting way to experience Ukrainian culture.

2. Royal Tyrrell Museum of Palaeontology (p614)

One of the preeminent dinosaur museums on the planet, this museum was made even better by a $5.9 million expansion project completed in 2019.

3. Miette Hot Springs (p607)

More remote than Banff's historic springs, Miette Hot Springs are surrounded by peaks and are especially enjoyable when the fall snow is drifting down.

4. Icefields Parkway (p592)

This 230km highway winds through the pristine wilderness of the Canadian Rockies.

Mercato
ITALIAN $$$

(☑403-263-5535; www.mercatogourmet.com; 2224 4th St SW; mains $21-55; ⊙11:30am-9pm Sun-Wed, to 9:30pm Thu, to 10pm Fri & Sat, deli from 9am daily) Attached to an open-plan Italian market-deli that sells everything from coffee to salami, Mercato is one of those local restaurants that gets everything right. Decor, service, atmosphere, food and price all hit the spot in a modern but authentic take on la dolce vita in the endearing Mission neighborhood.

Blink
FUSION $$$

(☑403-263-5330; www.blinkcalgary.com; 111 8th Ave SW; mains $24-42; ⊙11am-2pm Mon-Fri, 5-10pm Mon-Sat) 🍴 It's true: you could miss this small oasis tucked along a busy street and that would be a shame. Inside this trendy gastro haven, an acclaimed chef oversees an ever-evolving menu of fine dishes like smoked ricotta ravioli with walnuts and truffle vinaigrette or grilled striploin with caramelized shallots and red-wine sauce. Food is fresh and, wherever possible, locally sourced.

 Drinking & Nightlife

Craft cocktail, thy name is Calgary. Hit 17th Ave NW for a slew of martini lounges and crowded pubs, and 4th St SW for a lively after-work scene. There's even a password-protected speakeasy now. Other spots include Kensington Rd NW and Stephen Ave. Calgary's LGBTIQ+ scene is ever-improving; even the Stampede has a drag show now.

★ Betty Lou's Library
COCKTAIL BAR

(☑403-454-4774; www.bettylouslibrary.com; 908 17th Ave SW; ⊙5pm-12:30am Tue-Thu, to 2am Fri & Sat) Betty Lou's Library won't be for everyone, but if you like feeling like you've stepped back in time to Prohibition 1920s, then you'll get a kick out of coming here. The cocktails are superb; if you can't decide just ask one of the bartenders for a custom-crafted cup of yum. You'll need a password to enter, so call first.

The entrance is actually on 16th Ave, not 17th. Look for a red light, a bookshelf and a phone.

Note also that there are some house rules that are enforced – among them, no talking or making chitchat with other parties at the bar. That means this spot is best enjoyed with a friend or two, unless you like drinking alone.

★ Pr%f
COCKTAIL BAR

(☑403-246-2414; www.proofyyc.com; 1302 1st St SW; ⊙4pm-midnight Sun & Mon, to 1am Tue-Sat) No, that isn't a typo. Pr%f might be small but the bar is big enough to require a library ladder, and the drinks menu not only requires time, but also imagination. The menu itself is a beautiful thing to behold and the drinks look so stunning, you almost don't want to drink them. But you do. Trust us, you do.

Jusu
JUICE BAR

(☑403-452-2159; www.jusubar.com; 816 16th Ave SW; juice $7-12; ⊙9am-6pm) Cold-pressed juice is the latest craze in Calgary. Like a meal in a bottle, it can be found in trendy cafes or at this retail store. Some flavors are super-tasty, others more on the healthy side than flavorful, but you're sure to find something you like. At the end of each day, unused food is donated to local shelters.

Analog Coffee
COFFEE

(☑403-910-5959; www.analogcoffee.ca; 740 17th Ave SW; coffees $3-6; ⊙7am-10pm, to midnight Jul & Aug) The third-wave coffee scene is stirring in Calgary, led by companies like Fratello, which runs this narrow, overflowing hipsterish 17th Ave cafe. Beans of the day are displayed on a clipboard and there are rows of retro vinyl along the back wall. Teas are here, too, as are tasty desserts aplenty.

Barley Mill
PUB

(☑403-290-1500; www.barleymillcalgary.com; 201 Barclay Pde SW; ⊙11am-midnight, from 10am Sun) Built in a 1900s style, with the original distillery's lumber used for the top floor and an actual waterwheel churning outside, the Barley Mill draws crowds for its pub grub, long lineup of draft beers and a well-stocked bar. Two patios for when it's warm and a big stone fireplace for when it's not keep it busy in every season.

Twisted Element
GAY & LESBIAN

(☑403-802-0230; www.twistedelement.ca; 1006 11th Ave SW; ⊙9pm-2am Wed-Sun) Consistently voted the best queer dance venue by the local community, this club has weekly drag shows, karaoke nights and DJs spinning nightly.

☆ Entertainment

Calgary has a lively and varied entertainment scene, from comedy shows and improv theater to Shakespeare and indie films only a Canadian could love.

Ironwood Stage & Grill
LIVE MUSIC

(403-269-5581; www.ironwoodstage.ca; 1229 9th Ave SE, Inglewood; ⊙ shows 8pm Sun-Thu, 9pm Fri & Sat) Cross over into the hip universe of Inglewood to find the grassroots of Calgary's music scene, here inside the Garry Theatre. Local bands alternate with bigger touring acts for nightly music in the welcoming, woody confines of Ironwood. Country and folk are the staples. Events are all ages.

Calgary Flames
SPECTATOR SPORT

(403-777-2177; http://flames.nhl.com) Arch-rival of the Edmonton Oilers, the Calgary Flames play ice hockey from October to April at the Saddledome (403-777-4646; Stampede Park). Make sure you wear red to the game and head down to 17th Ave afterward, or the 'Red Mile,' as they call it during play-offs.

Loose Moose
Theatre Company
THEATER

(403-265-5682; www.loosemoose.com; 1235 26th Ave SE) Guaranteed to be a fun night out, Loose Moose has digs near the Inglewood neighborhood. It specializes in improv comedy and, at times, audience participation (you've been warned). You'll also find kids' theater.

Arts Commons
THEATER

(403-294-7455; https://artscommons.ca; 205 8th Ave SE) This is the hub for live theater in Calgary. With four theaters and one of the best concert halls in North America, you can see everything from ballet to Bollywood here.

Globe Cinema
CINEMA

(403-262-3309; www.globecinema.ca; 617 8th Ave SW; tickets $10; ⊙ 6:30-9:30pm, matinees Sat & Sun) This art-house theater specializes in foreign films and Canadian cinema – both often hard to find in mainstream movie houses. Look for discounts on Tuesdays and matinees on the weekend.

Broken City
Social Club
LIVE MUSIC

(403-262-9976; www.brokencity.ca; 613 11th Ave SW; ⊙ 11am-2am) There's something on stage here most nights – everything from jazz jams to hip-hop, along with comedy and quiz nights. The rooftop patio is ace in the summer, and the small but well-curated menu keeps you happy whether you're after a steak sandwich or vegan cauliflower wings.

Calgary Stampeders
SPECTATOR SPORT

(403-289-0258; www.stampeders.com) The Calgary Stampeders, part of the Canadian Football League (CFL), play from July to September at McMahon Stadium (1817 Crowchild Trail NW) in the University District, 6km northwest of downtown.

Pumphouse Theatres
THEATER

(403-263-0079; http://pumphousetheatre.ca; 2140 Pumphouse Ave SW) Set in what used to be, you guessed it, the pumphouse, this theater company puts on avant-garde, edgy productions like One Man Star Wars Trilogy.

🅰 Shopping

Calgary has several hot shopping spots, but these districts are reasonably far apart. The Kensington area and 17th Ave SW have a good selection of interesting, fashionable clothing shops and funky trinket outlets. Stephen Ave Walk is a pedestrian mall with shops, bookstores and atmosphere. Inglewood is good for antiques, junk, apothecaries, and secondhand books and vinyl.

Tea Trader
TEA

(403-264-0728; www.teatrader.com; 1228a 9th Ave SE, Inglewood; ⊙ 10am-5pm Tue-Sat, noon-4pm Sun) This wonderful shop is up a set of stairs and very easy to miss, but it's worth searching out for its lovely aroma wafting around the room, cheery, happy-to-help proprietors and wealth of tea options. Teas from all over the world line the shelves, as well as some local flavors. If you can't find what you're looking for, just ask!

Alberta Boot Co
SHOES

(403-263-4623; www.albertaboot.com; 50 50th Ave SE; ⊙ 9am-6pm Mon-Sat) Visit the factory and store run by the province's only Western boot manufacturer and pick up a pair of your choice made of kangaroo, bullhide or boring old cowhide, or just breathe in the aroma of leather and tanning oil. Over 200 hours of labor go into each boot, and prices range from $385 to $2100 or more.

If the boots are too pricey, there are free coasters at the door made from leather scraps that make a nice souvenir.

Smithbilt Hats
HATS

(403-244-9131; https://smithbilthats.com; 1015 11th St SE; ⊙ 9am-5pm Mon-Wed & Fri, to 7pm Thu, 10am-4pm Sat) Ever wondered how a cowboy hat is made? Here is your chance to find out. Smithbilt has been shaping hats in the traditional way since 1919 when you parked your horse out front. You can pick up one made of straw or beaver felt and priced accordingly, or just marvel at the artisans as they work, crafting, cutting and shaping.

Mountain Equipment Co-op SPORTS & OUTDOORS
(📞 403-269-2420; www.mec.ca; 830 10th Ave SW; ⊙10am-9pm Mon-Fri, 9am-6pm Sat, 10am-5pm Sun) MEC is the place to get your outdoor kit sorted before heading into the hills. It's a Canadian institution with a huge selection of outdoor equipment, travel gear, active clothing and books.

ⓘ Information

Rockyview General Hospital (📞 403-943-3000; 7007 14th St SW; ⊙24hr) Emergency room open 24 hours.

Visit Calgary (www.visitcalgary.com; 101 9th Ave SW; ⊙8am-5pm) Operates a visitor center in the base of the Calgary Tower (p575). The staff can help you find accommodations. Information booths are also available at both the arrivals and departures levels of the airport.

ⓘ Getting There & Away

AIR

Calgary International Airport (YYC; 📞 403-735-1200; www.yyc.com; 2000 Airport Rd NE) is about 15km northeast of the center off Barlow Trail, a 25-minute drive away.

BUS

Luxurious **Red Arrow** (https://redarrow.ca; 205 9th Ave SE) buses run to Edmonton ($76,

3½ hours, six daily) and Lethbridge ($53, three hours, two daily).

Canmore and Banff ($72, 2¼ hours, eight daily) and Lake Louise ($99, 2½ hours, eight daily) are served by **Brewster Express** (📞 403-762-6700; www.banffjaspercollection.com/brewster-express).

Red Arrow picks up downtown on the corner of 9th Ave SE and 1st Ave SE. Brewster Express buses pick up at various downtown hotels. Inquire when booking.

CAR & MOTORCYCLE

All the major car-rental firms are represented at the airport and downtown.

Alberta Motor Association (📞 403-240-5300; https://ama.ab.ca; 4700 17th Ave SW)

CanaDream (📞 888-480-9726, international calls 925-255-8383; www.canadream.com)

Cruise Canada (📞 403-291-4963; www.cruisecanada.com)

ⓘ Getting Around

TO/FROM THE AIRPORT

You can go between the airport and downtown on public transportation. From the airport, take bus 57 to the Whitehorn stop (northeast of the city center) and transfer to the C-Train; reverse that process coming from downtown. You can also take bus 300 from the city center all the way to the airport. Either way, the trip costs only $3.40, and takes between 45 minutes and an hour.

For transport to Banff or other places outside Calgary, the **Airporter Shuttle Express** (📞 403-509-4799; www.airportshuttleexpress.com; from $85) and **Banff Airport Taxi** (📞 403-720-5788;

WORTH A TRIP

TURNER VALLEY

As you head south on the Cowboy Trail (Hwy 22), you'll pass through Turner Valley. At first glance it looks like many of the small towns in this region, but it's definitely worth stopping here to fill both your belly and your liquor cabinet.

Chuck Wagon Cafe (📞 403-933-0003; 105 Sunset Blvd; mains $9-20; ⊙8am-2:30pm Mon-Fri, to 3:30pm Sat & Sun) Housed in a tiny red barn, this legendary cafe feels much like the homestead kitchen it is – it draws hungry diners from miles around. The enormous, all-day breakfast of smoked hash, triple-A steak and eggs Benedict will have you shouting 'Yeehaw!' This is ranch cooking at its best.

Eau Claire Distillery (📞 403-933-5408; www.eauclairedistillery.ca; 113 Sunset Blvd SW; tasting $8.50, tasting & tour $15, cocktails $15; ⊙11am-5pm Sun-Thu, to 8pm Fri & Sat, tours noon, 2pm & 4pm) Next door to the cafe, this is the province's first craft distillery, using Alberta grain and custom-crafted German stills. Having taken over the town's original movie theater and built on the site of the neighboring brothel, this award-winning place pours tastings of gin and vodka that are infused with natural flavors like prickly pear and lemon, as well as single-malt whiskey. Take a tour and sit yourself down at the bar for a cocktail, or try the flight of 'Seven Deadly Gins.'

www.banffairporttaxi.com) are useful options. The Airporter Shuttle Express can also drop you in Calgary for around $85.

A taxi to the airport costs between about $40 and $55 from downtown.

CAR & MOTORCYCLE

Parking in downtown Calgary is an expensive nightmare – a policy designed to push people to use public transportation. Luckily, downtown hotels generally have garages. Private lots charge about $20 per day. There is also some metered parking, which accepts coins and credit cards. Outside the downtown core, parking is free and easy to find.

PUBLIC TRANSPORTATION

Calgary Transit (www.calgarytransit.com) is efficient and clean. Use the website's handy plan-your-trip section to get where you're going. You can choose from the Light Rapid Transit (LRT) rail system, aka the C-Train, and ordinary buses. One fare ($3.40) entitles you to transfer to other buses or C-Trains. The C-Train is free in the downtown area along 7th Ave between 10th St SW and 3rd St SE. If you're going further or need a transfer, buy your ticket from a machine on the C-Train platform. Most buses run at 15- to 30-minute intervals daily. There is no late-night service.

TAXI

For a cab, call **Checker Cabs** (☑ 403-299-9999; www.thecheckergroup.com) or **Calgary United Cabs** (☑ 403-777-1111; https://calgarycabs.ca).

BANFF & JASPER NATIONAL PARKS

With the Rocky Mountains stretched across them, Banff and Jasper National Parks are filled with dramatic, untamed wilderness. Rugged mountaintops scrape the skyline while enormous glaciers cling to their precipices. Glassy lakes flash emerald, turquoise and sapphire, filled by waterfalls tumbling down cliff faces and thundering through bottomless canyons. Deep forests blanket wide valleys and lofty alpine meadows explode with vibrant flowers. It's the scenery that you only expect to see on postcards, right here at your fingertips. And through it wander a cast of elusive wildlife characters such as bears, elk, moose, wolves and bighorn sheep.

Of the thousands of national parks scattered around the world today, Banff, created in 1885, is the third oldest and Canada's first, while adjacent Jasper was only 22 years

behind. Situated on the eastern side of the Canadian Rockies, the two bordering parks were designated Unesco World Heritage sites in 1984. In contrast to some of North America's more remote parks, they both support small towns that lure from two to five million visitors each year.

Despite the throngs who come for the parks' more famous sites, like Lake Louise and Miette Hot Springs, it's by no means difficult to escape to a more tranquil experience of this sublime wonderland. However you choose to experience the parks, be it through hiking, backcountry skiing, paddling or simply sitting at a lake's edge beneath towering, castle-like mountains, the intensity and scale of these parks will bowl over even the most seasoned traveler. The more you see, the more you'll come to appreciate these parks' magic – and the more you'll want to discover.

Kananaskis Country

☑ 403 / POP 1350

The area collectively known as Kananaskis Country (or K-Country to the locals) covers a vast area to the south and east of Banff National Park, comprising several side-by-side provincial parks and protected areas, including Peter Lougheed Provincial Park, Elbow Valley, Sheep Valley, Ghost River Wilderness Area and Don Getty Wildland Provincial Park.

While visitors and tourists make a beeline for Banff's trails, many Albertans prefer to hike in K-Country, where the routes are quieter, the scenery is just as impressive and that all-important sense of wilderness is much easier to come by. It's less well known than Banff, but with a bit of research you'll find some fantastic hikes and trails, as well as plenty of sky-topping peaks, mountain lakes and outdoor pursuits. And with less traffic and no fencing, you are likely to encounter plenty of wildlife here.

🏃 Activities

★ **Peter Lougheed Provincial Park**   HIKING
(www.albertaparks.ca/peter-lougheed) Kananaski Country's quiet trails and backcountry offer superb hiking, especially around this 304-sq-km park on the west side of Kananaskis Valley, which includes the Upper and Lower Kananaskis lakes and the highest navigable vehicle pass in Canada. It's an excellent area

Banff National Park

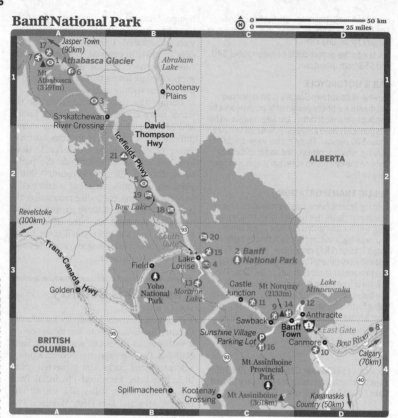

for wildlife spotting: watch for foxes, wolves, bears, lynx and coyotes.

This area is an important wildlife corridor and the valley has been subjected to very little development. Recommended half-day hikes include the 3km trail to **Boulton Creek** (one hour) and the loop hike to the natural bowl of Ptarmigan Cirque. Longer day routes include the 7.2km hike to **Mt Indefatigable** (four hours) and the 16km **Upper Kananaskis Lake Circuit** (five hours).

Trail leaflets and information on conditions are available from the park's **visitor center** (☏403-678-0760; www.albertaparks.ca/peter-lougheed; Kananaskis Lakes Trail; ☺9:30am-4:30pm Mon-Thu, to 5:30pm Fri-Sun Jul & Aug, 9:30am-4:30pm daily rest of year, closed mid-Mar-early May & mid-Oct-early Dec) near Kananaskis Lakes.

★ King Creek Ridge
HIKING

You have to be something of a masochist to tackle this 6.2km out-and-back trail, but

the views up top are beyond belief. Starting from the King Creek picnic area on the east side of Hwy 40, parallel the highway briefly north on a clear but unsignposted footpath to bypass a creek gully, then head northeast straight up into the hills.

Over the next 1.5km you'll gain about 500m as the trail climbs relentlessly up through a mix of forest and steep flowery meadows. After about 90 minutes your efforts are rewarded as you crest King Creek Ridge and wave after wave of knife-edged mountains unfolds to the east, with the entire Kananaskis Valley spread out below you to the north and south. Turn left (north) to continue along the ridgeline as long as you like. You'll reach the ridge's high point (2420m) about 3.1km into the hike. From here, retrace your steps down the mountain.

Ptarmigan Cirque
HIKING

This 5km, two-hour loop hike starts in the high country near Highwood Pass (at

Banff National Park

2206m, the highest paved pass in Canada; usually open from June to October) and just keeps getting higher. Park on the west side of Hwy 40 just south of the pass, then walk back north and cross east over the highway, following the signposted trail for Ptarmigan Cirque.

Kananaskis Outfitters   ADVENTURE
(☑ 403-591-7000; www.kananaskisoutfitters.com; 1 Mt Sparrowhawk Cres, Kananaskis Village; bike/ski rental per day from $50/30; ⊙ 9am-7pm Jul & Aug, shorter hours rest of year) This outfitter in Kananaskis Village rents out bikes, cross-country skis and fat bikes for winter rides. It also runs canoe tours in the summer on Barrier Lake and winter bike tours to the picturesquely frozen Troll Falls.

**Kananaskis
Nordic Spa**   SPA
(☑ 403-591-6800; www.knordicspa.com; 1 Centennial Dr, Kananaskis Village; day pass $85; ⊙ 9am-9pm Sun-Thu, to 11pm Fri & Sat) K-Country's splashiest attraction is this full-service spa with oodles of hot and cold pools, saunas, a steam cabin, an on-site bistro and a variety of massage treatments. A single pass grants all-day access to the grounds. It's first-come, first-served and you must be 18 or older to enter; prepare to join the waiting list during busy periods.

Nakiska   SKIING
(www.skinakiska.com; Hwy 40; day pass adult/youth $90/68; ⊙ 9am-4pm early Nov–mid-Apr) The K-Country's only ski resort was one of the main venues for the 1988 Winter Olym-

pics. It's still a popular place to hit the slopes, though the facilities and runs are much less developed than in nearby Banff. Shuttle buses run throughout winter from Canmore and Banff, making Nakiska a credible (and often quieter) alternative to the Big Three.

There are more than five dozen runs spread out over 413 hectares, with plenty of scope for off-piste riding on the slopes of Mt Allan. More than half of the runs are rated intermediate, so Nakiska is a good all-round resort for most mid-level skiers.

Snowboarders can tackle the challenging Najibska Rail Park. The resort also has some of the Rockies' only accessible areas for glade skiing.

Chinook Rafting   RAFTING
(Map p586; ☑ 866-330-7238; www.chinookrafting.com; Hwy 1A; rafting adult/child from $97/62; ⊙ mid-May–mid-Sep) A great company for families, Chinook runs four-hour trips on Class II and III sections of the beautiful Kananaskis River. Kids must be five years or older to participate.

🍽 Sleeping & Eating

★ **Sundance Lodges**   CAMPGROUND $
(☑ 403-591-7122; www.sundancelodges.com; Kananaskis Trail/Hwy 40; campsites $34, small tipis $70, large tipis or trappers' tents $94-99; ⊙ mid-May–Sep) For that authentic Canadian experience, try the hand-painted tipis and old-timey trappers' tents at this privately run campground. As you'd expect, facilities are basic – sleeping platforms and a kerosene lantern are about all you'll find inside

– so you'll need the usual camping gear, but kids are bound to lap up the John Muir vibe.

HI Kananaskis Wilderness Hostel HOSTEL $

(403-591-7333; www.hihostels.ca; 1 Ribbon Creek Rd, Kananaskis Village; dm/d $38/95; reception 5-9pm, closed late Oct-late Nov & 2 weeks in Apr; P) The rustic exterior at this place just north of Kananaskis Village might fool you into thinking you'll be roughing it, but inside you'll find HI's most luxurious wilderness hostel, with indoor plumbing, propane-heated showers, shiny pine floors, plush sofas, a fire-lit lounge and a kingly kitchen. Four private rooms supplement the 14-bed dorms, and the region-savvy manager is very welcoming.

Mt Kidd RV Park CAMPGROUND $

(403-591-7700; www.mountkiddrv.com; 1 Mt Kidd Dr; RV sites without/with hookups $37/54; year-round) Halfway along the Kananaskis Valley and handily placed for the facilities around Kananaskis Village, this place is the best option for trailer and RV campers, with full hookups and over 200 sites, plus comprehensive facilities, including tennis courts, a kids' wading pool, laundry, a basic grocery store and games rooms with ping pong, pool and foosball.

★Mt Engadine Lodge LODGE $$$

(587-807-0570; www.mountengadine.com; 1 Mt Shark Rd; s/d/q $199/525/549, glamping tent $525, d/q cabin $499/599; P) You can't get much more rural – or more peaceful – than this remote mountain lodge decorated with antler chandeliers and antique skis and snowshoes. Lodge rooms and family suites with balcony and sitting room overlook unspoiled meadows and a natural salt lick frequented by moose. Surrounding the lodge are cozy cabins and glamping tents sleeping two to four.

Lodge rates include four hearty meals, including a build-your-own lunch, afternoon tea and a gourmet dinner whipped up by a five-star chef. Look for the Mt Shark Rd turnoff on the west side of the Smith Dorrien/Spray Trail Rd, about 30km northwest of the Kananaskis Lakes or 40km south of Canmore.

Moose Family Kitchen CAFE $

(403-591-7979; mains $5-11; 8am-10pm daily) Presided over by its delightful Japanese chef-owner, this no-nonsense cafe in the heart of Kananaskis Village serves an eclectic mix of bagels, sandwiches, panini, milk-shakes, ramen, curry and teriyaki bowls. It's not fine dining, but it's all served with a smile, and it's one of the few budget options in K-Country.

★Mt Engadine
Lodge Dining Room CANADIAN $$

(587-807-0570; www.mountengadine.com; Smith Dorrien/Spray Trail, Kananaskis; brunch/afternoon tea/dinner $25/17.50/55; tea 2-5pm, dinner 7pm, brunch 10am-1pm Sun) It's worth detouring off the Smith Dorrien/Spray Trail for a bite at this charming backwoods lodge. Drop-ins are welcome for the daily afternoon tea, which features freshly baked goods, fancy cheeses, local meats and fresh fruit. With 24 hours' notice, day trippers can also enjoy the lodge's renowned multicourse family-style dinners (nightly) or the sumptuous Sunday brunch.

❶ Information

Elbow Valley Visitor Centre (403-678-0760; www.albertaparks.ca; Hwy 66; 9am-12:30pm & 1:30-4:30pm Fri-Sun mid-May–mid-Oct) Just west of Bragg Creek.

Kananaskis Information Centre at Barrier Lake (403-678-0760; www.albertaparks.ca; Hwy 40; 9am-5pm & 1:30-6pm mid-Jun–early Sep, shorter hours rest of year) Located 6.5km south of the junction of Hwys 1 and 40.

Peter Lougheed Information Centre (p588) Near the junction of Hwys 40 and 742, north of Kananaskis Lakes.

❶ Getting There & Away

Brewster Express (Map p596; 403-760-6934; www.banffjaspercollection.com/brewster-sightseeing; 100 Gopher St; 7am-9pm) runs buses between the Pomeroy Kananaskis Mountain Lodge in Kananaskis Village to Calgary's airport (adult/youth $72/36). You can also sometimes get a shuttle from the lodge to Nakoda Resort on Hwy 1, where you can meet up with Brewster buses to Banff or Jasper.

Navigating K-Country is much easier if you have your own wheels. There are two main roads through the area, which link up near the Kananaskis Lakes to form a convenient loop. The main Kananaskis Trail (Hwy 40) travels through the center of Kananaskis Valley from Barrier Lake, while the unpaved gravel Spray Lakes Trail (Hwy 742) heads northwest from the junction near Lower Kananaskis Lake all the way back to Canmore.

Be sure to double-check your policy if you're driving a rental; not all rental insurance will cover you on Hwy 742. Also be aware that there is virtually no cell-phone service along the route and no gas stations.

Canmore

📱 403 / POP 13,992

Canmore is Banff for locals, a former coal-mining town that reinvented itself as an outdoorsy hub during the 1988 Winter Olympics, when it hosted the cross-country skiing events. Spend time sitting in a downtown bar or cafe and you'll quickly intuit that most of the population lives here because they love it – and no wonder! The hiking, cycling, skiing and spiky mountain vistas are magnificent, and the rock climbing – Canmore acts as HQ for the Alpine Club of Canada – is world-class. Quieter, cheaper and more relaxed than Banff, Canmore makes a good launching pad for the national park or the more hidden pleasures of Kananaskis Country to the south.

While not officially part of Banff National Park, Canmore is a mere 24km southeast of Banff Town and 7km from the park's East Gate along Hwy 1.

◉ Sights & Actvities

Big Head   SCULPTURE
At the end of Main St, half-buried in gravel by the Bow River, sits the impressive sculpture known as the Big Head (for reasons that will quickly become obvious). Created by the artist Al Henderson, the sculpture was inspired by Canmore's name – the original town of Canmore in northwest Scotland was called *ceann mór*, a Gaelic word meaning 'great head' or 'chief.'

The sculpture has become a much-loved landmark, and the head's shiny pate is sometimes adorned to mark town festivities. It occasionally even gets its very own woolly toque in winter.

★ Canmore
Nordic Centre   MOUNTAIN BIKING, SKIING
(📱403-678-2400; www.canmorenordiccentre. ca; Olympic Way; winter day-pass adult/youth/ child $15/11.25/9, summer trail-use free; ☺9am-5:30pm) Nestled at the foot of Mt Rundle on the way to the Spray Lakes Reservoir, this huge trail center was originally developed for the Nordic events of the 1988 Winter Olympics. It's now one of western Canada's best mountain-biking and cross-country skiing centers, with over 100km of trails developed by some of the nation's top trail designers.

There are graded routes to suit all abilities, from easy rides on wide dirt roads to technical single tracks and full-on downhills. You can bring your own bike, or hire one from **Trail Sports** (📱403-678-6764; www. trailsports.ab.ca; Canmore Nordic Centre, 2003 Olympic Way; bike per 2hr/day from $40/60, ski package per 2hr/day $25/30; ☺9am-6pm), opposite the center's day lodge. If mountain biking is not your thing, most of the center's trails are also open to walkers, orienteerers and roller-skiers.

In winter, there are over 65km of ski trails – both machine-groomed and natural (ungroomed) – with 6.5km lit for night skiing.

Whatever the time of year, take precautions to avoid wildlife encounters, as the routes cross through areas of backcountry that form part of the Bow Valley Wildlife Corridor, and you might find that grizzlies, black bears and moose have decided to use the trails, too.

The center is a 4km drive from Canmore, just off Spray Lakes Rd. Cross the Bow River at the west edge of downtown, take Rundle Dr, continue south along Three Sisters Dr and follow signs to the Canmore Nordic Centre.

Gear Up   CYCLING
(📱403-678-1636; www.gearupsport.com; 1302 Bow Valley Trail; bike rental/ski rental per day from $50/20; ☺9am-6pm; 🖐) This easy-to-navigate Canmore rental shop is handy on account of its position within freewheeling distance of the start of the Legacy Trail (p591). As well as trail bikes, they've got junior, full-suspension and trailers, climbing gear, paddleboards (including blow-ups for easy transportation) and both alpine and Nordic skis. Bikes come with a handy repair kit, plus helmet and lock.

Elevation Place   HEALTH & FITNESS
(📱403-678-8920; www.elevationplace.ca; 700 Railway Ave; adult/child pool only $8/5, full facility $16/8; ☺9am-10pm Mon-Fri, to 9pm Sat & Sun; 🖐) Canmore's impressive sports center replicates many of the activities you can do outdoors, so if the weather's not cooperating, this is a fantastic place to escape the elements. The kid-friendly swimming pool is excellent, and the huge indoor climbing wall is an ideal place to get to grips with the basics before you tackle a real crag.

Snowy Owl Tours   DOG SLEDDING
(📱403-678-4369; www.snowyowltours.com; 829 10th St; 2hr tour 1-/2-person sled $425/475, 3- or 4-person sled $600) Dogsledding has been a traditional mode of travel in the Canadian

ALBERTA CANMORE

Rockies for centuries, and it's a wonderful way to see the wilderness. Snowy Owl offers sled trips ranging from two hours to two days on custom-built sleighs pulled by your own well-cared-for team of Siberian, Canadian and Alaskan huskies. The sledding season is usually from December to April.

On Top Mountaineering
CLIMBING

(☑ 403-678-2717; www.ontopmountaineering.com; 340 Canyon Close) This long-established, locally run outfit organizes outstanding outdoor adventures in the Rockies, including ice climbing, backpacking, classic peak ascents and five-day climbing courses. Other trips include trekking across glaciers from Bow Lake to Peyto Lake in summer and backcountry hut-to-hut skiing in winter. Alternatively, devise your own custom route with a private guide (from $520 per day for two people).

Canmore Cave Tours
ADVENTURE

(☑ 403-678-8819; www.canmorecavetours.com; 129 Bow Meadows Crescent, Unit 202) Buried deep beneath the Grotto Mountain near Canmore is a system of deep caves known as the **Rat's Nest**. Canmore Cave Tours runs guided trips into the maze of twisting passageways and claustrophobic caverns. Be prepared to get very wet and muddy, and brace yourself for chilly temperatures, as the caves stay at a constant 5°C (41°F) year-round.

🛏 Sleeping

★ Canmore Clubhouse
HOSTEL $

(☑ 403-678-3200; www.alpineclubofcanada.ca; Indian Flats Rd; dm $45, d & tr $100; ℗ 🤚 🛜) 🏊 Steeped in climbing history and mountain mystique, the Alpine Club of Canada's beautiful hostel sits on a rise 5km east of town, with stellar views of the Three Sisters through big picture windows. Dorms in the main building have access to a spacious guest kitchen and are supplemented by sweet, well-priced, three-person private rooms in the Boswell Cabin just uphill.

HI members and Alpine Club of Canada members get generous discounts. It's a great place to find climbing partners or just soak up the spirit of adventure. The Alpine Club, whose headquarters is located in the same building, sells bear spray and outdoor activity guides, offers classes in mountaineering and maintains several backcountry huts.

Canmore Downtown Hostel
HOSTEL $

(☑ 403-675-1000; www.canmoredowntownhostel. ca; 302 Old Canmore Rd; dm with shared/private bathroom $50/55, d/tr $185/216; 🛜) A welcome addition to Canmore, this bright modern hostel opened in 2019 and has won a loyal following. Its location at the far end of a parking lot adjoining the Trans-Canada Highway doesn't immediately inspire confidence, but climb to the spacious 2nd floor common room, the teal-walled guest kitchen and the clean wood-clad dorms and things quickly improve.

A sister project to the Jasper Downtown Hostel (p610), this place has the same friendly, community-minded vibe, with $8 bear-spray rental, a notice board to help you find hiking partners and comfy seats for lounging. The microbrewery just across the parking lot doesn't hurt, and it's only a short walk to the shops and restaurants of downtown Canmore.

Bow River Campground
CAMPGROUND $

(☑ 403-673-2163; www.bowvalleycampgrounds. com; Hwy 1; tent/RV sites $28/40; ⊙ May-Oct) The best option for camping close to Canmore is this riverside site 1.6km southeast along Hwy 1. It's sandwiched between the river and the highway, so it's not as peaceful as it could be, but it's pleasant enough if you can bag a spot by the water. Some sites offer full electrical and water hook-ups for RVs.

Canadian Artisans
B&B $$

(☑ 403-678-4138; www.canadianartisans.ca; 1016 9th Ave; d $250; ℗ 🛜) This quirky B&B is tucked away in the forest on the edge of Canmore. Two wooden suites are detached from the main house; they're comfortable, if not plush. The Treehouse Suite has picture windows, stained-glass door panels, a futuristic shower and a lovely vaulted roof. The Foresthouse is somewhat more cramped, with a whirlpool tub next to the queen-sized bed.

Windtower Lodge & Suites
HOTEL $$

(☑ 403-609-6600; www.windtower.ca; 160 Kananaskis Way; d/ste/2-room ste $199/319/509; ℗ @ 🛜) This modern, well-appointed hotel on a suburban backstreet is a good option if you're looking for a suite – both the one- and two-room options come with full kitchen, washing machine and dryer. Standard rooms are comfortable but small. Some rooms have fine views of the Three Sisters, and all have access to a fitness center and an outdoor hot tub.

BANFF LEGACY TRAIL

It's not often that getting from point A to B involves dazzling scenery, the possibility of spotting a moose and a huge dose of mountain air. The **Banff Legacy Trail** (www.pc.gc.ca/en/pn-np/ab/banff/activ/cyclisme-biking/Heritage-Legacy) is a 26.8km paved route that connects cyclists, pedestrians and skaters with Canmore and Banff Town. Shadowing Hwy 1 and gaining 30m of elevation, the trail takes most pedalers two or three hours round-trip. For those not up to cycling/walking in both directions, **Three Sisters Taxi** (☑403-493-9990) offers a handy shuttle service between the trailheads to get you back to your starting point.

Banff and Canmore are linked by two additional trails, the rugged **Rundle Riverside Trail** (for experienced mountain bikers) and the easier **Goat Creek Trail**. Check with Parks Canada (www.pc.gc.ca) for current conditions.

Paintbox Lodge   B&B $$$
(☑403-609-0482; www.paintboxlodge.com; 629 10th St; r $275-399; P☼) Run by ex-Olympic skiers Thomas Grandi and Sarah Renner, this B&B takes Canadian decor to a new level, right down to the tartan carpet. Its five unique suites offer a mix of country chic and luxury comfort. For maximum space ask for the Loft Suite, which sleeps four and features beamed ceilings, mountain-view balcony and sexy corner tub.

✴ Eating & Drinking

★**Communitea**   CAFE $
(☑403-688-2233; www.thecommunitea.com; 1001 6th Ave; mains $12-15; ☺8am-7pm Jun-Sep, 9am-5pm Oct-May; ☼) ✔ Ethically aware and all organic, this community cafe exudes a warm, relaxed vibe and colorful modern aesthetic. Food is fresh and local, with noodles, rice bowls, smoked salmon and avocado toast, wraps, salads, and plenty of vegan, veggie and gluten-free options. Sip fresh-pressed juices, well-executed coffee and, of course, every type of tea you can conceive of.

Old School Bus   ICE CREAM $
(621 Main St; 1/2/3 scoops $4.25/5.75/7.25, kid's scoop $2.50; ☺11am-10pm) Permanently parked just off Main St, this converted school bus is *the* place for ice cream in Canmore. The chalkboard hawks a tempting spectrum of flavors, from white chocolate to blackberry to peanut butter, and the milkshakes are heavenly too. Cash only.

Rocky Mountain Flatbread   ITALIAN $$
(☑403-609-5508; www.rockymountainflatbread.ca; 838 10th St; pizza $14-31; ☺11:30am-9pm Sun-Thu, to 10pm Fri & Sat; ☑) ✔ In this outdoorsy town where you naturally end up craving pizza, Rocky Mountain Flatbread is a fabu-lous apparition. The thin-crusted flatbreads start simple with organic tomato sauce and Canadian mozzarella, but you can rev things up with additional ingredients like smoked bison, fig and Brie, or lemon chicken and apple.

Grizzly Paw   PUB FOOD $$
(☑403-678-9983; www.thegrizzlypaw.com; 622 Main St; mains $18-25; ☺11am-11pm Sun-Thu, to midnight Fri & Sat) ✔ Alberta's best microbrewery (offering seven year-round beers plus seasonal specials) is hiding in the mountains of Canmore. With beer and food pairings, big burgers, hand-crafted sodas and a view-filled patio, it's a popular spot. The purveyors of Beavertail Raspberry Ale and Grumpy Bear Honey Wheat also have a nearby brewery and microdistillery where tours and tasters are available.

★**Crazyweed Kitchen**   INTERNATIONAL $$$
(☑403-609-2530; www.crazyweed.ca; 1600 Railway Ave; lunch mains $16-24, dinner mains $19-46; ☺11:30am-10pm Tue-Sun) This flashy bistro on the edge of town feels more big city than small town, with its sharp designer lines, funky artwork and globetrotting menu that takes in everything from wood-fired pizza, Malaysian noodles and Myanmar fish cakes to grass-fed Alberta rib eye. The tropical-themed cocktails lineup is equally inspired, with passion-fruit mojitos, grapefruit margaritas and tamarind whiskey sours.

★**Trough**   CANADIAN $$$
(☑403-678-2820; www.thetrough.ca; 725 9th St; mains $34-46; ☺5:30-9pm Tue-Sun) Canmore's slinkiest bistro is a bit tucked away on 9th St, but worth discovering for a romantic night out. The mother-son team creates amazing dishes like Prince Edward Island

(PEI) mussels with house-smoked tomatoes, grilled Alberta lamb chops with rosemary-black pepper marinade, and BC halibut with mango and sweet peppers. With just nine tables, it's wise to book ahead.

★ Tank 310
MICROBREWERY

(☑ 403-678-2487; www.thegrizzlypaw.com; 310 Old Canmore Rd; ☺ 11am-9pm Thu & Sun, to 9:30pm Fri & Sat) Soaring ceilings and in-your-face views of Mt Rundle and the Three Sisters greet you at this cool gastropub launched by Grizzly Paw Brewing. Views aside, your attention will quickly shift to the beer. A full lineup of Grizzly Paw drafts, from Powder Hound Blonde to Evolution IPA, comes complemented by a solid menu of upscale pub grub.

❶ Information

Travel Alberta Canmore Visitor Information Centre (☑ 403-678-5277; www.travelalberta. com; 2801 Bow Valley Trail; ☺ 9am-7pm May-Oct, to 5pm Nov-Apr; ☏) This regional visitor center with a free wi-fi lounge, just off the Trans-Canada Hwy northwest of town, focuses on the Canmore/Banff/Lake Louise area.

❶ Getting There & Away

Canmore is easily accessible from Banff Town (20 minutes) and Calgary (1¼ hours) via the Trans-Canada Highway (Hwy 1).

The **Banff Airporter** (☑ 403-762-3330; www.banffairporter.com; Coast Canmore Hotel, 511 Bow Valley Trail; Canmore to Calgary Airport adult/child $65/32.50) runs 11 buses daily between the Coast Canmore Hotel and Calgary Airport. **Brewster** (Map p596; ☑ 866-606-6700; www.banffjaspercollection.com/ brewster-express; 100 Gopher St) offers slightly more expensive and less frequent connections to the airport and downtown Calgary ($72, six to nine daily).

Bus 3, operated by **Roam** (☑ 403-762-0606; www.roamtransit.com; Canmore to Banff adult/ child $6/3), makes the 25-minute run between Canmore and Banff every 30 to 60 minutes. Buses stop downtown on 9th St near 7th Ave.

Icefields Parkway
☑ 403, 780

Nothing in North America compares to the Icefields Parkway. For much of its 230km length, this ribbon of highway winding through the heart of the Canadian Rockies is the lone sign of human influence in an otherwise pristine wilderness of jewel-hued

glacial lakes, unbroken virgin forest and otherworldly mountain crags.

Much of the route followed by the parkway was established over the millennia by indigenous people and later adopted by 19th-century fur traders. An early road was built during the 1930s as a Depression-era work project, and the present highway was opened in the early 1960s.

Nowadays it's used almost entirely by tourists, aside from the occasional elk, coyote or bighorn meandering along its perimeter. It can get busy in July and August, particularly with large recreational vehicles. Many also tackle it on a bike – the roadway is wide and sprinkled with plenty of strategically spaced campgrounds, hostels and lodges.

◉ Sights & Activities

There are two types of sights here: static (lakes, glaciers and mountains) and moving (elk, bears, moose etc). If you don't see at least one wild animal (look out for the inevitable 'bear jams') you'll be very unlucky.

★ Athabasca Glacier
GLACIER

(Map p586) The tongue of the Athabasca Glacier runs from the Columbia Icefield to within walking distance of the road opposite the Icefield Centre (p594). It can be visited on foot or in an Ice Explorer all-terrain vehicle. It has retreated about 2km since 1844, when it reached the rock moraine on the north side of the road. To reach its toe (bottom edge), walk from the Icefield Centre along the 1.8km **Forefield Trail**, then join the 1km **Toe of the Glacier Trail**.

You can also park at the start of the latter trail. While it is permitted to stand on a small roped section of the ice, do not attempt to cross the warning tape – many do, but the glacier is riddled with crevasses and there have been fatalities.

To walk safely on the Columbia Icefield, you'll need to enlist the help of **Athabasca Glacier Icewalks** (Map p586; ☑ 780-852-5595; www.icewalks.com; Icefield Centre, Icefields Pkwy; 3hr tour adult/child $110/60, 6hr tour $175/90; ☺ late May–Sep), which supplies all the gear you'll need and a guide to show you the ropes. Its basic tour is three hours; there's a six-hour option for those wanting to venture further out on the glacier. Hikers must be at least seven years of age.

The other, far easier (and more popular) way to get on the glacier is via the **Columbia Icefield Adventure** (Map p586; www.banff

jaspercollection.com/attractions/columbia-icefield; adult/child $114/57; ⊙9am-6pm Apr-Oct) tour. For many people this is the defining experience of their visit to the Canadian Rockies. The large hybrid bus-truck grinds a track onto the ice, where it stops to allow you to go for a 25-minute wander on the glacier. Dress warmly, wear good shoes and bring a water bottle to try some freshly melted glacial water. Tickets can be bought at the Icefield Centre or online; tours depart every 15 to 30 minutes.

Mt Edith Cavell
MOUNTAIN

(Map p608) Rising like a snowy sentinel over Jasper Town, Mt Edith Cavell (3363m) is one of the park's most distinctive and physically arresting peaks. What it lacks in height it makes up for in stark, ethereal beauty. Accessed via a winding, precipitous road that branches off the Icefields Pkwy 6km south of Jasper, the mountain is famous for its flower meadows and its wing-shaped **Angel Glacier**.

Athabasca Falls
WATERFALL

(Map p608) Despite being only 23m high, Athabasca Falls is Jasper's most dramatic and voluminous waterfall, a deafening combination of sound, spray and water. The thunderous Athabasca River has cut deeply into the soft limestone rock, carving potholes, canyons and water channels. Interpretive signs explain the basics of the local geology. Visitors crowd the large parking lot and short access trail. It's just west of the Icefields Pkwy, 30km south of Jasper Town, and at its most ferocious during summer.

Columbia Icefield
GLACIER

About halfway between Lake Louise village and Jasper Town, you'll glimpse the vast Columbia Icefield, covering an area the size of Vancouver and feeding eight glaciers. This remnant of the last ice age is up to 350m thick in places and stretches across the plateau between **Mt Columbia** (3747m) and **Mt Athabasca** (3491m). For serious hikers and climbers, this is also the only accessible area of the icefield. For information and conditions, visit Parks Canada (p594) at the Columbia Icefield Discovery Centre.

This is the largest icefield in the Rockies, feeding the North Saskatchewan, Columbia, Athabasca, Mackenzie and Fraser River systems with its meltwaters. The mountainous sides of this vast bowl of ice are some of the highest in the Rockies, with nine peaks higher than 3000m.

Peyto Lake
LAKE

(Map p586) You'll have already seen the indescribably vibrant blue color of Peyto Lake in a thousand publicity shots, but there's nothing like gazing at the real thing – especially since the viewing point for this lake is from a lofty vantage point several hundred feet above the water. The lake is best visited in early morning, between the time the sun first illuminates the water and the first tour bus arrives.

Weeping Wall
WATERFALL

(Map p586) This imposing rock wall towers above the east side of the Icefields Parkway, a few kilometers south of Sunwapta Pass and the Banff–Jasper border. In summer it's a sea of waterfalls, with tears of liquid pouring from the top, creating a veil of moisture. Come winter, the water freezes up solid to form an enormous sheet of ice. The vertical ice field is a popular playground for ice climbers, who travel from around the globe to test their mettle here.

Wilcox Ridge
HIKING

(Map p586) One of Jasper's most accessible high-country walks is the 9km out-and-back trail to Wilcox Ridge. Turn off the Icefields Pkwy 2km east of the Columbia Icefield Centre at Wilcox Campground. From the signposted trailhead, the path climbs rapidly above treeline, reaching a pair of red chairs after 30 minutes where you can sit and enjoy fine Athabasca Glacier views.

If you've had enough climbing, you can simply return from here to the parking lot. Otherwise continue ascending, gazing down over a river canyon on your left as you traverse wide-open meadows to reach **Wilcox Pass** (2370m) at the 3.2km mark. Here you'll turn left, following the undulating trail another 1.3km to reach the **Wilcox Ridge** viewpoint. Up top, dramatic, near-aerial views of the Athabasca Glacier unfold across the valley. To return to the parking lot simply retrace your steps downhill.

🍴 Sleeping & Eating

Waterfowl Lakes Campground
CAMPGROUND $

(Map p586; Icefields Pkwy; tent & RV sites $21.50; ⊙late Jun-early Sep) Tucked between two beautiful lakes about 60km north of Lake Louise, this campground just off the Icefields Pkwy has wooded sites and plenty of hiking opportunities. Facilities for the 116 first-come, first-served sites include flush toilets, hot water, BBQ shelters, food storage and interpretive programs, but no showers. Sites 1, 2, 4, 6 and 10 are all near the lakeshore.

HI Mt Edith Cavell
Wilderness Hostel
HOSTEL $

(Map p608; ☑780-852-3215; www.hihostels. ca; Cavell Rd; dm $38; ⊙reception 5-8pm mid-Feb–mid-Oct) 🏊 Secluded down a dead-end road near the base of Mt Edith Cavell and the Angel Glacier, this rustic place has wood-burning stoves in each of its two 16-bunk cabins and in the propane-lit kitchen-common room, where guests play cards and share stories of hikes to nearby Cavell Meadows and the remote Tonquin Valley (trailhead directly across the street).

HI Mosquito Creek
Wilderness Hostel
HOSTEL $

(Map p586; www.hihostels.ca; dm $38, private cabin for 2/3/4/5 people $95/115/135/155; ⊙reception 5-10pm, closed Oct & Tue Nov-Apr) Tucked away under the trees beside a rushing creek, this charming 34-bed backcountry hostel was originally built to house German POWs during WWII. There's a rustic wood-fired sauna, a stove-lit lounge and a pocket-sized (propane-powered) kitchen where you can cook up communal grub. Two 12-bed dorms are supplemented by two private rooms sleeping up to five. No showers or electricity.

Num-Ti-Jah Lodge
INN $$$

(Map p586; ☑403-522-2167; www.num-ti-jah.com; d with mountain/lake view $375/425; ⊙mid-May–mid-Oct; P🐾🌐) On the edge of Bow Lake, the historic Num-Ti-Jah Lodge is full to the brim with backcountry nostalgia. Built by pioneer Jimmy Simpson in 1923 (12 years before the highway), the carved-wood interior displays animal heads and photos from the golden age. The 16 rooms have big views, but show their age with worn furniture, dated decor and tiny bathrooms.

★Elkhorn Dining Room
CANADIAN $$$

(Map p586; ☑403-522-2167; www.num-ti-jah.com; Icefields Pkwy; breakfast buffet cold/hot $14/22, dinner mains $30-50; ⊙8-10am & 6:30-9pm mid-May–mid-Oct) Rustic yet elegant, the Num-Ti-Jah's historic Elkhorn Dining Room lets you step back in time to Jimmy Simpson's original hunting lodge, complete with stone fireplace and majestic views. Dine on elk burgers or crispy steelhead trout beneath the watchful eye of moose, wolverines and other hunting trophies. Guests get seating priority; if you're staying elsewhere make sure you reserve ahead.

You'll also find the Bow Lake Cafe (mains $8 to $13; 9am to 5pm) where you can refuel with a sandwich, soup or baked goods from tall wooden stools.

ℹ️ Information

Columbia Icefield Discovery Centre (Icefields Pkwy) Situated on the Icefields Pkwy, close to the toe of the Athabasca Glacier, the green-roofed Icefield Centre is a bit of a zoo in the summer, with tour coaches cramming the car

CYCLING THE ICEFIELDS PARKWAY

With its ancient geology, landscape-altering glaciers, and lakes bluer than Picasso paintings from his blue period, the 230km-long Icefields Parkway is one of the world's most spectacular roads, and, by definition, one of the world's most spectacular bicycle rides – if your legs and lungs are up to it. Aside from the distance, there are several long uphill drags, occasional stiff headwinds and two major passes to contend with, namely Bow Summit (2088m) and Sunwapta Pass (2035m). Notwithstanding these issues, the route is highly popular in July and August (don't even think about doing it in the winter), with aspiring cyclists lapping up its bicycle-friendly features. No commercial trucks are allowed on the parkway, there's a generous shoulder throughout, two-wheeled company is virtually guaranteed, and accommodations along the route (campgrounds, hostels and the occasional lodge or hotel) are plentiful and strategically placed. There's a choice of six HI hostels and four lodge/motel accommodations en route. Book ahead. Basic provisions can be procured at Saskatchewan River Crossing, 83km north of Lake Louise.

Sturdy road bikes can be rented from **Wilson Mountain Sports** (☑403-522-3636; www.wmsll.com; Samson Mall, Lake Louise village; bike/ski rental per day from $39/25; ⊙8am-7pm) in Lake Louise village. Brewster (p602) buses can sometimes transport bicycles, but always check ahead. **Backroads** (☑510-527-1555; www.backroads.com; 5-day tour from $3449) runs a Canadian Rockies Bike Tour, a six-day organized trip that incorporates cycling along the parkway.

park. Decamp here to purchase tickets and board buses for the Snocoaches and Glacier Skywalk. You'll also find a hotel, cafeteria, restaurant, gift shop and Parks Canada information desk.

South Gate The entrance to the Parkway north of Lake Louise, where you can purchase your park pass and pick up a map and brochures.

❶ Getting There & Away

Brewster Express (☑ 877-625-4372; www. banffjaspercollection.com/brewster-express) has buses plying the parkway between Banff, Lake Louise and Jasper, with stops at Saskatchewan River Crossing, Columbia Icefield Discovery Centre and Sunwapta Falls.

If you're driving, start out with a full tank of gas. It's fairly pricey to fill up at Saskatchewan River Crossing, the only gas station in the 230km-long stretch between Lake Louise and Jasper.

Banff Town

☑ 403 / POP 7847

It seems hard to believe when you first lay eyes on Banff Town, but this overgrown village of less than 10,000 souls is the largest metropolis in the entire national park. Thankfully, Banff has largely avoided North America's notorious penchant for sprawl – though its few city blocks *do* manage to squeeze in a surprising amount of commercial hustle and bustle.

A resort town with boutique shops, nightclubs, museums and fancy restaurants may seem incongruous in this wild setting. But Banff is no ordinary town. It developed as a service center for the park that surrounds it. Today it brings in busloads of tourists keen to commune with shops as much as with nature; artists and writers are also drawn to the Rockies' unparalleled majesty. Whether you love or loathe Banff's cosmopolitan edge, wander 15 minutes in any direction and you're back in wild country, a primeval world of bears, elk and wolves.

◉ Sights

★**Banff National Park**　　NATIONAL PARK
(Map p586; www.pc.gc.ca/banff; day pass adult/youth/family $9.80/free/19.60) Towering like giant castles in the sky, the mountains of Banff provide endless opportunities for wildlife-watching, hiking, boating, climbing, mountain biking, skiing or simply communing with nature. Rugged canyons compete for your attention with lush fields of alpine wildflowers, jewel-like blue-green lakes and dense emerald forests. Created in 1885 and ranging over 6641 sq km, Banff is the world's third-oldest national park – and was Canada's first.

★**Whyte Museum of the Canadian Rockies**　　MUSEUM
(Map p596; ☑ 403-762-2291; www.whyte.org; 111 Bear St; adult/student/child $10/5/free; ◉10am-5pm) Founded by local artists Catharine and Peter Whyte, the century-old Whyte Museum is more than just a rainy-day option. It boasts a beautiful, ever-changing gallery displaying art from 1800 to the present, by regional, Canadian and international artists, many with a focus on the Rockies. Watch for work by the Group of Seven (aka the Algonquin School). There's also a permanent collection telling the story of Banff and the hardy men and women who forged a home among the mountains.

Upper Hot Springs Pool　　HOT SPRINGS
(www.hotsprings.ca; Mountain Ave; adult/child/family $8.30/6.30/24.50; ◉9am-11pm mid-May–mid-Oct, 10am-10pm Sun-Thu, to 11pm Fri & Sat rest of year) Banff quite literally wouldn't be Banff if it weren't for its hot springs, which gush out from 2.5km beneath **Sulphur Mountain** at a constant temperature of between 32°C (90°F) and 46°C (114°F) – it was the springs that drew the first tourists to Banff. You can still sample the soothing mineral waters at the Upper Hot Springs Pool, near the Banff Gondola.

Fairmont Banff Springs　　HISTORIC BUILDING
(www.fairmont.com/banffsprings; 405 Spray Ave) Looming up beside the Bow River, the Banff Springs is a local landmark in more ways than one. Originally built in 1888, and remodeled in 1928 to resemble a cross between a Scottish baronial castle and a European château, the turret-topped exterior conceals an eye-poppingly extravagant selection of ballrooms, lounges, dining rooms and balustraded staircases that would make William Randolph Hearst green with envy.

Cave & Basin
National Historic Site　　HISTORIC SITE
(☑ 403-762-1566; www.pc.gc.ca/en/lhn-nhs/ab/caveandbasin; 311 Cave Ave; adult/child $3.90/free; ◉9:30am-5pm mid-May–mid-Oct, 11am-5pm Wed-Sun rest of year) The Canadian National Park system was effectively born at these hot springs, discovered accidentally by three Canadian Pacific Railway employees on their

ALBERTA BANFF TOWN

Banff Town

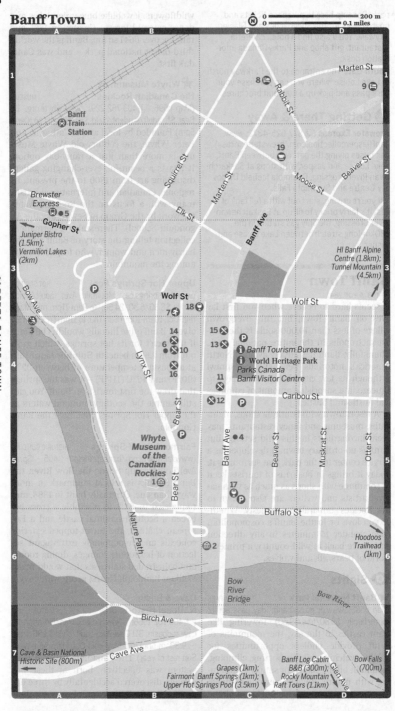

N 0   200 m
0   0.1 miles

Marten St

8 🍴

9 🍴

Rabbit St

Banff
Train
Station

19 🏧

Squirrel St

Beaver St

Moose St

Brewster
Express
● 5

Marten St

Gopher St

Elk St

Banff Ave

Juniper Bistro
(1.5km);
Vermilion Lakes
(2km)

HI Banff Alpine
Centre (1.8km);
Tunnel Mountain
(4.5km)

Bow Ave

Wolf St

7 ☩ 18 🍴

Wolf St

14 ✕
6 ● ✕ 10
16 ✕

15 ✕
13 ✕

i Banff Tourism Bureau
i World Heritage Park
Parks Canada
Banff Visitor Centre

Lynx St

11 ✕

Bear St

✕ 12

Caribou St

● 4

Whyte
Museum
of the
Canadian
Rockies

Beaver St

Muskrat St

Otter St

1 🏛

17 🍴

Nature Path

Buffalo St

2 🏛

Hoodoos
Trailhead
(1km)

Bow
River
Bridge

Bow River

Cave & Basin National
Historic Site (800m)

Birch Ave

Cave Ave

Grapes (1km);
Fairmont Banff Springs (1km);
Upper Hot Springs Pool (3.5km)

Banff Log Cabin
B&B (300m);
Rocky Mountain
Raft Tours (1.1km)

Bow Falls
(700m)

Glen Ave

Banff Town

day off in 1883 (though known to indigenous peoples for 10,000 years). The springs quickly spurred a flurry of private businesses offering facilities for bathers to enjoy the then-trendy thermal treatments. To avert an environmental catastrophe, the government stepped in, declaring Banff Canada's first national park in order to preserve the springs.

Bow Falls   WATERFALL
About 500m south of town, just before the junction with Spray River, the Bow River plunges into a churning melee of white water at Bow Falls. Though the drop is relatively small – just 9m at its highest point – Bow Falls is a dramatic sight, especially in spring following heavy snowmelt.

Vermilion Lakes   NATURE RESERVE
West of town, this trio of tranquil lakes is a great place for **wildlife spotting**: elk, beavers, owls, bald eagles and ospreys can often be seen around the lakeshore, especially at dawn and dusk. A paved path – part of the **Legacy bike trail** – parallels the lakes' northern edge for 5.9km, but the proximity

of the Trans-Canada Hwy/Hwy 1 means that it's not as peaceful as it could be.

Banff Park Museum   MUSEUM
(Map p596; ☑403-762-1558; www.pc.gc.ca/en/lhn-nhs/ab/banff; 91 Banff Ave; adult/child $3.90/free; ◉9:30am-5pm Wed-Sun) Occupying the oldest surviving federal building in a Canadian National Park and dating from 1903, this museum is a national historic site. Its exhibits – a taxidermic collection of local animals, including grizzly and black bears, plus a tree carved with graffiti dating from 1841 – was curated by Norman Sanson, who ran the museum and Banff weather station until 1932. A number of the animals originally resided in a long-ago zoo that was briefly located behind the museum.

🏃 Activities

Canoeing & Kayaking
Despite a modern penchant for big cars, canoe travel is still very much a quintessential Canadian method of transportation. The best options near Banff Town are **Lake Minnewanka** and nearby **Two Jack Lake**, both to the northeast, or – closer to the town itself – the **Vermilion Lakes**. Unless you have your own canoe, you'll need to rent one; try **Banff Canoe Club** (Map p596; ☑403-762-5005; www.banffcanoeclub.com; cnr Wolf St & Bow Ave; canoe & kayak rental per 1st/additional hour $45/25, SUP/bike rental per hour $30/12; ◉9am-9pm mid-Jun–Aug, reduced hours mid-May–mid-Jun & Sep).

Cycling
There are lots of riding options around Banff, both on the road and on selected trails. Popular routes around Banff Town include **Sundance** (7.4km round-trip) and **Spray River Loop** (12.5km); either is good for families. **Spray River & Goat Creek** (19km one way) and **Rundle Riverside** (14km one way) are both A-to-Bs with start/finish points near Canmore. The former is pretty straightforward; the latter is more challenging, with ups and downs and potential for thrills and spills.

Serious road cyclists should check out Hwy 1A (the Bow Valley Pkwy) between Banff and Lake Louise; the rolling hills and quiet road here are a roadie's dream. Parks Canada publishes the brochure *Mountain Biking & Cycling Guide – Banff National Park,* which describes trails and regulations. Pick it up at the Banff Visitor Centre (p602).

Snowtips/Bactrax (Map p596; ☎403-762-8177; www.snowtips-bactrax.com; 225 Bear St; bike rental per hour/day from \$10/35, cross-country/alpine ski rental per day from \$20/40; ⊗8am-8pm Jun–mid-Oct, 7am-9pm rest of year) has a barn full of town and trail bikes to rent and will deliver them to your hotel.

Hiking

Hiking is Banff's key attraction and therefore the focus of many travelers who visit the area. The trails are easy to find, well signposted and maintained enough to be comfortable to walk on, yet rugged enough to provide a wilderness experience.

In general, the closer to Banff Town you are, the more people you can expect to see and the more developed the trail will be. But regardless of where in the park you go walking, you are assured to be rewarded for your efforts.

Before you head out, check at the Banff Visitor Centre (p602) for trail conditions and possible closures. Keep in mind that trails are often snow-covered much later into the summer season than you might expect, and trail closures due to bears are a possibility, especially in berry season (July to September).

One of the best hikes from the town center is the **Bow River Falls & The Hoodoos Trail**, which starts by the Bow River Bridge and tracks past the falls to the Hoodoos – weird-looking rock spires caused by wind and water erosion. The trail works its way around the back of Tunnel Mountain through forest and some river meadows (10.2km round-trip).

You can track the north shore of Lake Minnewanka for kilometers on a multi-use trail that is sometimes closed due to bear activity. The classic hike is to walk as far as the **Aylmer Lookout**, nearly 12km one way. Less taxing is the 5.6km round-trip hike to **Stewart Canyon**, where you can clamber down rocks and boulders to the Cascade River.

Some of the best multiday hikes start at the Sunshine Village parking lot (where skiers grab the gondola in winter). From here you can plan two- to four-day sorties up over **Healy Pass** and down to **Egypt Lake**, or else catch the gondola up to Sunshine Village, where you can cross the border into BC and head out across Sunshine Meadows into **Mt Assiniboine Provincial Park**.

The best backcountry experience is arguably the **Sawback Trail**, which travels from Banff up to Lake Louise the back way – it's over 74km, with six primitive campsites and three spectacular mountain passes.

Check out Lonely Planet's *Banff, Jasper & Glacier National Parks* guide for more details about more single-day and multiday hikes.

★Cory Pass Loop   HIKING

(Map p586) By the time you reach the midpoint of this adventurous 13km loop, you'll have a hard time believing you started from the Trans-Canada Hwy/Hwy 1. The trail's relentless 920m ascent into spectacular, wild high country culminates at Cory Pass (2350m), where you'll round the corner of Mt Edith and descend through a barren scree-covered landscape before looping back through dense forest.

★Johnston Canyon
& the Inkpots   HIKING

(Map p586; 🚹) Aside from the Lake Louise shoreline, no place in Banff sees as much foot traffic as the wide, paved Johnston Canyon Trail. The crowds make total sense once you enter the canyon, where dramatic cliff faces vie for your attention with two gorgeous waterfalls. More intrepid hikers can climb to the Inkpots, colorful natural pools in a high mountain valley.

★Mt Assiniboine Trail   HIKING

Banff's most iconic backcountry hike is this three- to four-day, 55.7km odyssey to the pyramid-shaped peak of Mt Assiniboine, nicknamed the Matterhorn of the Rockies. Starting from the top of the Sunshine ski gondola, the trail takes in alpine meadows, rocky valleys, high mountain passes and a series of beautiful lakes en route to Assiniboine and the pristine Bryant Valley.

Horseback Riding

Banff's first European explorers – fur traders and railway engineers – penetrated the region primarily on horseback. You can recreate their pioneering spirit on guided rides with **Banff Trail Riders** (Map p596; ☎403-762-4551; www.horseback.com; 138 Banff Ave; guided rides per person \$64-196), which will fit you out with a trusty steed and lead you on a one- to three-hour day trip or bring you into the backcountry for an overnight adventure at its Sundance Lodge. Instruction and guiding are included; a sore backside is more or less mandatory for beginners. Grin and bear it.

Skiing & Snowboarding

There are three ski areas in the national park, two of them in the vicinity of Banff Town. Large, snowy Sunshine Village is considered world-class. Tiny Norquay, a mere 5km from the center, is your half-day, family-friendly option.

Sunshine Village (Map p586; www.skibanff.com; day ski pass adult/youth $114/89) straddles the Alberta–BC border. Though slightly smaller than Lake Louise in terms of skiable terrain, it gets much bigger dumpings of snow, or 'Champagne powder' as Albertans like to call it (up to 9m annually). Aficionados laud Sunshine's advanced runs and lengthy ski season, which lingers until Victoria Day weekend in late May. A high-speed gondola whisks skiers up in 17 minutes to the village, which sports Banff's only ski-in hotel, the Sunshine Mountain Lodge.

Mt Norquay (Map p586; ☑ 403-762-4421; www.banffnorquay.com; Mt Norquay Rd; day ski pass adult/youth/child $89/68/35; ⊙ 9am-4pm; ♿), a short distance uphill from downtown Banff, has a long history of entertaining Banff visitors. The smallest and least visited of the three local hills, this is a good place to body-swerve the major show-offs and hit the slopes for a succinct half-day.

Local buses shuttle riders from Banff hotels to both resorts (and Lake Louise) every 30 minutes during the season.

White-Water Rafting

The best rafting is outside the park (and province) on the **Kicking Horse River** in Yoho National Park, BC. There are Class IV rapids here, meaning big waves, swirling holes and a guaranteed soaking. Lesser rapids are found on the **Kananaskis River** and the Horseshoe Canyon section of the **Bow River**. The Bow River around Banff is better suited to mellower float trips.

Several rafting companies are located in the park, including Hydra River Guides (p600) and **Rocky Mountain Raft Tours** (☑ 403-762-3632; www.banffrafttours.com; Golf Course Loop Rd; ⊙ mid-May–late Sep; ♿). Tour prices start around $60 for a one-hour float.

☞ Tours

Via Ferrata   OUTDOORS
(Map p586; ☑ 844-667-7829; www.banffnorquay.com/summer/via-ferrata; Mt Norquay; ⊙ mid-Jun–mid-Oct) These fixed-protection climbing

---

THE MOUNTAIN MAN

Driving into Banff you might notice a distinctive face staring at you from the town-limits sign, sporting a jaunty hat, a drooping meerschaum pipe and a rather splendid handlebar moustache. Meet 'Wild' Bill Peyto, one of the great characters of the Canadian Rockies and the original wild man of the mountains.

Born in Kent, England, in 1869, young William was the third eldest of a family of nine children. Having left the cramped environs of the Peyto household at 17, Bill set out to find his fortune in Canada, arriving in Halifax in 1887, where he initially found work as a railway laborer, part-time rancher and government employee. But it wasn't long before Bill found his true calling – as a mountain guide working for the packing and outfitting business owned by Tom Wilson.

Over the next decade he proved himself a skilled trapper, huntsman and alpinist, exploring Mistaya Valley and Peyto Lake, making the first successful ascent of Bow Summit in 1894 and notching up the first (failed) attempt at Mt Assiniboine the following year (he eventually scaled it in 1902). He even found time for some book-larnin', schooling himself in paleontology and geology using secondhand textbooks. Within a matter of years he had become one of the most skilled amateur naturalists in the Rockies.

He was also a notorious showman with an eye for a natty outfit. One of his clients, Norman Collie, painted a vivid picture of Wild Bill: 'Peyto assumes a wild and picturesque though somewhat tattered attire. A sombrero, with a rakish tilt to one side, a blue shirt set off by a white kerchief (which may have served civilization for napkin), and a buckskin coat with a fringe border add to his cowboy appearance. A heavy belt containing a row of cartridges, hunting knife and six-shooter as well as the restless activity of his wicked blue eyes, give him an air of bravado...'

You can still visit one of Bill's original log cabins on the grounds of the Whyte Museum in Banff, and his action-packed diary – which is appropriately titled *Ain't It Hell: Bill Peyto's Mountain Journal* – is available from the museum shop.

routes on Mt Norquay let your test your head for heights. Choose from the Explorer ($169, 2½ hours), the Ridgewalker ($219, four hours), the Skyline ($279, five hours) and the Summiteer ($349, six hours), which includes a three-wire suspension bridge to the top of Mt Norquay. Prices include full safety kit, accompanying guide and passage up the Norquay chairlift to the start point.

Hydra River Guides   RAFTING

(Map p596; ☑ 403-762-4554; www.raftbanff.com; 211 Bear St; ⊙ 7:30am-9pm) This well-regarded company has been running rafting trips for over three decades. The most popular is the 20km Kicking Horse Classic ($149), with varied rapids (up to class IV) and a BBQ lunch; novices and families will appreciate the sedate Mild float trip (adult/child $79/59); for late risers there's the Last Waltz ($115), which doesn't get going until midafternoon.

Lake Minnewanka Cruises   CRUISE

(Map p586; ☑ 866-606-6700; www.banffjasper collection.com/attractions/lake-minnewanka-cruise; Minnewanka Loop Dr; adult/child classic cruise $58/29, explorer cruise $81/41; ⊙ classic cruise hourly 10am-6pm late Jun–mid-Sep, noon-5pm mid-Sep–mid-Oct; explorer cruise 10am late Jun-early Sep) Hop on board the standard cruise across emerald-hued Lake Minnewanka, or opt for an extended 'explorer' cruise between snowy peaked mountains to the glacial pass of **Devil's Gap**, where you can catch a glimpse of the Prairies. Crew will fill you in on local geology and history.

🛌 Sleeping

Accommodations in Banff Town are generally expensive, especially in summer. Booking ahead is strongly recommended.

For listings of available accommodations, check the Banff Tourism Bureau (p602) and the Parks Canada Visitor Centre (p602).

Parks Canada operates several popular campgrounds. Sites at Tunnel Mountain and Two Jack – the two closest to town – should be reserved months in advance; others along the Bow Valley Parkway/Hwy 1A are first-come, first-served.

★ Samesun Banff   HOSTEL $

(Map p596; ☑ 403-762-4499; www.banffhostel. com; 433 Banff Ave; dm incl breakfast from $65; P @ 🛜) Catering to a youthful international backpacker crowd, the welcoming Samesun offers a central Banff Ave location, a full line-

up of daily activities (hiking, cycling, canoeing, hot springs) and 112 dorm beds spread across modern, compact six- to 14-person rooms (some with fireplaces). A DIY breakfast is included, and the bustling on-site **Beaver** resto-bar keeps everyone happy with nightly drink specials.

Two Jack Lakeside   CAMPGROUND $

(Minnewanka Loop Dr; tent & RV sites $27.40; ⊙ May-Oct; P) Right on Two Jack Lake, 11km northeast of town, Two Jack Lakeside is the most scenic of the Banff-area campgrounds, usually filling its 74 reservable sites months in advance. You can now also 'glamp' at Two Jack in one of 10 'oTENTiks' – fully serviced A-frame 'tents' with hot showers and electricity, sleeping up to six people for $120 per night.

HI Banff Alpine Centre   HOSTEL $

(☑ 403-762-4123; www.hihostels.ca; 801 Hidden Ridge Way; dm from $55, d with shared/private bath from $177/214, private cabins from $238; P @ 🛜) Near the top of Tunnel Mountain, Banff's HI hostel is well away from the madness of Banff Ave. The classic mountain-lodge style buildings offer spick-and-span accommodations ranging from dorms to private doubles to cabins. Common areas are open and comfortable, with fireplaces, views and an on-site bar and restaurant. Public buses run by the front door, and passes are complimentary.

★ Buffaloberry   B&B $$$

(Map p596; ☑ 403-762-3750; www.buffaloberry. com; 417 Marten St; r $465; P ❄ 🛜) Centrally located and surrounded by colorful flowering plants, this purpose-built B&B makes a cheerful, comfortable home base. The four individually decorated bedrooms are heavy on homey charm, and the underfloor heating and nightly turn-down treats keep the pamper factor high. With an ever-changing menu (think baked Camembert egg custard or 'triple B' – blueberry, buttermilk and buckwheat – pancakes), breakfasts are divine.

★ Fairmont Banff Springs   HOTEL $$$

(☑ 403-762-2211; www.fairmont.com/banff-springs; 405 Spray Ave; r from $599; P ❄ @ 🛜 🏊) Rising like a Gaelic Balmoral above the trees at the base of Sulphur Mountain and visible from miles away, the Banff Springs is a wonder of early 1920s revivalist architecture and one of Canada's most iconic buildings. Wandering through its grand lobby and elegant lounge, wine bar and restaurant, it's easy to forget that it's also a hotel.

Banff Log Cabin B&B
B&B **$$$**

(☑ 403-762-3516; www.bannfflogcabin.ca; 222 Glen Cres; cabin incl breakfast $425; P ☎) If having your own cozy cabin only steps from the rush of Bow River Falls sounds appealing, you'll love this B&B. Wedding planner/photographer owners Sharon and Malcolm ply guests with a comfy bed, prosecco and handmade local chocolates, tea kettles, an outdoor fire pit for roasting marshmallows and loaner bikes for the short ride across the pedestrian bridge into town.

🍴 Eating

Wild Flour
CAFE **$**

(Map p596; ☑ 403-760-5074; www.wildflour bakery.ca; 211 Bear St; mains $5-10; ⊙7am-4pm; ☎☑) ✎ If you're searching for an inexpensive snack or a relatively guilt-free sugary treat, make a beeline for Banff's best bakery, where you'll find cheesecake, dark-chocolate torte and macaroons – along with breakfasts, delicious fresh-baked focaccia, well-stuffed sandwiches on homemade bread, and soups, all of it organic. Not surprisingly, the place gets busy – but outdoor courtyard seating helps alleviate the crush.

Evelyn's Coffee World
CAFE **$**

(Map p596; ☑ 403-762-0352; www.evelynscoffee bar.com; 215 Banff Ave; mains $6-10; ⊙7am-9pm, to 10pm Fri-Sun; ☎) Pushing Starbucks onto the periphery, Evelyn's cranks out some of Banff's best coffee, along with wraps, pies and – best of all – its own selection of giant homemade cookies, the saviour of many an exhausted hiker.

★ Eddie Burger Bar
BURGERS **$$**

(Map p596; ☑ 403-762-2230; www.eddieburger bar.ca; 6/137 Banff Ave; burgers $17-23; ⊙11am-2am, from 11:30am Oct-May) Not your average fast-food joint, Eddie's is devoted to building large, custom-made and crave-worthy burgers, from the usual classics to specialties like the elk burger with blueberry chutney. Add to this a hearty helping of poutine and an Oreo milkshake or a shaken Caesar (cocktail, not salad!) garnished with a chicken wing, and you're set – for the next week.

★ Bear Street Tavern
PUB FOOD **$$**

(Map p596; ☑ 403-762-2021; www.bearstreet tavern.ca; 211 Bear St; mains $15-25; ⊙11:30am-late) This gastropub hits a double whammy: ingeniously flavored pizzas washed down

with locally brewed pints. Banffites head here in droves for a plate of pulled-pork nachos or a bison-and-onion pizza, accompanied by pitchers of hoppy ale. The patio overlooking Bison Courtyard is the best place to linger if the weather cooperates.

Block Kitchen & Bar
TAPAS **$$**

(Map p596; ☑ 403-985-2887; www.banffblock. com; 201 Banff Ave; tapas $9-28; ⊙11am-11pm; ☑) This casual bar serves up tapas with heavy Asian and Mediterranean influences – or 'Mediterrasian,' as it calls it. The small but creative plates might not satisfy truly ravenous post-hiking appetites, but there are plenty of vegan and gluten-free options. The low-lit interior has a cool and quirky edge, while the breezy sidewalk terrace makes a pleasant perch in summertime.

Nourish
VEGETARIAN **$$**

(Map p596; ☑ 403-760-3933; www.nourishbis tro.com; 211 Bear St; mains $18-26; ⊙11:30am-10:30pm Mon-Thu, 7:30-10:30am & 11:30am-10:30pm Fri-Sun; ☑) Confronted by a strangely beautiful papier-mâché tree when you walk in the door, you instantly know this vegetarian bistro is not average. With locally sourced dishes like wild-mushroom ravioli, Moroccan cauliflower bites or 27-ingredient nachos with Canadian cheddar or vegan queso, Nourish has carved out a gourmet following in Banff. Dinner is served as shareable tapas and larger plates.

Juniper Bistro
BISTRO **$$$**

(☑ 403-763-6219; www.thejuniper.com/dining; 1 Juniper Way; breakfast & small plates from $14, mains $28-34; ⊙7am-11pm; ☑) Spectacular mountain views combine with an innovative, locally sourced menu at Juniper's, a surprisingly good hotel restaurant on Banff's northern outskirts. Beyond breakfasts and dinners, the midafternoon 'Graze' menu is also enticing – think small plates of orange and cardamom-poached beets or bison carpaccio with juniper berry and pink peppercorn, all accompanied by fab cocktails and 'mocktails'. Vegetarian, vegan and gluten-free options abound.

Park
AMERICAN **$$$**

(Map p596; ☑ 403-762-5114; www.parkdistillery. com; 219 Banff Ave; mains $19-52; ⊙11am-10pm) Banff gets hip with a microdistillery to complement its microbrewery, plying spirits (gin, vodka and whiskey) and beer made from Alberta's foothills' grain. It all goes down perfectly with a mesquite beef hoagie, fish tacos or anything off the excellent appetizer menu. Cocktails are creative, fun and ever-changing.

Drinking & Nightlife

★ Grapes
WINE BAR

(☑ 403-762-6860; www.fairmont.com/banff-springs/dining/grapeswinebar; Fairmont Banff Springs, 405 Spray Ave; 5-9:30pm Sun-Thu, from 3pm Fri & Sat) Sporting original crown molding and dark wood paneling from its early days as a ladies' writing salon, this intimate wine bar in Banff's Fairmont makes an elegant spot for afternoon aperitifs. British Columbian Meritage and Ontario Riesling share the menu with international vintages, while tapas of house-cured meats, cheeses, pickled veggies and candied steelhead will tempt you to linger for dinner.

Whitebark Cafe
COFFEE

(Map p596; ☑ 403-760-7298; www.whitebarkcafe.com; 401 Banff Ave; ⊙ 6:30am-7pm) Early risers in need of their java fix should head straight to this sleek corner cafe attached to the Aspen Lodge. It's renowned among locals not only for its superb coffee, but also for its muffins, snacks and sandwiches. For an unconventional (and inexpensive) breakfast, check out its bacon-and-egg breakfast cup, a mini-meal encased in delicious flaky pastry.

Banff Ave Brewing Co
MICROBREWERY

(Map p596; ☑ 403-762-1003; www.banffavebrewingco.ca; 110 Banff Ave; ⊙ 11am-2am) Banff Ave's sprawling 2nd-floor beer hall bustles day and night, slinging a dozen craft brews created on the premises alongside a wide range of nibbles: buttered soft pretzels, bratwurst, burgers and the like. Late-night half-price pizza specials offer welcome relief to late-returning hikers and help keep things hopping into the wee hours.

St James's Gate Olde Irish Pub
PUB

(Map p596; ☑ 403-762-9355; www.stjamesgatebanff.com; 207 Wolf St; ⊙ 11am-2am) Banff is a Celtic name, so it's hardly surprising to find an Irish pub here, and a rather good one at that. Check out the woodwork, crafted and shipped from the old country. Aside from stout on tap and a healthy selection of malts, there's classic pub grub, including an epic steak-and-Guinness pie.

Information

Banff Tourism Bureau (Map p596; ☑ 403-762-8421; www.banfflakelouise.com; 224 Banff Ave; ⊙ 8am-8pm mid-May–Sep, 9am-5pm rest of year) Opposite the Parks Canada desks in the Banff Visitor Centre, this info desk provides advice on accommodations, activities and attractions.

Parks Canada Banff Visitor Centre (Map p596; ☑ 403-762-1550; www.pc.gc.ca/banff; 224 Banff Ave; ⊙ 8am-8pm mid-May–Sep, 9am-5pm rest of year) The Parks Canada office provides park info and maps. This is where you can find current trail conditions and weather forecasts, and register for backcountry hiking and camping.

Getting There & Away

AIR

The nearest airport is Calgary International Airport (p584). Numerous year-round shuttle buses make the two-hour journey between the airport and Banff. Buses are less frequent in the spring and fall. Companies include **Banff Airporter** (☑ 403-762-3330; www.banffairporter.com; Banff to Calgary Airport adult/child $68/34), whose 11 daily buses can pick up and drop off passengers at virtually any Banff address, and the slightly more expensive Brewster Express, whose nine daily services (adult/child $72/36) also stop at most Banff hotels.

BUS

Brewster Express (☑ 403-221-8242; www.banffjaspercollection.com/brewster-express; 100 Gopher St; adult/child Banff to Calgary Airport $72/36, to Jasper $120/60, to Lake Louise $37/19) offers bus service from most Banff hotels to downtown Calgary ($72, 2½ hours), Jasper ($120, 4¾ hours) and Lake Louise ($37, one hour).

From late October through April, Jasper-based **SunDog Tour Company** (☑ 780-852-4056; www.sundogtours.com; 414 Connaught Dr, Jasper Town; ⊙ 8am-5pm) also runs buses from Banff to Jasper ($79, four hours).

CAR & MOTORCYCLE

Several major car-rental companies have branches in Banff Town. During summer all vehicles might be reserved in advance, so call ahead. If you're flying into Calgary, reserving a car at the airport (where the fleets are huge) may yield a better deal than waiting to pick up a car when you reach Banff Town. In winter, all-weather tires or snow chains are often required; inquire locally about current road conditions.

Getting Around

Roam (☑ 403-762-0606; www.roamtransit.com; adult/child local routes $2/1, regional routes $6/3) Roam runs Banff's excellent public bus network. Five local routes serve Banff Town and its immediate surroundings: route

1 to Banff Hot Springs, 2 to Tunnel Mountain, 4 to Cave and Basin, 6 to Lake Minnewanka and 7 to the Banff Centre. Additional regional buses serve Canmore (route 3), Lake Louise (8X express and 8S scenic) and Johnston Canyon (route 9).

Banff Taxi (☑ 403-762-0000; www.banfftransportation.com/banff-taxi-service.html) Taxi service for Banff and the surrounding area.

Lake Louise

☑ 403 / POP 1175

Considered by many to be the crown jewel of Banff National Park, Lake Louise is nearly impossible to describe without resorting to shameless clichés. Standing next to the serene, implausibly turquoise lake, Banff's wild grandeur feels (and is) tantalizingly close, with a surrounding amphitheater of finely chiseled mountains that hoist Victoria Glacier audaciously toward the heavens.

Famous for its teahouses, grizzly bears and hiking trails, Lake Louise is also renowned for its much-commented-on 'crowds,' plus the incongruous lump of towering concrete known as Chateau Lake Louise. But frankly, who cares? You don't come to Lake Louise to dodge other tourists. You come to share in one of the Rockies' most spectacular sights, one that has captured the imaginations of mountaineers, artists and visitors for more than a century.

Lake Louise 'village,' just off Trans-Canada Hwy/Hwy 1, is little more than an outdoor shopping mall, a gas station and a handful of hotels.

◉ Sights

★Moraine Lake   LAKE

The spectacular, deep teal waters of Moraine Lake are one of Banff's iconic sights. The lake's rugged and remote setting in the **Valley of the Ten Peaks**, accessed via a narrow winding road, only add to its allure, Many visitors actually prefer Moraine Lake to the more famous Lake Louise – so many, in fact, that you'll have to be lucky or an early riser to get a parking spot here; the lot often fills up by 5:30am in peak season.

For many, the quintessential Moraine Lake experience is watching sunrise from the **Rockpile**, the famous viewpoint on the lake's northern shore. From the parking lot, it's a steep but short 10-minute climb to the best views.

There are also some excellent day hikes from the lake, or you can rent a boat at the

Moraine Lake Boathouse (Map p586; www.morainelake.com/day-visits; boat rental per hour $120; ☉9am-5pm mid-Jun–mid-Sep, weather permitting) and paddle through the glacier-fed waters.

Moraine Lake Rd and its facilities are open from June to early October. In winter the access road is closed by snow.

★Lake Louise   LAKE

Named for Queen Victoria's fourth daughter (Princess Louise Caroline Alberta, who also lent her name to the province), the gob-smackingly gorgeous Lake Louise is a place that requires multiple viewings. Aside from the standard picture-postcard shot (blue sky, even bluer lake, glistening glacier), try visiting at six in the morning, at dusk in August, in the October rain or after a heavy winter storm.

Morant's Curve Viewpoint   VIEWPOINT

(Map p586) Evoking oohs, ahs and countless shutter clicks from every traveler who passes near, this pullover and viewpoint on the Bow Valley Pkwy/Hwy 1A sits at a scenic curve in the Bow River much favored by both the Canadian Pacific Railway and *National Geographic* photographer Nicholas Morant (1910–99), whose images helped publicize Banff during its early days as a national park.

Lake Louise Summer Gondola   CABLE CAR

(☑403-522-3555; www.lakelouisegondola.com; 1 Whitehorn Rd; adult/child $38/17; ☉9am-4pm mid-May–mid-Jun, 8am-5:30pm mid-Jun–Jul, to 6pm Aug, to 5pm Sep–mid-Oct; ☉) For a bird's-eye view of the Lake Louise area – and a good chance of spotting grizzly bears on the avalanche slopes – climb aboard the Lake Louise Gondola, which crawls up the side of **Whitehorn Mountain** via an open ski lift or enclosed gondola to a dizzying viewpoint 2088m above the valley floor. Look out for the imposing fang of 3544m-high **Mt Temple** piercing the skyline on the opposite side of the valley.

🏃 Activities

★Lake Agnes & the Beehives   HIKING

Two compelling attractions make this Lake Louise's most popular hike. First, the historic Lake Agnes Teahouse (p606), where hikers have been refueling since 1901, makes a supremely atmospheric spot to break for tea, sandwiches and baked goods at the

Lake Louise Area

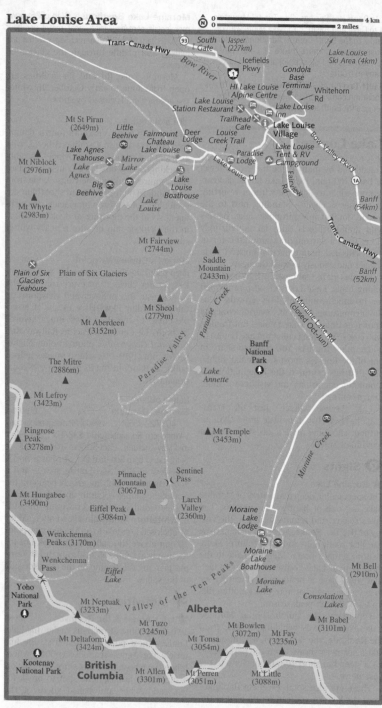

N

0 — 4 km
0 — 2 miles

Trans-Canada Hwy

93 South Gate

Jasper (227km)

Bow River

Icefields Pkwy

Lake Louise Ski Area (4km)

Gondola Base Terminal

HI Lake Louise Alpine Centre

Lake Louise Station Restaurant

Whitehorn Rd

Mt St Piran (2649m)

Little Beehive

Fairmount Chateau Lake Louise

Deer Lodge

Trailhead Cafe

Louise Creek Trail

Lake Louise Inn

Lake Louise Village

Lake Agnes Teahouse

Lake Agnes

Mirror Lake

Paradise Lodge

Lake Louise Tent & RV Campground

Bow Valley Pkwy

Mt Niblock (2976m)

Big Beehive

Lake Louise Boathouse

Lake Louise

Lake Louise Dr

Fairview Rd

1A

Banff (54km)

Mt Whyte (2983m)

Lake Louise

Trans-Canada Hwy

Banff (52km)

Mt Fairview (2744m)

Saddle Mountain (2433m)

Plain of Six Glaciers Teahouse

Plain of Six Glaciers

Paradise Creek

Moraine Lake Rd (closed Oct–Jun)

Mt Sheol (2779m)

Mt Aberdeen (3152m)

Paradise Valley

Banff National Park

The Mitre (2886m)

Lake Annette

Mt Lefroy (3423m)

Ringrose Peak (3278m)

Mt Temple (3453m)

Moraine Creek

Mt Hungabee (3490m)

Pinnacle Mountain (3067m)

Sentinel Pass

Eiffel Peak (3084m)

Larch Valley (2360m)

Moraine Lake Lodge

Wenkchemna Peaks (3170m)

Wenkchemna Pass

Eiffel Lake

Moraine Lake Boathouse

Mt Bell (2910m)

Yoho National Park

Mt Neptuak (3233m)

Valley of the Ten Peaks

Alberta

Moraine Lake

Consolation Lakes

Mt Tuzo (3245m)

Mt Bowlen (3072m)

Mt Fay (3235m)

Mt Babel (3101m)

Kootenay National Park

Mt Deltaform (3424m)

British Columbia

Mt Allen (3301m)

Mt Tonsa (3054m)

Mt Perren (3051m)

Mt Little (3088m)

3.4km mark. Second, the lake views from atop 2270m Big Beehive (the trail's ultimate destination) are phenomenal. Set off early to beat the crowds.

★ Skoki Valley Trail   WALKING

(Map p586) The beautiful multiday hike into Skoki Valley is one of Banff's classic backcountry adventures. Starting from Temple Lodge at Lake Louise ski resort, the trail leads over Boulder Pass and Deception Pass, past numerous lakes and around Fossil Mountain to the rustic 1930s-vintage **Skoki Lodge** (Map p586; ☑ 403-522-3555; www.skoki. com; r per person incl 3 meals & afternoon tea $240-305) and **Merlin Meadows** wilderness campground. From here, various loop hikes fan out into the wilderness.

Plain of Six
Glaciers Trail   HIKING

Combining magnificent lake and glacier perspectives with an afternoon tea break, this is one of Banff's most memorable hikes. Follow Lake Louise's western shore for 2km, then enter a long wooded valley flanked by crags popular with rock climbers and zigzag up to the historic Plain of Six Glaciers Teahouse (p606). A further 1km climb leads to impressive Victoria Glacier views.

Lake Louise
Ski Resort   SKIING

(☑ 403-522-3555; www.skilouise.com; 1 Whitehorn Rd; day pass adult/youth $114/98; 🚐) Lake Louise is the largest of Banff's 'Big Three' resorts (the other two being Sunshine and Norquay). It offers a humongous 1700 hectares of skiable land divided between 145 runs. It's great for families, with a good spread of beginner-rated (25%) runs on the Front Side/South Face (especially around the base area), along with plenty of intermediate-rated (45%) runs. The longest (8km) is on the Larch Face.

Lake Louise
Boathouse   BOATING

(☑ 403-522-3511; www.fairmont.com/lake-louise/ promotions/canoeing; canoe rental per 30min/1hr $115/125; ⊙ 8am-8:30pm Jun-Sep, weather permitting) Hire a canoe from the Lake Louise Boathouse and paddle across the icy waters – you can dislodge yourself from at least some of the lakeside crowds, although you'll pay handsomely for the experience. Boats can carry three adults or two adults and two children. Life jackets are included.

Wild Water Adventures   RAFTING

(☑ 403-522-2211; www.wildwater.com; 111 Lake Louise Dr; ⊙ 6am-8pm late May-early Oct) This operator will get you out on the Kicking Horse River rapids for everything from a gentle ride (adult/child $89/69) to the Maximum Horsepower trip ($169). Some trips will pick up from Lake Louise or Banff hotels; others require you to find your own way there (double-check when you book).

🛏 Sleeping

Lake Louise Tent & RV
Campground   CAMPGROUND $

(www.reservation.pc.gc.ca; Lake Louise village; tent/RV sites $27.40/32.30; ⊙ tent park Jun-Sep, RV park year-round) Near the village, this efficient, wooded 395-site campground accommodates RVs on one side of the river and tents and soft-sided vehicles on the other, protected from bears behind an electric fence. Choose a site away from the railway tracks to enjoy views of Mt Temple in relative peace. Book online through the Parks Canada website.

HI Lake Louise Alpine Centre   HOSTEL $

(☑ 403-522-2201; www.hihostels.ca; 203 Village Rd, Lake Louise village; dm/d $64/192; 🅿) This is what a hostel should be – clean, friendly and full of interesting travelers – and the rustic, comfortable lodge-style buildings, with plenty of raw timber and stone, are fine examples of Canadian Rockies architecture. Dorm rooms are fairly standard and the small private rooms are a bit overpriced, but this is as close as you'll get to budget in Lake Louise.

★ Moraine Lake Lodge   HOTEL $$$

(☑ 403-522-3733; www.morainelakelodge.com; 1 Moraine Lake Rd; r/cabin from $717/964; ⊙ Jun-Sep; 🅿🐾) 🌿 The experience here is intimate, personal and private, and the service is famously good. While billed as rustic (ie no TVs), the rooms and cabins offer mountain-inspired luxury with big picture windows, wood-burning or antique gas fireplaces, soaking tubs, feather comforters and balconies overlooking the lake. The fine-dining restaurant on-site wins equal plaudits. Canoe use is free for guests.

★ Paradise Lodge
& Bungalows   CABIN $$$

(☑ 403-522-3595; www.paradiselodge.com; Lake Louise Dr; cabins $345-488, r in lodge $415-475; ⊙ mid-May–Sep) These cozy, lovingly restored

1930s log cabins along the Lake Louise road are only moments from the lakeshore. Each is unique, but expect comfy beds, kitchens or kitchenettes and claw-foot soaking tubs. Newer lodge rooms are hotel-style. Cheerful flowery grounds and tree-shaded lawns provide ample lounging opportunities. Kids will love the playground and miniature doghouse cabin for Beau the pooch.

★ **Deer Lodge** HOTEL $$$
(☑ 403-410-7417; www.crmr.com; 109 Lake Louise Dr; r from $329; P ♠) Tucked demurely behind Chateau Lake Louise, historic Deer Lodge dates from the 1920s and has managed to keep its genuine alpine feel intact. The rustic exterior and maze of corridors can't have changed much since the days of bobbed hair and F Scott Fitzgerald. Lodge rooms are fairly small but quaint, while spacious Heritage rooms have smart, boutique-like furnishings.

The beautifully restored lounge and log-cabin sitting room, especially with its stone fireplace ablaze, make time travel feel like a real possibility. Tranquility here is ensured – you won't find a TV anywhere.

✗ Eating

★ **Lake Agnes Teahouse** TEAHOUSE $
(www.lakeagnesteahouse.com; lunch $7.50-15; ☺ 8am-5pm early Jun-early Oct) The 3.4km hike from Lake Louise to Lake Agnes is among the area's most popular – surely because it ends here. This fabulously rustic alpine teahouse perched at 2135m (7005ft) seems to hang in the clouds beside the ethereal lake and its adjacent waterfall. Homemade soup, thick-cut sandwiches and lake-water tea help fuel the jaunt back down. Cash only. Expect queues.

Trailhead Café SANDWICHES $
(☑ 403-522-2006; www.facebook.com/lakelouise AB; Samson Mall, Lake Louise village; sandwiches $6-10; ☺ 7am-6pm) This is *the* place to come for breakfast or a takeout lunch. Wraps and sandwiches are made to order, the staff are well versed in the espresso machine, and the omelets, buttermilk pancakes and lox cream-cheese bagels will fuel you for the trail without breaking the bank. Expect a queue.

Plain of Six
Glaciers Teahouse TEAHOUSE $$
(snacks & meals $9.50-25; ☺ 9am-5pm mid-Jun-early Oct) Constructed in 1927 as a way station for Swiss mountaineering guides leading clients up to the summit of Mt Victoria, this twin-level log chalet looks like something out of the pages of *Heidi*. Nestled in a quiet glade at 2100m, it dishes up homemade sandwiches, cakes, gourmet teas and hot chocolates to a steady stream of puffed-out hikers.

★ **Lake Louise**
Station Restaurant CANADIAN $$$
(☑ 403-522-2600; www.lakelouisestation.com; 200 Sentinel Rd, Lake Louise village; mains lunch $16-26, dinner $20-48; ☺ 11:30am-4pm & 5-9pm Jun-Sep, noon-4pm & 5-8:30pm Wed-Sun Oct-May) Lake Louise's historic train station is the most atmospheric place in town to have a meal. Details like stacks of turn-of-the-century luggage, the stationmaster's desk and the original dining cars out back transport you back to 1910, when the elegant edifice was first built. Dig into maple-glazed salmon, Wiener schnitzel or slow-braised bison ribs and soak up the vintage vibe. Reservations recommended.

ℹ Information

Lake Louise Backcountry Trails Office
(☑ 403-522-1264; Lake Louise Visitor Centre, Lake Louise village; ☺ 8:30am-7pm Jun-Sep, 9am-5pm Oct-May) Parks Canada desk offering specialist advice on exploring the backcountry area around Lake Louise.

Lake Louise Tourism Bureau (☑ 403-762-8421; www.banfflakelouise.com; Samson Mall, Lake Louise village; ☺ 8:30am-7pm Jun-Sep, 9am-5pm Oct-May) Information on activities and accommodations in Lake Louise village.

Parks Canada Lake Louise Visitors Centre
(☑ 403-522-3833; www.pc.gc.ca/en/pn-np/ab/banff; Samson Mall, Lake Louise village; ☺ 8:30am-7pm Jun-Sep, 9am-5pm Oct-May) Visit Parks Canada's newly renovated digs for national park info and to register for backcountry hikes.

ℹ Getting There & Away

Brewster (p592) runs bus services to Lake Louise from Calgary International Airport, Banff and Jasper; the bus terminal is a marked stop at Samson Mall.

For drivers, the quickest way to get to Lake Louise from Banff (55km, 40 minutes) is along the Trans-Canada Hwy/Hwy 1. Running parallel to the main highway, the Bow Valley Parkway is a slightly slower (one to 1¼ hours), but much more scenic alternative; as it isn't fenced, it's a great route for wildlife sightings.

Jasper Town & Around

📍 780 / POP 4590

Arriving in Jasper Town, the first thing you may notice is how low-key it all feels. Yes, Jasper is the most important town for kilometers around, and sees nearly two million visitors each year. Yet it feels far removed from the traffic jams of Lake Louise and retains an agreeable humility that seems more reflective of its workaday railway town roots than of its modern status as a national park hub.

With only two main thoroughfares, Patricia St and Connaught Dr, holding the lion's share of businesses, you can easily explore Jasper on foot in half an hour. Sit on the lawn outside the early 20th-century log cabin at the heart of town, meditate on the murmur of the freight trains running by, and soak up the unhurried vibe. You really couldn't ask for a friendlier, more relaxing base for exploring the awe-inspiring wilderness that surrounds you.

◎ Sights

★ **Jasper National Park** NATIONAL PARK
(Map p608; www.pc.gc.ca/jasper; day pass adult/child/family $9.80/free/19.60) Wolves, elk, caribou, beaver and bear roam freely; glaciers stretch out between stark mountain peaks; waterfalls thunder over slopes; and valleys are wide and lush, with rivers charging turbulently through them – this is Jasper National Park, covering a diverse 11,228 sq km. Jasper is far from built up: while activities like hiking and mountain biking are well established and deservedly popular, it's still easy to experience the solitude and remoteness that abound in this park.

Some of the most popular natural wonders, like Miette Hot Springs and Maligne Canyon, are easily accessible, and many more attractions are just a short hike away. Keep a little spare time in your itinerary to take advantage of the many diversions you stumble upon – a sparkling lake to admire, a snowshoe tour to explore or a moose to watch ambling by. As the largest of Canada's Rocky Mountain parks, Jasper will quickly captivate you with its beauty and serenity.

★ **Miette Hot Springs** HOT SPRINGS
(Map p608; www.pc.gc.ca/hotsprings; Miette Rd; adult/child/family $7.05/5.15/20.35; ⊙9am-11pm mid-Jun–Aug, 10:30am-9pm May–mid-Jun & Sep–mid-Oct) More remote than Banff's historic

springs, Miette Hot Springs ('discovered' in 1909) are 61km northeast of Jasper off Hwy 16, near the park's eastern boundary. The soothing waters, kept at a pleasant 37°C (98°F) to 40°C (104°F), are surrounded by peaks and are especially enjoyable when the fall snow is drifting down and steam envelops the crowd. Raining summer evenings also make for stunning, misty conditions.

Horseshoe Lake LAKE
(Map p608) This idyllic, blue-green horseshoe-shaped lake just off the Icefields Pkwy is missed by many visitors, making a stopover here all the more alluring. A choice spot for a bracing summer swim or a short stroll around the perimeter, the lake is surrounded by steep cliffs and is frequented by cliff divers. It's probably safer to watch than join in.

Maligne Lake LAKE
(Map p608) Almost 50km from Jasper at the end of a stunning road that bears its name, 22km-long Maligne Lake is the recipient of a lot of hype. It's the largest lake in the national park and there's no denying its appeal: the baby-blue water and a craning circle of rocky, photogenic peaks are a feast for the eyes.

Jasper Skytram CABLE CAR
(Map p608; 📍780-852-3093; www.jaspertramway.com; Whistlers Mountain Rd; adult/child/family $50/27/125; ⊙8am-9pm late Jun-Aug, 9am-8pm mid-May–late Jun, 10am-5pm late Mar–mid-May, Sep & Oct) If the average, boring views from Jasper just aren't blowing your hair back, go for a ride on this sightseeing gondola. The seven-minute journey (departures every nine minutes) zips up through various mountain life zones to the high barren slopes of the Whistlers. From the gondola's upper station a steep 1.25km hike leads to the mountain's true summit, where views stretch for 75km. Arrive early or late to avoid midday lines. There's a small restaurant and gift shop up top.

Pyramid Lake LAKE
(Map p608) Pyramid Lake is popular with canoers and kayakers in summer and ice-skaters in winter. From its eastern shore, a wooden pedestrian bridge leads out to Pyramid Island, a small nature preserve. At night, stargazers congregate on the bridge for unobstructed views of the heavens. It's roughly 7km northwest of Jasper Town.

Jasper National Park

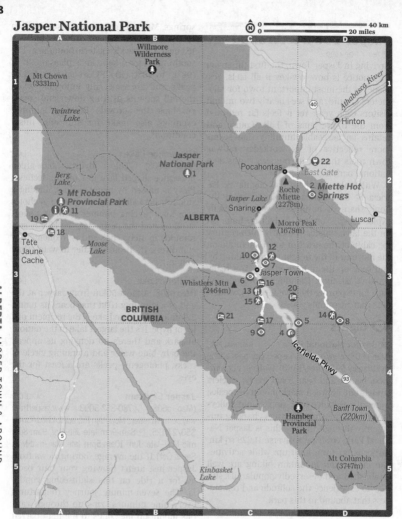

0 — 40 km
0 — 20 miles

Lake Edith
LAKE

(Map p608) On the east side of the highway opposite Jasper town, Lake Edith is a popular summer getaway, ringed by cycling and hiking trails and frequented by kayakers and other boaters. It's equipped with picnic spots and a small beach area.

Jasper Planetarium
OBSERVATORY

(☎ 780-931-3275; www.jasperplanetarium.com; 1 Old Lodge Rd, Jasper Town; adult/child $29/15, incl telescope stargazing $59/25; ⊙ shows 3:30, 4:30, 7:45 & 8:45pm mid-Jun–mid-Sep, 7:45pm mid-Sep–Apr, 8:45pm May–mid-Jun, closed Nov & last week of Apr) Relocated to the Fairmont Jasper Park Lodge on a year-round basis in 2019, Jasper's planetarium screens multiple shows daily in its 40-seat dome theater, whisking visitors off on a virtual tour of Jasper's Dark Sky Preserve. For an extra fee, you can also stargaze through the planetarium's giant telescope (billed as the largest in the Rockies).

🏃 Activities

Cycling

Jasper tops Banff for single-track mountain biking; in fact, it's one of the best places in Canada for the sport. Many rides are within striking distance of town. Flatter, on-road options include the long-distance

Jasper National Park

grunt along the Icefields Parkway. The holy grail for experienced off-road cyclists is the **Valley of the Five Lakes** – it's varied and scenic, with plenty of places where you can let it rip. For more information, get a copy of *Mountain Biking Guide, Jasper National Park* from the Jasper Information Centre (p613).

Vicious Cycle (☑780-852-1111; www.vicious canada.com; 630 Connaught Dr, Jasper Town; bike rental per hour/day from $8/32; ☺9am-6pm Sun-Thu, to 7pm Fri & Sat) and **The Bench Bike Shop** (☑780-852-7768; www.thebenchbikeshop. com; 606 Patricia St, Jasper Town; bike rental per hour/day from $10/30; ☺10am-6pm) can sort out bike rentals and offer additional trail tips.

Hiking

★**Skyline Trail**   HIKING
(Map p608) This 45.6km Canadian Rockies classic leads through awe-inspiringly rugged, wide-open high country along the crest of the Maligne Range. Most hikers allow two or three days to savor the expansive views, with overnight stops at a series of backcountry campsites or the rustic Shovel Pass Lodge (p611). A shuttle (p614) allows hikers to start at one trailhead and finish at the other.

★**Tonquin Valley Trail**   HIKING
(Map p608) For wilderness lovers, this 53.2km out-and-back into one of Jasper's most untouched lake valleys is the experience of a lifetime. Notorious for its mosquitoes and mud, it's not for the faint-hearted, but the access route through Maccarib Pass is highly scenic, while campgrounds and a backcoun-

try lodge offer accommodations with amazing views of Amethyst Lake and the sheer rock Ramparts.

★**Maligne Canyon**   HIKING
(Map p608) One of Jasper's most spectacular hikes is the easy amble through this steep, narrow gorge shaped by the torrential waters of the Maligne River. The canyon at its narrowest is only a few meters wide and drops a stomach-turning 50m beneath your feet. Crossed by six bridges, it's most easily accessed from the parking area on Maligne Lake Rd.

Horseback Riding
Tonquin Valley Backcountry Lodge (p612) runs incredible, fully guided summer pack trips into the roadless Tonquin Valley, including meals and accommodations at their backcountry lodge and complimentary use of boats on Amethyst Lake. For a more leisurely horseback experience, **Jasper Riding Stables** (☑780-852-7433; www.jasper stables.com; Stables Rd, Jasper Town; 1/2/3hr rides $52/95/135; ☺May–mid-Oct) offers enjoyable day rides lasting from one to three hours.

Skiing & Snowboarding
Jasper National Park's only downhill ski area is **Marmot Basin** (Map p608; www.ski marmot.com; Marmot Basin Rd; day pass adult/ child $110/89), which lies 19km southwest of town off Hwy 93A. Though not legendary, the presence of 95 runs and the longest high-speed quad chairlift in the Canadian Rockies mean Marmot is no pushover – and

its relative isolation compared to the trio of ski areas in Banff means shorter lift lines.

On-site are some cross-country trails and a predictably expensive day lodge, but no overnight accommodations. Regular shuttles link to Jasper Town in season. Seriously cold weather can drift in suddenly off the mountains, so dress appropriately.

☞ Tours

Jasper Adventure Centre OUTDOORS
(☏ 780-852-5595; www.jasperadventurecentre.com; 611 Patricia St, Jasper Town; ⊙ 8am-9pm late Jun-Aug, to 6pm May-late Jun & Sep–mid-Oct) Jasper's veteran guiding outfit runs numerous local tours, as well as some further afield to the Icefields and Lake Louise. One of their most popular trips is the three-hour Wildlife Discovery Tour (adult/child $69/35). In winter they share office space with **Sun-Dog Tour Company** (☏ 780-852-4056; www.sundogtours.com; 414 Connaught Dr, Jasper Town; ⊙ 8am-5pm), from where they organize dog-sledding and ice walks in addition to their many year-round tours.

Jasper Walks & Talks HIKING
(☏ 780-852-4994; www.walksntalks.com; 626 Connaught Dr, Jasper Town; walks per adult $65-90, per child $45-50) Longtime local resident and former Parks Canada guide Paula Beauchamp leads small groups on three- to six-hour tours with a focus on such local attractions as Maligne Canyon and Mt Edith Cavell Meadows. Bring a picnic lunch, good walking shoes, your camera and lots of questions for your very knowledgeable guide. Winter snowshoe adventures are also offered.

Maligne Lake Cruises CRUISE
(Map p608; www.banffjaspercollection.com/attractions/maligne-lake-cruise; Maligne Lake; adult/child 90min cruise $79/40, 2hr cruise $114/57; ⊙ May-Sep) These interpretive boat tours take you to the far end of Maligne Lake, to iconic Spirit Island (which, it should be noted, is not actually an island). En route, the lake shimmers in beguiling shades of blue as guides fill you in on local history and geology. Nevertheless, the price does seem rather high for the service provided.

🛏 Sleeping

Accommodations in Jasper are generally cheaper than Banff, but that's not really saying much. The town's limited hotel and hostel rooms fill up quickly in summer, as

do the cabins, bungalows and campgrounds in the surrounding countryside.

Jasper's 11 park campgrounds (four of which accept reservations) are open from mid-May to September or October, with one (Wapiti) staying open year-round. For information, visit the Parks Canada Jasper Information Centre (p613).

★ HI Jasper HOSTEL $
(☏ 587-870-2395; www.hihostels.ca; 708 Sleepy Hollow Rd, Jasper Town; dm/d from $50/167; P @ 🖥) 🅿 Jasper's 157-bed HI hostel, opened two blocks from downtown in 2019 to replace the aging Whistlers Mountain facility, is a gem. The sprawling lower level houses a bevy of bright, welcoming common spaces – a guest kitchen and dining area complete with cozy booth seating, pool table, cafe, laundry facilities, free parking with EV charging stations, and more.

Upstairs, pairs of four-bed dorms share their own shower, toilet and sink area, while family rooms, private quads and wheelchair-accessible units are also available. There's excellent wi-fi throughout, along with individual reading lights and charging stations above each bed. A potential downside for light sleepers are the train tracks right outside the back windows.

Jasper Downtown Hostel HOSTEL $
(☏ 780-852-2000; www.jasperdowntownhostel.ca; 400 Patricia St, Jasper Town; dm/d from $45/140; 🖥) With Jasper's town center smack on its doorstep, this former residence has been remodeled and expanded to create simple, modern two- to 10-bed dorms, many with en suite bathrooms, along with comfortable private rooms sleeping one to three. Upstairs rooms are brighter, with wooden floors, while common areas include a well-equipped kitchen, a spacious front patio and a simple lounge.

Athabasca Hotel HOTEL $$
(☏ 780-852-3386; www.athabascahotel.com; 510 Patricia St, Jasper Town; r without/with bath $139/239, 1-/2-bedroom ste $395/425; P @ 🖥) Around since 1929, the Atha-B (as it's known) is the best budget hotel in town. A taxidermist's dream, with animal heads crowding the lobby, it has small, clean rooms with wooden and brass furnishings and thick, wine-colored carpets. Less expensive rooms share a bathroom. Dated but not worn, it feels like you're staying at Grandma's (if Grandma liked to hunt).

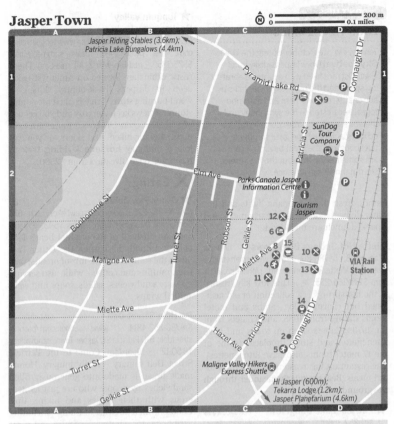

Jasper Town

Jasper Town

Activities, Courses & Tours
1	Jasper Adventure Centre	C3
2	Jasper Walks & Talks	C4
3	SunDog Tour Company	D2
4	The Bench Bike Shop	C3
5	Vicious Cycle	C4

Sleeping
6	Athabasca Hotel	C3
7	Jasper Downtown Hostel	D1

Eating
8	Coco's Cafe	C3
9	Olive Bistro	D1
10	Other Paw Bakery	D3
11	Patricia Street Deli	C3
12	Raven Bistro	C2
13	The Spice Joint	D3

Drinking & Nightlife
14	Jasper Brewing Co	D3
15	SnowDome Coffee Bar	C3

Becker's Chalets CHALET $$
(Map p608; ☑780-852-3779; www.beckers
chalets.com; Hwy 93; d/q chalet from $200/225;
P ☎) Just 6km south of Jasper Town and
paces from the northern entrance to the
Icefields Pwky, this complex of 118 chalets
has something for everyone – from 33 cute
1930s-vintage 'heritage' cabins to a block of
big modern four-plexes popular with fami-
lies and European tour groups. Rates here
are among Jasper's cheapest, even if it's a bit
of a mob scene.

Shovel Pass Lodge LODGE $$
(Map p608; ☑780-852-4215; www.skylinetrail.
com; per person incl meals $255; ◷late Jun-early
Sep) Built in 1921 and rebuilt in 1991, the
Shovel Pass Lodge is situated halfway along
the emblematic Skyline Trail (p609). The
seven guest cabins are basic, with log bed

LOOK TO THE SKIES

Ten days in late October during the **Dark Sky Festival** (www.jasperdarksky.travel; ☉late Oct) are filled with events celebrating space and the night sky. Hear talks by astronauts, astronomers and astrophotographers, listen to the symphony under the stars, see the aurora borealis reflected in a glacial lake and gaze through a telescope into the great beyond. There are some free events, but the big hitters sell out months in advance.

frames, fresh linen, propane lights and hot water delivered daily. Two hearty meals and a packed lunch are includedd.

Miette Hot Springs Bungalows   CABIN $$
(Map p608; ☑780-866-3750; www.miettebunga lows.com; Miette Hot Springs Rd; r/chalets/cabins from $135/165/235; ℗) This low-key 'resort' at the hot springs is a collection of old fashioned but charming log cabins and motel rooms dating from 1938, and chalets from the 1970s. Cabins sleep up to six and have kitchenettes and stone fireplaces (some of the 17 motel rooms also have kitchenettes). The restaurant has reasonably priced standard meals. **Bears regularly meander through the grounds.**

⭐**Patricia Lake Bungalows**   BUNGALOW $$$
(☑780-852-3560; www.patricialakebungalows. com; Patricia Lake Rd; bungalows $199-510) Reminiscent of an earlier era, this charming assemblage of bungalows sits placidly at the end of a dead-end road on the shores of lovely Patricia Lake, 5km north of Jasper Town. Owned by the same family for nearly half a century, it's the kind of place where you can truly leave the modern world behind.

⭐**Tekarra Lodge**   HOTEL $$$
(☑780-852-3058; www.tekarralodge.com; Hwy 93A; lodge/cabins from $249/289; ☉May-Oct; ℗🐾🐾) In business since 1947, these cabins – some of the most atmospheric in the park – sit 1km south of town near the Athabasca River amid tall trees and splendid tranquility. Hardwood floors, wood-paneled walls plus stone fireplaces and kitchenettes inspire coziness. Family-friendly amenities abound, including an on-site playground, evening s'mores and songs by the campfire, bike rentals and a guest laundry.

⭐**Tonquin Valley**
Backcountry Lodge   LODGE $$$
(Map p608; ☑780-852-3909; www.tonquinvalley. com; per person incl meals summer/winter $325/185; ☉mid-Feb–Mar & Jul–mid-Sep) These rustic cabins are located on Amethyst Lake, deep in Jasper's backcountry. Linen, a wood-burning stove, home-cooked meals and stunning views keep you cozy and you get use of a boat or canoe. There's a minimum two-night stay for hikers and skiers, or you can join a multiday **horseback-riding trek** to reach the lodge (five days from $2500).

🍴 Eating

⭐**Other Paw Bakery**   CAFE $
(☑780-852-2253; www.bearspawbakery.com; 610 Connaught Dr, Jasper Town; mains $5-13; ☉7am-6pm) An offshoot of the original Bear's Paw bakery around the corner, the Other Paw offers the same addictive mix of breads, pastries, muffins and coffee – while also serving up tasty sandwiches, salads, soups and well-stuffed wraps.

Patricia Street Deli   SANDWICHES $
(☑780-852-4814; www.facebook.com/patricia streetdeli; 610 Patricia St, Jasper Town; sandwiches $9.50-12; ☉10am-7pm) Come to the Patricia Street Deli hungry – really hungry. Homemade bread is made into generously filled sandwiches by people who are just as generous with their smiles and hiking tips. Choose from a huge list of fillings, including various pestos, chutneys, veggies and meat cuts. Join the queue and satiate your ravenous backcountry appetite.

Coco's Cafe   CAFE $
(☑780-852-4550; www.cocoscafe.ca; 608b Patricia St, Jasper Town; mains $9-15; ☉8am-4pm; 🍴)
🍴 If you're looking for breakfast, you can't go wrong at Coco's. There's not much room inside, but many are happy to cram in to plan hikes and trade bear sightings. There's plenty of locally sourced, vegan, veggie and celiac-friendly fare on the menu, while carnivores are kept happy with Montreal smoked meat, pulled pork and lox.

The Spice Joint   JAMAICAN $
(☑780-852-3615; www.facebook.com/thespice joint; 614 Connaught Dr, Jasper Town; mains $12-16; ☉10am-9pm) Since opening in 2018, this friendly snack shack decked out in red, yellow and green has brought a welcome dose of Caribbean flavor to Jasper's northern wilds. The menu revolves around Jamaican treats

like spicy jerk chicken, barbecued pork, Rasta greens and quinoa salad, all accompanied by fruit smoothies, ginger beer, rum, Red Stripe beer and Blue Mountain coffee.

Olive Bistro MEDITERRANEAN $$
(☑780-852-5222; www.olivebistro.ca; Pyramid Lake Rd, Jasper Town; mains $14-35; ⏱4-10pm May-Oct, 5-9pm Nov-Apr; ✍) This casual restaurant with big booths has a classy menu. Main dishes such as slow-braised organic lamb shank, elk rigatoni or a vegan 'dragon bowl' come sandwiched between appetizers of white truffle scallops and indulgent desserts like a gourmet banana split. In summer, enjoy excellent cocktails during the 4pm to 6pm happy hour; in winter, there's live music twice monthly.

★**Maligne Canyon Wilderness Kitchen** BARBECUE $$$
(Map p608; ☑844-762-6713; www.banffjasper collection.com; Maligne Canyon Rd; lunch mains $16-26, dinner $55; ⏱8am-10pm May-Sep, 9am-4pm Sun-Fri, to 10pm Sat Oct-Apr) The outdoor deck at the edge of gorgeous Maligne Canyon is temptation enough to dine at Jasper's newest restaurant. But the real clincher is the cornucopia of local meats, shown off to full advantage in the house special Maligne Canyon Platter: grilled venison sausage, smoked chicken, glazed baby back pork ribs, and barbecue Alberta beef brisket slow-cooked for 16 hours.

★**Raven Bistro** MEDITERRANEAN $$$
(☑780-852-5151; www.theravenbistro.com; 504 Patricia St, Jasper Town; lunch mains $16-27, dinner mains $28-46; ⏱11:30am-11pm; ✍) This cozy, tastefully designed bistro offers vegetarian dishes, encourages shared plates and earns a loyal clientele with sublime offerings like Kaffir lime–coconut seafood pot or lamb shank glazed with fresh mint, horseradish, honey and Dijon mustard. Not in a lunch-dinner mood? Try the 'late riser' breakfast skillet, or come for happy hour (3pm to 5:30pm daily).

🍸 Drinking & Nightlife

★**SnowDome Coffee Bar** COFFEE
(☑780-852-3852; http://snowdome.coffee; 607 Patricia St, Jasper Town; ⏱7am-8pm; 🛜) Some of Jasper's best damn coffee is – no joke! – served at this former Coin Clean Laundry, now reincarnated as a cafe-gallery-community hangout. Beyond the stellar espresso, SnowDome bakes killer muffins

(still oven-warm at opening time) and promotes good karma with its free mug basket and 'pay it forward' bulletin board where you can prepurchase coffee for an unsuspecting future customer.

Folding Mountain Taproom MICROBREWERY
(Map p608; ☑780-817-6287; www.foldingmoun tain.com; 49321 Hwy 16, Jasper East; ⏱11am-10pm) This up-and-coming microbrewery draws a boisterous mix of locals from nearby Hinton and travelers heading to or from the wilderness. Test the waters with a four-beer sampler (choose from Flash Flood IPA, Alpine Cranberry Sour or a dozen other brews on tap), then stick around for excellent burgers, salads and other pub grub. It's just 5km outside Jasper's eastern park gate.

Jasper Brewing Co BREWERY
(☑780-852-4111; www.jasperbrewingco.ca; 624 Connaught Dr, Jasper Town; ⏱11:30am-1am) 🍺 This brewpub was the first of its kind in a Canadian national park, using glacial water to make its fine ales, including the signature Rockhopper IPA and Jasper the Bear honey beer. It's a perennial favorite hangout for locals and tourists alike, with TVs and a good food menu.

ℹ️ Information

Parks Canada Jasper Information Centre
(☑780-852-6176; www.pc.gc.ca/jasper; 500 Connaught Dr, Jasper Town; ⏱9am-7pm mid-May–early Oct, to 5pm rest of year) Parks Canada operates a well-staffed and helpful info desk in this wonderful midtown building – Jasper's oldest, dating from 1913. Directly adjacent are the local tourist information stand, plus an excellent gift shop.

Tourism Jasper (☑780-852-6236; www. jasper.travel; 500 Connaught Dr, Jasper Town; ⏱9am-7pm mid-May–early Oct, to 5pm rest of year) Jasper's municipal tourist office, directly adjacent to the Parks Canada info center at the heart of town, offers a wealth of information about area activities and accommodations.

ℹ️ Getting There & Away

BUS

SunDog (p602) offers daily bus service year-round to Edmonton airport ($99, 5½ hours), along with winter service (late October through April) to Lake Louise ($69, four hours), Banff Town ($79, five hours) and Calgary airport ($135, seven hours).

From May through mid-October, **Brewster Express** (☑877-625-4372; www.banffjasper collection.com/brewster-express) runs its own daily express bus to Lake Louise ($97, 3½ hours), Banff ($120, 4¾ hours), Canmore ($144, 5¾ hours) and Calgary International Airport ($167, eight hours).

TRAIN

VIA Rail (☑888-842-7245; www.viarail.ca) offers tri-weekly train services west to Vancouver (from $148, 23½ hours) and bi-weekly services east to Toronto (from $367, 72 hours). In addition, there is a tri-weekly service to Prince Rupert, BC (from $156, 33 hours, with obligatory overnight stop in Prince George). Call or check in at the **train station** (607 Connaught Dr, Jasper Town) for exact schedule and fare details.

❶ Getting Around

Maligne Valley Hikers Express Shuttle (☑780-852-3331; www.maligneadventures. com; one way adult/child $35/17.50; ☉late Jun–late Sep) Runs a daily 45-minute shuttle from Jasper Town to Maligne Lake, stopping en route at the North Skyline trailhead, then returning from Maligne Lake to Jasper at 10am.

Caribou Cabs (☑780-931-2334; www.facebook.com/cariboucabs) offers dependable taxi service; call to arrange pickup. Ride-sharing services such as Uber and Lyft are not currently an option.

SOUTHERN ALBERTA

Alberta's national parks and cities grab most of the headlines, leaving the expansive south largely forgotten. This is true cowboy land, where the ghosts of herders like John Ware and the Sundance Kid are woven through the history of endless ranch land. It's often interrupted by deep, dramatic canyons carved in the last ice age, as well as towering hoodoos – funky, Dr Seuss–like rock sculptures. History abounds at Head-Smashed-In Buffalo Jump, and Writing-on-Stone and Dinosaur provincial parks, Unesco World Heritage areas that preserve the region's fascinating past.

Picture-perfect landscapes are plentiful here. The dusty badlands around Drumheller open up into wide open prairies that stretch east all the way to the Cyprus Hills of western Saskatchewan. To the west lies Waterton Lakes National Park, with some of the most spectacular scenery in the Rockies – utterly different from Banff and Jasper yet still under the radar of most visitors.

Drumheller

☑403 / POP 7982

As you approach Drumheller, the road dips down dramatically into the Red Deer Valley, looking like a big layered cake. This community was founded on coal but now thrives on another subterranean resource – dinosaur bones. A small town set amid Alberta's enigmatic badlands, it acts as the nexus of the so-called Dinosaur Trail. Paleontology is a serious business here (the nearby fantastic Royal Tyrrell Museum is as much research center as tourist site), and downtown the cartoon dino statues on most street corners add some color and character to an otherwise average town. Add in the museums in nearby East Coulee on the Hoodoo Drive and the ghosts of Wayne, and you're set.

The summers are hot, and the deep-cut river valley in which Drumheller sits provides a much-needed break to the monotony of the prairies. Hoodoos dominate this badlands landscape, which has featured in many a movie (mainly Westerns).

◎ Sights & Activities

★ **Royal Tyrrell Museum of Palaeontology**   MUSEUM
(☑403-823-7707; www.tyrrellmuseum.com; 1500 North Dinosaur Trail, Midlands Provincial Park; adult/child/family $19/10/48; ☉9am-9pm mid-May–Aug, 10am-5pm Sep, 10am-5pm Tue-Sun Oct–mid-May; ♿) This fantastic museum is one of the pre-eminent dinosaur museums on the planet, made even better by a $5.9 million expansion project completed in 2019. Even if you have no interest in dinos, you'll come out feeling like you missed your calling as a paleontologist. The exhibits are nothing short of mind-blowing. Unlike some other dinosaur exhibits, there's nothing dusty or musty about this super-modern place. Children will love the interactive displays.

Look for the skeleton of 'Hell-Boy,' a dinosaur discovered in 2005, and 'Black Beauty,' a 67-million-year-old *T rex* rearing its head into the sky. You can learn how the dinosaurs are extracted from the ground and even peer into the fossil lab.

There are also summertime opportunities to get among the badlands on a guided tour and discover your own dino treasures on a fossil search ($10) or a dinosaur dig ($15) – you'll feel like you've stepped right into your very own *Jurassic Park*.

Atlas Coal Mine
MINE

(☑403-822-2220; https://atlascoalmine.ab.ca; East Coulee; adult/family $12/35, tours $14-27; ⊙9:45am-5pm Sep-Jun, to 6:30pm Jul & Aug) Home to the last wooden tipple (a coal-loading structure) in Canada, Atlas Coal Mine closed its production in 1959. Today it's an engaging historic sight where you can check out the original mine buildings and chat with staff dressed as mine characters. Join an hourly tour to climb the tipple, don a lamp and head down a tunnel – or to learn about the darker, unmentionable side of mining.

Rosedale Suspension Bridge
BRIDGE

(Hwy 56, Rosedale) This suspension bridge isn't very long or particularly high, but it's definitely not for the faint of heart. Made of see-through wire mesh, it sways like a river reed in the wind. The bridge was used by miners from 1931 to 1957; on the far side of the Red Deer river, you can see the now-closed mines. Despite previous use of row-boats and aerial cable cars, it was the bridge that was considered dangerous due to high winds and floods.

East Coulee School Museum
MUSEUM

(☑403-822-3970; http://ecsmuseum.ca; 359 2nd Ave, East Coulee; $7; ⊙10am-5pm May-Sep) This original village school in art deco style doubled in size to eight rooms during the coal mining boom of the 1930s. Exhibits inside detail the history of East Coulee (once bigger than Drumheller) and of the school itself. In the recreated classroom, peruse the students' journals to get a sense of what life was like back then, both for them and their teachers.

World's Largest Dinosaur
LANDMARK

(60 1st Ave W; adult/family $4/10.50; ⊙10am-5:30pm; ⊕) In a town filled with dinosaurs, this *T rex* is the king of them all. Standing 26m high above a parking lot, it dominates the Drumheller skyline (and is featured in the *Guinness World Records*). It's worth climbing the 106 steps to the top for the novelty of standing in the dino's toothy jaws – plus the views are mighty good. Ironically, the dinosaur isn't technically very accurate: at 46m long, it's about 4.5 times bigger than its extinct counterpart.

Dinosaur Trail
& Hoodoo Drive
SCENIC DRIVE

Drumheller is on the Dinosaur Trail, a 48km loop that runs northwest from town and includes Hwys 837 and 838. The stunning scenery is worth the drive – badlands and river views await at every turn. The 25km Hoodoo Drive starts about 18km southeast of Drumheller on Hwy 10; it's usually done as an out-and-back, with Wayne as the turn-around point.

The Dinosaur Trail loop takes you past **Midland Provincial Park** (no camping), where you can take a self-guided hike, and past the vast **Horsethief Canyon** and its picturesque views. Glide peacefully across the Red Deer River on the free, cable-operated **Bleriot Ferry**, which has been running since 1913; watch for beavers, which have a dam here. This area is also frequented by moose, lynx and cougars. On the west side of the valley, pause at **Orkney Viewpoint**, which overlooks the area's impressive canyons.

Along the Hoodoo Drive between Rosedale and Lehigh you'll find the best examples of **hoodoos** – weird, eroded, mushroom-like columns of sandstone rock – there's also an interpretive trail.

This area was once the site of a prosperous coal-mining community; the historic Atlas Coal Mine and East Coulee School Museum are both worth a stop. Take the side trip on Hwy 10X (which includes 11 bridges within 6km) from Rosedale to the small community of **Wayne** (population 27) with its famous and supposedly haunted saloon.

🍴 Sleeping & Eating

★Rosedeer Hotel
HISTORIC HOTEL

(☑403-823-9189; http://visitlastchancesaloon. com; 555 Jewel St, Wayne; camping $20, rooms $65-80; ℗) If you've wondered what it's like to stay in a ghost town (or in what's rumored to be a haunted hotel!), this is your chance to find out. The Rosedeer is much like it was in yesteryear: small rooms, simple furnishings and a rip-roaring Wild West saloon downstairs. Don't come expecting frills and fanciness, and reserve ahead (it fills fast).

River Grove
Campground & Cabins
CAMPGROUND $

(☑403-823-6655; www.camprivergrove.com; 25 Poplar St; campsites/RV sites/cabins from $38/47/104; ⊙May-Sep; ℗⛱) Right in town and close to the big *T rex,* this shaded campground next to the river has lots of amenities, such as laundry machines and a big playground for kids. There's even an arcade for the surly teens among you.

ALBERTA DRUMHELLER

Taste the Past B&B
B&B **$$**

(☑403-823-5889; www.bbcanada.com/taste; 281 2nd St W; s/d $130/150; P❋🛜) This converted turn-of-the-century house has evolved into a cozy downtown B&B. All rooms have a private bathroom, and there is a communal living room that could have been airlifted straight from your Grandma's house. With only three rooms, a stay here feels more like visiting with friends.

★ Café Olé
CAFE **$**

(☑403-800-2090; www.facebook.com/cafeoledrum; 11 Railway Ave; sandwiches $8-13; ⊙8am-5pm Sun-Thu, to 7pm Fri & Sat; ☑) This quiet, darkly lit cafe serves up soups, sandwiches, coffees, teas and desserts that would hold their own in New York City. Flavorful and fresh, mains pair perfectly with a London Fog chai or a fruit smoothie. The waitstaff are kind, helpful and attentive, though when busy things can be slow – but worth the wait, for sure.

★ Last Chance Saloon
BAR

(☑403-823-9189; www.visitlastchancesaloon.com; 555 Jewel St, Wayne; ⊙11am-11pm Mon-Sat, to 7pm Sun) Last Chance is the real thing – a Western saloon from 1913, complete with bear skins, old kerosene lamps, antique photos and bullet holes in the wall. Since its original heyday, Wayne's population has dwindled from 2500 to 27, many of whom you'll find in this lively, eclectic place. Meat pies, maple-bacon burgers and chicken dinners go well with the beer.

❶ Information

Tourist Information Center (☑403-823-1331; https://traveldrumheller.com; 60 1st Ave W; ⊙9am-9pm mid-May–Sep, 10am-5:30pm Oct–mid-May) Located by the feet of the giant *T rex*, with lots of maps and brochures on offer.

❶ Getting There & Away

Hammerhead Tours (☑403-590-6930; www.hammerheadtours.com) runs a full-day tour ($141) from Calgary to the Drumheller badlands and the Royal Tyrrell Museum.

There is currently no public transportation to Drumheller.

Dinosaur Provincial Park

In no other place on earth has such a large number of dinosaur bones been found in such a small area – over 40 species and 400 skeletons. Set where *The Lost World* meets *Little House on the Prairie*, **Dinosaur Provincial Park** (☑403-378-4342; www.dinosaurpark.ca; off Hwy 544; ⊙9am-5pm Sun-Thu, to 7pm Fri & Sat) FREE – a Unesco World Heritage site – comes at you without warning, deep in a chasm that opens before your feet from the grassy plain. A dehydrated fantasy landscape, there are hoodoos, colorful rock formations and dinosaurs aplenty.

The 81-sq-km park begs to be explored, with wildflowers, the odd rattler in the rocks and, if you're lucky, maybe even a *T rex*. This isn't just a tourist attraction but a hotbed for science: paleontologists have uncovered countless skeletons here, which now reside in many of the finest museums around the globe.

There are five short interpretive hiking trails to choose from and a driving loop runs through part of the park, giving you the chance to see a number of dinosaur skeletons in their death positions. To preserve the fossils, access to 70% of the park is restricted and may be seen only on guided hikes or **bus tours** (adult/child $20/10), which operate from late May to October. (The hikes and tours are popular, so be sure to reserve a place.)

The park's **Dinosaur Visitors Centre** (☑403-378-4342; http://albertaparks.ca; gallery admission adult/child $6/3; ⊙9am-5pm Sun-Thu, to 7pm Fri & Sat mid-May–Aug, shorter hours rest of year) is a field station of the Royal Tyrrell Museum (p614) in Drumheller and has a small, yet excellent, series of dino displays, as well as exhibits on the realities of paleontology.

In a hollow by a small creek sits the park's **Dinosaur Campground** (☑403-378-4342; https://albertaparks.ca; campsites/RV sites $26/33, comfort camping $105-130, reservation fee $12; ⊙year-round; P). The ample tree cover is a welcome reprieve from the volcanic sun. Laundry facilities and hot showers are available, as are a small shop and cafe. This is a popular place, especially with the RV set, so phone ahead.

Though 75 million years ago dinosaurs cruised around a tropical landscape, it's now a hot and barren place – make sure you dress for the weather, with sunscreen and water at the ready. It's halfway between Calgary and Medicine Hat, and some 48km northeast of Brooks. From Hwy 1, take Secondary Hwy 873 to Hwy 544.

Head-Smashed-In Buffalo Jump

The story behind the place with the strangest name of any attraction in Alberta is one of ingenuity and resourcefulness – and is key to the First Nations' (and Canada's) cultural heritage. For thousands of years, the Blackfoot used the cliffs near the town of Fort Macleod to hunt bison. Head-Smashed-In Buffalo Jump ([✎] 403-553-2731; https:// headsmashedin.ca; Secondary Hwy 785; adult/child $15/10; ⊗ 10am-5pm) was a marvel of simple ingenuity. When the bison massed in the open prairie, braves from the tribe would gather and herd them toward the towering cliffs. As the animals got closer, they would be funneled to the edge and made to stampede over it to their doom, thus providing meat aplenty for the tribe. For the Blackfoot, the bison was sacred; to honor the fallen prey, every part of the animal was used.

The well-presented displays and films at the interpretive center built cleverly into the hillside are befitting of a Unesco World Heritage site, and it's definitely worth the excursion from Calgary or Lethbridge. You can walk along the cliff trail to the end of the drive land, the spot where the bison plummeted. The site, about 18km northwest of Fort Macleod and 16km west of Hwy 2, also has a cafe and a shop.

Lethbridge

[✎] 403 / POP 92,700

In the heart of southern Alberta farming country sits the former coal-mining city of Lethbridge, divided by the distinctive coulees of the Oldman River. Though there isn't much to bring you to the city, copious parkland, decent dining, and a few good historical sites and museums will help you to easily fill a day. There are ample hiking opportunities in the Oldman River Valley, a 100m-deep coulee bisected by the proverbial Eiffel Tower of steel railway bridges, the largest of its kind in the world. The cottonwoods and pines below the bridge are a prime spot to see porcupines, the infamous North American rodent second only to the beaver in size.

The downtown area, like many North American downtowns, has made a good stab at preserving its not-so-ancient history. To the east, less inspiring Mayor Magrath Dr (Hwy 5) is a chain-store-infested main drag that could be Anywhere, North America.

◉ Sights & Activities

Alberta Birds of Prey Foundation   ANIMAL SANCTUARY

([✎] 403-331-9520; www.burrowingowl.com; 2124 16th Ave, Coaldale; adult/child $12/8; ⊗ 9:30am-5pm mid-May–early Sep) This is a working rescue sanctuary that takes in raptors, owls and other birds of prey and – ideally – releases them promptly back into the wild. However, some animals that are non-releasable are used for trained demos, and the center allows kids and adults to get very close to birds they'd only see glimpses of otherwise. Owl on your shoulder, anyone?

Galt Museum & Archives   MUSEUM

([✎] 403-320-3954; www.galtmuseum.com; 502 1st St; adult/child $6/3; ⊗ 10am-5pm Mon-Sat, to 9pm Thu, 1-5pm Sun) The story of Lethbridge is told at the Sir Alexander Galt Museum, encased in an old hospital building (1910) on the bluff high above the river. Interactive kid-oriented displays let you sit in a streetcar and watch historical footage. The view from the lobby out onto the coulee is great – and free.

Southern Alberta Art Gallery   MUSEUM

([✎] 403-327-8770; www.saag.ca; 601 3rd Ave S; adult/child $5/free, Sun free; ⊗ 10am-5pm Tue-Sat, to 7pm Thu, 1-5pm Sun) With new temporary exhibits every three months, this small gallery focuses on contemporary art. Past exhibitions have included local artists as well as national and international ones, with everything from photography to installation art. The space itself is open and bright and the gift shop is ace.

Helen Schuler Nature Centre & Lethbridge Nature Reserve   NATURE RESERVE

([✎] 403-320-3064; www.lethbridge.ca/nature; Indian Battle Rd; by donation; ⊗ 10am-4pm Tue-Sun Apr, May, Sep & Oct, 10am-6pm Jun-Aug, 1-4pm Tue-Sun Nov-Mar) Permanent displays tell the story of the river valley and coulee, while temporary exhibits focus on bats, bees and the like. Check out Taco Charlie, the tiger salamander, or wander upstairs and see the living roof – in summer, it's filled with blooms. The surrounding trails give you the opportunity to see long-eared and great horned owls and plenty of porcupines sleeping in the trees.

🛏 Sleeping & Eating

Sandman Signature
Lethbridge Lodge   HOTEL $$

(☑ 403-328-1123; www.sandmanhotels.com; 320 Scenic Dr S; r from $139; P🐾😊@🛜🏊) Rooms here are clean and bright, if a little unmemorable; the atrium, on the other hand, is something else, making this a great deal. All of the rooms look down into the fake-foliage-filled tropical interior, complete with winding brick pathways, a kidney-shaped pool and water features.

Bread Milk & Honey   CAFE $

(☑ 403-381-8605; www.breadmilkhoney.ca; 427 5th St S; items $8-15; ⊙7am-5pm Mon-Fri, 9am-5pm Sat & Sun; 🛜) With excellent coffee and everything from oatmeal loaded with banana, cinnamon and almond to a bacon burrito, this is *the* place to come for breakfast. The interior is all exposed brick and wood; come and hang, get an avocado toast or a freshly baked scone, and enjoy the relaxed pace of a Lethbridge morn.

★Telegraph Tap House   PUB FOOD $$

(☑ 403-942-4136; https://taphouse.pub; 310 6th Street S; mains $15-23; ⊙11am-11pm Mon-Thu, to 1am Fri, 9am-1am Sat, 9am-10:30pm Sun) So this is where cool Lethbridgians go. Park yourself at the bar with a craft brew and pulled-pork sliders or chili-cheese fries. Is the stack of antique suitcases left over from others who dared try the Baked Ultimate Poutine and didn't make it out the door?

★Plum   COCKTAIL BAR

(☑ 403-394-1200; http://uncorkplum.com; 330 6th St; cocktails $9-12; ⊙11:30am-10pm, to midnight Fri & Sat) Lethbridge is not an elegant city, but Plum may make you rethink: it's got plush velour curtains, a marble bar with dim lighting and polished copper accents, dark wood and probably the tastiest cocktails you'll find for miles. The 'Baby Ben' is a big favorite, but all of the cocktails are delicious. And the bartenders are cheerful and fun.

It's also a tasty spot for dining. Don't be shy about coming for dinner or lunch.

ℹ Information

Chinook Country Tourist Association

(☑ 403-394-2403; https://tourismlethbridge.com; 2805 Scenic Dr S; ⊙9am-5pm Mon-Sat Oct-Apr, daily May-Sep) On the approach to Lethbridge from Hwy 5.

ℹ Getting There & Away

The **Lethbridge Airport** (☑ 403-329-4466; www.lethbridgeairport.ca; 417 Stubb Ross Rd), a short drive south on Hwy 5, is served by commuter affiliates of Air Canada. Six or seven flights per day go to Calgary.

Red Arrow (☑ 800-232-1958; www.redarrow.ca; 449 Mayor Magrath Dr S) buses connect once daily with Calgary ($53, three hours) and Fort Macleod ($36.50, 45 minutes).

Writing-on-Stone Provincial Park

Perhaps the best thing about this **park** (☑ 403-647-2364; www.albertaparks.ca) FREE is that it really isn't on the way to anywhere. For those willing to get off the main thoroughfare, all efforts will be rewarded. It's named for the extensive carvings and paintings made by the Blackfoot on the sandstone cliffs along the banks of Milk River – more than 3000 years ago. There is an excellent, self-guided interpretive trail that takes you to some of the spectacular viewpoints and accessible pictographs and petroglyphs.

(You *must* stay on the trails to prevent damage to the hoodoos. Many visitors feel the need to add their own marks to the hoodoos – don't be one of them. Not only are you vandalizing a piece of history, you're also desecrating a sacred First Nations site.)

The best art is found in a restricted area (to protect it from vandalism), which you can visit only on a **guided tour** (10am, 2pm and 6pm daily in summer; adult/youth/child $19/11/7) with the park ranger. Other activities include canoeing and swimming in the river in summer and cross-country skiing in winter. Park wildlife is ample, and the visitor center, built in the shape of a traditional tipi, blends perfectly with the region's natural and cultural heritage. Beware: it can get exceedingly hot in the summer and you must have close-toed shoes. (This is rattlesnake country!)

The park's riverside **campground** has 67 sites, running water, showers and flush toilets. It's popular on weekends.

The park is southeast of Lethbridge and close to the US border; the Sweetgrass Hills of northern Montana are visible to the south. To get to the park, take Hwy 501 east for 42km from the town of Milk River, on Hwy 4.

Waterton Lakes National Park

Here flat prairies collide dramatically with the Rockies, with a sparkling lake and a hilltop castle that may make you wonder if you've fallen into a fairy tale. However, **Waterton Lakes National Park** (www.pc.gc.ca/waterton; per day family/adult/child $15.70/7.80/free) is little known to outside visitors, remaining a pocket of sublime tranquility. Visitor numbers took a hit after the 2017 Kenow Wildfire that burned over 19,000 hectares of the park, destroying infrastructure and damaging 80% of the trail network.

Established in 1895 and now part of a Unesco World Heritage site, Unesco Biosphere Reserve and International Peace Park (with the USA's Glacier National Park), this 525-sq-km reserve lies in Alberta's southwestern corner. The park is a sanctuary for numerous iconic animals – grizzlies, elk, deer and cougar – along with 800-odd wildflower species.

The town of **Waterton**, a low-key alpine village with a winter population of about 40, provides a marked contrast to larger, flashier Banff. Its 1920s-era Prince of Wales Hotel stands regally above town on the lakefront.

◉ Sights & Actvities

Cameron Lake   LAKE
Backed by the sheer-sided slopes of Mt Custer, placid Cameron Lake is tucked tantalizingly beneath the Continental Divide at the three-way meeting point of Montana, Alberta and British Columbia. Poised at the end of the 16km Akamina Pkwy (currently closed due to fire damage), this is where day-trippers stop to picnic, hike and rent boats. From foam flowers to fireweed, copious wildflower species thrive here, while grizzly bears are known to frequent the lake's isolated southern shores.

Upper Waterton Lake   LAKE
Visible from all over town, this is the deepest lake in the Canadian Rockies, sinking to a murky 120m. One of the best vantage points is from the Prince of Wales Hotel, where a classic view is framed by an ethereal collection of Gothic mountains, including Mt Cleveland, Glacier National Park's highest peak. A more placid spot is **Emerald Bay**, famous for its turquoise waters and ever-popular with scuba divers.

Cameron Falls   WATERFALL
At the west end of Cameron Falls Dr (a short hop from the center of town) is this dramatically poised torrent of foaming water, notable among geologists for harboring the oldest exposed Precambrian rocks in the Canadian Rockies. Estimates suggest they are 1.5 billion years old, give or take the odd millennium. The lookout here is paved for wheelchair access and the falls are lit up at night.

Crypt Lake Trail   HIKING
Done in a day thanks to a water taxi with service to the trailhead, this thrilling obstacle-laden hike includes a climb up a ladder, a crawl through a narrow rocky tunnel and a sheer rock face with a cable for assistance, ending in gorgeous Crypt Lake. The ascent begins quickly and soon after you'll take in up-close views of waterfalls, mountains and lakes below. Allow enough time for your return trip down, as the boat is the only easy way back!

Waterton Shoreline Cruises   CRUISE
(☑403-859-2362;   www.watertoncruise.com; adult/youth/child $53/26/18; ☉May-Oct) Sail across the shimmering waters of Upper Waterton Lake to the far shore of Goat Haunt, Montana (USA). This family-owned business offers a scenic, 2¼-hour trip on the vintage MV *International* (1927), with lively commentary.

Bring your passport: it docks in the USA for about 30 minutes. July and August have four cruises daily (10am, 1pm, 4pm and 7pm).

Blakiston & Co
Adventure Rentals   BOATING
(☑800-456-0772;   www.blakistonandcompany.com; Crandell Mountain Lodge, 102 Mt View Rd; stand-up paddleboard rental per 1/4hr $30/85; ☉Jun-Aug) Offers stand-up paddleboard (SUP), canoe and kayak (including ones with glass bottoms) rentals for Emerald Bay, the mostly calm patch of water across the street from the Crandell Mountain Lodge (from where this shop operates). E-bikes are also now available (one/two hours $35/50).

🛏 Sleeping & Eating

★Northland Lodge   B&B $$
(☑403-859-2353;   www.northlandlodgecanada.com; 408 Evergreen Ave; r $196-249; ☉mid-May–mid-Oct; 🐾) On the edge of town within

BLACKFOOT CROSSING HISTORICAL PARK

Standing stoically in the center of a First Nations reserve, **Blackfoot Crossing Historical Park** (☑403-734-5171; www.blackfootcrossing.ca; Hwy 842; adult/child $15/10; ☺9am-6pm Jul & Aug, to 5pm Mon-Fri Mar-Jun, Sep & Oct, 10am-3pm Mon-Fri Nov-Feb) celebrates and embraces authentic Siksika (Blackfoot) culture and is entirely worth exploring.

The history of southern Alberta pre-1880 belongs to the Blackfoot confederacy, an amalgamation of the Peigan, Blood and Montana-based Blackfeet tribes. Blackfoot Crossing, long an important tribal nexus, was unique in that it was the only place where nomadic First Nations tribes built a semi-permanent settlement. It was here that the notorious Treaty 7 was signed by Chief Crowfoot in 1877, ceding land to the British crown and establishing the Siksika reservation. After a visit from Prince Charles in 1977, the idea for a historical site was hatched; after 30 years of planning, the park finally opened in 2007.

It's anchored by an architecturally stunning, ecofriendly main building that incorporates elements of tipis and feathered headdresses into its creative design. Within its walls lie a 100-seat theater showcasing cultural dances, a set of exhibits chronicling Blackfoot history and guided tours with local Siksika interpreters and storytellers. Outside, you can enjoy various trails, prairie viewpoints, and a tipi village where traditional crafts are practiced and taught.

To get here, head 100km east of Calgary on Hwy 1 and then 7km south on Hwy 842. The historical park hasn't yet made it onto the mainstream tourist track and remains curiously light on visitors.

earshot of gushing Cameron Falls is this cozy house that Louis Hill (the genius behind the Prince of Wales Hotel) built for himself. A B&B with a wide range of quaint rooms (some with shared bath) and a creaking staircase, it's steeped in character. The welcoming host's freshly baked breakfast is fabulous.

Crandell Mountain Lodge　　　HOTEL $$
(☑403-859-2288; www.crandellmountainlodge.com; 102 Mt View Rd; r from $200; P☎) With homemade cookies in the lobby, this 1940s lodge is doing a good impersonation of a Tudor cottage plucked from a quiet English village. The Crandell has old-fashioned rooms with quilts like Grandma used to make, fireplaces and a front deck facing Emerald Bay across the street. Service is very welcoming.

★**Prince of
Wales Hotel**　　　HISTORIC HOTEL $$$
(☑403-859-2231; www.princeofwaleswaterton.com; Prince of Wales Rd; r from $249; ☺May-Sep; P☎) With a Hogwarts-like setting on a wind-buffeted bluff overlooking Upper Waterton Lake, the grand Prince of Wales blends Swiss-style architecture with the atmosphere of a Scottish castle. The old-world charms extend to serving staff in kilts and high tea in the main lounge – very civilized.

The large lake-facing windows frame the wilderness that awaits.

★**Welch's Chocolates,
Ice Cream & Desserts**　　　DESSERTS $
(cnr Windflower Ave & Cameron Falls Dr; desserts $3-12; ☺9am-10pm May-Oct) In a ranch-style house at the end of Windflower Ave, this family-run Waterton institution is filled with a Willy Wonka's worth of homemade chocolates, fudge and candy. It's also been dishing out ice cream, pies and pastries for 50 plus years, all scoffed down on the wraparound deck.

★**49° North Pizza**　　　PIZZA $$
(☑403-859-3000; www.49degreesnorthpizza.com; 303 Windflower Ave; pizzas $12-30; ☺noon-9pm Mon-Fri, from 5pm Sat & Sun May-Sep) Seriously satisfying pizza with all of the expected renditions, plus some creative gourmet options such as bison and Saskatoon berries, as well as a choice of salads and a make-your-own 'power bowl' (brown rice with a bunch of vegetarian add-ons). Service is top-notch and there's a good beer selection; if the handful of tables and patio are full, you can get takeout.

❶ Information

Parks Canada Visitor Centre (☑403-859-2378; www.pc.gc.ca/waterton; Fountain Ave;

⊘8am-6pm May-Sep) The central stop for information on everything from trail conditions to hotels (and the place to pay your park fee if the entrance isn't staffed or you arrive after hours). It's in a temporary stucture until a new large, contemporary-designed building opens.

My Waterton (www.mywaterton.ca) Waterton Lakes' Chamber of Commerce website with up-to-date visitor information, including a listing of monthly events.

❶ Getting There & Away

The park is open 24 hours a day, 365 days a year, although many amenities and a couple of park roads close in winter. Entry costs are family/adult/child $15.70/7.80/free per day ($11.75/5.80/free during the shoulder seasons). An annual Waterton pass costs $39.20 (adult). Park admission is free on Canada Day (July 1) and Parks Day (third Saturday in July). Passes, to be displayed on your vehicle's windshield, are valid until 4pm on the date of expiration.

If you enter the park when the booth is shut, get a pass early the next morning at the Parks Canada Visitor Centre. Upon entering, you'll receive a map of Waterton Lakes and Glacier National Parks, and the quarterly information-packed newspaper Waterton-Glacier Guide.

Waterton lies in Alberta's southwestern corner, 130km from Lethbridge and 156km from Calgary. The one road entrance into the park is in its northeastern corner, along Hwy 5. Most visitors coming from Glacier and the USA reach the junction with Hwy 5 via Hwy 6 (Chief Mountain International Hwy) from the southeast, after crossing at the **Chief Mountain border crossing** (Chief Mountain Hwy; ⊘7am-10pm Jun-Labour Day, 9am-6pm mid-May–late May & Labour Day-Sep 30). A passport, enhanced driver's license or NEXUS card is required for US and Canadian citizens; all others must present passports and fill out an I-94 or I-94W form (available for $6 at the border).

From Calgary, to the north, Hwy 2 shoots south toward Hwy 5 into the park. From the east, Hwy 5, through Cardston, heads west and then south into the park.

There is no public transportation from Canadian cities outside the park. **Pincher Creek Taxi** (☎403-632-9738) does provide service from the town of Pincher Creek to Waterton town for $75. The shuttle service that previously connected the Prince of Wales Hotel and Glacier Park Lodge in Montana is no longer offered.

Crowsnest Pass

West of Fort Macleod the Crowsnest Hwy (Hwy 3) heads through the prairies and into the Rocky Mountains to Crowsnest Pass (1396m) and the BC border. The Pass, as it's known, is a string of small communities just to the east of the BC border. Of note is the story of the town of **Frank**. In 1903 Frank was almost completely buried when 30 million cu meters (some 82 million tonnes' worth) of nearby Turtle Mountain collapsed and killed around 70 people. Some believe the coal mine dug into the base of the mountain was to blame. But the mining didn't stop; this black gold was the ticket to fortune for the entire region some hundred years ago. Eventually the demand for coal decreased, and after yet more cave-ins and fear of a second slide, the mines shut down for good.

★Frank Slide Interpretive Centre   MUSEUM

(☎403-562-7388; www.frankslide.org; Hwy 3; adult/child $13/9; ⊘9am-6pm Jul & Aug, 10am-5pm Sep-Jun; ⊞) This excellent museum overlooks the Crowsnest Valley and helps put a human face on the tragedy of the Frank landslide. Displays bring mining, the railroad and the early days of this area to life; kids will enjoy having things to pull, push and jump on, as well as puzzles and other interactive activities. There's also a fantastic film dramatizing the tragic events of 1903. Trails from the museum take you out over the slide site itself.

Most of the staff can trace their roots to the area and thus have a personal connection to the slide. You'll find it 1.5km off Hwy 3 and 27km east of the BC border.

NORTHERN ALBERTA

Despite the presence of its increasingly infamous oil sands, the top half of Alberta is little visited and even less known. Once you travel north of Edmonton, the population drops off to Siberian levels. The sense of remoteness here is almost eerie.

If it's solitude you seek, then this is paradise found. Endless stretches of pine forests seem to go on forever, nighttime brings aurora borealis displays that are better than any chemical hallucinogens, and it's here you can still see herds of wild bison roaming.

The Cree, Slavey and Dene were the first peoples to inhabit the region, and many of them still depend on fishing, hunting and trapping for survival. The northeast has virtually no roads and is dominated by Wood

Buffalo National Park, the Athabasca River and Lake Athabasca. The northwest is more accessible, with a network of highways connecting Alberta with northern BC and the NWT.

Peace River & Around

Heading northwest along Hwy 43 leads to the town of Dawson Creek, BC, and mile zero of the Alaska Hwy. Dawson is a whopping 590km from Edmonton, so it's a long way to go to check out this isolated section of northern Alberta. Along the way you'll pass through **Grande Prairie**, the base of operations for the local agricultural industry and home to chuckwagon-racing legend Kelly Sutherland.

Peace River is so named because the warring Cree and Beaver indigenous groups made peace along its banks. The town of **Peace River** sits at the confluence of the Heart, Peace and Smoky Rivers. West out of town, Hwy 2 leads to the Mackenzie Hwy.

Mackenzie Highway

The small town of **Grimshaw** is the official starting point of the Mackenzie Hwy (Hwy 35) north to the NWT. There's not much here except for the mile-zero sign and a few shops. The relatively flat and straight road is mostly paved, though there are stretches of loose gravel where the road is being reconstructed.

The mainly agricultural landscape between Grimshaw and Manning gives way to endless stretches of spruce and pine forest. Come prepared – this is frontier territory: services become fewer (and more expensive) as you head northward through the wilderness. Make sure you fill your tank any time you see a gas station from here on.

High Level, the last settlement of any size before the NWT border, is a timber-industry center. Workers often stay in its motels during the week. The only gas station between High Level and Enterprise (in the NWT) is at Indian Cabins.

Lake District

From **St Paul**, more than 200km northeast of Edmonton, to the NWT border lies Alberta's immense lake district. Fishing is popular (even in winter, when there is ice fishing), but many of the lakes, especially further north, have no road access and you have to fly in.

St Paul is the place to go if you are looking for little green people. Its flying-saucer landing pad – which is still awaiting its first customer – is open for business. It's billed as the world's largest, and only, UFO landing pad and UFO enthusiasts have been visiting ever since.

Highway 63 is the main route into the province's northeastern wilderness interior. The highway, with a few small settlements and campgrounds on the way, leads to **Fort McMurray**. The town itself isn't particularly interesting; non-oil workers who do visit come to see the aurora borealis.

Oil Sands Discovery Centre   MUSEUM
(☑780-743-7167; http://history.alberta.ca/oil sands; 515 MacKenzie Blvd, Fort McMurray; adult/child/family $11/7/29; ⊙9am-5pm mid-May–early Sep, 10am-4pm Tue-Sun early Sep–mid-May) The Athabasca Oil Sands are the world's largest single oil deposit – and Alberta's economic bread and butter. Interactive displays at this museum get you up close with their history and the technology behind how crude oil is extracted from them.

This area was devastated by a forest fire in 2016. On the way you'll still see acres and acres of charred woodland. Amazingly, nobody was burned, though people were displaced for months and some areas have yet to be rebuilt.

**UFO Data Centre
& Tourist Information**   GIFTS & SOUVENIRS
(☑780-645-6800, UFO hotline 888-733-8367; www.town.stpaul.ab.ca/UFO-Landing-Pad; 50th Ave, St Paul; ⊙10am-6pm May-Sep) Next to the flying saucer landing pad, this information center has a space-themed gift shop and a book you can flip through to learn more about 137 recorded local sightings, along with images and accounts of local cattle mutilations, abductions and crop circles. There's also a UFO hotline for people to report new sightings.

National Parks

If there's one thing that Canada excels at in the global pecking order (other than hockey), it's national parks. An early pioneer in ecological management in the late 1800s, the nation flaunts 48 national parks, ranging from groundbreaking, user-friendly Banff to the vast, empty wildernesses of the Arctic.

Contents

Above Rocky Mountaineer (p561), Banff National Park

1. Glacier National Park (p742) 2. Yoho National Park (p744)
3. Waterton Lakes National Park (p619) 4. Jasper National Park (p607)

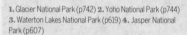

The Early Western Parks

The Canadian National Parks system has its roots in the imposing peaks and spires of the Rocky Mountains. Galvanized by the formation of Banff in 1885, the early parks were directly linked to the development of the cross-continental railway, which toted rich and curious tourists into previously unexplored wilderness areas.

Banff

Predated only by Yellowstone in the USA and Royal National Park in Australia, Banff's history is entwined with that of the national park movement and the pioneering Canadian Pacific Railway that helped pave its way.

Yoho

Named for the ancient Cree word for 'wonder and awe,' Yoho is one of the geological highlights of the Rocky Mountain parks, with its Burgess Shale fossil deposits exhibiting 120 marine species accumulated over a 500-million-year period.

Waterton Lakes

The Canadian Rockies' forgotten corner is a continuation of the Glacier National Park (USA) to the south, and is notable for its easily accessible high-alpine day hikes. Its trademark Prince of Wales hotel is linked by historic red buses to Amtrak's Seattle–Chicago *Empire Builder* train.

Jasper

Once a nexus for fur traders, Jasper welcomed two railroads in the 1910s. They are both still in operation, running passenger services to Prince Rupert and Vancouver and allowing easy access to this larger, quieter, more fauna-packed northern neighbor of Banff.

Glacier

Established just one year after Banff in 1886, Glacier was another 'railroad park.' These days it's better known for its legendary dumpings of powdery snow, ideal for heli-skiing and backcountry excursions.

Expanding East

With the formation in 1911 of Parks Canada, the world's first coherent national parks service, the park network spread east as the age of the motorcar brought Canada's spectacular natural beauty to the masses. While environmental-protection measures were always important, the early national parks were tailored more to a first-class 'visitor experience.'

Prince Edward Island

A park since 1937, PEI enhances its diminutive stature with dune-backed beaches, narrow wetlands and a gigantic literary legacy enshrined in the old farm 'Green Gables,' the inspiration for the 1908 novel *Anne of Green Gables* by Lucy Maud Montgomery.

Riding Mountain

A huge array of trails – more than 400km – pepper this forested Unesco Biosphere Reserve, which sits like a wooded island amid fertile agricultural land in southern Manitoba. In winter many trails are groomed for cross-country skiing.

Point Pelee

Geographically tiny but vital to birds (and bird-watchers), Point Pelee in Ontario on Canada's most southerly tip, and overlooking Lake Erie, is an important fly-through for more than 360 feathered species.

Cape Breton Highlands

The font of Nova Scotia's once distinct French-Acadian culture, Cape Breton –

1. Gros Morne National Park (p494) 2. Riding Mountain National Park (p528) 3. Black-throated Green Warbler in Point Pelee National Park (p155)

made a park in 1936 – is best accessed via 25 moderate day hikes that contour the coast near the Cabot Trail scenic highway.

Gros Morne

A spectacular jumble of fjords, headlands, sheer cliffs and waterfalls on the New-foundland coast, Gros Morne came late to the Parks Canada fold in 1973. It has since been listed by Unesco for its impor-tance in understanding the processes of continental drift.

Kejimkujik

Used since ancient times by local Mi'kmaq people, this pocket of unspoiled wilderness towards the eastern end of Nova Scotia is split into two parts.

There's an upland area, rich in petro-glyph sites, old growth forest and First Nations culture, and a seaside adjunct, which is best explored on foot or by kayak.

Bruce Peninsula

Ancient cedars, rare orchids, dramatic cliffs and turquoise waters make up this magnificent Unesco Biosphere Reserve straddling Georgian Bay and Lake Huron. Come here for loads of hiking, boul-dering, kayaking and postcard-perfect photos.

1. Auyuittuq National Park (p818) 2. Aulavik National Park (p810)
3. Ivvavik National Park (p790) 4. Polar bears in Wapusk National
Park (p530)

ALL CANADA PHOTOS/ALAMY STOCK PHOTO ©

Northern Exposure

By the 1980s, the national parks service had shifted its philosophy from a purely visitor-centric view of park management to a position that prioritized ecological integrity. Vast wildernesses in the north of Canada were gradually taken under the parks umbrella, often with the cooperation of local indigenous peoples.

Aulavik

More people have visited the moon than drop by Aulavik annually (official annual tourist numbers rarely exceed a dozen). Situated on arctic Banks Island, this land of musk oxen and 24-hour summer sunlight is the true 'back of beyond.'

Wapusk

Polar bears are Wapusk's raison d'être: its name means 'white bear' in Cree and it's the best place in the world to see these animals in the wild. Book a guided tour and head for Churchill, Manitoba.

Auyuittuq

A name few Canadians will recognize (or be able to pronounce), Auyuittuq ('the land that never melts') is another leave-your-car-at-home kind of park. Situated on Baffin Island, it is ideal for ski touring, climbing and backcountry camping.

Ivvavik

No services, no facilities, just miles of untamed tundra. Save some money, hone your backcountry survival skills and live out your expedition fantasies.

Wild horses on Sable Island

Young Parks

Parks Canada has always been an open-ended project with a long-term roll-out plan, and parks continue to be formed. Eight have gained federal approval since 2000 and the network now covers an impressive 3% of Canada's total land mass – roughly the size of Italy.

Nahanni

Nahanni in the Northwest Territories became a national park in the 1970s and had the honor of being made Unesco's first *natural* World Heritage site in 1978. After years of negotiations, it was significantly expanded in 2011. It is now Canada's third-largest national park, covering an area the size of Belgium.

Torngat Mountains

A stark mélange of glaciated mountains and roaming caribou on the wild coast of Labrador, Torngat Mountains was created in 2005 as Canada's 42nd national park.

Nááts'ihch'oh

This park, inaugurated in 2012, abuts the expanded Nahanni National Park and has a strong spiritual significance to the Métis and Dene First Nations, who played a role in the legal negotiations. It is also a northern roaming ground for grizzly bears, caribou and Dall sheep.

Sable Island

A sinuous sand spit 300km off Nova Scotia, grassy Sable Island is home to hundreds of feral horses, thought to be left over from the Great Acadian Expulsion in the 1750s. More than 350 ships have met their watery end on this hard-to-reach outpost.

British Columbia

Best Places to Eat

➜ Purebread (p669)

➜ Brasserie L'École (p686)

➜ Vij's (p653)

➜ St Lawrence Restaurant (p652)

Best Places to Stay

➜ Free Spirit Spheres (p698)

➜ Wickaninnish Inn (p704)

➜ Victorian Hotel (p646)

➜ Skwachàys Lodge (p646)

Why Go?

Visitors to Canada's westernmost province should pack a long list of superlatives with them; the words 'wow', 'amazing' and 'spectacular' will only go so far. Luckily, it's easy to wax lyrical about the mighty mountains, deep forests and dramatic coastlines that instantly lower heart rates to tranquil levels.

There's much more to British Columbia (BC) than nature-hugging dioramas, though. Cosmopolitan Vancouver fuses cuisines and cultures from Asia and beyond, while mid-sized cities such as Victoria and Kelowna have their own vibrant scenes. And it's hard to beat the welcoming, sometimes quirky character of smaller communities – from Cumberland to Powell River and Salt Spring – that are BC's beating heart.

Wherever you head, the great outdoors will always call: BC is unbeatable for life-enhancing skiing, kayaking and hiking experiences that can make this the trip of a lifetime.

When to Go
Vancouver, BC

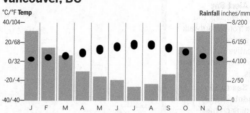

Dec–Mar Best powder action on the slopes of Whistler and Blackcomb mountains.

Jul & Aug Beaches, patios and a plethora of outdoor festivals in sun-dappled Vancouver.

Sep & Oct Dramatic surfing and early season storm-watching in beach-hugging Tofino.

British Columbia Highlights

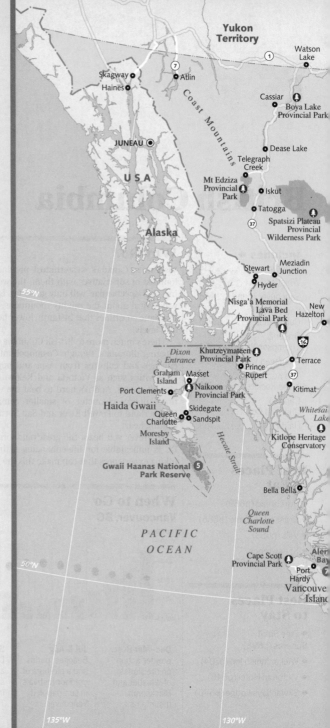

1 Stanley Park (p635) Stretching your legs on the curvaceous 8.8km seawall stroll.

2 Tofino (p702) Surfing up a storm (or just watching a storm) on Vancouver Island's wild west coast.

3 Okanagan Valley (p724) Slurping some celebrated tipples on an ever-winding winery tour.

4 Whistler (p665) Skiing the Olympian slopes, then enjoying a warming après-ski beverage in the village.

5 Gwaii Haanas National Park Reserve (p759) Exploring the ancient and ethereal rainforest and kayaking the coastline for a bird's-eye view of the region.

6 Salt Spring Island (p716) Puttering around the lively Saturday Market and scoffing more than a few treats.

7 Alert Bay (p712) Walking the waterfront boardwalk and exploring evocative First Nations art and totem poles.

8 Sea to Sky Gondola (p663) Hopping on the gondola near Squamish for panoramic up-top views of Howe Sound and its mountainous cousins.

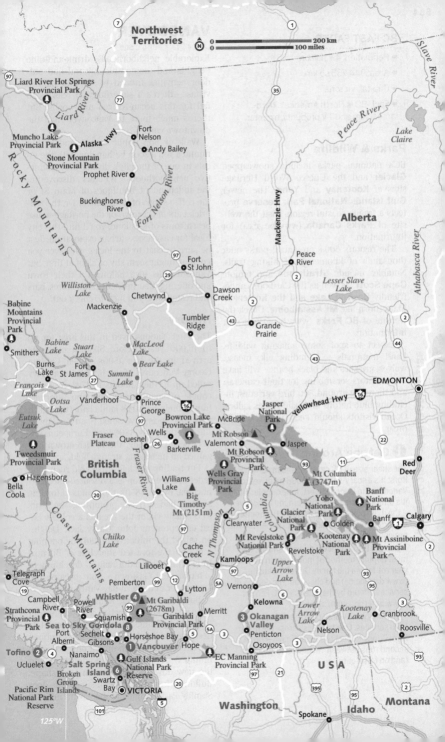

BC FAST FACTS

➡ Population: 4.7 million

➡ Area: 944,735 sq km

➡ Capital: Victoria

➡ Fact: BC is North America's third-largest film and TV production center.

Parks & Wildlife

BC's national parks include snowcapped **Glacier** and the Unesco World Heritage sites of **Kootenay** and **Yoho**. The newer **Gulf Islands National Park Reserve** protects a fragile coastal region. Visit the website of **Parks Canada** (www.pc.gc.ca) for information.

The region's 600+ provincial parks offer thousands of kilometers of hiking trails. Notables include **Strathcona** and remote **Cape Scott**, as well as the Cariboo's canoe-friendly **Bowron Lake** and the Kootenays' Matterhorn-like **Mt Assiniboine**. Check the website of **BC Parks** (www.bcparks.ca) for information.

Expect to spot some amazing wildlife. Land mammals – including elk, moose, wolves, grizzlies and black bears – will have most visitors scrambling for their cameras, and there are around 500 bird varieties, including blue herons and bald eagles galore. Ocean visitors should keep an eye out for orcas.

ⓘ Getting Around

The sheer size of BC can overwhelm some visitors: it's a scary-sounding 1508km drive from Vancouver to Prince Rupert, for example. While it's tempting to simply stick around Vancouver – the main point of entry for most BC-bound visitors – you won't really have experienced the province unless you head out of town.

Despite the distances, driving remains the most popular method of movement in BC. Plan your routes via the handy DriveBC website (www.drivebc.ca) and check out the dozens of services offered by the extensive BC Ferries (www.bcferries.com) system.

VIA Rail (www.viarail.com) operates two BC train services. One trundles across the north from Prince Rupert to Jasper (in Alberta). A second runs between Vancouver and Jasper (and on to Toronto).

VANCOUVER

📞 604, 778 / POP 631,500

Explorable neighborhoods, drink-and-dine delights and memorable cultural and outdoor activities framed by striking natural vistas – there's a superfluity of reasons to fall for this ocean-fringed metropolis. But there's much more to Vancouver than the downtown core.

Walk or hop public transit and within minutes you'll soon be hanging with the locals in one of the city's diverse and distinctive neighborhoods. Whether discovering the independent boutiques of Main St or the coffee shops of Commercial Dr, the redbrick bars of Gastown or the heritage-house beachfronts of Kitsilano, you'll find this city ideal for easy-access urban exploration. Just be sure to chat to the locals wherever you go: they might seem shy or aloof at first, but Vancouverites love talking up their town and offering their insider tips on stores, bars and restaurants you have to check out.

History

The First Nations lived in this area for up to 16,000 years before Spanish explorers arrived in the late 1500s. When Captain George Vancouver of the British Royal Navy sailed up to these shores in 1792, he met a couple of Spanish captains who informed him of their country's land claim (the beach they met on is now called Spanish Banks). But by the early 1800s, as European settlers began arriving, the British crown had gained an increasing stranglehold.

Fur trading and a feverish gold rush soon redefined the region as a resource-filled cornucopia. By the 1850s, thousands of fortune seekers had arrived, prompting the Brits to officially claim the area as a colony. Local entrepreneur John 'Gassy Jack' Deighton seized the initiative in 1867 by opening a bar on the forested shoreline of Burrard Inlet. This triggered a rash of development – nicknamed Gastown – that became the forerunner of modern-day Vancouver.

But not everything went to plan. While Vancouver rapidly reached a population of 1000, its buildings were almost completely destroyed in an 1886 blaze (quickly dubbed the Great Fire, even though it only lasted 20 minutes). A prompt rebuild followed and the new downtown core soon took shape. Buildings from this era still survive, as does Stanley Park. Originally the town's military reserve, it was opened as a public recreation area in 1888.

Relying on its port, the growing city became a hub of industry, importing thousands of immigrant workers to fuel economic development. The Chinatown built at this time is still one of the largest in North America. But WWI and the 1929 Wall Street crash brought deep depression and unemployment. The economy recovered during WWII, when shipbuilding and armaments manufacturing added to the traditional economic base of resource exploitation.

Growing steadily throughout the 1950s and 1960s, Vancouver added an NHL (National Hockey League) team and other accoutrements of a midsize North American city. Finally reflecting on its heritage, Gastown – by now a slum – was saved for gentrification in the 1970s, becoming a National Historic Site in 2010.

In 1986 the city hosted a highly successful World's Fair, sparking a wave of new development and adding the first of the mirrored skyscrapers that now define Vancouver's downtown core. A further economic lift arrived when the city staged the Olympic and Paralympic Winter Games in 2010, showcasing itself to a global audience of TV viewers. Recent years have seen a citywide tension between developer-driven house price surges and locals who say Vancouver's cost of living has risen too high. As the city grapples with its attempts to create sustainable growth, the next few years will be crucial.

◎ Sights

Few of Vancouver's main visitor attractions are downtown; the main museums are in Vanier Park and at the University of British Columbia (UBC). Other top sights and landmarks are in Stanley Park or Chinatown, while two major outdoor lures are on the North Shore. Luckily, most are easy to reach by car or transit hop from the city center.

◎ Downtown & West End

★**Stanley Park**   PARK
(Map p640; www.vancouver.ca/parks; West End; P💧; 🚌19) This magnificent 404-hectare park combines excellent attractions with a mystical natural aura. Don't miss a stroll or a cycle (rentals near the W Georgia St entrance) around the seawall: a kind of visual spa treatment fringed by a 150,000-tree temperate rainforest, it'll take you past the park's popular totem poles and alongside its shimmering oceanfront.

Lost Lagoon   LAKE
This rustic area near Stanley Park's entrance was originally part of Coal Harbour. But after a causeway was built in 1916, the new body of water was renamed, transforming itself into a freshwater lake a few years later. Today it's a **nature sanctuary** – keep your eyes peeled for beady-eyed herons – and its perimeter pathway is a favored stroll for nature-huggers.

The excellent **Stanley Park Nature House** (Map p640; ☑604-257-8544; www.stanleyparkecology.ca; north end of Alberni St, Lost Lagoon, Stanley Park; ⊘10am-5pm Tue-Sun Jul & Aug, 10am-4pm Sat & Sun Sep-Jun; 💧; 🚌19) **FREE** provides exhibits and illumination on the park's wildlife, history and ecology. Ask about its fascinating park walks, covering everything from bird-watching strolls to artsy ambles around the park.

Stanley Park Seawall   WATERFRONT
(Stanley Park; 🚌19) Built between 1917 and 1980, the 8.8km seawall trail is Vancouver's favorite outdoor hangout. Encircling the whole of Stanley Park, it offers spectacular waterfront, mountain-fringed vistas on one side and dense forest canopy on the other. You can walk the whole thing in around three blister-triggering hours or rent a bike from the Denman St operators near the park entrance to cover the route faster. But what's the rush? Slow down and slide into the natural side of life instead.

BEST SIGHTS

Stanley Park An oceanfront gem with seawall trails and visitor attractions.

Museum of Anthropology (p639) Vancouver's best cultural attraction, with exhibits from BC and beyond.

Science World (p639) Brilliant kid-friendly attraction under a landmark geodesic dome.

Capilano Suspension Bridge Park (p643) A leg-wobbling wooden walkway set in a forested park.

Vancouver Art Gallery (p637) Downtown art institution showcasing Canadian artists and blockbuster visiting exhibitions.

Vancouver

10 km
5 miles

N
0
0

Coquitlam River

Indian Arm
Provincial Park

Noons Creek

Massom River

Indian Arm

BELCARRA

ANMORE

Belcarra
Regional Park

Burnaby Mountain
Conservation Area

Barnston
Island

Douglas
Island

PORT
COQUITLAM

Fort Langley
(8km)

Tynehead
Regional Park

184thSt

COQUITLAM

Como Lake Ave

Mundy
Park

Austin Ave

Green
Timbers
Urban Forest

152nd St

Fraser Hwy

SURREY

88th Ave

King George Hwy

96th Ave

128th St

120th St

72nd Ave

Serpentine River

Mt Seymour
Pkwy

Dollarton Hwy

Confederation
Park

Second Narrows Burrard
Bridge

E Hastings St

Lynn Creek

BURNABY

Lougheed Hwy

Burnaby Lake
Regional Park

Burnaby Lake
Nature Park

10TH Ave

Canada Way

NEW
WESTMINSTER

New Media
Gallery 3

12

Nordel Way

Annacis
Island

Delta
Nature
Reserve

91

DELTA

Annacis Hwy

Horseshoe Bay (2km);
Bowen Island (7km);
Whistler (105km)

Upper Levels Hwy

West
Bay

Sandy
Cove

Marine Dr

Lions Gate
Bridge

Grouse Mountain
(1km)

1

NORTH
VANCOUVER

Capilano
Suspension
Bridge Park

Stanley
Park

7

10

11

4

Polygon
Gallery

Vancouver
Harbour

First
Narrows

Rupert St

Nanaimo St

Commercial Dr

Boundary Rd

Kingsway

Central
Park

Kerr St

Kingsway

Knight St

Mitchell
Island

Marine Way

North Arm Fraser River

River Rd

Fraser River

91

Richmond
Hwy

RICHMOND

George
Massey
Tunnel

Tsawwassen (15km);
Seattle (USA, 190km)

99

Blundell Rd

Steveston Hwy

STEVESTON

No1Rd

Richmond
Nature Park

Bridgeport
Rd

14

15

16

5

Richmond
Night Market

Westminster Hwy

Sea Island

Iona
Island

Musqueam Indian
Reserve 2

Vancouver
International
Airport

9

8

Pacific Spirit
Regional Park

Marine Drive
Foreshore Park

Musqueam Indian
Reserve 2

UNIVERSITY
OF BRITISH
COLUMBIA

6

7

13

KITSILANO

W Broadway

16th Ave W

Granville St

Cambie St

Oak St

Main St

Queen
Elizabeth
Park

W 41st Ave

SOUTH
MAIN

WEST
SIDE

See Downtown
Vancouver Map
(p640)

English
Bay

Spanish Banks
Beach Park

Point Grey

Museum of 2
Anthropology

Burrard Inlet

Strait of Georgia

Bowen
Island

Coquitlam River

Vancouver

★ **Vancouver Art Gallery**   GALLERY
(Map p640; ☑604-662-4700; www.vanart
gallery.bc.ca; 750 Hornby St, Downtown; adult/child
$24/6.50; ◷10am-5pm Wed-Mon, to 9pm Tue;
🚇5) Combining blockbuster international
shows with selections from its striking contemporary collection, the VAG is a magnet
for art fans. There are often three or four
different exhibitions on its public levels but
save time for the top-floor Emily Carr paintings, showcasing swirling nature-themed
works from BC's favorite historic artist.
Check ahead for FUSE ($29; ◷8pm-midnight),
a late-opening party with bars and live music. And if you're on a budget, consider the
by-donation entry after 5pm on Tuesdays
($10 suggested); expect a queue.

★ **Roedde House Museum**   MUSEUM
(Map p640; ☑604-684-7040; www.roedde
house.org; 1415 Barclay St, West End; $5, Sun $8;
◷1-4pm Tue-Fri & Sun; 🚇5) For a glimpse of

what the West End looked like before the
apartment blocks, visit this handsome 1893
Queen Anne–style mansion, now a lovingly
preserved museum. Designed by infamous
architect Francis Rattenbury, the yesteryear,
antique-studded rooms have a lived-in feel
while its guided tour (included with admission) tells you all about its middle-class
Roedde family residents. Look out for the
cylinder record player, 250-year-old grandfather clock and the taxidermied deer heads
that were hunted in Stanley Park in 1906.

Bill Reid Gallery of
Northwest Coast Art   GALLERY
(Map p640; ☑604-682-3455; www.billreid
gallery.ca; 639 Hornby St, Downtown; adult/youth/
child $13/6/free; ◷10am-5pm May-Sep, 11am-5pm
Wed-Sun Oct-Apr; Ⓢ Burrard) Showcasing detailed carvings, paintings, jewelry and more
from Canada's most revered Haida artists
and others around the region, this open-
plan gallery occupies a handsome bi-level
hall. Bookended by a totem pole at one end
and a ceiling-mounted copper-lined canoe
at the other, explore the cabinets of intricate creations and the stories behind them,
including some breathtaking gold artifacts.
On the mezzanine level, you'll come face-
to-face with an 8.5m-long bronze of intertwined magical creatures, complete with
impressively long tongues.

Canada Place   LANDMARK
(Map p640; ☑604-665-9000; www.canadaplace.
ca; 999 Canada Place Way, Downtown; 🅿🚻;
Ⓢ Waterfront) 🆓 Vancouver's version of
the Sydney Opera House – judging by the
number of postcards it appears on – this
iconic landmark is shaped like sails jutting
into the sky over the harbor. Both a cruise-
ship terminal and a convention center, it's
also a stroll-worthy pier, providing photogenic views of the busy floatplane action
and looming North Shore mountains. Here
for Canada Day on July 1? This is the center
of the city's festivities, with displays, live music and fireworks.

Vancouver Aquarium   AQUARIUM
(☑604-659-3400; www.vanaqua.org; 845 Avison
Way, Stanley Park; adult/child $38/21; ◷9:30am-
6pm Jul & Aug, 10am-5pm Sep-Jun; 🚻; 🚌19)
Stanley Park's biggest draw is home to 9000
critters – including sharks, wolf eels and a
somewhat shy octopus. There's also a small,
walk-through rainforest area of birds, turtles
and a statue-still sloth. The aquarium keeps
captive whales and dolphins and organizes

animal encounters with these and its other creatures, which may concern some visitors.

⊙ Gastown & Chinatown

★ Vancouver Police Museum & Archives MUSEUM

(Map p640; ☑ 604-665-3346; www.vancouverpolicemuseum.ca; 240 E Cordova St, Chinatown; adult/child $12/8; ☉ 9am-5pm Tue-Sat; 🖵 3) Illuminating Vancouver's crime-and-vice-addled history, this quirky museum has had a makeover, uncovering the former coroner's courtroom (spot the elaborate cross-hatched ceiling) and sprucing up exhibits including a spine-chilling gallery of real-life cases (weapons included). The star attraction is the old autopsy room, complete with preserved slivers of human tissue; bullet-damaged brain slices are among them. Add a Sins of the City (www.sinsofthecity.ca; adult/student $18/14; ☉ Apr-Oct) area walking tour to learn all about Vancouver's salacious olden days; tours include museum entry.

★ Dr Sun Yat-Sen Classical Chinese Garden & Park GARDENS

(Map p640; ☑ 604-662-3207; www.vancouverchinesegarden.com; 578 Carrall St, Chinatown; adult/child $14/10; ☉ 9:30am-7pm mid-Jun–Aug, 10am-6pm Sep & May–mid-Jun, 10am-4:30pm Oct-Apr; ⑤ Stadium-Chinatown) A tranquil break from bustling Chinatown, this intimate 'garden of ease' reflects Taoist principles of balance and harmony. Entry includes an optional 45-minute guided tour, in which you'll learn about the symbolism behind the placement of the gnarled pine trees, winding covered pathways and ancient limestone formations. Look out for the colorful carp and lazy turtles in the jade-colored water.

Chinatown Millennium Gate LANDMARK

(Map p640; cnr W Pender & Taylor Sts, Chinatown; ⑤ Stadium-Chinatown) Inaugurated in 2002, Chinatown's towering entrance is the landmark most visitors look for. Stand well back, since the decoration is mostly on its lofty upper reaches, an elaborately painted section topped with a terra-cotta-tiled roof. The characters inscribed on its eastern front implore you to 'Remember the past and look forward to the future.'

Steam Clock LANDMARK

(Map p640; cnr Water & Cambie Sts, Gastown; ⑤ Waterfront) Halfway along Water St, this oddly popular tourist magnet lures the cameras with its tooting steam whistle. Built in

1977, the clock's mechanism is actually driven by electricity; only the pipes on top are steam fueled (reveal that to the patiently waiting tourists and you might cause a riot). It sounds every 15 minutes, and marks each hour with little whistling symphonies.

⊙ Yaletown & Granville Island

★ Granville Island Public Market MARKET

(Map p640; ☑ 604-666-6655; www.granvilleisland.com/public-market; Johnston St, Granville Island; ☉ 9am-7pm; 🖵 50, 🚢 miniferries) Granville Island's highlight is the covered Public Market, a multisensory smorgasbord of fish, cheese, fruit, teas and bakery treats (near-legendary Lee's Donuts included). Pick up some fixings for a picnic at nearby Vanier Park or hit the market's international food court (dine off-peak and you're more likely to snag a table). It's not all about food; there are often stands here hawking all manner of arts and crafts, from filigree jewelry to knitted baby hats.

Engine 374 Pavilion MUSEUM

(Map p640; www.roundhouse.ca; 181 Roundhouse Mews, Roundhouse Community Arts & Recreation Centre, Yaletown; ☉ 10am-4pm, reduced hours off-season; ♿; ⑤ Yaletown-Roundhouse) FREE May 23, 1887, was an auspicious date for Vancouver. That's when Engine 374 pulled the very first transcontinental passenger train into the fledgling city, symbolically linking the country and kick-starting the eventual metropolis. Retired in 1945, the engine was, after many years of neglect, restored and placed in this splendid pavilion. The friendly volunteers here will show you the best angle for snapping photos and share a few yesteryear railroading stories at the same time.

BC Sports Hall of Fame & Museum MUSEUM

(Map p640; ☑ 604-687-5520; www.bcsportshalloffame.com; 777 Pacific Blvd, Gate A, BC Place Stadium, Yaletown; adult/child $15/12; ☉ 10am-5pm; ♿; ⑤ Stadium-Chinatown) Inside BC Place Stadium (☑ 604-669-2300; www.bcplace.com), this expertly curated attraction showcases top BC athletes, both amateur and professional, with an intriguing array of galleries crammed with fascinating memorabilia. There are medals, trophies and yesteryear sports uniforms on display (judging by the size of their shirts, hockey players were much smaller in the past), plus tonnes of hands-on activities to tire the kids out. Don't miss the **Indigenous Sport Gallery**, covering everything from hockey to lacrosse to traditional indigenous games.

◉ Main Street

★**Science World** MUSEUM
(Map p640; ☑604-443-7440; www.science world.ca; 1455 Quebec St; adult/child $27.15/18.10; ⊙10am-6pm Jul & Aug, reduced hours off-season; **P** ⚐; **S**Main St-Science World) Under Vancouver's favorite geodesic dome (OK, it's only one), this ever-popular science showcase has tonnes of hands-on galleries and a cool outdoor park crammed with rugged fun (yes, you *can* lift 2028kg). Inside, there are two floors of brilliant educational play, from plasma balls to whisper dishes. Check out the live critters in the **Sara Stern Gallery**, the bodily functions exhibits in the **BodyWorks** area, then fly over a city on the virtual-reality **Birdly** ride ($8 extra).

◉ Fairview & South Granville

★**VanDusen Botanical Garden** GARDENS
(☑604-257-8335; www.vandusengarden.org; 5251 Oak St; adult/child $11.25/5.50; ⊙9am-8pm Jun-Aug, 9am-6pm Apr & Sep, 9am-7pm May, hours reduced Oct-Mar; **P** ⚐; ⚌17) This highly popular green-thumbed oasis is a 22-hectare, 255,000-plant idyll that offers a strollable web of pathways weaving through specialized garden areas: the Rhododendron Walk blazes with color in spring, while the Korean Pavilion is a focal point for a fascinating Asian collection. Save time to get lost in the hedge maze and look out for the herons, owls and turtles that call the park and its ponds home. Informative guided tours are also offered here daily from April to October.

★**Bloedel Conservatory** GARDENS
(☑604-257-8584; www.vandusengarden.org; 4600 Cambie St, Queen Elizabeth Park; adult/child $6.75/3.30; ⊙10am-5pm Jan-Mar, Nov & Dec, 10am-6pm Apr, Sep & Oct, 10am-8pm May-Aug; **P** ⚐; ⚌15) Cresting the hill in Queen Elizabeth Park, this domed conservatory is a delightful rainy-day warm-up. At Vancouver's best-value paid attraction, you'll find tropical trees and plants bristling with hundreds of free-flying, bright-plumaged birds. Listen for the noisy resident parrots but also keep your eyes peeled for rainbow-hued Gouldian finches, shimmering African superb

DISCOUNTS GALORE

From cheap nights to free tours, there are several ways to keep your costs down in Vancouver.

Vancouver Art Gallery (p637) entry is by donation on Tuesday evenings from 5pm to 9pm.

Museum of Anthropology (p639) entry is reduced to $10 on Thursday evenings from 5pm to 9pm.

Grouse Grind (www.grousemountain. com; Grouse Mountain, North Shore; ⚌236) gives access to the attractions atop Grouse Mountain via this free hiking route; it's $15 to get back down via the gondola, though.

starlings and maybe even a dramatic Lady Amherst pheasant, snaking through the undergrowth. Ask nicely and the attendants might even let you feed the smaller birds from a bowl.

◉ Kitsilano & University of British Columbia

★**Museum of Anthropology** MUSEUM
(MOA; Map p636; ☑604-822-5087; www.moa. ubc.ca; 6393 NW Marine Dr, UBC; adult/child $18/16; ⊙10am-5pm Fri-Wed, 10am-9pm Thu, closed Mon Oct-May; **P**; ⚌99B-Line, then 68) Vancouver's best museum is studded with spectacular indigenous totem poles and breathtaking carvings – but it's also teeming with artifacts from cultures around the world, from intricate Swedish lace to bright Sri Lankan folk masks. Take one of the free daily tours (check ahead for times) for some context, but give yourself at least a couple of hours to explore on your own; it's easy to immerse yourself here. On a budget? Thursday evening entry is $10 (after 5pm).

Kitsilano Beach BEACH
(cnr Cornwall Ave & Arbutus St, Kitsilano; ⚌2) Facing English Bay, Kits Beach is one of Vancouver's favorite summertime hangouts. The wide, sandy expanse attracts buff Frisbee tossers and giggling volleyball players, and those who just like to preen while catching the rays. The ocean is fine for a dip, though serious swimmers should consider the heated **Kitsilano Pool** (☑604-731-0011;

Downtown Vancouver

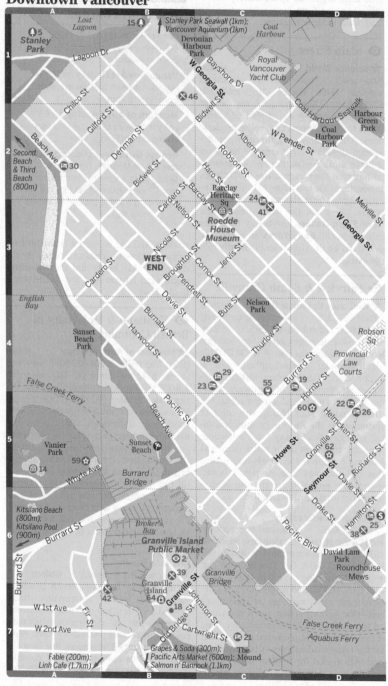

Stanley Park Seawall (1km);
Vancouver Aquarium (1km)

15

Lost Lagoon

5
Stanley
Park

Lagoon Dr

Chilco St

Gilford St

Devonian
Harbour
Park

Coal
Harbour

Royal
Vancouver
Yacht Club

W Georgia St

Bidwell St

46

Coal Harbour Seawalk

Harbour
Green
Park

Coal
Harbour
Park

Beach Ave

Second
Beach &
Third
Beach
(800m)

30

Denman St

Bidwell St

Haro St

Robson St

Alberni St

W Pender St

Melville St

W Georgia St

Cardero St

Barclay St

Nelson St

Barclay
Heritage
Sq

3

Roedde
House
Museum

24
41

English
Bay

Cardero St

Nicola St

Broughton St

Cornox St

Pendrell St

WEST
END

Jervis St

Bute St

Nelson
Park

Robson
Sq

Davie St

Burnaby St

Sunset
Beach
Park

Harwood St

Thurlow St

Provincial
Law
Courts

48

29

23

55

Burrard St

19

Hornby St

60

22

26

Helmcken St

Richards St

False Creek Ferry

Pacific St

Beach Ave

Howe St

Granville St

62

Seymour St

Davie St

Vanier
Park

59

14

Sunset
Beach

Whyte Ave

Burrard
Bridge

Drake St

Hamilton St

38

25

S

Kitsilano Beach
(800m);
Kitsilano Pool
(900m)

Burrard St

Burrard St

Pacific Blvd

David Lam
Park
Roundhouse
Mews

Broker's
Bay

Granville Island
Public Market

2

39

Granville
Island

42

64

18

Granville
Bridge

Granville St

Johnston St

False Creek Ferry

Aquabus Ferry

W 1st Ave

Fir St

W 2nd Ave

Cartwright St

Old Bridge St

21

Fable (200m);
Linh Cafe (1.7km)

Grapes & Soda (300m);
Pacific Arts Market (600m);
Salmon n' Bannock (1.1km)

The
Mound

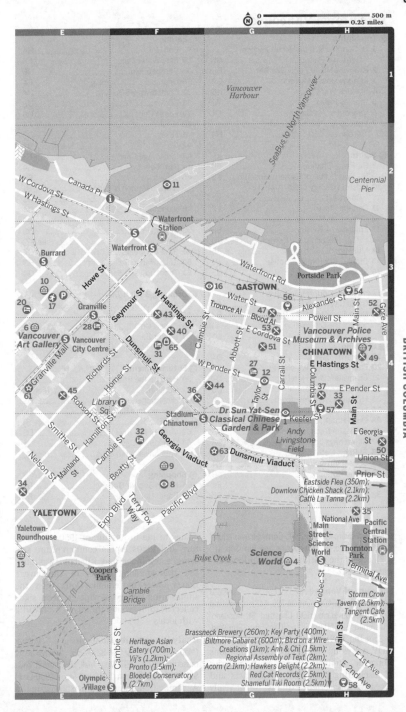

0   500 m
0   0.25 miles

BRITISH COLUMBIA

Vancouver
Harbour

SeaBus to North Vancouver

Centennial
Pier

W Cordova St

Canada Pl

W Hastings St

Waterfront
Station

Waterfront Rd

Portside Park

Burrard

Waterfront

10

17

20

6

28

Howe St

Seymour St

Granville

Vancouver
Art Gallery

Vancouver
City Centre

Richards St

Dunsmuir St

W Hastings St

16 GASTOWN

Water St

Trounce Al

Blood Al

E Cordova St

W Pender St

43

40

31

65

Cambie St

Abbott St

56

47

53

51

Alexander St

Powell St

Vancouver Police
Museum & Archives

CHINATOWN

E Hastings St

54

52

Gore Ave

Main St

7

49

61

45

Granville Mall

Homer St

Robson St

Smithe St

Hamilton St

Library
Sq

Cambie St

Beatty St

36

27

12

44

Taylor St

Carrall St

W Pender St

Stadium–
Chinatown

Georgia Viaduct

32

9

8

63

Dunsmuir Viaduct

Dr Sun Yat-Sen
Classical Chinese
Garden & Park

1

Keefer St

Andy
Livingstone
Field

E Columbia St

37

33

57

E Pender St

E Georgia
St

Union St

50

Main St

Nelson St

Mainland St

Smithe St

34

YALETOWN

Yaletown-
Roundhouse

13

Expo Blvd

Terry Fox Way

Pacific Blvd

Cooper's
Park

Cambie
Bridge

Cambie St

False Creek

Science
World

4

Prior St

Eastside Flea (350m);
Downlow Chicken Shack (2.1km);
Caffè La Tanna (2.2km)

National Ave

Main
Street–
Science
World

35

Pacific
Central
Station

Thornton
Park

50

Quebec St

Terminal Ave

Storm Crow
Tavern (2.5km);
Tangent Cafe
(2.5km)

Heritage Asian
Eatery (700m);
Vij's (1.2km);
Pronto (1.5km);
Bloedel Conservatory
(2.7km)

Olympic
Village

Brassneck Brewery (260m); Key Party (400m);
Biltmore Cabaret (600m); Bird on a Wire
Creations (1km); Anh & Chi (1.5km);
Regional Assembly of Text (2km);
Acorn (2.1km); Hawkers Delight (2.2km);
Red Cat Records (2.5km);
Shameful Tiki Room (2.5km)

Main St

E 1st Ave

E 2nd Ave

58

Downtown Vancouver

www.vancouverparks.ca; 2305 Cornwall Ave; adult/child $6.10/3.05; ⊙7am-evening mid-Jun–Sep; ♿; 🚇2), one of the world's largest outdoor saltwater pools.

Museum of Vancouver MUSEUM
(MOV; Map p640; ☑604-736-4431; www.museumofvancouver.ca; 1100 Chestnut St, Kitsilano; adult/child $20.50/9.75; ⊙10am-5pm Sun-Wed, to 8pm Thu, to 9pm Fri & Sat; 🅿♿; 🚇2) The MOV serves up cool temporary exhibitions alongside in-depth permanent galleries of fascinating First Nations artifacts and evocative pioneer-era exhibits. But it really

comes to life in its vibrant 1950s pop culture and 1960s hippie counterculture sections, a reminder that Kitsilano was once the grass-smoking center of Vancouver's flower-power movement. Don't miss the shimmering gallery of vintage neon signs collected from around the city; it's a favorite with locals.

Beaty Biodiversity Museum MUSEUM
(Map p636; ☑604-827-4955; www.beatymuseum.ubc.ca; 2212 Main Mall, UBC; adult/child $14/10; ⊙10am-5pm Tue-Sun; ♿; 🚍99B-Line) A family-friendly museum showcasing a

two-million-item natural-history collection including birds, fossils and herbarium displays. The highlight is the 25m blue-whale skeleton, artfully displayed in the two-story entranceway. Don't miss the first display case, which is crammed with a beady-eyed menagerie of tooth-and-claw taxidermy. Consider visiting on the third Thursday of the month when entry is by donation after 5pm and the museum stays open until 8:30pm; there's often a special theme or live performance for these monthly Nocturnal events.

UBC Botanical Garden GARDENS
(Map p636; ☑604-822-4208; www.botanical garden.ubc.ca; 6804 SW Marine Dr, UBC; adult/child $10/5; ⊙10am-4:30pm; ⋒; ☐99B-Line, then 68) You'll find a huge array of rhododendrons, a fascinating apothecary plot and a winter green space of off-season bloomers in this 28-hectare complex of themed gardens. Among the towering trees, look for northern flicker woodpeckers and chittering little Douglas squirrels. Also save time for the attraction's **Greenheart TreeWalk** (adult/child $23/10; ⊙Apr-Oct; ℗⋒), which elevates visitors up to 23m above the forest floor on a 310m guided ecotour. The combined garden and Greenheart ticket costs adult/child $23/10.

HR MacMillan Space Centre MUSEUM
(Map p640; ☑604-738-7827; www.spacecen tre.ca; 1100 Chestnut St, Kitsilano; adult/child $19.50/14; ⊙10am-5pm Jul & Aug, reduced hours off-season; ℗⋒; ☐2) Focusing on the wonderful world of space, admission to this kid-favorite museum includes a gallery of hands-on exhibits (don't miss the Mars section where you can drive across the surface in a simulator) as well as a menu of live science demonstrations in the small theater and a cool 45-minute planetarium show upstairs. Check the daily schedule of shows and presentations online before you arrive. The Saturday-night planetarium performances are popular with locals and typically draw a more adult crowd.

☉ North Shore

★Capilano Suspension Bridge Park PARK
(Map p636; ☑604-985-7474; www.capbridge. com; 3735 Capilano Rd, North Vancouver; adult/child $47/15; ⊙8am-8pm May-Aug, reduced hours off-season; ℗⋒; ☐236) As you inch gingerly across one of the world's longest (140m) and highest (70m) pedestrian suspension bridges, swaying gently over roiling Cap-

ilano Canyon, remember that its thick steel cables are firmly embedded in concrete. That should steady your feet – unless there are teenagers stamping across. Added park attractions include a glass-bottomed **cliff-side walkway** and an elevated **canopy trail** through the trees.

★Polygon Gallery GALLERY
(Map p636; ☑604-986-1351; www.thepolygon.ca; 101 Carrie Cates Ct, North Vancouver; ⊙10am-5pm Tue-Sun; ☒Lonsdale Quay SeaBus) North Van's former Presentation House Gallery renamed itself and relocated to this dramatic, sawtooth-roofed waterfront landmark in 2017, providing greatly increased wall space for the multiple exhibitions staged here throughout the year. Photo-conceptualism remains a focus but expect thought-provoking contemporary art installations and evocative Aboriginal exhibits as well. There are free 45-minute tours every Saturday at 2pm. A new North Vancouver Museum across the street was expected to open in late 2021.

Lynn Canyon Park PARK
(Map p636; www.lynncanyon.ca; Park Rd, North Vancouver; ⊙10am-5pm Jun-Sep, noon-4pm Oct-May; ℗⋒; ☐228 then 227) **FREE** Amid a dense bristling of century-old trees, the main lure of this popular park is its **Suspension Bridge**, a free alternative to Capilano. Not quite as big as its tourist-magnet rival, it nevertheless provokes the same jelly-legged reaction as you sway over the river that tumbles 50m below – and it's always far less crowded. Hiking trails, swimming areas and picnic spots will keep you busy, while there's also a cafe to fuel up.

The park's **Ecology Centre** (☑604-990-3755; www.lynncanyonecologycentre.ca; 3663 Park

---

VANCOUVER FOR CHILDREN

Family-friendly Vancouver is stuffed with activities and attractions for kids, including Science World (p639), HR MacMillan Space Centre and the Vancouver Aquarium (p637). Keen to get them outdoors? Don't miss Stanley Park (p635) or Capilano Suspension Bridge Park. Several city festivals are also especially kid-friendly, while local transport experiences such as SeaBus and SkyTrain are highlights for many youngsters.

Rd, North Vancouver; by donation; ⊘10am-5pm Jun-Sep, 10am-5pm Mon-Fri & noon-4pm Sat & Sun Oct-May; 🚻; 🚌227) ⚲ houses interesting displays, including dioramas on the area's rich biodiversity. There are also some fascinating free history-themed walking tours in the park on Wednesdays and Thursdays in July and August; check www.nvma.ca/programs for details.

Mt Seymour Provincial Park   PARK
(www.bcparks.ca; 1700 Mt Seymour Rd, North Vancouver; ⊘dawn-dusk) **FREE** A popular rustic retreat from the downtown clamor, this huge, tree-lined park is suffused with summertime **hiking trails** that suit walkers of most abilities (the easiest path is the 2km Goldie Lake Trail). Many trails wind past lakes and centuries-old Douglas firs. This is also one of the city's main winter playgrounds.

🏃 Activities

Vancouver's variety of outdoorsy activities is a huge hook: you can ski in the morning and hit the beach in the afternoon; hike or bike scenic forests; paddleboard along the coastline; or kayak to your heart's content – and it will be content, with grand mountain views as your backdrop.

There's also a full menu of spectator sports to catch here.

★**Grouse Mountain**   SNOW SPORTS
(☎604-980-9311; www.grousemountain.com; 6400 Nancy Greene Way, North Vancouver; lift ticket adult/child $47/42; ⊘9am-10pm mid-Nov–mid-Apr; 🚻; 🚌236) Vancouver's favorite winter hangout, family-friendly Grouse offers four chairlifts plus 33 ski and snowboard runs (including night runs). Classes and lessons are available for beginners and beyond, and the area's forested snowshoe trails are magical. There are also a couple of dining options if you just want to relax and watch the snow with a hot chocolate in hand.

Cypress Mountain   SNOW SPORTS
(☎604-926-5612; www.cypressmountain.com; 6000 Cypress Bowl Rd, West Vancouver; lift ticket adult/youth/child $79/56/36; ⊘9am-10pm mid-Dec–Mar, to 4pm Apr; 🚻) Around 8km north of West Van via Hwy 99, **Cypress Provincial Park** (www.bcparks.ca; Cypress Bowl Rd, West Vancouver; ⊘dawn-dusk) **FREE** transforms into Cypress Mountain resort in winter, attracting well-insulated locals with its 53 runs, cross-country ski access and a family-friendly snow-tubing course. There are also 11km of snowshoe trails, with several guided tours available (the $59 chocolate fondue option is recommended).

☞ Tours

★**Cycle City Tours**   CYCLING
(Map p640; ☎604-618-8626; www.cyclevancouver .com; 648 Hornby St, Downtown; tours from $65; bicycle rentals per hour/day $9.50/38; ⊘9am-6pm, reduced hours in winter; Ⓢ Burrard) Striped with bike lanes, Vancouver is a good city for two-wheeled exploring. But if you're not great at navigating, consider a guided tour with this popular operator. Its Grand Tour ($90) is a great city intro, while the Craft Beer Tour ($90) includes brunch and three breweries. Alternatively, go solo with a rental; there's a bike lane outside the store.

★**Vancouver Foodie Tours**   TOURS
(☎604-295-8844; www.foodietours.ca; tours from $65) A popular culinary-themed city stroll operator running three tasty tours in Vancouver; choose between Best of Downtown, Gastronomic Gastown and Granville Island tours. Friendly red-coated guides lead you on belly-pleasing ventures with plenty to eat

---

URBAN BIRDING

You don't have to go far to spot some beady-eyed locals in this city. Birding has become a popular pastime for many Vancouverites and if you're keen to join in the feather-fancying fun, consider spending an hour or two in Stanley Park (p635), **Vanier Park**, **Pacific Spirit Park** or **Queen Elizabeth Park**.

Many city streets are also lined with established trees that are home to a surprisingly diverse array of beaked critters: on our West End exploration, we spotted hummingbirds, barred owls and northern flicker woodpeckers. Heading into adjoining Stanley Park, you might also see wrens, chickadees, downy woodpeckers, bald eagles, coots, ducks, cormorants and herons – which are also famous for nesting in a large and noisy heronry here every spring.

and drink; the trick is not to dine before you arrive.

Forbidden Vancouver WALKING
(☎604-227-7570; www.forbiddenvancouver.ca; tours from $25) This quirky company offers highly entertaining tours, including a delve into Prohibition-era Vancouver, a Stanley Park 'secrets' tour and a combination chocolate-tasting and art-deco architecture walk. It also hosts regular behind-the-scenes tours of the infamous Penthouse nightclub as well as a recently added walk-and-talk around the city's LGBTIQ+ history.

Sewell's Marina BOATING
(☎604-921-3474; www.sewellsmarina.com; 6409 Bay St, Horseshoe Bay, West Vancouver; adult/child $93/60; ⏲8am-6pm Apr-Oct; 👪; 🚌257) West Vancouver's Horseshoe Bay is the departure point for Sewell's two-hour Sea Safari boat tours. Orcas are always a highlight, but even if they're not around you'll almost certainly spot harbor seals lolling on the rocks and pretending to ignore you. Seabirds and bald eagles are also big stars of the show.

Festivals & Events

Vancouver International Wine Festival WINE
(www.vanwinefest.ca; 999 Canada Pl, Convention Centre West, Downtown; tickets from $40; ⏲late Feb) The city's oldest and best annual wine celebration, with a different regional focus every year.

Vancouver Craft Beer Week BEER
(www.vancouvercraftbeerweek.com; event tickets from $15; ⏲late May) A showcase for BC's amazing craft-beer scene, with dozens of tasty events around the city.

Vancouver International Jazz Festival MUSIC
(www.coastaljazz.ca; ⏲Jun) City-wide cornucopia of superstar shows and free outdoor events from mid-June.

Vancouver Mural Festival ART
(www.vanmuralfest.ca; Main St; ⏲Aug) Mostly radiating along Main St and its tributaries, this annual event transforms city walls with huge, eye-popping artworks.

Pride Week LGBTIQ+
(www.vancouverpride.ca; West End; ⏲Aug) Parties, concerts and fashion shows, as well as the city's biggest annual street parade.

Pacific National Exhibition (PNE) CULTURAL
(www.pne.ca; 2901 E Hastings St, Hastings Park; adult/under-13s $18/free; ⏲mid-Aug–Sep; 👪; 🚌14) Family-friendly shows, music concerts and fairground fun (plus lots of calorific things to eat).

Vancouver International Film Festival FILM
(www.viff.org; ⏲late Sep) Popular two-week showcase of Canadian and international movies on screens throughout the city. Book ahead: tickets are hot items here.

Eastside Culture Crawl ART
(www.culturecrawl.ca; ⏲mid-Nov) Vancouver's best visual-arts festival: a four-day gallery and studio open house with hundreds of participants.

Sleeping

Metro Vancouver is home to more than 23,000 hotel, B&B and hostel rooms, the majority in or around the downtown core. Airbnb also operates here, although a regulatory crackdown has reduced their number in recent years. Book far ahead for summer, unless you fancy sleeping rough in Stanley Park. Rates peak in July and August, but there are good spring and fall deals here (alongside increased rainy days).

Downtown & West End

Samesun Backpackers Lodge HOSTEL $
(Map p640; ☎604-682-8226; www.samesun.com; 1018 Granville St, Downtown; dm/r incl breakfast from $62/180; @📶; 🚌10) Vancouver's liveliest hostel is right on the city's nightlife strip. Ask for a back room if you fancy a few hours of sleep or head down to the on-site bar (provocatively called the Beaver) to hang out with the partying throng. Dorms, including some pod beds, are comfortably small, and there are also private rooms plus a large shared kitchen.

HI Vancouver Central HOSTEL $
(Map p640; ☎604-685-5335; www.hihostels.ca/en/destinations/british-columbia/hi-vancouver-central; 1025 Granville St, Downtown; dm/r from $60/120; ❄@📶; 🚌10) On the Granville Strip, this warren-like hostel is more of a party joint than its **HI Downtown** (Map p640; ☎604-684-4565; www.hihostels.ca/en/destinations/british-columbia/hi-vancouver-downtown; 1114 Burnaby St, West End; dm/r from $62/135; @📶; 🚌6) sibling. Some of the

benefits of its past hotel incarnation remain, including air-conditioning and small rooms, some of which are now private, with the rest converted to dorms with up to four beds. There are dozens of two-bedded rooms (some en suite).

★ **Victorian Hotel** HOTEL **$$**
(Map p640; ☑ 604-681-6369; www.victorianhotel.ca; 514 Homer St, Downtown; d incl breakfast from $200; ⊖ @ �ʘ; Ⓢ Granville) The high-ceilinged rooms at this well-maintained heritage hotel combine glossy hardwood floors, a sprinkling of antiques, an occasional bay window and plenty of historical charm. The best rooms are in the extension, where raindrop showers, marble bathroom floors and flat-screen TVs add a slice of luxe. Rates include continental breakfast and rooms are provided with fans in summer.

★ **Sunset Inn & Suites** HOTEL **$$**
(Map p640; ☑ 604-688-2474; www.sunsetinn.com; 1111 Burnaby St, West End; d incl breakfast $225; �℗ ✲ @ �ʘ; ⬛ 6) A good-value cut above most of Vancouver's self-catering suite hotels, the popular Sunset Inn offers larger-than-average rooms with kitchens. Each has a balcony, and some – particularly those on south-facing higher floors – have partial views of English Bay. Rates include continental breakfast (with make-your-own waffles) and, rare for Vancouver, free parking. The attentive staff is among the best in the city.

Sylvia Hotel HOTEL **$$**
(Map p640; ☑ 604-681-9321; www.sylviahotel.com; 1154 Gilford St, West End; d from $199; �℗ @ �ʘ ✲; ⬛ 5) This ivy-covered 1912 charmer enjoys a prime location overlooking English Bay. Generations of guests keep coming back – many requesting the same room every year – for a dollop of old-world ambience, plus a side order of first-name service. The rooms, some with older furnishings, have an array of comfortable configurations; the best are the large suites with kitchens and waterfront views.

Burrard Hotel HOTEL **$$**
(Map p640; ☑ 604-681-2331; www.theburrard.com; 1100 Burrard St, Downtown; d from $240; �℗ ✲ �ʘ ✲; ⬛ 2) A groovy makeover a few years back transformed this 1950s downtown motel into a knowingly cool sleepover with a tongue-in-cheek retro feel (neon exterior sign included). Colorful, mostly compact rooms have been spruced up with modern flourishes and contemporary amenities such as refrigerators and flat-screen TVs. But not everything has changed; the hidden interior courtyard's towering palm trees echo yesteryear Vegas.

St Regis Hotel BOUTIQUE HOTEL **$$$**
(Map p640; ☑ 604-681-1135; www.stregishotel.com; 602 Dunsmuir St, Downtown; d incl breakfast from $325; ✲ @ �ʘ; Ⓢ Granville) An elegant art-lined boutique sleepover in a 1913 heritage shell. Befitting its age, almost all the rooms seem to be a different size, and they exhibit a loungey élan with deco-esque furniture, earth-toned bedspreads, flat-screen TVs and multimedia hubs.

Rates include value-added flourishes such as cooked breakfasts, access to the nearby gym and free long-distance and international phone calls.

Listel Hotel BOUTIQUE HOTEL **$$$**
(Map p640; ☑ 604-684-8461; www.thelistelhotel.com; 1300 Robson St, West End; d from $340; �℗ ✲ @ �ʘ; ⬛ 5) 🖉 A lounge-cool sleepover with famously friendly front-deskers. Rooms at the Listel have a relaxed West Coast feel and typically feature striking original artworks. But it's not all about looks; cool features include glass water bottles in the rooms, a daily wine reception (from 5pm) and the free use of loaner e-bikes if you want to explore nearby Stanley Park (p635).

Fairmont Hotel Vancouver HOTEL **$$$**
(Map p640; ☑ 604-684-3131; www.fairmont.com/hotel-vancouver; 900 W Georgia St, Downtown; d from $500; ℗ ✲ @ ⩙ ⩙ ✲; Ⓢ Vancouver City Centre) Opened in 1939 by visiting UK royals, this gargoyle-topped grand dame is a Vancouver historic landmark. Despite its vintage provenance, the hotel carefully balances comfort with elegance; the lobby is bedecked with crystal chandeliers but the rooms have an understated business-hotel feel.

If you have the budget, you can check into the Gold Floor for a raft of pampering extras.

🛏 Gastown & Chinatown

★ **Skwachàys Lodge** BOUTIQUE HOTEL **$$**
(Map p640; ☑ 604-687-3589; www.skwachays.com; 29 W Pender St, Chinatown; d from $300; ✲ �ʘ; Ⓢ Stadium-Chinatown) The 18 small but

elegantly designed rooms at this sparkling First Nations art hotel include the captivating Forest Spirits Suite, with floor-to-ceiling birch branches, and the sleek Longhouse Suite, with its illuminated metalwork frieze. Deluxe trappings, from plasma TVs to ecofriendly toiletries, are standard and there's an on-site gallery for purchasing one-of-a-kind artworks.

🛏 Yaletown & Granville Island

YWCA Hotel HOTEL $

(Map p640; ✆604-895-5830; www.ywcahotel. com; 733 Beatty St, Yaletown; s/d/tr without bath $106/118/173; P❄❋@🛜; S Stadium-Chinatown) A good-value, well-located option with nicely maintained (if spartan) rooms of the student-accommodations variety. There's a range of configurations, from singles to five-bed rooms, plus shared, semiprivate or private bathrooms. Each room has a TV and mini-refrigerator and there are TV lounges and communal kitchens too.

Rates include access to the YWCA Health & Fitness Centre, located a 15-minute walk away.

Opus Hotel BOUTIQUE HOTEL $$$

(Map p640; ✆604-642-6787; www.opushotel. com; 322 Davie St, Yaletown; d $500; P❋🛜❄; S Yaletown-Roundhouse) The 96-room Opus kick-started Vancouver's boutique-hotel scene and, with regular revamps, it's remained one of the city's top sleepover options. The designer rooms have contemporary-chic interiors with bold colors, mod furnishings and feng-shui bed placements, while many of the luxe bathrooms have clear windows overlooking the streets (visiting exhibitionists take note).

Granville Island Hotel BOUTIQUE HOTEL $$$

(Map p640; ✆604-683-7373; www.granville islandhotel.com; 1253 Johnston St, Granville Island; d $400; P❋@🛜❄; 🖵50) This gracious boutique property hugs Granville Island's quiet southeastern tip, enjoying tranquil views across False Creek to Yaletown's mirrored towers. You'll be a stroll from the Public Market, with shopping and theater options on your doorstep. Rooms have a West Coast feel with some exposed-wood flourishes. There's also a rooftop Jacuzzi, while the on-site brewpub-restaurant has one of the city's best patios.

VANCOUVER'S BEST BLOGS

Miss 604 (www.miss604.com) Vancouver's leading blogger, covering local events and happenings.

Scout Magazine (www.scoutmagazine. ca) Trendy site profiling the city's food and drinks scene.

Bored in Vancouver (www.boredin vancouver.com) Alternative take on multiple scenes around the city.

Daily Hive Vancouver (www.dailyhive. com/vancouver) City news and lifestyle happenings.

🛏 Kitsilano & University of British Columbia

HI Vancouver Jericho Beach HOSTEL $

(Map p636; ✆604-224-3208; www.hihostels.com; 1515 Discovery St, Kitsilano; dm/d $43/86; ☽May-Sep; P@🛜; 🖵4) One of Canada's largest hostels looks like a Victorian hospital but has a scenic near-the-beach location. Basic rooms make this the least palatial Vancouver HI hostel, but it has a large kitchen, bike rentals and a popular licenced cafe. Dorms are also larger here. Book ahead for the popular budget-hotel-style private rooms (with shared and private bathroom options).

🍴 Eating

Vancouver has an eye-popping array of generally good-value dine-out options: authentic Asian restaurants, finger-licking brunch spots, fresh-catch seafood joints and a locally sourced farm-to-table scene are all on the menu here. You don't have to be a local to indulge: just follow your taste buds and dinner will become the most talked-about highlight of your Vancouver visit.

🍴 Downtown & West End

Finch's CAFE $

(Map p640; ✆604-899-4040; www.finchtea house.com; 353 W Pender St, Downtown; mains $6-12; ☽9am-5pm Mon-Fri, 11am-4pm Sat; ✆; 🖵4) For a coveted seat at one of the dinged-ed old tables, arrive off-peak at this sunny, super-friendly corner cafe, which combines creaky wooden floors and a junk-shop bric-a-brac aesthetic. Join hipsters and office workers who've been calling this their local for years and who come mainly for the freshly prepared baguette sandwiches (pear, blue Brie, prosciutto and roasted walnuts recommended).

Japadog
JAPANESE $

(Map p640; ☑604-569-1158; www.japadog. com; 530 Robson St, Downtown; mains $6-12; ◎6:30am-10pm Mon-Fri, 7:30am-11pm Sat, 7:30am-9pm Sun; ☐10) You'll have spotted the lunchtime queues at the Japadog hot-dog stands around town, but this was their first storefront, opening back in 2010. The ever-*genki* Japanese expats serve up a menu of lip-smacking wonder wieners – think turkey smokies with miso sauce and crunchy shrimp tempura dogs – but there are also irresistible fries (try the butter and *shoyu* version).

Kintaro Ramen Noodle
RAMEN $

(Map p640; ☑604-682-7568; 788 Denman St, West End; mains $6-10; ◎11:30am-11pm; ☐5) One of Vancouver's oldest noodle shops, fancy-free Kintaro feels like a bustling ramen spot in backstreet Tokyo. Arrive off-peak to avoid queues and snag a counter seat to watch the steam-shrouded action. Miso ramen is recommended; a brimming bowl of sprouts, bamboo shoots and thick slices of barbecued pork. When you're done, walk off your noodle belly in Stanley Park.

★ Indigo Age Cafe
VEGAN $$

(Map p640; ☑604-622-1797; www.indigoage cafe.com; 436 Richards St, Downtown; mains $15-20; ◎11am-7pm Wed-Sun; ☎☑; ☐14) ⊘ The kind of woodsy subterranean cave a health-minded hobbit would enjoy, this small vegan and raw-food restaurant has legions of local fans. Snag a table (peak-time reservations recommended) and dive into hearty, savor-worthy dishes from cabbage rolls to the colorful, best-selling Fresh Addiction Burger. Fancy a unique high tea? It offers a cool raw vegan version here; book ahead.

★ Forage
CANADIAN $$

(Map p640; ☑604-661-1400; www.foragevancou ver.com; 1300 Robson St, West End; mains $16-35; ◎6:30-10am & 5-11pm Mon-Fri, 7am-2pm & 5-11pm Sat & Sun; ☎; ☐5) ⊘ A popular farm-to-table eatery, this sustainability-focused restaurant is the perfect way to sample regional flavors. Brunch has become a firm local favorite

(halibut eggs Benny recommended), and for dinner there's everything from bison steaks to slow-cooked salmon. Add a flight of BC craft beers, with top choices from the likes of Four Winds, Strange Fellows and more. Reservations recommended.

Jam Cafe
BREAKFAST $$

(Map p640; ☑778-379-1992; www.jamcafes.com; 556 Beatty St, Downtown; mains $9-17; ◎8am-3pm; ☎☑; ⑤Stadium-Chinatown) The Vancouver outpost of Victoria's wildly popular breakfast and brunch superstar lures the city's longest queues, especially on weekends. Reservations are not accepted so you're well advised to dine off-peak and during the week. You'll find a white-walled room studded with Canadian knickknacks and a huge array of satisfying options, from chicken and biscuits to red-velvet pancakes.

Mumbai Local
INDIAN $$

(Map p640; ☑604-423-3281; www.mumbai local.ca; 1148 Davie St, West End; mains $15-25; ◎11am-10pm; ☎☑; ☐5) Seated alongside a striking Mumbai-themed mural, dive into some street-food snacks and dishes inspired by the home-style cuisine of this bustling Indian city. We loved the *chaat* sampler of crunchy savory treats plus the chickpea and potato patties in a bun, but don't miss the *dabba* combo of condiments, stew, dal, bread and rice served in a multilayer tiffin tin.

Chambar
EUROPEAN $$$

(Map p640; ☑604-879-7119; www.chambar. com; 568 Beatty St, Downtown; mains $28-36; ◎8am-11pm; ℗; ⑤Stadium-Chinatown) This giant, brick-lined cave is a juggernaut of Vancouver's dining scene, serving an ever-changing all-day menu of sophisticated Belgian-esque dishes from morning waffles to excellent *moules frites* to a lip-smacking dinnertime lamb shank with figs and couscous. An impressive wine and cocktail list (try a blue-fig martini) is coupled with a great Belgian beer menu dripping with *tripels* and *lambics*.

✖ Gastown & Chinatown

★ Ovaltine Cafe
DINER $

(Map p640; ☑604-685-7021; www.facebook. com/ovaltinecafe; 251 E Hastings St, Chinatown; mains $7-10; ◎6:30am-2pm Mon-Sat, 6:30am-2pm Sun; ☐14) Like being inside Edward Hopper's *Nighthawks* diner painting, this time-capsule greasy spoon instantly transports you to the 1940s. Snag a booth alongside the hospital-green walls or, better yet, slide onto a tape-repaired spinning stool at the long counter. Truck-stop coffee is de rigueur here, alongside burgers, sandwiches and fried breakfasts that haven't changed in decades (yes, that's liver and onions on the menu).

Chinatown BBQ
CHINESE $

(Map p640; ☑604-428-2626; www.china townbbq.com; 130 E Pender St, Chinatown; mains $10-19; ☺11am-8pm Tue-Sun; ☐3) A modern-day version of this historic neighborhood's once-ubiquitous barbecue shops, this retro-feel eatery (vinyl booths, checkerboard floor and monochrome wall photos) serves simple, perfectly prepared platters of meat and rice plus more (we like the beef-brisket curry). Expect a soundtrack of traditional Chinese music and the thud of meat cleavers from the old dudes in the open kitchen.

Tacofino Taco Bar
MEXICAN $

(Map p640; ☑604-899-7907; www.tacofino. com; 15 W Cordova St, Gastown; tacos from $6; ☺11:30am-10pm Sun-Wed, 11:30am-midnight Thu-Sat; ☎☑; ☐14) Food-truck favorite Tacofino made an instant splash with this huge, handsome dining room (think stylish geometric-patterned floors, hive-like lampshades and a tiny back patio). The simple menu focuses on a handful of taco options plus nachos, soups and a selection of beer, agave and tequila flights. Fish tacos are the top seller, but we love the super-tender lamb *birria* version.

Save on Meats
DINER $

(Map p640; ☑604-569-3568; www.saveon meats.ca; 43 W Hastings St, Gastown; mains $6-15; ☺11am-7pm Sun-Thu, 11am-11pm Fri & Sat; ☎☑; ☐14) A former old-school butcher shop that's been transformed into a popular hipster diner. Slide into a booth or hop on a swivel chair at the super-long counter and tuck into comfort dishes. They range from a good-value $6 all-day breakfast to the satisfying SOM burger, paired with a heaping tangle of 'haystack' fries. Add a BC-brewed Persephone beer to keep things lively.

Phnom Penh
VIETNAMESE, CAMBODIAN $

(Map p640; ☑604-682-5777; www.phnom penhrestaurant.ca; 244 E Georgia St, Chinatown; mains $8-18; ☺10am-9pm Mon-Thu, 10am-10pm Fri-Sun; ☐3) The dishes at this bustling, local-legend joint are split between Cambodian and Vietnamese soul-food classics. It's the highly addictive chicken wings and their lovely pepper sauce that keep regulars loyal. Once you've piled up the bones, dive back in for round two: papaya salad, butter beef and spring rolls show just how good a street-food-inspired Asian menu can be.

★ Campagnolo
ITALIAN $$

(Map p640; ☑604-484-6018; www.cam pagnolorestaurant.ca; 1020 Main St, Chinatown; mains $18-25; ☺11:30am-2:30pm Mon-Fri, plus 5:30-10pm daily; ☑; ☐3) Eyebrows were raised when this contemporary, rustic-style Italian restaurant opened in a hitherto sketchy part of town. But Campagnolo has lured locals and inspired a miniwave of other restaurants in the vicinity. Reserve ahead and dive into reinvented comfort dishes such as shrimp gnocchetti and a fennel sausage-topped pizza that may induce you to eat your body weight in thin-crust.

MeeT in Gastown
VEGAN $$

(Map p640; ☑604-696-1111; www.meeton main.com; 12 Water St, Gastown; mains $10-16; ☺11am-11pm Sun-Thu, 11am-midnight Fri & Sat; ☑; Ⓜ Waterfront) Serving great vegan comfort dishes without the rabbit-food approach, this wildly popular spot can be clamorously busy at times. But it's worth the wait for a wide-ranging array of herbivore- and carnivore-pleasing dishes, from rice bowls and mac 'n' cheese (made from vegan cashew 'cheese') to hearty burgers and poutine-like fries slathered in nut-based miso gravy (our recommendation).

Bao Bei
CHINESE $$

(Map p640; ☑604-688-0876; www.bao-bei. ca; 163 Keefer St, Chinatown; small plates $6-23; ☺5:30pm-midnight Mon-Sat, 5:30-11pm Sun; ☐3) Reinterpreting a Chinatown heritage building with hipsteresque flourishes, this Chinese brasserie is a seductive dinner destination. Bringing a contemporary edge to Asian cuisine are tapas-sized, MSG-free dishes such as *shao bing* (stuffed Chinese flatbread), delectable dumplings and spicy-chicken steamed buns. There's also an enticing drinks menu guaranteed to make you linger, especially if you dive into the inventive cocktails.

AGUSTIN ESMORIS/SHUTTERSTOCK ©

1. Alert Bay (p712)
Home to the Namgis First Nation, there are lots of ways to experience Indigenous culture here.

2. Sea to Sky Gondola (p663)
Head to the top station of Squamish's spectacular gondola for stunning views.

3. Whistler (p665)
One of the world's largest, best-equipped and most popular ski resorts.

4. Salt Spring Island (p716)
The busiest and most developed of the Southern Gulf Islands.

Sai Woo
ASIAN $$

(Map p640; ☑ 604-568-1117; www.saiwoo.ca; 158 E Pender, Chinatown; mains $13-23; ⊘ 5pm-midnight Tue-Sat, 5-9pm Sun; ☐ 3) There's a film-set look to the exterior of this contemporary restaurant that resembles a replica of an old Hong Kong restaurant. But the long, slender interior is a candlelit cave with a lounge-like vibe. Expect a wide array of Asian dishes, from Szechuan spicy-beef noodles to Korean-style barbecued-pork pancakes, and consider the happy hour (5pm to 6pm) with half-price dumplings.

★ St Lawrence Restaurant
FRENCH $$$

(Map p640; ☑ 604-620-3800; www.stlawrencerestaurant.com; 269 Powell St, Railtown; mains $34-44; ⊘ 5:30-10:30pm Tue-Sun; ☐ 4) Resembling a handsome wood-floored bistro that's been teleported straight from Montréal, this sparkling, country-chic dining room is a Railtown superstar. The Québecois approach carries over onto a small menu of elevated, perfectly prepared old-school mains such as trout in brown-butter sauce and the utterly delicious duck-leg confit with sausage. French-Canadian special-occasion dining at its finest.

✖ Yaletown & Granville Island

DD Mau
VIETNAMESE $

(Map p640; ☑ 604-684-4446; www.ddmau.ca; 1239 Pacific Blvd, Yaletown; sandwiches $5-13; ⊘ 11am-4pm Mon-Sat; ☎; ⑤ Yaletown-Roundhouse) At the forefront of Vancouver's love affair with Vietnamese banh mi sandwiches, this tiny, often-busy spot serves daily specials (always check these first) alongside five made-to-order regulars. Expect crisp baguette sandwiches (in large or half-order options) with diverse fillings including barbecue pork and lemongrass chicken. Seating is extremely limited so aim for takeout or visit its larger Chinatown branch.

★ Go Fish
SEAFOOD $

(Map p640; ☑ 604-730-5040; 1505 W 1st Ave; mains $8-14; ⊘ 11:30am-6pm Mon-Fri, noon-6pm Sat & Sun; ☐ 50) A short stroll westward along the seawall from the Granville Island entrance, this almost-too-popular seafood stand is one of the city's fave fish-and-chip joints, offering halibut, salmon and cod encased in crispy golden batter. The smashing fish tacos are also recommended, while changing daily specials – brought in by the nearby fishing boats – often include scallop burgers or ahi tuna sandwiches.

Edible Canada
CANADIAN $$

(Map p640; ☑ 604-682-6681; www.ediblecanada.com; 1596 Johnston St, Granville Island; mains $12-35; ⊘ 8:30-8:30pm Mon-Fri, 9am-8:30pm Sat & Sun; ☐ 50) Granville Island's most popular bistro (book ahead) delivers a tempting menu of seasonal dishes. With ingredients from BC and across Canada, typical options include bison burgers, wild salmon or Québec-style duck poutine. Add a selection from the huge all-Canadian wine list (dominated by BC) or dive into a local beer flight that includes several Vancouver producers.

Blue Water Cafe
SEAFOOD $$$

(Map p640; ☑ 604-688-8078; www.bluewatercafe.net; 1095 Hamilton St, Yaletown; mains $30-45; ⊘ 5-11pm; ⑤ Yaletown-Roundhouse) Under celebrated executive chef Frank Pabst, this is one of Vancouver's best high-concept seafood restaurants. Gentle music fills the brick-lined, blue-hued interior, while top-notch char, sturgeon and butter-soft scallops grace the tables inside and on the patio. Not a seafood fan? There's also a small array of meaty 'principal plates' to sate your carnivorous appetite, including Kobe-style short ribs.

✖ Commercial Drive

★ Caffè La Tanna
ITALIAN $

(☑ 604-428-5462; www.caffelatana.ca; 635 Commercial Dr; mains $12-16; ⊘ 8am-6pm; ☐ 20) Like a 1950s neighborhood cafe in Rome, this handsome little hidden gem looks like it's been here for decades. But it's a newer addition to this quiet stretch of the Drive, luring delighted locals with its delicate housemade pastries and fresh pastas (watch the mesmerizing pasta production at the counter). Check the daily special and peruse the shelves of Italian groceries, too.

Downlow Chicken Shack
CHICKEN $

(☑ 604-283-1385; www.dlchickenshack.ca; 905 Commercial Dr; mains $8-32; ⊘ 11am-9pm Tue-Sat, 11am-4:30pm Sun; ☎; ☐ 20) Spicy, deep-fried, southern-style chicken is the menu foundation at this bright and buzzing spot with its surprisingly happy grinning-bird logo. Choose from a variety of cuts, including wings, boneless thighs and the popular-but-messy chicken-breast sandwich, then add your heat level plus tasty sides. Aim for a summertime deck seat and don't miss their $2 Wing Wednesday deal.

Tangent Cafe — DINER $

(☑604-558-4641; www.tangentcafe.ca; 2095 Commercial Dr; mains $11-19; ⊙8am-3pm Mon & Tue, 8am-midnight Wed & Thu, 8am-1am Fri & Sat, 8am-10pm Sun; 🛜🅿; 🖳20) Lined with retro wood paneling, this warm and welcoming Drive hangout combines comfort-classic wraps and burgers with several Malaysian curries and some good vegetarian options. But breakfast, served until mid-afternoon, is when you're most likely to meet the locals. A great craft-beer menu (check the corner chalkboard) and regular live music (mostly jazz) also make this a popular nighttime haunt.

🍴 Main Street

Hawkers Delight — ASIAN $

(☑604-709-8188; www.facebook.com/hawkers delightdeli; 4127 Main St; mains $5-13; ⊙noon-9pm Mon-Sat; 🅿; 🖳3) It's easy to miss this cash-only hole-in-the-wall, but it's worth retracing your steps for authentic Malaysian and Singaporean street food, made from scratch at this family-run favorite. Prices are temptingly low, so order to share – from spicy *mee pok* to noodle-heavy *mee goreng* and shrimp-packed *laksa*. Check the counter for addictive veggie fritters (just $1.45 for two).

★ Anh & Chi — VIETNAMESE $$

(☑604-878-8883; www.anhandchi.com; 3388 Main St; mains $16-25; ⊙11am-11pm; 🅿; 🖳3) You'll find warm and solicitous service at this delightful contemporary Vietnamese restaurant whose authentic, perfectly prepared dishes are a must for local foodies. Not sure what to order? Check out the menu's 'bucket list' dishes, including the highly recommended prawn-and-pork-packed crunchy crepe. Reservations are not accepted and waits here can be long; consider mid-afternoon weekday dining instead.

★ Acorn — VEGETARIAN $$

(☑604-566-9001; www.theacornrestaurant.ca; 3995 Main St; mains $18-22; ⊙5:30-10pm Mon-Thu, to 11pm Fri, 10am-2:30pm & 5:30-11pm Sat, to midnight Sun; 🅿; 🖳3) One of Vancouver's hottest vegetarian restaurants – hence the sometimes long wait for tables – the Acorn is ideal for those craving something more inventive than mung-bean soup. Consider seasonal, artfully presented treats such as

beer-battered haloumi or vanilla-almond-beet cake and stick around at night: the bar serves until midnight if you need to pull up a stool and set the world to rights.

🍴 Fairview & South Granville

★ Salmon n' Bannock — NORTHWESTERN US $$

(☑604-568-8971; www.facebook.com/salmonn bannockbistro; 1128 W Broadway, Fairview; mains $16-32; ⊙5-10pm Mon-Sat; 🖳9) Vancouver's only First Nations restaurant is an utterly delightful art-lined little bistro on an unassuming strip of Broadway shops. It's worth the easy bus trip, though, for fresh-made indigenous-influenced dishes made with local ingredients. The juicy salmon 'n' bannock burger has been a staple here for years but more elaborate, feast-like options include game sausages and bison pot roast.

Heritage Asian Eatery — ASIAN $$

(☑604-559-6058; www.eatheritage.ca; 382 W Broadway, Fairview; mains $12-18; ⊙11am-8pm; 🛜🅿; 🖳9) Bigger than its Pender St sibling, this bright, cafeteria-style spot serves a small, well-curated menu of comfort-food rice and noodle bowls. Serving top-notch dishes such as velvety pork belly and spicy lamb shank, it also offers a couple of flavor-hugging vegetarian options; go for the lip-smacking eggplant rice bowl. On your way out, add a warm egg-custard bun to your day.

★ Vij's — INDIAN $$$

(☑604-736-6664; www.vijs.ca; 3106 Cambie St, Cambie Village; mains $23-36; ⊙5:30-10pm; 🅿; 🖳15) Spicy aromas scent the air as you enter this warmly intimate dining space for Vancouver's finest Indian cuisine. Exemplary servers happily answer menu questions, while bringing over snacks and chai tea. There's a one-page array of tempting dishes but the trick is to order three or four to share (mains are all available as small plates and orders come with rice and naan).

🍴 Kitsilano & University of British Columbia

Jamjar Canteen — LEBANESE $

(Map p636; ☑604-620-5320; www.jamjarcan teen.ca; 6035 University Blvd, UBC; mains $10-12; ⊙10:30am-10pm Mon-Fri, to 9pm Sat & Sun; 🛜🅿; 🖳99B-Line) Visiting Canteen, a

simplified version of the city's highly popular Jamjar Lebanese comfort-food restaurants, means choosing from four mains
(lamb sausages or deep-fried cauliflower
recommended) then adding the approach:
rice bowl, salad bowl or wrap. Choices of
olives, veggies, hummus and more are then
requested before you can dive into your
hearty lunch or dinner.

Fable Kitchen CANADIAN $$
(604-732-1322; www.fablekitchen.ca; 1944 W
4th Ave, Kitsilano; mains $21-28; 11am-2:30pm
& 5:30-10pm Tue-Fri, 10am-2pm & 5-10pm Sat &
Sun; 4) One of Vancouver's favorite farm-
to-table restaurants is a lovely rustic-chic
room of exposed brick, wood beams and
prominently displayed red rooster logos.
But looks are just part of the appeal. Ex-
pect perfectly prepared bistro dishes show-
casing local seasonal ingredients such as
duck, pork and scallops. It's great gourmet
comfort food with little pretension, hence
the packed room most nights. Reservations
recommended.

Linh Cafe FRENCH, VIETNAMESE $$
(604-559-4668; www.linhcafe.com; 2836 W
4th Ave, Kitsilano; mains $14-45; 11am-9pm
Wed-Fri, 10am-9pm Sat & Sun; 4) Arrive
off-peak (limited reservations are also
available) at this chatty locals' favorite,
a friendly, red-tabled restaurant serving
French bistro classics and enticing Vietnamese specialties. You'll find everything
from escargot to *steak frites* on the eclectic
menu, but we recommend the deliciously
brothy beef pho. On your way out, add a
shiny little palmier pastry and a Vietnamese coffee to go.

Drinking & Nightlife

Vancouverites spend a lot of time drinking.
And while BC has a tasty wine sector and
is undergoing an artisanal distilling surge,
it's the regional craft-beer scene that keeps
many quaffers merry. For a night out with
locally made libations as your side dish, join
savvy city drinkers in the bars of Gastown,
Main St and beyond.

★Alibi Room PUB
(Map p640; 604-623-3383; www.alibi.ca; 157 Alexander St, Gastown; 5-11:30pm Mon-Thu, 5pm-
12:30am Fri, 10am-12:30am Sat, 10am-11:30pm Sun;
4) Vancouver's best craft-beer tavern
pours a near-legendary roster of 50-plus
drafts, many from celebrated BC breweries

including Four Winds, Yellow Dog and Dag-
eraad. Hipsters and veteran-ale fans alike
love the 'frat bat': choose your own four samples or ask to be surprised. Check the board
for new guest casks and stick around for a
gastropub dinner at one of the long communal tables.

Storm Crow Tavern PUB
(604-566-9669; www.stormcrowtavern.com;
1305 Commercial Dr; 11am-1am Mon-Sat, to midnight Sun; 20) Knowing the difference
between Narnia and *Neverwhere* is not a
prerequisite at this brilliant Commercial
Dr nerd pub. But if you do, you'll certainly
make new friends. With displays of *Doctor
Who* figures and steampunk ray guns – plus
TVs that might screen *Logan's Run* at any
moment – dive into the craft beer and settle
in for a fun evening.

Narrow Lounge BAR
(Map p640; 778-737-5206; www.narrowlounge.
com; 1898 Main St; 5pm-1am Mon-Fri, to 2am
Sat & Sun; 3) Enter through the doorway
on 3rd Ave – the red light tells you if it's
open or not – then descend the graffiti-
lined stairway into one of Vancouver's
coolest small bars. Little bigger than a
train carriage and lined with taxidermy
and junk-shop pictures, it's an atmospheric nook where it always feels like 2am. In
summer, try the hidden alfresco bar out
back.

Grapes & Soda WINE BAR
(604-336-2456; www.grapesandsoda.ca; 1541
W 6th Ave, South Granville; 5:30-11pm Tue-Sat;
10) A warm, small-table hangout that
self-identifies as a 'natural wine bar' (there's
a well-curated array of options from BC, Europe and beyond). This local favorite also
serves excellent cocktails: from the countless bottles behind the small bar, they can
seemingly concoct anything your taste buds
desire, whether or not it's on the menu.
Need help? Slide into a Scotch, ginger and
walnut Cortejo.

★Key Party BAR
(www.keyparty.ca; 2303 Main St; 5pm-1am
Mon-Thu, to 2am Fri & Sat, to 1am Sun; 3) Walk
through the doorway of a fake storefront
that looks like an accountancy office and
you'll find yourself in a candlelit, bou-
doir-red speakeasy dominated by a dramatic mural of frolicking women and animals.
Arrive early to avoid the queues, then fully
explore the entertaining cocktail program

(Kir Royale champagne jello shooters included).

Keefer Bar
COCKTAIL BAR

(Map p640; ✈604-688-1961; www.thekeeferbar.com; 135 Keefer St, Chinatown; ⊗5pm-1am Sun-Thu, 5pm-2am Fri & Sat; ⑤Stadium-Chinatown) This dark, narrow and atmospheric Chinatown bar has been claimed by local cocktail-loving coolsters since day one. Drop in for a full evening of liquid tasting and you'll have a blast. From perfectly prepared rosemary gimlets and tart blood moons to an excellent whiskey menu and some tasty tapas (we like the steam buns), it offers up a great night out.

★ Brassneck Brewery
MICROBREWERY

(✈604-259-7686; www.brassneck.ca; 2148 Main St; ⊗2-11pm Mon-Fri, noon-11pm Sat & Sun; ☐3) A beloved Vancouver microbrewery with a small, wood-lined tasting room. Peruse the ever-changing chalkboard of intriguing libations with names such as Pinky Promise, Silent Treatment and Faux Naive, or start with a delicious, highly accessible Passive Aggressive dry-hopped pale ale. It's often hard to find a seat here, so consider a weekday afternoon visit for a four-glass $8 tasting flight.

Shameful Tiki Room
BAR

(www.shamefultikiroom.com; 4362 Main St; ⊗5pm-midnight Sun-Thu, to 1am Fri & Sat; ☐3) This windowless snug instantly transports you to a Polynesian beach. The lighting – including glowing puffer-fish lampshades – is permanently set to dusk and the walls are lined with tiki masks and rattan coverings under a straw-shrouded ceiling. But it's the drinks that rock; seriously well-crafted classics from zombies to blue Hawaiis to a four-person Volcano Bowl (don't forget to share it).

Guilt & Co
BAR

(Map p640; www.guiltandcompany.com; 1 Alexander St, Gastown; ⊗7pm-late; ⑤Waterfront) This cavelike subterranean bar, beneath Gastown's brick-cobbled sidewalks, is also a brilliant venue to catch a tasty side dish of live music. Most shows are pay-what-you-can and can range from trumpet jazz to heartfelt singer-songwriters. Drinks-wise, there's a great cocktail list plus a small array of draft beers (and many more in cans and bottles). Avoid weekends when there are often long queues.

Fountainhead Pub
GAY

(Map p640; ✈604-687-2222; www.fthdpub.com; 1025 Davie St, West End; ⊗11am-midnight Mon-Thu & Sun, to 2am Fri & Sat; ☐6) The area's loudest and proudest gay neighborhood pub, this friendly joint is all about the patio, which spills onto Davie St like an overturned wine glass. Take part in the ongoing summer-evening pastime of ogling passersby or retreat to a quieter spot inside for a few lagers or a naughty cocktail: anyone for a Crispy Crotch or a Slippery Nipple?

☆ Entertainment

Live Music

★ Commodore Ballroom
LIVE MUSIC

(Map p640; ✈604-739-4550; www.commodoreballroom.com; 868 Granville St, Downtown; tickets from $30; ☐10) Local bands know they've made it when they play Vancouver's best mid-sized venue, a restored art-deco ballroom that still has the city's bounciest dance floor – courtesy of tires placed under its floorboards.

If you need a break from moshing, collapse at one of the tables lining the perimeter, catch your breath with a bottled brew and then plunge back in.

Biltmore Cabaret
LIVE MUSIC

(✈604-676-0541; www.biltmorecabaret.com; 2755 Prince Edward St; tickets from $15; ☐9) One of Vancouver's favorite alt venues, the intimate Biltmore is a firm fixture on the local indie scene. A low-ceilinged, good-vibe spot to mosh to local and touring musicians, it also has regular event nights; check the online calendar for upcoming happenings, including trivia nights and stand-up comedy shows.

Theater

★ Arts Club Theatre Company
THEATER

(✈604-687-1644; www.artsclub.com; tickets from $29; ⊗Sep-Jun) Vancouver's largest, most popular and most prolific theater company, the Arts Club stages shows at three venues around the city.

★ Bard on the Beach
PERFORMING ARTS

(Map p640; ✈604-739-0559; www.bardonthebeach.org; 1695 Whyte Ave, Vanier Park, Kitsilano; tickets from $24; ⊗Jun-Sep; ⊕; ☐2) Watching Shakespeare performed while the sun sets over the mountains beyond the tented main stage is a Vancouver summertime highlight. There are usually three Shakespeare plays, plus one Bard-related work (*Rosencrantz* and Guildenstern are Dead, for example), to choose from during the season. Q&A talks are staged after some Tuesday performances; also opera, fireworks and wine-tasting special nights are held throughout the season.

Cinema

★ **Cinematheque** CINEMA
(Map p640; ☑ 604-688-8202; www.thecine matheque.ca; 1131 Howe St, Downtown; tickets $12, double bills $16; 🖵 10) This beloved cinema operates like an ongoing film festival with a daily-changing program of movies. A $3 annual membership is required – organize it at the door – before you can skulk in the dark with other chin-stroking movie buffs who probably named their children (or pets) after Fellini and Bergman.

Vancity Theatre CINEMA
(Map p640; ☑ 604-683-3456; www.viff.org; 1181 Seymour St, Downtown; tickets $13, double bills $20; 🖵 10) The state-of-the-art headquarters of the Vancouver International Film Festival (p645) screens a wide array of movies throughout the year in the kind of auditorium that cinephiles dream of: generous legroom, wide armrests and great sight lines from each of its 175 seats. It's a place where you can watch a four-hour subtitled epic about paint drying and still feel comfortable.

Sports

Vancouver Whitecaps SOCCER
(Map p640; ☑ 604-669-9283; www.whitecapsfc. com; 777 Pacific Blvd, BC Place Stadium, Yaletown; tickets from $45; ☉ Mar-Oct; 🚇; Ⓢ Stadium-Chinatown) Using BC Place Stadium (p638) as its home, Vancouver's professional soccer team plays in North America's top-tier Major League Soccer (MLS). Their on-field fortunes have ebbed and flowed since being promoted to the league in 2011, but they've been finding their feet (useful for soccer players) lately. Make time to buy a souvenir soccer shirt to impress everyone back home.

Vancouver Canucks HOCKEY
(Map p640; ☑ 604-899-7400; www.nhl.com/ca nucks; 800 Griffiths Way, Rogers Arena, Downtown; tickets from $47; ☉ Sep-Apr; Ⓢ Stadium-Chinatown) Recent years haven't been hugely successful for Vancouver's National Hockey League (NHL) team, which means it's sometimes easy to snag tickets to a game if you're simply visiting and want to see what 'ice hockey' (no one calls it that here) is all about. You'll hear

'go Canucks, go!' booming from the seats and in local bars on game nights.

BC Lions FOOTBALL
(Map p640; ☑ 604-589-7627; www.bclions.com; 777 Pacific Blvd, BC Place Stadium, Yaletown; tickets from $20; ☉ Jun-Nov; 🚇; Ⓢ Stadium-Chinatown) Founded in 1954, the Lions are Vancouver's team in the Canadian Football League (CFL), which is arguably more exciting than its US counterpart, the NFL. The team has had some decent showings lately, but hasn't won the all-important Grey Cup since 2011. Tickets are easy to come by – unless the boys are laying into their arch enemies, the Calgary Stampeders.

🛍 Shopping

Vancouver's retail scene has developed dramatically in recent years. Hit Robson St's mainstream chains, then discover the hip, independent shops of Gastown, Main St and Commercial Dr. Granville Island is stuffed with artsy stores and studios, while South Granville and Kitsilano's 4th Ave serve up a wide range of tempting boutiques.

★ **Pacific Arts Market** ARTS & CRAFTS
(☑ 778-877-6449; www.pacificartsmarket.ca; 1448 W Broadway, South Granville; ☉ noon-5:30pm Tue & Wed, noon-7pm Thu & Fri, 11am-7pm Sat, 1-5pm Sun; 🖵 9) Head upstairs to this large, under-the-radar gallery space and you'll find a kaleidoscopic array of stands showcasing the work of 40+ Vancouver and BC artists. From paintings to jewelry and from fiber arts to handmade chocolate bars, it's the perfect spot to find authentic souvenirs to take back home. The artists change regularly and there's something for every budget here.

★ **Regional Assembly of Text** ARTS & CRAFTS
(☑ 604-877-2247; www.assemblyoftext.com; 3934 Main St; ☉ 11am-6pm Mon-Sat, noon-5pm Sun; 🖵 3) This ironic antidote to the digital age lures ink-stained locals with its journals, handmade pencil boxes and T-shirts printed with typewriter motifs. Check out the tiny under-the-stairs gallery showcasing global zines and don't miss the monthly Letter Writing Club (7pm, first Thursday of every month), where you can hammer on vintage typewriters, crafting erudite missives to faraway loved ones.

Paper Hound BOOKS
(Map p640; ☑ 604-428-1344; www.paperhound. ca; 344 W Pender St, Downtown; ☉ 10am-7pm Sun-Thu, to 8pm Fri & Sat; 🖵 14) Proving the print-

ed word is alive and kicking, this small but perfectly curated secondhand bookstore is a dog-eared favorite among locals. A perfect spot for browsing, you'll find tempting tomes (mostly used but some new) on everything from nature to poetry to chaos theory. Ask for recommendations; they really know their stuff here. Don't miss the bargain rack out front.

Red Cat Records MUSIC
(☑604-708-9422; www.redcat.ca; 4332 Main St; ⊙11am-7pm Mon-Thu, to 8pm Fri & Sat, to 6pm Sun; ▣3) Arguably Vancouver's coolest record store and certainly the only one named after a much-missed cat... There's a brilliantly curated collection of new and used vinyl and CDs, and it's co-owned by musicians; ask them for tips on where to see great local acts such as Loscil and Nick Krgovich or peruse the huge list of shows in the window.

Kitsilano Farmers Market MARKET
(www.eatlocal.org; 2690 Larch St, Kitsilano Community Centre, Kitsilano; ⊙10am-2pm Sun May-Oct; ▣9) ✔ This seasonal farmers market is one of the city's most popular and is Kitsilano's best excuse to get out and hang with the locals. Arrive early for the best selection and you'll have the pick of freshly plucked local fruit and veg, such as sweet strawberries or spectacularly flavorful heirloom tomatoes. You'll likely never want to shop in a mainstream supermarket again.

Eastside Flea MARKET
(www.eastsideflea.com; 550 Malkin Ave, Eastside Studios; $3-5; ⊙11am-5pm Sat & Sun, once or twice a month; ▣22) A size upgrade from its previous venue has delivered a cavernous market hall of hip arts and crafts-isans hawking everything from handmade chocolate bars to intricate jewelry and a humungous array of cool-ass vintage clothing. Give yourself plenty of time to hang out here; there's a pool table and retro arcade machines plus food trucks and a long bar serving local craft beer.

Bird on a Wire Creations ARTS & CRAFTS
(☑604-874-7415; www.birdonawirecreations.com; 2535 Main St; ⊙10am-6pm Mon-Sat, 11am-5pm Sun; ▣3) Specializing in BC artisans, there's an eminently browsable and surprisingly diverse array of tasteful handmade goodies at this ever-friendly store. Your credit cards will start to sweat as you move among the cute jewelry, artsy T-shirts, ceramic tea tankards and fiber arts kids' toys (that adults want, too). But it's not just for show; there are regular craft classes here too.

★**Karen Cooper Gallery** ART
(Map p640; ☑604-559-5112; www.karencooper gallery.com; 1506 Duranleau St, Granville Island; ⊙10am-6pm, reduced hours in winter; ▣50) You'll feel like you've entered a tranquil forest clearing when you open the door of this delightful nature-themed photography gallery. Cooper's striking work focuses on BC's jaw-dropping wild beauty, from coniferous trees to grizzly bears. Take your time and don't be surprised if you fall in love with a handsome image of a bald eagle perched on a mountain tree.

ℹ️ Information

MEDICAL SERVICES

Shoppers Drug Mart (☑604-669-2424; 1125 Davie St, West End; ⊙24hr; ▣6) Pharmacy chain.

Ultima Medicentre (☑604-683-8138; 1055 Dunsmuir St, Downtown; ⊙8am-5pm Mon-Fri; ⑤Burrard) Full range of walk-in clinic medical services. Appointments not essential.

Vancouver General Hospital (☑604-875-4111; www.vch.ca; 855 W 12th Ave, Fairview; Ⓜ️Broadway-City Hall)

MONEY

Vancouver Bullion & Currency Exchange (☑604-685-1008; www.vbce.ca; 800 W Pender St, Downtown; ⊙8:30am-5pm Mon-Fri; ⑤Granville) Aside from the banks, try Vancouver Bullion & Currency Exchange for currency exchange. It often has a wider range of currencies and competitive rates.

TOURIST INFORMATION

Tourism Vancouver Visitor Centre (Map p640; ☑604-683-2000; www.tourism vancouver.com; 200 Burrard St, Downtown; ⊙9am-5pm; ⑤Waterfront) A large repository of resources for visitors, with a staff of helpful advisers ready to assist in planning your trip in the city and around the area. Services and info available include free maps, visitor guides, accommodation and tour bookings, plus a host of glossy brochures on the city and the wider BC region.

ℹ️ Getting There & Away

AIR

Canada's second-busiest airport, **Vancouver International Airport** (YVR; Map p636; ☑604-207-7077; www.yvr.ca; 3211 Grant McConachie Way, Richmond; 🚇) is 13km south of downtown in the city of Richmond. There are two main terminals – international (including flights to the US) and domestic – just a short indoor stroll apart. A third (and much smaller) South Terminal is located a quick drive away; free shuttle-bus links are provided. This terminal services floatplanes, helicopters and smaller aircraft traveling to small communities in BC and beyond. In addition, short-hop **floatplane** (www.harbourair.com) and **helicopter services** (www.helijet.com) to and from Vancouver Island and beyond also depart from the city's downtown waterfront, near Canada Place. Baggage carts are free (no deposit required) and there is also free wi-fi.

BOAT

BC Ferries (250-386-3431; www.bcferries. com) services arrive at Tsawwassen, an hour south of Vancouver, and at Horseshoe Bay, 30 minutes from downtown in West Vancouver. The company operates one of the world's largest ferry networks, including some spectacular routes throughout the province.

Main services to Tsawwassen arrive from Vancouver Island's Swartz Bay, near Victoria, and Duke Point, near Nanaimo. Services also arrive from the Southern Gulf Islands.

Services to Horseshoe Bay arrive from Nanaimo's Departure Bay. Services also arrive here from Bowen Island and from Langdale on the Sunshine Coast.

To depart Tsawwassen via transit, take bus 620 (adult/child $5.70/3.90) to Bridgeport Station in Richmond and transfer to the Canada Line. It takes about an hour to reach downtown.

From Horseshoe Bay to downtown, take bus 257 (adult/child $4.20/2.90), which is faster than bus 250. It takes about 40 minutes.

BUS

Intercity nontransit buses trundle into Vancouver's neon-signed **Pacific Central Station** (1150 Station St, Chinatown; Main St-Science World). Almost all Greyhound bus services (www.greyhound.com) into Vancouver have been cancelled in recent years; the only remaining route is from Seattle (from $20, four hours). **BC Connector** (www.bcconnector.com) operates bus services from Kelowna, Kamloops and Whistler as well as Victoria (via BC Ferries). Cross-border services from **Bolt Bus** (www.boltbus.com) and **Quick Shuttle** (www.quickcoach.com) also arrive here.

CAR & MOTORCYCLE

If you've rented a car in the US and are driving it into Canada, bring a copy of the rental agreement to save any possible hassles with border officials.

Gas is generally cheaper in the US, so be sure to fill up before you cross into Canada.

TRAIN

Pacific Central Station is the city's main terminus for long-distance trains from across Canada on **VIA Rail** (www.viarail.com), and from Seattle (just south of the border) and beyond on **Amtrak** (www.amtrak.com).

The Main St-Science World SkyTrain station is just across the street for connections to downtown and beyond.

There are car-rental desks in the station and cabs are also available just outside the building.

Getting Around

TO/FROM THE AIRPORT

Taxi

➨ Follow the signs from inside the airport terminal to the cab stand just outside. A system of zone fares operates from YVR; your fare will typically be between $20 and $45 (most downtown Vancouver destinations cost $35). Confirm your fare with the driver before you set off.

➨ Rates do not include tips; 15% is the norm.

➨ Limo-car services are also available close to the main taxi stand. Expect to pay around $20 more for your ride to the city if you want to arrive in style.

Train

SkyTrain's 16-station **Canada Line** (see the route maps at www.translink.ca) operates a rapid-transit train service from the airport to downtown. Trains run every few minutes from early morning until after midnight and take around 25 minutes to reach downtown's Waterfront Station. The airport station is located just outside, between the domestic and international terminals. Follow the signs from inside either terminal and buy your ticket from the platform vending machines. These accept cash and credit cards – look for green-jacketed Canada Line staff if you're bleary-eyed and need assistance after your long-haul flight. Fares from the airport cost between $8 and $10.75, depending on your destination and the time of day.

BICYCLE

➨ Vancouver is a relatively good cycling city, with more than 300km of designated routes crisscrossing the region.

➨ Cyclists can take their bikes for free on SkyTrains, SeaBuses and transit buses, which are all now fitted with bike racks. Cyclists are required by law to wear helmets.

➨ There are dedicated bike lanes in the city, and locals and visitors alike can use **Mobi** (778-655-1800; www.mobibikes.ca), a public bike-share scheme.

➨ Download free cycle route maps from the TransLink website (www.translink.ca) or plan your route using https://vancouver.bikeroute planner.com.

➨ If you're traveling sans bike, you can also rent wheels from businesses around the city, especially on Denman St near Stanley Park – home of Vancouver's most popular scenic cycling route.

CAR & MOTORCYCLE

For sightseeing in the city, you'll be fine without a car (the city center is especially easy to explore on foot and transit routes are extensive). For visits that incorporate the wider region's mountains and communities, however, a vehicle makes life much simpler: the further you travel from downtown, the more limited your transit options become. There are car-rental desks in Pacific Central Station.

PUBLIC TRANSPORTATION
Bus

Vancouver's **TransLink** (www.translink.ca) bus network is extensive. All vehicles are equipped with bike racks and all are wheelchair accessible. Exact change (or more) is required; buses use fare machines and change is not given. Fares cost adult/child $3/1.95 and are valid for up to 90 minutes of transfer travel. While Vancouver's transit system covers three geographic fare zones, all bus trips are regarded as one-zone fares.

Bus services operate from early morning to after midnight in central areas. There is also an additional 12-route NightBus system that runs from 2am. Look for NightBus signs at designated stops.

SeaBus

The iconic SeaBus shuttle is part of the TransLink transit system (regular transit fares apply) and it operates throughout the day, taking around 15 minutes to cross Burrard Inlet between Waterfront Station and North Vancouver's Lonsdale Quay. At Lonsdale you can then connect to buses servicing North Vancouver and West Vancouver; this is where you pick up bus 236 to both Capilano Suspension Bridge and Grouse Mountain.

SeaBus services leave from Waterfront Station between 6:16am and 1:22am, Monday to Saturday (8:16am to 11:16pm on Sunday). Vessels are wheelchair accessible and bike-friendly.

Tickets must be purchased from vending machines on either side of the route before boarding. The machines take credit and debit cards, and also give change up to $20 for cash transactions.

SkyTrain

TransLink's SkyTrain rapid-transit network is a great way to move around the region, especially beyond the city center. A new route to the University of BC campus is expected to open in the coming years.

Compass tickets for SkyTrain trips can be purchased from station vending machines (change is given; machines also accept debit and credit cards) prior to boarding.

SkyTrain journeys cost $3 to $5.75 (plus $5 more if you're traveling from the airport), depending on how far you are journeying.

TAXI

At the time of research, Vancouver was in the process of paving the way for ride-hailing schemes such as Uber and Lyft. Until then, try the following long-established taxi companies:

Black Top & Checker Cabs (604-731-1111; www.btccabs.ca; 📞)

Vancouver Taxi (604-871-1111; www.vancouvertaxi.cab)

Yellow Cab (604-681-1111; www.yellowcabonline.com; 📞)

LOWER MAINLAND

Stretching from coastal Horseshoe Bay as far inland as the verdant Fraser Valley, this region encompasses the towns and suburbs within an hour or two of downtown Vancouver, including those communities immediately adjoining the city that together are known as Metro Vancouver. Ideal for day trips, the area is striped with forested coastal parks, wildlife sanctuaries and an increasing number of wineries.

The snow-capped dome-shaped mountain dominating the skyline to the south is Mt Baker (3286m), an active volcano just across the border in the US.

Richmond & Steveston

The region's modern-day Chinatown is easy to reach via Canada Line SkyTrain from Vancouver, making for an easy half-day excursion. There are two distinctly different experiences to be had here. Richmond proper is a utilitarian grid of Asian shopping malls, car parks and (with a bit of delving) some of the best Asian restaurants outside Asia. A little to the south, waterfront Steveston village is second only to Fort Langley in its historical significance, harboring two museums, an afternoon's worth of blustery dyke walks and legendary fish-and-chips.

👁 Sights

⭐**Richmond Night Market**　　　MARKET
(Map p636; 604-244-8448; www.richmondnightmarket.com; 8351 River Rd, Richmond; adult/child $5/free; ⊙7pm-midnight Fri-Sun mid-May–mid-Oct; 🚊Bridgeport) Arguably Richmond's biggest lure is this atmospheric, always

busy, Asian-flavored night market that has grown from humble beginnings in 2000 to become the largest night market in North America. Beyond the predictable (but fun) trinket stalls and fairground attractions, the complex is best known for its abundance of steam-billowing food stalls that ply everything from *poke* bowls to fried octopus. The live entertainment is equally diverse with punk rock alternating with martial-arts displays.

Gulf of Georgia Cannery
MUSEUM
(Map p636; ☑604-664-9009; www.gulfofgeorgia cannery.org; 12138 4th Ave, Steveston; adult/child $12/free; ☉10am-5pm; ⊕; ☐401, ⑤Richmond-Brighouse) British Columbia's best 'industrial museum' illuminates the sights and sounds of the region's bygone era of labor-intensive fish processing. Most of the machinery remains and there's an evocative focus on the people who used to work here; you'll hear recorded testimonies from old employees percolating through the air like ghosts, bringing to life the days they spent immersed in entrails as thousands of cans rolled down the production line. Take one of the excellent, free, volunteer-led tours for the full story.

Britannia Shipyard
MUSEUM
(☑640-718-8038; www.britanniashipyard.ca; 5180 Westwater Dr, Steveston; ☉10am-5pm, from noon Oct-Apr; ☐402, ⑤Richmond-Brighouse) FREE A riverfront complex of historic sheds housing dusty tools, boats and reminders of the region's maritime past, this is one of the most evocative, fancy-free historic sites in the region. Check out the preserved Murakami House, where a large Japanese family lived before being unceremoniously interned during the war. Interpretive boards tell the story; well-versed volunteers fill in the gaps.

Iona Beach
Regional Park
PARK
(Map p636; ☑604-224-5739; 900 Ferguson Rd, Richmond; ☉dawn-dusk) This long, slender sand-and-grass isthmus at the mouth of the Fraser River, which can be reached by car or bike, is one of the region's best birding destinations. Look out for migrating avian critters (snow geese included) plus 'locals' such as kinglets, hummingbirds, bald eagles and many more. Turtles also call this park home and you'll have great shoreline views to point your camera at, especially from the 4km-long Iona Jetty.

 ## Eating

President Plaza Food Court
FOOD HALL $
(Map p636; ☑604-270-8677; 8181 Cambie Rd, Richmond; mains $5-8; ☉10am-7pm; ⑤Aberdeen) Richmond's bustling shopping-mall food courts echo the hawker stands found in many Asian cities, and one of the most authentic is this upstairs hidden gem that's lined with independent vendors. Order a few plates to share and you'll soon be diving into savory pancakes, silken-tofu soup and chewy Beijing donut bread.

Shibuyatei
RAMEN $
(Map p636; ☑778-297-1777; 2971 Sexsmith Rd, Richmond; mains $7-14; ☉11:30am-2pm & 5-9pm Thu-Tue; ⑤Bridgeport) Inauspiciously located next to a car wash a couple of long-jumps from Bridgeport station, this unadorned hole-in-the-wall serves sushi but it's really all about great ramen bowls (with no MSG) and Japanese curries, served with chicken or pork *katsu* (deep-fried). It's a one-man operation so avoid peak times if you don't want to wait too long.

Pajo's
SEAFOOD $
(Map p636; ☑604-272-1588; www.pajos.com; The Wharf, Steveston; mains $12-20; ☉11am-8pm, reduced hours off-season; ☐401, ⑤Richmond-Brighouse) This weather-dependent floating fish shack nestled amid the fishing boats offers a three-way choice of salmon, cod and halibut to have with your chips. They also offer burgers, but seriously you didn't come here for that! If it's raining, try Dave's, a bricks-and-mortar place in Moncton St around the corner.

★Shanghai River Restaurant
CHINESE $$
(Map p636; ☑604-233-8885; www.shanghai riverrestaurant.com; 7381 Westminster Hwy, Richmond; mains $10-22; ☉11am-3pm & 5:30-10pm; ⑤Richmond-Brighouse) Dining at Shanghai River is like attending a jam-packed Asian-style banquet brimming with an array of food. Fried eel arrive in hot stone bowls, whole fish adorn overstuffed plates, while smaller dishes of crispy pot stickers, prawns with candied walnuts, Szechuan smoked duck and soup dumplings fly by.

ⓘ Information

Tourism Richmond Visitor Centre (Map p636; ☑604-271-8280; www.tourismrichmond.com; 3811 Moncton St, Steveston; ☉9:30am-6pm Jul & Aug, 9:30am-5pm Mon-Sat, noon-4pm Sun Sep-Jun; ☐401, ⑤Richmond-Brighouse)

Super-helpful spot inside old Steveston post office with a small affiliated museum.

ℹ Getting There & Away

TransLink's (www.translink.ca) Canada Line SkyTrains trundle in from Vancouver every few minutes throughout the day. The service splits at Bridgeport station, with some trains heading to the airport and others winding further into Richmond; make sure you're on the right one. Transit buses (including those to Steveston) connect to the Canada Line at Bridgeport and other stations.

New Westminster

POP 76,000

A short SkyTrain ride from downtown Vancouver, 'New West' is one of BC's most historic communities – in theory, at least. It was briefly the capital of the new Colony of British Columbia in 1859. Its star faded during much of the last century, but recent years have seen attempts at revival. A small but succinct museum catalogs its brief moment in the limelight while (in the same building) an inventive media gallery deftly snaps you back to the 21st century.

⊙ Sights

★**New Media Gallery**　　　　　　GALLERY
(Map p636; ☑604-875-1865; www.newmediagallery.ca; 777 Columbia St, Anvil Centre; ⊙10am-5pm Tue-Sun, to 8pm Thu; ⑤New Westminster) **FREE** With the right curators and a foresighted arts community, it's amazing what you can do with 200 sq meters of space. This small gallery in New West's super-modern Anvil Centre puts together what are, arguably, the most cutting-edge exhibitions on the Lower Mainland. The bent is unashamedly modern – we're talking 21st-century art that lights up, talks back and interacts with the observer rather than traditional two-dimensional paintings. All visitors receive a free tour explaining more about what they're seeing.

Westminster Pier Park　　　　　　PARK
(Map p636; ☑604-521-3711; www.newwestcity.ca/parks-and-recreation/parks; 1 Sixth St; ⑤Columbia) Sandwiched between railway tracks and the mighty Fraser River, this linear boardwalk park is an excellent New West addition. Join the locals for a breezy promenade stroll and check out the public art, water-facing seats (heron-sightings are common) and stepped wall of screen-printed photos detailing the city's past. There's also a seasonal concession stand serving ice-cream and more.

New Westminster Museum & Archives　　　　MUSEUM
(Map p636; ☑604-527-4640; www.anvilcentre.com; 777 Columbia St, Anvile Centre; ⊙10am-5pm, to 8pm Thu; ⑤New Westminster) **FREE** On the 3rd floor of the swish Anvil Centre, this well-presented small museum illuminates New West's tumultuous history, from its First Nations origins and later pioneer era to its shiny postwar boom and slow economic decline. Look for the mailbox-red stagecoach that carried VIPs around the region and make time to peruse the evocative, wall-mounted photos of the yesteryear city.

✕ Eating

Re-Up BBQ　　　　　　BARBECUE $
(Map p636; ☑604-553-3997; www.reupbbq.com; 810 Quayside Dr, River Market; mains $9-14; ⊙10am-7pm; ⑤New Westminster) A one-time pioneer of the Vancouver food-truck scene now touring its own permanent eatery, this is the place to sink your choppers into heaping servings of ribs, brisket and pulled pork. Arrive hungry and save room for housemade 'slaw and beans plus a refreshing southern sweet tea.

★**El Santo**　　　　　　MEXICAN $$
(Map p636; ☑604-553-1849; www.elsanto.ca; 680 Columbia St; mains $16-30; ⊙11:30am-10pm, to

---

WORTH A TRIP

WHERE BC BEGAN

Located 40km east of Vancouver, the historic village of Fort Langley is where BC's colonial story began. The original **fort** (☑604-513-4777; www.parkscanada.gc.ca/fortlangley; adult/child $8/4; ⊙10am-5pm; ♿; ☒562), built in 1827 and now a National Historic Site, predated the founding of Vancouver by well over half a century, and it was from here that, in 1858, James Douglas announced the province's creation. The fort is well worth a visit: with its preserved buildings and costumer interpreters, it's a popular attraction for families. Today, Fort Langley is a pretty little village within the wider Langley township, but with its tree-lined avenues and boutique shops it harbors its own distinct character and atmosphere. It's a rewarding day or half-day trip from central Vancouver.

11pm Fri & Sat; ⑤ New Wesminster) Way more sophisticated than your typical nachos 'n' burritos Mexican restaurant, El Santo is the mark of a trend in New West's culinary renaissance. Presenting menu items in Spanish with English translations, it offers a minimalist take on Latino favorites using BC ingredients – such as Fraser valley chicken with a Mexican mole rub and BC perch with a mezcal-chipotle glaze.

Bruncheria Cafe BREAKFAST $$

(Map p636; ☑604-544-0018; 656 Columbia St; mains $15-22; ⊘7:30am-3:30pm; 🖰🖉; ⑤New Westminster) Offering healthy artisan breakfasts in a comfy interior encased in one of New West's older heritage buildings. The cafe is a spirited venture and includes some more unusual early morning offerings such as yogurt, granola and fruit served in a coconut shell.

❶ Information

Tourism New Westminster (Map p636; ☑604-526-1905; www.tourismnewwest minster.com; 777 Columbia St, Anvil Centre; ⊘10am-5pm Mon-Sat, to 4pm Oct-May)

❶ Getting There & Away

Frequent TransLink (www.translink.ca) SkyTrain services from downtown Vancouver take about 25 minutes to whisk you to New West. It's a two-zone fare ($4.20).

BOWEN ISLAND

POP 3600

One of the best days out you can have from Vancouver – it's just a 20-minute boat hop from Horseshoe Bay, but it feels a million miles from downtown – Bowen is like British Columbia in miniature. Time slows down a notch here in yoga retreats, boutique apothecaries and the handsome heritage buildings of the cozy harbor, appropriately called Snug Cove.

Bowen Island Sea Kayaking KAYAKING

(☑604-947-9266; www.bowenislandkayaking.com; Bowen Island Marina, Snug Cove; rentals/tours from $52/$82; ⊘10am-6pm Apr-Oct) Handily tucked along the boardwalk jetty just steps from the ferry dock, this congenial operation is a one-stop shop if you're looking to kayak or paddleboard around the area. Rentals are popular, of course, but they also offer guided tours – we love the all-day Pasley Island tour ($185).

Bowen Island Tours TOURS

(☑604-812-5041; www.bowenislandtours.com; adult/child from $25/12) A series of tour options run by a friendly Bowen guide. The best of the bunch is the history-themed weave that regales participants with stories of the old steamship resort days. Your friendly guide also has plenty of suggestions for the rest of your visit on Bowen.

Doc Morgan's Restaurant & Pub BISTRO $$

(☑604-947-0808; www.docmorgans.ca; 437 Bowen Island Trunk Rd; mains $16-23; ⊘11:30am-9pm, to 10pm Sat & Sun) Doc's wood-paneled yester-year interior is an ideal rainy day hangout, while the outdoor deck is perfect for languid sunny day-dining perusing the maritime action in Snug Cove. Service is exemplary, delivering a typical pub menu with a few less predictable flourishes. Start with a healthy salad and then tear up the diet-sheet for sticky toffee pudding.

❶ Information

Visitors Center (☑604-200-2399; www.tourism bowenisland.com; 432 Cardena Rd; ⊘9am-4pm mid-May–Sep) Drop into the visitors center, just steps from the ferry dock, for insider tips.

❶ Getting There & Away

Take a TransLink (www.translink.ca) transit bus from downtown Vancouver – the 257 express bus is best – and you'll be at the Horseshoe Bay BC Ferries (www.bcferries.com) terminal in around 40 minutes. Ferry services depart from here to Bowen Island's Snug Cove throughout the day (adult/child/car $11/5/30, 20 minutes).

SEA TO SKY HIGHWAY

Otherwise known as Hwy 99, this unforgettably spectacular cliffside roadway links a string of communities between West Vancouver and Lillooet and is the main route to Squamish and Whistler from Metro Vancouver. If you can take your eyes off the collage of mountains and sea, the winding road has several worthwhile stops, especially if you're in the market for hiking, climbing, mining history or – at the opposite end of the spectrum – imbibing small-batch alcoholic beverages.

Squamish & Around

Watch out Whistler, Squamish is awakening. A one-time coffee stop on the way to

BC's famous skiing capital, this small former logging town has become a destination in its own right in the last 10 years. Climbers from around the world converge on the town to tackle the intimidating rock-walls of the Chief, while kitesurfers brave the stiff winds of Howe Sound, and hikers enjoy the steep network of paths that stretch between Shannon Falls and the top of the cable-car station.

Beware: 30-minute coffee stops can easily morph into seven-day adventure frenzies.

◉ Sights

★ **Sea to Sky Gondola**   CABLE CAR
(📞 604-892-2551; www.seatoskygondola.com; 36800 Hwy 99, Squamish; adult/child $42/14; ⊙ 10am-6pm May-Oct, reduced hours Nov-Apr) On a warm summer's evening, with a 7.5km ascent under your belt and a pint of craft beer on the table in front of you, there are few better places in Canada than the top station of Squamish's spectacular gondola. The glorious glass-and-wood Summit Lodge is a triumph of environmentally congruous Northwest architecture while the views – Howe Sound on one side and the 100m-long Sky Pilot suspension bridge on the other – are unforgettable.

For an active day out, hike up from Shannon Falls on the Sea to Summit Trail and take the gondola down afterwards (down-only gondola tickets cost $15). There is a whole network of additional trails heading out from the Summit Lodge – some easy, others forging further up the mountain. You can also enjoy the wobbly suspension bridge, several viewing platforms and the lodge restaurant with its alfresco deck where the hills are alive with the sound of (live) music in the summer.

★ **Garibaldi Provincial Park**   PARK
(www.env.gov.bc.ca/bcparks/explore/parkpgs/garibaldi; Hwy 99) This 1950-sq-km park is justly renowned for hiking trails colored by diverse flora, abundant wildlife and panoramic vistas. Summer hikers seem magnetically drawn here but the trails also double as cross-country ski routes in winter. There are five main trail areas – directions to each are marked by the blue-and-white signs you'll see off Hwy 99. Among the park's most popular trails, the Cheakamus Lake hike (3km) is relatively easy, with minimal elevation.

The Elfin Lakes trail (11km) is a lovely, relatively easy day hike. The Garibaldi Lake hike (9km) is an outstanding introduction to 'Beautiful BC' wilderness, fusing scenic alpine meadows and breathtaking mountain vistas.

Britannia Mine Museum   MUSEUM
(📞 604-896-2260; www.britanniaminemuseum.ca; Hwy 99, Britannia Beach; adult/child $30/19; ⊙ 9am-5pm; 👪) Once the British Empire's largest copper mine, this giant and superbly restored industrial museum is just 10 minutes before Squamish on Hwy 99. The rattling underground train tour is highly recommended (included with entry) and there are plenty of kid-friendly exhibits, including hands-on gold panning. You'll never moan about your boss again as you discover just how grim it was to work a *real* job back in the day. Save time for the gift shop and a sparkly pyrite souvenir.

Shannon Falls Provincial Park   WATERFALL
(www.bcparks.ca; Hwy 99, Squamish) About 4km before you reach Squamish, you'll hear the pounding waters of Shannon Falls Provincial Park. Pull into the parking lot and stroll the short trail to BC's third-highest waterfall, where water cascades down a 335m drop. A few picnic tables make this a lovely spot for an alfresco lunch.

**Stawamus Chief
Provincial Park**   PARK
(www.bcparks.ca; Hwy 99, Squamish) On the way into Squamish from Vancouver, you'll see a sheer, 652m-high granite rock face looming ahead. Attracting hardy climbers the world over, it's called the 'Chief' and it's the highlight of Stawamus Chief Provincial Park. You don't have to gear up to experience the summit's vistas: there are hiking routes up the back for anyone who wants to have a go. Consider Squamish Rock Guides (p54) for climbing assistance or lessons.

**West Coast Railway
Heritage Park**   MUSEUM
(📞 604-898-9336; www.wcra.org; 39645 Government Rd, Squamish; adult/child $25/15; ⊙ 10am-3pm; 👪) Train nuts should continue just past central Squamish to this large, mostly alfresco museum that's lined with clapboard buildings and several historic locomotives and carriages – including BC's legendary Royal Hudson steam engine, housed in the purpose-built Roundhouse. There's also an old walk-through mail train and an erstwhile stationmaster's house. Check ahead for kid-friendly special events, particularly during Christmas and school holidays.

HIKING AROUND SQUAMISH

The installation of the Sea to Sky gondola in 2014 massively improved Squamish's hiking potential. A new trail now winds its way up to the spectacular summit station perched 885m above Howe Sound from where several other trails crisscross above the treeline. Meanwhile, glowering to the north sits the moodily magnificent Stawamus Chief.

Activities

★ Sea to Sky Trail HIKING
A 7.5km trail that climbs from Shannon Falls to the top of the Sea to Sky Gondola (p663), this relatively new path is rated 'intermediate' save for a couple of steeper sections where cables and ropes are provided for assistance. Pack plenty of water and snacks for the ascent and enjoy a drink and canteen-style meal at the summit lodge.

Stawamus Chief Trail HIKING
A short, but steep climb up the side of Squamish's sentinel mountain so beloved by rock climbers. The path provides access to all three of the Chief's summits (between 1.3km and 3.4km one-way) and is rated 'hard' due to its unrelenting steepness and scrambling sections. Hand supports are provided near the top.

Sea to Sky Air TOURS
(☑604-898-1975; www.seatoskyair.ca; Squamish Airport; from $96; ⊙9am-5pm Apr-Sep, 9am-4pm Wed-Sun Oct-Mar) Running a series of small airplane tours from the town's forest-fringed little airport, the friendly folk here will soon have you snapping photos over snow-peaked valleys and glittering glacier-fed lakes. But the best option is the Introductory Flight Experience ($249), where you'll start with a runway plane inspection, shimmy up into the sky alongside the pilot and then take the controls.

Squamish Spit KITESURFING
(www.squamishwindsports.com; per day $20) A popular kiteboarding (and windsurfing) hot spot from May to October. The Squamish Windsports Society manages the spit's launching and landing facility; see their website for weather and water conditions and information on access to the spit.

🛏 Sleeping & Eating

Alice Lake Provincial Park CAMPGROUND $
(www.discovercamping.ca; Hwy 99, Brackendale; campsites $43) This large, family-friendly campground, 13km north of Squamish, has more than 100 sites. There are two shower buildings with flush toilets, and campers often indulge in swimming, hiking and biking (rentals available). Consider an interpretive ranger tour through the woods (July and August only). Reserve far ahead; this is one of BC's most popular campgrounds.

Sunwolf CABIN $$
(☑604-898-1537; www.sunwolf.net; 70002 Squamish Valley Rd, Brackendale; cabin from $130; 🔊🐾) This idyllic place – a former logging resort – has a clutch of 12 comfortable, well-maintained cabins along a forested riverbank. The owners also run year-round rafting and eagle-viewing trips (adult/child $119/79).

The well-loved on-site cafe, Fergie's has partially reopened since sustaining fire damage. It traditionally serves potent coffee and fortifying breakfasts.

The resort is near Brackendale, 14km north of Squamish.

Howe Sound Inn INN $$
(☑604-892-2603; www.howesoundinn.com; 37801 Cleveland Ave, Squamish; d $145; 🔊) Quality rustic is the approach at this comfortable inn, where the rooms are warm and inviting with plenty of wooden furnishings. Recover from your climbing escapades in the property's popular sauna – or just head to the downstairs **brewpub** (☑778-654-3358; mains $15-26; ⊙11am-midnight, to 1am Fri, from 8am Sat & Sun), which serves some of BC's best housemade beers. Inn guests can request free brewery tours.

Even if you're not staying, it's worth stopping in at the restaurant here for great pub grub with a gourmet twist.

Backcountry Brewing BREWERY
(☑604-567-2739; www.backcountrybrewing.com; 405/1201 Commercial Way, Squamsih; ⊙noon-11pm, to midnight Fri, from 11am Sat & Sun) One of the newest micro-businesses to populate the commercial district north of Squamish, this brewery is equipped with a large tasting room designed (in their own words) with the feel of a 1970s ski cabin. There's also a full-blown kitchen dispatching that finest of beer accompaniments, pizza ($15 to $20). Beer-wise, you'd be unwise to miss the punchy Widowmaker IPA.

ℹ️ Information

Squamish Adventure Centre (☑604-815-5084; www.exploresquamish.com; 38551 Loggers Lane, Squamish; ⊙8am-6pm mid-May–mid-Sep, reduced hours rest of year; 🛜) One of several astoundingly good visitor centers in southern BC, this gracefully curvaceous building beside Hwy 99 is part museum, part cafe and part information portal. You can spend half a morning here, perusing maps, browsing the outdoor museum or sipping coffee inside.

ℹ️ Getting There & Away

Skylynx (www.yvrskylynx.com) buses connect with Vancouver airport ($55, two hours, eight daily)

The comfortable **Squamish Connector** (☑604-802-2119; www.squamishconnector. com) minibus shuttle heads north to Whistler ($25, one hour) and south to Vancouver ($25, one hour) twice daily. It stops outside the Squamish Adventure Centre.

WHISTLER

POP 11,800

Named for the furry marmots that populate the area and whistle like deflating balloons, this gabled alpine village and 2010 Olympics venue is one of the world's largest, best-equipped and most popular ski resorts. Colonizing two mountains – Whistler and Blackcomb – and lying a mere 90 minutes north of Vancouver, the Village, which dates from the late 1970s, is a poster child for attractive design with nary an ugly building or piece of litter to pierce the natural beauty. Skiing may be Whistler's raison d'être, but these days summer visitors with their BMXs and SUPs outnumber their ski-season equivalents. Adding more diversity, the resort has recently developed an art scene worthy of a small European city. The caveat? Whistler is busy (2.3 million visitors a year) and expensive. For a quieter, more economical experience, be selective with your dates and don't follow the herd.

👁️ Sights

⭐ **Audain Art Museum** GALLERY
(☑604-962-0413; www.audainartmuseum. com; 4350 Blackcomb Way; adult/child $18/free; ⊙10am-5pm, to 9pm Fri, closed Tue) The opening of the Audain in 2016 elevated Whistler from 'world-class ski resort' to 'world-class ski resort with serious art credentials'. With two-dozen works by iconic painter Emily Carr, a priceless collection of indigenous masks, and sparkling photoconceptualist images by Jeff Wall, Rodney Graham et al, this is no rainy-day filler. BC artists take center stage. Alongside Carr you'll spot material from the 'Group of Seven' modernists, plus works by contemporary First Nations artists including Robert Davidson.

Peak 2 Peak Gondola CABLE CAR
(☑604-967-8950; www.whistlerblackcomb.com/ discover/360-experience; 4545 Blackcomb Way; adult/child $63/32; ⊙10am-5pm) Built to link the area's two main mountaintops, the world's second-longest free-span gondola eases passengers along a lofty and ethereally peaceful 4.4km ride that takes around 11 minutes to complete. En route, you can gaze down on forest, crags, skiers and bears – especially if you snag one of the two glass-bottomed cars. The gondola's completion in 2008 effectively joined Whistler and Blackcomb into one giant ski area, making it one of the world's largest.

Squamish Lil'wat Cultural Centre MUSEUM
(☑604-964-0990; www.slcc.ca; 4584 Blackcomb Way; adult/child $18/5; ⊙10am-5pm daily Apr-Oct, Tue-Sun Nov-Mar) This handsome, wood-beamed facility showcases two quite different First Nations groups – the Lil'wat and the Squamish – who have inhabited this region for eons. Take a tour for the vital context behind the museumlike exhibits and keep your eyes open for on-site artist demonstrations during the summer, when there are also Tuesday-night barbecue dinners. There's also an on-site cafe serving bannock tacos.

Whistler Museum & Archives MUSEUM
(☑604-932-2019; www.whistlermuseum.org; 4333 Main St; suggested donation $5; ⊙11am-5pm, to 9pm Thu) Tucked into an anonymous green shed behind the library building, this great little museum traces Whistler's development from 1970s hippy hangout to 21st-century resort. The story is as compelling as it is short, speckled with interesting exhibits such as the original 1965 ski-lift gondola and a 2010 Olympic torch. Don't leave without digesting the story of the infamous 1973 'Toad Hall' photo.

Cloudraker Skybridge BRIDGE
The newest attraction on Whistler Mountain is this 130m-long suspension bridge

Whistler

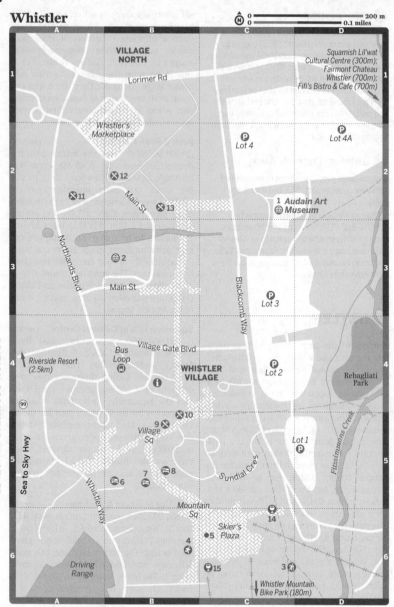

with a see-through base that connects the top of Whistler Peak with the Raven's Eye viewing platform on the West Ridge. Opened in summer 2018, the bridge is accessed by hiking downhill for 15 minutes from the Roundhouse Lodge and then tak-ing the Peak Empress chairlift to the top of Whistler Mountain.

If you are a vertigo sufferer, bear in mind that both chairlift and suspension bridge are mildly exposed.

Entrance is included with the Peak 2 Peak Gondola (p665) ticket.

Whistler

🏃 Activities

★ **Whistler-Blackcomb**   SNOW SPORTS
(🕿604-967-8950; www.whistlerblackcomb.com; day pass adult/child $178/89) Comprising 37 lifts and crisscrossed with over 200 runs, the Whistler-Blackcomb sister mountains, physically linked by the resort's mammoth 4.4km Peak 2 Peak Gondola (p665) are, indisputably, one of the largest and best ski areas in North America. The variety and quality of the facilities here is staggering and regular upgrades have maintained the resort's Olympian edge.

More than half the resort's runs are aimed at intermediate-level skiers, and the season typically runs from late November to April on Whistler and November to June on Blackcomb – December to February is the peak for both.

You can beat the crowds with an early-morning Fresh Tracks ticket ($23.95), available in advance at the Whistler Village gondola. Coupled with your regular lift ticket, it gets you an extra hour on the slopes (boarding from 7:15pm) and the ticket includes a buffet breakfast at the Roundhouse Lodge up top.

Snowboarders should also check out the freestyle terrain parks, mostly located on Blackcomb, including the Snow Cross and the Big Easy Terrain Garden. There's also the popular Habitat Terrain Park on Whistler.

Whistler Olympic Park   SNOW SPORTS
(🕿604-964-0060; www.whistlersportlegacies.com; 5 Callaghan Valley Rd; trail pass skiing/snowshoeing $28/17; ⊙9am-4:30pm mid-Dec–late Mar) Just 25km southwest of the village via Hwy 99, the pristine, snow-swathed Callaghan Valley hosted several 2010 Olympic Nordic events. There are essentially two cross-country skiing areas here: the Whistler Olympic Park (where you can sample the Nordic and biathlon courses) and Ski Callaghan, which predates it. One pass covers both.

A modern, rarely overcrowded day lodge at the end of the road rents skis and snowshoes and has an economical cafe. There are 90km of trails leading out from the lodge plus around 40km of snowshoe trails. Several are pet-friendly. For an altogether more unique experience, it is possible to partake in biathlon lessons ($99, weekends only) at the nearby Olympic shooting range and race circuit.

A shuttle bus from Whistler Village ($10 round-trip) serves the park with one drop-off and two pickups per day in season. Book via the website.

Whistler Mountain
Bike Park   MOUNTAIN BIKING
(🕿604-967-8950; http://bike.whistlerblackcomb.com; half-day lift ticket adult/child $59/32; ⊙May-Oct) Colonizing the melted ski slopes in summer and accessed via lifts at the village's south end, this park offers barreling downhill runs and an orgy of jumps and bridges twisting through well-maintained forested trails. Luckily, you don't have to be a bike courier to stand the knee-buckling pace: easier routes are marked in green, while blue intermediate trails and black-diamond advanced paths are also offered.

BYO bike, or hire from **Summit Sport** (🕿604-932-9225; www.summitsport.com; 4293 Mountain Sq; downhill/trail per day $150/80; ⊙9am-8:30pm).

Outside the park area, regional trails include Comfortably Numb (a tough 26km with steep climbs and bridges), A River

BRITISH COLUMBIA WHISTLER

Runs Through It (suitable for all skill levels, it has teeter-totters and log obstacles) and the gentle Valley Trail (an easy 14km loop that encircles the village and its lake, meadow and mountain chateau surroundings, and is recommended for first-timers).

Singing Pass Trail
HIKING

Your best bet for a challenging multi-terrain hike departing directly from Whistler village is the 11.5km (one-way) Singing Pass trail which takes you up above the tree line and subsequently offers a couple of continuation hikes for those with energy to burn.

One extension carries on to beautiful Russet Lake (an extra 3km one-way), another undulates over the so-called 'musical bumps' to the Roundhouse Lodge (21km from the village) close to the top of Whistler Mountain. From here you can catch the gondola back down.

Ziptrek Ecotours
ADVENTURE SPORTS

(☑604-935-0001; www.ziptrek.com; 4280 Mountain Sq, Carleton Lodge; adult/child from $119/99; ⏺) Not content with having one of the world's longest gondolas, Whistler opened North America's longest zip line in 2016, the super-scary Sasquatch (open June to September) – a 2.2km-long catapult between Whistler and Blackcomb Mountains where it's possible to attain speeds of up to 100km/h. They also have several less dramatic zip lines, some aimed at kids, plus a great canopy walking tour ($49).

Wedge Rafting
RAFTING

(☑604-932-7171; www.wedgerafting.com; 4293 Mountain Sq; tours adult/child from $119/79; ⏺) A great way to wet your pants and still have fun, Wedge offers three white-water rafting tours around the region, including the kid-friendly Cheakamus River excursion.

⭐ Festivals & Events

Winterpride
LGBTIQ+

(www.whistlerpride.com; ⊘Jan) A week of gay-friendly snow action and late-night partying.

World Ski & Snowboard Festival
SPORTS

(www.wssf.com; ⊘Apr) A multi-day showcase of pro ski and snowboard competitions, plus partying.

Crankworx
SPORTS

(www.crankworx.com; ⊘Aug) An adrenaline-filled celebration of bike stunts, speed contests and mud-splattered shenanigans.

Cornucopia
FOOD & DRINK

(www.whistlercornucopia.com; ⊘Nov) Bacchanalian food and wine fest crammed with parties.

🛏 Sleeping

Accommodation in Whistler is expensive but of a high quality (even the HI hostel is plush). Most hotels offer deluxe rooms with kitchenettes, fireplaces and balconies. Many are also equipped with sofa beds and hot tubs and are classified as studios or suites. The bigger hotels have gyms, spas, outdoor pools and hot tubs. Parking, if available, costs up to $40 extra. Breakfast is seldom included in room rates.

HI Whistler Hostel
HOSTEL $

(☑604-962-0025; www.hihostels.ca/whistler; 1035 Legacy Way; dm/r $43/120; @🛜) Built as athletes' accommodation for the 2010 Winter Olympics, this sparkling hostel is 7km south of the village, near Function Junction. Transit buses to/from town stop right outside. Book ahead for private rooms (with private baths and TVs) or save by staying in a small dorm. Eschewing the sometimes institutionalized HI hostel feel, this one has IKEA-style furnishings, art-lined walls and a licensed cafe.

There's also a great TV room for rainy-day hunkering. If it's fine, hit the nearby biking and hiking trails or barbecue on one of the two mountain-view decks.

Pangea Pod Hotel
HOTEL $$

(☑604-962-1011; www.pangeapod.com; 4333 Sunrise Alley; pods from $140; ❄🛜) Posing as a smarter, more private version of a hostel, Canada's first capsule hotel is based on the Japanese model, offering bed-sized 'pods' equipped with double futons, privacy curtains, individual air-con units, reading lights, lockers and mirrors. Colorfully tiled showers, powder rooms and loos are shared, but kept scrupulously clean.

Add in a happening bar/restaurant, ample gear storage and young, helpful staff and you've got a rare Whistler bargain bang in the center of the village.

Riverside Resort
CAMPGROUND, CABIN $$

(☑604-905-5533; www.parkbridge.com/en-ca/rv-cottages/riverside-resort; 8018 Mons Rd; campsites/yurts/cabins $43/130/235; 🛜🍽) Just a few minutes past Whistler on Hwy 99, this facility-packed, family-friendly campground and RV park has elevated itself in

CROSS-COUNTRY SKIING AROUND WHISTLER

Whistler has 120km of cross-country skiing trails spread over two areas: Lost Lake Park, a short walk from the Village, and the interlinked Olympic Park–Callaghan Country network, 25km by road to the west. Both areas offer groomed trails appropriate for classic and skate skiing and are graded easy (green) to advanced (black). Lost Lake is a pretty but relatively benign area with placid vistas and 30km of trails that partially utilize the snowed-in Chateau Whistler golf course. The Olympic Park has more technical terrain including the Nordic and Biathlon Olympic courses. The adjacent Callaghan Valley has a wilder flavor, including an opportunity to ski to the backcountry Journeyman Lodge, where you can dine and/or spend the night.

recent years by adding cozy cabin and yurt options. The yurts come with basic furnishings, electricity and bedding provided, and are especially recommended. The resort's on-site Riverside Junction Cafe serves great breakfasts.

Yurts and cabins have a two-night minimum stay.

Crystal Lodge & Suites — HOTEL $$

(☑604-932-2221; www.crystal-lodge.com; 4154 Village Green; d/ste from $160/210; ❄️🌐💲🐾) Not all rooms are created equal at the Crystal, forged from the fusion of two quite different hotel towers. Cheaper rooms in the South Tower are standard style – baths and fridges are the highlight – but those in the Lodge Wing match the handsome rock-and-beam lobby, complete with small balconies. Both share excellent proximity to restaurants and ski lifts.

Adara Hotel — BOUTIQUE HOTEL $$

(☑604-905-4009; www.adarahotel.com; 4122 Village Green; r from $219; 🌐💲🐾) Unlike all those lodges now claiming to be boutique hotels, the sophisticated and blissfully affordable Adara is the real deal. With warm wood furnishings studded with orange exclamation marks, the rooms offer spa-like baths, cool aesthetics and 'floating' fireplaces that look like TVs. Boutique extras include fresh cookies and in-room boot dryers. Prices dip significantly in shoulder season.

★ Nita Lake Lodge — BOUTIQUE HOTEL $$$

(☑604-966-5700; www.nitalakelodge.com; 2135 Lake Placid Rd; d $289; 🌐💲) Adjoining the handsome Creekside railway station, this chic timber-framed lodge offers 'suites' rather than mere rooms, the smallest of which is an ample 45 sq meters. Hugging the lakeside, the swankier suites feature individual patios, rock fireplaces and baths with heated floors and large tubs; some also have handy kitchens.

Creekside's ski lifts are a walkable few minutes away and there's an on-site spa. The hotel also has an excellent West Coast restaurant and a free shuttle to whisk you to the village if you'd prefer to dine further afield. Check the website for weekday bargains.

Fairmont Chateau Whistler — HOTEL $$$

(☑604-938-8000; www.fairmont.com/whistler; 4599 Chateau Blvd; d $480; ❄️🌐💲) Enjoying ski-in, gondola-out privileges at the foot of Blackcomb Mountain, the Fairmont is like a 'village' within *the* Village. Chateau-esque in nature and grand in scale, it's not nearly as old as other Canadian landmark hotels, although the huge campus includes designer shops, a spa, gym, pools (it's plural here!) and a sprawling bar worthy of a baronial castle.

✖️ Eating

★ Purebread — BAKERY $

(☑604-962-1182; www.purebread.ca; 4338 Main St; baked goods $3-6; ⊙8am-6pm) Imagine the best bakery you've ever visited, elevate the quality by the power of 10 and you might just get Purebread. Founded as a pinprick-sized business in Whistler's Function Junction business park in 2010, this slice of baking heaven has since expanded to fill this larger cafe in the central village.

It's hard to overstate the ambrosial perfection of the melt-in-your-mouth scones, wonderfully stodgy cakes and doorstep-sized sandwiches. Rather like a Whistler 'black diamond,' it will remain etched in your memory long after you leave.

La Cantina
Urban Taco Bar — MEXICAN $

(☑604-962-9950; www.tacoslacantina.ca; 4340 Lorimer Rd; mains $8-14; ⊙11:30am-9pm; 🐾) A busy corner eatery where you order at the

WORTH A TRIP

DETOUR TO COWBOY COUNTRY

If you're craving an alternative to tourist-heavy Whistler Village (but you don't want to head into the wilderness like Grizzly Adams on a day out), head for Pemberton – the next community north along Hwy 99. Founded as a farming and cowboy town, it still has a distant-outpost feel, with enough to keep you occupied for a half-day. The 99 Pemberton Commuter transit bus runs here from Whistler ($4.50, 30 minutes, four times daily), but a car will enable you to explore much more effectively. Plan ahead via www.tourism pemberton.com.

Start with coffee and a giant cinnamon bun at the woodsy little **Blackbird Bakery** (☑604-894-6226; www.blackbirdbread.com; 7424 Frontier St; baked goods & sandwiches $3-8; ⊘6am-8pm, from 7am Sun) in the former train station, then walk over to **Pemberton Museum** (☑604-894-5504; www.pembertonmuseum.org; 7455 Prospect St; by donation; ⊘10am-5pm May-Oct) for the lowdown on how this quirky little town started. Ask them about the Pemberton mascot, a neckerchief-wearing potato dressed like a cowboy.

Next, head over to **Pemberton Distillery** (☑604-894-0222; www.pembertondistillery. ca; 1954 Venture Pl; ⊘noon-5pm Wed & Thu, to 6pm Fri & Sat Jun-early Sep, reduced hours rest of year). A pioneer of BC's latter-day artisan booze movement, it has tours and a tasting room. And while it started with silky potato vodka, it has expanded production to include top-selling gin and a seductive whiskey and wild-honey liqueur. Next – with designated driver at the wheel – trundle 20 minutes out of town and uphill to **Joffre Lakes**. There's a lovely two-hour hike from the trailhead here or you can just snap some glacier photos from the parking lot.

Finally, when dinner beckons, weave back into town and find a table at the rustic, red-walled **Pony** (☑604-894-5700; www.theponyrestaurant.ca; 1392 Portage Rd; mains $22-38; ⊘6:30am-late; 🖋). The town's main dining hangout, it serves an elevated comfort-food menu (pizzas recommended) and some choice BC craft beers.

counter and then grab a perch (the high stools down the side usually have some empty spots), aim for a selection of $3 tacos or dive into a bulging burrito if you're really hungry. This place gets jam-packed at peak times so consider a takeout rather than resorting to fisticuffs to find a seat.

★ **Hunter Gather** CANADIAN $$
(☑604-966-2372; www.huntergatherwhistler.com; 4368 Main St; mains $15-29; ⊘noon-10pm) A noisy but cheerful emporium of local food, this place is known for its smoked meats (the 'hunter' part) and local veg (the 'gather' part). Relish the beef brisket (smoked for 18 hours) and the golden-brown Pemberton potatoes, pan-fried to a state of crispy deliciousness. Punters must order and pay upfront and then grab a pew.

The scene inside is all action, from the busy open-to-view kitchen to tipsy diners sharing backcountry stories over long wooden tables. Good selection of craft beers too.

Bar Oso SPANISH $$
(☑604-962-4540; www.baroso.ca; 4222 Village Sq; small plates $9-27; ⊘11:30am-late) Affiliated with Araxi a couple of doors away, Bar Oso takes a casual Spanish approach to dining creating small *pintxos* (Basque tapas) and *raciones* (shared plates) that dabble in Mediterranean flavors. You can load up the cured hams on the charcuterie board or go full-on Spanish with the *tortilla patata* (Spanish omelet).

Red Door Bistro FRENCH $$$
(☑604-962-6262; www.reddoorbistro.ca; 2129 Lake Placid Rd; mains $26-43; ⊘5-10pm) As soon as you know you're coming to Whistler, call for a reservation at this hot little Creekside eatery, largely a local residents' domain. Taking a French-bistro approach to fine, mostly West Coast ingredients means juniper-rubbed elk with mint pesto, or a seafood bouillabaisse – the menu is a changeable feast (check the blackboard). Food presentation is artistic and the service is spot on.

Araxi Restaurant & Bar CANADIAN $$$
(☑604-932-4540; www.araxi.com; 4222 Village Sq; mains $28-48; ⊘from 5pm) Whistler's best gourmet restaurant, Araxi cooks up an inventive and exquisite Pacific Northwest menu and has charming and courteous ser-

vice. Try the diver-caught scallops and enjoy a bottle or two from the 15,000-bottle wine selection, but allow space for dessert: an artisanal cheese plate or the dreamy hazelnut panna cotta...or both.

Drinking & Nightlife

Garibaldi Lift Company   PUB
(☑604-905-2220; 4165 Springs Lane; ☉11am-1am) The closest bar to the slopes. You can smell the sweat of the skiers (or mountain bikers) hurtling past the patio at this cavernous bar that's known by every local as the GLC. The furnishings have the scuffs and dings of a well-worn pub, and the best time to come is when DJs or bands turn the place into a clubbish mosh pit.

Dubh Linn Gate   PUB
(☑604-905-4047; www.dubhlinngate.com; 4320 Sundial Cres; ☉8am-1am, from 7am Sat & Sun) Arguably the best pub at the bottom of the Whistler Village gondola (after all, it's Irish), this dark-wood-lined joint would feel just like an authentic Galway watering hole if not for the alfresco firepits and dudes wielding snowboards. Tuck yourself into a shady corner table inside and revive yourself with a stout – there's Guinness as well as Murphy's.

❶ Information

Whistler Visitors Centre (☑604-935-3357; www.whistler.com; 4230 Gateway Dr; ☉8am-8pm Sun-Wed, to 10pm Thu-Sat Jun-Aug, reduced hours Sep-May) Flyer-lined visitor center with friendly staff right next to the bus station.

Check out Whistler Insider Blog (www.whistler.com/blog) for more info.

❶ Getting There & Away

While most visitors arrive by car from Vancouver via Hwy 99, there are several economical buses from Vancouver, including the following:

Skylynx (www.yvrskylynx.com) Seven services a day between Vancouver Airport and Whistler Village (from $58.50, three hours). Buses are modern with seat belts, toilets and wi-fi, and drivers are congenial and safe. En route, the bus stops at the Hyatt Hotel in Downtown Vancouver and, by request, at Whistler Creekside. Book online.

Snowbus (www.snowbus.com) Two buses a day from YVR Airport ($40) via Vancouver's Hyatt Hotel to Whistler, including a dawn service that gets you to the slopes before 8am. Winter only.

Buses pull into the village's outdoor **Bus Loop** next to the Whistler Visitors Centre.

SUNSHINE COAST

Fringing the forested coastline for 139km from Langdale in the south to Lund in the north, the Sunshine Coast – separated from the Lower Mainland by the Coast Mountains and the Strait of Georgia – has an independent, island-like mentality that belies the fact it's just a short hop by ferry or plane from Metro Vancouver. Hwy 101 handily strings together the key communities of Gibsons, Roberts Creek, Sechelt and Powell River, making this an easy and leisurely region to explore. Popular with hikers, kayakers and mountain bikers, it also has a small-scale arts scene.

Gibsons
POP 4600

If you're arriving on the Sunshine Coast via BC Ferries from Horseshoe Bay, your first port of call after docking in Langdale and driving or busing into town will be the pretty waterfront strip called Gibsons Landing. A rainbow of painted wooden buildings overlooking the marina, its streets are lined with browsable boutiques and eclectic eateries while its wharf is a summer-hugging promenade for languid boat watching.

Transformation is coming to the Gibsons Landing waterfront in the form of a controversial new harbor complex consisting of a hotel, luxury condos and a conference center. Despite initial approval, the project stalled in 2018 due to environmental concerns and has yet to reach fruition. Drop in to the **visitor center** (☑604-886-2374; www.gibsonsvisitorinfo.com; 417 Marine Dr; ☉10am-4pm Wed-Sun) for the latest news.

◉ Sights & Activities

Gibsons Public Art Gallery   GALLERY
(☑604-886-0531; www.gpag.ca; 431 Marine Dr; ☉11am-4pm Jun-Aug, Thu-Mon only Sep-May) **FREE** A delightful little gallery with a firm focus on showcasing Sunshine Coast works, from painting to sculpture and fiber art. The diverse roster of shows changes every month – opening nights are a good time to meet creative Gibsonites – and this is also a great spot to buy locally produced artworks at reasonable prices. If you're here in August, check out the town's Art Stroll event, which includes this and other galleries and stores.

Sunshine Kayaking KAYAKING
(☑604-886-9760; www.sunshinekayaking.com; Molly's Lane; rentals per 2/24hr $49/98; ☉9am-7pm)
Expanding over the years from its kayak-renting early days, these friendly folks now also offer diving, SUP and even fishing charters. But it's the guided kayaking tours that many visitors aim for – book ahead for one of the monthly Full Moon Tours, an unforgettable way to experience the tranquil beauty of the West Coast. Call ahead for reservations.

Talaysay Tours TOURS
(☑604-628-8555; www.talaysay.com; Porpoise Bay Provincial Park; tours $199; ☉May-Sep) For a First Nations take on the Salish Sea and the Pacific Northwest region, take a boat trip around the islands and channels of Howe Sound. Four-hour boat trips depart from Gibsons and are led by an indigenous guide who points out the flora, fauna and fascinating cultural history of the area.

Sleeping & Eating

Arcturus Retreat Bed & Breakfast B&B $$
(☑604-886-1940; www.arcturusretreat.ca; 160 Pike Rd; d from $160; ☎) Well located just up the hill from the Langdale ferry dock, this is one of the most convenient places to stay in Gibsons – no car required (they'll pick you up from the ferry). The homely quarters and warm welcome add to the appeal and the owners are also full of suggestions for what to do on the Sunshine Coast.

Bonniebrook Lodge HOTEL $$
(☑604-886-2887; www.bonniebrook.com; 1532 Ocean Beach Esplanade; d from $249; ☎) A handsome, wood-built retreat constructed in 1929 but luxuriously updated, this historic charmer occupies a tranquil waterfront stretch that feels like a million miles from any city. All the rooms are delightfully sumptuous with fireplaces and hot tubs, but if you pay extra for one of the two top-floor penthouse suites, you'll have your own balcony overlooking the ocean.

Smitty's Oyster House SEAFOOD $$
(☑604-886-4665; www.smittysoysterhouse.com; 643 School Rd Wharf; mains $18-29; ☉noon-late Tue-Sat, to 8pm Sun, reduced hours in winter) The best spot for seafood in Gibsons (especially if you snag a seat at the communal long table alongside the marina boardwalk), Smitty's sparked a renaissance in local dining when it opened a few years back. It's as popular as ever, especially on summer evenings when

this is the perfect place to scoff a pile of fresh-shucked bivalves.

Drift Cafe & Bistro BISTRO $$$
(☑604-886-5858; www.drift-gibsons.ca; 546 Gibsons Way; mains $19-28; ☉10am-2pm & 5-9pm Fri-Tue) Residing in a cute little cottage no larger than a two-car garage, Drift (formerly Nova Kitchen) continues to impress, serving everything from egg-and-bacon breakfasts to sweet seared scallops with bacon risotto. On warm days, the deck overlooking the water practically doubles the restaurant's size and is a great spot to enjoy a Persephone beer with your gourmet grub.

★ Persephone Brewing Company BREWERY
(☑778-462-3007; www.persephonebrewing.com; 1053 Stewart Rd; ☉10am-9pm late May-early Sep, 11am-7pm early Sep-late May) Welcome to one of Canada's only farm-to-barrel microbreweries. Among numerous sustainable practices, Persephone grows its own hops at an on-site 11-acre farm and harvests them specifically for its home-brewed beer. Try them in a pint of crisp Coast Life Lager in the brewery's big red barn of a tasting room or add a sample to your four-taster flight.

Hops are only half of it. Persephone also grow apples for cider and vegetables for food. The veg are served out of a sleek silver food truck either spread over crispy pizzas or hidden in well-stuffed tacos. All in all, this is an idyllic spot to imbibe, located five minutes from the ferry terminal, with picnic tables, a gabled barn and rows of hops blowing in the breeze. Tours are offered on Sundays. Kids are welcome (for homemade lemonade).

Getting There & Away

BC Ferries (www.bcferries.com) services arrive at Langdale, 6km northeast of Gibsons, from West Vancouver's Horseshoe Bay (passenger/vehicle $14/46, 40 minutes, nine daily).

Sunshine Coast Regional Transit System (www.busonline.ca) buses arrive in Gibsons from the Langdale ferry terminal and other Sunshine Coast communities (one-way/day pass $2/5).

Roberts Creek

Just off Hwy 101 via Roberts Creek Rd, the funky 'downtown' here looks like a little hobbit community, if hobbits had gone through a hippie phase. Poke around the wood-built, shack-like stores and eateries and then wander downhill to the beach, checking out the huge, ever-changing Community Mandala painted on the ground.

🛏 Sleeping & Eating

Up the Creek Backpackers B&B HOSTEL **$**
(📞604-837-5943; www.upthecreek.ca; 1261 Roberts Creek Rd; dm/r $28/84; 🛜) 🚲 Run by a round-the-world cyclist, Up the Creek has incorporated all the best facets of a classic hostel: a place where you can relax but still meet people and feel at home. Take your pick from small dorms, private rooms aimed at couples and families, a back-garden cabin and a tent pitch in the grounds ($15).

They'll even rent you a two-person tent if you've left yours at home ($28). The small shared kitchen is well equipped and there's an active eco approach including rigorous recycling.

Cyclists are welcomed and public transport users actively encouraged. They offer free loaner bikes (helmets included) if you fancy exploring Roberts Creek's network of quiet lanes and cycling trails on your own.

Shades of Jade Inn & Spa B&B **$$**
(📞604-885-3211; www.shadesofjade.ca; 1489 Henderson Rd; d from $199; 🛜) Aimed at tranquility-craving adults, this luxe two-unit B&B – with its Asian–West Coast decor – couldn't be more relaxing. Each spacious room (including the Tall Cedars Suite with its secluded deck) is equipped with a kitchen and steam shower while there's an outdoor hot tub plus on-site spa treatments to provide you with multiple reasons to never leave.

Gumboot Cafe CAFE **$**
(www.thegumbootcafe.com; 1057 Roberts Creek Rd; mains $7-11; ⏰7am-5pm, from 8am Sat & Sun; 🛜) A cool, wood-floored hangout that's ideal for eavesdropping on local gossip – or just perusing the ever-changing art lining the walls. Either way, drop by for coffee and a breakfast fuel-up (the Italian baked eggs work wonders) or arrange to be here for lunch when bulging sandwiches jostle for attention with thin crust pizzas (look for the daily special).

Regular live music is on the creative side – think psychedelic folk and ukulele jams.

Gumboot Restaurant CANADIAN **$$**
(📞604-885-4216; www.gumbootrestaurant.com; 1041 Roberts Creek Rd; mains $14-27; ⏰10am-8:30pm Mon-Thu, 9am-9pm Fri & Sat, 9am-8:30pm

SUNSHINE COAST GALLERY CRAWL

Pick up the free *Purple Banner* flyer at area visitor centers for the location of dozens of studios and galleries throughout the region. Many are open for drop-in visitors (especially in summer) – look out for the purple flags along the road on your travels – and they're a great way to meet the locals and find unique souvenirs. For further information, see www.suncoastarts.com. Also, if you're here in October, don't miss the three-day **Sunshine Coast Art Crawl** (www.sunshinecoastartcrawl.com), a party-like showcase of local studios, galleries and events.

Sun; 🅿) 🚲 Talk about a West Coast classic! This delightful bistro (with gorgeous garden patio) combines an old-school welcome with a lovingly prepared menu backed up by Sunshine Coast beers and Vancouver Island wines. Eye-catching dishes include curried pierogi (dumplings), boo-tine (like poutine, but with gnocchi rather than fries) and the Korean-style chicken wings.

❶ Getting There & Away

Regular Sunshine Coast Regional Transit System (www.busonline.ca) buses run from the ferry terminal at Langdale into Roberts Creek and beyond ($2).

Sechelt

POP 10,000

Not quite as alluring as Gibsons, Roberts Creek or Powell River, Sechelt is nevertheless a good stop-off on your Sunshine Coast jaunt: there are several places to fuel up (both your car and your body) plus access to some cool outdoor activities – kayaking and off-road cycling are particularly well represented.

◉ Sights & Activities

Porpoise Bay Provincial Park PARK
(www.env.gov.bc.ca/bcparks/explore/parkpgs/porpoise; Hwy 101) A forest-backed oceanfront park popular with families, campers and kayakers venturing out into Sechelt Inlet, visiting tree-huggers will also enjoy communing with the towering Douglas fir and western hemlock that call this place home.

Looking for a hike? Head to Angus Creek where abundant birds hang around the estuary as if they own the place.

Pedals & Paddles
KAYAKING

(☑604-885-6440; www.pedalspaddles.com; 7425 Sechelt Inlet Rd; rentals per 2/24hr $34/80) Kayak rentals (and guided kayak tours) are the mainstay of this popular operation but if you're here in July and August – and your looking for something less strenuous – try their zodiac tours that will zip you around the natural sights and sounds of the inlet.

Sechelt Farmers & Artisans Market
MARKET

(Cowrie St; ⊙9am-2:30pm Sat Easter-Sep) Combining fresh local produce (look out for seasonal BC peaches and cherries) with cool arts and crafts, this market is Sechelt's liveliest community hub – especially during its mid-summer peak. Food trucks and food stands add to the appeal.

🛏 Sleeping & Eating

Beachside by the Bay
B&B $$

(☑604-741-0771; www.beachsidebythebay.com; 5005 Sunshine Coast Hwy; d from $212; 🐾) This tranquil property comprises two spacious suites and a cottage where communing with the ocean is guaranteed. There's a three-night minimum stay in July and August, but that will give you plenty of time to experience the alfresco hot tub, watch the sunset (and passing eagles) or prepare your own dinner using your private kitchen or barbecue.

DON'T MISS

THE OTHER WEST COAST TRAIL

Vancouver Island's West Coast Trail is so popular it's hard not to run into other hikers en route. But the Sunshine Coast offers its own under-the-radar version that many West Coasters have only just started discovering. Running from Sarah Point to Saltery Bay, the 180km-long **Sunshine Coast Trail** is a wilderness paradise of ancient forests, eagle-dotted waterfronts and snowcapped vistas. Unlike the West Coast Trail, this one is free and reservations are not required – there are also 15 free-use sleeping huts dotted along the route. For more information, visit www.sunshinecoasttrail.com.

★ Painted Boat Resort Spa & Marina
RESORT $$$

(☑604-883-2122; www.paintedboat.com; 12849 Lagoon Rd; d from $440; 🐾🏊) A boutique waterfront resort where the spacious villa accommodations look like a West Coast dream home. One- and two-bedroom units hug the waterfront showing off decor that's top-of-the-line contemporary. Rooms include kitchens, and there's a deluxe on-site spa with its own garden and an outdoor infinity pool, plus kayak rental at the marina.

★ Basted Baker
CAFE $

(☑604-885-1368; www.bastedbaker.com; 5685 Cowrie St; $9-14; ⊙8am-4pm Mon-Fri, 9am-3pm Sun; 🐾🖊) Sechelt's best dining option is a slightly out of the ordinary bakery that retains the ambience of a casual bistro and specializes in biscuit sandwiches. With an unlimited appetite, you could effectively stay here all day, demolishing eggs benny, salad bowls and individually tailored quiches. And did we mention the perfectly confected coffee and the gloriously sticky cinnamon buns?

Biscuit-wise, we're talking American-style – fresh, crumbly creations that resemble giant scones and require a small stick to hold savory fillings (such as smoked salmon and poached egg) in place. Hash browns make perfect bedfellows.

ℹ Getting There & Away

Regular Sunshine Coast Regional Transit System (www.busonline.ca) buses arrive in Sechelt from the Langdale ferry terminal and other Sunshine Coast communities ($2).

Harbour Air (☑604-885-2111; www.harbour air.com) flies floatplanes from downtown Vancouver to Sechelt twice a day ($118, 20 minutes).

Powell River

POP 13,100

The last significant settlement as you head north on the Sunshine Coast retains an idiosyncratic end-of-the-road flavor. Surrounded by mossy rainforest and lapped by the sheltered waters of Malaspina Strait, Powell River's prettiness is tempered by the presence of a smoke-belching paper factory and a harbor full of permanently barking sea lions. On the waterfront, a fleet of 10 concrete ships dating from the 1940s acts as an improvised breakwater. Anyone familiar with the offbeat, surreal world of 1990s TV series *Twin Peaks* will feel instantly at home.

There are two main hubs in Powell River: the 'new town' (Westview) where you disembark from the ferry and the best restaurants are located, and the Powell River Historic District consisting of a small assemblage of heritage buildings gathered incongruously around the paper mill and embellished by a brewpub and Canada's oldest continuously operating cinema. It's 5km between the two.

Activities

Pick up a free walking-tour flyer from the visitor centre and wander the Townsite's heritage buildings, including many carefully restored arts-and-crafts constructions. Highlights include **Dr Henderson's House** (6211 Walnut Ave) and the lovely **Patricia Theatre** (604-483-9345; www.patriciatheatre. com; 5848 Ash Ave), Canada's oldest continually operating cinema.

Powell River Sea Kayak　　　　KAYAKING
(604-483-2160; www.bcseakayak.com; 10676 Crowther Rd; rental per 3/8hr $50/65) Arguably the best way to view the natural splendors of this region is from the water. And if you've already done the ferry, it's time for some quality kayak time. Book a rental via these guys and explore around Cortes Island, Savary Island or up to Lund. Or let someone else do the navigating on a guided tour.

Dive deeper into the wilderness by staying at their Cabana Desolation Eco Resort. The company is based in end-of-the-road Lund, 27km north of Powell River.

Sleeping & Eating

Old Courthouse Inn　　　　HOTEL $$
(604-483-4000; www.oldcourthouseinn.ca; 6243 Walnut St; s/d from $119/139;) A wonderful slice of yesteryear or an old-fashioned over-cluttered inn, depending on your penchant for antiques, this mock-Tudor hotel keeps one foot in the past, reliving its glory days as the town courthouse. The eight rooms retain the feel of the 1940s, but with modern amenities (wi-fi, TVs) thrown in, and a generous hot breakfast is included in the on-site cafe.

Base Camp　　　　CAFE $
(604-485-5826; www.basecamp-coffee.com; 4548 Marine Dr; mains $8-16; 7am-5pm;) The town's quintessential community coffee hangout has, no doubt, served as base camp for many energetic Sunshine Coast excursions judging by the breakfasts – be it the maple granola parfait or the curried tofu scramble. The communal tables are great for eavesdropping and the large local map on the wall will help get you oriented while you enjoy the java.

Costa del Sol　　　　MEXICAN $
(604-485-2227; www.costadelsollatincuisine. com; 4578 Marine Ave; mains $10-16; 11:30am-late Wed-Mon;) Arriving off-peak is the best way to avoid the crush and maybe even snag a table at this bright-painted former police station with a striking Emiliano Zapata mural within. The menu is Latin with a strong Mexican bent (gourmet tacos are the mainstays) though there's a nod to Louisiana in the jam-packed jambalaya bowl.

Coastal Cookery　　　　BISTRO $$
(604-485-5568; www.coastalcookery.com; 4553 Marine Ave; mains $12-28; 11:30am-late) This casual dining favorite has the town's best patio plus a great menu of tweaked classics and seasonal specials – with a strong focus on BC ingredients. If Salt Spring mussels are on the menu, order them immediately or just dive headfirst into the chicken-and-waffle sandwich (especially if you have a marathon to run).

★ **Townsite Brewing**　　　　BREWERY
(604-483-2111; www.townsitebrewing.com; 5824 Ash Ave; 11am-9pm) An elder statesman of BC's craft-beer scene (which means it's more than five years old), this brilliant, Belgian-focused brewery occupies a heritage post office building. Take a free 3pm tour on Saturdays or sidle up to the tasting bar for a sip or three of Tinhat, Zunga or the only-available-here Suncoast Pale Ale. A four-glass tasting flight costs $8.

Information

Visitors Centre (604-485-4701; www.powell river.info; 4670 Joyce Ave; 9am-6pm Jul & Aug, to 5pm Mon-Sat Sep-Jun) Close to Powell River's main shopping mall.

Getting There & Away

Pacific Coastal Airlines (www.pacificcoastal. com) flies into Powell River from the South Terminal of Vancouver International Airport between three and five times daily (from $145, 35 minutes).

If you're driving here from the lower Sunshine Coast, you'll hop the BC Ferries (www.bcferries. com) service between Earls Cove and Saltery Bay en route (passenger/vehicle $14/45, 50 minutes, up to seven daily). From there, it's a 40-minute drive to Powell River. The company also operates

BRITISH COLUMBIA POWELL RIVER

Powell River services to and from Texada Island (passenger/vehicle $10/23, 35 minutes, up to nine daily) and Vancouver Island's Comox (passenger/vehicle $14/42, 90 minutes, up to five daily). Powell River's ferry terminal is in Westview.

VANCOUVER ISLAND

Vancouver Island is studded with colorful, quirky communities, many founded on logging or fishing and featuring the word 'Port' in their names.

Locals are a friendly bunch, proud of their region and its distinct differences. The island is the largest populated landmass between western North America and New Zealand – around 500km long and 100km wide – and hosts a broad range of attractions, experiences and activities that feel many miles from the bustle of mainland Vancouver.

While the history-wrapped BC capital Victoria is the arrival point for many, it shouldn't be the only place you visit here. (And, to make a good impression, don't mistakenly refer to the place as 'Victoria Island.') Food and wine fans will love the Cowichan Valley farm region; outdoor-activity enthusiasts shouldn't miss the surf-loving, wild West Coast radiating from Tofino; and visitors venturing north will find an uncrowded region of independent communities fringed by rugged wilderness.

❶ Information

For an introduction to the island, contact **Tourism Vancouver Island** (☑250-754-3500; www.vancouverisland.travel) for listings and resources.

Victoria

☑ 250 / POP 88,000

Double-decker buses, afternoon tea, homes that look like castles, and pubs with names such as the Sticky Wicket and the Penny Farthing... Victoria has long traded on its British

Vancouver Island

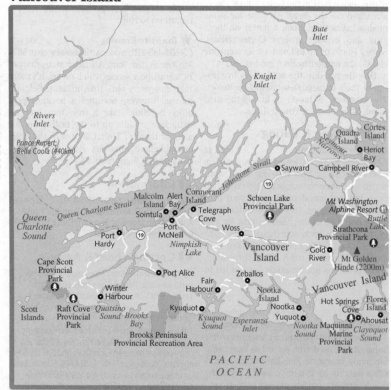

affiliations. But while the fish-and-chips remain first class and cricket games still enliven Beacon Hill Park, the days when Victoria was more British than Britain are long gone. In Victoria 2.0, the food culture embraces fusion, the beer leans toward craft brews and the abundance of bicycles seems to have more in common with Holland than England.

Compared to the glassy skyscrapers of Vancouver, Victoria is more laid-back and low-rise. On balmy summer days, a distinct holiday atmosphere takes over as people pile off the ferries to escape the mayhem of the mainland and forget work. Sure, Victoria might have become trendier and more sophisticated in recent years but, in pace and essence, it remains comfortably old-fashioned.

◉ Sights

★**Royal BC Museum**   MUSEUM
(Map p680; ☑250-356-7226; www.royalbcmuse um.bc.ca; 675 Belleville St; adult/child $17/11, incl IMAX $26.95/21.25; ☺10am-5pm daily, to 10pm Fri

& Sat mid-May–Sep; ⊕; ☐70) Arguably the finest museum in British Columbia and carrier of a 'royal' prefix since 1987, Victoria's flagship sight mixes the cream of BC's provincial exhibits with a revolving lineup of world-class temporary exhibitions. Adding value is an **IMAX Theatre** (☑250-480-4887; www. imaxvictoria.com; tickets $11.95) and a small park replete with indigenous and early pioneer history. Permanent fixtures inside the museum are split into natural history (2nd floor) and human history (3rd floor). Both focus almost exclusively on BC.

The natural history section beautifully recreates some of BC's classic ecosystems, peppered with a selection of taxidermied animals. Highlights include hyper-realistic sea lions and a life-size woolly mammoth with meter-long fur.

The human history section illuminates BC's First Nations with a recreated Kwak-waka'wakw clanhouse and a sonic exhibit that greets you in 34 different indigenous

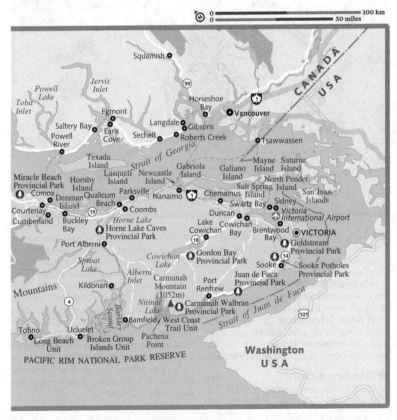

Victoria

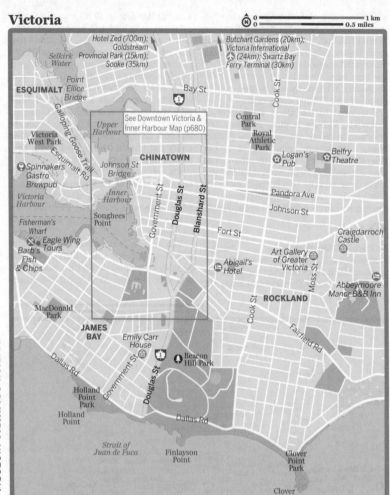

languages. Further on, you'll encounter a diorama of an early-20th-century BC street complete with a cinema showing Charlie Chaplin movies.

In adjacent **Thunderbird Park**, behind a line of weathered totem poles, lie two of the province's oldest buildings. The small log cabin **St Ann's Schoolhouse** dates from 1844 when it served as a fur trading post. Next door, the **Helmcken House** is the former home of fur-trade-era doctor, John Helmcken.

⭐**Craigdarroch Castle**   MUSEUM
(📞250-592-5323; www.thecastle.ca; 1050 Joan Cres; adult/child $14.60/5.10; ⊙9am-7pm mid-

Jun–early Sep, 10am-4:30pm early Sep–mid-Jun; 🅿; 🚌14) More ostentatious country mansion than fortified castle, Craigdarroch, with its turrets, stained-glass windows and palatial interior, looks like it might have been teleported over from the Scottish Highlands. Beautifully preserved by a local historical society, the interior is filled with rich period detail and notable for its spectacular wood-paneled staircase that ascends from the entry vestibule. You'll need at least an hour to admire the four floors of rooms, including a dining room, smoking room, billiard room and dance hall.

Surrounded today by an attractive assemblage of lesser mansions in a Victoria suburb, Craigdarroch once stood on 28 acres of woodland. Built in the late 1880s, it drew its architectural inspiration from a medieval Gothic style known as 'Scottish Baronial', then experiencing a Victorian revival.

The property is also interesting for the complex family dramas that once played out here courtesy of the feuding Dunsmuir clan, led by a Scottish coal-mining baron named Robert Dunsmuir who died before the house was finished. One room is dedicated to telling the Dunsmuir story: the family lived here until 1908 and their squabbles over money and inheritance became legendary. Before you leave, climb the tower's 87 steps for distant views of the Olympic Mountains.

Parliament Buildings HISTORIC BUILDING
(Map p680; ☑250-387-3046; www.leg.bc.ca; 501 Belleville St; ⊙tours 9am-5pm mid-May–Aug, from 8:30am Mon-Fri Sep–mid-May; ☐70) FREE
This dramatically handsome confection of turrets, domes and stained glass is British Columbia's working legislature and is also open to visitors. You can go behind the facade on a free 45-minute guided tour then stop for lunch at the 'secret' politicians' restaurant (p686) inside. Return in the evening when the elegant exterior is illuminated like a Christmas tree.

The buildings were constructed in the 1890s in a mix of renaissance, Romanesque and classical styles after the government had outgrown the original legislature, the less illustriously named 'Birdcages.' The current ceremonial entrance has a mosaic floor and is embellished with Italian marble, while the graceful dome is topped on the outside by a gold-encrusted statue of George Vancouver (an early explorer of BC's coastal regions).

Miniature World MUSEUM
(Map p680; ☑250-385-9731; www.miniature world.com; 649 Humboldt St; adult/child $16/8; ⊙9am-9pm mid-May–mid-Sep, to 5pm mid-Sep–mid-May; ⛟; ☐70) Tucked along the side of the Fairmont Empress Hotel, this huge collection of skillfully crafted models depicting important battles, historic towns and popular stories is far more fascinating than it sounds. Lined with dozens of diminutive diorama scenes, divided into themes ranging from Camelot to space and from fairyland to Olde England, it has plenty of push-button action, several trundling trains and the chance to see yourself on a miniature movie-theater screen. An immaculately maintained reminder of innocent yesteryear attractions.

Victoria Bug Zoo ZOO
(Map p680; ☑250-384-2847; www.victoria bugzoo.com; 631 Courtney St; adult/child $12/8; ⊙10am-5pm Mon-Fri, to 6pm Sat & Sun, reduced hours Sep-May; ⛟; ☐70) It's not big, nor are its resident critters (although some of them are alarmingly colossal by insect standards); however, this diminutive indoor 'zoo' is a small marvel thanks to the enthusiasm and knowledge of its guides. Atlas beetles, dragon-headed crickets and thorny devils are all explained, admired and – on occasion – lifted out of their tanks to be handed around for closer inspection. Children are the main audience, but this is a hugely entertaining and educational experience on any level.

Beacon Hill Park PARK
(www.victoria.ca/EN/main/residents/parks/beacon hill.html; Douglas St; ⊞⛟; ☐3) Fringed by crashing ocean, this waterfront park is ideal for feeling the breeze in your hair – check out the windswept trees along the cliff top. You'll also find a gigantic totem pole, Victorian

BRITISH COLUMBIA VICTORIA

CYCLING AROUND VICTORIA

Victoria is a progressive city when it comes to cycling and its biking infrastructure has improved by leaps and bounds in recent years. In 2017, the first proper downtown bike lane (with its own traffic lights and signage) was laid on Pandora St. The plan is to have another 32km of separated bike lanes in place by the end of 2022.

The bike-friendliness dates from the 1990s when two regional hiking-biking trails were developed to connect Victoria with the surrounding countryside. The 55km Galloping Goose Trail runs along an old railway line to Sooke and beyond, while the 33km Lochside Regional Trail connects downtown Victoria with the Swartz Bay Ferry Terminal. Both trails allow cyclists to pedal unmolested by traffic right into the heart of the city. They share a southern nexus on the downtown side of the Johnson St Bridge, recently equipped with a designated bike lane.

Downtown Victoria & Inner Harbour

N

0   200 m
0   0.1 miles

BRITISH COLUMBIA VICTORIA

Princess Ave

Pembroke St

Discovery St

Chatham St

CHINATOWN

Herald St

Fisgard St

Cormorant St

Pandora Ave

Johnson St

Yates St

View St

Fort St

Broughton St

Courtney St

Burdett Ave

Fairfield Rd

Upper Harbour

Store St

Government St

Douglas St

Blanshard St

Fan Tan Al

Swift St

Johnson St Bridge

Esquimalt Rd

Harbour Rd

Johnson St

Pandora Ave

Market Sq

Store St

Broad St

Ped Mall

Trounce Al

Langley St

Fort St

Wharf St

Government St

Douglas St

Blanshard St

Songhees Point

Inner Harbour

Ferry to Port Angeles & Seattle (USA)

Laurel Point Park

Victoria Clipper

Belleville St

Black Ball Transport

James Bay

Victoria Harbour Ferry

Courtney St

Humboldt St

Tofino Bus

Cridge Park

Humboldt St

Quebec St

Kingston St

Menzies St

Government St

Royal BC Museum

JAMES BAY

Superior St

Michigan St

Southgate St

Beacon Hill Park

22

17

38

8

16 32

37

30

35

23 14

21

12

31

34

27

7

20

18 24

19

26

36

5 28

6

33

2

29

25 9

13

15

4

10

1

3

11

Downtown Victoria & Inner Harbour

cricket pitch and a marker for Mile 0 of Hwy 1, alongside a statue of the Canadian legend Terry Fox, who ran across the country in 1980 for cancer research. If you're here with kids, consider the popular **children's farm** (www.beaconhillchildrensfarm.ca) as well.

Robert Bateman Centre   GALLERY
(Map p680; ☑ 250-940-3630; www.bateman centre.org; 470 Belleville St; adult/child $10/6; ☺ 10am-5pm daily, to 9pm Fri & Sat Jun-Aug; ☐ 70) Colonizing part of the Inner Harbour's landmark Steamship Terminal building, this gallery showcases the photo-realistic work of Canada's most celebrated nature painter, the eponymous Bateman, along with a revolving roster of works by other artists. Start with the five-minute intro movie, then check out the dozens of achingly beautiful paintings showing animals in their natural surroundings in BC and beyond.

Emily Carr House   MUSEUM
(☑ 250-383-5843; www.emilycarr.com; 207 Government St; adult/child $6.75/4.50; ☺ 11am-4pm Tue-Sat May-Sep; 🅿; ☐ 3) The birthplace of BC's best-known painter, this bright-yellow gingerbread-style house has plenty of period rooms, plus displays on the artist's life and career. There are changing displays of local

contemporary works, but head to the Art Gallery of Greater Victoria if you want to see more of Carr's paintings. On your visit here, look out for the friendly house cats.

Art Gallery of Greater Victoria   GALLERY
(☑ 250-384-4171; www.aggv.ca; 1040 Moss St; adult/child $13/2.50; ☺ 10am-5pm Tue, Wed, Fri & Sat, to 9pm Thu, noon-5pm Sun; ☐ 14) Granted, it's not the Louvre, or even Vancouver Art Gallery for that matter, but this east-of-downtown art nook does harbor one of Canada's best Emily Carr collections. Aside from the Victoria-born painter's swirling nature canvases, you'll find an immersive display of Asian art and changing temporary exhibitions. Check online for events, including lectures and frequent guided tours. Admission is by donation on the first Tuesday of every month.

🏃 Activities

★ **Galloping Goose Trail**   CYCLING
Victoria's best-loved trail follows the grade of an old railway line and is named for an erstwhile train carriage that rattled through these parts in the early 20th century. As a result, the trail is flat, passable on a hybrid bike, and flecked with remnants of

Vancouver Island's pioneering railroad history, including several trestles and a smattering of explanatory boards.

The first 13km is on concrete and relatively urban. Further west, the trail becomes increasingly rural, with pastoral sections interspersing with woodland and regular glimpses of water (both bays and lakes).

Lochside Regional Trail CYCLING

A semi-rural hiking-biking trail linking Victoria's downtown core with the main ferry terminal 33km to the north, the Lochside bisects pastoral fields, woodland and quiet suburbs. It's pancake-flat, family-friendly and well-utilized by both tourists and locals, particularly in the summer. The trail – a mixture of gravel, concrete and quiet roads – is marked with kilometer posts.

Ocean River Sports KAYAKING

(Map p680; ☑ 250-381-4233; www.oceanriver. com; 1630 Store St; rentals per 2hr $40, tours from $79; ☉ 10am-5pm Mon-Sat, from 11am Sun) Offers kayak rentals and organizes popular kayak day tours in the area (including evening options). Harbor tours cast off from the dock behind the shop. Stand-up paddling and multiday tours are also available.

Tours

★ **Pedaler** CYCLING

(Map p680; ☑ 778-265-7433; www.thepedaler. ca; 321 Belleville St; tours from $50, rentals per day $30; ☉ 9am-6pm, reduced hours Nov–mid-Mar) Pedaler offers bike rentals and several guided two-wheeled tours around the city, including the 'Hoppy Hour Ride' with its craft-beer-sampling focus. Get kitted out with a sturdy hybrid at the office in the 'olde' Huntingdon Manor building and go explore the Galloping Goose Trail (p681). Helmets, locks and rain ponchos are thrown in.

Eagle Wing Tours WHALE-WATCHING

(☑ 250-384-8008; www.eaglewingtours.ca; 12 Erie St, Fisherman's Wharf; adult/child from $115/75; ☉ Mar-Oct) Popular and long-established operator of whale-watching boat tours.

Harbour Air SCENIC FLIGHTS

(Map p680; ☑ 250-384-2215; www.harbourair.com; 950 Wharf St; tours from $119) For a bird's-eye Victoria view, these floatplane tours from the Inner Harbour are fab, especially when they dive-bomb the water on landing.

Architectural Institute of BC WALKING

(Map p680; ☑ ext 325 604-683-8588; www.aibc.ca; tours $10; ☉ 10am & 1pm Tue-Sun Jul & Aug) The institute puts on three great-value history- and building-themed walking tours, covering Chinatown, the James Bay residential district and the little-touched-upon history of the now demolished Fort Victoria. All tours start at the downtown visitor center (p689).

Festivals & Events

Victoria Day Parade PARADE

(www.gvfs.ca; ☉ mid-May) Street fiesta, with dancers, marching bands and 50,000-plus spectators. It usually starts on the corner of Douglas and Finlayson Sts and runs down Douglas St to the intersection with Courtenay St.

Victoria Ska & Reggae Fest MUSIC

(www.victoriaskafest.ca; ☉ mid-Jun) The largest music festival of its kind in Canada.

Victoria Fringe Theatre Festival THEATER

(www.victoriafringe.com; ☉ late Aug) Two weeks of quirky short plays and stand-up performances throughout the city.

Victoria International Buskers Festival PERFORMING ARTS

(☉ early Sep) Five days of street-performing action from local and international artists in Bastion and Market Sqs.

Rifflandia MUSIC

(www.rifflandia.com; ☉ Sep) Victoria's coolest music festival sees indie bands playing around the city.

Sleeping

From heritage B&Bs to cool boutiques and swanky high-end options, Victoria is stuffed with accommodations for all budgets. Off-season sees great deals. Tourism Victoria's **room-reservation service** (☑ 800-663-3883, 250-953-2033; www.tourism victoria.com/hotels) can show you what's available. Keep in mind that most downtown accommodations also charge for parking.

★ **Ocean Island Inn** HOSTEL $

(Map p680; ☑ 250-385-1789; www.oceanisland. com; 791 Pandora Ave; dm/d from $36/56; @ 🛜 ☐70) The kind of hostel that'll make you

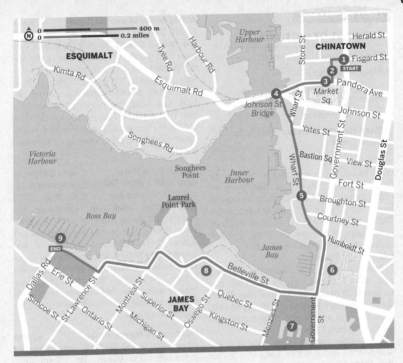

Walking Tour
Chinatown & the Inner Harbour

START CHINATOWN GATE
END FISHERMAN'S WHARF
LENGTH 2KM; 1½ HOURS

Victoria's Chinatown might not be as large, but it's the second-oldest Chinese neighborhood in North America after San Francisco.

A handsome **1 gate** near the corner of Government and Fisgard Sts marks its entrance. Beyond, lies Fisgard, the most ostensibly Chinese of the quarter's compact streets.

Leading off it on the south side is **2 Fan Tan Alley**, a narrow passageway connecting with Pandora Ave. Once a muddle of opium dens and gambling clubs, today it's home to used record stores and trinket shops.

3 Pandora Ave was the first street in Victoria to have a separated bike lane. Cross the road, before turning right and strolling past vintage clothes shops and a couple of pubs.

The bridge right in front of you as you approach the water is the **4 Johnson St Bridge**, a bascule (lifting) bridge that was completely remodeled in 2018. It now has dedicated pedestrian and bike lanes and is the de facto starting point for the Lochside and Galloping Goose interurban trails.

Turn left into Wharf St and look out for a small **5 monument** overlooking the harbor near the junction of Broughton St. This is where Fort Victoria once stood, a fur trading post built in 1843.

Curve on round to the Inner Harbour dominated by the palatial **6 Fairmont Empress Hotel** (p685) built in 1908 on former mudflats. If you're feeling thirsty (and rich), pop inside for afternoon tea.

At right-angles to the Empress and looking equally regal is BC's **7 Parliament building** (p679). Follow Belleville St west past a string of harborside accommodations including the Queen Anne–style **8 Huntingdon Manor Hotel** (p684), fronted by one of Victoria's oldest heritage buildings.

The main road kinks inland and dips deeper into the quiet James Bay neighborhood, before emerging at **9 Fisherman's Wharf** (www.fishermanswharfvictoria.com) where the homes float, and fish-and-chips are de rigueur.

684

LOCAL KNOWLEDGE

THE BEST OF VICTORIA

Place to sleep Abigail's Hotel (p684)

Place for dinner Brasserie
L'École (p686)

Place to drink Drake (p687)

Place for breakfast Jam Cafe (p686)

Place for afternoon tea Pendray Tea
House (p686)

want to become a backpacker (again), the
Ocean is a fabulous blitz of sharp color accents, global travel memorabilia and more
handy extras than a deluxe five-star hotel.
Bank on free breakfast (including waffles!),
free dinner, a free nightly drink, free bag
storage (handy for the West Coast Trail) and
free friendly advice.

Funky rooms are available in single-sex
and mixed dorms, micro doubles and
queens with private bathrooms, plus there's
a shared modern kitchen and plenty of common space to mingle and swap travel escapades with new friends.

The same owners also have private,
self-catering suites across town in a James
Bay character house from $135; see www.
oisuites.com for information.

HI Victoria Hostel
HOSTEL $

(Map p680; ☑250-385-4511; www.hihostels.ca/
victoria; 516 Yates St; dm/d $33/80; @🛜; 🖵70)
This quiet downtown hostel in a high-
ceilinged heritage building has two large
single-sex dorms (sleeping 44 guests, no
less), three small mixed dorms and a couple
of private rooms. There's a games room and
a book-lined reading area, but you're also
in the heart of the action if you want to do
your own thing. Free breakfast, tea and coffee included.

Hotel Zed
MOTEL $$

(☑250-388-4345; www.hotelzed.com; 3110 Doug-
las St; d from $209; P🛜🏊🐾; 🖵70) If you
like an accommodations that – in its own
words – likes to 'rebel against the ordinary'
then you'll love the Zed, an eccentric motel
that has been given a tongue-in-cheek retro
makeover, complete with rainbow paint-
work and free VW-van rides to downtown (a
20-minute walk away). The rooms are also
fun: 1970s phones, bathroom comic books
and brightly painted walls.

Abbeymoore Manor B&B Inn
B&B $$

(☑250-370-1470; www.abbeymoore.com; 1470
Rockland Ave; d from $239; P@🛜; 🖵14) A Vic-
toria B&B worthy of Queen Victoria, the Ab-
beymoore has a decidedly posh address and
was designed in the arts-and-crafts style in
1912. Seven deluxe rooms mix period details with satisfying modern touches in a
way that is grand rather than kitschy. Hot
breakfasts are equally creative and you're
never far from a complimentary coffee and
cookie.

Swans Suite Hotel
BOUTIQUE HOTEL $$

(Map p680; ☑250-361-3310; www.swanshotel.
com; 506 Pandora Ave; ste $195; 🛜🐾; 🖵70)
This former brick-built warehouse has
been transformed into an art-lined bou-
tique hotel. Most rooms are spacious loft
suites where you climb upstairs to bed
down in a gabled nook, and each is deco-
rated with a comfy combination of wood
beams, rustic-chic furniture and deep
leather sofas. The full kitchens are handy
but there's also a brewpub downstairs for
liquid sustenance.

Huntingdon Manor Hotel
HOTEL $$

(Map p680; ☑250-381-3456; www.huntingdon
manor.com; 330 Quebec St; r from $195;
P🌸@🛜🐾; 🖵30) The noticeably 'olde'
white clapboard edifice along the harbor
hides a comfortable, well-priced hotel
that mixes stiff wood-paneling with large,
modern rooms. Book online and you'll
get a hot breakfast included in the rate.
There's a traditional tearoom on-site (in
one of Victoria's oldest structures) should
you get the afternoon munchies. Staff are
extra-courteous.

Helm's Inn
HOTEL $$

(Map p680; ☑250-385-5767; www.helmsinn.com;
600 Douglas St; d from $140; P@🛜; 🖵70)
One of downtown's best-value hotels, this
three-building, motel-style property has 42
surprisingly large rooms, all with handy
kitchen facilities (either full kitchens or
refrigerators and microwaves). Family-run
for three decades, it also has a coin laundry,
cookies in the lobby and a communal seat-
ing nook around a fireplace. It's sandwiched
between the Royal BC Museum and Beacon
Hill Park.

★ Abigail's Hotel
B&B $$$

(☑250-388-5363; www.abigailshotel.com; 906
McClure St; d from $249; P@🛜; 🖵7) A bou-
tique hotel with the ambience of a B&B, the

historic, regal and faintly English Abigail's is Victoria's most Victorian accommodations despite the fact it was only built in 1930 with a mock Tudor facade. Near-perfect rooms come with heavy drapes, shapely furniture and marble bathrooms. In the morning, you can swan downstairs for a spectacular breakfast.

Complimentary afternoon appetizers are also laid on and guests have the run of a country-mansion-style library and lounge with a crackling fireplace. No guests under 13 years of age.

Fairmont Empress Hotel
HOTEL $$$

(Map p680; ☑250-384-8111; www.fairmont.com/empress-victoria; 721 Government St; d from $340; P★@🤝🐾; 📵70) One of the most famous hotels in Canada, the Empress was built in 1908 in French-chateau-esque style. There have been numerous renovations and a who's-who of famous guests, from movie stars to royalty, prancing through in the years since. Modern-day guests can still expect classic decor and effortlessly solicitous service.

It's as much a historic monument as an accommodations option, so expect plenty of company (read: tourists) in the grandiose communal areas.

Oswego Hotel
BOUTIQUE HOTEL $$$

(Map p680; ☑250-294-7500; www.oswegohotelvictoria.com; 500 Oswego St; d $265; P🤝🐾; 📵30) Well hidden on a residential side street a short stroll from the Inner Harbour, this contemporary boutique sleepover is an in-the-know favorite. Suite rooms have granite floors, cedar beams and, in most units, small balconies. All have kitchens (with dishwashers) and deep baths, making them more like apartments than hotel rooms. Cleverly, the smaller studio rooms have space-saving high-end Murphy beds.

✖ Eating

Crust Bakery
BAKERY $

(Map p680; ☑250-978-2253; www.crustbakery.ca; 730 Fort St; baked goods $3-6; ☺8am-5:30pm; 📵14) There are several bakeries on this stretch of Fort St, but the Crust jumps out at you first. Maybe it's the deliciousness of the aromas, or the delicate presentation, or the rich buttery-ness of the croissants, savory pastries and sweet tartlets with flavors like chocolate mousse and crème brûlée.

La Taqueria
MEXICAN $

(Map p680; ☑778-265-6255; www.lataqueria.com; 766 Fort St; tacos up to $3; ☺11am-8:30pm Mon-Sat, noon-6pm Sun; ☑; 📵14) A huge, aquamarine-painted satellite of Vancouver's popular and authentic Mexican joint, this ultra-friendly spot specializes in offering a wide array of soft-taco options (choose four for $10.50, less for vegetarian), including different specials every day. Quesadillas are also available and you can wash everything down with margaritas, Mexican beer or mezcal – or all three.

Red Fish Blue Fish
SEAFOOD $

(Map p680; ☑250-298-6877; www.redfish-bluefish.com; 1006 Wharf St; mains $6-18; ☺11am-7pm Mar-Oct; 📵70) 🐾 On the waterfront boardwalk at the foot of Broughton St, this freight-container takeout shack serves fresh-made, finger-licking sustainable seafood. Highlights include jerk fish poutine, amazing chowder and tempura-battered oysters (you can also get traditional fish-and-chips, of course).

Expanded seating has added to the appeal but watch out for hovering gull mobsters as you try to eat.

Foo Asian Street Food
ASIAN $

(Map p680; ☑250-383-3111; www.foofood.ca; 769 Yates St; mains $14-15; ☺11:30am-10pm Mon-Sat, to 9pm Sun; P; 📵70) Like a food truck that grew roots in a car park, this local-fave shack focuses on quickly rendered dishes inspired by Asian hawker stalls. Grab a perch inside or out, check the specials board and dive into fresh-cooked, good-value options, from saag paneer to papaya salad. Beer-wise, there's a love for local brews from the likes of Hoyne and Driftwood.

John's Place
DINER $

(Map p680; ☑250-389-0711; www.johnsplace.ca; 723 Pandora Ave; mains $9-17; ☺7am-3pm Mon-Fri, from 8am Sat & Sun; 🤝☑; 📵70) This friendly, diner-style hangout is lined with memorabilia (complete with obligatory jukebox), while its enormous menu is a cut above standard diner fare. Start off with a basket of addictive housemade bread then load up on generous pasta dishes, piled-high salad mains or pancakes that come with a stupendous cream-cheese-and-syrup dip.

★ **Jam Cafe** BREAKFAST $$

(Map p680; ☑778-440-4489; http://jamcafes.com; 542 Herald St; breakfast $13-17; ⊙8am-3pm; 🛜🍴; 🚇70) No need to conduct an opinion poll: the perennial lines in the street outside Jam suggest that this is the best breakfast spot in Victoria. The reasons? Tasteful vintage decor (if you'll excuse them the moose's head); fast, discreet service; and the kind of creative breakfast dishes that you'd never have the energy or ingenuity to cook yourself.

Jam classics include the 'cracker jack' (a banana-and-nutella brioche sandwich), the 'three pigs' (sausages fried in pancake batter) and the naan burrito (eggs, goat's cheese, avocado and spices). It's first-come, first-served, so join the line.

Fishhook SEAFOOD $$

(Map p680; ☑250-477-0470; www.fishhookvic. com; 805 Fort St; mains $13-24; ⊙11am-9pm; 🚇14) 🍴 Don't miss the smoky, coconutty chowder at this tiny Indian- and French-influenced seafood restaurant, but make sure you add a tartine open-faced sandwich: it's the house specialty. If you still have room (and you're reluctant to give up your place at the communal table), split a seafood biryani platter with your dining partner. Focused on local and sustainable fish.

Pendray Tea House TEAHOUSE $$

(Map p680; ☑250-388-3892; www.pendray innandteahouse.com; 309 Belleville St; afternoon tea $24; ⊙11am-2pm Mon-Sat, to 7pm Sun; 🚇30) A decorous little tearoom in one of Victoria's oldest houses in front of the Huntingdon Manor hotel where you can get the full monty – 'high tea' – with all the trimmings for $54, or a lighter version for $24. Reservations recommended.

Pink Bicycle BURGERS $$

(Map p680; ☑250-384-1008; www.pinkbicycle burger.com; 1008 Blanshard St; mains $13-17; ⊙11:30am-9pm Mon-Sat; 🛜; 🚇14) A long way from the greasy patties of yore, the Pink Bicycle (named for the machine that has pride of place in the window) deals in gourmet burgers served in sesame-seed buns and filled idiosyncratically with seared ahi tuna or free-range bison with smoked cheddar. The diminutive interior shimmers with candlelight at night adding nuance to the framed art-nouveau prints.

Barb's Fish & Chips FISH & CHIPS $$

(☑250-384-6515; www.barbsfishandchips.com; 1 Dallas Rd, Fisherman's Wharf; meals $10-23; ⊙11am-dusk mid-Mar–Oct; 🚇30) With its British antecedents and proximity to the sea, Victoria knows how to fry up fine fish-and-chips and this Fisherman's Wharf institution, in business for more than 30 years, is a good place to start taste-testing. Enjoy the batter-fried goodness alongside the bobbing boats with beady-eyed gulls for company.

Legislative Dining Room CANADIAN $$

(Map p680; ☑250-387-3959; www.leg.bc.ca; 501 Belleville St, Parliament Buildings; mains $9-18; ⊙8am-3pm Mon-Thu, to 2pm Fri; 🚇70) One of Victoria's best-kept dining secrets, the Parliament Buildings (p679) have their own subsidized, old-school restaurant where both MLAs and the public can drop by for a silver-service menu of regional dishes, ranging from salmon salads to velvety steaks and a BC-only wine list. Entry is via the security desk just inside the building's main entrance; photo ID is required.

★ **Il Terrazzo** ITALIAN $$$

(Map p680; ☑250-361-0028; www.ilterrazzo.com; 555 Johnson St; mains $21-44; ⊙11:30am-3pm & 5pm-late Mon-Fri, 5pm-late Sat & Sun; 🚇24) Authentic Italian flavors melded with a laid-back Victoria spirit make a devastatingly good combo. If you don't believe us, come to Il Terrazzo, a restaurant that's as much about its atmosphere and service as it is about its Italian-inspired, locally nurtured food. Aside from the usual suspects (seafood linguine, margherita pizza), there is a handful of more unusual renditions.

★ **Brasserie L'École** FRENCH $$$

(Map p680; ☑250-475-6260; www.lecole.ca; 1715 Government St; mains $20-50; ⊙5:30-10pm Tue-Thu, to 11pm Fri & Sat; 🚇70) *Bonsoir!* You may have just arrived at the best restaurant in Victoria, a small but wonderfully elegant bistro discreetly furnished in *la mode français*, but without any of the infamous Parisian pretension. Service is warm and impeccable, and the renditions of classic French dishes are exquisitely executed. *Moules frites* (mussels and fries), duck confit and superb Bordeaux wines all hit the spot.

The restaurant operates on a first-come, first-served basis and there's often a line when it opens at 5:30pm. Join it!

🍸 **Drinking & Nightlife**

Victoria is one of BC's best beer towns; look out for local craft brews at pubs around the city. There is also a good smattering of traditional pubs, some of which wouldn't look out of place in England.

★**Drake** BAR
(Map p680; ☑ 250-590-9075; www.drakeeatery. com; 517 Pandora Ave; ⊙ 11:30am-midnight; 🔊; 🖵 70) Victoria's best tap house, this red-brick hangout has more than 30 amazing craft drafts, typically including revered BC producers Townsite, Driftwood and Four Winds. Arrive on a rainy afternoon and you'll find yourself still here several hours later. Food-wise, the smoked tuna club is a top seller but the cheese and meat boards are ideal for grazing.

★**Garrick's Head Pub** PUB
(Map p680; ☑ 250-384-6835; www.garrickshead. com; 66 Bastion Sq; ⊙ 11am-late; 🖵 70) A great spot to dive into BC's brilliant craft-beer scene. Pull up a seat at the long bar with its 55-plus taps – a comprehensive menu of beers from Driftwood, Phillips, Hoyne and beyond. There are always 10 rotating lines with intriguing tipples (ask for samples) plus a comfort-grub menu of burgers and such to line your boozy stomach.

Habit Coffee COFFEE
(Map p680; ☑ 250-294-1127; www.habitcoffee.com; 552 Pandora Ave; ⊙ 7am-6pm Mon-Fri, from 8am Sat & Sun; 🔊; 🖵 70) 🖋 If you like your coffee ethically sourced and sustainably produced, hit Habit, where the potent brews and simple snacks are made with practically zero waste and the staff use bicycles to transport goods between two Victoria locations.

Clive's Classic Lounge LOUNGE
(Map p680; ☑ 250-361-5684; www.clivesclassic lounge.com; 740 Burdett Ave; ⊙ 5pm-midnight Sun-Thu, to 1am Fri & Sat; 🖵 70) Tucked into the lobby level of the Chateau Victoria Hotel, this is the best spot in town for perfectly prepared cocktails. Completely lacking the snobbishness of most big-city cocktail haunts, this ever-cozy spot is totally dedicated to its mixed-drinks menu, which means timeless classic cocktails, as well as cool fusion tipples that are a revelation.

Spinnakers Gastro Brewpub PUB
(☑ 250-386-2739; www.spinnakers.com; 308 Catherine St; ⊙ 11am-11pm; 🔊; 🖵 15) One of Canada's first craft brewers, this wood-floored smasher is a short hop from downtown via Victoria Harbour Ferry (p689). Sail in for copper-colored Nut Brown Ale or the lip-smacking Lion's Head Cascadia Dark Ale, and check out the daily casks to see what's on special. Save room to eat: the menu here is true gourmet gastropub grub.

Big Bad John's PUB
(Map p680; ☑ 250-383-7137; www.strathcona hotel.com; 919 Douglas St; ⊙ noon-2am; 🖵 70) Easily missed from the outside, this dark little hillbilly-themed bar feels like you've stepped into the backwoods. But rather than some dodgy banjo players with mismatched ears, you'll find good-time locals enjoying the cave-like ambience of peanut-shell-covered floors and a ceiling dotted with old bras. A good spot to say you've been to, at least once.

BRITISH COLUMBIA VICTORIA

AFTERNOON TEA

Victoria may have jumped on the third-wave-coffee bandwagon in recent years, but the city still harbors a devout love for afternoon tea, a habit it inherited from its orange-pekoe-swilling British founders. For every trendy cafe full of hipsters ordering avocado on toast, there exists at least one refined tearoom with walls the color of clotted cream and patrons sipping daintily from china teacups as if they've just stepped out of an episode of *Downton Abbey*.

The cathedral of afternoon tea in Victoria (and possibly all Canada) is the Fairmont Empress Hotel, where a full spread, served in the elegant lobby-lounge to a tinkling piano accompaniment, goes for a weighty $82 per person. Your substantial investment will be rewarded by three-tier trays loaded up with finger sandwiches, homemade pastries, fresh scones (with obligatory Devon-style clotted cream), and optional flutes of champagne. Make sure you cancel any dinner plans.

For those not in the market for pricey afternoon indulgences, tea needn't always be so expansive or expensive. Numerous tearooms and cafes around Victoria offer more modest versions of the repast, sometimes referred to as 'cream tea' (ie a pot of tea with an accompaniment of scones, jam and cream).

KINSOL TRESTLE

Standing as a testament to 20th-century railroad engineering, the Kinsol Trestle emerges out of Vancouver Island's misty forest like a giant Meccano set made from wood. Welcome to one of the largest timber trestles in the world.

Built between 1911 and 1920, and named after the local King Solomon mines, the Kinsol once carried log-dragging locomotives across the deeply cut Koksilah River. With changing patterns in industry, the last train crossed the trestle in 1979 and the wooden railway bridge was subsequently left to rot. A concerted community campaign between 2007 and 2011 raised the funds to refurbish and reopen the trestle as a multiuse path.

Today, it is possible to experience this glorious structure by walking or cycling along a trail that starts from a car park a kilometer from its southern end (take the Shawnigan Lake road west for 10km from Hwy 1 just north of Mill Bay). Signs at the site explain the history and engineering behind the structure while, on the trestle's north side, a steep path winds down to the river.

The Kinsol is approximately 50 minutes' drive from Victoria heading north and easily done as a day trip.

☆ Entertainment

Check the weekly freebie *Monday Magazine* for the lowdown on local happenings. Entertainment resources online include **Live Victoria** (www.livevictoria.com) and **Play in Victoria** (www.playinvictoria.net).

Vic Theatre   CINEMA
(Map p680; ☑ 250-389-0440; www.thevic.ca; 808 Douglas St; ☐70) Screening art-house and festival movies in the heart of downtown, the Vic charges a $2 membership alongside your ticket admission.

Belfry Theatre   THEATER
(☑ 250-385-6815; www.belfry.bc.ca; 1291 Gladstone Ave; ☐22) The celebrated Belfry Theatre showcases contemporary plays in its lovely former church-building venue, a 20-minute stroll from downtown.

Logan's Pub   LIVE MUSIC
(☑ 250-360-2711; www.loganspub.com; 1821 Cook St; ☑3pm-1am Mon-Fri, from 10am Sat, 10am-midnight Sun; ☐6) This no-nonsense pub looks like nothing special from the outside, but since 1997 the Logan has been the hotbed of Victoria's alt-rock scene. Come here to see bands with names like Alcoholic White Trash and Acid Mothers Temple. Fridays and Saturdays are best. Check the online calendar to see what's coming up. It's a 10-minute walk from downtown.

🛍 Shopping

While Government St is a souvenir-shopping magnet, those looking for more original purchases should head to the Johnson St stretch between Store and Government Sts, which is lined with cool independent stores.

★ Munro's Books   BOOKS
(Map p680; ☑ 250-382-2464; www.munrobooks. com; 1108 Government St; ☑9am-6pm Mon-Wed, to 9pm Thu-Sat, 9:30am-6pm Sun; ☐70) The name is no coincidence. Victoria's cathedral to reading was established in 1963 by Nobel-prize-winning Canadian author Alice Munro and her husband Jim. Encased in a heritage building on the city's famous Government St, it's an obligatory pilgrimage for bibliophiles with its high ceilings, wide array of local-interest tomes and well-read staff, some of whom have worked here for decades.

Regional Assembly of Text   STATIONERY
(Map p680; ☑ 778-265-6067; www.assemblyof text.com; 560 Johnson St; ☑11am-6pm Mon-Sat, noon-5pm Sun; ☐70) This branch of Vancouver's charming hipster stationery store is socked into a quirky space resembling a hotel lobby from 1968. You'll find the same clever greeting cards and cool journals, plus the best Victoria postcards ever. Add the button-making table, typewriter stations and a *Mister Mitten* chapbook purchase and you'll be beaming brighter than a shiny new paper clip.

Victoria Public Market   MARKET
(Map p680; ☑ 778-433-2787; www.victoriapublic market.com; 1701 Douglas St; ☑10am-6pm Mon-Sat, 11am-5pm Sun; ☐4) At this indoor market lined with artisan food businesses, tempting deli counters and food-court dining, you'll find everything from chocolate to cheese to

challenge your diet. Check the website for upcoming events, too.

Rogers' Chocolates   FOOD
(Map p680; ☑250-881-8771; www.rogerschoc olates.com; 913 Government St; ⊙9:30am-7pm; ⌨70) This charming, museum-like confectioner serves the best ice-cream bars, but repeat offenders usually spend their time hitting the 20-flavor-strong menu of rich Victoria Creams (soft-centered chocolates), one of which is usually enough to substitute for lunch. Varieties range from peppermint to seasonal specialties and they're good souvenirs, if you don't eat them all before you get home (which you will).

Silk Road   TEA
(Map p680; ☑250-704-2688; https://silkroad teastore.com; 1624 Government St; ⊙10am-5:30pm Mon-Sat, 11am-5pm Sun; ⌨70) A pilgrimage spot for fans of regular and exotic teas, where you can pick up all manner of leafy paraphernalia. Alternatively, sidle up to the tasting bar to quaff some adventurous brews. There's also a small on-site spa, where you can indulge in oil treatments and aromatherapy.

ℹ Information

Downtown Medical Centre (☑250-380-2210; 622 Courtney St; ⊙8:30am-5pm Mon-Fri; ⌨70) Handy walk-in clinic.

Main Post Office (Map p680; 709 Yates St; ⊙9am-5pm Mon-Fri; ⌨70) Near the corner of Yates and Douglas Sts.

Tourism Victoria Visitor Centre (Map p680; ☑250-953-2033; www.tourismvictoria.com; 812 Wharf St; ⊙8:30am-8:30pm mid-May–Aug, 9am-5pm Sep–mid-May; ⌨70) Tons of brochures, plenty of staff, ample help.

ℹ Getting There & Away

AIR

Victoria International Airport (☑250-953-7500; www.victoriaairport.com) is 26km north of the city via Hwy 17. Frequent **Air Canada** (www.aircanada.com) flights arrive from Vancouver ($193, 25 minutes) and Calgary ($285, 1¾ hours). **WestJet** (www.westjet.com) offers similar services. **Alaska Airlines** (www.alaskaair.com) links to Seattle (US$246, 45 minutes) five times a week.

YYJ Airport Shuttle (☑778-351-4995; www.yyjairportshuttle.com) buses run between the airport and downtown Victoria ($25, 30 minutes). In contrast, a taxi to downtown costs around $50.

Harbour Air (☑250-384-2215; www.harbour air.com; 950 Wharf St) flies into the Inner Harbour from downtown Vancouver ($242, 30 minutes) throughout the day. Similar **Helijet** (www.helijet.com) helicopter services arrive from Vancouver ($245, 35 minutes).

BOAT

BC Ferries (☑250-386-3431; www.bcferries. com) Runs large car ferries from mainland Tsawwassen (adult/vehicle $17.20/57.50, 1½ hours) to Swartz Bay, 33km north of Victoria via Hwy 17. Services run eight to 12 times a day. There are additional ferry services from Swartz Bay to and from the Southern Gulf Islands.

Black Ball Transport (Map p680; ☑250-386-2202; www.cohoferry.com; 430 Belleville St) Car ferries operate from the Inner Harbour to and from Port Angeles in the US (adult/child/ vehicle US$18.50/9.25/65.50, 1½ hours, up to four daily).

Victoria Clipper (Map p680; ☑250-382-8100; www.clippervacations.com) Has a dock in the Inner Harbour from where it runs a passenger-only catamaran to and from Seattle (adult/ child US$124/74, three hours, up to two daily).

BUS

With Greyhound no longer serving Vancouver Island, the best transportation company is **Tofino Bus** (Map p680; ☑250-725-2871; www.tofin obus.com), which runs three daily services via Nanaimo ($33, two hours) to all points north as far as Campbell River ($65, 5¼ hours) with bus 1 carrying on to Port Hardy ($115, nine hours). A separate service runs to and from Tofino ($75, 6½ hours, one daily) via Port Alberni ($60, 4½ hours, two daily).

Frequent **BC Ferries Connector** (☑778-265-9474; www.bcfconnector.com) services, via the ferry, arrive from Vancouver (from $49.50, 3½ hours) and Vancouver International Airport ($58, four hours).

ℹ Getting Around

BICYCLE

Victoria is a great cycling capital, with routes crisscrossing the city and beyond. Check the website of the **Greater Victoria Cycling Coalition** (www. gvcc.bc.ca) for local resources. Bike rentals are offered by **Cycle BC Rentals** (☑250-380-2453; www.cyclebc.ca; 685 Humboldt St; per hour/day $8/28; ⊙10am-4pm; ⌨1) or Pedaler (p682).

BOAT

Victoria Harbour Ferry (Map p680; ☑250-708-0201; www.victoriaharbourferry.com; fares from $7; ⊙Mar-Oct) calls in at over a dozen docks around the Inner Harbour and beyond with its colorful armada of little boats.

BUS

Victoria Regional Transit (www.bctransit.com/victoria) buses (single fare/day pass $2.50/5) cover a wide area from Sidney to Sooke, with some routes served by modern-day double-deckers. Children under five travel free.

Buses 70 and 72 link downtown with the Swartz Bay Ferry Terminal. Bus 75 goes to Butchart Gardens. Bus 61 goes to Sooke.

TAXI

BlueBird Cabs (☑ 250-382-2222; www.taxicab.com)
Yellow Cab (☑ 250-381-2222; www.yellowcabvictoria.com)

Southern Vancouver Island

Not far from Victoria's madding crowds, Southern Vancouver Island is a laid-back region of quirky little towns that are never far from tree-lined cycle routes, waterfront hiking trails and rocky outcrops bristling with gnarled Garry oaks. The wildlife here is abundant and you'll likely spot bald eagles swooping overhead, sea otters cavorting on the beaches and perhaps the occasional orca sliding silently by just off the coast.

Saanich Peninsula & Around

Home to Vancouver Island's main airport and busiest ferry terminal, this peninsula north of Victoria has plenty to offer day-trippers looking to escape from the city. Pencil in time for Canada's finest botanical gardens and the bookshop bonanza of seaside Sidney.

SIDNEY

Seafront Sidney is a pleasant afternoon diversion with a walkable waterfront and enough bookstores to satisfy a far larger city. Located at the Saanich Peninsula's northern end, it's a popular retirement community.

◉ Sights & Actvities

Shaw Centre for the Salish Sea AQUARIUM
(☑ 250-665-7511; www.salishseacentre.org; 9811 Seaport Pl; adult/child $17.50/12; ☺ 10am-4:30pm; ▣) Sidney's kid-luring highlight, this aquarium is accessed through a dramatic Disney-style entrance that makes you think you're descending below the waves. Then you'll step into a gallery of aquatic exhibits, including alien-like jellyfish, a large touch tank with purple starfish and an octopus

that likes to unscrew a glass jar to snag its fresh crab dinner.

Sidney Whale Watching WHALE-WATCHING
(☑ 250-656-7599; www.sidneywhalewatching.com; 2537 Beacon Ave; adult/child $129/95; ☺ Mar-Oct) With luck on your side, you could spot orcas and gray whales (minkes and fin whales are also possible) on a salt-licked boat jaunt with this outfit. If not, there are usually seals and seabirds aplenty to crane your neck toward. Boats zigzag through the Southern Gulf Island and San Juan Island archipelagos searching for the best whale foraging grounds.

The company also rents out kayaks and stand-up paddleboards for $60 per day.

🛏 Sleeping & Eating

Sidney Pier Hotel & Spa HOTEL $$
(☑ 250-655-9445; www.sidneypier.com; 9805 Seaport Pl; d/ste $245/275; @🕸🛜🐾) This swish waterfront property fuses West Coast lounge cool with beach pastel colors and is a worthy alternative to staying in Victoria. Many rooms have shoreline views, and each has local artworks lining the walls. A spa and large gym add value, plus you're steps from a rather good micro-distillery. There's also an on-site deli-cafe and West Coast–themed restaurant.

Beacon Cafe CAFE $
(☑ 778-426-3663; 2505 Beacon Ave; snacks $6-11; ☺ 8am-4pm) A steadfastly local corner cafe with a few regal touches. The chairs owe a nod to the elegant 'Louis Quinze' epoch while the mantlepiece pays ceramic homage to the British royal family with Jubilee mugs and royal wedding plates. Pastries and sandwiches abound, but the place is best enjoyed for its hot smoothies (including apple-pie flavor) and all-day high tea.

Sabhai Thai THAI $$
(☑ 250-655-4085; www.sabhai.ca; 2493 Beacon Ave; mains $11-19; ☺ 11:30am-2pm & 4:30-9pm Mon-Sat, 4:30-9pm Sun) A cozy locals' favorite with a bonus patio and a good line in authentic curry dishes and pad Thai. The lunch combos ($11 to $13) are good value and include rice and spring rolls.

🔒 Shopping

Sidney is an official 'booktown,' one of only two in Canada. At least half-a-dozen bookstores lie on or around Beacon Ave and all are locally owned.

★ **Haunted Books** BOOKS
(☑250-656-8805; 9807 3rd St; ⊙10am-5pm)
An agreeably Dickensian bookstore stuffed
to the rafters with random busts, faded old
maps, a grandfather clock and piles of dusty
old tomes. Despite its name, Haunted's eclectic book collection extends way beyond
ghost stories. It's by far the most atmospheric of Sidney's half-dozen book nooks – and
the oldest.

Tanner's Books BOOKS
(☑250-656-2345; www.tannersbooks.com; 2436
Beacon Ave; ⊙8am-8pm Mon-Sat, to 6pm Sun;
🖾) You can easily spend a leisurely afternoon perusing the selection at this cavernous corner bookstore with its large array of
magazines and comprehensive travel-book
section. Tanner's also organizes evening
book readings, typically at the Red Brick
Cafe across the street – check the bookstore's
website for listings.

Beacon Books BOOKS
(☑250-655-4447; 2372 Beacon Ave; ⊙10am-5pm
Mon-Sat, 11am-4pm Sun) A multi-room town-
center bookstore piled high with used books,
all guarded by a house cat that may or may
not let you stroke her (probably not). Look
out for the collection of vintage postcards,
then send one home, pretending you're va-
cationing in 1942.

ℹ️ **Information**

Visitor Center (☑250-665-7362; www.sidney.
ca; 2281 Beacon Ave; ⊙9am-5pm, reduced
hours Nov-Mar) Comprehensive coverage of the
whole Saanich Peninsula.

ℹ️ **Getting There & Away**

It takes around an hour to get here by **Victoria
Regional Transit System** (☑250-382-6161;
www.bctransit.com/victoria) bus from Victoria
($2.50, bus 70 or 72). Buses carry on to the
Swartz Bay BC Ferries Terminal (☑250-386-
3431; www.bcferries.com), 6km to the north,
and to Victoria International Airport (p689), 5km
to the west.

BRENTWOOD BAY

This countryside swath a 30-minute drive
from Victoria has some attractions of its
own. You can cycle across it on the ur-
ban-to-rural Lochside Regional Trail, upgrade your book collection in seaside Sidney
and admire one of the finest gardens in Canada – and one of BC's most popular visitor
attractions – at Butchart Gardens.

★ **Butchart Gardens** GARDENS
(☑250-652-5256; www.butchartgardens.com; 800
Benvenuto Ave; adult/teen/child $33.80/16.90/3;
⊙8:45am-10pm Jun-Aug, reduced hours Sep-
May; 🖾75) Far more than just another
pretty flower arrangement, Butchart is a
national historic site and a triumph of ear-
ly-20th-century gardening aesthetics. With
its well-tended blooms, ornate fountains
and diverse international flavor (from Japanese to Italian), it's hard to imagine that
this land was once an abandoned limestone quarry. Tour buses roll in relentlessly
throughout the summer, but the gardens
with their undulating topography are big
enough to absorb the melee.

Food outlets and gift shops crowd the entrance, including the **Dining Room Restaurant**, which serves a smashing afternoon tea.

Butchart is open year-round, although
summer is, arguably, the best (and busiest)
season to visit: there are Saturday-night fireworks in July and August. The Christmas-
lights season from early December to early
January is another highlight.

The gardens were the brainchild of Jen-
nie Butchart, whose husband founded the
limestone quarry. She began planting and
landscaping over the old quarry in 1912.
Expanded and manicured throughout the
course of a century, the site now counts over
one million blooms to cater for its one million annual visitors. Passed down through
several generations, the gardens are still
owned by the Butchart family.

Victoria Butterfly Gardens GARDENS
(☑250-652-3822; www.butterflygardens.com;
1461 Benvenuto Ave; adult/child $16.50/6.50;
⊙10am-4pm mid-Mar–Sep, to 3pm Oct–mid-Mar)
These gardens offer a kaleidoscope of thousands of fluttering critters, from around 75
species, in a free-flying environment. As well
as watching them flit about and land on
your head, you can learn about ecosystem
lifecycles, and eyeball exotic fish, plants and
birds. Look out for Spike, the long-beaked
puna ibis, who struts around the garden
trails as if he owns the place.

Sooke & Around

Only a 45-minute drive from Victoria, Sooke
is the gateway to some of South Vancouver
Island's best wilderness areas, but still has
enough facilities to offer choice and comfort.
You can cycle to the town from Victoria on
the Galloping Goose Trail or catch a metro

bus along Hwy 14. Twisted Garry oaks and unkempt hedgerows signal your arrival in a more rural domain.

◉ Sights & Activities

Sooke Region Museum   MUSEUM
(☑ 250-642-6351; www.sookeregionmuseum.com; 2070 Phillips Rd; ☺ 9am-5pm Tue-Sun) **FREE**
This jam-packed community museum is like a 100-year-old attic turned inside-out. It illuminates the area's rugged pioneer days with dioramas, glass cases, clothing and old newspapers. Check out Moss Cottage in the museum grounds – built in 1869, it's the oldest residence west of Victoria – and the Douglas fir cut-out that's older than 1200 years. The museum shares the same building and hours as the visitor center.

Sooke Potholes Provincial Park   PARK
(☑ 250-474-1336; www.bcparks.ca; Sooke River Rd)
This relaxed park has been a favorite natural hangout among locals for generations. With the potholes (natural rock pools) carved into the river base during the last ice age, it's ideal for summertime swimming and tube-floating. It's 5km drive from Hwy 14 along River Rd, or even better, a short ride on the Galloping Goose Trail (p681).

Juan de Fuca Marine Trail   HIKING
Rivaling the West Coast Trail as a must-do trek, the 47km Juan de Fuca Marine Trail is located in **Juan de Fuca Provincial Park**

(☑ 250-474-1336; www.env.gov.bc.ca/bcparks/explore/parkpgs/juan_de_fuca; Hwy 14) and takes around four days to complete, though you don't have to do the whole thing. Some sections are often muddy and difficult to hike, while bear sightings and swift weather changes are not uncommon.

From east to west, the trailhead access points are China Beach, Sombrio Beach, Parkinson Creek and Botanical Beach. The most difficult stretch is between Bear Beach and China Beach.

The route has several basic backcountry campsites and you can pay your camping fee ($10 per adult) at any of the trailheads. The most popular spot to pitch your tent is the more salubrious, family-friendly China Beach Campground, which has pit toilets and cold-water taps but no showers. There's a waterfall at the western end of the beach and booking ahead in summer is essential.

Booking ahead is also required on the West Coast Trail Express minibus that runs between Victoria, the trailheads and Port Renfrew.

Adrena LINE   ZIP-LINING
(☑ 250-642-1933; www.adrenalinezip.com; 5128 Sooke Rd; adult/child from $89/70; ☺ 9am-5pm Mar-Oct) If you're craving some thrills, find your inner screamer on a forested zip-line tour. The full-moon zips are the most fun but book ahead since they run irregularly, depending on the lunar schedule. If you

VANCOUVER ISLAND BOOZE TRAIL

Vancouver Island's blossoming local-food movement has spread to booze, with wineries, breweries, cideries and distilleries popping up across the region, giving visitors plenty of reason to appoint a designated driver. But unless you know where to go, many of these artisanal operators can be hard to find. Here are some thirst-slaking recommendations for visitors.

In the Comox Valley, Cumberland Brewing (p709) is one of the island's tastiest beer makers – don't miss the Red Tape Pale Ale. A weave around the Cowichan region delivers you to **Cherry Point Vineyards** (☑ 250-743-1272; www.cherrypointvineyards.com; 840 Cherry Point Rd, Cobble Hill; ☺ 10am-5pm), with its lip-smacking blackberry port; **Averill Creek** (☑ 250-709-9986; www.averillcreek.ca; 6552 North Rd, Duncan; tastings $5; ☺ 11am-5pm Mar-Dec), with its patio views and lovely pinot noirs; and the rustic-chic **Merridale Estate Cidery** (☑ 250-743-4293; www.merridalecider.com; 1230 Merridale Rd, Cobble Hill; ☺ 11am-5pm, reduced hours Oct-Mar), an inviting apple-cider producer that also makes brandy and has a great patio bistro.

Further south in Saanich – just a short drive from Victoria – organic apples are also on the tasting menu at **Sea Cider** (☑ 250-544-4824; www.seacider.ca; 2487 Mt St Michael Rd, Saanichton; ☺ 11am-4pm). Booze of a stronger hue is the approach at Sidney's **Victoria Distillers** (☑ 250-544-8218; www.victoriadistillers.com; 9891 Seaport Pl; tours $7; ☺ noon-5pm Wed & Thu, to 6pm Fri-Sun), where the lovely Oaken Gin is recommended. Both offer tours and tastings.

don't have your own transport, Adrena can also shuttle you to and from Victoria for an extra $20.

Sleeping & Eating

China Beach Campground
CAMPGROUND $
(☑519-826-6850, 800-689-9025; www.discover camping.ca; campsites $20; ⊘mid-May–mid-Sep) A popular forested campground with vehicle-accessible sites – the only one in Juan de Fuca Provincial Park. It's not far from the waterfront.

Sooke Harbour House
HOTEL $$$
(☑250-642-3421; www.sookeharbourhouse. com; 1528 Whiffen Spit Rd; d from $329; 🐾🖥) Whether you opt for the Emily Carr or the Blue Heron, each of the 28 guest rooms here has a decadent tub or steam shower, while most also have wood-burning fireplaces, balconies and expansive sea views. Expect a decanter of blackberry port to be waiting in your room when you arrive; try not to drink it all in one go.

Stick in the Mud Cafe
CAFE $
(☑250-642-5635; www.stickinthemud.ca; 6715 Eustace Rd; snacks $5-10; ⊘6am-5pm Mon-Fri, from 7:30am Sat & Sun) Fortify yourself with an 'eggamajig' (a tangy egg-filled English muffin) before hitting the Galloping Goose Trail (p681) – it'll carry you an extra few miles. For more energy add a smoothie. The cafe is hidden behind a boring strip mall and embellished by a colorful alfresco mural.

❶ Getting There & Away

Victoria Regional Transit System (☑250-382-6161; www.bctransit.com/victoria; $2.50) Bus 61 goes direct from the city to Sooke.

PORT RENFREW

Conveniently nestled between the Juan de Fuca and West Coast Trails, delightfully remote Port Renfrew is a great access point for either route. There are several places to rest your weary head and fuel up with non-gourmet grub.

Sleeping & Eating

Wild Renfrew
HOTEL, CABIN $$
(☑250-647-5541; www.wildrenfrew.com; 17310 Parkinson Rd; d/cabins from $139/199; 🐾🖥) With woodland cabins and lodge rooms recently upgraded, there are many ways to unplug from the city and sink into the retreat-like feel of the rainforest here. The luxury wood seaside cottages are best and each includes a

kitchen for preparing your alfresco balcony breakfast in the morning – there's also a pub nearby if you're feeling lazy.

Coastal Kitchen Cafe
CAFE $
(☑250-647-5545; 17245 Parkinson Rd; mains $8-19; ⊘8am-4pm May-Sep) For a respite from campground pasta, this laid-back, locally loved hangout serves food to satisfy a post–West Coast Trail appetite with BC craft beers to wash it down. The menu highlight? Avocado toast with poached egg and smoked salmon.

Renfrew Pub
PUB
(☑250-647-5541; 17310 Parkinson Rd; ⊘11:30-8pm Sun-Fri, to 9pm Sat) Summer drinking here is all about snagging a spot on the patio alongside the wharf. On lazy days, it's hard to peel yourself away from the shimmering shoreline views, especially if you've a round or two of BC craft ale. Pure joy, especially if you've just emerged from a hike on the West Coast Trail. The food's good too.

❶ Getting There & Away

It's hard to miss Port Renfrew if you're driving around Vancouver Island: it's located at the western end of Hwy 14.

West Coast Trail Express (☑888-999-2288, 250-477-8700; www.trailbus.com) shuttle-bus services arrive at the West Coast Trail trailhead at Port Renfrew from Sooke ($50), Victoria ($55) and Nanaimo ($125). The bus runs daily from mid-May to late September. Book ahead.

Cowichan Valley

A swift drive northwest of Victoria on Hwy 1, the mild, almost Mediterranean climate of the Cowichan Valley has helped it develop as the island's major farming region. There's also a growing number of vineyards, cider-makers and even a tea farm.

Cowichan Bay

'Cow Bay' to the locals, the region's most attractive pit stop is a colorful string of wooden buildings perched over a mountain-framed ocean inlet. It's well worth an afternoon of your time, although it might take that long to find parking on a busy summer day.

Maritime Centre
MUSEUM
(☑250-746-4955; www.classicboats.org; 1761 Cowichan Bay Rd; suggested donation $5; ⊘9am-4pm Wed-Sun) A lovely pier-length attraction aimed at anyone with more than a passing

interest in salty history, this folksy facility is lined with intricate models, seafaring displays and usually at least one or two locals working on some kind of boat-building or repairing project. It's all wonderfully sprawling and random.

True Grain Bread   FOOD
(☑250-746-7664; www.truegrain.ca; 1725 Cowichan Bay Rd; ⊗8am-6pm, closed Mon Nov-Feb) Adding the welcome aroma of baking bread to the oily harbor smells, True Grain is part of a three-shop island chain. From sourdough to raisin, the bread is all handcrafted, organic and milled on-site (from BC-farmed grain). Homemade crackers and cookies will add to your picnic hamper – if it's not already too weighed-down with the chocolate buns.

Masthead Restaurant   NORTHWESTERN US $$$
(☑250-748-3714;   www.themastheadrestaurant.com; 1705 Cowichan Bay Rd; mains $22-54; ⊗5-10pm) The patio deck of this charming, 1863 heritage-building restaurant is a fine place for a splurge, and the $37 three-course BC-sourced tasting menu is surprisingly good value. Seasonal ingredients form the approach here and there are also some good Cowichan Valley wines to try if you're feeling boozily adventurous.

⊙ Getting There & Away

Driving the island's main Hwy 1 thoroughfare, take the Cowichan Bay Rd turnoff (it's about 45 minutes away from Victoria). This leads right into the village. Parking is challenging here in summer so arrive early to find a roadside spot.

Tofino Bus (www.tofinobus.com) stops at the Koksilah Transit Exchange on Hwy 1, 2.5km from the waterfront community. Four buses a day head north to Nanaimo ($25, 1¼ hours) and south to Victoria ($20, 50 minutes). Reserve in advance.

Chemainus

POP 3900

After its last big sawmill shut down in 1983, tiny Chemainus became the model for BC communities dealing with declining natural-resource jobs. Instead of submitting to a slow death, town officials commissioned a giant wall-mural depicting local history. More than 45 artworks were later added and street art, along with an excellent local theater, remains the mainstay of Chemainus' modern tourism industry.

Stroll the Chemainus streets (expect a permanent aroma of fresh-cut logs from the small sawmill nearby) on a mural hunt and you'll pass artsy boutiques and tempting ice-cream shops, some housed in heritage buildings and others in attractive faux-historic piles. In the evening, the surprisingly large **Chemainus Theatre** (www.chemainustheatrefestival.ca; 9737 Chemainus Rd; tickets from $25) stages professional productions, mostly popular plays and musicals, to keep you occupied.

Chemainus is more a place for a quick bite than a protracted dinner. Its best spot for a repast is the **Willow Street Cafe** (☑250-246-2434; www.willowstreetcafe.com; 9749 Willow St; mains $12-15; ⊗8am-5pm; 🛜).

Check in at the **visitor center** (☑250-246-3944; www.visitchemainus.ca; 9799 Waterwheel Cres; ⊗9:30am-5pm mid-Jun–Aug, reduced hours in winter) for mural maps and further information, plus the little community museum in the same building.

⊙ Getting There & Away

Chemainus is an hour's drive north from Victoria via Hwy 1; look for the exit after you pass through Duncan.

Tofino Bus (www.tofinobus.com) calls in at least three times daily on its way between Victoria ($25, one hour) and Nanaimo ($20, one hour). Reserve ahead. The bus stops on Hwy 1, 2.5km from the town center.

Nanaimo

☑250 / POP 90,000

Vancouver Island's 'second metropolis,' Nanaimo will never have the allure of tourist-magnet Victoria, but the Harbour City has undergone some quiet upgrades since the 1990s. It's seen the emergence, especially on Commercial St, of some good shops and eateries, plus a popular museum. With dedicated ferry services from the mainland, the city is also a handy hub for exploring the rest of the island.

⊙ Sights & Activities

Nanaimo Museum   MUSEUM
(☑250-753-1821; www.nanaimomuseum.ca; 100 Museum Way; adult/child $2/75¢; ⊗10am-5pm daily, closed Sun Sep–mid-May) This popular museum just off the Commercial St main drag showcases the region's heritage, from First Nations to colonial, maritime, sporting and beyond. Highlights of the eclectic collec-

Nanaimo

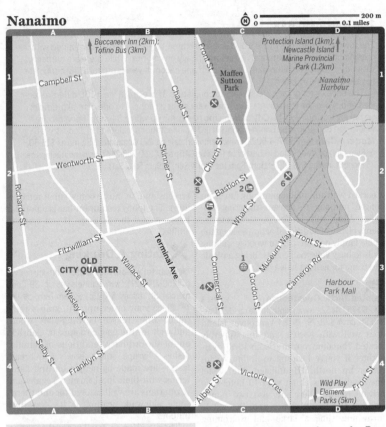

Nanaimo

⊙ Sights
1 Nanaimo Museum...................................C3

🛏 Sleeping
2 Coast Bastion Hotel.............................C2
3 Painted Turtle
  Guesthouse...C2

⊗ Eating
4 Gabriel's Gourmet Cafe........................C3
5 Modern Cafe..C2
6 Penny's Palapa......................................C2
7 Pirate Chips...C1
8 Vault Cafe..C4

tion include exhibits on the local sweet treat, Nanaimo bars (p696), and bathtub racing – plus a carved golden beaver from an 1890s tugboat. Ask at the front desk about the museum's guided walking-tour program as well

as summertime entry to the nearby **Bastion**, an 1853 wooden tower fortification.

Newcastle Island
Marine Provincial Park   PARK
(www.newcastleisland.ca) 🌿 Nanaimo's rustic outdoor getaway (also known as Saysutshun in the indigenous language) offers 22km of **hiking** and **biking** trails, plus beaches and wildlife-spotting. Traditional Coast Salish land, it was the site of shipyards and coal mines before becoming a popular summer excursion for locals in the 1930s when a tea pavilion was added. Accessed by a 10-minute ferry hop from the harbor (adult/child return $8/5), the island has a seasonal eatery and regular First Nations dancing displays.

Wild Play Element Parks   AMUSEMENT PARK
(📞250-716-7874; www.wildplay.com; 35 Nanaimo River Rd; ⊙10am-6pm mid-May–Sep, reduced hours Oct–mid-May; 👶) The perfect spot to tire your kids out, this tree-lined adventure playground

THE NANAIMO BAR

The town's culinary gift to the world is a small three-layered slab of wafer topped with cream and icing that's intensely sweet and heavy on calories. While there are numerous varieties, classic Nanaimo bars usually combine coconut, vanilla custard and chocolate flavors to dramatic effect.

The bar's exact origins are subject to conjecture. There are at least 100 different recipes and, while the ingredients vary, the sweet slabs all adhere to one central premise: no baking is required. The City of Nanaimo has come up with a 34-stop 'Nanaimo Trail' where you can enjoy the bar in myriad weird manifestations including in a cocktail at **Modern Cafe** (☑250-754-5022; www.themoderncafe.ca; 221 Commercial St; mains $15-30; ☺8am-late) or deep-fried in batter at **Pirate Chips** (☑250-753-2447; www.piratechips.ca; 75 Front St; mains $10-21; ☺11am-8pm Tue-Thu & Sun, to 9pm Fri & Sat).

is packed with adrenaline-pumping fun, from bungee jumping to scream-triggering ziplining. Along with its fun obstacle courses, there's plenty of additional action to keep the whole family occupied, from woodsy walking trails to busy volleyball courts. Bring a picnic and come for at least half a day.

SLEEPING

Painted Turtle Guesthouse   HOSTEL $
(☑250-753-4432; www.paintedturtle.ca; 121 Bastion St; dm/r $38/79; @ ☎) Vancouver Island does well with hostels and this superbly located Nanaimo venture is an ideal overnighter if you're heading to Tofino, Victoria or up north. HI-affiliated, the hostel has small dorms along with 10 hotel-style private rooms (there are also two family rooms). Hardwood floors and IKEA-style furnishings line a large and welcoming kitchen-lounge combo.

Buccaneer Inn   MOTEL $$
(☑250-753-1246; www.buccaneerinn.com; 1577 Stewart Ave; d/ste from $99/169; P☎) This friendly, family-run motel has a gleaming white exterior that makes it hard to pass by. It's worth staying in as the neat-and-tidy approach is carried over into the maritime-themed rooms, most of which have kitchen facilities. Splurge on a spacious suite and you'll have a fireplace, full kitchen and flat-screen TV. It's handy for the Departure Bay ferry terminal.

Coast Bastion Hotel   HOTEL $$
(☑250-753-6601; www.coasthotels.com; 11 Bastion St; d from $185; ❄@☎☀) Downtown's best hotel has an unbeatable location overlooking the harbor, with most guests enjoying sparkling waterfront views – when it's not foggy. Rooms have been well refurbished with a lounge-modern élan in recent years. Bank on wall-mounted flat-

screens and, in most rooms, small refrigerators. The lobby restaurant-bar is a popular hangout and there's a spa if you want to chillax.

Eating & Drinking

★ **Gabriel's Gourmet Cafe**   INTERNATIONAL $
(☑250-714-0271; www.gabrielscafe.ca; 39 Commercial St; mains $10-15; ☺8am-7pm; ☎ ✐) ✐ Place your order upfront, grab a table (made from reused bowling-alley wood) and wait for the magic to appear. Gabriel's out-of-the-ordinary renditions of familiar dishes – wraps, soups, bowls and breakfasts – are made by people on first-name terms with their local farmer. Vegans and vegetarians are well catered for and there's some sidewalk seating if it's too busy indoors.

The attention to detail is equal to the attention to ethical sourcing. Try the spoon-licking-good Malaysian-peanut-sauce chicken rice bowl or the quinoa-and-chickpea fritter with hummus. It's hard to believe that this busy hub was run out of a wheel-less food truck until relatively recently.

Vault Cafe   CAFE $
(☑778-441-2950; 499 Wallace St; mains $13-16; ☺7am-10pm Mon & Tue, to midnight Wed-Fri, 8am-midnight Sat, 9am-4pm Sun; ☎) This old bank building reborn in bright pink might have floated over from bohemian Paris in the age of Joyce and Hemingway. There's plenty to gaze at inside, from the romantic lamps to the elegant sofas to the Toulouse-Lautrec style prints. Good coffee, bagels and regular live music are the icing on top.

Penny's Palapa   MEXICAN $$
(☑250-753-2150; www.pennyspalapa.com; 10 Wharf St, Dock H; mains $9-19; ☺11am-8pm May-

Sep; ✍) This flower-and-flag-bedecked floating hut and patio in the harbor is lovely for an alfresco meal among the jostling boats. The inventive, well-priced menu of Mexican delights includes seasonal seafood specials (the signature halibut tacos are great) plus some good vegan options. The dining area fills rapidly on balmy summer evenings. When it comes to drinks, it's all about the margaritas.

★ **Crow and Gate**   PUB
(✆250-722-3731; www.crowandgate.ca; 2313 Yellow Point Rd, Cedra; ⊙11am-11pm) Taking you back to dear ole Blighty (England) is this out-of-town Brit-style pub with a dark, wood-beam interior and a wonderfully stodgy menu of housemade pies, Scotch eggs and bangers and mash. Providing a beery backup is a formidable lineup of foamy drafts including Guinness and English-style (but BC-brewed) Blue Buck Ale.

It's 13km from town, but insanely popular, especially in the summer when you can sit in the idyllic country garden and quaff to your heart's content. No minors.

❶ Information

Nanaimo Visitor Centre (✆250-751-1556; www.tourismnanaimo.com; 2450 Northfield Rd; ⊙9am-6pm Apr-Sep, reduced hours Oct-Mar) The main visitor center is 6km northwest of the city center, but there's also a smaller booth overlooking the harbor that gives out information in the summer.

❶ Getting There & Away

AIR

Nanaimo Airport (YCD; ✆250-924-2157; www.nanaimoairport.com) is 18km south of town via Hwy 1. Frequent **Air Canada** (www.aircanada.com) and **WestJet** (www.westjet.com) flights arrive here from Vancouver (from $175, 25 minutes) throughout the day. There are also a couple of flights to and from Calgary ($220, 1½ hours).

Frequent and convenient **Harbour Air** (✆250-714-0900; www.harbourair.com) floatplane services arrive in the inner harbor from downtown Vancouver ($110, 20 minutes).

BOAT

Nanaimo has two different ferry terminals located 19km apart by road.

BC Ferries (✆250-386-3431; www.bcferries.com) from Tsawwassen (passenger/vehicle $17.20/57.50, two hours) arrive at Duke Point, 14km south of Nanaimo. Services from West Vancouver's Horseshoe Bay (passenger/vehicle $17.20/57.50, 95 minutes) arrive at Departure Bay, 3km north of the city center via Hwy 1.

BUS

Tofino Bus (✆866-986-3466; www.tofinobus.com) serves all points north, west and south, including Campbell River ($42, 2½ hours, three daily), Tofino ($53, four hours, two daily) and Victoria ($32, 2¼ hours, three daily). Services pick up at Woodgrove Mall and the Departure Bay ferry terminal.

❶ Getting Around

Downtown Nanaimo, around the harbor, is highly walkable, but after that the city spreads out and a car or strong biking legs are required. Be aware that taxis are expensive here.

Nanaimo Airporter (www.nanaimoairporter.com; from $26) Provides door-to-door service to downtown from both ferry terminals, as well as handy airport drop-off and pickup.

Nanaimo Regional Transit (www.bctransit.com; single trip/day pass $2.50/6.25) Buses stop along Gordon St, west of Harbour Park Mall. Bus 2 goes to the Departure Bay ferry terminal. No city buses run to Duke Point.

Parksville & Qualicum

Qualicum Beach is not without its rebellious spirit, despite having the oldest demographic in Canada (average age: 60). Strict planning laws mean there are no big shops or restaurant franchises in this small seaside settlement, with its handsome timber-framed houses and strong community vibe.

Anchored by a historic hotel where John Wayne once laid his Stetson, Qualicum is known for its golf courses, long pebbly beach and pastoral surroundings that produce high-quality Qualicum cheeses (sold in supermarkets throughout southern BC). Otherwise, this is primarily a place to chill out, sip tea in manicured gardens and plan sorties to nearby caves and provincial parks.

Parksville, 15 minutes south of Qualicum, has the best of the area's beaches and is hence a little busier and more popular with families.

◉ Sights

Morningstar Farm   FARM
(✆250-954-3931; www.morningstarfarm.ca; 403 Lowrys Rd; ⊙9am-5pm; 🅿) **FREE** Check out the region's 'locavore' credentials at this delightful and highly welcoming working

farmstead. Let your kids run wild – most will quickly fall in love with the rabbits – then hunt down some samples from the on-site Little Qualicum Cheeseworks and Mooberry Winery: the 'Bleu Claire' cheese is recommended, along with a bottle of velvety blueberry wine to go.

The farm is located roughly halfway between Parksville and Qualicum Beach.

Coombs Old Country Market MARKET
(☑ 250-248-6272; www.oldcountrymarket.com; 2326 Alberni Hwy, Coombs; ☺ 9am-6pm Feb-Dec) The mother of all pit stops, this wood-framed and turf-roofed food and crafts menagerie is stuffed with bakery and produce delectables. It attracts huge numbers of visitors on summer days, when cameras are pointed at the grassy roof where a herd of goats spends the season. Nip inside for giant ice-cream cones, heaping pizzas and the deli makings of a great picnic. Need a souvenir? Grab a Billy Gruff chocolate bar.

Save some time to explore the attendant store and attractions clustered around the site, from clothing emporiums to an Italian trattoria.

Milner Gardens & Woodland GARDENS
(☑ 250-752-6153; www2.viu.ca/milnergardens; 2179 W Island Hwy, Qualicum Beach; adult/youth/child $12/7/free; ☺ 10am-5pm mid-Apr–Aug, reduced hours Feb-Apr, Sep-Oct, closed Nov-Jan) This idyllic outdoor attraction combines rambling forest trails shaded by centuries-old trees with flower-packed gardens planted with magnificent trilliums and rhododendrons.

Meander down to the 1930s **tearoom** on a bluff overlooking the water. Then tuck into tea and scones ($13.50) on the porch and drink in views of the bird-lined shore and snowcapped peaks shimmering on the horizon.

Horne Lake Caves & Outdoor Centre PARK
(☑ 250-248-7829; www.hornelake.com; tours from $27; ☺ 9am-5pm) BC's best spelunking, a 45-minute drive from Parksville. Some caves are open to the public for self-exploration, though the excellent guided tours are recommended, ranging from family-friendly to extreme; book ahead for these. To get there, take Hwy 19 toward Courtenay, then take exit 75 and proceed for 12km on the gravel road; if you get lost en route give the outdoor center a call.

🛏 Sleeping & Eating

★ **Crown Mansion** BOUTIQUE HOTEL $$
(☑ 250-752-5776; www.crownmansion.com; 292 E Crescent Rd, Qualicum Beach; d from $179; [P][☎]) The effortlessly regal Crown Mansion is easily worthy of its name. Dating from 1914, this country hotel mixes modern comforts with handsome historical features: check out the elaborate wooden fireplace complete with family crest. The suite rooms on the ground floor of a newer wing are the best deal with their humongous bathrooms (with heated floors) and four-poster beds.

Famous past guests include American actors John Wayne and Rita Hayworth, as well as the King of Siam. Complimentary continental breakfast is served in a music room complete with bay window near the entrance.

Blue Willow Guest House B&B $$
(☑ 250-752-9052; www.bluewillowguesthouse. com; 524 Quatna Rd, Qualicum Beach; d from $155) A surprisingly spacious, delightfully tranquil Victorian-style cottage, this lovely B&B has a book-lined lounge, exposed beams and a fragrant country garden. The two rooms and one self-contained suite are lined with antiques and each is extremely homey. The attention to detail carries over to the gourmet breakfast: served in the conservatory, it's accompanied by finger-licking home-baked treats.

★ **Free Spirit Spheres** CABIN $$$
(☑ 250-757-9445; www.freespiritspheres.com; 420 Horne Lake Rd, Qualicum Beach; spheres from $314) When it comes to extravagantly unconventional accommodations, these three wooden spheres, handmade by owner-inventor Tom Chudleigh and suspended like giant eyes within the forest canopy, score 10 out of 10. Compact two- to three-person spheres have pull-down beds, built-in cabinets and mini-libraries rather than TVs and are a perfect way to commune with BC's giant trees.

Named 'Eve' (the smallest and most basic), 'Eryn' and 'Melody,' each sphere is reached by a wooden spiral staircase with an outhouse situated at the bottom (oh, those nighttime walks!). There's also a ground-level facilities block with a surprisingly deluxe sauna, BBQ and hotel-quality showers.

The spheres are located 18km northwest of Qualicum Beach, but are well hidden in the forest and hard to find. Book ahead and ask for directions.

Tom is in the process of building another sphere and moving the whole project to another site. Check online for updates.

Bistro 694   CANADIAN $$$

(📞250-752-0301; www.bistro694.com; 694 Memorial Ave, Qualicum Beach; mains $22-32; ⏱4-9pm Thu-Sun) Any local will tell you to cancel your other dinner plans and head straight here. You'll find an intimate, candlelit dining room little bigger than a train carriage and a big-city menu fusing top-notch regional ingredients with knowing international nods. It's worth taking the seafood route, especially if the Balinese prawn curry or highly addictive seafood crepes are available.

❶ Information

For more information on the area, visit www.parksvillequalicumbeach.com.

❶ Getting There & Away

Tofino Bus services arrive in Parksville from Victoria ($42, 3½ hours, four daily) and Nanaimo ($19, 30 minutes, four daily), among other destinations.

Port Alberni

📞250 / POP 18,000

With resource jobs declining, Alberni – located on Hwy 4 between the island's east and west coasts – has been dipping its toe into tourism in recent years. And while the downtown core is a little run-down, there are some good historical attractions and outdoor activities to consider before you drive on through.

◉ Sights & Acivities

Cathedral Grove   PARK

(www.bcparks.ca; MacMillan Provincial Park; 🅿) This spiritual home of tree-huggers is the mystical highlight of **MacMillan Provincial Park**. Located between Parksville and Port Alberni, it's often overrun with summer visitors – try not to knock them down as they scamper across the highway in front of you. Short accessible trails on either side of the road wind through a dense canopy of vegetation, offering glimpses of some of BC's oldest trees, including centuries-old Douglas firs more than 3m in diameter. Only huggable in groups.

Alberni Valley Museum   MUSEUM

(📞250-723-2181; www.alberniheritage.com; 4255 Wallace St; by donation; ⏱10am-5pm Tue-Sat, to 8pm Thu) Don't be put off by the unassuming concrete exterior: this is one of Vancouver Island's best community museums. Studded with fascinating First Nations displays – plus an eclectic array of vintage exhibits ranging from bottle caps to dresses and old-school toys – it's worth an hour of anyone's time.

History buffs should also hop aboard the summertime **Alberni Pacific Railway steam train** (www.alberniheritage.com/alberni-pacific-railway), likewise operated by the Alberni Valley Heritage Network, for a trundle to McLean Mill; it's a National Historic Site.

MV Frances Barkley   CRUISE

(📞250-723-8313; www.ladyrosemarine.com; 5425 Argyle St; round-trip Bamfield/Ucluelet $84/88) This historic boat service is a vital link for the region's remote communities, ferrying freight, supplies and passengers between Alberni and Bamfield thrice weekly. In summer, with its route extended to Ucluelet and the utterly beautiful Broken Group Islands, it lures kayakers and mountain bikers – as well as those who just fancy an idyllic day cruise up Barkley Sound.

Port Alberni–Bamfield takes 4½ hours one-way. The summer run to the Broken Group Islands and Ucluelet takes three and five hours respectively. The company also runs a lodge on the Broken Group Islands that can be booked through the website.

Batstar Adventure Tours   KAYAKING

(📞250-724-2050; www.batstar.com; 6360 Springfield Rd) If you're unsure about exploring the beautiful but undeniably remote Broken Group Islands by kayak on your own, this outfit can sort you out. From long-weekend jaunts to multiday odysseys of the life-changing variety, all the details, including food and accommodations, are taken care of on these guided adventures.

🛏 Sleeping & Eating

Hummingbird Guesthouse   B&B $$

(📞250-720-2111; www.hummingbirdguesthouse.com; 5769 River Rd; ste from $150; 🛜) With four large suites and a huge deck with its own hot tub, this modern B&B has a home-away-from-home feel. There's a shared kitchen

THE DOPE ON POT RULES

Canada became the second country in the world to legalize non-medicinal marijuana in October 2018. Federal law allows public possession of up to 30g of marijuana, but its consumption is generally limited to places where cigarette smoking is permitted. The product can either be bought from licensed private or government-run stores, or purchased from registered online vendors. Private individuals are legally permitted to grow up to four marijuana plants.

The legal age for marijuana consumption is 19 in BC and the Yukon and 18 in Alberta. Driving under the influence of the drug and transporting it across international boundaries is illegal.

Some cities have local bylaws concerning the drug's use. For example, in Calgary it is illegal to consume marijuana in public places. Wise up before you travel to avoid getting caught out.

on each of the two floors and each suite has satellite TV; one has its own sauna. For families, there's a teen-friendly game room out back.

Hummingbirds in the garden are laid on free of charge.

Mountain View Bakery & Deli BAKERY $
(☑ 250-724-1813; 4561 Gertrude St; snacks $4-10; ☉ 7:30am-6pm Tue-Sat) If you're making a transportation connection in Port Alberni, pray you have time to dash across the road to this traditional bakery with a huge selection of pies, samosas, wraps, sandwiches, pastries, brownies, cheesecakes, muffins, buns and...there goes your bus!

Bare Bones Fish & Chips FISH & CHIPS $$
(☑ 250-720-0900; 4824 Johnston Rd; mains $9-21; ☉ 11:30am-7:30pm Sun-Thu, to 8pm Fri & Sat) Occupying a decommissioned wooden church, this smashing fry-joint serves cod, salmon and halibut in three different styles (beer-battered recommended), adding a tangle of delicious chips and the restaurant's own lemon-dill dip. Arrive off-peak to avoid the rush (this place is a true local favorite) and add a prawn side dish if you're still hungry (you won't be).

ⓘ Information

For more on what to do in the region, visit www. albernivalleytourism.com.

ⓘ Getting There & Away

Tofino Bus (☑ 866-986-3466; www.tofinobus. com; 4541 Margaret St) services arrive here from Victoria ($60, 4½ hours, two daily) and Tofino ($36, 2½ hours, two daily), among other places.

Pacific Rim National Park Reserve

Dramatic, wave-whipped beaches and brooding, mist-licked forests make the Pacific Rim National Park Reserve a must-see for anyone interested in encountering BC's raw West Coast wilderness. The 500-sq-km park comprises the northern Long Beach Unit, between Tofino and Ucluelet; the Broken Group Islands Unit in Barkley Sound; and, to the south, the ever-popular West Coast Trail Unit. If you're stopping in the park, you'll need to pay and display a pass, available from the visitor center or from the yellow dispensers dotted along the highway.

Long Beach Unit

Attracting the lion's share of park visitors, Long Beach Unit is easily accessible by car along the Pacific Rim Hwy, or you can walk or cycle in from Tofino and Ucluelet. Wide sandy beaches, untamed surf, lots of beach-combing nooks, plus a living museum of dense, old-growth rainforest, are the main reasons for the summer tourist clamor. Cox Bay Beach alone is an ideal hangout for surfers and families. Seabirds, sand dollars and purple-and-orange starfish abound.

For an introduction to the area's natural history and First Nations heritage, visit the Kwisitis Visitor Centre (Wick Rd; ☉ 10am-5pm May-Oct, Fri-Sun only Mar, Apr, Nov & Dec) FREE overlooking Wickaninnish Beach. If you're suddenly inspired to plunge in for a stroll, try one of the following walking trails, keeping your eyes peeled for bald eagles and giant banana slugs. Safety precautions apply: tread carefully over slippery surfaces and never turn your back on the mischievous surf.

Long Beach Great scenery along the sandy shore (1.2km; easy).

Rainforest Trail Two interpretive loops through old-growth forest (1km; moderate).

Schooner Trail Passes through old- and second-growth forests with beach access (1km; moderate).

Shorepine Bog Loops around a moss-layered bog (800m; easy and wheelchair-accessible).

West Coast Trail Unit

The 75km West Coast Trail is BC's best-known hiking route. It's also one of the toughest, not for the uninitiated. There are two things you'll need to know before tackling it: it might hurt and you'll want to do it again next year.

The trail winds along the wave-lapped rainforest shoreline between trailhead information centers at Pachena Bay, 5km south of Bamfield on the north end, and Gordon River, 5km north of Port Renfrew on the southern tip. The entire stretch takes between five and seven days to complete. Alternatively, a midpoint entrance at Nitinat Lake, operated by the **Ditidaht First Nation** (📞250-745-3999; www.westcoasttrail.com), can cut your visit to a two- or three-day adventure. Check the website for packages.

Open from May to the end of September, access to the route is limited to 75 overnight backpackers each day and **reservations** (📞519-826-5391, 877-737-3783; www.reservation. pc.gc.ca; nonrefundable reservation fee $11) are required. Book as far ahead as you can – reservations open in January each year. All overnighters must pay a trail-user fee ($127.50), plus a per-person reservation fee ($24.50) and the price of the short ferry crossings along the length of the route. All overnighters must attend a detailed orientation session before departing. If you don't have a reservation on the day you arrive, your name can be added to a standby list for any remaining spots (don't count on this, though, especially during the summer peak).

If you don't want to go the whole hog (you wimp), you can do a day hike or hike half the trail from Pachena Bay, considered the easier end of the route. Overnight hikers who only hike this end of the trail can exit from Nitinat Lake. Day hikers are exempt from the pricey trail-user fee, but they need to get a day-use permit at one of the trailheads.

West Coast Trail walkers must be able to manage rough, slippery terrain, stream crossings and adverse, suddenly changing weather. There are more than 100 little, and some not-so-little, bridges and 70 ladders. Be prepared to treat or boil all water and cook on a lightweight camping stove; you'll be bringing in all your own food. Hikers can rest their weary muscles at any of the basic campsites along the route, most of which have solar-composting outhouses. It's recommended that you set out from a trailhead at least five hours before sundown to ensure you reach a campsite before nightfall – stumbling around in the dark is the prime cause of accidents on this route.

West Coast Trail Express (p702) runs a handy shuttle service to and from the trailheads. Book ahead.

Broken Groups Islands Unit

Comprising some 300 islands and rocks scattered across 80 sq km around the entrance to Barkley Sound, this serene natural wilderness is beloved of visiting kayakers – especially those who enjoy close-up views of whales, porpoises and multitudinous birdlife. Compasses are required for navigating here, unless you fancy paddling to Hawaii.

If you're up for a trek, Lady Rose Marine Services (p702) will ship you and your kayak from Port Alberni to its Sechart Lodge three hours away in Barkley Sound. The lodge rents kayaks if you'd rather travel light and it also offers accommodations (single/double $211/357, including meals).

From there, popular paddle destinations include **Gibraltar Island**, one hour away, with its sheltered campground and explorable beaches and tidal pools. **Willis Island** (1½ hours from Sechart) is also popular. It has a campground and, at low tide, you can walk to the surrounding islands. Remote **Benson Island** (four hours from Sechart) has a campground, grazing deer and a blowhole.

Camping fees are $9.80 per night, payable at Sechart or to the boat-based staff who patrol the region – they can collect additional fees from you if you decide to stay longer. The campgrounds are predictably basic and have solar composting toilets, but you must carry out all your garbage. Bring your own drinking water since island creeks are often dry in summer.

ⓘ Information

Pacific Rim Visitors Centre (☑ 250-726-4600; www.pacificrimvisitor.ca; 2791 Pacific Rim Hwy, Ucuelet; ⊙10am-4:30pm Tue-Sat) At the junction of Hwy 4 and the Tofino–Ucluelet road, 8km north of Ucluelet and 32km south of Tofino.

ⓘ Getting There & Away

West Coast Trail Express (☑ 250-477-8700; www.trailbus.com) shuttle-bus services arrive at West Coast Trail Unit trailheads at Bamfield and Port Renfrew from Victoria ($55 to $110) and Nanaimo ($125). The bus runs daily from mid-May to late September. Book ahead.

The kayakers paradise of the Broken Group Islands Unit can be accessed by boat via **Lady Rose Marine Services** (☑ 250-723-8313; www.ladyrosemarine.com) from Port Alberni and Ucluelet.

The Long Beach Unit can be accessed from Tofino and Ucluelet on foot, by bicycle or by car.

Tofino

☑ 250 / POP 1950

Christened 'Tuff City' by its early inhabitants due to its isolation and heavy reliance on logging, 21st-century Tofino remains a diminutive end-of-the-road town bordered by rugged wilderness on one side and the raging Pacific on the other. Although less than 2000 Tofitians live here permanently, the population swells tenfold in the summer when visitors from far and wide arrive for whale-watching, kayaking, fishing and – best of all – surfing.

Tofino is the undisputed surfing capital of Canada and the annual inundation of wave-riding surf bums gives the place a laid-back, modern-hippie flavor. Eschewing international chains and restaurant franchises, the town supports a burgeoning farm-to-table food movement and counts on a strong history of environmental activism.

◎ Sights

Meares Island   PARK
Visible across Clayoquot Sound and accessible via kayak or water taxi from the Tofino waterfront, Meares Island was the site of the key 1984 Clayoquot Sound anti-logging protest that kicked off the region's latter-day environmental movement. As a result, it preserves some geriatric trees including a 1500-year-old red cedar, called the 'Hanging Garden,' that would have been a sapling not long after the Roman Empire fell. There are two hiking trails on Meares.

The **Big Tree Trail** is a 4.2km loop, some of it on boardwalk, that takes in the Hanging Garden and other impressively large trees. The **Lone Cone Trail** is a steep scramble to the top of the distinctive crinkled mountain visible from Tofino. It's 7km round-trip with 730m of ascent. The trails start in different places. A water taxi costs $25 for the Big Tree and $40 for the Lone Cone.

Ahousat   PARK
(www.wildsidetrail.com; trail fee $25) Situated on remote Flores Island and accessed by tour boat or kayak, Ahousat is the mystical location of the spectacular **Wild Side Heritage Trail**, a moderately difficult path that traverses 11km of forests, beaches and headlands between Ahousat and Cow Bay. There's a natural warm spring on the island and it's also home to a First Nations band. A popular destination for kayakers, camping (no facilities) is allowed.

There's a twice-daily water taxi in the summer to Flores Island ($20, 30 minutes). At a push the 22km round-trip hike can be done in a long nine-hour day.

**Tofino Botanical
Gardens**   GARDENS
(☑ 250-725-1220; www.tbgf.org; 1084 Pacific Rim Hwy; 3-days adult/child $12/free; ⊙8am-dusk) Explore what coastal temperate rainforests are all about by checking out the frog pond, forest boardwalk, native plants and educational workshops at this smashing, bird-packed attraction. New sculptures have been added to the garden in recent years, many by local artists. Pick up a field guide from the front desk to illuminate your self-guided exploration. There's a $1 discount on admission if you arrive car-free.

**Maquinna Marine
Provincial Park**   HOT SPRINGS
(www.bcparks.ca) One of the most popular day trips from Tofino, the highlight here is **Hot Spring Cove**. Tranquility-minded trekkers travel to the park by Zodiac boat or seaplane, watching for whales and other sea critters en route. From the boat landing, 2km of boardwalks lead to the natural hot pools.

Eagle Aerie Gallery   GALLERY
(☑ 250-725-3235; www.royhenryvickers.com; 350 Campbell St; ⊙10am-5pm) **FREE** Showcasing the work of First Nations artist Roy Hen-

ry Vickers, this dramatic, longhouse-style building is a downtown landmark. Inside you'll find beautifully presented paintings and carvings (most of them for sale) as well as occasional opportunities to meet the man himself.

🏃 Activities

⭐Tonquin Trail HIKING

If you're freshly arrived in Tofino and want to know what makes this place so special, head down First St and join the undulating gravel trail to **Tonquin Beach** (1.2km one-way) where a magical parting of the trees reveals a rock-punctuated swath of sand known for its life-affirming sunsets.

If you can drag yourself away from the natural light show, the trail leads further south along the coast to **Third Beach** and **Middle Beach** with several peek-a-boo look-outs on the way.

Ocean Outfitters BOATING

(📞250-725-2866; www.oceanoutfitters.bc.ca; 368 Main St; adult/child $109/89) The largest of the local water-excursion operators (judging by its slick office, which also contains a coffee bar), Ocean Outfitters offers the popular Tofino tour triumvirate of whale-watching, bear-viewing and hot-springs treks. It also runs water taxis to Meares Island as well as multiday kayaking excursions up Tofino Inlet.

Pacific Surf School SURFING

(www.pacificsurfschool.com; 430 Campbell St; board rental 6/24hr $20/25) Offers rentals, camps and lessons for beginners and board rental for old hands.

T'ashii Paddle School CANOEING

(📞250-266-3787; www.tofinopaddle.com; 1258 Pacific Rim Hwy; tours from $65) Tour the regional waters in a canoe (you'll be doing the paddling) with a First Nations guide who provides an evocative interpretive narration. Walking tours also available.

Tofino Sea Kayaking KAYAKING

(📞250-725-4222; www.tofinoseakayaking.com; 320 Main St; tours from $69) Evocative guided paddles around Clayoquot Sound, over to Meares Island and further up the coast. The outfit offers rentals ($50 per day) for go-it-aloners and multiday excursions with camping for adventurers.

🛏 Sleeping

Whalers on the Point Guesthouse HOSTEL $

(📞250-725-3443; www.hihostels.ca; 81 West St; dm/r $59/169; 🛜) Close to the action, but with a secluded waterfront location, this excellent HI hostel is a comfy, wood-lined retreat. Dorms are mercifully small (the female-only one has the best waterfront views) and there are some highly sought-after private rooms. Facilities include a BBQ patio, games room and a wet sauna. Reservations are essential in summer.

Ocean Village Beach Resort CABIN $$

(📞250-725-3755; www.oceanvillageresort.com; 555 Hellesen Dr; ste from $239; 🅿🛜😿🐕) This immaculate beachside resort of bee-hive-shaped cedar cabins – hence the woodsy aroma when you step in the door – is a family favorite with a Scandinavian look. All units face the nearby shoreline and have handy kitchens. If your kids tire of the beach, there's an indoor saltwater pool and lots of board games to keep them occupied.

Ecolodge HOSTEL $$

(📞250-725-1220; www.tbgf.org; 1084 Pacific Rim Hwy; r incl breakfast from $159; 🅿@🛜) 🍃 This quiet, wood-built education center on the grounds of the botanical gardens is popular with families and groups for its selection of rooms, large kitchen and on-site laundry. There's a bunk room that's around $45 per

BRITISH COLUMBIA TOFINO

STORMING TOFINO

Started as a clever marketing ploy to lure off-season visitors, **storm-watching** has become a popular reason to visit the island's wild West Coast between November and March. View spectacularly crashing winter waves, then scamper back inside for hot chocolate with a face freckled by sea salt. There are usually good off-peak accommodations deals during storm-watching season and many hotels can supply you with loaner 'Tofino tuxedos,' otherwise known as waterproof gear. The best spots to catch a few crashing spectacles are Cox Bay, Chesterman Beach, Long Beach, Second Bay and Wickaninnish Beach. Just remember not to get too close or turn your back on the waves: these gigantic swells can have you in the water within seconds.

person per night in summer for groups of four. Rates include garden entry.

Tofino Resort & Marina HOTEL $$

(☑1-855-615-7592; www.tofinoresortandmarina.com; 634 Campbell St; r from $159; ☎) All mod cons greet you at this updated small resort with an affiliated bar and restaurant overlooking the marina. Even the viewless rooms have king-sized beds, snazzy bathrooms (with sensor-activated lights), and blown-up aerial photos of Tofino's coastline accented on one wall.

★ Wickaninnish Inn HOTEL $$$

(☑250-725-3100; www.wickinn.com; Chesterman Beach; d $360-840; P ☎ ☎) ✔ Cornering the market in luxury winter storm-watching packages, 'the Wick' is worth a stay any time of year. Embodying nature with its recycled-wood furnishings, natural stone tiles and the ambience of a place grown rather than constructed, the sumptuous guest rooms have push-button TVs that rise out of the furniture, two-person hot tubs, gas fireplaces, floor-to-ceiling windows and wave-whipped balconies.

A litany of deluxe extras includes raincoats and umbrellas for outside, bathrobes and slippers if you're staying indoors, a fitness center, a gourmet restaurant and 42 different room types. Despite the obvious lure for romantics, the Wick is also proactively child-friendly and pet-friendly.

Wildpod CABIN $$$

(☑250-725-2020; www.wildpod.ca; 174 West St; d $295-375; P ☎) Luxury 'glamping' comes to Tofino in the shape of these six yurt-like pods made out of PVC that sit perched on the waterside at Grice Point in full view of passing whales. The individually themed pods (named sand, rock, wave, wood, nest and leaf) all have mega-comfortable beds, deluxe toiletries, propane fireplaces and mini-kitchenettes and sit on raised cedar decks.

✖ Eating & Drinking

Shed CANADIAN $

(☑250-725-7433; www.shedtofino.com; 461 Campbell St; mains $11-16; ⊙8:30am-10pm; ☑) True, it's a shed of sorts, albeit a very nice one with candles, an open kitchen, lovely wood furnishings – and quite decent food: count on quick-fire burgers, salads and creative 'bowls' headlined by the standout Pachamama bowl, a deft melange of squash, kale, ricotta and brussels sprouts. Coming in a worthy runner-up is the tuna *poke* bowl.

Rhino Coffee House CAFE $

(☑250-725-2558; www.rhinocoffeehouse.com; 430 Campbell St; doughnuts $2-4; ⊙7:30am-4pm; ☎) In outdoor-orientated Tofino, it's easy to justify a doughnut for breakfast, and the best place in Tofino to procure one is at Rhino. Toss a coin to decide whether you'll opt for the cinnamon-beer flavor or the less boozy sour cream.

Sobo CANADIAN $$

(☑250-725-2341; www.sobo.ca; 311 Neill St; mains $17-36; ⊙11:30am-9pm) It's hard not to love a restaurant whose name is short for

---

DON'T MISS

TOFINO'S INDIE SHOPPING MALL

Most shopping malls host a predictable gaggle of well-known brands housed in functional boxy buildings that look like they were designed by an eighth-grade technical-drawing student. Not so in Tofino where the timber-framed **Beaches Shopping Centre** looks as if it grew organically out of the forest and is home to a sweet consortium of independent homegrown businesses. Located 4km south of Tofino proper, you could easily spend a happy half-day here imbibing java at **Tofitian** (www.tofitian.com; 1180 Pacific Rim Hwy; snacks $3-8; ⊙7am-4pm Apr-Oct, to 3pm Nov-Mar; ☎) or gobbling sweets and ice cream at **Chocolate Tofino** (☑250-725-2526; www.chocolatetofino.com; ice cream $4-8; ⊙10am-9pm Jun-Aug, reduced hours Sep-May) just around the corner (salted caramels recommended). When lunch beckons, join the line or call your order in at **Tacofino** (☑250-726-8288; www.tacofino.com; mains $11-12; ⊙11am-7pm, reduced hours Nov-Mar), or avoid queuing completely by heading to **Wildside Grill** (☑250-725-9453; www.wildsidegrill.com; mains $13-15; ⊙9am-9pm, reduced hours Sep-May) for panko-fried fish. With its proximity to Tofino's surf beaches, the shopping center is also a good place to rent a board, or a bicycle, before continuing on your merry way.

'sophisticated bohemian,' a label that might have been invented with Tofino in mind. Once a humble food truck, Sobo is now an ultra-contemporary bricks-and-mortar bistro with floor-to-ceiling windows. The salads are exceptional and the pizzas (especially the exotic mushroom) aren't far behind.

The menu's showstopper, though, is the broiled oysters with miso mayonnaise.

Shelter CANADIAN $$
(☑250-725-3353; www.shelterrestaurant.com; 601 Campbell St; mains $12-32; ☺11am-midnight) This low-ceilinged designer 'shed' has kept expanding over the years, but has never lost its welcoming locals' hangout feel. The perfect spot to grab lunch (fish tacos and a patio seat will do nicely), Shelter becomes an intimate dinner venue every evening, when the menu ratchets up. *Steak-frites* and the 'Tofino surf' bowl (salmon, chicken and veg) call loudly.

★**Wolf in the Fog** CANADIAN $$$
(☑250-725-9653; www.wolfinthefog.com; 150 Fourth St; mains $21-45; ☺10am-late, dinner from 5pm) Reserve ahead for your table at this sparkling regional- and seasonal-focused restaurant that was recognised on Canada's 100 Best Restaurants list. The menu is split into single and sharing plates.

The bar is open for coffee and a light menu during the day, but head upstairs for dinner from 5pm.

Tofino Brewing Company BREWERY
(☑250-725-2899; www.tofinobrewingco.com; 681 Industrial Way; ☺11am-10pm) Slip into this recently renovated tasting room in an industrial park and enjoy a $7 'flight' of taster suds amid the polished beer vats and au naturel pine furnishings. For a true beach-to-table experience ask for the kelp stout made using locally foraged Pacific seaweed.

Like at all good tasting rooms, there are no TVs or obnoxious jukeboxes to distract you, just the light chatter of people enjoying their beer.

❶ Information

Tourism Tofino Visitor Centre (☑250-725-3414; www.tourismtofino.com; 1426 Pacific Rim Hwy; ☺9am-8pm Jun-Aug, reduced hours Sep-May) This visitor center (with handy washrooms) 6.5km south of town has detailed information on area accommodations, hiking trails and hot surf spots. There's also a kiosk in the town center in summer that dispenses advice to out-of-towners.

❶ Getting There & Away

Pacific Coastal Airlines (☑800-663-2872; www.pacificcoastal.com) Flights arrive at **Tofino–Long Beach Airport** (☑250-725-3751; www.tofinoairport.com) from Vancouver ($145, 40 minutes, one daily).

Tofino Bus (www.tofinobus.com; 346 Campbell St) runs one bus per day to and from Ucluelet ($18, 40 minutes), Port Alberni ($36, 2½ hours), Nanaimo ($51, three to four hours), Victoria ($75, 6½ hours) and Vancouver ($61, 7¼ hours) via the Nanaimo–Horseshoe Bay ferry.

❶ Getting Around

Cycling is popular in Tofino. You can cycle to most of the beaches (and along them too) via the MUP (multiuse path), a paved bike trail that leads south from town to Cox Bay and now extends to Pacific Rim National Park Reserve. Bike rental is around $35 per day and the roads are mostly flat. **Tofino Bike Co** (☑250-266-7655; www.tofinobike.com; 1180 Pacific Rim Hwy, Beaches Shopping Centre; full-day rental $35; ☺10am-5pm) can set you up.

From June to September, there's a free shuttle running hourly between 8am and 10pm to and from town and the visitor center.

Ucluelet

☑250 / POP 1700

Both the cousin of Tofino and the antidote to it, Ucluelet ('Ukee' to its friends) is situated on a similarly spectacular slice of Pacific Coast 40km to the south. But while Tofino is trendy, tourist-focused and challenging on the credit card, Ukee is blue-collar, less manicured and more down-to-earth.

Still largely undiscovered by the international set, 95% of whom head directly to Tofino, Ukee has plenty of fans, most of them loyal islanders who dig the sleepy rhythms, cheap motels and reliable snack shacks. And, lest we forget, those iconic surf beaches are still a short drive or bike ride away.

◉ Sights & Activities

Ucluelet Aquarium AQUARIUM
(☑250-726-2782; www.uclueletaquarium.org; Main St Waterfront Promenade; adult/child $15/8; ☺10am-5pm mid-Mar–Nov; ♠) 🖉 This excellent catch-and-release facility on the waterfront focuses on illuminating the marine critters found in the region's local

waters, which can mean anything from alien-looking sea cucumbers to a squirming, and frankly mesmerizing, Pacific octopus or two. But it's the enthusiasm of the young staff that sets this place apart, along with the ability to educate on issues of conservation without browbeating. A great kid-friendly facility – expect to walk away with renewed excitement about the wonders of ocean wildlife.

★ **Wild Pacific Trail**　　　　　HIKING
(www.wildpacifictrail.com) Where the temperate rainforest comes down to kiss the ocean, the citizens of Ukee have built a magnificent 10km trail that can be equally spectacular in both the sun and (stormy) rain. It starts with a 2.6km loop that winds past a 1915 Amphitrite lighthouse and progresses northwest as far as the Ancient Cedars loop and the Rocky Bluffs beyond.

The trail is well signposted and fastidiously mapped. To complete the whole 10km you'll need to take a couple of interconnecting paths along quiet roads calling in at several attractive beaches on the way. Various information boards provide background on the area's history and nature, and the path is dotted with benches, lookouts and so-called 'artist's loops' equipped with viewing platforms. Pack your easel.

Check the website for the latest news on the trail, included the summertime guided-walk program.

Subtidal Adventures　　　　WILDLIFE
(☑ 250-726-7336; www.subtidaladventures.com; 1950 Peninsula Rd; adult/child $109/89) A long-established local company offering open-to-the-elements Zodiac boat tours that show off the regional wildlife scene, with options including a summer favorite that often includes sightings of bears, several types of whales, lots of seabirds and maybe a sea otter (if you're lucky).

**Majestic
Ocean Kayaking**　　　　　KAYAKING
(☑ 250-726-2868; www.oceankayaking.com; 1167 Helen Rd; tours from $79) Majestic Ocean Kayaking leads day trips around the area. The easiest and shortest trips stick to Ucluelet's sheltered harbor. Highly recommended are the single-day and multiday trips south into Barkley Sound, and the Broken Group Islands, an archipelago of 100-plus islands that's part of Pacific Rim National Park.

 Sleeping

C&N Backpackers　　　　　HOSTEL $
(☑ 250-726-7416; www.cnnbackpackers.com; 2081 Peninsula Rd; dm/r $39/90; ☺ Apr-Oct; @ 🛜) Take your shoes off at the door and slide into this large timber hostel, where the gigantic back garden is the best place to hang (in a hammock) on lazy evenings. A spacious downstairs kitchen and up-to-date bathrooms with parquet floors add to the appeal, while the dorms are joined by three sought-after private rooms.

Surfs Inn Guesthouse　　CABIN, HOSTEL $$
(☑ 250-726-4426; www.surfsinn.ca; 1874 Peninsula Rd; ste/2-/3-/4-bedroom cottages $129/199/250/300; P 🛜) Hidden from the road behind vegetation, this funky collection of brightly painted houses and cottages hosts four choices of lovely accommodations, ranging from a loft suite to a four-bedroom house. All have kitchens or kitchenettes and three of them have outdoor BBQs and decks. The town and its supermarket is a short hop away on foot.

West Coast Motel　　　　　MOTEL $$
(☑ 250-726-7732; www.westcoastmotel.com; 279 Hemlock St; d from $99; P 🛜 🏊) The best motel in town juxtaposes its standard rooms (refrigerator, coffee machine, TV) with free access to the town's main fitness center, with which it shares a building. There's also a pool and sauna and friendly service to boot.

★ **Black Rock Oceanfront Resort**　HOTEL $$$
(☑ 250-726-4800; www.blackrockresort.com; 596 Marine Dr; studios/1-/2-bedroom ste from $345/450/700; P 🛜 🏊) Ucluelet's fanciest hotel feels like a transplant from Tofino. Set dramatically on the Pacific waterfront and painted the same gray hue as the rocks, it curves around the jagged shoreline seemingly oblivious to the stormy surf. On offer are kitchen-equipped suites wrapped in contemporary West Coast wood-and-stone and deluxe bathrooms the size of entire Vancouver apartments.

Many rooms have great views of the choppy surf and, just in case yours doesn't, there's a vista-hugging **restaurant** specializing in regional nosh. The lobby-level bar is shaped like a rolling wave.

✕ **Eating**

★ **Zoe's Bakery & Cafe**　　　BAKERY $
(☑ 250-726-2253; www.zoesbakeryandcafe.com; 250 Main St; sandwiches $8-10; ☺ 7am-5pm, re-

duced hours Nov-Mar) Ukee has about three places to refuel your car and at least another three to refuel your brain and legs while sating your sugar addiction, including the reliable Zoe's where the coffee goes down like maple syrup with bread-pudding egg bakes and cinnamon buns topped with generous dollops of icing.

Ravenlady
SEAFOOD $$

(www.ravenlady.ca; 1801 Bay St; mains $15-18; ⊙noon-2pm & 5-8pm Fri-Tue) The sole exponent of Ucluelet's food-truck scene is far superior to many bricks-and-mortar seafood restaurants. Specializing in fresh-shucked regional oysters, there are also gourmet delights from seared-tuna tacos to baguette po'boys stuffed to the gills with albacore tuna or panko-fried oysters. The truck is named after a magnificent stainless-steel sculpture vaguely reminiscent of Botticelli's *Venus* that stands beside it.

Frankie's Resto-Bar
BARBECUE $$

(☑250-726-2225; www.frankiesrestobar.com; 1576 Imperial Lane; mains $15-25; ⊙5-9:30pm) Not a lot else has changed at the establishment formerly known as Hanks, still a fount of carnivorous comfort grub where the key word is 'pork.' The menu offers ample opportunities to face-plant into generous portions of pork belly, pork mac 'n' cheese, pulled pork and good old sausages. A week's worth of calories in a single, highly satisfying sitting.

Norwoods
CANADIAN $$$

(☑250-726-7001; www.norwoods.ca; 1714 Peninsula Rd; mains $28-48; ⊙5-10pm) Showing how far Ucluelet's dining scene has elevated itself in recent years, this lovely candlelit room would easily be at home in Tofino. The ever-changing menu focuses on seasonal regional ingredients; think halibut and duck breast. All are prepared with a sophisticated international approach, plus there's a full menu of BC (and beyond) wines, many offered by the glass.

❶ Information

Ucluelet Visitor Centre (www.ucluelet.ca; 1604 Peninsula Rd; ⊙9am-5pm Jun-Aug, 9:30am-4:30pm Mon-Fri Sep-May) To learn a few good reasons to stick around in Ukee, including a dining scene that finally has some great options, make for the downtown visitor center.

❶ Getting There & Away

Tofino Bus (www.tofinobus.com) Buses to Port Alberni, Nanaimo, Victoria and Tofino leave from outside Murray's Grocery Store.

Denman & Hornby Islands

The main Northern Gulf Islands, Denman and Hornby share laid-back attitudes, artistic flair and some tranquil outdoor activities. You'll arrive by ferry at Denman first from Buckley Bay on Vancouver Island, then hop from Denman across to Hornby. Stop at Denman Village, near the first ferry dock, and pick up a free map and attractions guide for both islands.

Denman has three provincial parks: **Fillongley**, with easy hiking and beachcombing; **Boyle Point**, with a beautiful lighthouse walk; and **Sandy Island**.

Among Hornby's provincial parks, **Tribune Bay** features a long sandy beach with safe swimming, while **Helliwell** has notable hiking and **Ford's Cove** offers the chance to dive with sharks. Hiking and mountain-biking trails crisscross large **Mt Geoffrey Regional Park**.

Denman Hornby Canoes & Kayaks
KAYAKING

(☑250-335-0079; www.denmanpaddling.ca; 4005 East Rd, Denman Island; ⊙half-day rental/tour from $50/120) The perfect way to explore the idyllic waters around and between the two islands. You can rent kayaks or stand-up paddleboards from this family-run operator based in a water-side house on Denman's eastern shore. The outfit also hosts guided tours, aimed at paddlers of all skill levels. The staff are happy to customize tours.

⟮ Sleeping & Eating

Blue Owl
B&B $$

(☑250-335-3440; www.blueowlondenman.ca; 8850 Owl Cres, Denman Island; s/d $125/140; ☏❄) An idyllically rustic retreat for those craving an escape from city life, this woodsy little cottage is a short walk from the ocean. Loaner bikes are freely available if you fancy exploring (there's a swimmable lake nearby), but you might want to just cozy up in your room (or in the sauna!). There's a two-night minimum stay.

Sea Breeze Lodge
HOTEL $$

(☑250-335-2321; www.seabreezelodge.com; 5205 Fowler Rd, Hornby Island; adult/child $215/100) This 12-acre retreat, with 16 cottages overlooking the ocean, is a popular island fixture. Rooms are comfortable rather than palatial, though some have fireplaces and full kitchens. You can swim, kayak and fish or just flop lazily around in the oceanside hot tub. Rates are per person.

Thatch Pub & Restaurant   PUB FOOD $
(☑250-335-0136; www.thatchpub.ca; 4325 Shingle Spit Rd, Hornby Island; mains $12-18; ⊙11:30am-9pm Jul & Aug; reduced hours Sep-Jun) Hornby Island's only pub is also its most reliable place for a bite. It's open year-round, through only three nights a week in the off-season. The food's a cheerful mix of sandwiches, tacos, burgers and flatbreads with a roast-beef buffet on Fridays. Beer-wise, it serves Cumberland Brewing's Forest Fog on tap.

ⓘ Information

For more information on the islands, check out www.visitdenmanisland.ca and www.hornby island.com.

ⓘ Getting There & Away

BC Ferries (☑250-386-3431; www.bcferries. com) Hourly services travel between Denman and Buckley Bay or Hornby Island (passenger/vehicle $8.90/20.65, 10 minutes).

Comox Valley

This region of rolling mountains, alpine meadows and colorful communities, comprises the towns of Comox and Courtenay as well as the hipster-favorite village of Cumberland. It's a good outdoor-adventure base and a hotbed for mountain biking, with Mt Washington as its activity highlight.

◉ Sights & Activities

Courtenay and District Museum & Palaeontology Centre   MUSEUM
(☑250-334-0686; www.courtenaymuseum.ca; 207 4th St, Courtenay; by donation; ⊙10am-5pm Mon-Sat, noon-4pm Sun, closed Mon & Sun in winter; ⊞) With its life-size replica of an elasmosaur (a prehistoric marine reptile first discovered in the area), this excellent small museum also houses pioneer and First Nations exhibits. Pick up a dino-themed chocolate bar from the gift shop: the perfect edible souvenir.

Cumberland Museum   MUSEUM
(☑250-336-2445; www.cumberlandmuseum. ca; 2680 Dunsmuir Ave, Cumberland; adult/child $5/4; ⊙10am-5pm Jun-Aug, closed Mon Sep-May) A wonderfully quirky museum located on a row of false-fronted buildings that looks like a Dodge City movie set, with evocative exhibits on the area's pioneer past and its Japanese and Chinese communities. There's also a walk-through mine tunnel that offers a glimpse of just how tough the job would have been (the frightening iron lung exhibited upstairs does the same).

Dodge City Cycles   CYCLING
(☑250-336-2200; www.dodgecitycycles.com; 2705 Dunsmuir Ave, Cumberland; bike rentals per 2/24hr $50/120; ⊙9am-6pm Mon-Sat, 10am-2:30pm Sun) Mega-friendly and informative bike shop with rentals and insider tips on the local terrain. It sells comprehensive color-coded bike-trail maps for $6.95. From the front door, it's practically one pedal-turn to a nirvana of singletrack.

Mt Washington Alpine Resort   OUTDOORS
(☑250-338-1386; www.mountwashington.ca; winter lift ticket adult/child $95/52) The island's only major ski area is something of a local secret cherished by the type of crowd-avoiding skier who doesn't care for the busy conveyor belt of Whistler. It's less than one-third the size of Whistler, but can claim higher snowfall (up to 10m in a season) and lower prices by nearly half.

⌂ Sleeping

★ **Riding Fool Hostel**   HOSTEL $
(☑250-336-8250; www.ridingfool.com; 2705 Dunsmuir Ave, Cumberland; dm/r $32/68; @ 🖗) One of BC's finest hostels colonizes a restored Cumberland heritage building with its rustic wooden interiors, large kitchen and lounge areas and, along with small dorms, the kind of immaculate family and private rooms often found in midrange hotels. Bicycle rentals are available from the excellent Dodge City Cycles out front.

Old House Village Hotel & Spa   HOTEL $$
(☑250-703-0202; www.oldhousevillage.com; 1730 Riverside Lane, Courtenay; d $179; 🖗▨) There's nothing particularly old about this high-quality modern hotel with slick rooms, slick service and a steamy year-round outdoor pool. Raising the bar is an on-site spa, an expansive basement gym and thoughtful little extras such as free cookies in a glass jar by reception next to a fancy coffee machine. Rooms have a gleaming, straight-out-of-the-catalog look.

Eating & Drinking

Cooks Restaurant FAST FOOD $
(250-400-4222; www.cooksrestaurant.ca; 3273
3rd St, Cumberland; mains $9-12; ⊗noon-8pm
Tue-Sat) In a town that trades on its outdoor affiliations, there's always a place for
guilty-pleasure eating indulgences which, in
the case of this snack shack, means burgers.
The ultra-simple menu narrows things down
to a three-way choice between fried-chicken
sandwiches, grilled-cheese sandwiches and
the default burgers. It's all unashamedly un-
complicated and old-school with everything
made from scratch.

Waverley Hotel Pub BURGERS $$
(250-336-8322; www.waverleyhotel.ca; 2692
Dunsmuir Ave, Cumberland; mains $13-18;
⊗10:30am-10pm Sun, from 11am Mon & Tue,
11am-late Wed-Sat; 🐾) Hit this historic, ant-
ler-studded saloon for a pub-grub dinner
while you flick through a copy of glossy local
magazine *CV Collective*. There are a dozen
or so craft drafts to keep you company, while
the menu covers all tastes from avowed car-
nivores (elk burgers) to strict vegetarians
(quinoa salad). The honey teriyaki chicken
wings have a fanatical following.

Locals Restaurant CANADIAN $$$
(250-338-6493; www.localscomoxvalley.com;
1760 Riverside Lane, Courtenay; mains $30-38;
⊗11am-9pm;) 'Locally produced' is a
mantra you hear a lot on Vancouver Island
and it's taken particularly seriously at this
attractive, if pricey, wooden restaurant on
the river just south of Courtenay's town
center. A checklist on the back of the menu
highlights the nearby farms and vineyards
that have contributed to the creative dishes.

Cumberland Brewing BREWERY
(250-400-2739; www.cumberlandbrewing.com;
2732 Dunsmuir Ave, Cumberland; ⊗noon-9pm Sun,
Tue & Wed, to 10pm Thu-Sat) A microbrewery
that's mastered the neighborhood-pub vibe,
this tasty spot combines a woodsy little tasting room with a larger outdoor seating area
striped with communal tables. Dive into a
tasting flight of four beers; make sure it includes the Red Tape Pale Ale.

Information

Vancouver Island Visitors Centre (885-
400-2882; www.discovercomoxvalley.com;
3607 Small Rd, Cumberland; ⊗9am-5pm)
Super-slick visitor center with mega-
helpful staff, museum-worthy exhibits and
surgery-clean toilets. It's 2km northeast of
Cumberland, just off Hwy 19.

Getting There & Away

If you're flying in from the mainland, **Pacific
Coastal Airlines** (604-273-8666; www.paci
ficcoastal.com) services arrive at **Comox Valley
Airport** (250-890-0829; www.comoxairport.
com) from Vancouver's South Terminal ($125,
35 minutes, two to three daily).

BC Ferries (www.bcferries.com) runs services
between Comox and Powell River (passenger/
car $13.50/42.20, 1½ hours, four daily) on the
Sunshine Coast.

The area's three main communities are linked
by easy-to-explore highway routes, while **Tofino
Bus** (250-725-2871; www.tofinobus.com;
2663 Kilpatrick Ave, Courtenay) services trundle
into Courtenay at least twice a day from towns
across the island, including Port Hardy ($62, five
hours, one daily) and Nanaimo ($38, 1½ hours,
three daily).

Campbell River

250 / POP 35,400
Southerners will tell you this marks the
end of civilization on Vancouver Island, but
Campbell River is a handy drop-off point for
wilderness tourism in Strathcona Provincial
Park. While the town's core isn't the island's
prettiest, it benefits from a sheltered waterside location (Quadra Island lies across the
strait) and an impressively proactive Rotary
Club that has initiated numerous rejuvenation projects. These include a Maritime Heritage Centre and a spectacular suspension
bridge in nearby Elk Falls Provincial Park.

Campbell River used to dub itself the
'Salmon Capital of the World' and though
the industry has diminished in the 21st
century, fishing remains entrenched in the
town's heritage. You can even rent a rod and
try your luck fishing from the pier.

Sights

Museum at Campbell River MUSEUM
(250-287-3103; www.crmuseum.ca; 470 Island
Hwy; adult/child $8/5; ⊗10am-5pm mid-May–Sep,
from noon Tue-Sun Oct–mid-May) This fascinating museum is worth an hour of anyone's
time. Its diverse collection showcases indigenous masks, an 1890s pioneer cabin and
video footage of the world's largest artificial,
non-nuclear blast (an underwater mountain
in Seymour Narrows that caused dozens of
shipwrecks before it was blown apart in a
controlled explosion in 1958). In summer,

ask about the museum's daylong, history-themed boat cruises around the area.

Maritime Heritage Centre

MUSEUM

(📞250-286-3161; www.maritimeheritagecentre.ca; 621 Island Way; adult/child $7/3.50; ⊘10am-4pm Mon-Fri) A labor of love for the local Rotary Club, this small museum anchored by a restored Seine fishing boat stands as a testament to Campbell River's salmon-fishing heritage. Volunteer guides walk you around the exhibits (boat included), imparting fascinating snippets of fishing history in the process. The restored Seine vessel once featured on Canada's $5 bill.

Elk Falls Provincial Park

STATE PARK

(www.env.gov.bc.ca/bcparks/explore/parkpgs/elk_falls; Hwy 28) This small but nature-packed provincial park was given fresh impetus for visitors with the building of a new centerpiece, a 60m-long suspension bridge over the Campbell River just east of the gushing torrent of Elk Falls. The green pocket is barely 5km from the city center and well endowed with trails, a campground and a salmon hatchery. The suspension bridge was conceived and partially funded by Campbell River's proactive Rotary Club.

🛏 Sleeping & Eating

Heron's Landing Hotel

HOTEL $$

(📞250-923-2848; www.heronslandinghotel.com; 492 S Island Hwy; d from $130; @ 🛜 🐾) Superior motel-style accommodations with renovated rooms, including large loft suites ideal for families. Rates include breakfast but rooms also have their own kitchens if you want to cook up your own eggs-and-bacon special. There are also handy coin-operated

laundry facilities on-site. Some rooms have water-facing balconies.

Dick's Fish & Chips

FISH & CHIPS $$

(📞250-287-3336; www.dicksfishandchips.com; 660 Island Hwy; mains $12-18; ⊘11am-dusk) A steamy-windowed fish-and-chips shop, this restaurant a short walk from Discover Pier is often busy, so consider an off-peak visit. Alongside the usual golden-battered meals, you'll find popular salmon, oyster and halibut burgers, as well as housemade mushy peas that some Vancouver Islanders just can't live without.

FoggDukkers Coffee

COFFEE

(907 S Island Hwy; ⊘6am-7pm) A wonderfully disheveled beach shack that doubles as an ultra-friendly coffee bar. Inside there are humorous signposts, a jumble of seats and a wood-fire stove usually commandeered by a bevy of gossiping locals. On warmer evenings you can adjourn outside with your coffee and cookies to a firepit overlooking the beach.

ℹ Information

Campbell River Visitor Centre (1235 Shoppers Row; ⊘9am-5pm Tue-Sun) Staff here will fill you in on what to do in Campbell River and around the nearby region.

ℹ Getting There & Away

Campbell River Transit (📞250-287-7433; www.bctransit.com; fare $2) Operates buses throughout the area.

Pacific Coastal Airlines (📞604-273-8666; www.pacificcoastal.com) Operates flights from Vancouver YVR airport's South Terminal ($145, 45 minutes, up to five daily).

Tofino Bus (📞250-725-2871; www.tofinobus.com) All Island Express buses roll in from Port Hardy, Nanaimo and Victoria at least once daily, stopping next to the Coast Discovery Inn.

THE TYEE CLUB

Anyone can have a go at fishing in Campbell River – just rent a rod, hang it over the Discovery Pier and wait for something to bite. But to become a member of the prestigious Tyee Club, you'll need a little extra skill – or luck. Founded in 1924, the club only admits fishers who have reeled in a prized Chinook 'tyee' salmon weighing 30lb or more using light tackle from a non-motorized rowing boat.

It's not an easy proposition. An average season sees only around 40 to 50 tyees caught and, for every success, there are many disappointments. Hollywood actor and avid fisher John Wayne famously never achieved the honor despite many enthusiastic attempts. If the legendary Duke's failure doesn't deter you, the tyee season runs from mid-July to mid-September. See www.tyeeclub.org for more details.

WORTH A TRIP

QUADRA ISLAND HOP

For a day out with a difference, take your bike on the 10-minute BC Ferries (p697) trip from Campbell River to rustic **Quadra Island**. There's an extensive network of trails across the island; maps are sold in local stores. Many of the forested trails are former logging routes, and the local community has spent a lot of time building and maintaining the trails for mountain bikers of all skill levels. If you don't have your wheels, you can rent a bike on the island or in Campbell River. For more information on visiting the island, see www.quadraisland.ca.

Quadra's fascinating **Nuyumbalees Cultural Centre** (www.nuyumbalees.com; 34 Weway Rd; adult/child $10/5; ⊙10am-5pm May-Sep) illuminates the heritage and traditions of the local Kwakwaka'wakw First Nations people, showcasing carvings and artifacts and staging traditional dance performances. But if you just want to chill out with the locals, head to **Spirit Sq**, where performers entertain in summer.

If you decide to stick around for dinner, head for the waterfront pub or restaurant at the handsome **Heriot Bay Inn & Marina** (☑250-285-3322; www.heriotbayinn.com; Heriot Bay; d/cabins from $109/229; ▣⑨) where, if you have a few too many drinks, you might also choose to stay the night. The hotel has motel-style rooms and charming rustic cabins.

Strathcona Provincial Park

Centered on Mt Golden Hinde (2200m), the island's highest point, **Strathcona Provincial Park** (☑250-474-1336; www.env.gov.bc.ca/bcparks/explore/parkpgs/strath) is a magnificent pristine wilderness crisscrossed with enticing trail systems. Give yourself plenty of time and you'll soon be communing with waterfalls, alpine meadows, glacial lakes and mountain crags.

There are two main areas: Butte Lake, accessible from Campbell River, and the Forbidden Plateau, a network of trails close to the Mt Washington Ski Resort, a short drive west of Courtenay.

On arrival at the park's main entrance, get your bearings at **Strathcona Park Lodge & Outdoor Education Centre**. It's a one-stop shop for park activities, including kayaking, zip-lining, guided treks and rock climbing. All-in adventure packages are available, some aimed specifically at families. Head to the **Whale Room** or **Myrna's** for a yummy fuel-up before you get too active.

Notable park hiking trails include **Paradise Meadows Loop** (2.2km), an easy amble in a delicate wildflower and evergreen ecosystem, and **Mt Becher** (5km), with its great views over the Comox Valley and mountain-lined Strait of Georgia. Around Buttle Lake, easier walks include **Lady Falls** (900m) and the trail along **Karst Creek** (2km), which winds past sinkholes, streams and tumbling waterfalls.

The park's **lodge** (☑250-286-3122; www.strathconaparklodge.com/escape/accommodation; 41040 Gold River Hwy; r/cabins from $139/250; ▣) offers good accommodations, ranging from rooms in the main building to secluded timber-framed cottages. If you're a true back-to-nature fan, there are five campsites available in the park. Consider pitching your tent at **Buttle Lake Campground** (☑519-826-6850, 800-689-9025; www.discovercamping.ca; campsites $20; ⊙Apr-Oct); the swimming area and playground alone make it a great choice for families.

There are a couple of good dining options in the Strathcona Park Lodge just outside the park or you can cook your own grub at your campsite spot or self-catering cabin.

❶ Getting There & Away

If you're driving around the island, you'll reach the park via Hwy 28 from Campbell River. To access the Forbidden Plateau area, take the Mt Washington ski resort road just north of Courtenay (exit number 13 of Hwy 19).

Public transport is limited. A ski shuttle runs daily December to April from Comox/Courtenay to the Mt Washington ski resort. Another bus serves Victoria (www.mtwskibus.com).

North Vancouver Island

In this remote region of outstanding natural beauty, the infrastructure is best described as rudimentary. Like anything north of Campbell River, it's what islanders call the real 'north.' With its light scattering of people and wild islet-buffered coastline battling rough, temperamental seas, the area is faintly reminiscent of the Scottish Highlands, but with more trees. (Indeed several local landmarks are named after Scots – including the most northwesterly point, Cape Scott.) Trees are big business in these parts. The north island is known for its logging, indigenous culture and glaring lack of paved roads. The only notable settlements – Port Hardy and Port McNeill – are little more than large villages.

Port McNeill

Barreling down the hill almost into the harbor, Port McNeill is a useful pit stop for those heading to Port Hardy or craving a coffee before boarding the ferry to delightful (and highly recommended) Alert Bay.

Check out the **museum** (351 Shelley Cres; donations accepted; ⊙10am-5pm Jul-Sep, 1-4pm Sat & Sun Oct-Jun) for the region's backstory and don't miss the **World's Biggest Burl** as you stroll toward the entrance. A giant warty outgrowth from a huge tree, it's the best selfie opportunity in the area.

🛏 Sleeping & Eating

Black Bear Resort   MOTEL **$$**
(☑250-956-4900; www.port-mcneill-accommodation.com; 1812 Campbell Way; d/cabin incl breakfast from $162/212; @🜚🗶) More a superior motel than a resort, this hillside spot overlooks the town and is conveniently located across from the town's shops and restaurants. Standard rooms are small but clean and include microwaves and refrigerators; full-kitchen units are also available, as are a string of roadside cabins. Big bonus: there's an indoor pool, small gym and sauna.

Archipelagos Bistro   MEDITERRANEAN **$$**
(☑250-956-4553; 1703 Broughton Blvd; mains $14-37; ⊙5-8pm Sun, Mon, Wed & Thu, to 9pm Fri & Sat) Granted, it's not a bistro in the European sense, but that doesn't stop Archipelagos being a welcome addition to Port McNeill's limited dining scene. Skip the burgers and opt instead for the Mediterranean-influenced 'planks' (cheese, smoked meat or vegetable boards) and the best risottos north of Victoria.

❶ Information

Visitor Center (☑250-956-3881; www.town. portmcneill.bc.ca; 1594 Beach Dr; ⊙8:30am-5:30pm May-Sep, reduced hours in winter) Super-helpful office on the waterfront.

❶ Getting There & Away

Tofino Bus (☑250-287-7151; www.tofinobus. com) Buses stop next to the Alert Bay ferry terminal.

Alert Bay

One of the region's best days out is just a 45-minute ferry ride from Port McNeill. Located on Cormorant Island and radiating from the ferry dock along easily strolled waterfront boardwalks, Alert Bay's brightly painted shacks and houses-on-piles are highly photogenic – even the ones that are crumbling into the briny sea. Home to the Namgis First Nation, there are lots of ways to experience indigenous culture here, plus some cozy spots to eat or sleep. Expect eagles and ravens to be whirling overhead.

◉ Sights & Activities

★U'mista Cultural Centre   MUSEUM
(☑250-974-5403; www.umista.ca; 1 Front St; adult/child $12/5; ⊙9am-5pm Tue-Sat Sep-Jun, daily Jul & Aug) This must-see longhouse-like facility proudly displays dozens of culturally priceless Kwakwaka'wakw artifacts confiscated when potlatch ceremonies were outlawed in Canada, and distributed to museums and collections around the world. The cultural center has been slowly negotiating their return and the main gallery here is a wonderful manifestation of their efforts (and ongoing work). The mask collection is especially haunting. Summer programs include book readings and cedar-bark-weaving demonstrations, while the on-site gift shop brims with ethically sourced First Nations art.

Namgis Big House   PERFORMING ARTS
(cnr Wood St & Hill St; ⊙Thu-Sat Jul & Aug) This traditional clan house hosts dance performances by Alert Bay's local Namgis community in summer. Ask at the visitor center for performance times and current ticket prices. Head up Park St from the waterfront to find the house, which is next to a soccer field and behind a gigantic (if dilapidated) totem pole.

Ecological Park   PARK
A big draw on tiny Cormorant Island, this hidden nature park consists of a small marsh guarded by a clutch of starkly beautiful dead trees (most of them still standing) that eerily resemble totem poles. Nature trails wind through the sodden grounds, some of them

on boardwalks. It's a mystical spot that is faintly redolent of Florida's everglades.

Seasmoke Whale Watching   WHALE-WATCHING
(☑250-974-5225; www.seasmokewhalewatching. com; 69 Fir St; adult/child $119/99; ⊙tours mid-Jun–Sep) Killer whales, humpbacks and even minke whales can be part of the mix during these seasonal sailboat tours from Alert Bay. A relaxing way to experience the region (expect abundant marine birds en route), the 3½-hour tours also keep an eye out for eagles, seals and anything else that is interesting and moves.

🍴 Sleeping & Eating

Seine Boat Inn   INN $$
(☑877-334-9465; www.seineboatinn.com; 60 Fir St; r from $135; 🛜) Named for a local fishing style utilizing weighted nets, the Seine sits on a forest of pilings above the water in an attractive dockside building. The cabin-sized rooms with rich wood finishes and water views make you feel as if you're sleeping in a docked ship, although the potted plants and trellis-covered decks quickly remind you you're on terra firma.

Alert Bay Cabins   CABIN $$
(☑604-974-5457;   www.alertbaycabins.net; 390 Poplar Rd; cabins $145-200) A clutch of well-maintained cabins, each with kitchen or kitchenette, this is a great retreat-like option if you want to get away from it all. Cabins accommodate four to six people. Call ahead and the staff will even pick you up from the ferry (otherwise it's a 2.5km walk).

Pass 'n Thyme   BISTRO $$
(☑250-974-2670; 4 Maple Rd; mains $13-21; ⊙11am-8pm Tue-Thu & Sat, to 9pm Fri) Head up the ramp alongside and aim for a picture-window table overlooking shimmering, boat-bobbling Broughton Strait. You'll soon be diving into some excellent grilled halibut and chips alongside everyone else who was on the ferry (this is one of Alert Bay's few eateries). Burgers, wraps and made-from-scratch soups round out the menu. The deep-fried ice-cream tops it off.

ℹ️ Information

Visitor Center (☑250-974-5024; www.alert bay.ca; 118 Fir St; ⊙9am-5pm Mon-Fri Jun, Sep & Oct, daily Jul & Aug) One of the friendliest visitor centers around. Head here first when you arrive (turn right along the boardwalk from the ferry) and ask for tips on what to see and do. The staff will point you toward the island's top totem-pole spots and also give you some handy hints on where to eat.

ℹ️ Getting There & Away

BC Ferries (☑250-386-3431; www.bcferries. com) Services arrive in Alert Bay from Port McNeill (adult/vehicle $12.35/28.40, 45 minutes, up to six daily).

Telegraph Cove

Built as a one-shack telegraph station, this former fishing village and cannery has since expanded into one of the north's main visitor lures. Its pioneer-outpost feel is enhanced by the dozens of brightly painted wooden buildings perched around the marina on stilts. Be aware, although the permanent population consists of around 20 people, it can get very crowded with summer day-trippers.

🅞 Sights & Activities

Whale Interpretive Centre   MUSEUM
(☑250-928-3129;   www.killerwhalecentre.org; adult/child $5/3;   ⊙9:30am-5:30pm mid-May–Oct) This unique, beautifully rustic barn-like museum is bristling with hands-on artifacts and artfully displayed skeletons of cougars and sea otters, but the main hooks are the many whale skeletons, mostly hanging from the ceiling. Minke, grey, fin and pygmy are part the menagerie but give yourself plenty of time to peruse everything carefully.

Tide Rip Grizzly Tours   BOATING
(☑250-339-5320; www.tiderip.com; tours $320-370; ⊙May-Sep) For a magical all-day boat tour to commune with the region's Knight Inlet grizzly bears, book ahead with this popular Telegraph Cove operator. Knight Inlet is on the BC mainland as grizzlies don't traditionally live on Vancouver Island (although the occasional bear has been known to swim across).

North Island Kayaks   KAYAKING
(☑250-928-3114; www.kayakbc.ca; Lagoon Rd; 2hr trip from $65) Wildlife-watching kayak trips with guides are offered from June to September, ranging from two-hour family jaunts to eight-day excursions in search of humpback whales, sea lions and First Nations culture.

🍴 Sleeping & Eating

Telegraph Cove Resort   RESORT $$
(☑250-928-3131;   www.telegraphcoveresort.com; campsites/cabins/r   from $38/150/220)   The

dominant business in Telegraph Cove, this well-established heritage resort provides accommodations in forested tent spaces as well as a string of rustic, highly popular cabins on stilts overlooking the marina. A new 24-room lodge built from local wood to resemble the nearby Whale Interpretive Centre (p713) manages to look fabulous without spoiling the fishing-village ambience.

Killer Whale Cafe
BISTRO $$

(☑250-928-3155; www.telegraphcoveresort.com/dining; mains $14-20; ⊙11am-11pm mid-May–mid-October) Part of the sprawling Telegraph Cove Resort (p713), Killer Whale Cafe is the cove's best eatery – the salmon, mussel and prawn linguine is recommended. Aim for a window seat in this creaky-floored heritage building so you can gaze over the marina. There's usually a salmon barbecue fired up outside in the summer.

❶ Getting There & Away

Telegraph Cove is a winding but well-signposted turnoff drive from Hwy 19. There is no scheduled public transport. Car-less travelers should hop on the **Tofino Bus** (www.tofinobus.com) to Port McNeill and take a taxi from there (approximately $40 one-way). **Waivin Flags Taxi** (☑250-230-7655; www.waivinflags.com) offers a reliable service.

Port Hardy
☑250 / POP 4000

The last semblance of settlement heading north on Vancouver Island, Port Hardy is little more than a large village, but it has a strong First Nations culture and acts as a hub for those keen to explore the north's many rugged outdoor experiences. It's named somewhat bizarrely for Horatio Nelson's flag captain at the Battle of Trafalgar.

◎ Sights & Activities

Storey Beach
BEACH

If you haven't got time to hit the epic beaches of Cape Scott, decamp to this closer-to-town option mixing urban comforts (picnic tables and parking) with typical north island ruggedness (expect occasional wildlife visits in summer). It's particularly good at low tide. For a day trip, pack a picnic and walk in from Port Hardy via the **Fort Rupert Trail**.

North Island Lanes
BOWLING

(☑250-949-6307; 7210 Market St; per game incl shoes $6; ⊙1-3pm Tue, 5-9:30pm Wed-Sun, 5-10pm Fri & Sat) With old-school bowling alleys tumbling like knocked-over pins across BC, this immaculately preserved six-lane hangout is a must-see even if you don't want to play. The yellow-painted walls and retro-cool backlights make it like a living 1970s museum. But rather than being a mothballed old exhibit, it's also one of the friendliest and liveliest evening hangouts in town.

Nakwakto
Rapids Tours
BOATING

(☑250-230-3574; www.nakwaktorapidstours.com; 154 Tsulquate Reserve; adult/child $195/135; ⊙by appointment) There's more to this four-hour boat tour than experiencing the roiling waters of 'the world's fastest tidal surge.' Your First Nations guides will also provide a rich interpretive narration as well as taking you to some of the region's most remote areas. You'll feel like you're a million miles away from the big city. Check the website for trip dates.

🛏 Sleeping & Eating

North Coast Trail
Backpackers Hostel
HOSTEL $

(☑250-949-9441; www.northcoasthostel.com; 8635 Granville St; dm/r $32/69; @🛜) This well-used, well-loved hostel is a warren of small and larger dorms, overseen by friendly owners with plenty of tips for exploring the region. The hostel's hub is a large rec room and, while the kitchen is small, the adjoining mural-painted cafe can keep you well fueled. Small, simple private rooms are available and traveling families are also welcomed.

★ Kwa'lilas Hotel
HOTEL $$

(☑855-949-8525; www.kwalilashotel.ca; 9040 Granville St; r from $182; P❄🛜) A beautiful manifestation of Kwakwaka'wakw culture, this cedar-wood hotel is rich with indigenous art. The modern, uncluttered look extends to the rooms, which are clean, bright and decorated with indigenous motifs. Value-for-money extras include air-con (unusual in these parts), an on-site pub and cafe, a tribal gift shop and great service.

Cafe Guido
CAFE $

(☑250-949-9808; www.cafeguido.com; 7135 Market St; mains $6-9; ⊙7am-6pm Mon-Fri, from 8am Sat, 8am-5pm Sun; 🛜) This three-pronged business (craft shop upstairs, bookstore below decks) is Port Hardy's local hub, dispatching the best coffee north of Campbell River and serving flaky scones that you'll have to visit Tofino to emulate. Backing it all up are grilled pesto-flatbread sandwiches and service that is at once laid-back and efficient.

Sporty Bar & Grill PUB FOOD $$
(☑250-949-7811; www.sportybar.ca; 8700 Hastings St; mains $11-24; ☺11:30am-11pm; 🐾) Great service and pub grub push this regular-looking neighborhood bar to the top of the Port Hardy dine-out tree. Sporty's (as everyone calls it) offers hearty burgers, pizzas and fish-and-chips – and also a great-value Cobb salad ($14) that's well worth face-planting into. Beer-wise, eschew the Lucky Lager (the north's traditional favorite) and go for Victoria-brewed Hermann's Dark Lager.

ℹ Information

Port Hardy Visitor Information Centre
(☑250-949-7622; www.visitporthardy.com; 7250 Market St; ☺9am-6pm Jun-Sep, 8am-4pm Mon-Fri Oct-May) Lined with flyers and staffed by locals who can help you plan your visit in town and beyond, this should be your first port of call in Port Hardy. The staff are especially adept with area hiking tips.

ℹ Getting There & Away

BC Ferries (☑250-386-3431; www.bcferries.com) Ferries arrive from mainland Prince Rupert (passenger/vehicle $175/399, 16 hours) via the scenically splendid Inside Passage. The ferry terminal is 10km by road from the town center at Bear Cove.

Pacific Coastal Airlines (www.pacificcoastal.com) Services arrive from Vancouver's South Terminal ($265, 65 minutes, two to three daily).

Tofino Bus (☑250-725-2871; www.tofinobus.com) Currently the only bus service connecting Port Hardy to the rest of Vancouver Island. Office is underneath the Pier Side Landing (8600 Granville St).

Cape Scott Provincial Park

This should be your number-one destination if you really want to experience the raw, ravishing beauty of BC, especially its unkempt shorelines, breeze-licked rainforests and lonely sandy bays animated with tumbling waves and beady-eyed seabirds. The nature-hugging trailhead of this remote park on the island's crenulated northern tip is more than 550km from Victoria.

Hike the park's well-maintained 2.5km **San Josef Bay Trail** and you'll pass from the shady confines of the trees right onto one of the best beaches in BC, a windswept expanse of roiling water, forested crags and the kind of age-old caves that could easily harbor lost smugglers. You can camp right here on the beach or just admire the passing ospreys before plunging back into the trees.

From the same parking lot, a trail leads 23km to Cape Scott. You can make a day hike out of the first 3km as far as **Eric Lake**.

If you really like a challenge, consider the 59km **North Coast Trail**, which typically takes between five and eight days. The trail is basically an extension of the Cape Scott Trail, but is usually done east to west finishing at the San Josef Bay trailhead parking lot.

One of the area's shortest trails (2km), in adjoining **Raft Cove Provincial Park** (www.env.gov.bc.ca/bcparks/explore/parkpgs/raft_cove), brings you to the wide, crescent beach and the beautiful lagoons of Raft Cove. You're likely to have the entire 1.3km expanse to yourself, although the locals also like to surf here – it's their secret, so don't tell anyone.

Cove Adventures HIKING
(☑250-230-4575; www.coveadventuretours.com; 8640 Granville St; adult/child $195/145) If you don't fancy driving the rutted road to Cape Scott, join a tour with this excellent company that runs daily minibuses from Port Hardy between May and mid-October. The staff will take you along the San Josef Bay Trail and beyond and furnish you with stories of First Nations inhabitants and early Danish settlers. Expect to see wildlife.

ℹ Information

For additional information on visiting Cape Scott Provincial Park and the North Coast Trail, visit www.capescottpark.com.

ℹ Getting There & Away

It's 70km of rough gravel road between Port Hardy and Cape Scott Provincial Park. Throw in logging trucks and inclement weather and the going can be tough. Be prepared.

If you're aiming to tackle the North Coast Trail, take an early morning **Cape Scott Water Taxi** (☑250-949-6541; www.capescottwatertaxi.ca; 6555 Port Hardy Bay Rd) service to Shushartie Bay and, after your hike, hop the **North Coast Trail Shuttle** (☑250-949-6541; www.northcoasttrailshuttle.com) minibus back to Port Hardy. Book ahead for both services. The boat/bus costs $100/80 per person.

SOUTHERN GULF ISLANDS

Stressed Vancouverites love escaping into the restorative arms of these laid-back islands, strung like a shimmering necklace between the mainland and Vancouver Island. Formerly colonized by hippies and US draft dodgers, Salt Spring, Galiano, Mayne, Saturna, and North and South Pender deliver on their promise of rustic, sigh-triggering getaways. For more visitor information, see www.sgislands.com.

Salt Spring Island

POP 10,500

The busiest and most developed of the Southern Gulf Islands, Salt Spring has a reputation for palatial vacation homes, but it's also lined with artist studios and artisan food-and-drink producers who welcome visitors. Well worth a long weekend visit, the heart of the community is Ganges, home of Salt Spring's awesome summer market.

◎ Sights & Actvities

★ **Saturday Market**   MARKET
(www.saltspringmarket.com; Centennial Park, Ganges; ⊙9am-4pm Sat Apr-Oct) At the best market in British Columbia, the gigantic cornucopia of produce, edible goodies and locally made artworks lures everyone like a magnet on summer Saturdays. Arrive in the morning; it can be oppressively jam-packed at times. Alternatively, join the locals at the smaller, produce-only Tuesday market. Everything at both markets is made, baked or grown on the island.

Salt Spring Island Cheese   FARM
(☑250-653-2300; www.saltspringcheese.com; 285 Reynolds Rd; ⊙11am-5pm, to 4pm Oct-Apr; ♠) A family-friendly farmstead with a strollable garden, wandering chickens and a winery-like tasting room and shop, this quintessential Salt Spring spot produces goat- and sheep-milk chèvres, feta and Camembert styles; the soft goat-cheese rounds in several flavors (the peppercorn one packs a punch) are the farm's specialty. You can watch the handmade production through special windows but look out for the farm's gamboling goats.

Ruckle Provincial Park   PARK
(www.bcparks.ca) A pocket of ragged shoreline and gnarly arbutus forest on Salt Spring's southeastern rump contains around 16km of trails and the oldest active farm in BC. Yeo Point is an ideal pit stop.

Salt Spring Adventure Co   KAYAKING
(☑250-537-2764; www.saltspringadventures.com; 125 Rainbow Rd, Ganges; rentals/tours from $40/65; ⊙9am-6pm May-Sep) When it's time to hit the water, touch base with this well-established local operator. They can kit you out for a bobbling kayak tour around Ganges Harbour, but they also serve the SUP crowd. Bike rentals and half-day whale-watching tours ($130) are also on the menu.

🛏 Sleeping & Eating

Wisteria Guest House   B&B $$
(☑250-537-5899; www.wisteriaguesthouse.com; 268 Park Dr; d/cottage from $120/180; ♠) This home-away-from-home B&B has brightly painted guest rooms in the main building, some with shared baths. There is also a pair of private-entrance studios and a small cottage with a compact kitchen – the immaculate studio 1 is our favorite. Breakfast is served in the large communal lounge, surrounded by a rambling, flower-strewn garden. A two-night minimum stay sometimes applies; check ahead.

★ **Hastings House Hotel**   HOTEL $$$
(☑800-661-9255; www.hastingshouse.com; 160 Upper Ganges Rd, Ganges; d from $485; ♠) This smashing rustic-chic hotel with 17 rooms is just up the hill from the main Ganges action, but it feels like staying in a country cottage estate in England – indeed it was built by an Englishman in 1939 to resemble his historic Sussex home. The immaculate grounds are strewn with locally made artworks and the waterfront views are like a pastoral watercolor.

Cottages on Salt Spring Island COTTAGE $$$
(☑250-931-7258; www.cottagesonsaltspring.com; 315 Robinson Rd; cottages from $300; ₱♠♠) A small 'village' of deluxe cottages spread over lakeside grounds 3km northeast of Ganges. The semi-detached cottage units have huge modern interiors (most have three levels) with king-size beds, full kitchens and spectacular bathrooms equipped with tubs and separate showers. There are four different cottage configurations with the largest measuring 150 sq meters. All have two bedrooms.

Buzzy's Luncheonette   JEWISH $
(☑250-222-8650; 122 Fulford-Ganges Rd; sandwiches $8-12; ⊙11am-4pm Mon-Sat) It's

Southern Gulf Islands

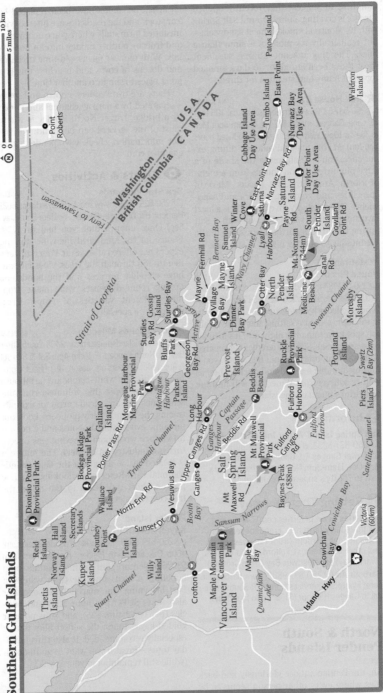

0 ... 10 km
0 ... 5 miles

Reid Island
Thetis Island
Hall Island
Norway Island
Kuper Island
Tent Island
Willy Island
Secretary Islands
Wallace Island
Southey Point
North End Rd
Vesuvius Bay
Booth Bay
Sunset Dr
Stuart Channel
Crofton
Maple Mountain Centennial Park
Vancouver Island
Quamichan Lake
Maple Bay
Sansum Narrows
Island Hwy
Cowichan Bay
Victoria (60km)

Dionisio Point Provincial Park
Bodega Ridge Provincial Park
Galiano Island
Portlier Pass Rd
Montague Harbour Marine Provincial Park
Montague Harbour
Parker Island
Trincomali Channel
Upper Ganges Rd
Ganges
Salt Spring Island
Mt Maxwell Rd
Mt Maxwell Provincial Park
Baynes Peak (588m)
Ganges Rd
Fulford Ganges Rd

Sturdies Bay Rd
Gossip Island
Sturdies Bay
Bluffs Park
Georgeson Bay Rd
Active Pass
Mayne
Fernhill Rd
Bennett Bay
Samuel Island
Mayne Island
Village
Bay
Dinner Bay Park
Prevost Island
Captain Passage
Beddis Rd
Beddis Beach
Long Harbour
Ganges Harbour

Winter Cove
Saturna Island
Payne Rd
Saturna
Lyall Harbour
Otter Bay
North Pender Island
Mt Norman (244m)
Medicine Beach
Canal Rd
South Pender Island
Gowland Point Rd
Moresby Island
Swanson Channel
Ruckle Provincial Park
Fulford Harbour
Portland Island
Swartz Bay (2km)
Piers Island
Satellite Channel
Cowichan Bay

East Point Rd
Cabbage Island Day Use Area
Tumbo Island
East Point
Narvaez Bay
Narvaez Bay Day Use Area
Taylor Point Day Use Area
Patos Island
Waldron Island

Point Roberts
Washington
British Columbia
USA
CANADA
Ferry to Tsawwassen
Strait of Georgia

Navy Channel
Fulford Harbour

tempting to suggest that recently opened Buzzy's is creating a buzz around Salt Spring with its Montreal smoked-meat sandwiches, but realistically it's more of a siren than a buzz. The tiny takeout utilizes succulent meat that's been cured for 10 days, smoked for eight hours and steamed for three.

★ **Tree House Cafe**   CANADIAN $$
(☑ 250-537-5379; www.treehousecafe.ca; 106 Purvis Lane, Ganges; mains $12-18; ⊙ 8am-4pm Mon to Tue, to 10pm Wed-Sun Jul & Aug, reduced hours Sep-Jun) At this magical outdoor dining experience, you'll be sitting in the shade of a large plum tree as you choose from a menu of North American–style pastas, Mexican specialties and gourmet burgers and sandwiches. The roasted-yam quesadilla is a local favorite, perhaps washed down with a Salt Spring Island Ales porter. There's live music Wednesday to Sunday nights in summer.

Restaurant

House Piccolo   CANADIAN $$$
(☑ 250-537-1844; www.housepiccolo.com; 108 Hereford Ave, Ganges; mains $35-42; ⊙ 5-10pm Wed-Sun) White-tablecloth dining in a beautifully intimate heritage-house setting, this is the locals' top spot for a romantic night out. It's focused on seasonal Salt Spring ingredients prepared with knowing international flourishes; you'll find memorable seafood and duck dishes, as well as soft venison. Wine fans will find the best drinks menu on the island.

ℹ Information

Salt Spring Island Visitor Information Centre
(☑ 250-537-5252; www.saltspringtourism.com; 121 Lower Ganges Rd, Ganges; ⊙ 9am-4pm May-Oct, 11am-3pm Nov-Apr) In the car park next to Thrifty's supermarket in Ganges.

ℹ Getting There & Away

BC Ferries (www.bcferries.com) Salt Spring has three ferry terminals. Frequent services arrive at Long Harbour (from Tsawwassen and other Gulf Islands), Fulford Harbour (from Swartz Bay) and Vesuvius Bay (from Crofton).

Harbour Air (☑ 250-537-9880; www.harbourair.com) Floatplane services from YVR South terminal to Ganges Harbour ($135, up to four daily).

North & South Pender Islands

POP 2250

Ah, the Penders...those gloriously laid-back isles where every other person seems to be an artist, bus stops have been replaced by 'car stops' and the roadsides are littered with unstaffed farm stalls where you can buy eggs and fruit by putting money into an honesty box. With pioneer farms, old-time orchards and dozens of coves and beaches, this is a great place to slip into another time.

There are two Penders – north and south – separated by a narrow channel and joined by a bridge. Larger North Pender is where most of the services can be found. For visitor information, check www.penderislandchamber.com.

◎ Sights & Activities

Sea Star Vineyards   WINERY
(☑ 250-629-6960; www.seastarvineyards.ca; 6621 Harbour Hill Dr, North Pender; ⊙ 11am-5pm May-Sep) Once upon a time you had to fly to France for the kind of idyllic wine-supping experience offered at Sea Star. Water glistens like tin-foil through the trees, vines cling to huge step-like terraces and the handsome tasting room dispenses wine made from nine different varieties of grape. Crisp whites are a specialty.

Pender Islands Museum   MUSEUM
(www.penderislandsmuseum.ca; 2408 South Otter Bay Rd, North Pender; ⊙ 10am-4pm Sat & Sun Jul & Aug, reduced hours off-season; Ⓟ) FREE Colonizing a historic white-clapboard farmhouse dating from 1908, this volunteer-run museum includes an eclectic array of exhibits tracing the island's early pioneers. Look out for some evocative old photos and a beautiful vintage wool loom (weaving was once a thriving industry on Pender). The museum is located inside a tract of the Gulf Islands National Park Reserve overlooking tiny Roe Islet. A short trail leads to the tip of the tree-covered islet.

Pender Island
Kayak Adventures   KAYAKING
(☑ 250-629-6939; www.kayakpenderisland.com; 4605 Oak Rd, North Pender; rentals/tours from $30/65) Venture out with a paddle (and hopefully a boat) into the calm waters of Port Browning. The marina-based operator also rents SUPs (per hour $25) and bicycles (per two hours $25), and runs popular guided kayak tours; the sunset bliss tour is especially recommended. It also runs multiday tours – great if you want to go in-depth (while still remaining in your kayak).

🛏 Sleeping & Eating

Woods on Pender CABIN **$$**

(📞250-629-3353; www.woodsonpender.com; 4709 Canal Rd, North Pender; d/cabin/caravan from $130/220/275; 🛜🐾) With lodge rooms and rustic cabins also available, the stars here are the six self-catering Airstream caravans, each with its own barbecue-equipped deck. The tree-lined site also includes hot tubs, outdoor games and a restaurant serving farm-to-table food. There's a three-night minimum stay in summer.

Poet's Cove Resort & Spa HOTEL **$$$**

(📞250-629-2100; www.poetscove.com; 9801 Spalding Rd, South Pender; d from $350; 🅿🛜🐾) This luxurious harbor-front lodge has arts-and-crafts-accented rooms plus larger cabins and villas curved around a gorgeous marina. The elegant lobby sets the tone and it's backed up by a range of other activities including swimming pools (two of them), basketball nets, a tennis court, kayak rentals, a gym and a full-treatment spa, complete with that all-important steam cave.

Jo's Place CANADIAN **$$**

(📞250-629-6033; www.josplacepender.com; 4605 Bedwell Harbour Rd, North Pender; mains $15-24; ⊗8am-2pm, plus 5-8pm Fri-Sun) It's worth making Jo's your first stop after the ferry, so good is the food, service and ambience, especially if you're in the mood for brunch when the eclectic menu parades bubble and squeak, and pear and Gorgonzola omelets.

ℹ Getting There & Away

BC Ferries (www.bcferries.com) Frequent services arrive from Tsawwassen (adult/child/car $18/9/67), Swartz Bay (adult/child/car $12/6/36) and other islands.

Seair Seaplanes (📞604-273-8900; www.seairseaplanes.com) Services arrive on North Pender from Vancouver International Airport ($125, three daily).

Galiano Island

POP 1150

With the most ecological diversity of the Southern Gulf Islands, this skinny landmass – named after a 1790s Spanish explorer – offers activities for marine enthusiasts and landlubbers alike.

The Sturdies Bay ferry end is busier than the rest of the island (with restaurants and shops to match) while the island becomes ever more forested and tranquil as you drive away from the dock.

🏃 Activities

Once you've got your bearings – that is, driven off the ferry – head for Montague Harbour Marine Provincial Park for trails to beaches, meadows and a cliff carved by glaciers. In contrast, Bodega Ridge Provincial Park is renowned for eagle and cormorant birdlife plus spectacular vistas.

You can hike up the island's highest hill, Mt Galiano, from a trailhead on the Georgeson Bay Rd.

The protected waters of Trincomali Channel and the more chaotic waters of Active Pass satisfy paddlers of all skill levels. **Galiano Kayaks** (📞250-539-2442; www.seakayak.ca; 3451 Montague Rd; per 2hr/day from $35/60, tours from $60) can help with rentals and guided tours.

🛏 Sleeping & Eating

⭐**Galiano Inn** HOTEL **$$**

(📞250-539-3388; www.galianoinn.com; 134 Madrona Dr; d from $249; 🛜🐾) The island's most deluxe accommodations occupies a small unobtrusive collection of buildings right next to the ferry dock, complete with spa, manicured lawns and the casual-gourmet **Atrevida Restaurant** (mains $22-32; ⊗6-9pm Jun-Sep, reduced hours Oct-May). All rooms face the placid water and the one-bedroom villas positively spoil you with multi-jet showers, wine coolers and outdoor patios furnished with hot tubs, barbecues and wood-burning fireplaces.

Bodega Ridge CABIN **$$$**

(📞250-539-2677; www.bodegaridge.com; 120 Manastee Rd; cabins $300; 🛜) Those craving a nature retreat will love this tranquil woodland clutch of seven cedar cabins at the quieter end of Galiano. It's a also a great base for hiking the island's tree-lined backcountry. Each cabin has a full kitchen.

Sturdies Bay Bakery CAFE **$**

(📞250-539-2004; 2450 Sturdies Bay Rd; mains $6-12; ⊗7am-3pm Mon-Thu, to 5pm Fri-Sun; 🛜) For your first taste of Galiano (both literally and figuratively), take the first left off the ferry and hit this cafe-bakery for meat pies, apple turnovers and cake-like scones washed down with island-roasted coffee. Popular with locals and visitors alike.

ℹ Information

Drop into the **visitors info booth** (www.ga-lianoisland.com; 2590 Sturdies Bay Rd; ☉10am-5pm Mon-Sat Jun-Aug, reduced hours Sep-May) before you leave the ferry area. Nearby **Galiano Island Books** (☑250-539-3340; www.galiano islandbooks.com; 76 Mardona Dr; ☉10am-5pm) also has friendly staff who can point you in the right direction.

ℹ Getting There & Away

BC Ferries (www.bcferries.com) Frequent services arrive at the Sturdies Bay dock from Tsawwassen (adult/child/car $18/8/67, 55 minutes), Swartz Bay (adult/child/car $12/6/36, 1¼ hours) and other islands.

Seair Seaplanes (p719) has flights from Vancouver International Airport arrive at Montague Harbour ($119, two daily).

Saturna Island

POP 350

Tranquil, tiny Saturna is a natural retreat remote enough to deter casual visitors. Almost half the island, laced with curving bays, stunning rock bluffs and towering arbutus trees, is part of the Gulf Islands National Park Reserve and the only crowds you'll see are feral goats that call this area home. If you've had enough of civilization, this is the place to be.

On the north side of the island, Winter Cove has a white-sand beach that's popular for swimming, boating and fishing. Great for a hike is Mt Warburton Pike (497m), where you'll spot wild goats, soaring eagles and restorative panoramic views of the surrounding islands: focus your binoculars and you might spy a whale or two sailing quietly along the coast.

If you're here on Canada Day (July 1), join the locals at the annual **Lamb Barbecue** (www.saturnalambbarbeque.com; adult/child $25/12; ☉Jul 1). It's the biggest party on the island.

Alongside campsites and B&Bs, you'll find a small selection of additional sleeping options. Aim for **Saturna Lodge** (☑250-539-2254; www.saturna.ca; 130 Payne Rd; d $159-199; ☏), a peaceful respite surrounded by a tree-fringed garden.

Saturna only has two regular places to eat: a cafe in a grocery store and a dockside pub. There's also a restaurant in the Saturna Lodge open Thursday to Saturdays for dinner; book ahead.

ℹ Information

Visit the Saturna Island Tourism Association website (www.saturnatourism.com) for more information.

ℹ Getting There & Away

BC Ferries (www.bcferries.com) Services dock at Lyall Harbour on the west of the island from Tsawwassen (adult/child/car $18/9/67), Swartz Bay (adult/child/car $12/6/36) and other islands.

Seair Seaplane (p719) services arrive at Lyall Harbour from Vancouver International Airport ($125, three daily).

Mayne Island

POP 1100

One of the smaller and quieter Gulf Islands, Mayne wasn't always so soporific. In the 1850s, gold-seeking miners made camp here on their way to the Cariboo in the BC interior. These days the biggest racket is probably the sound of a folksy guitarist strumming at the summer farmers market.

Measuring 21 sq km, Mayne is conveniently compact (you can circumnavigate it on foot in half a day) but ideal for crowd-escaping travelers who are happy with life's simple pleasures – a good bakery, a tasteful small resort and perfect kayaking waters off Bennett Bay.

For further visitor information, see www.mayneislandchamber.ca.

◉ Sights & Actvities

The heritage Agricultural Hall in Miners Bay hosts a summer Farmers Market of local crafts and produce. Elsewhere, the south shore's Dinner Bay Park has a lovely sandy beach, as well as an immaculate Japanese Garden.

Japanese Garden   GARDENS
(Dinner Point Rd, Dinner Bay Community Park) **FREE** This immaculate Japanese Garden was built by locals to commemorate the island's early-20th-century Japanese residents, most of whom were interred in BC's interior during WWII. With its pond, stone lanterns, trees and large bell, it's a meditative place even by easygoing Mayne standards.

Kayaking Gulf Islands   KAYAKING
(☑250-539-0864; www.bennettbaykayaking.com; 494 Arbutus Dr; kayak rentals/tours from $39/66; ☉Apr-Oct) This popular operator rents kayaks and SUPs, and many visitors also go for their

BRITISH COLUMBIA SATURNA ISLAND

guided tours. We recommend the Sea Lion Tour, which offers plenty of opportunities to view the lolling marine critters on rocks.

Sleeping & Eating

Mayne Island Resort HOTEL $$
(☑250-539-3122; www.mayneislandresort.com; 494 Arbutus Dr; d/villa $159/299; 🛜🖩🍽) Superbly inviting option with lots of deluxe flourishes, there are cottages and inn rooms to choose from here. You'll also find a **restaurant** (www.bennettbaybistro.com; mains $15-28; ⊙11:30am-8:30pm), on-site spa and beach proximity at this top-notch hotel.

Fairview Farm B&B B&B $$
(☑250-539-5582; www.fairviewonmayne.net; 601 Bell Bay Rd; d $135-150) A delightful escape from the city, this yellow clapboard Victorian heritage house once stood in downtown Vancouver but was floated over to Mayne Island in 1980. The two lovely guest rooms will make you feel like you're immersed in a rustic idyll, and are backed up by heaping home-cooked breakfasts. Wildlife roam the surroundings and the beach is just steps away.

Sunny Mayne Bakery Cafe CAFE $
(☑250-539-2323; www.sunnymaynebakery.com; 472 Village Bay Rd; mains $4-10; ⊙6am-6pm) All Mayne visitors should make a beeline for the island's most reliable eating joint (open year-round with earlier closing in the winter), a source of immense muffins, custom cakes, homemade pizzas and thick soups.

❶ Getting There & Away

BC Ferries (www.bcferries.com) Frequent services arrive at Village Bay from Tsawwassen (adult/child/car $18/9/67), Swartz Bay (adult/child/car $12/6/36) and other islands.

Seair Seaplanes (p719) Flights arrive from Vancouver International Airport at Miners Bay ($125, two daily).

FRASER & THOMPSON VALLEYS

Those looking for an inland escape from Vancouver can shoot east on Hwy 1 through the fertile plains of the Fraser River valley. Mostly people just whiz past this farmland, and you should too, unless you have a hankering to see a turnip in the rough. That said, Harrison Hot Springs makes a pleasant stop.

From Hope, if you're heading to Kamloops you have a choice. Take the faster, more direct route on Hwy 5, or the old Hwy 1. If you decide on the latter, the Fraser Canyon will thrill with stunning river-gorge beauty and the Thompson River looks little changed in decades.

EC Manning Provincial Park

This 708-sq-km **provincial park** (www.env. gov.bc.ca/bcparks; P), 30km southeast of Hope, is a hint of bigger – much bigger – things to come as you head east, away from the farmlands of the Lower Mainland, towards the Rocky Mountains. It packs in a lot: dry valleys, dark mountainous forests; roiling rivers and alpine meadows. The park makes a good pause along Hwy 3, but don't expect solitude, as there are scores of folk from the burgs west seeking the same thing.

◎ Sights & Activities

Manning is a four-seasons playground. Manning Park Resort has winter sports. In summer, boat rentals are available on Lightning Lake, and you can enjoy the alpine splendor on day hikes.

The following walks are easily reached from Hwy 3.

Dry Ridge Trail Crosses from the dry interior into an alpine climate; excellent views and wildflowers (3km round-trip, one hour).

Canyon Nature Trail Nice loop trail with a river crossing on a bridge (2km, 45 minutes).

Lightning Lake Loop The perfect intro: a level loop around this central lake (9km, two hours). Look for critters in the evening.

Sleeping

Lightning Lake Campground CAMPGROUND $
(☑reservations 800-689-9025; www.discover camping.ca; tent & RV sites $35; P) A popular campground that accepts advance reservations.

Manning Park Resort RESORT $$
(☑800-330-3321; www.manningpark.com; 7500 Hwy 3; dm/r from $35/120; P🖩🛜🍽) Sprawling Manning Park Resort has the only indoor accommodations in the park, with lodges and cabins, plus a variety of eating options,

Fraser & Thompson Valleys

British Columbia

Mahood Falls · Mahood Lake
100 Mile House · Clearwater
Clinton · Sun Peaks Resort
Cache Creek
Lillooet · Kamloops
Stein Valley Nlaka'pamux Heritage Park · Paul Lake Provincial Park
Whistler · Lytton
Squamish · Alexandra Bridge Provincial Park · Spuzzum · Merritt
Harrison · Osoyoos (50km)
Vancouver · Harrison Hot Springs · Hope · Princeton
Chilliwack · EC Manning Provincial Park
Abbotsford
Washington USA

and a grocery and liquor store. There are hot tubs, requisite after a day of downhill skiing and snowboarding (adult/child day pass $57/37). The resort also boasts 100km of groomed trails for cross-country skiing and snowshoeing.

❶ Information

EC Manning Provincial Park Visitor Center (☏604-668-5953; Hwy 3; ☺9am-6pm mid-Jun–mid-Sep) The park's visitor center is 30km inside the western boundary. It has detailed hiking descriptions, and a relief model of the park and nearby beaver ponds.

Fraser River Canyon

At the height of the Fraser River Gold Rush of 1858, it is said that the now-tiny town of Yale reached a population of 30,000, making it the largest city north of San Francisco and west of Chicago. It's certainly hard to believe these days as although the signs read Hwy 1, you feel like you're in a backwater of Canada as you head north from Hope to Cache Creek, 85km west of Kamloops. The first road was completed in 1926 and the present highway dates from the 1960s. The road shadows the swiftly flowing Fraser River through the eponymous canyon and, as you'd expect, white-water rafting is huge

here. Grand scenery and several good provincial parks make this a winning trip.

◉ Sights & Activities

Alexandra Bridge Provincial Park HISTORIC SITE
(www.env.gov.bc.ca/bcparks; off Hwy 1; ℗) Alexandra Bridge Provincial Park, 2km north of Spuzzum, makes for a scenic stop, where you can picnic while gazing up at the old bridge's historic 1926 span.

Fraser River Raft Expeditions RAFTING
(☑604-863-2336; www.fraserraft.com; 30950 Hwy 1, Yale; day trips from $179) This rafting outfit based in Yale covers all the main waterways in the area.

Lytton

☏250, 778 / POP 260

At the confluence of the Fraser and Thompson rivers, the area around Lytton has been inhabited by the Nlaka'pamux people for over 10,000 years. They call it Kumsheen, meaning 'river meeting.' It was originally known as 'The Forks' to Europeans, then renamed Lytton at the height of the gold rush in 1858 after Sir Edward Bulwer-Lytton, Britain's Secretary of State and the writer who coined the saying 'the pen is mightier than the sword.'

These days Lytton is a small but interesting town with a number of historic buildings and the surprising reputation as being the hottest spot in Canada during summer heat waves. The free Lytton Ferry connects First Nation communities on the west side of the river with Lytton township, while there is also pedestrian access via a walkway on the Canadian National Railway bridge crossing the river.

◉ Sights & Activities

Stein Valley Nlaka'pamux Heritage Park PARK
(www.env.gov.bc.ca/bcparks; Stein Valley Rd; ℗) This ecologically diverse park is co-managed by BC Parks and the Lytton First Nation. It offers some excellent long-distance hiking through dry valleys and snow-clad peaks amid one of the best-preserved watersheds in lower BC. The main trail head is on the west side of the Fraser River by Lytton, accessed via the free Lytton Ferry. After disembarking the ferry, follow the road to the right

for 5km to Stein Valley Rd. Vehicles are not allowed in the park.

Kumsheen Rafting Resort   RAFTING
(☑800-663-6667; www.kumsheen.com; Hwy 1, 5km east of Lytton; half-/full-day rafting from $139/189) Offers a variety of half- and full-day rafting trips on the Thompson, Fraser and Nicola rivers and has two-day packages. It also offers funky accommodations such as canvas cabins and tipis.

🛌 Sleeping & Eating

Totem Motel   MOTEL $
(☑250-455-2321; www.totemmotellytton.com; 320 Fraser St; r from $85; ⊕🅿🕾) This cute place a block back from Lytton's main street is based in a 1912 building that was originally the town's post office until the 1950s. The lodge has three self-contained units, while there are 12 cottage-style units with kitchen and bathroom. In a good spot overlooking the Fraser River.

Klowa Art Café   CAFE $
(☑778-765-4450; www.klowa.ca; 350 Main St; snacks from $3; ⊙8am-5pm Mon-Fri, from 10am Sat & Sun) Lovely family-run place on Lytton's main street combining local art, knitwear and a cafe in a cheerful atmosphere. Great coffee, cookies and baked goods.

ℹ Information

Lytton Visitor Info Centre (☑250-455-2523; www.lytton.ca; 400 Fraser St; ⊙9am-5pm mid-May–mid-Sep) All you need to know, with maps and brochures, is here at the friendly visitor center.

Kamloops

☑250,778 / POP 90,300

If you've opted to follow Hwy 1 from Vancouver east to the Rockies and Banff, Kamloops makes a useful break in the journey. Motels abound, and there's a walkable heritage center. Historically, the Shuswap First Nation found the area's many rivers and lakes useful for transportation and salmon fishing. Traders set up camp for fur hunting in 1811.

The focus of the downtown area is tree-lined Victoria St, which is a lively place on sunny days; very busy train tracks separate the wide Thompson River from downtown. Franchises and malls line the highlands along Hwy 1.

◉ Sights

Kamloops Art Gallery   GALLERY
(☑250-377-2400; www.kag.bc.ca; 465 Victoria St; adult/child $5/3; ⊙10am-5pm Mon-Sat Mon, Tue, Fri & Sat, to 8pm Wed & Thu) Suitably loft-like in feel, this gallery, which shares the civic building with the town library, has an emphasis on contemporary Western and indigenous works by regional artists.

Kamloops Museum & Archives   MUSEUM
(☑250-828-3576; www.kamloops.ca/museum; cnr Seymour St & 2nd Ave; adult/child $3/1; ⊙9:30am-4:30pm Tue-Sat; 🅿) Kamloops Museum is in a vintage building and has a fitting collection of historic photographs. Come here for the scoop on river-namesake David Thompson, and an entire floor dedicated to exhibits for kids.

Riverside Park   PARK
A short stroll from the center of town and sitting, as its name suggests, on the banks of the Thomson River, lovely Riverside Park is a source of pride for locals. Lots going on here, with walking trails, sports facilities and 'music in the park' held nightly during summer.

Kamloops Heritage Railway   HISTORIC SITE
(☑250-374-2141; www.kamrail.com; 510 Lorne St; 🅿) Across the train tracks from downtown, the Kamloops Heritage Railway runs steam-engine-powered excursions. Check the website for a variety of trips throughout the year.

🛌 Sleeping & Eating

★Plaza Hotel   HOTEL $$
(☑877-977-5292, 250-377-8075; www.theplazahotel.ca; 405 Victoria St; r from $99; 🅿⊕🅿🕾) In a town of bland modernity as far as lodgings go, the Plaza reeks of character. This 67-room, six-story classic has changed little on the outside since its opening in 1928. Rooms are nicely redone in a chic heritage style, though, and the included breakfast is excellent. Use of the nearby YMCA's pool and gym is included too.

South Thompson
Inn Guest Ranch   LODGE $$
(☑250-573-3777; www.stigr.com; 3438 Shuswap Rd E; r from $180; 🅿⊕🅿🕾🏊) Some 20km east of town off Shuswap Rd on the north side of the South Thompson River, this luxe waterfront lodge is set amid rolling grasslands. Its 58 rooms are spread between the

wood-framed main building, a small manor house and some converted stables. Plenty of things to do and the Rivershore Golf Links are right next door.

Scott's Inn
MOTEL **$$**

(☑ 250-372-8221; www.scottsinnkamloops.ca; 551 11th Ave; r from $118; P⊖🅿️✳️@🛜🏊) Unlike many of its competitors, Scott's is close to the center and very well run. The 51 rooms are nicely furnished for a motel, and extras include an indoor pool, hot tub, cafe and rooftop sundeck.

Art We Are
CAFE **$**

(☑ 250-828-7998; www.theartweare.com; 246 Victoria St; mains from $8; ⊙ 9am-9pm Mon-Sat; 🛜☑) Tea joint, local artist venue, hangout, bakery and more – this funky cafe is a great place to let some Kamloops hours slip by. The organic menu changes daily. Saturday night has live rock or blues.

★ Noble Pig
PUB FOOD **$$**

(☑ 778-471-5999; www.thenoblepig.ca; 650 Victoria St; mains from $14; ⊙ 11:30am-11pm Mon-Wed, to midnight Thu-Sat, 3-10pm Sun) This slick microbrewery has a rotating lineup of its own beers (its excellent IPA is always on tap) plus other top BC brews. The food is equally good and includes salads, burgers, pizza and various specials. The inside is warm and welcoming; in summer you can't beat the huge patio.

Brownstone Restaurant
CANADIAN **$$$**

(☑ 250-851-9939; www.brownstone-restaurant. com; 118 Victoria St; mains from $22; ⊙ 5-11pm) Top-notch dining at its own historic site, the atmospheric 1904 Canadian Bank of Commerce building, said to have once been the workplace of poet Robert Service. The menu, excellently prepared and presented with attention to detail, features innovative dishes such as bacon-wrapped elk meatloaf ($29).

❶ Information

Kamloops Visitors Center (☑ 250-374-3377, 800-662-1994; www.tourismkamloops.com; 1290 W Hwy 1, exit 368; ⊙ 8am-6pm; 🛜) Just off Hwy 1, overlooking town.

❶ Getting There & Away

VIA Rail (www.viarail.ca) serves Kamloops North Station with tri-weekly services from Vancouver (9½ hours) to Jasper, AB (another 9½ hours) and beyond.

Rider Express (www.riderexpress.ca) runs buses connecting Vancouver, Kamloops, Calgary and places in-between, with a bus in each direction daily.

Ebus (www.myebus.ca) runs buses connecting Vancouver, Kamloops and Kelowna.

Adventure Charters (www.adventurecharters. ca) has buses south to Hope and Surrey, and north to Williams Lake and Prince George.

Sun Peaks

The hills looming northeast of Kamloops are home to the **Sun Peaks Resort** (☑ 800-807-3257; www.sunpeaksresort.com; 1280 Alpine Rd; lift tickets adult/child $115/58, mountain biking $56/34). This ever-growing resort, proudly the second-largest ski area in Canada, boasts 135 ski runs (including some 8km-long powder trails), eight lifts and a pleasant base-area village. In summer, lifts provide access to more than two dozen mountain-bike trails.

Sun Peaks has many lodges, B&Bs and luxury condos.

The resort area has several eateries for all budgets.

❶ Getting There & Away

Sun Peaks is 50km northeast of Kamloops via Hwy 5. In winter there are shuttles from Kamloops ($20).

OKANAGAN VALLEY

It's hard to know which harvest is growing faster in this fertile and beautiful valley midway between Vancouver and Alberta: tourists or fruit. The 180km-long Okanagan Valley is home to orchards of peaches and apricots, and scores of excellent wineries whose vines spread across the terraced hills, soaking up some of Canada's sunniest weather.

The valley has provided a summer escape for generations of Canadians, who frolic in the string of lakes linking the Okanagan's towns.

Osoyoos, near the US border, is almost arid, but things become greener heading north. Central Kelowna is a fast-growing city that's a heady mix of lakeside beauty and fun.

In July and August the entire valley is as overburdened as a grapevine before harvest; the best times to visit are late spring and early fall, when the crowds lessen. Snowy winters also make nearby Big White resort an attraction for skiers and snowboarders.

Osoyoos

✍ 250, 778 / POP 5100

Once-modest Osoyoos has embraced an upscale future. The town takes its name from the First Nations word *soyoos,* which means 'sand bar across'; even if the translation is a bit rough, the definition is not: much of the town is indeed on a narrow spit of land that divides Osoyoos Lake. It is ringed with beaches, and the waters irrigate the lush farms, orchards and vineyards that line Hwy 97 going north out of town.

Nature's bounty aside, this is the arid end of the Okanagan Valley and locals like to say that the town marks the northern end of Mexico's Sonoran Desert; much of the town is done up in a style that loses something across borders. From the cactus-speckled sands to the town's cheesy faux-tile-and-stucco architecture, it's a big change from the BC image of pine trees and mountains found in both directions on Hwy 3.

◉ Sights & Activities

Osoyoos Lake is one of the warmest in the country. That, together with Osoyoos' sandy beaches, means great swimming, a huge relief when the summer temp hits 42°C (108°F). Many lakeside motels and campgrounds hire out kayaks, canoes and small boats.

Osoyoos Desert Centre   PARK
(✍250-495-2470; www.desert.org; 14580 146 Ave, off Hwy 97; adult/child $8/6; ⊗9:30am-4:30pm mid-May–mid-Sep, shorter hours mid-Sep–mid-May; ℗) Hear the rattle of a snake and the songs of birds at the Osoyoos Desert Centre, 3km north of town, where interpretive kiosks along raised boardwalks meander through the dry land. The nonprofit center offers 90-minute **guided tours**. Special gardens focus on delights such as delicate wildflowers.

Nk'Mip Desert & Heritage Centre   MUSEUM
(✍250-495-7901; www.nkmipdesert.com; 1000 Rancher Creek Rd; adult/child $12/8; ⊗9:30am-4:30pm May-Sep, shorter hours Oct-Apr; ℗) Part of a First Nations empire, the Nk'Mip Desert

& Heritage Centre features cultural demonstrations and tours of the arid ecology. Located off 45th St north of Hwy 3, it also has a desert **golf course**, the noted winery **Nk'Mip Cellars**, a resort and more.

Orchard Hill Estate Cidery   CIDERY
(✍778-437-2335;   www.orchardhillcidery.com; 3480 Fruitvale Way; ⊗10am-5pm) **FREE** All wined out? Stop on the side of Hwy 97 at this family roadside place for a free tasting of their excellent cider. Our pick: the Red Roof Apple Cider ($12.50 a bottle).

🛏 Sleeping & Eating

**Nk'Mip Campground
& RV Resort**   CAMPGROUND $
(✍250-495-7279; www.campingosoyoos.com; 8000 45th St; tent/RV sites from $35/48; ℗ 🐾) Choose from more than 300 sites at this year-round lakeside resort off Hwy 3. There is a good campground store.

★**Watermark Beach Resort**   RESORT $$
(✍250-495-5500;   www.watermarkbeachresort. com; 15 Park Pl; r from $150; ℗ ☺ ❋ 🐾 ☎ ☲) A top spot right on the water in Osoyoos, perfect for couples and families. Facilities include a heated outdoor swimming pool, hot tubs, spa, restaurants and access to a gorgeous beach right out front. It also has two-bedroom townhouses.

Walnut Beach Resort   RESORT $$
(✍250-495-5400; www.walnutbeachresort.com; 4200 Lakeshore Dr; r from $150; ℗ ☺ ❋ 🐾 ☲) This large resort is an upscale addition to the east shore of the southern half of the lake. There are 112 large suites (some with two bedrooms) and a vast terrace surrounding a pool.

Jojo's Café   CAFE $
(✍250-495-6652; www.jojoscafe.ca; 8316 Main St; pastries from $1.50; ⊗7am-4pm) Definitely the most happening spot in the morning in Osoyoos. Battle the locals for an inside table or grab a seat out on the sidewalk after ordering a set breakfast (from $5.95), or just settle for a muffin and coffee. Jojo's exudes a cool vibe and everyone knows it.

❶ Information

Osoyoos Visitors Center (✍250-495-5070; www.destinationosoyoos.com; cnr Hwys 3 & 97; ⊗9am-6pm; ☎) This large center has info, maps and books.

OKANAGAN VALLEY WINERIES

The abundance of sunshine, fertile soil and cool winters have allowed the local wine industry to thrive. Kelowna and the region in the valley's north are known for whites, such as Pinot Grigio. South, near Penticton and Oliver, reds are the stars, especially ever-popular Merlot.

A majority of the more than 120 wineries are close to Hwy 97, which makes tasting a breeze. Most offer tours and all will gladly sell you a bottle or 20; in fact, many of the best wines are only sold at the cellar door. Some wineries feature excellent cafes and bistros that offer fine views and complex regional fare to complement what's in the glass.

Festivals

Okanagan seasonal **wine festivals** (www.thewinefestivals.com) are major events, especially the one in fall.

The usual dates are fall (early October), winter (mid-January), spring (early May) and summer (early August). Events take place at wineries across the valley.

Information

Good sources of information on Okanagan Valley wines include the **BC Wine Information Centre** in Penticton's visitor center (p731) and the Okanagan Wine & Orchard Museum (p733) in Kelowna. *John Schreiner's Okanagan Wine Tour Guide* is an authoritative guidebook.

Tours

Numerous companies allow you to do the sipping while they do the driving.

Club Wine Tours (☎250-762-9951; www.clubwinetours.com; 1152 Sunset Dr, Kelowna; tours from $75) The 'signature' tour includes four wineries and lunch in a vineyard.

Distinctly Kelowna Tours (p733) Offers winery tours by valley region; many include stops for lunch.

Visiting the Wineries

Wine tastings at those wineries open to visitors vary greatly. Some places have just a couple of wines on offer; others offer dozens of vintages. Some tasting rooms are glorified sales areas; others have magnificent views of the vineyards, valley and lakes. Some charge; others are free.

Among the dozens of options, the following (listed north to south) are recommended. Summerhill Pyramid and Cedar Creek Estate are south of Kelowna along the lake's east shore. The rest of the wineries can be reached via Hwy 97.

Sandhill Wines (☎250-979-4211; www.sandhillwines.ca; 1125 Richter St; ⊙10am-6pm; P) Formerly known as Calona Vineyards, Sandhill Wines was the Okanagan's first winery when it kicked off production in 1932. Its architecturally striking tasting room is an atmospheric spot to try its ever-popular, melon-note Pinot Blanc.

Summerhill Pyramid Winery (☎250-764-8000; www.summerhill.bc.ca; 4870 Chute Lake Rd; ⊙9am-6pm; P) In the hills along the lake's eastern shore is one of the Okanagan's most colorful wineries. Summerhill Pyramid Winery combines a traditional tasting room with a huge pyramid where every Summerhill wine is aged in barrels. The winery's **Summerhill Pyramid Bistro** (mains from $15; ⊙11am-11pm) 🍷 offers locally sourced dishes; the wines are organic.

CedarCreek Estate Winery (☎778-738-1020; www.cedarcreek.bc.ca; 5445 Lakeshore Rd; ⊙10am-7pm Jul & Aug, 11am-5pm Sep-Jun; P) Known for excellent tours, its Riesling and its Ehrenfelser, a refreshing fruity white wine. Its **Home Block at CedarCreek** (☎250-980-

4663; mains from $24; ◎10am-9pm Jun–mid-Sep) has the kind of view that makes you want to eat here twice.

Quails' Gate Winery (☑250-769-4451; www.quailsgate.com; 3303 Boucherie Rd, West Kelowna; ◎10am-8pm; P) A small winery with a huge reputation; it's known for its Pinot Noir, Chardonnay and Chenin Blanc. The **Old Vines Restaurant** (☑250-769-2500; mains from $23; ◎11am-10pm) is among the best.

Mission Hill Family Estate (☑250-768-6400; www.missionhillwinery.com; 1730 Mission Hill Rd, West Kelowna; ◎10am-7pm; P) As if it were a Tuscan hill town, this winery's architecture wows. Go for a taste of one of the blended reds (try the Bordeaux) or the excellent Syrah. Terrace (p732) is one of the valley's best restaurants and sources fine foods locally; book ahead.

Haywire Winery at Okanagan Crush Pad (☑250-494-4445; www.okanagancrushpad. com; 16576 Fosbery Rd, Summerland; ◎11am-5pm; P) Ages many of its wines in concrete tanks, reviving a centuries-old practice that largely died out when the industry shifted to stainless steel. Tastings range across more than 20 varieties from the multiple labels produced here.

Hester Creek (☑250-498-4435; www.hestercreek.com; 877 Road 8; ◎10am-7pm; P) Has a sweeping location and a great tasting room and is known for its reds, especially its richly flavored Cabernet Franc. Terrafina at Hester Creek by RauDZ (p729) has a Med accent.

Inniskillin (☑866-455-0559; www.inniskillin.com; 7857 Tucelnuit Dr; ◎10am-5pm; P) BC's first producer of Zinfandel is also home to the elixirs known as ice wines, which are harvested when the grapes are frozen on the vine; go for the golden-hued Riesling.

Road 13 (☑250-498-8330; www.road13vineyards.com; 799 Ponderosa Rd; ◎10am-5:30pm; P) Its very drinkable reds (Pinot Noir) and whites (Chenin Blanc) win plaudits. The no-frills vibe extends to its picnic tables with gorgeous views and the motto 'It's all about dirt.' The attractive lounge has views of the grapes.

Rust Wine Co (☑250-498-3276; www.rustwine.com; 4444 Golden Mile Dr; ◎10:30am-7pm; P) Recently rebranded, these guys produce excellent whites, reds and rosé, though it's best known for the Zinfandel. Breathtaking views in the valley overlook the Black Sage Bench to the east and Osoyoos to the south.

Black Hills Estate (☑250-498-0666; www.blackhillswinery.com; 4190 Black Sage Rd; guided tastings from $10; ◎10am-6pm; P) The tasting room here is an arresting vision of glass and metal, with deeply shaded patios for sunset tippling. Besides vintages such as Viognier, there are many blends, including Alibi, a blend of Sauvignon Blanc and Semillon.

Church & State Wines (☑250-498-2700; www.churchandstatewines.com; 4516 Ryegrass Rd; ◎11am-6pm; P) Making a big splash at its Coyote Bowl vineyards, especially with its full-bodied, luscious Syrahs. Also home to the Lost Inhibitions label, which produces popularly priced wines with names such as Chill the F*uck Out and I Freakin' Love You.

Burrowing Owl Estate Winery (☑250-498-0620; www.burrowingowlwine.ca; 500 Burrowing Owl Pl; ◎10am-6pm mid-Fed–mid-Dec; P) ⬬ Wine with an eco-accent that includes organic farm techniques; try the Syrah. Other award-winners include the Cabernet Franc and Meritage. This Golden Mile landmark includes a hotel and the excellent **Sonora Room** (mains from $24; ◎11:30am-9pm) restaurant.

LaStella Winery (☑250-495-8180; www.lastella.ca; 8123 148 Ave; ◎11am-5pm; P) A beautiful vision of Italy rises up near Osoyoos Lake. Terra-cotta roof tiles and floors and granite touches combine for one of the valley's most beautiful wineries. The Cabernet Sauvignon–based Maestoso is highly regarded.

Okanagan Valley

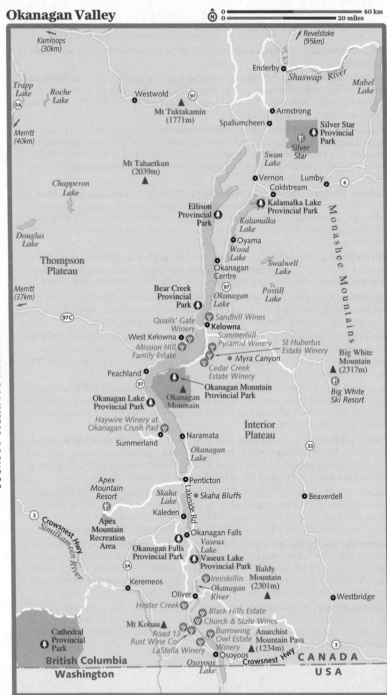

N

0 — 40 km
0 — 20 miles

Kamloops
(30km)

Revelstoke
(95km)

Enderby

Shuswap River

Mabel
Lake

Trapp
Lake

Roche
Lake

Westwold

97

Mt Tuktakamin
(1771m)

Spallumcheen

Armstrong

Silver Star
Provincial
Park

Silver
Star

Merritt
(40km)

5A

Swan
Lake

Mt Tahaetkun
(2039m)

Vernon

Coldstream

Lumby

6

Chapperon
Lake

Ellison
Provincial
Park

Kalamalka Lake
Provincial Park

Kalamalka
Lake

Douglas
Lake

Thompson
Plateau

Oyama

Wood
Lake

Swalwell
Lake

Merritt
(37km)

97C

Okanagan
Centre

97

Bear Creek
Provincial
Park

Okanagan
Lake

Postill
Lake

Monashee Mountains

Quails' Gate
Winery

Sandhill Wines

Kelowna

West Kelowna

Summerhill
Pyramid Winery

St Hubertus
Estate Winery

Big White
Mountain
(2317m)

Mission Hill
Family Estate

Myra Canyon

Peachland

97

Cedar Creek
Estate Winery

Okanagan Mountain
Provincial Park

Big White
Ski Resort

Okanagan Lake
Provincial Park

Okanagan
Mountain

Haywire Winery at
Okanagan Crush Pad

Naramata

Interior
Plateau

Summerland

Okanagan
Lake

33

Apex
Mountain
Resort

Penticton

Skaha
Lake

Skaha Bluffs

Beaverdell

3

Crowsnest Hwy

Simikameen River

Apex
Mountain
Recreation
Area

Kaleden

Lakeside Rd

Okanagan Falls
Provincial Park

3A

Okanagan Falls

Vaseux
Lake

Vaseux Lake
Provincial Park

Baldy
Mountain
(2301m)

Westbridge

Keremeos

Inniskillin

Okanagan
River

Oliver

Hester Creek

Black Hills Estate

Church & State Wines

Mt Kobau

Road 13

Rust Wine Co

Burrowing
Owl Estate
Winery

Anarchist
Mountain Pass
(1234m)

3

LaStella Winery

Osoyoos

Cathedral
Provincial
Park

British Columbia

Washington

Osoyoos
Lake

Crowsnest Hwy

CANADA

USA

Oliver

📱 250, 778 / POP 4920

Oliver has emerged as a hub of excellent wineries and other natural bounty and is, without doubt, a very cheeky little town. The Tourism Association has managed to trademark the slogan 'Wine Capital of Canada', much to the chagrin of its rivals, and you'll find signboards claiming such at the entry to town. They've also laid claim to the website www.winecapitalofcanada. com and it will be interesting to see what comes next.

Over the 20km drive between Oliver and Osoyoos, Hwy 97 plunges through orchard after orchard laden with lush fruits, earning it the moniker 'The Golden Mile.' Roadside stands display the ripe bounty and many places will let you pick your own. This little town enjoys life with a twinkle in its eye.

🛏 Sleeping & Eating

Mount View Motel   MOTEL $
(📱 250-498-3446; www.mountviewmotel.com; 5856 Main St; r from $80; 🅿😊❄🛜) Close to the center of town, seven units sunbathe around a flower-bedecked vintage motor court. All have kitchens – and corkscrews. The decor features wood floors and a contemporary style.

⭐**Burrowing Owl**
Guest House   BOUTIQUE HOTEL $$$
(📱 250-498-0620; www.burrowingowlwine.ca; 500 Burrowing Owl Pl, off Black Sage Rd; r from $170; 🅿😊❄🛜🏊) One of the Okanagan's best wineries (p727) has 10 rooms with patios facing southwest over the vineyards. There's a big pool, a hot tub, king-size beds and corporate Mission-style decor. The Sonora Room (p727) is noted for its fusion cuisine. It's 13km south of Oliver, off Hwy 97.

Villa at Hester Creek   INN $$$
(📱 250-498-4435; www.hestercreek.com/visit/villa; 877 Road 8; r from $200; 🅿😊❄🛜) One of the valley's top wineries, Hester Creek (p727) has six suites in a Mediterranean-style villa with a sweeping view over the vineyards. The trappings are plush, with fireplaces, soaking tubs and more.

On-site Terrafina serves excellent Tuscan-accented fare using foods from the region.

⭐**Terrafina at Hester**
Creek by RauDZ   ITALIAN $$$
(📱 250-498-2229; www.terrafinabyraudz.com; 887 Road 8; mains from $23; ⏰11:30am-9pm) This intimate Tuscan-style restaurant at Hester Creek Estate Winery (p727) is run by the creative minds behind RauDZ Regional Table (p735) in Kelowna. Its outdoor terrace is one of the valley's finest.

ℹ Information

Oliver Visitor Center (📱778-439-2363; www. winecapitalofcanada.com; 6431 Station St; ⏰10am-4pm) Located in the old train station near the center of town. It has affable staff, excellent regional info, and walking and biking maps.

Vaseux Lake

About 10km north of Oliver on Hwy 97, nature reasserts itself at this lake – an azure gem, framed by sheer granite cliffs.

If you're not in a hurry, the small roads on the east side of Skaha Lake between Okanagan Falls and Penticton are much more interesting for their wineries and views than Hwy 97.

Vaseux Lake Provincial Park   PARK
(www.env.gov.bc.ca/bcparks; Hwy 97) This lakeside park has a 300m boardwalk for viewing oodles of birds, bighorn sheep, mountain goats and some of the 14 species of bat. You can also hike to the **Bighorn National Wildlife Area** and the **Vaseux Lake National Migratory Bird Sanctuary**, which has more than 160 bird species.

Penticton

📱 250, 778 / POP 37,035

Penticton combines the idle pleasures of a beach resort with its own edgy vibe. It's long been a final stop in life for Canadian retirees, which adds a certain spin to its Salish-derived name Pen-Tak-Tin, meaning 'place to stay forever.' The town today is growing fast, along with the rest of the Okanagan Valley.

Penticton makes a good base for your valley pleasures. There are plenty of activities and diversions to fill your days, even if you don't travel further afield.

Ditch Hwy 97, which runs west of the center, for Main St and the attractively walkable downtown area, which extends about

10 blocks southward from the picture-perfect lakefront; avert your eyes from the long stretch of strip malls and high-rise condos further south.

◉ Sights

Okanagan Beach boasts about 1.3km of sand, with average summer water temperatures of about 22°C (72°F). If things are jammed, quieter shores are often found at 1.5km-long **Skaha Beach** on Skaha Lake, south of the center.

★ SS Sicamous
Heritage Park   HISTORIC SITE
(☑ 250-492-0403; www.sssicamous.ca; 1099 Lakeshore Dr W; adult/child $6/3; ⊙ 10am-5:30pm Fri-Mon) Back when the best way to get around inland BC was by boat, the SS *Sicamous* hauled passengers and freight on Okanagan Lake from 1914 to 1936. Now the boat has been restored and permanently moored; a tour is an evocative self-guided ramble.

Skaha Bluffs
Provincial Park   PARK
(www.env.gov.bc.ca/bcparks; Smythe Dr; ⊙ Mar-Nov) Propelled by the dry weather and compact gneiss rock, climbers from all over the world come to this park to enjoy climbing on more than 400 bolted routes. For comprehensive info on the bluffs, which are off Lakeside Rd on the east side of Skaha Lake, visit www.offtracktravel.ca/climbing-skaha-bluffs-guide.

A climbing area trails map is on the BC Parks website.

Penticton Museum   MUSEUM
(☑ 250-490-2451; www.pentictonmuseum.com; 785 Main St; by donation; ⊙ 10am-5pm Tue-Sat) Inside the library, the Penticton Museum has delightfully eclectic displays, including the de rigueur natural-history exhibit with stuffed animals and birds, and everything

you'd want to know about the juicy fruits of the **Peach Festival** (www.peachfest.com; ⊙ early Aug).

🏃 Activities

★ Coyote Cruises   WATER SPORTS
(☑ 250-492-2115; www.coyotecruises.ca; 215 Riverside Dr; rentals & shuttle $18; ⊙ 11am-4pm mid-Jun–Sep) Coyote Cruises rents out inner-tubes (single, double, quad or for a party of 10) that you can float in 7km down the Okanagan River Channel to Skaha Lake. It then buses you back to the start near Okanagan Lake.

If you have your own floatable, it's $5 for the bus ride.

Apex Mountain Resort   SKIING
(☑ 250-292-8222, condition report 250-487-4848; www.apexresort.com; off Green Mountain Rd; lift tickets adult/child $87/54) One of Canada's best small ski resorts is 37km west of Penticton. It has more than 68 downhill runs for all ability levels, but the mountain is known for its plethora of double-black-diamond and technical runs; the drop is more than 600m. It is usually quieter than nearby **Big White** (☑ 250-765-8888, snow report 250-765-7669; www.bigwhite.com; off Hwy 33; 1-day lift pass adult/child $105/64).

Freedom the Bike Shop   CYCLING
(☑ 250-493-0686; www.freedombikeshop.com; 533 Main St; bicycle rental per day from $45; ⊙ 9:30am-5:30pm Mon-Sat) Rents bikes and offers a wealth of information. Can arrange transport to/from the Kettle Valley Rail Trail (p736).

🛏 Sleeping

Penticton Lakeside Resort   HOTEL $$
(☑ 250-493-8221; www.pentictonlakesideresort.com; 21 Lakeshore Dr W; r from $150; 🅿 ➷ ❋ 🛜 ⛄) Plush Penticton Lakeside Resort & Conference Centre, lakefront and at the foot of Main St, may be described by some as a

---

ON YER BIKE

Long dry days and rolling hills add up to perfect conditions for mountain biking. Get to popular rides by heading east out of town, toward Naramata. Follow signs to the city dump and **Campbell's Mountain**, where you'll find a singletrack and dual-slalom course, both of which aren't too technical. Once you get there, the riding is mostly on the right-hand side, but once you pass the cattle guard, it opens up and you can ride anywhere.

Cyclists can try the route through Naramata and onto the Kettle Valley Rail Trail (p736). Other good options include the small, winery-lined roads south of town and east of Skaha Lake.

six-floor monstrosity. Indoor pool, hot tub, restaurants, panoramic views and, undoubtedly, the top location in town – though it might just feel a tad sterile.

Bowmont Motel
MOTEL **$$**

(☑ 250-490-0231; www.bowmontmotel.com; 80 Riverside Dr; r from $87; P⊖❄🐕🏊) Look past the dubious faux-Southwestern facade and you'll find an excellent indie motel near the lake. The 45 rooms are immaculate and all share terraces or balconies. Each has a full kitchen, there is a gas barbecue near the pool and off-season room rates plummet.

Crooked Tree Guest Suites
B&B **$$**

(☑ 250-490-8022; www.crooked-tree.com; 1278 Spiller Rd; ste from $195; P⊖❄🏊) Okanagan Lake glistens below from this mountainside retreat, 9km east of downtown Penticton. The three large apartments have multiple decks amid this woodsy aerie and are well stocked with luxuries. Minimum stay is two nights.

🍴 Eating & Drinking

★ Penticton Farmers Market
MARKET **$**

(☑ 250-493-8540; www.pentictonfarmersmarket.org; 100 Main St; ⊙8:30am-1pm Sat May-Oct) Penticton definitely has its share of good eats. The farmers market, based at Gyro Park on Main St, has large numbers of local organic producers.

Bench Market
CAFE **$**

(☑ 250-492-2222; www.thebenchmarket.com; 368 Vancouver Ave; meals from $9; ⊙7am-4pm Mon-Fri, from 8am Sat & Sun) Always buzzing – and not just because of the excellent organic coffee – this neighborhood fave is consistently busy. The patio is where locals meet and exchange gossip. Egg dishes star at breakfast; lunch is about sandwiches and salads. Great baked goods and other deli items are sold through the day.

Il Vecchio Deli
DELI **$**

(☑ 250-492-7610; 317 Robinson St; sandwiches from $6; ⊙9am-5pm Mon-Sat) The smell that greets you as you enter confirms your choice. The best lunch sandwiches in town can be consumed at a couple of tables in this atmospheric deli, but will taste better on a picnic. Choices are many; we like the sandwich with garlic salami and marinated eggplant.

ℹ FRUIT-A-PALOOZA

Roadside stands and farms where you can buy and even pick your own fruit line Hwy 97 between Osoyoos and Penticton. Major Okanagan Valley crops and their harvest times are as follows.

Cherries Mid-June to late July

Apricots Mid-July to mid-August

Peaches Mid-July to mid-September

Pears Mid-August to late September

Apples Early September to late October

Table grapes Early September to late October

★ Dream Cafe
FUSION **$$**

(☑ 250-490-9012; www.thedreamcafe.ca; 67 Front St; mains from $12; ⊙6-11pm daily, 11am-2pm Sat & Sun; 🎵) The heady aroma of spices hits as you enter this pillow-bedecked, upscale-yet-funky bistro. Asian and Indian flavors mix on the menu, which has numerous veggie options. There's live acoustic music by touring pros on many nights; tables outside hum all summer long.

★ Bad Tattoo Brewing
MICROBREWERY

(☑ 250-493-8686; www.facebook.com/badtattoo brewing; 169 Estabrook Ave; ⊙11am-10pm Sun-Thu, to 11pm Fri & Sat) There's a 'born to be bad' attitude going on here along with some great beer. Get a flight of five brews ($10) then go for what you like. Locals are refilling growlers, while the pizzas are good if you're here for something solid. The Los Muertos Cerveza Negra, a dark lager brew, gets raves reviews.

ℹ Information

Penticton & Wine Country Visitor Centre
(☑ 250-276-2170; www.visitpenticton.com; 888 Westminster Ave W; ⊙9am-5pm; 🎵) Has a full range of info on area activities and wine.

ℹ Getting There & Away

Penticton Regional Airport (CYYF) is 3km south of town and has daily flights to Vancouver and Calgary with Air Canada (www.aircanada.com) and Westjet (www.westjet.com).

Penticton is on Hwy 97, 63km south of Kelowna and 62km north of Osoyoos. You'll want your own wheels.

Penticton to Kelowna

Lakeside resort town **Summerland**, 18km north of Penticton on Hwy 97, features some fine 19th-century heritage buildings on the hillside above the ever-widening and busy highway. There are some good wineries here, too.

Hugging the lake below Hwy 97, some 25km south of Kelowna, the little town of **Peachland** is good for a quick, breezy stroll along the water amid parks and interesting shops. Try not to lose your lunch on Canada's highest zip line.

Between Peachland and Kelowna, urban sprawl becomes unavoidable, especially through the billboard-lined nightmare of **West Kelowna** (aka Westbank).

Activities

Kettle Valley Steam Railway　　RAIL
(☑877-494-8424; www.kettlevalleyrail.org; 18404 Bathville Rd, Summerland; adult/child $25/16; ☺May-Oct) The Kettle Valley Steam Railway is an operating, 16km remnant of the famous tracks. Ride behind an old steam locomotive in open-air cars and enjoy orchard views.

Zipzone Peachland　　ADVENTURE SPORTS
(☑855-947-9663; www.zipzone.ca; 5875 Brenda Mines Rd, Peachland; adult/child from $114/84; ☺9:30am-6pm May-Oct) Zoom along Canada's highest freestyle zip lines here, where you can sail high over Deep Creek Canyon.

Sleeping & Eating

A View of the Lake　　B&B $$
(☑250-769-7854; www.aviewofthelake.com; 1877 Horizon Dr, West Kelowna; r from $130; P❧❄🛜) Set on the west side of Okanagan Lake, this B&B offers privacy and magnificent views. Book the Grandview Suite for a lake vista that extends even to the air-jet bathtub. Rooms are peaceful, beds are comfy and the three-course breakfast on the deck is gourmet.

★**Peach Pitt**　　MARKET $
(☑778-516-7003; cnr Hwy 97 & Jones Flat Rd, Summerland; treats from $3; ☺9am-6pm May-Oct) Amid oodles of competition, this roadside stand on Hwy 97 on the north side of Summerland stands out. The owners have an orchard right behind the market. They also have deals with some of the valley's best producers (the $3 tub of raspberries will have you checking local real-estate

prices) and they create wonderful baked goods.

★**Terrace Restaurant**　　MODERN AMERICAN $$$
(☑250-768-6467; www.missionhillwinery.com; 1730 Mission Hill Rd, Mission Hill Family Estate, West Kelowna; mains from $25; ☺noon-8:30pm Jun-Oct) A suitably impressive restaurant to go with a very impressive winery. Terrace (yes, there are views) exemplifies farm-to-table with its fresh and inventive menu.

Kelowna

☑250, 778 / POP 127,380

A kayaker paddles past scores of new tract houses on a hillside: it's an iconic image for ever-growing Kelowna, the unofficial 'capital' of the Okanagan and the sprawling center of all that's good and not-so-good with the region.

Entering from the north, the ever-lengthening urban sprawl of tree-lined Hwy 97/ Harvey Ave seems to go on forever. Once past the ceaseless waves of chains and strip malls, the downtown is a welcome respite. Museums, culture, nightlife and the parklined lakefront feature. You can spend a day strolling here. About 2km south of the center is **Pandosy Village**, a charming and upscale lakeside enclave.

Sights

The focal point of the city's shoreline, the immaculate downtown **Kelowna City Park** (waterfront) is home to manicured gardens, water features and **Hot Sands Beach** (Waterfront Park), where the water is a respite from the hot summer air.

Restaurants and pubs take advantage of the uninterrupted views of the lake and forested shore opposite. North of the marina, **Waterfront Park** (lakefront) has a variegated shoreline and a popular open-air stage.

Among the many outdoor statues near the lake, look for the one of the **Ogopogo** (Kelowna City Park), the lake's mythical – and hokey – monster. More prosaic is **Bear** (Water St), a huge, lacy confection in metal. The visitor center has a lavish public art guide.

Be sure to pick up the **Cultural District** walking-tour brochures at the visitor center (p736) and visit www.kelownamuseums.ca for exhibitions info.

BC Tree Fruits Cidery & Tasting Bar　　WINERY
(☑250-979-2629; www.bctreefruitscider.com; 880 Vaughan Ave; tasting $5; ☺11am-5pm)

The cidery division of BC Tree Fruits, a 400-family BC cooperative, is booming. Head to the Cidery & Tasting Bar, next to its fruit and vegetable **market** (☑250-763-8872; www.bctree.com; 826 Vaughan Ave; prices by the kg; ☺9am-5pm Mon-Sat) on Vaughan St to try innovative ciders such as Apple & Hops, Pears & Peaches and Rosé. Locals bring refillable growlers (glass jars) and buy by the liter, though visitors can purchase by the can.

Carmelis Goat
Cheese Artisan   FARM
(☑250-764-9033; www.carmelisgoatcheese.com; 170 Timberline Rd; ☺10am-6pm May-Sep, 11am-5pm Mar, Apr & Oct; [P][♿]) **FREE** At Carmelis you can sample soft-ripened cheeses with names such as Moonlight and Heavenly, or the hard-ripened Smoked Carmel or Goatgonzola. For those with a milder palate, there are supersoft unripened versions, such as feta and yogurt cheese. And then there's the delectable goat's-milk gelato!

Okanagan Wine &
Orchard Museum   MUSEUM
(☑778-478-0325; www.kelownamuseums.ca; 1304 Ellis St; by donation; ☺10am-5pm Mon-Sat, 11am-4pm Sun) Located in the historic Laurel Packing House, the Okanagan Wine & Orchard Museum recounts the Okanagan Valley from its ranchland past, grazed by cows, to its present, grazed by tourists. The old fruit-packing-crate labels are works of art.

Okanagan Lavender Farm   FARM
(☑250-764-7795; www.okanaganlavender.com; 4380 Takla Rd; tours $5-15; ☺10am-5pm, tours 10:15am, 11:30am & 2:30pm Jun-Aug; [P][♿]) Visiting Okanagan Lavender Farm is a heady experience. Rows and rows of more than 60 types of lavender waft in the breeze against a backdrop of the Okanagan Lake. Enjoy a guided or self-guided tour of the aromatic acres, and pop into the shop for everything from bath products to lavender lemonade.

The farm is 9km south of the center.

🏃 Activities

The balmy weather makes Kelowna ideal for fresh-air fun, whether on the lake or in the surrounding hills.

You'll find great **hiking** and **mountain-biking** opportunities all around town. The 17km **Mission Creek Greenway** is a meandering, wooded path following the creek along the south edge of town. The western half is a wide and easy expanse, but to the east the route becomes sinuous as it climbs into the hills.

Knox Mountain, which sits at the northern end of the city, is another good place to hike or ride. Populated with bobcats and snakes, the 235-hectare park has well-maintained trails and rewards visitors with excellent views from the top.

Cycling on the Kettle Valley Rail Trail (p736) and amid the vineyards is hugely popular.

Okanagan Rent A Boat   BOATING
(☑250-862-2469; www.lakefrontsports.com; 1350b Water St, Delta Grand Okanagan Resort; kayak rental per 2hr $40; ☺May-Sep) Rent speedboats (starting at $259 per hour), Jet Skis, kayaks, wakeboards, pedal boats and much more from this seasonal booth on the lakefront.

Myra Canyon Bike Rentals   CYCLING
(☑250-878-8763; www.myracanyonrental.com; Myra Canyon; bicycle rental per half-day adult/child from $39/30, bike tours from $70; ☺9am-5:30pm mid-May–mid-Oct) Offers bike rentals and tours in the Myra Canyon.

Distinctly Kelowna Tours   WINE
(☑250-979-1211; www.distinctlykelownawinetours. ca; 875 Wardlaw Ave, Kelowna; tours from $100) Offers winery tours by valley region; many include stops for lunch.

DON'T MISS

SCENIC DRIVE TO NARAMATA

On all but the busiest summer weekends, you can escape many of Penticton's mobs by taking the road less traveled, 18km north from town along the east shore of Okanagan Lake. The route through the **Naramata Bench** (www.naramatabench.com) is lined with countless wineries, as well as farms producing organic lavender and the like. This is a good route for cycling and at several points you can access the Kettle Valley Rail Trail (p736). There are numerous places to hike, picnic, bird-watch or do whatever else occurs to you in beautiful and often secluded surroundings. Naramata itself is a cute little village.

Kelowna

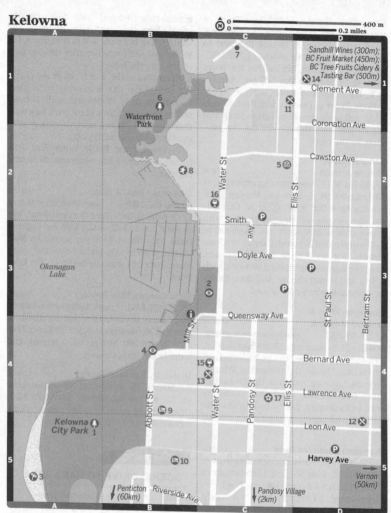

Sandhill Wines (300m);
BC Fruit Market (450m);
BC Tree Fruits Cidery &
Tasting Bar (500m)

Clement Ave

Coronation Ave

Cawston Ave

Water St

Ellis St

Smith Ave

Doyle Ave

St Paul St

Bertram St

Queensway Ave

Bernard Ave

Mill St

Abbott St

Water St

Pandosy St

Ellis St

Lawrence Ave

Leon Ave

Harvey Ave

Vernon (50km)

Penticton (60km)

Riverside Ave

Pandosy Village (2km)

Waterfront Park

Okanagan Lake

Kelowna City Park

Sleeping

★ Hotel Zed
MOTEL **$$**

(📞250-763-7771; www.hotelzed.com; 1627 Abbott St; r from $90; 🅿😑❄🐕📶) An old Travelodge has been reborn as this funky throwback to a 1960s that never existed. The rooms come in many shapes and sizes; all are in cheery colors. Extras such as free bike rentals, Ping-Pong, hot tub, comic books in the bathrooms and much more are way cool. It's perfectly located downtown, across from City Park (p732).

★ Hotel Eldorado
HOTEL **$$**

(📞250-763-7500; www.hoteleldoradokelowna. com; 500 Cook Rd; r from $180; 🅿😑❄🐕📶🐕) This historic lakeshore retreat, south of Pandosy Village, has 19 heritage rooms where you can bask in antique-filled luxury. A modern, low-key wing has 30 more rooms and six opulent waterfront suites. It's classy, artful and funky all at once. Definitely the choice spot for a luxurious getaway.

Lakeshore Bed & Breakfast
B&B **$$**

(📞250-764-4375; www.lakeshorebb.ca; 4186 Lakeshore Rd; r from $115; 🅿😑❄📶) This bright, two-room B&B has a prime lakefront loca-

Kelowna

tion, 6km south of the center, complete with its own tiny strip of sand. The larger of the two rooms is a real deal, with broad water views and a private outdoor sitting area. Furnishings are modern and upscale.

Samesun Kelowna HOSTEL **$$**
(☑250-763-9814; www.samesun.com; 245 Harvey Ave; dm/r from $57/140; P◉❂❂) Near the center and the lake, this purpose-built hostel has 88 dorm beds in four- and eight-bed dorms, plus private rooms. There is a hot tub; activities include various group outings.

 Eating

Little Hobo Soup & Sandwich Shop CAFE **$**
(☑778-478-0411; www.facebook.com/littlehobo kelowna; 596 Leon Ave; mains from $7; ◉8am-2pm Mon-Fri) This unadorned sandwich shop is hugely popular and for good reason: the food is excellent. Custom sandwiches are good, but the daily specials really shine (meatloaf, pasta, pierogi etc) and the variety of soups is simply superb.

Kelowna Farmers Market MARKET **$**
(☑250-878-5029; www.kelownafarmersand craftersmarket.com; cnr Springfield Rd & Dilworth Dr; ◉8am-1pm Wed & Sat Apr-Oct) The farmers market has more than 150 vendors, including many with prepared foods. Local artisans also display their wares. It's east of downtown near the Orchard Park Shopping Centre, off Hwy 97.

★**BNA Brewing Co & Eatery** CANADIAN **$$**
(☑236-420-0025; www.bnabrewing.com; 1250 Ellis St; mains from $14; ◉4pm-late) While the beer tasting room is open from midday to 6pm daily, dining kicks in from 4pm at this welcoming spot in a historic building. There's a good line of tapas-like plates for sharing, as well as a wide range of main courses. If you've come for the beer, try the Don't Lose Your Dinosaur IPA.

★**RauDZ Regional Table** FUSION **$$**
(☑250-868-8805; www.raudz.com; 1560 Water St; mains from $17; ◉5-10pm) Noted chef Rod Butters has defined the farm-to-table movement with his casual bistro that's a temple to Okanagan produce and wine. The dining room is as airy and open as the kitchen. The seasonal menu takes global inspiration for its Mediterranean-infused dishes, which are good for sharing, and serves steaks and seafood. Suppliers include locally renowned Carmelis goat's cheese.

★**Train Station Pub** PUB FOOD **$$**
(☑778-484-5558; www.thetrainstationpub.com; 1177 Ellis St; mains from $12; ◉9:30am-late) The long-disused 1926 Canadian National train station has been reborn as an upscale pub with an excellent selection of beers. The usual pub-food standards show color and flair; enjoy the wide terrace on balmy days.

🍷 **Drinking & Nightlife**

★**Tree Brewing Beer Institute** BREWERY
(☑778-484-0306; www.treebrewingbeerinstitute. com; 1346 Water St; ◉11am-11pm) These guys feature tank to tap craft beer, including experimental brews in an unfiltered state. Intriguing stuff if you like checking out new tastes. There are seven tanks on the go with an array of lagers, Kölsch, ales and various IPAs, while there are pizzas and sandwiches to choose from too.

BRITISH COLUMBIA KELOWNA

Micro Bar & Bites PUB

(☑778-484-3500; www.microkelowna.com; 1500 Water St; ☺2pm-midnight) This great small bar just off Bernard Ave is hard to leave. Craft beers, local wines and fine cocktails are served. Small bites are fresh and inventive, good for sharing – or for lunch. Gather at the beautiful wood-block bar or at a side-walk table.

Blue Gator Bar & Grill LIVE MUSIC

(☑250-860-1529; www.bluegator.net; 441 Lawrence Ave; ☺10am-6pm Mon-Wed, to late Thu-Sat) Head for blues, rock, acoustic jam and more at the valley's sweaty dive for live music and cold beer.

❶ Information

Tourism Kelowna (☑250-861-1515; www.tourismkelowna.com; 238 Queensway Ave; ☺8:30am-8:30pm) In an impressive facility on the waterfront; excellent source for free maps and tour info.

❶ Getting There & Away

Kelowna International Airport (☑250-807-4300; www.kelownaairport.com; 5533 Airport Way, off Hwy 97) The airport is 20km north of the center on Hwy 97 and handles over 70 flights daily to a growing number of destinations.

Ebus (www.myebus.ca) runs buses connecting Vancouver, Kamloops and Kelowna.

Vernon

☑250, 778 / POP 40,100

The Okanagan glitz is reaching north to Vernon, though winters have more of the traditional inland BC bite here and there are fewer wineries. The orchard-scented valley is surrounded by three lakes – Kalamalka, Okanagan and Swan – that attract fun-seekers all summer long.

Downtown life is found along busy 30th Ave, known as Main St. Confusingly, 30th Ave is intersected by 30th St in the middle of downtown, so mind your streets and avenues.

◉ Sights & Activities

★ **Planet Bee Honey Farm & Meadery** FARM

(☑250-542-8088; www.planetbee.com; 5011 Bella Vista Rd; ☺8am-6pm; ℗) **FREE** At Planet Bee you can learn all the sweet secrets of the golden nectar, taste 25 different honeys

DON'T MISS

KETTLE VALLEY RAIL TRAIL

The famous **Kettle Valley Rail Trail** vies with wine-drinking and peach-picking as the attraction of choice for the region's visitors – smart ones do all three.

Once stretching 525km in curving, meandering length, the railway was built so that silver ore could be transported from the southern Kootenays to Vancouver. Finished in 1916, it remains one of the most expensive railways ever built, on a per-kilometer basis. It was entirely shut by 1989, but it wasn't long before its easy grades (never more than 2.2%) and dozens of bridges were incorporated into the **Trans Canada Trail (TCT)**.

Of the entire Kettle Valley Rail Trail, the most spectacular stretch is close to Kelowna. The 24km section through the **Myra Canyon** has fantastic views of the sinuous canyon from **18 trestles** that span the gorge for the cliff-hugging path. That you can enjoy the route at all is something of a miracle, as 12 of the wooden trestles were destroyed by fire in 2003. All have been rebuilt; much credit goes to the **Myra Canyon Trestle Restoration Society** (www.myra-trestles.com), the website of which has downloadable maps and info. The broad views sweep down to Kelowna and the lake, more than 900m below. You can see alpine meadows reclaiming the fire-cleared landscape.

To reach the area closest to the most spectacular trestles from Kelowna, follow Harvey Ave (Hwy 97) east to Gordon Dr. Turn south and then go east 2.6km on KLO Rd and then join McCulloch Rd for 7.4km after the junction. Look for the Myra Forest Service Rd; turn south and make a winding 8.7km climb on a car-friendly gravel road to the parking lot. It's about a 40-minute drive from Kelowna's center.

Myra Canyon is just part of an overall 174km network of trails in the Okanagan that follows the old railway through tunnels, past Naramata and as far south as Penticton and beyond. You can easily access the trail at many points, or book hiking and cycling tours. Myra Canyon Bike Rentals (p733) offers bike rentals and tours at the main trailhead.

and see a working hive up close. Even better, taste the selection of delicious meads, a wine made from honey. Follow 30th Ave west from downtown for 3km.

Davison Orchards FARM
(📱250-549-3266; www.davisonorchards.ca; 3111 Davison Rd; ⊙8am-8pm Apr-Oct; P 🚗) FREE
Has tractor rides, homemade ice cream, fresh apple juice, a cafe, winsome barnyard animals and more. Great for the family, but definitely on the beaten path. Follow 30th Ave west from downtown for 3km.

Kalamalka Lake Provincial Park PARK
(www.env.gov.bc.ca/bcparks; off Hwy 6; P) The beautiful 9-sq-km Kalamalka Lake Provincial Park lies south of town on the eastern side of the warm, shallow lake. The park offers great swimming at Jade and Kalamalka Beaches, good fishing and a network of mountain-biking and hiking trails. Innerspace Watersports operates a seasonal booth in the park.

Innerspace Watersports WATER SPORTS
(📱250-549-2040; www.innerspacewatersports. com; 3006 32nd St; canoe rental per hour $25; ⊙10am-5:30pm Mon-Sat) Offers canoe and stand-up paddleboard rentals at Kalamalka Lake Provincial Park. Its full-service store in town has scuba gear. Park location is open mid-June to August.

🛏️ Sleeping & Eating

Ellison Provincial Park CAMPGROUND $
(📱info 250-494-6500, reservations 800-689-9025; www.discovercamping.ca; Okanagan Landing Rd; tent & RV sites $32; ⊙Apr-Oct; P) Some 16km southwest of Vernon, this is a great tree-shaded, 219-acre place near the lake. The 71 campsites fill up early, so reserve in advance.

Beaver Lake Mountain Resort LODGE $$
(📱250-762-2225; www.beaverlakeresort.com; 6350 Beaver Lake Rd; tent & RV sites from $37, cabins from $100; P 🍽️@🐾) Set high in the hills east of Hwy 97, about midway between Vernon and Kelowna, this postcard-perfect lakeside resort has a range of rustic log cabins and some more luxurious cabins that sleep up to six people.

Tiki Village Motor Inn MOTEL $$
(📱250-503-5566; www.tikivillagevernon.com; 2408 34th St; r from $109; P🍽️🐾🌊🏊) An ode to the glory days of decorative concrete blocks, the Tiki has suitably expansive plantings and 30 rooms with a vaguely Polynesian minimalist theme. All rooms have a fridge; some have a kitchenette.

★**Naked Pig Kitchen** BARBECUE $$
(📱778-475-5475; www.nakedpig.ca; 2933 30th Ave; mains from $13; ⊙11am-9pm) It doesn't get much better than this if you're into smokehouse BBQ. This is slow craft-style cooking using local produce and the Naked Pig's own tasty BBQ sauces. It's not all about meat though, with the veggie burger a menu favorite and the Naked Pig boasting its own line of coffee, the Naked Pig Roast.

Bamboo Beach Fusion Grille FUSION $$
(📱250-542-7701; www.bamboobeach.ca; 3313 30th Ave; mains from $13; ⊙11:30am-2pm & 5-8pm Tue-Fri, 5-8.30pm Sat; 🍴) Flavors from across Asia season popular local foods at this sprightly restaurant. Look for Japanese, Korean and Thai influences in the halibut curry, fish-and-chips and much more. The curry soba noodles show the talent of the Japanese-trained chef.

ℹ️ Information

Vernon Visitor Center (📱250-542-1415; www. tourismvernon.com; 3004 39th Ave; ⊙9am-6pm; 🕾) North of the town center.

ℹ️ Getting There & Away

Ebus (www.myebus.ca) Links Vernon with Kamloops and Kelowna, with connections to Vancouver.

Vernon Regional Transit System (📱250-545-7221; www.transitbc.com; fares from $2) Buses leave from the Downtown Exchange bus stop at the corner of 31st Ave and 30th St. For Kalamalka Lake, catch bus 1; for Okanagan Lake, bus 7.

North of Vernon

Just north of Vernon, beautiful Hwy 97 heads northwest to Kamloops via tree-clad valleys punctuated by lakes. **Armstrong**, 23km north of Vernon, is a cute little village. Attractions are few in this area, which is more notable for its major highway connections.

Silver Star (p738) is one of the region's top ski resorts, 24km northeast of Vernon.

◎ Sights & Activities

Historic O'Keefe Ranch HISTORIC SITE
(📱250-542-7868; www.okeeferanch.ca; 9380 Hwy 97N; adult/child $13.50/8.50; ⊙10am-5pm

May, Jun & Sep, to 6pm Jul & Aug) Home to the O'Keefe family between 1867 and 1977, the O'Keefe Ranch retains its original log cabin, and has lots of live displays of old ranching techniques. Before orchards – and later grapes – covered the valley, ranching as portrayed here was the typical way of life. The ranch is 12km north of Vernon, 4km after Hwy 97 splits from Hwy 97A, which continues northeast to Sicamous and Hwy 1.

Silver Star   SKIING

(☑250-542-0224; www.skisilverstar.com; 123 Shortt St, Silver Star Mountain; 1-day lift ticket adult/child $95/50) Silver Star, 24km northeast of Vernon and 75km from Kelowna, is extremely popular with skiers and snowboarders in winter. In summer the lifts haul mountain bikers and hikers up to the lofty green vistas.

There are lots of lodges and hotels, cafes, restaurants and pubs.

Shuttles come via Vernon from Kelowna and Kelowna Airport.

Shuswap Region

Rorschach-test-like **Shuswap Lake** anchors a somewhat bland but pleasing region of green, wooded hills, some farms and two small towns, **Sicamous** and **Salmon Arm**. The former has a lakefront park that's good for picnics, just northwest of Hwy 1.

The entire area is home to several lake-based provincial parks and is a popular destination for families looking for outdoor fun. Many explore the sinuous lakes via houseboats.

Roderick Haig-Brown Provincial Park PARK

(www.env.gov.bc.ca/bcparks; off Hwy 1, Saquilax) The main attraction here is the annual spawning of sockeye salmon. The 10.59-sq-km park protects both sides of the Adams River between Shuswap Lake and Adams Lake, a natural bottleneck for the bright-red sockeye when they run upriver every October. The fish population peaks every four years, when as many as four million salmon crowd the Adams' shallow riverbed.

D Dutchmen Dairy   ICE CREAM $

(☑250-836-4304; www.dutchmendairy.ca; 1321 Maeir Rd, Sicamous; treats from $3; ⊗8am-9pm Jun-Sep) Meet the cows, then lick the ice cream at this offbeat dairy close to Hwy 1. There are 40 flavors of ice cream and traditional frozen treats to choose from.

THE KOOTENAYS & THE ROCKIES

You can't help sighing as you ponder the plethora of snow-covered peaks in BC's Kootenay region. Deep river valleys cleaved by white-water rivers, impossibly sheer rock faces, alpine meadows and a sawtooth of white-dappled mountains stretching across the horizon inspire awe, action and contemplation.

Coming from the west, the mountain majesty builds as if choreographed. The roughly parallel ranges of the Monashees and the Selkirks striate the West Kootenays, with the Arrow Lakes adding texture. Appealing towns such as Revelstoke and Nelson nestle against the mountains and are outdoor fun centers year-round. The East Kootenays cover the Purcell Mountains region below Golden, taking in Radium Hot Springs and delightful Fernie.

BC's Rocky Mountains national parks (Mt Revelstoke, Glacier, Yoho and Kootenay) don't have the profile of Banff and Jasper over the border, but for many that's an advantage: each has its own spectacular qualities, often relatively unexploited by Banff-bound hordes.

Revelstoke

☑250, 778 / POP 7950

Gateway to serious mountains, Revelstoke doesn't need to toot its own horn – the ceaseless procession of trains through the center does that. Built as an important point on the Canadian Pacific Transcontinental Railroad that first linked eastern and western Canada, Revelstoke echoes not just with whistles but with history. The compact center is lined with heritage buildings, yet it's more than a museum piece. There's a vibrant local arts community, and most locals take full advantage of the boundless opportunities for hiking, kayaking and, most of all, skiing.

It's more than worth a long pause as you pass on Hwy 1, which bypasses the town center to the northeast. The main streets include 1st St and Mackenzie Ave.

◉ Sights

Grizzly Plaza, between Mackenzie and Orton Aves, is a pedestrian precinct and the heart of downtown, where free live-music performances take place every evening in July and August.

While outdoor activities are Revelstoke's real drawcard, a stroll of the center and a moment spent at the museums is a must. Pick up the *Public Art* and *Heritage* walking-tour brochures at the visitor center (p742).

★**Mt Revelstoke National Park** PARK
(www.pc.gc.ca/revelstoke; off Hwy 1; adult/child incl Glacier National Park $7.80/free) Grand in beauty if not in size, this 260-sq-km national park, just northeast of its namesake town, is a vision of peaks and valleys – many all but untrodden.

There are several good **hiking trails** from the summit. To overnight in the wild, you must have a Wilderness Pass camping permit ($10, in addition to your park pass), available from **Parks Canada Revelstoke Office** (☑250-837-7500; www.pc.gc.ca; 301 3rd St; ☺8am-4:30pm Mon-Fri) or Rogers Pass Centre (p742) inside Glacier National Park (p742).

★**Jones Distilling** DISTILLERY
(www.jonesdistilling.com; 616 3 St W; ☺noon-6pm Thu-Sun) In what was the 1914-built brick Mountain View School building, over the road from the Columbia River, Jones Distillery is making a name with its award-winning Revelstoke Gin Series and Mr Jones Vodka. Focusing on local ingredients and Revelstoke enthusiasm, the rewards are coming. Book tastings and tours through the Canadian Gin Guild (www.canadian ginguild.com).

Revelstoke Railway Museum MUSEUM
(☑250-837-6060; www.railwaymuseum.com; 719 Track St W; adult/child $10/5; ☺9am-5pm May-Sep, shorter hours Oct-Apr; P) In an attractive building across the tracks from the town center, Revelstoke Railway Museum contains restored steam locomotives, including one of the largest steam engines ever used on Canadian Pacific Railway (CPR) lines. Photographs and artifacts document the construction of the CPR, which was instrumental – actually, essential – in linking eastern and western Canada.

🏃 **Activities**

Sandwiched between the vast but relatively unknown Selkirk and Monashee mountain ranges, Revelstoke draws serious snow buffs looking for vast landscapes of crowd-free

powder. It's where North America's first ski jump was built, in 1915.

For **cross-country skiing**, head to the 22km of groomed trails at Mt MacPherson Ski Area, 7km south of town on Hwy 23; see www.revelstokenordic.org for information.

All that white snow turns into white water come spring and **rafting** is big here. **Mountain biking** is also huge; pick up trail maps from the visitor center (p742).

Revelstoke Mountain Resort SKIING
(☑866-373-4754; www.revelstokemountainresort. com; Camozzi Rd; 1-day lift ticket adult/child $88/30) Just 6km southeast of town, the Revelstoke Mountain Resort has ambitions to become the biggest ski resort this side of the Alps. It has seemingly endless virgin slopes and 65 runs. In one run you can ski both 700m of bowl and 700m of trees. At 1713m, the vertical drop is the greatest in North America.

Apex Rafting Co RAFTING
(☑250-837-6376; www.apexrafting.com; 112 1st St E; adult/child $124/99; ☺Jun-Aug; ⚙) Runs kid-friendly two-hour guided trips on the Illecillewaet River in spring and summer.

Wandering Wheels CYCLING
(☑250-814-7609; www.wanderingwheels.ca; 120 MacKenzie Ave; lessons per hour from $35, tours from $60; ☺Jun-Oct) Offers bike shuttle services, lessons, heli-bike and tours.

🛏 **Sleeping**

Revelstoke Backpacker Hostel HOSTEL **$**
(☑250-837-4050; www.revyhostel.com; 400 2nd St W; dm/r from $35/65; P☺☎) Ramble though the numerous rooms online for this perennial backpacker favorite. The dorms are popular so book ahead. It has bike and ski storage, plus summer barbecues, free passes to the town's aquatic center and free resort shuttle in winter.

★**Regent Hotel** HOTEL **$$**
(☑250-837-2107; www.regenthotel.ca; 112 1st St E; r from $110; P☺❄☎♨) The poshest place in the center is not lavish, but it is comfy. The 42 modern rooms bear no traces of the hotel's 1914 roots and exterior. The restaurant and lounge are justifiably popular. Many guests bob the night away in the outdoor hot tub.

Swiss Chalet Motel MOTEL **$$**
(☑877-837-4650; www.swisschaletmotel.com; 1101 West Victoria Rd; r from $96; P☺❄☎)

The Kootenays & The Rockies

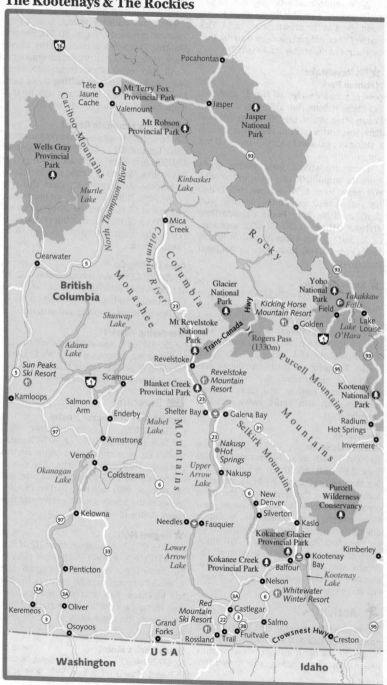

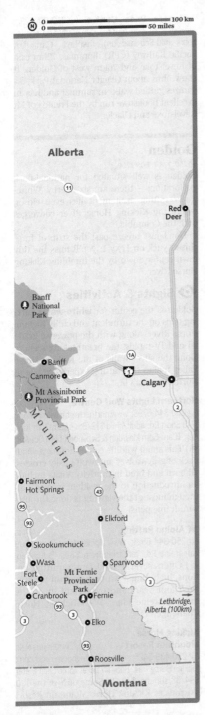

Alberta

Red ●
Deer

Banff ●
Q National
Park

● Banff

Canmore ●

Q Mt Assiniboine
Provincial Park

Calgary ●

● Fairmont
Hot Springs

● Elkford

● Skookumchuck

● Wasa   ● Sparwood

Fort ●
Steele   Mt Fernie
Provincial
● Cranbrook Park
         Q ● Fernie

Lethbridge,
Alberta (100km)

● Elko

● Roosville

Montana

Rooms may be small, but they're clean and comfy at this place on the main road, a 10-minute walk from the center of Revelstoke. Perks include a complimentary breakfast, tickets to the aquatic center, guest laundry and a free shuttle service during ski season to Revelstoke Mountain Resort (p739).

Courthouse Inn   B&B $$
(📞250-837-3369; www.courthouseinnrevelstoke.com; 312 Kootenay St; r from $129; P⊝❄🐾) A posh 10-room B&B close to the center. Extras include a lavish breakfast, boot and glove driers for winter and lots of personal service. You can't beat the quiet location; rooms have no TV or phone.

✕ Eating & Drinking

★ **Modern Bakeshop & Café**   CAFE $
(📞250-837-6886; www.themodernbakeshopandcafe.com; 212 Mackenzie Ave; mains from $6; ⏲6:30am-5pm Mon-Sat; 🐾) Try a croque monsieur (grilled ham-and-cheese sandwich) or an elaborate pastry for a taste of Europe at this cute art-deco cafe. Many items, such as the muffins, are made with organic ingredients. Discover the baked 'boofy uptrack bar' for a treat. Nice seating outside.

Taco Club   MEXICAN $
(📞250-837-0988; www.thetacoclub.ca; 206 MacKenzie Ave; mains from $6; ⏲11am-10pm) Once Revelstoke's favorite food truck, Taco Club has now laid down some roots in a vintage building downtown. Tacos and burritos are excellent, and all the usual suspects for sides are available. Enjoy the outside seating on long summer evenings.

Old School Eatery   CANADIAN $$
(📞250-814-4144; www.oldschooleatery.ca; 616 3 St W; dinner mains from $14; ⏲11am-9pm Tue-Fri, from 9am Sat & Sun) Sharing the old Mountain View School building of 1914 with Jones Distilling (p739), the Old School Eatery is becoming a favorite in Revelstoke, particularly for brunch in the weekends. With what they describe as 'sophisticated comfort food', you'll find top dinner options too, such as Creole pork chop ($28) and Moroccan lamb chops ($32), all in an old school room.

★ **Mt Begbie Brewing**   MICROBREWERY
(📞250-837-2756; www.mt-begbie.com; 2155 Oak Dr; ⏲11:30am-9pm Mon-Sat, tours at 4pm) Head out just east of town to Mt Begbie's tasting area and store to try the popular local brews.

The Powerhouse Pale Ale and the Brave Liver, a seasonal winter Scottish pale ale (at 6.5%), should put a smile on your face. There's decent food plus both indoor and outdoor seating.

❶ Information

Revelstoke Visitor Center (☑ 250-837-5345; www.seerevelstoke.com; 301 Victoria Rd; ☺ 8:30am-7pm) Excellent source for hiking and mountain-biking info and maps.

❶ Getting There & Away

Riders Express (www.riderexpress.ca) runs buses connecting Vancouver, Kamloops and Calgary, with a bus stopping daily in Revelstoke and Golden in both directions.

Revelstoke to Golden

Keep your eyes on the road or, better yet, let someone else drive as you traverse the Trans-Canada Hwy (Hwy 1) for 148km between Revelstoke and Golden. Stunning mountain peaks follow one after another as you go.

Glacier National Park   PARK
(www.pc.gc.ca; adult/child incl Mt Revelstoke National Park $8/4) To be accurate, this 1350-sq-km park should be called '430 Glaciers National Park'. The annual snowfall can be as much as 23m, and due to the sheer mountain slopes, this is one of the world's most active avalanche areas. For this reason, skiing, caving and mountaineering are regulated; you must register with park wardens before venturing into the backcountry. Check the weather and get an avalanche report. **Rogers Pass** ranks as one of the world's most beautiful mountain passes.

Be sure to pause at the **Hemlock Grove Trail**, 54km east of Revelstoke, where a 400m boardwalk winds through an ancient hemlock rainforest.

Glacier National Park has good camping options at **Illecillewaet Campground** (www.pc.gc.ca; Rogers Pass, off Hwy 1; tent & RV sites from $16; ☺ late Jun–early Oct) and **Loop Brook Campground** (www.pc.gc.ca; Rogers Pass, off Hwy 1; tent & RV sites from $16; ☺ Jul–late Sep), both on the Revelstoke side of Rogers Pass. Sites are available on a first-come, first-served basis. Otherwise, you'll need to stay in either Revelstoke or Golden.

Rogers Pass Centre (☑ 250-814-5233; off Hwy 1; ☺ 8am-7pm mid-Jun–early Sep, shorter hours mid-Sep–mid-Jun) displays Canadian Pacific Railway (CPR) dioramas, 72km east of Revelstoke and 76km west of Golden. It show films about Glacier National Park, organizes guided walks in summer and has an excellent bookstore run by the Friends of Mt Revelstoke and Glacier.

Golden

☑ 250, 778 / POP 3700

Golden is well situated for national-park explorations – there are six nearby. White-water rafting excitement lies even closer, where the Kicking Horse River converges with the Columbia.

Don't just breeze past the strip of franchised yuck on Hwy 1: you'll miss the tidy town center down by the tumbling Kicking Horse River.

◉ Sights & Activities

Golden is the center for **white-water rafting** trips on the turbulent and chilly Kicking Horse River. Along with the powerful grade III and IV rapids, the breathtaking scenery along the sheer walls of the Kicking Horse Valley makes this rafting experience one of North America's best.

Northern Lights Wolf Centre   PARK
(☑ 250-344-6798; www.northernlightswildlife.com; 1745 Short Rd; adult/child $12/6; ☺ 9am-7pm Jul & Aug, 10am-6pm May, Jun & Sep, noon-5pm Oct-Apr; ⓟ) This small wildlife center houses a small pack of gray wolves and wolf-husky crosses, all born and bred in captivity. Visits include an introduction to the resident wolves – although most of the viewing is done through wire-frame pens.

★ **Alpine Rafting**   RAFTING
(☑ 250-344-6521; www.alpinerafting.com; 1509 Lafontaine Rd; raft trips from $89; ☺ Jun-Sep; ⊛) Offers several good family rafting options, including a white-water run for kids aged four years and over, right up to the more extreme class IV+ 'Kicking Horse Challenge.'

Kicking Horse Mountain Resort   SKIING, MOUNTAIN BIKING
(☑ 250-439-5425; www.kickinghorseresort.com; Kicking Horse Trail; 1-day lift ticket adult/child winter $94/38, summer $42/21) Some 60% of the 120 ski runs at Kicking Horse Mountain Resort

are rated advanced or expert. With a 1260m (4133ft) vertical drop and a snowy position between the Rockies and the Purcells, the resort's popularity grows each year. It's renowned for its summer mountain biking, which includes the longest cycling descent in Canada.

🛏 Sleeping

★ **Dreamcatcher Hostel** HOSTEL **$**
(📞 250-439-1090; www.dreamcatcherhostel.com; 528 9th Ave N; dm/r from $32/90; P ➲ 🛜) Run by two veteran travelers, this centrally located hostel has everything a budget traveler could hope for. There are three dorm rooms, five private rooms, as well as a vast kitchen and a comfy common room with a stone fireplace. Outside there's a garden and a barbecue.

Kicking Horse Canyon B&B GUESTHOUSE **$$**
(📞 250-899-0840; www.kickinghorsecanyonbb.com; 644 Lapp Rd; d from $120; P ➲ 🛜) Hidden away among the hills to the east of Golden, this endearingly offbeat B&B takes you into the bosom of the family the minute you cross the threshold. Run by genial host Jeannie Cook and her husband, Jerry, it's a real alpine home-away-from-home, surrounded by private grassy grounds with views across the mountains.

Chancellor Peak Chalets LODGE **$$$**
(📞 250-344-7038; www.chancellorpeakchalets.com; 2924 Kicking Horse Rd; cabins from $289; P ➲ ✳ 🛜) The 11 log chalets at this riverside retreat have two levels and sleep up to six. There are soaker tubs, full kitchens and all the nature you can breathe in. The chalets are 25km southeast of Golden, just outside Yoho National Park.

🍴 Eating & Drinking

★ **Bacchus Books & Cafe** CAFE **$**
(📞 250-344-5600; www.bacchusbooks.ca; 409 9th Ave N; mains from $8; ⊙ 9am-5:30pm) This bohemian hideaway at the end of 8th St is a favorite haunt for Golden's artsy crowd. Browse for books (new and secondhand) in the downstairs bookstore, then head upstairs to find a table for tea among the higgledy-piggledy shelves. Sandwiches, salads and cakes are made on the premises, and the coffee is as good as you'll find in Golden.

ℹ AVALANCHE WARNING

The Kootenays are the heart of avalanche country. Such events kill more people in BC each year than any other natural phenomenon – the annual toll is stubbornly high.

Avalanches can occur at any time, even on terrain that seems relatively flat. Roughly half the people caught in one don't survive. It's vital that people venturing out onto the snow ask about conditions first; if an area is closed, don't go there. Whether you're backcountry ski touring or simply hiking in the alpine region, you'll want to rent a homing beacon; most outdoors shops can supply one.

In Revelstoke, **Avalanche Canada** (📞 250-837-2141; www.avalanche.ca) tracks avalanche reports and offers forecasts for BC and the Canadian Rockies. It has a vital website and a phone app.

★ **Island Restaurant** INTERNATIONAL **$$**
(📞 250-344-2400; www.islandrestaurant.ca; 101 10th Ave; dinner mains from $14; ⊙ 9am-9pm) On a small river island in the middle of Kicking Horse River in the center of Golden, this place features a flower-embellished riverside patio and international dishes and drinks. The food wears many hats, from a Jamaican-jerk chicken sandwich to Thai Thursdays and full-on Mexican nights on Mondays and Tuesdays.

Wolf Den PUB FOOD **$$**
(📞 250-344-9863; www.thewolfsdengolden.ca; 1105 9th St; dinner mains from $14; ⊙ 4-10pm) An excellent pub with live music on Sundays. It's hugely popular with locals, who love the burgers and hearty fare, which are way above average. The beer menu includes some of BC's best on tap. It's just south of the river from downtown.

★ **Whitetooth Brewing Company** MICROBREWERY
(📞 250-344-2838; www.whitetoothbrewing.com; 623 8th Ave N; ⊙ 2-10pm) Golden's microbrewery features tank-to-tap brews and a marvelous sunny patio for those long summer evenings. Whitetooth is a hit with locals who come to fill their growlers and relax on the patio. We like the Icefields Belgian-inspired pale ale.

ℹ Information

Golden Visitor Information Centre (☑ 250-439-7290; www.tourismgolden.com; 1000 Hwy 1; ☺ 9am-7pm Jun-Sep) In a purpose-built building on Hwy 1 and Hwy 95 into town from the southeast.

ℹ Getting There & Away

Riders Express (www.riderexpress.ca) Runs buses connecting Vancouver, Kamloops and Calgary, with a bus stopping daily in Revelstoke and Golden in both directions.

Yoho National Park

The surging waters of glacier-fed, ice-blue Kicking Horse River that plow through a valley of the same name are an apt image for dramatic Yoho National Park. This spectacular park is home to looming peaks, pounding waterfalls, glacial lakes and patches of pretty meadows.

◉ Sights & Activities

★ **Yoho National Park**   NATIONAL PARK
(☑ 250-343-6783; www.pc.gc.ca; off Hwy 1; adult/child $10/5) Although the smallest (1310 sq km) of the four national parks in the Rockies, Yoho is a diamond in the (very) rough. This wilderness is the real deal; it's some of the continent's least tarnished.

East of Field on Hwy 1 is the Takakkaw Falls road, open from late June to early October. At 255m, Takakkaw Falls is one of the highest waterfalls in Canada. From here the **Iceline Trail**, a 20km hiking loop, passes many glaciers and spectacular scenery.

Near the south gate of the park, you can reach pretty **Wapta Falls** along a 2.4km trail. The easy walk takes about 45 minutes each way.

Don't miss the surging waters at Natural Bridge, which you can admire on the short drive from Hwy 1 near Field to iconic Emerald Lake.

★ **Burgess Shale**
Fossil Beds   NATIONAL PARK
This World Heritage site protects the amazing Cambrian-age fossil beds on Mt Stephen and Mt Field. These 515-million-year-old fossils preserve the remains of marine creatures that were some of the earliest forms of life on earth. You can only get to the fossil beds by guided hikes, which are led by naturalists from the Burgess Shale

Geoscience Foundation. Reservations are essential.

Kicking Horse Pass
& Spiral Tunnels   VIEWPOINT
The historic Kicking Horse Pass between Banff and Yoho National Parks is one of the most important passes in the Canadian Rockies. It was discovered in 1858 by the Palliser Expedition, which was tasked with discovering a possible route across the Rockies for the Canadian Pacific Railway. Accessible 8km east of Field from the westbound lanes of Hwy 1, the viewing area is often closed and the view obscured by vegetation.

Takakkaw Falls   WATERFALL
A thundering torrent of water tumbles from its source in the nearby Daly Glacier over a sheer cliff face for 255m (836ft), making it the second-highest waterfall in Canada. At the end of the road, a trail leads for around 800m (half a mile) from the Takakkaw parking lot to the base of the falls. The road is open from late June to early October.

Emerald Lake   LAKE
For most visitors, this vividly colored lake is Yoho's most unmissable sight. Ringed by forest and silhouetted by impressive mountains, including the iconic profile of **Mt Burgess** to the southeast, it's a truly beautiful – if incredibly busy – spot. Escape the mobs in a rental canoe. The lake road is signed off Hwy 1 just to the southwest of Field and continues for 10km (6.2 miles) to the lake shore.

🛏 Sleeping

Kicking Horse
Campground   CAMPGROUND **$**
(www.reservation.pc.gc.ca; Yoho Valley Rd; tent & RV sites $27.40; ☺ May 23–Oct 14; 🅿 🛜) This is probably the most popular campground in Yoho. It's in a nice forested location, with plenty of space between the 88 sites, and there are showers. Riverside sites (especially 68 to 74) are the pick of the bunch.

HI-Yoho National Park   HOSTEL **$**
(Whiskey Jack Hostel; ☑ 403-670-7580; www.hi hostels.ca; Yoho Valley Rd; dm from $28; ☺ Jun 29–Sep 23) Yoho National Park's Takakkaw Falls are so close you can see them from the hostel's timber deck. Three nine-bed dorms and a basic kitchen comprise the ru-

dimentary facilities; it's usually booked out in summer.

Lake O'Hara usually remains covered with snow or else stays very muddy until mid-July.

Lake O'Hara

Perched high in the mountains, Lake O'Hara is an encapsulation of the Rockies region, and worth the significant hassle to reach it. Compact wooded hillsides, alpine meadows, snow-covered passes, mountain vistas and glaciers wrap around the stunning lake. A day trip is rewarding, but if you stay overnight in the backcountry you'll be able to access many **hiking trails** – some quite difficult, and all quite spectacular. The **Alpine Circuit** (12km) has a bit of everything.

🛏 Sleeping

Lake O'Hara Campground   CAMPGROUND **$**
(☑ reservations 250-343-6433; www.pc.gc.ca; Yoho National Park; tent sites $10, reservation fee $12; ☺ mid-Jun–Sep) Reserve three months in advance to snare one of 30 campsites. Available spots are often taken in the first hour that reservation phone lines are open (from 8am Mountain time). If you don't have advance reservations, three to five campsites are set aside for 'standby' users; call at 8am the day before you wish to stay.

★ Lake O'Hara Lodge   LODGE **$$$**
(☑ 250-343-6418; www.lakeohara.com; Yoho National Park; s/d from $500/665, cabins $940; ☺ Jan-Apr & Jun-Oct; ☺☎) ✏ Leaving guests slack-jawed for more than 90 years, the lodge is the only place to stay at the lake if you're not traveling with a tent. It's luxurious in a rustic way, and its environmental practices are lauded. Food comes from BC producers and is excellent. Minimum stay is two nights.

ℹ Getting There & Away

To reach the lake, take the **shuttle bus** (☑ reservations 877-737-3783; www.pc.gc.ca; adult/child return $15/8, reservation fee $12; ☺ mid-Jun–Sep) from the Lake O'Hara parking lot, 15km east of Field on Hwy 1. A quota system governs bus access to the lake. Given the lake's popularity, reservations are basically mandatory, unless you want to walk. That said, if you don't have advance reservations, six day-use seats on the bus are set aside for 'standby' users. Call at 8am the day before and think 'lucky.'

You can freely walk the 11km from the parking area, but no bikes are allowed. The area around

Field

Right off Hwy 1, this historic railroad town is worth a stop for its dramatic overlook of the river and quaint yet unfussy atmosphere. Many buildings date from the early days of the railways, when the town was the Canadian Pacific Railway's headquarters for exploration and, later, for strategic planning, when engineers were working on the problem of moving trains over Kicking Horse Pass.

Burgess Shale Geoscience Foundation   HIKING
(☑ 800-343-3006; www.burgess-shale.bc.ca; 201 Kicking Horse Ave; tours adult/child from $94.50/65; ☺ 9am-4pm Tue-Sat mid-Jun–mid-Sep) The only way to visit the amazing 515-million-year-old Burgess Shale fossil beds is on a hike led by the Burgess Shale Geoscience Foundation. Book online and follow instructions for the morning meeting location. There are two core hikes, one to Walcott Quarry and another to the adjacent fossil fields on Mt Stephen.

Both are strenuous full-day trips with plenty of elevation gain, so you'll need to be fit and wear proper footwear.

★ Truffle Pigs Lodge   HOTEL **$$**
(☑ 250-343-6303; www.trufflepigs.com; 100 Centre St; r from $120; ☺ Jun-Sep; ☻☀☎) ✏ Field's only hotel is a timber building with heritage charm. The 14 rooms are fairly simply decked out, though. Some have small kitchens. The owners run the town's well-known restaurant, **Truffle Pigs bistro** (mains from $12; ☺ 8am-9pm; ☎) ✏, in the same attractive building.

ℹ Information

Yoho National Park Information Centre
(☑ 250-343-6783; www.pc.gc.ca; off Hwy 1; ☺ 9am-7pm May-Oct) Pick up maps and trail descriptions. Rangers can advise on itineraries and conditions. Alberta Tourism staffs a desk here in summer and Friends of Yoho maintains a book shop.

Kootenay National Park

Kootenay is the the only national park in Canada with both glaciers and cacti. From Radium Hot Springs you can create a fine driving loop through Kootenay into Alberta's Banff National Park, then back into BC at Golden through Yoho National Park; many of the top sights are easily reached by car.

The very remote Mt Assiniboine Provincial Park offers true adventurers a remarkable wilderness experience.

◉ Sights

Kootenay National Park NATIONAL PARK

(☑250-347-9505; www.pc.gc.ca/kootenay; Hwy 93; adult/child $9.80/free, tent/RV sites $21.50/38.20; ☺camping May-Oct) Shaped like a lightning bolt, 1406-sq-km Kootenay National Park is centered on a long, wide, tree-covered valley shadowed by cold, gray peaks. It has a more moderate climate than other Rocky Mountains parks and, in the southern regions especially, summers can be hot and dry, which is a factor in the frequent fires.

The interpretive **Fireweed Trails** (500m or 2km) loop through the surrounding forest at the north end of Hwy 93. Panels explain how nature is recovering from a 1968 fire. Some 7km further on, **Marble Canyon** has a pounding creek flowing through a nascent forest. Another 3km south on the main road you'll find the easy 2km trail through forest to ocher pools known as the **Paint Pots**. Panels describe both the mining history of this rusty earth and its importance to Indigenous people.

Learn how the park's appearance has changed over time at the **Kootenay Valley Viewpoint**, where informative panels vie with the view. Just 3km south, **Olive Lake** makes a perfect picnic or rest stop. A 500m lakeside interpretive trail describes some of the visitors who've come before you.

Mt Assiniboine
Provincial Park PARK

(www.env.gov.bc.ca/bcparks) Between Kootenay and Banff National Parks lies this lesser-known and smaller (39-sq-km) provincial park, part of the Rockies' Unesco World Heritage site. The pointed peak of Mt Assiniboine (3618m), often referred to as Canada's Matterhorn, and its near neighbors have become a magnet for experienced rock climbers and mountaineers. Backcountry hikers revel in its meadows and glaciers.

The park's main focus is crystal-clear **Lake Magog**, which is reachable on a 27km trek from Banff National Park or by helicopter. At the lake, there's a lodge, camping and huts.

🛏 Sleeping

★Kootenay Park Lodge CABIN $$

(☑403-762-9196; www.kootenayparklodge.com; Hwy 93, Vermilion Crossing, Kootenay National Park; d cabins from $125; ☺mid-May–late Sep; P❄❀🐾) The pick of the few places to stay inside the park, this lodge has a range of cute log cabins complete with verandah, fridge and hot plates. Think rustic charm. There is a restaurant open June 1 through mid-September, a general store selling coffee and snacks, and for those who can't do without it, spotty wi-fi.

Assiniboine Lodge LODGE $$$

(☑403-678-2883; www.assiniboinelodge.com; Mt Assiniboine Provincial Park; r per person $350, shared & private cabin per person from $350; ☺Feb, Mar & Jun-Oct; 🐾) The only lodge in Assiniboine is also the oldest ski lodge in the Canadian Rockies, surrounded by mountain meadows and gloriously backed by Mt Assiniboine. Rustic rooms sleep one or two people (solo travelers usually must share), plus there are shared (three to five people) or private cabins. Rates include meals and hiking-guide service. Helicopter transport is $175 each way.

❶ Information

The main **Kootenay National Park visitor center** (☑250-347-9331; www.radiumhotsprings.com; 7556 Main St E; ☺ visitor center 9am-5pm year-round, Parks Canada May-Oct, later in summer; 🐾) is in Radium Hot Springs. It has excellent resources for hikers.

Radium Hot Springs

Lying just outside the southwest corner of Kootenay National Park, Radium Hot Springs is a major gateway to the entire Rocky Mountains national park area.

Radium boasts a large resident population of bighorn sheep, which often wander through town, but the big attraction is the namesake hot springs, 3km northeast of town.

There's a definite German-Austrian vibe here with accommodations such as Motel Tyrol, Alpen Motel, Motel Bavaria, restaurants like the Old Salzburg and Helna Stube, and even an Edelweiss St.

Radium Hot Springs HOT SPRINGS

(☑250-347-9485; www.pc.gc.ca/hotsprings; off Hwy 93; adult/child $7.30/4.95; ☺9am-11pm) The large hot springs pools have just been modernized and can get very busy in summer. The water comes from the ground at 44°C, enters the first pool at 39°C and hits the cooler one at 29°C. It's 3km northeast of the township, inside the park gate, with plenty of parking.

Radium Park Lodge   MOTEL $
(☑778-527-4857; www.radiumparklodge.com; 4873 Stanley St; r from $79; P❷❀❁☎) Clean and comfortable motel rooms at Radium Hot Springs, near the entrance to the parks. Continental breakfast is included and there's plenty of parking a couple of blocks back from the highway.

Inn on Canyon   GUESTHOUSE $$
(☑250-347-9392; www.villagecountryinn.bc.ca; 7557 Canyon Ave; r from $109; P❷❀) A cute gabled house just off the main drag. Its rooms are sparkling clean and decked out in country fashion.

Big Horn Cafe   CAFE $
(☑403-861-2978; www.bighorncafe.net; 7527 Main St; snacks from $3; ❷6am-4:30pm; ❀) An ideal road-trip breaker where you can refuel with coffee and a cinnamon bun or something more savory.

Radium Hot Springs to Fernie

South from Radium Hot Springs, Hwy 93/95 follows the wide Columbia River valley between the Purcell and Rocky Mountains. It's not especially interesting, unless you're into the area's industry (ski-resort construction), agriculture (golf courses) or wild game (condo buyers).

South of Skookumchuck on Hwy 93/95, the road forks. Go left on Hwy 95 and you'll come to **Fort Steele Heritage Town** (☑250-426-7342; www.fortsteele.ca; 9851 Hwy 93/95; adult/youth $18/12; ❷10am-5pm mid-Jun–Aug, shorter hours winter).

From Fort Steele, it's 95km to Fernie along Hwys 93 and 3.

Fernie

☑250 / POP 5250
Surrounded by mountains on four sides – that's the sheer granite Lizard Range you see looking west – Fernie defines cool. Once devoted solely to lumber and coal, the town has used its sensational setting to branch out. Skiers love the 8m-plus of dry powder

that annually blankets the runs seen from town. In summer, this same dramatic setting lures scores of hikers and mountain bikers.

Despite the town's discovery by pleasure seekers, it still retains a down-to-earth, vintage-brick vibe, best felt in the cafes, bars, shops and galleries along Victoria (2nd) Ave in the historic center, three blocks south of Hwy 3 (7th Ave).

◉ Sights & Activities

Fernie Museum   MUSEUM
(☑250-423-7016; www.ferniemuseum.com; 491 2nd Ave; adult/child $5/free; ❷10am-5:30pm) Impressively housed in a 1909 bank building, the Fernie Museum has engaging displays and is an excellent source of info about the town and region. Experience the fires, floods, booms and busts that have shaped the town.

Mt Fernie Provincial Park   PARK
(☑250-422-3003; www.env.gov.bc.ca/bcparks; Mt Fernie Park Rd, off Hwy 3) Mountain biking is popular at Mt Fernie Provincial Park, just 3km south of town. It also offers hikes for all skills and interests, plus camping.

★Fernie Alpine Resort   SKIING
(☑250-423-4655; www.skifernie.com; 5339 Ski Area Rd; 1-day pass adult/child $94/38) In fall, all eyes turn to the mountains for more than just their beauty: they're looking for snow. A five-minute drive from downtown, fast-growing Fernie Alpine Resort boasts 142 runs, five bowls and almost endless dumps of powder. Most hotels run shuttles here daily.

Guide's Hut   CYCLING
(☑250-423-3650; www.theguideshut.ca; 671 2 Ave; guiding per hour $30; ❷10am-6pm) Raise your mountain-biking game with expert coaching and instruction, and let them show you the far reaches of the Elk Valley.

Mountain High River Adventures   RAFTING
(☑250-423-5008; www.raftfernie.com; 2001 6th Ave; trips adult/child from $140/100; ❷8am-6pm May-Sep) The Elk River is a classic white-water river, with three grade IV rapids and 11 grade III rapids. In addition to rafting, Mountain High offers kayaking, floats, rentals and more on the surging waters. Its Adventure Centre is at Fernie RV Resort.

ℹ CHECK YOUR WATCH

It is a constant source of confusion that the East Kootenays lie in the Mountain time zone, along with Alberta, unlike the rest of BC, which falls within the Pacific time zone. West on Hwy 1 from Golden, the time changes at the east gate of Glacier National Park. Going west on Hwy 3, the time changes between Cranbrook and Creston. Mountain time is one hour later than Pacific time.

🛏 Sleeping

HI Raging Elk Hostel   HOSTEL $
(☎250-423-6811; www.ragingelk.com; 892 6th Ave; dm/r from $30/85; P⊜⊚) Wide decks allow plenty of inspirational mountain-gazing at this well-run central hostel. Raging Elk has good advice for those hoping to mix time on the slopes or trails with seasonal work. The pub (open 4pm to midnight) is a hoot (and offers cheap beer).

★Park Place Lodge   HOTEL $$
(☎250-423-6871; www.parkplacelodge.com; 742 Hwy 3; r from $130; P⊜✳⊚≋) The nicest lodging close to the center, Park Place offers 64 comfortable rooms with fridge and microwave, and access to an indoor pool and hot tub. Some have balcony and views.

Snow Valley Lodging   MOTEL $$
(☎877-696-7669; www.snowvalleymotel.com; 1041 7th Ave/Hwy 3; r from $99; P⊜✳⊚) Great value in the middle of town. There are rooms, 'tiny homes' and suites that you can pick online and book direct. Throw in complimentary laundry facilities, bike use, BBQ area and hot tub and you have a great place to stay in Fernie.

🍴 Eating & Drinking

Blue Toque Diner   CAFE $
(☎250-423-4637; www.bluetoquediner.com; 601 1st Ave; mains from $12; ⊙9am-2:30pm Thu-Mon; ⊿) Part of the Arts Station community gallery, this is *the* place for breakfast. The menu features lots of seasonal and organic vegetarian specials.

★Nevados Tapas & Tequila   LATIN AMERICAN $$
(☎250-423-5566; www.nevados.ca; 531 2 Ave; tapas from $4.50; ⊙5-10pm) The hottest spot in Fernie, Nevados is invitingly dark inside with century-old exposed-brick walls and a lovely outside terrace for long summer eve-

nings. It's all on here, with a two-page tequila menu, local craft beers and a delightful selection of Latin tapas and full meals. Try the pork *arepa,* street food from Venezuela.

★Yamagoya   JAPANESE $$
(☎250-430-0090; www.yamagoya.ca; 741 7th Ave/ Hwy 3; small dishes from $4, mains from $11; ⊙5-10pm) As compact as a California roll, this gem of a sushi place serves a wide range of classics, from sashimi to tempura. The miso soup is good, especially after a day of skiing. In addition to sake, there's a great beer selection. Also has outdoor seating.

Fernie Distillers   DISTILLERY
(www.ferniedistillers.com; 531 1st Ave; ⊙4-10pm Wed-Fri, from 2pm Sat & Sun) Fernie's distillery sits next to the old station building and produces small-batch (200 bottles per batch) hand-crafted gin and vodka. Turn up, view the stills, chat with the owners, sip the product and enjoy an extremely convivial laid-back atmosphere. The Prospector Gin and No 9 Mine Vodka are great, but don't forget to ask about the 'seasonal spirit'.

ℹ Information

Visitor Center (☎250-423-6868; www.fernie chamber.com; 102 Commerce Rd; ⊙9am-5pm Mon-Fri) Located east of town off Hwy 3, just past the Elk River crossing.

Kimberley

🗺 250, 778 / POP 7425

When big-time mining left Kimberley in 1973, a plan was hatched to transform the little mountain village at 1113m altitude into the Bavarian City of the Rockies. The center became a pedestrian zone named the Platzl; locals were encouraged to prance about in lederhosen and dirndl; and sausage was added to many a menu. Now, more than three decades later, that shtick is long-gone, though the city still claims to have the largest freestanding cuckoo clock in Canada. There's still a bit of fake half-timbering here and there, but for the most part Kimberley is a diverse place that makes a worthwhile detour off Hwy 95 between Cranbrook and Radium Hot Springs.

Kimberley Alpine Resort   SKIING
(☎250-427-4881; www.skikimberley.com; 301 N Star Blvd; 1-day lift pass adult/child $75/30) In winter this popular resort has more than 700 hectares of skiable terrain, including

80 runs, and mild weather. Lots going on in summer including hiking, mountain biking, golf, canoeing, kayaking, rafting and fly-fishing.

Kimberley's Underground Mining Railway   RAIL
(☑250-427-7365; www.kimberleysunderground miningrailway.ca; Gerry Sorensen Way; adult/child $25/10; ☺tours 11am, 1pm & 3pm May-Sep, trains to resort 10am Sat & Sun) Take a ride on Kimberley's Underground Mining Railway, where the tiny train putters through the steep-walled Mark Creek Valley toward some sweeping mountain vistas.

❶ Information

Kimberley Visitor Centre (☑778-481-1891; www.tourismkimberley.com; 270 Kimberley Ave; ☺10am-5pm daily Jul & Aug, closed Sun Sep-Jun) The visitor centre has everything you need to know.

Cranbrook

☑250, 778 / POP 19,250

The region's main center, 31km southeast of Kimberley, Cranbrook is a modest crossroads. Hwy 3/95 bisects the town and is lined with a charmless array of strip malls.

★Cranbrook History Centre   MUSEUM
(☑250-489-3918; www.cranbrookhistorycentre. com; 57 Van Horne St S, Hwy 3/95; adult/child $5/3; ☺10am-5pm Tue-Sun) The one great reason for stopping in Cranbrook? This museum, which includes the **Canadian Museum of Rail Travel**. It has some fine examples of classic Canadian trains, including the luxurious 1929 edition of the Trans-Canada Limited, a legendary train that ran from Montréal to Vancouver.

Lazy Bear Lodge   MOTEL $
(☑250-426-6086; www.lazybear.ca; 621 Cranbrook Street N; r from $75; P❂❋☎) Unlike most of the chain places along Hwy 95, locally owned Lazy Bear has been catering to visitors for nigh on 50 years. Nothing fancy, but its motel-type rooms are clean and affordable, plus there's a nice outdoor pool.

★Fire Hall Kitchen & Tap   GASTROPUB $$
(☑778-520-0911; www.irehallcbk.ca; 37 11 Ave St; dinner mains from $12; ☺8am-10pm Sun-Thu, to midnight Fri & Sat) Top BC craft beers (20 on tap!) and great food all day in what used to be Cranbrook's fire station. Rooftop and streetside seating, plus a beautifully reno-

vated interior, make this an extremely atmospheric place to eat and drink.

Cranbrook to Rossland

Hwy 3 twists and turns its way 300km from Cranbrook to Osoyoos at the south end of the Okanagan Valley. Along the way it hugs the hills close to the US border and passes eight border crossings.

Creston, 123km west of Cranbrook, is known for its many orchards and as the home of Columbia Brewing Co's Kokanee True Ale. Hwy 3A heads north from here for a scenic 80km to the free **Kootenay Lake Ferry**, which connects to Nelson. This is a fun and scenic journey.

Some 85km west of Creston, **Salmo** is notable mostly as the junction with Hwy 6, which runs north for a bland 40km to Nelson. The Crowsnest Hwy splits 10km to the west. Hwy 3 bumps north through **Castlegar**, which has the closest large airport to Nelson and a very large pulp mill. Hwy 3B dips down through cute cafe-filled town **Fruitvale** and industrial **Trail**.

🛏 Sleeping & Eating

Valley View Motel   MOTEL $
(☑250-428-2336; www.valleyviewmotel.info; 216 Valley View Dr, Creston; r from $75; P❂❋☎) In motel-ville Creston, this is your best bet. On a view-splayed hillside, it's clean, comfortable and quiet.

Retro Cafe   FRENCH $
(☑250-428-2726; www.retrocafe.ca; 1431 NW Blvd, Creston; mains from $8; ☺7am-4pm Mon-Fri, to 3pm Sat) A French mirage in Creston, 'retro' will probably be the last thing on your mind as you scour the hand-scrawled blackboard and tuck into *très délicieux* crepes.

Rossland

☑250, 778 / POP 3730

Rossland is a world apart. High in the Southern Monashee Mountains (1023m), this old mining village is one of Canada's best places for **mountain biking**. A long history of mining has left the hills crisscrossed with old trails and abandoned rail lines, all of which are perfect for riding.

Free-riding is all the rage as the ridgelines are easily accessed and there are lots of rocky paths for plunging downhill. The **Seven Summits & Dewdney Trail** is a 35.8km singletrack along the crest of the Rossland Range. The **Kootenay Columbia Trails Society** (www.kcts.ca) has good maps online.

Red Mountain Ski Resort
SKIING

(☑ 250-362-7384, snow report 250-362-5500; www.redresort.com; Hwy 3B; 1-day lift pass adult/child $96/48) Red Mountain Ski Resort draws mountain bikers in summer and plenty of ski enthusiasts in winter. Red, as it's called, includes the 1590m-high Red Mountain, the 2075m-high Granite Mountain and the 2048m-high Grey Mountain, for a total of 1670 hectares of challenging, powdery terrain and 110 runs. Plenty going on with heli-, cat-, cross-country and backcountry skiing too.

Flying Steamshovel Gastropub & Inn
INN $

(☑ 250-362-7323; www.theflyingsteamshovel.com; 2003 2 Ave; r from $80; ☺ ☎) Lots going on here at the Flying Steamshovel, from the main street in Rossland. Great location, comfortable rooms, free parking – and if you're into craft beer, 14 different brews on tap. The restaurant offers a huge variety from its *poke* bowl to yellow coconut curry to the John Candy burger. Check the website for live concert listings.

❶ Information

Rossland Visitor Centre (☑ 250-362-7722; www.rosslandmuseum.ca; 1100 Hwy 3B, Rossland Museum; ☺ 11am-5pm May-Sep) Located in the Rossland Museum building, at the junction of Hwy 22 (coming from the US border) and Hwy 3B.

Nelson

☑ 250, 778 / POP 10,660

Nelson is an excellent reason to visit the Kootenays and should feature on any itinerary in the region. Tidy brick buildings climb the side of a hill overlooking the west arm of deep-blue Kootenay Lake, and the waterfront is lined with parks and beaches. The thriving cafe, culture and nightlife scene is a bonus. However, what really propels Nelson is its personality: a funky mix of hippies, creative types and rugged individualists. You can find all these along Baker St, the pedestrian-friendly main drag where wafts of patchouli mingle with hints of fresh-roasted coffee.

Born as a mining town in the late 1800s, Nelson embarked on a decades-long heritage-preservation project in 1977. Today there are more than 350 carefully preserved and restored period buildings. The town is also an excellent base for hiking, skiing and kayaking the nearby lakes and hills.

◉ Sights

Almost a third of Nelson's **historic buildings** have been restored to their high- and late-Victorian architectural splendor. Pick up the superb *Heritage Walking Tour* from the visitor center (p752). It gives details of more than 30 buildings in the center and offers a good lesson in Victorian architecture.

Lakeside Park
PARK

(Lakeside Dr; ℗) By the iconic Nelson Bridge, Lakeside Park is a flower-filled, shady park and a beach, and has a great summer cafe.

Touchstones Nelson Museum of Art & History
MUSEUM

(☑ 250-352-9813; www.touchstonesnelson.ca; 502 Vernon St; adult/child $8/6; ☺ 10am-5pm Mon-Wed, Fri & Sat, to 8pm Thu, to 4pm Sun Jun-Aug, closed Mon Sep-May) An enormous renovation transformed what was once a baronial old city hall (1902) into Touchstones Nelson, a museum of local history and art. Every month brings new exhibitions, many of which celebrate local artists. The history displays are engaging and interactive, banishing images of musty piles of poorly labeled artifacts.

Activities

★ Kokanee Glacier Provincial Park
HIKING

(www.env.gov.bc.ca/bcparks; Kokanee Glacier Rd) This park boasts 85km of some of the area's most superb hiking trails. The fantastic summer-only 2.5km (two-hour) round-trip hike to **Kokanee Lake** on a well-marked trail can be continued to the treeless, boulder-strewn expanse around the glacier. Turn off Hwy 3A 20.5km northeast of Nelson, then head another 16km on Kokanee Glacier Rd.

Whitewater Winter Resort
SKIING

(☑ 250-354-4944, snow report 250-352-7669; www.skiwhitewater.com; off Hwy 6; 1-day lift ticket adult/child $76/38) Known for its heavy powdery snowfall, this laid-back resort 12km south of Nelson off Hwy 6 has small-town charm. Lifts are few, but so are the crowds, who enjoy a drop of 623m on 81 runs. There are 11 groomed Nordic trails.

Sacred Ride MOUNTAIN BIKING
(☑250-354-3831; www.sacredride.ca; 213 Baker St; bicycle rental per day from $45; ⏲9am-5:30pm Mon-Sat) The Sacred Ride has a wide variety of rentals. Also sells *Your Ticket to Ride,* an extensive trail map.

ROAM KAYAKING
(Rivers, Oceans & Mountains; ☑250-354-2056; www.roamshop.com; 639 Baker St; kayak rental per day $40; ⏲8am-7pm Mon-Sat, to 5pm Sun) ROAM sells and rents gear and offers advice. Book **Kootenay Kayak Company** (☑250-505-4549; www.kootenaykayak.com; kayak rentals per day $40-50, tours from $55) tours here.

Streetcar 23 RAIL
(☑250-352-7672; www.nelsonstreetcar.org; Waterfront Pathway; adult/child $3/2; ⏲11am-4:30pm mid-May–mid-Nov) One of the town's originals, streetcar 23 follows a 2km track from Lakeside Park to the wharf at the foot of Hall St.

🛏 Sleeping

★**Dancing Bear Inn** HOSTEL $
(☑250-352-7573; www.dancingbearinn.com; 171 Baker St; dm/r from $29/59; P😀🤏) The brilliant management here offers advice and smooths the stay of guests in the 14 shared and private rooms, all of which share baths. There's a gourmet kitchen, library, patio and laundry.

★**Adventure Hotel** HOTEL $$
(☑250-352-7211; www.adventurehotel.ca; 616 Vernon St; r from $95; P😀❄🤏) Rooms come in three flavors at this well-located, slick, renovated hotel: budget (tiny, two bunk beds, shower down the hall), economy (full private bath) and deluxe (a choice of beds). Common areas include a lounge, patio, gym and rooftop sauna. The building also features the hotel's Uptown Sports Bar, Louie's Steakhouse and Empire Coffee café.

Hume Hotel & Spa HOTEL $$
(☑250-352-5331; www.humehotel.com; 422 Vernon St; r incl breakfast from $120; P😀❄🤏) This 1898 classic hotel maintains its period grandeur. The 43 rooms vary greatly in shape and size; ask for the huge corner rooms with views of the hills and lake. Rates include a delicious breakfast. It has several appealing nightlife venues.

Victoria Falls Guest House INN $$
(☑250-551-3663; www.victoriafallsguesthouse. com; 213 Victoria St; r from $95; P😀🤏) The wide porch wraps right around this festive, yellow, renovated Victorian. The five suites have sitting areas and cooking facilities. Decor ranges from cozy antiques to family-friendly bunk beds. There is a barbecue.

BC MASCOTS

Some BC towns have their own quirky mascots, which sometimes appear at community events. On your travels, look out for **Knuckles** the grey whale in Ucluelet; **Peter Pine** the tree in Princeton; **Mr PG** in Prince George; and, our favorite, **Potato Jack** in Pemberton – a jaunty tuber dressed as a cowboy, complete with spurs and a neckerchief.

🍴 Eating & Drinking

Cottonwood Community Market MARKET $
(www.ecosociety.ca; 199 Carbonate St, Cottonwood Falls Park; ⏲9:30am-3pm Sat mid-May–Oct) Close to downtown and next to the surging Cottonwood waterfall, this market encapsulates Nelson. There's great organic produce; fine baked goods, many with heretofore-unheard-of grains; and various craft items with artistic roots in tie-dyeing. A second event is the **Downtown Market** (Hall St; ⏲9:30am-3pm Wed mid-Jun–Sep).

Full Circle Cafe DINER $
(☑250-354-4458; www.facebook.com/fullcirclecafe; 402 Baker S; mains from $8; ⏲6:30am-2:30pm) A downtown diner beloved for its omelets, the Full Circle will have you doing just that as you return for skillfully made breakfast classics, such as eggs Benedict. It gets popular on weekends, so prepare for a wait.

★**Jackson's Hole & Grill** CANADIAN $$
(☑250-354-1919; www.jacksonsgrill.ca; 524 Vernon St; dinner mains from $14; ⏲11:30am-9pm Sun-Tue, to 10pm Wed & Thu, to midnight Fri & Sat) In a historic building that has been around since 1897, this place is both lively and friendly. Used as Dixie's Café in the Steve Martin and Darryl Hannah Hollywood classic *Roxanne* in 1986, Jackson's serves soups, salads, sandwiches, wraps, burgers and pastas. Plenty to choose from in a very convivial atmosphere.

★**All Seasons Cafe** FUSION $$$
(☑250-352-0101; www.allseasonscafe.com; 620 Herridge Lane; mains from $22; ⏲5-10pm) Sitting on the patio here beneath little lights

twinkling in the huge maple above you is a Nelson highlight; in winter, candles inside provide the same romantic flair. The eclectic menu changes with the seasons but always celebrates BC foods. Presentations are artful; service is gracious.

★ Backroads Brewing Company
MICROBREWERY

(☑778-463-3361; www.backroadsbrewing.com; 460 Baker St; ☺noon-10pm Mon-Thu, to 11pm Fri & Sat, to 8pm Sun) Nelson's local brews from tank to tap on Baker St. Small-batch, hand-crafted ales and lagers such as the El Dorado Golden Ale and Navigator Irish Red keep the locals coming back for more. Limited food apart from bar snacks, but that's not what you're here for, right?

Royal on Baker
BAR

(☑250-354-7014; www.royalgrillnelson.com; 330 Baker St; ☺5pm-2am) This gritty old pub on Baker gets some of the region's best music acts. It has a whole section of tables outside on the street and serves decent pub food.

Oso Negro Café
CAFE

(☑250-532-7761; www.osonegrocoffee.com; 604 Ward St; ☺7am-6pm; 🛜) This local favorite corner cafe roasts its own coffee in 20 blends. Outside there are tables in a garden that burbles with water features amid statues. Enjoy baked goods and other snacks.

ℹ Information

Discover Nelson Visitor Centre (☑250-352-3433; www.discovernelson.com; 90 Baker St; ☺8:30am-6pm daily May-Oct, to 5pm Mon-Fri Nov-Apr) Housed in the beautifully restored train station, it offers excellent brochures detailing driving and walking tours, plus has an excellent cafe.

ℹ Getting There & Away

West Kootenay Regional Airport (www.wkrairport.ca; Hwy 3A) The closest major airport to Nelson is 42km southwest at Castlegar.

West Kootenay Transit System (☑855-993-3100; www.bctransit.com; fares $2) The main stop is at the corner of Ward and Baker Sts.

Nelson to Revelstoke

Heading north from Nelson to Revelstoke, there are two options, both scenic. Hwy 6 heads west for 16km before turning north at **South Slocan**. The road eventually runs alongside pretty Slocan Lake for about

30km before reaching New Denver, 97km from Nelson.

The most interesting route is north and east from Nelson on Hwy 3A. Head 34km northeast to Balfour, where the free **Kootenay Lake Ferry** (☑250-229-4215; www2.gov.bc.ca/gov/content/transportation/passenger-travel) connects to Kootenay Bay. The ferry's worthwhile for its long lake vistas of blue mountains rising sharply from the water. From Kootenay Bay, Hwy 3A heads 80km south to Creston. Continuing north from the ferry at Balfour, the road becomes Hwy 31 and follows the lake 34km to Kaslo, passing cute towns. West from Kaslo to New Denver on Rte 31A is spectacular. North of there you pass Nakusp village and another free ferry before reaching Revelstoke. This is a great all-day trip.

Kaslo

A cute little town, Kaslo is an underrated gem with a beautiful lakeside setting.

SS Moyie
HISTORIC SITE

(☑250-353-2525; www.klhs.bc.ca; 324 Front St; adult/child $12/5; ☺10am-5pm mid-May–mid-Oct) Don't miss the restored 1898 lake steamer SS *Moyie*. It also has tourist info on the myriad ways to kayak and canoe the sparkling-blue waters.

Kaslo Hotel & Pub
HOTEL $$

(☑250-353-7714; www.kaslohotel.com; 430 Front St; r from $125; ☻✳🛜) This appealing three-story downtown veteran (1896) has lake views and a good pub. Rooms have balcony and porch.

New Denver

Wild mountain streams are just some of the spectacular highlights on Hwy 31A, which goes up and over some rugged hills west of Kaslo. At the end of this twisting 47km road, you reach New Denver, which seems about five years away from ghost-town status. But that's not necessarily bad, as this historic little gem slumbers away peacefully right on the clear waters of Slocan Lake. The equally sleepy old mining town of **Silverton** is just south.

Silvery Slocan Museum
MUSEUM

(☑250-358-2201; www.newdenver.ca/silvery-slocan-museum; 202 6th Ave; by donation; ☺9am-5pm daily Jul & Aug, Sat & Sun only Sep-Jun) Housed in the 1897 Bank of Montreal building, this museum features well-done displays from the booming mining days, a tiny vault and an untouched tin ceiling. It also has visitor info.

Nakusp

250, 778 / POP 1570

Situated right on Upper Arrow Lake, Nakusp was forever changed by BC's orgy of dam building in the 1950s and 1960s. The water level here was raised and the town was relocated to its current spot, which is why it has a 1960s-era look. It has some attractive cafes and a tiny museum.

Nakusp Hot Springs HOT SPRINGS

(🗷 250-265-4528; www.nakusphotsprings.com; 8500 Hot Springs Rd; adult/child $10.50/9.50; ⊘9:30am-9:30pm) These hot springs, 12km northeast of Nakusp off Hwy 23, feel a bit artificial after receiving a revamp. However, you'll forget this as you soak away your cares amid an amphitheater of trees.

CARIBOO CHILCOTIN COAST

This vast and beautiful region covers a huge swath of BC north of Whistler. It comprises three very distinct areas. The Cariboo region includes numerous ranches, and terrain that's little changed from the 1850s, when the 'Gold Rush Trail' passed through from Lillooet to Barkerville.

Populated with more moose than people, the Chilcotin lies to the west of Hwy 97, the region's north–south spine. Its mostly wild, rolling landscape has a few ranches and some indigenous villages. Traveling west along Hwy 20 from Williams Lake leads you to the Bella Coola Valley, a spectacular bear-and-wildlife-filled inlet along the coast.

Much of the region can be reached via Hwy 97, enabling you to build a circle itinerary to other parts of BC via Prince George in the north.

❶ Getting There & Away

Adventure Charter (www.adventurecharters. ca/) runs buses north from Kamloops to Williams Lake and on to Prince George.

Hwy 97 forms the spine of the region; it's a good-quality road that continues to be improved.

Williams Lake to Prince George

Cattle and lumber have shaped **Williams Lake** as the hub for the region. At 205km north of the junction of Hwys 1 and 97 at Cache Creek, this small town is a busy three-way crossroads.

Dead-end Hwy 20 heads 450km west to coastal **Bella Coola**; Hwy 97 heads south to Cache Creek and north for 124km to **Quesnel**. There's not much character on the highways in Williams Lake. Head west on Oliver St into the old part of town to escape the chain stores, restaurants and hotels.

From Quesnel, Hwy 26 leads east to the area's main attractions, **Barkerville Historic Park** and **Bowron Lake Provincial Park**. North from Quesnel, it's 116km on Hwy 97 to Prince George.

Lakeside Motel MOTEL $$

(🗷 250-392-4181; www.lakesidemotelwilliamslake. net; 1505 Cariboo Hwy; r from $90; 🅿️⊖❋🛜) A good option if you like avoiding rather charmless chain hotels, Lakeside Motel is like its name suggests, beside the lake. The rooms are basic, but they have patios and there's plenty of grass outside. Rooms have microwave, refrigerator and flat-screen TV, and guests can use the laundry facilities, BBQ and picnic area.

❶ Information

Williams Lake Visitor Centre (🗷 250-392-5025; www.williamslake.ca; 1660 Broadway S, off Hwy 97; ⊘9am-6pm) Located in a massive log building as you come into town from the south, this place has excellent regional information. In the same building you'll find the **Museum of the Cariboo Chilcotin** (entry by donation).

Barkerville & Around

In 1862 Billy Barker, previously of Cornwall, struck gold deep in the Cariboo. **Barkerville** soon sprung up, populated by the usual fly-by-night crowds of prostitutes, dupes, tricksters and just plain prospectors. Today it's a compelling attraction, a time capsule of the Old West.

Barkerville lies 82km east of Quesnel along Hwy 26. Historic **Cottonwood House**, a parklike area, makes an atmospheric stop on the way. Nearby **Wells**, which you'll pass through on Hwy 26, has a top eating option.

Barkerville Historic Town HISTORIC SITE

(☑888-994-3332; www.barkerville.ca; Hwy 26; adult/child $16/6; ⊙8am-8pm mid-Jun–Aug, 8:30am-4pm mid-May–mid-Jun & Sep) You can visit more than 125 restored heritage buildings in Barkerville Historic Town, which also has shops, cafes and a couple of B&Bs. In summer, people dressed in period garb roam through town and, if you can tune out the crowds, it feels more authentic than forced. At other times of the year, you can wander the town for free, but don't expect to find much open.

★ Bear's Paw Cafe CAFE $

(☑250-994-3538; www.thebearspawcafe.com; Hwy 26, Wells; lunch mains from $10; ⊙9am-8pm Thu-Tue) If some of the clientele are a tad wiffy, it's because this is the spot that outdoors types head straight to when dropping back into civilization. The cafe boasts freshly made foods, locally roasted espresso and treats to die for, while right outside there's a food truck (June to September) on the patio.

❶ Information

Wells Visitor Centre (☑250-994-2323; www.wells.ca/tourism/visitor-information-centre; 11900 Hwy 26, Wells; ⊙9am-5pm May-Sep) Has regional info.

Bowron Lake

The place heaven-bound canoeists go when they die, Bowron Lake Provincial Park is a fantasyland of 10 lakes surrounded by snow-capped peaks.

★ Bowron Lake Provincial Park PARK

(www.env.gov.bc.ca/bcparks; off Hwy 26; ⊙May-Sep; 🅿) Forming a natural circle with sections of the Isaac, Cariboo and Bowron Rivers, the park's 116km canoe circuit (permits $30 to $60) is one of the world's finest. There are eight portages, with the longest (2km) over well-defined trails.

The park website has maps, and details everything you'll need to know for planning your trip, including mandatory reservations, which sometimes book up in advance. Campsites cost $18. Check out Bowron Lake Canoe Rentals (www.bowronlakecanoe.com).

The whole canoe circuit takes between six and 10 days, and you'll need to be completely self-sufficient. September is a good time to visit, both for the bold colors of changing leaves and the lack of summer crowds.

Wells Gray Provincial Park

Plunging 141m onto rocks below, **Helmcken Falls** may only be Canada's fourth-highest waterfall but it is one of the undiscovered facets of Wells Gray Provincial Park, itself an underappreciated gem. **Clearwater**, 123km north of Kamloops on Hwy 5, is the town near the park entrance and has everything you'll need for a visit.

◉ Sights & Activities

Wells Gray Provincial Park PARK
(www.env.gov.bc.ca/bcparks; Wells Gray Rd) BC's fourth-largest park is bounded by the Clearwater River and its tributaries, which define the park's boundaries. Highlights for visitors include five major lakes, two large river systems, scores of waterfalls such as **Helmcken Falls** and most every kind of BC land-based wildlife. Many hiking trails and sights, such as Helmcken Falls, are accessible off the main park road, which ends at **Clearwater Lake**.

You'll find opportunities for **hiking**, **cross-country skiing** and **horseback riding** along more than 20 trails of varying lengths. Rustic backcountry campgrounds dot the area around four of the lakes.

Clearwater Lake Tours OUTDOORS
(☑250-674-2121; www.clearwaterlaketours.com; canoe/kayak rental per day from $60) Rents canoes and kayaks, leads tours of the park and runs taxi-boats to Azure Lake and Rainbow Falls. Based at Osprey Cafe at Clearwater Lake, the only cafe and the only wi-fi in the park.

🛏 Sleeping & Eating

Wells Grey Provincial Park Campgrounds CAMPGROUND $
(☑800-689-9025; www.discovercamping.ca; Wells Grey Provincial Park; campsites from $20; 🅿) There are three vehicle-accessible yet simple campgrounds in the park. Woodsy **Pyramid Campground** is close to Helmcken Falls. There's also plenty of **backcountry camping** ($5).

★ **Lake House**   B&B **$$**
(☑ 250-674-5198; www.thelakehouseclearwater.
com; 309 Harby Rd; r from $195; P ⊜ ❀ 🛜) This
lovely B&B sits right on the edge of Dutch
Lake and features three exquisite rooms in
a large log house, handmade rustic wood-
en furniture, an attractive common lounge
area and a delicious breakfast. Guests have
complimentary use of canoes, paddleboards
and a rowboat from the Lake House's private
jetty.

All rooms have a private terrace overlook-
ing the lake.

★ **Hop 'N' Hog Tap &**
Smokehouse   CANADIAN **$$**
(☑ 250-674-3654; www.canadiansmokehouse.
com; 424 Clearwater Valley Rd, Clearwater; mains
from $20; ⊙ 5-9:30pm May-Oct) One for the
hard-core carnivores among us, Hop 'N' Hog
specializes in smoked meats and sausages
and has 10 rotating taps of BC craft beer.
The smoked beef brisket ($26.50) is a doozy,
while herbivores are not forgotten with the
smoked vegetarian platter ($25). Wine and
liquor options abound.

ⓘ Information

Clearwater Wells Gray Park Visitors Centre
(☑ 250-674-3334; www.wellsgraypark.info; 416
Eden Rd, off Hwy 5, Clearwater; ⊙ 9am-7pm
May-Oct; 🛜) Has full park and regional info.

Chilcotin & Highway 20

Meandering over the lonely hills west of the
Chilcotin, Hwy 20 runs 450km from Williams Lake to the Bella Coola Valley. You'll
come across a few indigenous villages, as
well as gravel roads that lead off to the odd
provincial park and deserted lake.

Long spoken about by drivers in hushed
and concerned tones, Hwy 20 has received
steady improvement and is now more than
90% paved.

However, the unpaved section remains a
doozy: The Hill is a 30km stretch of gravel
386km west of Williams Lake. It descends
1524m from Heckman's Pass to the valley,
which is nearly at sea level, through a series
of sharp switchbacks and 11% grades. But by
taking your time and using low gear, you'll
actually enjoy the stunning views. It's safe
for all vehicles – visitors in rented SUVs will
be humbled when a local in a Ford beater
zips past.

★ **Eagle's Nest Resort**   LODGE **$$**
(☑ 250-742-3707; www.eaglesnest-resort.com;
Anahim Lake; r from $100; P ⊜ 🛜) At Anahim
Lake, 320km west of Williams Lake and
130km east of Bella Coola, this small resort
lodge has a variety of rooms, cabins and a
cottage. Enjoy birds and wildlife, meals in
the lakeside dining room, and the outdoor
hot tub, or rent a boat or canoe.

KiNiKiNiK Restaurant
& Store   CANADIAN **$$**
(☑ 250-394-6000; www.pasturetoplate.ca; 9391
Hwy 20, Redstone; mains from $12; ⊙ 10am-5pm
Jun-Sep) This is a good stop on the long Hwy
20 drive, 145km west of Williams Lake and
305km east of Bella Coola, featuring a sod
roof, restaurant and cabin accommodation.
KiNiKiNiK uses organic ingredients and
meats for sausages, salads and sandwiches. Rooms, available year-round, run from
$120; you'll want to book ahead.

Bella Coola Valley

The verdant Bella Coola Valley is at the
heart of Great Bear Rainforest, a lush land
of huge stands of trees, surging white water and lots of bears. It's a spiritual place:
Nuxalk First Nation artists are active here
and, for many creative types from elsewhere, this is literally the end of the road.
The valley lies west of the dry expanses of
the Chilcotin.

The valley stretches 53km to the shores
of the **North Bentinck Arm**, a deep, glacier-fed fjord that runs 40km inland from
the Pacific Ocean. The two main towns,
Bella Coola on the water and **Hagensborg**
15km east, almost seem as one, with most
places of interest in or between the two.

⊙ Sights & Activities

Tweedsmuir Provincial Park   PARK
(www.env.gov.bc.ca/bcparks; off Hwy 20) Spanning the Chilcotin and the east end of the
valley, the southern portion of Tweedsmuir
Provincial Park is the second-largest provincial park in BC. It's a seemingly barely
charted place, perfect for challenging backcountry adventures. Day hikes off Hwy 20
in the valley follow trails into lush and untouched coastal rainforest. Campsites are
$20.

Kynoch Adventures   ADVENTURE, WILDLIFE
(☑ 250-982-2298;   https://kynoch-adventures.
business.site;   1896   Hwy   20,   Hagensborg)

Specializes in critter-spotting trips down local rivers and wilderness hikes. Highly recommended float trips to spot the valley's renowned **grizzly bear** population run from late August into October ($150 per person).

🛏️ Sleeping & Eating

Rip Rap Campsite   CAMPGROUND **$**
(☑ 250-982-2752; www.riprapcamp.com; 1854 Hwy 20, Hagensborg; campsites/cabins from $22/75; ☺ May-Oct; 🅿🛜) A much-lauded campground, Rip Rap has plenty of services and a great viewing deck overlooking the river, 15km east of Bella Coola village. Four cabins, two with private toilet and shower, two with shared facilities.

★ Bella Coola Mountain Lodge   INN **$$**
(☑ 250-982-2298;   www.bcmountainlodge.com; 1900 Hwy 20, Hagensborg; r from $140; 🅿😊@🛜) The rooms, many with kitchen facilities, are huge and there's an excellent espresso bar at this lodge 15km east of Bella Coola village. The owners also run Kynoch Adventures (p755), which offers river tours and wilderness hikes.

Bella Coola Valley Restaurant   CANADIAN **$$**
(☑ 250-799-0045; MacKenzie St, Bella Coola; dinner mains from $14; ☺ 7am-8pm) It's simple and unfussy, but you won't go hungry in the village of Bella Coola. Choose from sandwiches and Valley favorites such as fish-and-chips ($12.95) for lunch, or pastas and steak for dinner.

ℹ️ Information

Bella Coola Valley Tourism (☑ 250-799-5202; https://bellacoola.ca; 442 MacKenzie St, Bella Coola; ☺ 10am-6pm Jun-Sep) Oodles of info and advice (get the trail guide).

ℹ️ Getting There & Away

BC Ferries (☑ 888-223-3779; www.bcferries. com) runs direct ferries connecting Port Hardy to Bella Coola, but to get to Prince Rupert from Bella Coola requires a transfer in Bella Bella, a small Inside Passage town – a major inconvenience. Schedules allow a trip every few days in summer (much less often in winter).

There are no buses along Hwy 20 from Williams Lake, but you can get to Bella Coola by charter plane. **Pacific Coastal Airlines** (☑ 800-663-2872; www.pacificcoastal.com) has daily one-hour flights from Vancouver.

NORTHERN BRITISH COLUMBIA

Northern British Columbia is where you'll truly feel that you've crossed that ethereal border into some place different. Nowhere else are the rich cultures of Canada's indigenous people so keenly felt, from the Haida on Haida Gwaii to the Tsimshian on the mainland. Nowhere else does land so exude mystery, whether it's the storm-shrouded coast and islands or the silent majesty of glaciers carving passages through entire mountain ranges. And nowhere else is so alive with fabled fauna, from orcas to moose to grizzlies.

It's also a region of promise. Highways such as the fabled Alaska or the awe-inspiring Stewart-Cassiar encourage adventure, discovery or even a new life. Here, your

---

GREAT BEAR RAINFOREST

It's the last major tract of coastal temperate rainforest left on the planet. The Great Bear Rainforest is a wild region of islands, fjords and towering peaks. Covering 64,000 sq km (7% of British Columbia), it stretches south from Alaska along the BC coast and Haida Gwaii to roughly Campbell River on Vancouver Island (which isn't itself part of the forest). The forests and waters are remarkably rich in life: whales, salmon, eagles, elk, otters and more thrive. Remote river valleys are lined with forests of old Sitka spruce, Pacific silver fir and various cedars that are often 100m tall and 1500 years old.

In 2016, BC's provincial government announced that 85% of the Great Bear Rainforest region would be permanently protected from industrial logging. For an introduction to the continuing campaign to save this area, head to www.savethegreatbear.org.

From Bella Coola you can arrange boat trips and treks to magical places in the Great Bear, including hidden rivers where you might see a rare **Kermode bear**, a white-furred offshoot of the black bear known in tribal legend as the 'spirit bear' and the namesake of the rainforest.

place next to nature will never be in doubt; you'll revel in your own insignificance.

Prince Rupert

📞 250, 778 / POP 12,220

People are always 'discovering' Prince Rupert, and realizing what a find it is. This intriguing town with a gorgeous harbor is not just a transportation hub for ferries heading south to Vancouver Island, west to Haida Gwaii and north to Alaska: it's a destination in its own right. It has two excellent museums, fine restaurants and a culture that draws much from its indigenous heritage. It may rain 220 days a year, but that doesn't stop the drip-dry locals enjoying activities in the misty mountains and waterways.

Prince Rupert's economic driver is its deep, ice-free anchorage and port. International freighters use the container port year-round and an increasing number of cruise ships turn up in summer. Plentiful salmon drew dozens of canneries to the coast in the 1800s, while Prince Rupert once enjoyed the title of 'halibut capital of the world'.

◉ Sights & Activities

A short walk from the center, **Cow Bay** is a delightful place for a stroll. The eponymous spotted decor is everywhere, but somehow avoids seeming clichéd. There are shops, cafes and a good view of the waterfront, especially from the docks at the Atlin Terminal.

You'll see **totem poles** all around town; two flank the statue of Charlie Hays beside City Hall on 3rd Ave. Also watch around town for more than 30 huge **murals** adorning buildings. Noted artist Jeff King paints history and nature.

Among the many local walks, a good place to start is the **Butze Rapids Trail**, a 4.5km loop beginning 6km south of town. It has interpretive signs.

Further afield, **Khutzeymateen Grizzly Bear Sanctuary** is a natural area home to more than 50 of the giants; it can be visited through Prince Rupert Adventure Tours.

★**North Pacific Cannery National Historic Site** HISTORIC SITE
(📞250-628-3538; www.northpacificcannery.ca; 1889 Skeena Dr; adult/child $12/8; ⊙10am-5pm daily Jul & Aug, Tue-Sun May, Jun & Sep) Explore the history of fishing and canning along the Skeena River. This fascinating all-wood complex was used from 1889 to 1968; exhib-

its document the miserable conditions of the workers, and tours cover the industrial process or cannery life. Prince Rupert Transit has bus service to the site. Situated about 20km south of Prince Rupert, near the town of Port Edward.

★**Museum of Northern BC** MUSEUM
(📞250-624-3207; www.museumofnorthernbc. com; 100 1st Ave W; adult/child $6/2; ⊙9am-5pm daily Jun-Aug, Tue-Sat Sep-May) Residing in a building styled after an indigenous longhouse, this museum is a must-see. It shows how local civilizations enjoyed sustainable cultures that lasted for thousands of years. The displays include a wealth of excellent Haida, Gitksan and Tsimshian art and plenty of info on totem poles. The bookstore is excellent.

★**Prince Rupert Adventure Tours** WILDLIFE
(📞250-627-9166; www.adventuretours.net; 205 Cow Bay Rd; bear tours $290, whale tours $145) Excellent boat tours include Khutzeymateen grizzly-watching trips (from mid-May to early August) and whale tours (August and September). Trips can last many hours as you track the region's rich wildlife.

🛏 Sleeping

Black Rooster Inn & Apartments INN $
(📞250-627-5337; www.blackrooster.ca; 501 6th Ave W; r from $85; 🅿😊❄🛜) This bright and friendly renovated house just 400m up the hill from the center has a patio and an appealing common room. Rooms range from spartan singles to large apartments.

Cow Bay Pioneer Guesthouse HOSTEL $
(📞250-624-2334; www.pioneerprincerupert.com; 167 3rd Ave E; dm/r from $30/70; 🅿😊🛜) Located between Cow Bay and downtown, bright blue Pioneer Guesthouse has spotless, compact rooms accented with vibrant colors. Besides the mixed dorms there are two rooms with en suite and a two-bedroom master suite. There's a small kitchen and barbecue facilities out back.

★**Eagle Bluff B&B** B&B $$
(📞250-627-4955; www.eaglebluff.ca; 201 Cow Bay Rd; r from $95; 😊❄🛜) In an ideal location on Cow Bay, this pier-side B&B is in a heritage building that has a striking red-and-white paint job. Inside, the seven rooms have harbor views – some quite spectacular; two share baths.

★ Crest Hotel
HOTEL $$

(📞 250-624-6771; www.cresthotel.bc.ca; 222 1st Ave W; r from $130; 🅿️ ➡️ ❄️ 🛜) Prince Rupert's premier hotel has harbor-view rooms that are worth every penny, right down to the built-in bay-window seats with loaner binoculars. Avoid the smallish rooms overlooking the parking lot. Suites are opulent.

✖️ Eating & Drinking

Cowpuccino's
CAFE $

(📞 250-627-1395; 25 Cow Bay Rd; coffee from $2.50; ⏰ 7am-9pm, to 6pm Sat & Sun; 🛜) This woodsy local cafe will make you forget the rain with its coffee and fine selection of baked goods (great cookies) and sandwiches. Good for picnics or eating in.

★ Dolly's Fish Market
SEAFOOD $$

(📞 250-624-6090; www.dollysfishmarket.com; 7 Cow Bay Rd; chowder from $4.95; ⏰ 11am-9pm) It's hard to miss bright red Dolly's as you wander around Cow Bay. This is seafood country and you can't go wrong with Dolly's legendary chowders, in three different sizes ($4.95 to $10.95), cream or tomato base, or go for the superb Boston clam chowder. Lots of other options too, such as oysters, prawns and classic fish-and-chips.

★ Charley's Lounge
PUB FOOD $$

(📞 250-624-6771; www.cresthotel.bc.ca; 222 1st Ave W, Crest Hotel; mains from $14; ⏰ noon-10pm) Locals flock to trade gossip while gazing out over the harbor from the heated patio. The food matches the view: the pub menu features some of Rupert's best seafood.

Fukasaku
JAPANESE $$

(📞 250-627-7874; www.fukasaku.ca; 215 Cow Bay Rd, Atlin Terminal; mains from $15; ⏰ noon-2pm & 5-8:30pm Tue-Sat) 🍴 This excellent sushi place has a menu crafted with certified sustainability in mind. Enjoy uberfresh seafood in rolls, sashimi, *donburi* etc. The dining area is properly minimalist.

★ Wheelhouse Brewing Company
MICROBREWERY

(📞 250-624-2739; www.wheelhousebrewing.com; 217 1 Ave E; ⏰ 4pm-late Wed-Fri, from noon Sat, to 9pm Sun) This rollicking little brewpub is the project of three buddies who are knocking out some of Northern BC's best microbrews. You can find their beer all over town, but here at home base they serve fresh beer right from the taps. Strictly a drinking spot with minimal snacks.

ℹ️ Information

Prince Rupert Visitor Center (📞 250-624-5637; www.visitprincerupert.com; 215 Cow Bay Rd, Atlin Terminal; ⏰ 9am-6pm) Has regional info.

ℹ️ Getting There & Away

AIR

Prince Rupert Airport (📞 250-624-6274; www.ypr.ca) is located on Digby Island, across the harbor from town. The trip involves a bus and ferry; pickup is at the Prince Rupert Hotel about two hours before flight time. Confirm all the details with your airline or the airport. Call 250-622-2222 for up-to-date details.

Air Canada (www.aircanada.com) flies to Vancouver.

BOAT

BC Ferries (📞 250-386-3431; www.bcferries.com) Sails the Inside Passage run to Port Hardy, hailed for its amazing scenery. There are three services per week in summer and one per week in winter. There is also service to Haida Gwaii.

BUS

BC Bus North (📞 1-844-564-7494; www.bcbus.ca) runs twice per week return along Hwy 16 connecting Prince George, Smithers and Prince Rupert.

TRAIN

VIA Rail (www.viarail.ca) operates tri-weekly services to Prince George (12½ hours) and, after an overnight stop, on to Jasper, AB (another 7½ hours).

Haida Gwaii

Haida Gwaii forms a dagger-shaped archipelago of some 450 islands lying 80km west of the BC coast, and offers a magical trip for those who make the effort. The number-one attraction here is remote Gwaii Haanas National Park, which makes up the bottom third of the archipelago. Attention has long focused on the many unique species of flora and fauna to the extent that 'Canada's Galápagos' is a popular moniker. But each year it becomes more apparent that the real soul of the islands is the Haida culture itself.

Haida reverence for the environment is protecting the last stands of superb old-growth rainforests, where the spruce and cedars are some of the world's largest. Amid this sparsely populated, wild and rainy place are bald eagles, bears and much more wildlife. Offshore in marine-protected waters, sea lions, whales and orcas abound, and once-rare right whales and sea otters have been spotted.

⊙ Sights

★ Gwaii Haanas National Park Reserve, National Marine Conservation Area Reserve & Haida Heritage Site NATIONAL PARK

(☑250-559-8818; www.pc.gc.ca/en/pn-np/bc/gwaiihaanas) This huge Unesco World Heritage site encompasses Moresby and 137 smaller islands at its southern end. It combines a time-capsule look at abandoned Haida villages with hot springs, amazing natural beauty and some of the continents best kayaking. A visit demands advance planning as the number of visitors entering the park each day is limited. The easiest way is to take a guided trip with a licensed operator; access to the park is by boat or floatplane only.

Archaeological finds have documented more than 500 ancient Haida sites, including villages and burial caves throughout the islands. The most famous village is **SGang Gwaay** (Ninstints) on Anthony Island, where rows of weathered totem poles stare eerily out to sea. Other major sights include the ancient village of **Skedans**, on Louise Island, and **Hotspring Island**, whose natural hot springs are back on after being disrupted by earthquakes in 2012. The sites are protected by Haida Gwaii caretakers, who live on the islands in summer.

In 2013 the magnificent **Gwaii Haanas Legacy Pole** was raised at Windy Bay, the first new pole in the protected area in 130 years.

The easiest way to get into the park is with a tour company. Parks Canada (p761) has a lists of licensed operators on its website. Many operators can also set you up with rental kayaks (average per day/week $60/300) and gear for independent travel.

To visit independently, you must make a reservation, pay a visitor use fee (adult $20 per day, child free) and attend a 90-minute orientation. The number of daily reservations is limited, so plan well in advance, especially for the busiest period of July to mid-August. Details of the requirements are on the excellent Parks Canada website, which has links to the essential annual trip planner. The Parks Canada office is next to the Haida Heritage Centre at Kay Llnagaay.

★ Haida Heritage Centre at Kay Llnagaay MUSEUM

(☑250-559-7885; www.haidaheritagecentre.com; Second Beach Rd. Hwy 16, Skidegate; adult/child $16/5; ⊙9am-5pm Jul & Aug, reduced hours Sep-Jun) One of the top attractions in the north is this marvelous cultural center. With exhibits on history, wildlife and culture, it would be enough reason to visit the islands just by itself. The rich traditions of the Haida are fully explored in galleries, programs and work areas, where contemporary artists create works such as the totem poles lining the shore. Look for the remarkable model of Skidegate before colonial times.

Crystal Cabin GALLERY

(☑250-557-4383; www.crystalcabingallery.com; 778a Richardson Rd, Tlell; ⊙9am-6pm May-Sep, reduced hours Oct-Apr) The works of 20 Haida artists are featured at the jewelry workshop of April and Sarah Dutheil, second-generation artisans and sisters who were taught by their father, local legend and authority on island geology, Dutes. April has written on Haida Gwaii agate collecting and is happy to explain Dutes' Tlell Stone Circle, which is just outside the cabin. There are many forms of art here, including carvings from argillite, a local rock that can only be carved by Haida artisans.

Naikoon Provincial Park PARK

(☑250-626-5115; www.env.gov.bc.ca/bcparks; off Hwy 16) Much of the island's northeastern side is devoted to the beautiful 726-sq-km Naikoon Provincial Park, which combines sand dunes and low sphagnum bogs, surrounded by stunted and gnarled lodgepole pine, and red and yellow cedar. The starkly beautiful **beaches** on the north coast feature strong winds, pounding surf and flotsam from across the Pacific. They can be reached via the stunning 26km-long Tow Hill Rd, east of Masset.

Wooden steps and a boardwalk make visiting the **Tow Hill Lookout** and **Blow Hole** near the end of Tow Hill Rd easy. Allow about one hour for a looping walk with many steps. A 21km loop trail traverses a good bit of the park to/from **Fife Beach** at the end of the road. The park has campsites ($18).

⚡ Activities

Away from the park, Haida Gwaii has myriad other natural places to explore on land and sea.

★ **Golden Spruce Trail** WALKING
Just south of Port Clements, this is an excellent short walk (30 minutes return) through moss-covered forest featuring huge red cedar and Sitka spruce to the Yakoun River. Across the river is where the legendary Golden Spruce used to stand. To get to the trailhead, carry on through Port Clements on Bayview Dr, then for 3.5km on the gravel road.

★ **Moresby Explorers** ADVENTURE
(☑250-637-2215, 800-806-7633; www.moresby explorers.com; 365 Beach Rd, Sandspit; day tours from $250) Offers one-day Zodiac tours, including the Louise Island trip that takes in the town of Skedans and its important totem poles, as well as much longer trips (the four-day trip is highly recommended). Also rents kayaks and gear, and provides logistics.

Haida Style Expeditions CULTURAL
(☑250-637-1151; www.haidastyle.com; Second Beach Rd/Hwy 16, Skidegate; tours per person from $250; ☺Apr-Sep) Buzz through the Gwaii Haanas National Park Reserve (p759) in a large inflatable boat. This Haida-run outfit runs four different day tours (eight to 12 hours) that together take in the most important sights in the park.

🛌 Sleeping

★ **Premier Creek Lodging** INN $
(☑888-322-3388, 250-559-8415; www.haidagwaii. net/premier; 3101 Oceanview Dr, QCC; s/d from $45/75; P☺❄🛜) Dating from 1910, this is the top place to stay in the town of Queen Charlotte. The lodge has 14 rooms that range from tiny but great-value singles to spacious rooms with views, kitchen and porch.

Agate Beach Campground CAMPGROUND $
(☑250-557-4390; www.env.gov.bc.ca/bcparks; Tow Hill Rd, North Shore, Naikoon Provincial Park; tent & RV sites $18; P) This stunning, wind-whipped campground is right on the beach on the north shore. Frolic on the sand, hunt for its namesake rocks and see if you can snare some flotsam.

★ **Cacilia's B&B** B&B $$
(☑250-557-4664; www.facebook.com/caciliasbed breakfast; 36914 Hwy 16, Tlell; r incl breakfast from $110; P☺❄🛜) Cacilia's is in a lovely spot in Tlell, a 30-minute drive north from the ferry landing. There are seven rooms, four with private bath, in a big log building, with patchy wi-fi and a friendly family atmos-

phere among guests. Cacilia prepares a tasty breakfast each morning using local produce, and the beach is a short walk away through the dunes.

All the Beach You Can Eat CABIN $$
(☑250-626-9091; www.allthebeachyoucaneat. com; Km 15, Tow Hill Rd, North Shore; cabins from $120; P) 🌊 On beautiful North Beach, five cabins are perched in the dunes, back from the wide swath of sand that runs for miles east and west. Like other properties with rental cabins out here, there is no electricity; cooking and lighting are fueled by propane. It's off the grid and out of this world.

🍴 Eating & Drinking

The best selection of restaurants is in Queen Charlotte (QCC), and there are also a few in Skidegate and Masset. There is a simple pub with food in Port Clements. Good supermarkets are found in QCC and Masset.

★ **Jags Beanstalk Bistro & Beds** CANADIAN $
(☑250-559-8826; www.jagsbeanstalk.com; 100 16 Hwy, Skidegate; mains from $10; ☺7:30am-4pm Mon-Fri, 9am-4pm Sat) Fresh, wholesome food delivered with speedy, friendly service about 1.5km north of the ferry terminal. Great coffee, pizzas, tacos and salads, with an effort to source ingredients locally. It also has cozy guest rooms above the coffee shop.

Moon Over Naikoon Bakery BAKERY $
(☑250-626-5064; 16443 Tow Hill Rd, Masset; snacks from $3; ☺8am-5pm Jun-Aug) Embodying the spirit of its location, on a road to the end of everything, this tiny community center and bakery is housed in an old school bus in a clearing about 6km east of Masset. The baked goods and coffee are brilliant. Keep your eyes open for the sign as the bus can't be seen from the road.

Queen B's CAFE $
(☑250-559-4463; www.facebook.com/queenbs cafe; 3201 Wharf St, QCC; mains from $3; ☺8am-5pm Mon-Sat) This funky place in Queen Charlotte excels at baked goods, which emerge from the oven all day long. There are tables with water views outside, and lots of local art inside.

Haida House at Tllaal SEAFOOD $$
(☑855-557-4600; www.haidahouse.com; 2087 Beitush Rd, Tlell; mains from $20; ☺5-7:30pm Tue-Sun mid-May–mid-Sep) This Haida-run restaurant

next to the river in Tlell at the end of Beitush Rd has excellent, creative seafood and other dishes with island accents, such as Haida favorites with berries. Also rents plush rooms at this magical spot in the forest.

★**Daddy Cool's Public House at Mile Zero** PUB

(☑250-626-3210; www.daddycools.ca; Collison Ave, Masset; ⊙9am-2am, hours can vary) Can't go wrong at Daddy Cool's in Masset with a popular pub on one side and a quiet dining room specializing in pub grub on the other. The eating side is family-friendly, while the pub side usually stays open until everyone has gone home. These guys are onto it and also run a liquor store and a taxi service.

❶ Information

Parks Canada (☑250-559-8818, reservations 877-559-8818; www.pc.gc.ca/en/pn-np/bc/gwaiihaanas; Haida Heritage Centre at Kay LInagaay, Skidegate; ⊙office 8:30am-noon & 1-4:30pm Mon-Fri) Main Parks Canada office for Haida Gwaii. Download the Gwaii Haanas National Park trip planner from the website.

Queen Charlotte Visitor Centre (☑250-559-8316; www.queencharlottevisitorcentre.com; 3220 Wharf St, QCC; ⊙9am-7pm Mon-Sat, noon-6pm Sun May-Sep, shorter hours other times; 🐧) This handy visitor center can make advance excursion bookings by phone. There's a gift shop, toilets and wi-fi.

❶ Getting There & Away

The main airport for Haida Gwaii is at Sandspit on Moresby Island, 12km east of the ferry landing at Aliford Bay. Note that reaching the airport from Graham Island is time-consuming: eg if your flight is at 3:30pm, you'll need to line up at the car ferry at Skidegate Landing at 12:30pm (earlier in summer). **Air Canada** (www.aircanada.com) flies daily between Sandspit and Vancouver.

There's also a small airport 2km east of Masset that has daily flights from Vancouver with **Pacific Coastal Air** (www.pacificcoastal.com). Daily seaplane services between Prince Rupert and Masset are flown by **Inland Air** (www.inlandair.bc.ca).

BC Ferries (☑250-386-3431; www.bcferries.com) is the most popular way to reach the islands. Mainland ferries dock at Skidegate Landing on Graham Island, which houses 80% of residents. Services run between Prince Rupert and Skidegate Landing five times a week in summer and three times a week in winter (adult $39 to $48, children half-price, cars $139 to $169; six to seven hours). Cabins are useful for overnight schedules (from $90).

❶ Getting Around

The main road on Graham Island is Hwy 16, the first part of the Yellowhead Hwy, which is fully paved. It links Skidegate with Masset, 101km north, passing the small towns of Tlell and Port Clements. The principal town is Queen Charlotte (previously Queen Charlotte City and still known by its old QCC acronym), 7km west of Skidegate. Off paved Hwy 16, most roads are gravel or worse. There is no public transit.

BC Ferries, with its MV Kwuna car ferry, links Graham and Moresby Islands at Skidegate Landing and Alliford Bay (adult/child $11/5.50, cars from $25, 20 minutes, from 7am to 6pm).

Eagle Transit (☑250-559-4461, 877-747-4461; www.eagletransit.net; airport shuttle adult/child $30/15) buses meet Sandspit flights and serve Skidegate and QCC.

Renting a car can cost roughly the same ($60 to $100 per day) as bringing one over on the ferry. There are several small, locally owned firms, but the number of rental cars on Haida Gwaii is limited, so think ahead.

You can rent bikes at the small **Sandspit Airport Visitor Center** (☑250-637-5362; Sandspit Airport; ⊙9:30-11:30am & 1.30-4pm) for $30 per day. **Green Coast** (☑250-637-1093; www.gck-ayaking.com; 3302 Oceanview Dr, QCC; per day $30) rents bikes in Queen Charlotte, while **Masset Bikes** (☑250-626-8939; www.massetbikes.com; 1900 Towhill Rd, Masset; per day from $30) has a good selection of rentals at Masset Airport.

Prince Rupert to Prince George

You can cover the 725km on Hwy 16 between BC's Princes in a day or a week. There's nothing that's an absolute must-see, but there's much to divert and cause you to pause if so inclined. With the notable exception of

Skeena River, the scenery along much of the road won't fill your memory card, but it is a pleasing mix of mountains and rivers.

Prince Rupert to Smithers

For the first 145km out of Prince Rupert to Terrace, the Yellowhead Hwy (Hwy 16) hugs the wide and wild **Skeena River**. This is four-star scenic driving and you'll see glaciers and jagged peaks across the waters. Keep an eye out for anglers fishing for salmon on the Skeena River 10 months of the year – and also for a Kermodei or 'spirit bear', a cream-colored subspecies of black bear that is becoming increasingly imperiled by habitat loss.

The industrial timber town of **Terrace** doesn't have much to interest visitors. From there, Hwy 16 continues following the narrowing Skeena River valley 93km east to Kitwanga Junction, where the Stewart-Cassiar Hwy (Hwy 37) strikes north toward the Yukon and Alaska.

From Kitwanga Junction, the Yellowhead Hwy (Hwy 16) continues 115km to Smithers, following first the Skeena River, then the Bulkley River from where it joins the Skeena at Hazelton.

'Ksan Historical
Village & Museum   HISTORIC SITE
(🚶 250-842-5544; www.ksan.org; off Hwy 16, Hazelton; from $2; ⊙10am-9pm Jun-Aug, shorter hours Sep-May) Just east of Kitwanga and the start of Hwy 37 is the Hazelton area, the center of some interesting indigenous sites, including this historical village. The re-created site of the Gitksan people features longhouses, a museum, various outbuildings and totem poles. The Eagle House Cafe is open 10am to 3pm daily.

Smithers

🚶 250, 778 / POP 10,600

Smithers is an appealing town with a cute old downtown area, roughly halfway between Prince Rupert and Prince George. It's the hub of the surprisingly vibrant Bulkley Valley cultural scene and makes for a good overnight stop. Make sure to get off Hwy 16 on Main St and have a wander around downtown.

Bulkley Valley Museum   MUSEUM
(🚶 250-847-5322; www.bvmuseum.org; 1425 Main St; by donation; ⊙9am-5pm Mon-Sat) **FREE**
Sharing the lovely old Smithers Court House

building of 1925 with the **Smithers Art Gallery** on the corner of Main St and Hwy 16, this museum does a great job of making local history interesting and engaging. Lots of old photos plus a number of changing exhibitions.

This is the traditional territory of the Witsuwit'en people and a permanent exhibit features artifacts, images and information about their history and culture.

Prestige Hudson
Bay Lodge   HOTEL **$$**
(🚶 250-847-4581; www.prestigehotelsandresorts.com; 3251 E Hwy 16; r from $125; 🅿️❄️🐾❄️🛜) Part of a BC-wide chain, this place has a variety of well-appointed guest rooms and suites at the southern entrance to town on Hwy 16. Two on-site restaurants cover fine dining and a sports bar and grill, while there are complimentary bicycles, laundry and fitness room.

⭐ **Telly's Grill**   MEDITERRANEAN **$$**
(🚶 250-847-001; www.facebook.com/tellysgrill; 3843 4 Ave; mains from $15; ⊙4:30-9:30pm Mon-Sat) Don't let the drab exterior of the building fool you, this is one of the top places to eat in Northern BC. The Canadian-Mediterranean fusion menu offers a stunning array of mains including a Hot Chicken Caesar and Telly's mum's lasagne. Telly's comes complete with a photo of Telly Savalas sucking a lollipop and a Kojak burger on the menu.

⭐ **Smithers Brewing Co**   MICROBREWERY
(🚶 778-640-2739; www.smithersbrewing.com; 3832 3 Ave; ⊙2-8pm) Try the local brews just off Main St at Smithers Brewing Co in the custom-made taproom with timber framing and stunning bar tops. Ten taps pour mainstay beers and rotating seasonal offerings, as well as cider and an in-house kombucha. Our favorite is the Scatterbrain IPA.

ℹ️ Information

Smithers Visitor Centre (🚶 250-847-5072; www.tourismsmithers.com; 1411 Court St; ⊙9am-5pm; 🛜) Can steer you to excellent mountain biking, white-water rafting and climbing.

ℹ️ Getting There & Away

Central Mountain Air (🚶 888-865-8585; www.flycma.com) With its home base at Smithers Airport, CMA serves 16 communities across BC and Alberta, including Vancouver, Calgary and Edmonton.

VIA Rail (www.viarail.ca) trains stop in Smithers on runs between Prince Rupert and Prince George.

BC Bus North (p758) runs twice per week return connecting Prince George, Smithers and Prince Rupert.

Smithers is on Hwy 16, the Yellowhead Hwy, 371km west of Prince George and 347km east of Prince Rupert.

Smithers to Prince George

Heading south and then east from Smithers along the Yellowhead Hwy (Hwy 16) for 146km will have you passing through **Burns Lake**, the center of a popular fishing district. Continue another 128km toward **Vanderhoof**, where you can either detour north on Hwy 27 to Fort St James or carry on along Hwy 16 for 100km to Prince George.

Fort St James National Historic Site
HISTORIC SITE

(☑ 250-996-7191; www.pc.gc.ca; Kwah Rd; adult/child $7.80/free; ☉ 9am-5pm Jun-Sep) From Vanderhoof, Hwy 27 heads 66km north to Fort St James National Historic Site. The former Hudson's Bay Company trading post that's on the tranquil southeastern shore of Stuart Lake has been restored to its 1896 glory.

Prince George

☑ 250, 778 / POP 78,675

In First Nations times, before outsiders arrived, Prince George was called Lheidli T'Enneh, which means 'people of the confluence,' an appropriate name given that the Nechako and Fraser Rivers converge here. Today the name would be just as fitting, although it's the confluence of highways that matters most. A mill town since 1807, it is a vital BC crossroads, and you're unlikely to visit the north without passing through at least once.

Hwy 97 from the south cuts through the center of town on its way north to Dawson Creek (360km) and the Alaska Hwy. Hwy 16 becomes Victoria St as it runs through town westward to Prince Rupert (724km), and east to Jasper (380km) and Edmonton.

The downtown, no beauty-contest winner, is compact and is home to some good restaurants.

◎ Sights

★ **Northern Lights Estate Winery** WINERY

(☑ 250-564-1112; www.northernlightswinery.ca; 745 Prince George Pulpmill Rd; tastings $5; ☉ 10am-9pm Mon-Thu, to 10pm Fri & Sat, to 5pm Sun) On the northern banks of the Nechako River, this is BC's northernmost winery, specializing in wines made from fruit produced on-site, including blueberry, strawberry, haskap, gooseberry, apple, cherry, raspberry, blackcurrant and rhubarb. Try Seduction, its tasty strawberry and rhubarb special. Taste four wines for $5, or better yet, savor a bottle with a meal at its popular riverside **bistro**.

Two Rivers Gallery ARTS CENTER

(☑ 250-614-7800; www.tworiversgallery.ca; 725 Canada Games Way; adult/child $7.50/3; ☉ 10am-5pm Mon-Wed, Fri & Sat, to 9pm Thu, noon-5pm Sun) PG's public art gallery is housed in the architecturally impressive Two Rivers Gallery building at the Civic Centre and has permanent collections, changing exhibitions and a lovely gift shop. The focus is on local art, encouraging local artisans, plus teaching creativity with classes for children. Admission is free on Thursdays.

Prince George Railway & Forestry Museum MUSEUM

(☑ 250-563-7351; www.pgrfm.bc.ca; 850 River Rd, Cottonwood Island Nature Park; adult/child $8/5; ☉ 10am-5pm daily Jun-Aug, 11am-4pm Tue-Sat Sep-May) This museum honors trains, the beaver and local lore. It's located in **Cottonwood Island Nature Park**, north of the train station, which has sylvan walks alongside the river.

🛏 Sleeping & Eating

Coast Inn of the North HOTEL $$

(☑ 250-563-0121; www.coasthotels.com; 770 Brunswick St; r from $100; P ❂ ✲ 🛜 🛋) One of the nicest stays in a town with few options, the Coast is a high-rise with 153 very comfy rooms, some with balcony. There's an indoor pool, which is handy during the long months of cold temperatures. It's close to the center and its nightlife.

Nancy O's PUB FOOD $$

(☑ 250-562-8066; www.nancyos.ca; 1261 3rd Ave; mains from $15; ☉ 11am-late Mon-Fri, from 10am Sat, to 3pm Sun) Locally sourced ingredients are combined to create fabulous food at Nancy O's: burgers, veggie specials, a great avocado salad and a truly amazing *steak frites*. The bottled beer selection is fab

(Belgian and BC), and there's live music and DJs many nights.

★ Twisted Cork
CANADIAN $$$

(☑ 250-561-5550; www.twisted-cork.com; 1157 5 Ave; dinner mains from $25; ☺ 11am-9pm Mon-Thu, to 11pm Fri & Sat, 5-9pm Sun) As good as it gets in PG, the Twisted Cork will grab your attention with its gorgeous stone building and attractive wooden decor. The meals are superb. For dinner, mains include the elk tenderloin ($50), bison pie ($27) and wild-game burger ($27).

★ CrossRoads Brewing
MICROBREWERY

(☑ 250-614-2337; www.crossroadscraft.com; 508 George St; ☺ 11.30am-late) PG's local microbrewery features an impressive taproom, allowing you to see into the production facility. There are nine standard brews plus seasonal favorites, a kitchen producing everything from snacks to pizzas to Kobe beef ribs and an extremely convivial atmosphere. Try the Fast Lane IPA, heavy on hops, and head outside to the patio if the weather is playing ball.

❶ Information

Prince George Visitor Centre (☑ 250-562-3700; www.tourismpg.com; 1300 1st Ave, VIA Rail station; ☺ 8am-6pm Jun-Aug, shorter hours other times; ☏) This excellent visitor center in the VIA Rail station building has info on Northern BC and can make bookings such as ferry tickets. Loans out free bikes and fishing rods.

❶ Getting There & Away

Prince George Airport (☑ 250-963-2400; www.pgairport.ca; 4141 Airport Rd) is off Hwy 97. **Air Canada** (☑ 888-247-2262; www.aircanada.com) and **Westjet** (☑ 888-937-8538; www.westjet.com) serve Vancouver.

VIA Rail (www.viarail.ca; 1300 1st Ave) trains head west three times a week to Prince Rupert (12½ hours) and east three times a week to Jasper, AB (7½ hours). Through-passengers from either direction must overnight in Prince George.

Adventure Charters (www.adventurecharters.ca) operates buses south from Prince George to Williams Lake, Kamloops, Hope and Surrey.

BC Bus North (p758) runs buses either twice or once weekly on four routes:

➡ Prince George–Smithers–Prince Rupert
➡ Prince George–Dawson Creek–Fort St John
➡ Prince George–Valemount
➡ Dawson Creek–Fort Nelson

Prince George to Alberta

Look for lots of wildlife as well as some good parks along the 375km stretch of Hwy 16 that links Prince George with Jasper, just over the Alberta border. McBride, 208km east of Prince George, is the only township of any size along the way and a good spot for food and gas. Monster Mt Robson, 3954m and highest peak in the Canadian Rockies, dominates the drive up the Yellowhead Hwy to the provincial park of the same name, while the Robson Valley is also the birthplace of the mighty Fraser River that flows all the way out to the sea at Vancouver. From the Mt Robson Visitor Centre allow an hour to get to Jasper.

◉ Sights & Activities

★ Ancient Forest / Chun T'oh Whudujut Park
PARK

(www.env.gov.bc.ca/bcparks; off Hwy 16) About 113km east of Prince George is the site of BC's newest park, established in 2016. The Ancient Forest features two trails – a 900m boardwalk (return) and a 2.3km loop trail – both of which reveal some real behemoths of the temperate inland rainforest: old-growth red cedars and hemlocks, some reaching heights of 60m, that are more than 1000 years old.

★ Mt Robson Provincial Park
PARK

(Map p608; ☑ 250-964-2243; www.env.gov.bc.ca/bcparks; off Hwy 16) Northern BC's major mountain attraction abuts Jasper National Park, but on the BC side of the border. Uncrowded Mt Robson Provincial Park has steep glaciers, prolific wildlife and superb hiking highlighted by the Kinney Lake & Berg Lake Trails. Mt Robson itself, highest peak in the Canadian Rockies, is a stunner. Campsites are available (from $22).

★ Kinney Lake & Berg Lake Trails
HIKING

(Map p608; www.env.gov.bc.ca/bcparks) The trailhead for this easy 2½-hour round-trip hike into gorgeous Kinney Lake (4.5km one-way; www.valemounttrails.com/kinney-lake) is 3km north of the Mt Robson Visitor Centre. A longer hike carries on from Kinney Lake to Berg Lake (23km each way; www.env.gov.bc.ca), with seven camping areas along the way. All Berg Lake hikers must check into Mt Robson Visitor Centre before heading out.

🛏 Sleeping

**Mt Robson Lodge
& Campground**　　　　CABIN, CAMPING **$$**
(Map p608; 📞250-566-4821; www.mountrobson
lodge.com; 16895 Fransworth Rd; tent & RV sites
from $30, cabins from $139; ☺mid-May–Sep;
🅿😊) This place, 5km west of Mt Robson
Park, has a number of comfortable cabins,
all with private bath, and lovely tent and RV
sites down by the Fraser River, each with a
firepit. There are stunning views of Mt Rob-
son, plus they also run **rafting** (from $99)
and scenic **float trips** ($59).

Mt Robson Mountain River Lodge　　LODGE **$$**
(Map p608; 📞250-566-9899; www.mtrobson.com;
cnr Hwy 16 & Swift Current Creek Rd, Mt Robson;
lodges/cabins from $150/180; 🅿😊📶) On the
western border of Mt Robson Provincial
Park, this lodge commands stunning views
of the eponymous giant peak. There's a main
building and a couple of cabins that share a
cozy, away-from-it-all atmosphere.

ℹ Information

Mt Robson Visitor Centre (Map p608; 📞250-
566-4038; www.env.gov.bc.ca; Hwy 16; ☺8am-
5pm) Great information on the park in full view
of Mt Robson. There is also a cafe (8am to
6pm), a gift shop a petrol station here.

Stewart-Cassiar Highway

The 724km Stewart-Cassiar Hwy (Hwy 37)
is a viable and ever-more-popular route between BC and the Yukon and Alaska. But it's
more than just a means to get from Hwy 16
in BC to the Alaska Hwy in the Yukon (west
of Watson Lake) – it's a window onto one of
the largest remaining wild and woolly parts
of the province. It's also the road to Stewart
(p766), a near-mandatory detour to glaciers
and more.

Gitanyow, a mere 15km north of Hwy
16, has an unparalleled collection of totem
poles and you can often see carvers creating
more.

🛏 Sleeping & Eating

★**Bell 2 Lodge**　　　　　LODGE **$$**
(📞888-499-4354; www.bell2lodge.com; 249
Hwy 37; tent/RV sites from $25/32, r from $190;
🅿😊❄📶) This northern oasis is at the
248km mark on the Stewart-Cassiar Hwy,
241km south of Dease Lake, where Hwy
37 crosses the Bell-Irving River. There are
tent sites, RV hook-ups, plus standard and

deluxe rooms in five log chalets. There's a
restaurant and coffee shop (8am to 8pm in
summer), a hot tub and sauna complex, and
a gas station.

★**Ripley Creek Inn**　　　　GUESTHOUSE **$$**
(📞250-636-2344; www.ripleycreekinn.com; 306
5th Ave, Stewart; r from $115; 🅿😊📶) The 40
rooms in various heritage buildings are decorated with new and old items; decor varies greatly. The Peterson House is a former
brothel. Check out the great range of options
online.

Bus　　　　　　　　　SEAFOOD **$**
(📞250-636-9011; 6th St, Hyder, AK; mains from
$11; ☺noon-8pm Tue-Sun Jun-Sep) Also known
as Seafood Express, the Bus serves the tastiest seafood ever cooked in a school bus on
6th St in tiny Hyder.

ℹ Information

Check out www.stewartcassiarhighway.com.

ℹ Getting There & Away

All major roads linking to the Stewart-Cassiar Hwy
are in excellent condition. Except for areas of construction, the highway is sealed and suitable for all
vehicles. At any point, you should not be surprised
to see bears, moose and other large mammals.

There's never a distance greater than 150km
between gas stations. BC provides **road condition reports** (📞800-550-4997; www.drivebc.
ca). When it's dry in summer, people drive from
Stewart to Whitehorse (1043km) or from Smithers to Watson Lake (854km) in a single day,
taking advantage of the long hours of daylight.
This a real haul, so be prepared.

Alaska Highway

Even in Prince George you can start to smell
the Alaska Hwy. As you travel north along
Hwy 97, the mountains and forests give way
to gentle rolling hills and farmland. Nearing
Dawson Creek (360km), the landscape resembles the prairies of Alberta. There's no
need to dawdle.

From **Chetwynd** you can take Hwy 29
along the wide vistas of the Peace River valley north via Hudson's Hope to join the Alaska Hwy north of Fort St John.

Dawson Creek is *the* starting point
(Mile 0) for the Alaska Hwy and it capital-
izes on this at the **Alaska Highway House**
(📞250-782-4714; www.tourismdawsoncreek.com;
10201 10th St, Dawson Creek; by donation; ☺8am-
4pm), an engaging museum in a vintage

STEWART & HYDER

Awesome. Yes, the word is almost an automatic cliché, but when you gaze upon the **Salmon Glacier**, you'll understand why it was coined in the first place. This horizon-spanning expanse of ice is more than enough reason to make the 67km detour off Hwy 37 at Meziadin Junction, 156km north of Kitwanga. In fact, your first confirmation comes when you encounter the iridescent blue expanse of the **Bear Glacier** looming over Hwy 37A.

The sibling border towns of **Stewart** and **Hyder**, AK, perch on the coast at the head of the Portland Canal. Stewart, once a boomtown of 10,000 thanks to gold and silver mines, is the much more businesslike of the pair, and has excellent places to stay and eat.

Among several campgrounds and motels, Stewart's real star is Ripley Creek Inn (p765). The 40 rooms in various heritage buildings are stylishly decorated with new and old items, and there's a huge collection of vintage toasters. For more information on Stewart see www.districtofstewart.com.

Hyder ekes out an existence as a 'ghost town.' Some 40,000 tourists come through every summer, avoiding any border hassle from US customs officers (because there aren't any), although going back to Stewart you'll pass through beady-eyed Canadian customs. It has muddy streets and two businesses of note: the **Glacier Inn** (☑250-636-9248; International St, Hyder, Alaska; ☉noon-late), a bar you'll enjoy if you ignore the touristy 'get Hyderized' shot-swilling shtick; and the Bus (p765), which has the tastiest seafood ever cooked in a school bus. *This* is Hyder.

The enormous, horizon-filling Salmon Glacier is 37km beyond Hyder, up a winding dirt road that's OK for cars when it's dry. Some 3km into the drive, you'll pass the **Fish Creek viewpoint**, an area alive with bears and doomed salmon in late summer.

building overlooking the milepost. The nearby downtown blocks make a good stroll and have free wi-fi, and there's a **walking tour** of the old buildings. The **visitor center** (☑250-782-9595; www.tourismdawsoncreek.com; 900 Alaska Ave, Dawson Creek; ☉7:30am-6pm mid-May–Sep, shorter hours other times; ☎) is housed in the old train station and has lots of Alaska Hwy info. Note that this corner of BC stays on Mountain Standard Time year-round. So in winter, the time is the same as Alberta, one hour later than BC. In summer, the time is the same as Vancouver.

Now begins the big drive. Heading northwest from Dawson Creek, you'll pass through Fort St John on the 430km stretch to **Fort Nelson** – it gives little hint of the wonders to come.

Fort Nelson has seen boom and bust in recent years with the fluctuation of oil prices. This is the last place of any size on the Alaska Hwy until Whitehorse in the Yukon – most 'towns' along the route are little more than a gas station and motel or two.

Around 140km west of Fort Nelson, **Stone Mountain Provincial Park** (www.env.gov.bc.ca/bcparks; Alaska Hwy) has hiking trails, with backcountry camping and a campground. The stretches of road often have dense concentrations of wildlife: moose, bears, bison, wolves, elk and much more. From here, the Alaska Hwy rewards whatever effort it took getting this far.

A further 75km brings you to **Muncho Lake Provincial Park** (www.env.gov.bc.ca/bcparks; Alaska Hwy), centered on the emerald-green lake of the same name and boasting spruce forests, vast rolling mountains and some truly breathtaking scenery. There are two campgrounds by the lake, plus a few lodges scattered along the highway.

Finally, **Liard River Hot Springs Provincial Park** (☑250-427-5452; www.env.gov.bc.ca/bcparks; 75100-81198 Alaska Hwy; adult/child $5/3) has a steamy ecosystem that allows a whopping 250 species of plants to thrive. After a long day in the car, you'll thrive, too, in the soothing waters. From here it's 220km to Watson Lake and the Yukon.

Yukon Territory

Best Places to Eat

➡ Joe's Wood-fired Pizza (p788)

➡ Klondike Kate's (p788)

➡ Klondike Rib & Salmon (p773)

➡ Antoinette's (p774)

Best Places to Stay

➡ Coast High Country Inn (p773)

➡ Moose Creek Lodge (p784)

➡ Bombay Peggy's (p788)

➡ Klondike Kate's Cabins (p788)

Why Go?

This vast and thinly populated wilderness, where most four-legged species far outnumber humans, has a grandeur and beauty only appreciated by experience. Few places in the world today have been so unchanged over the course of time. Indigenous people, having eked out survival for thousands of years, hunt and trap as they always have. The Klondike Gold Rush of 1898 was the Yukon's high point of population, yet even its heritage is ephemeral, easily erased by time.

Any visit will mean much time outdoors: Canada's five tallest mountains and the world's largest ice fields below the Arctic are all within Kluane National Park, while canoe expeditions down the Yukon River are epic. And don't forget the people: get set to appreciate the offbeat vibe of Dawson City and the bustle of Whitehorse, and join the growing numbers of people who've discovered the Yukon thanks to TV shows such as *Yukon Gold* and *Dr Oakley: Yukon Vet*.

When to Go
Dawson City

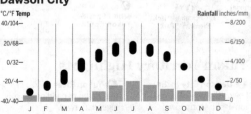

Nov–Apr Days of snowy winter solitude end when the river ice breaks up.

Jun–Aug Summers are short but warm, with long hours of daylight.

Sep You can feel the north winds coming. Trees erupt in color, crowds thin and places close.

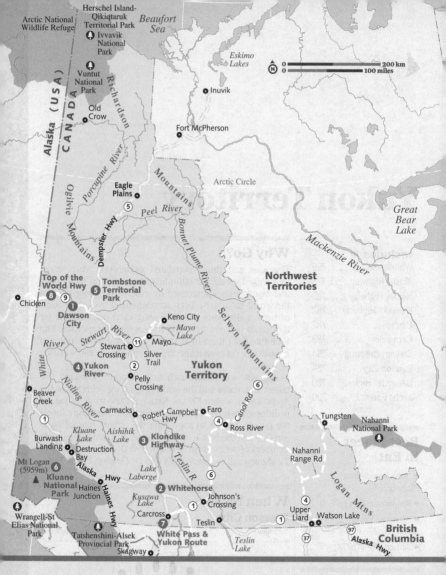

Yukon Territory Highlights

1 Dawson City (p784)
Loving the vibe of Canada's funkiest historic town.

2 Whitehorse (p769)
Spending an extra day in this surprising, culture-filled city.

3 Klondike Hwy (p782)
Spotting moose and bears along this stunning road – they may outnumber cars.

4 Yukon River (p772) Living the dream of paddlers on this legendary river.

5 Tombstone Territorial Park (p790) Losing yourself in this vast park, where the grandeur of the North envelops you.

6 Kluane National Park (p780) Naming one of the

100 unnamed glaciers in this Unesco-listed park.

7 White Pass & Yukon Route (p771) Enjoying the ride on the fabled gold rush–era railroad.

8 Top of the World Highway (p789) Marveling at the wilderness from Dawson City to Chicken, Alaska.

History

There's evidence that humans were eating animals in the Yukon some 15,000 to 30,000 years ago, depending on your carbon-dating method of choice. However, it's widely agreed that these people were descended from those who crossed over from today's Siberia while the land bridge was in place. There's little recorded history otherwise, although it's known that a volcanic eruption in 800 CE covered much of the southern Yukon in ash. Similarities to the Athapaskan people of the southwest United States have suggested that these groups may have left the Yukon after the volcano ruined hunting and fishing.

In the 1840s Robert Campbell, a Hudson's Bay Company explorer, was the first European to travel the district. Fur traders, prospectors, whalers and missionaries all followed. In 1870 the region became part of the Northwest Territories (NWT). But it was 1896 when the Yukon literally hit the map, after gold was found in a tributary of the Klondike River, near what was to become Dawson City. The ensuing gold rush attracted upward of 40,000 hopefuls from around the world. Towns sprouted overnight to support the numerous wealth seekers, who were quite unprepared for the ensuing depravities.

In 1898 the Yukon became a separate territory, with Dawson City as its capital. Building the Alaska Hwy (Hwy 1) in 1942 opened up the territory to development. In 1953 Whitehorse became the capital, because it had the railway and the highway. Mining continues to be the main industry, followed by tourism, which accounts for over 350,000 visitors a year.

Parks

The Yukon has a major Unesco World Heritage site in raw and forbidding Kluane National Park, which sits solidly within the Yukon abutting Tatshenshini-Alsek Provincial Park in British Columbia. Glacier Bay

> **YUKON TERRITORY FAST FACTS**
>
> ➡ Population: 38,300
>
> ➡ Area: 482,443 sq km
>
> ➡ Capital: Whitehorse
>
> ➡ Quirky fact: twice the area of the UK, but with only 38,300 people compared to the UK's 66 million!

and Wrangell-St Elias National Parks are found in adjoining Alaska.

The Yukon has a dozen parks and protected areas (www.yukonparks.ca), but much of the territory itself is parklike and government campgrounds can be found throughout. Tombstone Territorial Park is remote yet accessible via the Dempster Hwy, so you can absorb the horizon-sweeping beauty of the tundra and the majesty of vast mountain ranges.

ℹ Information

There are excellent visitor information centers (VICs) covering every entry point in the Yukon: Beaver Creek, Carcross, Dawson City, Haines Junction, Watson Lake and Whitehorse.

The Yukon government produces enough literature and information to supply a holiday's worth of reading. Among the highlights are *Camping on Yukon Time, Art Adventures on Yukon Time,* the very useful *Yukon Wildlife Viewing Guide* and lavish walking guides to pretty much every town with a population greater than 50. Start your collection at the various visitor centers online (www.travelyukon.com). Another good internet resource is www.yukoninfo.com.

ℹ Getting There & Around

Whitehorse is served by Air Canada Jazz, WestJet and Air North (p789). There are direct flights to Vancouver and Calgary. There are even flights nonstop to Germany during summer. Air North serves Whitehorse, and Dawson City has flights to Mayo, Old Crow and to Inuvik and Yellowknife in the NWT.

There are three major ways to reach the Yukon:
➡ initially by ferry, using the **Alaska Marine Highway System** (☑ 250-627-1744, 800-642-0066; www.dot.state.ak.us) to the entry points of Skagway and Haines, AK, and then by road.
➡ by the Alaska Hwy from Dawson Creek, BC.
➡ by the Stewart-Cassiar Hwy from northwest BC, which joins the Alaska Hwy near Watson Lake.

Rental cars (and RVs) are expensive and only available in Whitehorse and Dawson City. The Alaska Hwy and Klondike Hwy are paved and have services every 100km to 200km.

To check the territory's road conditions, contact **511Yukon** (☑ 511; www.511yukon.ca).

WHITEHORSE

The capital city of the Yukon Territory (since 1953, to the continuing regret of much smaller and isolated Dawson City), Whitehorse

Whitehorse

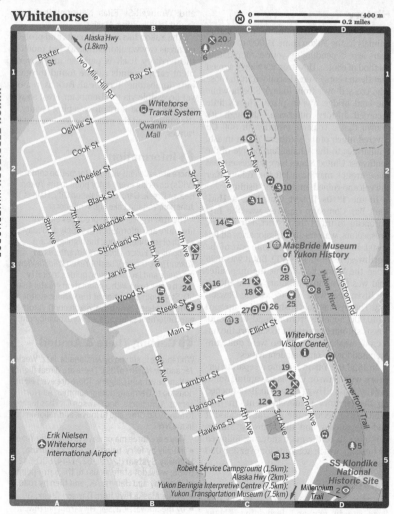

will likely have a prominent role in your journey. The territory's two great highways, the Alaska and the Klondike, cross here, making it a hub for transportation (it was a terminus for the White Pass & Yukon Route railway from Skagway in the early 1900s, and during WWII was a major center for work on the Alaska Hwy). You'll find all manner of outfitters and services for explorations across the territory.

Not immediately appealing, Whitehorse rewards the curious. It has a well-funded arts community (with an especially vibrant visual arts community), good restaurants and a range of motels. Exploring the sights

within earshot of the rushing Yukon River can easily take a day or more. Look past the bland commercial buildings and you'll see many heritage ones awaiting discovery.

◎ Sights

You can explore Whitehorse's main sights in a day, mostly on foot.

★ MacBride Museum
of Yukon History   MUSEUM
(☑ 867-667-2709;   www.macbridemuseum.com;
1124 Front St; adult/child $10/5; ◌ 9:30am-5pm)
This is the Yukon's pre-eminent museum, preserving and presenting the Yukon's his-

Whitehorse

tory since 1952. Recently expanded, the museum offers a comprehensive view of the resilient people and groundbreaking events that have shaped the Yukon Territory's history and should not be missed.

★ **SS Klondike**
National Historic Site HISTORIC SITE
(☑867-667-4511; www.pc.gc.ca; cnr South Access Rd & 2nd Ave; ⊙9:30am-5pm May-Aug) FREE Carefully restored, this was one of the largest stern-wheelers used on the Yukon River. Built in 1937, it made its final run upriver to Dawson in 1955 and is now a national historic site.

Whitehorse Waterfront AREA
One look at the surging Yukon River and you'll want to spend time strolling its bank. The beautiful **White Pass & Yukon Route Station** (1109 1st Ave) has been restored and anchors an area that's in the midst of a revitalization. **Rotary Peace Park** (off 2nd Ave) at the southern end is a great picnic spot, the **Kwanlin Dün Cultural Centre** (☑867-456-5322; www.kwanlindunculturalcentre.com; 1171 1st Ave; by donation; ⊙10am-6pm Mon-Sat) is a dramatic addition in the middle, and **Shipyards Park** (off 2nd Ave) at the northern end has a growing collection of historic structures moved here from other parts of the Yukon.

Whitehorse Fish Ladder LANDMARK
(☑867-633-5965; Nisutlin Dr; by donation; ⊙9am-9pm Jun-Aug) Stare down a salmon at the

Whitehorse Fishway, a 366m wooden fish ladder (the world's longest) past the hydroelectric plant south of town. Large viewing windows let you see Chinook salmon swim past, starting in late July (before that it's grayling). The fishway is easily reached on foot via the Millennium Trail.

Arts Underground GALLERY
(☑867-667-4080; www.artsunderground.ca; 305 Main St, Hougen Centre lower level; ⊙10am-5pm Tue-Sat) Operated by the Yukon Arts Society. There are carefully selected and well-curated rotating exhibits of work by local Yukon artists.

Yukon Transportation Museum MUSEUM
(☑867-668-4792; www.goytm.ca; 30 Electra Cres; adult/child $10/5; ⊙10am-6pm mid-May–Sep) Find out what the Alaska Hwy was really like back in the day; let's just say mud was a dirty word. Exhibits cover planes, trains and dogsleds. The museum is near the airport and Beringia Centre. Look for the iconic **DC-3 weather vane** (yes, it spins!) out front.

Yukon Beringia
Interpretive Centre MUSEUM
(☑867-667-8855; www.beringia.com; Km 1473 Alaska Hwy; adult/child $6/4; ⊙9am-6pm) This place focuses on Beringia, a mostly ice-free area that encompassed the Yukon, Alaska and eastern Siberia during the last ice age. Engaging exhibits recreate the era, right down to the actual skeleton of a 3m-long giant ground sloth – although some prefer the giant beaver.

Activities

The visitor center can guide you to numerous local hikes and activities year-round. Otherwise, Whitehorse is a major outfitting center for adventures on Yukon waterways.

Canoeing & Kayaking

Whitehorse is the starting place for popular canoeing and kayaking trips from half-day trips on the Yukon River to full-on expeditions to Carmacks or on to Dawson City. It takes an average of eight days to the former and 16 days to the latter. Outfitters offer gear of all kinds (canoes and kayaks are about $40 to $50 per day), guides, tours, lessons and planning services, and can arrange transportation back to Whitehorse. Most paddlers use the map *The Yukon River: Marsh Lake to Dawson City*; available at www.yukonbooks.com.

Kanoe People CANOEING
(☎867-668-4899; www.kanoepeople.com; cnr 1st Ave & Strickland St; half-day from $70) At the river's edge, these guys can arrange any type of trip including paddles down the Yukon, Teslin and Big Salmon Rivers. Gear, maps and guides for sale; also has bikes for rent. Lots of winter options at its wilderness facility, Fox Bay Retreat.

Up North Adventures CANOEING
(☎867-667-7035; www.upnorthadventures.com; 103 Strickland St; canoeing half-day from $70; ⊙9am-7pm) Offers guided tours, rentals and transportation on the major rivers. Also paddling lessons, fishing trips and winter activities such as snowmobiling, snowshoeing, ice fishing and aurora-watching.

Cycling

Whitehorse has scores of bike trails along the Yukon River and into the surrounding hills. The visitor center has maps.

Cadence Cycle CYCLING
(☎867-633-5600; www.cadencecycle.squarespace.com; 505 Steele St; per day bike/electric bike from $35/45; ⊙10am-6pm Mon-Sat) Sells and rents good used mountain bikes. Also does repairs.

Walking & Hiking

You can walk a scenic 5km loop around Whitehorse's waters that includes a stop at the fishway. From the SS *Klondike* go south on the **Millennium Trail** until you reach the Robert Service Campground and the **Rotary Centennial Footbridge** over the river. The fishway is just south. Head north along the water and cross the Robert Campbell Bridge and you are back in the town center.

Yukon Conservation Society HIKING
(☎867-668-5678; www.yukonconservation.org; 302 Hawkins St; ⊙Tue-Sat Jun-Aug) FREE Discover the natural beauty all around Whitehorse with a free Yukon Conservation Society nature hike. There are various itineraries ranging from easy to hard.

Sleeping

Whitehorse can get almost full during the peak of summer, so book ahead. It has a lot of midrange motels that earn the sobriquet 'veteran.' Check a room first before you commit.

★ **Robert Service Campground** CAMPGROUND $
(☎867-668-3721; www.robertservicecampground.com; 120 Robert Service Way; tent sites $20; ⊙mid-May–Sep; P 🛜) It's a pretty 15-minute walk from town on the Millennium Trail to the 70 sites at this tents-only campground on the river 1km south of town. Sites have picnic tables and fire pits. The on-site cafe

CANOEING 101

If the outdoors is something you've always wanted to get into but you're short on experience, consider taking a 25km, four-hour paddle in a canoe down the Yukon River. Kanoe People are right on the river in Whitehorse and you have a couple of options. For those feeling confident, you get a canoe, all the necessary safety gear, instructions and a pickup 25km downriver at the Takhini River bridge on the Klondike Hwy, all for $70 per person. Alternatively, go with a guide for $140 per person. Both options have a minimum of two people. The paddling is easy, the river serene and wildlife spotting is supreme. Expect to see eagles, a beaver or two, and if you're lucky, something on four legs. Remember, they wouldn't let you go out there by yourself if it was remotely dangerous.

has excellent coffee, baked goods and ice cream.

★**Historical Guest House** B&B $$
(☑867-668-3907; www.historicalguesthouse.com; 5128 5th Ave; r from $105; ☻☎) A classic wooden home from 1907 with three guest rooms. Top-floor options have individual bathrooms one floor down and angled ceilings. A larger unit has a huge kitchen. Rooms have high-speed internet, and there's a nice garden. A good option with character.

★**Coast High Country Inn** HOTEL $$
(☑867-667-4471; www.highcountryinn.yk.ca; 4051 4th Ave; r from $110; P☻✳☎) Towering over Whitehorse (four stories!), the High Country is popular with business travelers and groups. The 84 rooms are large – some have huge Jacuzzis right in the room. The pub is popular.

Elite Hotel HOTEL $$
(☑867-668-4567; www.elitehotel.ca; 206 Jarvis St; r from $99; ☻✳☎) Don't let the name have you expecting more than you're going to get. Elite Hotel probably doesn't fit in many people's 'elite' category, but it is a good cheaper option with clean, spacious rooms in a convenient location. There are restaurants and a bar in the same building and Main St is a short stroll away.

Boréale Ranch GUESTHOUSE $$
(☑888-488-8489; www.be-yukon.com; 1827 Klondike Hwy S; r from $110; P☻☎) A lodge with an emphasis on cycling, 30 minutes' drive south of Whitehorse. There are four rooms in the appealingly minimalist main building, plus detached suites. Outside there's a hot tub. Guests can use fat-tire bikes for free and there are numerous cycling programs. There are also summer-only yurts and tents with hardwood floors. The food wins plaudits.

✖ Eating & Drinking

★**Deli Yukon** DELI $
(☑867-667-6077; 203 Hanson St; sandwiches from $7; ⊙9am-5:30pm Mon-Fri) The smell of smoked meat wafts out to the street; inside there's a huge selection of prepared items and custom-made sandwiches. Offers great picnic fare, or dine in the simple table area. The spicy elk sausage rolls for $3.95 are addictive. Attached to Yukon Meat & Sausage.

Fireweed Community Market MARKET $
(☑867-333-2255; www.fireweedmarket.ca; Shipyards Park; ⊙3-7pm Thu mid-May–early Sep) The Fireweed Community Market draws vendors from the region; the berries are fabulous.

★**Klondike Rib & Salmon** CANADIAN $$
(☑867-667-7554; www.klondikerib.com; 2116 2nd Ave; mains from $14; ⊙11am-9pm May-Sep) The food is superb at this sprawling casual half-tent restaurant in a place originally opened as a tent-frame bakery in 1900. Besides the namesakes (the salmon skewers and smoked pork ribs are tops), there are other local faves.

This is a great place to try bison steak ($34) or Yukon Arctic char ($28). It's half-tent, so closed when winter temperatures turn up.

Asahiya JAPANESE $$
(☑867-668-2828; www.asahiya.ca; 309 Jarvis St; dinner mains from $12; ⊙11am-3pm & 4:30-10pm Mon-Sat, 4-10pm Sun) Top-notch Japanese prepared by Japanese chefs in downtown Whitehorse. Think sashimi, sushi and rolls, noodle dishes such as udon and soba, plus curry and meat dishes. Good bento box combinations at lunchtime, and all very reasonably priced.

Wood Street Ramen FUSION $$
(www.facebook.com/woodstreetramen; 302 Wood St; mains from $14; ⊙11am-3pm & 5-9pm Tue-Sat) This colorful place is going its own way with an intriguing Yukon-Asian fusion that is proving extremely popular. While there are ramen faves such as *tonkotsu ramen* (ramen in pork bone broth), it also has dishes like crispy pork noodles ($16), Bangkok bowl ($16), and sandwiches and wraps (from $12).

A top spot in Whitehorse.

Pickapeppa CARIBBEAN $$
(☑867-456-4990; www.pickapeppayukon.com; 2074 2nd Ave; mains from $15; ⊙11:30am-2:30pm & 5-8pm Mon-Fri, 5-9pm Sat) Nothing like a bit of Caribbean soul food to cheer you up when things are cooling down. Pickapeppa is bright, casual and vegetarian-friendly. On the menu you'll find dishes like jerk pork ribs ($22.95), curried goat ($22.95) and, for nonmeat eaters, chickpea curry ($14.95). The Jamaican rum balls for dessert really hit the spot.

Burnt Toast   BISTRO $$
(☑867-393-2605; www.burnttoastcafe.ca; 2112 2nd Ave; lunch mains from $11; ☺7am-4pm Mon-Fri, 9:30am-2pm Sat & Sun) The food is far better than the coy name suggests! Brunch is excellent at this inviting bistro (try the French toast) and lunch specials abound. Food is local and seasonal; consult the blackboard. Good salads, sandwiches and Yukon meats.

You'll find lots of locals in here.

Sanchez Cantina   MEXICAN $$
(☑867-668-5858; www.yukonweb.com/tourism/sanchez; 211 Hanson St; mains from $14; ☺11:30am-2pm & 5-9pm Mon-Sat) You'd think you would have to head south across two borders to find Mexican this authentic. Burritos here are the real thing – get them with the spicy mix of red and green sauces. Settle in for what may be a wait on the broad patio.

★**Antoinette's**   FUSION $$$
(☑867-668-3505; www.antoinettesrestaurant. com; 4121 4th Ave; dinner mains from $22; ☺3:30-10pm Mon-Sat) Antoinette Greenoliph runs one of the most creative kitchens in the Yukon. Her eponymous restaurant has an ever-changing, locally sourced menu. Many dishes have a Caribbean flair. There is often live bluesy, loungey music on weekends.

★**Dirty Northern Public House**   PUB
(☑867-633-3305; www.facebook.com/dirtynorthernpublichouse; 103 Main St; ☺3pm-late) There are hints of style at this upscale pub, which has a great draft-beer selection and makes excellent mixed drinks. Grab a booth and chase the booze with a wood-fired pizza. Top local acts perform many nights and the food comes from the sister-restaurant next door, Miner's Daughter.

Deck   PUB
(☑867-667-4471; www.coasthotels.com; 4051 4th Ave, Coast High Country Inn; ☺noon-midnight) The eponymous covered deck here draws

crowds of locals, tourists and guides through the season. Good beer list, plus fine burgers and the like (mains from $10). How often can you have a beer at a place that stays open late and still closes before sunset?

🛍 Shopping

★**Mac's Fireweed Books**   BOOKS
(☑867-668-2434; www.macsbooks.ca; 203 Main St; ☺8am-9pm Mon-Sat, from 10am Sun) Mac's has an unrivaled selection of Yukon titles. It also stocks topographical maps, road maps and periodicals.

Midnight Sun Emporium   ARTS & CRAFTS
(☑867-668-4350; www.midnightsunemporium. com; 205c Main St; ☺9am-6pm Mon-Sat) Has a good selection of Yukon arts, crafts and products.

North End Gallery   ARTS & CRAFTS
(☑867-393-3590; www.yukonart.ca; 1116 Front St; ☺9am-6:30pm Mon-Sat, 11am-5pm Sun) High-end Canadian art featuring top Yukon artists.

ℹ️ Information

Whitehorse Visitor Center (☑867-667-3084; www.travelyukon.com; 2nd Ave & Lambert St; ☺8am-8pm) An essential stop with vast amounts of territory-wide information.
Whitehorse General Hospital (☑867-393-8700; www.yukonhospitals.ca; 5 Hospital Rd; ☺24hr) The top hospital in the territory.

ℹ️ Getting There & Away

Whitehorse is the transportation hub of the Yukon.

AIR
Erik Nielsen Whitehorse International Airport (YXY; ☑867-667-8440; www.hpw. gov.yk.ca/whitehorse_airport.html; off Alaska Hwy; 🛜) is five minutes west of downtown. Air Canada and WestJet serve Vancouver. Locally owned **Air North** (www.flyairnorth. com) serves Dawson City, Mayo and Old Crow, and has flights to Inuvik, NWT, plus Vancouver, Kelowna, Edmonton and Calgary. **Condor** (www.condor.com) has weekly summer flights to/from Frankfurt, Germany.

BUS
Bus services, er, come and go; check the latest with the visitor center.

Husky Bus (📞 867-993-3821; www.klondike experience.com) Serves Dawson City ($119, thrice weekly) and makes all stops along the Klondike Hwy. Departures are from the visitor center. It will do pickups of paddlers and canoes along the Klondike Hwy with advance arrangement.

Alaska/Yukon Trails (📞 907-479-2277; www.alaskashuttle.com) Serves Fairbanks, AK (US$385, thrice weekly June to mid-September), via Dawson City.

White Pass & Yukon Route (📞 867-633-5710; www.wpyr.com; 1109 1st Ave; adult/child one way US$144/72; ⊘ ticket office 9am-5pm Mon-Sat mid-May–mid-Sep) Offers a jaw-droppingly scenic daily 10-hour rail and bus connection to/ from Skagway, AK, via Fraser, BC, in season. On some days, the bus meets the train in Carcross, which maximizes the beautiful train ride (this is the preferred option).

🛈 Getting Around

TO/FROM THE AIRPORT

A **Yellow Cab** (📞 867-668-4811) taxi to the center (10 minutes) will cost around $22.

BUS

Whitehorse Transit System (📞 867-668-7433; www.whitehorse.ca; $2.50; ⊘ Mon-Sat) runs through the center. Route 3 serves the airport, Route 5 passes the Robert Service Campground.

CAR & RECREATIONAL VEHICLE

Check your rental rate very carefully, as it's common for a mileage charge to be added after the first 200km per day, which will not get you far in the Yukon.

Also understand your insurance coverage and ask whether windscreen and tire damage from Yukon's rugged roads is included.

Budget (📞 867-667-6200; www.budget.com; Erik Nielsen Whitehorse International Airport) The only one of the worldwide rental car companies in Whitehorse.

Driving Force (📞 867-322-0255; www.driving force.ca; Erik Nielsen Whitehorse International Airport; ⊘ 8am-6pm) These guys have cars, trucks, vans and SUVs.

Fraserway RV Rentals (📞 867-668-3438; www.fraserway.com; 9039 Quartz Rd) Rents all shapes and sizes of RV from $200 per day depending on size (it matters) and season. Mileage extra; rates can quickly add up.

Whitehorse Subaru (📞 867-393-6550; www. whitehorsesubaru.com; 17 Chilkoot Way) Has good rates; most cars have manual transmissions.

ALASKA HIGHWAY

It may be called the Alaska Hwy, but given that its longest stretch (958km) is in the Yukon, perhaps another name is in order...

Roughly 2224km in length from Dawson Creek, BC, to Delta Junction, far inside Alaska, the Alaska Hwy has a meaning well beyond just a road; it's also a badge, an honor, an accomplishment. Even though today it's a modern thoroughfare, the very name still evokes images of big adventure and getting away from it all.

As you drive the Alaska Hwy in the Yukon, you're on the most scenic and varied part of the road. From little villages to the city of Whitehorse, from meandering rivers to the upthrust drama of the St Elias Mountains, the scenery will overwhelm you.

British Columbia to Whitehorse

You'll never be far from an excuse to stop on this stretch of the highway. Towns, small parks and various roadside attractions appear at regular intervals. None are a massive draw, but overall it's a pretty drive made compelling by the locale.

Watson Lake

Originally named after Frank Watson, a British trapper, Watson Lake is the first town in the Yukon on the Alaska Hwy and is just over the border from British Columbia (BC). It's mostly just a good rest stop, except for the superb **Visitor Center** (📞 867-536-7469; www.travelyukon.com; Km 980 Alaska Hwy; ⊘ 8am-8pm May-Sep), which has a good museum about the highway and a passel of territory-wide info.

The town is famous for its **Sign Post Forest** just outside the VIC. The first signpost, 'Danville, Illinois,' was nailed up in 1942. Others were added and now there are over 77,000 signs, many purloined late at night from municipalities worldwide.

Some 136km west on the Alaska Hwy, past the Km 1112 marker, look for the **Rancheria Falls Recreation Site**. A boardwalk leads to powerful twin waterfalls. It's an excellent stop.

Nugget City LODGE $
(📞 867-536-2307; www.nuggetcity.com; Km 1003 Alaska Hwy; tent & RV sites $25; r from $85; P⊘🛜) Just west of the junction with the

Stewart-Cassiar Hwy (Hwy 37), family-run Nugget City has cabins and rooms, the Baby Nugget RV park, the Wolf It Down Restaurant and Bakery, the Northern Beaver Post gift shop and fuel. Not much going on for a while west of here.

Air Force Lodge MOTEL $$
(☑867-536-2890; www.airforcelodge.com; Km 978 Alaska Hwy; s/d from $89/99; ☺May-Sep; Ⓟ☻☎) The Air Force Lodge has spotless rooms with shared bathrooms in a historic 1942 barracks for pilots. While the exterior is still original, the inside has been totally refurbished.

Kathy's Kitchen CAFE $$
(☑867-536-2400; 805 Frank Trail; dinner mains from $14; ☺6:30am-8pm) Offering good home-style cooking with options to sit inside or out, Kathy's is popular with locals.

Teslin

Teslin, on the long, narrow lake of the same name, is 260km west of Watson Lake. It's long been a home to the Tlingits (lin-*kits*), and the Alaska Hwy brought both prosperity and rapid change to this Indigenous population.

★**Teslin Tlingit**
Heritage Center CULTURAL CENTRE
(☑867-390-2532; www.ttc-teslin.com; Km 1248 Alaska Hwy; adult/child $5/3; ☺9am-5pm Jun-Aug) On the shores of beautiful Teslin Lake, 5km north of Teslin, this cultural center greets visitors with five totem poles and features exhibits of modern and traditional Tlingit arts, cultural demonstrations and a canoe exhibit by the lake. The gift shop has locally made crafts and gifts.

Yukon Motel & RV Park MOTEL $
(☑867-390-2575; www.yukonmotel.com; Km 1244 Alaska Hwy; r from $80; Ⓟ☻☎) Just over the bridge and on the shore of Nisutlin Bay in Teslin, the Yukon Motel offers simple motel rooms, an RV park with 70 sites, a licensed restaurant (7am to 9pm), a small shop, the Northern Wildlife Gallery (worth seeing) and a gas station (24 hours).

Johnson's Crossing

Some 50km northwest of Teslin and 127km south of Whitehorse is Johnson's Crossing, at the junction of the Alaska Hwy and Canol Rd (Hwy 6). During WWII the US Army built the Canol pipeline at tremendous human and financial expense to pump oil from Norman Wells in the NWT to Whitehorse. It was abandoned after countless hundreds of millions of dollars (in 1943 money, no less) were spent.

The Teslin River Bridge offers sweeping views.

Johnson's Crossing Lodge MOTEL $$
(☑867-390-2607; www.johnsonscrossinglodge. com; Km 1295 Alaska Hwy; tent sites/RV sites/r from $27/35/95; ☺year-round; Ⓟ☻☎) Lots going on here at Johnson's Crossing Lodge, just after crossing the Teslin River on the bridge, with motel rooms, RV sites, campsites, restaurant and fuel.

Whitehorse to Alaska

West of Whitehorse, the Alaska Hwy is relatively flat as far as Haines Junction. From here the road parallels legendary Kluane National Park and the St Elias Mountains. The 300km to Beaver Creek is the most scenic part of the entire highway.

Haines Junction

It's goodbye flatlands when you reach Haines Junction and see the sweep of imposing peaks looming over town. You've reached the stunning Kluane National Park and this is the gateway. The town makes an excellent base for exploring the park or for staging a serious four-star mountaineering, backcountry or river adventure.

The magnificent Haines Hwy heads south from here to Alaska. The four-hour drive to Haines, traversing raw alpine splendor, is one of the North's most beautiful.

☺ Sights & Activities

Although Kluane National Park will most likely be your focus, there are some good activities locally. For a hike after hours of driving, there's a pretty 5.5km **nature walk** along Dezadeash River where Hwy 3 crosses it at the southern end of town.

Our Lady of the Way CHURCH
(Km 1578 Alaska Hwy) This much-photographed Catholic church was constructed in 1954 from an old US Army Quonset hut used during the building of the Alaska Hwy. It was split down the middle and had a height extension and windows inserted to make it

look more church-like and to allow light into the building.

Da Kų Cultural Centre CULTURAL CENTER
(☑867-634-3300; www.cafn.ca/da-ku-cultural-centre; Km 1578 Alaska Hwy; ⊙8:30am-6pm mid-May–Aug) FREE This large and impressive facility has a variety of exhibit areas that showcase the culture and history of the Champagne and Aishihik people. It has a picnic area.

Tatshenshini Expediting RAFTING
(☑867-633-2742; www.tatshenshiniyukon.com; rafting trip from $165, kayak rental per day $35; ⊙May-Sep) Tatshenshini Expediting leads white-water rafting trips on the nearby Tatshenshini River, which has rapids from grade II to grade IV. Trips leave from Haines Junction and Whitehorse. It also arranges custom river trips and rents gear. Based in Whitehorse and out of Village Bakery & Deli in Haines Junction.

★**Kluane Glacier Air Tours** TOURS
(☑867-634-2916; www.kluaneglacierairtours.com; off Alaska Hwy, Haines Junction Airport; tours from $270) Kluane Glacier Air Tours offers flight-seeing of Kluane and its glaciers that will leave you limp with amazement. There are four options taking in truly spectacular mountains and glaciers, beginning with a one-hour tour.

🛏 Sleeping & Eating

There's a cluster of motels and RV parks in Haines Junction. There's also a beach and shade at Pine Lake, a territorial campground 6km east of town on the Alaska Hwy.

Parkside Inn MOTEL $$
(☑867-634-2900; www.parksidekluaneyukon. com; 137 Haines Hwy; r from $145; P😊❄🐾) Five good self-catering units in the middle of town with fully equipped kitchens, open year-round. A good pick.

★**Village Bakery & Deli** BAKERY $
(☑867-634-2867; www.villagebakeryyukon.com; cnr Kluane & Logan Sts; mains from $8; ⊙7am-8pm May-Sep; 📶) The bakery here turns out excellent goods all day, while the deli counter has tasty sandwiches you can enjoy on the large deck. On Friday night there's a popular barbecue with live folk music. It has milk, other very basic groceries, and even a gift shop.

WORTH A TRIP

ROBERT CAMPBELL HIGHWAY

To get right off the beaten path, consider this lonely gravel road (Hwy 4), which runs 585km from Watson Lake north and west to Carmacks, where you can join the Klondike Hwy (Hwy 2) for Dawson City. Along its length, the highway parallels various rivers and lakes. Wilderness campers will be thrilled.

Around 370km from Watson Lake, at the junction with Canol Rd (Hwy 6), is **Ross River**, home to the Kaska First Nation and a supply center for the local mining industry. About 62km further west is **Faro**. There is a hotel and guesthouses in Faro, as well as six campgrounds along the highway.

Guys & Dolls Bistro FOOD TRUCK $
(☑867-634-2300; www.facebook.com/Guysand-DollsBistro; Steel St; mains from $12; ⊙4-9pm Tue-Sun) Stunning views from this food truck with attached outdoor seating that serves up pizzas and Greek classics. Proving very popular among locals in Haines Junction.

★**Mile 1016 Pub** PUB
(☑867-634-2093; 118 Marshall Creek Rd; ⊙noon-2am) *The* place to head to in Haines Junction for decent pub meals, drinks and a good night out. Sit outside and check out the mountains. Also check out the Facebook page.

ℹ Information

Visitor Center (☑867-634-2345; www. travelyukon.com; Km 1578 Alaska Hwy, Da Kų Cultural Centre; ⊙8am-8pm May-Sep) Offers region-wide info.
Parks Canada Visitor Centre (☑867-634-7250; www.parkscanada.gc.ca/kluane; Km 1578 Alaska Hwy, Da Kų Cultural Centre; ⊙9am-7pm) Has park details, maps, brochures and displays; get hiking info here.

ℹ Getting There & Away

Haines Junction is a hub of highways: the Haines Hwy (Hwy 3) and the Alaska Hwy (Hwy 1) meet here, 160km west of Whitehorse.

Who What Where Tours (☑867-333-0475; www.whitehorsetours.com) offers the only public service between Whitehorse and Haines Junction (one way $75, twice weekly June to September).

JUSTIN FOULKES/LONELY PLANET ©

JUSTIN FOULKES/LONELY PLANET ©

1. Kluane National Park (p780)

Unesco-recognized as an 'empire of mountains and ice,' this magnificent wilderness covers 22,015 sq km.

2. Dawson City (p784)

The center of the Klondike Gold Rush, today Dawson has a seductive and funky vibe.

3. Yukon River (p772)

Kayakers and canoeists are drawn to this legendary river for its beauty and wildlife-spotting opportunities.

4. SS Klondike National Historic Site (p771)

The SS *Klondike* was one of the largest stern-wheelers used on the Yukon River.

Kluane National Park & Reserve

Unesco-recognized as an 'empire of mountains and ice,' Kluane National Park and Reserve looms south of the Alaska Hwy much of the way to the Alaska border. This rugged and magnificent wilderness covers 22,015 sq km of the southwest corner of the territory. Kluane (kloo-wah-nee) gets its far-too-modest name from the Southern Tutchone word for 'Lake with Many Fish.'

With British Columbia's Tatshenshini-Alsek Provincial Park to the south and Alaska's Wrangell-St Elias National Park to the west, this is one of the largest protected wilderness areas in the world. Deep beyond the mountains you see from the Alaska Hwy are over 100 named glaciers and as many unnamed ones.

Winters are long and harsh. Summers are short, making mid-June to early September the best time to visit. Note that wintery conditions can occur at any time, especially in the backcountry.

◉ Sights

The park consists primarily of the **St Elias Mountains** and the world's largest non-polar **ice fields**. Two-thirds of the park is glacier interspersed with valleys, glacial lakes, alpine forest, meadows and tundra. The **Kluane Ranges** (averaging a height of 2500m) are seen along the western edge of the Alaska Hwy. A greenbelt wraps around the base of these mountains, where most of the animals and vegetation live. Turquoise **Kluane Lake** is the Yukon's largest. Hidden are the immense ice fields and towering peaks, including **Mt Logan** (5959m), Canada's highest mountain, and **Mt St Elias** (5489m), the second highest. Partial glimpses of the interior peaks can be found at the Km 1622 **viewpoint** on the Alaska Hwy and also around the **Donjek River Bridge**, but the best views are from the air.

In Haines Junction, Kluane Glacier Air Tours (p777) offers highly recommended flight-seeing of Kluane and its glaciers.

🏃 Activities

There's excellent hiking in the forested lands at the base of the mountains, along either marked trails or less defined routes. There are about a dozen in each category, some following old mining roads, others traditional Indigenous paths. Detailed trail guides and topographical maps are available at the information centers. Talk to the rangers before setting out. They will help select a hike and can provide updates on areas that may be closed due to bear activity. Overnight hikes require backcountry permits ($10 per person per night).

A good pause during an Alaska Hwy drive is the **Soldier's Summit Trail**, an easy 1km return hike from near the Thechàl Dhâl information center. It has views across the park and plaques commemorating the inauguration of the Alaska Hwy at this point on November 20, 1942. You can listen to the original CBC broadcast of the opening.

The Thechàl Dhâl information center is also the starting point for **Ä'äy Chù (Slim's West)**, a popular 45km round-trip trek to **Kaskawulsh Glacier** – one of the few that can be reached on foot. This is a difficult route that takes from two to four days to complete and includes sweeping views from Observation Mountain (2114m).

A moderate four- to six-hour trip is the 15km **Auriol loop**, which goes from spruce forest to subalpine barrens and includes a wilderness campground. It's 7km south of Haines Junction.

Fishing is good and wildlife-watching plentiful. Most noteworthy are the Dall sheep that can be seen on **Sheep Mountain** in June and September. There's a large and diverse population of grizzly bears, as well as

---

EXTREME YUKON

Tough conditions spawn tough contests:

Yukon Quest (www.yukonquest.com; ◷ Feb) This legendary 1600km dogsled race goes from Whitehorse to Fairbanks, AK, braving winter darkness and -50°C temperatures. Record time: eight days, 14 hours, 21 minutes, set in 2014.

Yukon River Quest (www.yukon riverquest.com; ◷ late Jun) The world's premier canoe and kayak race, which covers the classic 742km run of the Yukon River from Whitehorse to Dawson City. Record times include team canoe (39 hours, 32 minutes) and solo kayak (42 hours, 49 minutes).

Klondike Trail of '98 Road Relay (www.klondikeroadrelay.com; ◷ early Sep) Some 100 running teams of 10 athletes each complete the overnight course from Skagway to Whitehorse.

black bears, moose, caribou, goats and 150 varieties of birds, among them eagles and the rare peregrine falcon.

🛏 Sleeping

★ Kathleen Lake Campground   CAMPGROUND $

(www.parkscanada.gc.ca/kluane; off Haines Hwy; tent & RV sites $15.70; P) Cerulean waters highlight Kathleen Lake, which has a campground and is 24km south of Haines Junction. The lake is a good stop by day and there are frequent ranger tours and programs in summer. Parks Canada also has five oTENTik, a cross between an A-frame cabin and a prospector tent mounted on a raised wooden floor, for $120 per night.

ℹ️ Information

Thechàl Dhâl Visitor Centre (Sheep Mountain; Km 1648 Alaska Hwy; ⊙9am-4pm mid-May–Aug) An excellent resource with views of Sheep Mountain. Rangers have wildlife info, hiking info and binoculars set up on tripods focused on groups of sheep for visitors to peer through.

Destruction Bay

This small village on the shore of huge Kluane Lake is 106km northwest of Haines Junction. It was given its evocative name after a storm tore through the area during construction of the highway during WWII. Most of the residents are First Nations, who live off the land through the year.

Talbot Arm Motel   MOTEL $$
(☑867-841-4461; www.talbotarm.com; Km 1684 Alaska Hwy; r from $90; P🐕📶) Given its monopoly on service, this motel/diner/gas station/general store is much better than it needs to be. The 32 rooms are large and comfortable; opt for one on the 2nd floor with a lake view. Meals in the restaurant (open 7am to 10pm) are straight-forward – eggs, burgers, pasta – but well prepared (mains from $10). Walk off dinner with a lakeside stroll.

Burwash Landing

Burwash Landing, 17km northwest of Destruction Bay, boasts a spectacular setting, with Kluane National Park on one side and Kluane Lake on the other. It's a good place to stretch those legs and visit the excellent museum. Next to the museum is what is said

to be the world's largest gold pan. The town was established by fur traders in 1909.

★ Kluane Museum   MUSEUM
(☑867-841-5561; www.kluanemuseum.ca; Km 1700 Alaska Hwy; adult/child $5/3; ⊙9am-6:30pm mid-May–mid-Sep) Commune with an enormous, albeit stuffed, moose at the excellent Kluane Museum. Enjoy intriguing wildlife exhibits and displays on natural and Indigenous history. It may not look like much from the outside, but this is a surprising gem in terms of museums. The gift shop features works by local Yukon artists.

Rocking Star Adventures   SCENIC FLIGHTS
(☑867-841-4322; www.rockingstar.ca; Burwash Airport; per person from $160) Flying out of Burwash Airport, 2km west of Burwash Landing, these guys operate a variety of scenic flights taking in the Kaskawulsh, Donjek and Kluane Glaciers. You can also get views of Mt Logan, Canada's highest peak.

Beaver Creek

Wide-spot-in-the-road Beaver Creek, 291km northwest from Haines Junction, is a beacon for sleepy travelers or those who just want to get gas. The Canadian border checkpoint is 2km north of town; the US border checkpoint is 27km further west. Both are open 24 hours.

Beaver Creek is the most westerly community in Canada and is the spot where northbound (from Whitehorse) and southbound (from Fairbanks) construction crews met up when completing the Alaska Hwy on October 20, 1942.

Church of Our Lady of Grace   CHURCH
(Km 1870 Alaska Hwy) Heading into Beaver Creek from the south, you'll find this cute little Catholic church on the left. It was built using a US Army Quonset hut left over from the construction of the Alaska Hwy. If you want to go in, ask at the visitor center about the key.

1202 Motor Inn   MOTEL $
(☑867-862-7600; www.1202motorinn.ca; Km 1870 Alaska Hwy; r from $90; ⊙8am-10pm; P🐕❄️📶) The 1202 Motor Inn is at the northern end of town and is reasonably appealing with basic but functional rooms. For meals, head to Buckshot Betty's just down the road. There are fuel pumps (discount if you're staying), some groceries and gifts.

Buckshot Betty's
Restaurant and Cafe   CANADIAN $$
(☑ 867-862-7111; www.buckshotbettys.ca; Km 1870 Alaska Hwy; mains from $12; ☺ 7am-10pm) Your best bet for a decent feed in Beaver Creek. Pizzas and main dinner courses such as pork cutlet and chicken parmesan (both $16.95). Betty's also has a bakery, cabins (from $100) and gifts.

Visitor Center   TOURIST INFORMATION
(☑ 867-862-7321; www.travelyukon.com; Km 1870 Alaska Hwy; ☺ 8am-8pm May-Sep) Being a gateway town to the Yukon, the visitor center has information on all of the territory.

HAINES HIGHWAY

If you're doing only a short loop between Haines and Skagway in Alaska via Whitehorse, this 259km road could be the highlight of your trip. In fact, no matter what length your Yukon adventure, the Haines Hwy (Hwy 3) might be the high point. In a relatively short distance you'll see glaciers, looming snow-clad peaks, lush and wild river valleys, windswept alpine meadows and a river delta dotted with the shadows of bald eagles.

Heading south of Haines Junction, look west for a close-up of the St Elias Mountains, those glaciers glimpsed at the top stretch all the way to the Pacific Ocean. About 80km south, look for the **Tatshenshini River viewpoint**. This white-water river flows through protected bear country and a valley that seems timeless.

About 10km further, you'll come to **Million Dollar Falls**. For once the sight lives up to the billing, as water thunders through a narrow chasm. As you drive, watch for glacier views.

The highway crosses into British Columbia for a mere 70km, but you'll hope for more as you traverse high and barren alpine wilderness, where sudden snow squalls happen year-round. At the 1070m **Chilkat Pass**, an ancient Indigenous route into the Yukon, the road suddenly plunges down for a steep descent into Alaska. The US border is 72km north of Haines, along the wide Chilkat River Delta.

The delta is home to scores of bald eagles year-round; the handsome birds flock like pigeons each fall when they amass in the trees overlooking the rivers, drawn by the comparatively mild weather and steady supply of fish. Pullouts line the Haines Hwy (Hwy 7 in Alaska), especially between mileposts 19 and 26. Take your time driving and find a place to park. Just a few feet from the road it's quiet, and when you see a small tree covered with 20 pensive – and sizable – bald eagles, you can enjoy your own raptor version of *The Birds*.

KLONDIKE HIGHWAY

Beginning seaside in Skagway, AK, the 714km Klondike Hwy climbs high to the forbidding Chilkoot Pass before crossing into stunning alpine scenery on the way to Carcross. For much of its length, the road generally follows the **Gold Rush Trail**, the route of the Klondike prospectors. You'll have a much easier time of it than they did.

North of Whitehorse, the road passes through often-gentle terrain that has been scorched by wildfires through the years. Signs showing the dates let you chart nature's recovery.

Carcross

Long a forgotten gold-rush town, cute little Carcross (the name was shortened from Caribou Crossing in 1902), 73km south of Whitehorse, is an evocative stop. There's a growing artisan community, old buildings are being restored and the site on Lake Bennett is superb – although Klondike prospectors who had to build boats here to cross the lake and head on to Dawson City didn't think so. The old train station has good displays on local history.

Carcross Desert   DESERT
Proudly claimed as the world's smallest desert, Carcross Desert, 2km north of town, is actually the exposed sandy bed of a glacial lake. There are a few pine trees among the 260 hectares of sand.

★ White Pass & Yukon Route   RAIL
(☑ 800-343-7373; www.wpyr.com; one way from Skagway adult/child $165/82.50; ☺ mid-May–mid-Sep) There are five trains weekly in summer from Skagway to Carcross (and vice versa). These five-hour rides over White Pass access a lot of remote scenery that the shorter regular trips to Bennett don't cover. There are packages that include bus transport in one direction to allow Skagway-based day trips.

Information

Visitor Center (☎867-821-4431; www.travelyukon.com; 7 Austin St; ⏲8am-8pm May-Sep) The VIC is in a modern complex with seasonal shops and cafes. Get the excellent walking-tour brochure.

Carmacks

This small village sits right on the Yukon River and is named for one of the discoverers of gold in 1896, George Washington Carmack. A rogue seaman wandering the Yukon, it was almost by luck that Carmack (with Robert Henderson, Tagish Charlie and Keish – aka Skookum Jim Mason) made a claim on Bonanza Creek. Soon he was living the high life and it wasn't long before he abandoned his First Nations family and headed south to the US. Given his record as a husband and father, it's fitting that Carmack be honored by this uninspired collection of gas stations and places to stay. Like elsewhere in the territory, residents here are keenly attuned to the land, which supplies them with game and fish throughout the year. A pretty 15-minute interpretive walk by the river provides a glimmer of insight into this life.

Sights

Besides the interpretive center, there are things to see on the Klondike Hwy north and south of Carmacks.

About 25km north of Carmacks, the **Five Finger Rapids Recreation Site** has excellent views of the treacherous stretch of the rapids that once tested the wits of riverboat captains traveling between Whitehorse and Dawson. There's a steep 1.5km walk down to the rapids.

South, there are a series of water features starting with **Twin Lakes**, 23km from Carmacks, followed by **Fox Lake**. Another 24km south, you can't miss serene **Lake Laberge**. The final 40km to Whitehorse is marked by low trees and a few cattle ranches.

Tagé Cho Hudän Interpretive Centre MUSEUM
(☎867-863-5831; www.yukonmuseums.ca; off Hwy 2; by donation; ⏲9am-6pm May-Sep) This super-friendly interpretive center has knowledgeable volunteers who explain their Indigenous life past and present.

Sleeping & Eating

Hotel & RV Park Carmacks HOTEL $$
(☎867-863-5221; www.hotelcarmacks.com; 35607 Klondike Hwy N; tent & RV sites/cabins/r from $40/95/179; P ⊖ ❄ ☰) It's all here, 177km north of Whitehorse, with the largest accommodations place on the Klondike Hwy between Whitehorse and Dawson City. Hotel Carmacks offers a good standard of rooms and also features the Gold Panner Restaurant and Gold Dust Lounge. The RV Park offers campsites, power and internet. Nothing like this further north.

THE KLONDIKE GOLD RUSH

The Klondike Gold Rush continues to be the defining moment for the Yukon. Certainly it was the population high point. Around 40,000 gold seekers washed ashore (some literally) in Skagway, hoping to strike it rich in the goldfields of Dawson City, some 700km north.

To say that most were ill-prepared for the enterprise is an understatement. Although some were veterans of other gold rushes, a high percentage were American men looking for adventure. Clerks, lawyers and waiters were among those who thought they'd just pop up North and get rich. The reality was different. Landing in Skagway, they were set upon by all manner of flimflam artists, most working for the incorrigible Soapy Smith. Next came dozens of trips hefting their 1000lb of required supplies over the frozen Chilkoot Pass. Then they had to build boats from scratch and make their way across lakes and the Yukon River to Dawson. Scores died trying.

Besides more scamsters, there was another harsh reality awaiting in Dawson: by the summer of 1897 when the first ships reached the West Coast of the US with news of the discoveries on Dawson's Bonanza Creek, the best sites had all been claimed. The Klondike gold-rush mobs were mostly too late to the action by at least a year. Sick and broke, the survivors glumly made their way back to the US. Few found any gold and most sold their gear for pennies to merchants who in turn resold it to incoming gold seekers for top dollar. Several family fortunes in the Yukon today can be traced to this trade.

Tatchun Centre General Store FOOD
(☑867-863-6171; 35607 Klondike Hwy; ☺7:30am-10pm) This is the biggest store between Whitehorse and Dawson City, and offers the opportunity to purchase grocery and food items, drinks, gifts and souvenirs. There are also gas pumps outside.

ⓘ Information

Carmacks Visitor Centre (☺9am-5pm Jun-Sep) This cute little hut at the entrance to Carmacks was built in 1903 as a telegraph station. It has no electricity or phone but is staffed during the season and has helpful maps and brochures to hand out. Pick up the Historical Building Walking Tour pamphlet.

Stewart Crossing

Another popular place to get your canoe wet, Stewart Crossing is on the Stewart River, which affords a narrow and somewhat more rugged experience before it joins the Yukon to the west for the trip to Dawson.

Little more than a petrol station and store, the village is at the junction of the Klondike Hwy (Hwy 2) and the Silver Trail (Hwy 11), which makes a 225km round-trip northeast to the nearly abandoned town of Keno City and the tiny village of Mayo.

Keno City Mining Museum MUSEUM
(☑867-995-3103; www.yukonmuseums.ca; Main St, Keno City; ☺10am-6pm Jun-Sep) In Jackson Hall, built in the 1920s when Keno City was booming, the Mining Museum shows what life was like during silver- and gold-mining times with some superb old photographs, tools and equipment.

★**Moose Creek Lodge** LODGE $$
(☑867-996-2550; www.moosecreek-lodge.com; 561 Klondike Hwy N; cabins from $125; 🅿⊜🛜) If you're after a bit of seclusion, head here to Moose Creek, about 24km north of Stewart Crossing. These comfy little cabins are set back in the forest with communal toilet and shower facilities nearby. The lodge restaurant uses homegrown vegetables and produce, and the gift shop offers a good selection of pieces by local artists.

ⓘ Information

Visitor Information Center (Klondike Hwy N, Stewart Crossing; ☺9am-5pm Jun-Sep) Run by the village and small towns of Mayo and Keno on Hwy 11 to the northwest, you'll find maps, pamphlets and friendly help.

DAWSON CITY

If you didn't know its history, Dawson City would be an atmospheric place to pause for a while, with a seductive, funky vibe. That it's one of the most historic and evocative towns in Canada is like gold dust on a cake: unnecessary but damn nice.

Set on a narrow shelf at the confluence of the Yukon and Klondike Rivers, a mere

---

WORTH A TRIP

THE SILVER TRAIL

As prospectors found it harder and harder to become rich and stake gold claims around Bonanza Creek at Dawson City after 1898, others searched further afield and by 1920 silver had been found at Keno Hill and 600 claims staked. Shipping the heavy ore was a problem though and horse-drawn sleighs were used to haul it to the Stewart River, where it was picked up by specially designed stern-wheeler paddle steamers and shipped out, initially downriver to Dawson City, then all the way to a smelter in San Francisco. The small town of Mayo developed as a transportation center on the Stewart River where supplies were dropped off and the ore was picked up.

These days, those wanting to see these small former mining communities can take the dead-end Silver Trail (Hwy 11) northeast from Stewart Crossing. **Mayo** (population 450; www.villageofmayo.ca), formerly known as Mayo Landing, is 51km up paved Hwy 11. It is the largest community in the region and its airport is serviced by Air North (www.flyairnorth.com). The **North Star Motel** (☑867-996-2231; https://northstarmotel.business.site; 212 Fourth Ave, Mayo; r from $95; 🅿⊜✳🛜) is a good place to stay here.

A further 61km up the now gravel road you'll find **Keno City**, site of the silver mine camp, the Keno City Mining Museum and, these days, about 50 people. The only way out is back down the road you came on.

240km south of the Arctic Circle, Dawson was the center of the Klondike Gold Rush. Today, you can wander the dirt streets of town, passing old buildings with dubious permafrost foundations, and discover Dawson's rich cultural life (that person passing by may be a dancer, filmmaker, painter or miner).

Dawson can be busy in the summer, especially during its festivals. But by September the days are getting short, the seasonal workers have fled south and the 1400 year-round residents are settling in for another long, dark winter.

History

In 1898 more than 30,000 prospectors milled the streets of Dawson – a few newly rich, but most without prospects and at odds with themselves and the world. Shops, bars and prostitutes relieved these hordes of what money they had, but Dawson's fortunes were tied to the gold miners and, as the boom ended, the town began a decades-long slow fade.

The territorial capital was moved to Whitehorse in 1952 and the town lingered on, surviving on the low-key but ongoing gold-mining industry. By 1970 the population was under 900. But then a funny thing happened on the way to Dawson's demise: it was rediscovered.

Improvements to the Klondike Hwy and links to Alaska allowed the first major influx of summertime tourists, who found a charmingly moldering time capsule from the gold rush. Parks Canada designated much of the town as historic and began restorations.

⊙ Sights

Dawson is small enough to walk around in a few hours, but you can easily fill two or more days with the many local things to see and do. If the summertime hordes get you down, head uphill for a few blocks to find timeless old houses and streets. Parks Canada operates programs and restorations with great vigor in Dawson. Check out the pass options, good for the many Parks Canada sites.

★ Klondike National Historic Sites   HISTORIC SITE

(☑ 867-993-7210; www.pc.gc.ca/dawson; Parks Canada passes adult $7-31) It's easy to relive the gold rush at myriad preserved and restored places. Parks Canada runs walking tours (p787) through the day that allow access to various examples of the 26 restored buildings. Take several tours so you can see a wide variety. Outside of tours, various buildings such as the Palace Grand Theatre are open for free on a rotating basis, usually 4:30pm to 5:30pm.

★ Bonanza Creek Discovery Site   HISTORIC SITE

(Bonanza Creek Rd) [FREE] Some 1.5km up the valley from Dredge No 4, this national historic site is roughly where gold was first found in 1896. It's a quiet site today with a little water burbling through the rubble. A fascinating 500m-long walk passes interpretive displays. Pick up a guide at the visitor center.

★ Dredge No 4   LANDMARK

(☑ 867-993-5023; Bonanza Creek Rd; adult/child $20/10, return transport from Dawson $10; ☉ 10am-4pm May-Sep, tour times vary) The scarred valleys around Dawson speak to the vast amounts of toil that went into the gold hunt. Most emblematic is Bonanza Creek, where gold was first found and which still yields some today. Dredge No 4, 13km off the Klondike Hwy, is a massive dredging machine that tore up the Klondike Valley and left the tailings, which remain as a blight on the landscape. Tours of this Parks Canada site are run by Goldbottom Tours (p787).

★ Jack London Museum   MUSEUM

(☑ 867-993-5575; www.jacklondonmuseum.ca; 600 Firth St; adult/child $5/free; ☉ 11am-6pm May-Aug) In 1898 Jack London lived in the Yukon, the setting for his most popular stories, including *Call of the Wild* and *White Fang*. At the writer's cabin there are excellent daily interpretive talks. A labor of love by the late historian Dick North, Dawne Mitchell and others, this place is a treasure trove of stories – including the search for the original cabin.

Midnight Dome   VIEWPOINT

(New Dome Rd) The slide-scarred face of this hill overlooks the town to the north, but to reach the top you must travel south of town about 1km, turn left off the Klondike Hwy onto New Dome Rd, and continue for about 7km. The Midnight Dome, at 880m above sea level, offers great views of the Klondike

Dawson City

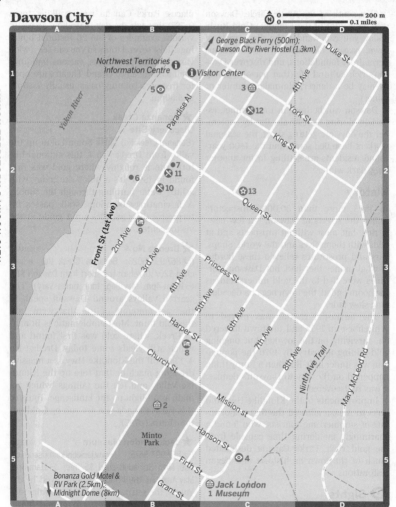

George Black Ferry (500m);
Dawson City River Hostel (1.3km)

Northwest Territories
Information Centre
Visitor Center

Yukon River

Bonanza Gold Motel &
RV Park (2.5km);
Midnight Dome (8km)

Jack London
Museum

Valley, Yukon River and Dawson City. There's also a steep **trail** that takes 90 minutes from Judge St in town; maps are available at the visitor center.

Fortymile Gold Workshop/Studio GALLERY
(☑ 867-993-5690; www.fortymilegoldworkshop.ca; 1131 3rd Ave; ☺ 9am-6pm May-Sep) Watch as jewelry is made from local refined gold, which is silky and has a rich yellow color, as opposed to the bling you see peddled on late-night TV. Examples of gold from various local claims and locations shows how old miners could tell where gold originated.

Dawson City Museum MUSEUM
(☑ 867-993-5291; www.dawsonmuseum.ca; 595 5th Ave; adult/child $9/7; ☺ 10am-6pm May-Aug) Make your own discoveries among the 25,000 gold-rush artifacts at this museum. Engaging exhibits walk you through the grim lives of the miners. The museum is housed in the landmark 1901 Old Territorial Administration building.

SS Keno HISTORIC SITE
(☑ 867-993-7200; www.pc.gc.ca; cnr Front & Queen Sts; Parks Canada admission $7; ☺ noon-4pm May-Aug) The SS *Keno* was one of a fleet of paddle wheelers that worked the Yukon's rivers for

Dawson City

◉ Top Sights
1 Jack London Museum C5

◎ Sights
2 Dawson City Museum.............................B4
3 Fortymile Gold Workshop/Studio C1
4 Robert Service Cabin.............................C5
5 SS Keno..B1

◉ Activities, Courses & Tours
6 Goldbottom Tours...................................B2
7 Klondike Experience B2

◎ Sleeping
8 Aurora Inn B4
9 Bombay Peggy's......................................B3
Klondike Kate's Cabins.................(see 12)

◈ Eating
10 Drunken Goat Taverna............................B2
11 Joe's Wood-fired Pizza B2
12 Klondike Kate's C1

◎ Drinking & Nightlife
Billy Goat's Pub ....(see 10)
Bombay Peggy's ....(see 9)

◎ Entertainment
13 Diamond Tooth Gertie's
Gambling Hall......................................C2

❶ Transport
Husky Bus...(see 7)

more than half a century. Grounded along the waterfront, the boat recreates a time before any highways.

Robert Service Cabin   HISTORIC SITE
(☑ 867-993-7200; www.pc.gc.ca; cnr 8th Ave & Hanson St; Parks Canada admission $7; ☺ several events daily May-Aug) The 'Bard of the Yukon,' poet and writer Robert W Service, lived in this typical gold-rush cabin from 1909 to 1912. Each day in season there are dramatic readings, guided walks and tours.

☀ Activities

Dawson City River Hostel   CANOEING
(www.yukonhostels.com; bike rental per day from $25; ☺ May-Sep) Arranges all manner of canoe rentals, trips and transportation from Whitehorse and points further downstream to Dawson and from Dawson to the Alaskan towns of Eagle and Circle. Canoe rental for the 16-day trip from Whitehorse to Dawson City costs $395 plus freight; you can also rent bicycles by the day. On the far side of the Yukon River from downtown Dawson City.

★ Parks Canada Walking Tours   WALKING
(☑ 867-993-7200; www.pc.gc.ca; single tour $7, unlimited tours $31; ☺ May-Aug) Parks Canada docents, often in period garb, lead excellent walking tours. On each tour, learn about a few of the 26 restored buildings and the many characters that walked the streets (many of whom could be called 'streetwalkers'). There are also self-guided 90-minute audio tours (adult $7, 9am to 5pm).

★ Goldbottom Tours   HISTORY
(☑ 867-993-5023; www.goldbottom.com; 966 Front St; tours with/without transport from Dawson $55/45; ☺ May-Sep) Run by the legendary Millar mining family. Tour the placer mine 15km up Hunker Creek Rd, which meets Hwy 2 just north of the airport. The three-hour tours include a gold-panning lesson; you get to keep what you find. You can also just pan for gold on the site for $20. The ticket office is on Front St.

Klondike Experience   TOURS
(☑ 867-993-3821; www.klondikeexperience.com; 954 2nd Ave; mountain bike rentals per day/week $39/150; ☺ May-Sep) Runs various tours that include Midnight Dome (75 minutes; $29), the Goldfields (three hours; $59) and Tombstone Park (7½ hours; $129). It also rents mountain bikes.

☀ Festivals & Events

★ Discovery Days   CULTURAL
(www.dawsoncity.ca; ☺ mid-Aug) Celebrates the you-know-what of 1896, with parades and picnics. Events begin days before, including an excellent art show. It's a hoot!

Dawson City Music Festival   MUSIC
(☑ 867-993-5584; www.dcmf.com; ☺ mid-Jul) Going for over 40 years and popular – tickets sell out months in advance and the city fills up; reservations are essential.

⊨ Sleeping

Reservations are a good idea in July and August. Many places will pick you up at the airport; ask in advance.

Dawson City River Hostel HOTEL $

(☑867-993-6823; www.yukonhostels.com; dm $22, r from $48; ☺May-Sep; P☺☎) ✔ This delightfully eccentric hostel is across the river from town and five minutes up the hill from the ferry landing. It has good views, cabins, platforms for tents, and a communal bathhouse. Tent sites are $14. Owner Dieter Reinmuth is a noted Yukon author and all-around character.

★ **Klondike Kate's Cabins** LODGE $$

(☑867-993-6527; www.klondikekates.ca; cnr King St & 3rd Ave; cabins from $175; ☺Apr-Sep; P☺☎) The 15 cabins behind the excellent restaurant of the same name are rustic without the rusticisms. Some units have microwaves and fridges. All have porches, perfect for decompressing.

★ **Bombay Peggy's** INN $$

(☑867-993-6969; www.bombaypeggys.com; cnr 2nd Ave & Princess St; r from $110; ☺Mar-Nov; P☺☎) ✔ A renovated former brothel with alluring period furnishings and spunky attitude. Budget 'snug' rooms share bathrooms. Rooms are plush in a way that will make you want to wear a garter. The bar is a classy oasis.

★ **Aurora Inn** INN $$

(☑867-993-6860; www.aurorainn.ca; 5th Ave; r from $120; P☺❄☎) All 20 rooms in this European-style inn are large and comfortable. And if there's such a thing as old-world cleanliness, it's here: the admonishments to remove your (invariably) muddy shoes start at the entrance.

Bonanza Gold Motel & RV Park MOTEL $$

(☑867-993-6789; www.bonanzagold.ca; Klondike Hwy N; r from $129; P☺❄☎) Lots of options at this massive place out near the entrance to town on the Klondike Hwy. Motel rooms (from $119) are simple yet functional, the RV Park (from $24) packs in all those RVs racing around the Yukon, and the facilities meet the needs of travelers on the move. Think wi-fi, laundry, car wash.

✖ Eating

★ **Joe's Wood-fired Pizza** PIZZA $$

(☑867-993-5326; 978 2nd Ave; pizzas from $15; ☺4-9:30pm Mon-Fri) Surprisingly authentic Italian in downtown Dawson City. Pizza options include Italian favorites and house specialties, the wine list has bottles from all over the globe, while the atmosphere is friendly, relaxed and comfortable.

★ **Klondike Kate's** CANADIAN $$

(☑867-993-6527; www.klondikekates.ca; cnr King St & 3rd Ave; dinner mains from $14; ☺11am-10pm Mon-Fri, from 8am Sat & Sun May-Oct) Two ways to know spring has arrived: the river cracks up and Kate's reopens. Locals in the know prefer the latter. The long and inventive menu has fine sandwiches, pastas and fresh Yukon fish. Look for great specials. Excellent list of Canadian craft brews.

Drunken Goat Taverna GREEK $$

(☑867-993-5800; 2nd Ave; mains from $14; ☺5pm-late) Follow your eyes to the flowers, your ears to the Aegean music and your nose to the excellent Greek food, served year-round by the legendary Tony Dovas. A terrace out back is a fine place to while away an evening.

🍷 Drinking & Nightlife

The spirit(s) of the prospectors lives on in several saloons. On summer nights the action goes on until dawn, which would mean something if it weren't light all night.

★ **Bombay Peggy's** PUB

(☑867-993-6969; www.bombaypeggys.com; cnr 2nd Ave & Princess St; ☺11am-11pm Mar-Nov) There's always a hint of pleasures to come swirling around the tables of Dawson's most inviting bar.

Enjoy good beers, wines and mixed drinks inside or out.

Billy Goat's Pub PUB

(☑867-993-5868; www.facebook.com/billygoat pub; 950 2nd Ave; ☺5pm-late) Not a branch of the famed Chicago original, but a friendly lounge from Tony of Drunken Goat fame. Serves food from the Drunken Goat menu until late. Note the murals on the walls.

★ **Diamond Tooth Gertie's Gambling Hall** CASINO

(☑867-993-5575; www.dawsoncity.ca; cnr Queen St & 4th Ave; $15; ☺7pm-2am) This popular recreation of an 1898 saloon is complete with small-time gambling, a honky-tonk piano and dancing girls. The casino helps promote the town and fund culture. Each night there are three different floor shows with singing and dancing, which are often surprisingly contemporary.

DAWSON CITY TO ALASKA

From Dawson City, the **George Black** (www.yukoninfo.com/dawson-city-yukon; ⊘24hr) **FREE** free car ferry crosses the Yukon River from the end of Front St to the scenic **Top of the World Highway** (Hwy 9). Only open in summer, the mostly gravel 107km-long road to the US border has superb vistas across the region.

You'll continue to feel on top of the world as you cross at the most northerly US–Canada border crossing. The land is barren alpine meadows with jutting rocks and often grazing caribou. The border crossing at Poker Creek (open 9am to 9pm Yukon time, 8am to 8pm Alaska time May 15 to September 15) has strict hours – if you're late you'll have to wait until the next day.

On the US side, Alaska shows its xenophobic side, as the first 19km connection to the intersection with the Taylor Hwy (Hwy 5) is newly sealed and gives the impression that the easy road may last forever. The old gold-mining town of Eagle on the Yukon River is 105km from the intersection.

It's time to go back to the gravel! Some further 48km south from the intersection, over unsealed roads, you encounter **Chicken**, a delightful place of free thinkers happy to sell you a stupid T-shirt at one of the gas-station cafes or offer their views regarding government bureaucrats. The town was going to be called Ptarmigan, but locals didn't trust their spelling and pronunciation skills so went for Chicken instead.

Another 119km south and you reach the Alaska Hwy, where a turn east takes you to the Yukon. Just a tick west, **Tok** has services and motels. Alaska time is one hour earlier than the Yukon. The only place between Dawson City and the Alaska Hwy to get fuel or food is in Chicken, so prepare well.

ⓘ Information

Much of Dawson is closed October to May. The bi-weekly, volunteer-run *Klondike Sun* (www.klondikesun.com) covers special events and activities.

Northwest Territories Information Centre (📞867-993-6167; www.spectacularnwt.com; 1123 Front St; ⊘9am-7pm May-Sep) Maps and information on the NWT and the Dempster Hwy.

Visitor Center (📞867-993-5566; www.travelyukon.com; cnr Front & King Sts; ⊘8am-8pm May-Sep) A veritable mine of tourist and Parks Canada information (buy activity tickets and passes here). It also has essential schedules of events and activities.

ⓘ Getting There & Away

Dawson City is 527km from Whitehorse. Public transportation to/from Whitehorse is often in flux.

Yukon Dawson Airport (Km 694 Klondike Hwy) is 15km east of Dawson. **Air North** (📞800-661-0407; www.flyairnorth.com) serves Whitehorse and Old Crow in the Yukon, Inuvik in the NWT, and flies to Vancouver, Calgary, Edmonton and other cities.

Alaska/Yukon Trails (www.alaskashuttle.com) runs buses to Fairbanks, AK ($315, thrice weekly June to mid-September).

Husky Bus (📞867-993-3821; www.huskybus.ca) serves Whitehorse ($119, thrice weekly) and makes all stops along the Klondike Hwy. Departures are from the visitor center. Husky will do pickups of paddlers and canoes along the Klondike Hwy with advance arrangement. Also does airport transfers. Uses the Klondike Experience (p787) office.

DEMPSTER HIGHWAY

Rather than name this road for an obscure Mountie (William Dempster), it should be named the Michelin Hwy or the Goodyear Hwy for the number of tires it's sent to an explosive demise. The 736km thrill ride to Inuvik is one of North America's great adventure roads, winding through stark mountains and emerald valleys, across huge tracts of tundra, and passing through Tombstone Territorial Park. And it recently got even better, with a 144km extension north to Tuktoyaktuk on the shores of the Beaufort Sea and Arctic Ocean.

The Dempster (Hwy 5 in the Yukon, Hwy 8 in the NWT) starts 40km southeast of Dawson City, off the Klondike Hwy.

Built on a thick base of gravel to insulate the permafrost underneath (which would otherwise melt, causing the road to sink without a trace), the Dempster is open most of the year, but the best time to travel is between early June and late October, when the ferries over the Peel and Mackenzie Rivers operate. In winter, ice forms a natural bridge over the rivers, which become ice roads. The Dempster is closed during the spring thaw and the winter freeze-up; the timing of these vary by the year and can occur from mid-April to June and mid-October to December, respectively.

Check road conditions in the Yukon (p769) and the NWT (☑800-661-0750; www.dot.gov.nt.ca); the Northwest Territories Information Centre (p789) in Dawson City is a good resource. It takes 10 to 12 hours to drive to Inuvik without stopping for a break. (Given that William Dempster regularly made 700km dogsled journeys in subzero weather, this rugged and challenging road is properly named after all.)

Tombstone Territorial Park   PARK

(☑867-667-5648; www.yukonparks.ca; Dempster Hwy) Tombstone Territorial Park, which lies along Dempster Hwy for about 50km, is an easy day trip from Dawson City. Shades of green and charcoal color the wide valleys here, and steep ridges are dotted with small glaciers and alpine lakes. Summer feels tentative but makes its statement with a burst of purple wildflowers in July. Clouds sweep across the tundra, bringing squalls punctuated by brilliant sun. Stand amid this and you'll know the meaning of the sound of silence.

The park's excellent **interpretive centre** (Dempster Hwy; ⊙9am-7pm Jun-early Sep), which offers walks and talks, is 71km from the start of Hwy 5.

Tombstone Mountain
Campground   CAMPGROUND $

(http://yukon.goingtocamp.com; Dempster Hwy; tent & RV sites $12; P) The park's only formal campground is at the excellent interpretive centre. There are also three backcountry campsites at Grizzly Lake, Divide Lake and Talus Lake, with tent pads and outhouses. These require permits from June to mid-September; buy permits through the website.

Eagle Plains Hotel
& Service Station   MOTEL $$

(☑867-993-2453; www.eagleplainshotel.ca; Dempster Hwy; r from $120; P 😊 🛜) The Eagle Plains Hotel, at the 370km mark and only 35km from the Arctic Circle, is open year-round and offers 32 rooms in a low-rise building in a stark setting. The next service station is 180km further north at Fort McPherson in the NWT.

ARCTIC PARKS

North of the Arctic Circle, the Yukon's population numbers a few hundred. It's a lonely land and only the hardiest venture here during the short summers.

The 300-person village of **Old Crow** is home to the Vuntut Gwitch'in First Nations and is unreachable by vehicle, although Air North flies there. It's at the confluence of the Crow and Porcupine Rivers and is the only village in the Yukon Territory that does not have road access. Locals subsist on caribou from the legendary 130,000-strong Porcupine herd, which migrates each year between the Arctic National Wildlife Refuge (ANWR) in Alaska and the Yukon.

A large swath of land is now protected in the adjoining **Vuntut National Park** and **Ivvavik National Park**. Information on both can be obtained from the Parks Canada office (p809) in Inuvik, NWT. There are very limited options for organizing visits to the parks and no facilities of any kind.

Herschel Island-Qikiqtaruk
Territorial Park   PARK

(☑867-777-4058; www.yukonparks.ca) The Indigenous name of Herschel Island-Qikiqtaruk Territorial Park means 'it is island' and indeed it is. Barely rising above the waters of Mackenzie Bay on the Beaufort Sea, the park has a long tradition of human habitation. In the late 1800s, American whalers set up shop at Pauline Cove. Abandoned in 1907, the whalers left behind several surviving wooden buildings. Summer visits to Herschel Island are possible via tours from Inuvik.

Northwest Territories

Best Places to Eat

➡ Woodyard Brewhouse & Eatery (p800)

➡ Alestine's (p808)

➡ Birchwood Coffee Ko (p798)

➡ Bullocks Bistro (p799)

➡ Zehabesha (p799)

Best Places to Stay

➡ Blachford Lake Lodge (p799)

➡ Mackenzie Rest Inn (p805)

➡ Whooping Crane Guest House (p803)

➡ Arctic Chalet (p808)

Why Go?

On a planet containing seven billion people, it's difficult to imagine that there are still places as sparsely populated as the Northwest Territories (NWT). A vast swath of boreal forest and Arctic tundra five times the size of the UK, it has a population of a small provincial town. In the 19th century, gold prospectors passed it over as too remote; modern Canadians, if they head north at all, prefer to romanticize about iconic Nunavut or the grandiose Yukon. More people orbit the earth each year than visit lonely Aulavik, one of the territory's four national parks.

What they're missing is something unique: a potent combo of epic, remarkably beautiful, accessible terrain, singular indigenous culture and a vibrant, cosmopolitan regional capital. With one of the world's greatest waterfalls and North America's deepest lake, it has enough brutal wilderness to keep a modern-day David Livingstone happy for a couple of lifetimes.

When to Go
Yellowknife

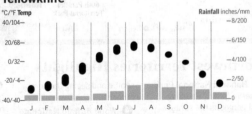

Jun See the midnight sun and go hiking before the horseflies hatch.

Jul & Aug Hyperactive summer, good for fishing and canoeing. Aurora sightings in late August.

Mar Best winter visits, with aurora viewing, husky mushing and Yellowknife's Snowking festival.

Northwest Territories Highlights

1 **Nahanni National Park Reserve** (p805) Paddling past gorgeous hot springs or flying over Canada's most iconic waterfall.

2 **Dempster Hwy** (p808) Embarking on one of Canada's iconic road trips.

3 **Yellowknife** (p794) Enjoying NWT's cosmopolitan capital and seeing the aurora borealis.

4 **Wood Buffalo National Park** (p803) Being dazzled by herds of bison and the brilliant night sky.

5 **Inuvik** (p807) Visiting the Western Arctic's remotest communities.

6 **Canol Heritage Trail** (p807) Hiking where few have hiked before.

7 **Great Slave Lake** (p795) Paddleboarding past floatplanes and houseboats.

8 **Norman Wells** (p806) Embarking on a canoeing adventure down the mighty Mackenzie.

History

The first NWT residents, ancestors of today's Dene, tramped here from Asia about 14,000 years ago. The Inuvialuit (Western Canadian Inuit), who migrated from Alaska, showed up more recently. Fur-hunting Europeans, followed by missionaries, penetrated the area in the 18th and 19th centuries. After oil turned up near Tulita in the 1920s, a territorial government was formed. Gold near Yellowknife and radium near Great Bear Lake brought a population influx in the 1930s. In 1999 the territory was cut in half with the formation of Nunavut: NWT is now evenly divided between Indigenous and non-Indigenous. The latter group, and to a smaller extent the former, have benefited from oil, gas and diamond development.

Land & Climate

The NWT is a supersized wilderness reaching poleward from the 60th parallel. The south is evergreen flatlands, the east is the boulder-filled landscape of the Canadian Shield, and toothy mountains rear up from the west. Canada's biggest river, the Mackenzie, bisects the territory, draining two gargantuan lakes, Great Slave and Great Bear.

Summers have been warm recently but can bring anything. One sure thing is daylight: from May through July there's no end of it. June's the driest summer month, but lake ice can linger until the month's end. Most visitors come in July, when much of the region is plagued with horseflies and mosquitoes, and August.

Winters are long and punishing. In January, lows in Yellowknife collapse to -40°C and daylight is feeble. If you're keen on a winter visit, try March or April, when the sun climbs and the mercury follows suit.

ℹ Getting There & Away

AIR

Edmonton International Airport (p571) in Alberta is the main gateway to NWT. Edmonton–Yellowknife flights, starting at around $499 return, are offered by First Air (www.firstair.ca), Canadian North (www.canadiannorth.com), Air Canada (www.aircanada.com), Northwestern Air (www.nwal.ca) and WestJet (www.westjet.com). Canadian North also flies from Edmonton to Inuvik ($1360 return) via Norman Wells ($1390). Northwestern Air serves Hay River ($1200 return) and Fort Smith ($1600 return) direct from Edmonton. Air Canada and WestJet also serve Yellowknife from Calgary ($548 return).

NORTHWEST TERRITORIES FAST FACTS
....
➡ Population: 44,541

➡ Area: 1,141,000 sq km

➡ Capital: Yellowknife

➡ Quirky fact: The world's first 'grolar bear' (grizzly and polar bear hybrid) was discovered in the wild here in 2006.

From Whitehorse, Yukon, Air North (www.flyairnorth.com) flies via Dawson City to Inuvik ($650 return).

From Iqaluit, Nunavut, First Air and Canadian North fly to Yellowknife ($3400 return) via Rankin Inlet.

BUS

At the time of writing, there were no bus services to the NWT.

CAR & MOTORCYCLE

There are two overland routes into NWT from the south. From Edmonton, Alberta, a 924km drive up Hwy 35 brings you to the NWT border, 84km shy of Enterprise. From Fort Nelson, British Columbia, the Liard Trail runs 137km to the border. Fort Liard is another 38km north.

If you're heading up to the Mackenzie Delta, you can set out from Dawson City, Yukon, on the shockingly scenic but challenging Dempster Hwy, which reaches the NWT border after 465km.

ℹ Getting Around

AIR

Half of the NWT's 32 communities are fly-in only, and are accessed from Yellowknife Airport (p800) with Air Tindi (www.airtindi.com), Norman Wells with North-Wright Air (www.north-wrightairways.com) and Inuvik with Aklak Air (www.aklakair.ca). First Air (www.firstair.ca) and Canadian North (www.canadiannorth.com) cover the major destinations.

BUS

There were no bus services within NWT at research time.

CAR & MOTORCYCLE

To best appreciate the NWT, you need wheels. Cars can be rented in all major communities.

The territory has two highway networks: a southern system, linking most communities in the North Slave, South Slave and Deh Cho regions; and the Dempster Hwy, which winds through the Mackenzie Delta. Getting to the Delta from southern NWT requires a two-day

CLIMATE CHANGE IN THE ARCTIC

The Arctic is warming at twice the rate of the rest of the planet and climate change is making itself felt. Its effects are many and diverse.

➡ Shorter, warmer winters affect ice roads that connect remote communities to main towns and transport to the mines.

➡ Hotter, drier summers turn boreal forests into tinderboxes and wildfires are becoming more frequent and bigger in scale, affecting air quality and driving up CO_2 emissions.

➡ Longer, hotter summers also mean longer mosquito and biting fly seasons, an annoyance to humans and a key factor in declining numbers of caribou, whose reproductive cycles they disrupt.

➡ Later freeze-up means more hungry and desperate polar bears near northern settlements, posing a danger to humans.

➡ Changing weather patterns are affecting the migration patterns of wildlife – or 'country food' – on which many remote Inuit communities still depend.

➡ The melting of the permafrost has potentially catastrophic implications for buildings and other infrastructure, not to mention the rising levels of CO_2 in the atmosphere, which in turn means hotter summers and escalating cycles of wildfires and swifter melting of the permafrost.

➡ Southern wildlife, such as grizzlies, foxes, deer, moose, magpies and killer whales, are encroaching on the territory of Arctic wildlife, making its existence more precarious.

detour through BC and the Yukon. Roads are either sealed or are good gravel roads.

In summer free ferries cross several rivers; in winter vehicles drive across ice that's more than 1m thick. Travel is interrupted for several weeks during spring thaw (April and May) and freeze-up (October and November). High river levels can interrupt ferry services on the Dempster Hwy for days. Check www.dot.gov.nt.ca for current conditions.

If traveling by yourself, make a trip plan and share it with someone responsible. Bring the right gear for the season and extra food, water and a sleeping bag in case you break down. If you do break down, stay with your vehicle. There is no phone reception along most of the Dempster Hwy and along some other remote roads, so a satellite phone is also recommended.

YELLOWKNIFE

POP 19,569

Amid the droning bush planes and picturesque houseboats of Yellowknife's Old Town, bordering Great Slave Lake, it's still possible to detect a palpable frontier spirit. It's as if you're standing on the edge of a large, undiscovered and barely comprehensible wilderness – and you *are*. Draw a line north from Yellowknife to the Arctic Ocean and you won't cross a single road.

Friendly, multicultural, subarctic Yellowknife supports 50% of the NWT population and is a blend of Dene and Métis from across the territory; Inuit and Inuvialuit from further north; grizzled non-Indigenous pioneers; get-rich-quick newcomers from southern Canada; and a sizable selection of more recent immigrants from different parts of the world.

Named Somba K'e (Place of Money) in the local Tlicho language, the city, a mining hub and surprisingly artsy place, has been the territorial capital since 1967 and is unsurpassed in winter for views of the northern lights.

History

When the first Europeans reached Great Slave Lake in 1771, the north shore was home to the Tetsot'ine, who were dubbed the Yellowknives due to their penchant for copper blades. Wars and disease eradicated them, but the moniker remained.

Over a century later, Klondike-bound prospectors on Yellowknife Bay unearthed gold. By the mid-1930s, bush planes had made the area accessible to commercial mining. Yellowknife became a boomtown.

In 1967, when Ottawa devolved management of the NWT, Yellowknife became the capital. Though gold mining ceased in the early 21st century, diamonds were discovered nearby in 1991, with subsequent diamond mines fueling a new boom, and turning Yellowknife into the cosmopolitan place it now is. Though plans for more diamond exploration are afoot, locals are wondering what's next when the stones run low in a decade or so.

◉ Sights

Uphill from the Old Town, Yellowknife's less characterful downtown was built – quite literally – on gold in the 1940s and '50s.

★ Prince of Wales
Northern Heritage Centre   MUSEUM
(Map p796; ☑ 867-873-7551; www.pwnhc.ca; ⊙ 10:30am-5pm; ℗ ♿) FREE Acting as NWT's historical and cultural archive, this well-laid-out museum overlooks Frame Lake. Expertly assembled displays address natural history, European exploration, Northern aviation, diamond mining and, especially, Dene and Inuit history and culture, their symbiotic relationship with their environment and their dependance on game for shelter, clothing, transport and food. Temporary exhibits include exceptional soapstone and whalebone sculpture by Inuvialuit artist Abraham Anghik Ruben. There's a terrific cafe and a good play zone for younger kids.

★ Great Slave Lake   LAKE
Yellowknife sits on the shores of Great Slave Lake – the 10th largest lake in the world and the deepest in North America. It takes its name from the Slavey First Nations, who've lived on its shores for millennia, and it has played a crucial part in the fur trade by the Hudson Trading Company. These days, it's a water-sports hub, a favorite of canoeists and a take-off and landing strip for floatplanes.

Yellowknife Cultural Crossroads   PUBLIC ART
(Map p796; Franklin Ave) On a huge boulder by the road there's a striking work of art: a soaring eagle, a whirl of colorful handprints and the skeletal outline of a tipi. In front there's a bronze replica sculpture of the one found inside the Legislative Assembly, and another stone sculpture. This work is a collaboration between Métis, Dene, Inuvialuit, French- and English-Canadian artists.

NWT Diamond Centre   NOTABLE BUILDING
(Map p796; ☑ 867-920-7108; www.nwtdiamond centre.com; 5105 49th St; ⊙ 10am-5:45pm Tue-Sat) A great place to buy your diamond bling, this gallery also provides a good overview of diamond mining in Canada's frigid north. The accompanying video explains the difference between diamond types and why they truly are forever. Diamond-polishing sessions are held from 2:30pm to 3:30pm. Striking aerial photos of the Lac de Gras mines too.

Old Town   HISTORIC SITE
(Map p796) Many living people are older than Yellowknife but, despite the fact the Old Town only dates from the mid-1930s, its ramshackle streets wedged between Back and Yellowknife Bays have a tangible gold-rush-era atmosphere. Funky cabins and eye-catching mansions share views with floating homes and fish shacks. Beyond, picturesque Latham Island includes N'Dilo ('End of the Road'), Yellowknife's Dene village.

Legislative Assembly   NOTABLE BUILDING
(Map p796; ☑ 867-669-2230; www.assembly.gov. nt.ca; 4570 48th St; ⊙ 9am-6pm Mon-Fri) FREE In the impressive, igloo-shaped Legislative Assembly, you can learn about the territory's indigenous-style government by joining their free hour-long tour (10:30am, 1:30pm and 3:30pm June to August). There's excellent Northern art throughout, you get to peek into the chamber where debates happen, and you learn the story of the Speaker's Mace, the symbol of authority engraved with the slogan 'One land, many voices.'

🏃 Activities

There are various hikes around town. Longest and best is the 7km Frame Lake Trail, a favorite with runners. Start downtown in Capital Area Park; spurs connect to the 1.2km Range Lake Trail and precipitous Jackfish Lake Trail. There's also the 3.2km Prospector Trail, in Fred Henne Territorial Park.

Borealis Bike Tours Unlimited   CYCLING
(Map p796; ☑ 867-447-0037; www.borealisbike tours-unlimited.com; 4708 Hamilton St; tours $120-140; ⊙ tours 6pm Tue-Fri, 10am, 2pm & 6:30pm Sat & Sun) Want to cycle on snow? Then go for one of the three-hour fat-bike tours run by an enthusiastic Ontario expat. Tours in the fall are cheaper. Book in advance via email.

My Backyard Tours   OUTDOORS
(Map p796; ☑ 867-920-4654; www.myback yard-tours.com; 65 Rycon Dr; tours from $89) Recommended city walking tours ($89) and artists'-studio tours in summer and northern-lights tour packages in winter ($149). Can also organize multiday Arctic photography workshops and trout fishing at Point Lake.

Yellowknife

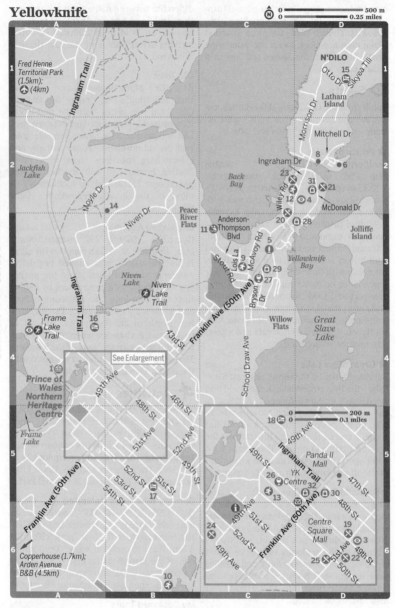

0 500 m
0 0.25 miles

N'DILO

Fred Henne
Territorial Park
(1.5km);
(4km)

Ingraham Trail

Otto Dr
Skyea Tili
15

Latham
Island

Morrison Dr

Mitchell Dr

Ingraham Dr
8
6

Jackfish
Lake

Moyle Dr

14

Niven Dr

Back
Bay

23
31
21
12
4
McDonald Dr

Peace
River
Flats

Anderson-
Thompson
Blvd
11

20
28

Jolliffe
Island

Stout Rd

McAvoy Rd
Lois La
9
5

Yellowknife
Bay

Niven
Lake

Niven
Lake
Trail

27
29

Bryson
Dr

Franklin Ave (50th Ave)

43rd St

Willow
Flats

Great
Slave
Lake

Frame
Lake
Trail

16

School Draw Ave

Prince of
Wales
Northern
Heritage
Centre

2

1

49th Ave

48th St

46th St

51st Ave

52nd Ave

49th St

*Frame
Lake*

See Enlargement

52nd St
53rd St
54th St

51st St
17

10

Copperhouse (1.7km);
Arden Avenue
B&B (4.5km)

Franklin Ave (50th Ave)

A   B   C   D

Enlargement

0 200 m
0 0.1 miles

18

Ingraham Trail

49th Ave

49th St

Panda II
Mall

47th St

26
YK
Centre
32
7

13
30
48th St

49th Ave
51st St

Franklin Ave (50th Ave)

Centre
Square
Mall

19
3

24

52nd St

49th Ave

25
22
50th St
51st Ave

Old Town Paddle & Co WATER SPORTS
(Map p796; 867-447-4927; www.oldtownpad dle.
com; 3506 Racine Rd; SUP rental per day $50; Wed
& Fri-Sun) Rent your SUP here to explore the
vast wateriness of Great Slave Lake. Courses
($85) available; check website for dates.

Overlander Sports OUTDOORS
(Map p796; 867-873-2474; www.overlander
sports.com; 4909 50th St; kayak/skis rental per day
$45/25; 9:30am-6pm Mon-Fri, to 5pm Sat) Yel-
lowknife's main outfitter store rents canoes
and kayaks in summer and cross-country

Yellowknife

skis in winter, as well as fat-tire bikes ($35 for three hours).

Narwal Northern Adventures   KAYAKING
(Map p796; ☑867-873-6443; www.narwal.ca; 4702 Anderson-Thompson Blvd; kayak rental per day $45) Located on Back Bay (part of Great Slave Lake), this friendly, indigenous family business rents canoes, SUPs and kayaks, and also offers entertaining floating dinner-theater tours, multiday kayaking along the North Arm of the lake and paddling under the aurora ($240). Call ahead.

⌖ Tours

Dogsledding, a Dene fish barbecue, overnighting in a trapper's tent, sightseeing from a bush plane: Yellowknife offers plenty of 'only in the NWT' experiences.

★**Sean's Aurora Tours**   OUTDOORS
(Map p796; ☑867-444-1211; www.seannorman. com; per person $140) Travelers are raving about Sean and his outings into the countryside to chase the northern lights from August to April. Expect an intimate, small-group outing and a very enthusiastic photographer and guide.

★**North Star Adventures**   OUTDOORS
(☑867-446-2900; www.northstaradventures. ca) This indigenous-run company offers a bit of everything – excellent Dene cultural

tours ($130), boat tours ($67), fishing trips ($109), aurora-viewing trips ($130) and snowmobiling on Great Slave Lake (2½ hours, $200).

★**Air Tindi**   SCENIC FLIGHTS
(Map p796; ☑867-669-8218; www.airtindi.com; 23 Mitchell Dr; per person 30min $159) Offers excellent 30-minute tours over the city, Ingraham Trail and Yellowknife Bay. There's also a dramatic four-hour tour to Great Slave Lake's cliff-flanked East Arm, with an hour-long stop for hiking. Very occasionally, it runs an 11-hour scenic flight trip to Nahanni National Park ($1449).

B Dene Adventures   CULTURAL
(☑867-444-0451; www.bdene.com) ✈ These recommended summer and winter tours have a focus on Northern experiences and, particularly, Dene cultural tours that guide you through the N'diloh and Dettah communities (per person from $120). The base for activities is a lakeside camp.

Aurora Village   TOURS
(Map p796; ☑867-669-0006; www.auroravillage. com; 4709 Franklin Ave) This tour operator does the lion's share of aurora bus tours, making for an efficient rather than intimate experience, with special heated seats ($126). They also offer dogsledding ($100) and snowshoeing ($100), and boating on Great Slave Lake ($63) in summer. The lodge and

the viewing areas are located just off the first section of the Ingraham Trail; pickup from hotels.

Bluefish Services FISHING
(Map p796; ☑867-873-4818; www.bluefishservices.ca; Mitchell Dr) Bluefish takes you out on Great Slave Lake to battle grayling, pike and lake trout. Prices range from $150 (4½ hours) up to $330 (10 hours). They also have simple one-hour boat tours ($55) and 3½-hour bird-watching excursions ($145).

🎊 Festivals & Events

★ Folk on the Rocks MUSIC
(www.folkontherocks.com; Yellowknife Hwy; day/4-day VIP pass $80/380; ☉mid-Jul) This stellar four-day event on Long Lake features everything from hip-hop and rock to Dene drumming. It draws musicians from throughout Canada and is voted one of the country's top 10 music festivals.

★ Snowking
Winter Festival PERFORMING ARTS
(www.snowking.ca; $10; ☉Mar) The Snowking, a grizzled houseboater, organizes this great winter event, hosting concerts, theatrical performances and hockey games right through March at a giant ice castle he builds on Yellowknife Bay.

🛏 Sleeping

Chateau Nova BUSINESS HOTEL $$
(Map p796; ☑867-766-6682; www.novahotels.ca/chateau-nova-yellowknife; 4571 48th St; r from $199, ste $329; P☀🛜) This smart business hotel appeals to visiting government workers and aurora chasers alike. Rooms come with king-sized beds, artfully mismatched furniture and a slew of mod cons, while the luxury suites feature in-room hot tubs.

Arden Avenue B&B B&B $$
(☑867-446-5656; www.ardenbnb.ca; 120 Arden Ave; s/d from $100/110; P🛜) Tucked away west of Old Airport Rd, the three rooms inside this spacious residential house are snug, carpeted, warm and appealingly decorated in neutral shades; one is en suite. Owner Ian is on hand to help or advise, and the continental breakfast spread is fairly extensive. Downtown is easily reachable on bus route B.

Blue Raven B&B B&B $$
(Map p796; ☑867-873-6328; tmacfoto@me.com; 37 Otto Dr Hill; s/d $100/115; 🛜) In a quiet,

idyllic location on Latham Island, with great bay views from the lounge and deck, this welcoming spot feels like a rural retreat. There are three neat, compact rooms, two of which have a 'ladder loft' with an extra sleeping area. You can use the kitchen and you'll generally feel like you're staying at a friend's place.

Embleton House B&B B&B $$
(Map p796; ☑867-873-2892; www.embletonhouse.com; 5203 52nd St; s/d $120/175, without bath $100/155; P🛜) This well-kitted-out downtown B&B offers two options: compact, cozy rooms with shared bathroom and kitchen, or fabulous decorative themed suites with private whirlpool baths, robes and well-equipped kitchenettes. In both, ingredients are supplied for you to make your own breakfast. The owners are sociable and extremely congenial and both price and facilities outweigh any downtown hotel. Under-12s stay free.

Explorer Hotel HOTEL $$
(Map p796; ☑867-873-3531; www.explorerhotel.ca; 4825 49th Ave; s/d from $110/120, ste $215; P☀🛜🏊) Looming over downtown, this generic high-rise is arguably the best in-town hotel, with comfortable, slightly dated rooms, a good restaurant and lounge, plus an imposing lobby polar bear. Odd-numbered rooms have a slightly nicer view. Standard suites are much larger for not a great deal extra. The airport shuttle stops here.

🍴 Eating

Yellowknife Farmers Market MARKET
(Map p796; www.yellowknifefarmersmarket.ca; Somba K'e Civic Plaza; ☉5:15-7:30pm Tue early Jun–late Sep; 🖉) If you're in Yellowknife on a Tuesday, you're in for a treat. The farmers market is a great place to hang out, shop for artisanal baked goods and preserves, and munch on Somalian dishes, Vietnamese spring rolls, Korean chicken wings and corn on the cob. There's a DJ by the lake, too.

★ Birchwood Coffee Ko CAFE $
(Map p796; ☑867-873-5466; www.birchwoodcoffeeko.com; 5021 49th St; mains $7-12; ☉7:30am-6pm Mon-Fri, 11am-5pm Sun) This great addition to Yellowknife's cafe scene has become the local epicenter for leisurely brunches, laptop-tapping over a seriously good coffee or just gathering to catch up

BLACHFORD LAKE LODGE

The excellent **Blachford Lake Lodge** (☑867-873-3303; www.blachfordlakelodge.com; d cottage/lodge 2 nights incl transport & meals $2225/3378; ☎) sits on a pristine lake a half-hour floatplane flight from Yellowknife. It's a stunning spot to get away from it all, offering numerous summer and winter activities. You can stay either in rustic wood cabins or in the lodge itself, where smart, colorful rooms give you the chance to see the aurora from under the covers.

Sociable common areas include lounges, decks, the dining room and an outdoor hot tub. There are skis, skates, snowshoes, kayaks, canoes, hiking paths and more at your disposal and fishing, snowmobiling and husky-sledding excursions are easily arranged.

It's a friendly, relaxed place and they're often looking for volunteer staff, including WWOOFers for the organic vegetable garden.

on local gossip over a lunchtime sandwich. Super-central locale and sunny outdoor terrace, too.

★**Zehabesha** ETHIOPIAN **$$**
(Map p796; ☑867-873-6400; 5030 50th St; mains $12-23; ☉11am-2pm & 4-9pm Mon-Sat; ☎☑) Authentic Ethiopian food? In northern Canada? As unexpected as it is welcome, this unpretentious restaurant has earned itself a loyal clientele with generous portions of curried goat, *doro wot* (chicken stew) and other flavorful offerings. The *mahiberawi* (combination) is a great way to try a little of each dish with *injera* (spongy sourdough flatbread).

Copperhouse BISTRO **$$**
(☑867-920-5500; www.copperhouse.ca; 484 Range Lake Rd; mains $18-38; ☉noon-9pm Tue-Fri, 10am-10pm Sat, 10am-9pm Sun; ☎☑) At this epitome of an urban bistro, the succinct menu revolves around a handful of family-favorite virtues: wood-fired pizzas, brisket sandwiches, ribs and burgers, all smartly executed under a canopy of a myriad twinkling lightbulbs.

There's a separate bar area serving craft beer and it's worth driving out here for brunch, too.

Korea House KOREAN **$$**
(Map p796; ☑867-669-0188; 5103 50th St; mains $11-19; ☉11:30am-7pm Mon-Sat; ❄☑) What this place lacks in atmosphere – it's a brightly lit, canteen-style setup – it makes up for with authentic Korean flavors. The spicy tofu stew is a fantastic cold-weather warmer, the bibimbap (mixed rice bowl) comes with lots of fresh veggies, and the bulgogi (grilled beef) and the veggie dumplings hit the spot too.

Dancing Moose Café CAFE **$$**
(Map p796; ☑867-669-8842; www.baysidenorth.com; 3505 McDonald Dr; mains $14-22; ☉8am-3pm Tue-Sun; ☎☑) ✐ Watch floatplanes taking off as you kick back in the backyard of this pleasant cafe. The interior gets busy at lunchtime, with soups, salads and sandwich specials. It's also a good breakfast choice, with ingredients locally sourced as much as possible.

Art exhibitions and a cheery ambience make it a winner.

Wildcat Café CANADIAN **$$**
(Map p796; ☑867-873-8850; www.facebook.com/wildcatyellowknife; cnr Wiley Rd & Doornbos Lane; mains $18-44; ☉11am-10pm Jun-Sep) A beloved local landmark, this refurbished Old Town log cabin has been churning out food since 1937, though today's fare is more sophisticated, ranging from smoked Arctic char bagel to bison rib eyes and epic burgers.

The summer deck is mighty nice for kicking back with a brew on a warm evening.

★**Bullocks Bistro** SEAFOOD **$$$**
(Map p796; ☑867-873-3474; 3534 Weaver Dr; mains $26-39; ☉11:30am-9pm, from 4pm Sun) This legendary shack, brimful of bumper stickers, happy diners, diners' graffiti, and mix-and-match furniture, is a sassy, humorous place specializing in huge portions of fish. It comes pan-fried, grilled or deep-fried with chips, salad and a secret home-made sauce. Slabs of grilled Arctic char are superb, as is the blue-cheese dressing. Stews are the focus at lunchtime.

Expect serve-yourself drinks, to wait and wait some more for service, and saucy back-chat from the staff.

Drinking & Nightlife

★ Woodyard Brewhouse & Eatery MICROBREWERY
(Map p796; ☑867-873-2337; www.nwtbrewingco.com; 3905 Franklin Ave; ⊙5-11pm Mon, 11:30am-11pm Tue-Thu, to 1am Fri & Sat, 10:30am-2pm Sun; 🖥) This award-winning microbrewery is the star of both Yellowknife's dining scene and nightlife. Consistently packed, it does many things right: the food (thin-crust pizza, mac 'n' cheese) is great, the decor is industrial-meets-hunter's-cabin and there's an outdoor patio for kicking back with a pint of one of Ragged Pine pale ale, Turbid Wit or a seasonal IPA.

Black Knight Pub PUB
(Map p796; ☑867-920-4041; www.facebook.com/blackknightNWT; 4910 49th St; ⊙11am-11pm Mon-Thu, to 2am Fri & Sat) Among the more straight-laced drinkeries, this local favorite is a sociable place with a Scottish theme. They pour a good pint and do decent pub food, with various special evenings – wings on Wednesdays are very popular – and a barrage of 'knight' puns.

Shopping

★ Northern Images ARTS & CRAFTS
(Map p796; ☑867-873-5944; www.northernimages.ca; 4801 Franklin Ave; ⊙10am-6pm Mon-Fri, noon-5pm Sat & Sun) Owned by indigenous art-and-crafts cooperatives, this excellent place carries the famed Inuit prints and lithographs from Cape Dorset, Pangnirtung and Ulukhaktok, along with splendid Inuit sculptures, Dene birch-bark baskets and moccasins, prints by Yukon and NWT artists and merchandise featuring the striking designs of Inuit artist Kenojuak Ashevak. Prices are fair and shipping can be arranged.

★ Barren Ground Coffee COFFEE
(Map p796; www.barrengroundcoffee.com; 3532 McDonald Drive; ⊙4:30-6:30pm Thu, 11am-3pm Sat & Sun) These guys run the only coffee roastery in NWT, specialising in small-batch roasts of single origin, mostly organic beans that you may spot in gift shops all over the province. There are plans to open an espresso bar downtown...

★ Yellowknife Book Cellar BOOKS
(Map p796; ☑867-920-2220; www.yellowknifebooks.com; 4923 49th St; ⊙10am-8pm, to 6pm Sat, noon-5pm Sun; 🖥) This bookstore stocks a great selection of titles on Northern and indigenous subjects; it also sells maps and children's books.

Down to Earth Gallery ARTS & CRAFTS
(Map p796; ☑867-920-0711; www.facebook.com/downtoearthgallery; 5007 Bryson Dr; ⊙noon-5pm Tue-Fri, from 11am Sat, noon-4pm Sun) Stop by for splendid panoramic photos of Yellowknife, bags of Barren Ground gourmet coffee, CDs by northern First Nations artists and bands, striking art by Yellowknife resident Robbie Craig, Dene felt art and caribou moccasins, plus local edibles such as birch syrup.

ℹ Information

MEDICAL SERVICES
Stanton Territorial Hospital (☑867-669-4111; www.stha.ca; 550 Byrne Rd; ⊙24hr)

MONEY
You'll find the big banks downtown on Franklin Ave.

POST
Post office (Map p796; www.canadapost.ca; 4902 Franklin Ave; ⊙9am-5:30pm Mon-Fri)

TOURIST INFORMATION
Up Here (www.uphere.ca) Look out for copies of this terrific locally based magazine with articles on all things Northern.
Visitor Center (Map p796; ☑867-920-8687; www.visityellowknife.com; 49th Ave, Town Hall; ⊙10am-6pm, to 5pm Sun; 🖥) In a temporary home inside the Town Hall, with helpful maps and brochures, plus the indispensable annual *Explorers' Guide*.
Yellowknike Old Town Soundwalk (https://experienceyellowknife.com) An excellent downloadable app that takes you on a guided tour of Old Town.

ℹ Getting There & Away

AIR
Yellowknife Airport (☑867-767-9091; 1 Yellowknife Hwy) is NWT's hub. From here First Air (www.firstair.ca) flies to Hay River ($267, 40 minutes, one or two daily) and Fort Simpson ($818, one hour, daily except Sunday), as well as Cambridge Bay ($1039, 1¾ hours, five weekly) and Iqaluit ($2198, five hours, four weekly) via Rankin Inlet ($1370, two hours). Both First Air and Canadian North (www.canadiannorth.com) fly to Inuvik ($408, 2½ hours, daily) via Norman Wells ($406, one hour); the latter is also served by the North-Wright Air (www.north-wrightairways.com; $886, 2½ hours, daily except Sunday). Smaller airlines

sometimes offer good specials. Northwestern Air (www.nwal.ca) hits Fort Smith ($455, one hour, two daily except Saturday); and Air Tindi (www.airtindi.com) serves Fort Simpson ($535, 80 minutes, daily except Sunday). All fares quoted here are one way.

CAR

Car rental is expensive. A small car typically costs about $70 per day, $450 per week, *plus* 35¢ per kilometer (with a free 250km thrown in with weekly rentals). If you'l be covering major distances, consider renting in Edmonton and driving up.

Big-name agencies are at the airport.

ⓘ Getting Around

TO/FROM AIRPORT

Yellowknife's airport is 2km west of downtown. Taxis charge about $15. A free shuttle bus runs to the Explorer Hotel and Yellowknife Inn, among other central hotels.

BIKE

Old Town Glassworks (Map p796; ☑ 867-669-7654; www.oldtownglassworks.com; 3510 McDonald Dr; ☉10am-6pm, noon-5pm Sat & Sun) rents bicycles (including electric ones) from early June until early September, while Overlander Sports (p796) has fat-tire bikes for rent during the winter months ($35 for three hours).

BUS

Yellowknife City Transit (☑ 867-920-5600; www.yellowknife.ca; adult/child $3/2) runs three bus routes. Route A serves Old Airport Rd and downtown. Route B circles the Range Lake community and runs downtown. Route C connects downtown and Old Town. Buses run every half-hour, roughly 7:15am to 7pm Monday to Saturday.

TAXI

Download the **City Cab** (☑ 867-873-4444; http://ykcitycab.com) app.

NORTH SLAVE

The North Slave region, between Great Slave and Great Bear Lakes, is rocky, densely forested, lake-strewn and rich in minerals. Save for the people in Yellowknife, most people here are Tlicho, living traditional (and non-tourist-oriented) lives. This is a true land o' lakes – a wonderland for canoeists, kayakers, fishers and nature lovers.

Highway 3

From Yellowknife, Hwy 3 runs northwest, rounds the North Arm of Great Slave Lake, and dives off to Fort Providence (314km).

The first stretch winds through bogs, taiga and pinkish outcrops of the Canadian Shield. Watch out for roller-coaster bumps, caused by the road's heat, which melts the permafrost in summer. **Behchokò** (population 1926), 10km north of Hwy 3 on an access road, is the largest of NWT's First Nations' settlements, with a gas station, lodgings and indigenous art for sale.

Later, the land becomes flat boreal forest, ubiquitous in the southern NWT. The **Mackenzie Bison Sanctuary**, home to Canada's northernmost population of around 4000 free-ranging wood bison, flanks the road for around 150km. The animals outweigh your

---

LOCAL KNOWLEDGE

INGRAHAM TRAIL

The Ingraham Trail (Hwy 4), 69km east of Yellowknife, is where locals go to play. The mostly sealed route reveals scenic, lake-dotted, pine-covered Canadian Shield topography, and offers good fishing, hiking, camping, paddling and, in winter, skiing and snowmobiling.

Prelude Lake, 28km from Yellowknife, has a vast campground, boat launch (rentals available) and two nature trails. At **Hidden Lake Territorial Park**, 46km from Yellowknife, a 1.2km trail leads to popular **Cameron Falls**. You can crawl to the brink of this marvelous cascade. At Km 56, a 400m woodland trail goes to Cameron River Ramparts, the falls' smaller cousin. At **Reid Lake**, 61km from Yellowknife, you can canoe or fish for pike, whitefish and trout. The friendly campground has a good beach and walking trail, plus ridge-top campsites with lake views.

In summer Ingraham Trail ends at the Tibbitt Lake fishing spot, 70km from town.

car and have tempers, so give them plenty of room.

South of here, a 5km access road leads to Fort Providence. A few kilometers further, the **Deh Cho Bridge** spans the mighty Mackenzie River.

SOUTH SLAVE

The South Slave region, encompassing the area south of Great Slave Lake, is mostly flat forestland. It's cut through by big rivers and numerous spectacular waterfalls, and is home to mighty herds of bison and the historic fur-trading outposts of Hay River and Fort Smith.

Mackenzie Highway

From the Hwy 3 junction, 23km south of the Mackenzie River, the Mackenzie Hwy (Hwy 1) branches west into the Dehcho region and southeast into the South Slave. The latter Alberta-bound branch is dubbed the Waterfalls Route.

Lady Evelyn Falls Territorial Park, 7km down the access road to Kakisa, is worth a stop. There's a short path to the 17m falls, which pour over an ancient, crescent-shaped coral reef, and a campground.

From here, it's 83km to **Enterprise**, a crossroads settlement.

South of Enterprise, the Mackenzie Hwy parallels impressive Twin Falls Gorge Territorial Park. A 2km forested trail links the tiered, 15m Louise Falls on the Hay River with splendid Alexandra Falls (33m). There's also a campground here.

At the Alberta border, 72km south, is the 60th Parallel Territorial Park. The visitor center displays indigenous crafts; there's a small campground as well.

ℹ Information

The helpful **visitor center** (☑ 867-984-3811; Hwy 1, Km 0; ⊙ 8:30am-8:30pm mid-May–mid-Sep; ☎) at the 60th Parallel Territorial Park can advise on road conditions and river crossings in the Dencho region.

Hay River

POP 3528

Settled as a fur-trading post in 1868, Hay River is the territory's second-largest town and an important rail terminus, lake harbor

and freight-distribution nexus. It's a useful service center rather than a drawcard in itself. The nicest part of town is the original settled area, Vale Island, with a picturesque beach on the impossibly large Great Slave Lake. There's good fishing, boating and dogsledding available. Downtown is dominated by the highway and an out-of-place residential tower. Across the river is a Dene reserve.

🏃 Activities

The interpretive **Kiwanis Nature Trail** starts in Riverview Dr and runs for 5km along the Hay River and the West Channel of Great Slave Lake. **2 Seasons Adventures** (☑ 867-875-7112; Lagoon Rd; ⊙ Jun-Sep) runs boat trips to Louise Falls and also rents out canoes, kayak and paddleboards. The visitor center can provide information on hiking, flightseeing, fishing and canoe rentals.

🛏 Sleeping

Eileen's Bed & Breakfast   B&B $$
(☑ 867-875-7607;   www.eileensbedandbreakfast.com; 3 Wright Cres; r $158; ☎) This well-appointed three-bedroom residential home, run by the friendly Eileen, is located down a quiet street a 15-minute walk south of the center. Guests share the bathroom and kitchen.

ℹ Information

Visitor Information Center (☑ 867-874-3180; www.hayriver.com; cnr Mackenzie Hwy & McBryan Dr; ⊙ 8am-8pm Mon-Thu, 8:30am-9pm Fri-Sun, reduced hours Oct–mid-May) On the highway in the center of town.

ℹ Getting There & Away

AIR

First Air (www.firstair.ca) flies to Yellowknife for $267 (40 minutes) once or twice daily. Northwestern Air (www.nwal.ca) serves Edmonton ($595, three hours) and Fort Smith ($286, 40 minutes). No flights on Saturdays. Fares listed here are one-way.

CAR & MOTORCYCLE

By road, it's a paved 38km to Enterprise, 179km to Fort Providence and 431km of partially paved road to Fort Simpson. About 5km out of town is the turnoff to the paved Hwy 5, leading 267km to Fort Smith. Fill up on gas in Hay River since there was no gas station at Enterprise at research time.

Fort Smith

POP 2542

On a high bluff above the Slave River, friendly Fort Smith has been the gateway to the North for years, situated at the end of a portage route around the Slave River rapids. The Hudson's Bay Company set up shop here in 1874 and, until Yellowknife became the territorial capital in 1967, it was the administrative center for most of Canada's northern territories. Today it remains a government hub and headquarters of Wood Buffalo National Park, Canada's largest protected area. Two-thirds of the residents are Cree, Chipewyan or Métis.

◎ Sights

★ Pelican Rapids   RIVER

Twelve kilometers south of Fort Smith, an old road leads east towards the river, with a footpath dipping down to a creek and ascending a bluff overlooking the tumultuous river. There are not that many pelicans here, but you can wander out onto the great slabs of pink granite rising from the water. The trip makes for a great bike ride.

★ Rapids of the Drowned   RIVER

Named after a fatal 19th-century boat accident, these turbulent rapids are the northernmost pelican nesting site in the world. Walk 10 minutes from the top of Portage St to observe the birds snatching fish out of the swirling waters. Keep your distance to avoid disturbing them.

🛏 Sleeping & Eating

★ Whooping Crane Guest House   B&B $$

(☑ 867-872-3426; www.whoopingcraneguesthouse.com; 13 Cassette Cres; r $115-140; ☎) Luxurious, stylish and welcoming, this B&B occupies an intriguing octagonal wooden building down a very quiet street off Calder Ave. Helpful hosts, delicious breakfasts, artistic quilting on the walls, and an abundance of books, bikes and hammocks. One spacious suite has a kitchen and dining area, while two enchantingly decorated rooms boast magnificent private (exterior) bathrooms.

Wood Buffalo Inn   MOTEL $$

(☑ 867-872-3222; www.woodbuffaloinn.com; 123 Simpson St; r $200; P✶☎) This neat apart-motel, centrally located and set back from the main street, consists of 10 self-contained, compact apartments. All come with fully equipped kitchenettes – ideal for self-caterers – and nice touches include potted plants on the balconies and satellite TV. The owner goes out of his way to be helpful.

★ Anna's Home Cooking   CAFE $$

(☑ 867-872-2582; www.facebook.com/north heathy living; 338 Calder Ave; lunch/dinner mains from $7/14; ⊙ 8am-8pm Mon-Fri; ☑) 🍴 Home cooking prepared with care is the key here, with a range of mighty breakfasts, delicious salads, panini, tasty fresh juices, stone-baked pizzas and lunchtime specials such as chili. Dinner is burgers and more substantial BBQ mains. It's a casual, cozy place with a yoga-healing vibe (massages and more available) and outdoor seating.

ℹ Information

Town of Fort Smith (www.fortsmith.ca) A good resource for local information.

Wood Buffalo National Park Information Centre (☑ 867-872-7960; www.pc.gc.ca; 149 McDougal Rd; ⊙ 9am-6pm; ☎) Located in Fort Smith, this national park information point also doubles as the town visitor center. Interesting exhibitions on local ecology and inspiring audiovisual displays of the park. Runs guided walks in the park in summer.

ℹ Getting There & Away

From the **airport** (☑ 867-872-2007; McDougal Rd), Northwestern Air (www.nwal.ca) flies into Fort Smith from Yellowknife ($455 one way, one hour, two daily except Saturday) and Edmonton ($750 one way, 3½ to 4¼ hours, two to three daily except Saturday) via Hay River ($286 one way, 40 minutes).

There were no bus services to Fort Smith at research time.

Paved Hwy 5 cuts through part of Wood Buffalo National Park en route from Fort Smith to Hay River.

Wood Buffalo National Park

Straddling the Alberta–NWT border Wood Buffalo is one of the world's largest national parks (44,000 sq km): a vast expanse of taiga forest, karstic formations and enormous freshwater systems. The wilderness is best experienced from the air, by river or on foot.

The park was established in 1922 to protect a large, dark and distinctly Northern

NORTHWEST TERRITORIES FORT SMITH

subspecies of bison. Thousands inhabit the region and you'll likely see them grazing along roadsides. Their interaction with wolves here was memorably filmed in the BBC's *Frozen Planet* and David Suzuki's *The Nature of Things*.

Also protected is the last wild migratory flock of whooping cranes on earth. These birds nearly disappeared, but are now rebounding. Along with millions of ducks and geese, they avail themselves of the wetlands including the Peace-Athabasca Delta – one of the world's largest freshwater deltas. Moose, caribou, bears and lynx are also residents, along with, in summer, countless mosquitoes and horseflies.

🏃 Activities

★ Highway 5
SCENIC DRIVE

(Hwy 5) Bisecting Wood Buffalo National Park from Hay River to Fort Smith, Hwy 5 passes the enormous **Angus Sinkhole** (Angus Fire Tower), disappearing **Nyarling River**, and **Little Buffalo River Falls**, which has an unstaffed **campground** (📷 867-872-2602; www.campingnwt.ca; tent/RV sites $15/22.50; ☺May-Sep) and 2km nature trail. Further on, there's an 11km side road to **Salt Plains Lookout** (off Hwy 5); a short trail leads down to a vast white salt field.

Canoeing
CANOEING

Feeling adventurous? Canoe from Peace Point, then hike 13km in to the Sweetgrass area, where there are vast grasslands, old bison corrals and camping and simple cabins available. Here you'll see herds of bison and possibly wolves.

Hiking
HIKING

There are eight walking trails in the park, ranging from easy to moderate and varying in length from 500m to 13km. Particularly rewarding are the North Loop (7.5km) and South Loop (9km) at Salt River. The former for its sinkholes, the latter for its salt meadows and salt flats at Grosbeak Lake.

Peace Point Road
SCENIC DRIVE

Between Fort Smith and Peace Point is **Salt River Day-Use Area**, home to a snake hibernaculum (they only have group sex in late April), and the trailhead for excellent day hikes to salt flats and sinkholes. About 60km south of Fort Smith, at popular **Pine Lake Campground** (www.pc.gc.ca; tent & RV sites $15.70; ☺May-Sep; 🐾), you can bask on

white-sand beaches and swim in the aquamarine water.

ℹ️ Getting There & Away

Some 25km west of Fort Smith, Hwy 5 passes through a section of the park en route to Hay River. From Fort Smith, a decent gravel road runs south, reaching the park roughly 20km later and passing all the way through it. You need your own wheels to access the park and a 4WD for Parson's Lake Road, which is sometimes closed.

DEHCHO

Dehcho (Big River) in the southwest of NWT is awash in waterways, most notably the Mackenzie, Liard and Nahanni Rivers. The area is also blessed with one of Canada's remotest and most spectacular national parks, bisected by the Mackenzie Mountains, with warmer temperatures and a rich Dene culture.

Fort Simpson

POP 1202

Fort Simpson (Liidlii Kue; Where Two Rivers Meet) is located where the voluminous Liard and Mackenzie Rivers meet. For centuries, the Dene used to gather here to trade, before the Hudson Bay Company established a fur-trading post in 1822, who were then followed by the priests and the gold-seekers. Today, with an easygoing blend of Dene, Métis and European cultures, this laid-back town is the regional hub and gateway to the incredible Nahanni National Park Reserve.

🔘 Sights

OSC Gallery
GALLERY

(📷 867-695-3005; www.openskycreativesociety.com; cnr 97th Ave & 100th St; ☺1-4pm Mon-Fri) This gallery, located in the town's library building, displays contemporary and traditional Dehcho art, some of it for sale.

👉 Tours

★ Simpson Air
SCENIC FLIGHTS

(📷 867-695-2505; www.simpsonair.ca; Antoine Dr; ☺8:30am-5pm Jun-Sep) Excellent operator that handles most flightseeing excursions to Nahanni National Park Reserve, including Virginia Falls (per person $518) and Glacier Lake (per person $676). Three-person minimum or else you charter the whole plane. Flyovers without landing are cheaper.

Pilot owner Ted runs the remote fly-in Nahanni Mountain Lodge (p806) on Little Doctor Lake.

South Nahanni Airways SCENIC FLIGHTS
(☑867-695-2263; https://southnahanniairways.ca; Antoine Dr; ⊙8am-5pm Jun-Sep) Friendly operator offering flights to Nahanni National Park Reserve, some with landings at Virginia Falls ($1670, 5½ hours) and Glacier Lake ($2170, seven hours). Price is per plane; maximum four passengers.

🛏 Sleeping

★ Mackenzie Rest Inn B&B $$
(☑867-695-2357; www.mackenzierest.ca; 10518 99th St; s/d with shared bath $150/180; 🛜) A charming, well-furnished B&B in a land of floatplanes and giant rivers. Faultless hospitality is matched with very cute, stylish rooms in a characterful, nobly furnished house with great river views, books and magazines on Canada's North, and relaxing deck spaces. Rooms are all different – the top one is our favorite – and share spotless modern bathrooms. Breakfast cooked to order.

Willows Inn MOTEL $$
(☑867-695-2077; www.janor.ca; cnr of 103 Ave & Antoine Dr; r $170-210; ❄🛜) This spotless motel comprises six self-sufficient, spacious rooms geared toward all seasons, with air-con and in-floor heating, and all with coffeemakers, fridges and microwaves. There's also a fully equipped guest kitchen and appealing patio with deck chairs and a BBQ. Guests receive an entrance code when they make a reservation.

ℹ Information

At the entrance to town, the helpful **visitor center** (☑867-695-3182; www.fortsimpson. com; 100th St; ⊙9am-8pm Jun-Sep) has brochures on Fort Simpson and the surrounding area. A separate Parks Canada **visitor center** (☑867-695-7750; www.parkscanada.gc.ca/nahanni; cnr 100th St & 100 Ave; ⊙8:30am-noon & 1-5pm mid-Jun–Sep) provides information on the Nahanni National Park Reserve and is the place to pay your park fees.

ℹ Getting There & Away

Fort Simpson Airport (Mackenzie Hwy) is 12km southeast of town on the Mackenzie Hwy. Air Tindi (www.airtindi.com) serves Yellowknife ($535 one-way, 80 minutes, daily except Sunday). First Air (www.firstair.ca) offers nonstop flights to Yellowknife ($818, daily except Sunday), plus connecting flights to Edmonton, Hay River, Inuvik and Ottawa.

Fill up on gas here; the nearest gas stations are in Fort Liard (287km south), Enterprise (398km east) and Fort Providence (324km east).

Nahanni National Park Reserve

To many, Nahanni means wilderness. Situated in the southwestern NWT near the Yukon border, this 30,000-sq-km **park** (day/year $24.50/147.20) embraces its namesake, the epic South Nahanni River. This untamed river tumbles more than 500km through the jagged Mackenzie Mountains. It's a dream destination for canoeing and one of Canada's most spectacular places.

The Nahanni is a Canadian Heritage river, and the park is a Unesco World Heritage site. In 2009 the federal government and Dehcho First Nations signed an agreement increasing the park's size more than sixfold.

◉ Sights

★ Virginia Falls WATERFALL
Yes, there is a higher set of falls in British Columbia, but for the sheer gushing power of two mighty torrents of water, falling from a height of 96m (twice the height of Niagara Falls), and for the remote, spectacular setting, Virginia Falls is the most impressive waterfall in Canada.

Glacier Lake LAKE
Flanked by the Britnell Glacier in the northwest reaches of the park, this spectacular lake is surrounded by the granite mountains of the Ragged Range and is the gateway to the climbers' mecca known as the Cirque of the Unclimbables.

🏃 Activities

Climbing
Cirque of the Unclimbables CLIMBING
There's world-class rock climbing in these granite peaks around Glacier Lake. The Lotus Flower Tower, an 18-pitch 5.11 monolith known as one of the most beautiful big-wall routes in the world, throws down the gauntlet to experienced climbers.

Hiking
There is some excellent hiking in the Nahanni River Valley, from the boardwalk

leading to the waterfall lookout to the full-day hike to the peak of Sunblood Mountain, across the river from Virginia Falls campground. The Ragged Range around Glacier Lake offers days of hiking and challenging rock-climbing routes.

Hot Springs

There are two sets of hot springs in the park: **Rabbitkettle Hot Springs**, surrounded by the largest tufa mounds in the northern world, and the smaller, smellier, sulfur-rich **Kraus Hot Springs**. You can soak in both.

 Tours

Raft and canoe trips can be arranged with a licensed outfitter. Prices start from $6640, depending on distance and number of days. Try to book months in advance. Canoes require some basic experience; white-water canoeing adventures are for experienced and fit travelers only. Rafts, steered by a guide, are relaxing and suitable for all.

Most trips begin at Moose Ponds, Rabbitkettle Lake or Virginia Falls, because those are where floatplanes can land. From Moose Ponds to Rabbitkettle is about 160km, much of it Class III white water. For the 118km from Rabbitkettle to the falls, the river meanders placidly through broad valleys. Once the falls are portaged, it's another 252km to **Blackstone Territorial Park** (Hwy 7), first through steep-sided, turbulent canyons, and then along the broad Liard River. The lower-river trip takes seven to 10 days. From Rabbitkettle it's around 14 days, from Moose Ponds 21.

★ **Black Feather** KAYAKING, CANOEING
(☑705-746-1372; www.blackfeather.com) This excellent operator's offerings include special family and women-only trips. Guided canoeing on the Nahanni is what they do best; a 14-day Nahanni Classic costs $7095.

Nahanni Wilderness Adventures CANOEING, RAFTING
(☑1-888-897-5223; www.nahanniwild.com) 🖉 Eco-conscious operator committed to minimizing carbon footprint through shorter charter flights. David has been paddling the South Nahanni River since 1989 and arranges trips ranging from 10 ($7245) to 22 ($7980) days.

🛏 Sleeping

★ **Nahanni Mountain Lodge** LODGE $$$
(☑867-695-2505; www.simpsonair.ca; lodge from $400, plus drop-off $932) Sitting on the shore of Little Doctor Lake, right outside the national-park boundary, this fly-in lodge accommodates a single party of up to 20 people in four wooden cabins (price varies depending on number). It's just you and the wilderness, with nothing to do but swim, fish or float. Lodge stays, combined with Nahanni Park visits, are booked through Simpson Air (p804).

ℹ Information

You can obtain park information and permits at the Parks Canada visitor center (p805) in Fort Simpson. The day-use fee is $24.50; the Backcountry Pass, valid for a year, costs $147.20. Nahanni National Park Reserve is open to fly-in visitors between mid-June and mid-September.

ℹ Getting There & Away

The park is only accessible by floatplane.

SAHTU

Mountain-studded Sahtu, centered on the Great Bear Lake, is accesible by plane year-round and by ice road in winter. The Mackenzie River, swollen by water draining from one-fifth of Canada, cuts its way through here, in places more than 3km wide. Either side, bald-headed peaks arise, guarding some of the wildest country – and best hiking and paddling – left in the world.

Norman Wells

POP 778

This historic oil town springs from the boreal frontier, halfway between Fort Simpson and Inuvik. It's a launchpad for canoeists, hikers tackling the Canol Heritage Trail, adventurers heading into the Mackenzie Mountains and fisherfolk heading for Great Bear Lake.

◉ Sights & Activities

Norman Wells Historical Centre MUSEUM
(☑867-587-2415; www.normanwellsmuseum.com; Mackenzie Dr; ⊙10am-5:30pm, to 4pm Sat, noon-4pm Sun) FREE A labor of love, this small museum showcases regional history, geology, arts and crafts, and has information on the rivers and the Canol Heritage Trail. There's a cool gift shop too.

★ Canol Heritage Trail   HIKING

The wild, challenging Canol Heritage Trail leads 358km southwest to the Yukon border, traversing peaks, canyons and barrens. Wildlife is abundant and there are numerous deep river crossings. The only shelter is provided by old Quonset huts. Hiking the whole length takes three to four weeks and most people arrange food drops. Contact Northwest Territories Tourism (www.gov. nt.ca/services/visitors) for outfitters.

Some visitors helicopter in from Norman Wells to reach the most interesting sections.

Past the Yukon border, an unpaved road leads to Ross River and the Yukon highway system.

The trail was built at enormous monetary and human cost during WWII to transport oil to Whitehorse; 'Canol' is shorthand for 'Canadian Oil.' The huge project was abandoned in 1945, with the war nearly over and cheaper oil sources found.

Courses

★ Canoe North Adventures   CANOEING

(☑867-587-4440; www.canoenorthadventures. com; 9 Beaver Lane; multiday trips from $6500; ☺mid-May–mid-Sep) This excellent setup has decades of experience organizing rugged canoeing trips on the Nahanni, Mountain, Coppermine, Keele and other mighty northern rivers, lasting from 10 to 12 days. At their base at the North-Wright floatplane dock they hire out all necessary equipment for self-guided trips and offer accommodation in private and bunk rooms with cooking facilities.

Sleeping

★ Canoe North Lodge B&B   B&B $$

(☑867-587-4440; www.canoenorthadventures. com; 8 Beaver Ln; per person $90-135; ☎) Right at their floatbase, this excellent canoeing and hiking outfitter has a cozy lodge for active travelers. You have a choice of private rooms in the award-winning lodge and cheaper bunkrooms; ample breakfasts are thrown in and lunch ($20) and dinner ($40) can be arranged. In between bouts of canoeing, hang out in the common areas or use the kitchen for meals.

ⓘ Getting There & Away

Canadian North (www.canadiannorth.com) connects with Yellowknife (from $412, 1¼ hours, daily) and Inuvik (from $427, one hour, daily except Monday) while North-Wright Air (www.

north-wrightairways.com) serves smaller communities in the region, as well as Yellowknife ($886, 2½ hours, daily except Sunday).

In winter, an ice road runs 333km from Wrigley to Norman Wells and continues north as far as Colville Lake. There are plans to connect Norman Wells to Fort Simpson and Inuvik by all-season road in the next decade.

OFF THE BEATEN TRACK

TUKTUT NOGAIT NATIONAL PARK

The **Tuktut Nogait National Park** (day/year $24.50/147.20) is a major calving ground for bluenose caribou. It's an excellent place to observe birds of prey and has spectacular pingos, beautiful canyons and a magnificent waterfall. Parks Canada in Inuvik occasionally offers six-day adventures in the park (around $7500 per person), using the limited infrastructure at Uyarsivik Lake Base Camp and led by an Inuvialuit cultural guide, and can help you make travel arrangements. Access is by charter flight with Kenn Borek (www.borek air.com) from Inuvik.

Pay your fees and register at the Inuvik Parks Canada office.

WESTERN ARCTIC

Comprising the Mackenzie Delta, the Richardson Mountains and several High Arctic islands, this is the NWT's most diverse region. Several remote national parks are here, plus indigenous hamlets whose residents still maintain a largely traditional lifestyle of whaling, trapping and hunting. The region's 'metropolis' is prefabricated Inuvik, reached via the heart-wrenchingly beautiful Dempster Hwy.

Inuvik

POP 3243

Inuvik, a few dozen kilometers from the mouth of the Mackenzie River, was founded in 1955 as an administrative post to replace the inconveniently located Aklavik (www. aklavik.ca). With its rainbow-colored rows of houses and warren of above-ground heated pipes, this close-knit community still feels like a work in progress. During the summer's constant daylight, lots of visitors arrive in search of Arctic adventure via the rugged, awesome 737km Dempster Hwy from the Yukon, and many continue all the way to Tuktoyaktuk, on the shore of the Arctic Ocean.

Activities

Our Lady of Victory Church CHURCH
(☑ 867-777-2236; 174 Mackenzie Rd; donation $5; ⊙ tours 6:30pm Mon, Wed, Fri & Sat, noon Sun Jun-Aug) The town landmark is the wooden Our Lady of Victory Church, also called the Igloo Church, designed to reflect the local Inuvialuit culture. It has a resplendent gleaming dome and its appealing interior is decorated with scenes from the Rapture, painted by Inuvialuit artist Mona Thresher.

★ Dempster Highway SCENIC DRIVE
The 737km road that leads south into Yukon is the notorious Dempster Hwy, a most worthy contender for Canada's most scenic and challenging drive. It passes through dense boreal forest and bare tundra, and rises gently between snow-tipped mountains. It's an unpaved, partially potholed road with treacherous muddy sections, potential delays at ferry crossings and no phone signal. Likely wildlife sightings.

Inuvik–Tuktoyaktuk Highway SCENIC DRIVE
Open to the public since 2017, this scenic 150km gravel road takes you all the way to the Arctic Ocean, passing multiple pingos (hillocks) rising from the tundra.

Tours

Tundra North Tours ADVENTURE
(☑ 867-993-3323, 800-420-9652; http://tundranorthtours.com; 185 Mackenzie Rd; ⊙ 9am-5pm) This professional operator offers flights to Tuktoyaktuk on the Arctic coast ($750 per person) to view pingos and the town itself, scenic flights to remote Herschel Island ($1500 per person), summer boating in the Mackenzie Delta ($400 per person) and drives along the Dempster Hwy (from $1100). Winter guests get to herd reindeer and drive the Aklavik ice road.

Arctic Adventures ADVENTURE
(White Huskies; ☑ 867-777-3535; www.whitehuskies.com; 25 Carn St) Highly recommended summertime excursions – six-day chauffeured runs on the Dempster Hwy ($2600), day trips up the Inuvik–Tuktoyaktuk Hwy ($400 per person), opportunities to meet their beautiful snow-white huskies ($45) – and, in winter,

daily dogsled tours, snowmobiling outings and ice-road drives to Aklavik. They also rent vehicles and canoes.

Sleeping

★ Andre's Place B&B $$
(☑ 867-777-3177; www.facebook.com/Andresplace inuvik; 55 Wolverine Rd; s/d $215/245; 🐾) Run by an affable French-Chilean couple, this B&B consists of a single bedroom with an adjoining immaculate bathroom. Guests get the benefit of Andre's fantastic cooked breakfasts and the hosts are happy to share their insight into life in the far north.

★ Arctic Chalet GUESTHOUSE $$
(☑ 867-777-3535; www.arcticchalet.com; 25 Carn St; s/d/tr from $135/140/145, cabin $200-250; 🐾🐾) In a boreal glade 3km from town, the main house showcases local fauna in the form of animal skins and piles of antlers. Satellite cabins, sleeping up to four, have simple kitchens. Some of the wood-paneled rooms are en suite. The affable owners rent canoes, kayaks and cars, run dogsledding and other tours and are a good source of local info.

Eating

★ Alestine's CANADIAN $$
(☑ 867-777-3702; www.facebook.com/alestines; 48 Franklin Rd; mains $13-25; ⊙ noon-2pm & 5-8pm Tue-Sat) This fantastic mom-and-pop place has single-handedly elevated Inuvik's dining scene. The menu is succinct and makes the most of fresh local produce. Feast on whitefish tacos, grilled salmon and reindeer chili on the upstairs deck or inside the cube-like interior, decked out with local prints. Your meals are cooked in an old school bus.

★ Andre's Place FRENCH $$$
(☑ 867-777-3177; 55 Wolverine Rd; 4-course menu $75; ⊙ 6:30pm Wed & Fri) Andre is a classically trained chef who learned his craft in Paris. Expect fine dining in an intimate setting; the menu changes weekly (see the updated menu at the visitor center), but may include the likes of rack of lamb with Provençal sauce and tarte tatin. Advance reservations essential.

Shopping

★ Originals ARTS & CRAFTS
(☑ 867-777-2433; www.nwtarts.com; 2 Berger St; ⊙ 9am-5pm Mon-Sat) The best arts-and-crafts

shop in town, stocking plenty of soapstone and whalebone carvings as well as jewelry made of NWT diamonds. The art section focuses heavily on the dramatic, moody prints and cards by Yukon artist Nathalie Parenteau, and it's well worth asking to see the shop's excellent selection of Ulukhaktok (Holman) prints.

❶ Information

Parks Canada (☑ 867-777-8800; www.pc.gc. ca; 81 Kingmingya Rd; ⊘ 8:30am-noon & 1-4:30pm Mon-Fri Jun-Aug) Has info on Tuktut Nogait, Ivvavik and Aulavik National Parks. Park visitors must register and deregister here. Staff organize multiday trips into Ivvavik and Tuktut Nogait.

Western Arctic Regional Visitors Centre (☑ 867-777-4727, info off-season 867-777-7237; www.inuvik.ca; 284 Mackenzie Rd; ⊘ 9am-7pm, from 10am Sat & Sun May-Sep) Has tourism literature, eager staff and a nature display.

❶ Getting There & Away

AIR

Inuvik Airport (Dempster Hwy) is 14km south of town. **Town Cab** (☑ 867-777-4777) and **Delta Cab** (☑ 867-777-5100) charge $30/36 for one/two people to downtown.

Air North (www.flyairnorth.com) flies here from Dawson City ($161, five weekly), Old Crow ($83, five weekly) and Whitehorse ($248, daily). Aklak Air (www.aklakair.ca) connects with Tuktoyaktuk, Paulatuk and Sachs Harbour three times weekly and provides charters to the national parks. Canadian North (www.cana diannorth.com) and North-Wright Air (www. north-wrightairways.com) service Norman Wells ($413, one hour, six weekly) and Yellowknife ($408, 2½ hours, daily).

CAR

Driving Force (☑ 867-777-2346; www.driving force.ca; 60 King Rd; per day from $170; ⊘ 8am-noon & 1-5pm Mon-Fri) and **Arctic Chalet Car Rental** (☑ 867-777-3535; www. arcticchalet.com; 25 Carn St; per day from $1000) rent vehicles and have airport counters. There's a 100km daily limit. If you are driving, it's vital that you check Dempster Hwy **road and ferry conditions** (800-661-0750; www.dot.gov.nt.ca and www.511yukon.ca); the road is closed during the initial fall freeze-up and spring thaw and raised water levels occasionally stop the ferry from running. The all-season gravel road now connects Inuvik to Tuktoyaktuk (150km). Petrol is by far the most expensive in the NWT.

Tuktoyaktuk

POP 898

Some 150km northeast of Inuvik on the Arctic coast is Tuktoyaktuk ('Place Resembling Caribou'), long home of the whale-hunting Inuvialuit, and now also a land base for Beaufort Sea gas explorations.

Pods of belugas may be seen in summer. Visible year-round are pingos, of which the Tuk Peninsula has the Western Arctic's highest concentration. Some 1400 of these huge mounds of earth and ice dot the land; the largest two have been designated the Pingo Canadian Landmark.

In Tuk, notable buildings include two replica sod houses – traditional Inuvialuit dwellings – and the Icehouse, a natural freezer dug into the permafrost where villagers keep their catch. Near the two is the beautifully restored Our Lady of Lourdes schooner; it delivered supplies to far-flung Catholic missions in the Arctic in the 1930s and '40s.

◉ Sights

★ **Pingo Canadian Landmark**   HILL
The Tuk Peninsula has the world's highest concentration of pingos. Some 1350 of these huge mounds of earth-covered ice, that form only in a permafrost environment, dot the land. Two of these, nearest to Tuktoyaktuk, have been designated the Pingo Canadian Landmark. You get great views of the village from one of them.

☞ Tours

★ **Arctic Ocean Tuk Tours**   CULTURAL
(☑ 867-977-2406; eileenjacobson@hotmail.com) Eileen Jacobson is an excellent local guide who offers detailed insights into traditional Inuvialuit life, especially since she still lives it herself. She lives off the land, hunting, trapping and fishing, and her cultural tours include a visit to her home where you can taste smoked whale meat, musk ox and dried fish.

🛏 Sleeping & Eating

★ **Hunter's B&B**   B&B $$$
(☑ 867-977-2558; www.huntersbbtuk.ca; Oceanview Dr; s/d $200/400; 🖧) Friendly, knowledgeable Maureen and Patsy are happy to fill guests in on the settlement's history and they run a tight ship: their spotless little B&B overlooks an Arctic beach and the

rooms come with down comforters, local art and access to a well-equipped guest kitchen.

Grandma's Kitchen CANADIAN **$$**
(☑ 867-678-5226; www.facebook.com/Grandmas KitchenTuk; 330 Ocean View Rd; mains from $15; ⊙ noon-midnight, to 10pm Sat, 1-9pm Sun) The only place to eat in town, this family-run restaurant serves musk-ox burgers, platters of local delicacies and cinnamon buns, with a side order of ocean views.

ℹ Information

Hamlet office (☑ 867-977-2286; www.tuk.ca; ⊙ 9am-noon & 1-5pm) Can provide information on the village's services.

ℹ Getting There & Away

There are at least two daily flights to **Tuk-toyaktuk airport** (off Inuvik-Tuktoyaktuk Hwy) from Inuvik with Aklak Air (www.aklakair.ca). Some visitors come either with aerial or boat tours from Inuvik, though they've decreased in number compared to motorists since the Inuvik–Tuktoyaktuk Hwy was completed; it's a good all-season, gravel road, and it's now possible to drive North America's only road to the Arctic Ocean in around two hours.

Banks Island

Adrift in the Arctic Ocean, Banks Island has abundant wildlife by polar standards, and is one of the world's best places to see musk oxen. The island has two bird sanctuaries with summer flocks of snow geese and sea-birds. **Sachs Harbour**, a small hunting, fishing and trapping Inuvialuit community on the south coast, is the only settlement. On the north end of the island, seldom-visited Aulavik National Park covers 12,275 sq km. It has the world's largest concentration of musk oxen, as well as badlands, tundra and archaeological sites.

⊙ Sights

★ **Aulavik National Park** NATIONAL PARK
(day/year $24.50/147.20) This seldom-visited park has the world's largest concentration of musk ox, as well as tundra and archaeological sites. This is true Arctic wilderness, with zero infrastructure. Contact Parks Canada (p809) in Inuvik for details about visiting, as they run summer trips here. You can also come independently by chartering a flight with Kenn Borek Air (www.borekair.com) in Inuvik, but still have to register and pay the fees at the Parks Canada office.

Nunavut

Best Places to Eat

➜ Black Heart Cafe (p815)

➜ Granite Room (p816)

➜ Kuugaq Cafe (p822)

➜ Big Racks Barbecue (p816)

Best Places to Stay

➜ Dorset Suites (p818)

➜ Accommodations by the Sea (p815)

➜ Discovery (p815)

➜ Arctic Circle Paws & Paddles B&B (p821)

➜ Nanuq Lodge (p821)

➜ Ublu Inn (p822)

Why Go?

Picture a treeless, ice-encrusted wilderness lashed by unrelenting weather with a population density that makes Greenland seem claustrophobic. Add polar bears, narwhals, beluga whales and a scattered Inuit population who have successfully mastered a landscape so harsh that foreigners could not colonize it.

Nunavut is Canada's largest and most lightly populated subdivision, a mythical assortment of uninhabited islands and frigid ocean that exists on the planet's climatic and geographic extremes. Visitors here face multiple obstacles, not least perennial blizzards, no roads and massive travel costs. But those that do get through have the benefit of welcoming communities and awe-inspiring natural wonders, as well as the privilege of joining a small band of intrepid trailblazers, safe in the knowledge that they are setting foot where few have trodden before.

When to Go
Iqaluit

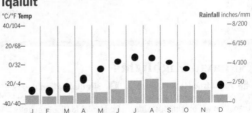

Aug & Sep Prime visiting time during the short hyperactive summer season.

Apr & May The ideal time for dogsledding and other snow sports and activities.

Jun The midnight sun coincides with Iqaluit's Alianait Arts Festival.

Nunavut Highlights

1 Auyuittuq National Park (p818) Feeling small beside the planet's most precipitous cliffs.

2 Cape Dorset (p818) Encountering colourful Inuit prints in this art mecca.

3 Quttinirpaaq National Park (p820) Going on a once-in-a-lifetime musk-ox-watching adventure.

4 Sirmilik National Park (p820) Hitting spectacular Pond Inlet for floe's-edge wildlife-watching.

5 Iqaluit (p813) Enjoying Nunavut's unexpectedly cosmopolitan, friendly capital.

6 Resolute (p820) Walking this awesomely lunar place.

7 Katannilik Territorial Park (p819) Canoeing amid cascades and caribou.

8 Ukkusiksalik National Park (p821) Seeing polar bears up close from the safety of a boat.

History

Nunavut has been populated for over 4000 years, first by the Dorset people, who were gradually pushed out by the Thule, the ancestors of the Inuit, who arrived from the west just a millennium ago.

Vikings likely visited Baffin Island (Helluland in the sagas); later, in 1576, Martin Frobisher came seeking the Northwest Passage. Over the centuries came more explorers (including Sir John Franklin, who disappeared here in 1845), and Roald Amundsen, who finally traversed the Passage between 1903 and 1906, with whalers, traders and missionaries hot on their heels.

After WWII, Canada finally recognized the Arctic's strategic importance. In the 1950s and '60s Inuit were settled into villages, while the northernmost communities of Resolute Bay and Grise Fjord were created when a number of Inuit families were relocated there by deceit, to bolster national sovereignty.

In the 1960s and '70s rising political awareness inspired dreams of Inuit self-government. Nunavut split from the Northwest Territories in 1999 to become a separate territory and negotiations are underway regarding Nunavut's eventual devolution from Ottawa, which will enable the territory to exercise jurisdiction over the land and its natural resources.

Land & Climate

Gargantuan Nunavut sprawls across Canada's northeast. About half – the mainland – is the 'Barrenlands,' an expanse of undulating rock and tundra cut through by major rivers. Even more barren is the Arctic archipelago, scattering north to Ellesmere Island, just shy of the Pole, and east to enormous Baffin Island, home to skyscraping mountains.

It's chilly. Snow holds sway from September to June; relentless winds create hard-to-fathom chill factors. July to mid-August is summer, when seas thaw beneath the perpetual sun.

The territory's 26 communities are incredibly isolated and rely on air transport and the July 'sealift,' when ships bring a year's worth of supplies to otherwise inaccessible harbors. Houses sit on stilts to negate ferocious winds and slow the thawing of the permafrost. Water is rationed and delivered daily from a central village deposit by truck.

ⓘ Getting There & Away

Nunavut is essentially roadless; the easiest way to get here and around is via (extremely pricey) flights. Iqaluit is served from Montréal, Ottawa and Yellowknife. Cambridge Bay is linked to Yellowknife, and Rankin Inlet to Yellowknife and Winnipeg. Smaller communities are reached from those three hubs. Flights are operated by Canadian North (www.canadiannorth.com), Calm Air (www.calmair.com) and First Air (www.firstair.ca); Iqaluit-based Kenn Borek Air (www.borekair.com) offers charter flights.

Flying standby halves the price of normal flights. In winter medical staff and fish get priority and there are lots of weather-induced cancellations (also the case in fog in spring and fall), but in summer (if you're flexible), you've a chance of saving some money.

Cruise ships ply the Northwest Passage, calling at communities such as Pond Inlet, Cambridge Bay, Gjoa Haven and Kimmirut.

IQALUIT

POP 7740

Nunavut's capital, Iqaluit (ee-*kal*-oo-eet), feels like a different country. All the signs are in Inuktitut and you'll hear it widely spoken in the street. This, scruffy, dusty, colorful Arctic town, with its spectacular natural setting around the bay and its moon-base buildings, houses a fascinating mixture of Inuit professionals, politicians and dropouts, Johnny-come-latelies from around Canada (and beyond) drawn by high salaries from government and construction jobs, enormous SUVs with elaborately courteous drivers limited by a few short kilometers of road, and barking dogs contesting territory with huge bossy ravens. It's surprisingly cosmopolitan, a good introduction to the region, and has good places to stay and eat, as well as some wilderness-lite to explore on the outskirts of town.

◉ Sights

★ Nunatta Sunakkutaangit Museum
MUSEUM

(☑ 867-979-5537; Sinaa St; ⊙ 1-5pm Tue-Sun; P) 🆓FREE This friendly little museum in an old Hudson's Bay Company building showcases an engaging permanent collection of traditional Inuit clothing, tools, children's toys, weaponry and methods of transport, including a full-size sealskin canoe, plus splendid soapstone and whalebone carvings. Upstairs are Thule artifacts (including some early snow-goggles) dating back hundreds of years.

★ Legislative Assembly
NOTABLE BUILDING

(☑ 867-975-5000; www.assembly.nu.ca; 926 Federal Rd; ⊙ 9am-5pm Mon-Fri) 🆓FREE It's well worth taking an entertaining free tour (by appointment) of Nunavut's prefab parliament to learn about all manner of Inuit art displayed throughout the building, as well as about the chamber, with its aboriginal touches, such as the igloo-like interior, sealskin benches and seats for community elders. You'll encounter two maces: the diamond-tipped Working Mace and the original, made of narwhal tusk.

Sculpture Garden
SCULPTURE

(Queen Elizabeth St) There's an extensive range of mostly stone sculpture by local artists right near the post office, with northern themes well represented. Our favorite? A thuggish-looking Sedna (sea goddess) with raised fist and a raven made of scrap metal.

St Jude's Igloo Cathedral
CHURCH

(☑ 867-979-5595; Mattaq Cres; P) This igloo-shaped Anglican cathedral was designed to reflect Inuit culture. This recent incarnation was built in 2012 to replace the 1972 original, burnt down in a 2005 arson fire, and is bright and airy inside, thanks to the skylight. Sunday services are held in both English (9:45am) and Inuktitut (11am).

Qaummaarviit Territorial Park
STATE PARK

(http://nunavutparks.com/parks-special-places/ qaummaarviit-territorial-park) This tiny bay island is a 12km boat or snowmobile ride west of Iqaluit and preserves a 750-year-old Inuit (Thule) winter camp. You can see 11 well-preserved traditional sod houses and a grave site; a huge number of bones and hunting and household artifacts were found here, testifying to the site's significance for

Thule hunters. It's a great half-day trip; to get there, contact Iqaluit outfitters.

Apex
AREA

Located 5km from downtown, Apex is now Iqaluit's beach suburb, but was where nomadic Inuit began to settle when modern Iqaluit was an airbase. On the shore is the photogenic Hudson Bay Trading Post complex, dating back to 1949. It's a beautiful 40-minute walk along the waterfront from downtown; the trail starts at the Iqaluit cemetery. On the southeast side of Apex, two whale ribs by the tiny cemetery frame the tundra.

Sylvia Grinnell Territorial Park
STATE PARK

(www.nunavutparks.ca; Iqaluit Rd; P) The viewpoint at this bleakly beautiful park, 2km southwest of town and divided by the river of the same name, overlooks the snow-flecked tundra and the rapids that Arctic char swim up. Various short paths (25 to 45 minutes one way) lead to a waterfall and escarpments.

🏃 Activities

Apex Trail
WALKING

This picturesque 4km seaside trail starts at the cemetery in town and leads to the historic Hudson Bay Company buildings in Apex across a picturesquely barren landscape of lichen-covered rock, with great views of offshore islands and great chunks of ice floating in the bay and with cawing ravens as your only companions. The trail is easy to follow.

👉 Tours

★ Arctic Kingdom
OUTDOORS

(☑ 888-737-6818; www.arctickingdom.com) This professional setup can organize half-day hiking, boating, 4WD, kayaking and snowmobiling trips around Iqaluit plus multiday wildlife-watching adventures throughout Nunavut, such as the nine-day polar-bear safari ($16,734) and eight-day Arctic diving excursions to Pond Inlet ($22,342). The best bet for something at short notice.

Inukpak Outfitting
OUTDOORS

(☑ 867-222-6489; www.inukpakoutfitting.ca; 3310 Niaqunngusiariaq, Apex) Rents inflatable canoes, camping equipment, satellite phones and polar clothing. Also runs winter dog-sledding (half-day $200), snowmobiling (half-day $240), and igloo-building, plus summer hiking, canoeing (day trip $170

ARCTIC PACKAGES

Independent travel offers the chance for trailblazing, saving cash and seeing the reality. Except, perhaps, in Nunavut. Here you should consider teaming up with other travelers: only groups can achieve the economies of scale that make the Arctic affordable.

Black Feather (☑toll-free 888-849-7668; www.blackfeather.com) Highly esteemed, Ontario-based wilderness outfitter running expert trips to some of Canada's wildest corners, from multiday floe-edge adventures out of Pond Inlet ($8000) to hiking expeditions in Auyuittuq ($6000), Sirmilik ($6400) and Quttinirpaaq ($15,400) National Parks.

Adventure Canada (☑905-271-4000; www.adventurecanada.com) Arctic cruise specialist, with highly recommended two-week cruises along the Northwest Passage (from $7000).

Great Canadian Adventure Company (☑780-414-1676; www.adventures.ca) Organizes a multitude of Nunavut-based trips, including adventure tours from Iqaluit, spring caribou migration safaris, and polar bear, walrus and whale-spotting from base camp in Foxe Basin.

---

per person) and sea kayaking. Also runs trekking expeditions to Auyuittuq National Park (p818).

Festivals & Events

★ **Alianait Arts Festival**   CULTURAL
(www.alianait.ca; ⊙late Jun–early Jul) A midsummer celebration of Inuit culture in several venues around town, encompassing art, live music, film, storytelling, performances from Nunavut's Got Talent, and a community feast. Events like seal thanksgiving and concerts around National Aboriginal Day (June 21) are sometimes tied in.

Sleeping

Iqaluit has the best range of accommodations in Nunavut, but that's not much of a horse race. Camping is the only cheap option; there are more and more room-sharing services, but they are not much cheaper than hotels. Hotels are few, overpriced and booked in advance; free airport pickup.

★ **Accommodations by the Sea**   B&B $$
(☑867-979-0131; https://staybythesea.ca; 2536 Paurngaq Cr; r incl breakfast $220-250; ☜) A half-hour walk from downtown, this end-of-the-road spot has a lovely bay outlook. It's a comfortable, modern place decked out in ski-chalet style. Guests have use of a kitchen, with breakfast supplies, and a great lounge with DVDs and views. The two cheapest rooms share a bathroom. Airport pickup available.

Apex B&B   B&B $$
(☑867-222-4546; www.apexbnb.com; 3037 Niaqunngusiariaq, Apex; r $200) A clutch of

smart rooms, sparsely decorated in a contemporary fashion, plus a guest kitchen and a verandah for tundra-watching make this a great offbeat choice. It's in Apex, a 5km walk or taxi ride from central Iqaluit; free airport pickup offered. Two-night minimum.

Nunattaq Suites   B&B $$
(☑867-975-2745; www.nunattaqsuites.com; 4141 Imiqtarviminiq Rd; r $226; ℗☜) This spotless, large, well-equipped grey-blue house overlooks a lake, a 15-minute walk from town. The suite with the claw-foot tub has the best lake views; all four rooms come with excellent modern bathrooms. Guests also have the run of the kitchen, laundry facilities and a lounge-balcony area with BBQ. The friendly host stops by daily and makes you very welcome.

★ **Discovery**   BOUTIQUE HOTEL $$$
(☑867-979-4433; www.thediscoveryiqaluit.com; 1056 Mivvik St; s/d/ste $250/295/350; ℗☜) Located between the airport and downtown, this stylish single-story boutique place is all creams, browns and slate inside, with a cozy guest lounge and artistic touches. Big flat-screen TVs, well-equipped bathrooms, and a great restaurant make this an appealing stay.

Eating

★ **Black Heart Cafe**   CAFE $
(☑867-222-1660; www.facebook.com/BlackHeart Cafe; 1405 Masak Ct; sandwiches from $9; ⊙7am-5pm, 10am-4pm Sat & Sun; ℗☝) This great cafe was exactly what the town needed and has rapidly become Iqaluit's most popular

gathering place. There's excellent coffee from the Equator roastery in Ottawa, artisan teas, kombucha, great cakes, plus a cracking selection of lunchtime sandwiches (reuben, Arctic char club, croque monsieur), a kiddie corner, book exchange and Inuit art on the walls.

Big Racks Barbecue
BARBECUE $$

(☑867-979-5555; www.facebook.com/bigracksiqal uit; 810 Aviq St; mains $18-35; ☺11am-9pm) The carnivore-pleasing menu of ribs, wings, country fried chicken, burgers, beef brisket and pulled-pork sandwiches has quickly endeared itself to locals at this buzzing spot. The vibe? Brisk cafeteria. Portion sizes? Enormous. Takeout available.

Yummy Shawarma & Pizza
KEBAB $$

(☑867-979-1515; 1085E Mivvik St; shawarmas $12-16, pizzas $18-54; ☺11am-11pm) Nunavut has a bona-fide kebab joint, with a pleasant, Lebanese-themed dining area. You can diverge from the shawarma/pizza core of the menu to vine leaves, tabbouleh and baklava. Delivery available.

Frob Kitchen
CANADIAN $$$

(☑867-979-2222; Astro Hill Tce; mains $18-54; ☺7-10:30am, 11:30am-1:30pm & 5-8:30pm Mon-Fri, from 8am Sat & Sun; ℗) The perpetually popular upmarket restaurant at the Frobisher Inn (☑867-979-2222; www.frobisherinn. com; Astro Hill Tce; r $268-288, ste $311-328; ℗⎙) serves the likes of Arctic char wraps, pad Thai and musk-ox burgers at lunchtime. Dinner is equally globe-spanning, but more refined: steak tartare, fresh Vietnamese spring rolls, prime ribs and bison steak. Try to get a window seat.

Granite Room
FUSION $$$

(☑867-979-4433; www.thediscoveryiqaluit.com; 1056 Mivvik St; mains lunch/dinner from $17/42; ☺6:30-9am, noon-2pm & 6-9pm; ℗) At the Discovery hotel (p815), the French-influenced fare offers specials to complement à la carte offerings that include northern delights such as Arctic char and caribou. Homemade desserts are excellent. The all-you-can-eat Sunday brunch buffet ($46) is terrific value.

🍷 Drinking & Nightlife

★NuBrewCo
BREWERY

(☑867-979-2337; www.facebook.com/NuBrewCo; 2025 Iqaluit Ln; ☺4-10pm Mon-Thu, to midnight Fri, noon-midnight Sat) Near the Sylvia Grinnell Territorial Park, Canada's northernmost craft brewery has ambitious plans to utilise the water from the Sylvia Grinnell River in the production of their five very palatable brews, including a porter, pale ale and red ale. Ask the friendly owner for a tour and stay to watch the game on the big screen.

★Royal Canadian Legion
CLUB

(☑867-979-6215; Mivvik St; ☺7pm-late Fri & Sat) The Legion doubles as a club on weekends and becomes the most hopping place in Iqaluit, with a mixed crowd of Inuit, Somalians and other party-goers dancing to Top 40 tunes. To get in, either get a member to sign you in or call ahead for a visitor's pass. Friday night is steak night.

🛍 Shopping

★Carvings Nunavut
ARTS & CRAFTS

(☑867-979-0650; www.carvingsnunavut.com; 626 Queen Elizabeth Way; ☺10am-6pm Mon-Sat, to 3pm Sun) 🖉 Inside the Tumiit Plaza building, this place has Nunavut's most diverse selection of Inuit serpentine, black and white marble and whalebone sculpture for sale – from souvenir size to true collectors' items – as well as prints by Nunavut's renowned artists, such as Andrew Qappik from Pangnirtung.

★Northern Collectables
ART

(☑877-344-6848; http://northerncollectables.com; 1324 Ulu Ln; ☺10am-noon & 1-5pm Mon-Sat) Bryan's little treasure cave is overflowing with stone carvings (mostly from south Baffin, but also more abstract ones from a Toronto-based Inuit artist), appliqué and felt art pieces from Baker Lake and Rankin Inlet, prints from Cape Dorset, plus fur parkas, Inuit art calendars and popular merchandise featuring the designs of Kenojuak Ashevak and some other Cape Dorset luminaries.

Victoria's Arctic Fashion
CLOTHING

(☑867-222-9215; www.facebook.com/Victorias ArcticFashion; 1517 Federal Rd; ☺10am-5pm Wed-Fri, 1-5pm Sat & Sun) High-end, custom-made Inuit parkas with a contemporary twist by local designer Victoria Kakuktinniq. (Bear in mind that sealskin cannot be imported into many countries – including the US and all of the EU.)

ℹ Information

Parks Canada (☑867-975-4673; www.pg.gc. ca; 1104b Qamaniqtuaq St; ☺9am-noon & 1-5pm Mon-Fri) This extremely helpful office has information on all of Nunavut's national parks. Find it on the ground floor of the green apartment building behind Yummy Shawarma.

Qikiqtani General Hospital (☑ 867-979-8600; Niaqunngusiaq Rd; ⊘ 24hr) The only hospital in Nunavut, with emergency services. Check out the colorful murals outside.

Unikkaarvik Visitor Center (☑ 867-979-4636; 220 Sinaa St; ⊘ 9am-5pm Mon-Fri, 10am-4pm Sat, often closed noon-1pm) Offers pamphlets, an informative museum and nature display on the six seasons of the Inuit, and a reference collection of Nunavut books and videos that you can browse or watch in comfort. Arctic-themed movie screenings on Thursdays at 7.30pm.

❶ Getting There & Away

From **Iqaluit Airport** (☑ 867-979-5224; 1126 Mivvik St), around 2km from downtown, Canadian North (www.canadiannorth.com) and First Air (www.firstair.ca) have direct flights to a number of Nunavut communities, as well as Ottawa, Ontario and Yellowknife, NT. Kenn Borek Air (www.borekair.com) offers charter flights.

BAFFIN REGION

Comprising Nunavut's eastern and High Arctic islands, this region reaches from the swampy, forested isles of James Bay to the glaciers and jagged peaks of Ellesmere Island, 3000km north. Encompassing four of Nunavut's five remarkable national parks and with unparalleled opportunities for viewing Arctic wildlife and wilderness trekking, this region also has the best infrastructure, centered on the surprisingly cosmopolitan capital, Iqaluit.

Pangnirtung

POP 1550

An ancient Thule settlement and former whale-blubber processing station for the Hudson Bay Company, Pangnirtung, or 'Pang,' is renowned for its thriving artistic scene. Located 50km south of the Arctic Circle, Pang benefits from a dramatic setting on the banks of a fjord, towered over by Mt Duval – which can be summited for spectacular views. Pang is also the main gateway to even more spectacular scenery at Auyuittuq National Park.

◉ Sights & Activities

★**Uqqurmiut Centre for Arts & Crafts**   GALLERY
(☑ 867-473-8669; www.uqqurmiut.ca; ⊘ 9am-noon & 1-5pm Mon-Fri) 🖉 Pang is famous for its lithographs, prints and tapestries, and this extraordinary place brings it all together. There are few tapestry studios in the world, but one is here and you can watch the weavers at work. Artists create prints via a variety of techniques in the adjacent workshop, and there's a stunning archived collection available to browse and buy. Famous crocheted hats and hand-woven scarves are another highlight, as are the soapstone, marble and bone carvings and jewelry.

★**Angmarlik Visitor Centre**   MUSEUM
(☑ 867-473-8737; oarnaqaq1@gov.nu.ca; ⊘ 8:30am-noon & 1-8pm) 🖉 This enthusiastically run place near the waterfront features a replica Inuit tent made of whalebone and animal skins, sealskin canoes and interesting displays on Inuit culture, with traditional hunting, fishing and household implements, plus archaeological finds from Kekerten Island. Another exhibition charts local whaling history and its effect on Inuit life. Elders congregate in a separate room here on Mondays, Wednesdays and Fridays. Make sure staff explain the game of seal flipperbone Monopoly.

★**Mt Duval**   HIKING
Looming high above Pang, Mt Duval (850m) affords tremendous views of the fjord and the settlement from its summit. There's not much of a trail but no chance of getting lost; start at the reservoir and navigate your way up among the boulders. Allow four hours' round-trip.

☞ Tours

★**PEO Services**   OUTDOORS
(☑ 867-473-4060; www.kilabukoutfitting.com) From June to October, Peter Kilabuk, knowledgable former speaker of Nunavut Legislative Assembly, offers transport to Auyuittuq National Park (from $125 per person) and Kekerten Historic Park (from $250 per person), wildlife-spotting boat trips on Cumberland Sound and fishing trips.

🛏 Sleeping

★**Fjordview B&B**   B&B $$
(☑ 867-473-8039; www.beconnectedservices.ca; r $200; 🛜) Run by affable Markus, this cheerful yellow B&B overlooks the fjord in central Pang. Besides the terrific location, there are hearty breakfasts, Inuit art on walls, a cozy guest lounge that encourages camaraderie among travelers and plenty of help and advice from the host. The two singles and a double share a bathroom.

❶ Information

Angmarlik Visitor Centre (p817) Come here for in-depth displays on Inuit culture and whaling history and info on local outfitters. You can also have a cup of tea with an elder and a game of seal flipperbone Monopoly.

You can register and deregister at **Parks Canada** (☑ 867-473-2500; www.parkscanada. gc.ca; ⊙ 8:30am-noon & 1-5pm) for Auyuittuq National Park and pay the park fee. Plenty of info on the park, plus maps. Next to Angmarlik Visitor Centre.

For more information visit www.pangnirtung.ca.

❶ Getting There & Away

There are at least two flights daily to Iqaluit with Canadian North (www.canadiannorth. com) and First Air (www.firstair.ca) from Pangnirtung Airport, and six flights weekly to Qikitarjuaq.

Auyuittuq National Park

★ **Auyuittuq**
National Park   NATIONAL PARK
(www.pc.gc.ca/en/pn-np/nu/auyuittuq; day/over-night/maximum $12/24.50/147.20) Among the globe's most flabbergasting places, Auyuit-tuq (ah-you-ee-tuk) means 'the land that never melts.' Appropriately, there are plenty of glaciers in this 19,500-sq-km park, plus jagged peaks, vertiginous cliffs and deep valleys. Hikers trek the 97km Akshayuk Pass (crossing the Arctic Circle) in summer, when it's snow-free. Access is by boat either from Pangnirtung (per person one way $150) or Qikiqtarjuaq ($275); arrange pickup in advance. Camp in any safe, windproof, ecologically appropriate spot. Nine emergency shelters dot the pass.Register and pay park fees at Parks Canada.

In the park, experienced climbers and base jumpers scale Mt Thor (1500m), the earth's highest sheer cliff, and twin-peaked Mt Asgard (2015m), famed for the parachute scene from *The Spy Who Loved Me*.

Parks Canada sell maps ($17), though the valley route is relatively intuitive.

While wondrous, Auyuittuq is also brutal and isolated. To hike it you need to be an experienced wilderness operator, and fit. Ten days is average for the route. Rivers must be crossed; polar bears are seen most seasons. The trail follows the valley, so it's difficult to get lost.

Cape Dorset
POP 1441

On a small rocky island just off Baffin Island's Foxe Peninsula, Cape Dorset (Kinngait; meaning 'Mountains') is a beautifully situated, hilly little settlement next to a bay, renowned as the epicenter of Inuit art. In the late 1950s residents pioneered modern printmaking, marketing it to the world with remarkable success. Dorset boasts numerous artists, with skills passed down in the family, and some, such as Pudlo Pudlat, Pitseolak Ashoona and Kenojuak Ashevak, have achieved international recognition. Walk around town and you'll see carvers at work at makeshift tables outdoors.

◉ Sights

★ **Kenojuak Cultural**
Centre & Print Shop   GALLERY
(Kinngait Arts; ☑ 867-897-8965; www.dorsetfine arts.com; ⊙ 9am-noon & 1-5pm Mon-Fri) ✍ Though many Inuit communities now generate world-class artworks, Cape Dorset's remain the most revered. The Kenojuak Cultural Centre, named after Kenojuak Ashevak, is split into exhibition space and a state-of-the-art print workshop where you can watch artists work. The most activity occurs from September to May; manager Joemee is happy to explain the stonecut, lithograph and stencil techniques in the print shop and there's a good selection of prints and souvenirs for sale.

Mallikjuaq Historic Park   ARCHAEOLOGICAL SITE
(www.nunavutparks.ca) Mallikjuaq Historic Park is an island reachable via a low-tide land bridge from Dorset's metal dump; it's a 20-minute crossing and you need rubber boots. A half-day hike across spongy tundra takes in the remains of thousand-year-old Thule stone houses, a 200-year-old grave of stranded whalers and a fox trap used by Inuit women until the 1940s. Go with a guide carrying a rifle; bears are afoot.

⌸ Sleeping

★ **Dorset Suites**   BOUTIQUE HOTEL $$$
(☑ 867-897-8806; www.dorsetsuites.com; r from $300; 🖥) Nunavut's most appealing hotel has spacious rooms with balconies and views, warm wood furnishings and kitchenettes; the interior is decked out with local art. The restaurant (lunch/dinner mains

from \$12/45) is open to nonguests and serves up sandwiches and salads for lunch and the likes of caribou meat loaf and Arctic char for dinner; reserve ahead.

Staff can arrange tours with **Huit Huit Tours** (☑867-897-8806; www.capedorsettours. com; 4-day tour per person \$1500). You'll also find a comprehensive selection of stone carvings for sale here.

❶ Getting There & Away

First Air (www.firstair.ca) and Canadian North (www.canadiannorth.com) serve Cape Dorset airport from Iqaluit (one hour, one or two daily). Good chance of getting a standby seat.

Pond Inlet

POP 1617

Sitting on the perpetually icy Lancaster Sound, against a backdrop of snow-covered mountains, Pond Inlet (Mittimatalik, named after an Inuit ancestor) is the gateway to Sirmilik National Park: bird-watching paradise and glacier-draped arctic marvel. Make arrangements with outfitters beforehand for memorable nature-watching experiences.

🏃 Activities

Black Feather (p815) runs multiday trips to nearby Sirmilik National Park. Arctic Kingdom (p814), the only diving operator in the Arctic, runs annual dive safaris around Bylot Island, and both Arctic Kingdom and Black Feather operate narwhal-watching trips to the floe's edge. Pond Inlet–based **Inuarak Outfitting** (☑867-899-8551; inuarak@gmail. com) and **Tagak Outfitting Service** (☑867-899-8932) can help with logistics.

❶ Information

Nattinnak Centre (☑867-899-8225; www. pondinlet.ca; ⊙10am-noon & 1-5pm Tue, Thu & Fri, 1-5pm & 7-9pm Wed, 2-4pm Sun) Info on activities and outfitters, plus a mini-museum with wildlife and Inuit culture displays.

Parks Canada (☑867-899-8092; www.pc.gc. ca/sirmilik; ⊙8:30am-noon & 1-5pm Mon-Fri) Supplies information on Sirmilik National Park; register for the park here.

❶ Getting There & Away

First Air (www.firstair.ca) flies from Iqaluit (\$1300, 2¾ hours, one or two daily).

Kimmirut

POP 389

Baffin Island's southernmost and still very traditional Inuit community sits at the mouth of Soper River, overlooking Glasgow Inlet. The area has been continuously inhabited by the ancestors of the Inuit for around 4000 years. The hamlet is a stop on cruise-ship routes and the gateway to Katannilik Territorial Park and a good place to buy kamiks (traditional boots).

◉ Sights

★**Katannilik
Territorial Park**   STATE PARK
(http://nunavutparks.com/parks-special-places/ katannilik-territorial-park; day/year \$24.50/147.20) Near Iqaluit and one of Nunavut's finest parks, Katannilik means 'Place of Waterfalls' and comprises two main features. A Canadian Heritage waterway, aquamarine **Soper River** splashes a navigable 50km through a deep, fertile valley, past cascades, caribou, gemstone deposits and dwarf-willow forest to Kimmirut, attracting paddlers. Hikers and skiers take the **Itijjagiaq Trail**, a traditional 120km route (one week) over the tablelands of the Meta Incognita Peninsula and through the Soper valley to the Frobisher Bay trailhead, 10km west of Iqaluit.

Most paddlers charter a plane from Iqaluit to the riverside airstrip at Mt Joy, float three to five days from the put-in to Kimmirut, and then fly back to Iqaluit. Kenn Borek Air (www.borekair.com) does charters. Iqaluit outfitters can take hikers to the trailhead by boat.

Before entering Katannilik Territorial Park, you have to register either at the visitor center (p817) in Iqaluit (which stocks the invaluable *The Itijjagiaq Trail* guide) or at the Katannilik Park Centre in Kimmirut.

❶ Information

Katannilik Park Center (☑867-939-2416; www.nunavutparks.com; ⊙9am-5pm Mon-Fri) Register here for Katannilik Territorial Park.

❶ Getting There & Away

First Air (www.firstair.ca) links Kimmirut and Iqaluit four times weekly (\$315 one way, 35 minutes).

Resolute

POP 198

This clutch of minuscule homes, Resolute (Qausuittuq; 'Place with no Dawn'), in a wind-lashed gravel desert on Cornwallis Island, is the launchpad for expeditions to the North Pole, as well as trips to Quttinirpaaq National Park and scenic Grise Fiord – Canada's northernmost civilian community.

The settlement was founded in 1953, when several Inuit families were lured here from Pond Inlet, as well as Inukjuak, Québec, with false promises of a better life, in order to shore up national sovereignty. During the last month of winter, known locally as 'silly season,' Resolute becomes a hive of activity as adventurers and scientific research teams arrive. In April and May, local guides can take you wildlife-watching on the ice.

Look for marine fossils at **Tupirvik Territorial Park** or fly to National Historic Site **Beechey Island**, where the ill-fated Franklin expedition wintered in 1845–46 before vanishing with little trace.

Sleeping

South Camp Inn HOTEL $$$

(☑ 867-252-3737; www.southcampinn.com; Summerside; s/d $300/400; ☎) This large, two-story hotel, Resolute's nerve center, is run by local legend Ozzie, a Tanzanian who arrived in the 1970s with barely a dollar to his name. It's a friendly, labyrinthine place with a gym and spacious rooms, popular with North Pole adventurers. Full board included.

OFF THE BEATEN TRACK

SIRMILIK NATIONAL PARK

Pond Inlet is the base for visits to the spectacular **Sirmilik National Park** (www.pc.gc.ca/en/pn-np/nu/sirmilik; day/year $24.50/147.20), a breeding ground for countless seabirds including the planet's largest flock of snow geese. The park has three main areas: Bylot Island, a glacier-draped bird sanctuary; Oliver Sound, a fjord with exciting canoeing; and Borden Peninsula with its striking hoodoos (eroded red sandstone towers). Sirmilik's logistics are challenging, so most people choose to go on some kind of tour. Contact the Pond Inlet parks office (p819) for info and to register.

Getting There & Away

First Air (www.firstair.ca) flies from Iqaluit via Pond Inlet and Arctic Bay (from $2540 one way, five hours, daily) to Resolute, while Kenn Borek Air (www.borekair.com) does charters.

Quttinirpaaq National Park

★ **Quttinirpaaq National Park** NATIONAL PARK

(www.pc.gc.ca/en/pn-np/nu/quttinirpaaq; day/year $24.50/147.20) The northernmost and most mountainous of Nunavut's national parks, 37,775-sq-km Quttinirpaaq is Canada's second-largest, way up on Ellesmere Island. Now the mass of frozen crags, topped with age-old ice caps, deep fjords, vast glaciers and sheltered valleys are home to musk ox, wolverine and Peary caribou. Highlights include 24-hour daylight, Mt Barbeau (2616m), eastern North America's highest peak, and Lake Hazen Basin. Multiday treks are offered by Black Feather (p815), which also runs a joint trip with Parks Canada.

A charter from Resolute costs around $60,000 round-trip for up to nine people and 1200kg of gear. Pay your fees and register at the **Parks Canada office** (☑ 867-252-3000; Clinic St; ☺ 9am-noon & 1-5pm Mon-Fri mid-May–mid-Aug) in Resolute.

KIVALLIQ REGION

This region, a flat, windswept area, cut through by wild rivers and a refuge for caribou and waterfowl, takes in the Hudson Bay coast and the Barrenlands to the west. Ukkusiksalik National Park, reachable from Rankin Inlet or Naujaat (formerly Repulse Bay), is the prize here, with its cornucopia of wildlife and one of the world's greatest concentrations of polar bears.

Rankin Inlet

POP 2842

With an enormous *inukshuk* (humanoid stone cairn) as the town's symbol, Rankin Inlet (Kangiqtiniq; Deep Inlet) grew up around nickel mining in the late '50s and is the Kivalliq region's largest community. New gold mines and mineral exploration means it's still an important center. It's also an arty place and a base for accessing Kivalliq, and there's good char and grayling fishing close to town. The town's other claim to fame is that it's the home of Jordin Tootoo, the only Inuk player in the National Hockey League.

◉ Sights

★ Matchbox Gallery
GALLERY

(📞 867-645-2674; info@matchboxgallery.com; In-ukshuk St; ⊙ hours vary) 🖎 This small space is famed for having pioneered Inuit ceramic art. Watch artists at work, and browse and buy a wide range of beautiful handicrafts, including prints and soapstone and antler carvings.

Iqalugaarjuup Nunanga Territorial Park
STATE PARK

(www.nunavutparks.com) This tongue twister of a park is located 5km from town and is popular for hiking and berry-picking. Near the Meliadine River's mouth are archaeological sites where the pre-Inuit Dorset people dwelled, as well as a re-creation of a traditional sod dwelling.

🛏 Sleeping

★ Nanuq Lodge
B&B $$

(📞 867-645-2650; nanuq@qiniq.com; 1 Atausiq St; s/d $160/210; 📶) This big, friendly, sunny B&B is the region's best place to stay. It rents kayaks, loans bicycles and arranges tours, especially dogsledding. Enjoy comfortable en-suite rooms adorned with Inuit art, or trade polar-bear stories in the communal lounge. Its alternative accommodation, Nanuq Suites, has upmarket doubles with kitchenette and great modern facilities.

Katimavik Suites
BUSINESS HOTEL $$$

(📞 867-857-2752; www.katimaviksuites.com; Tupirvik Ave; r $260; 📶) This comfy hotel comprises a clutch of spacious suites with kitchenettes and splashes of bright colours to liven the place up. Continental breakfast is thrown in, and the really helpful management can arrange car rental.

ℹ Information

There's a **visitor center** (📞 867-645-3838; kivalliqtourism@qiniq.com; Sivulliq Ave; ⊙ 8:30am-5pm Mon-Fri) in town where you can purchase some local art. For more information see www.rankininlet.ca and www.nunavuttourism.com.

ℹ Getting There & Away

Canadian North (www.canadiannorth.com) and First Air (www.firstair.ca) fly from Yellowknife (from $1370, two hours, Monday, Wednesday, Friday and Sunday) and Iqaluit (from $1400, two

---

UKKUSIKSALIK NATIONAL PARK

Surrounding Wager Bay, a vast inlet off Hudson Bay, **Ukkusiksalik National Park** (www.pc.gc.ca/en/pn-np/nu/ukkusiksalik; day/year $24.50/147.20) comprises 20,500 sq km of bleak uninhabited tundra and is one of the world's best places to observe polar bears as well as other arctic wildlife. July and early August are best for visits and an Inuit guide is highly recommended.

Charter flights from Baker Lake or motorboats from Naujaat (formerly Repulse Bay) are the way in: Rankin Inlet has flights to both. Boat trips offers terrific wildlife-watching opportunities.

Highlights include abundant animals and birds, great hiking and boating, and a spectacular reversing waterfall. Fees payable at the **Naujaat park office** (📞 867-462-4500; ⊙ 8:30am-noon & 1-5pm Mon-Fri).

---

hours, Monday, Wednesday, Friday and Saturday). First Air and Calm Air (www.calmair.com) serve Churchill ($721, one hours, two daily) and Winnipeg ($1056, 2½ hours, one or two daily).

Naujaat
POP 1082

Appropriately named 'Resting Place of Seagulls', the cliffs around Naujaat (formerly Repulse Bay; www.repulsebay.ca) are important nesting places for thousands of seagulls, snowbirds and other winged creatures. The bay provided shelter to whaling ships overwintering here during the 19th century; today this small community on the Arctic Circle is the gateway to Ukkusiksalik National Park and is an excellent place to fish for Arctic char.

🛏 Sleeping

Arctic Circle Paws & Paddles B&B
B&B $$

(📞 867-462-4482; http://arcticcirclepawsandpaddles.weebly.com; r per person incl breakfast $210; 📶) Carol and Bill are friendly hosts, and guests are served a full breakfast and have access to their ample collection of Northern literature. Accommodation is in two snug rooms with twin beds. Depending on the season, dogsledding or kayaking tours can be arranged for $75 per person.

ℹ Getting There & Away

There are First Air (www.firstair.ca) and Calm Air (www.calmair.com) flights to Naujaat from Rankin Inlet ($711 one way, 1½ hours), as well as Winnipeg, Manitoba via Churchill, Rankin Inlet and Coral Harbor (from $1836 one way, seven hours).

KITIKMEOT REGION

Nunavut's least populated region occupies the mainland's Arctic coast and the islands north of there. Between them runs the fabled Northwest Passage, plied by cruise ships during the short but intense summer season. Cambridge Bay and Gjoa Haven are both on the cruise-ship route, and the Kitikmeot Region has repeatedly made the news since the finding of Franklin's lost ships – HMS *Erebus* in 2014 and HMS *Terror* in 2016.

Cambridge Bay

POP 1766

Wind-wracked Cambridge Bay (Iqaluktut-tiaq; 'Place of Good Fishing') on Victoria Island is the regional center and stop for cruise ships navigating the Northwest Passage. The federal **Canadian High Arctic Research Station** (CHARS; info@polar.gc.ca; Natik St; ⊙2pm Wed) opened here in 2017, attracting scientists worldwide to monitor climate change. The Inuinnaqtun dialect is spoken here and Cambridge Bay is known for its crafts, including clothing made out of *qiviut* (supremely warm musk-ox down).

Explorers seeking the Northwest Passage often sheltered here; the remains of Roald Amundsen's schooner *Maud* lie in the harbor.

⊙ Sights

★**Ovayok Territorial Park**   STATE PARK
Ovayok Territorial Park, accessible via a rough road or 15km hike, is a prime place to see musk ox and offers good views from Mt Pelly (200m). It has some 20km worth of walking trails and good camping spots. Accommodations can help arrange transport.

🛏 Sleeping & Eating

Ublu Inn   BOUTIQUE HOTEL $$
(☎867-983-3214; www.theubluinn.com; 16 Koihok Mahagak Cres; r $250; 🖱) Decked out with prints of the northern lights, these five in-dividually styled rooms are located above Cambridge Bay's best restaurant, making them a win-win prospect. The hotel and cafe feature some stunning local photography and the helpful owners are happy to share their local knowledge.

★**Kuugaq Cafe**   FUSION $$
(☎867-983-2662; www.facebook.com/kuugaqcafe; 16 Koihok Mahagak Cres; mains $16-25; ⊙11am-7pm Tue-Fri, 10am-3pm Sat & Sun; 🖱) This un-expectedly gourmet spot is the community meeting place and most popular dining venue in town, courtesy of good old Canadian favorites (pulled-pork poutine), Northern flavors (musk-ox chili, musk-ox burgers, char chowder) and global touches, courtesy of one of the owners, who happens to be Trinidad-ian. There's good coffee, local art on walls, and an air of happy anticipation.

ℹ Getting There & Away

Canadian North (www.canadiannorth.com) and First Air (www.firstair.ca) fly from Yellowknife (from $1039 one way, 1¾ hours, five weekly).

Gjoa Haven

POP 1324

Named after the ship used by Norwegian explorer Amundsen, the first person to successfully traverse the Northwest Passage, this hamlet (www.gjoahaven.net) grew around a Hudson's Bay Company trading post that was setup here in the 1920s. Since September 2014, Gjoa Haven has been the epicenter of excitement, generated by Parks Canada finally locating HMS *Erebus*, one of the two ships of the vanished Franklin expedition of 1845, just south of King William Island, off the coast of the Adelaide Penin-sula. This was followed by the discovery of HMS *Terror* in 2016. History buffs may follow the Northwest Passage Trail around the settlement to learn about its pivotal role in Arctic exploration, while naturalists will be drawn to the **Queen Maud Migratory Bird Sanctuary**.

ℹ Getting There & Away

There are direct flights with Canadian North (www.canadiannorth.com) from Yellowknife ($1555 one way, 2¾ hours, five weekly) and Cambridge Bay ($825 one way, one hour, twice weekly).

Understand Canada

History

The human story of Canada begins around 15,000 years ago, when indigenous locals began carving thriving communities from the abundant wilderness. Everything changed, though, when the Europeans rolled in from the late 15th century onward, staking claims that triggered rumbling conflicts and eventually shaped a vast new nation. Much of this colorful heritage is accessible to visitors, with more than 950 national historic sites covering everything from forts to battlefields to famous homes.

The First Inhabitants

Canada's first inhabitants were most likely hunter-nomads who, in hungry pursuit of caribou, elk and bison, crossed over from Asia on the land bridge that once linked Siberia and Alaska. As the earth warmed and the glaciers retreated, these immigrants began to trickle across the Americas.

About 4500 years ago, a second major wave of migration from Siberia brought the ancestors of the Inuit to Canada. The new arrivals took one look at the North, sized it up as a tasty icebox filled with fish-and-seal dinners, and decided to hang around. These early Inuit were members of the Dorset Culture, named after Cape Dorset on Baffin Island, where its remains were first unearthed. Around 1000 CE a separate Inuit culture, the whale-hunting Thule of northern Alaska, began making its way east through the Canadian Arctic. As these people spread, they overtook the Dorset Culture. The Thule are the direct ancestors of the modern Inuit.

By the late 15th century, when the first Europeans arrived, indigenous peoples had spread beyond the Arctic into four other major locations across Canada: the Pacific, the Plains, the southern Ontario/St Lawrence River area and the Northeast woodlands.

The Vikings & European Explorers

Viking celebrity Leif Eriksson was the first European to reach Canada's shores. In fact, he and his band of Scandinavian seafarers were the first Europeans in all of North America. Around 1000 CE they poked around the eastern shores of Canada, establishing winter settlements and way stations for repairing ships and restocking supplies, such as at L'Anse

Atlantic Canada had a notorious history of pirates. Peter Easton was the first in 1602, plundering around Newfoundland. Black Bart, aka Bartholomew Roberts, was another, c 1720. He disliked booze and gambling and encouraged prayer among his employees. In Halifax pirates were called 'privateers' and were sanctioned by the government.

TIMELINE	c 70 million BCE	c 25,000 BCE	1000 BCE
	Dinosaurs enjoy the warm, coastal climate that exists in southern Alberta (the hefty creatures think of it like today's Victoria).	Hot on the hoofs of juicy caribou and bison, the first humans arrive in Canada by crossing the land bridge that once connected Siberia to North America.	After hanging around for a few thousand years, the Maritime Archaic Indians, known for their ceremonial burials at sites such as Port aux Choix, inexplicably disappear.

aux Meadows in Newfoundland. The locals didn't exactly roll out the welcome mat for these intruders, who eventually tired of the hostilities and went home. There would be no more visits from the outside for another 300 to 400 years.

The action heated up again in the late 15th century. In 1492, backed by the Spanish crown, Christopher Columbus went searching for a western sea route to Asia and instead stumbled upon some small islands in the Bahamas. Other European monarchs, excited by his 'discovery', quickly sponsored expeditions of their own. In 1497, Giovanni Caboto, better known as John Cabot, sailed under a British flag as far west as Newfoundland and Cape Breton.

Cabot didn't find a passage to China, but he did find cod, a much-coveted commodity in Europe at the time. In short order, hundreds of boats were shuttling between Europe and the fertile new fishing grounds. Basque whalers from northern Spain soon followed. Several were based at Red Bay in Labrador, which became the biggest whaling port in the world during the 16th century.

King François I of France looked over the fence at his neighbors, stroked his beard, then snapped his fingers and ordered Jacques Cartier to appear before him. By this time, the hunt was on not only for the Northwest Passage but also for gold, given the findings by Spanish conquistadors among the Aztec and Inca civilizations. François hoped for similar riches in the frosty North.

Upon arrival in Labrador, Cartier found only 'stones and horrible rugged rocks,' as he wrote in his journal in 1534. He dutifully kept exploring and soon went ashore on Québec's Gaspé Peninsula to claim the land for France. The local Iroquois thought Cartier a good neighbor, until he kidnapped two of the chief's sons and took them back to Europe. To his credit, Cartier returned them a year later when sailing up the St Lawrence River to Stadacona (present-day Québec City) and Hochelaga (today's Montréal). Here he got wind of a land called Saguenay that was full of gold and silver. The rumor prompted Cartier's third voyage, in 1541, but alas, the mythical riches remained elusive.

Fur Trade Ignites

François I became bored with his distant colony, which wasn't producing the wealth he wanted. But his interest perked up a few decades later when fur hats became all the rage. Everyone who was anyone was wearing one and, as the fashion mavens knew, there was no finer *chapeau* than one made from beaver pelts. With beavers pretty much extinct in the Old World, the demand for a fresh supply was strong.

In 1588, the French crown granted the first trading monopoly in Canada, only to have other merchants promptly challenge the claim. And so

France retains a token of its early exploits in Canada: St Pierre and Miquelon, two small islands off Newfoundland's coast, remain staunchly French to this day.

Explorer Jacques Cartier bestowed Canada with its name. Scholars say it comes from *kanata,* a Huron-Iroquois word for 'village' or 'settlement,' which was written in Cartier's journal and later transformed by mapmakers to 'Canada.'

1000 CE	1497	1528	1534
Viking Leif Eriksson and crew wash up at L'Anse aux Meadows, where they build sod houses. They're the first Europeans in North America, beating Columbus by 500 years.	John Cabot sails over from Britain and finds Newfoundland instead of China. It's not a bad trade-off because the waters are filled with fat, delicious codfish.	St John's, Newfoundland, bobs up as North America's first town. It belongs to no nation; rather it serves fishing fleets from all over Europe.	Jacques Cartier sails into what is now Québec. He searches for gold and precious metals, but finds only chilled rocks. He claims the land for France anyway.

the race for control of the fur trade was officially on. The economic value of this enterprise and, by extension, its role in shaping Canadian history, cannot be underestimated. It was the main reason behind the country's European settlement, at the root of the struggle for dominance between the French and the British, and the source of strife and division between indigenous groups. All because of a hat.

The Canadian Military History Gateway (www.cmhg.gc.ca) provides access to digitized resources on Canada's military history, including audio links to old CBC war broadcasts.

In order to gain control of the distant lands, the first order of business was to put European bodies on the ground. In the summer of 1604, a group of French pioneers established a tentative foothold on Île Ste-Croix (a tiny islet in the river on the present US border with Maine). They moved to Port Royal (today's Annapolis Royal) in Nova Scotia the following spring. Exposed and difficult to defend, neither site made a good base for controlling the inland fur trade. As the would-be colonists moved up the St Lawrence River, they finally came upon a spot their leader, Samuel de Champlain, considered prime real estate – where today's Québec City stands. It was 1608 and 'New France' had become a reality.

French vs English

The French enjoyed their plush fur monopoly for several decades, but in 1670 the British mounted a formidable challenge. They caught a lucky break when a pair of disillusioned French explorers, Radisson and Des Groseilliers, confided that the best fur country actually lay to the north and west of Lake Superior, which was easily accessible via Hudson Bay. King Charles II quickly formed the Hudson's Bay Company and granted it a trade monopoly over all the lands whose rivers and streams drained into the bay. This vast territory, called Rupert's Land, encompassed about 40% of present-day Canada, including Labrador, western Québec, northwestern Ontario, Manitoba, most of Saskatchewan and Alberta, and part of the Northwest Territories.

The English infuriated the French with such moves, and so the French kept right on galling the English by settling further inland. Both countries had claims to the land, but each wanted regional dominance. They skirmished back and forth in hostilities that mirrored those in Europe, where wars raged throughout the first half of the 18th century.

Top Historic Sites: West

Klondike sites, Yukon

Batoche, Saskatchewan

Head-Smashed-In Buffalo Jump, Alberta

Fort Edmonton, Alberta

Things came to a head with the Treaty of Utrecht, which ended Queen Anne's War (1701–13) overseas. Under its provisions, the French had to officially recognize British claims to Hudson Bay and Newfoundland, and give up all of Nova Scotia (then called Acadia) except for Cape Breton Island.

The conflict simmered for a few decades, then ramped up to a new level in 1754 when the two countries battled each other in the French and Indian Wars (also known as the Seven Years' War). The tide soon turned in the Brits' favor with the capture of the Louisbourg fortress,

1608	1610	1670	1755
After four years of moving around, Samuel de Champlain finds his dream-home site, putting down stakes at Québec City and giving New France its first permanent settlement.	The British take their turn: merchant John Guy builds a plantation at Cupids, Newfoundland. It's England's first colony in Canada (and second in the New World after Jamestown).	King Charles II creates the Hudson's Bay Company to shore up the local fur trade for the Brits. Years later, the company morphs into the Bay department store chain.	The English deport some 14,000 French Acadians from the Bay of Fundy region. They're forced onto ships during the Great Expulsion; many head to Louisiana in the USA.

giving them control of a strategically important entrance to the St Lawrence River.

In 1759 the British besieged Québec, scaling the cliffs in a surprise attack and quickly defeating the stunned French; it was one of Canada's bloodiest and most famous battles, and left both commanding generals dead. At the Treaty of Paris (1763), France handed Canada over to Britain.

Growing Pains

Managing the newly acquired territory presented quite a challenge for the British. First, they had to quell uprisings by First Nations groups, such as the attack on Detroit by Ottawa chief Pontiac. The British government issued the Royal Proclamation of 1763, which prevented colonists from settling west of the Appalachian Mountains and regulated purchases of indigenous land. Though well-intentioned, the proclamation was largely ignored.

The French Canadians caused the next headache. Tensions arose when the new rulers imposed British law that heavily restricted the rights of Roman Catholics (the religion of the French), including the rights to vote and hold office. The British hoped their discriminatory policy would launch a mass exodus and make it easier to anglicize the remaining settlers. The plan didn't work – the French just crossed their arms and further dug in their heels.

As if the indigenous peoples and French weren't problems enough, the American colonies started making revolutionary rumbles to the south. The British governor, Guy Carleton, wisely reasoned that winning the French settlers' political allegiance was more valuable than turning them

Manual laborers from China built much of the Canadian Pacific Railway's western stretch. They earned $0.75 to $1.25 per day, and often were given the most dangerous, explosive-laden jobs.

1759	1763	1775	1793
Canada's most famous battle, a beauty between the French and English, happens on the Plains of Abraham at Québec City. It lasts less than an hour. France loses.	The Treaty of Paris boots France out of Canada after France loses the Seven Years' War. Thus, Canada ceases to ping-pong between power-mongering France and Britain.	American rebels invade Canada and try to entice Québec to join the revolt against the British in the American Revolution, but the locals refuse.	Explorer Alexander Mackenzie makes the first transcontinental journey across the land. He scrawls 'from Canada by land' on a rock near Bella Coola, BC.

into tea drinkers. This led to the passage of the Québec Act of 1774. The act confirmed French Canadians' right to their religion, allowed them to assume political office and restored the use of French civil law. Indeed, during the American Revolution (1775–83) most French Canadians refused to take up arms for the American cause, although not many willingly defended the British either.

After the revolution, the English-speaking population exploded when some 50,000 settlers from the newly independent US migrated northward. Called United Empire Loyalists due to their presumed allegiance to Britain, many settlers were motivated more by cheap land than by love of king and crown. The majority ended up in Nova Scotia and New Brunswick, while a smaller group settled along the northern shore of Lake Ontario and in the Ottawa River Valley (forming the nucleus of what became Ontario). About 8000 people moved to Québec, creating the first sizeable Anglophone community in the French-speaking bastion.

The Nation Splits: Upper & Lower Canada

Partly in order to accommodate the interests of Loyalist settlers, the British government passed the Constitutional Act of 1791, which divided the colony into Upper Canada (today's southern Ontario) and Lower Canada (now southern Québec). Lower Canada retained French civil laws, but both provinces were governed by the British criminal code.

The British crown installed a governor to direct each colony. The governor in turn appointed the members of his 'cabinet,' then called the Executive Council. The legislative branch consisted of an appointed Legislative Council and an elected Assembly, which ostensibly represented the interests of the colonists. In reality, though, the Assembly held very little power, since the governor could veto its decisions. Not surprisingly, this was a recipe for friction and resentment. This was especially the case in Lower Canada, where an English governor and an English-dominated Council held sway over a French-dominated Assembly.

The USA has invaded Canada twice – in 1775 and 1812 – both times to no avail.

THE MAPLE LEAF SYMBOL

It's on the penny, on Air Canada planes, on Toronto hockey-team jerseys, and on every Canadian traveler's backpack – you can't escape the maple leaf. The leaf has been considered a national symbol for almost two centuries. In 1836, *Le Canadien* newspaper, published in Lower Canada, wrote about it as a suitable emblem for the nation. Ontario and Québec both were using it on their coat of arms by 1868. The Canadian Armed Forces used it during the world wars. And finally, after much wrangling over the design (one leaf? three leaves? 13 points?), the current 11-point leaf was granted national-symbol status and went on the flag in 1965.

1812	1818	1858	1864
The War of 1812, though between American and British opponents, was often fought on (and over!) Canadian soil, at the expense of the local pioneers and indigenous peoples.	The USA and Britain hash out the Treaty of 1818. The upshot: Canada's border is defined as the 49th Parallel from Lake of the Woods to the Rocky Mountains.	Yee-haw! Prospectors discover gold along the Fraser River in BC, spurring thousands of get-rich-quick dreamers to move north and start panning. Most remain poor.	The Fathers of the Confederation meet in Charlottetown, PEI, and mold a new country called Canada from the group of loosely knit colonies that now comprise the land.

Rampant cronyism made matters worse. Members of the conservative British merchant elite dominated the Executive and Legislative Councils and showed little interest in French-Canadian matters. Called the Family Compact in Upper Canada and the Château Clique in Lower Canada, their ranks included brewer John Molson and university founder James McGill. The group's influence grew especially strong after the War of 1812, an ultimately futile attempt by the US to take over its northern neighbor.

In 1837, frustration over these entrenched elites reached a boiling point. Parti Canadien leader Louis-Joseph Papineau and his Upper Canadian counterpart, Reform Party leader William Lyon Mackenzie, launched open rebellions against the government. Although both uprisings were quickly crushed, the incident signaled to the British that the status quo wasn't going to cut it any longer.

Cautious Reunion

The British dispatched John Lambton, the Earl of Durham, to investigate the causes of the rebellions. He correctly identified ethnic tensions as the root of the problem, calling the French and British 'two nations warring in the bosom of a single state.' He then earned the nickname 'Radical Jack' by asserting that French culture and society were inferior and obstacles to expansion and greatness – only assimilation of British laws, language and institutions would quash French nationalism and bring long-lasting peace. These ideas were adopted into the Union Act of 1840.

Upper and Lower Canada soon merged into the Province of Canada and became governed by a single legislature, the new Parliament of Canada. Each ex-colony had the same number of representatives, which wasn't exactly fair to Lower Canada (ie Québec), where the population was much larger. On the plus side, the new system brought responsible government that restricted the governor's powers and eliminated nepotism.

While most British Canadians welcomed the new system, the French were less than thrilled. If anything, the union's underlying objective of destroying French culture, language and identity made Francophones cling together even more tenaciously. The provisions of the act left deep wounds that still haven't fully healed.

Thus the united province was built on slippery ground. The decade or so following unification was marked by political instability as one government replaced another in fairly rapid succession. Meanwhile, the USA had grown into a self-confident economic powerhouse, while British North America was still a loose patchwork of independent colonies. The American Civil War (1861–65) and the USA's purchase of Alaska from Russia in 1867 raised fears of annexation. It became clear that only a less volatile political system would stave off these challenges, and the movement toward federal union gained momentum.

Gold Diggers (2010), by Charlotte Gray, tells of the last great gold rush in history. Between 1896 and 1899 Dawson City, in the Yukon, boomed from 400 people to 30,000 people. The author uses letters and newspaper articles by resident journalists, bankers, prostitutes, priests and lawmen to depict the era.

Searching for your Cajun roots? The Acadian Genealogy Homepage (www.acadian.org) has compiled census reports harking back to 1671, plus maps and histories of local Acadian communities.

1867	1885	1893	1896
It's official: the British North America Act unites the colonies under the Dominion of Canada, a card-carrying member of the British Empire. Queen Victoria celebrates with Canadian bacon for breakfast.	Canada's first national park opens in Banff, Alberta; meanwhile, in Craigellachie, BC, workers drive in the spike that completes the Canadian Pacific Railway.	The Montréal AAA hockey team accepts the first Stanley Cup (donated by one Lord Stanley of Preston). It's now the oldest trophy North American pro sports teams compete for.	Prospectors find more of the shiny stuff, this time in the Yukon. The Klondike Gold Rush is on, with 40,000 hopefuls bringing their picks and pans to Dawson City.

Confederation

In 1864, Charlottetown, Prince Edward Island (PEI), served as the birthing room for modern Canada. At the town's Province House, the 'Fathers of Confederation' – a group of representatives from Nova Scotia, New Brunswick, PEI, Ontario and Québec – hammered out the framework for a new nation. It took two more meetings before Parliament passed the British North America Act in 1867. And so began the modern, self-governing state of Canada, originally known as the Dominion of Canada. The day the act became official, July 1, is celebrated as Canada's national holiday; it was called Dominion Day until it was renamed Canada Day in 1982.

How the West Was Won

Task one on the infant dominion's to-do list was to bring the remaining land and colonies into the confederation. Under its first prime minister, John A Macdonald, the government acquired vast Rupert's Land in 1869 for the paltry sum of £300,000 (about $11.5 million in today's money) from the Hudson's Bay Company. Now called the Northwest Territories (NWT), the land was only sparsely populated, mostly by Plains First Nations and several thousand Métis (may-*tee*), a racial blend of Cree, Ojibwe or Saulteaux and French-Canadian or Scottish fur traders, who spoke French as their main language. Their biggest settlement was the Red River Colony around Fort Garry (today's Winnipeg).

The Canadian government immediately clashed with the Métis people over land-use rights, causing the latter to form a provisional government led by the charismatic Louis Riel. He sent the Ottawa-appointed governor packing and, in November 1869, seized control of Upper Fort Garry, thereby forcing Ottawa to the negotiating table. However, with his delegation already en route, Riel impulsively executed a Canadian prisoner he was holding at the fort. Although the murder caused widespread uproar in Canada, the government was so keen to bring the west into the fold it agreed to most of Riel's demands, including special language and religious protections for the Métis. As a result, the then-pint-sized province of Manitoba was carved out of the NWT and entered the dominion in July 1870. Macdonald sent troops after Riel but he narrowly managed to escape to the USA. He was formally exiled for five years in 1875.

British Columbia (BC), created in 1866 by merging the colonies of New Caledonia and Vancouver Island, was the next frontier. The discovery of gold along the Fraser River in 1858 and in the Cariboo region in 1862 had brought an enormous influx of settlers to such gold-mine boom towns as Williams Lake and Barkerville. Once the gold mines petered out, though, BC was plunged into poverty. In 1871 it joined the dominion in exchange

Delegates to the Charlottetown Conference in 1864 had to sleep on their steamships because the circus was in town and all the inns were fully booked.

Best Historic Neighborhoods

....

Gastown, Vancouver

....

Vieux-Québec, Québec

....

Old Montréal, Montréal

....

Downtown Halifax, Nova Scotia

....

Charlottetown, PEI

....

Downtown Niagara-on-the-Lake, Ontario

1931	1933	1942	early 1960s
The residential school system peaks. First Nations, Inuit and Métis children are removed from their communities and forced to attend schools (most operated by churches) far from home to 'assimilate.'	Three out of 10 people are out of work, as Canada feels the effects of the Great Depression. The prairies are especially hard hit by the drought-induced Dust Bowl.	Newfoundland becomes the only North American site directly attacked by German forces during WWII, when a U-boat launches a torpedo that strikes inland at Bell Island.	It's a time of change: the Quiet Revolution modernizes, secularizes and liberalizes Québec, while indigenous peoples are finally granted citizenship nationwide.

for the Canadian government assuming all its debt and promising to link
it with the east within 10 years via a transcontinental railroad.

The construction of the Canadian Pacific Railway is one of the most
impressive chapters in Canadian history. Macdonald rightly regarded the
railroad as crucial in unifying the country, spurring immigration and
stimulating business and manufacturing. It was a costly proposition,
made even more challenging by the rough and rugged terrain the tracks
had to traverse. To entice investors, the government offered major benefits, including vast land grants in western Canada. Workers drove the
final spike into the track at Craigellachie, BC, on November 7, 1885.

To bring law and order to the 'wild west,' the government created the
North-West Mounted Police (NWMP) in 1873, which later became the
Royal Canadian Mounted Police (RCMP). Nicknamed 'Mounties,' they still
serve as Canada's national police force today. Although they were effective,
the NWMP couldn't prevent trouble from brewing on the prairies, where
the Plains First Nations had been forced to sign various treaties relegating
them to reserves. Soon these groups began to challenge their status.

Meanwhile, many Métis had moved to Saskatchewan and settled
around Batoche. As in Manitoba, they quickly clashed with government
surveyors over land issues. In 1884, after their repeated appeals to Ottawa had been ignored, they coaxed Louis Riel out of exile to represent
their cause. Rebuffed, Riel responded the only way he knew: by forming
a provisional government and leading the Métis in revolt. Riel had the
backing of the Cree, but times had changed: with the railroad nearly
complete, government troops arrived within days. Riel surrendered in
May and was hanged for treason later that year.

Cutting Ties with England

Canada rang in the 20th century on a high note. Industrialization was in
full swing, prospectors had discovered gold in the Yukon, and Canadian
resources – from wheat to lumber – were increasingly in demand. In
addition, the new railroad opened the floodgates to immigration.

The Nova Scotia government maintains a website (http://titanic.gov.ns.ca) of all things *Titanic*, including a list of passengers buried in local graveyards and artifacts housed in local museums. The province played a vital role in the tragedy, as ships from Halifax were sent out to recover victims.

1961	1962	1967	1982
The kind and neighborly folks of Saskatchewan introduce the first universal health-care plan, an idea that soon spreads to the rest of Canada.	Canada becomes the third nation in space, after the Soviet Union and the USA, when it launches the *Alouette* satellite into the stratosphere.	The Great Canadian Oil Sands plant opens at Fort McMurray, Alberta, and starts pumping out black gold. It's reputed to hold more oil than all of Saudi Arabia.	Queen Elizabeth II signs the Canada Act, giving Canada complete sovereignty. However, she retains the right to keep her face on the money and to appoint a governor general.

Between 1885 and 1914 about 4.5 million people arrived in Canada. This included large groups of Americans and Eastern Europeans, especially Ukrainians, who went to work cultivating the prairies. Optimism reigned: a buoyant Prime Minister Wilfrid Laurier said 'The 19th century was the century of the United States. I think we can claim that it is Canada that shall fill the 20th century.' It was only natural that this new-found self-confidence would put the country on track to autonomy from Britain. The issue took on even greater urgency when WWI broke out in 1914.

Canada – as a member of the British Empire – found itself automatically drawn into the conflict. In the war's first years, more than 300,000 volunteers went off to European battlefields. As the war dragged on and thousands returned in coffins, recruitment ground to a halt. The gov-

QUÉBEC'S SEPARATIST MOVEMENT

Québec's separatist movement began in earnest in 1968, when René Lévesque founded the sovereigntist Parti Québecois (PQ).

The issue intensified quickly. In October 1970, the radical Front de Libération du Québec (FLQ; Québec Liberation Front) kidnapped Québec's labor minister Pierre Laporte and a British trade official in an attempt to force the independence issue. Prime Minister Pierre Trudeau declared a state of emergency and called in the army to protect government officials. Two weeks later, Laporte's body was found in the trunk of a car. The murder discredited the FLQ in the eyes of many erstwhile supporters and the movement quickly faded.

Still, Lévesque's PQ won the 1976 Québec provincial election and quickly pushed through a bill that made French the province's sole official language. His 1980 referendum on secession, however, was resoundingly defeated, with almost 60% voting *non*. The issue was put on the back burner for much of the 1980s.

Lévesque's successor, Robert Bourassa, agreed to a constitution-led solution – but only if Québec was recognized as a 'distinct society' with special rights. In 1987 Prime Minister Brian Mulroney unveiled an accord that met most of Québec's demands. To take effect, the so-called Meech Lake Accord needed to be ratified by all 10 provinces and both houses of parliament by 1990. Dissenting premiers in three provinces eventually pledged their support but, incredibly, the accord collapsed when a single member of Manitoba's legislature refused to sign.

Relations between Anglos and Francophones hit new lows, and support for independence was rekindled. Only one year after returning to power in 1994, the PQ, under Premier Lucien Bouchard, launched a second referendum. This was a cliff-hanger: Québecois decided by 52,000 votes – a majority of less than 1% – to remain within Canada.

The issue lost some of its luster in the years that followed, though the PQ remained a viable force. In 2012, the PQ won 32% of the vote in Québec's elections, enough to form a minority government. But by 2013, the party was losing ground again after its controversial proposal that public workers be banned from wearing religious headgear.

1990	1992	1998	1999
The Oka Crisis, a violent standoff between the government and a band of Mohawk activists near Montréal, is sparked by a land claim over a golf course. One person dies.	The government imposes the Atlantic cod moratorium, and thousands of fisherfolk lose their livelihoods. The ban was supposed to be lifted within a few years, but depleted stocks never rebounded.	The Canadian government apologizes to indigenous peoples, saying 'attitudes of racial and cultural superiority led to a suppression of Indigenous culture and values.' It vows not to repeat past mistakes.	Nunavut, Canada's newest province, is chiseled from the icy eastern Arctic, giving about one-fifth of Canadian soil to the 28,000 Inuit who live there.

ernment, intent on replenishing its depleted forces, introduced the draft in 1917. This was very unpopular, especially among French Canadians. Animosity toward Ottawa was already at a high since the government had abolished bilingual schools in Manitoba and restricted the use of French in Ontario's schools. The conscription issue fanned the flames of nationalism. Thousands of Québecois took to the streets in protest.

By the time the guns of WWI fell silent in 1918, most Canadians were fed up with sending their sons and husbands to fight in distant wars for Britain. Under the government of William Lyon Mackenzie King, Canada began asserting its independence. Mackenzie King made it clear that Britain could no longer automatically draw upon the Canadian military, started signing treaties without British approval, and sent a Canadian ambassador to Washington. This forcefulness led to the Statute of Westminster, passed by the British Parliament in 1931. The statute formalized the independence of Canada and other Commonwealth nations, although Britain retained the right to pass amendments to those countries' constitutions.

That right remained on the books until the 1982 Canada Act. Today, Canada is a constitutional monarchy with a parliament consisting of an appointed upper house, or Senate, and an elected lower house, the House of Commons. The British monarch remains Canada's head of state, although this is predominantly a ceremonial role and does not diminish the country's sovereignty. Within Canada, the appointed governor general is the monarch's representative.

It was Newfoundland's Beothuk people and their ceremonially ocher-coated faces who were dubbed 'red men' by arriving Europeans, a name soon applied to all of North America's indigenous groups. Tragically, the Beothuk died out (some argue were exterminated) by 1829.

Modern-Day Canada

The period after WWII brought another wave of economic expansion and immigration, especially from Europe.

Newfoundland finally joined Canada in 1949. Joey Smallwood, the politician who persuaded the island to sign up, claimed it would bring economic prosperity. Once he became Newfoundland's premier, he helped this prosperity along by forcing a resettlement program upon citizens. People living in small, isolated fishing communities (aka outports) were strongly encouraged to pack up and move inland where the government could deliver schools, health care and other services more economically. One method for 'encouraging' villagers was to cut ferry services to their communities, thus making them inaccessible since there were no roads.

The only province truly left behind during the 1950s boom years was Québec. For a quarter century, it remained in the grip of ultra-conservative Maurice Duplessis and his Union Nationale party, with support from the Catholic Church and various business interests. Only after Duplessis' death did the province finally start getting up to speed during the 'Quiet Revolution' of the 1960s. Advances included expanding the public sector, investing in public education and nationalizing the provincial hydroelectric

More than one million Canadians served in the armed forces during WWII from a population of approximately 11.5 million; 42,000 died.

2003	2005	2006	2010
Canada becomes the world's third-largest diamond producer (after Botswana and Russia), thanks to riches discovered in the NWT. The baubles spark a modern-day boom similar to gold-rush times.	Canada legalizes gay marriage throughout the country. Most provinces and territories had permitted it, but now hold-outs Alberta, PEI, Nunavut and the NWT join the ranks.	The census shows almost 20% of the population is foreign-born – the highest proportion in 75 years. Immigrants from Asia (including the Middle East) make up the largest proportion of newcomers.	Vancouver and Whistler showcase the west coast's gorgeous mountains and cool urbanity when they host the 2010 Winter Olympics. Team Canada wins the gold medal for hockey.

companies. Still, progress wasn't swift enough for radical nationalists who claimed independence was the only way to ensure Francophone rights. Québec has spent the ensuing years flirting with separatism.

In 1960, Canada's indigenous peoples were finally granted Canadian citizenship. Issues involving land rights and discrimination played out in the decades that followed. In 1990, indigenous frustration reached boiling point with the Oka Crisis, a standoff between the government and a group of Mohawk activists near Montréal. The conflict was set off by a land claim: the town of Oka was planning to expand a golf course onto land that the Mohawk considered sacred. A 78-day clash ensued, and one policeman died of gunshot wounds. The event shook Canada.

In the aftermath of Oka, the Royal Commission on Aboriginal Peoples issued a report recommending a complete overhaul of relations between the government and indigenous peoples. In 1998 the Ministry of Indian and Northern Affairs issued an official Statement of Reconciliation that accepted responsibility for past injustices toward indigenous peoples. In 1999, the government resolved its biggest land claim, creating the new territory of Nunavut and handing it over to the Inuit people who have long lived in the northern region. Recent disputes have focused on re-naming landmarks, such as Mt Douglas near Victoria, BC, which indigenous people want returned to its original name of Pkols.

In 1985, Canada became the first country in the world to pass a national multicultural act. Today, more than 20% of Canada's population is foreign-born. BC has a long history of welcoming Japanese, Chinese and South Asian immigrants. The prairie provinces have traditionally been the destination of large numbers of Ukrainians, and Ontario, which has sizable Caribbean and Russian populations, is also home to 60% of Canada's Muslims.

The new millennium has been kind to Canada. The loonie took off around 2003 – thanks to the oil, diamonds and other natural resources fueling the economy – and tolerance marches onward, with marijuana and gay marriage both legalized. The country showed off its abundant assets to the world when it successfully hosted the 2010 Winter Olympics in Vancouver.

In many ways, Canada's domestic challenges in the 21st century reflect the planet's wider battles: coping with the COVID-19 pandemic; the side-effects of climate change (seen most dramatically in forest fires), the over-dependence on oil and its economic fall-out (most marked in Alberta); and the notion that, despite the country's success in cementing a stable multicultural society, Canada is still dealing with the ghosts of a less tolerant past, particularly with regard to its indigenous people.

In *Canadian History for Dummies*, best-selling author Will Ferguson uses his irreverent, opinionated and energetic style to take you on an entertaining cruise through his country's wild and wacky past.

Canadian Inventions

Foghorn (1854)

Basketball (1892)

Insulin (1922)

Peanut butter (1884)

Egg carton (1911)

IMAX (1967)

Telephone (1874)

2013	2018	2019	2021
Calgary is hit by epic floods; four people die and 100,000 others are forced from their homes. It's the costliest natural disaster in Canadian history.	Anti-independence Coalition Avenir Québec (Coalition for Québec's Future) party wins a landslide victory in the Québec assembly, gaining 74 of the 125 seats.	After a closely fought General Election, incumbent Prime Minister Justin Trudeau hangs onto power and forms a minority government.	The remains of up to 1000 indigenous children are found at the sites of several former residential schools in Western Canada.

Indigenous Cultures

Canada's original inhabitants began living on the land more than 15,000 years ago. The term 'indigenous' refers to the descendants of these earliest residents, which now comprise three groups: First Nations (those of North American Indian descent), Métis (those with 'mixed blood' ancestry) and Inuit (those in the Arctic). Together they make up 4.9% of Canada's total population. The growing popularity of indigenous tourism is an indicator of native people's determination to retain or regain their traditional cultural roots.

The People

First Nations

This broad term applies to all indigenous groups except the Métis and Inuit. Almost 978,000 First Nations people live in Canada (about 3% of the total population), comprising more than 600 communities (sometimes called bands). British Columbia (BC) is home to the most First Nations (198 groups), while Ontario is second (126 groups).

Pacific

Historically, the people along the Pacific Coast built cedar-plank houses and carved elaborate totem poles and canoes. The potlatch, a ritual feast where the host gives away lavish gifts and possessions, is a renowned facet of many local cultures. The Canadian government banned the practice from 1885 to 1951 for being 'uncivilized.'

The Haida of Haida Gwaii, a group of islands off BC's northern shore, are perhaps the region's best-known First Nations group. Their artistic traditions are extraordinary, and they're famed for their wood carvings, totem poles and stylized prints of animals. Many other groups along the coast have similar art forms.

Plains

The Plains First Nations, which traditionally included the Sioux, Cree and Blackfoot, occupied the prairies from Lake Winnipeg to the Rocky Mountain foothills. Primarily buffalo hunters, they cunningly killed their prey by driving them over cliffs, such as at Head-Smashed-In Buffalo Jump in southern Alberta.

The Plains today still have a strong First Nations (and Métis) presence. Winnipeg has the largest number of First Nations people in Canada, with Edmonton not far behind. In Regina, First Nations University of Canada (www.fnuniv.ca) is the only First Nations–run institution of higher learning in the country.

Great Lakes & St Lawrence River Area

Present-day southern Ontario and the area along the St Lawrence River are the time-honored home of the Iroquoian-speaking peoples, who were once divided into the Five Nations (including the Mohawk, Oneida and Seneca), the Huron, the Erie and the Neutral confederacies. Although often at war with one another, they were relatively modern societies who

Indigenous Peoples

....

Pacific: Haida, Tsimshian, Tlingit, Salisan, Nuu-chah-nulth

....

Plains: Sioux, Cree, Blackfoot

....

Great Lakes/St Lawrence: Ojibwe, Huron, Iroquois, Mohawk, Oneida, Onondaga, Cayuga, Seneca

....

Maritimes: Mi'kmaq, Maliseet

....

Québec, Labrador: Innu

....

Northern Ontario, Québec, Manitoba, Saskatchewan: Cree

....

Yukon, Northwest Territories: Dene, Gwich'in

....

Arctic: Inuit

lived in large farming communities, built sturdy longhouses and traded with other indigenous groups.

Today Manitoulin Island, floating in Lake Huron, preserves Ojibwe culture through its several reserves, where visitors can attend powwows and participate in other cultural tourism opportunities with local tour guides.

Maritime Provinces

The Mi'kmaq and Maliseets are the main First Nations in the Maritimes. Traditionally they fished the shores in summer, and moved inland to hunt moose and caribou in winter.

In New Brunswick, the Maliseets (renowned basket-makers) live in the upper St John River valley in the west, while the Mi'kmaq live to the east. In Nova Scotia, the Mi'kmaq live in 14 communities, mostly around Bras d'Or Lake on Cape Breton and near Truro. A small group also lives on Prince Edward Island (PEI).

The Maritimes have experienced a revival of traditional song and dance, language programs, and healing and ritual ceremonies. Public powwows often take place, especially around Truro.

Northeastern Québec & Labrador

The Innu are the long-time inhabitants of the cold boreal forest stretching across the north of Québec and Labrador. The Innu are often confused with the Inuit, but they are not related. Rather, two First Nations – the Naskapi and the Montagnais – make up the Innu. In the past, they were fairly nomadic, and survived by hunting caribou and moose for food and skins.

About 80% of Innu live in Québec, with 20% in Labrador.

Northern Ontario, Manitoba & Saskatchewan

The Cree dominate this chilly landscape. As one of Canada's largest First Nations, they also extend west into the Plains and east into Québec. There's a well-known reserve in Ontario at Moose Factory (a former Hudson Bay fur-trading post), which built the hemisphere's first indigenous eco-lodge. Many Cree also live in polar-bear epicenter Churchill, Manitoba, where they make up about one-third of the local population; it's not uncommon to hear people speaking Cree in Churchill. The Cree have a reputation for being gifted healers.

Yukon & Northwest Territories

The Dene were the first people to settle in what is now the Northwest Territories. Today many live in Yellowknife, as well as villages throughout the Mackenzie Delta, west into the Yukon and Alaska, east toward Nunavut and south into the prairies. Traditionally they're hunters, fishers and trappers and known for their birch-bark basket weaving.

The Gwich'in First Nations people live further north and rely on caribou for a major part of their diet and lifestyle. They've actively protested drilling in the Arctic National Wildlife Refuge, saying it will deplete the

Indigenous Population Percentages

Nunavut *86%*

Northwest Territories *51%*

Yukon Territory *23%*

Manitoba *18%*

Saskatchewan *16%*

Newfoundland & Labrador *9%*

Alberta *6.5%*

British Columbia *6%*

Ontario *3%*

Urban Indigenous Populations

Winnipeg *92,810*

Edmonton *76,205*

Vancouver *61,455*

Toronto *46,315*

Saskatoon *31,350*

Montréal *34,745*

Regina *21,650*

INDIGENOUS MEDIA

First Nations Drum (www.firstnationsdrum.com) National newspaper.

CBC Indigenous (www.cbc.ca/news/indigenous) The broadcaster's online page devoted to indigenous news and culture, with links to regional programming in native languages.

Aboriginal Peoples Television Network (www.aptn.ca) National cable/satellite network that produces and airs indigenous programming.

caribou herd there that they depend on for food. The economy of their communities is based mostly on hunting and fishing.

Métis

Métis is the French word for 'mixed blood.' Historically, the term was applied to the children of French fur traders and Cree women in the prairies, and English and Scottish traders and Dene women in the north. Today the term is used broadly to describe people with mixed First Nations and European ancestry.

Métis account for about one-third of the overall indigenous population. They are largely based in western Canada. Winnipeg and Edmonton are the cities with the highest number of Métis.

Louis Riel (1844–1885) is the culture's most famous individual. He battled for the rights of Métis, who were often trampled during Canada's westward expansion. Riel led two resistance movements against the government, the last at Batoche, Saskatchewan, in 1885. He was caught and convicted of treason, though today he's considered a hero by most Canadians.

Unlike First Nations people, Métis were never placed on reserves.

Inuit

The Inuit are indigenous to Arctic Canada. Today they number 65,025 (4% of the overall indigenous population) and are spread throughout four Arctic regions: Nunavut, the Inuvialuit area in the Northwest Territories, Nunavik (northern Québec) and Nunatsiavut (Labrador). All in all, they cover one-third of Canada.

Inuit have never been placed on reserves as their frozen territory was not carved up in the same way. Instead they live in small communities: 38% of their villages have a population of fewer than 500 people. About 29% have between 500 and 999 people, while 33% have 1000 or more residents.

Traditionally, Inuit hunted whales and big game, traveled by kayak and dogsled, and spent winters in igloos. Snowmobiles and houses have replaced the sleds and igloos these days, but subsistence hunting is still a big part of the economy, as is traditional soapstone carving and printmaking.

The Inuit language is Inuktitut, a system of syllabics versus letters.

'Eskimo' was the term given to Inuit by European explorers. It's now rarely used in Canada. It derives from an Algonquian term meaning 'raw meat eaters,' and many find it offensive.

Recent History

Canada never experienced the all-out massacres that marred the European–Native American clashes in the USA. Nevertheless, Canada's indigenous population still suffered massive discrimination, loss of territory and serious civil rights violations throughout the country's history.

In 1993 Canada's biggest land claim was settled when Prime Minister Brian Mulroney signed into existence the new territory of Nunavut,

TOP MUSEUMS FOR INDIGENOUS ARTS

➡ Art Gallery of Ontario, Toronto

➡ Royal Alberta Museum, Edmonton

➡ Canadian Museum of History, Gatineau

➡ National Gallery, Ottawa

➡ UBC Museum of Anthropology, Vancouver

➡ Musée National des Beaux-Arts du Québec, Québec City

➡ Huron-Wendat Museum, Wendak

➡ Bill Reid Gallery of Northwest Coast Art, Vancouver

➡ McMichael Canadian Art Collection, Kleinburg

➡ Audain Art Museum, Whistler

➡ Winnipeg Art Gallery, Winnipeg

Top First Nations Cultural Centers

Museum of Northern British Columbia, BC

Blackfoot Crossing Historical Park, Alberta

Haida Heritage Centre, BC

Squamish Lil'wat Cultural Centre, BC

Dänojà Zho Centre, Yukon

Wanuskewin Heritage Park, Saskatchewan

Woodland Cultural Centre, Ontario

which took effect in 1999, giving the Inuit self-government after more than 20 years of negotiations. The 28,000 people of the far north now have control over about one-fifth of Canadian soil.

Following this, in 2010 the government formally apologized for the relocation of Inuit families to the high Arctic during the 1950s. At the time, the government promised the families a better life by moving to the region, but it didn't follow through in providing them with necessary supports such as adequate shelter and supplies. As a result, the families struggled greatly to survive. Many have argued the government moved the families not to help them, as stated, but to establish Canada's Arctic sovereignty during the Cold War. The apology was a follow-up to a 1996 settlement, in which the government agreed to pay $10 million into a trust fund to compensate the families.

Apology and compensation were also given to the 150,000 First Nations people, Métis and Inuit who were forced into Residential Schools from 1880 until the last closed in 1996. Taken from their homes and not allowed to speak their languages or practice their culture, the students were often subjected to abuse and severe mistreatment (more than 6000 died while attending). In 2007, the federal government granted a $1.9 billion compensation pack and an official apology the following year.

Indigenous Tourism

From learning to paddle a traditional canoe in Tofino, BC and sampling bannock bread in a Mi'kmaq cafe on PEI's Lennox Island to perusing the Great Northern Arts Festival in Inuvik in the Northwest Territories and attending a powwow on Manitoulin Island, there are many opportunities to immerse yourself in indigenous culture.

The further north in Canada you head, the more your travel dollars benefit indigenous communities. First Air (www.firstair.ca) and Air Creebec (www.aircreebec.ca) are indigenous-owned, as are Inns North hotels (www.innsnorth.com), located in several communities throughout Nunavut and the Northwest Territories.

A good website with links to indigenous tourism opportunities nationwide is run by the Indigenous Tourism Association of Canada (http://indigenouscanada.travel). Several provinces have their own organizations with the lowdown on the region's indigenous-owned businesses, including BC (www.indigenousbc.com), Ontario (http://indigenoustourismontario.ca), and Québec (www.quebecaboriginal.com).

Wildlife

On land, in the water and in the air, Canada is teeming with the kind of camera-worthy critters that make visitors wonder if they haven't stepped into a safari park by mistake. And when we say 'critters,' we're not talking small fry: this is the home of grizzlies, polar bears, wolverine, moose and bald eagles, and the coast offers perfect viewing spots for a roll call of huge whales. Extra camera batteries are heartily recommended.

Grizzly Bears & Black Bears

Grizzly bears – *Ursus arctos horribilis* to all you Latin scholars out there – are commonly found in the Rocky Mountain regions of British Columbia (BC) and Alberta, though they are now moving up further into the Arctic. Standing up to 3m tall, they have a distinctive shoulder hump and labrador-like snout. Solitary animals with no natural enemies (except humans), they enjoy crunching on elk, moose and caribou, but they're

Above American black bear and cubs, Jasper National Park (p607)

Best Bear-Spotting

Churchill,
Manitoba – polar
bears

Khutzeymateen
Grizzly Bear
Sanctuary, Prince
Rupert, BC –
grizzlies

Icefields Parkway,
Alberta – black
bears

Lake Louise
Gondola, Alberta –
grizzlies

Alaska Highway,
Yukon Territory –
grizzlies

usually content to fill their bellies with berries and, if available, fresh salmon. Keep in mind that you should never approach any bear. And in remote areas, be sure to travel in groups.

In 1994, coastal BC's Khutzeymateen Grizzly Bear Sanctuary (near the northern town of Prince Rupert) was officially designated with protected status. More than 50 grizzlies currently live on this 450-sq-km refuge. A few ecotour operators have permits for viewing the animals.

Just to confuse you, grizzlies can be brown or black, while their smaller, more prevalent relative, the black bear, can be brown. Canada is home to around half a million black bears and they're spread out across the country, except for Prince Edward Island, southern Alberta and southern Saskatchewan. In regions such as northern BC, as well as in Banff and Jasper National Parks, seeing black bears feasting on berries or dandelions as you drive past on the highway is surprisingly common.

The world's only white-colored black bears roam in northern BC. Born with a recessive gene, there are approximately 400 of these 'spirit bears' living in mostly coastal areas.

Polar Bears

Weighing less than a kilogram at birth, the fiercest member of the bear clan is not quite so cute when it grows up to be a hulking 600kg. But these mesmerizing animals still pack a huge visual punch for visitors. If your visit to Canada won't be complete until you've seen one, there's really only one place to go: Churchill, Manitoba, on the shores of Hudson Bay (late September to early November is the viewing season). About 900 of the planet's roughly 20,000 white-furred beasts prowl the tundra here.

Just remember: the carnivorous, ever-watchful predators are not cuddly cartoon critters. Unlike grizzlies and black bears, polar bears actively prey on people.

Moose

Canada's iconic shrub-nibbler, the moose is a massive member of the deer family that owes its popularity to its distinctively odd appearance: skinny legs supporting a humongous body and a cartoonish face that looks permanently inquisitive and clueless at the same time. And then there are the antlers: males grow a spectacular rack every summer, only to discard them come November.

Best Moose-Viewing

Northern
Peninsula,
Newfoundland

Cape Breton
Highlands National
Park, Nova Scotia

Algonquin
Provincial Park,
Ontario

Maligne Lake,
Jasper National
Park, Alberta

Kananaskis,
Alberta

Adding to their *Rocky and Bullwinkle Show* appeal, a moose can move at more than 50km/h and easily outswim two adults paddling a canoe – all on a vegetarian diet comprised mostly of tasty leaves and twigs.

You'll spot moose foraging for food near lakes, muskegs and streams, as well as in the forests of the western mountain ranges in the Rockies and the Yukon. Newfoundland is perhaps the moosiest place of all. In 1904, the province imported and released four beasts into the wild. They evidently enjoyed the good life of shrub-eating and hot sex, ultimately spawning the 120,000 inhabitants that now roam the woods.

During mating season (September), the males can become belligerent, as can a mother with her calves, so keep your distance.

Elk, Deer & Caribou

Moose are not the only animals that can exhibit a Mr Hyde personality change during rutting season. Usually placid, male elk have been known to charge vehicles in Jasper National Park, believing their reflection in the shiny paintwork to be a rival for their harem of eligible females. It's rare, though, and Jasper is generally one of the best places in Canada to see this large deer species wandering around attracting camera-toting travelers on the edge of town.

Moose on Cape Breton Island (p377)

White-tailed deer can be found anywhere from Nova Scotia's Cape Breton to the Northwest Territories' Great Slave Lake. Its bigger relative, the caribou, is unusual in that both males and females sport enormous antlers. Barren-ground caribou feed on lichen and spend most of the year on the tundra from Baffin Island to Alaska. Woodland caribou roam further south, with some of the biggest herds trekking across northern Québec and Labrador. These beasts, which have a reputation for not being especially smart, also show up in the mountain parks of BC, Alberta and Newfoundland, where many visitors see them. In 2009, the small herd in Banff National Park set off an avalanche that ultimately wiped out the population. Also known as reindeer, the caribou is on the Canadian 25-cent coin.

Whales

More than 22 species of whale and porpoise lurk offshore in Atlantic Canada, including superstars such as the humpback whale, which averages 15m and 36 tons; the North Atlantic right whale, the world's most endangered leviathan, with an estimated population of just 350; and the mighty blue whale, the largest animal on earth at 25m and around 100 tons. Then there's the the minke, which grows to 10m and often approaches boats, delighting passengers with acrobatics as it shows off. Whale-watching tours are very popular throughout the region: the Bay of Fundy and Cape Breton are both whale-watching hot spots.

You can also spot humpbacks and gray whales off the west coast, but it's the orca that dominates viewing here. Their aerodynamic bodies, signature black-and-white coloration and incredible speed (up to 40km/h) make them the Ferraris of the aquatic world, and their diet includes seals, belugas and other whales (hence the killer whale nickname). The waters around Vancouver Island, particularly in the Strait of Juan de Fuca, teem with orcas every summer. Whale-watching tours depart from points throughout the

Whale Hot Spots

Witless Bay, Newfoundland

Digby Neck, Nova Scotia

Victoria, BC

Tofino, BC

Tadoussac, Québec

Cabot Trail, Nova Scotia

Orca (killer whale)

region; Tofino and Victoria are particular hot spots for operators. It's also not uncommon to see them from the decks of the BC ferries.

Belugas glide in Arctic waters to the north. These ghostly white whales are one of the smallest members of the whale family, typically measuring no more than 4m and weighing about 1 ton. They are chatty fellows who squeak, chirp and peep while traveling in close-knit family pods. Churchill, Manitoba, is a good place to view them, as is Tadoussac, Québec (the only population outside the Arctic resides here).

Birds

Best Birding

Cape St Mary's, Newfoundland

Point Pelee National Park, Ontario

Witless Bay, Newfoundland

Grand Manan Island, New Brunswick

Brackendale, BC

Cap Tourmente National Wildlife Area, Québec

Iona Beach Regional Park, BC

Canada's wide skies are home to 462 bird species, with BC and Ontario boasting the greatest diversity. The most famous feathered resident is the common loon, Canada's national bird – if you don't spot one in the wild, you'll see it on the back of the $1 coin. Rivaling it in the ubiquity stakes are Canada geese, a hardy fowl that can fly up to 1000km per day and seems to have successfully colonized parks throughout the world.

The most visually arresting of Canada's birds are its eagles, especially the bald variety, whose wingspan can reach up to 2m. Good viewing sites include Brackendale, between Vancouver and Whistler in BC, where up to 4000 eagles nest in winter. Also train your binoculars on Bras d'Or Lake on Cape Breton Island, Nova Scotia and on Vancouver Island's southern and western shorelines.

Seabirds flock to Atlantic Canada to breed. Think razorbills, kittiwakes, Arctic terns, common murres and, yes, puffins. Everyone loves these cute little guys, a sort of waddling penguin-meets-parrot, with black-and-white feathers and an orange beak. They nest around Newfoundland in particular. The preeminent places to get feathered are New Brunswick's Grand Manan Island and Newfoundland's Witless Bay and Cape St Mary's (both on the Avalon Peninsula near St John's). The best time is May through August, before the birds fly away for the winter.

Cuisines of Canada

Canadian cuisine is nothing if not eclectic, a casserole of food cultures blended together from centuries of immigration. Poutine (French fries topped with gravy and cheese curds), Montréal-style bagels, salmon jerky and pierogi jostle for comfort-food attention. For something more refined, Montréal, Toronto and Vancouver have well-seasoned fine-dining scenes, while regions across the country have rediscovered the unique ingredients grown, foraged and produced on their doorsteps – bringing distinctive seafood, artisan cheeses and lip-smacking produce to menus.

Local Flavors
The Maritimes

If you're starting from the east, the main dish of the Maritime provinces is lobster – boiled in the pot and served with a little butter – and the best place to sample it is a community hall 'kitchen party' on Prince Edward Island. Dip into some chunky potato salad and hearty seafood chowder while waiting for your crustacean to arrive, but don't eat too much; you'll need room for the mountainous fruit pie coming your way afterwards.

Next door, Nova Scotia visitors should save their appetites for butter-soft Digby scallops and rustic Lunenberg sausage, while the favored meals of nearby Newfoundland and Labrador often combine rib-sticking dishes of cod cheeks and sweet snow crab. If you're feeling really ravenous, gnaw on a slice of seal-flipper pie – a dish you're unlikely to forget in a hurry.

Québec

Québec is the world's largest maple-syrup producer, processing an annual 6.5 million gallons of the syrup used on pancakes and as an ingredient in myriad other dishes. In this French-influenced province, fine food is a lifeblood for the locals, who happily sit down to lengthy dinners where the accompanying wine and conversation flow in equal measures.

The province's cosmopolitan Montréal has long claimed to be the nation's fine-dining capital, but there's an appreciation of food here at all levels that also includes hearty pea soups, exquisite cheeses and tasty pâtés sold at bustling markets. In addition, there's also that national dish, poutine, waiting to clog your arteries, plus smoked-meat deli sandwiches so large you'll have to dislocate your jaw to fit them in your mouth.

Ontario

Ontario – especially Toronto – is a microcosm of Canada's melting pot of cuisines. As in Québec, maple syrup is a super-sweet flavoring of choice here, and it's found in decadent desserts such as beavertails (fried, sugared dough) and on breakfast pancakes the size of Frisbees. Head south to the Niagara Peninsula wine region and you'll also discover restaurants fusing contemporary approaches and traditional local ingredients, such as fish from the Great Lakes.

Foodie Festivals

International Shellfish Festival (www.peishellfish.com), Prince Edward Island

Shediac Lobster Festival (www.shediaclobsterfestival.ca), New Brunswick

Feast Tofino (www.feasttofino.com), British Columbia

Ribfest (www.canadaslargestribfest.com), Ontario

Calgary Stampede (www.calgarystampede.com), Alberta

Barbecued teriyaki salmon dish

Nunavut

Far north from here, Nunavut in the Arctic Circle is Canada's newest territory, but it has a long history of Inuit food, offering a culinary adventure for extreme-cuisine travelers. Served in some restaurants (but more often in family homes), regional specialties include boiled seal, raw frozen char and *maktaaq* – whale skin cut into small pieces and swallowed whole.

Central Canada

In contrast, the central provinces of Manitoba, Saskatchewan and Alberta have their own deep-seated culinary ways. The latter, Canada's cowboy country, is the nation's beef capital – you'll find top-notch Alberta steak on menus at leading restaurants across the country. If you're offered 'prairie oysters' here, though, you might want to know (or maybe you'd prefer not to!) that they're bull's testicles, prepared in a variety of ways designed to take your mind off their origin. In the Rockies things get wilder – try elk, bison and even moose.

There's an old Eastern European influence over the border in Manitoba, where immigrant Ukrainians have added comfort food staples such as pierogi and thick, spicy sausages. Head next door to prairie-land Saskatchewan for dessert. The province's heaping fruit pies are its most striking culinary contribution, especially when prepared with tart Saskatoon berries.

British Columbia

In the far west, British Columbians have traditionally fed themselves from the sea and the fertile farmlands of the interior. Okanagan Valley peaches, cherries and blueberries – best purchased from seasonal roadside stands throughout the region – are the staple of many summer diets. But it's the seafood that attracts the lion's share of culinary fans. Tuck into succulent wild salmon, juicy Fanny Bay oysters and velvet-soft scallops and you may decide you've stumbled on foodie nirvana. There's also a large and ever-growing influence of Asian food in British Columbia's Lower Mainland.

Top City Dining

Ask anyone in Toronto, Montréal or Vancouver to name Canada's leading foodie city and they'll likely inform you that you've just found it. But while each of the big three claims to be at the top table when it comes to dining, their strengths are so diverse they're more accurately defined as complementary courses in one great meal.

Montreal

First dish on the table is Montréal, which was Canada's sole dine-out capital long before the upstarts threw off their fried-meat-and-mashed-potato shackles. Renowned for bringing North America's finest French-influenced cuisine to local palates, it hasn't given up its crown lightly. Chefs here are often treated like rock stars as they challenge old-world conventions with daring, even artistic, approaches – expect clever, fusion-esque gastronomy. You should also expect a great restaurant experience: Montréalers have a bacchanalian love for eating out, with lively rooms ranging from cozy old-town restaurants to the animated patios of Rue Prince Arthur and the sophisticated, often funky eateries of the Plateau.

Toronto

If Montréal serves as an ideal starter, that makes Toronto the main course – although that's a reflection of its recent elevation rather than its prominence. Fusion is also the default approach in Canada's largest city, although it's been taken even further here, with a wave of contemporary immigration adding modern influences from Asia to a foundation of European cuisines. With a bewildering 7000 restaurants to choose from, it can be a tough choice figuring out where to unleash your top-end dining budget. The best approach is to hit the neighborhoods: both the Financial District and Old Town are studded with classy, high-end joints.

Vancouver

And while that appears to make Vancouver the dessert, it could be argued this glass-towered, west-coast metropolis is the best of the bunch. In recent years, some of the country's most innovative chefs have set up shop here, inspired by the twin influences of an abundant local larder and Canada's most cosmopolitan population. Fusion is the starting point here in fine-dining districts such as Yaletown and Kitsilano. But there's also a high level of authenticity in the top-notch Asian dining: the best sushi bars and izakayas outside Japan jostle for attention with superb Vietnamese and Korean eateries.

Tasty Blogs

Dinner with Julie (www.dinnerwith julie.com)

Seasonal Ontario Food (www.sea sonalontariofood. blogspot.com)

Vancouver Foodster (www. vancouverfoodster. com)

Food Bloggers of Canada (www.food bloggersofcanada. com)

CUISINES OF CANADA TOP CITY DINING

Wine Regions

While many international visitors – especially those who think Canadians live under a permanent blanket of snow – are surprised to learn that wine is produced here, their suspicion is always tempered after a drink or two. Canada's wines have gained ever-greater kudos in recent years and, while their small-scale production and the industry dominance of other wine regions mean they will never be global market leaders, these wines could definitely hold their own in an international taste-off.

Regional Wine List

Depending on how thirsty you are, you're rarely too far from a wine region in Canada. Which means that most visitors can easily add a mini tasting tour to their visit if they'd like to meet a few producers and sample some intriguing local flavors. Here's a rundown of the best areas, including the magnum-sized larger regions and the thimble-sized smaller locales – why not stay all summer and visit them all?

Okanagan Valley, British Columbia

The rolling hills of this lakeside region are well worth the five-hour drive from Vancouver. Studded among the vine-striped slopes are more than 100 wineries enjoying a diverse climate that fosters both crisp whites and bold reds. With varietals including pinot noir, pinot gris, pinot blanc, merlot and chardonnay, there's a wine here to suit almost every palate. Most visitors base themselves in Kelowna, the Okanagan's wine capital, before fanning out to well-known blockbuster wineries, such as Mission Hill, Quail's Gate, Cedar Creek and Summerhill Pyramid Winery (yes, it has a pyramid). Many of them also have excellent restaurants.

Further south in the valley, the small town of Oliver has cunningly trademarked its slogan, 'Wine Capital of Canada,' and controversially registered the website www.winecapitalofcanada.com, much to the chagrin of its rivals. There are huge signs emphasizing the point at the entrance to town.

Find out more about British Columbia's wine regions and annual festivals and download free touring maps at www.winebc.com.

Niagara Peninsula, Ontario

This picture-perfect region of country inns and charming old towns offers more than 60 wineries and grows more than three quarters of Canada's grapes. Neatly divided between the low-lying Niagara-on-the-Lake area and the higher Niagara Escarpment, its complex mix of soils and climates – often likened to the Loire Valley – is ideal for chardonnay, riesling, pinot noir and cabernet-franc varietals. This is also the production center for Canadian ice wine, that potently sweet dessert libation. Although it's home to some of Canada's biggest wineries, including Inniskillin, Jackson-Triggs and Peller Estates, don't miss smaller pit stops such as Magnotta, Cave Spring Cellars and Tawse.

Grapevine at a vineyard on the Niagara Peninsula

Prince Edward County, Ontario

Proving that not all Ontario's wineries are clustered in Niagara, this comparatively new grape-growing region – located in the province's southeastern corner – is a charming alternative if you want to avoid the tour buses winding through the main wine area. A long-established fruit-growing district with generally lower temperatures than Niagara, cooler-climate wines are favored here, including chardonnay and pinot noir. The most intriguing wineries include Closson Chase, Black Prince Winery and Grange of Prince Edward. If your taste buds are piqued, consider checking out other Ontario wine regions such as Pelee Island and Lake Erie North Shore.

Eastern Townships, Québec

Starting around 80km southeast of Montréal, this idyllic farmland region is studded with quiet villages, leafy woodlands, crystal-clear lakes and winding country roads. A rising tide of wineries has joined the traditional farm operations here in recent years, with rieslings and chardonnays particularly suited to the area's cool climate and soil conditions. But it's the local ice wines, dessert wines and fruit wines that are the area's main specialties, so make sure you come with a sweet tooth. Wineries to perk up your taste buds here include Domaine Félibre, Vignoble de L'Orpailleur and Vignoble Le Cep d'Argent.

Montérégie, Québec

The dominant player in Québec's wider Eastern Townships, this bumpy and bucolic area is packed with vineyards and orchards (not to mention a surfeit of maple groves). As a major fruit-farming region – this is an

Find out more about Nova Scotia's wine region, including information on courses and festivals, at www. winesofnova scotia.ca. Explore Ontario further by downloading a free map and wine country visitor guide from http://wine country ontario.ca.

ideal spot to try ciders and flavor-packed fruit wines – growers here are happy to try just about any red or white varietal, but it's their rosés that are particularly memorable. Recommended wineries include Domaine St-Jacques, Les Petits Cailloux and Vignoble des Pins; and keep in mind that Québécois restaurants often encourage diners to bring their own bottles, so fill your car as you explore the region.

Wine Online

·····················

Wines of Canada (www.winesof canada.com)

John Schreiner on Wine (www. johnschreiner. blogspot.com)

·····················

Dr Vino (www. drvino.com)

Nova Scotia

Divided into six boutique wine-producing regions – from the warm shoreline of Northumberland Strait to the verdant Annapolis Valley – Nova Scotia's two-dozen wineries are mostly just a couple of hours' drive from Halifax. One of the world's coldest grape-growing areas, cool-climate whites are a staple here, including a unique varietal known as l'Acadie Blanc. Innovative sparkling wines are a Nova Scotia specialty and they tend to dominate the drops on offer at the province's popular stops, such as the excellent Benjamin Bridge Vineyards. Other highly recommended destinations include Gaspereau Vineyards, Jost Vineyards and Domaine de Grand Pré.

Wine Festivals

Canada is dripping with palate-pleasing wine events, which makes it especially important to check the dates of your trip: raising a few glasses with celebratory locals is one of the best ways to encounter the country.

If you're in British Columbia, it's hard to miss one of the Okanagan's three main festivals – see www.thewinefestivals.com for dates. If you prefer not to leave the big city, check out February's Vancouver International Wine Festival (www.vanwinefest.ca).

Across the country in Ontario, Niagara also stages more than one annual event to celebrate its winey wealth, including January's Niagara Icewine Festival and September's giant Niagara Grape and Wine Festival. For information, visit www.niagarawinefestival.com.

Québec-bound oenophiles should drop into the annual Montréal Passion Vin (www.montrealpassionvin.ca), a swish two-day charity fundraiser focused on unique and rare vintages. For regional food as well as wine, the Eastern Townships' Magog-Orford area hosts the multiday Fête des Vendanges (www.fetedesvendanges.com) in September.

Visitors to the east coast are not left out. Nova Scotia hosts the NSLC Festival of Wines (www.mynslc.com) in September.

Survival Guide

Directory A–Z

Accessible Travel

Canada is making progress when it comes to easing the everyday challenges facing people with disabilities, especially the mobility-impaired.

➜ Many public buildings, including museums, tourist offices, train stations, shopping malls and cinemas, have access ramps and/or lifts. Most public restrooms feature extra-wide stalls equipped with hand rails. Many pedestrian crossings have sloping curbs.

➜ Newer and recently remodeled hotels, especially chain hotels, have rooms with extra-wide doors and spacious bathrooms.

➜ Interpretive centers at national and provincial parks are usually accessible, and many parks have trails that can be navigated in wheelchairs.

➜ Car rental agencies offer hand-controlled vehicles and vans with wheelchair lifts at no additional charge, but you must reserve them well in advance.

➜ Download Lonely Planet's free Accessible Travel guides from https://shop.lonelyplanet.com/categories/accessible-travel.com.

➜ For accessible air, bus, rail and ferry transportation, check **Access to Travel** (www.accesstotravel.gc.ca),

the federal government's website. In general, most transportation agencies can accommodate people with disabilities if you make your needs known when booking.

Other organizations specializing in the needs of travelers with disabilities:

Mobility International (www.miusa.org) Advises travelers with disabilities on mobility issues and runs an educational exchange program.

Society for Accessible Travel & Hospitality (www.sath.org) Travelers with disabilities share tips and blogs.

Accommodations

Seasons

➜ Peak season is summer, basically June through August, when prices are highest.

➜ It's best to book ahead during summer, as well as during ski season at winter resorts, and during holidays and major events, as rooms can be scarce.

➜ Some properties close down altogether in the off-season.

Amenities

➜ At many budget properties (campgrounds, hostels, simple B&Bs) bathrooms are shared.

➜ Midrange accommodations, such as most B&Bs, inns (auberges in French), motels and some hotels, generally offer the best value for money. Expect a private bathroom, cable TV and, in some cases, free breakfast.

➜ Top-end accommodations offer an international standard of amenities, with fitness and business centers and on-site dining.

➜ Most properties offer in-room wi-fi. It's typically free in budget and midrange lodgings, while top-end hotels often charge a fee.

➜ Many smaller properties, especially B&Bs, ban smoking. Marriott and Westin hotels are 100% smoke-free. Other properties have rooms set aside for nonsmokers.

➜ Note that tobacco, cannabis and vaping are all considered 'smoking,' so do not plan on doing any in

PLAN YOUR STAY ONLINE

For more accommodations reviews by Lonely Planet authors, check out www.lonelyplanet.com. You'll find independent reviews, as well as recommendations on the best places to stay.

a nonsmoking room. At a minimum, you risk a (often hefty) fine.

➡ Air-conditioning is not a standard amenity at most budget and midrange places. If you want it, be sure to ask about it when you book.

Discounts

➡ In winter (or hotel off-seasons), prices can plummet by as much as 50%.

➡ Membership of the American Automobile Association (AAA), the American Association of Retired Persons (AARP) or other organizations also yields modest savings (usually 10%).

B&Bs

➡ Bed & Breakfast Online (http://m.bbcanada.com) is the main booking agency for properties nationwide.

➡ In Canada, B&Bs (gîtes in French) are essentially converted or purpose-built private homes whose owners live on-site. People who like privacy may find B&Bs too intimate, as walls are rarely soundproof and it's usual to mingle with your hosts and other guests.

➡ Standards vary widely, sometimes even within a single B&B. The cheapest rooms tend to be small, with few amenities and a shared bathroom. Nicer ones have added features such as a balcony, a fireplace and an en suite bathroom.

➡ Breakfast is always included in the rates (though it might be continental instead of a full cooked affair).

➡ Not all B&Bs accept children.

➡ Minimum stays (usually two nights) are common, and many B&Bs are only open seasonally.

Camping

➡ Canada is filled with campgrounds – some federal or provincial, others privately owned.

➡ The official season runs from May to September, but exact dates vary by location.

➡ Facilities vary widely. Backcountry sites offer little more than pit toilets and fire rings, and have no potable water. Unserviced (tent) campgrounds come with access to drinking water and a washroom with toilets and sometimes showers. The best-equipped sites feature flush toilets and hot showers, and water, electrical and sewer hookups for recreational vehicles (RVs).

➡ Private campgrounds sometimes cater only to trailers (caravans) and RVs, and may feature convenience stores, playgrounds and swimming pools. It is a good idea to phone ahead to make sure the size of sites and the services provided at a particular campground are suitable for your vehicle.

➡ Most government-run sites are available on a first-come, first-served basis and fill up quickly, especially in July and August. Several national parks participate in Parks Canada's **camping reservation program** (☏519-826-5391; http://reservation.pc.gc.ca; reservation fee online/call center $11/13.50), which is a convenient way to make sure you get a spot.

➡ Nightly camping fees in national and provincial parks range from $25 to $35 (a bit more for full-hookup sites); fire permits often cost a few dollars extra. Backcountry camping costs about $10 per night. Private campgrounds tend to be a bit pricier. British Columbia's parks, in particular, have seen a hefty rate increase in recent years.

➡ Some campgrounds remain open for maintenance year-round and may let you camp at a reduced rate in the off-season. This can be great in late autumn or early spring, when there's hardly a soul about. Winter camping, though, is only for the hardy.

Homestays

How do you feel about staying on the couch of a complete stranger? If it's not a problem, consider joining an organization that arranges homestays. The following groups charge no fees to become a member, and the stay itself is also free.

Couch Surfing (www.couchsurfing.org)

Hospitality Club (www.hospitalityclub.org)

Hostels

Canada has independent hostels as well as those affiliated with Hostelling International (HI). All have dorms ($25 to $40 per person on average), which can sleep from two to 10 people, and many have private rooms (from $70) for couples and families. Rooms in HI hostels are often gender-segregated. Nonmembers pay a surcharge of about $4 per night.

Bathrooms are usually shared, and facilities include

PRACTICALITIES

Newspapers The most widely available newspaper is the Toronto-based *Globe and Mail*. Other principal dailies are the *Montréal Gazette, Ottawa Citizen, Toronto Star* and *Vancouver Sun*. *Maclean's* is Canada's weekly news magazine.

Radio & TV The Canadian Broadcasting Corporation (CBC) is the dominant nationwide network for both radio and TV. The CTV Television Network is its major competition.

Smoking Banned in all restaurants, bars and other public venues nationwide. This includes tobacco, vaping and cannabis.

Weights & Measures Canada officially uses the metric system, but imperial measurements are used for many day-to-day purposes.

a kitchen, lockers, free wi-fi, internet access, a laundry room and a shared TV room. Many also include a free continental breakfast. Some hostels allow alcohol, others don't; smoking is prohibited.

Most hostels, especially those in the big cities, are open 24 hours a day. If they are not, ask if you can make special arrangements if you are arriving late.

Backpackers Hostels Canada (www.backpackers.ca) Independent hostels.

Hostelling International Canada (www.hihostels.ca)

Hostels.com (www.hostels.com) Includes independent and HI hostels.

Hotels & Motels

Most hotels are part of international chains, and the newer ones are designed for either the luxury market or businesspeople, with in-room cable TV and wi-fi. Many also have swimming pools and fitness and business centers. Rooms with two double or queen-sized beds sleep up to four people, although there is usually a small surcharge for the third and fourth people. Many places advertise 'kids stay free,' but sometimes you have to pay extra for a crib or a rollaway (portable bed).

In Canada, like the USA (both lands of the automobile), motels are ubiquitous. They dot the highways and cluster in groups on the outskirts of towns and cities. Although most motel rooms won't win any style awards, they're usually clean and comfortable and offer good value for travelers. Many regional motels remain typical mom-and-pop operations, but plenty of North American chains have also opened up across the country.

University Accommodations

In the lecture-free summer months, some universities and colleges rent beds in their student dormitories to travelers of all ages. Most rooms are quite basic, with rates ranging from $40 to $70 per night, depending on the city, and often including breakfast. Students can usually qualify for small discounts.

Customs Regulations

The Canada Border Services Agency (www.cbsa-asfc.gc.ca) website has the customs lowdown. A few regulations to note:

Alcohol You can bring in 1.5L of wine, 1.14L of liquor or 24 355mL beers duty-free.

Gifts You can bring in gifts totaling up to $60.

Money You can bring in/take out up to $10,000; larger amounts must be reported to customs.

Personal effects Camping gear, sports equipment, cameras, drones and laptop computers can be brought in without much trouble. Declaring these to customs as you cross the border might save you some hassle when you leave, especially if you'll be crossing the US–Canadian border multiple times.

Pets You must carry a signed and dated certificate from a veterinarian to prove your dog or cat has had a rabies shot in the past 36 months.

Prescription drugs You can bring in/take out a 90-day supply for personal use (though if you're taking it to the USA, know it's technically illegal, but usually overlooked for individuals).

Tobacco You can bring in 200 cigarettes, 50 cigars, 200g of tobacco and 200 tobacco sticks duty-free.

Cannabis Though legal for personal use in Canada, you cannot transport the drug across borders, either into or out of Canada.

Discount Cards

Discounts are commonly offered for seniors, children, families and people with disabilities, though no special cards are issued (you get the savings on-site when you pay). AAA and other automobile association members can also receive various travel-related discounts.

International Student Identity Card (www.isic.org) Provides students with discounts on travel insurance and admission to museums and other sights. There are also cards for those who are under 26 but not students, and for full-time teachers.

Parks Canada Discovery Pass (www.pc.gc.ca; adult/family $68/137) Provides access to more than 100 national parks and historic sites for a year. Can pay for itself in as few as seven visits; also provides quicker entry into sites. Note that there's no charge for kids under 18, and a 'family' can include up to seven people in a vehicle, even if they're unrelated.

Many cities have discount cards for local attractions, such as:

Montréal Museum Pass (www.museesmontreal.org; $75)

Ottawa Museums Passport (www.museumspassport.ca; $35)

Toronto CityPASS (www.citypass.com/toronto; adult/child $73/50)

Vanier Park ExplorePass (Vancouver; www.spacecentre.ca/explore-pass; adult/child $42.50/36.50)

Electricity

Type A
120V/60Hz

Type B
120V/60Hz

Embassies & Consulates

All countries have their embassies in Ottawa, including those listed here, and maintain consulates in such cities as Montréal, Vancouver, Calgary and Toronto. Contact the relevant embassy to find out which consulate is closest to you.

Australian High Commission (☑613-236-0841; www.canada.embassy.gov.au; Suite 1301, 50 O'Connor St)

British High Commission (☑613-237-1530; www.gov.uk/government/world/canada; 80 Elgin St)

French Embassy (☑613-789-1795; www.ambafrance-ca.org; 42 Sussex Dr)

German Embassy (☑613-232-1101; www.ottawa.diplo.de; 1 Waverley St)

Irish Embassy (☑613-233-6281; www.embassyofireland.ca; 130 Albert St, Suite 1105, 11th fl)

Italian Embassy (☑613-232-2401; www.ambottawa.esteri.it; 275 Slater St, 21st fl)

Japanese Embassy (☑613-241-8541; www.ca.emb-japan.go.jp; 255 Sussex Dr)

Mexican Embassy (☑613-787-5177; https://embamex.sre.gob.mx/canada/index.php/en; World Exchange Plaza, 45 O'Connor St, Suite 1000)

Netherlands Embassy (☑613-237-5031; www.netherlandsandyou.nl/your-country-and-the-netherlands/canada; Suite 2020, 350 Albert St)

New Zealand High Commission (☑613-238-5991; www.nzembassy.com/canada; Suite 1401, 150 Elgin St)

US Embassy (☑613-688-5335; https://ca.usembassy.gov; 490 Sussex Dr)

Etiquette

Canadians are a fairly relaxed crowd and don't offend easily; however, some rules of etiquette do apply.

Politeness Canadians value their pleases and thank-yous. Bumping into someone without apologizing or not thanking someone for holding the door will earned shocked looks.

Patriotism Commenting that Canadians and Americans aren't much different is considered highly offensive.

Language In French-speaking areas, always attempt to speak French before English (regardless of how poor your French is).

Lining up While Canadians usually tut rather than speak out, jumping ahead in line can cause a full-blown argument.

Exiting buildings In winter, when someone is about to enter the place you're exiting, let them in first; they're much colder than you are.

Removing dirty footwear In winter remove your shoes or boots and place them in the tray (plateau) provided. Winter footwear is covered in grit, mud and salt, which can soil and harm carpets and wooden floors.

Food & Drink

It's worth booking ahead for popular places, especially on the weekend – which, in the Canadian restaurant world (p843), includes Thursdays. Most cafes and budget restaurants don't accept reservations.

Restaurants Diverse selection, from steakhouses to vegan raw-food joints. Many are family-friendly and casual; some are not.

Cafes Often serve sandwiches, soups and baked goods, as well as coffee, and offer counter service.

Bistros Small and often classy, with home-cooked food.

Delis Choose your food, have it wrapped and take it with you. Usually have sandwiches and wraps.

Diners Brunches and lunches, sometimes served 24 hours; often family-friendly.

Pubs Home-cooked fish and chips, burgers and salads.

Health

Before You Go
HEALTH INSURANCE

Canada offers some of the finest health care in the world. However, unless you are a Canadian citizen, it can be prohibitively expensive. It's essential to purchase travel health insurance if your regular policy doesn't cover you when you're abroad. Check www.lonelyplanet.com/travel-insurance for supplemental insurance information.

Bring medications you may need clearly labeled in their original containers. A signed, dated letter from your physician that describes your medical conditions and medications, including generic names, is also a good idea.

MEDICAL CHECKLIST

➜ acetaminophen (eg Tylenol) or aspirin

➜ anti-inflammatory drugs (eg ibuprofen)

➜ antihistamines (for hay fever and allergic reactions)

➜ antibacterial ointment (eg Neosporin) for cuts and abrasions

➜ steroid cream or cortisone (for poison ivy and other allergic rashes)

➜ bandages, gauze, gauze rolls

➜ adhesive or paper tape

➜ safety pins, tweezers

➜ thermometer

➜ insect repellent

➜ permethrin-containing insect spray for clothing, tents and bed nets

➜ sunblock

➜ motion-sickness medication

RECOMMENDED VACCINATIONS

No special vaccines are required or recommended for travel to Canada. All travelers should be up to date on routine immunizations.

USEFUL WEBSITES

Government travel-health websites are available for Australia (www.smarttraveller.gov.au), the United Kingdom (www.nhs.uk/healthcareabroad) and the United States (www.cdc.gov/travel).

MD Travel Health (http://redplanet.travel/mdtravelhealth) General health resources.

Public Health Agency of Canada (www.phac-aspc.gc.ca) Canadian health resources.

World Health Organization (www.who.int) General health resources.

In Canada
AVAILABILITY & COST OF HEALTH CARE

Medical services are widely available. For emergencies, the best bet is to find the nearest hospital and go to its emergency room. If the problem isn't urgent, call a nearby hospital and ask for a referral to a local physician, which is usually cheaper than a trip to the emergency room (where costs can be $500 or so before any treatment).

Pharmacies are abundant, but prescriptions can be expensive without insurance. However, Americans may find Canadian prescription drugs to be cheaper than drugs at home. You're allowed to take out a 90-day supply for personal use (it's technically illegal to bring them into the USA, but often overlooked for individuals).

ENVIRONMENTAL HAZARDS

Cold exposure This can be a significant problem, especially in the northern regions. Keep all body surfaces covered, including the head and neck. Watch out for the 'Umbles' – stumbles, mumbles, fumbles and grumbles – which are signs of impending hypothermia.

Heat exhaustion Dehydration is the main contributor. Symptoms include feeling weak, headache, nausea and sweaty skin. Lay the victim flat with their legs raised; apply cool, wet cloths to the skin; and rehydrate.

INFECTIOUS DISEASES

Most are acquired by mosquito or tick bites, or environmental exposure. The Public Health Agency of Canada (www.phac-aspc.gc.ca) has details on all listed below.

Giardiasis Intestinal infection. Avoid drinking directly from lakes, ponds, streams and rivers.

Lyme Disease Occurs mostly in southern Canada. Transmitted by deer ticks in late spring and summer. Perform a tick check after you've been outdoors.

Severe Acute Respiratory Syndrome (SARS) At the time of writing, SARS had been brought under control in Canada.

West Nile Virus Mosquito-transmitted in late summer and early fall. Prevent by keeping covered (wear long sleeves, long pants, hats, and shoes rather than sandals) and applying a good insect repellent, preferably one containing DEET, to exposed skin and clothing.

TAP WATER

Tap water in Canada is potable and generally safe to drink; however, many people prefer bottled.

Insurance

Make sure you have adequate travel insurance, whatever the length of your trip. At a minimum, you need coverage for medical emergencies and treatment, including hospital stays and an emergency flight home.

Medical treatment for non-Canadians is very expensive.

Also consider insurance for luggage theft or loss. If you already have a homeowners or renters policy, check what it will cover and get only supplemental insurance to protect the rest. If you have prepaid a large portion of your vacation, trip cancellation insurance is worthwhile.

Check out the following providers:

Insure.com (www.insure.com)

Travel Guard (www.travelguard.com)

Travelex (www.travelexinsurance.com)

Internet Access

➡ It's easy to find internet access. Libraries and community agencies in practically every town provide free wi-fi and computers for public use. The only downsides are that usage time is limited (usually 30 minutes), and some facilities have erratic hours.

➡ Internet cafes are scarce, limited to the main tourist areas in only certain towns; access generally starts around $2 per hour.

➡ Wi-fi is widely available. Most lodgings have it (in-room, with good speed), as do many restaurants, bars and Tim Hortons coffee shops.

Legal Matters
Drugs & Alcohol

➡ The blood-alcohol limit is 0.08% federally, but can be 0.06% or lower provincially, and driving cars, motorcycles, boats and snowmobiles while drunk or high is a criminal offense. If you are caught, you may face stiff fines, license suspension and possibly prison.

➡ Consuming alcohol anywhere other than at a residence or licensed premises is also a no-no, which puts parks, beaches and the rest of the great outdoors off-limits.

➡ Avoid illegal drugs, as penalties may entail heavy fines, possible jail time and a criminal record. While cannabis for personal and medical use is legal, driving while high is certainly not, and police can stop you and request a breathalyzer even if you're behind the wheel of a parked vehicle.

Police

If you are arrested or charged with an offense, you have the right to keep your mouth shut and to hire any lawyer you wish (contact your embassy for a referral, if necessary).

If you cannot afford one, ask to be represented by public counsel. There is a presumption of innocence.

LGBTIQ+ Travelers

Canada is tolerant when it comes to gays and lesbians, though this outlook is more common in the big cities than in rural areas. Same-sex marriage is legal throughout the country (Canada is one of 29 nations worldwide that permit this, up from 21 a few years ago).

Montréal, Toronto and Vancouver are by far Canada's gayest cities, each with a humming nightlife scene, publications and lots of associations and support groups. All have sizeable Pride celebrations, too, which attract big crowds.

Attitudes remain more conservative in the northern regions. Throughout Nunavut, and to a lesser extent in the indigenous communities of the Northwest Territories, there are some retrogressive attitudes toward homosexuality. The Yukon, in contrast, is more like British Columbia, with a live-and-let-live West Coast attitude.

The following are good resources for LGBTIQ+ travel; they include Canadian information, though not all are exclusive to the region:

Damron (www.damron.com) Publishes several travel guides, including *Men's Travel Guide*, *Women's Traveller* and *Damron Accommodations;* gay-friendly tour operators are listed on the website, too.

Out Traveler (www.outtraveler.com) Gay travel magazine.

Purple Roofs (www.purpleroofs.com) Website listing queer accommodations, travel agencies and tours worldwide.

Queer Events (www.queerevents.ca) A general resource for finding events to attend that are aimed at the gay community.

TAX RATES BY PROVINCE

Percentages represent federal and provincial taxes combined:

PROVINCES & TERRITORIES	TAX RATE
Alberta	5%
British Columbia	12%
Manitoba	13%
New Brunswick	15%
Newfoundland & Labrador	15%
Northwest Territories	5%
Nova Scotia	15%
Nunavut	5%
Ontario	13%
Prince Edward Island	14%
Québec	15%
Saskatchewan	10%
Yukon Territory	5%

Xtra (www.xtra.ca) Source for gay and lesbian news nationwide.

Maps

➡ Most tourist offices distribute free provincial road maps.

➡ For extended hikes or multiday backcountry treks, it's a good idea to carry a topographic map. The best are the series of 1:50,000 scale maps published by the government's Centre for Topographic Information. These are sold by bookstores and parks around the country.

➡ You can also download and print maps from GeoBase (http://geogratis.gc.ca).

Money

➡ All prices quoted are in Canadian dollars ($), unless stated otherwise.

➡ Canadian coins come in 5¢ (nickel), 10¢ (dime), 25¢ (quarter), $1 (loonie) and $2 (toonie or twoonie) denominations. The gold-colored loonie features the loon, a common Canadian waterbird, while the two-toned toonie is decorated with a polar bear. Canada phased out its 1¢ (penny) coin in 2012.

➡ Paper currency comes in $5 (blue), $10 (purple), $20 (green) and $50 (red) denominations. The $100 (brown) and larger bills are less common. The newest bills in circulation – which have enhanced security features – are actually a polymer-based material; they feel more like plastic than paper.

➡ For changing money in the larger cities, currency exchange offices may offer better conditions than banks.

ATMs

➡ Many grocery and convenience stores, airports and bus, train and ferry stations have ATMs. Most are linked to international networks, the most common being Cirrus, Plus, Star and Maestro.

➡ Most ATMs also spit out cash if you use a major credit card. This method tends to be more expensive because, in addition to a service fee, you'll be charged interest immediately (in other words, there's no interest-free period as with purchases). For exact fees, check with your own bank or credit card company.

➡ Visitors heading to Canada's truly remote regions won't find an abundance of ATMs, so it is wise to cash up beforehand.

➡ Scotiabank, common throughout Canada, is part of the Global ATM Alliance. If your home bank is a member, fees may be less if you withdraw from Scotiabank ATMs.

Cash

Most Canadians don't carry large amounts of cash for everyday use, relying instead on credit and debit cards. Still, carrying some cash, say $100 or less, comes in handy when making small purchases. In some cases, cash is necessary to pay for rural B&Bs and shuttle vans; inquire in advance to avoid surprises. Shops and businesses rarely accept personal checks.

Credit Cards

Major credit cards such as MasterCard, Visa and American Express are widely accepted in Canada, except in remote, rural communities, where cash is king. You'll find it difficult or impossible to rent a car, book a room or order tickets over the phone without having a piece of plastic. Note that some credit card companies charge a 'transaction fee' (around 3% of whatever you purchased); check with your provider to avoid surprises. If you are given an option to pay in your home currency, it is usually better to NOT accept, as they charge a higher interest rate for the point-of-sale transaction.

For lost or stolen cards, these numbers operate 24 hours:

American Express (☑800-869-3016; www.americanexpress.com)

MasterCard (☎800-307-7309; www.mastercard.com)

Visa (☎416-367-8472; www. visa.com)

Taxes & Refunds

Canada's federal goods and services tax (GST), aka the 'gouge and screw' or 'grab and steal' tax, adds 5% to just about every transaction. Most provinces also charge a provincial sales tax (PST) on top of it. Several provinces have combined the GST and PST into a harmonized sales tax (HST). Expect to pay 10% to 15% in most cases.

You might be eligible for a rebate on some of the taxes. If you've booked your accommodations in conjunction with a rental car, plane ticket or other service (ie if it all appears on the same bill from a 'tour operator'), you should be eligible to get 50% of the tax refunded from your accommodations. Fill out the GST/HST Refund Application for Tour Packages form, available from the Canada Revenue Agency (www.cra-arc.gc.ca).

Tipping

Tipping is a standard practice. Generally you can expect to tip:

Restaurant waitstaff 15% to 20%

Bar staff $1 per drink

Hotel bellhop $1 to $2 per bag

Hotel room cleaners From $2 per day (depending on room size and messiness)

Taxis 10% to 15%

Opening Hours

Opening hours vary throughout the year. We've provided high-season opening hours; hours will generally decrease in the shoulder and low seasons.

Banks 10am–5pm Monday to Friday; some open 9am–noon Saturday

Restaurants breakfast 8–11am, lunch 11:30am–2:30pm Monday to Friday, dinner 5–9:30pm daily; some open for brunch 8am–1pm Saturday and Sunday

Bars 5pm–2am daily

Clubs 9pm–2am Wednesday to Saturday

Shops 10am–6pm Monday to Saturday, noon–5pm Sunday; some open to 8pm or 9pm Thursday and/or Friday

Supermarkets 9am–8pm; some open 24 hours

Post

➡ Canada's national postal service, Canada Post/Postes Canada (www.canadapost. ca), is neither quick nor cheap, but it is reliable. Stamps are available at post offices, drugstores, convenience stores and hotels.

➡ Standard 1st-class airmail letters or postcards up to 30g cost 90¢ within Canada, $1.27 to the US and $2.65 to all other destinations.

➡ Travelers often find they have to pay high duties on items sent to them while in Canada, so beware.

Public Holidays

Canada observes 10 national public holidays and more at the provincial level. Banks, schools and government offices close on these days.

National Holidays

New Year's Day January 1

Good Friday March or April

Easter Monday March or April

Victoria Day Monday before May 25; called National Patriots Day in Québec

Canada Day July 1; called Memorial Day in Newfoundland

Labour Day First Monday of September

Thanksgiving Second Monday of October

Remembrance Day November 11

Christmas Day December 25

Boxing Day December 26

Provincial Holidays

Some provinces observe local holidays, with Newfoundland leading the pack.

Family Day Third Monday of February in Alberta, Ontario, Saskatchewan, Manitoba and British Columbia; known as Louis Riel Day in Manitoba

POSTAL ABBREVIATIONS

PROVINCES & TERRITORIES	ABBREVIATION
Alberta	AB
British Columbia	BC
Manitoba	MB
New Brunswick	NB
Newfoundland & Labrador	NL
Northwest Territories	NT
Nova Scotia	NS
Nunavut	NU
Ontario	ON
Prince Edward Island	PE
Québec	QC
Saskatchewan	SK
Yukon Territory	YT

St Patrick's Day Monday nearest to March 17

St George's Day Monday nearest to April 23

National Day Monday nearest to June 24 in Newfoundland; June 24 in Québec (aka St-Jean Baptiste Day)

Orangemen's Day Monday nearest to July 12 in Newfoundland

Civic Holiday First Monday of August everywhere except Newfoundland, Québec and Yukon Territory

Discovery Day Third Monday of August in Yukon Territory

School Holidays

Kids break for summer holidays in late June and don't return to school until early September. University students get even more time off, usually from May to early or mid-September. Most people take their big annual vacation during these months.

Safe Travel

Canada is one of the safest countries in the world. Pickpocketing and muggings are rare, especially if you take common sense precautions. Panhandling is common, but usually not dangerous or aggressive.

➡ Stay in your car at all times when photographing wildlife.

➡ Drink spiking is rare but solo travelers should be cautious.

➡ With the exception of cannabis, recreational drug use in Canada is illegal, including magic mushrooms, and police can stop you any time you're behind the wheel.

➡ Forest fires, though rare, are a possible threat and should be treated seriously, as they can shift and turn quickly into unexpected areas.

Telephone

Canada's phone system is extensive and landlines reach most places; however, cell service can be spotty. Truly remote areas may not have any phone service at all.

Cell Phones

➡ If you have an unlocked GSM phone, you should be able to buy a SIM card from local providers such as Telus (www.telus.com), Rogers (www.rogers.com) or Bell (www.bell.ca). Bell has the best data coverage.

➡ US residents can often upgrade their domestic cell phone plan to extend to Canada. Verizon (www.verizonwireless.com) provides good results.

➡ Reception is poor and often nonexistent in rural areas no matter who your service provider is. Some companies' plans do not reach all parts of Canada, so check coverage maps prior to purchase.

➡ SIM cards that work for a set period, such as seven, 14, 20 or 30 days, can be purchased online, often with United States and Canada voice, SMS and data bundled together.

Domestic & International Dialling

➡ Canadian phone numbers consist of a three-digit area code followed by a seven-digit local number. In many parts of Canada, you must dial all 10 digits preceded by 1, even if you're calling across the street. In other parts of the country, when you're calling within the same area code, you can dial the seven-digit number only, but this is slowly changing.

➡ For direct international calls, dial 011 + country code + area code + local phone number. The country code for Canada is 1 (the same as for the USA, although international rates still apply for all calls made between the two countries).

➡ Toll-free numbers begin with 800, 877, 866, 855, 844 or 833 and must be preceded by 1. Some of these numbers are good throughout Canada and the USA, others only work within Canada, and some work in just one province.

Emergency Numbers

Dial 911. This is *not* the emergency number in the Northwest Territories, which is usually the regional three-digit code and then 2222 for fire, or 1111 for police.

Public Phones

Coin-operated public pay phones are fewer than previously, but still out there. Local calls cost 50¢; many phones also accept prepaid phonecards and credit cards. Dialing the operator (0) or directory assistance (411 for local calls, 1 + area code + 555-1212 for long-distance calls) is free of charge from public phones; it may incur a charge from private phones.

Phonecards

➡ Prepaid phonecards usually offer the best per-minute rates for long-distance and international calling.

➡ Cards come in denominations of $5, $10 or $20 and are widely sold in drugstores, supermarkets and convenience stores.

➡ Beware of cards with hidden charges, such as 'activation fees' or a per-call connection fee.

➡ A surcharge ranging from 30¢ to 85¢ for calls made from public pay phones is common.

Time

➡ Canada spans six of the world's 24 time zones. The Eastern zone in Newfoundland is unusual in that it's only 30 minutes different from the adjacent zone. The time difference from coast to coast is 4½ hours.

➡ Canada observes daylight saving time, which comes into effect on the second

Sunday in March, when clocks are put forward one hour, and ends on the first Sunday in November. Saskatchewan and small pockets of Québec, Ontario and British Columbia are the only areas that do not switch to daylight saving time.

➡ In Québec especially, times for shop hours, train schedules, film screenings etc are usually indicated by the 24-hour clock.

Tourist Information

➡ The Canadian Tourism Commission (www.canada. travel) is loaded with general information, packages and links.

➡ All provincial tourist offices maintain comprehensive websites packed with information helpful in planning your trip. Staff also field telephone inquiries and, on request, will mail out free maps and directories about accommodations, attractions and events. Some offices can also help with making hotel, tour or other reservations.

➡ For detailed information about a specific area, contact the local tourist office, aka visitor center. Just about every city and town has at least a seasonal branch with helpful staff, racks of free pamphlets and books and maps for sale.

Provincial Tourist Offices

Newfoundland & Labrador Tourism (www.newfoundland labrador.com)

Northwest Territories Tourism (www.spectacularnwt.com)

Nunavut Tourism (www. nunavuttourism.com)

Ontario Tourism (www.ontario travel.net)

Prince Edward Island Tourism (www.tourismpei.com)

Tourism British Columbia (www.hellobc.com)

Tourism New Brunswick (www. tourismnewbrunswick.ca)

Tourism Nova Scotia (www. novascotia.com)

Tourism Saskatchewan (www. tourismsaskatchewan.com)

Tourisme Québec (www.quebec original.com/en)

Travel Alberta (www.travel alberta.com)

Travel Manitoba (www.travel manitoba.com)

Yukon Department of Tourism (www.travelyukon.com)

Visas

Currently, visas are not required for citizens of 46 countries – including most EU members, Australia and New Zealand – for visits of up to six months.

To find out if you need an Electronic Travel Authorisation (eTA) or are required to apply for a formal visa, go to www.cic.gc.ca/english/visit/visas.asp.

Visitor visas – aka Temporary Resident Visas (TRVs) – can now be applied for online at: www.cic.gc.ca/english/information/applications/visa.asp. Single-entry TRVs ($100) are usually valid for a maximum stay of six months from the date of your arrival in Canada. In most cases your biometric data (such as fingerprints) will be taken. Note that you don't need a Canadian multiple-entry TRV for repeated entries into Canada from the USA, unless you have visited a third country.

A separate visa is required for all nationalities if you plan to study or work in Canada.

Visiting the USA

Admission requirements are subject to rapid change, especially with COVID-19. The US State Department (http://travel.state.gov) has the latest information; you can also check with a US consulate in your home country. See p862 for info on border crossings.

Under the US visa-waiver program, visas are not required for citizens of 38 countries – including most EU members, Australia and New Zealand – for visits of up to 90 days (no extensions allowed), as long as you can present a machine-readable passport and are approved under the Electronic System for Travel Authorization (www.cbp.gov/esta). Note that you must register at least 72 hours before arrival with an e-passport, and there's a $14 fee for processing and authorization.

Canadians do not need visas to enter the USA, though they do need a passport or document approved by the Western Hemisphere Travel Initiative (http://www.cbp.gov/travel/us-citizens/western-hemisphere-travel-initiative). Citizens of all other countries need to apply for a US visa in their home country before arriving in Canada.

All foreign visitors (except Canadians) must pay a US$6 processing fee when entering at land borders.

Volunteering

Volunteering provides the opportunity to interact with local folks and the land in ways you never would just passing through. Many organizations charge a fee, which varies depending on the program's length and the type of food and lodging it provides. The fees usually do not cover travel to Canada. Groups that use volunteers:

Churchill Northern Studies Centre (http://churchillscience.ca) Volunteer for six hours per day (anything from stringing wires to cleaning) and get free room and board at this center for polar bear and other wildlife research.

Earthwatch (www.earthwatch.org) Help scientists track whales off the coast of British Columbia, track moose and deer in Nova Scotia, and monitor climate change in Churchill, Manitoba or the Mackenzie Mountains of the Northwest Territories. Trips last from seven to 14 days and cost from $2250 to $5050.

Volunteers for Peace (www.vfp.org) Offers tutoring stints in indigenous communities in Canada's far north, as well as projects in Québec.

World-Wide Opportunities on Organic Farms (www.wwoof.ca) Work on an organic farm, usually in exchange for free room and board; check the website for locations throughout Canada.

Women Travelers

Canada is generally a safe place for women to travel, even alone and even in the cities. Simply use the same common sense as you would at home.

In bars and nightclubs, solo women are likely to attract a lot of attention, but

if you don't want company, most men will respect a firm 'no, thank you.' If you feel threatened, protesting loudly will often make the offender slink away – or will at least spur other people to come to your defense. Note that carrying mace or pepper spray is illegal in Canada.

Physical attacks are unlikely, but if you are assaulted, call the police immediately – dial 911 except in the Northwest Territories (p858) – or contact a rape crisis center. A complete list is available from the **Canadian Association of Sexual Assault Centres** (www.casac.ca).

Resources for women travelers include:

Her Own Way (www.travel.gc.ca/travelling/publications/her-own-way) Published by the Canadian government for Canadian travelers, but contains a great deal of general advice.

Journeywoman (www.journeywoman.com) Travel links and tips for women with a section on Canada.

Work
Permits

In almost all cases, you need a valid work permit to work in Canada. Obtaining one may be difficult, as employment opportunities go to Canadians first. Before you can even apply, you'll need a specific job offer from an employer, who in turn must have been granted permission from the government to give the position to a foreign national. Applications must be filed

at a visa office of a Canadian embassy or consulate in your home country. Some jobs are exempt from the permit requirement. For full details, check with Citizenship & Immigration Canada (www.cic.gc.ca).

Employers hiring temporary service workers (for hotels, bars, restaurants and resorts) and construction, farm or forestry workers sometimes don't ask for a permit. If you get caught, however, you can kiss Canada goodbye.

Finding Work

Students aged 18 to 30 from more than a dozen countries, including the USA, UK, Australia, New Zealand, Ireland and South Africa, are eligible to apply for a spot in the Student Work Abroad Program (www.swap.ca). If successful, you get a six-to-12-month, nonextendable visa that allows you to work anywhere in Canada in any job you can get. Most 'Swappers' find work in the service industry as waiters or bartenders.

Even if you're not a student, you may be able to spend up to a year in Canada on a 'working holiday program' with International Experience Canada (www.canada.ca). The Canadian government has an arrangement with several countries for people aged 18 to 35 to come over and get a job; check the website for participants. The Canadian embassy in each country runs the program, but basically there are quotas and spaces are filled on a first-come, first-served basis.

Transportation

GETTING THERE & AWAY

Flights, cars and tours can be booked online at www.lonely-planet.com/bookings.

Entering the Country

Visitors to Canada must hold a valid passport with at least six months remaining before its expiration. Visitors from visa-exempt countries (with the exception of the US) are required to purchase an Electronic Travel Authorization (eTA; $7), similar to the USA's ESTA visa waiver, before departing their home country. Visitors from non-visa-waiver countries must apply for the appropriate visa prior to arriving in Canada.

Note that questioning may be more intense at land border crossings and your car may be searched.

For updates (particularly regarding land border-crossing rules), check the websites for the **US State Department** (http://travel.state.gov) and **Citizenship & Immigration Canada** (www.cic.gc.ca).

Passport

Most international visitors require a passport to enter Canada. US citizens at land and sea borders have other options, such as an enhanced driver's license, permanent resident card or NEXUS card. See **Canada Border Services Agency** (www.cbsa-asfc.gc.ca) for approved identification documents.

Air

Toronto is far and away Canada's busiest airport, followed by Vancouver. The international gateways you're most likely to use:

Calgary (Calgary International Airport; www.yyc.com)

Edmonton (Edmonton International Airport; http://flyeia.com)

Halifax (Halifax Stanfield International Airport; http://halifaxstanfield.ca)

Montréal (Montréal Trudeau International Airport; www.admtl.com)

Ottawa (Ottawa International Airport; http://yow.ca)

St John's (St John's International Airport; http://stjohnsairport.com)

Toronto (Toronto Pearson International Airport; www.torontopearson.com)

Vancouver (Vancouver International Airport; www.yvr.ca)

Winnipeg (Winnipeg International Airport; www.waa.ca)

The national flagship carrier **Air Canada** (www.aircanada.com) is considered one of the world's safest airlines. All major global airlines fly to Canada. Other companies

CLIMATE CHANGE & TRAVEL

Every form of transport that relies on carbon-based fuel generates CO_2, the main cause of human-induced climate change. Modern travel is dependent on aeroplanes, which might use less fuel per kilometer per person than most cars but travel much greater distances. The altitude at which aircraft emit gases (including CO_2) and particles also contributes to their climate change impact. Many websites offer 'carbon calculators' that allow people to estimate the carbon emissions generated by their journey and, for those who wish to do so, to offset the impact of the greenhouse gases emitted with contributions to portfolios of climate-friendly initiatives throughout the world. Lonely Planet offsets the carbon footprint of all staff and author travel.

based in the country and serving international destinations include:

WestJet (www.westjet.com) Calgary-based low-cost carrier serving destinations throughout Canada as well as across the US and Caribbean.

Porter Airlines (www.flyporter. com) Flies around eastern Canada and to US cities, including Boston, Chicago, Washington, DC, and New York.

Air Transat (www.airtransat. com) Charter airline from major Canadian cities to holiday destinations (ie southern USA and Caribbean in winter, Europe in summer).

Land
Border Crossings

There are around 25 official border crossings along the US–Canadian border, from New Brunswick to British Columbia. Borders were closed due to COVID-19 but were poised to reopen in late 2021 to fully vaccinated travelers. Check the website of the **Canadian Border Services Agency** (www. cbsa-asfc.gc.ca), which also shows current wait times at each border.

In general, waits rarely exceed 30 minutes, except during the summer peak, and on Friday and Sunday after-

noons, especially on holiday weekends. Some entry points are especially busy:

➡ Windsor, Ontario, to Detroit, Michigan

➡ Fort Erie, Ontario, to Buffalo, New York

➡ Niagara Falls, Ontario, to Niagara Falls, New York

➡ St Bernard de Lacolle, Québec to Rouse's Point / Champlain, New York

➡ Surrey, British Columbia, to Blaine, Washington

Organize your Canadian visa or Electronic Travel Authorization (eTA; www.cic.gc.ca/english/visit/eta-start.asp) in advance. When returning to the USA, check the website for the **US Department for Homeland Security** (http://bwt.cbp.gov) for border wait times.

All foreign visitors (except Canadians) must pay a $6 processing fee when entering the USA by land.

Bus

Greyhound Canada stopped operating all domestic services permanently in mid-2021, but the US **Greyhound** (www.greyhound.com) planned to continue to run services from Toronto to New York and Buffalo, Montreal to New York and Boston and Vancouver to Seattle. Most

international buses have free wi-fi on board. Other notable international bus companies (with free wi-fi) include:

Megabus (www.megabus.com) Runs between Toronto and US cities, including New York City, Philadelphia and Washington, DC. Tickets can only be purchased online.

Quick Coach (www.quickcoach. com) Runs between Seattle and Vancouver; typically a bit quicker than Greyhound.

Car & Motorcycle

The highway system of the continental USA connects directly with the Canadian highway system at numerous points along the border. These Canadian highways then meet up with the east–west Trans-Canada Hwy further north. Between the Yukon Territory and Alaska, the main routes are the Alaska, Klondike and Haines Hwys.

If you're driving into Canada, you'll need the vehicle's registration papers, proof of liability insurance and your home driver's license. Cars rented in the USA can usually be driven into Canada and back, but make sure your rental agreement says so. If you're driving a car registered in someone else's name, bring a letter from the owner authorizing use of the vehicle in Canada.

TRAIN ROUTES & FARES

ROUTE	DURATION (HR)	FREQUENCY (DAILY)	FARE (US$)
New York–Toronto (*Maple Leaf*)	13¾	1	$131
New York–Montréal (*Adirondack*)	12	1	$70
Seattle–Vancouver (*Cascades*)	4	2	$44

GREYHOUND BUS ROUTES & FARES

ROUTE	DURATION (HR)	FREQUENCY (DAILY)	FARE (C$)
Boston–Montréal	7-9	6	$75
New York–Montréal	9-10	6-11	$86
Seattle–Vancouver	4½	6	$46

Train

Amtrak (www.amtrak.com) and **VIA Rail Canada** (www. viarail.ca) run three routes between the USA and Canada: two in the east and one in the west. Customs inspections happen at the border, not upon boarding.

Sea

Various ferry services on the coasts connect the USA and Canada:

➡ Bar Harbor, Maine, to Yarmouth, NS: **Bay Ferries Limited** (www.ferries.ca/thecat)

➡ Eastport, Maine, to Deer Island, NB: **East Coast Ferries** (www.eastcoastferriesltd.com)

➡ Seattle, WA, to Victoria, BC: **Victoria Clipper** (www.clippervacations.com)

➡ Ketchikan, Alaska, to Prince Rupert, BC: **Alaska Marine Highway System** (www.ferryalaska.com)

➡ Bella Bella, BC, to Prince Rupert, BC: **BC Ferries** (www.bcferries.com)

➡ Sandusky, Ohio, to Pelee Island, ON: **Pelee Island Transportation Service** (www.ontarioferries.com)

➡ Port Angeles, WA, to Victoria, BC: **Black Ball Ferry** (www.cohoferry.com)

➡ Anacortes, WA, to Sidney, BC; **Washington State Ferries** (www.wsdot.wa.gov/ferries)

GETTING AROUND

Air

As well as Air Canada, the Canadian aviation arena includes many independent regional and local airlines, which tend to focus on small, remote regions, mostly in the North. Depending on the destination, fares in such

noncompetitive markets can be high.

Air Canada (☑888-247-2262; www.aircanada.com) Operates the largest domestic-flight network in the country, serving some 150 destinations nationwide.

Air Creebec (☑800-567-6567; www.aircreebec.ca) Serves northern Québec and Ontario, including Chisasibi and Chibougamau, from Montréal and other cities.

Air Inuit (☑800-361-2965; www.airinuit.com) Flies from Montréal to all 14 Inuit communities in Nunavik (northern Québec), including Kuujjuaq and Puvirnituq.

Air North (☑toll free 800-661-0407; www.flyairnorth.com) Flies from the Yukon to British Columbia, Alberta, Northwest Territories and Alaska.

Air St-Pierre (☑709-726-9700; www.airsaintpierre.com) Flies from eastern Canada to the French territories off Newfoundland's coast.

Air Tindi (☑867-669-8260; www.airtindi.com) Serves the Northwest Territories' North Slave region.

Aklak Air (☑867-777-3555; www.aklakair.ca) Serves the Northwest Territories' Mackenzie Delta.

Bearskin Airlines (☑800-465-2327; www.bearskinairlines.com) Serves destinations throughout Ontario and eastern Manitoba.

Calm Air (☑800-839-2256; www.calmair.com) Flights throughout Manitoba and Nunavut.

Canadian North (☑800-661-1505; www.canadiannorth.com) Flights to, from and within the Northwest Territories and Nunavut.

Central Mountain Air (☑888-865-8585; www.flycma.com) Destinations throughout British Columbia and Alberta.

First Air (☑800-267-1247; www.firstair.ca) Flies from Ottawa, Montréal, Winnipeg and

Edmonton to 24 Arctic destinations, including Iqaluit.

Harbour Air (☑604-274-1277; www.harbourair.com) Seaplane service from the city of Vancouver to Vancouver Island, Gulf Islands and the Sunshine Coast.

Northwestern Air Lease (☑877-872-2216; http://nwal.ca) Flies in Alberta and the Northwest Territories.

North-Wright Air (☑867-587-2288; http://north-wrightairways.com) Serves the Northwest Territories' Mackenzie Valley.

Pacific Coastal Airlines (☑604-273-8666; www.pacific-coastal.com) Vancouver-based airline with service to many British Columbia locales.

PAL Airlines (☑800-563-2800; www.palairlines.ca) Serves Newfoundland and northern Québec from its base in St John's.

Porter Airlines (☑416-619-8622; www.flyporter.com) Turboprop planes from eastern Canadian cities to Toronto's convenient Billy Bishop City Airport downtown.

Seair Seaplanes (☑604-273-8900; www.seairseaplanes.com) Flies from Vancouver to Nanaimo and the Southern Gulf Islands in British Columbia.

Transwest Air (☑306-764-1404; www.transwestair.com) Service within Saskatchewan.

WestJet (☑toll free 888-937-8538; www.westjet.com) Calgary-based airline serving destinations throughout Canada and some locations in the US, Mexico, the Caribbean and Europe.

Air Passes

Star Alliance (www.staralliance.com) members can use their 'Round the World' trip planner to make up to 16 different flights at a discounted fare.

Air North has an **Arctic Circle Air Pass** (www.flyairnorth.com) for those traveling around the Yukon and Northwest Territories.

Bicycle

Much of Canada is great for cycling. Long-distance trips can be done entirely on quiet back roads, and many of the large cities (including Edmonton, Montréal, Ottawa, Toronto, Vancouver and Victoria) have designated bike routes.

➡ Cyclists must follow the same rules of the road as vehicles, but don't expect drivers to always respect your right of way.

➡ Helmets are mandatory for all cyclists in British Columbia, New Brunswick, Prince Edward Island and Nova Scotia, as well as for anyone under 18 in Alberta and Ontario.

➡ The **Better World Club** (www.betterworldclub. com) provides emergency roadside assistance. Membership costs $40 per year, plus a $12 enrollment fee; it entitles you to two free pickups, and transport to the nearest repair shop, or home, within a 50km radius of where you're picked up.

Transportation

By air Most airlines will carry bikes as checked luggage without charge on international flights, as long as they're in a box. On domestic flights they usually charge between $30 and $65. Always check details before you buy the ticket.

By train VIA Rail will transport your bicycle for $25, but only on trains offering checked-baggage service (which include all long-distance and many regional trains).

Rental

➡ Outfitters renting bicycles exist in most tourist towns.

➡ Rentals cost around $20 per day for touring bikes and $35 or more per day for mountain bikes. The price usually includes a helmet and lock.

➡ Most companies require a security deposit of $20 to $200.

Boat

Ferry services are extensive, especially throughout the Atlantic provinces and in British Columbia.

Walk-ons and cyclists should be able to get aboard at any time, but call ahead for vehicle reservations or if you require a cabin berth. This is especially important during summer peak season and holidays. Main operators:

Bay Ferries (☎877-762-7245; www.ferries.ca) Year-round service between Saint John, New Brunswick, and Digby, Nova Scotia.

BC Ferries (☎250-386-3431; www.bcferries.com) Huge passenger-ferry network with 25 routes and 47 ports of call, including Vancouver Island, the Gulf Islands, the Sechelt Peninsula along the Sunshine Coast and the islands of Haida Gwaii – all in British Columbia.

Coastal Transport (☎506-662-3724; www.coastaltransport. ca) Ferry from Blacks Harbour to Grand Manan in the Fundy Isles, New Brunswick.

CTMA Ferries (☎418-986-3278; www.ctma.ca/en) Daily ferries to Québec's Îles de la Madeleine from Souris, Prince Edward Island.

East Coast Ferries (☎506-747-2159; www.eastcoastferriesltd. com) Connects Deer Island to Campobello Island, both in the Fundy Isles, New Brunswick.

Labrador Marine (☎709 535 0811; www.labradormarine. com) Connects Newfoundland to Labrador.

Marine Atlantic (☎902-794-5254; www.marineatlantic.ca) Connects Port aux Basques and Argentia in Newfoundland with North Sydney, Nova Scotia.

Northumberland Ferries (☎902-566-3838; www.ferries. ca) Connects Wood Islands (PEI) and Caribou, Nova Scotia.

Ontario Ferries (☎800-265-3163; www.ontarioferries.com; adult/child/car $17/9/38; ☺May-late Oct) Connects Tobermory to South Baymouth (Manitoulin Island) and Pelee Island to Leamington, Kingsville and Sandusky.

Provincial Ferry Services (☎888-638-5454; www.tw.gov. nl.ca/ferryservices) Operates coastal ferries throughout Newfoundland.

Traversiers (☎toll free 877-787-7483; www.traversiers.com) Operates many of the ferries in Québec's St Lawrence regions.

Bus

Greyhound Canada stopped operations in 2021 and regional carriers have picked up the slack.

Buses are generally clean, comfortable and reliable. Amenities may include onboard toilets, air-conditioning (bring a sweater), reclining seats, free wi-fi and onboard movies. Smoking is not permitted. On long journeys, buses make meal stops every few hours, usually at highway service stations.

Autobus Maheux (☎888-797-0011; www.autobusmaheux.

LONG DISTANCE BUS FARES

ROUTE	DURATION (HR)	FARE (US$)
Vancouver–Calgary	3-15	$118
Montréal-Toronto	9	$17

Road Distances (km)

	Banff	Calgary	Edmonton	Halifax	Inuvik	Jasper	Montréal	Ottawa	Québec City	St John's	Toronto	Vancouver	Whitehorse	Winnipeg
Calgary	130													
Edmonton	410	290												
Halifax	4900	4810	4850											
Inuvik	3440	3515	3220	8110										
Jasper	280	415	370	5250	3150									
Montréal	3700	3550	3605	1240	6820	3950								
Ottawa	3450	3340	3410	1440	6620	3770	200							
Québec City	3900	3800	3880	1020	7060	4210	250							
St John's	6200	6100	6150	1480	9350	6480	2530	2730	2310					
Toronto	3400	3400	3470	1790	6680	3820	550	450	800	3090				
Vancouver	850	970	1160	5880	3630	790	4580	4350	4830	7130	4360			
Whitehorse	2210	2290	2010	6830	1220	1930	5620	5390	5840	8150	5450	2400		
Winnipeg	1450	1325	1330	3520	4550	1670	2280	2140	2520	4820	2220	2290	3340	
Yellowknife	1800	1790	1510	6340	3770	1590	5050	4900	5350	7620	4950	2370	2540	2800

These distances are approximate only.

qc.ca) Service from Montréal to Québec's northwest regions.

Coach Canada (☏705-748-6411; www.coachcanada.com) Scheduled service within Ontario and from Toronto to Montréal.

DRL Coachlines (☏709-263-2171; www.drl-lr.com) Service throughout Newfoundland.

Ebus (http://myebus.ca) Connects Vancouver, Kamloops and Kelowna.

Intercar (☏800-806-2167; http://intercar.ca) Connects Québec City, Montréal and Tadoussac, among other towns in Québec.

Limocar (☏819-562-8899; http://limocar.ca) Regional service in Québec.

Maritime Bus (☏800-575-1807; http://maritimebus.com) For New Brunswick, Prince Edward Island and Nova Scotia.

Megabus (www.megabus.com) Service between Toronto and Montréal via Kingston; tickets can only be purchased online.

Ontario Northland (☏705-472-4500; www.ontarionorthland.ca) Operates bus and train routes that service northern Ontario from Toronto.

Orléans Express (☏833-449-6444; www.orleansexpress.com) Service to eastern Québec.

Parkbus (☏800-928-7101; www.parkbus.ca) Runs from Toronto to Algonquin, Killarney and other Ontario parks.

Red Arrow (☏403-531-0350; http://redarrow.ca) Serves all the major cities in Alberta, with free wi-fi, snacks, drinks and plug-ins.

Skylynx (www.yvrskylynx.com) Several daily buses between Vancouver and Whistler.

Tofino Bus (☏250-725-2871; www.tofinobus.com) Connects all main population centers on Vancouver Island and also offers connections (via ferry) to Vancouver.

Reservations

Some companies, such as Megabus, take reservations online only. The earlier you buy a ticket online, the cheaper your fare.

Show up at least 30 to 45 minutes prior to departure.

Car & Motorcycle
Automobile Associations

Autoclub membership is a handy thing to have in Canada. The **Canadian Automobile Association** (www.caa.ca) offers services, including 24-hour emergency roadside assistance, to members of international affiliates, such as AAA in the USA, AA in the UK and ADAC in Germany. The club also offers trip-planning advice, free maps, travel-agency services and a range of discounts on hotels, car rentals etc.

The **Better World Club** (www.betterworldclub.com), which donates 1% of its annual revenue to environmental cleanup efforts, has emerged as an alternative. It offers service throughout the USA and Canada, and has a roadside-assistance program for bicycles.

Bringing Your Own Vehicle

There's minimal hassle driving into Canada from the USA, as long as you have your vehicle's registration papers, proof of liability insurance and your home driver's license.

Driver's Licenses

In most provinces, visitors can legally drive for up to three months with their home driver's license. In some, such as British Columbia, this is extended to six months.

If you're spending considerable time in Canada, think about getting an International Driving Permit (IDP), which is valid for one year. Your automobile association at home can issue one for a small fee. Always carry your home license together with the IDP.

Fuel

Gas is sold in liters. Prices are higher in remote areas, with Yellowknife usually setting the national record; drivers in Calgary typically pay the least for gas.

Fuel prices are usually lower in the USA, so fill up south of the border if that's an option.

Insurance

Canadian law requires liability insurance for all vehicles, to cover you for damage caused to property and people.

➡ The minimum requirement is $200,000 in all provinces except Québec, where it is $50,000.

➡ Americans traveling to Canada in their own car should ask their insurance company for a Nonresident Interprovince Motor Vehicle Liability Insurance Card (commonly known as a 'yellow card'), which is accepted as evidence of financial responsibility anywhere in Canada. Although not mandatory, it may come in handy in an accident.

➡ Car-rental agencies offer liability insurance. Collision Damage Waivers (CDW) reduce or eliminate the amount you'll have to reimburse the rental company if there's damage to the car itself. Some credit cards cover CDW for a certain rental period if you use the card to pay for the rental and decline the policy offered by the rental company. Always check with your card issuer to see what coverage it offers in Canada.

➡ Personal accident insurance (PAI) covers you and any passengers for medical costs incurred as a result of an accident. If your travel insurance or your health-insurance policy at home does this as well (and most do, but check), then this is one expense you can do without.

Rental

CAR

To rent a car in Canada you generally need to:

➡ be at least 25 years old (some companies will rent to drivers between the ages of 21 and 24 for an additional charge)

➡ hold a valid driver's license (an international one may be required if you're not from an English- or French-speaking country)

➡ have a major credit card. You should be able to get an economy-size vehicle for about $45 to $75 per day. Child safety seats are compulsory (reserve them when you book) and cost about $15 per day.

Major international car-rental companies usually have branches at airports, train stations and in city centers.

In Canada, on-the-spot rentals often are more expensive than pre-booked packages (ie cars booked with a flight or in advance).

Avis (☑800-230-4898; www. avis.com)

Budget (☑800-268-8900, French 800-268-8970; www. budget.com)

Dollar (☑800-800-5252; www. dollarcanada.ca)

Enterprise (☑844-307-8008; www.enterprise.ca)

Hertz (☑800-654-3131; www. hertz.com)

National (☑toll free 844-307-8014; www.nationalcar.ca)

Practicar (☑toll free 800-327-0116; www.practicar.ca) Often has lower rates. It's also affiliated with Backpackers Hostels Canada and Hostelling International.

Thrifty (☑800-334-1705; www. thriftycanada.ca)

CAR-SHARING

Car2Go (www.car2go.com) operates in Vancouver, Calgary, Montreal and Toronto. It costs $5 to join and then 41¢ per minute or $15 per hour to use a vehicle. You locate the cars with a smartphone app and then can park and leave them anywhere within the designated downtown zone.

MOTORCYCLE

Several companies offer motorcycle rentals and tours. A Harley Heritage Softail Classic costs about $210 per day, including liability insurance and 200km mileage. Some companies have minimum rental periods, which can be as much as seven days. Riding a hog is especially popular in British Columbia.

Cycle BC (☑604-709-5663; http://cyclebc.ca) Tours and rentals out of Victoria and Vancouver in British Columbia.

McScoots Motorcycle & Scooter Rentals (☑250-763-4668; www.mcscoots.com) Big selection of Harleys; also operates motorcycle tours. It's based in Kelowna, British Columbia.

RECREATIONAL VEHICLES

The RV market is biggest in the west, with specialized agencies in Calgary, Edmonton, Whitehorse and Vancouver. For summer travel, book as early as possible. The base cost is roughly $250 per day in high season for smaller vehicles, although insurance, fees and taxes add a hefty chunk to that. Diesel-fueled RVs have considerably lower running costs.

Canadream Campers (☑925-255-8383; www.canadream. com) Based in Calgary, with rentals (including one-way rentals) in eight cities, including Vancouver, Whitehorse, Toronto and Halifax.

Cruise Canada (☑403-291-4963; www.cruisecanada. com) Offers three sizes of RVs. Locations in Halifax, and in central and western Canada; offers one-way rentals.

Road Conditions & Hazards

Road conditions are generally good, but there are a few things to keep in mind:

➡ Fierce winters can leave potholes the size of landmine craters. Be prepared to swerve. Winter travel in general can be hazardous due to heavy snow and ice, which may cause roads and bridges to close periodically.
Transport Canada (☑613-990-2309; www.tc.gc.ca/en/transport-canada.html) provides links to road conditions and construction zones for each province.

➡ If you're driving in winter or in remote areas, make sure your vehicle is equipped with four-season radial or snow tires, and emergency supplies in case you're stranded.

➡ Distances between services can be long in sparsely populated areas, such as the Yukon, Newfoundland or northern

Québec, so top up your gas whenever possible.

➡ Moose, deer and elk are common on rural roadways, especially at night. There's no contest between a 534kg bull moose and a Subaru, so keep your eyes peeled.

➡ In some areas you can drive for hours without cell service, so plan carefully for emergencies.

Road Rules

➡ Canadians drive on the right-hand side of the road.

➡ Seat belt use is compulsory. Children who weigh less than 18kg must be strapped into child-booster seats, except infants, who must be in a rear-facing safety seat.

➡ Motorcyclists must wear helmets and drive with their headlights on.

➡ Distances and speed limits are posted in kilometers. The speed limit is generally 40km/h to 50km/h in cities and 90km/h to 110km/h outside town.

➡ Slow down to 60km/h when passing emergency vehicles (such as police cars and ambulances) stopped on the roadside with their lights flashing.

➡ Turning right at red lights after coming to a full stop is permitted in all provinces (except where road signs prohibit it, and on the island of Montréal, where it's always a no-no). There's a national propensity for running red lights, however, so don't assume 'right of way' at intersections.

➡ Driving while using a hand-held cell phone is illegal in Canada. Fines are hefty.

➡ Radar detectors are not allowed in most of Canada (Alberta, British Columbia and Saskatchewan are the exceptions). If you're caught driving with a radar detector, even one that isn't

being operated, you could receive a fine of $1000 and your device may be confiscated.

➡ The blood-alcohol limit for drivers is 0.08%, but provincial limits can be lower. Driving while drunk or high is a criminal offense.

Hitchhiking

Hitching is never entirely safe in any country and we don't recommend it. That said, in remote and rural areas in Canada it is not uncommon to see people thumbing for a ride.

➡ If you do decide to hitch or offer a ride, understand that you are taking a small but potentially serious risk. Remember that it's safer to travel in pairs and let someone know where you are planning to go.

➡ Hitchhiking is illegal on some highways (ie the 400-series roads in Ontario), as well as in the provinces of Nova Scotia and New Brunswick.

Ride-Sharing

Ride-share services link drivers and paying passengers headed in the same direction. **Kangaride** (www.kangaride. com) is a Québec City–based service that is rapidly expanding across Canada. It costs $7.50 per year for membership and $5 per ride (on top of what the driver charges).

Local Transportation

Bicycle

Cycling is a popular means of getting around during the warmer months, and many cities have hundreds of kilometers of dedicated bike paths. Bicycles typically can be taken on public transportation (although some cities have restrictions during peak travel times). All the major cities have shops renting bikes. Vancouver, Toronto and Montréal have bike-share programs.

Bus

Buses are the most common form of public transportation, and practically all towns have their own systems. Most are commuter-oriented, and offer only limited or no services in the evenings and on weekends.

Taxi

Most of the main cities have taxis and smaller towns have one or two. They are usually metered, with a flag-fall fee of roughly $3.50 and a per-kilometer charge of around $1.75. Drivers expect a tip of between 10% and 15%. Taxis can be flagged down or ordered by phone.

Train

Toronto and Montréal are the two Canadian cities with subway systems. Vancouver's version is mostly an above-ground monorail. Calgary, Edmonton and Ottawa have efficient light-rail systems. Route maps are posted in all stations.

Tours

Using tour companies is an easy way to get around this great big country.

Arctic Odysseys (☑20 6-325-1977; www.arcticodys-seys.com) Experience Arctic Canada up close on tours chasing the northern lights in the Northwest Territories, heli-skiing on Baffin Island or polar-bear spotting on Hudson Bay.

Backroads (☑510-527-1555; www.backroads.com) Guided cycling, walking and paddling tours in the Rockies, Nova Scotia and Québec.

Moose Travel Network (☑888-244-6673; http://moosebus.travel) Operates backpacker-type tours in small

buses covering British Columbia, Alberta and beyond.

Road Scholar (☑800-454-5768; www.roadscholar.org) This nonprofit organization offers study tours in nearly all provinces for active older adults, including train trips, cruises, and bus and walking tours.

Train

VIA Rail (☑514-871-6000; www.viarail.ca) operates most of Canada's intercity and transcontinental passenger trains, chugging over 14,000km of track. In some remote parts of the country, such as Churchill, Manitoba, trains provide the only overland access.

➡ Rail service is most efficient in the corridor between Québec City and Windsor, Ontario – particularly between Montréal and Toronto, the two major hubs.

➡ The rail network does not extend to Newfoundland, Prince Edward Island or the Northwest Territories.

➡ Free wi-fi is available on most trains.

➡ Smoking, including vaping and smoking cannabis, is prohibited on all trains.

Classes

There are four main classes:

➡ Economy class buys you a fairly basic, if indeed quite comfortable, reclining seat with a headrest. Blankets and pillows are provided for overnight travel.

➡ Business class operates in the southern Ontario/Québec corridor. Seats are more spacious and have outlets for plugging in laptops. You also get a meal and priority boarding.

➡ Sleeper class is available on shorter overnight routes. You can choose from compartments with upper or lower pullout berths, and private single, double or triple roomettes, all with a bathroom.

➡ Touring class is available on long-distance routes and includes sleeper-class accommodations plus meals, access to the sightseeing car and sometimes a tour guide.

Costs

Taking the train is more expensive than the bus and often comparable to flying, but most people find it a fun, comfortable way to travel. June to mid-October is peak season, when prices are about 40% higher. Buying tickets in advance (even just five days before) can yield significant savings.

Long-Distance Routes

VIA Rail has several classic trains:

Canadian A 1950s stainless-steel beauty between Toronto and Vancouver, zipping through the northern Ontario lake country, the western plains via Winnipeg and Saskatoon, and Jasper in the Rockies over three days.

Hudson Bay From the prairie (slowly) to the subarctic: Winnipeg to polar-bear hangout Churchill.

Ocean Chugs from Montréal along the St Lawrence River through New Brunswick and Nova Scotia.

Jasper to Prince Rupert An all-daylight route from Jasper, Alberta, to coastal Prince Rupert, British Columbia; there's an overnight stop in Prince George (you make your own hotel reservations).

Privately run regional train companies offer additional rail-touring opportunities:

Algoma Central Railway (www.agawatrain.com) Access to northern Ontario wilderness areas.

Ontario Northland (www.ontarionorthland.ca) Operates the seasonal *Polar Bear Express* from Cochrane to Moosonee on James Bay (round-trip $119).

Royal Canadian Pacific (☑403-319-4690; www.royalcanadian-pacific.com) A cruise-ship-like luxury line running between and around the Rockies via Calgary.

Rocky Mountaineer Railtours
(www.rockymountaineer.com)
Gape at Canadian Rockies scenery on swanky trains between Vancouver, Kamloops and Calgary (two days from $1247).

White Pass & Yukon Route
(www.wpyr.com) Gorgeous route paralleling the original White Pass trail from Whitehorse, Yukon, to Fraser, British Columbia (round-trip $175).

Reservations

Seat reservations are highly recommended, especially in summer, on weekends and around holidays. During peak season (June to mid-October), some of the most popular sleeping arrangements are sold out months in advance, especially on long-distance trains such as the *Canadian*. The *Hudson Bay* often books solid during polar-bear season (around late September to early November).

Train Passes

VIA Rail offers a variety of passes that provide good savings, but the 'System' Canrailpass ($649 to $1518) is often the best for travelers. It's good for six, 12 or unlimited trips on all trains during a 15-, 30- or 60-day period. All seats are in economy class; upgrades are not permitted. You must book each leg at least three days in advance (which you can do online).

Language

English and French are the official languages of Canada. You'll see both on highway signs, maps, tourist brochures, packaging etc. In Québec the preservation of French is a major concern and fuels the separatist movement. Here, English can be hard to find, and road signs and visitor information is often in French only. Outside Montréal and Québec City, you'll need French at least some of the time.

New Brunswick is the only officially bilingual province. French is widely spoken, particularly in the north and east. It is somewhat different from the French of Québec. Nova Scotia and Manitoba also have significant French-speaking populations, and there are pockets in most other provinces. In the west of Canada, French isn't as prevalent.

The French spoken in Canada is essentially the same as in France. Although many English-speaking (and most French-speaking) students in Québec are still taught the French of France, the local tongue is known as 'Québecois' or *joual*. Announcers and broadcasters on Québec TV and radio tend to speak a more refined, European style of French, as does the upper class. Québecois people will have no problem understanding more formal French.

French sounds can almost all be found in English. The exceptions are nasal vowels (represented in our pronunciation guides by o or u followed by an almost inaudible nasal consonant sound m, n or ng), the 'funny' *u* (ew in our guides) and the deep-in-the-throat *r*. Bearing this in mind and reading the pronunciation guides in this chapter as if they were English, you'll be understood just fine.

WANT MORE?

For in-depth language information and handy phrases, check out Lonely Planet's *French Phrasebook*. You'll find it at **shop.lonelyplanet.com**, or you can buy Lonely Planet's iPhone phrasebooks at the Apple App Store.

BASICS

Hello.	*Bonjour.*	bon·zhoor
Goodbye.	*Au revoir.*	o·rer·vwa
Excuse me.	*Excusez-moi.*	ek·skew·zay·mwa
Sorry.	*Pardon.*	par·don
Yes./No.	*Oui./Non.*	wee/non
Please.	*S'il vous plaît.*	seel voo play
Thank you.	*Merci.*	mair·see
You're welcome.	*De rien.*	der ree·en

How are you?
Comment allez-vous? ko·mon ta·lay·voo

Fine, and you?
Bien, merci. Et vous? byun mair·see ay voo

My name is ...
Je m'appelle ... zher ma·pel ...

What's your name?
Comment vous appelez-vous? ko·mon voo· za·play voo

Do you speak English?
Parlez-vous anglais? par·lay·voo ong·glay

I don't understand.
Je ne comprends pas. zher ner kom·pron pa

ACCOMMODATIONS

Do you have any rooms available?
Est-ce que vous avez des chambres libres? es·ker voo za·vay day shom·brer lee·brer

How much is it per night/person?
Quel est le prix par nuit/personne? kel ay ler pree par nwee/per·son

Is breakfast included?
Est-ce que le petit déjeuner est inclus? es·ker ler per·tee day·zher·nay ayt en·klew

a ... room	*une chambre ...*	ewn shom·brer ...
single	*à un lit*	a un lee
double	*avec un grand lit*	a·vek un gron lee

air-con	climatiseur	klee·ma·tee·zer
bathroom	salle de bains	sal der bun
campsite	camping	kom·peeng
dorm	dortoir	dor·twar
guesthouse	pension	pon·syon
hotel	hôtel	o·tel
window	fenêtre	fer·nay·trer
youth hostel	auberge de jeunesse	o·berzh der zher·nes

DIRECTIONS

Where's ...?
Où est ...? oo ay ...

What's the address?
Quelle est l'adresse? kel ay la·dres

Could you write the address, please?
Est-ce que vous pourriez écrire l'adresse, s'il vous plaît? es·ker voo poo·ryay ay·kreer la·dres seel voo play

Can you show me (on the map)?
Pouvez-vous m'indiquer (sur la carte)? poo·vay·voo mun·dee·kay (sewr la kart)

at the corner	au coin	o kwun
at the traffic lights	aux feux	o fer
behind	derrière	dair·ryair
in front of ...	devant ...	der·von ...
far (from ...)	loin (de ...)	lwun (der ...)
left	gauche	gosh
near (to ...)	près (de ...)	pray (der ...)
next to ...	à côté de ...	a ko·tay der...
opposite ...	en face de ...	on fas der ...
right	droite	drwat
straight ahead	tout droit	too drwa

EATING & DRINKING

A table for (two), please.
Une table pour (deux), s'il vous plaît. ewn ta·bler poor (der) seel voo play

What would you recommend?
Qu'est-ce que vous conseillez? kes·ker voo kon·say·yay

What's in that dish?
Quels sont les ingrédients? kel son lay zun·gray·dyon

I'm a vegetarian.
Je suis végétarien/ végétarienne. zher swee vay·zhay·ta·ryun/ vay·zhay·ta·ryen (m/f)

I don't eat ...
Je ne mange pas ... zher ner monzh pa ...

To get by in French, mix and match these simple patterns with words of your choice:

Where's (the entry)?
Où est (l'entrée)? oo ay (lon·tray)

Where can I (buy a ticket)?
Où est-ce que je peux (acheter un billet)? oo es·ker zher per (ash·tay un bee·yay)

When's (the next train)?
Quand est (le prochain train)? kon ay (ler pro·shun trun)

How much is (a room)?
C'est combien pour (une chambre)? say kom·buyn poor (ewn shom·brer)

Do you have (a map)?
Avez-vous (une carte)? a·vay voo (ewn kart)

Is there (a toilet)?
Y a-t-il (des toilettes)? ee a teel (day twa·let)

I'd like (to book a room).
Je voudrais (réserver une chambre). zher voo·dray (ray·ser·vay ewn shom·brer)

Can I (enter)?
Puis-je (entrer)? pweezh (on·tray)

Could you please (help)?
Pouvez-vous (m'aider), s'il vous plaît? poo·vay voo (may·day) seel voo play

Do I have to (book a seat)?
Faut-il (réserver une place)? fo·teel (ray·ser·vay ewn plas)

Cheers!
Santé! son·tay

That was delicious.
C'était délicieux! say·tay day·lee·syer

Please bring the bill.
Apportez-moi l'addition, s'il vous plaît. a·por·tay·mwa la·dee·syon seel voo play

Key Words

appetiser	entrée	on·tray
bottle	bouteille	boo·tay
breakfast	déjeuner	day·zher·nay
children's menu	menu pour enfants	mer·new poor on·fon
cold	froid	frwa
delicatessen	traiteur	tray·ter
dinner	souper	soo·pay
dish	plat	pla
food	nourriture	noo·ree·tewr

SIGNS

Entrée	Entrance
Femmes	Women
Fermé	Closed
Hommes	Men
Interdit	Prohibited
Ouvert	Open
Renseignements	Information
Sortie	Exit
Toilettes/WC	Toilets

fork	fourchette	foor·shet
glass	verre	vair
grocery store	épicerie	ay·pees·ree
highchair	chaise haute	shay zot
hot	chaud	sho
knife	couteau	koo·to
local specialty	spécialité locale	spay·sya·lee·tay lo·kal
lunch	dîner	dee·nay
main course	plat principal	pla prun·see·pal
market	marché	mar·shay
menu (in English)	carte (en anglais)	kart (on ong·glay)
plate	assiette	a·syet
spoon	cuillère	kwee·yair
wine list	carte des vins	kart day vun
with	avec	a·vek
without	sans	son

Meat & Fish

beef	bœuf	berf
chicken	poulet	poo·lay
fish	poisson	pwa·son
lamb	agneau	a·nyo
pork	porc	por
turkey	dinde	dund
veal	veau	vo

Fruit & Vegetables

apple	pomme	pom
apricot	abricot	ab·ree·ko
asparagus	asperge	a·spairzh
beans	haricots	a·ree·ko
beetroot	betterave	be·trav
cabbage	chou	shoo
celery	céleri	sel·ree

cherry	cerise	ser·reez
corn	maïs	ma·ees
cucumber	concombre	kong·kom·brer
gherkin (pickle)	cornichon	kor·nee·shon
grape	raisin	ray·zun
leek	poireau	pwa·ro
lemon	citron	see·tron
lettuce	laitue	lay·tew
mushroom	champignon	shom·pee·nyon
peach	pêche	pesh
peas	petit pois	per·tee pwa
(red/green) pepper	poivron (rouge/vert)	pwa·vron (roozh/vair)
pineapple	ananas	a·na·nas
plum	prune	prewn
potato	pomme de terre	pom der tair
prune	pruneau	prew·no
pumpkin	citrouille	see·troo·yer
shallot	échalote	eh·sha·lot
spinach	épinards	eh·pee·nar
strawberry	fraise	frez
tomato	tomate	to·mat
turnip	navet	na·vay
vegetable	légume	lay·gewm

Other

bread	pain	pun
butter	beurre	ber
cheese	fromage	fro·mazh
egg	œuf	erf
honey	miel	myel
jam	confiture	kon·fee·tewr
lentils	lentilles	lon·tee·yer
oil	huile	weel
pasta/noodles	pâtes	pat
pepper	poivre	pwa·vrer
rice	riz	ree
salt	sel	sel
sugar	sucre	sew·krer

QUESTION WORDS

How?	Comment?	ko·mon
What?	Quoi?	kwa
When?	Quand?	kon
Where?	Où?	oo
Who?	Qui?	kee
Why?	Pourquoi?	poor·kwa

Drinks

beer	*bière*	bee·yair
coffee	*café*	ka·fay
(orange) juice	*jus (d'orange)*	zhew (do·ronzh)
milk	*lait*	lay
red wine	*vin rouge*	vun roozh
tea	*thé*	tay
(mineral) water	*eau (minérale)*	o (mee·nay·ral)
white wine	*vin blanc*	vun blong

EMERGENCIES

Help!
Au secours! — o skoor

I'm lost.
Je suis perdu/perdue. — zhe swee pair·dew (m/f)

Leave me alone!
Fichez-moi la paix! — fee·shay·mwa la pay

There's been an accident.
Il y a eu un accident. — eel ya ew un ak·see·don

Call a doctor.
Appelez un médecin. — a·play un mayd·sun

Call the police.
Appelez la police. — a·play la po·lees

I'm ill.
Je suis malade. — zher swee ma·lad

It hurts here.
J'ai une douleur ici. — zhay ewn doo·ler ee·see

I'm allergic to ...
Je suis allergique ... — zher swee za·lair·zheek ...

Where are the toilets?
Où sont les toilettes? — oo son lay twa·let

SHOPPING & SERVICES

I'd like to buy ...
Je voudrais acheter ... — zher voo·dray ash·tay ...

May I look at it?
Est-ce que je peux le voir? — es·ker zher per ler vwar

I'm just looking.
Je regarde. — zher rer·gard

I don't like it.
Cela ne me plaît pas. — ser·la ner mer play pa

How much is it?
C'est combien? — say kom·byun

It's too expensive.
C'est trop cher. — say tro shair

Can you lower the price?
Vous pouvez baisser le prix? — voo poo·vay bay·say ler pree

1	*un*	un
2	*deux*	der
3	*trois*	trwa
4	*quatre*	ka·trer
5	*cinq*	sungk
6	*six*	sees
7	*sept*	set
8	*huit*	weet
9	*neuf*	nerf
10	*dix*	dees
20	*vingt*	vung
30	*trente*	tront
40	*quarante*	ka·ront
50	*cinquante*	sung·kont
60	*soixante*	swa·sont
70	*soixante-dix*	swa·son·dees
80	*quatre-vingts*	ka·trer·vung
90	*quatre-vingt-dix*	ka·trer·vung·dees
100	*cent*	son
1000	*mille*	meel

There's a mistake in the bill.
Il y a une erreur dans la note. — eel ya ewn ay·rer don la not

ATM	*guichet automatique de banque*	gee·shay o·to·ma·teek der bonk
credit card	*carte de crédit*	kart der kray·dee
internet cafe	*cybercafé*	see·bair·ka·fay
post office	*bureau de poste*	bew·ro der post
tourist office	*office de tourisme*	o·fees der too·rees·mer

TIME & DATES

What time is it?
Quelle heure est-il? — kel er ay til

It's (eight) o'clock.
Il est (huit) heures. — il ay (weet) er

It's half past (10).
Il est (dix) heures et demie. — il ay (deez) er ay day·mee

morning	*matin*	ma·tun
afternoon	*après-midi*	a·pray·mee·dee
evening	*soir*	swar
yesterday	*hier*	yair
today	*aujourd'hui*	o·zhoor·dwee
tomorrow	*demain*	der·mun

Monday	lundi	lun·dee
Tuesday	mardi	mar·dee
Wednesday	mercredi	mair·krer·dee
Thursday	jeudi	zher·dee
Friday	vendredi	von·drer·dee
Saturday	samedi	sam·dee
Sunday	dimanche	dee·monsh

January	janvier	zhon·vyay
February	février	fayv·ryay
March	mars	mars
April	avril	a·vreel
May	mai	may
June	juin	zhwun
July	juillet	zhwee·yay
August	août	oot
September	septembre	sep·tom·brer
October	octobre	ok·to·brer
November	novembre	no·vom·brer
December	décembre	day·som·brer

TRANSPORTATION

Public Transportation

boat	bateau	ba·to
bus	bus	bews
plane	avion	a·vyon
train	train	trun

I want to go to ...
Je voudrais aller à ... zher voo·dray a·lay a ...

Does it stop at ...?
Est-ce qu'il s'arrête à ...? es·kil sa·ret a ...

At what time does it leave/arrive?
À quelle heure est-ce a kel er es
qu'il part/arrive? kil par/a·reev

Can you tell me when we get to ...?
Pouvez-vous me poo·vay·voo mer
dire quand deer kon
nous arrivons à ...? noo za·ree·von a ...

I want to get off here.
Je veux descendre zher ver day·son·drer
ici. ee·see

first	premier	prer·myay
last	dernier	dair·nyay
next	prochain	pro·shun

a ... ticket	un billet ...	un bee·yay ...
1st-class	de première classe	der prem·yair klas
2nd-class	de deuxième classe	der der·zyem las
one-way	simple	sum·pler
return	aller et retour	a·lay ay rer·toor

aisle seat	côté couloir	ko·tay kool·war
cancelled	annulé	a·new·lay
delayed	en retard	on rer·tar
platform	quai	kay
ticket office	guichet	gee·shay
timetable	horaire	o·rair
train station	gare	gar
window seat	côté fenêtre	ko·tay fe·ne·trer

Driving & Cycling

I'd like to hire a ...	Je voudrais louer ...	zher voo·dray loo·way ...
car	une voiture	ewn vwa·tewr
bicycle	un vélo	un vay·lo
motorcycle	une moto	ewn mo·to

child seat	siège-enfant	syezh·on·fon
diesel	diesel	dyay·zel
helmet	casque	kask
mechanic	mécanicien	may·ka·nee·syun
petrol/gas	essence	ay·sons
service station	station-service	sta·syon·ser·vees

Is this the road to ...?
C'est la route pour ...? say la root poor ...

(How long) Can I park here?
(Combien de temps) (kom·byun der tom)
Est-ce que je peux es·ker zher per
stationner ici? sta·syo·nay ee·see

The car/motorbike has broken down (at ...).
La voiture/moto est la vwa·tewr/mo·to ay
tombée en panne (à ...). tom·bay on pan (a ...)

I have a flat tire.
Mon pneu est à plat. mom pner ay ta pla

I've run out of petrol.
Je suis en panne zher swee zon pan
d'essence. day·sons

I've lost my car keys.
J'ai perdu les clés de zhay per·dew lay klay der
ma voiture. ma vwa·tewr

Where can I have my bicycle repaired?
Où est-ce que je peux oo es·ker zher per
faire réparer mon vélo? fair ray·pa·ray mon vay·lo

Behind the Scenes

SEND US YOUR FEEDBACK

We love to hear from travelers – your comments keep us on our toes and help make our books better. Our well-traveled team reads every word on what you loved or loathed about this book. Although we cannot reply individually to your submissions, we always guarantee that your feedback goes straight to the appropriate authors, in time for the next edition. Each person who sends us information is thanked in the next edition – the most useful submissions are rewarded with a selection of digital PDF chapters.

Visit **lonelyplanet.com/contact** to submit your updates and suggestions or to ask for help. Our award-winning website also features inspirational travel stories, news and discussions.

Note: We may edit, reproduce and incorporate your comments in Lonely Planet products such as guidebooks, websites and digital products, so let us know if you don't want your comments reproduced or your name acknowledged. For a copy of our privacy policy visit lonelyplanet.com/privacy.

OUR READERS

Many thanks to the travelers who used the last edition and wrote to us with helpful hints, useful advice and interesting anecdotes:

Anne Cayer, Cheryl Ferguson, Dan Hunter, Diane Beckett, Elisa Maria Garattoni, Emiliano E. Lareu, Emill Spilchak, Erin Howe, Graham Leggett, Greta, Dania & Robert Rauer, Janine Hancock, Jérémie Robichaud, Leon Brass, Linda James, Mark Hughes, Miguel Prohaska, Nicki Gay, Sara Raiola, Sharon V

Whims, Stacie McGugan, Stacy Kermode, Susan Kantor, Tom Kelly, Win Hill, Yvette Snackers.

WRITER THANKS

Brendan Sainsbury

Many thanks to all the skilled bus drivers, helpful tourist information staff, generous hotel owners, expert burger flippers, unobtrusive bears and numerous passers-by who helped me, unwittingly or otherwise, during

THIS BOOK

This 15th edition of Lonely Planet's *Canada* guidebook was curated by Brendan Sainsbury, Oliver Berry, John Lee and Regis St Louis, and researched and written by Brendan, Oliver and John, and Ray Bartlett, Gregor Clark, Shawn Duthie, Steve Fallon, Carolyn B Heller, Anna Kaminski, Adam Karlin, Craig McLachlan, Korina Miller, Liza Prado and Phillip Tang. This guidebook was produced by the following:

Destination Editor Ben Buckner

Senior Product Editors Daniel Bolger, Grace Dobell, Saralinda Turner

Regional Senior Cartographer Corey Hutchison

Cartographer Mark Griffiths

Product Editors Sasha Drew, Kate Kiely

Book Designer Clara Monitto

Assisting Editors Sarah Bailey, Andrew Bain, James Bainbridge, Judith Bamber, Michelle Bennett, Hannah Cartmel, Samantha Cook, Joel Cotterell, Lucy Cowie, Melanie

Dankel, Bruce Evans, Emma Gibbs, Shona Gray, Carly Hall, Jennifer Hattam, Gabrielle Innes, Kellie Langdon, Jodie Martire, Lou McGregor, Christopher Pitts, Sarah Reid, Tamara Sheward, Ross Taylor, Simon Williamson

Assisting Cartographers Julie Dodkins, Mick Garrett

Cover Researcher Gwen Cotter

Thanks to Imogen Bannister, Kate Chapman, Bailey Freeman, Andi Jones, Martine Power, Lauren O'Connell, Kirsten Rawlings

my research trip. Special thanks to my wife Liz, my son Kieran and my mother-in-law Ammy for their company (and patience) on the road.

Oliver Berry

Big thanks to Ben Buckner for the chance to return to write about Canada, to the Lonely Planet editors for whipping my work into shape, and to my fellow writers for making this book what it is. Heartfelt thanks to Rosie Hillier for putting up with my wanderlust, and to Susie Berry for long-distance correspondence. Thanks also to Sam White, Justin Foulkes, Deborah Gill, Anna Louis and many others for useful Canadian tips and much-needed hospitality.

John Lee

Heartfelt thanks to Maggie for joining me at all those restaurants and for keeping me calm during the brain-throbbing final write-up phase of this project. Thanks also to Max, our crazy-whiskered ginger cat, for sticking by my desk and also reminding me to chase him around the house every once in a while. Cheers also to my brother Michael for visiting from England and checking out some local breweries with me: you really know how to go the extra mile.

Ray Bartlett

Thanks first and foremost, to Buck, for the chance to work on this, and to each of the editors who will peek at it afterwards, and to the great team of co-authors. Thanks as well to my family, friends, and to the incredible collage of folks I met along the way: Kristina, Vera, Rubí, Miro, Allan & Dan, Cat and Greg, Louise and Melva, Alice H, Molly and Spencer (congrats!), Morgan, William Flenders, Josh W, Char, the Lindsays, Riya and many more.

Gregor Clark

Heartfelt thanks to all of the kind Albertans and fellow travelers who shared their love and knowledge of Banff and Jasper – especially Karina Birch, Kate Williams, Ken Wood, Paul Krywicki, Erin Wilkinson, Ed and Vanessa, Shauna and Lindsay. Thanks also to the family and friends who helped me explore Banff and Jasper's trails: Chloe, Sophie, Wes and Ted, that means you! Couldn't have asked for a more delightful research crew.

Shawn Duthie

It was great to reconnect with my home province and my deepest thanks to Vivek, Danny and Stefan for allowing me to sleep on your couch, driving too many kilometres to count and just making the research even more fun than usual. Of course, my biggest thank you is to my wife and son who put up with all my traveling!

Steve Fallon

Un très grand merci to the folk who offered assistance, ideas and/or hospitality along the way, including Gabriel d'Anjou Drouin and Maxime Aubin in Québec City; Vicky Drolet in Malbaie; Sylvie Senécal & Pierre Lachance in Ville de Mont-Tremblant; and Carolyne Cyr and Pierre-André Guichoud in Ste-Adèle. *Et à mon cher 'pays d'hiver' qui a combattu le bon combat et gagné!* (And to my beloved 'land of winter' that fought the good fight and won!). As always, my share is dedicated to my now spouse and almost Quebecer, Michael Rothschild.

Carolyn B Heller

Many thanks to all the friends and colleagues who shared their Québec tips, especially Kim Huard-Carette and Emily Dunn. Special thanks to Ben Buckner for signing me onto the Canada team, to Suzie Loiselle and Étienne Fiola for all the advice and the crêpes, and to Michaela Albert, ace travel buddy, snow hiker and champion lobster eater.

Anna Kaminski

Huge thanks to Ben for entrusting me with Nunavut, NWT and Manitoba, and to everyone who's helped me along the way. In particular: Theresa and the merry crew of medics, plus Stephen, Alan and Brian in Iqaluit, Markus in Pangnirtung, Joamie, Pootoogook and Silaqqi in Cape Dorset, Don and Christine in Fort Smith, Sherry in Valleyview, Jacob and Herb in Yellowknife, John and Gina in Fort Providence, Lois in Fort Simpson, Wayne at Checkpoint and Minerva in Inuvik.

Adam Karlin

Big thanks: Ben Buckner, for getting me on this project; Anna Kaminski, my commiserator in chief; my fellow co-authors; Carolyn and Adam in St John's; Gordon in Bonavista; the construction crews of the New-Wes-Valley; mom and dad; my wild little Isaac; and my favorite traveling companions, Rachel, who can layer for anything, and Sanda, who endures the road better than her daddy.

Craig McLachlan

A hearty thanks to all those who helped out on the road, but most of all, to my exceptionally beautiful wife, Yuriko, who maintained semi-control of my craft beer intake.

Korina Miller

Thank you to Ben Buckner for inviting me to join this project, to my fellow authors for their enthusiasm and to Imogen Bannister for her support. Huge thanks to my parents who kept things ticking along while I was away, to Kirk for being my rock, and to my daughters,

Simone and Monique, who make coming home the best part of traveling. To the people of New Brunswick, *merci* for sharing your truly beautiful province with me.

Liza Prado

A shout out to the extraordinary Lonely Planet team: Ben Buckner, the production crew, my co-authors – I'm so proud to be able to work with you. *Mil gracias* to Mom and Dad for your boundless support, love, and curiosity about places so close to home. Big thanks to Eva and Leo for waiting so patiently for 'Fun...With Mom.' And Gary, my love, there is absolutely no way I could do my job without you. Your support, your understanding, your cheerleading. Thank you, always.

Phillip Tang

Thank you to Ben Buckner and the Destination Editors for your expertise and legacy. *Muchas gracias a Lalo* (José Eduardo García Sánchez) *por tu apoyo y consejo sobre estilo y mucho más desde lejos*. Thank you to Felix, Nick Zhang and all the other Montréalers who offered guidance; and to Manuelle González Goretti for advice on the Eastern Townships and adventures in the Village.

ACKNOWLEDGEMENTS

Climate map data adapted from Peel MC, Finlayson BL & McMahon TA (2007) 'Updated World Map of the Köppen-Geiger Climate Classification', *Hydrology and Earth System Sciences*, 11, 1633–44.

Cover photograph: West Point Lighthouse, Prince Edward Island, Aurélien Pottier/Getty Images©

BEHIND THE SCENES

Index

Map Legend

Sights

- Beach
- Bird Sanctuary
- Buddhist
- Castle/Palace
- Christian
- Confucian
- Hindu
- Islamic
- Jain
- Jewish
- Monument
- Museum/Gallery/Historic Building
- Ruin
- Shinto
- Sikh
- Taoist
- Winery/Vineyard
- Zoo/Wildlife Sanctuary
- Other Sight

Activities, Courses & Tours

- Bodysurfing
- Diving
- Canoeing/Kayaking
- Course/Tour
- Sento Hot Baths/Onsen
- Skiing
- Snorkeling
- Surfing
- Swimming/Pool
- Walking
- Windsurfing
- Other Activity

Sleeping

- Sleeping
- Camping
- Hut/Shelter

Eating

- Eating

Drinking & Nightlife

- Drinking & Nightlife
- Cafe

Entertainment

- Entertainment

Shopping

- Shopping

Information

- Bank
- Embassy/Consulate
- Hospital/Medical
- @ Internet
- Police
- Post Office
- Telephone
- Toilet
- Tourist Information
- • Other Information

Geographic

- Beach
- Gate
- Hut/Shelter
- Lighthouse
- Lookout
- ▲ Mountain/Volcano
- Oasis
- Park
-)(Pass
- Picnic Area
- Waterfall

Population

- Capital (National)
- Capital (State/Province)
- City/Large Town
- Town/Village

Transport

- Airport
- BART station
- Border crossing
- Boston T station
- Bus
- Cable car/Funicular
- Cycling
- Ferry
- Metro/Muni station
- Monorail
- Parking
- Petrol station
- Subway/SkyTrain station
- Taxi
- Train station/Railway
- Tram
- Underground station
- • Other Transport

Routes

- Tollway
- Freeway
- Primary
- Secondary
- Tertiary
- Lane
- Unsealed road
- Road under construction
- Plaza/Mall
- Steps
- Tunnel
- Pedestrian overpass
- Walking Tour
- Walking Tour detour
- Path/Walking Trail

Boundaries

- International
- State/Province
- Disputed
- Regional/Suburb
- Marine Park
- Cliff
- Wall

Hydrography

- River, Creek
- Intermittent River
- Canal
- Water
- Dry/Salt/Intermittent Lake
- Reef

Areas

- Airport/Runway
- Beach/Desert
- Cemetery (Christian)
- Cemetery (Other)
- Glacier
- Mudflat
- Park/Forest
- Sight (Building)
- Sportsground
- Swamp/Mangrove

Note: Not all symbols displayed above appear on the maps in this book

Anna Kaminski

Manitoba, Northwest Territories, Nunavut Originally from the Soviet Union, Anna grew up in Cambridge, UK. She graduated from the University of Warwick with a degree in Comparative American Studies, a background in the history, culture and literature of the Americas and the Caribbean, and an enduring love of Latin America. Her restless wanderings led her to settle briefly in Oaxaca and Bangkok and her flirtation with criminal law saw her volunteering as a lawyer's assistant in the courts, ghettos and prisons of Kingston, Jamaica. Anna has contributed to almost 30 Lonely Planet titles. When not on the road, Anna calls London home.

Adam Karlin

Newfoundland & Labrador Adam has contributed to dozens of Lonely Planet guidebooks, covering an alphabetical spread that ranges from the Andaman Islands to the Zimbabwe Border. As a journalist, he has written on travel, crime, politics, archeology and the Sri Lankan Civil War, among other topics. He has sent dispatches from every continent barring Antarctica (one day!) and his essays and articles have featured in the BBC, NPR and multiple nonfiction anthologies. Adam is based out of New Orleans, which helps explain his love of wetlands, food and good music. Learn more at http://walkonfine.com/ or follow on Instagram @adamwalkonfine.

Craig McLachlan

British Columbia, Saskatchewan, Yukon Territory Craig has covered destinations all over the globe for Lonely Planet for two decades. Based in Queenstown, New Zealand for half the year, he runs an outdoor activities company and a sake brewery, then moonlights overseas for the other half, leading tours and writing for Lonely Planet. Craig has completed a number of adventures in Japan and his books are available on Amazon. Describing himself as a 'freelance anything', Craig has an MBA from the University of Hawai'i and is also a Japanese interpreter, pilot, hiking guide, tour leader, karate instructor, marriage celebrant and budding novelist. Check out www.craigmclachlan.com

Korina Miller

New Brunswick Korina grew up on Vancouver Island and has been exploring the globe independently since she was 16, visiting or living in 36 countries and picking up a degree in Communications and Canadian Studies, an MA in Migration Studies and a diploma in Visual Arts en route. As a writer and editor, Korina has worked on nearly 60 titles for Lonely Planet and has also worked with lonelyplanet.com, BBC, the *Independent*, the *Guardian*, BBC5 and CBC, as well as many independent magazines, covering travel, art and culture. She has currently set up camp back in Victoria, soaking up the mountain views and the pounding surf.

Liza Prado

Ontario Liza has been a travel writer since 2003, when she made a move from being a corporate lawyer to travel writing (and never looked back). She's written dozens of guidebooks and articles as well as apps and blogs to destinations throughout the Americas. She takes decent photos too. Liza is a graduate of Brown University and Stanford Law School. She lives very happily in Denver, Colorado, with her husband and fellow Lonely Planet writer, Gary Chandler, and their two kids.

Phillip Tang

Québec Phillip grew up on a typically Australian diet of pho and fish'n'chips before moving to Mexico City. A degree in Chinese- and Latin-American cultures launched him into travel and then writing about it for Lonely Planet's *Canada*, *China*, *Japan*, *Korea*, *Mexico*, *Peru* and *Vietnam* guides. You can see more of his writing at hellophillip.com, photos @mrtangtangtang and tweets @philliptang.

Contributing Writer

Michael Grosberg researched and wrote about the Waterton Lakes National Park in Alberta.

Regis St Louis

Regis grew up in a small town in the American Midwest – the kind of place that fuels big dreams of travel – and he developed an early fascination with foreign dialects and world cultures. He spent his formative years learning Russian and a handful of Romance languages, which served him well on journeys across much of the globe. Regis has contributed to more than 50 Lonely Planet titles, covering destinations across six continents. His travels have taken him from the mountains of Kamchatka to remote island villages in Melanesia, and to many grand urban landscapes. When not on the road, he lives in New Orleans. Follow him on www.instagram.com/regisstlouis.

Ray Bartlett

Alberta Ray has been travel writing for nearly two decades, bringing Japan, Korea, Mexico, Tanzania, Guatemala, Indonesia and many parts of the United States to life in rich detail for top publishers, newspapers and magazines. His acclaimed debut novel, *Sunsets of Tulum*, set in Yucatán, was a Midwest Book Review 2016 Fiction pick. Among other pursuits, he surfs regularly and is an accomplished Argentine tango dancer. Follow him on Facebook, Twitter, Instagram, or contact him for questions or motivational speaking opportunities via www.kaisora.com, his website. Ray also wrote the Plan, Understand and Survival sections.

Gregor Clark

Alberta Gregor is a US-based writer whose love of foreign languages and curiosity about what's around the next bend have taken him to dozens of countries on five continents. Chronic wanderlust has also led him to visit all 50 states and most Canadian provinces on countless road trips through his native North America. Since 2000, Gregor has regularly contributed to Lonely Planet guides, with a focus on Europe and the Americas. Titles include *Italy*, *France*, *Brazil*, *Costa Rica*, *Argentina*, *Portugal*, *Switzerland*, *Mexico*, *South America*, *Montréal & Québec City*, *France's Best Trips*, *New England's Best Trips*, cycling guides to Italy and California and coffee-table pictorials such as *Food Trails*, the *USA Book* and the *Lonely Planet Guide to the Middle of Nowhere*.

Shawn Duthie

Ontario Originally from Canada, Shawn has been traveling, studying and working around the world for the past 13 years. A love of travel merged with an interest in international politics, which led to several years of lecturing at the University of Cape Town and now working as a freelance political risk consultant specializing in African countries. Shawn lives in South Africa and takes any excuse to travel around this amazing continent.

Steve Fallon

Québec A native of Boston, Massachusetts, Steve graduated from Georgetown University with a Bachelor of Science in modern languages. After working for several years for an American daily newspaper and earning a master's degree in journalism, his fascination with the 'new' Asia led him to Hong Kong, where he lived for over a dozen years, working for a variety of media and running his own travel bookshop. Steve lived in Budapest for three years before moving to London in 1994. He has written or contributed to more than 100 Lonely Planet titles. Steve is a qualified London Blue Badge Tourist Guide. Visit his website on www.steveslondon.com.

Carolyn B Heller

Québec Carolyn has been a full-time travel, food and feature writer since 1996, writing for publications including lonelyplanet.com, *Forbes Travel Guide*, *Boston Globe* and *Los Angeles Times*, amongst others. Carolyn has also contributed to 50-plus travel and restaurant guides for Lonely Planet and other publishers. She's eaten her way across more than 40 countries on six continents, and when she's not traveling, you can find her running on the beach, in the theatre, or trying to learn enough Mandarin to decipher menus on Chinese restaurant walls.

OUR STORY

...beat-up old car, a few dollars in the pocket and a sense of ... 1972 that's all Tony and Maureen Wheeler needed ... cross Europe and Asia overland to ... the end – broke but ... g and stapling ... on the Cheap. ... lanet was born. ... land and China, with a network of over 2000 contributo... y's belief that 'a great guidebook should do three things: inform, edu...

OUR WRITERS

Brendan Sainsbury

British Columbia Born and raised in the UK in a town that never merits a mention in any guidebook (Andover, Hampshire), Brendan spent the holidays of his youth caravanning in the English Lake District and didn't leave Blighty until he was 19. Making up for lost time, he's since squeezed 70 countries into a sometimes precarious existence as a writer and professional vagabond. His rocking chair memories will probably include staging a performance of *A Comedy of Errors* at a school in war-torn Angola, running 150 miles across the Sahara Desert in the Marathon des Sables, and hitchhiking from Cape Town to Kilimanjaro with an early, dog-eared copy of Lonely Planet's *Africa on a Shoestring*. He has written more than 40 books for Lonely Planet.

Oliver Berry

Nova Scotia, New Brunswick, Prince Edward Island, Québec Oliver is a writer and photographer from Cornwall. He has worked for Lonely Planet for more than a decade, covering destinations from Cornwall to the Cook Islands, and has worked on more than 30 guidebooks. He is also a regular contributor to many newspapers and magazines, including Lonely Planet magazine. His writing has won several awards, including the *Guardian* Young Travel Writer of the Year and the *TNT Magazine* People's Choice Award. His latest work is published at www.oliverberry.com.

John Lee

British Columbia Born and raised in the historic UK city of St Albans, John grew up in London, gorging on the capital's rich diet of museums and galleries. Slowly succumbing to the lure of overseas exotica, he arrived on Canada's West Coast in 1993 to begin an MA in Political Science at the University of Victoria. Regular trips home to Britain ensued, along with stints living in Tokyo and Montréal, before he returned to British Columbia to become a full-time freelance writer in 1999. Now living in Vancouver, John specializes in travel writing and has contributed to more than 150 different publications around the world. You can read some of his stories (and see some of his videos) online at www.johnleewriter.com. John has worked on more than 25 Lonely Planet books, including *Canada*, *British Columbia & the Canadian Rockies*, *Western Europe* and *Vancouver*.

> OVER MORE
> PAGE WRITERS

Published by Lonely Planet Global Limited
CRN 554153
15th edition – Jan 2022
ISBN 978 1 78868 460 6
© Lonely Planet 2022   Photographs © as indicated 2022
10 9 8 7 6 5 4 3 2 1
Printed in Singapore